HOW TO USE THIS BOOK

Explore Australia by Four-Wheel Drive is arranged in 6 sections.

BEFORE YOU GO All you will need to know to get ready and be prepared: how to plan your trip; how to select and equip your vehicle; what to take; how to deal with emergency situations, both medical and mechanical.

TOURS OUT OF CAPITAL CITIES These are loop **tours** that vary from a day's travel to 2 weeks. Each has its own sketch map, detailed route directions, camping and permits information, and is cross-referenced to the Australia-wide map coverage section of the book.

TREKS AROUND AUSTRALIA The complete four-wheel drive journey around Australia is divided into a number of **treks**, starting and ending at major population centres, so you can join in or leave when you wish. There are reverse route directions, printed in red, for people travelling in the opposite direction. Treks are divided into **sections**, corresponding roughly to a day's travel. Each section has its own sketch map, route directions and camping and permits information, and is cross-referenced to the Australia-wide map section of the book.

OUTBACK DESERT TREKS The desert treks may be undertaken individually or linked together. Each has its own sketch map, detailed route directions and camping and permits information, and is cross-referenced to the Australia-wide map coverage section of the book.

ROAD MAPS Map pages are numbered **2–65**. Use maps to get to/from start/end points of every tour.

INDEX This lists places mentioned in text and on maps.

INFORMATION FOR EACH TOUR AND TREK SECTIONS INCLUDES:
▶ total number of kilometres covered, and unsealed distance;
▶ degree of difficulty;
▶ approximate driving time – which does not include stops;
▶ best time of year to do the trip;
▶ warnings about road conditions, permits needed to camp or traverse land and where to obtain these, touring information; camping sites – denoted by *italic* type in the section description;
▶ road and topographic map references and any other information you might use, such as local and regional maps.

HOW TO FOLLOW THE ROUTE DIRECTIONS

Route directions for the tours and trek sections are based on trip meter (odometer) readings linked to features along the way (intersections, bridges, rivers and so on).
▶ Read the trip notes carefully **before** you set out.
▶ Use the road maps to get to the start point.
▶ Set your trip meter to zero according to the instructions included in the route directions.
▶ Note as you pass each trip meter reading point; if you miss more than one point retrace your tracks and start again from the last registered reading point.
▶ The intermediate (point to point) readings shown are a useful means of checking that you are on track.
▶ **Trip meters vary slightly from vehicle to vehicle.** Make a trial run to test your meter and see how much your readings vary from those in the book. You will soon learn to allow for any slight variation.
▶ If you diverge from the route, zero your trip meter and note your position. You can then pick up the point-to-point directions when you rejoin the route.
▶ Use the sketch maps when planning your tour or trek and as an adjunct to navigation.
▶ We recommend the use of additional topographic maps as an aid to navigation.
▶ Unsealed roads can vary from good gravel to rough potholed tracks, sand or mud.
▶ Read the reverse directions from the bottom of the page to the top. They give cumulative trip meter readings.

ABBREVIATIONS USED IN ROUTE DIRECTIONS

SO	Straight on	**KL**	Keep left
TR	Turn right	**P**	Petrol
TL	Turn left	**D**	Diesel
KR	Keep right	**PD**	Petrol, diesel

PUBLISHER'S NOTE Every effort has been made to ensure that the information in this book is accurate at the time of going to press. We welcome information and suggestions for correction or improvement.

WARNING The condition of four-wheel drive tracks varies greatly, depending on the weather, the number of vehicles using them and how frequently they are graded. Please use common sense before setting out on any of the trips in this book. Many tracks in Far North Queensland and the Northern Territory are impassable during the wet season; it is inadvisable to attempt four-wheel drive mountain routes after snow. Always equip your vehicle properly for the conditions you expect to meet and check ahead with relevant authorities before departure.

Ford Raider makes a trip to Kakadu, the Kimberleys or Mt Kosciusko almost as easy as a shopping expedition to the supermarket.

Because when Raider becomes part of the family, all those weekend and holiday trips you promised to do together start to become possible.

FOR THE FAMILY THAT PLAYS TOGETHER.

Choosing a vehicle to suit the needs of a family usually comes down to either a people mover or a station wagon. Highly practical but hardly exciting.

Now there's an alternative: Ford Raider, the 4WD family wagon that seats seven in beautifully quiet, smooth riding comfort.

You can run all over town all week.

Yet when the weekend rolls around, you can engage the Raider's remote locking front hubs, select 4WD and put yourself on the road to excitement and adventure.

And with a seating plan as flexible as Raider's you can make arrangements that exactly fulfil your ever-changing passenger and cargo requirements.

FORD RAIDER

EXPLORE AUSTRALIA
BY
FOUR-WHEEL DRIVE

A Claremont Book
487 Maroondah Highway, PO Box 257
Ringwood, Victoria 3134, Australia

This edition published 1995
10 9 8 7 6 5 4 3 2 1
Copyright © Penguin Books Australia 1995
ISBN 0 670 86381 5

Front cover photography: *Background* Bill Bachman / Stock Photos;
Car Craig Robinson / Palermo Studios

Printed and bound in China through Bookbuilders Limited, Hong Kong

EXPLORE AUSTRALIA
BY
FOUR-WHEEL DRIVE

Peter and Kim Wherrett

VIKING

CONTENTS

Creek crossing, Gunbarrel Highway

Around Indian Head, Fraser Island

Bullita Stock Route

ACKNOWLEDGEMENTS

The authors and publisher thank the following people and organisations without whose help this book could not have been produced.

SPONSORS Special thanks are due to: *Ford Australia Ltd* (Jac Nasser, Ian Vaughan, Mike Jarvis, Ian McLean, David Hosking and Adrian Ryan) who provided the Maverick; and *BP Australia Ltd* (Michael Garnett).

Dunlop Australia (Geoff Moorhead, Alan Finney); *Segal Media*; *Codan Pty Ltd* (Roger Smith, Bob Potter); *Long Distance Communications Pty Ltd* (Peter Linden); *Toshiba Australia Pty Ltd* (Lesley McLennan, David Bierwerth); *Bush Boy Refrigeration* (Mike Clayton); *Shippshape Tents* (Eric Shipp); *Hayman Reece Pty Ltd* (Bob Buck, Tim Wood); *Opposite Lock Pty Ltd* (Adrian Stafford, Lionel Sewart, Ralph Martel); *Alltrack Services* and *DB Swags* (Peter Young); *Wilderness Publications*; *Tri-Star Motors* (Bryant Stafford).

ADVICE AND RESEARCH *The Australian National Four Wheel Drive Council* and especially Vice Chairman Jan Scudamore and Ivan Scudamore, and the state four-wheel drive associations: *Western Australia* (Steve and Marg Wilke); *South Australia* (Steve Charles); *Queensland* (Graeme and Di Smith). *National Parks, forestry and tourism* services in all states and especially: *New South Wales: National Parks and Wildlife Service*; *NSW Forestry Commission* (Wyong office); *Shoalhaven Shire Council* (Tom Phillips); *NSW Travel Centre*. *Queensland: National Parks and Wildlife Service* (Barry and Di Kubala: Lawn Hill; Terry Vowles and Andrea Dobbyn: Brisbane; Mark Swart and Seamus Conway: Mackay; Scotty McVeigh: Eungella); *Queensland Forest Service* (Merv Venz: Beerburrum; Diane McLean, Geoff Clare and Vic Bishop: Brisbane; Bruce Erlich: Mt Mee); *Water Resources Commission* (Robert Engstrom: Townsville); *Gulf Local Authorities Development Association* (John Courtenay, Sandy Whyte); *Tourism Mackay* (Joanne Libline); *Queensland Tourist and Travel Corporation* (Karen Peace); *Townsville Enterprises* (Kerrie Kent); *Inland Queensland Tourism and Development Association* (Bronwyn Staddon); *Golden Mermaid Caravan Park Clairview*

(Mary Kilamoff); *Mirani Shire Council*. **Northern Territory:** *Northern Territory Tourist Commission* (George Dunne, Lisa Bell, Chrissie Barry); *Pungalina Station* (Judy Retter); *Conservation Commission of the Northern Territory* (Ross Belcher: Gregory National Park). **Western Australia:** *The Wilderness Society of Western Australia* (Peter Robinson, Jon Rowdon) for advice on the Kimberley; *Department of Conservation and Land Management* (Ron Shepherd, Caris Bailey; Steep Point: Graeme Reagan; Dwellingup: Mike Tagliaferri; Nambung National Park: Keith Hockey; Moora District: Ken Borland and David Rose; Corporate Relations Division: John Hunter and Marg Wilke; *Department of Land Administration* (Kerry Smyth); *Useless Loop Saltworks Joint Venture* (Joe Twiss); *Peoples Park Caravan Village, Coral Bay* (Norman Monch); *Western Australian Tourism Commission* (Bernie Whewell, Kathie Wylie, Bart Boden); *El Questro Station* (Will Burrell, Celia Shelmerdine). **South Australia:** *South Australian Department of Environment and Planning* (Dick Olezinski); *The Pink Roadhouse, Oodnadatta* (Adam and Lynnie Plate). **Victoria:** *Department of Conservation and Environment* (Frank Noble; Powelltown: Ross Potter; Colac: Bob Brinkman, Jack Holden, Des Peters); *Bowyangs Maps* (Kew). **Tasmania:** *Department of Parks, Wildlife and Heritage* (Steve Robertson, Chris Boden, Frank Morley; Queenstown: Terry Reid); *Forestry Commission Tasmania* (Simon Cubin; Triabunna: John Cunningham); *Broughtons Map Shop* (Hobart). *The Royal Flying Doctor Service* and *Storry Walton*, National Public Affairs Manager.

PHOTOGRAPHS *New South Wales: Philip Green* (Watagan Mountain photographs, Cedar forest); *Shoalhaven Shire Council* (Tianjara Falls, Hamden Bridge); *Richard I'Anson* (Fitzroy Falls, Kangaroo Valley, Lake Jindabyne); *Ken Stepnell* (Mt Kosciusko); *NSW Travel Centre* (Southern Highlands forest); *Peter McNeill* (Outback desert). **Queensland:** *Trezise Bush Guide Service* and *Ian Brown* photographer (Jowalbinna Bush Camp); *Water Resources Commission* and *Robert Engstrom* (Burdekin Falls Dam); *Jan Scudamore* (Isla Gorge, Bottle trees, Delusion Creek, Blackdown Tableland National Park); *Queensland Tourist and Travel Corporation* (Millaa Millaa Falls, Barron Falls, Blue Ulysses butterfly); *GLADA* (Lawn Hill National Park, Lagoon on Dorunda Station, Prawn trawlers, Einasleigh Gorge, Undara lava tube, Hot springs on Tallaroo Station, Welcome to Burketown, Road train on a Gulf road, *Inland Queensland Tourism Development Association* (Pyramid at Porcupine Gorge, Prairie Hotel, Sunset Lawn Hill National Park); *Townsville Enter-*

Signpost, Windjana Gorge

Cape York river crossing

Walkers on Kallaranga lookout

prise (Charters Towers City Hall, Church in Ravenswood); *National Parks and Wildlife Service* (Donna Cave, Paradise Waterhole, Limestone formations at Chillagoe, Broken River, Eungella National Park); *Tourism Mackay* (Victoria Street Mackay, Blacks Beach Mackay, Pioneer Valley). **Northern Territory:** *Northern Territory Tourist Commission* (Nitmiluk, Roper River, Mataranka Thermal Pool); *Philip Green* (Victoria River Crossing, Escarpment along Victoria River); *Richard I'Anson* (Nourlangie rock art). **Western Australia:** Ian Johnson and Peter Carwardine of the *WA Tourism Commission Library* (Millstream, Yardie Creek Gorge, Northampton, Geraldton, Coalseam National Park, Dongara, Coral Bay beach, Nornalup Inlet, Albany, Hellfire Bay, York Motor Museum, Buckland Homestead, Nanga Pool, Wave Rock, Pinnacles Desert, Western Australian wildflowers, Abbey Church New Norcia, Sturt Desert Pea, Flock of galahs, Freshwater and saltwater crocodiles, Frill-necked lizard, Fruit bat, Traditional Aboriginal dancers, Aboriginal rock paintings, Pentecost River crossing, Kimberley station hands, Kimberley coastline, Mitchell Falls, Lower Manning Gorge, Windjana Gorge, Geikie Gorge); *Jill McIntyre* and the *Norseman Tourist Bureau* (Norseman, Wagin Historical Village); *Peta Halleen* and *Contact Point*, the management of *El Questro Station* and *Bill Bachman* (Wandjina rock paintings, Blue pool at Emma Gorge). **South Australia:** *Eva Niebrzydowski* and *Tourism South Australia* (Wildflowers in the Gawler Ranges, Salt lakes, Thurlga homestead, Ancient rock formations, Gawler sunset, Wiluna Almond Blossom Festival, Fleurieu coast, Goolwa, Murray River). **Victoria:** *Ken Stepnell* (Grampians, Mt Buffalo National Park, Kiewa River, Bogong High Plains, Goldwashing near Omeo, Alpine road); *Rudi Paoletti* (Big Desert); *Richard I'Anson* (Tree ferns, Yarra Valley). **Tasmania:** *Ken Stepnell* (Huon Valley, Huon pine forest, Maria Island); *Department of Parks, Wildlife and Heritage* (South-eastern forest).

EDITORIAL ACKNOWLEDGEMENTS

Project Manager: Janet Bunny. **Editors:** Barbara Whiter, Janice Hockey, Deborah Doyle, Bettina Stevenson. **In-house editor:** Clare Coney. **Design:** George Dale. **Sketch maps:** Bill Farr, Chris Crook. **Cartographic consultants:** Fran Church, Colin Critchell. **Word processing:** Margedd Heliosz. **Typesetting:** Barry Walters, Supertype.

PREFACE

Peter and Kim Wherrett

'Don't you smell it, boys? Don't you smell it? It's Australia.'
TOM ROBERTS (Thomas William Roberts) 1856–1931
(on smelling eucalyptus leaves in Spain).

Australia is a land of stunning images, rich and stark; of vibrant colours – with green, red, blue and brown predominating. Wide, vast and underpopulated, it offers itself for exploration and contemplation.

Of the hundreds of thousands of navigable routes in Australia, a large percentage are little more than bush and outback tracks. Even some major roads severely test the modern family sedan. To see Australia, to really experience its extremes, it is necessary to utilise the strength and high ground-clearance of a four-wheel drive vehicle.

You don't have to travel for days to experience this get-away-from-it-all feeling. Just an hour and a half out of Melbourne it is possible to pick up a track, drive for a further 3 hours and not see another vehicle, while less than 10 kilometres away is a major highway carrying 1000 vehicles a day. Under 2 hours from Brisbane is rainforest so dense it is almost necessary to use headlights.

On the other side of the continent lies the Kimberley region of red gorges and sand-topped mesas. From east to west across Australia you will find vast deserts and glistening winter snowscapes – all available to the four-wheel drive explorer.

The place names on these treks evoke the continent's history as often you will be following the paths of the great explorers. On the Strzelecki Track in South Australia, for instance, you follow some of the route taken by Edward Eyre and then you can join up with Burke and Wills and trek to the Gulf of Carpentaria. On Cape York Peninsula you will overlap Edmund Kennedy's disastrous expedition of 1848 and Ludwig Leichhardt's successful overlander to the Northern Territory.

But in no circumstances ought any four-wheel drive exploration of Australia be undertaken lightly, or without a thorough preparation. The remoteness and climatic extremes can be dangerous. However, these will pose no problems to those who are well prepared, and who exercise common sense.

If you don't own a four-wheel drive, enterprising operators have outback explorer trips available by four-wheel drive coach or four-wheel drive vehicles. If you have your own vehicle but feel a little intimidated – and there is some truth in the safety-in-numbers idea – join a convoy expedition, one of those put together by four-wheel drive clubs, motoring organisations or private operators.

But in our opinion nothing quite compares with seeing Australia as a family. Just you and yours; taking your time to see what you want for as long as you want.

Take time to read through both the shorter capital-city based tours and long treks described in this book. It will be obvious when you look at the routes that you need not plan to travel all of Australia. The short tours are based on a major capital city and there are some that can easily be completed within a day. All the long treks which are part of the 'Around Australia' route are arranged in sections, so it is simple to join and leave at convenient places.

If, however, you do have 6 months or more, this guide can also take you right around our amazing land – the four-wheel drive way. It is possible to circumnavigate Australia today without leaving the bitumen, but that is not what this book is about.

Primarily, we are concerned with driving for pleasure, with sightseeing and experiences, and in providing travel options. Not every bush track in Australia is included, and there are bound to be some you know that are not detailed. We had to draw a limit somewhere, but we have included major excursions, and some diversions, providing enormous diversity of country, scenery and experience.

Most importantly, please note that all the tours and treks in this publication cover existing roads and formed tracks. We strongly advise against bush bashing – making new tracks through virgin country. Please study the Australian Association of Four Wheel Drive Clubs code of ethics in the front of the book and follow it as you drive. Remember that just about all the territory you will cover is in someone's care – make sure you leave it as you found it so that your children and their children will enjoy it too.

Good luck!

PETER AND KIM WHERRETT

BEFORE YOU GO

Use this part of the book to help you get started on your four-wheel drive adventures. We have provided lists of government and other organisations to contact for more detailed information if you need it.

FOUR-WHEEL DRIVING IN AUSTRALIA

FOUR-WHEEL DRIVING IN AUSTRALIA

WHAT IS FOUR-WHEEL DRIVE? There was a time when the description 'four-wheel drive' implied a vehicle designed mainly for rural or military purposes – the Land Rover and the Jeep, for example – capable of handling off-road conditions. Since the mid-1980s this description alone is barely valid. Modern technology and the need for even safer, better-handling cars has made four-wheel drive an increasingly commonplace feature in passenger cars not designed to leave the bitumen.

The technological advantage of four-wheel, or all-wheel, drive is simply that driving all the wheels provides better traction in all conditions but, most importantly, on road surfaces that are wet or greasy and therefore slippery.

Today, the essential differences between an all-wheel drive passenger saloon and a vehicle capable of tackling Australia's outback are the latter's mix of rugged construction, high ground clearance, large, lug-style tyres and, of course, a transmission transfer case that provides a low-range gearbox for crawling over and through difficult terrain.

If adventure is where your heart lies, remember the hazards of Australian motoring earlier this century: it is easy to emulate these journeys in today's cars. Murray Aunger and H.H. Dutton, for instance, made the first serious motorised crossing of Australia in 1908 travelling from south to north – Adelaide to Darwin. They had attempted it the year before but their Talbot became bogged in the Northern Territory. Returning with a more powerful Talbot, they found and retrieved the first car and successfully arrived in Darwin after 40 days on the track. Today you could do this trip in an easy 3 days.

Not all vehicles capable of off-road performance are permanently locked into four-wheel drive mode. Most require the engagement of the front hubs before the four-wheel drive transmission is effective. Some do this automatically as soon as four-wheel drive is selected at the gearbox but others require manual selection. With the vast range of four-wheel drive vehicles now available, you should choose the one best suited to your needs very carefully. Read the advice in 'Choosing your Vehicle' before committing yourself.

HANDLING YOUR FOUR-WHEEL DRIVE Let's be clear about four-wheel drive vehicles. They are *not* indestructible or unbreakable, nor will they go anywhere. They need to be maintained properly and demand considerate, realistic driving, especially when using them in difficult terrain.

Learning to use a winch

Vehicle setup and preparation are keys to successful outback touring, but driver confidence is as important, and that can be gained by taking an appropriate four-wheel driving advanced course before setting out anywhere. Having a licence to drive a car and several years' experience does not mean that the intricacies of four-wheel driving will come easily. Far better to bog your new vehicle in company of other

FOUR-WHEEL DRIVING IN AUSTRALIA

learners on a course near to home than to be on your own in the outback having a similar learning experience!

If you haven't time to get to a hands-on course, there are videos available from car manufacturers. They include *Getting Through* by Toyota, *4WD to Adventure* by Mitsubishi (with a handbook for the glovebox) and a similar product from Range Rover. The Forestry Commission of New South Wales has produced an easy-to-understand booklet, *The Glovebox Guide to 4-Wheel Driving* by Bernard R. Kestel, available from the Forestry Commission of NSW, Locked Bag 23, Pennant Hills NSW 2120.

Private individuals and four-wheel drive magazines also have produced videos to help drivers. *Four Wheel Driving – the Right Way*, presented by Grahame Maxwell, aims to talk the novice four-wheel driver through hazardous driving situations. It covers many techniques including water crossings, hill climbs, negotiating mud and sand and recovery equipment. Telephone Cape Enterprises Pty Ltd toll free

(008) 81 0030 for details. *4x4 Australia* magazine has produced its own video with similar information, from GPO Box 628E, Melbourne 3001. It has been endorsed by the Victoria Association of Four Wheel Drive Clubs – another source of hands-on experience as the association also runs driving training programmes.

Another easy way to learn is to buy the information-packed monthly or quarterly four-wheel driving magazines. Feature articles are included from time to time on basic four-wheel driving skills and techniques for getting out of trouble, and they are loaded with information covering access, touring, road tests, towing hints and tests, camping gear and accessories for the vehicle.

However, there really is nothing like getting out and doing, so do consider a day or weekend course. State by state we've listed motoring organisations, private driver training companies and individuals as well as appropriate associations of four-wheel drive clubs which run driver-education courses.

FOUR-WHEEL DRIVE COURSES

NSW and ACT
Australian National Four Wheel
   Drive Council, (Head Office)
PO Box 79, Canberra 2601

Four Wheel Drive Club Association of NSW and ACT
PO Box 3870, Sydney 2000

4WD Off Road Driver Training
Lot 5, Cherry Tree Close, Moss Vale
NSW 2577, (048) 69 1235

Dynamic Safety
17 Central Park Drive, Bow Bowing
NSW 2577, (048) 69 1235

New South Wales Traffic
Education Centre
Mann Street East, Armidale
NSW 2350, (067) 72 8688

Northern Territory
Northern Territory Four Wheel
   Drive Club Association
PO Box 37476, Winnellie NT 5789

South Australia
South Australian Association of
   Four Wheel Drive Clubs
PO Box 178, Blair Athol SA 5084

Western Australia
Western Australia Association of
   Four Wheel Drive Clubs
PO Box 6029, East Perth WA 6004

Royal Automobile Club of
   Western Australia Inc. (RAC)
228 Adelaide Terrace, Perth 6000

Queensland
Jan Scudamore
Queensland Association of Four Wheel
   Drive Clubs Inc.
PO Box 174, Brisbane Markets
QLD 4106, (07) 379 9129

Victoria
Peter Greenham
Victoria Association of Four
   Wheel Drive Clubs Inc.
PO Box 401C, Melbourne 3001
(03) 872 4610

Metropolitan Traffic Education
   Centre (METEC)
PO Box 231, Ringwood
VIC 3134, (03) 725 4758

Jim Murcott's Advanced Driving
   Centre
41–43 Miles Street, Mulgrave
VIC 3170, (03) 562 0400

DECA Four-Wheel
   Drive Courses
PO Box 1034, Shepparton
VIC 3630, (058) 21 1099

Cape Enterprises
PO Box 169, Wodonga VIC 3690
(008) 81 0030

Tasmania
Tasmanian Recreational
   Vehicles Association
22 Elliott Road
Glenorchy TAS 7010

RAC Tasmania Driving School
Cnr Patrick and Murray Streets
Hobart TAS 7000, (002) 38 2299

PLANNING AHEAD

PREPARATION AND PLANNING It sounds easy: decide on a destination and just go. However, by being impulsive some of the enjoyment of a tour, as well as time to iron out any problems, will be missed – we're talking about the planning stage. For a long trek, planning will begin months before the trip itself: maps and brochures will be spread out, destinations marked, lists made, full of possibilities.

The shorter tours in this book, all based on capital cities, need less planning. However, the principles of four-wheel drive touring remain the same, and the first consideration is the condition of the road or track you want to use. Obviously there is no point planning a trip on a road under metres of snow – or water – or recently ravaged by bushfire.

Even if your aim is to turn straight to the treks around Australia, you need to know that what you want to achieve is possible. *Read the trip notes carefully.* Estimate the journey, short or long, on a large map of Australia, or use our road maps. Taking into consideration the degree of difficulty and the distances to be travelled, estimate an average speed and check that each section of the trip is possible within a realistic time frame – for you. Being pushed for time over distance could mean inappropriate speeding and possible trouble.

Join your state motoring body and obtain relevant numbers for interstate affiliates in case of emergency breakdowns. Members have reciprocal rights with interstate organisations around Australia.

Supplement our route directions by using the following contacts to obtain up-to-date background information about the chosen trip and state: tourist bureau, motoring organisation and four-wheel drive association are detailed. Bear in mind that there are regional tourist offices, as well as local, more specialised four-wheel drive clubs, so ask for the specific information you require when contacting central office.

PERMITS AND REGULATIONS Keep in mind as you travel that even the most desolate-looking land is under someone's care. This may mean that permits and/or permissions need to be obtained before you can camp or fish.

If you plan to stay in or travel through national or state park areas check our introductions to the trip notes as well as with the controlling body in question. General rules, regulations and restrictions apply within these parks covering four-wheel drive access, camping, water, wood collection, fires, pets, hunting and fishing.

Equally, if you plan on trekking across designated Abo-

Camp setup with all comforts

Mosquito-netted swag

riginal Land you *must* obtain permission. In Queensland, notification of a route, time of travel and preferred campsite to the appropriate local Aboriginal council as you travel is all that is required; but Aboriginal councils in other states issue a permit for a specific journey. It is best to telephone before taking to the road to find out exact requirements for these states. Permits can take up to 6 weeks to process, so pre-planning here will prevent frustration or disappointment.

The following list contains the addresses of the national parks' controlling body in each state; ask for specific regional information if you already know where you would like to go. Also listed are the contacts for Aboriginal Land permits where relevant.

WHEN TO GO? Weather conditions (if making a short tour out of a capital city) or the seasons (if you are setting out on a longer trek) are the next consideration. For example, Australia's north should not be attempted in the wet season (November – May). Remember too that heavy rain will raise creek and stream levels and may render them impassable; snow in highland areas makes roads and

TOURING INFORMATION

Tourist Bureau

Australian Capital Territory
ACT Tourism Commission
Northbourne Avenue
Dickson ACT 2602
(06) 249 7577

New South Wales
New South Wales Travel Centre
19 Castlereagh Street
Sydney 2000
(02) 231 4444

Queensland
Queensland Government
  Travel Centre
196 Adelaide Street
Brisbane 4000, (07) 221 6111

Northern Territory
NT Tourist Commission
(008) 80 8244 (reservations)
CATIA (Alice Springs)
(089) 52 5199 (information)

Western Australia
WA Tourist Centre
Cnr Forrest Place and
  Wellington Street
Perth 6000, (09) 483 1111

South Australia
Tourism SA Travel Centre,
1 King William St
Adelaide 5000
(08) 212 1505, (008) 822 092

Victoria
Victorian Travel Centre
230 Collins Street
Melbourne 3000
(03) 650 1522

Tasmania
Tasmanian Travel Centre
Elizabeth Street
Hobart 7000
(002) 30 8250

Motoring Organisation

National Roads and Motorists'
  Association (NRMA)
92 Northbourne Avenue
Braddon ACT 2601
(06) 243 8805

National Roads and Motorists'
  Association (NRMA)
151 Clarence Street
Sydney 2000
(02) 260 9222

Royal Automobile Club
  of Queensland (RACQ)
300 St Pauls Terrace
Brisbane 4000
(07) 361 2444

Automobile Association of
  Northern Territory Inc. (AANT)
79–81 Smith Street
Darwin 0800
(089) 81 3837

Royal Automobile Club of Western
  Australia Inc. (RAC)
228 Adelaide Terrace
Perth 6000
(09) 421 4444

Royal Automobile Association of
  South Australia Inc. (RAA)
41 Hindmarsh Square
Adelaide 5000
(08) 223 4555

Royal Automobile Club
  of Victoria (RACV)
422 Little Collins Street
Melbourne 3000
(03) 790 2211

Royal Automobile Club
  of Tasmania (RACT)
Cnr Patrick and Murray Streets
Hobart 7000, (002) 38 2200

Four-Wheel Drive Association

Four Wheel Drive Clubs Association of
  New South Wales and Australian
  Capital Territory
GPO Box 3870
Sydney 2001

Four Wheel Drive Clubs Association
  of New South Wales and
  Australian Capital Territory
GPO Box 3870
Sydney 2001

Queensland Association of
  Four Wheel Drive Clubs Inc.
PO Box 174
Brisbane Markets
QLD 4106

Northern Territory Association of
  Four Wheel Driving
PO Box 37476
Winnellie NT 0821

Western Australia Association of
  Four Wheel Drive Clubs
PO Box 6029
East Perth WA 6004

South Australian Association of
  Four Wheel Drive Clubs
GPO Box 178
Blair Athol SA 5084

Victoria Association of
  Four Wheel Drive Clubs Inc.
552 Whitehorse Road
Mitcham VIC 3132
(03) 872 4610

Tasmanian Recreational
  Vehicles Association
22 Elliott Road
Glenorchy TAS 7010

tracks unsuitable; and very hot weather gives a good reason to bypass the deserts. You must take weather and seasons into account when planning.

Local media provide precise forecasts, often up to 4 days in advance. However, you can phone recorded information services for weather checks outside your area. The weather on a trip of any length will help you decided what you must take. Cold weather requires more gear than warm weather, as bulky sleeping bags and extra clothing are needed. This must *not* mean that recovery gear is jettisoned.

WHAT TO SEE? This is an absolutely personal piece of planning, to be linked with the where and when to go, as well as who is travelling with you. Set your trip limits (not necessarily distance, but what the journey will entail in time and anticipated enjoyment) to fit your available time and money: there is no point in deciding it's Melbourne to Cape York and back in three weeks.

Another consideration is what you may find happening along your route. Depending upon your interests, your local contacts may give information about shows, events and competitions in your area of enjoyment. However, most towns and regions throughout Australia hold sporting competitions, regattas and rodeos, arts and craft and trade exhibitions, agricultural and flower shows, music festivals and such events annually. Details are available from tourism outlets in each state. Refer back to the beginning of this chapter and write to or telephone the tourist office of your destination state as well as check through the trip notes of the journey you plan on taking, to ask for advice to be forwarded about what there is to see on the way and nearby, both natural and manmade attractions.

MAPS AND NAVIGATION Maps and guides are an essential part of four-wheel drive touring. Pack them so that they are easily accessible during a driving day in a waterproof, preferably clear plastic cover, with pencil, notebook, ruler and possibly a pocket calculator.

In the routes we refer to the road maps at the end of this book, and our simple sketch maps will get you to the start and end points of trips. However, you should supplement these with the suggested local guides and, most importantly, topographic maps. We have listed national parks' office addresses – they will help with specific maps and information for parks under their control. Tourism offices will usually post brochures and touring maps on request. Check that information is current – the date it is printed – and this applies to maps also. Don't discount general stores, newsagents and pubs as sources of up-to-date information when you are travelling through an area. Four-wheel drive tracks are notoriously subject to change.

Topographic maps, which show largely unchanging geographic features, are helpful navigation aids. We strongly recommend them for outback and remote areas

NATIONAL PARKS

Head Office
Australian Capital Territory
Australian National Parks and
   Wildlife Service
GPO Box 636, Canberra 2601
(06) 250 0200

New South Wales
National Parks and Wildlife
   Service
43 Bridge Street
Hurstville NSW 2220
(02) 585 6333

Queensland
National Parks and Wildlife
   Service
160 Ann Street
Brisbane QLD 4000
(07) 227 8185

Northern Territory
Australian National Parks and
   Wildlife Service
5th floor, MLC Building, Smith
   Street, Darwin 0801
(089) 81 5299

Conservation Commission of NT
Gaymark Building
Palmerston NT 0831
(089) 89 4411

Kakadu National Park
PO Box 71, Jabiru NT 0886
(089) 79 2101

Uluru (Ayers Rock–Mt Olga)
   National Park
PO Box 119, Yulara NT 0872
(089) 65 2299

Western Australia
Department of Conservation
   and Land Management
   (CALM)
50 Hayman Road
Como WA 6152
(09) 367 0333

South Australia
National Parks and Wildlife
   Service
55 Grenfell Street
Adelaide 5000, (08) 207 2000

Tasmania
Department of Parks, Wildlife
   and Heritage
134 Macquarie Street
Hobart 7000, (002) 33 8011

– the larger the scale the better. Australia is now covered by the Auslig 1:250 000 and 1:100 000 series, in printed maps and compilation sheets, and there is an excellent index sheet showing the areas covered by each map. State mapping authorities also publish maps on a larger scale which are useful for the shorter tours and will add to your fun by pointing up physical features. *Australian Geographic* magazine produces excellent maps available through retail outlets. For enquiries write to P.O. Box 321, Terry Hills, NSW 2084.

Spend some time reading and interpreting the information on your maps before you venture into a remote area like the Simpson Desert, or even onto a winding forest track closer to home. Note both natural features, such as hills, mountains, rivers, forests, and also constructed landmarks such as roads, towns and railways crossings. Also, by understanding contours, which show the shape of the ground, you will be able to read your topographic maps and understand the immediate landscape much better. You should also be able to read grid references in case you need to let others know where you are. Topographic maps have directions for plotting a point on the margin. We strongly recommend you invest in an inexpensive guide like Gregory's *Four Wheel Drive Handbook*, for detailed instructions on map reading before setting out.

If you have around $2000, you can purchase your own personal, hand-held navigation tool to determine the latitude, longitude and altitude of wherever you are. It utilises the Global Positioning System, a 24-satellite system encircling the earth. Signals from the four nearest satellites help to determine your position. The tiny instrument fits comfortably in the palm of a hand and it doesn't need fitting; the antenna however should be mounted on the car roof. There is a 12-volt power supply included, and there are now several brands available. Enquire at electrical retailers and communications specialists.

A TRIAL RUN Although it is exciting to plan a wonderful trip, especially a longer trek, the journey will entail a complete lifestyle change. Let's face it, a four-wheel drive home for an extended time means compromise, so how much compromise? How does it all fit together?

If you are not yet committed to a vehicle, consider renting a vehicle similar to that which you are considering buying. You will never be able to set it up, prepare it and be as certain of its maintenance as you would be with your own vehicle, but it is an ideal stepping stone into the experience of four-wheel driving and to understanding the needs of your travelling companions.

A trial short tour for, say, a weekend before setting out on anything longer, is certain to sort out many queries, including whether you will be tenting the whole way, taking a trailer/camper or even a full-sized caravan with you. See the section on towing for more discussion about these options.

TRAVELLING WITH CHILDREN Children, whether infants, toddlers or school-age, need special consideration. If it is to be a long trek, schooling must be weighed

ABORIGINAL LAND AUTHORITIES

Aboriginal Land Councils
NORTHERN TERRITORY
Alice Springs and Tennant
  Creek regions
Central Land Council
33 Stuart Highway
(PO Box 3321)
Alice Springs NT 0871
(089) 52 3800

Melville and Bathurst Islands
Tiwi Land Council
Nguiu, Bathurst Island
via Darwin 0822
(089) 78 3957; or Darwin office
(089) 41 0224

Darwin, Nhulunbuy and
  Katherine regions
Northern Land Council
9 Rowling Street
(PO Box 42921)
Casuarina NT 0810
(089) 81 7011

Aboriginal Affairs
WESTERN AUSTRALIA
Aboriginal Affairs Planning
  Authority
PO Box 628
West Perth WA 6005
(09) 483 1222

Tribal Councils
SOUTH AUSTRALIA
Pitjanjatjara Tribal Council
PO Box 2584
Alice Springs NT 0871
(089) 50 5411
(for Pitjanjatjara Land within South Australia, Western Australia and Northern Territory)

Maralinga Tjarutja Tribal
  Council
PO Box 435
Ceduna SA 5690
(086) 25 2946

up. For primary school children the first step is to talk to the child's teacher and principal, who may well advise that each child make a daily journal of the trip. Into a scrapbook will go weather reports, admission tickets, pressed flowers, photos, postcards or drawings plus a little description of the day's events. Be careful not to edit, it needs to be the child's experiences.

For older children, further discussion may be needed regarding correspondence schooling or taking along work.

Most children are good travellers, and consider every trip an adventure. Remember that this will be a highlight of your child's life. They will be overexcited and, as the long car trips add up, could get bored. Again, planning will save the day by easing the strain on all.

Before setting out make a list of dos and don'ts for the children and explain seriously why their cooperation is necessary. Make it quite clear that these are safety issues and you expect them to observe the rules at all times. Reinforce this message at the time of departure. Your list will be your own, but here are a few points to get the ball rolling.

▶ *Do not* fight or yell loudly while the car is moving as it distracts the driver. This could cause a collision and bring the holiday to an abrupt end.
▶ *Do not* play with door handles or locks. (Set childproof locks on rear doors before departure.)
▶ *Do not* lean out of windows – ever. Head, hands and arms are to be kept inside the car.
▶ *Do not* unbuckle seat belts or restraints while the car is in motion.

Although your main concern will be to keep the children happy during the car trip, it is also important to take along some games, such as Snakes and Ladders, Monopoly, Pictionary or Scrabble and a pack or two of cards, to keep everyone amused around the camp fire, in the tent or caravan.

Older children may work on their diaries and younger ones will love a rubber ball and skipping rope to play outdoors without annoying everyone else in the campsite!

PETS Four-legged friends need to be found a reliable, comfortable home-away-from-home while you are travelling. That is, unless you are prepared to be turned away from a large percentage of caravan parks and national parks. Dogs and cats chase native birds and wildlife. Check with friends for good kennels and catteries and take time to visit the shortlist to check the facilities: then book your pet in for the holiday of their life.

HOBBIES If you are making a once-in-a-lifetime trip you will probably carry a camera, even if you've never touched one before, because you will want to record the highlights. Ensure you know how your new – or underused – camera works, keep the instructions close by and take a test film *before* you set out.

Weather and light conditions vary, so carry films with a range of speeds. Your local dealer will advise on the varieties available. Stock up on film, batteries, a lens brush, flash holder and spare bulbs if required. Other useful accessories include a close-up lens, exposure meter, lens hood and filters.

Safeguard this equipment in a camera bag. In a hot closed car, keep the camera in the shade. High temperatures and humidity can damage colour film, so keep it in the

BUREAU OF METEOROLOGY RECORDED INFORMATION SERVICES

Australia-wide	**Telephone**		**In Perth:**	metropolitan	1196
Interstate cities	0055 33221			south-west	1195
Three-month outlook	0055 33551			north-west	11698
				boating	11541
In Canberra: metropolitan	1196			WA severe weather	11542
In Sydney: metropolitan	0055 19800		**In Adelaide:**	metropolitan	1196
coastal	0055 29111			boating	11541
country	0055 29321				
			In Melbourne:	metropolitan	0055 19800
In Brisbane: south-east Queensland	1196			state bays/coast . . .	0055 15111
warnings	1190			Victorian cities . . .	0055 15321
boating	1182				
			In Hobart:	metropolitan	1196
In Darwin: forecasts/warnings	82 4726			boating	11541
cyclone information	11542				

coolest possible place, and once the film is used *get it processed quickly.*

If you are a painter, don't take oils as they take so long to dry and collect dust. Use acrylics, watercolours, inks, pencil or charcoal instead. Canvasses take lots of space, so try canvas board or drawing paper in blocks, including different shapes and sizes of paper wrapped in large plastic

bags and/or a cardboard folder to keep them flat and as dustfree as possible.

There are many opportunities for keen anglers to enjoy great sport on our trips. Remember if you are intending to fish in Victoria or Tasmania you need to obtain an inland fishing licence. Contact: Department of Conservation and Environment, 240 Victoria Parade, East Melbourne VIC

SPECIALITY MAP SHOPS: Government

Australian Capital Territory
Australian Surveying and Land
  Information Group (AUSLIG)
Head Office
Scrivenor Building, Dunlop Court
Bruce ACT 2617
(PO Box 2 Belconnen ACT 2616)
(06) 201 4300, (008) 800 173 (enquiries)

New South Wales
Department of Lands
  Central Mapping Authority
Panorama Avenue
Bathurst NSW 2795
(063) 31 5344, (063) 32 8200

Department of Lands Central
  Mapping Authority
23–33 Bridge Street
Sydney 2000
(02) 228 6111

Queensland
Lands Department
Sunmap Centre
Cnr Main and Vulture Streets
Woolloongabba QLD 4102
(07) 896 3333

Department of Primary Industries
Queensland Forestry Service
160 Mary Street, Brisbane 4000
(07) 234 0184

Sunmap Centre
State Government Building
Adelaide Street (Anzac Square)
Brisbane 4000
(07) 227 6892

Sunmap Centre
South Coast Region
108 George Street
Beenleigh QLD 4207
(07) 807 4045

Northern Territory
Department of Lands and Housing
Moonta House, 43 Mitchell Street
Darwin 0800
(089) 89 7032

Department of Lands and Housing
Sturt House, Linton Street
Casuarina NT 0810
(089) 89 8440

Northern Territory
  Government Centre
5 First Street, Katherine NT 0850
(089) 73 8940

Northern Territory
Government Centre
99 Patterson Street
Tennant Creek NT 0860
(089) 62 2405

Northern Territory
  Government Centre
AFT Building
21 Gregory Terrace
Alice Springs NT 0870
(089) 51 5746

Conservation Commission of the
  Northern Territory
Head Office
Palmerston NT 0830
(089) 89 5511

Western Australia
Department of Land
  Administration (DOLA)
Mapping and Survey Division
Central Map Agency
Central Government Building
Cathedral Avenue
Perth 6000
(09) 323 1370

South Australia
Department of Lands
Land Information
Bureau Mapland
12 Pirie Street
Adelaide 5000
(08) 226 3895, (08) 226 3905

Victoria
AUSLIG
Dandenong Office
280 Thomas Street
Dandenong VIC 3175
(03) 794 4500

Department of Conservation
  and Environment
240 Victoria Parade
East Melbourne VIC 3004
(03) 412 4011

Tasmania
Department of Environment
  and Planning
Mapping Division
Tasmap Sales Centre
134 Macquarie Street
Hobart 7000
(002) 33 8011

PLANNING AHEAD

3002; tel. (03) 412 4011 or Department of Primary Industry, Inland Fisheries Commission, 127 Davey Street, Hobart 7000; tel. (002) 23 6622. In any other state you must enquire locally about season and bag limitations before you throw that line in. The same sources will probably give you a hint about where they're biting too!

Other hobbies, such as bushwalking, gem and mineral fossicking, birdwatching and all water sports, need careful consideration about space and care for necessary equipment as well.

HOW WILL YOU TRAVEL? Most travellers swear by the travel slowly, see more and listen better motto. It stands to reason that if you are travelling more slowly your vehicle will consume less fuel, running costs and repairs will be kept to a minimum and you will see more. It usually means too, that you are not keeping strictly to an itinerary and can divert to that wonderful bush camp you were told about at the roadhouse where you found the cheapest fuel for kilometres; certainly it makes for more relaxing travel.

SPECIALITY MAP SHOPS: Retail

New South Wales
Rex Map Centre
Prudential Arcade
Cnr Castlereagh Street
  and Martin Place
Sydney 2000
(02) 235 3017

Rex Map Centre
868a Princes Highway
Tempe NSW 2044
(02) 559 1665

Rex Map Centre
246 Pacific Highway
Crows Nest NSW 2065
(02) 906 5233

Rex Map Centre
128 Parramatta Road
Granville NSW 2142
(02) 637 9763

The Travel Bookshop
20 Bridge Street, Sydney 2000
(02) 241 3554

Queensland
Jacaranda Cartographic
33 Park Road, Milton QLD 4064
(07) 369 9755

The Map Shop
1 Manning Street
Sth Brisbane QLD 4101
(07) 844 1051

Hema Maps Pty Ltd
239 George Street
Brisbane 4000
(07) 221 4330

Northern Territory
The Northern Territory General Store
42 Cavenagh Street, Darwin 0800
(089) 81 8242

Western Australia
The Map Shop
38a Walters Drive
Osborne Park WA 6017
(09) 244 2488

Perth Map Centre
891 Hay Street, Perth 6000
(09) 322 5733

South Australia
Adelaide Booksellers
6a Rundle Mall
Adelaide 5000
(08) 410 0216

The Map Shop
16a Peel Street
Adelaide 5000
(08) 231 2033

Victoria
Melbourne Map Centre
740 Waverley Road
Chadstone VIC 3148
(03) 569 5472

A-Roving Travel Things
Level 2, The Promenade
279 Toorak Road
South Yarra VIC 3141
(03) 824 1714

Bowyangs
372 Little Bourke Street
Melbourne 3000
(03) 670 4383

The Map Shop
318 Little Bourke Street
Melbourne 3000
(03) 651 4130

Bowyangs
259 High Street, Kew VIC 3101
(03) 862 3526

Wilderness Shop Pty Ltd
1 Carrington Road
Box Hill VIC 3128
(03) 890 0710

Tasmania
Map Supplies
27 Pearl Place, Blackmans Bay
TAS 7052
(002) 29 2784

J Walch & Sons
130 Macquarie Street
Hobart 7000
(002) 23 3444

INSURANCE AND FINANCES Finally but certainly not least important, we're going to talk about personal finances and insurance.

The days of needing to carry wads of cash are gone. However, remember that automatic teller machines are only found in larger centres. If you can, try to use a credit card, such as Bankcard, Mastercard or Visa, for all fuel purchases to give you a record of your spending on this one large, unavoidable item. Arrange to have your credit card bill paid while you are away, either by automatic deductions from your account or by someone on your behalf. Try not to spend to your limit every month, so you have an emergency reserve. (Or keep 2 cards – one for fuel purchases only and one for emergencies.)

In plenty of time before travelling (that means weeks, not the day before you leave), talk to your bank about how to get cash in remote areas. A Commonwealth Bank savings account is useful because it can be operated at post offices around Australia.

Check every clause in your home and contents insurance well before you leave, especially if the house is to be left vacant, or rented. And while on the paper work, you should also look at vehicle, caravan, or trailer insurance and possibly travel insurance.

For queries about insurance, telephone or visit the local office of the Insurance Council of Australia in the capital cities of all states and listed in the White Pages.

Don't take shortcuts with insurance. If you check your vehicle

Storage solutions: built-in shelving

and/or home contents insurance and find they don't cover your possessions further than 100 kilometres from home, they are not adequate and you may need travel insurance. With caravan insurance only *some* companies will be able to help – shop around. There are specialist four-wheel drive vehicle insurers; ask your dealer at time of purchase, your state association of four-wheel drive clubs or friends who already run four-wheel drives.

Finally, are you and your family members of your state's ambulance service? By carrying a valid membership card you are entitled to ambulance benefits in all Australian states and territories. Look under Ambulance Service in your capital city's White Pages telephone directory.

HINTS ON TRAVELLING WITH CHILDREN

You know your children best and what keeps them happy, but read on, there may be something here which you've not thought about before.
▶ *To keep children as comfortable as possible, curtains, towels, sunscreen blinds on windows are advisable.*
▶ *Babies and pre-schoolers will need a blanket, bottle or toy to save the day when they are tired or upset.*
▶ *Keep a small bag nearby packed with moist towelettes or a damp facecloth.*
▶ *First-aid kit ought to contain junior paracetamol as well as supplies of any other medication taken by the children.*
▶ *Insect repellent and Factor 15 sun block need to be handy. (Have you thought of taking mosquito nets for everyone, but especially your baby's bassinet at night?)*
▶ *Make up a 'busy box', perhaps in a shoe box, and keep it on the back seat, easily reached. Include small notepads, activity books, crayons, pencils, sharpener, or washable felt-tipped pens.*

▶ *Try breakfast trays, or if not enough room, clipboards, for colouring-in supports.*
▶ *Favourite storybooks need a place of their own.*
▶ *Even if your car does have a radio, a cassette with headphones would be good for the back-seat passengers. Tapes of children's stories and songs soothe overtired children.*
▶ *Stop every hour or so, for young children to let off steam and go to the toilet.*
▶ *If they feel sick, stop as soon as possible and let them out for some fresh air. Persuade them to have a sip of water before continuing.*
▶ *Even though there will be set mealtimes, pack some snack food and drinks in the children's own lunchboxes. Cartons of drinks with straws are easy to handle while in a moving car.*
▶ *Take a supply of car-sized rubbish bags for the inevitable mess.*

SELECTING YOUR VEHICLE

THE CHOICE Once the decision has been taken to buy a four-wheel drive vehicle, the process is not very different from buying any car for private use.

There are certain clear-cut factors to be considered. The first consideration, of course, will be cost. Any current copy of the major specialist four-wheel drive magazines will include a price list, so select possible vehicles within your budget. Bear in mind you should set aside some of the budget for 'extras'. You may need to equip your vehicle for special purposes, so be aware that it is not difficult to spend $10–15 000 on such extras. Check the following chapter for more detailed information on such equipment.

Don't forget registration and insurance costs and, for Victorian purchasers, from 1 January 1992 there has been an annual fee of $40 payable to VicRoads for four-wheel drive vehicles in addition to the normal annual registration fee. There are exemptions for concession cardholders and those engaged in primary production. Enquiries to VicRoads on (03) 345 6811.

After price, size is the next consideration. How many people will travel in the vehicle? How much gear will you need to carry with you? Do you want to tow a trailer, camper or caravan?

Then there is the question of usage. Some people will be buying a four-wheel drive as a mixed workhorse and passenger vehicle; others just for occasional short jaunts into four-wheel drive country; yet others will have in mind the grand circular tour, maybe a long-service leave or retirement trek around the real Australia.

Other considerations include the choice of manual or automatic transmission, automatic or manual hub locking, diesel or petrol.

TRANSMISSIONS Almost all four-wheel drive vehicles offer the option of three- or four-speed automatics or five-speed manuals. If the vehicle is to be often used in rugged outback-style conditions it is better to choose a manual, because it has a wider selection of gears, and therefore a more appropriate set of gear ratios. It is also better for the driver to be making the gear selection rather than allowing the vehicle to do so. If, on the other hand, the vehicle will mainly be used on bitumen with only occasional sojourns into rough country, automatic transmission will be perfectly OK.

HUB LOCKING Automatic hub locking is not available, yet, on all four-wheel drives but is becoming more common. If there is no automatic locking it will be necessary to get out of the vehicle to lock in the hubs before engaging four-wheel drive.

DIESEL OR PETROL New diesel-engined vehicles are more expensive to buy than petrol ones but use less fuel and generally enjoy a longer life. On the other hand, injector maintenance is important and dirty fuel can play havoc. If you intend going through water crossings and want a diesel engine, ensure there is a snorkel fitted to the air intake. Petrol and water don't mix well, but diesel and water mean *real* trouble with major mechanical failure.

Electronically controlled, efficient, turbo-charged diesel engines are becoming a sound choice for the new buyer. However, petrol engines usually respond faster to the throttle and provide livelier performance. Long-distance operators tend to prefer diesels but this is not necessarily a recommendation. Availability of fuels other than super was once a real worry on long outback trips. These days, however, both unleaded and super petrol, diesel and the newest cost-saver, auto gas, are all fairly well represented at bowsers except in extremely remote areas. Many travellers with petrol engines have spent up to $2000 to have their vehicles converted to enable both petrol and auto gas to be used, reporting considerable savings on long trips.

BODY OPTIONS Most four-wheel drives can be classified under the short-wheelbase or long-wheelbase category as only one or two manufacturers actually have medium-sized vehicles; the long wheelbase wagons are preferred by most families and, in fact, most travellers, because of the extra space involved.

Short and long wheelbases are defined from the length between each axle. With the long wheelbase models there are usually 4 doors seating at least 4 adults, plus storage space, while the shorter wheelbases usually only have the small passenger cab (plenty for 2 on short trips) plus storage. It could well be practical for long-haul touring with just 2 people to choose the long-wheelbase model and fold down the rear seats to provide extra storage and sleeping space.

The smaller vehicles, such as Suzuki Sierra and Vitara, Daihatsu Feroza and Lada Niva, are best suited to short tours. Not that they can't handle the long stuff, but they provide less overall comfort and have smaller fuel tanks, reducing the range between fuel stops. This can be a problem when there are not filling stations on every corner.

SEVEN SEATS.

TWO OPTIONS.

Every Ford Raider comes equipped with two options you don't often find together in a family wagon.

City and country. On-road or off. Work or play.

During the week, it's a seven seat people mover. With the creature comforts you'd expect in a passenger car.

Luxuries like power windows, electric sunroof, central locking, and a premium sound system.

It's easy to park, thanks to power steering.

And the secure feeling you get from riding higher than the traffic, makes Raider a comforting car to drive around town.

On the weekends, that's a different story. You can

Automatic or manual transmissions available.

shift into four-wheel drive without getting out of the driver's seat. Which makes it easier to get into the bush or out of trouble.

And Raider's powerful 2.6 litre EFI engine makes for effortless and economical cruising on the open road.

Phone 008 035 666 for more information on Ford Raider, or see your local Ford Dealer for a test drive. When you see the kind of deal he can give you on a Ford Raider . . . well, you might decide that other cars aren't really an option at all.

HAVE YOU DRIVEN A FORD...LATELY?

BEFORE YOU GO
SELECTING YOUR VEHICLE

Outside the Birdsville Hotel

Camping with a trailer

The mid-range vehicles, for example the Toyota Fore-runner, Nissan Navara, Mitsubishi Pajero and Holden Jackeroo, will take you anywhere, anytime in more than adequate comfort and style. Even more spacious and comfortable are the full-size long-wheelbase wagons, such as the Ford Raider, Nissan Patrol, Toyota Land Cruiser and the Range Rover.

It is also possible to mix a real workhorse utility with a good-sized passenger cab by selecting a Toyota Hi Lux, Nissan Navara, Ford Courier, Mitsubishi Triton or similar.

More expensive is not necessarily better in terms of performance when it comes to four-wheel drives. In a few cases the extra money spent is buying luxury. If you can afford it, well and good, but outback travelling causes heavy wear and tear on expensive finishes. You can, however, get plenty of serious four-wheel driving in for under $50 000 and still have the right mix of comfort and performance. You might even be able to do it for considerably less if you buy a used vehicle.

BUYING SECONDHAND Secondhand buying is worth considering as you can save yourself up to $30 000, against a similar new vehicle. Up to 30 per cent of all privately owned four-wheel drive vehicles spend little or no time actually off the bitumen. Such a vehicle may make an excellent buy for someone who wants to tour. However, buying any used vehicle can be fraught with danger, and you will need to be careful.

Remember, city-owned four-wheel drives are usually better buys than those from country centres because they are less likely to have been off the road. Another fair guide to usage is what has been fitted to the vehicle as extras and accessories. People don't usually fit bull-bars, driving lights and winches to drive around the city. However, if such accessories are fitted and the vehicle is in good overall condition, having them already installed will also save you money.

Your potential vehicle should have under 100 000 kilometres on the clock, should have no rust anywhere, should feel tight to drive and perform well. The under-body should be free from dings in sumps and floorpan which might have been caused by rocks. Both ranges of the transmission should be tried during the road test which, of course, is compulsory. (This means you need to find a gravel road to test four-wheel drive as it should not be used on bitumen.) If you have little mechanical knowledge, take a friend along who does. If you belong to one of the motoring clubs – RACV, NRMA for instance – it will pay to have them carry out an inspection for you.

In our opinion, private sales are better than dealer sales because private owners are less likely to know how to cover up wear and tear and damage. Although with a private buy there are no warranties, in some states in some circumstances there are no warranties with a dealer either. Check on what you are entitled to; this legislation is usually administered by the Department of Consumer Affairs; you will find addresses in the White Pages of the telephone directory.

TRY BEFORE YOU BUY – ANYTHING If you have never owned or driven a four-wheel drive before and you are still not absolutely sure it's the vehicle for you, hire a vehicle and do one, or some, of the capital-city based tours in this book to establish some good driving experience.

SETTING UP: ACCESSORIES AND EQUIPMENT

SETTING UP: ACCESSORIES AND EQUIPMENT

The Maverick set up to go

VEHICLE PREPARATION For all four-wheel drive trips your vehicle will require some preparation, more for the longer journeys than the short. Let's assume your vehicle is new or has never been on a serious bush track. (If your vehicle is set up for bush touring you may compare what is suggested here with has been done.)

BODY There is no real *need* to change anything on the body provided by the maker except that you may want to protect certain areas from damage. The bullbar is the most popular accessory in this regard. It acts as a mounting place for extra lights (long-range or fog), for a power winch and for aerials for citizen band and long-range radio and, to a certain extent, it also protects against damage to the front of the vehicle – lights and radiators – in case of contact with an animal or vegetation. However, a bullbar does not make the front of the vehicle invulnerable and a substantial front-end hit may well cause more damage with a bullbar than without. It also adds weight over the front springs which may require up-rating to cope.

Front: bullbar (aluminium); snorkel; high-frequency radio; automatic tuning whip antenna; winch control box and cable; headlamp protectors; car-top tent

Bullbars are made in steel or aluminium. Both provide about equal protection. Aluminium costs more but weighs less. If overall weight is important and a bullbar is considered necessary, choose aluminium; remember though that few people in the outback can weld aluminium if your bullbar were to break.

There are other forms of body protection available, up to completely surrounding the vehicle – on sides, rear and top. They all add weight, offer only limited protection and, in my opinion, are not necessary for most outback touring.

MECHANICAL PROTECTION The vehicle will come with some form of underbody protection already fitted. Most have a protection plate for the fuel tank, some have sump guards, some have skid-plates to protect the gearbox and transfer case against rock damage. All are desirable, but not necessary.

Where considerable amounts of fine dust and numbers of water crossings are contemplated, a snorkel is

Rear: spare wheel; towbar; taps for interior water tanks

SETTING UP: ACCESSORIES AND EQUIPMENT

strongly advisable. This device raises the height of the air-intake to protect against water entering the engine. At the same time, it offers improved air filtration, protecting against dust. Snorkels can be fitted to both petrol and diesel engines and are *essential* for diesels.

TYRES AND WHEELS The standard tyre on most four-wheel drives is a compromise one, designed for bitumen road and smooth gravel, and with limited capabilities in mud, sand and snow. Lug-type tyres are better for bogs and really hard going over rocks, but they are often noisy and not very good for bitumen driving. Choose tyres that will suit your purpose.

If you fit a genuine off-road tyre, accept the fact that any bitumen-road travel must be at lower speeds than normal and will require more careful driving in the wet. The sacrifice may be worthwhile. Compromise tyres may give problems in the really hard going, although performance can be enhanced in boggy conditions by a set of snow chains fitted to the front wheels. An alternative to chains is the Bog-Claw, a device with three metal claws which attaches to the outside of the wheels. However, a Bog-Claw cannot be driven on once the vehicle is clear of the actual bog, whereas chains can remain fitted for as long as the boggy conditions might be expected to continue.

Tubes or tubeless? It will not matter much if you puncture a tyre on a short tour or weekender. You have a spare and you will probably be close to somewhere the puncture can be repaired. But a long trek in remote areas means you need to repair punctures yourself, to maintain a spare wheel in good condition. Tubed tyres are easier to repair efficiently.

This raises another point. How many spares and what type of rims? It is possible to travel for weeks on end without a puncture and then have 3 in a day. It is for this reason that many people carry 2 spare wheels and tyres – but this is extra weight and takes up a lot of space. Carrying spare wheels does not protect against punctures, so a repair kit must be carried, also a pump to reinflate a repaired tyre. A good quality hand pump is fine; alternatively you can buy a small 12-volt air compressor.

Basic models of the larger four-wheel drives fit split rims as standard equipment. More expensive versions fit one-piece rims because they look nicer, but split rims are easier to handle when repairing tyres.

Also remember that a standard tyre size – such as a 750 x 16, commonly used on farm and station vehicles – will be more easily replaced in an emergency in an isolated place than an unusual urban tyre.

So, for long expeditions, our recommendation would be a good quality steel-radial lug tyre, with a second

spare, fitted with tubes and mounted on split rims. Carry tyre levers, tyre valve tool and a tyre rubber hammer as well as a tube repair kit. And drive to avoid tyre damage in the first place – it is expensive, can be frustrating and is probably dangerous.

TOOLS AND SPARES There is no point in carrying tools you can't use, and the electronic engine control of modern vehicles makes roadside repairs effectively impossible. However, the following items, in a steel toolbox properly strapped down, will be of value. Even if you can't use them, you may meet someone who can. Don't forget any special tools for your own vehicle also.

Heavy duty torch, spare batteries
Tyre levers, tyre rubber hammer, tube repair kit
Tyre pump or compressor, tyre pressure gauge
Basic set of sockets; open-end and ring spanners
Standard pliers, long-nose pliers, multigrip pliers
Small pipe wrench and a set of vice-grips
Side-cutters
Ball pein hammer, sledge hammer
Set of screwdrivers; flat tip and Phillips head
Two shifting spanners
Wheel-nut cross brace
Bow saw, hacksaw and fretsaw, and blades
Soldering iron, 12 volt and solder
Sharp knife, perhaps two: small and hunting size
Empty can and old paint brush (for washing parts)
Roll of tie wire
Ball of string
Wire brush
Electrical insulation tape
Can of dewatering fluid

Other items we consider you need to take, but which will not necessarily fit into the toolbox, include the following.

Workshop manual
Strong shovel
Two or more star pickets
Tomahawk and axe
Some fencing wire
Grease gun
Machete
High lift jack (in addition to standard jack) plus wood, 30 centimetres x 30 centimetres x 5 centimetres, or flat steel plate to use as a secure base
Jump leads
Fire extinguisher
Snow chains

Carefully consider the spare parts you carry. There is an excellent list in Gregorys *Four Wheel Drive Handbook*. What you take will depend on terrain and engine type, but if appropriate include the following.

SETTING UP: ACCESSORIES AND EQUIPMENT

Air cleaner elements
Appropriate driver belts
Distributor cap
Fuel filters
Fuses
Extra ignition key (outside vehicle)
Globes for head and tail lights
Ignition coils, plugs, condenser, points
Oil filters
Radiator and heater hoses and clips
Radiator pressure cap

Most importantly, know your vehicle. Read the manual (and make sure it is in your glovebox). A basic course in vehicle maintenance is a good idea and essential if you are intending to travel far from civilization. Contact the appropriate motoring organisation in your state for information on these; see 'Planning Ahead'.

RECOVERY GEAR A full set of recovery gear is essential on long treks and won't go astray on some short tours as well. On long treks you must expect to have to pull the vehicle out of a bog or creek. What follows is just the gear to take; how to use it is included in 'On the Road'.

The **winch** (hand or electric) and its fittings are the most important recovery gear. Winches range in size and effectiveness from a capacity of 5400 kilograms down to 660 kilograms capacity. Around 3700 kilograms capacity is a good average. Talk to experienced people to assess your needs and buy the best you can – it could save your life. It is also worthwhile having it attached to your vehicle with a professionally produced and fitted winch-mounting system.

Made-up kits of recovery gear packed in a specially designed carrybag are available: *Opposite Lock* have one that includes a **length of chain**, secondary **length of winch cable**, **snatch strap**, **tow rope** and **D shackles**, while *Warn* package an accessory kit through *ARB* outlets Australia-wide that includes a **snatch block**, **shackle**, **tree trunk protector** and **choker chain** with **hooks** and **gloves**.

Possibly you have not come across a snatch strap before. Well, a standard braided tow rope can be used for pulling another vehicle out of a bog but is better when towing on flat ground. The snatch strap is a length of super-strong nylon webbing with considerable elasticity. You attach the strap between pulling vehicle and bogged vehicle, the pulling vehicle accelerates to about 5 kilometres per hour against the strap which stretches until all the slack is taken up and then, almost literally, it helps pop the bogged vehicle out of the bog. Continue to use it to pull the bogged vehicle to hard stand but not for towing on the flat.

The secondary length of winch cable and D shackles in your recovery gear are used to add length to a standard winch cable.

SUSPENSION All today's four-wheel drive vehicles are fitted with suspension which is perfectly adequate for no load or light loads, and some suspension systems work well fully laden. Others need assistance if they are to handle rough terrain and heavy loads day in and out for months.

Leaf spring vehicles can benefit from a resetting of the leaves and adding an extra leaf. A helper spring – one which only comes into operation when the vehicle is fully laden – might suffice. Vehicles with coil springs may benefit, at the rear at least, from heavy-duty rubber airbags which fit inside the coils.

Some people change shock absorbers for heavy duty dampers (perhaps gas) which last longer, but if the standard units are in good condition they may suffice.

Suspension modifications should not be undertaken lightly as some may be seen as illegal for roadworthy certificate purposes. Non-standard parts are difficult to obtain away from big cities; thus repairs can become specialist jobs. Detailed advice ought to be taken from a genuine off-road suspension specialist. This also raises the question of vehicle servicing.

VEHICLE SERVICING AND ENERGY EQUIPMENT
Preparing for a short tour of a day or even a week demands no more than a routine check of brakes, suspension, steering and electrics to ensure the vehicle is ready, especially if it is used regularly as normal transport. But a long trek is something different and will need all of these checks, plus a few extra ones.

Items to be thoroughly checked include: tyres, suspension, brakes, all electrical connections (some of which may need to be made more secure), the complete fuel supply system, the cooling system, the transmission and drive shafts and the lubrication system.

If you intend to go into cold regions, ensure that anti-freeze is added to the cooling system and a rust-inhibitor needs to be added as a matter of course. You should carry a container of engine oil in case of a ruptured sump and, for the same reason, a method to stop an oil leak and a similar product for sealing a fuel tank leak.

For long trekking an important feature of the vehicle will be its capacity to supply electricity. Your vehicle will be required to power equipment such as a long-range radio, a refrigerator and extra lighting. It is almost mandatory, therefore, to fit a dual battery system – that is, a backup to the normal battery with an isolation switch or relays that disconnect the main battery when the engine is not running. With the engine on, the

SETTING UP: ACCESSORIES AND EQUIPMENT

The high-lift jack, an essential repair item

vehicle's alternator will recharge both batteries but make sure that the only battery supplying current when the engine is off is the secondary one.

There are various options but a deep-cycle battery is probably the way to go for the backup battery plus a reliable isolation switch – which may either be manual or automatic. Consult a qualified auto electrician; preferably one who has had experience with four-wheel drive automatic systems used for outback touring. Remember, even with this dual battery system you need to take the vehicle for a drive or run the engine to recharge the battery every other day at least, which can be a bit of a nuisance.

Generators are an alternative, but they need fuel, servicing and maintenance – and they are noisy. They are also banned at many national parks. So, why not consider a solar electric panel? They are light, silent, take up little room, require no fuel apart from the sun and maintenance is minimal. They are perfect for mounting on the roof because they are long and wide. They need to be easily moved so your car can stay in the shade while the panel sits in the sun, providing power. We had a folding panel which could be conveniently collapsed for travelling and it was a great asset.

Obviously the solar panels are somewhat restricted in poor light. But springtime Victorian weather will keep a refrigerator running well over several days; an outback sunny day is ideal.

Another consideration in vehicle setup is that cool travellers are calmer and happier. Think about fitting air-conditioning for trips into hot country. The extra weight, strain on the engine and fuel consumption need to be taken into account, along with the comfort of passengers, but the $1500 or so outlayed may be well worth it depending on your priorities.

FUEL AND WATER There will be times when extra fuel and water must be carried. Fuel can be carried in jerrycans outside the passenger compartment of the vehicle. Avoid plastic containers. Special mounts are available from four-wheel drive accessory suppliers. And don't forget to take an adequate funnel! *It is important to schedule the stages of any long trip to take fuel supply into account.* We have indicated where fuel is available in the route directions for all trips in this book. You *must* work out the fuel consumption of your vehicle in both hard and easy going and determine what sorts of conditions are most likely to be encountered on upcoming terrain.

For example, if the easy-going consumption rate is 14 litres per 100 kilometres and the hard-going rate is 18 litres per 100 kilometres, and the next planned section is going to be a mix of both, you should estimate fuel usage closer to the hard-going figure. For this exercise, then, 17 litres per 100 kilometres would be the figure to work on. With a tank capacity of 90 litres, the range of the vehicle will be 100 x 90 divided by 17, which equals 529 kilometres. Then deduct a conservative 10 per cent for non-recoverable fuel from the tank; this gives you a range of 476 kilometres per tank of fuel. There is a safety margin built into these calculations, but assume that if you are about to undertake a section in which the distance between refuelling points is over 480 kilometres, you must carry extra fuel.

Travellers who will need extra fuel on several trips may feel it worth considering supplementary or replacement long-distance fuel tanks. They are available for almost all four-wheel drive vehicles. Remember, however, that this is yet another way to add weight to the vehicle.

Finally, a vital ingredient in outback touring: water. If it is not readily available on your journey into remote places, it must be carried. Read our route directions carefully before heading off, to establish where water may be scarce. The quantity required is not less than 5 litres per person per day, plus enough to refill a holed

SETTING UP: ACCESSORIES AND EQUIPMENT

radiator. (Carry this spare radiator water separately.) This can be a lot of water; water is heavy, and water containers take up a lot of space. Two people on a five-day trip without water replenishment, for example, will mean carrying at least 50 litres for the humans and another 20 litres for the radiator. Build in a safety margin and it's about 80 litres in total, which means four 20-litre jerrycans. *Make room for them.* Never head off into arid zones without sufficient water. Opposite Lock have a 40-litre aluminium water container which is fitted inside the vehicle with a tap to the outside – neat and convenient!

COMMUNICATIONS Some form of communication is absolutely essential in the remote areas of outback Australia. Citizens Band (CB) radios are better than nothing but generally provide only short-range communication – possible long-range at night. If you intend to go into remote areas, arrange a radio-transceiver with a top supplier and installer. Ideally all outback travellers should carry a high-frequency single sideband radio to contact the network of Royal Flying Doctor Service bases all around Australia and the Australia-wide Australian and Overseas Telecommunications Corporation (AOTC) Radphone network.

The **Radphone** network is a public radio telephone service available to any vessel or land mobile equipped with a suitable radio fitted with AOTC Radphone frequencies and whose operator is currently licensed by the Department of Transport and Communication. Several stations are strategically placed around the coast of Australia to enable contact to be made 24 hours a day and seven days a week. The stations maintain a dedicated distress and safety watch, broadcast regular coastal and high seas weather forecasts, navigation warnings and traffic lists. More information can be obtained from AOTC offices throughout Australia.

Contact your local office of the Commonwealth Department of Transport and Communications to obtain information about radio operator's licences, appropriate radio bases and their frequencies. They have offices in every State capital and are listed in the front of the White Pages of the telephone directory.

The **Royal Flying Doctor Service** (RFDS) is an organisation well known to Australians. While travelling through outback areas and towns you will often be asked to support its work through t-shirt buying or a stall – give as generously as you can, you never know when you may be a customer! The Service's Bases and Visitors' Centres can provide advice on outback touring and on proper emergency procedures. Bases at Broken Hill, Charleville and Jandakot also provide transceiver sets, at a very reason-

able cost, with a fixed emergency call button in case of accident or sickness. Other bases, while not hiring out transceiver sets themselves, can suggest local outlets.

The RFDS network connects to immediate medical advice and aid even to the point of evacuation arrangements. But as well, if you have previously arranged the service, the RFDS can patch the caller into the Radphone service and thus enable telephone calls to be made around the country – or more importantly to someone who can give advice on how to repair a breakdown.

So, before you depart, contact the appropriate office of the Royal Flying Doctor Service to register your name, home or base address and radio call sign with them so you can make Radphone calls through them. Obtain the guide.setting out all the bases, radio call signs and broadcast frequencies.

RFDS bases are usually staffed full-time only during the day (there are possible exceptions) but access can be obtained after hours if your radio is fitted with the emergency call button that automatically turns on a transmitter and connects further help. Such calls, of course, must be made only in the case of a genuine emergency. RFDS calls are free, but there are charges for all Radphone connections.

In an emergency requiring RFDS assistance it will be necessary for them to know exactly where you are. In some cases the RFDS will direct you to the nearest airstrip for evacuation, if an aircraft is needed. Where it is impossible to move either the vehicle (in the case of a serious collision), or the patient, the RFDS may arrange a helicopter charter. They still need to be able to locate you, so give your position as precisely as you can and consider lighting an oily fire which will give off dense black smoke to help them find you. See the section on Maps and Navigation in 'Planning Ahead'.

PEOPLE SETUP AND CAMPING GEAR Unless your plans include a caravan or trailer, or a budget for staying in hotels or motels, you will need to equip yourself with camping gear. Our choice was to spend many nights under the stars and this is the emphasis in the book. You will enjoy it thoroughly too, if you plan beforehand.

Once again, consider the differences between the demands of short tours and longer treks, between spending a few nights on the ground and making your vehicle your home for months at a time. Either way, you will rarely be spending more than 2 nights at the same location, so you will not want to spend too much time setting up and breaking a camp. The faster it is established and you are ready to eat, relax and sleep, the better for the whole trip.

SETTING UP: ACCESSORIES AND EQUIPMENT

SLEEPING SPACES You may get by on short tours with nothing more than an enclosed swag or small tent, neither of which takes much time to set up. There are swags today which are much more than just the old rolled mattress and blankets; they are like expanded sleeping bags with a raised section, enclosed by either zip-in flyscreen, or canvas, or both. There is a wide choice also of small, portable tents offering excellent comfort and protection.

These can of course be chosen for long treks too, but another option is to carry your home on your back. Car-toppers are excellent for two: a comfortable bed on the top of your car sheltered by an easily erected mini tent. Many expand into ground-level living areas as well, to provide extra space for sleepers or for living accommodation in inclement weather. Remember though, if you want to drive to the nearest shop for supplies, you must take your camp with you!

If you choose to carry a car-top tent, as we did, it will be mounted to a roof rack, which must be securely mounted and of sturdy design. It will probably be provided as part of the tent package. With the living space on top of the vehicle, you will have only limited space to stow gear and equipment on the roof, but on the other hand you will not have tents and sleeping equipment taking up space inside.

If you are travelling in a station wagon, all your equipment will be behind you. In an accident it could fly round, causing injury, so it must be strapped down. We recommend the gear is separated from the passenger section by a cargo barrier: a wire mesh screen fitting between floor and roof behind either the front or rear seats.

The more passengers you carry, the less room there is for stowage. You can tow a trailer (see the following chapter for more details), but in our opinion towing is not a good idea unless no other solution can be found. On many four-wheel drive tracks anything pulled along behind is going to cause difficulties, even making some particularly appealing places inaccessible.

With or without a trailer, it is not difficult to see how the overall weight is going to increase dramatically. Fully laden, the vehicle is going to lose some of its vital ground clearance and spring travel, so check back to those earlier paragraphs in this chapter regarding suspension modifications.

ROYAL FLYING DOCTOR SERVICE BASES

For information regarding all the services offered by the RFDS contact: Australian Council of the Royal Flying Doctor Service of Australia, Level 5, 15-17 Young Street, NSW 2000; tel. (02) 241 2411. The bases are listed here.

New South Wales
Airport, Broken Hill NSW 2880
(080) 88 0777

Queensland
1 Junction Street, Cairns QLD 4870
(070) 53 1952 (base)
(070) 53 5419 (medical assistance)
Barkly Highway, Mount Isa QLD 4825
(077) 43 2800 (base)
(077) 43 2802 (medical assistance)
Old Cunnamulla Road, Charleville QLD 4470
(076) 54 1233 (base)
(076) 54 1443 (medical assistance)

Northern Territory
Stuart Terrace, Alice Springs NT 0870
(089) 52 1033
(089) 52 5733 (after hours)

Western Australia
29 Douglas Street, Carnarvon WA 6701
(099) 41 1758 (base)
(099) 41 2399 (medical assistance)
Clarendon Street, Derby WA 6728
(091) 91 1211
3 Eagle Drive, Jandakot Airport WA 6164
(09) 332 7733
46 Picadilly Street, Kalgoorlie WA 6430
(090) 21 2211
Main Street, Meekatharra WA 6642
(099) 81 1107
The Esplanade, Port Hedland WA 6721
(091) 73 1386

South Australia
4 Vincent Street, Port Augusta SA 5700
(086) 42 2044

Tasmania
9 Adelaide Street, Launceston TAS 7250
(003) 31 2121

SETTING UP: ACCESSORIES AND EQUIPMENT

CREATURE COMFORTS Apart from tent or swag protection, creature comforts for campers need to include good quality sleeping bags (rated for the climate you will be travelling) or your preferred bedding, some type of mattress, folding chairs, a lightweight table, a kitchen 'bench' with a wash basin, gas stove, portable refrigerator and some form of lighting, probably gas-fuelled so 2 gas bottles will be needed. A good quality ground sheet is a must. Deciding what to leave behind is probably more difficult than deciding what to take. Remember that weight is still an important factor and overloading the vehicle can cause problems. Go for lightweight products but do not buy flimsy ones, sacrificing strength for weight.

Look critically at the seats in your vehicle. Are they up to the journey? It would be worth investigating some options for new, improved, perhaps orthopaedic, seats. Equally, storage problems for radio, plus all the things to be kept handy in the cabin need to be solved now. Roof or centre-seat consoles, drawers and boxes are the choices. See your accessory dealer.

REFRIGERATION The different portable refrigerators on the market provide a choice of size, capacity and power sources: 240 volts, 12 volts, gas, liquid fuel or a combination. Of course, only you can decide if a refrigerator is necessary for your trip; perhaps an insulated icebox will be fine.

We chose to take a 90-litre Bush Boy refrigerator/freezer with a 240/12-volt option because its design suited our purposes perfectly. Bush Boy also produce a refrigerator which has two sections – part fridge, part freezer. This compartmentalisation is an advantage in that not all fresh foods carried should be frozen. The single compartment unit is either a freezer or a refrigerator, depending upon thermostat setting. Bush Boy provide a system of easily accessed plastic-coated wire storage baskets, so that all available space is utilised. Within this system, we carried perishables in assorted sealable plastic containers to prolong life and to make access easier. You can also buy insulated plastic bags in most supermarkets which extend the life of refrigerated fruit and vegetables for up to 2 weeks.

We do not recommend using gas or liquid fuel refrigeration when the refrigerator is carried within the passenger compartment of the vehicle, but these systems can suit those travelling in utilities or panel vans when the passengers are separated. Many people choose three-way refrigeration because they plan to camp in one spot for more than a couple of nights where 240 volts will not be available and 12 volts will be a constant drain on the battery, even when a dual battery is fitted.

The travelling kitchen with built-in shelving system

Lightweight table and choice of gas cookers

COOKERS Cooking methods range from varying sizes of open fire grill plates through to elaborate but compact three-burner gas stoves.

If you decide to rely on an open fire with grill plate, take another energy source as well, because at times of fire restrictions you will be prevented from using an open fire. Most national parks prefer you to use portable gas-fired stoves rather than open fires. Also, wood is a precious resource, a home to various animals, and is not always available.

FIRE EXTINGUISHERS At least one carbon dioxide or dry chemical one-kilo fire extinguisher ought to be carried, supplemented by a smothering blanket for possible kitchen fires. Carbon dioxide and dry chemical are both electrically non-conductive so are approved for use on electrical equipment fires, plus they are perfect for flammable liquids, wood, paper, textiles, cooking oils and fats too.

▶ *Remember to switch off power or fuel sources before tackling any fire.*

TOWING

CARAVANS, CAMPERS AND TRAILERS Many people use a four-wheel drive vehicle and drag along a caravan, campervan or trailer behind them. There are certainly some advantages. A caravan or camper, or a convertible camper trailer, provides excellent accommodation and extra facilities in varying degrees which are not available to those camping out. Where a number of passengers are travelling, the trailer, whatever shape or size it might be, will take some and perhaps most of the gear and equipment which might otherwise have been carried within the vehicle.

However, there are disadvantages too, and they need to be considered. For a start, there are certain tracks over which it is impossible to pull trailers (for simplicity in this chapter, anything towed is a trailer).

On long treks this might be overcome by arriving at a destination and parking the trailer for a few days while you take short tours around the region. For example, it's possible to do this in Cairns while you explore Cape York, because it is likely you will return to Cairns before proceeding further 'across the top'. You then need to carry camping gear as well, to use while the trailer is parked – and you have to pay site rental for the trailer while you are away.

In many areas, though, having elected to tow your sleeping quarters means you will be limited to short, one-day tours during stopovers or to better roads to proceed to your next destination. Your freedom to move around becomes limited.

Other major disadvantages, particularly with caravans and campervans (pop-tops), are that they dramatically increase fuel consumption and they can present greater road safety dangers than an unencumbered vehicle. So, if you decide to tow a trailer, remember that the smaller the towed vehicle the better – keep the size, mass and frontal area to a reasonable minimum.

HITCHING The quality of towing hitches varies between those made in the backyard by a handyman and those manufactured by a reputable organisation such as Hayman-Reece who, in our opinion, produce the best hitches in Australia.

There are a number of factors to consider when setting up a tow. The towbar itself must be strong enough to stand an often substantial load, which will vary constantly according to road conditions – ascents, descents, side winds, undulations, bumps – almost all of which are exaggerated in four-wheel driving operations. The bar and its components should be adjustable

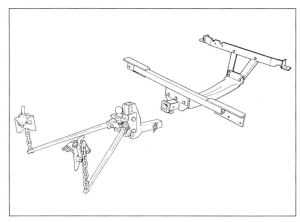

Weight distribution hitch

within certain parameters in order to balance the load at the bar itself, and, therefore, on the suspension of the towing vehicle. A weight-distribution hitch will distribute weight equally to the wheels of the towing vehicle and to those of the caravan or trailer.

According to the safety regulation requirements for the use of motor vehicles and trailers in combination (this includes caravans), the trailer must be 'properly set up'. This means that the trailer's load is concentrated as much as possible just forward of the axle centre so that there is a downward load of about 10 per cent of its total mass on the coupling and the rear of the towing vehicle is not excessively depressed on its suspension. There are varying load-levelling devices available, including flexible couplers which may be necessary to achieve this, so they should be investigated.

A vital part of the hitch is the trailer braking system. Again a number of options are available – mechanical override, hydraulic and electric, for example – and once again we recommend taking expert advice.

Last, we couldn't leave this section on hitching without a warning to ensure all lights and turning indicators are wired up correctly each and every time you stop, unhitch and re-hitch your trailer. Actually *see* them all working: don't leave it to chance.

TOWING LAWS It is imperative to consult your own home state motor traffic handbook (available from your state motoring organisation, Department of Transport and many newsagents and bookshops) for information regarding the laws concerning trailers before committing yourself to any of the wide range of towable living quarters available. For instance, Victorians ought to know that if they tow an unregistered vehicle in another state, the registration number of the towing vehicle must be displayed on the rear of the trailer. A pamphlet, *Towing Trailers*, gives practical advice and towing requirements and is available

A trailer bogged in sand, Cooloola National Park

free at any RACV branch and VicRoads office. And in South Australia, 5B(E) rated dry powder fire extinguishers are compulsory equipment in caravans.

DRIVING SAFELY WITH TRAILERS Although you need some special driving techniques to drive with trailers, the essential ingredients of concentration, observation and common sense apply.

If you have not previously towed anything you will notice immediately that the vehicle is not as lively a performer as it was, especially when larger vans are towed. You will need to think ahead even more and to plan your driving more carefully so that you are in the right gear at the right time to provide a steady forward momentum with the rig.

Gears? We prefer manual transmission for four-wheel drive vehicles and, if you are towing, manual is even more useful. But if you do drive an automatic, remember you can still preselect lower gears in anticipation of needing them. This is valuable when you are towing because you then lose less momentum on hills than if you wait for the load to tell the transmission to shift down. And on long steep descents, preselecting the lower gear and allowing

the vehicle to drive against it helps to retard speed and conserve brakes – although once again, this technique is much more effective with a manual gearbox.

Because the performance of the vehicle is down, hills will be slow and steady going and you will often hold up traffic behind you, especially on steep climbs. As soon as there is a safe opportunity, it is courteous to pull over and allow following traffic to clear. It also contributes to road safety because it prevents someone impatient behind you doing something rash.

Larger caravans, with high slab sides, are often badly affected by strong crosswinds, producing trailer sway. Trailer sway is dangerous. Its first indication will probably be that you feel the back of the vehicle being pulled from side to side; the situation may steadily get worse.

There is a classic method of correcting trailer sway, although it is not always appropriate or even possible to use it, and that is by accelerating. By making the vehicle go faster you pull the trailer straight again. This is the ideal method, but of course there are times when going faster is just not practical: in traffic, or travelling downhill with curves approaching, or uphill where the power is barely enough, this corrective procedure cannot be used. In this

23

case, ease off the accelerator instead, not suddenly but gently, and try to hold the steering steady until the danger is past and the trailer is back in line.

Trailer sway is unlikely to occur with a properly hitched and balanced trailer – which brings us back to the importance of setting up correctly in the first place.

DISTANCES AND AVERAGES
Towing restricts how far and how fast you can go. Big vans reduce average cruising speeds considerably; indeed, there are towing speed limits in some states depending upon weight towed. Lowering speeds will reduce daily average runs, which is unlikely to matter if only a few days' travel is involved, but on longer journeys might become the difference between seeing everything you want to or not.

For example, travelling 4 days in every 7 and averaging 200 kilometres a day instead of 300, you will lose 400 kilometres per week or 4800 kilometres in a four-month trek. That is a fair slice of Australia you will be giving up in exchange for the travelling comforts of home, but only you can weigh up the importance of what you see and how you see it!

A conclusion might be that four-wheel drive, long-distance holidays are best without towing your bed behind. Today's camping equipment can usually satisfy just about everyone's comfort level. Check back to 'Setting Up' for some tips on camping comforts.

TOWING INFORMATION

A trailer or caravan must conform to the rules of every state it travels through, not just to its home state regulations

New South Wales
National Roads and
 Motorists' Association
151 Clarence Street
Sydney 2000
(02) 260 9222
The mass of trailer or caravan must not exceed the unladen mass of the towing vehicle. There is also an 80 km/h speed limit if the laden mass of the trailer exceeds 750 kilograms.

Queensland
Royal Automobile Club
 of Queensland
300 St Pauls Terrace
Brisbane 4000
(07) 361 2444
Queensland does not have defined towing limits. The laws are similar to those applying in South Australia, although it appears the 'rule of thumb' is that the mass of the trailer should not exceed 1.5 times the unladen mass of the towing vehicle. Caution is needed however, if you are travelling from southern states into Queensland via New South Wales as you must then comply with the law in that state.

Northern Territory
Automobile Association of the
 Northern Territory
79–81 Smith Street
Darwin 0800
(089) 81 3837
In NT the mass of the trailer must not exceed the mass of the towing vehicle.

Western Australia
Royal Automobile Club of
 Western Australia Inc.
228 Adelaide Terrace
Perth 6000
(09) 421 4444
Western Australia does not have defined towing limits. There is, however, a 90 km/h speed limit if the highway-laden mass of the trailer exceeds 750 kilograms.

South Australia
Royal Automobile Association of
 South Australia
41 Hindmarsh Square
Adelaide 5000
(08) 223 4555
There are no defined towing limits in SA. The driver must be able to control the combination and be able to stop it within prescribed stopping distances.

Victoria
Royal Automobile Club
 of Victoria
422 Little Collins Street
Melbourne 3000
(03) 790 2211
A trailer up to 1.5 times the unladen (tare) mass may be towed provided the load limits of the towing equipment are not exceeded and the combination is properly set up and suitably braked. Caution should also be exercised if the mass of the trailer exceeds the towing vehicle manufacturer's recommended towing limits, even if the trailer mass falls within the above policy.

Tasmania
Royal Automobile Club
 of Tasmania
Cnr Patrick and Murray Streets
Hobart 7000
(002) 38 2200
In Tasmania the mass of the trailer must not exceed the laden mass of the towing vehicle. In addition there is an 80 km/h speed limit when towing any trailer.

ON THE ROAD

So, you're off? Everything for the journey is as prepared as it can be, you're in the car waving goodbye – off for that dream break.

Terrific. Are you sitting comfortably? We're not kidding, because you will be spending quite a bit of time just sitting, looking out of windows and admiring scenery. Sitting comfortably really means being supported upright in your seat, seatbelt comfortably across you, that feet and legs can be moved occasionally to ensure circulation stays normal and that your back and spine feel supported by the seat. Taking a short break every couple of hours is a good idea for the passengers literally to stretch their legs, but probably imperative to keep the driver alert.

What you keep easily accessible in the driving cabin will vary as much as people vary. However, we feel that money and valuables, a small first-aid kit, moist towelettes, sun block, tissues or a couple of small towels, pens and paper, package of maps and guides for the immediate destination, instructions for radio operation and maintenance, music or book-length story cassettes all ought to be fairly handy. And anything else *you* can't live without!

DRIVING PROCEDURES

All driving is potentially hazardous. Bush driving is no less so but the potential difficulties are different from those in built-up areas or on highways. It is not traffic and speed that are likely to present a threat, but the terrain – ill-formed tracks, sometimes badly shaped and most badly maintained. These are a challenge, but alone they are usually not a problem if handled with care.

A mix of bad road, sand, mud, rocks and water, though, can cause mishaps the city driver would never encounter. The crash and bump of some tracks can break components; being bogged in sand, mud or snow is another form of hazard; and being stranded midstream with a drowned engine is no joke.

This is why our chapters on planning ahead and vehicle setup are so thorough. But, as no-one can guarantee a trouble-free trip, read on for some tips to cope with unexpected challenges.

First, assuming that you have some warning that there may be problems on the track ahead, stop the car, get out and examine the hazard before driving headlong into or over it. Check the going and determine whether it is, in fact, passable, or if there is an alternative route.

In difficult circumstances such as steep slopes or rocky terrain, go carefully in the correct gears picking your way to clearer ground. The only safe way to descend a steep slope is in a straight line; if this isn't possible try an alternative route. There are times when a rocky but dry creek bed crossing still might necessitate someone walking on ahead, guiding the driver around the worst sections.

In boggy or sandy terrain, pick ground that looks most likely to give reasonable traction. When you feel confident that the hazard can be successfully negotiated, engage the front hubs (where this does not occur automatically), select low-range four-wheel drive and, where it is possible to do so, back up enough to have some momentum when you enter the hazard. Do not accelerate nor brake hard as spinning or locking the wheels will slow progress, perhaps to a halt. What is required is steady forward progress, counter-steering against any rear axle slippage to keep the front wheels pointed in the desired direction.

RECOVERY If the vehicle stops it is almost certain that you will be bogged, whether it is sand, mud or snow you are tackling, and then the exercise is how to extract your vehicle. The fastest and easiest way is to winch the vehicle out – precisely the reason you equipped the vehicle with a power or manual winch back home. And that it is where you ought to have familiarised yourself with its operation.

GENERAL GOOD HANDLING TIPS FOR WINCHES

▶ Always carry spare manufacturer-recommended shear pins. ▶ Don't winch with less than 5 wraps of cable on the drum. ▶ Always pull as straight as possible in line with the vehicle. ▶ Use leather gloves when handling the cable – lacerations from steel splinters are to be avoided. ▶ Keep people clear of the cable under tension – if it breaks it could cut someone in half – and before you start winching, throw a heavy piece of material over the cable about a metre from the hook. ▶ Keep the winch disengaged when not in use and when the cable is slack use the switch occasionally to bring the cable under tension. ▶ Increase the vehicle engine idle speed when using a winch – it prevents flattening the battery.

Now, most importantly, a winch needs something to pull against. In some conditions there may well be no trees or scrub to hook up to, so just one of the reasons you packed a shovel becomes obvious.

Dig a shallow pit, perhaps 50 or 60 centimetres deep, directly ahead of the vehicle, on the nearest hard stand within reach of the winch cable (and its extension if you carry one). Undercut the trench about 15 or 20 centimetres on the edge nearest the vehicle. Set into the trench a strong log of wood, if you can find one, or perhaps a spare tyre and wheel. Pass the winch cable around it at a point nearest the full depth and undercut of the trench. Use this as the anchor to pull against and slowly and steadily extract the vehicle from the bog or sand. Undercutting the trench stops the anchor pulling out under the load stress.

Or you can use the star picket system, which will only work if there is a solid base to the hazard, something the picket will bite into deeply and hold. Hammer 3 pickets deeply into the ground at the extension of the winch cable, one behind the other and about 30 centimetres apart, until there is only about a third of the pickets above the ground. They should be angled away from the load direction. Tie them together at ground level. Hook the winch cable up to the front picket at ground level and operate the winch to extract the vehicle.

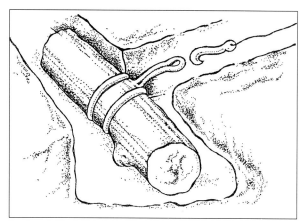

Log anchor

CREEK CROSSING When you are tackling a creek crossing it is obviously necessary to know the depth of the water and, at least to a certain extent, the consistency of the track under water before you enter it. In most cases this is simply a matter of walking the crossing first, feeling around for a grip for the tyres and the shallowest route. If the water is above tyre level, look for an alternative route. Where none is possible and if the water seems likely to lap up to the bonnet, it is as well to wrap the front of the vehicle with a groundsheet before entering the creek, to prevent water flowing back around the radiator and drowning the engine.

Then enter the water slowly and proceed at a constant speed, perhaps slipping the clutch in a manual vehicle to keep engine revs higher than the equivalent road speed. If the base of the creek is soft or rocky choose low-range four-wheel drive.

Watch the exit. If it is steep or soft or both, keep going by gunning the engine once clear of the water until higher, flatter ground is reached.

If the vehicle stalls in the water and will not immediately restart, stop trying; you will have to winch it out. Refer to the winch procedures detailed above regarding clearing bogs. Once clear of the water check to see that no water has entered the air intake, filling one or more cylinders with water. If this has happened, you will have a major mechanical job on your hands.

In some areas of northern Australia the creeks may be inhabited by crocodiles, in which case we certainly do *not* recommend that anyone checks the depth by wading across! Where possible, choose an alternative route and do not enter the water – in or out of your vehicle.

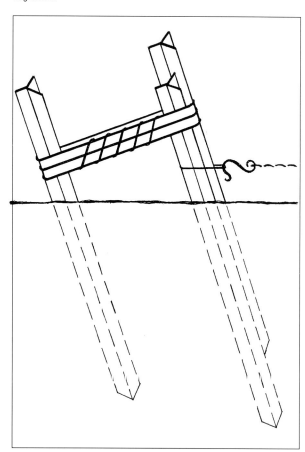

Star picket anchor

In and out of trouble, Cape York

However you still should not drive into water where depth and bottom track quality are unknown. Here is a way to check the depth, at least, without getting wet, or worse. Find and cut 4 or 5 straight thin poles or branches. Sharpen the points at the heaviest end or, if of even thickness, weight one end. What you are trying to do is make a javelin. Mark the javelin with a contrasting colour (perhaps with plastic tape) in bands at intervals of about a metre, 1.2 and 1.5 metres from the pointed end.

Toss the javelin in a high loop so that it falls vertically, towards the centre of the creek on the line of your track. With any luck it will stick in the creek bottom and give you an immediate depth indicator. Even if it doesn't stick, if you keep a sharp watch you'll be able to see the depth by your markers when the javelin bottoms (or doesn't as the case may be). Use the remaining javelins to try to mark the track at about a quarter and three-quarter distance, as well as trying to finish the path a couple of metres either side of the first.

If the creek looks impassable it probably is, but if the markers seem to indicate that it is possible to cross, follow the above procedure, preferably with someone sitting on the bonnet to retrieve the first javelin and depth-sound as you go.

SAND The key to driving a four-wheel drive vehicle safely over sand is flotation, which is gained by a combination of travelling slowly without stopping and low tyre pressures. Soft, dry sand often means that the vehicle needs power to keep travelling without digging in or stalling. Stick to existing wheel tracks where possible as the sand there is already compacted and less damage to the surrounding environment will result. *Remember that vegetated sand dunes are extremely fragile so avoid them.*

When travelling in sandy country or on a beach, always carry a tyre gauge to measure the air pressures accurately. If there is to be much sand driving an on-board air compressor will earn its keep quickly. Many travellers say that for hard-packed sand, tyres can stay at road-going pressures, but if in doubt, lower them to around 20 psi; on very soft sand you may need to go as low as 15 psi. Reinflate the tyres as soon as hard ground is reached.

For sand driving, whether beach or desert, don't overload the vehicle, and especially don't load up the roof rack as this can alter the centre of gravity of your vehicle and be extremely dangerous. Carry spare water and fuel if required of course but be abstemious with weighty items.

Generally speaking, selecting four-wheel drive high-range second gear is good for sand driving. Low range shouldn't be necessary, but if your vehicle's revs drop to around 1000 rpm, change down to a lower gear quickly to keep up the momentum.

Turning around on sand? Where possible turn down the beach toward the water and not toward the softer sand above. *Watch tides when beach driving*; it's easy to get bogged and then perhaps drown the engine in salt water, when you are caught by a returning tide.

A few extra checks for sand driving ▶ High temperatures can built up in engine oils so unless you have an oil temperature gauge in your vehicle and use it, avoid driving for hours in sand without stopping. ▶ Sand in the air filter and air intake isn't good – check frequently if doing much sand driving. ▶ Hose the underbody of your vehicle after all beach driving to minimise the risk of salt corrosion.

BULLDUST 'Bulldust' occurs in some outback areas when the surface of the track breaks up into a fine talc-like dust. It can cause damage if sucked into engines, or, because of its sandpaper-like characteristics, when it accumulates around greasy engine components.

Even more dangerous is the badly damaged road surface below the deceptively smooth dust. Drive slowly through bulldust patches to avoid raising the dust and damaging your undercarriage.

SNOW Chains are the first thing most drivers think of for alpine driving. So where and how do you fit them? For a four-wheel drive vehicle with four-wheel drive engaged, they ought to be fitted to the front wheels, which aids steering too. In heavy conditions however, you may need chains on all wheels.

Loosely fitted chains can work off and damage underbody parts such as brake lines. So drive a hundred metres or so after fitting chains and check their security. When driving with chains drive slowly and expect to feel the wheels out of balance. And quickly remove the chains once the danger has passed, as they damage tracks. You can use chains in soft sand and mud if you need extra traction, but again, remember the damage they can cause. Choose an alternative route where possible.

Other tips for alpine driving ▶ Keep to a speed where changing down gears will slow you down on icy roads. ▶ Avoid using the brakes to minimise the risk of skidding. ▶ Equally, when accelerating avoid jerky movements on the accelerator as you might cause wheelspin. ▶ Keep fuel tanks as full as possible in freezing conditions to minimise water condensation and regularly top up radiator with coolant/antifreeze. ▶ Check for snow build up after driving through heavy snow. Underbonnet wiring is particularly vulnerable, as are steering arms under the vehicle, which can

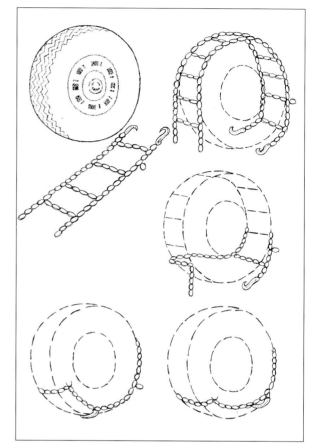

Fitting chains

stiffen if left coated with ice. ▶ Add methylated spirits to the windscreen washer bottles to keep washer jets working in below average temperatures and extend the wipers out from the windscreen when parking at night so they don't freeze to the glass. ▶ Don't park at night in freezing conditions leaving the handbrake on as it too can freeze and immobilise the vehicle until it thaws. Better to leave the car in gear.

ROADSIDE REPAIRS Many breakdowns can be cured by knowing how to carry out a running roadside repair. Success will depend on having that knowledge, the right tools and the right spares – or something temporary that will get you to mechanical assistance.

Even on holidays, a day needs to be set aside at regular intervals, with adequate time and at an appropriate location, for an overall service of the vehicle. Keep watching the warning gauges: do daily checks of fuel, oil, water and check tension and condition of the fan belt. You should have read your vehicle manual thoroughly, and the basic vehicle maintenance course we suggested will help you spot potential troubles.

Many modern cars are fitted with electronic engine management systems, or with electronic ignition and fuel injection. Generally, these are more reliable than older systems and often, in case of partial failure of the system, they have a 'limp home' mode, which enables travelling a limited distance at limited speed. However, total failure of such a system is difficult, perhaps impossible, to remedy at the roadside without expert knowledge and equipment. And this is a major reason for the long-range radio you have installed.

Here is some basic advice on problems with wheels and tyres, brakes, suspension and steering. Your vehicle manual will have additional information.

▶ Tyre stuck? If a tyre is stuck to the rim and nothing seems to remove it, pour soapy water into the crack and let it soak in. Alternatively, drive over the wheel to break the bead. ▶ Rear wheel damaged? If it is so bad the vehicle cannot be moved, jack up the vehicle and lash a large beam of wood below the side of the chassis so that it passes below the axle of the damaged vehicle and acts as a skid. Remove the wheel. The vehicle may be able to move under its own power in four-wheel drive; if not, it can at least be towed a short distance out of the way of further danger or damage. ▶ Broken spring? Jack up the vehicle and bring the spring into correct alignment. Apply wood strips as splints and bind them on with wire or rope. Put a block of wood between the top of the spring and the chassis and lash into place. Next heavy rope goes around the axle and nearest cross member of the chassis and is pulled tight and fixed. Drive very slowly. ▶ Steering linkage bent? Remove and straighten as much as possible; replace and drive slowly. ▶ Brake line broken? Flatten the end of the line on the master cylinder side of the split and bend it back on itself twice, crimping the end tight by hammering or with pliers. Check there is no fluid leakage when the brake pedal is pressed. ▶ Spring on the brake shoe damaged? Make a temporary repair by wiring end of the spring to the shoe or fixing a piece of inner tube in place of the broken spring.

KIM WHERRETT'S TRAVELLING LARDER There are many options for preparing meals on the road and you will need to experiment to find the best for you. We chose to carry all cooking equipment and non-perishable foodstuffs in a large lightweight metal box. This larder contained dried and canned foods, sauces, grains and cereals in assorted plastic containers – all square cornered so as to fit neatly and to double as shelving.

Cooking utensils such as knives, forks, spoons – table, wooden and slotted – can openers, corkscrews and so

Kim prepares a meal in the 'kitchen'

Kim Wherrett's travelling larder

on, we carried in a large soft plasticised fabric pencil case, divided into compartments, which kept sharp objects separately.

You can choose utensils made from lightweight aluminium, cast-iron or stainless steel. We took a small number of quality pots, a stainless steel billy, a large cast-iron frying pan and a medium size cast-iron camp oven. Personal preferences and the number of people travelling will make a difference to the pots and pans necessary. We think a cast-iron camp oven is an essential item, being both versatile and durable, allowing you to cook dampers, cakes, curries and stews on an open fire or to use it as a normal cooking pot on a gas stove or ring.

Many people carry woks, as Asian food is easy to prepare. However, they are large and can be cumbersome, although often other pots will stack into them easily; this is where the personal decision-making has to occur. We found the frying pan and camp oven just right for our needs. And a good quality metal thermos is useful, allowing hot or cold liquids to be carried at any time. Just remember the amount and weight of all your gear means everything you choose needs to be absolutely useful and necessary.

You will, of course, stock up well as you set up from home but food will be an ongoing item on the shopping list so it is worth deciding early what type of foods you prefer to carry. This will often depend upon the driving time between fresh food sources.

Try to carry as much fresh fruit and vegetables as possible, including those that do not need refrigeration such as potatoes, onions, sweet potatoes, pumpkin, whole watermelon, apples, oranges and green bananas. To supplement these fresh foods a selection of dried vegetables can be added to the larder: dried peas, corn, mushrooms, carrots and dried fruit, nuts and seeds.

You may prefer canned vegetables but remember cans, jars and bottles are bulky and heavy (and glass can break if not packed well) so should be kept to a minimum. They also increase the rubbish disposal problem. However, most travelling larders will include canned tomatoes, asparagus, beetroot and fruit.

There are alternative goods which can be carried for use when fresh or frozen meat, chicken and fish run out. Smoked and salted meats have a longer shelf life than fresh and can be added to dishes such as rice, noodles and eggs. Canned ham, tuna, sausages, nut meat (soy protein) and camp pie or corned beef can make up the balance.

You can supplement your larder by hunting, fishing and gathering (when the appropriate permissions or permits have been obtained), and some of our favourite meals on the road were created like this. Take advantage of the speciality foods of various regions to make delicious dishes.

We have to make mention of rubbish disposal here. These days with so many people travelling it is even more important to remember that what you take in with you, you take out with you again. The rubbish 'bin' in the vehicle should be airtight to prevent unwelcome smells. Dispose of all your rubbish in a legitimate dump – found on the outskirts of most towns – or in bins provided. Many outback and remote national parks have no bins for rubbish at bush campsites, and burying rubbish is not a satisfactory solution: there's nothing worse than arriving to find a place which has been 'turned over' by scavenging animals. So, take your rubbish out with you and, if necessary, take other people's too.

RECIPES FROM AROUND AUSTRALIA
Each recipe serves at least two

Shelburne Bay Oyster Chowder
On the coast (or near rivers) the obvious food source is seafood and fish and in many parts of the country this is abundant. On Cape York, where the large but delicious blacklipped oyster is prevalent, we cooked up this oyster chowder on the shores of Shelburne Bay.
  3 cups fish stock (see below)
  3 tablespoons butter
  2 leeks, chopped
  3 tablespoons flour
  1 teaspoon dried tarragon
  1 teaspoon cajun spices
  4 strands saffron
  $\frac{1}{2}$ cup milk
  salt and pepper to taste
  2 dozen large blacklipped oysters, shelled
Fish Stock
  head and skeleton of one fish
  1 onion, roughly chopped
  2 sticks celery, chopped
  1 bay leaf
  4 cups water
  salt and pepper to taste

First, make fish stock with bones and fish bits and head. Place in a billy with chopped onion, celery, bay leaf and water. Boil for 30 minutes until reduced to three cups. Season. Allow to cool and strain leaving clear stock.

In a camp oven (or suitable utensil) melt butter and gently sauté leeks until opaque. Add flour and stir until a light roux is formed. To this add tarragon, cajun spices, saffron and fish stock. Simmer for 30 minutes, add milk and season to taste. Finally add oysters and simmer for 2 minutes, do not boil. Serve immediately.

Nemus
  2 fish fillets
  juice of 2 lemons
  1 tablespoon salt
  4 tablespoons red wine vinegar
  1 onion, thinly sliced

Marinate fish fillets in lemon juice and salt for 1 hour or until opaque, and then chill. Drain off lemon juice and mix vinegar and onion with fish and chill.

Arnhem Land Barra

Along the coast and in the estuaries and rivers of Arnhem Land – and for that matter all across the north – the famous barramundi abounds. This delicate white-fleshed fish is actually best if taken from salt water rather than fresh as they can have a muddy flavour after long periods in fresh water. It has superb flavour prepared just about any way but we prefer to keep it simple. The Aborigines of Arnhem Land cook barramundi similarly to our recipe, although they do not gut the fish and they wrap it in the bark of the paperbark, then place it directly onto the hot coals. This is delicious as the fish takes on a slight eucalyptus flavour.

Gut the barramundi but leave the rest intact including the scales (which serve to keep the juices within the fish during cooking). In the stomach cavity place slices of lemon. Place the fish on a grill plate over an open fire of glowing coals and allow to cook for between 20 and 30 minutes on each side depending on size of the fish. Test to see if fish is cooked through to the bone. The scales will peel off in a piece with the skin. Sections of the meat can easily be lifted from the bone with an egglifter or a broad-bladed knife.

Tahitian Fish Salad

At the mouth of the Pennefather River in Cape York there is a wide choice of fish available, both offshore and from the embankments. At this stunning campsite we prepared a meal of raw fish dishes and shared them with a group of surprised but delighted fellow campers. Almost any firm-fleshed fish will suffice but we used queenfish for the recipe given.

   2 fish fillets
   juice of 2 lemons
   $\frac{1}{2}$ cup coconut milk
   1 chilli, seeded and finely chopped
   1 onion, finely chopped
   1 capsicum, finely chopped
   1 tablespoon red wine vinegar

Marinate fish fillets in lemon juice for about 1 hour or until opaque. Drain off all lemon juice and place fish in bowl. Into this bowl mix in coconut milk, chilli, onion, capsicum and vinegar. Chill.

Billabong Mussel Soup

In the billabongs of central Australia freshwater mussels are found and are easily collected. This recipe was enjoyed in the cool shade on the banks of one such billabong.

   1 onion, chopped
   1 clove garlic, finely chopped
   olive oil
   1 teaspoon dried mixed herbs
   1 dried birdseye chilli or chilli sauce to taste
   1 cup white wine or 1 cup water
   1 450 g can tomato soup
   1 450 g can tomato pieces
   salt and pepper to taste
   30 freshwater mussels

Lightly sauté onion and garlic in a small amount of olive oil until opaque. Add herbs, chilli, white wine or water, tomato soup and tomato pieces, and bring to the boil. Allow to boil for five minutes, season to taste and add mussels to cook for about 2 minutes until tender.

Wetherby Damper

The staff on Wetherby Station, one of the oldest cattle properties in Far North Queensland, supplied us with this tried, tested and delicious recipe for damper, an outback staple.

   1 kg self-raising flour
   1 tablespoon herbs (parsley, fresh or dried is good)
   1 clove garlic, chopped
   salt to taste
   2 tablespoons butter or margarine
   $\frac{1}{4}$ cup milk
   1 cup beer
   water
   extra milk for glaze

Put self-raising flour into bowl, add herbs and garlic. Add salt to taste and stir into flour. Work butter into flour with finger-tips and add milk, stir into mix. Add beer and stir in. Drink the rest of the beer before it goes flat. Stir in enough water until a dough the consistency of porridge is reached. Place into camp oven, glaze with a little milk and cook over coals, placing coals on lid of camp oven too for an even temperature. It takes around 30 minutes, but check after 20 minutes by sticking in a knife; if no dough sticks, damper is cooked. (You could instead shape the damper mix into patties and fry on the barbecue plate.)

SURVIVAL

This is the chapter we hope none of you ever have to turn to except in the comfort of an armchair before you leave. However, there are skills you can learn theoretically about survival and if you take the appropriate equipment and misfortune befall you, you will stay calm in the knowledge that you can help yourself.

The main reasons you could be stuck in a remote place are a major mechanical breakdown, or becoming hopelessly bogged. If you follow our route directions and take the right maps, getting lost is only a remote possibility. However, should a disaster occur, you need to be properly equipped to be able to wait with your vehicle until you are found.

So, someone needs to know you're missing first. This is why, when travelling through remote areas, you *must* give your itinerary to either the police or national parks ranger or a member of your family, any of whom will raise the alarm if you don't report in within an agreed limit. You can also report yourself stranded via the high-frequency radio already installed (see 'Setting Up'). If you are using the right maps, you should be able to tell fairly accurately where you are with just a few navigation skills.

And you won't panic in arid outback areas, because you will be carrying at least a minimum of 20 litres *per head* spare water with you for just such an emergency.

PROTECTION   If you are assured help is on its way, there are things to do to ensure you are still in good condition when it arrives. Protect yourself and your party from extremes of temperature once you have attended to any necessary first aid.

This means in cold weather to rug up in the warmest, driest clothes you have, including a hat, as we lose most heat from our heads in the cold. Plastic bags or newspapers can help with insulation if bedding is wet. In snow, digging a cave may be warmer than staying actually in the vehicle. Remember to use a metal pipe or similar to provide air and ventilation and take a heat source and shovel inside with you. If the heat source is a gas stove or light good ventilation is necessary as carbon monoxide poisoning is a danger. The shovel could be necessary to dig yourself out. Before entering the cave leave a brightly coloured flag or piece of material outside to alert rescuers.

In warm or hot conditions do not exert yourself; if work is needed on the vehicle or on survival techniques try to wait until the cooler evening. Improvise shade with tarpaulin, sheets or blankets anchored by rocks or spare tyres

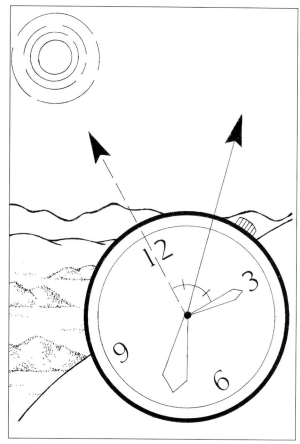

Direction finding

over the coolest side of the vehicle. Keep your body covered with light clothing and do as little as possible.

LOCATION BY RESCUERS   The most important rule is that *no-one leaves the vehicle*: this is only to be broken if you are positive you are close enough to walk to a homestead or town. Many people have put themselves in far greater danger by thinking they could walk to safety. It is far easier to find a vehicle than lone figures so stay with your car.

Build up scrub or add oil or tyres to a pyre of scrub to provide a signal fire to rescuers; ensure a bushfire won't be started by the fire however. White smoke will be produced by vegetation and black by oil or rubber; try to contrast the smoke colour to the terrain and sky.

Without a compass it is still possible to orient yourself if you are lost. A dial watch or the Southern Cross at night will guide you to due north or south. Using a watch (or by drawing a watch dial on the ground), point the 12 of the dial towards the sun. North will be halfway between 12 and the hour hand.

Near the Southern Cross are 2 bright pointer stars. Imagine a line extending out at right angles from the mid-point between the pointers and another line passing through the head and tail of the Southern Cross. Where these 2 imaginary lines cross is south.

WATER Water rationing seems to do nothing to prolong life. Drink what you need when the signs of exhaustion appear and use a little energy in the cool of the evening to construct a desert still, or even better 2 or 3. It is nearly as crucial as drinking water that you keep your perspiration rate as low as possible and so conserve body water loss.

It is important that you do not attempt to drink radiator coolant to survive – it is not pure water but chemical-based and even if you try to put only water in the radiator there are bound to be impurities in it.

In vegetated areas, you can construct a desert still. In cool of the evening, dig a hole about a metre wide and around half a metre deep. Put a container at the hole's centre to collect water. Surround the container with cut green vegetation (if there is a choice, fleshy plants such as succulents will be more efficient than drier plants such as saltbush), and then cover the hole with a plastic sheet held down and completely sealed with rocks. Place a smaller rock or pebble in the centre of this plastic sheet, directly above the container.

The sun's heat will evaporate moisture from the plants, which will condense on the inside of the plastic, run down to the centre and drip into the container. In continuous sunlight about 2 litres a day can be collected in this way, so you can see the sense in having 2 or more dug at once. Replace the plants every day.

If there are leafy trees or shrubs about, secure large plastic bags over several branches and watch the water collect in them too. Drain each bag daily and place them on fresh branches.

Other tips for finding water include watching out for animal and bird tracks or flights as they visit waterholes. If you are near the sea or a desert lake, fresh water is often found by digging just a few metres above the high tide mark; the water may taste brackish but will be fairly free from salt. In a dry creek bed, try digging down for about a metre or so at the lowest point of an outside bend in the channel (an outside bend will usually have steeper sides) and there could be a useful fresh water soak.

FOOD As you can last about 3 weeks without food, it is a lower priority than shelter and water. It is probably better to go hungry than to experiment by eating strange plants. Do not believe a plant is edible if you see animals eating it – it could be highly toxic to humans. However, a body without adequate nourishment is prone to sickness. If animals can be caught and cooked they are usually safe to eat, but avoid their offal.

FIRE AND FLOOD Australia, being a country of extremes, can be in flood in one area while burning up in another. Daily checks with local authorities where such natural phenomena are possible will warn you against travelling into such areas at critical times, see 'Planning Ahead'.

You can help prevent fires by thoroughly checking your exhaust system daily, especially when travelling in dry grassy country. Dry grass gets trapped around the exhaust shielding and can be a lethal combination with the hot temperature of the vehicle.

Bushfires travel fast, so if you are caught in the path of an approaching fire, find the clearest possible area with few trees and little or short grass. Turn on the vehicle's hazard lights to warn other vehicles of your presence and sit it out in the comparative safety of your vehicle while the worst passes.

Prepare by closing all windows of the vehicle, wrap yourself in a woollen blanket and lie on the floor or as low down as you can get. It is extremely unlikely that the car will catch fire; petrol in the tank will not burn unless it is somehow exposed to direct flame, and, unless it is a grass fire, most of the fire will pass overhead quickly as it is usually driven by strong winds. When the worse has passed check that no part of the car is alight. Use the fire extinguisher we have recommended as necessary. Then drive away from the fire front to clear ground.

Flash flooding is only likely to be a problem if you are driving or parked in a steep sided valley or creek and it has been raining heavily upstream or close to where you are. Usually you will get some warning. You may hear of storms and rain upstream, or there may be heavy rain in the immediate vicinity, in which case don't drive in creek beds or narrow valleys until the rain and its potential flood has gone. *Never* camp in dry creek beds for this reason.

If you are caught in a flash flood there is a good chance you will lose some possessions and perhaps the car. However, your life is more important than both, so get yourself out of the car and on to high ground and worry about the car and possessions later. If the car is washed away it is not likely to travel far before being stopped by a tree or rock, or stranding itself on shallow ground.

If the car is engulfed while you are in it (or if you drive into deep water by accident) the windows should be up, in which case the car will fill with water slowly. Wait until the water pressure inside and out are equalised or nearly so (you won't be able to open the doors until this happens anyway), then take a deep breath, open the necessary doors to gain egress for all passengers and swim to the surface. Help children or older people do the same.

Swim or float with fast-running water and not against it and look out for a projecting embankment or overhanging limb to help the climb to higher ground.

When the flood has past you may be able to retrieve the vehicle, dry it out on higher ground and continue. This is more likely if you have a manually operated (Tirfor) winch and not a battery-operated unit, as your battery might no longer work, or at least not with enough power for a winch. Any power remaining in the battery would be probably best conserved to operate the high-frequency radio you are carrying to call help. (See 'Setting Up'.)

FIRST AID We recommend that at least one of the passengers in your vehicle attend a St John Ambulance Association, Red Cross or similarly well-respected first-aid course before you set off on long trips. Emergencies involving people are usually the results of accidents of some kind, but can also be as a result of an illness. In either case there are procedures to follow which will help the sufferer and those around who also may be in shock. See the back end paper of this book for information about accident action.

For less grave emergencies, each vehicle needs to carry a personal first-aid kit with enough supplies to cover whoever is travelling and where you are travelling; include some extra items if spending a long time in remote areas.

Many motoring organisations and car accessory outlets have a selection of made-up kits to choose from, however, the drawback here is that you will be paying for items you will never use and will still need to buy personal preferences to include. If you make up your own kit, begin with an unbreakable plastic lunch box with strong lid attached, and the following items.

▶ *gauze dressing* ▶ *cotton wool* ▶ *antiseptic fluid* ▶ *antiseptic cream* ▶ *adhesive strips* ▶ *adhesive plaster bandages (both 75 millimetre and 25 millimetre width)* ▶ *medicated bandages (for sprains)* ▶ *pain relieving tablets* ▶ *diarrhoea tablets* ▶ *nausea relieving tablets* ▶ *travel sickness tablets* ▶ *burn relief cream* ▶ *drawing cream* ▶ *small scissors* ▶ *tweezers* ▶ *eye wash and bath* ▶ *calamine lotion* ▶ *methylated spirits* ▶ *safety pins* ▶ *thermometer* ▶ *suitable child preparations if travelling with small children*

Add to this list any items you feel are personally necessary, including penicillin (do not give unless you know patient is not allergic) or strong pain relievers if travelling in remote areas.

A book we recommend keeping in the kit or the glovebox is *First Aid in the Australian Bush* by Bruce Wilson, and

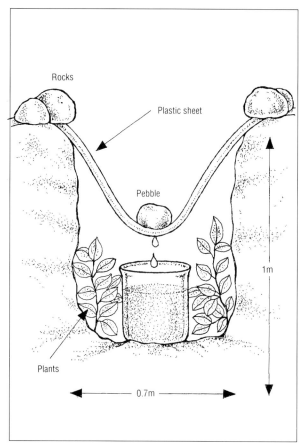

A desert still

it is available for $19.95 posted from Freepost No 4, Wilderness Publications, PO Box 444, Blackburn VIC 3130; (03) 878 4281.

ROYAL FLYING DOCTOR SERVICE For general information regarding all the services offered by the RFDS, contact: Royal Flying Doctor Service of Australia Federal Office, PO Box 345, Hurstville NSW 2220; (02) 580 9711. See 'Setting Up' for list of RFDS bases and telephone numbers.

TAKE CARE

● Don't take short cuts over virgin ground. You will destroy the vegetation. Stick to tracks open for use.

TOURS OUT OF CAPITAL CITIES

These are one-way tours which vary from a day's travel to a week or more. Each tour has its own sketch map, detailed route directions and camping and permits information and is also cross-referenced to the Australia-wide map coverage section of the book.

Southern Highlands view, Morton National Park

TOURS OUT OF SYDNEY

The lower mountains and valleys of the New South Wales section of the Great Dividing Range, the forests around Sydney and the tablelands of the south coast offer an excellent range of possibilities to the four-wheel drive explorer. We have plotted tours which are all easily accessed from the harbour city on good highways; the temperate climate of these regions means that aside from periods of heavy rainfall, which will make some tracks impassable, they are all-year-round propositions.

THE WATAGAN MOUNTAINS (a day tour: 104 kilometres). Relatively short and a good beginners' trip, this tour is through cool, green coastal forests of both native and introduced species. However, we suggest you make it a leisurely weekend expedition, to enjoy the beauty of the area and the forest camping. It is an excellent summer escape. Forest roads are passable but very slippery after rain.

THE SOUTH COAST HINTERLAND (tour over 2 or 3 days: 194 kilometres). This tour strikes into the diverse and very beautiful hinterland of the New South Wales coast below Sydney. It includes the dramatic Macquarie Pass, Fitzroy Falls, Kangaroo Valley and the picturesque holiday township of Robertson. The great plateau regions of Yalwal and Tianjara provide an interesting and challenging four-wheel drive section, which may be boggy due to the fact that the flat country holds water for long periods.

THE SYDNEY MOUNTAINS (tour over a minimum of 4 days: 636 kilometres). Our longest tour is this spectacular and historic trip through east-central New South Wales. Due to the areas of close population the actual four-wheel drive component is comparatively small, but the tour is on good mix of roads and tracks which take advantage of the social and natural history and geography of the region.

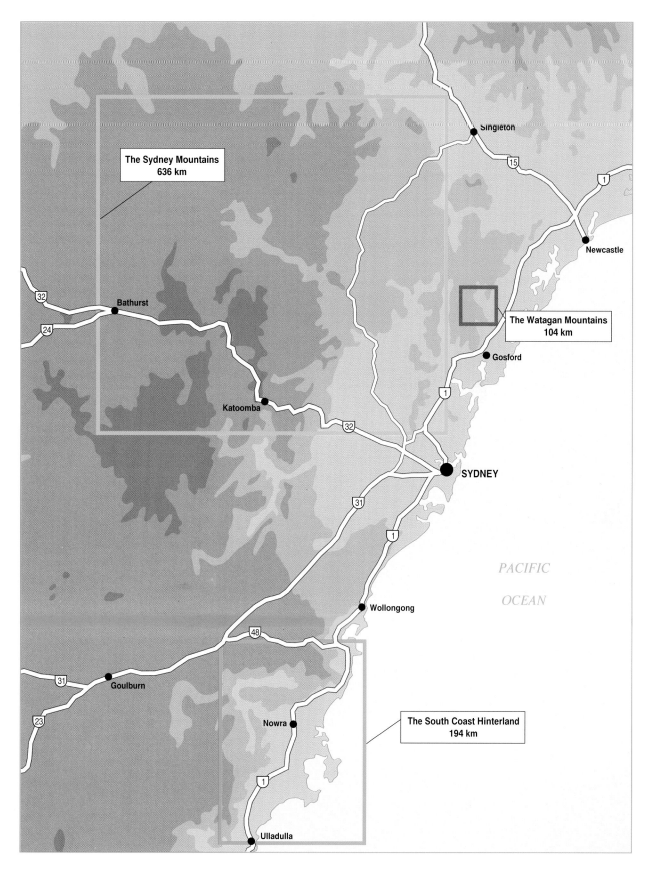

The Sydney Mountains
636 km

Singleton

15

1

Newcastle

32

Bathurst

24

The Watagan Mountains
104 km

Gosford

1

Katoomba

32

31

SYDNEY

1

PACIFIC

OCEAN

Wollongong

48

31

Goulburn

23

Nowra

The South Coast Hinterland
194 km

1

Ulladulla

NEW SOUTH WALES STATE FORESTS AND NATIONAL PARKS

The state forests of New South Wales are managed by the Forestry Commission for the production of timber, as a protection for wildlife and for recreational use. The national parks protect wilderness areas, endangered species and relics of Aboriginal culture. Both park systems offer many enjoyable four-wheel driving and camping-out opportunities in developed and undeveloped sites. Formed tracks lead to walking trails, fishing spots and secluded gorges of great beauty; brochures are available describing the attractions and facilities of individual parks. For state forests information contact the NSW Forestry Commission head office, Building 2, 423 Pennant Hills Road, Pennant Hills NSW 2120; tel. (02) 980 4100. For national parks information contact NPWS head office, 43 Bridge Street, Hurstville NSW 2220; PO Box 1967; tel. (02) 585 6333. Addresses and phone numbers of local offices are given in the tour description. When in state forests and national parks, observe the following code.

▶ *Do not divert from formed roads and tracks.*
▶ *Camp at least 20 metres from any watercourse.*

▶ *Use existing clearings; do not remove or damage vegetation.*
▶ *Do not camp in established picnic areas.*
▶ *Use rubbish bins provided, or take your rubbish with you.*
▶ *When bush camping, make sure that latrines are at least 50 metres from streams or rivers and are well covered when you leave.*
▶ *Light fires only in properly constructed fireplaces and never within 4.5 metres of a tree or a log. Flammable material should be cleared to at least 1.5 metres, and a fire must never be left unattended. Do not enter parks and forests during periods of total fire ban.*
▶ *Do not disturb native plants or animals; all are protected.*
▶ *Some areas in state forests are privately leased; respect owners' property. Do not damage or disturb evidence of Aboriginal culture.*
▶ *Fossicking is prohibited, except in certain specified areas.*
▶ *No pets or firearms in national parks. Keep pets under control at all times in forest areas.*

THE COASTAL FORESTS The lower slopes of the Great Dividing Range north of Newcastle offer great four-wheel drive challenges through dramatic scenery. They are accessed from the Pacific Highway. *For route directions and information see 'Sydney to Brisbane' in the Treks Around Australia.*

BEFORE YOU SET OUT ▶ Read the tour description carefully. ▶ Check that you have obtained any necessary permits. ▶ Check weather conditions with local authorities or Bureau of Meteorology. ▶ Make sure you have the appropriate maps and information for the tour. ▶ Check that your vehicle is in good order for the conditions ahead. Have you the necessary spare parts? ▶ If you are camping, have you the right equipment?

USEFUL INFORMATION

For general touring information contact:
New South Wales Travel Centre
19 Castlereagh Street
Sydney 2000
(02) 231 4444.

For motoring information contact:
National Roads and Motorists Association (NRMA)
151 Clarence Street
Sydney 2000
(02) 260 9222.

For four-wheel driving information contact:
Four Wheel Drive Clubs Association of New South Wales and Australian Capital Territory
GPO Box 3870
Sydney 2001.

THE WATAGAN MOUNTAINS

START POINT Map page 3, K6

TOTAL KM 104. Does not include 83 km Sydney to start point and 90 km end point to Sydney. *See Route Directions.*
UNSEALED KM 83.
DEGREE OF DIFFICULTY Easy.
DRIVING TIME Tour over 1 – 3 days. Allow extra time to/from start/end points. *See Route Directions.*
LONGEST DISTANCE NO FUEL 81 km (Yarramalong to Wyong).
TOPOGRAPHIC MAP Auslig 1:250 000 series: *Sydney.* See also 1:100 000 series.
LOCAL/SPECIALITY MAP NSW Forestry Commission map: *Newcastle State Forests.*
OTHER USEFUL INFORMATION NSW Forestry Commission brochure: *Forests of the Watagan Mountains*; also detailed forestry maps for walks.
BEST TIME OF YEAR TO TRAVEL Any time but heavy rain makes some sections of track impassable.

TOUR DESCRIPTION This tour is a good introduction to four-wheel driving on forest tracks. Close proximity to Sydney and easy access make it an excellent one-day trip, although the pleasant and varied scenery and excellent camping facilities suggest it would be enjoyed more over a weekend. Roads are mostly well-made gravel along ridge tops, although sometimes slippery and narrow, *see Warnings.* The tour is not suitable for caravans.

The best way to observe the native wildlife and vegetation of the Watagans is via the walking tracks, which are clearly marked, so take some time to explore them. The Rock Lily and Lyrebird tracks are both centred on The Basin Camping Area and wind through moss walls, cool rainforest and dense eucalypts with glimpses of Wollombi Creek. The Pines Track from the Pines Forest Reserve takes you to a fern-lined creek; the Wildflower Track leads through a dry forest understorey where there are spectacular wildflowers in spring. You'll enjoy great views of the coastal region from Muirs Lookout Picnic Area, just off the route along Prickly Ridge Forest Road.

The Watagan Mountains are managed by the NSW Forestry Commission for commercial timber production. Red cedar was the first target of the loggers in early days and only scattered pockets remain, easily distin-

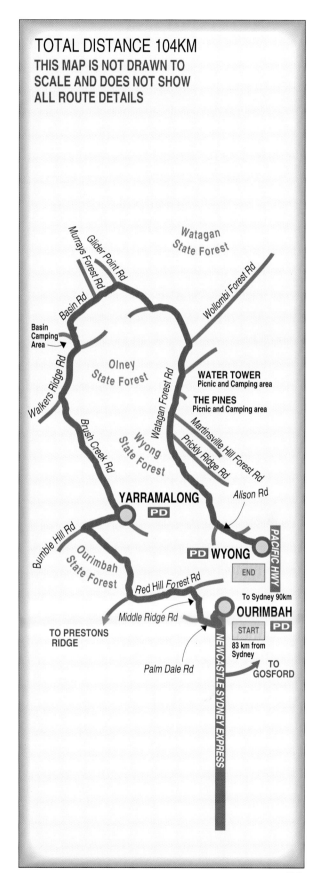

TOTAL DISTANCE 104KM
THIS MAP IS NOT DRAWN TO SCALE AND DOES NOT SHOW ALL ROUTE DETAILS

Walking trail, near the Pines Picnic Area

guishable in spring by the coppery tint of the new foliage. Now blackbutt, blue gum and turpentine are harvested, and there is a continuous programme of reforestation evident along the tracks throughout our tour. Recreational use of the forest areas is encouraged and there are many attractive spots to picnic and enjoy magnificent vistas of the coast and surrounding forests. Bush camping is permitted and there are camping and picnic facilities at the *Basin Camping Area* and the *Pines Camping Area* along our route; both are in open grassy clearings.

WARNINGS ▶ Beware of logging trucks on forest tracks. ▶ Some sections of tracks are closed or impassable after heavy rain. If in doubt, check with NSW Forestry Commission office at Wyong, 31 Alison Road, Wyong NSW 2259; tel. (043) 52 1188. ▶ Stick to formed tracks at all times and observe forestry regulations.

BOOKINGS AND PERMITS ▶ No bookings necessary to camp in state forests, but observe all regulations. For information about the area, contact NSW Forestry Commission head office in Sydney, or Wyong office, *see*

Warnings. ▶ Tourist information available from centre at Palm Dale Road and Pacific Highway intersection.

ROUTE DIRECTIONS

Depart Sydney north via Pacific Hwy and Sydney–Newcastle Expressway past the Gosford turnoff at Ourimbah (approx. 83 km). **PD**

START TOUR

0.0 km Zero trip meter at s'post: Palm Dale. **TL.**
(0.1 km)

0.1 km S'post: Palm Dale Rd. **TL.**
(1.9 km)

2.0 km Gravel.
(0.6 km)

2.6 km S'post: Middle Ridge Forest Rd. **TR.**

> *Sign: Ourimbah State Forest. Logging trucks use this road.*

(4.7 km)

7.3 km   S'post: Kulnura. **TL** onto Red Hill Forest Rd.

> *Wyong off to right.*

(3.8 km)

11.1 km   T intersection. **TR**.

> *Prestons Ridge Rd on left.*

(5.5 km)

16.6 km   Bitumen.

(3.3 km)

19.9 km   S'post: Bumble Hill Rd. **TR** at T intersection.

(3.3 km)

23.2 km   S'post: Newcastle. **TL** into Yarramalong village onto Great North Walk Track and Brush Creek Rd.

> PD *Cleared countryside in this section, small rural holdings.*

(7.1 km)

30.3 km   Gravel.

(9.7 km)

40.0 km   S'post: Walkers Ridge Forest Rd. **TR** at T intersection.

> *Kulnura off to left.*

(3.7 km)

43.7 km   S'post: Basin Camping Area. **TL** onto Basin Rd.

(1.3 km)

45.0 km   **SO** through camping area. **KR** at Y intersection and cross causeway.

> *Basin Camping Area on both sides of track. Barbecues, toilets, fresh water and picnic facilities. Open grassed campsites. Walking trails through rainforest and eucalypt stands.*

(4.3 km)

49.3 km   Y intersection. **KR**.

> *Murrays Forest Rd on left.*

(1.8 km)

51.1 km   Intersection. **KR**.

> *Glider Point Rd on left.*

(6.5 km)

57.6 km   S'post: Walkers Ridge Forest Rd. **TL** at T intersection.

(5.0 km)

62.6 km   S'post: Walkers Ridge Forest Rd. **KR** at Y intersection.

> *Wollombi Forest Rd on left.*

(3.7 km)

66.3 km   S'post: Cooranbong. **TR** onto Watagan Forest Rd at T intersection.

> *Water Tower Picnic Area on left. The Pines Camping Area 1 km off to left. Barbecues, toilets, fresh water. Open grassy sites. Walking trails.*

0.0 km   Zero trip meter at above intersection.

(1.0 km)

1.0 km   Intersection. **SO**.

> *The Pines Picnic Area 1 km off to left.*

0.0 km   Zero trip meter at above intersection.

(2.4 km)

2.4 km   S'post: Watagan Forest Rd. **TR** at intersection.

> *Martinsville Hill Forest Rd on left, to Wishing Well Forest Park. Barbecues, picnic facilities.*

(1.0 km)

3.4 km   S'post: Watagan Forest Rd. **KR** at Y intersection.

> *Prickly Ridge Rd on left. To Muirs Lookout and picnic area and spectacular views of coastal region.*

(27.9 km)

31.3 km   S'post: Wyong. **TR** at T intersection onto bitumen.

(1.6 km)

32.9 km   S'post: Wyong. **TR** at T intersection.

> *Wyee off to left.*

(1.8 km)

34.7 km   S'post: Wyong. **TL** onto Alison Rd and pass over expressway.

> *Yarramalong off to right.*

(1.5 km)

36.2 km   Y intersection. **KR** along Alison Rd.

(0.7 km)

36.9 km   S'post: Sydney. **TR** at T intersection in Wyong onto Pacific Hwy. Zero trip meter. PD

> *Newcastle off to left.*

END TOUR

Return to Sydney via Pacific Hwy and Sydney–Newcastle Expressway (approx. 90 km).

THE SOUTH COAST HINTERLAND

Kangaroo Valley

START POINT Map page 2, I10; map page 3, J10.

TOTAL KM 194. Does not include 105 km Sydney to start point and 250 km end point to Sydney. *See Route Directions.*
UNSEALED KM 94.
DRIVING TIME Tour over 2 or 3 days. Allow extra time to/from start/end points. *See Route Directions.*
LONGEST DISTANCE NO FUEL 106 km (Nowra to Ulladulla).
DEGREE OF DIFFICULTY Moderate. *See Warnings.*
TOPOGRAPHIC MAPS Auslig 1:250 000 series: *Ulladulla*; *Wollongong*. See also 1:100 000 series.
LOCAL/SPECIALITY MAPS NSW Forestry Commission map: *Nowra*; CMA map: *South Coast.*
OTHER USEFUL INFORMATION NSW NPWS: *Visitor Guide* and information sheets: *Morton National Park*; *Camping in Morton National Park; Fitzroy Falls*; NSW Forestry Commission leaflet: *State Forests of the Nowra Area*; *State Forests of the South Coast*; Shoalhaven City Council brochure and map: *Shoalhaven.*
BEST TIME OF YEAR TO TRAVEL Spring and early summer for wildflower season, but best before mid-summer rains which can make tracks impassable. A dry winter is a good time, but can be very cold.

TOUR DESCRIPTION Striking inland from the south coast road onto the Illawarra Highway, this tour takes you through the Macquarie Pass to Morton National Park, one of the larger parks in New South Wales. Our route offers the chance to enjoy many views from the dramatic sandstone cliffs over lightly wooded valleys or dense eucalypt forest. A visit to Fitzroy Falls, which plunge 81 metres from the escarpment, is worthwhile. There is a variety of wildlife to be seen and heard in Morton, including lyrebirds, if you are careful, and plenty of scenic walking trails.

The route south tracks through picturesque Kangaroo Valley farmland and historic Hampden back to the coast at Nowra. This pleasant resort town owes its development to the timber industry and to the Shoalhaven River, which provided a waterway to transport logs to the coast. The valuable red cedar first attracted loggers, who soon saw the value of other local timbers including blackbutt and spotted gum. The forests in the area still supply timber for sawmilling products. We visited the Naval Aviation Museum at HMAS *Albatross* and explored a few of the magnificent beaches in the region before tackling the true four-wheel drive tracks through the forests of the Yalwal and Tianjara sandstone plateaus. Vegetation here varies from low forest and heathlands to pockets of rainforest in the gullies, and taller eucalypt stands as you near the coast.

You can bush camp in *Morton National Park*, except where otherwise indicated, and there is a designated camping area with facilities at *Fitzroy Falls*. Bush camping is also permitted in state forests and there are excellent camping facilities at or near *Nowra, Milton* and *Ulladulla* at the end of the route, if you wish to extend the trip.

WARNINGS ▶ Parts of this tour not suitable for caravans. ▶ Four-wheel drive tracks impassable after heavy rain. Water lies for considerable periods on the soft flat sections of the Yarramunmun and Tianjara Fire Trails. Beware of washaways. If in doubt, check with forestry office at Nowra, 24 Berry Street, Nowra NSW 2541; tel. (044) 21 8833. ▶ Beware of logging trucks on forest tracks. ▶ Observe all regulations on driving, camping, lighting of fires, protection of native flora and fauna and rubbish removal when using state forests and national parks.

BOOKINGS AND PERMITS ▶ Bush camping permitted in state forests, but observe regulations. For information contact the forestry office in Sydney or Nowra, see address above. ▶ Bush camping in Morton National Park, or camp at designated site at Fitzroy Falls. Permit necessary, obtain on site. For information on camping and facilities in Morton National Park, contact NSW NPWS office in Nowra, 24 Berry Street, Nowra NSW 2541: PO Box 707, Nowra NSW 2540; tel. (044) 31 9969; contact Fitzroy Falls Visitor Information Centre direct on (048) 87 7270. ▶ For touring and camping information, contact: Shoalhaven Tourist Information Centre, Princes Highway, Bomaderry; tel. (044) 21 0778 or (008) 02 4261.

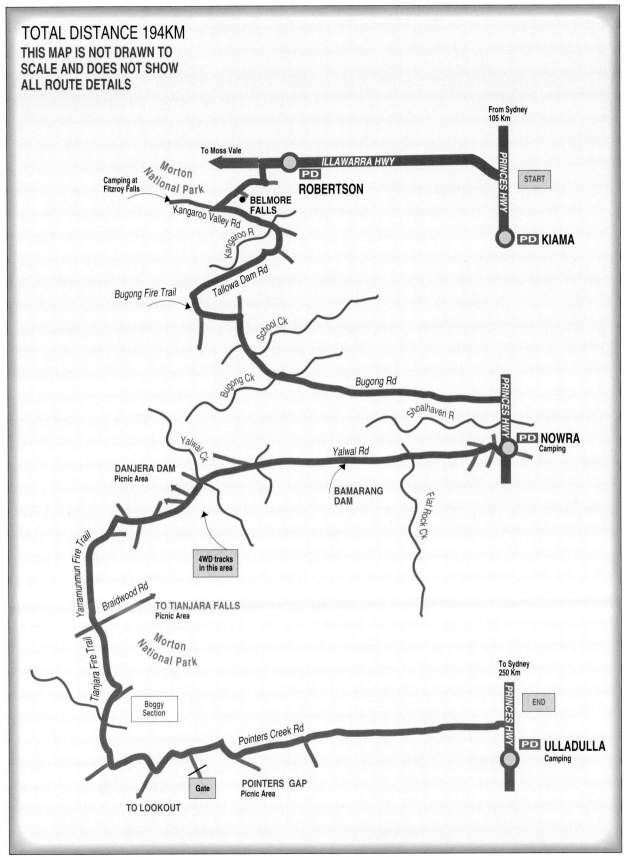

TOTAL DISTANCE 194KM
THIS MAP IS NOT DRAWN TO
SCALE AND DOES NOT SHOW
ALL ROUTE DETAILS

From Sydney
105 Km

To Moss Vale

Morton National Park

Camping at Fitzroy Falls

PD START

ILLAWARRA HWY

PRINCES HWY

PD
ROBERTSON

BELMORE FALLS

PD **KIAMA**

Kangaroo Valley Rd

Kangaroo R

Tallowa Dam Rd

Bugong Fire Trail

School Ck

Bugong Ck

Bugong Rd

PRINCES HWY

Shoalhaven R

PD **NOWRA**
Camping

Yalwal Ck

Yalwal Rd

DANJERA DAM
Picnic Area

BAMARANG DAM

Flat Rock Ck

Yarramunmun Fire Trail

4WD tracks
in this area

Braidwood Rd

TO TIANJARA FALLS
Picnic Area

Tianjara Fire Trail

Morton National Park

To Sydney
250 Km

END

Boggy Section

PRINCES HWY

Pointers Creek Rd

PD **ULLADULLA**
Camping

Gate

POINTERS GAP
Picnic Area

TO LOOKOUT

ROUTE DIRECTIONS

Depart Sydney CBD south on Princes Hwy via Bulli Pass and Wollongong to Princes Hwy and Illawarra Hwy intersection (approx. 105 km).

START TOUR

0.0 km Zero trip meter at s'post: Moss Vale. **TR** onto Illawarra Hwy.

(2.7 km)

2.7 km S'post: Moss Vale. **TR** in Albion Park, continuing along Illawarra Hwy.

> *Route traverses subtropical rainforest of Macquarie Pass National Park. Walking trails, no camping in this park.*

(24.9 km)

27.6 km Robertson town centre, adjacent to general store. **SO.**

> **PD** *Supplies.*

(1.1 km)

28.7 km Cross railway line.

(1.5 km)

30.2 km S'post: Wildes Meadow. **TL** onto Pearsons Road.

> *Moss Vale straight ahead.*

(5.0 km)

35.2 km S'post: Fitzroy Falls. **TR** onto Myra Vale Road.

> *Belmore Falls off to left. Short walk to lookout.*

(4.4 km)

39.6 km Fitzroy Falls Reservoir on right. **SO.**

(3.3 km)

42.9 km S'post: Kangaroo Valley.

> *Fitzroy Falls 1 km off to right. Camping and picnic area at Yarrunga Creek: barbecues and toilets. Obtain permit to camp at Morton National Park Information Centre in picnic area. No advance bookings necessary. Scenic walks through light bush and rainforest to lookouts over falls.*

0.0 km Zero trip meter at above s'post. **TL** onto Kangaroo Valley Rd.

(14.5 km)

14.5 km Kangaroo River. Cross Hampden Bridge.

Forest track, near Nowra

> *Hampden Bridge oldest suspension bridge in Australia. Pioneer Farm Museum on right. Tearooms and picnic area on left. Hampden Bridge Caravan Park and general store on left.* **PD**

(0.9 km)

15.4 km S'post: Mt Scanzi Rd. **TR.**

(4.9 km)

20.3 km Intersection. S'post: Tallowa Dam Picnic Ground. **SO.**

> *Mt Scanzi Rd on left.*

(9.4 km)

29.7 km S'post: Bugong Fire Trail. **TL** onto gravel.

(2.6 km)

32.3 km Intersection. **SO.**

> *Ruins Fire Trail on right.*

(5.2 km)

37.5 km T intersection. **TR** onto Bugong Rd.

(0.5 km)

38.0 km   School Creek. Cross bridge.
(2.0 km)
40.0 km   Bugong Creek. Cross causeway.
(7.9 km)
47.9 km   Bitumen.
(12.5 km)
60.4 km   T intersection. **TR** onto Princes Hwy and immediately cross bridge over Shoalhaven River into Nowra.

> PD *Supplies, caravan parks and camping in many attractive locations close to Nowra. Shoalhaven River excellent for fishing, water skiing, canoeing and sailing. Beautiful beaches in area.*

0.0 km   Zero trip meter on north bank of Shoalhaven River heading south. **SO.**
(1.1 km)
1.1 km   S'post: Ulladulla.

> *Nowra town centre off to right.*

0.0 km   Zero trip meter. **SO** at traffic lights.
(1.7 km)
1.7 km   S'post: HMAS *Albatross*. **TR** into Kalandar Rd at traffic lights.

> *Greenwell Point off to left.*

(0.3 km)
2.0 km   At roundabout take second exit: s'post: Albatross Rd.

> *Batemans Bay straight ahead.*

(0.9 km)
2.9 km   S'post: Danjera Dam/Historic Yalwal. **TR** onto Yalwal Rd.
(1.6 km)
4.5 km   Flat Rock Creek. Cross bridge.
(5.9 km)
10.4 km   Bamarang Dam on left. **SO.**
(1.3 km)
11.7 km   Gravel.
(1.0 km)
12.7 km   Cross bridge.
(0.5 km)
13.2 km   S'post: Yalwal Rd. **KL.**

> *Burrier Rd on right.*

(15.0 km)
28.2 km   Yalwal Creek. Cross wooden bridge.
(0.1 km)

28.3 km   Y intersection. **KL.**

> *Information Board on right. Track on right to Danjera Dam Picnic Area.*

(0.1 km)
28.4 km   Y intersection. **KL.**

> *Track on right to Danjera Dam.*

(0.1 km)
28.5 km   Intersection. **SO.**

> *Track on right. Sign: tourist drive. One-way traffic.*

(1.1 km)
29.6 km   Intersection. **SO.**

> *Track enters on right: tourist drive from Danjera Dam.*

(0.2 km)
29.8 km   Sign: Old Mining Rd 1872. **KR.**

> *S'post on track on left. Private property.*

(0.3 km)
30.1 km   Intersection. **TL** onto Yarramunmun Trail.
(2.1 km)
32.2 km   Intersection. **SO.**

> *Track enters on right. This area of Crown land set aside for 4WD recreation.*

(3.8 km)
36.0 km   T intersection. **TR.**
(20.1 km)
56.1 km   Crossroads.

> *Tianjara Falls 1.5 km off to left. Lookout and picnic area with great views of Morton National Park.*

0.0 km   Zero trip meter. **SO** over Braidwood Rd.
(0.5 km)
0.5 km   **SO** along Tianjara Fire Trail and immediately pass under transmission lines.

> *Radio tower mast on left.*

(6.3 km)
6.8 km   Kangaroo Hill on left. **SO.**
(0.5 km)
7.3 km   T intersection. **TR.**
(3.0 km)
10.3 km   Creek crossing.
(0.3 km)
10.6 km   Boggy section.
(3.7 km)

Fitzroy Falls

Historic Hampden Suspension Bridge

14.3 km Long boggy section.
(4.3 km)
18.6 km T intersection. **TL**.
(1.4 km)
20.0 km T intersection. **TL**.

Lookout on right.

(3.7 km)
23.7 km Intersection. **SO**.

Track on right leads to gate.

(0.2 km)
23.9 km Intersection. **TL**.
(1.2 km)
25.1 km Intersection.

Pointers Gap off to right. Picnic Area.

0.0 km Zero trip meter at above intersection. **SO**.
(0.1 km)
0.1 km Bitumen.
(2.6 km)
2.7 km Gravel.
(6.0 km)
8.7 km T intersection. Princes Hwy. Zero trip meter.
END TOUR
TL to return to Sydney via Princes Hwy (approx. 250 km). **TR** to Ulladulla (approx. 15 km).

PD *Supplies, camping, attractive fishing and resort town.*

THE SYDNEY MOUNTAINS

START POINT Map page 3, J4.

TOTAL KM 636. Does not include 245 km Sydney to start point and 60 km end point to Sydney. *See Route Directions.*

UNSEALED KM 222.

DEGREE OF DIFFICULTY Easy.

DRIVING TIME Tour over a minimum of 5 days. Allow extra time to/from start/end points.

LONGEST DISTANCE NO FUEL 103 km (Jerrys Plains to Bylong).

TOPOGRAPHIC MAPS Auslig 1:250 000 series: *Sydney; Bathurst.*

LOCAL/SPECIALITY MAPS CMA map: *Wollemi National Park* (Windsor–Kandos); NSW Forestry Commission map: *Bathurst* (Bathurst–Windsor).

OTHER USEFUL INFORMATION NSW NPWS: *Visitor Guide* and information sheets: *Hill End; Wollemi National Park.*

BEST TIME OF YEAR TO TRAVEL Autumn and spring when deciduous trees are at their best.

TOUR DESCRIPTION This long tour should be undertaken over a break such as Easter, to experience the wide range of experiences and activities it offers. This is an opportunity to take in a feast of Australian history and geography, to learn at first hand of the difficulties experienced by the pioneer explorers of the Blue Mountains and the settlers and gold miners of the Hawkesbury region.

Take the Windsor Road north of Sydney to reach the start of our tour. If you have the time, it's worth spending a day on the way exploring tranquil Windsor's old buildings and churches. Route directions proper start in historic Jerrys Plains and we travel through small farming communities such as Bylong, picturesque Rylstone, and Kandos, the home of the Portland Cement Company. This section also skirts Wollemi National Park, a vast wilderness area of peaks and gorges and diverse vegetation including rainforest. Although four-wheel driving is restricted in the park, it has beautiful walking trails for the energetic enthusiast. Further west, we traverse early goldmining regions; stop and wander through the old towns of Sofala and Hill End, once the largest inland town in Australia. Most Hill

Upper Bylong church

End buildings date back to around 1872, when the town was a thriving community of 8000 miners and tradespeople. We then follow the Bridle Track, the original access road from Bathurst, along the rapids of the Turon and Macquarie rivers and through parkland reserves with access to shaded riverside campsites and excellent fishing. Spend a day exploring Bathurst, the first Australian town west of the Great Divide, and drive around the famous Mt Panorama racing circuit.

Head south to Oberon, famous for the trout fishing at Oberon Dam and in the surrounding streams, and then on to Jenolan Caves, perhaps with a detour on the way to view the dramatic Kanangra Walls escarpment. The Jenolan Caves were first opened to the public 100 years ago; they form the most spectacular underground limestone cave complex in Australia. Our tour then briefly links with the Great Western Highway and climbs Mt Victoria Pass following the original route of Blaxland, Lawson and Wentworth. You have the opportunity to visit the beautiful gardens and homes of Mt Wilson and the botanic gardens at Mt Tomah before cutting across the mountains to Bells Line of Road to link with Mt Lagoon Road in Bilpin, centre of the famous fruit-growing district and home of Bilpin apples. We descend to the Hawkesbury and Colo river valleys and track through the parks of the river playground enjoyed by water skiers and boating enthusiasts, to cross the Hawkesbury at Wisemans Ferry. Skirting the sandstone cliffs of Dharug National Park, we join the Sydney–Newcastle Expressway to return to Sydney.

There is a plethora of camping opportunities along this tour. There is a camping and caravan park at *Rylstone,* three excellent camping areas at *Hill End,* superb riverside camping at the *Macquarie/Turon Parkland* reserve, camping and caravan parks at *Bathurst* and *Oberon,* camping at *Jenolan Caves,* many camping and caravan parks along the *Colo* and *Hawkes-*

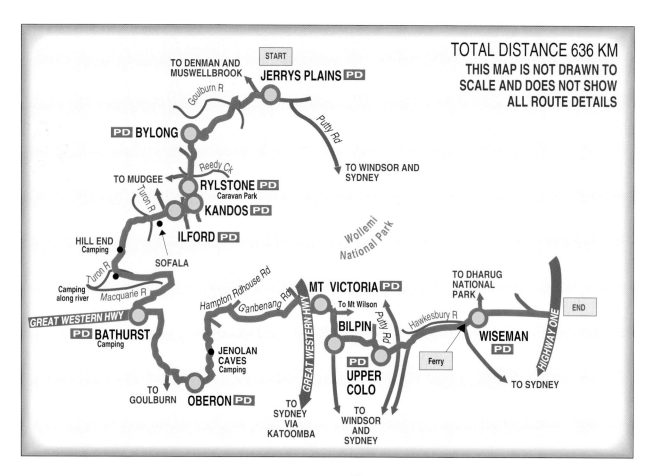

TOTAL DISTANCE 636 KM
THIS MAP IS NOT DRAWN TO
SCALE AND DOES NOT SHOW
ALL ROUTE DETAILS

bury rivers and at *Wisemans Ferry*, and camping in both Wollemi National Park, *Wheeney Creek, Newnes, or Dunns Swamp)* and Dharug National Park (*Ten Mile Creek* or *Ten Mile Hollow).*

WARNING ▶ Sections of road can be narrow and winding, take care.

BOOKINGS AND PERMITS ▶ For touring information and camping and accommodation guide to the area contact New South Wales Travel Centre or Bathurst Tourist Information Centre, Court House, Russell Street, Bathurst NSW 2795; tel. (063) 33 6288. ▶ For information and permits to camp in Dharug National Park, contact NSW NPWS, 207 Albany Street, PO Box 1393, Gosford South NSW 2250; tel. (043) 24 4911. ▶ For information on Wollemi National Park contact NSW NPWS, Putty Road, Bulga NSW 2330; tel. (065) 74 5275. ▶ For Hill End information and camping advice, contact NSW NPWS Visitor Centre, Hill End NSW 2850; tel. (063) 37 8206. ▶ For information and camping advice on Jenolan Caves area, contact Jenolan Caves Reserve Trust, PO Box 453, Oberon NSW 2787; tel. (063) 36 1070.

ROUTE DIRECTIONS

Depart Sydney on Great Western Hwy and Windsor Rd to Windsor (approx. 60 km), then north along the Putty Rd for approx. 160 km to link with Singleton–Denman Rd. **TL** to Jerrys Plains (approx. 25 km).
START TOUR
Historic buildings.

0.0 km Zero trip meter in Jerrys Plains (adjacent to post office) on Singleton–Denman Rd. **SO.**

PD *Supplies.*

(0.7 km)

0.7 km S'post: Doyles Creek. **SO.**

Muswellbrook off to right.

(0.1 km)

0.8 km S'post: Doyles Creek. **TL** at crossroads.
(4.6 km)

5.4 km Appletree Creek. Cross bridge.
(4.9 km)

10.3 km S'post: Denman. **SO**.

> *Doyles Creek off to left.*

(18.8 km)

29.1 km S'post: Denman: **TR** at T intersection onto Martindale Rd.

> *Martindale off to left.*

(0.8 km)

29.9 km Goulburn River. Cross bridge.

(3.5 km)

33.4 km S'post: Yarrawa. **TL** at T intersection onto Yarrawa Rd.

> *Denman 4 km off to right.* **PD** *Supplies.*

(2.3 km)

35.7 km Goulburn River. Cross bridge.

(9.1 km)

44.8 km Gravel.

(3.9 km)

48.7 km S'post: Rylstone. **TL** onto bitumen at T intersection.

> *Muswellbrook off to right.*

(15.7 km)

64.4 km Gravel.

(1.7 km)

66.1 km S'post: Rylstone. **SO**.

> *Widden Valley off to left.*

(0.9 km)

67.0 km Widden Creek. Cross bridge.

(1.2 km)

68.2 km Bitumen.

(3.3 km)

71.5 km Gravel.

(1.5 km)

73.0 km Bitumen.

(9.7 km)

82.7 km Honeysuckle Creek Picnic Area on left. **SO**.

> *Barbecue and toilets.*

(1.0 km)

83.7 km Gravel.

(15.6 km)

99.3 km Bitumen.

(1.5 km)

100.8 km Cross railway line. S'post: Rylstone. **SO**.

> *Mudgee off to right.*

(2.0 km)

102.8 km S'post: Upper Bylong. **TL** in Bylong village.

> **PD** *Rylstone straight ahead.*

(5.6 km)

108.4 km Gravel road in Upper Bylong village.

> *Lush valley, dairying country.*

(9.6 km)

118.0 km Lee Creek. Cross bridge. T intersection. **TL**.

(2.7 km)

120.7 km Intersection. **SO**.

> *Track enters on right.*

(4.4 km)

125.1 km Gate. T intersection. **TL** onto Bylong Rd.

(6.6 km)

131.7 km Growee Creek. Cross bridge.

(9.1 km)

140.8 km Bitumen.

(5.1 km)

145.9 km Reedy Creek. Cross bridge.

(7.1 km)

153.0 km S'post: Rylstone. **SO**.

> *Mudgee off to right.*

(3.7 km)

156.7 km Cudgegong River. Cross bridge.

(0.6 km)

157.3 km Rylstone town centre adjacent to post office.

> **PD** *Supplies, caravan park. Attractive and historic buildings.*

0.0 km Zero trip meter at above point. **SO**.

(0.1 km)

0.1 km S'post: Kandos. **TL** at T intersection.

> *Lake Windamere off to right.*

(6.7 km)

6.8 km S'post: Lithgow. **SO**.

> *Kandos town centre on left.* **PD** *Supplies.*

0.0 km Zero trip meter at above intersection. **SO**.

(0.3 km)

0.3 km S'post: Lithgow. **TR**.

> *Charbon straight ahead.*

(7.2 km)

7.5 km Intersection. **SO**.

> *Carwell Creek Picnic Area 3.5 km off to right. Barbecues.*

Avenue of trees, Hill End

0.0 km   Zero trip meter at above intersection.
(1.9 km)
1.9 km   Carwell Creek. Cross bridge.
(8.8 km)
10.7 km   S'post: Lithgow. **TL** at T intersection.

> *Mudgee off to right.*

(2.0 km)
12.7 km   Ilford village centre adjacent to general store/post office.

> **PD** *Supplies.*

(0.2 km)
12.9 km   S'post: Sofala/Bathurst. **TR**.

> *Lithgow straight ahead.*

(13.9 km)
26.8 km   Gravel.
(2.9 km)
29.7 km   Flaggy Creek. Cross bridge.
(8.5 km)
38.2 km   Four Mile Creek. Cross bridge. Bitumen.
(3.6 km)

41.8 km   Turon River. Cross bridge. Intersection. S'post: Hill End. **TR** onto gravel.

> *Sofala township on left. Old gold-mining town, historic buildings. Picnic area, barbecues, toilets.*

0.0 km   Zero trip meter at above intersection.
(3.2 km)
3.2 km   Bells Creek. Cross bridge.
(1.3 km)
4.5 km   Turon River. Cross bridge.
(6.2 km)
10.7 km   Intersection. **SO**.

> *Crudine 3 km off to right.*

(0.1 km)
10.8 km   S'post: Hill End. **SO**.

> *Turondale 6 km off to left.*

(8.7 km)
19.5 km   S'post: Hill End. **SO**.

> *Pyramul 16 km off to right.*

(16.7 km)

50

Old cottage, Hill End Road

36.2 km S'post: Hill End Visitors Centre. **TL** in Hill End.
(0.2 km)

36.4 km Hill End Visitors Centre and NPWS museum.

> *Explore Hill End at leisure. This old gold-mining town now administered by NPWS. Guided tours avail. through historic buildings and mine. Visitors Centre open Tuesday–Sunday for information and tour bookings. Camping with facilities at 3 areas: barbecues, toilets, water. Bush camping outside village on the Common.*

0.0 km Zero trip meter adjacent to Royal Hotel facing south. **SO** 50 metres. **KR** at Y intersection, Remembrance Memorial.
(0.5 km)

0.5 km S'post: Bridle Track. **SO**.

> *Hill End Post Office on left.*

(0.1 km)

0.6 km S'post: Bridle Track. **TL** onto Thomas St.

> *Hawkins Hill off to right.*

(0.2 km)

0.8 km S'post: Hill End Holiday Ranch. **SO** at crossroads.
(0.3 km)

1.1 km Intersection. **TR** onto Bridle Track.

> *Warning sign: Bridle Track unsuitable for caravans. This track once used by packhorses bringing supplies to Hill End from Bathurst.*

(2.1 km)

3.2 km Lookout on right. **SO**.
(4.5 km)

7.7 km Intersection. **SO**.

> *Sign: Turon Parkland and Reserve. Camping and picnic area, barbecues, toilets, water. Riverside campsites, fishing.*

(1.1 km)

8.8 km Turon River. Cross causeway.
(0.3 km)

9.1 km Intersection. **SO**.

> *Cave Hole Reserve on right. Riverside camping and picnic area, barbecues, toilets, water.*

(1.1 km)

10.2 km Intersection. **SO**.

> *Sailors Bluff Reserve on right. Camping and picnic area as above.*

(5.7 km)

15.9 km Intersection. **SO**.

> *Grimleys Hole Reserve on right. Camping and picnic area as above.*

(0.5 km)

16.4 km Intersection. **SO**.

> *Randwick Hole Reserve on right. Camping and picnic area as above.*

(1.9 km)

18.3 km Intersection. **SO**.

> *Johnsons Hole Reserve on right. Camping and picnic area as above.*

(4.4 km)

22.7 km Intersection. **SO**.

> *Black Gate Reserve on right. Camping and picnic area as above.*

(0.9 km)

23.6 km Intersection. **SO**.

> *Tattersalls Hole Reserve on right. Camping and picnic area as above.*

(1.8 km)

25.4 km Intersection. **SO**.

> *May Anderson Reserve on right. Camping and picnic area as above.*

(1.3 km)

The Bridle Track, near Hill End

26.7 km Intersection. **SO**.

> *Bruinbun Reserve on right. Camping and picnic area as above.*

(4.5 km)

31.2 km S'post: Bathurst. **SO**.

> *Willow Glen off to left.*

(6.8 km)

38.0 km Winburn Rivulet. Cross bridge onto bitumen.
(15.5 km)

53.5 km S'post: Bathurst. **TR** at T intersection.

> *Hill End/Turondale off to left.*

(7.6 km)

61.1 km S'post: Bathurst. **TL** at T intersection.

> *Freemantle off to right.*

(0.7 km)

61.8 km S'post: Bathurst. **TR**.
(0.9 km)

62.7 km S'post: Bathurst. **TL**.
(0.4 km)

63.1 km Macquarie River. Cross Rankin Bridge.
(1.1 km)

64.2 km S'post: Bathurst. **TL** at T intersection.

> *Dunkeld off to right.*

(3.4 km)

67.6 km S'post: Lithgow.

> *Bathurst town centre straight ahead.* **PD** *Supplies, caravan park. Nearby is Bathurst Gold Diggings (at Mt Panorama): authentic reconstruction of goldmining area.*

0.0 km Zero trip meter at above intersection. **SO** onto Great Western Hwy in Bathurst.
(1.7 km)

1.7 km Macquarie River. Cross bridge.
(2.0 km)

3.7 km S'post: Oberon/Jenolan Caves. **TR**.

> *Lithgow straight ahead.*

(16.7 km)

20.4 km Fish River. Cross bridge.
(25.2 km)
45.6 km S'post: Oberon/Jenolan Caves. **TL**.

> *Goulburn straight ahead.*

(1.0 km)
46.6 km Oberon town centre adjacent to post office.

> **PD** *Supplies, caravan park. Excellent trout fishing in Oberon Dam and local streams.*

0.0 km Zero trip meter at above point. **SO**.
(0.1 km)
0.1 km S'post: Jenolan Caves. **TR** into Ross St.

> *Katoomba straight ahead.*

(0.4 km)
0.5 km S'post: Jenolan Caves. **TL**.

> *Oberon Dam straight ahead. Forestry Commission office on left. Information on state forests in area.*

(11.3 km)
11.8 km Duckmaloi River. Cross bridge.
(1.9 km)
13.7 km Gravel.
(9.1 km)
22.8 km Y intersection. **KL**.
(1.2 km)
24.0 km T intersection. S'post: Jenolan Caves.

> *Kanangra Walls 27 km off to right. Sign: unsuitable for caravans, steep decline.*

0.0 km Zero trip meter at above intersection. **TL**.
(1.8 km)
1.8 km Bitumen.
(3.0 km)
4.8 km Intersection. **SO**.

> *Carpark and toilets on left. Walking track to Devils Coachhouse.*

(0.4 km)
5.2 km Carpark No. 1 on right. **SO**.
(0.2 km)
5.4 km Jenolan Caves Trust office on left.
0.0 km Zero trip meter at above point. **SO** through Grand Arch.
(1.6 km)
1.6 km Intersection. **SO**.

> *Jenolan Camping Area on right. Barbecues, toilets.*

(2.5 km)

Upper Colo Valley scene

The valley and township of Sofala

4.1 km Inspiration Lookout on right. **SO**.
(8.9 km)
13.0 km Intersection. **SO**.

> *Picnic ground on left. Barbecues, toilets.*

(4.7 km)
17.7 km Intersection. **SO**.

> *Mini Mini Rd on right.*

(4.6 km)
22.3 km S'post: Katoomba. **SO**.

> *Oberon off to left.*

(3.9 km)
26.2 km Hampton Roadhouse on left.
SO. **PD**
(6.0 km)
32.2 km S'post: Marsden Swamp Road. **TR** onto gravel.
(11.0 km)

43.2 km   Intersection. **SO**.

> *Redfern off to right.*

(3.5 km)

46.7 km   Ganbenang Creek. Cross causeway.

(1.1 km)

47.8 km   S'post: Hartley. **SO** along Ganbenang Rd.

> *Lowther Siding Rd on left.*

(3.7 km)

51.5 km   Cox River. Cross Duddewarra Bridge onto bitumen.

(1.0 km)

52.5 km   Intersection. **SO** along Ganbenang Rd.

> *Kanimbla Drive on right.*

(4.0 km)

56.5 km   S'post: Hartley. **TL** at T intersection.

> *Blackheath Rd on right.*

(4.5 km)

61.0 km   S'post: Katoomba. **TR** onto Great Western Hwy.

> *Lithgow off to left.*

(5.9 km)

66.9 km   Intersection. S'post: Bell in Mt Victoria village.

> **PD** *Supplies, caravan park. Great views.*

0.0 km   Zero trip meter at above intersection. **TL**.

(10.0 km)

10.0 km   S'post: Windsor.

> *Lithgow off to left. Zig Zag historic railway 7 km off to left.*

0.0 km   Zero trip meter at above intersection. **TR** onto Bells Line of Road.

(7.5 km)

7.5 km   S'post: Windsor.

> *Mt Wilson 7 km off to left. Beautiful homes. Gardens open to public: both native and exotic species.*

0.0 km   Zero trip meter at above intersection. **SO**.

(13.5 km)

13.5 km   S'post: Windsor. **SO**.

> *Sign on right: Mt Tomah Botanic Gardens.*

(12.6 km)

26.1 km   S'post: Mt Lagoon Rd. **TL** in Bilpin village.

> *Windsor straight ahead.*

(9.9 km)

36.0 km   Gravel.

(2.6 km)

38.6 km   Y intersection. **KR**.

> *Sams Way off to left.*

(1.1 km)

39.7 km   Intersection. Small s'post: Fire Trail to Upper Colo Rd. **SO**.

> *Sams Way off to left.*

(2.1 km)

41.8 km   Intersection. **SO**.

(5.8 km)

47.6 km   T intersection. Sign: Wollemi National Park. **TL**.

(4.0 km)

51.6 km   T intersection. S'post: Singleton. **TR** onto bitumen in Upper Colo village. Upper Colo Rd. **PD**

(4.5 km)

56.1 km   Cross single-lane bridge onto gravel.

(4.4 km)

60.5 km   Bitumen.

(5.6 km)

66.1 km   Crossroads. **SO** over Putty Rd onto gravel.

> *Colo village to left past Colo River Caravan Park.* **PD**

(10.0 km)

76.1 km   T intersection. **TL** onto bitumen: West Portland Rd.

(2.6 km)

78.7 km   S'post: ferry 200 m. **TR**.

> *Bridge over Colo River straight ahead.*

(0.3 km)

79.0 km   Lower Portland Ferry across Hawkesbury River.

> *Ferry operates 24 hours daily.*

(0.1 km)

79.1 km   S'post: Wisemans Ferry. **TL** at T intersection.

> *Windsor off to right.*

(1.7 km)

80.8 km Caravan park on left. **SO**.

> *Many camping areas and caravan parks along river. Water skiing and boating paradise.*

(2.3 km)

83.1 km Big Al's Caravan Park on left. **SO**.

(1.9 km)

85.0 km Gravel.

(2.1 km)

87.1 km Clifton Lodge Picnic Area on left. **SO**.

> *Cabin hire and kiosk.*

(5.3 km)

92.4 km Leetvale Caravan Park on left. **SO**.

(4.4 km)

96.8 km Torrens Caravan park on left. **SO**.

(3.4 km)

100.2 km Ko-veda Caravan Park on left. **SO**.

(1.3 km)

101.5 km S'post: Wisemans Ferry.

> *St Albans via Webb Creek Ferry on left.*

(0.3 km)

101.8 km S'post: Wisemans Ferry. **TL** at T intersection onto bitumen: Wisemans Ferry Rd.

> *Castle Hill off to right.*

(0.9 km)

102.7 km Wisemans Ferry. Cross Hawkesbury River. **TR** off ferry at s'post: Gosford.

> *Wisemans Ferry Park Reserve.* **PD** *Picnic area, barbecues, toilets. Ferry operates 24 hours daily. St Albans off to left over river.*

(4.6 km)

107.3 km Hazeldell Picnic Area. **SO**.

> *Barbecues, toilets. Dharug National Park and Mill Creek Camping and Picnic Area 1.7 km off to left. Barbecues, toilets. Permit to camp necessary.*

(16.8 km)

152.4 km S'post: Gosford. **SO**.

> *Cessnock off to left.*

(3.5 km)

Jenolan Caves House

155.9 km S'post: Sydney. **TR** onto George Downes Drive.

> *Singleton off to left.*

(2.2 km)

158.1 km S'post: Sydney. **TR** onto Hwy One.

> *Gosford off to left.*

END TOUR
Return to Sydney via freeway (approx. 76 km).

TOURS OUT OF BRISBANE

Queensland offers a huge diversity of attractive and challenging four-wheel drive opportunities, ranging from the ultimate adventures in the far north, only practicable in the dry season, to shorter tours based on Brisbane. Aside from times of heavy rainfall, when unsealed roads become impassable, all these shorter trips can be all-year-round expeditions. Our route directions plot a mixture of beach driving, inland sand tracks, forestry roads and the spectacular scenery of the Great Dividing Range where it joins the coast near Brisbane.

THE D'AGUILAR AND BLACKALL RANGES (a day tour: 207 kilometres). With the exception of the northern part of the D'Aguilar Range, four-wheel driving in state forests near Brisbane is restricted to regulation State Forest Drives. On this tour we have made the most of the non-restricted area and you can enjoy some serious four-wheel driving tracks together with great mountain views.

COOLOOLA NATIONAL PARK (tour over at least two days: 247 kilometres). Boating, swimming, fishing, surfing, bushwalking and wildlife observation provide extra enjoyment along the route. This tour could be a stepping stone and practice ground for Fraser Island, the world's largest sand island.

Mt Warning, NSW, seen from Tweed Scenic Drive

QUEENSLAND'S NATIONAL PARKS

From mountain tops to beaches, dense rainforest to heathlands, Queensland's national parks total more than 1 000 000 hectares. Where appropriate, we suggest you use park facilities for overnight camping. Permits are necessary to camp in all parks and, although self-registration is available at many, it is advisable to book ahead at busy holiday times. For information, contact Queensland National Parks and Wildlife Service (QNPWS), 160 Ann Street, Brisbane 4000; PO Box 155, North Quay 4002; tel. (07) 227 8185. Addresses and phone numbers for local and regional offices are given in the tour descriptions. When using national parks observe the following code.

▶ Drive only on roads and identifiable tracks and obey all notices.
▶ No domestic animals are allowed.
▶ When walking, keep to the tracks. Shortcutting causes erosion.
▶ Don't disturb or feed native animals. All are protected.
▶ Leave all plants, living or dead, undamaged.
▶ Don't collect firewood from the park. Bring your own or – preferably – use a fuel stove.
▶ No firearms, generators, petrol-engined fridges or chainsaws allowed.
▶ Never leave a campfire unattended and put your fire out with water.
▶ Take your rubbish with you or leave in the bins provided. Leave your campsite clean.

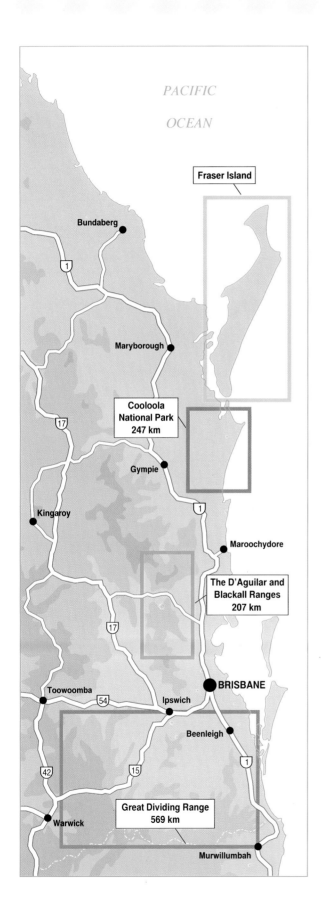

FRASER ISLAND (tour over a minimum of 3 days). Fraser is probably Australia's best-known four-wheel drive adventure. Although the beaches are great driving, the inland tracks are difficult and diverse and open up some wonderful scenic opportunities. Our tour does not provide detailed route charts as a plethora of information on tracks is available from Queensland National Parks and Wildlife Service.

THE GREAT DIVIDING RANGE (tour over 3 days: 569 kilometres). This tour includes sections of the range in south-east Queensland and northern New South Wales, and parts of the rich grazing country of the famed Darling Downs. Spicers Gap and Condamine Gorge are highlights, both genuine four-wheel drive tracks.

BEFORE YOU SET OUT ▶ Read the tour description carefully. ▶ Check that you have obtained any necessary permits. ▶ Check weather conditions with local authorities or Bureau of Meteorology. ▶ Make sure you have the appropriate maps and information for the tour. ▶ Check that your vehicle is in good order for the conditions ahead. Have you the necessary spare parts? ▶ If you are camping, have you the right equipment?

USEFUL INFORMATION

For touring information contact:
Queensland Government Travel Centre
196 Adelaide Street, Brisbane 4000
(07) 221 6111.

For touring and motoring information contact:
Royal Automobile Club of Queensland (RACQ)
300 St Pauls Terrace, Brisbane 4000
(07) 253 2444.

For four-wheel driving information contact:
Queensland Association of Four Wheel Drive Clubs Inc.
PO Box 174, Brisbane Markets 4106
(07) 379 9129.

For information on driving and camping in state forests contact:
Queensland Forest Service
Forestry House
160 Mary Street, Brisbane 4001
(07) 234 0157.

THE D'AGUILAR AND BLACKALL RANGES

START POINT Map page 13, N6.

TOTAL KM 207. Does not include 12 km to start point and approximately 55 km end point to Brisbane. **See Route Directions.**

UNSEALED KM 84.

DEGREE OF DIFFICULTY Easy.

DRIVING TIME A day tour (approximately 7 hours). Allow time to/from start/end points. **See Route Directions.**

LONGEST DISTANCE NO FUEL 130 km (Dayboro to Maleny).

TOPOGRAPHIC MAPS Auslig 1: 250 000 series: *Ipswich*; *Gympie*.

LOCAL/SPECIALITY MAPS Department of Forestry: *Mt Mee State Forest*; Sunmaps: *South-east Queensland*; *Ipswich* and *West Moreton*; *Sunshine Coast and Hinterland*.

OTHER USEFUL INFORMATION Queensland Forest Service booklet: *Recreation in State Forests.*

BEST TIME OF YEAR TO TRAVEL Best on a bright day. Heavy rain makes sections of road impassable.

TOUR DESCRIPTION This tour takes in the picturesque high country of the D'Aguilar and Blackall ranges, north-west of Brisbane. It is a comfortable day's drive with unforgettable scenery. Much of the tour winds through state forests, initially Brisbane Forest parkland near Samford, then through patches of rainforest and eucalypt in Mt Mee State Forest, the only forest in the Brisbane district to allow four-wheel drive access by permit. This forest is multi-use, with areas for timber and honey production, grazing and recreation. There is a day use picnic area, a camping area and walking tracks, and a swimming hole right on the edge of the forest on Neurum Creek.

From Mt Mee you briefly link onto the D'Aguilar Highway before turning off to Bellthorpe State Forest. The Stony Creek picnic area is situated beside a swimming hole in a gully, surrounded by rainforest. The road climbs over foothills before crossing the Conondale Range to Maleny, the centre of a major dairying region. Your trip back to Brisbane passes the Glass

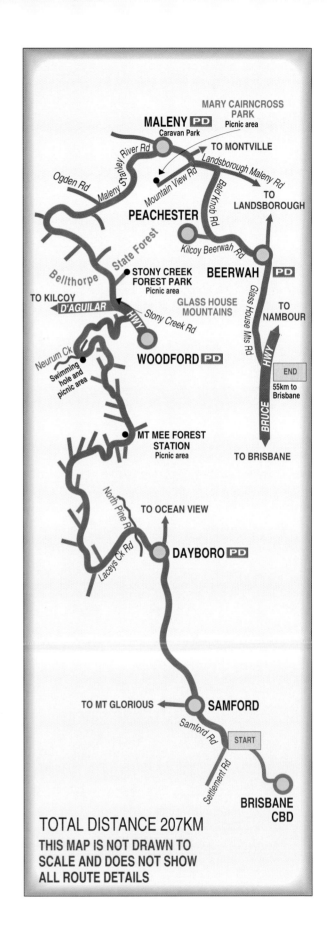

TOTAL DISTANCE 207KM

THIS MAP IS NOT DRAWN TO SCALE AND DOES NOT SHOW ALL ROUTE DETAILS

Mt Mee pine plantation track

House Mountains, 13 distinct peaks formed by volcanic activity over 20 million years ago, and named in 1770 by Captain Cook. These mountains retain their Aboriginal names and are important in Aboriginal folklore.

WARNINGS ▶ This tour is unsuitable for caravans and trailers. ▶ Creek crossings are subject to flooding after heavy rain.

BOOKINGS AND PERMITS ▶ A permit is required to traverse the D'Aguilar Range and Mt Mee section. Obtain from Queensland Forest Service, Brisbane District Office, 160 Mary Street, Brisbane 4000; tel. (07) 234 0205.

ROUTE DIRECTIONS

Depart Brisbane CBD north-west for 12 km approx. via Kelvin Grove Rd, Enoggera Rd and Samford Rd.
START TOUR

0.0 km Zero trip meter at the corner of Samford Rd and Settlement Rd after crossing Settlement Rd. **SO** along Samford Rd.
(0.5 km)

0.5 km S'post: Samford/Dayboro. **KR** along Samford Rd.
(8.5 km)

9.0 km S'post: Dayboro/Samford. **TR** onto Mt Samson Rd. **SO** through Samford.

> Samford Museum: large photographic collection. Display of farm equipment.

(0.6 km)

9.6 km S'post: Dayboro 23. **SO**.
(2.2 km)

11.8 km S'post: Dayboro 20. **SO**.
(20.9 km)

32.7 km Dayboro town centre, adjacent to Dayboro Crown Hotel. **SO** through Dayboro.

> **PD** *Hay Cottage in Roderick Cruice Park was built (of red cedar and beech) in 1872.*

(2.2 km)

34.9 km S'post: Laceys Creek Rd. **KL**.
(0.9 km)

35.8 km North Pine River. Cross bridge.
(6.4 km)

42.2 km Cross causeway onto gravel.
(3.8 km)

46.0 km Intersection. **KL**.

> *Sign on right: crossing subject to flooding.*

(1.8 km)

47.8 km Creek crossing. T intersection. **KR**.
(1.3 km)

49.1 km Y intersection. **KR**.

> *Sign: restricted vehicle access. Permit required.*

(2.7 km)

51.8 km T intersection. **TR**.
(1.6 km)

53.4 km Y intersection. **KR**.
(5.3 km)

58.7 km Intersection. **SO**.
(1.1 km)

59.8 km Intersection. **KL**.

> *S'post: Dayboro via May Creek Rd on right.*

(0.8 km)

60.6 km Y intersection. **KR**.
(1.1 km)

61.7 km Y intersection. **KR**. Follow main track.
(1.1 km)

62.8 km Intersection. **KR**. Follow main track.
(2.5 km)

65.3 km Y intersection. **KR**.
(4.9 km)

70.2 km Intersection. **KR**.

> *S'post: Byron Creek Rd on left.*

(0.5 km)

70.7 km S'post: Peggs Rd. **KL**. Follow main track.

> *S'post: Dayboro via Chambers Rd on right.*

(5.6 km)

76.3 km T intersection. **TL**.
(0.7 km)

THE D'AGUILAR AND BLACKALL RANGES

77.0 km Intersection. **KR**. Follow main track.
(0.4 km)
77.4 km S'post: Lovedays Rd. **SO** along main track.

> *S'post: Mt Mee Forest Station on left. Day use picnic area: tables, barbecues, water, toilets. Walking tracks.*

(1.1 km)
78.5 km Y intersection. **KL**.
(0.7 km)
79.2 km Y intersection. **KR**.
(0.4 km)
79.6 km Y intersection. **KR**.
(0.5 km)
80.1 km Intersection. **KL** onto main track.
(4.8 km)
84.9 km Y intersection. **KR** on main track.
(1.0 km)
85.9 km Y intersection. **KR**.
(0.2 km)
86.1 km Intersection. S'post: Lovedays Rd. **KL**.

> *Gate on right.*

(3.6 km)
89.7 km Grid.
(0.4 km)
90.1 km Intersection. **SO**.
(0.7 km)
90.8 km Intersection. **SO**.
(1.0 km)
91.8 km Y intersection. **KL**.
(0.6 km)
92.4 km Grid.
(1.4 km)
93.8 km Causeway.
(0.1 km)
93.9 km Swimming hole and picnic area on left.

> *No facilities.*

0.0 km Zero trip meter at entrance to picnic area. **SO**.
(1.3 km)
1.3 km Causeway.
(4.3 km)
5.6 km T intersection. **TL** onto bitumen.
(2.5 km)
8.1 km T intersection. **TR**.
(9.2 km)
17.3 km Intersection. **TL** onto D'Aguilar Hwy.

> *Woodford off to right.* PD

(2.7 km)

20.0 km Intersection. **SO**.

> *Beerwah/Kilcoy turnoff on right.*

(3.3 km)
23.3 km S'post: Stony Creek. **TR** onto Stony Creek Rd. 200 m to gravel.
(2.9 km)
26.2 km Intersection. S'post: Bellthorpe 15.

> *Stony Creek Forest Park and swimming hole 3 km straight ahead along Fletchers Rd. Recommended picnic area: tables, barbecues, water and toilets.*

0.0 km Zero trip meter at above intersection. **KL**.
(0.2 km)
0.2 km Cross causeway onto gravel.

> *Gradual climb over foothills in Bellthorpe State Forest.*

(7.2 km)
7.4 km S'post: Bellthorpe. **SO**.

> *S'post: Branch Creek on right.*

(4.2 km)
11.6 km Intersection. **SO**.

> *S'post: Beacon Rd on left.*

(0.7 km)
12.3 km S'post: Bellthorpe. **SO**.
(0.9 km)
13.2 km Intersection. **TR**.
(3.7 km)
16.9 km Bitumen.
(4.9 km)
21.8 km Y intersection. S'post: Maleny. **KL**.
(1.6 km)
23.4 km S'post: Maleny. **KR** onto Gap Rd: gravel.
(4.6 km)
28.0 km Intersection. S'post: Maleny. **KL**.
(0.9 km)
28.9 km Intersection. **KR** onto Maleny–Stanley River Rd.

> *S'post: Ogden Rd on left.*

(2.5 km)
31.4 km Bitumen.
(11.1 km)
42.5 km S'post: Landsborough 15. **TR** into Maleny.
(0.4 km)
42.9 km Maleny town centre adjacent post office.

Glass House Mountains from Peachester Road

> **PD** *Caravan parks, private guest house. Pretty village at the southern end of the Blackall Range surrounded by lush dairy country.*

0.0 km Zero trip meter adjacent to Maleny Post Office. **SO** along Landsborough–Maleny Rd.
(4.0 km)

4.0 km Intersection. **SO**.

> *Montville 11 km off to left along Maleny–Montville Rd.*

> *Striking views of Diamond Valley and the Sunshine Coast hinterland as you descend the range. Turn right onto Mountain View Rd (6 km from Maleny) for superb views of the Glass House Mts from Mary Cairncross Park: picnic tables, barbecues, toilets, water. Rainforest walking track.*

(5.2 km)

9.2 km S'post: Peachester 10. **TR** onto Bald Knob Rd.
(9.6 km)

18.8 km T Intersection. S'post: Beerwah 10. **KL** onto Kilcoy–Beerwah Rd.
(9.4 km)

28.2 km S'post: Nambour/Brisbane. **TR** in Beerwah.
PD
(0.1 km)

28.3 km S'post: Nambour/Brisbane. **TL** and cross railway line and immediately **TR**.
(0.7 km)

29.0 km S'post: Glass House Mts Rd/Brisbane. **TR** onto Glass House Mts Rd.

> *Views of spectacular Mt Tibrogargan. Roadside tropical fruit stalls.*

(14.9 km)

43.9 km Join Bruce Hwy. Zero trip meter.
END TOUR
Return to Brisbane via Bruce Hwy (approx. 55 km).

COOLOOLA NATIONAL PARK

START POINT Map page 13, N3.

TOTAL KM 247. Does not include 160 km Brisbane to start point and 250 km end point to Brisbane. **See Route Directions.**
UNSEALED KM 192.
DEGREE OF DIFFICULTY Moderate. Involves beach driving at low tide. **See Warnings.**
DRIVING TIME Tour over 2 or 3 days. Allow time to/from start/end points. **See Route Directions.**
LONGEST DISTANCE NO FUEL 66 km (Lake Cooroibah Resort to Rainbow Beach).
TOPOGRAPHIC MAPS Auslig 1:250 000 series: *Gympie; Maryborough.*
LOCAL/SPECIALITY MAPS Sunmaps: *Cooloola Region; South-east Queensland.*
OTHER USEFUL INFORMATION QNPWS visitor information sheets: *Southern Cooloola and Northern Cooloola National Park; Coastal sand-driving: Cooloola National Park.*
BEST TIME OF YEAR TO TRAVEL Avoid peak holiday times for most enjoyment and least traffic. Following heavy rain some sections are impassable.

TOUR DESCRIPTION This tour takes you through Cooloola National Park – 45 000 hectares of coastal land which protects wildlife and plants threatened elsewhere on the coast by rapid development. It is a complex and beautiful landscape of long sandy beaches, high sand dunes, mangroves, forests, lakes and rivers. You travel the entire length of the wide, wild Teewah and Cooloola beaches past the Teewah coloured sand dunes and cross Double Island Point onto Rainbow Beach. From here you tour inland, heading back towards the coastline to Freshwater Lake, along a 16-kilometre four-wheel drive track, past Bymien Picnic Area and Burwilla Lookout. The walk to the lookout is rewarded with stunning views of Rainbow Beach and Fraser Island. The tour then takes you through Southern Cooloola to Harrys Hut before looping back past Toolara State Forest to Poverty Point on Tin Can Inlet. It is a scenic tour which gives you a bit of everything: beach and forest driving; over a dozen walking tracks through rainforest, woodlands and around lakes; surf and lake swimming; beach and river fishing.

Camp in relative isolation in designated areas on the 13-kilometre stretch of Cooloola Beach between the Noosa Shire boundary and *Little Freshwater Creek* (no facilities). You can camp near the lake at *Freshwater*, on the banks of the Noosa River at *Harrys Hut*, or on the shores of Tin Can Inlet at *Poverty Point*. All these sites have a special beauty, but try to stop at least a night at Harrys Hut. There are a few small sites north of here on the river, accessible only by boat or in some cases by walking, and privately owned camping grounds at *Elanda, Boreen Point* and *Lake Cooroibah Resort.* There is a caravan park at this resort and in Rainbow Beach village. You have the option of visiting Tin Can Bay, where the sheltered waters in the inlet create a fishing and boating haven. There are a number of caravan parks in the town.

WARNINGS ▶ Check tide times and beach access with Rainbow Beach QNPWS; tel. (074) 86 3160; or Noosa Heads QNPWS; tel. (074) 47 3243. ▶ Take underbody protection and wash and reduce tyres to 15-20 psi before beach driving. ▶ Drive on the beach only at low tide and observe road rules. ▶ Slow down when approaching people and vehicles: surf noise impedes hearing. ▶ Detour via Freshwater Road if the Leisha Track is impassable and if Mudlo Rocks on Rainbow Beach are exposed and impassable.

BOOKINGS AND PERMITS ▶ Camp only in designated areas in the park. Obtain permits to traverse the park and to camp, from Brisbane QNPWS head office, or from QNPWS, Park Road, Noosa Heads QLD 4567; tel. (074) 47 3243; or QNPWS, Rainbow Beach Rd, Rainbow Beach QLD 4581; tel. (074) 86 3160. Self-registration is available near the ferry departure point, Moorindal St, Tewantin. Camping permits are for a maximum of 6 persons per site. ▶ Obtain permit to traverse Toolara State Forest from Toolara Forest Station, Tin Can Bay Road, Toolara, via Gympie QLD 4570; tel. (074) 86 5220; or from the Queensland Forest Service head office in Brisbane.

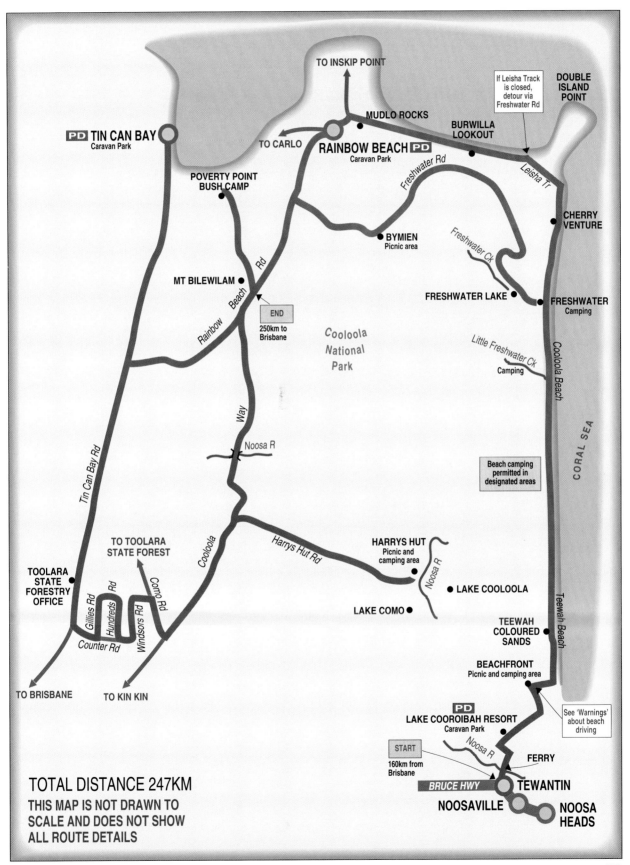

TO INSKIP POINT

If Leisha Track is closed, detour via Freshwater Rd

DOUBLE ISLAND POINT

MUDLO ROCKS

BURWILLA LOOKOUT

PD TIN CAN BAY
Caravan Park

TO CARLO

RAINBOW BEACH PD
Caravan Park

Freshwater Rd

Leisha Tr

POVERTY POINT
BUSH CAMP

CHERRY VENTURE

BYMIEN
Picnic area

Freshwater Ck

Rainbow Beach Rd

MT BILEWILAM

FRESHWATER LAKE

FRESHWATER
Camping

END
250km to Brisbane

Cooloola National Park

Little Freshwater Ck
Camping

Cooloola Beach

Way

Noosa R

CORAL SEA

Beach camping permitted in designated areas

Tin Can Bay Rd

Cooloola Way

Harrys Hut Rd

HARRYS HUT
Picnic and camping area

Noosa R

TOOLARA STATE FORESTRY OFFICE

TO TOOLARA STATE FOREST

Hundreds Rd

Como Rd

LAKE COOLOOLA

Gillies Rd

Windsors Rd

LAKE COMO

TEEWAH COLOURED SANDS

Counter Rd

Teewah Beach

TO BRISBANE

TO KIN KIN

BEACHFRONT
Picnic and camping area

PD
LAKE COOROIBAH RESORT
Caravan Park

See 'Warnings' about beach driving

START
160km from Brisbane

Noosa R

FERRY

BRUCE HWY

TEWANTIN

NOOSAVILLE

NOOSA HEADS

TOTAL DISTANCE 247KM
THIS MAP IS NOT DRAWN TO SCALE AND DOES NOT SHOW ALL ROUTE DETAILS

ROUTE DIRECTIONS

Depart Brisbane north via Bruce Hwy to Cooroy. **TR** onto Cooroy–Noosa Rd. **SO**. Follow signs to Tewantin, approx. 160 km. **PD** Before leaving Tewantin check beach access and tides with Rainbow Beach QNPWS.

START TOUR

0.0 km   Zero trip meter in Tewantin opposite Royal Mail Hotel. S'post: Bruce Hwy. **SO** along Poinciana Ave.
(0.4 km)

0.4 km   S'post: Noosa River Ferry. **TR** into Moorindil St.
(1.8 km)

2.2 km   Gravel. **SO**.

> Self-registration point in Moorindil St for Cooloola camping permits.

(0.2 km)

2.4 km   Noosa River Ferry. Cross Noosa River.
(0.4 km)

2.8 km   Intersection. S'post: Maximillian Rd. **TL**.
(0.7 km)

3.5 km   Bitumen. **SO**.
(0.6 km)

4.1 km   Gravel. **SO**.
(0.6 km)

4.7 km   S'post: To Beach. **TR**.

> Lake Cooroibah Resort on left. **PD** Caravan park, campsites. Underbody wash and oil avail. Warning: apply oil here before venturing onto beach.

(2.2 km)

6.9 km   Intersection. **SO** to beach.

> Beachfront Camping and Picnic Area off to left. Warning: before driving onto beach reduce tyre pressure to 15-20 psi and engage 4WD.

(0.2 km)

7.1 km   Drive onto beach and **TL**. **SO** towards Double Island Point.
(22.5 km)

29.6 km   S'post: Cooloola National Park. **SO**.

> Beach camping in designated areas. Permit required. Teewah coloured sands rise in cliffs to over 200 m.

(14.7 km)

44.3 km   S'post: Little Freshwater Creek. **SO**.

> Beach campsite on left. No facilities. Beach camping not permitted beyond this point.

(3.1 km)

47.4 km   S'post: Freshwater Camping Area.

> Turn left to campsite: picnic tables, barbecues, toilets, water. Firewood avail.

0.0 km   Zero trip meter at above s'post. **SO** along beach.
(5.4 km)

5.4 km   Cherry Venture wreck. **SO**.

> Rusting freighter wreck. Worth close inspection.

(0.5 km)

5.9 km   S'post: Leisha Track/Rainbow Beach. **TL** off beach onto Leisha Track to cross Double Island Point.

> Warning: if track or Mudlo Rocks are impassable take Freshwater Rd to Rainbow Beach village.

(1.2 km)

7.1 km   S'post: Rainbow Beach. **TL** onto beach.

> Coloured sandcliffs on Rainbow Beach.

(10.1 km)

17.2 km   Beach exit. **KL** onto bitumen.
(0.5 km)

17.7 km   S'post: Clarkeson Drive. **TL**.

> Warning: re-inflate tyres if finished with beach driving. Apply underbody wash.

(0.4 km)

18.1 km   T intersection. S'post: Rainbow Beach Rd.

> Rainbow Beach village on left. **PD** Caravan park straight ahead.

0.0 km   Zero trip meter at above intersection. **TR** onto Rainbow Beach Rd.

> QNWPS office 0.5 km ahead on Rainbow Beach Rd: camping permits and park information.

(4.4 km)

4.4 km   Intersection. S'post: Freshwater Rd. **TL** onto gravel.
(0.1 km)

4.5 km   Information sign. **SO**.

A bogged trailer

Boat builders, Tin Can Bay

Poverty Point bush campsite

Bymien Picnic Area 3 km/Burwilla Lookout 7.6 km. Freshwater Camping Ground 16 km. 4WD access only. Permit required.

(3.0 km)

7.5 km Y intersection. **KL** on Freshwater Rd.

Bymien Picnic Area on right. Day use only: picnic tables, barbecues, toilets. No camping.

(2.3 km)

9.8 km Intersection. **KL**.

(2.3 km)

12.1 km Intersection. **SO** along Freshwater Rd. Burwilla Lookout parking area on left.

Walk 700 m to Burwilla Lookout: 20-minute round trip. Leads to the top of the coloured sandcliffs 100 m above the beach. Impressive views of Rainbow Beach, Double Island Point and Fraser Island.

(7.5 km)

19.6 km Intersection. **KL** along Freshwater Rd.

Freshwater Lake Carpark on right.

(0.8 km)

20.4 km S'post: Freshwater Camping Area. **TL**.

(0.2 km)

20.6 km Freshwater Camping Area.

Picnic tables, barbecues, toilets, water, hot showers. Telephones. Firewood avail. Good fishing on beach. Circuit walk of 2.7 km around lake. Surf and lake swimming.

0.0 km Zero trip meter at camping area exit. **TR** onto Freshwater Rd. Return to Rainbow Beach Rd.

(15.9 km)

15.9 km T intersection. **TL** onto Rainbow Beach Rd: bitumen.

(12.0 km)

27.9 km S'post: Brisbane 199. **TL** onto Cooloola Way: gravel.

(6.1 km)

34.0 km S'post: Noosa River. Cross wooden bridge. Follow main track.

(18.6 km)

52.6 km Y intersection. **KL** on main track.

(1.2 km)

53.8 km Intersection. S'post: Harrys Hut Rd. **TL**.

(0.7 km)

54.5 km Information sign. **KR**.

> *Dry-weather road only. Sign relates to information on park use. Permit required to camp at Harrys Hut Camping Area. Self-registration point is located at site.*

(10.0 km)

64.5 km Harry Springs Hut on right. **SO**.
(0.1 km)

64.6 km Harrys Hut Picnic and Camping Area. **TL**.

> *Beautiful picnic and camping ground on Noosa River: picnic tables, barbecues, toilets, water. Fascinating animal and bird life. Excellent boating and fishing. Walking tracks. Well worth a visit.*

0.0 km Zero trip meter at turnaround in picnic area. **TR** onto Harrys Hut Rd. **SO** to Cooloola Way.
(10.9 km)

10.9 km Cooloola Way. **TL**.
(3.3 km)

14.2 km S'post: Tarangau. **TR**.

> *S'post on turning corner: Toolara–Como Forestry Rd. Permit from Forestry Service required to traverse.*

(3.2 km)

17.4 km Intersection. S'post: Tarangau. **SO**.
(0.1 km)

17.5 km Intersection. **SO**.

> *Tarangau off to right.*

(1.5 km)

19.0 km Y intersection. **KL**.
(0.7 km)

19.7 km Crossroads. S'post: Machinery Corner. **SO**.
(3.4 km)

23.1 km Crossroads. **TL** onto Windsors Rd.
(4.1 km)

27.2 km S'post: Counter Rd. **TR**.
(4.5 km)

31.7 km S'post: Hundreds Rd. **TR**.
(5.6 km)

37.3 km T intersection. **TL**.
(2.8 km)

40.1 km Y intersection. S'post: Gillies Rd. **TL**.
(2.4 km)

42.5 km Y intersection. **KR**.
(2.2 km)

44.7 km T intersection. **TR** onto Counter Rd (no sign).
(4.9 km)

49.6 km T intersection. S'post: Gympie/Tin Can Bay. **TR** onto bitumen: Tin Can Bay Rd.
(5.9 km)

55.5 km Toolara State Forestry Office on left.

> *Free permits to use forestry tracks can be obtained here.*

(11.9 km)

67.4 km Intersection. S'post: Rainbow Beach.

> *Tin Can Bay 11 km straight ahead.* **PD** *Caravan parks. Attractive fishing and boating centre worth a visit. Charter houseboats and vessels. Fresh seafood co-operatives.*

0.0 km Zero trip meter at above intersection. **TR** onto Rainbow Beach Rd.
(13.1 km)

13.1 km Intersection. **SO**.

> *Cooloola Way on right.*

(3.1 km)

16.2 km Intersection. **TL** after quarry onto narrow obscured gravel track.

> *Information s'post for Poverty Point Bush Camping Area 50 m along track. 4WD access only.*

(0.1 km)

16.3 km Y intersection. **KR**.
(6.1 km)

22.4 km Poverty Point Bush Camping Area.

> *Cleared bush campsite on Tin Can Inlet. No facilities.*

0.0 km Zero trip meter. Return to Rainbow Beach Rd via gravel track.
(6.1 km)

6.1 km Rainbow Beach Rd. Zero trip meter.
END TOUR
TR to return to Brisbane via Tin Can Bay Rd to Gympie and Bruce Hwy to Brisbane, approx. 250 km. Or **TL** to Rainbow Beach village, the starting point for Fraser Island tour.

FRASER ISLAND

START POINT Map page 13, N2.

DEGREE OF DIFFICULTY Moderate. Involves beach driving at low tide. *See Warnings.*
DRIVING TIME Tour over a minimum of 3 days.
LONGEST DISTANCE NO FUEL Fuel at Eurong and Happy Valley. Petrol only at Cathedral Beach Resort and Orchid Beach Resort.
LOCAL/SPECIALITY MAP Sunmap: *Fraser Island.*
OTHER USEFUL INFORMATION QNPWS brochure and map: *Fraser Island Recreation Area* (issued with permit); QNPWS information sheets: *Fraser Island; Coastal Sand Driving in Great Sandy National Park;* QNPWS booklet: *The Great Sandy Adventure.*
BEST TIME OF YEAR TO TRAVEL Any time of year but avoid peak holiday times.

TOUR DESCRIPTION The world's largest sand island, measuring 123 kilometres from southern to northern tips, Fraser is a great adventure as the only practical way to explore it fully is with a four-wheel drive vehicle. With the exception of a short bitumen section bypassing Hook Point, all roads are unsealed. Fraser's natural attractions include endless beaches, coloured sand cliffs, freshwater creeks, unspoiled vegetation and tangled rainforests sheltering a variety of plant and animal life, including dingoes of a pure strain not found anywhere on the mainland. Anglers will enjoy great sport during the tailor season in August and September; walkers can follow the many trails which criss-cross the island and the surf beaches and fresh-water lakes offer many opportunities to swim.

Declared a 'recreation area' to ensure the protection of its resources for nature-based recreation, Fraser is jointly managed by the QNPWS and the Queensland Forest Service. Permits are necessary to enter the island and to camp in the Fraser Island Recreation Area. *See Bookings and Permits.* Make sure you adhere to the environmental codes and suggestions in the excellent brochure issued by QNPWS when you buy access and camping permits. There are general stores at Happy Valley, Eurong and Cathedral Beach Resort which are well stocked with everything from groceries to camping and fishing equipment, bait and ice. Take a well-stocked first aid kit and plenty of insect repellent; Fraser Island does not have a resident doctor.

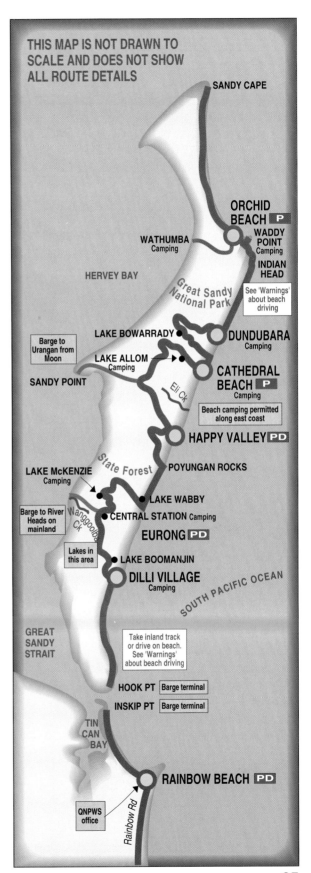

THIS MAP IS NOT DRAWN TO SCALE AND DOES NOT SHOW ALL ROUTE DETAILS

Champagne Pools, Fraser Island

There are developed camping areas at *Central Station, Lake Boomanjin, Lake McKenzie, Lake Allom, Dundubara, Waddy Point* and *Wathumba*; beach camping is permitted along the east coast and at some points on the west coast; commercial camping areas are at *Dilli Village* and *Cathedral Beach* where you do not need a permit.

The best way to approach Fraser is by way of our Cooloola National Park tour. However, if time restrictions prevent this, fastest access to the island from Brisbane is via the Bruce Highway to Gympie for 150 kilometres. Then take the Gympie–Tin Can Bay Road and Rainbow Beach Road for 60 kilometres to Rainbow Beach Village. Follow Inskip Point Road north to the barge terminal, approximately 13 kilometres. Barges to Hook Point on Fraser operate every day between 7.00 am and 4.30 pm.

From Hook Point we found the fastest and smoothest route to the centre and north of the island is 24 kilometres along the beach to Dilli Village. A tough alternative is the centre bush track via Figtree, but this is little used and overgrown and though just navigable will cause scratches to your paintwork. When you take

into account that the beach route to Central Station may take about 1.5 hours and the inland route as long as 6 hours, the choice for an interesting and easy beach drive is obvious. However, check tide charts before taking to the beach and alter your pressure to 15–20 psi. There is an alternative inland route bypassing Hook Point if the tides make the beach impassable in this section.

Use the designated scenic routes to explore the island, and take care not to attempt other tracks. Many lead nowhere, or are not navigable for their entire length. Designated tracks will take you from Dilli to Central Station via Lake Boomanjin or via Eurong, then north through Poyungan Valley and Happy Valley to the Pinnacles. You can head inland via Lake Bowarrady, then to the coast at Dundubara. Follow the beach north for 19 kilometres to Indian Head, Waddy Point and Orchid Beach. A final 30-kilometre stretch of beach driving will bring you to Sandy Cape, Fraser's northernmost tip.

An alternative to returning to the mainland on the southern barge is the barges operating from Wanggoolba Creek to River Heads, and Moon Point to Urangan, south of Hervey Bay.

Coming off the barge, Fraser Island

Wreck of the *Maheno*, Fraser Island

Dingo, Fraser Island

WARNINGS ▶ Be aware of the dangers and skills necessary when beach driving and drive on them only during two-hour period before and after low tide. Take tide charts obtainable from QNPWS office, Rainbow Beach Road, Rainbow Beach; tel. (074) 86 3160. Adjust tyre pressure to 15–20 psi before beach driving. Take underbody protection for your vehicle. Observe beach driving code for coastal sand driving suggested in QNPWS information sheets. ▶ Stay on designated or authorised tracks to protect your vehicle and the environment. ▶ Observe rules for camping as set out in QNPWS information sheets. ▶ Do not feed native animals.

BOOKINGS AND PERMITS Obtain information about Fraser Island, access permits and camping permits for Fraser Island Recreation Area from head offices of QNPWS and QFS, or from QNPWS office in Rainbow Beach. ▶ Information about private camping facilities available from Queensland Government Travel Centre in Brisbane. ▶ Obtain information on barge services from QNPWS offices, or ring (071) 27 9122 for *Rainbow Venture* (Inskip Point to Hook Point); (074) 86 3227 for Fraser Island Ferry Service (Inskip Point to Hook Point); (071) 24 1900 (Wanggoolba Creek to River Heads); (071) 24 1300 (Moon Point to Urangan).

TREAD LIGHTLY!
ON PUBLIC AND PRIVATE LAND

■ Take your rubbish home with you. Do not bury it.

■ Leave gates as you found them – open or shut.

■ Do not damage swamps, steep hills or creekbanks which can be easily scarred by churning wheels.

■ Ford creeks at designated crossings.

■ Comply with signs and closures.

■ Observe firelighting regulations and total fire ban days.

THE GREAT DIVIDING RANGE

START POINT Map page 13, N6.

TOTAL KM 569 (including option). Does not include 33 km Brisbane to start point and 80 km end point to Brisbane. *See Route Directions.*

UNSEALED KM 215.

DEGREE OF DIFFICULTY Moderate. Spicers Gap 9-km track difficult.

DRIVING TIME Tour over 3 days. Includes optional visit to Glenrow Station. Allow time to/from start/end points. *See Route Directions.*

LONGEST DISTANCE NO FUEL 123 km (Beenleigh to Boonah).

TOPOGRAPHIC MAPS Auslig 1:250 000 series: *Warwick*; *Tweed Heads*.

LOCAL/SPECIALITY MAPS Sunmaps: *Ipswich and West Moreton*; *Gold Coast and Hinterland*; *South-east Queensland*; NSW Forestry Commission map: *Casino State Forests*.

OTHER USEFUL INFORMATION QNPWS park guide: *Southern Inland National and Environmental Parks*; QNPWS visitor information sheets: *Main Range* and *Mt Mistake* national parks; *Queen Mary Falls National Park*; *Moogerah Peaks National Park*.

BEST TIME OF YEAR TO TRAVEL All year round except after heavy rain which makes some sections of road impassable.

TOUR DESCRIPTION This tour offers an interesting blend of road surfaces through scenic country: lush grazing lands, the spectacular valleys and rainforests of the Great Dividing Range, and the picturesque Tweed Valley. Highlights of the tour include Main Range and Border Ranges national parks which form part of the Scenic Rim – a sweeping arc of mountains stretching from the Gold Coast hinterland to the Darling Downs. Maroon Dam is an ideal picnic and refreshment stop on your first day of touring, with access to boating and fishing. From the dam you enter Main Range National Park where open eucalypt forest and rainforest cover rugged peaks and ridges. *Spicers Gap Camping Ground*, in a grassy clearing with views of Spicers Peak and Mt Alphen, is adjacent to the Pioneer Picnic Area and Pioneer Graves and is worth an overnight stop. Only 2 kilometres away you pass the day use area of Governors Chair Picnic Ground. Take the walking track to Moss's Well Picnic Area where bellbirds, cockatoos and rosellas harmonise, and to Governors Chair Lookout for stunning views of Fassifern Valley.

The Spicers Gap track to the Cunningham Highway takes you out of the park (**see Warnings**) through private property. From Gladfield visit *Glenrow Station* camping and four-wheel drive resort near Goomburra. With four-wheel drive and bushwalking tracks and opportunities to fish, swim and canoe, Glenrow is a recommended stopover. At Queen Mary Falls National Park 10 kilometres south of Killarney, the sound of the falls can be heard from the picnic grounds at the park entrance and intensifies to a roar as you near the gorge and falls on the circuit track. *Queen Mary Falls* privately-owned caravan park and kiosk are just outside the gates of the park.

After skirting the southern tip of Main Range National Park your final day of touring takes you down the range into New South Wales. On the Tweed Range Scenic Drive through Border Ranges National Park there are plenty of picnic areas to break the drive. As the name suggests, the views are breathtaking and there are excellent walking tracks through rainforest to waterfalls and lookouts. Stop at Blackbutt Picnic Area for fabulous views over the Tweed Valley to Mt Warning, an impressive 1156 metre volcanic peak which erupted millions of years ago.

WARNINGS ▶ Sections of the tour are not suitable for caravans. ▶ The Spicers Gap track is difficult and requires low range 4WD. It is closed in wet weather. Check with the QNPWS Ranger, Southern Downs District Office, MS 394, Warwick QLD 4370; tel. (076) 66 1133. ▶ A section of track between Queen Mary Falls and Teviot Falls Lookout is narrow: watch for oncoming traffic. There are many creek crossings, impassable after heavy rain. ▶ Beware logging trucks in Border Ranges National Park.

BOOKINGS AND PERMITS ▶ Obtain a camping permit for Spicers Gap from the Warwick QNPWS office, or from Brisbane head office. ▶ To book at Glenrow Station, tel. (076) 66 6176. ▶ To book at Queen Mary Falls Caravan Park, tel. (076) 64 7151.

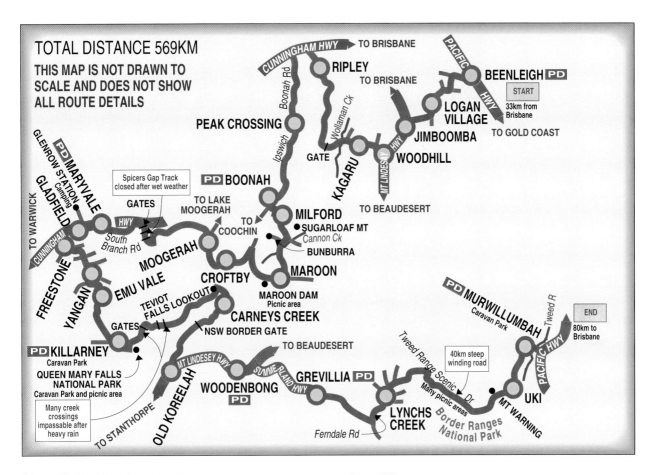

TOTAL DISTANCE 569KM

THIS MAP IS NOT DRAWN TO SCALE AND DOES NOT SHOW ALL ROUTE DETAILS

ROUTE DIRECTIONS

Depart Brisbane CBD for approx. 33 km along SE Fwy and/or Pacific Hwy to Beenleigh. **PD**
START TOUR

0.0 km Zero trip meter at Beenleigh Plaza shopping mall entrance. **SO** along City Road.
(0.2 km)

0.2 km Roundabout. **TR** into George St.
(0.4 km)

0.6 km Roundabout. **SO** along George St.
(0.4 km)

1.0 km Roundabout. S'post: Kingston. **SO**.
(3.4 km)

4.4 km S'post: Gardiner Rd. **TL**.
(1.3 km)

5.7 km S'post: Dairy Creek Rd. **TR**.
(3.0 km)

8.7 km Waterford–Tamborine Rd. **TL**.
(6.6 km)

15.3 km Logan Village town centre adjacent to shopping centre. **SO**.
(4.1 km)

19.4 km S'post: Jimboomba 9. **TR**.
(7.5 km)

26.9 km S'post: Beaudesert. **TL** onto Mt Lindesay Hwy.
(10.9 km)

37.8 km S'post: Kagaru 7. **TR**.
(3.7 km)

41.5 km S'post: Kagaru. **TL**.
(3.5 km)

45.0 km Railway bridge. **SO**.
(1.3 km)

46.3 km Gravel.
(2.5 km)

48.8 km Intersection. **SO**.
(1.7 km)

50.5 km Wollaman Creek crossing.
(4.0 km)

54.5 km Gate.

Leave as found.

(0.5 km)

55.0 km Y intersection. **KR**.
(11.9 km)

66.9 km Bitumen.
(1.7 km)

68.6 km Gravel.
    (1.7 km)
70.3 km Bitumen.
    (5.1 km)
75.4 km Ripley 60 km/h sign. **SO**.
    (1.6 km)
77.0 km S'post: Warwick. **TL** onto Cunningham Hwy.
    (3.5 km)
80.5 km S'post: Boonah. **TL** off Cunningham Hwy.
    (0.5 km)
81.0 km S'post: Boonah. **TL** onto Ipswich–Boonah Rd.
    (13.1 km)
94.1 km Peak Crossing town centre adjacent to state school. **SO**.
    (28.2 km)
122.3 km S'post: Boonah/Rathdowney. **TL** in Boonah.
    (0.7 km)
123.0 km Boonah town centre adjacent to police station. **PD**
0.0 km Zero trip meter at police station. **SO**.
    (1.1 km)
1.1 km S'post: Milford 5. **TL**.
    (3.7 km)
4.8 km T intersection. S'post: Evans Rd. **TL**.
    (1.0 km)
5.8 km Intersection. **KR** on bitumen.
    (1.7 km)
7.5 km S'post: Cannon Creek. **SO**.

> *Mt Sugarloaf straight ahead.*

    (3.4 km)
10.9 km Gravel. Immediately cross causeway.
    (1.6 km)
12.5 km Y intersection. **KR**.
    (2.4 km)
14.9 km S'post: Cannon Creek–Maroon Rd. **SO**.

> *Warning: no through road in wet weather. Alternative route through Bunburra via Boonah–Rathdowney Rd.*

    (9.9 km)
24.8 km S'post: Maroon Dam 10. **TR** onto bitumen.
    (8.1 km)
32.9 km Intersection. S'post: Boonah.

> *Maroon Dam Picnic Area 3.4 km off to left. Spectacular views of valleys, Mt Toowoonan and Mt May. Attractive day use picnic area: tables, barbecues, toilets, water. Swimming. Boat ramp.*

0.0 km Zero trip meter at above intersection. **SO** along Boonah–Rathdowney Rd.
    (6.3 km)
6.3 km S'post: Carneys Creek/Croftby. **TL**.
    (9.3 km)
15.6 km S'post: Moogerah. **TR** onto Croftby–Lake Moogerah Rd.
    (0.4 km)
16.0 km Gravel.
    (10.8 km)
26.8 km S'post: Spicers Gap 13. **TL**.
    (5.8 km)
32.6 km S'post: Spicers Gap 7. **TL**.

> *Information sign: Spicers Gap Camping Area. Part of Main Range National Park. Dry weather road only.*

    (2.7 km)
35.3 km Intersection. **SO**.
    (4.1 km)
39.4 km Intersection. S'post: Spicers Gap Camping Ground.

> *Turn left to this recommended camping area: barbecues, toilets, water. Permit required. Self-registration on site. Great walks.*

0.0 km Zero trip meter at above s'post. **TL** from entrance of camping area onto Governors Chair Rd.
    (1.6 km)
1.6 km S'post: Governors Chair Picnic Ground. **SO**.
    (0.5 km)
2.1 km Governors Chair Picnic Ground. S'post: Cunningham Hwy 9. **TR** onto Spicers Gap track.

> *Walking track to Moss's Well off to left. The 150-m walking track to Governors Chair Lookout has stunning views. Warning: Spicers Gap track is a 9-km 4WD dry weather road only beyond Governors Chair. Difficult, requires low range. Closed following wet weather. Check with Warwick QNPWS ranger if in doubt about condition of this track.*

    (4.1 km)
6.2 km Gate.

> *Leave as found.*

    (3.1 km)

Fassifern Valley from Governors Chair Lookout

9.3 km Gate.

> *Leave as found.*

(0.6 km)

9.9 km Gate.

> *Leave as found.*

(0.6 km)

10.5 km Gate.

> *Leave as found.*

(0.1 km)

10.6 km T intersection. **TL** onto Cunningham Hwy.
(2.4 km)

13.0 km S'post: South Branch Rd. **TL** off Cunningham Hwy onto gravel.
(2.0 km)

15.0 km Intersection. **SO**.
(7.4 km)

22.4 km Bitumen.
(3.3 km)

25.7 km T intersection. **TL** onto Cunningham Hwy.

> *Maryvale general store 100 m off to right.* **PD**

(5.8 km)

31.5 km Intersection in Gladfield.

> *Bitumen road on right leads to Glenrow Station camping and 4WD resort (17.5 km). Follow signs. Fully equipped tents, toilets, hot showers, water, gas, ice, kiosk. 4WD and bushwalking tracks. Canoeing, swimming, fishing. Book ahead.*

0.0 km Zero trip meter at above intersection in Gladfield. **SO** along Cunningham Hwy.
(4.3 km)

4.3 km S'post: Freestone 5. **TL**.
(4.1 km)

8.4 km S'post: Upper Freestone Rd. **TL**.
(1.6 km)

10.0 km Gravel.
(3.8 km)

13.8 km Intersection. **TR**.
(1.9 km)

15.7 km Crossroads. S'post: Yangan 8. **SO** over crossroads towards Yangan.
(1.7 km)

17.4 km Intersection. **KR**.
(0.4 km)

17.8 km Intersection. **KL**.
(2.1 km)

19.9 km Bitumen.
(0.6 km)

20.5 km Gravel.
(1.6 km)

22.1 km T intersection. **TR** onto bitumen.
(1.7 km)

23.8 km Yangan. S'post: Killarney 23. **KL**. **PD**
(4.8 km)

28.6 km Emu Vale State School on left. **SO** to s'post: Killarney 19. **TR**.
(14.5 km)

43.1 km T intersection. S'post: Killarney 3. **TL**.
(2.6 km)

45.7 km S'post: Killarney Falls/Legume. **TR** in Killarney.

> **PD** *Caravan park.*

(4.2 km)

49.9 km S'post: Queen Mary Falls 7. **TL**.
(6.7 km)

56.6 km Queen Mary Falls National Park Carpark on left.

> *No camping: day use only. Picnic tables, barbecues, toilets, water. Return walk of 2 km to gorge and the breathtaking falls. Queen Mary Falls Caravan Park opposite parking area: campsites, hot showers, laundry, kiosk.*

0.0 km Zero trip meter at Queen Mary Falls Picnic Ground exit and head back towards Killarney.
(6.6 km)

6.6 km S'post: Killarney 4. **TR**.
(1.0 km)

7.6 km Intersection. **TR** onto side road (no signpost).
(1.6 km)

9.2 km Intersection. **SO.**
(1.0 km)

10.2 km Gravel. **SO.**
(0.9 km)

11.1 km Intersection. **SO.**
(0.2 km)

11.3 km Creek crossing.
(0.3 km)

11.6 km Creek crossing.
(0.7 km)

12.3 km S'post: Dry Weather Road Only. **SO.**

Warning: road closed after wet weather.

(0.5 km)

12.8 km Creek crossing.

Track follows Condamine Gorge. Warning: narrow, watch for oncoming traffic. Many creek crossings, impassable after heavy rain.

(0.8 km)

13.6 km Creek crossing.
(0.5 km)

14.1 km Creek crossing.
(0.6 km)

14.7 km Creek crossing.
(0.2 km)

14.9 km Creek crossing.
(0.5 km)

15.4 km Creek crossing.
(0.3 km)

15.7 km Creek crossing.
(0.3 km)

16.0 km Creek crossing.
(0.4 km)

16.4 km Gate.

Leave as found.

(1.1 km)

17.5 km Creek crossing.
(0.3 km)

17.8 km Creek crossing.
(1.3 km)

19.1 km Gate.

Leave as found.

(1.2 km)

20.3 km Creek crossing.

Beautiful scenery.

(0.2 km)

20.5 km Creek crossing.
(1.7 km)

22.2 km Gate.

Leave as found.

(1.1 km)

23.3 km Gate.

Leave as found.

(1.1 km)

24.4 km Gate.

Leave as found.

(2.0 km)

26.4 km Intersection. S'post: Boonah. **SO** across grid.
(6.6 km)

33.0 km S'post: Main Range National Park/Teviot Falls Lookout.

Spectacular views. Steep descent.

(10.8 km)

43.8 km T intersection. S'post: New South Wales. **TR** onto bitumen.
(1.5 km)

45.3 km Gravel.
(5.6 km)

50.9 km S'post: New South Wales Border. **SO.**
(6.6 km)

57.5 km NSW border gate and agriculture inspection point. **SO.**
(7.3 km)

64.8 km S'post: Old Koreelah. **KL** along White Swamp Rd.
(9.5 km)

74.3 km Bitumen.
(5.7 km)

80.0 km S'post: Woodenbong 23. **TL** onto Mt Lindesay Hwy.
(23.1 km)

103.1 km Woodenbong town centre adjacent to Woodenbong Public Hall. **PD**

0.0 km Zero trip meter at public hall. **SO.**
(0.1 km)

0.1 km S'post: Brisbane. **SO** along Mt Lindesay Hwy.
(4.6 km)

4.7 km S'post: Kyogle 56. **TR** onto Summerland Hwy.
(23.6 km)

28.3 km Grevillia town centre adjacent to general store. **SO** along Summerland Way. **PD**
(17.6 km)

45.9 km S'post: Ferndale Rd. **TL.**
(0.5 km)

46.4 km Intersection. **TR** onto gravel and immediately cross wooden bridge.
(2.9 km)

49.3 km **KR** over wooden bridge.
(0.4 km)

49.7 km T intersection. **TL** onto bitumen.
(2.0 km)

51.7 km S'post: Lynchs Creek. **SO** along gravel towards Border Ranges National Park.
(2.7 km)

54.4 km S'post: Lynchs Creek. **TL**.

> *Sign: Border Ranges Scenic Drive 8/Tweed Range Scenic Drive.*

(1.3 km)

55.7 km S'post: Border Ranges National Park. **TL**.

> *Warning: beware logging trucks.*

(1.9 km)

57.6 km S'post: Border Ranges National Park 4. **KR** at Y intersection.
(4.3 km)

61.9 km Intersection. S'post: Tweed Range Scenic Drive.

> *Caution: 40 km of narrow, steep, winding road. Sheep Station Creek Picnic Area 200 m off to left: tables, barbecues, toilets, water.*

0.0 km Zero trip meter at above intersection. **KR**.

> *There are various picnic areas and walks along the Tweed Range Scenic Drive.*

(6.4 km)

6.4 km Intersection. **SO**.

> *Forest Tops Picnic Area on left: tables, barbecues, toilets, water.*

(0.3 km)

6.7 km S'post: One Way Road. Tweed Valley Lookout 9. **TL**.
(1.9 km)

8.6 km Brindle Creek Picnic Area. **SO**.

> *Picnic area on both sides of road: tables, barbecues, toilets, water. Red Cedar Rainforest Walk 750 m return. Brindle Creek Walk 5 km return.*

(5.0 km)

13.6 km Antarctic Beech Picnic Area. **SO**.

> *Picnic area on left: tables, barbecues, toilets, water.*

(2.0 km)

15.6 km Tweed Valley Lookout.

> *View Mt Warning (1156 m), the peak which receives the first Australian sun each day.*

(0.8 km)

16.4 km S'post: Murwillumbah 70. **TL**.
(11.4 km)

27.8 km Blackbutt Picnic Area and Lookout. **SO**.

> *Lookout and picnic area on left: tables, barbecues, toilets, water.*

(3.0 km)

30.8 km Intersection. **SO**.

> *Bar Mountain Picnic Area 150 m off to right: tables, barbecues, toilets, water. Walking tracks.*

(13.2 km)

44.0 km T intersection. **TL**.
(2.8 km)

46.8 km S'post: Murwillumbah 44. **TL** onto bitumen.
(5.4 km)

52.2 km S'post: Murwillumbah 38. **SO**.
(17.4 km)

69.6 km Uki town centre adjacent to post office. **SO**.
(8.6 km)

78.2 km Tweed River Bridge. **SO**.
(5.0 km)

83.2 km Murwillumbah. S'post: Tweed Heads. **TR**.
(0.4 km)

83.6 km Murwillumbah town centre adjacent to Sunnyside Mall. **SO**.

> **PD** *Caravan park. Attractive town in the Tweed Valley on the banks of the Tweed River. Sugar cane, bananas, tea and coffee are all grown in this area.*

(0.3 km)

83.9 km Cross Tweed River Bridge.
(0.4 km)

84.3 km S'post: Pacific Hwy/Tweed Heads. **TL**. Zero trip meter.
END TOUR
Return to Brisbane on Pacific Hwy via Gold Coast (approx. 80 km).

Sandy Creek Falls, Litchfield National Park

TOURS OUT OF DARWIN

The rugged and tropical top end of the Northern Territory is still largely untamed and a paradise for the recreational driver in search of great scenery and diverse travelling experiences. It is magnificent country, with sandstone escarpments, woodlands, wetlands and mangrove swamps, pockets of rainforest and a dramatic coastline. The variety of wildlife is extraordinary and you could spend endless hours fishing, bushwalking, bird watching and boating. The seasonal extremes of the wet and dry season restrict travel to the months between May and September. In the wet, unsealed roads become rivers or bogs and high humidity makes driving and sightseeing uncomfortable.

Darwin, with a fine harbour and beautiful beaches, is a perfect base for exploring the top end. The Stuart Highway, linking the city with Alice Springs, and the Arnhem Highway, stretching across Kakadu, are excellent access roads for our tours.

LITCHFIELD NATIONAL PARK (tour over 3 days: 236 kilometres). Only a short distance from Darwin, Litchfield is spectacularly beautiful and less travelled than other Northern Territory parks. It offers camping in a beautiful rainforest, bushwalks on the Tabletop Range, swimming in deep rock pools near stunning waterfalls and plenty of wildlife. There are also challenging four-wheel drive tracks to the fascinating Lost City rock formations and Sandy Creek Falls.

GURIG NATIONAL PARK (tour over a minimum of 4 days: 619 kilometres). Gurig, on the Cobourg Peninsula, is a coastal wilderness park surrounded by tropical waters with abundant aquatic life. This is an angler's mecca, with superb beach fishing within walking distance of the camping area behind Smith Point. The track to Gurig, branching out of Kakadu and across the edge of Arnhem Land, is long and solitary, making this the Territory's most remote tour.

KAKADU NATIONAL PARK (tour over a minimum of 2 days: 855 kilometres). This best known of all national

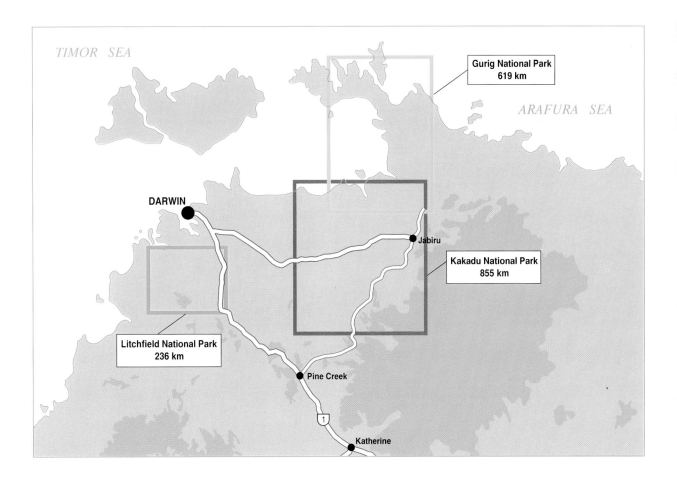

parks is not to be missed. Although sealed roads are developed for tourist access, we offer 3 interesting four-wheel drive options to more secluded destinations. Try to visit Kakadu soon after the wet season when the beautiful Jim Jim Falls are still flowing and the wetlands abound with tropical waterbirds. Kakadu is steeped in Aboriginal history and the rock art here is among the finest in the world, tracing the enormous changes in climate, geology and culture that have shaped this region over the last 25 000 years.

BEFORE YOU SET OUT ▶ Read the tour description carefully. ▶ Check that you have obtained necessary permits. ▶ Check weather conditions with local authorities or the Bureau of Meteorology. ▶ Make sure you have the appropriate maps and information for the tour. ▶ Check that your vehicle is in good order for the conditions ahead. Have you the necessary spare parts? ▶ If you are camping have the right equipment and adequate fuel and supplies. ▶ Carry high-frequency radio and guide listing Radphone call signs and frequencies.

USEFUL INFORMATION

For road conditions and motoring information contact:
Automobile Association of Northern
 Territory Inc. (AANT)
MLC Building, 79–81 Smith Street
Darwin 0800, (089) 81 3837.

For four-wheel driving information contact:
Northern Territory Association of Four Wheel Driving
PO Box 37476, Winnellie NT 0821.

For fishing regulations contact:
Department of Primary Industry and Fisheries (DPIF)
GPO Box 990, Darwin 0801, (089) 89 4322.

For emergency medical assistance contact:
Aerial Medical Services (Airmed)
(089) 22 8888 (Darwin Hospital)
(089) 72 9211 (Katherine Hospital).

Fishing trip from Smith Point, Gurig National Park

HOW TO BE CROCODILE-WISE

Of the two crocodile species found in Australia's north, the saltwater or estuarine crocodile is dangerous. It lives in salt water and fresh water, usually in tidal sections of rivers and creeks, floodplain waterholes and freshwater swamps and is found as far inland as 100 kilometres. The freshwater crocodile, while not dangerous, can deliver a savage bite if interfered with. Treat all crocodiles longer than 1.5 metres as dangerous, and obey the following rules.

▶ *Seek local advice before swimming, camping, fishing or boating.*
▶ *Swim, canoe and use small boats only in shallow rapids.*
▶ *Watch children and pets in the water or at the water's edge where large crocodiles might live.*
▶ *Fill a bucket with water and prepare food or clean fish at least 5 metres from the water's edge.*
▶ *Do not lean from boats or hang articles over the edge.*
▶ *When fishing stand at least a few metres back from the water's edge. Do not stand on overhanging logs.*
▶ *Burn or remove from your campsite food scraps, fish offal and other wastes.*

TOP END NATIONAL PARKS

Our 3 top end tours in national parks all have four-wheel drive tracks and are inaccessible in the wet season when rainfall is torrential. It is not necessary to book ahead to camp in the parks but in the peak dry season months of June and July roads and camping areas in Kakadu can be congested. Camping fees apply at each park but arrangements differ. You can self-register at Litchfield and at Kakadu where you also pay a park use fee at Park Headquarters or at camping areas. Permits are required for bush camping, also available at headquarters in the park. A permit is required to enter Gurig National Park, obtainable at the head office of the Conservation Commission of the Northern Territory (CCNT), Gaymark Building, Francis Mall, Palmerston Circuit, Palmerston NT; PO Box 496, Palmerston NT 0831; tel. (089) 89 4555 or 89 4559. Kakadu is administered by the Australian National Parks and Wildlife Service (ANPWS). Contact ANPWS, MLC Building, 79–81 Smith Street, Darwin NT: GPO Box 1260, Darwin NT 0801; tel. (089) 79 9110.

Kakadu and Gurig are both on Aboriginal land. When using all these parks observe the following rules.
▶ *Drive and walk along designated tracks only.*
▶ *Light fires only in barbecues and fireplaces provided. Extinguish fires completely before leaving campsites.*
▶ *Place rubbish in bins provided or take it away with you.*
▶ *Pets, firearms and spearguns are prohibited.*
▶ *All plants, animals, natural and cultural features within park boundaries are protected. Do not feed the wildlife.*
▶ *Help stop the spread of the noxious weed salvinia: check undercarriage of your vehicle, boat and trailer, and your fishing gear, and report any findings of the weed immediately.*
▶ *Avoid damaging rock paintings through touching or accidental brushing.*
▶ *Observe all Department of Primary Industry and Fisheries (DPIF) fishing regulations.*

LITCHFIELD NATIONAL PARK

The old Blyth Homestead

START POINT Map page 24, E5.

TOTAL KM 236. Does not include 10 km Darwin to start point and 85 km end point to Darwin. **See Route Directions.**

UNSEALED KM 136.

DEGREE OF DIFFICULTY Easy, except for extremely difficult optional short section to Lost City.

DRIVING TIME Tour over 3 days. Allow extra time to/from start/end points. **See Route Directions.**

LONGEST DISTANCE NO FUEL 121 km (Finnis River Store to Batchelor).

TOPOGRAPHIC MAP Auslig 1:250 000 series: *Darwin.* See also 1:100 000 series.

LOCAL/SPECIALITY MAPS Gregorys *Northern Territory*; DPIF: *Northern Territory Fishing Map*; CCNT map: *Litchfield Park.*

BEST TIME OF YEAR TO TRAVEL May–September as sections of road may be flooded in the wet season.

TOUR DESCRIPTION South-west of Darwin lies Litchfield Park, one of the most rewarding of our four-wheel drive destinations and within a short distance of this northern city. Litchfield's sandstone plateau, covered in dry woodland and open forest, offers great bushwalking opportunities and, where all-year-round flowing creeks plunge from the escarpment, there are pockets of lush rainforest, spectacular falls and cool swimming holes easily accessed from nearby camping areas. Litchfield's permanent water is one of its main attractions.

A highlight of this tour is an optional four-wheel drive hike to the Lost City, a huge freestanding sandstone formation near Tolmer Falls, and to the old Blyth Homestead, once the site of a tin mine, then a grazing lease. You can also see the famous magnetic termite mounds which dot the flat plain areas, and on the way to the park we allow time to visit the Territory Wildlife Park, a natural bushland habitat for animals and birds native and feral to the Northern Territory. Of interest on the return journey is the Rum Jungle Uranium Mine site, now undergoing rehabilitation. Batchelor, once the mine's town, is a major centre for training Aboriginal teachers.

There are a number of attractive camping possibilities on this tour and sites with facilities at *Wangi Falls*, *Sandy Creek Falls*, *Florence Falls*. There is a private facility (no bookings necessary) at *Pethericks Rainforest Reserve*.

WARNINGS ▶ Section of track between Lost City and Blyth Homestead extremely difficult and requires skill and caution. If in doubt take alternative route. ▶ After heavy rain check with AANT, MLC Building, 79–81 Smith Street, Darwin 0800; tel. (089) 81 3837. ▶ Crocodiles may inhabit streams and waterways in Litchfield Park. Be crocodile-wise. Swim only at Wangi Falls, Florence Falls, Sandy Creek Falls and in the Upper Walker Creek area. ▶ Sections of this tour not suitable for caravans. ▶ Bushwalkers should stick to defined trails and inform someone of intended destinations and time of return.

BOOKINGS AND PERMITS ▶ Permits are necessary to camp in Litchfield National Park: you can self-register and pay fees at the various designated sites. Observe all park regulations on lighting of fires, rubbish disposal, sanitation, pets and firearms. For information on Litchfield, contact CCNT office, Gaymark Building, Francis Mall, Palmerston Circuit, Palmerston; PO Box 496 NT 0831; tel. (089) 89 4555 or 89 4559. ▶ Collect dead timber for campfires from the roadside before reaching your camping destination. ▶ Obtain permit to visit Rum Jungle, Uranium Mine Rehabilitation Site from CCNT.

LITCHFIELD NATIONAL PARK

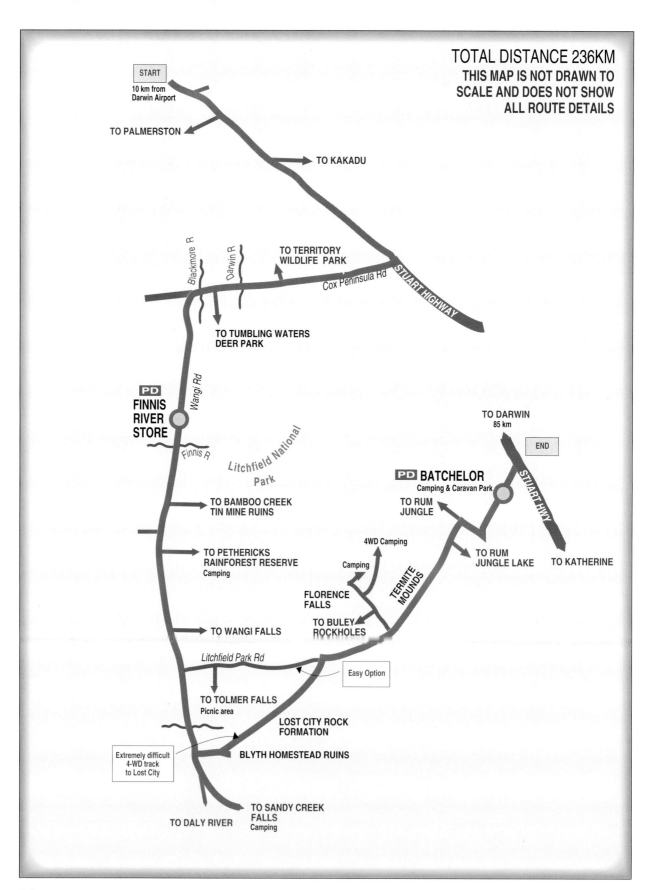

TOTAL DISTANCE 236KM
THIS MAP IS NOT DRAWN TO
SCALE AND DOES NOT SHOW
ALL ROUTE DETAILS

START
10 km from
Darwin Airport

TO PALMERSTON

TO KAKADU

Blackmore R

Darwin R

TO TERRITORY
WILDLIFE PARK

Cox Peninsula Rd

STUART HIGHWAY

TO TUMBLING WATERS
DEER PARK

Wangi Rd

PD
FINNIS
RIVER
STORE

Finnis R

Litchfield National
Park

TO DARWIN
85 km

END

PD BATCHELOR
Camping & Caravan Park

STUART HWY

TO RUM
JUNGLE

TO BAMBOO CREEK
TIN MINE RUINS

4WD Camping

TO RUM
JUNGLE LAKE

TO KATHERINE

TO PETHERICKS
RAINFOREST RESERVE
Camping

Camping

FLORENCE
FALLS

TERMITE
MOUNDS

TO WANGI FALLS

TO BULEY
ROCKHOLES

Litchfield Park Rd

Easy Option

TO TOLMER FALLS
Picnic area

LOST CITY ROCK
FORMATION

Extremely difficult
4-WD track
to Lost City

BLYTH HOMESTEAD RUINS

TO SANDY CREEK
FALLS
Camping

TO DALY RIVER

The track to the Lost City

ROUTE DIRECTIONS

Depart Darwin CBD via Stuart Hwy to
Darwin Airport entrance (approx. 10 km).
START TOUR

0.0 km Zero trip meter at above intersection. **SO**.
(13.3 km)

13.3 km S'post: Stuart Hwy. **KL**.

> *Palmerston off to right.*

(16.0 km)

29.3 km S'post: Alice Springs. **SO**.

> *Kakadu turnoff on left.*

(12.1 km)

41.4 km S'post: Berry Springs/Territory Wildlife
Park. **TR** onto Cox Peninsula Rd.
(10.7 km)

52.1 km S'post: Territory Wildlife Park.

> *Park on right. Allow 3 hrs to visit. Native
> and feral animals, moated enclosures,
> aquarium and aviary.*

0.0 km Zero trip meter at above intersection.
S'post: Mandorah. **SO** along Cox Peninsula
Rd.
(4.6 km)

4.6 km Darwin River. Cross bridge.
(2.8 km)

7.4 km S'post: Mandorah. **SO**.

> *Tumbling Waters Deer Park 3 km off to left.
> Private facility. Camping and picnic area,
> toilets, barbecues.*

(0.9 km)

8.3 km Blackmore River. Cross bridge.
(5.8 km)

14.1 km S'post: Litchfield Park. **TL** onto gravel:
Wangi Rd.
(30.2 km)

44.3 km Finnis River Store on right. **SO**.

> **PD** *Supplies. Next fuel Batchelor 120 km.*

(5.9 km)

50.2 km Finnis River. Cross bridge.
(8.8 km)

Wangi Falls and the pool

Wangi Falls 1.5 km off to left. Collect firewood on way in. Camping and picnic area, toilets, barbecues, cold showers. Permit necessary to camp, self-register on site. Excellent swimming in a large natural waterhole. Steep walking track to lookout above falls.

0.0 km   Zero trip meter at above s'post. **SO** along Litchfield Park Rd.
(6.6 km)
6.6 km   S'post: Sandy Creek Falls/Blyth Homestead. **TR.**

4WD access only. Road deteriorates to narrow track. Batchelor off to left.

(0.8 km)
7.4 km   Creek crossing.
(4.6 km)
12.0 km   S'post: Sandy Creek Falls/Daly River Rd. **SO.**

Blyth Homestead/Lost City off to left.

(1.6 km)
13.6 km   S'post: Sandy Creek Falls. **SO.**

Daly River Rd on right.

(1.6 km)
15.2 km   S'post: Sandy Creek Camping Ground and Carpark.

Collect firewood on way in. Camping and picnic area, toilets, barbecues, cold showers. Permit necessary to camp. Self-register on site. Walk to falls and natural swimming hole (1.7 km).

0.0 km   Zero trip meter at above s'post. Return via same track for 3.2 km as far as s'post: Blyth Homestead/Lost City.
Optional Lost City visit. **TR.**

Warning: the Lost City track is extremely difficult and requires skill and great care to traverse rocky outcrops and rutted tracks. Alternative route: Return 5.4 km to Litchfield Park Rd and turn right at s'post: Batchelor. Visit Tolmer Falls, a further 3.2 km along Litchfield Park Road and 400 m off to right. No camping at Tolmer Falls. Good walking tracks. Continue 10.4 km along Litchfield Park Rd and link with route directions at intersection and s'post: Batchelor.

(1.5 km)

59.0 km   S'post: Litchfield Park Entrance. **SO.**
(4.2 km)
63.2 km   Abandoned Bamboo Creek Tin Mine ruins off to left. **SO.**

4WD access. Attractive rockholes.

(2.3 km)
65.5 km   Walker Creek walking track on left. **SO.**
(0.3 km)
73.8 km   Crossroads. **SO.**

Labelle Station on right.

(2.0 km)
75.8 km   S'post: Batchelor.

Pethericks Rainforest Reserve 1 km off to left. Private facility. Camping, picnic area, barbecues, toilets. Thermal pool, cascades, rainforest, Mt Ford Gorge walking track. Further details from caretaker on site.

0.0 km   Zero trip meter at above s'post. **SO.**
(5.3 km)
5.3 km   S'post: Batchelor.

1.5 km S'post: Lost City. **TL**. Engage 4WD low range.

> *Blyth Homestead straight ahead. Visit to view only.*

(5.8 km)

7.3 km Lost City rock formations. **SO**.

> *No camping.*

(10.9 km)

18.2 km S'post: Batchelor.

> *Alternative route directions link up here.*

End option.

0.0 km Zero trip meter at above s'post. **TR** onto bitumen: Litchfield Park Rd.

(4.3 km)

4.3 km S'post: Florence Falls/Buley Rockholes. **TL** onto gravel.

> *Collect firewood along roadside.*

(2.1 km)

6.4 km S'post: Florence Falls.

> *Buley Rockholes 0.7 km off to left. Camping and picnic area, toilets, barbecues. Permit to camp necessary, self-register on site. Buley Rockholes, a sequence of cascades and deep rock pools suitable for diving and swimming, 50 m from campsites. Walking track leads up the creek to Florence Falls (1.5 km).*

0.0 km Zero trip meter at above s'post. **SO**.

(1.8 km)

1.8 km S'post: 4WD camping area.

> *Main Florence Falls camping area 50 m ahead on right. Toilets, barbecues, cold showers. Permit to camp necessary, self-register on site. Walk to Florence Falls (1.5 km). Florence Falls carpark is 500 m further on. Picnic area, barbecues, toilets. Steep 20-min. walk to falls and swimming hole or longer loop walk through rainforest.*

0.0 km Zero trip meter at 4WD camping area turnoff. **TR**.

(1.3 km)

1.3 km 4WD camping area.

> *Camping and picnic area. Barbecues, toilets. Permit to camp necessary, self-register on site. Walking track to Florence Falls.*

0.0 km Zero trip meter at above point. Return to Litchfield Park Rd via same track.

(5.2 km)

5.2 km S'post: Batchelor.

0.0 km Zero trip meter at above s'post. **TL** onto bitumen.

(0.6 km)

0.6 km Gravel.

(1.6 km)

2.2 km Bitumen.

(0.6 km)

2.8 km Gravel.

(3.2 km)

6.0 km Magnetic termite mounds field on left. **SO**.

(16.3 km)

22.3 km Bitumen.

(8.3 km)

30.6 km Bayan Tree Caravan Park and Store on right (no fuel). **SO**.

(1.2 km)

31.8 km S'post: Batchelor.

> *Rum Jungle Lake 2 km off to right. Picnic table, barbecue.*

0.0 km Zero trip meter at above s'post. **SO**.

(3.3 km)

3.3 km T intersection. S'post: Batchelor. **TR**.

> *Rum Jungle off to left. Permit required from CCNT to visit Rum Jungle Mine Rehabilitation Site.*

(5.9 km)

9.2 km S'post: Stuart Hwy. **SO**.

> *Batchelor town centre to left. Caravillage Caravan Park and camping area on right. **PD** Supplies, mechanical repairs.*

(0.6 km)

9.8 km T intersection. S'post: Stuart Hwy. **TL**.

(12.6 km)

22.4 km T intersection. S'post: Darwin. Zero trip meter.

END TOUR

TL onto Stuart Hwy to return to Darwin via Stuart Hwy (approx. 85 km).

Port Essington, Gurig National Park

GURIG NATIONAL PARK

START POINT Map page 24, I5.

TOTAL KM 619. Does not include 251 km Darwin to/from start/end point on Arnhem Highway. **See Route Directions.**

UNSEALED KM 575.

DEGREE OF DIFFICULTY Moderately difficult.

DRIVING TIME Tour over a minimum of 4 days. Allow extra time to/from start/end point. **See Route Directions.**

LONGEST DISTANCE NO FUEL No diesel between Jabiru and Black Point (623 km return). Petrol only at Border Store.

TOPOGRAPHIC MAPS Auslig 1:250 000 series: *Alligator River*; *Cobourg Peninsula*. See also 1:100 000 series.

LOCAL/SPECIALITY MAPS DPIF *Northern Territory Fishing Map*; ANPWS visitor guide: *Kakadu National Park*; Auslig: *Northern Australia*; CCNT: *Route to Gurig National Park.*

OTHER USEFUL INFORMATION CCNT visitor information sheets: *Gurig National Park*; *Cobourg Marine Park*; *Information Notes for Travellers by Road to Cobourg Peninsula.*

BEST TIME OF YEAR TO TRAVEL May–September (the dry season). Track through the park is impassable in the wet season.

TOUR DESCRIPTION The Cobourg Peninsula, in Gurig National Park, juts westwards from the coastal margins of Arnhem Land. It is a remote wilderness area, surrounded by the warm waters of the Arafura Sea. These waters, with their stunning coral reefs, sand beds and rich aquatic life, comprise Cobourg Marine Park: a major source of food for local Aborigines and an area of great cultural and spiritual importance to them. Gurig National Park is coastal Aboriginal land, managed as a wildlife sanctuary. You need a permit to enter the park, obtainable from the CCNT in Palmerston. Apply for your permit at least a week in advance, particularly if you are planning your tour for the peak dry season months of June and July.

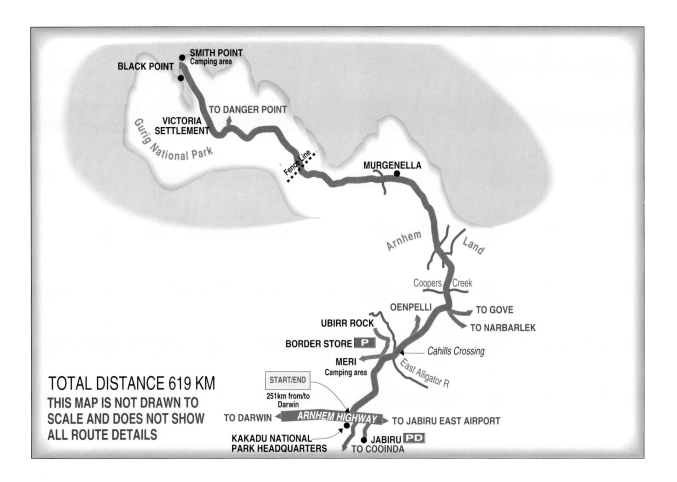

TOTAL DISTANCE 619 KM
THIS MAP IS NOT DRAWN TO SCALE AND DOES NOT SHOW ALL ROUTE DETAILS

Our tour starts at the Ubirr Rock turnoff on the Arnhem Highway in Kakadu National Park, 251 kilometres from Darwin. You must carry extra fuel beyond this point, as there are no towns after Jabiru. From the turnoff you drive out of Kakadu across the western edge of Arnhem Land and up to Smith Point on the tip of the Cobourg Peninsula. The unsealed road beyond Kakadu is generally well maintained and, provided there is no unseasonal rain, is only moderately difficult with some corrugated sections and sporadic patches of bulldust. Gurig is a fairly flat landscape covered by tropical eucalypt forest (mainly stringybark and woollybutt), broken by patches of monsoon rainforest, swampy paperbark woodlands, mangrove forests and kentia palm thickets. Banteng and sambar deer roam and graze on open land in the park. Present your permit at the Ranger Station at Black Point. *Smith Point* camping area, surrounded by casuarina trees, is 3 kilometres on, behind the wide sandy beach. Beach fishing here is superb: coral trout, mackerel, trevally and moon fish. Turtles, dugong and manta rays are often seen offshore, as well as more dangerous marine species including sharks, stingers and crocodiles.

Gurig Store, near the Ranger Station, has some supplies and the owners rent out the *Gurig Cabins* at Smith Point. They also conduct boat tours across Port Essington to Victoria Settlement: the ruins on the southwestern rim of the deep harbour. In the early 1800s the British tried unsuccessfully to establish a major tropical port here, and used the settlement as a base for botanical research. Darwin was finally selected in 1869 as a more appropriate port site. Drop in at the Cultural Centre next to the Ranger Station for a detailed account of the effect of Aboriginal, Macassan and European cultures on this isolated and beautiful part of the Northern Territory.

WARNINGS ▶ The 4WD road to the park is impassable October–April. Caravans are not permitted. Watch for corrugated sections and patches of bulldust. ▶ Fuel is not available beyond Jabiru. Have a full tank and take at least 100 litres extra. There is limited emergency fuel at Black Point. ▶ Be self-sufficient. Carry supplies of food and water, spare tyres and vehicle parts, and first aid and tool kits. Some food is available at Gurig Store and drinking water is available at Murgenella and

Marker cairn, Smith Point, Gurig National Park

Victoria Settlement ruins, Port Essington

Smith Point. ▶ Do not swim in the sea or in inland waterways at Gurig: beware sharks, crocodiles, blue-ringed octopus, stone fish, and box jellyfish.

BOOKINGS AND PERMITS ▶ Obtain a park permit from the Permits Officer, CCNT, Gaymark Building, Francis Mall, Palmerston Circuit, Palmerston NT; PO Box 196, Palmerston NT 0831; tel. (080) 80 4555 or 80 4559. Present the permit to the rangers at Murgenella and Black Point. Entry and camping fees are charged. ▶ Black Point Ranger Station can be contacted on (089) 79 0246. ▶ For enquiries about Gurig Cabins contact Gurig Store on (089) 79 0263. ▶ Camping is permitted only at Smith Point. Do not camp between Cahills Crossing and Black Point, en route to the park. ▶ Vehicle access is restricted to the designated track. Observe the list of conditions supplied by the CCNT with your permit.

ROUTE DIRECTIONS

Depart Darwin south along Stuart Hwy. **TL** onto Arnhem Hwy and proceed through Kakadu National Park to Ubirr/Oenpelli turnoff (approx. 251 km).

> *Jabiru 4 km straight ahead off Arnhem Hwy.* **PD** *Supplies. Last diesel for 623 km.*

START TOUR

0.0 km Zero trip meter at s'post: Ubirr/Oenpelli. **TL** off Arnhem Hwy onto gravel.
(8.9 km)

8.9 km S'post: Oenpelli. **KL.**

> *Mudginberri off to right.*

(5.8 km)
14.7 km Bitumen.
(21.8 km)
36.5 km Y intersection. S'post: Cahills Crossing.

> *Border Store 2 km off to left.* **P** *Limited supplies. Last petrol for 585 km. Ubirr Rock art carpark 0.5 km beyond store. Meri Camping Area 0.5 km off to left: toilets, hot showers, drinking water.*

0.0 km Zero trip meter at above intersection. **KR** onto gravel.
(0.4 km)

0.4 km East Alligator River / Cahills Crossing. Cross causeway.

> *Tidal river. Check tide chart provided by CCNT with permit.*

(12.7 km)
13.1 km Y intersection. S'post: Gurig National Park/Cobourg Peninsula. **KR.**

> *Oenpelli off to left.*

(22.6 km)
35.7 km Intersection. S'post: Gurig National Park/Cobourg Peninsula. **TL.**

> *Maningrida/Gove off to right.*

(100.8 km)
136.5 km Creek. Cross causeway.
(1.7 km)
138.2 km S'post: Cobourg Peninsula 135 km.

> *Ranger Station, solar phone. Present permit to ranger or deposit copy in post box at the station if ranger is absent.*

0.0 km Zero trip meter at above s'post. **KL** through Murgenella.
(18.3 km)

18.3 km S'post: Cobourg Peninsula. **KR**.
(1.7 km)

20.0 km S'post: Cobourg Peninsula. **KL**.
(21.2 km)

41.2 km S'post: Cobourg Aboriginal Land and Sanctuary. **SO** through gate.

> *Keep gate closed. Cobourg Peninsula and nearby offshore islands form Gurig National Park, on Aboriginal-owned land. Permit required. No camping before Smith Point.*

(9.4 km)

50.6 km Gate.

> *Leave as found.*

(34.7 km)

85.3 km S'post: Black Point Ranger Station. **KL**.

> *Danger Point Rd off to right. Private: no access without permit.*

(9.5 km)

94.8 km Intersection. **SO**.

> *Cape Don Road off to left. Private: no access without permit.*

(38.9 km)

133.7 km S'post: Park Office. **TL**.
(0.9 km)

134.6 km Gurig National Park Ranger Station, Black Point.

> *Check in at Ranger Station on arrival to present permit and to obtain printed and verbal information about Gurig. Cultural Centre adjacent to station. Gurig Store: open 3–4 pm daily. Limited supplies and limited fuel (for emergencies only). Enquire at store about boat tours across Port Essington to the Victoria Settlement ruins, and about Gurig Cabins at Smith Point. Smith Point Camping Area 3 km on from station behind beach: toilets, showers and drinking water. Excellent fishing off wide, sandy beach. Fascinating marine life, including dugongs and turtles.*

0.0 km Zero trip meter at Black Point and return via same track to East Alligator River / Cahills Crossing (approx. 273 km).

Port Essington from Gurig National Park

> *Tidal river. Check tide chart provided by CCNT with permit.*

0.0 km Zero trip meter at Cahills Crossing.
(0.4 km)

0.4 km Intersection. S'post: Jabiru.

> *Border Store 2 km off to right. **P** Limited supplies. Meri Camping Area 0.5 km off to right: toilets, hot showers, drinking water.*

0.0 km Zero trip meter at above intersection. **TL** onto bitumen.
(21.8 km)

21.8 km Gravel.
(14.7 km)

36.5km Arnhem Hwy. S'post: Darwin. Zero trip meter.

> *Jabiru 4 km off to left. **PD** Supplies, caravan park, mechanical repairs.*

END TOUR
TR onto hwy and proceed through Kakadu National Park to Stuart Hwy and Darwin (approx. 251 km).

Jim Jim Falls Gorge

KAKADU NATIONAL PARK

START POINT Map page 24, E5.

TOTAL KM 855 (includes optional tracks in park). Does not include 10 km Darwin to start point and 250 km end point to Darwin. *See Route Directions.*

UNSEALED KM 385.

DEGREE OF DIFFICULTY Easy. Optional 4WD tracks: difficult to extremely difficult.

DRIVING TIME Tour over a minimum of 2 days. Allow extra time to/from start/end points. *See Route Directions.*

LONGEST DISTANCE NO FUEL Within Kakadu National Park fuel is available at: Kakadu Holiday Village, Jabiru, Border Store, Gagudju Lodge Cooinda.

TOPOGRAPHIC MAPS Auslig 1:250 000 series: *Alligator River; Mount Evelyn.* See also 1:100 000 series.

LOCAL/SPECIALITY MAPS DPIF: *Northern Territory Fishing Map;* Australian Geographic: *Kakadu and Surrounds;* ANPWS visitor guide and map: *Kakadu National Park.*

OTHER USEFUL INFORMATION ANPWS park notes: *A Driver's Guide to Kakadu; Walking Tracks in Kakadu National Park; Animals of Kakadu.* Park notes on walking tracks are available from Kakadu Park Headquarters.

BEST TIME OF YEAR TO TRAVEL May–September (the dry season) when temperatures and humidity are relatively low.

TOUR DESCRIPTION Kakadu National Park is 250 kilometres from Darwin in the dense and wild Alligator rivers region, bordering Arnhem Land. The tour through this large park is mainly via the sealed Arnhem and Kakadu highways, through tropical woodlands which are a deceptively quiet and complex habitat for an incredible variety of wildlife. Woodlands cover over half the park which extends from the craggy red escarpment wall of the Arnhem Land plateau, across forests, floodplains and wetlands, to the mangrove swamps along Van Diemen Gulf. It is best seen as soon after the wet season as possible, when the landscape is lush and the roads, camping areas and walking tracks are the least congested.

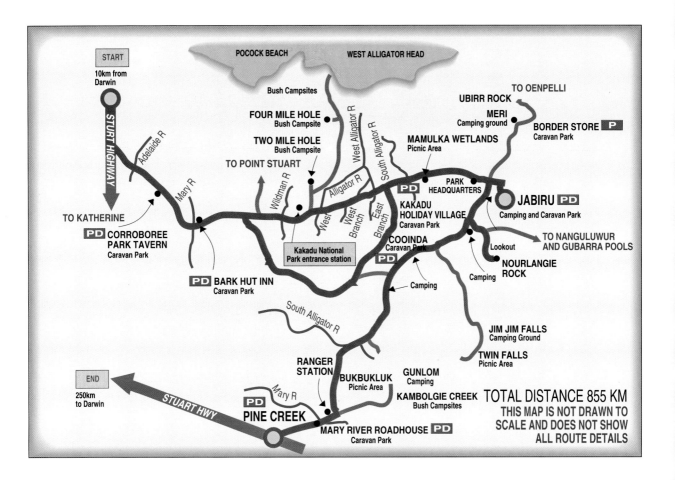

Park roads are heavily trafficked in the dry winter months. Our 3 plotted four-wheel drive tracks – to West Alligator Head, Red Lily and Alligator billabongs, and Jim Jim Falls – give you some solitude. The difficult track to remote West Alligator Head on Pocock Beach is often corrugated and becomes narrow and twisting near the head. It is a remote location, absolutely perfect for anglers. Red Lily and Alligator billabongs are excellent bush campsites and fishing spots where you can watch magpie geese, brolgas, jabirus, pelicans and other waterbirds which flock to billabongs as the wetlands recede. The track to the billabongs is only moderately difficult but be alert for washaways. Check with a ranger before taking the Jim Jim Falls track. It is an extremely difficult drive due to corrugation and, if the normally spectacular falls are dry, perhaps not worth the time and effort.

Kakadu is jointly managed by the ANPWS and descendants of Aboriginal tribes who have lived in the region for well over 25 000 years. The ancient art sites here are regarded as among the finest in the world, recording changes in climate, geology and Aboriginal culture. There are thousands of sites scattered through the park but the most accessible are Ubirr and Nourlangie rocks. Both are reached by walking tracks. Kakadu has 23 walking tracks of various lengths: along billabongs, through wetlands, woodlands and rainforests to caves, shelters and lookouts. Visit Park Headquarters Visitor Centre early in the tour. They have printed information as well as displays and videos which will help you choose which sights are of most interest. Peruse our sketch map and route directions when planning your trip. A park use fee is charged (valid for 2 weeks) and camping permits are necessary for bush camping.

Fuel and food can be obtained within the park at Jabiru and at 3 other locations and there are 17 camping grounds and plenty of caravan sites. *Muirella Park*, *Meri* and *Mardugal* are the most crowded camp-grounds. *Burdulba* and *Gunlom* camping grounds and *Red Lily* and *Alligator* billabongs are generally quieter. It is worth foregoing hot showers and flushing toilets to camp beside a billabong in relative isolation, but remember that you are sharing this habitat with crocodiles. A quarter of Australia's freshwater fish species are found in Kakadu and in the clear creek water at Gunlom you see many.

89

Crocodile warning at Alligator Billabong

WARNINGS ▶ Sections of park roads may be impassable in the wet season. ▶ Do not walk alone when bushwalking and enquire at park headquarters for advice on safety precautions. ▶ Drinking water is provided at park headquarters and at Meri, Muirella Park, Mardugal and Gunlom camping areas. Boil other water before drinking. ▶ Help stop the spread of the salvinia fern weed: check undercarriage of vehicles, boats and trailers when leaving waterways. ▶ Observe speed limits. Watch for wildlife if night driving. ▶ Crocodiles inhabit coastline and inland waterways in Kakadu. Be crocodile-wise. Do not swim. ▶ Observe all park regulations on sanitation, pets, firearms and lighting fires. Do not touch or disturb flora, fauna or Aboriginal cultural sites.

BOOKINGS AND PERMITS ▶ Pay park use fee at Park Headquarters, hotels or camping grounds (valid 14 days). ▶ Obtain a camping permit from Park Headquarters if bush camping. ▶ For information on Kakadu contact: ANPWS, MLC Building, 79–81 Smith Street, Darwin; GPO Box 1260, Darwin 0801; tel. (089) 81 5299; or Park Manager, Kakadu National Park, PO Box 71, Jabiru NT 0886; tel. (089) 79 9110.

ROUTE DIRECTIONS

Depart Darwin CBD via Stuart Hwy to Darwin Airport entrance (approx. 10 km).
START TOUR

0.0 km Zero trip meter at above intersection. **SO** along Stuart Hwy.
(13.1 km)

13.1 km S'post: Stuart Hwy. **KL**.

> *Palmerston off to right.*

(16.1 km)

29.2 km Intersection. S'post: Kakadu National Park/Jabiru.

0.0 km Zero trip meter at above intersection. **TL** onto Arnhem Hwy.
(32.4 km)

32.4 km Adelaide River Queen Pavilion on right. **SO**.

> *Cruises down the Alligator River.*

(0.1 km)

32.5 km Adelaide River. Cross bridge.
(22.1 km)

54.6 km Corroboree Park Tavern on right. **SO**.

> **PD** *Caravan park.*

(24.4 km)

79.0 km Mary River. Cross bridge.

> *Picnic facilities and boat ramp. Day use only.*

(3.3 km)

82.3 km The Bark Hut Inn on left. **SO**.

> **PD** *Caravan park.*

(17.8 km)

100.1 km S'post: Jabiru/Kakadu National Park.

> *Cooinda off to right along Jim Jim Rd.*

(0.8 km)

100.9 km S'post: Jabiru/Kakadu National Park.

> *Point Stuart off to left.*

0.0 km Zero trip meter at above s'post. **SO** along Arnhem Hwy.
(17.0 km)

17.0 km S'post: Kakadu National Park World Heritage Area. **SO**.
(5.7 km)

22.7 km Wildman River. Cross bridge.
(12.4 km)

35.1 km Kakadu National Park Entrance Station on left. **SO**.

> *Entrance to Kakadu National Park. Pay park fee (valid 14 days). Obtain park and walking track maps. Rest area, toilets.*

(1.6 km)

36.7 km Intersection. S'post: West Alligator Head 82 km/Two Mile Hole 38 km/Four Mile Hole 12 km.
Option: West Alligator Head 4WD Track.

0.0 km Zero trip meter at above intersection. **TL**.

> *Warning: firearms, traps and nets prohibited. Difficult track to remote West Alligator Head on Van Diemen Gulf.*

(8.1 km)

Sandy Billabong campsite

8.1 km Intersection. S'post: West Alligator Head.

> *Two Mile Hole 13.7 km off to left. Bush campsite near billabong.*

0.0 km Zero trip meter at above intersection. **SO.**
(26.1 km)

26.1 km Intersection. S'post: West Alligator Head.

> *Four Mile Hole 4.4 km off to left. Bush campsite near billabong.*

0.0 km Zero trip meter at above intersection. **SO.**
(48.6 km)

48.6 km West Alligator Head.

> *Pocock Beach 500 m off to left. Beach bush campsites under shade trees. Excellent fishing.*

Return to Arnhem Hwy via same track and continue with route directions.
End option.

0.0 km Zero trip meter at turnoff to West Alligator Head. **SO** along Arnhem Hwy.
(3.9 km)

3.9 km West Alligator River. Cross bridge.
(4.6 km)

8.5 km West Alligator River west branch. Cross bridge.

> *At Kapalga Field Research Station on left the CSIRO are investigating the effect of bushfires on wildlife.*

(8.6 km)

17.1 km West Alligator River east branch. Cross bridge.
(12.5 km)

29.6 km Intersection. S'post: Red Lily Billabong 23 km/Alligator Billabong 25 km.
Option: Red Lily and Alligator Billabongs 4WD Track.

0.0 km Zero trip meter at above intersection. **TR.**

> *Warning: moderately difficult track. Beware of washaways.*

(20.2 km)

20.2 km S'post: Alligator Billabong. **KR.**

Burning off in Kakadu

| **PD** *Caravan park, motel, limited supplies at general store. Swimming pool. Boat hire. Cruises up South Alligator River. Gungarra Nature Trail.* |

0.0 km Zero trip meter opposite Kakadu Holiday Village. **SO** along Arnhem Hwy.
(3.0 km)
3.0 km Picnic area on left. **SO**.

| *River access and boat ramp. Day use only.* |

(0.4 km)
3.4 km South Alligator River. Cross bridge.

| *River flows from Arnhem Land escarpment through woodlands, paperbark forests and floodplains, downstream to mangroves along Van Diemen Gulf. Binirrinj (Goanna Dreaming) rock outcrop in view (0.5 km north).* |

(7.5 km)
10.9 km Intersection.

| *Mamukala Wetlands Picnic Area and observation building 1 km off to right. Mamukala Wetlands Walk (3 km return).* |

0.0 km Zero trip meter at above intersection. **SO** along Arnhem Hwy.
(28.1 km)
28.1 km Intersection. S'post: Park Headquarters/Jabiru.

| *Ubirr Rock 39 km off to left. Oenpelli 52 km off to left.* |

0.0 km Zero trip meter at above intersection. **SO** along Arnhem Hwy.
(1.2 km)
1.2 km Intersection. S'post: Jabiru.

| *Park Headquarters Visitor Centre 2.3 km off to right along Kakadu Hwy. Park and walking track maps, videos and displays. Permits required for bush camping. Ranger guided walks May–September.* |

0.0 km Zero trip meter at above intersection. **SO** along Arnhem Hwy.
(1.5 km)
1.5 km S'post: Jabiru. **TR**.
(0.6 km)
2.1 km Kakadu Frontier Lodge and Caravan Park on right. **SO**.

| *Swimming pool, restaurant.* |

(0.5 km)

| *Red Lily Billabong 3.3 km off to left. Bush campsites near billabong.* |

(4.9 km)
25.1 km Intersection. **KL**.

| *Alligator Billabong first bush campsite 300 m off to right.* |

(1.3 km)
26.4 km Intersection. **KL**.

| *Alligator Billabong second bush campsite 1 km off to right.* |

Either turn around and return to Arnhem Hwy by same track to pick up route directions, or continue straight ahead 26 km to Jim Jim Rd. Turn right to return to Darwin, turn left to link with Kakadu Hwy. **End option.**
0.0 km Zero trip meter at turnoff to Red Lily and Alligator billabongs. **SO** along Arnhem Hwy.
(5.1 km)
5.1 km Kakadu Holiday Village on right.

2.6 km   Intersection. S'post: Leichhardt St.

> *Jabiru township on left.* **PD** *Supplies, mechanical repairs. Gagudju Crocodile Hotel. Mining town administered under strict environmental requirements.*

0.0 km   Zero trip meter at above intersection and return 1 km to Arnhem Hwy.

0.0 km   Zero trip meter at s'post Darwin. **TL**. **SO** along Arnhem Hwy.
           (1.5 km)

1.5 km   Intersection. **SO** over Kakadu Hwy.

> *Park Headquarters 2.3 km off to left along Kakadu Hwy.*

           (1.2 km)

2.7 km   Intersection. S'post: Ubirr Rock 39 km/ Oenpelli 52 km. **TR** onto gravel.
           (8.9 km)

11.6 km   S'post: Oenpelli. **KL**.

> *Mudginberri off to right.*

           (5.8 km)

17.4 km   Bitumen. **SO**.
           (21.8 km)

39.2 km   Y intersection. S'post: Ubirr Rock Art Sites/Meri Camp Ground.

> *Meri Camping Ground 0.5 km off to left: picnic tables, barbecues, toilets, showers, drinking water. Ranger collects fees. Border Store 2 km ahead on left.* **P** *Limited supplies. Manngarre Monsoon Rainforest walking track opposite store. Ubirr Rock art sites accessible from carpark, 0.5 km beyond store. Ancient ochre and x-ray paintings of human, animal and mimi spirit figures.*

0.0 km   Zero trip meter at above intersection and return 39.2 km to Arnhem Hwy via same track. S'post: Jabiru. **TL**.
           (1.2 km)

1.2 km   S'post: Pine Creek/Park Headquarters. **TR** onto Kakadu Hwy.
           (2.3 km)

3.5 km   Park Headquarters on right. **SO**.

> *Videos, displays and information at Visitor Centre. Permit required for bush camping.*

           (13.0 km)

16.5 km   Intersection.

> *Malabanjbanjdju bush campsite near billabong 1 km off to right. Tents only. Iligadjarr Nature Trail across grassy floodplains, past billabongs and through shrubland. Traditional Aboriginal hunting grounds.*

0.0 km   Zero trip meter at above intersection. **SO** along Kakadu Hwy.
           (1.2 km)

1.2 km   Intersection.

> *Malabanjbanjdju Camping Ground 4 km off to right near billabong: caravan sites, pit toilets. Access to Iligadjarr Nature Trail.*

0.0 km   Zero trip meter at above intersection. **SO** along Kakadu Hwy.
           (0.6 km)

0.6 km   Intersection.

> *Burdulba Camping Ground 1 km off to right near billabong. Pit toilets. Access to Iligadjarr Nature Trail.*

0.0 km   Zero trip meter at above intersection. **SO** along Kakadu Hwy.
           (3.6 km)

3.6 km   Intersection. S'post: Pine Creek.
           Option: Nourlangie Rock.

0.0 km   Zero trip meter at above intersection. **TL**.
           (6.2 km)

6.2 km   Intersection. **SO**.

> *Nanguluwur carpark 1.3 km off to left: 4-km circuit walk through woodlands to impressive rock art gallery. Gubara Pools carpark is 7.2 km further on: circuit walk past sandstone formations to Gubara Pools in a shady monsoon forest.*

           (3.8 km)

10.0 km   Intersection. **SO**.

> *Carpark for Nawurlandja Lookout Walk 0.5 km off to right: circuit walk to beautiful views of the Nourlangie area.*

           (1.3 km)

11.3 km   Intersection. **SO**.

> *Anbangbang Billabong Picnic Area 1 km off to right. Lovely billabong surrounded by paperbark and itchy bush trees. Watch for flying foxes, black cockatoos, magpie geese, pelicans and spoonbills. Circuit walk from picnic area to Anbangbang gallery and shelter, used in the wet season by tribes hunting in Kakadu thousands of years ago.*

           (0.7 km)

12.0 km   Nourlangie Rock carpark.

> *Take 1.5 km circuit walk to view outstanding art sites and shelters around the base of the rocky outcrop.*

Return to Kakadu Hwy via same route and continue with route directions
End option.

0.0 km   Zero trip meter at s'post Pine Creek on Kakadu Hwy. **SO**.
   (7.2 km)

7.2 km   Intersection. S'post: Pine Creek.

> *Muirella Park Camping Ground 6.5 km off to left near billabong: picnic tables, barbecues, hot showers, toilets, drinking water. Ranger collects camping fee. Bubba Wetlands Walk is a circuit through creekbeds, paperbark forests and open woodlands to Bubba Billabong and swamps, fringed with lilies.*

0.0 km   Zero trip meter at above intersection. **SO** along Kakadu Hwy.
   (2.3 km)

2.3 km   Intersection. S'post: Pine Creek.

> *Mirrai Lookout carpark 0.5 km off to left: steep 1.8 km circuit walk to Mirrai hilltop lookout with 360 degree views of central Kakadu.*

0.0 km   Zero trip meter at above intersection. **SO** along Kakadu Hwy.
   (10.3 km)

10.3 km   S'post: Pine Creek/Jim Jim Falls.
   Option: Jim Jim Falls 4WD Track.

0.0 km   Zero trip meter at above intersection on Kakadu Hwy. **TL** onto gravel.

> *Warning: corrugated track. Last 10 km extremely difficult. 4WD only. Road is not suitable for caravans and trailers. Collect firewood from roadside on way in. Falls may be dry May–September. Check with ranger.*

   (57.5 km)

57.5 km   S'post: Jim Jim Falls. **SO**.

> *Jim Jim Falls Camping Ground 1.4 km off to right: picnic tables, barbecues, pit toilets. Further 10 km to Twin Falls day use area.*

   (2.0 km)

59.5 km   Jim Jim Falls car park.

> *Day use picnic area. Three circuit walks: Budjmii Lookout walk 1 km; Jim Jim Falls Plunge Pool walk 1 km; Barrk Malam 6 km walk to Jim Jim Creek above the falls.*

Return to Kakadu Hwy by same gravel track. Continue with route directions.
End option.

0.0 km   Zero trip meter on Kakadu Hwy at s'post: Pine Creek/Jim Jim Falls. **SO**.
   (7.7 km)

7.7 km   Intersection. S'post: Cooinda.

> *Jim Jim Billabong Camping Ground 6 km off to left. Pit toilets, boat ramp.*

0.0 km   Zero trip meter at above intersection. **SO** along Kakadu Hwy.
   (0.5 km)

0.5 km   Intersection. S'post: Pine Creek.

> *Gagudju Lodge Cooinda 4 km off to right.* **PD** *Caravan park, limited supplies. Book here for cruise on Yellow Waters Billabong: crocodiles, variety birds and wildlife.*

0.0 km   Zero trip meter at above intersection. **SO** along Kakadu Hwy.
   (1.7 km)

1.7 km   Intersection. S'post: Pine Creek.

> *Mardugal Camping Ground 0.5 km off to right: picnic tables, barbecues, toilets, hot showers, drinking water. Ranger collects fee. Kunkardun Woodland Walk guides you through Kakadu's most productive woodlands. Watch for kingfishers, echidnas and wallabies.*

0.0 km   Zero trip meter at above intersection. **SO** along Kakadu Hwy.
   (4.3 km)

4.3 km   Gravel.
   (2.1 km)

6.4 km   Intersection. Kakadu Hwy and Jim Jim Rd. S'post: Darwin.
   Options: Either return to Darwin via Jim Jim Rd and Arnhem Hwy (approx. 220 km) or continue with route directions.

0.0 km   Zero trip meter at intersection Kakadu Hwy and Jim Jim Rd. **SO** along Kakadu Hwy heading south.
   (39.5 km)

39.5 km   S'post: Pine Creek.

Nourlangie Rock art

Maguk Camping Ground near Barramundi Gorge 9.5 km off to left: picnic tables, barbecues, pit toilets. Gorge carpark a further 1.7 km. Day use only. Walk to plunge pool.

0.0 km Zero trip meter at above intersection. **SO** along Kakadu Hwy.
(5.6 km)
5.6 km Cross South Alligator River.
(26.8 km)
32.4 km Bukbukluk Lookout on right.

Day use picnic area.

(8.5 km)
40.9 km Intersection. S'post: Pine Creek.

Kambolgie Creek bush campsites 13.4 km off to left. Gunlom (Waterfall Creek) Camping Ground and Picnic Area 36.1 km off to left: picnic tables, barbecues, toilets, hot showers, drinking water. Steep circuit walk to top of Gunlom Falls, featured in Crocodile Dundee.

0.0 km Zero trip meter at above intersection. **SO** along Kakadu Hwy.
(1.6 km)
1.6 km S'post: Pine Creek. **SO**.

Ranger Station on right.

(9.7 km)
11.3 km Mary River. Cross bridge.

Exit Kakadu National Park.

(0.3 km)
11.6 km Mary River Roadhouse.

PD *Caravan park.*

(59.0 km)
70.6 km Pine Creek. Zero trip meter.

PD *Caravan park. Small copper mining town on the Stuart Hwy.*

END TOUR
TR to return to Darwin via Stuart Hwy (approx. 250 km).

TOURS OUT OF PERTH

The vast state of Western Australia stretches from the virgin wilderness of the Kimberley in the north through central desert frontiers to Perth and the heartlands of the south. Our tours encompass a wide variety of landscapes throughout the south west: majestic jarrah–marri forests, coastal sand tracks, fishing holiday towns, salt-lake systems, wheatlands, goldmining regions and beautifully restored historic settlements. Wildflowers bloom and abound in spring – the best time to travel. Most of their natural settings are accessible to four-wheel drives.

THE JARRAH FOREST (tour over 2 or 3 days: 231 kilometres). An easy tour that visits the major timber town of Dwellingup and many camping and picnicking spots in Lane-Poole Reserve. You can bushwalk, swim, canoe, fish and explore the rock pools of the Murray River and see a wealth of forest plants and wildlife at close range.

YANCHEP TO NEW NORCIA (tour over a minimum of 3 days: 448 kilometres). Follow a difficult and challenging four-wheel drive route north through sand-dune and limestone tracks to the coastal fishing towns of Lancelin, Cervantes and Jurien.

Beach fishing, Wedge Island

Other highlights include Yanchep and Nambung national parks, the latter including the famous Pinnacles Desert, and the New Norcia monastic settlement with its splendid collection of religious art.

NORSEMAN AND THE SOUTH WEST (tour over 4 or 5 days: 1163 kilometres). A longer but only moderately difficult adventure along four-wheel drive tracks punctuated by wheat country, salt-lake systems, fields of wildflowers and ancient rock formations such as Wave Rock. You can stay in caravan parks in the many towns including Norseman, a fascinating goldmining settlement, and camp at Peak Charles and Frank Hann national parks if you are totally self-sufficient.

WESTERN AUSTRALIA'S NATIONAL PARKS, STATE FORESTS AND NATURE RESERVES

Western Australia has a wide range of natural and developed settings for camping enthusiasts: arid scrublands that become wildflower havens in spring, some of Australia's oldest landforms, virgin forests, and banks of rivers, creeks and lakes. Basic facilities are usually provided. Though no permits are necessary to traverse most national parks, camping fees usually apply and are payable to rangers on site or at ranger headquarters. Bush camping is also permitted by arrangement, and length of stay is restricted in some areas. Book ahead to camp during the peak seasons of Christmas and Easter. Contact the Department of Conservation and Land Management (CALM), State Operations Headquarters, 50 Hayman Road, Como WA 6152; tel. (09) 367 0333. Addresses and phone numbers for regional and district offices are given in the tour descriptions. When using lands managed by CALM obey the following rules.

▶ *Drive and walk along the designated tracks only, to prevent erosion and spread of dieback, a fungal disease that destroys vegetation.*
▶ *Light fires only in barbecues and fireplaces provided. Extinguish fires completely before leaving campsites. Preferably bring your portable gas stove.*
▶ *Place rubbish in bins provided or take it away with you.*
▶ *Pets, firearms and spearguns are prohibited. A permit is required to keep or move protected wildlife and flora.*
▶ *Follow signs and stay on roads marked in brochures and information shelters. Normal road rules apply.*
▶ *Promptly contact rangers and forest officers for all information relating to road surfaces, alternative routes, fire and flood danger, bushwalking tracks, facilities and campsites.*

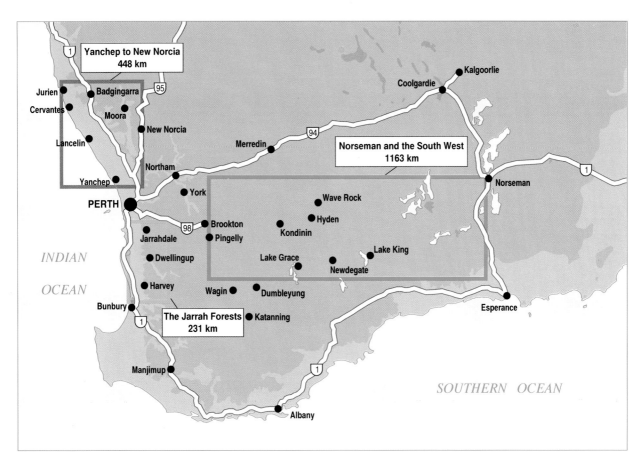

BEFORE YOU SET OUT ▶ Read the tour description carefully. ▶ Check that you have obtained any necessary permits. ▶ Check weather conditions with local authorities or Bureau of Meteorology. ▶ Make sure you have the appropriate maps and information for the tour. ▶ Check that your vehicle is in good order for the conditions ahead. Have you the necessary spare parts? ▶ If you are camping, have you the right equipment?

USEFUL INFORMATION

For touring information contact:
Western Australian Tourist Centre
Albert Facey House
Cnr Forest Place and Wellington Street
Perth 6000
(09) 483 1111.

For motoring information contact:
The Royal Automobile Club
  of Western Australia Inc. (RAC)
228 Adelaide Terrace, Perth 6000
(09) 421 4444.

For four-wheel driving information contact:
Western Australian Association
  of Four Wheel Drive Clubs Inc.
PO Box 6029
East Perth 6004.

For fishing regulations contact:
The Fisheries Department
  of Western Australia
108 Adelaide Terrace
East Perth 6004
(09) 220 5333.

THE JARRAH FOREST

START POINT Map page 30, E8.

TOTAL KM 231. Does not include 29 km Perth to start point and 140 km end point to Perth. **See Route Directions.**

UNSEALED KM 150.

DEGREE OF DIFFICULTY Easy.

DRIVING TIME Tour over 2 or 3 days. Allow time to/from start/end points. **See Route Directions.**

LONGEST DISTANCE NO FUEL 119 km (Dwellingup to Harvey–Quindanning Road and South Western Highway intersection).

TOPOGRAPHIC MAPS Auslig 1:250 000 series: *Perth; Pinjarra.*

LOCAL/SPECIALITY MAPS *Robinsons Western Australia.*

OTHER USEFUL INFORMATION CALM *Discover* series booklet: *Wild Places, Quiet Places: a Guide to the Natural Highlights of the South-West* and booklet: *Perth Outdoors: Recreation and Conservation Spots in Perth and Environs;* CALM brochure: *Dwellingup and Lane-Poole Reserve.*

BEST TIME OF YEAR TO TRAVEL September –December (spring–early summer) for the wildflowers, and December–March (summer–early autumn) for the cool of the forests and its streams and rivers.

TOUR DESCRIPTION This tour takes you in and around the Darling Ranges forest and catchment area that backs onto the eastern edge of the Swan Coastal Plain. Rainfall is about double that of the coastal belt. The rich deep soils of the valley have produced tall stands of jarrah, marri (redgum), blackbutt, bullich and wandoo. Though the area has few permanent rivers or streams, its many dams supply water to the Perth metropolitan area – only 100 kilometres away.

Though the tour covers a relatively short distance, the landscape is picturesque and diversified and deserves a few days to capture its moods. Much of the region has been set aside for public recreation for both day use and overnight stays. Dwellingup is the major forest town in the northern jarrah forest and is still the centre of a timber-mill network. Most of the town was rebuilt after 1961 when a fierce bushfire devastated the area, leaving only Dwellingup Hotel and a few houses un-

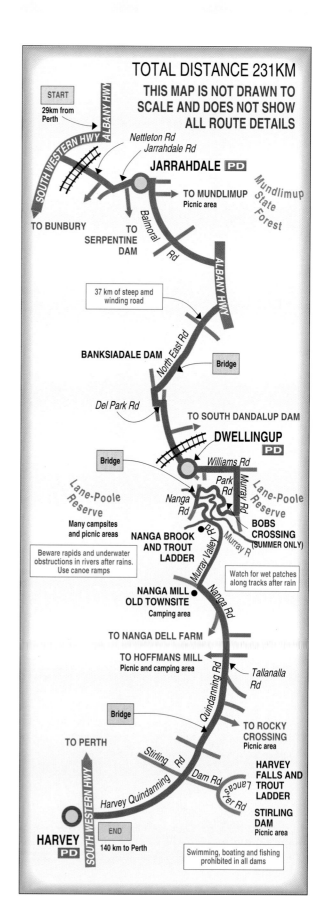

Camping at Nanga Pool

scathed. You also visit the old Nanga sawmill and townsite later in the tour.

Lane-Poole Reserve was established in 1983 and named after C. E. Lane-Poole, the state's first Conservator of Forests and a devoted conservationist. Covering 52 000 hectares, it offers several attractive camping and picnic areas. The tour's designated campsites are *Yarragil, Tonys Bend, Charlies Flat, Baden Powell, Nanga Mill, Nanga Townsite* and *The Stringers*.

The Murray is the longest permanent river, and also remains undammed. Activities centred on the river include fishing, swimming, canoeing and rock-pool exploration. Bushwalking tracks and lookouts reveal plants of the forest understorey such as bull banksias, zamia palms, blackboys and acacias. You can also enjoy the summer eucalypts, winter wattles and spring wildflowers when in bloom. See and hear a wealth of wildlife – birds, lizards and insects – as you walk through the jarrah forest.

WARNINGS ▶ Fire danger increases December to April. Total fire bans on days of very high or extreme fire danger. Obtain daily fire information weekdays

from CALM Dwellingup District Office, Banksiadale Road, Dwellingup WA 6213; tel. (09) 538 1078; from CALM Jarrahdale District Office, George Street, Jarrahdale WA 6203; tel. (09) 525 5004; from CALM State Operations Headquarters in Perth, or from local radio broadcasts. ▶ Tracks mainly good-quality gravel, but under forest-canopy cover maintain moisture; slippery after rain. Watch for wet patches. ▶ Obtain advice on road conditions and other useful information weekdays from CALM Dwellingup or Jarrahdale office. ▶ The dams are a main source of Perth's water supply – swimming, boating and fishing prohibited. ▶ Be particularly careful of rapids or underwater obstructions if swimming or canoeing in rivers after winter rains. Use canoe ramps provided to minimise bank erosion. ▶ Anglers contact the Fisheries Department, 108 Adelaide Terrace, East Perth 6004; tel. (09) 220 5333 for information about fishing regulations and restrictions in Lane-Poole Reserve.

BOOKINGS AND PERMITS ▶ No prior permits required to traverse region but camping fee payable in designated areas. Pay rangers or forest officers on site. Obtain camping information brochure from CALM Dwellingup office or State Operations Headquarters in Perth. If sites full, contact ranger at CALM Dwellingup office for advice on possible alternatives.

ROUTE DIRECTIONS

Depart Perth CBD south-east approx. 29 km via Adelaide Terrace, the Causeway and Albany Hwy.
START TOUR

0.0 km   Zero trip meter at s'post: Bunbury at Albany Hwy and South Western Hwy intersection. **SO** along South Western Hwy. **(8.9 km)**

8.9 km   S'post: Nettleton Rd/Scenic Drive via Jarrahdale. **TL**. **(15.6 km)**

24.5 km   Cross railway line. **(0.6 km)**

25.1 km   Intersection.

> *Langford Park Picnic Area on right. Picnic tables, barbecues, toilets. Walking tracks.*

0.0 km   Zero trip meter at above intersection. **SO**. **(1.9 km)**

1.9 km   S'post: Jarrahdale Rd. **TL**. **(2.0 km)**

3.9 km   S'post: Albany Hwy.

> *Serpentine Dam 10 km off to right. Picnic area and tearooms overlooking hills and landscaped wildflower gardens around dam. Camping, swimming and boating prohibited.*

0.0 km   Zero trip meter at s'post: Albany Hwy. **SO** through Jarrahdale along Jarrahdale Rd. **PD**
(0.5 km)

0.5 km   S'post: Balmoral Rd. **TR.**

> *Sign: Mundlimup State Forest.*

(0.5 km)

1.0 km   Intersection. **SO.**

> *Mundlimup Picnic Area off to left. Picnic tables, barbecues, toilets.*

(0.9 km)

1.9 km   Gravel.
(9.6 km)

11.5 km   Intersection. **SO.**
(2.0 km)

13.5 km   Intersection. **SO.**
(6.6 km)

20.1 km   T intersection. **TR** onto Albany Hwy.
(13.3 km)

33.4 km   Intersection. **TR** onto gravel.

> *Sign: 37 km of steep and winding road.*

(11.0 km)

44.4 km   Crossroads. S'post: North East Rd. **SO.**
(23.8 km)

68.2 km   Cross bridge.

> *Banksiadale Dam on right.*

(4.2 km)

72.4 km   T intersection. **TL** onto bitumen.
(1.7 km)

74.1 km   S'post: Del Park Rd. **TL** and immediately **TR** at s'post: Dwellingup.
(0.5 km)

74.5 km   Intersection.

> *South Dandalup Dam 1 km off to left. Day use only, closed at night. Picnic tables, barbecues, toilets, drinking water. Lookout. Camping, swimming and boating prohibited.*

0.0 km   Zero trip meter at above intersection. **SO.**
(9.1 km)

9.1 km   Cross railway line and enter Dwellingup. **PD**
(0.2 km)

9.3 km   S'post: Williams Rd.

0.0 km   Zero trip meter at town centre, adjacent to post office. **TL.**
(1.0 km)

1.0 km   Intersection. **SO.**

> *Nanga Rd on right. Enter Lane-Poole Reserve.*

(14.9 km)

15.9 km   S'post: To Dwellingup via Murray River. **TR** onto gravel: Murray Rd.
(5.8 km)

21.7 km   S'post: Yarragil Formation. **TR.**
(7.1 km)

28.8 km   S'post: Yarragil Picnic and Camping Area. **SO** along River Rd.

> *Permit to camp obtainable on site. Picnic tables, barbecues, toilets. Fishing, swimming, canoeing. Track begins to follow Murray River.*

(3.0 km)

31.8 km   Tonys Bend Camping Area.

> *Permit to camp obtainable on site. Picnic tables, barbecues, toilets. Fishing, swimming.*

0.0 km   Zero trip meter at Tonys Bend Camping Area. **SO.**
(0.4 km)

0.4 km   Island Pool Picnic Area on left. **SO.**

> *Picnic tables, barbecues, toilets. Fishing, swimming, canoeing. Walking track*

(2.2 km)

2.6 km   Charlies Flat Camping and Picnic Area. **SO.**

> *Permit to camp obtainable on site. Picnic tables, barbecues, toilets. Canoeing, swimming.*

0.0 km   Zero trip meter at Charlies Flat Camping and Picnic Area. **SO.**
(1.7 km)

1.7 km   S'post: Bobs Crossing. **SO.**

> *Crossing available in summer only. Nanga Mill off to left.*

(1.1 km)

Fishing for trout on the Murray River

2.8 km   S'post: Baden Powell. **TL** onto Park Rd.

> *Dwellingup straight ahead.*

(0.1 km)

2.9 km   S'post: Baden Powell. **KL.**
(1.9 km)

4.8 km   S'post: Baden Powell Camping and Picnic Area.

> *Permit to camp obtainable on site. Picnic tables, barbecues, toilets. Camera. Fishing, swimming, canoeing.*

0.0 km   Zero trip meter at s'post: Baden Powell Camping and Picnic Area. **SO.**
(0.7 km)

0.7 km   Intersection. **TL** onto Nanga Rd.
(0.2 km)

0.9 km   Intersection. **SO.**

> *Track on left leads to river.*

(1.3 km)

2.2 km   S'post: Nanga Mill. **TL** at T intersection and immediately cross bridge over Murray River.
(0.3 km)

2.5 km   Intersection. **SO.**

> *Nanga Bush Camp on left, private facility.*

(0.7 km)

3.2 km   S'post: Murray Valley Rd. **TL.**
(3.6 km)

6.8 km   S'post: Nanga Mill. **SO.**

> *Track on left leads to Bobs Crossing.*

(5.6 km)

12.4 km   Intersection. **SO.**
(0.1 km)

12.5 km   Nanga Brook. Cross bridge.

> *Trout Ladder on left.*

(0.1 km)

12.6 km   Intersection.

0.0 km   Zero trip meter at above intersection. **TR.**

THE JARRAH FOREST

> *Nanga Mill Camping and Picnic Area on right. Permit to camp obtainable on site. Picnic tables, barbecues, toilets, drinking water. Information. Swimming, canoeing. From Nanga Mill the King Jarrah Track begins, an 18-km walk through the reserve; an ancient majestic 'king' jarrah tree is a highlight. The Stringers Camping and Picnic Area off to left. Permit to camp obtainable on site. Picnic tables, barbecues, toilets. Fishing, swimming, canoeing.*

(1.1 km)

1.1 km   T intersection. S'post: Waroona. **TL** onto Nanga Rd.

> *Dwellingup off to right.*

(0.3 km)

1.4 km   S'post: Nanga Mill Old Townsite. **SO.**

> *Camping area on right. Group camping. Permit to camp obtainable on site. Picnic tables, barbecues, toilets. Walking track.*

(1.2 km)

2.6 km   Intersection. **SO.**

> *Nanga Dell Farm 5 km off to right along Waroona–Nanga Brook Rd.*

(3.6 km)

6.2 km   Intersection. **SO.**

> *Dawn Creek Rd on left.*

(23.2 km)

29.4 km   Crossroads. S'post: Tallanalla Rd.

> *Hoffmans Mill Picnic and Camping Area off to right along Clarke Rd. Permit to camp obtainable on site. Picnic tables, barbecues, toilets. Fishing. Walking track.*

0.0 km   Zero trip meter at s'post: Tallanalla Rd. **SO.**
(12.3 km)

12.3 km   S'post: Quindanning Rd. **KR.**
(0.7 km)

13.0 km   Intersection. **SO.**
(7.6 km)

20.6 km   Intersection.

> *Rocky Crossing Picnic Area 3 km off to left. Picnic tables, barbecues, toilets.*

0.0 km   Zero trip meter at above intersection. **SO.**
(0.1 km)

Dwellingup Hotel

0.1 km   Cross bridge.
(2.5 km)

2.6 km   Crossroads. S'post: Harvey–Quindanning Rd. **SO.**
(3.9 km)

6.5 km   Intersection.

> *Stirling Dam Rd on left continues 4.2 km to Lancaster Rd T intersection. Turn right, 2.5 km to Stirling Dam Picnic Area. Turn left, 2.3 km to Harvey Falls and Trout Ladder.*

0.0 km   Zero trip meter at above intersection. **SO** onto bitumen.
(10.2 km)

10.2 km   S'post: Perth.

> *Harvey straight ahead.*

PD Zero trip meter.
END TOUR
TR to return to Perth approx. 140 km via South Western Hwy, Albany Hwy, the Causeway and Adelaide Terrace.

YANCHEP TO NEW NORCIA

START POINT Map page 30, D7

TOTAL KM 448. Does not include 24 km Perth to start point and 132 km end point to Perth. *See Route Directions.*
UNSEALED KM 129.
DEGREE OF DIFFICULTY Difficult.
DRIVING TIME 10 hours over a minimum of 3 days. Allow time to/from start/end points. *See Route Directions.*
LONGEST DISTANCE NO FUEL 76 km (Lancelin to Cervantes).
TOPOGRAPHIC MAPS Auslig 1:250 000 series: *Perth*; *Hill River*; *Moora*. See also 1:100 000 series.
LOCAL/SPECIALITY MAPS Western Australian Tourism Commission map and brochure: *Western Australia Traveller's Guide*; Department of Land Administration Perth *StreetSmart Touring Map* and brochure: *Batavia Coast*; *Robinsons Western Australia*; local regional maps.
OTHER USEFUL INFORMATION Western Australian Tourist Centre booklet: *Western Australia's Golden Heartlands*; Department of Land Administration Perth booklet: *Geraldton and the Central West Coast*; CALM booklets: *Perth Outdoors: Recreation and Conservation Spots in Perth and Environs* and *Wildflower Country*; CALM brochures: *Nambung National Park*, *Lesueur National Park (Eastern Portion) Self-guided Tour with Description of Stops* and *Badgingarra Nature Trail*; Victoria Plains Tourist Association brochure: *New Norcia, Victoria Plains, Western Australia*; local regional brochures.
BEST TIME OF YEAR TO TRAVEL September–November (spring) for the wildflowers, otherwise any time of year.

TOUR DESCRIPTION
If you are truly adventurous you will enjoy this tour, not so much because of the degree of difficulty but because it requires careful plotting and navigation. For the first half you follow coastal tracks north through three lovely fishing–holiday towns: Lancelin, Cervantes and Jurien; you also pass through Yanchep and Nambung national parks and Nilgen and Wanagarren nature reserves.

Lancelin is the state's windsurfing capital, ideal for all water sports and swimming. Cervantes is a smaller but thriving fishing–resort village, named after an American whaling ship that was wrecked off the nearby island (of the same name) in 1844. Jurien is a renowned rock-lobster fishing town. Located on a sheltered bay, its climate, beaches and fishing are all excellent.

In Yanchep National Park you can enjoy unchanged bushlands, forests of massive tuart trees, wildflower walks, underground limestone caves and the amusingly named Loch McNess. All the parks are for day use only – camping is prohibited. Caravan parks, however, are located at *Two Rocks*, *Ledge Point*, *Lancelin*, *Cervantes*, *Jurien*, *Waddi Farms* and *Moora*.

The defence-force range stretches between Nilgen and Wanagarren nature reserves. The ecosystem of these reserves is very fragile; proceed with care and caution. Vegetation is also undergoing regeneration in the wake of bushfire damage that occurred in April 1991. Animals abound, and though most are nocturnal, you may come across bobtail skinks, blue-tongued lizards, snakes, emus and kangaroos on the tracks during the daytime.

Nambung National Park's most popular attraction is the Pinnacles Desert: thousands of limestone pillars up to 4 metres tall rising out of shifting yellow sands.

Between Lancelin and Jurien you drive approximately 104 kilometres through sand-dune country on tracks of limestone and sand. Wind and water movement sometimes demand minor redirections but reduced tyre pressures are not necessary; check local information before embarking *(see Warnings)*. North of the Wedge Island fishing community you drive through a section of beach, but the sand is firm and negotiable on most tides. The Hill River crossing, north of Cervantes, is usually easy to negotiate but tricky to find.

The roads generally improve after Jurien for the second half of the tour. An exception is Sandy Cape Track and its branch track that leads to the rough limestone country of Drovers Cave National Park. All cave entrances are locked in order to maintain public safety and avoid vandalism. Internal roads and walking tracks are limited to fire breaks because understorey vegetation is generally very thick. There are no rangers in this park, and Sandy Cape Track is used most often by local people fishing for rock lobsters.

You then pass alongside Lesueur National Park which boasts a diversity of inland plants including kwongan, hakea, southern cross, staghorn bush and black kangaroo paw. Four-wheel drive access is provided only in

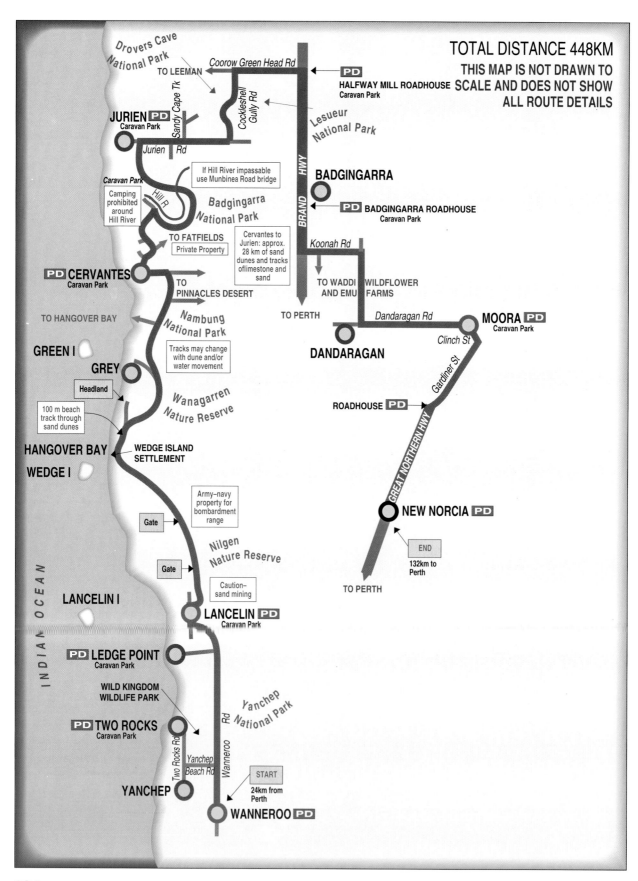

TOTAL DISTANCE 448KM

THIS MAP IS NOT DRAWN TO SCALE AND DOES NOT SHOW ALL ROUTE DETAILS

Drovers Cave National Park

TO LEEMAN

Coorow Green Head Rd

PD
HALFWAY MILL ROADHOUSE
Caravan Park

Sandy Cape Tk

Cockleshell Gully Rd

Lesueur National Park

JURIEN PD
Caravan Park

Jurien Rd

BRAND HWY

BADGINGARRA

Caravan Park

If Hill River impassable use Munbinea Road bridge

PD BADGINGARRA ROADHOUSE
Caravan Park

Camping prohibited around Hill River

Hill R

Badgingarra National Park

TO FATFIELDS
Private Property

Koonah Rd

Cervantes to Jurien: approx. 28 km of sand dunes and tracks of limestone and sand

PD CERVANTES
Caravan Park

TO PINNACLES DESERT

TO WADDI WILDFLOWER AND EMU FARMS

TO PERTH

TO HANGOVER BAY

Nambung National Park

Dandaragan Rd

MOORA PD
Caravan Park

Clinch St

GREEN I

Tracks may change with dune and/or water movement

DANDARAGAN

GREY

Headland

Wanagarren Nature Reserve

100 m beach track through sand dunes

ROADHOUSE **PD**

Gardiner St

GREAT NORTHERN HWY

HANGOVER BAY

WEDGE ISLAND SETTLEMENT

WEDGE I

Army–navy property for bombardment range

Gate

Nilgen Nature Reserve

NEW NORCIA PD

END
132km to Perth

Gate

Caution– sand mining

INDIAN OCEAN

LANCELIN I

LANCELIN PD
Caravan Park

TO PERTH

PD LEDGE POINT
Caravan Park

WILD KINGDOM WILDLIFE PARK

Yanchep National Park

Wanneroo Rd

Yanchep Rd

PD TWO ROCKS
Caravan Park

Two Rocks Rd

Yanchep Beach Rd

START
24km from Perth

YANCHEP

WANNEROO PD

Rowing on Loch McNess, Yanchep National Park

the eastern section. Bushwalkers and picnickers are welcome although there are no facilities. Heading south along the Brand Highway you then pass Badgingarra National Park. No four-wheel drive access is provided but walkers can undertake a nature trail beginning and ending at the Badgingarra Roadhouse.

The next township is Moora situated on the banks of the Moore River in an area that used to be virgin salmon-gum forest. Conclude the tour with a visit to New Norcia, a Benedictine monastic community established in 1846. This is a working community that still operates as a monastery and a boys' boarding school. Highlights are the Abbey Church and the museum and art gallery which house original paintings by Spanish and Italian masters as well as the state's best collection of modern Australian religious art.

WARNINGS ▶ Between Lancelin and Jurien stay on

designated tracks to avoid getting lost and spreading dieback. Sand dunes may change shape with wind and water movement but generally do not churn up. For information about dune movement, contact CALM Nambung National Park Ranger Headquarters, PO Box 62, Cervantes WA 6511; tel. (096) 52 7043, emergency tel. (096) 52 7320. ▶ North of Lancelin is defence-force range used as gunnery by army and for bombing by navy. Closed when in use, but sentries advise alternative route. Check ahead by phoning Lancelin police on (096) 55 1144. ▶ Total fire bans apply from 1 November to 14 February; ground fires always prohibited. Light fires only in barbecue areas provided and bring portable gas stove if possible. Obtain daily fire information for entire central west coastal zone, from Wanneroo to Geraldton, from ABC morning-radio broadcasts. ▶ For information on fire danger, ask at local service stations or contact CALM Perth District Office, 5 Dundebar Road, Wanneroo WA 6065; tel. (09)

405 1222 (for Yanchep National Park to Lancelin section of tour); CALM Moora District Office, Main Roads Department Building, Moora WA 6510; PO Box 328, Moora WA 6510; tel. (096) 51 1424 (for Lancelin to New Norcia section of tour), or CALM State Operations Headquarters in Perth. ▶ Don't travel after or during persistent heavy rain; from May to July, Hill River north of Cervantes may be too deep to cross. If crossing impassable, take alternative route via Munbinea Road. Camping also prohibited around Hill River – fishing and day use only. ▶ Beware of snakes in national parks and nature reserves, also kangaroo ticks occur in summer. Apply insect repellent liberally, but if you do get ticks, seek medical attention to have them removed.

BOOKINGS AND PERMITS ▶ No prior permits

required to traverse the national parks or reserves. Camping strictly prohibited. ▶ Stay in caravan parks in towns. For information about caravan parks, other accommodation, local conditions and activities, contact the Centre Store, Gin-Gin Road, Lancelin WA 6044; tel. (096) 55 1054; Shell Service Station, Cnr Aragon and Seville Streets, Cervantes WA 6511; tel. (096) 52 7041; Jurien Tourist Centre, BP Service Station, Jurien WA 6516; tel. (096) 52 1444; Moora Tourist Centre, 34 Padbury Street, Moora WA 6510; tel. (096) 51 1401; Victoria Plains Tourist Centre, Shell Roadhouse, Great Northern Highway, New Norcia WA 6509; tel. (096) 54 8020.

ROUTE DIRECTIONS

Depart Perth CBD north approx. 24 km via Mitchell Fwy, Charles St and Wanneroo Rd.
START TOUR

0.0 km   Zero trip meter at Wanneroo Rd and Hastings St intersection, adjacent to Wanneroo Shopping Centre. **SO** through Wanneroo along Wanneroo Rd. `PD` **(22.8 km)**

22.8 km   Sign: Yanchep National Park. **SO.** **(2.5 km)**

25.3 km   S'post: Yanchep National Park.

> *Yanchep and Two Rocks off to left: Yanchep Beach Rd continues 6.2 km to Two Rocks Rd T intersection. Turn left to Yanchep Lagoon. Turn right 3 km to Wild Kingdom Wildlife Park on right; Two Rocks and marina a further 3.6 km on left.* `PD` *Supplies, caravan park.*

Pinnacles desert, Nambung National Park

Cervantes coastal track

0.0 km Zero trip meter at s'post: Yanchep National Park. **SO.**
(0.1 km)

0.1 km S'post: Yanchep National Park.

> *Picnic tables, barbecues, septic toilets, running water. Walking tracks, cave tours, heritage trail, koala enclosure, horseriding, boat hire, underwater exploration.*

0.0 km Zero trip meter at s'post: Yanchep National Park. **SO.**
(63.6 km)

63.6 km S'post: Lancelin. **SO.**

> *Ledge Point 5 km off to left.* **PD** *Supplies, caravan park. Beach access.*

(12.3 km)
75.9 km T intersection. **TR** onto Gin-Gin Rd in Lancelin.

> **PD** *Supplies, caravan park.*

(1.1 km)
77.0 km **SO** through Lancelin.

> *Post office and tavern on left. Information at the Centre Store on right. Fishing, swimming, boating, windsurfing, surfskiing, beach buggies.*

(0.8 km)
77.8 km S'post: North St. **TR.**
(0.1 km)
77.9 km S'post: Bootoo St. **TL.**
(0.3 km)
78.2 km **TR** onto gravel through fence line. **KL** and follow low dune scrub.

> *Sign: Caution – sand mining 700 m north-east. Track on right leads to sand-mine site.*

(2.5 km)
80.7 km Intersection. **SO.**

> *Beach access on left. Enter Nilgen Nature Reserve.*

(1.4 km)
82.1 km Intersection. **KL.**

> *Tracks on right.*

(4.0 km)
86.1 km Intersection. **SO.**

Beach access on left.

(1.5 km)
87.6 km **SO** through gate.

Exit Nilgen Nature Reserve. Sentry box for defence-force range. Sign: Navy property for bombardment range. Parallel tracks for approx. 10 km: use track on left.

(1.2 km)
88.8 km Intersection. **SO.**
(10.5 km)
99.3 km Handmade s'post: Wedge – next left/Lancelin. **SO.**

Track on left.

(1.6 km)
100.9 km Y intersection. **KL.**
(1.5 km)
102.4 km **SO** through gate.

Sentry box. Exit defence-force range. Enter Wanagarren Nature Reserve.

(0.8 km)
103.2 km Handmade s'post: Wedge Is. **TL.**
(7.1 km)
110.3 km
T intersection. **TR** around dune.
(1.3 km)
111.6 km Y intersection. **KL** over dune.
(1.3 km)
112.9 km T intersection. **TR.**
(1.2 km)
114.1 km Y intersection. **KL** into and through Wedge Island settlement.
(0.5 km)
114.6 km Sign: Welcome to Wedge Island. **SO.**

Fishing, lobster fishing, swimming, windsurfing. Information board.

(0.4 km)
115.0 km Exit settlement onto beach. Take 100 m track through dunes and **TR** onto beach.
(7.8 km)
122.8 km **TR** off beach at headland opposite Flat Rock.
(3.2 km)
126.0 km Y intersection. **KL** between dunes, 100 m, then **KR.**
(1.6 km)
127.6 km Handmade s'post: Grey/Cervantes. **SO.**
(4.3 km)

131.9 km Sign: Nambung National Park. **SO.**

Picnic tables, barbecues, pit toilets. Exit Wanagarren Nature Reserve.

(1.8 km)
133.7 km Y intersection. **KR.**

Grey off to left.

(1.5 km)
135.2 km T intersection. **TR.**
(0.9 km)
136.1 km Sign: Pinnacles Desert 14/Cervantes 19. **SO.**
(7.5 km)
143.6 km S'post: Cervantes. **TR.**

Hangover Bay 1 km off to left. Picnic tables, barbecues, toilets. Fishing, swimming. Camping prohibited.

(0.1 km)
143.7 km S'post: Cervantes.

Pinnacles Desert 6 km off to right. Pay entrance fee to ranger on site. Information, toilets, carpark. Walking track, one-way loop driving track. Camping prohibited.

0.0 km Zero trip meter at s'post: Cervantes. **TL** onto gravel then bitumen: Grey Rd.
(11.9 km)
11.9 km T intersection. **TL** onto bitumen: Cervantes Rd.
(0.2 km)
12.1 km S'post: Aragon St. **TR** into Cervantes.

PD Caravan park. Diving, fishing, water sports. Many wildflowers on surrounding coastal plains.

(0.8 km)
12.9 km S'post: Catalonia St.

Caravan park on left.

0.0 km Zero trip meter at s'post: Catalonia St. **TR.**
(0.8 km)
0.8 km **SO** along gravel for 50 m then **TR.**
(2.5 km)
3.3 km Y intersection. **KL.**

Sign on right: Fatfields south boundary – no through road. Private property.

(0.6 km)
3.9 km Y intersection. **KR.**
(1.3 km)
5.2 km Intersection. **KR.**

YANCHEP TO NEW NORCIA

Western Australian wildflowers

Track straight ahead crosses sand dune.

(1.4 km)
6.6 km Intersection. **SO.**

Two high-hill tracks on left.

(0.1 km)
6.7 km Intersection. **KR.**

Salt lagoon on right.

(0.6 km)
7.3 km Intersection. **KR.**

Loop track on left rejoins after 100 m.

(0.4 km)
7.7 km

Three-way intersection. **KR.**

Two tracks on left cross sand dune.

(1.2 km)
8.9 km Intersection. **KR.**

Track on left crosses sand dune.

(1.1 km)
10.0 km Intersection. **SO.**
(2.6 km)
12.6 km Intersection. **SO.**

Beach access on left.

(0.9 km)
13.5 km Intersection. **SO.**
(0.6 km)
14.1 km Intersection. **SO.**
(0.2 km)
14.3 km Intersection. **TL.**
(0.2 km)
14.5 km Intersection. **KR.**
(0.2 km)
14.7 km Intersection. **TR.**
(1.4 km)
16.1 km T intersection. **TL.**
(1.3 km)
17.4 km Intersection. **TR.**
(0.4 km)

17.8 km Cross Hill River and immediately **TL**.

> *If river crossing impassable after heavy rains, use Munbinea Rd bridge instead.*

(0.4 km)

18.2 km Y intersection. **KR**.

(0.2 km)

18.4 km Intersection. **SO**.

> *Track joins route on left.*

(5.4 km)

23.8 km Y intersection. **KR**.

(1.0 km)

24.8 km T intersection. **TL**.

(3.6 km)

28.4 km T intersection.

> *Jurien 2 km off to left.* **PD** *Caravan park. Fishing, lobster fishing, swimming, boating, diving, windsurfing.*

0.0 km Zero trip meter at above T intersection. **TR** onto bitumen: Jurien Rd.

(2.6 km)

2.6 km Intersection. **SO**.

> *Canover Rd on right.*

(0.1 km)

2.7 km Intersection.

> *Sandy Cape Track on left continues for 5.1 km, then track on right leads to Drovers Cave National Park. Sign obscured. Access via soft sandy tracks. Day use only, picnicking unsuitable, camping prohibited. Walking restricted to fire breaks. No rangers present. Entrances to all caves locked.*

0.0 km Zero trip meter at above intersection. **SO**.

(10.5 km)

10.5 km S'post: Cockleshell Gully Rd. **TL** onto gravel.

> *Road passes through Lesueur National Park, a spectacular wildflower reserve. Some 4WD access provided in eastern section. Bushwalking and picnicking welcome. No facilities. Camping prohibited.*

(23.7 km)

34.2 km S'post: Brand Hwy. **TR** onto bitumen: Coorow–Green Head Rd.

(21.9 km)

56.1 km S'post: Perth. **TR** onto Brand Hwy.

> *Roadhouse on left.* **PD** *Caravan park.*

(41.7 km)

97.8 km Roadhouse on left. **SO**.

> **PD** *Caravan park. Sign on right: Badgingarra National Park. A wildflower haven. No 4WD access.*

(15.3 km)

113.1 km S'post: Waddi Farms. **TL** onto Koonah Rd.

(2.1 km)

115.2 km Intersection.

> *Waddi Wildflower and Emu Farms – private development – 5 km off to right. Caravan park. Wildflower cultivation, flowers for sale, emu farming, farm products for sale. Tearooms, restaurant.*

0.0 km Zero trip meter at above intersection. **SO**.

(12.5 km)

12.5 km S'post: Dandaragan. **TR** onto Badgingarra Rd.

(18.6 km)

31.1 km S'post: Moora. **TL** onto Dandaragan Rd.

> *Dandaragan off to right.*

(31.6 km)

62.7 km S'post: New Norcia. **TR** onto Roberts St in Moora. **PD**

> *Caravan park.*

(0.2 km)

62.9 km S'post: New Norcia. **TL** onto Clinch St.

(0.3 km)

63.2 km S'post: New Norcia. **TR** onto Gardiner St.

(22.0 km)

85.2 km S'post: New Norcia. **TR** onto Great Northern Hwy.

(0.3 km)

85.5 km Roadhouse on right. **SO**. **PD**

(34.6 km)

120.1 km New Norcia private town, adjacent to museum, art gallery and shop on right. Zero trip meter.

> *Australia's only monastic town, founded in 1846 by Spanish Benedictine monks. Heritage trail, tours, accomm.* **PD**

END TOUR

SO to return to Perth 132 km via Great Northern Hwy, Great Eastern Hwy, James St, Guildford Rd and Lord St.

NORSEMAN AND THE SOUTH WEST

START POINT Map page 30, E8.

TOTAL KM 1163. Does not include 22 km Perth to start point and 200 km end point to Perth. **See Route Directions.**

UNSEALED KM 468.

DEGREE OF DIFFICULTY Moderate.

DRIVING TIME Tour over 4 or 5 days. Allow time to/from start/end points. **See Route Directions.**

LONGEST DISTANCE NO FUEL 261 km (Norseman to Lake King: petrol only); 377 km (Norseman to Lake Grace: petrol and diesel).

TOPOGRAPHIC MAPS Auslig 1:250 000 series: *Perth*; *Corrigin*; *Hyden*; *Lake Johnston*; *Norseman*; *Newdegate*; *Dumbleyung*. See also 1:100 000 series.

LOCAL/SPECIALITY MAPS Department of Land Administration Perth *StreetSmart Touring Maps* and brochures: *Goldfields* and *The Greater South West*; Western Australian Tourism Commission map and brochure: *Western Australia Travellers Guide*; *Robinsons Western Australia*; local regional maps.

OTHER USEFUL INFORMATION Western Australian Tourist Centre booklet: *Western Australia's Golden Heartlands*; CALM brochures: *Esperance National Parks: Peak Charles, Cape Le Grand, Stokes* and *Fitzgerald River and Frank Hann National Parks*; CALM booklet: *Wildflower Country*; local regional brochures.

BEST TIME OF YEAR TO TRAVEL September–December (spring–early summer) for the wildflowers. **See Warnings.**

TOUR DESCRIPTION Visual interest is maintained on this long tour as you pass through a variety of landscapes covered by the wheatbelt, goldfields and south-coast regions. The countryside regularly varies between pasturelands, woodlands, salt-lake systems and arid scrub that changes to spectacular fields of wildflowers in spring. You also visit some of the region's most famous landmarks, the many ancient granite formations such as Boyagin Rock, Wave Rock, the Breakaway, Peak Eleanora and Peak Charles.

Only two suitable and permissible camping areas are included, at *Peak Charles* and *Frank Hann* national parks, where total self-sufficiency is required. There is plenty of alternative accommodation, though, at the caravan parks in the towns: *Brookton*, *Pingelly*, *Kondinin*, *Wave Rock*, *Norseman*, *Lake King*, *Newdegate*, *Lake Grace*, *Dumbleyung* and *Wagin*.

Brookton is the centre of a rich mixed-farming district; attractions include the Old Railway Station, Old Police Station Museum, two heritage trails, and colourful displays of native flora. A few kilometres away is Boyagin Rock Picnic Ground and reserve, an important remnant of natural bushland on the western edge of the central wheatbelt.

Sandalwood forests were once the focus of local industry at Pingelly, but their place has been taken by sheep and wheat farms; see the shearers in action at local farms. Bullaring is the next optional stopping place for fuel or supplies.

Gorge Rock offers excellent views of the surrounding wheatlands, then you pass through the small settlement of Kondinin. Further on, Hyden is the centre of the rich fertile land that has produced wheat since 1927. Just past Hyden is Wave Rock, the most famous rock formation in this semi-arid land. Sculpted and coloured by chemicals over 2700 million years, its beautiful bands of colour range from rusty reds to ochres to greys. Wave Rock also has a picnic area, wildlife park and the Wildflower Shop, incorporating the Lace Place – the largest collection of lace in the Southern Hemisphere.

At the rabbit-proof fence – a grid rather than a fence – the tour temporarily diverges from wheat to salt-lake country, and the next major rock formation is the Breakaway, a shallow sunken valley with a colourful rock-face cliff edge. Further on again is McDermid Rock, lower in height than Wave Rock but longer. The clay track then leads onto Coolgardie–Esperance Highway, which takes you to Norseman, the first major town at the end of the Nullarbor Plain route from the eastern states. A century of goldmining has given the town its most striking feature: a 40 metre-tall 'mesa' made up of some $50 million worth of mine tailings. Norseman remains Australia's richest quartz reef, second only to Kalgoorlie's Golden Mile in the volume of gold produced. Take time to tour the spectacular open-cut and underground mine. You can also fossick for gemstones amid rich mineral deposits.

Along the highway, you turn right onto Lake King–Norseman Road, and off to the left is Peak Charles National Park. Peak Charles and Peak Eleanora are highly weathered granite mountains that were islands some 40 million years ago. You will see wave-cut platforms on their upper slopes which offer panoramic views of the dry woodlands, sandplain heaths and

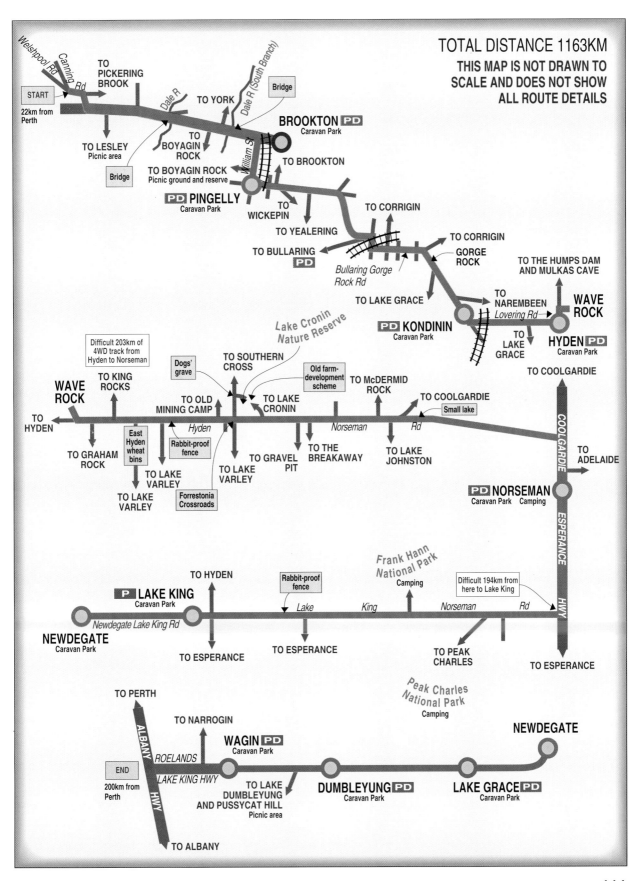

TOTAL DISTANCE 1163KM

THIS MAP IS NOT DRAWN TO
SCALE AND DOES NOT SHOW
ALL ROUTE DETAILS

Welshpool Rd

Canning Rd

TO PICKERING
BROOK

START
22km from
Perth

TO YORK

Dale R

Dale R (South Branch)

Bridge

BROOKTON **PD**
Caravan Park

TO LESLEY
Picnic area

TO BOYAGIN
ROCK

TO BROOKTON

Bridge

TO BOYAGIN ROCK
Picnic ground and reserve

William St

PD PINGELLY
Caravan Park

TO
WICKEPIN

TO CORRIGIN

TO YEALERING

TO CORRIGIN

GORGE
ROCK

TO THE HUMPS DAM
AND MULKAS CAVE

TO BULLARING
PD

Bullaring Gorge
Rock Rd

TO LAKE GRACE

TO NAREMBEEN

Lovering Rd

WAVE
ROCK

PD KONDININ
Caravan Park

TO
LAKE
GRACE

HYDEN **PD**
Caravan Park

Lake Cronin
Nature Reserve

TO COOLGARDIE

Difficult 203km of
4WD track from
Hyden to Norseman

Dogs'
grave

TO SOUTHERN
CROSS

Old farm-
development
scheme

TO McDERMID
ROCK

WAVE
ROCK

TO KING
ROCKS

TO OLD
MINING CAMP

TO LAKE
CRONIN

TO COOLGARDIE

Small lake

COOLGARDIE

TO
HYDEN

Hyden

Norseman   Rd

TO
ADELAIDE

East
Hyden
wheat
bins

Rabbit-proof
fence

TO GRAVEL
PIT

TO THE
BREAKAWAY

TO LAKE
JOHNSTON

TO GRAHAM
ROCK

TO LAKE
VARLEY

TO LAKE
VARLEY

PD NORSEMAN
Caravan Park   Camping

TO LAKE
VARLEY

Forrestonia
Crossroads

ESPERANCE

Frank Hann
National Park

Camping

Difficult 194km from
here to Lake King

TO HYDEN

Rabbit-proof
fence

P LAKE KING
Caravan Park

Lake   King   Norseman   Rd

HWY

NEWDEGATE
Caravan Park

Newgate Lake King Rd

TO ESPERANCE

TO ESPERANCE

TO PEAK
CHARLES

TO ESPERANCE

Peak Charles
National Park

Camping

TO PERTH

ALBANY

TO NARROGIN

WAGIN **PD**
Caravan Park

NEWDEGATE

ROELANDS

END
200km from
Perth

LAKE KING HWY

TO LAKE
DUMBLEYUNG
AND PUSSYCAT HILL
Picnic area

DUMBLEYUNG **PD**
Caravan Park

LAKE GRACE **PD**
Caravan Park

HWY

TO ALBANY

NORSEMAN AND THE SOUTH WEST

salt-lake vegetation. The national park has a bushwalking track from the carpark to a point on the south-east ridge that allows extensive views of Peak Eleanora. Further along the route is Frank Hann National Park. In December 1990–January 1991, bushfires badly damaged both these national parks. Regeneration is progressing well and they have an abundance of spring wildflowers.

At the second section of rabbit-proof fence you re-enter wheat country. Lake King is a crossroads centre that has a tavern, general store, and petrol but not diesel. In the early 1960s it was a control point for the first London–Sydney car rally.

You then pass through Newdegate and on to Lake Grace. Have a look at Hollands Track, cut from Broomehill to Coolgardie by John Holland and four mates, enabling them to reach the goldfields in record time. The wagon-wheel marks subsequently made by prospectors can still be seen on the road.

Lake Dumbleyung appears as a beautiful splash of blue amid the semi-arid landscape. One of the state's largest inland lakes, it owes its fame to (Sir) Donald Campbell, who broke the world water-speed record on it in *Bluebird* in 1964.

Wagin is an important railway junction for the grain and merino-stud industry. Every March is 'Woolorama', the state's biggest rural show attended by sheep farmers from all over Australia and over 25 000 people.

WARNINGS ▶ Do not attempt this tour during wet winters or hot summers: it includes two long sections of gravel and clay track that may be impassable after heavy rain. Most rain falls April– October, but severe thunderstorms occur May–August. The first difficult section is 55 kilometres of gravel between East Hyden Wheat Bins and Forrestonia Crossroads, followed by 203 kilometres of clay track leading to Coolgardie–Esperance Highway – surface quality varies from good to moderately difficult. Rain can make surfaces very slippery; heavy rain creates difficult bog patches. Clay track is particularly deceptive and conceals ruts, dips and washaways. Contact Norseman Police Station on (090) 39 1000 for road surface information. Second difficult section is 194 kilometres of gravel between intersection of Coolgardie–Esperance Highway and Lake King–Norseman Road – road leading to Lake King. For information contact Lake Grace Police Station on (098) 65 1007. For road conditions and other useful information, contact CALM Esperance District Office, 92 Dempster Street, Esperance WA 6450; PO Box 234, Esperance WA 6450; tel. (090) 71 3733; CALM South Coast Regional and District Office, 44 Serpentine Road, Albany WA 6330; tel.

(098) 41 7133, or CALM State Operations Headquarters in Perth. ▶ Fuel and/or supplies are scarce along these two sections: no fuel stops or supplies for 317 kilometres between Hyden and Norseman; no petrol for 261 kilometres between Norseman and Lake King; no petrol or diesel for 377 kilometres between Norseman and Lake Grace. ▶ In Peak Charles and Frank Hann national parks do not light fires; use portable gas stove. ▶ Neither park has barbecues, drinking water or any other facilities, although Peak Charles has pit toilets.

BOOKINGS AND PERMITS ▶ No prior permits required to enter or traverse Peak Charles and Frank Hann national parks. Camping allowed only in designated areas. ▶ For all information about Peak Charles National Park, contact CALM District Office. For Frank Hann National Park, contact CALM South Coast Regional and District Office. For both parks, contact CALM State Operations Headquarters in Perth. ▶ To stay in caravan parks in towns, book ahead for peak seasons of Christmas and Easter. Contact following places for information about caravan parks: Brookton Information Centre, Old Railway Station, Robinson Road, Brookton WA 6306; tel. (096) 42 1316; Pingelly Information Centre, Community Craft Centre, 22 Parade Street, Pingelly WA 6308; tel. (098) 87 1351; Kondinin Shire Offices, Gordon Street, Kondinin WA 6367; PO Box 7, Kondinin WA 6367; tel. (098) 89 1006; Hyden Tourist Information Centre, Wave Rock Wildflower Shop, Wave Rock, Hyden WA 6359; tel. (098) 80 5182; Norseman Tourist Bureau, 76 Roberts Street, Norseman WA 6443; tel. (090) 39 1071; Lake Grace Information Centre, Lake Grace Newsagency, Lake Grace WA 6353; tel. (098) 65 1029; Dumbleyung Tourist Information Centre, Shire Office, Harvey Street, Dumbleyung WA 6350; tel. (098) 63 4012; Wagin Tourist Information Centre, Wagin Historical Village, Ballagin Street, Wagin WA 6315; tel. (098) 61 1177.

▼▼▼▼▼▼▼▼
TAKE CARE

● In a bushfire, drive to an open area away from trees, stay in the vehicle, cover all bare skin with non-flammable clothing, preferably wool, or a woollen blanket, and keep low.

ROUTE DIRECTIONS

Depart Perth CBD south-east approx. 22 km via Adelaide Terrace, the Causeway, Albany Hwy and Welshpool Rd.

START TOUR

0.0 km Zero trip meter at Welshpool Rd and Canning Rd intersection. **TR** onto Canning Rd.

(4.0 km)

4.0 km S'post: to Brookton Hwy. **TR**.

> *Pickering Brook straight ahead.*

(8.1 km)

12.1 km T intersection. S'post: Brookton Hwy. **TL**.

(9.4 km)

21.5 km Intersection. **SO**.

> *Lesley Picnic Area on right. Picnic tables, barbecues, toilets. Walking tracks.*

(26.4 km)

47.9 km Intersection. **SO**.

> *Yarra Rd on left.*

(19.7 km)

67.6 km S'post: Brookton. **KR**.

> *Dale Mawson Rd on left continues 40 km to Avondale Research Station and Agricultural Museum.*

(2.2 km)

69.8 km Dale River. Cross bridge.

(24.4 km)

94.2 km Intersection. **SO**.

> *Boyagin Rock 17 km off to right.*

(0.4 km)

94.6 km S'post: Brookton. **SO**.

> *York off to left.*

(0.8 km)

95.4 km Dale River south branch. Cross bridge.

(17.8 km)

113.2 km S'post: Pingelly.

> *Brookton town centre straight ahead across railway line.* **PD** *Caravan park.*

0.0 km Zero trip meter at s'post: Pingelly. **TR** into William St.

(11.5 km)

11.5 km Intersection. **SO**.

> *Boyagin Rock Picnic Ground and reserve 10 km off to right. Picnic tables, barbecues, pit toilets.*

(9.2 km)

20.7 km S'post: Wickepin.

0.0 km Zero trip meter at s'post: Wickepin. **TL** in Pingelly, adjacent to post office.

> **PD** *Caravan park.*

(0.1 km)

0.1 km Cross railway line.

(0.6 km)

0.7 km Crossroads. S'post: Yealering. **SO**.

(7.4 km)

8.1 km S'post: Yealering. **SO**.

> *Brookton off to left.*

(1.2 km)

9.3 km S'post: Yealering. **KL**.

> *Wickepin straight ahead.*

(25.2 km)

34.5 km Intersection. **SO**.

> *Yealering off to right.*

(5.8 km)

40.3 km

S'post: Bullaring 34. **KR**.

(27.6 km)

67.9 km Crossroads. **TR** and immediately cross railway line.

> *Bullaring off to right.* **PD** *Supplies.*

(0.1 km)

68.0 km S'post: Hyden/Wave Rock. **TL** onto Bullaring–Gorge Rock Rd.

(8.6 km)

76.6 km Crossroads. S'post: Kondinin 45. **SO**.

> *Corrigin off to left.*

(4.9 km)

81.5 km Crossroads. **SO** onto gravel.

(11.3 km)

92.8 km Crossroads. **SO**.

(0.3 km)

93.1 km S'post: Kondinin. **TR** onto bitumen.

> *Corrigin off to left.*

(0.2 km)

NORSEMAN AND THE SOUTH WEST

A flock of galahs, a common sight

93.3 km Intersection.

> *Gorge Rock 500 m off to left.*

0.0 km Zero trip meter at above intersection. **SO.**
(4.6 km)
4.6 km S'post: Kondinin. **SO.**

> *Lake Grace off to right.*

(21.1 km)
25.7 km S'post: Kondinin. **KR.**

> *Narembeen off to left.*

(4.3 km)
30.0 km S'post: Hyden.
0.0 km Zero trip meter at s'post: Hyden. **SO**
through Kondinin.

> **PD** *Supplies, caravan park.*

(0.4 km)
0.4 km S'post: Hyden/Wave Rock. **TL.**
(0.4 km)
0.8 km Cross railway line.
(42.7 km)

43.5 km S'post: Hyden. **KL.**

> *Lake Grace off to right.*

(17.9 km)
61.4 km Hyden town centre, adjacent to Hyden
Trading Co., a post office–general store. **SO.**

> **PD** *Supplies. Next fuel Norseman 317 km.*

(2.1 km)
63.5 km S'post: Wave Rock. **TL** onto Lovering Rd.
(1.0 km)
64.5 km S'post: Wave Rock. **TR** onto Wave Rock Rd.

> *The Humps and Mulkas Cave 18 km
> straight ahead.*

(0.8 km)
65.3 km Intersection. **SO.**

> *Picnic ground on right. Picnic tables,
> barbecues, toilets.*

(0.2 km)
65.5 km S'post: Wave Rock 100 m.

> *Straight ahead 100 m to Wave Rock, the Breakers and Hippos Yawn on right. Caravan park. Picnic tables, barbecues, toilets. Information centre with Wildflower Shop, wildlife park and the Lace Place on left. Signposted round tour of region.*

0.0 km   Zero trip meter at s'post: Wave Rock 100 m. **SO.**
(1.2 km)

1.2 km   S'post: Lake King. **TL** onto Hyden–Norseman Rd.

> *Hyden off to right.*

(9.0 km)

10.2 km   S'post: King Rocks. **SO.**

> *Graham Rock 14 km off to right.*

(8.8 km)

19.0 km   S'post: Lake Varley. **SO.**

> *King Rocks 14 km off to left.*

(9.2 km)

28.2 km   Intersection. **SO** onto gravel.

> *East Hyden Wheat Bins on right. Lake Varley off to right.*

(15.5 km)

43.7 km   Intersection. **SO.**

> *Lake Varley 33 km off to right.*

(5.9 km)

49.6 km   **SO** over rabbit-proof fence.

> *End of wheat country.*

(27.1 km)

76.7 km

Intersection. **SO.**

> *Track on left leads to old mining camp.*

(6.3 km)

83.0 km   Forrestonia Crossroads. S'post: Norseman.

> *Lake Varley off to right. Track on left leads to Southern Cross: 3.7 km to crest of hill; turn right at track 1.2 km to Lake Cronin and nature reserve. Includes a rock-faced dam, relic of a 1930s farm scheme. On left is a small grave, tribute to a bush dweller's dogs.*

0.0 km   Zero trip meter at s'post: Norseman. **SO** onto clay track.

> *Track continues 203.3 km to Coolgardie–Esperance Hwy T intersection.*

(2.9 km)

2.9 km   Intersection. **SO.**

> *Track on left leads to Lake Cronin.*

(48.0 km)

50.9 km   Intersection. **SO.**

> *Track and gravel pit on right.*

(0.2 km)

51.1 km   Intersection. **SO.**

> *Track on right continues to the Breakaway.*

(19.9 km)

71.0 km   Intersection. **SO.**

> *Track on left.*

(36.6 km)

107.6 km   Intersection.

> *Track on left continues 1.5 km to McDermid Rock.*

0.0 km   Zero trip meter at above intersection. **SO.**
(5.9 km)

5.9 km   Intersection.

> *Track on right continues 1 km to Lake Johnston.*

0.0 km   Zero trip meter at above intersection. **SO.**
(2.4 km)

2.4 km   Intersection. **SO.**

> *Track on left leads to Coolgardie.*

(3.1 km)

5.5 km   Small lake on left. **SO.**
(84.3 km)

89.8 km   T intersection. **TR** onto Coolgardie–Esperance Hwy.
(25.3 km)

115.1 km   S'post: Esperance. **SO.**

> *Eyre Hwy on left continues to Adelaide.*

(1.5 km)

116.6 km   Norseman town centre, adjacent to post office.

> **PD** *Supplies, caravan park. Picnic tables, barbecues, toilets. Tourist bureau has barbecue facilities, hot showers and caravan parking spaces. Next petrol Lake King 261 km. Next diesel Lake Grace 377 km.*

Wave Rock

Breakaway on Hyden–Norseman Road

0.0 km Zero trip meter at post office. **SO.**
(56.0 km)

56.0 km S'post: Peak Charles. **TR** onto gravel: Lake King–Norseman Rd.
(25.8 km)

81.8 km Intersection. **SO.**

> *Kumarl Rd on left.*

(4.2 km)

86.0 km S'post: Lake King.

> *Road on left continues 20 km to Peak Charles. Sign at 15.1 km: Peak Charles National Park. Y intersection at 19.8 km. Turn right 300 m to carpark and camping area. No facilities, no water. Pit toilets. Bushwalking track begins, a 3-hr return trip. Turn left to 4WD track that skirts part of Peak Charles; impassable in wet.*

0.0 km Zero trip meter at s'post: Lake King. **SO.**
(59.3 km)

59.3 km Sign: Frank Hann National Park. **SO.**

> *No facilities, no water. Lake King–Norseman Rd traverses park; impassable in wet. Bushwalking.*

(80.4 km)

139.7 km Intersection. **SO.**

> *Track on left leads to Esperance.*

(1.9 km)

141.6 km **SO** over rabbit-proof fence.
(26.1 km)

167.7 km End of gravel. **SO** onto bitumen.
(6.2 km)

173.9 km Crossroads. S'post: Newdegate. **SO.**

> *Hyden off to right. Esperance off to left. Re-enter wheat country.*

(1.2 km)

175.1 km Lake King town centre, adjacent to general store. **SO** onto Newdegate–Lake King Rd.

> **P** *Caravan park. Heritage trail takes in historic sites, panoramic views.*

(63.0 km)

238.1 km S'post: Lake Grace. **TL** in Newdegate onto Lake Grace– Newdegate Rd.

> **P** *Caravan park.*

(53.8 km)

291.9 km Lake Grace town centre, adjacent to post office.

'Mesa' of mine tailings, Norseman

PD Supplies, caravan park. Service facilities. Hollands Track.

0.0 km Zero trip meter at post office. **SO.**
(80.2 km)

80.2 km Dumbleyung town centre, adjacent to Westpac Bank.

PD Supplies, caravan park.

0.0 km Zero trip meter at Westpac Bank. **SO.**
(8.9 km)

8.9 km Intersection.

Dumbleyung Lake Scenic Drive, around part of lake, continues 4.0 km to yacht club. Barbecues, pit toilets. Swimming, boating. Picnic tables, barbecues also at Bairstow Drive. Camping prohibited. Scenic drive also includes a 1-km detour to Pussycat Hill Lookout.

0.0 km Zero trip meter at above intersection. **SO.**
(31.0 km)

31.0 km Wagin town centre, adjacent to post office.

PD Supplies, caravan park.

0.0 km Zero trip meter at post office. **SO** onto Roelands–Lake King Hwy.
(1.4 km)

1.4 km S'post: Perth. **SO.**

Narrogin off to right.

(28.2 km)

29.6 km S'post: Perth. Zero trip meter.
END TOUR
TR to return to Perth via Albany Hwy, the Causeway and Adelaide Terrace, approx. 200 km.

TOURS OUT OF ADELAIDE

South Australia is a state of extreme contrasts ranging from mild and temperate gulf lands to the stern and challenging north, and we have planned tours of varying difficulty to encompass them all: pastoral land, mountain ranges and the semi-arid regions on the northern desert fringes. There are unique opportunities to combine four-wheel driving with visits to historic towns, to time a tour to coincide with one of the many events that take place in the Festival State or – with the mighty Murray as central feature – to participate in all kinds of water sports.

THE MT LOFTY RANGES AND THE BAROSSA VALLEY

(a day tour: 257 kilometres). This is an alternative and unique way to visit the Barossa. You will travel the well-known Adelaide Hills and the historic winelands, but return via a circuitous route through a less frequented and contrasting landscape.

THE RIVERLAND AND MURRAY RIVER VALLEY

(tour over 3 days: 749 kilometres). A tour centred on the Murray River must be an absorbing one: paddlesteamers still ply the river, and of particular interest are the wetlands and the irrigation system that has transformed semi-desert country into the nation's major citrus-growing region.

THE FLINDERS AND GAMMON RANGES **(tour over 3 or 4 days: 746 kilometres)**. This tour takes in the central and northern sections of the ranges and is a challenge for the experienced driver; the outstanding feature is the rugged, often isolated but beautiful and ancient terrain. Because much of the land outside the national parks is privately owned, particular care must be taken when off the plotted route.

BEFORE YOU SET OUT ▶ Read the tour description carefully. ▶ Check that you have obtained any necessary permits. ▶ Check weather conditions with local authorities or Bureau of Meteorology. ▶ Make sure you have the appropriate maps and information for the tour. ▶ Check that your vehicle is in good order for the conditions ahead. Have you the necessary spare parts? ▶ If you are camping, have you the right equipment?

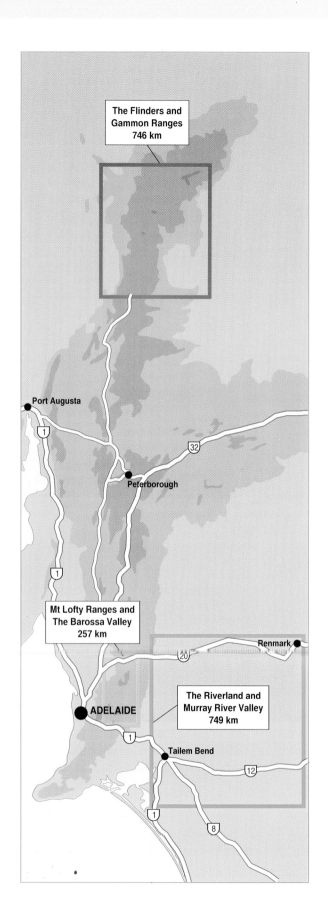

The Flinders and Gammon Ranges
746 km

Port Augusta

Peterborough

Mt Lofty Ranges and The Barossa Valley
257 km

Renmark

The Riverland and Murray River Valley
749 km

ADELAIDE

Tailem Bend

USEFUL INFORMATION

For touring information contact:
Tourism South Australia
Travel Centre
1 King William Street
Adelaide 5000
(08) 212 1505
(008) 88 2092.

For motoring and touring information contact:
Royal Automobile Association of South Australia
  Inc. (RAA)
41 Hindmarsh Square
Adelaide 5000
(08) 223 4555.

For four-wheel driving information contact:
South Australian Association of FWDC
GPO Box 178
Blair Athol SA 5084.

WARNING ▶ Unauthorised use of private roads and abuse of private property is causing considerable concern in South Australia and may result in certain roads being closed. Take particular care when off the plotted route, particularly on four-wheel drive tracks.

The Flinders Ranges

In Brachina Gorge, Flinders Ranges

SOUTH AUSTRALIA'S NATIONAL AND CONSERVATION PARKS

These parks are established in regions as diverse as mallee and semi-arid land, floodplains and remote mountain areas, and together give remarkable opportunities to observe the varied and often rare wildlife at close quarters. Camping facilities vary and it is wise to check in advance with local authorities, although bush camping is generally permitted. Contact National Parks and Wildlife Service (NPWS), 55 Grenfell Street, Adelaide 5000; tel. (08) 207 2300. Fees are reasonable and permits are required both to enter and to camp in Flinders Ranges and Gammon parks. Phone numbers for local and regional offices are given in the tour directions. In all parks, observe the following code.

▶ *Use fireplaces where provided. Preserve native timber; use portable stoves or bring your own firewood.*
▶ *Do not disturb or collect earth or rock formations, wildflowers or vegetation; it is an offence to remove material from parks.*
▶ *Do not disturb or collect artefacts from Aboriginal sites.*
▶ *Domestic animals and firearms are not permitted.*
▶ *Drive carefully and observe all notices; keep to designated tracks.*
▶ *Use litter bins or take your rubbish away with you.*
▶ *Contact rangers for advice on bushwalking.*
▶ *Remember that all native animals and plants are protected.*

THE MT LOFTY RANGES AND THE BAROSSA VALLEY

THE MT LOFTY RANGES AND THE BAROSSA VALLEY

START POINT Map page 41, L8.

TOTAL KM 257. Does not include 11 km Adelaide to start point and 30 km end point to Adelaide. **See Route Directions.**

UNSEALED KM 137.

DEGREE OF DIFFICULTY Easy.

DRIVING TIME A day tour. Allow time to/from start/end points. **See Route Directions.**

LONGEST DISTANCE NO FUEL 137 km (Truro to Mt Barker).

TOPOGRAPHIC MAP Auslig 1:250 000 series: *Adelaide.*

LOCAL/SPECIALITY MAPS RAA regional series: *Central*; UBD Tourist series: *Barossa Valley.*

OTHER USEFUL INFORMATION Adelaide Hills Regional Tourist Association booklet: *Your Guide to the Beautiful Adelaide Hills*; Barossa Tourist Association booklet: *The Barossa ... unforgettable*; Barossa Wine & Tourism Association pamphlet: *Barossa Region Fast Fact Finder.*

BEST TIME OF YEAR TO TRAVEL Possible at any time, but heavy rain makes some unsealed roads impassable.

TOUR DESCRIPTION This is a pleasant day tour through the northern Mt Lofty Ranges and the Barossa Valley, Australia's most famous wine-producing region. The country is extraordinarily beautiful, with rolling green hills, huge eucalypts and some wonderful old stone buildings and fences. The roads are mostly well-surfaced gravel, but may be narrow or winding (*see Warnings*).

The route starts in the Onkaparinga Valley, a region of orchards, pasture and meadowland, passing through towns such as Oakbank, which annually holds Australia's biggest picnic race meeting, and Woodside, where a complex of historic buildings at Heritage Park is being developed as a tourist centre. Should you wish to extend your trip beyond a day, a camping stopover at *Tanunda* gives access to walking trails, to Menglers Hill lookout and its superb views over much of the valley and to the nearby village of Bethany, Barossa's oldest German settlement. The German heritage is par-

ticularly strong in the Tanunda–Nuriootpa region – for instance, in the Barossa Valley Vintage Festival, traditionally a harvest thanksgiving celebration held biennially in the week following Easter. In Tanunda itself there are many wineries, historic buildings, the Barossa Folk Museum and the Kev Rohrlach Technology and Heritage Museum in the old Siegersdorf Winery, and for children Story Book Cottage and Whacky Wood is a must. Nuriootpa offers the Old Wine Heritage Museum, Linke's and Sobotta's bakeries, delightful picnic areas in Coulthard Reserve, and the Luhrs Pioneer Cottage and schoolhouse.

Returning to Adelaide through Truro and Keyneton, and following a fascinating, meandering southward route, you pass eventually through Mt Barker, the state's oldest town, where buildings are virtually unchanged since the earliest days.

WARNING ▶ After rain, check road conditions before departure with Adelaide Police Communications Department, tel. (08) 207 4444, and at local stations en route.

BOOKINGS AND PERMITS ▶ For caravan parks and camping contact Barossa Information Centre, 66 Murray Street, Nuriootpa SA 5355; tel. (085) 62 1866. ▶ For walking trails contact State Information Centre, 25 Grenfell Street, Adelaide 5000; tel. (08) 226 0000.

ROUTE DIRECTIONS

Depart Adelaide CBD south-east via Glen Osmond Rd–Mt Barker Rd (approx. 11 km).
START TOUR

0.0 km Zero trip meter adjacent to Eagle on the Hill Hotel, Mt Barker Rd. **SO.**
(12.2 km)

12.2 km S'post: Woodside/Hahndorf. **TL** off freeway.
(0.7 km)

12.9 km S'post: Verdun. **TL.**
(0.5 km)

13.4 km S'post: Verdun. **TR.**

Sign: Onkaparinga Valley Scenic Drive.

(1.1 km)

14.5 km Verdun town centre, adjacent to Stanley Ridge Hotel. **SO.** **PD**
(0.3 km)

14.8 km Cross Onkaparinga River.
(2.5 km)

17.3 km Cross railway line.
(1.4 km)

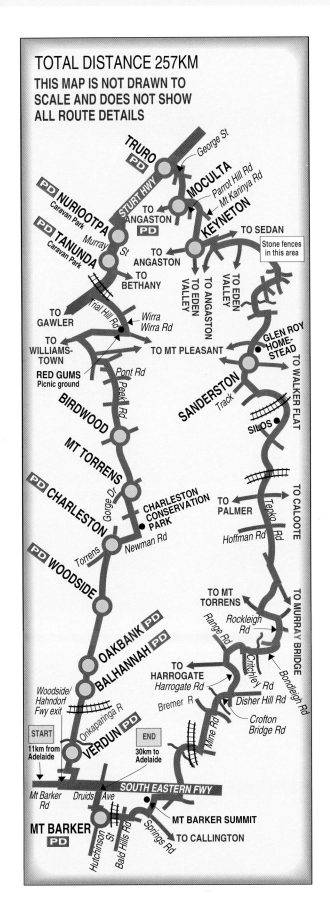

TOTAL DISTANCE 257KM

THIS MAP IS NOT DRAWN TO SCALE AND DOES NOT SHOW ALL ROUTE DETAILS

18.7 km	Balhannah town centre, adjacent to post office. **SO.** PD
	(1.6 km)
20.3 km	Oakbank town centre, adjacent to post office. **SO.** PD
	(4.8 km)
25.1 km	Woodside town centre, adjacent to post office. **SO.** PD
	(4.6 km)
29.7 km	Charleston town centre. S'post: Harrogate.

> PD *Torrens Gorge straight ahead. Charleston Conservation Park 5 km off to right. Picnic areas, no facilities.*

0.0 km	Zero trip meter at above town centre. **TR** onto Newman Rd.
	(3.4 km)
3.4 km	T intersection. **TL** onto gravel.
	(2.5 km)
5.9 km	Crossroads. **SO** over bitumen.
	(1.8 km)
7.7 km	T intersection. **TR** onto bitumen.
	(1.3 km)
9.0 km	Mt Torrens village. S'post: Birdwood. **TL.**
	(6.5 km)
15.5 km	Crossroads in Birdwood. S'post: Cromer Rd. **SO.**
	(0.3 km)
15.8 km	Cross causeway.
	(2.9 km)
18.7 km	Crossroads. **SO** onto gravel: Peek Rd.
	(2.6 km)
21.3 km	Crossroads. **SO** over Pont Rd.
	(0.7 km)
22.0 km	Y intersection. **KR.**

> *Road to private property on left.*

	(0.8 km)
22.8 km	T intersection. **TL.**
	(1.7 km)
24.5 km	T intersection. **TR** onto bitumen.
	(2.1 km)
26.6 km	S'post: Williamstown. **SO.**

> *Mt Pleasant 11 km off to right.*

	(9.2 km)
35.8 km	T intersection. **TR.**
	(7.6 km)
43.4 km	S'post: Wirra Wirra Rd. **TL** onto gravel.

Stone fences, Keyneton

> *Mt Pleasant straight ahead. Red Gums Picnic Ground 200 m on left.*

(4.7 km)
48.1 km S'post: Trial Hill. **SO**.

> *Track enters on right.*

(5.2 km)
53.3 km Bitumen.
(0.4 km)
53.7 km Gravel.
(3.0 km)
56.7 km Bitumen.
(0.7 km)
57.4 km Intersection. **TR** onto Barossa Valley Hwy.

> *Gawler off to left.*

(1.2 km)
58.6 km Cross railway line.
(7.0 km)
65.6 km T intersection. S'post: Tanunda. **TL**.

> *Bethany off to right.*

(1.5 km)
67.1 km Tanunda town centre, Murray St, adjacent post office.

> **PD** *Caravan park.*

(2.8 km)
60.0 km Cross railway line.
(4.3 km)
74.2 km Nuriootpa town centre, adjacent to post office.

> **PD** *Caravan park.*

0.0 km Zero trip meter at post office. **SO**.
(0.4 km)
0.4 km Coulthard House on right.

> *Major information centre for the valley.*

(1.4 km)
1.8 km T intersection. S'post: Blanchetown. **TR** onto Sturt Hwy.
(13.2 km)

THE MT LOFTY RANGES AND THE BAROSSA VALLEY

15.0 km Truro town centre, adjacent to post office. **SO**. PD

(0.3 km)

15.3 km S'post: Moculta. **TR**. After 100 m, s'post: Moculta. **TL**.

(1.0 km)

16.3 km S'post: Angaston via Moculta. **TL** onto George St.

(0.6 km)

16.9 km Crossroads. S'post: Moculta. **TR**.

(0.3 km)

17.2 km Gravel.

(5.4 km)

22.6 km Bitumen.

(0.8 km)

23.4 km In Moculta township, s'post: Keyneton.

> Angaston off to right.

0.0 km Zero trip meter at above s'post. **TL**.

(0.1 km)

0.1 km Gravel.

(1.0 km)

1.1 km Intersection. **KL** across culvert along Mt Karinya Rd.

> Parrot Hill Rd to right.

(0.9 km)

2.0 km S'post: Keyneton. **TR**.

(8.6 km)

10.6 km Bitumen.

(0.7 km)

11.3 km Crossroads in Keyneton. S'post: Sedan. **TL**.

> Eden Valley straight ahead. Angaston off to right. Magnificent eucalypts in this region.

(3.0 km)

14.3 km S'post: Eden Valley. **TR**.

(0.3 km)

14.6 km

Intersection. **TL** (hard left) onto gravel.

> Angaston straight ahead.

(5.0 km)

19.6 km Y intersection. **KL**.

> Eden Valley off to right. There are a number of remarkable hand-built stone fences throughout this region.

(8.9 km)

28.5 km Intersection. **SO**.

(0.1 km)

28.6 km

Y intersection. **KR**.

(0.6 km)

29.2 km Crossroads. S'post: Cambrai. **TR**.

> Sedan straight ahead.

(2.8 km)

32.0 km

Intersection. **SO** over crossroads.

(4.2 km)

36.2 km Creek crossing.

(0.2 km)

36.4 km T intersection. **TL**.

(1.1 km)

37.5 km S'post: Sanderston. **TR**.

(9.2 km)

46.7 km Crossroads. S'post: Sanderston. **SO**.

> Mt Pleasant off to right. Glen Roy homestead on left.

(2.0 km)

48.7 km Crossroads in Sanderston. **SO**.

> Mt Pleasant off to right. Walker Flat off to left.

(1.9 km)

50.6 km Intersection. **SO**.

> Track on right.

(2.0 km)

52.6 km T intersection. **TL**.

(5.8 km)

58.4 km Cross abandoned railway line.

(2.5 km)

60.9 km Bitumen.

> Silos on right.

(1.1 km)

62.0 km Crossroads. **SO** onto gravel.

(4.9 km)

66.9 km Cross abandoned railway line.

(1.4 km)

68.3 km Crossroads. S'post: Tepko. **SO** along Tepko Rd.

> Caloote off to left. Palmer off to right.

(3.2 km)

71.5 km Crossroads. **SO** over Hoffman Rd.

(3.2 km)

74.7 km Intersection. **KL** onto bitumen.

(1.2 km)

75.9 km S'post: Monarto. **TR** onto gravel.

Glen Roy homestead, near Sanderston

> *Murray Bridge straight ahead.*

(1.4 km)
77.3 km Intersection. S'post: Monarto South. **SO**.

> *Murray Bridge off to left.*

(2.0 km)
79.3 km T intersection. S'post: Monarto. **TL**.

> *Mt Torrens off to right.*

(2.5 km)
81.8 km S'post: Rockleigh Rd. **KR**.
(0.6 km)
82.4 km S'post: Rockleigh. **KR** along Rockleigh Rd.

> *Panican Hill Rd on left.*

(2.8 km)
85.2 km Cross causeway, then s'post: Bondleigh. **TL** onto Bondleigh Rd.
(2.9 km)
88.1 km Creek crossing.
(0.8 km)
88.9 km Intersection. **TR** continuing along Bondleigh Rd.

> *Critchley Rd on left.*

(2.0 km)
90.9 km S'post: Bondleigh Rd. **TL**.

> *Range Rd on right.*

(1.4 km)
92.3 km T intersection. S'post: Harrogate Rd. **TL**.

> *Harrogate off to right.*

(7.1 km)
99.4 km Crossroads. S'post: Crofton Bridge Rd. **TR**.

> *Disher Hill Rd on left.*

(1.6 km)
101.0 km Bremer River. Cross bridge.
(1.8 km)
102.8 km T intersection. **TR** onto bitumen.
(0.8 km)
103.6 km S'post: Mine Rd. **TL**.
(3.0 km)
106.6 km Gravel.
(1.5 km)
108.1 km Crossroads. **TR**.
(0.3 km)
108.4 km Cross railway line.
(1.4 km)
109.8 km Creek crossing.
(2.3 km)
112.1 km Freeway underpass. **SO** 100 m. S'post: Mt Barker. **TR**.
(0.5 km)
112.6 km Y intersection. **KR**.
(5.8 km)
118.4 km T intersection. **TL** onto bitumen.
(0.2 km)
118.6 km Intersection.

> *Mt Barker summit 1 km off to right.*

0.0 km Zero trip meter at above intersection. **SO**.
(2.4 km)
2.4 km T intersection. **TR** onto Springs Rd.

> *Callington off to left.*

(2.3 km)
4.7 km T intersection. **TR** continuing along Springs Rd.
(1.8 km)
6.5 km Crossroads. **SO** over Bald Hills Rd.
(2.5 km)
9.0 km Cross railway line.
(0.7 km)
9.7 km T intersection in Mt Barker town centre. **TR** into Hutchinson St.

> **PD** *Mt Barker is the state's oldest town.*

(0.4 km)
10.1 km Intersection. **TL** onto Druids Ave.
(0.3 km)
10.4 km Intersection. **TR**.
(0.7 km)
11.1 km Intersection. South Eastern Fwy entrance. Zero trip meter.
END TOUR
TL onto freeway. Return to Adelaide (approx. 30 km).

THE RIVERLAND AND MURRAY RIVER VALLEY

START POINT Map page 41, L8.

TOTAL KM 749. Does not include 11 km Adelaide to start point and approximately 98 km end point to Adelaide. *See Route Directions.*
UNSEALED KM 449.
DEGREE OF DIFFICULTY Easy.
DRIVING TIME Tour over 3 days. Allow time to/from start/end points. *See Route Directions.*
LONGEST DISTANCE NO FUEL 129 km (Loxton to Paruna).
TOPOGRAPHIC MAPS Auslig 1:250 000 series: *Adelaide; Renmark; Pinnaroo.*
LOCAL/SPECIALITY MAPS RAA regional series: *Riverland and Central Murray; Central.*
OTHER USEFUL INFORMATION Tourism South Australia booklet: *South Australia – Touring Guide*; Murraylands Regional Tourist Association booklet: *South Australia's Murraylands – Visitors' Guide*; Dept of Environment and Planning booklet: *The Riverland.*
BEST TIME OF YEAR TO TRAVEL Most pleasant in spring and summer, but in any season should be avoided after periods of heavy rain.

TOUR DESCRIPTION A pleasant and leisurely tour through the Murray Valley and the Riverland is an ideal family trip. You pass through semi-arid mallee country, regions producing wine and citrus fruits and some wheatlands. Gravel roads are good, although some are mushy and slippery after heavy rain. Along the Murray River there are many opportunities to swim, water ski, fish, or go boating and canoeing; you could break your driving time by taking a riverboat cruise or hiring a houseboat, and there are conservation parks and reserves either on or near the plotted route.

Murray Bridge could be explored either at the beginning of the tour or at the end. Visit Mary the Blacksmith, a tourism-award winner, or walk among hundreds of living tropical butterflies in the Butterfly House. Puzzle Park contains Australia's largest maze (not just for children) and a brilliant display of the state emblem can be seen at Sturt's Desert Pea Garden. (Not all places of interest are open continuously, so check with the Tourist Information Centre.) North of Murray Bridge is the historic town of Mannum. Discover the history of the paddlesteamers in the floating museum, PS *Marion*, or walk through the Halidon Bird Sanctuary, adjacent to the caravan park and extending along the Purnong road. Near Walker Flat the river is sheltered by high cliffs; canoes can be hired here, and a ferry gives access to a lookout. Farther along the Mannum–Swan Reach road and extending almost to the Punyelroo turnoff is *Ridley Conservation Park*, where birdlovers may find the striped honeyeater, rarely seen in South Australia. Brookfield Conservation Park, west of Blanchetown and best known as the habitat of the hairy-nosed wombat, is also a centre for research into arid-land ecology. Visitors should check with the ranger about access areas, the nature trail and bushwalking generally, and water supplies must always be carried.

Waikerie is the Riverland centre for 5000 hectares of orchards and vineyards, and you could take a less usual view of the fruitlands and the river by visiting the Waikerie Gliding Club, an important gliding centre that has hosted world championship competition. The river here is flanked by striking sandstone cliffs, and birdlife abounds. The garden city of Loxton is a centre for wine, wheat and wool industries, and its past is recreated in the Historical Village; across the Murray is *Katarapko Game Reserve*, noted for bush camping, fishing and birdwatching. The southward journey takes you through wheatlands that stretch towards the Victorian border and through Billiatt Conservation Park to the farming and grazing towns of Lameroo and Tintinara, and finally to Tailem Bend, where you could end the tour with a visit to Old Tailem Town, a pioneer village 5 kilometres along the road to Adelaide.

On this tour bush camping is limited but is permitted in *Ridley* and *Maize Island* conservation parks and in *Katarapko* and *Moorook* game reserves, and there are caravan parks in the main towns (**see Route Directions**).

BOOKINGS AND PERMITS ▶ For Murraylands, Murray Bridge Tourist Information Centre, 3 South Terrace, Murray Bridge SA 5253, tel. (085) 32 6660; Mannum Tourist Information Centre, Randell Street, Mannum SA 5238, tel. (085) 69 1303; Tailem Bend Tourist Information Centre, 15B Railway Terrace, Tailem Bend SA 5260, tel. (085) 72 3537. ▶ For the Riverland, Loxton Tourist & Travel Centre, East Terrace, Loxton SA 5333; Waikerie Travel Centre, 20 McCoy Street, Waikerie SA 5330, tel. (085) 41 2295.

THE RIVERLAND AND MURRAY RIVER VALLEY

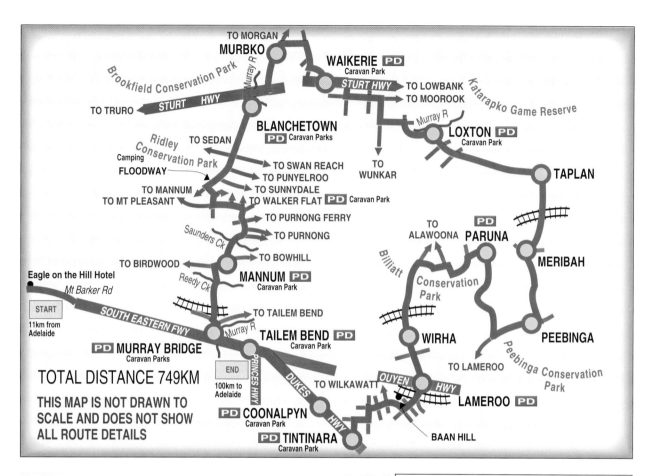

TO MORGAN
MURBKO
WAIKERIE PD
Caravan Park
Brookfield Conservation Park
STURT HWY
TO LOWBANK
TO MOOROOK
Katarapko Game Reserve
STURT HWY
TO TRURO
Murray R
Murray R
LOXTON PD
Caravan Park
BLANCHETOWN
PD Caravan Parks
Ridley Conservation Park
TO SEDAN
TAPLAN
Camping
FLOODWAY
TO SWAN REACH
TO PUNYELROO
TO WUNKAR
TO SUNNYDALE
TO MANNUM
TO WALKER FLAT PD Caravan Park
TO MT PLEASANT
TO PURNONG FERRY
PARUNA PD
Saunders Ck
TO PURNONG
TO ALAWOONA
MERIBAH
TO BIRDWOOD
TO BOWHILL
Billiatt
Conservation Park
Reedy Ck
MANNUM PD
Caravan Park
Eagle on the Hill Hotel
Mt Barker Rd
PEEBINGA
START
11km from Adelaide
SOUTH EASTERN FWY
Murray R
TO TAILEM BEND
WIRHA
PD MURRAY BRIDGE
Caravan Parks
Princes Hwy
TAILEM BEND PD
Caravan Park
Peebinga Conservation Park
TO LAMEROO
TOTAL DISTANCE 749KM
END
100km to Adelaide
TO WILKAWATT
OUYEN HWY
THIS MAP IS NOT DRAWN TO SCALE AND DOES NOT SHOW ALL ROUTE DETAILS
PD COONALPYN
Caravan Park
Dukes Hwy
LAMEROO PD
PD TINTINARA
Caravan Park
BAAN HILL

ROUTE DIRECTIONS

Depart Adelaide CBD south-east via Glen Osmond and Mt Barker roads (approx. 11 km).

START TOUR

0.0 km Zero trip meter adjacent to Eagle on the Hill Hotel, Mt Barker Rd. **SO**, continuing along South Eastern Fwy.
(60.0 km)

60.0 km S'post: Murray Bridge. **KL** off freeway.
(5.6 km)

65.6 km Murray Bridge town centre, adjacent to Telecom Building, cnr Adelaide Rd and McHenry St. **SO**.

> PD *Caravan parks, many riverfront picnic areas, fishing and boating, water skiing, houseboats, riverboat cruises. Puzzle Park, Butterfly House, Sturt's Desert Pea Garden, Mary the Blacksmith, Captain's Cottage Museum.*

(0.1 km)

65.7 km S'post: Mannum. **TL**.

> *Tailem Bend off to right.*

(1.0 km)

66.7 km S'post: Mannum. **KR** and immediately cross railway line.
(21.9 km)

88.6 km Reedy Creek. Cross bridge.
(6.5 km)

95.1 km T intersection. S'post: Mannum. **TR**.

> *Birdwood off to left.*

(3.4 km)

98.5 km Mannum town centre, adjacent to post office.

> PD *Caravan park, picnic area. Fishing, swimming, water skiing, boating. Houseboats for hire. The floating museum, PS Marion. The Bird Sanctuary extends 15 km along the Purnong road. Scenic walking tracks in Mannum Waterfalls Reserve, 10 km south.*

0.0 km Zero trip meter at post office. **SO**.
(0.4 km)

0.4 km S'post: Walker Flat. **SO.**

> *Bowhill off to right.*

(9.5 km)

9.9 km Saunders Creek. Cross bridge.

(5.1 km)

15.0 km Gravel.

(1.2 km)

16.2 km S'post: Walker Flat. **TL.**

> *Purnong off to right.*

(10.6 km)

26.8 km **SO** at crossroads.

> *Purnong ferry off to right.*

(2.8 km)

29.6 km Intersection. **KL.**

(1.2 km)

30.8 km Bitumen.

(0.8 km)

31.6 km S'post: Mt Pleasant. **TL.**

> *Walker Flat 1 km straight ahead.* **PD** *Ferry crossing, canoes for hire. Ngautngaut Conservation Park, 3 km north of Walker Flat, includes Devon Downs archaeological excavation, Aboriginal relics, canoe tree.*

(1.7 km)

33.3 km Intersection. **TL.**

> *Wongulla straight ahead.*

(2.8 km)

36.1 km Crossroads. **TR** onto gravel.

> *Alternative route to Purnong ferry off to left.*

(4.2 km)

40.3 km Intersection. **SO.**

> *Wongulla off to right.*

(1.2 km)

41.5 km S'post: Swan Reach. **TR.**

> *Mannum off to left.*

(1.2 km)

42.7 km Cross floodway.

> *Ridley Conservation Park extends along left of road. Camping, bushwalking.*

(6.0 km)

48.7 km Intersection. **SO.**

The River Murray at Mannum

Near Murray Bridge

Punyelroo Caravan Park on the Murray, downstream from Swan Reach

> *Sunnydale off to right.*

(7.0 km)

55.7 km Intersection.

> *Punyelroo Caravan Park 2 km to right.* **PD**

0.0 km Zero trip meter at above intersection. **SO.**
(5.1 km)

5.1 km Crossroads. S'post: Blanchetown. **SO.**

> *Sedan off to left. Swan Reach off to right.*

(24.4 km)

29.5 km Bitumen.
(0.5 km)

30.0 km T intersection. **TL.**

> *Blanchetown off to right.* **PD** *Caravan parks.*

(0.5 km)

30.5 km S'post: Waikerie. **TR** onto Sturt Hwy.

> *Truro off to left. Brookfield Conservation Park 11 km off to left. Picnic area, toilets. No camping. Ranger on site, 3 km from entrance; check regarding restricted areas.*

(1.3 km)

31.8 km Murray River. Cross bridge.
(3.8 km)

35.6 km S'post: Morgan. **TL** off Sturt Hwy.
(16.2 km)

51.8 km S'post: Murbko. **SO** onto gravel.

> *Waikerie off to right.*

(4.7 km)

56.5 km S'post: Oxford Landing Rd. **TR.**
(19.2 km)

75.7 km T intersection. **TR.** S'post: Murray View. **TL.**
(8.0 km)

83.7 km Intersection. **KL** passing Ramco road on left.
(3.6 km)

87.3 km T intersection. **TL.**
(9.4 km)

96.7 km Intersection. **TR** into Waikerie town centre.

> **PD** *Caravan parks. Picnic areas, barbecues in Lions Pioneer Park. Irrigation area, orchards and vineyards. Houseboats for hire; water skiing in Holden Bend Reserve. Major gliding centre. Notable fossil deposits on north side of river, near Lock 2. Camping in Maize Island Conservation Park. Clifftop lookout gives panoramic views of river, cliffs and surrounding region.*

0.0 km Zero trip meter at town centre. **TL** into White St.

> *Post office immediately on right.*

(0.1 km)

0.1 km S'post: Loxton. **TR.**
(0.1 km)

0.2 km S'post: Loxton. **TL.**
(1.6 km)

1.8 km S'post: Loxton. **TL** onto Sturt Hwy.
(6.9 km)

8.7 km S'post: Lowbank Rd. **TR** onto gravel.
(15.3 km)

24.0 km Crossroads. **TL.**
(9.1 km)

33.1 km Crossroads. **SO.**
(12.1 km)

45.2 km Intersection. S'post: Wunkar. **TR.**

> *Moorook straight ahead. Moorook Game Reserve an important waterbird area. Nature trail. Camping, fishing, canoeing; hunting in proclaimed season.*

(10.2 km)

55.4 km Crossroads. **TL.**
(8.0 km)

63.4 km Crossroads. **TR** onto bitumen.
(20.3 km)

83.7 km Loxton roundabout, town centre to left. Enter via Bookpurnong Rd.

> **PD** *Caravan parks. Historical Village, Penfolds Loxton Winery, Mike Elvey wood sculpture display. Canoeing; houseboats for hire. Camping in Katarapko Game Reserve.*

0.0 km Zero trip meter at roundabout. Take Taplan exit (Kokoda Tce).
(0.9 km)

0.9 km Cross railway line.
(0.1 km)

1.0 km Crossroads. **SO.**
(7.4 km)

8.4 km Intersection. S'post: Taplan. **SO** onto gravel.
(25.2 km)

33.6 km Taplan town centre, adjacent to Taplan Institute building. **SO.**
(0.1 km)

33.7 km S'post: Meribah. **TR.**
(11.5 km)

45.2 km Cross railway line.
(7.6 km)

THE RIVERLAND AND MURRAY RIVER VALLEY

52.8 km Intersection. **SO.**
(0.6 km)
53.4 km T intersection. **TL.**

> Meribah off to right.

(28.0 km)
81.4 km T intersection. **TR.**
(0.7 km)
82.1 km S'post: Pinnaroo. **SO.**
(4.6 km)
86.7 km T intersection. **TR** onto bitumen.
(0.1 km)
86.8 km Cross railway line and immediately s'post: Kringin. **TL** onto gravel.

> Paruna off to right. Section skirts Peebinga Conservation Park; stabilised dunes of a sand plain support mallee and tea tree, orchids, mallee birds.

(9.4 km)
96.2 km S'post: Paruna. **TR.**
(33.6 km)
129.8 km Intersection. **TL.**

> Paruna 2 km straight ahead. **PD**

(9.4 km)
139.2 T intersection. **TL.**
(22.8 km)
162.0 km Crossroads. S'post: Lameroo. **TL.**

> Alawoona off to right. The Lameroo road passes through Billiatt Conservation Park. Fauna includes mallee fowl, hopping mouse, pygmy possum. Views from Trig Hill, 1-km walk from road.

(44.1 km)
206.1 km Cross railway line.

> Wirha on right.

(6.5 km)
212.6 km Crossroads. S'post: Lameroo. **SO.**
(9.3 km)
221.9 km Bitumen.
(5.6 km)
227.5 km S'post: Pinnaroo. **SO** into Lameroo township.
(0.4 km)
227.9 km Roundabout. **SO** and immediately cross railway line.

> Lameroo town centre to left. **PD**
> No caravan park.

0.0 km Zero trip meter at railway line.
(3.7 km)
3.7 km S'post: Baan Hill. **KR.**
(0.7 km)
4.4 km Gravel.
(8.8 km)
13.2 km Crossroads. **SO.**

> Baan Hill Reserve 10 km to right. Picnic area, barbecues, toilets.

(1.9 km)
15.1 km Crossroads. **TR.**
(5.0 km)
20.1 km Crossroads. **SO.**
Wilkawatt off to right.
(5.7 km)
25.8 km Crossroads. S'post: Coonalpyn. **SO.**
(4.3 km)
30.1 km Crossroads. S'post: Coonalpyn. **TL.**
(7.5 km)
37.6 km S'post: Coonalpyn. **TR.**
(13.2 km)
50.8 km S'post: Tintinara. **TL.**
(38.1 km)
88.9 km Bitumen.
(4.3 km)
93.2 km Dukes Hwy intersection in Tintinara.

> **PD** Caravan park.

0.0 km Zero trip meter at above intersection. **TR** onto Dukes Hwy.
(28.1 km)
28.1 km Coonalpyn town centre, on Dukes Hwy.

> **PD** Caravan park.

0.0 km Zero trip meter at Coonalpyn town centre. **SO.**
(65.6 km)
65.6 km Tailem Bend, adjacent to Riverbend Motel on Princes Hwy. Zero trip meter.

> **PD** Town centre off highway to right. Caravan park. Old Tailem Town 5 km along Princes Hwy.

END TOUR

Proceed to Adelaide via Princes Hwy and South Eastern Fwy, approx. 100 km.

THE FLINDERS AND GAMMON RANGES

START POINT Map page 41, L4.

TOTAL KM 746. Does not include 135 km Adelaide to start point and approx. 425 km end point to Adelaide. *See Route Directions.*
UNSEALED KM 495.
DEGREE OF DIFFICULTY Moderate.
DRIVING TIME Tour over 3 or 4 days. Allow time to/from start/end points. *See Route Directions.*
LONGEST DISTANCE NO FUEL 269 km (Copley to Wilpena) or 133 km (Copley to Arkaroola, 32 km off route).
TOPOGRAPHIC MAPS Auslig 1:250 000 series: *Burra; Ororoo; Parachilna; Copley.*
LOCAL/SPECIALITY MAPS RAA regional series: *Mid North; Flinders Ranges*; Flinders Ranges and Outback Regional Tourist Association (FRORTA): *The Flinders Ranges.*
OTHER USEFUL INFORMATION FRORTA booklet: *Flinders Ranges and Outback South Australia*; information sheet: *Wilpena Pound.* RAA booklet: *Touring the Flinders Ranges*; Mid North Tourist Association booklet: *South Australia's Mid North*; NPWS brochures: *Flinders Ranges National Park; Gammon Ranges National Park; Bushwalking in the Flinders Ranges*; Conservation Council booklet: *Flinders Ranges Walks.*
BEST TIME OF YEAR TO TRAVEL April–October to avoid the heat of summer and to see wildflowers in bloom.

TOUR DESCRIPTION The Flinders Ranges region is semi-arid, harsh and very beautiful, with many unique and extraordinary natural features – gorges, ramparts and dry creekbeds. Flora include the massive river red gums Hans Heysen loved to paint and huge numbers of native cypress pines once used for hut construction; wildflowers bloom profusely after spring rains. Wildlife is abundant and often unique. Bushwalking trails range from short and gentle walks to challenging expeditions. For the most part the roads are good-surface gravel although sections may become impassable after heavy rain, some gorges are rough and stony and certain track sections are narrow and twisting. The popularity of the ranges makes it particularly necessary to tread carefully; also, with the exception of the national parks, most of the land consists of privately owned pastoral properties (**see Warnings**).

The trip begins at Clare, and runs north through wheat and grazing lands to Hawker. You pass by historic Bungaree homestead – a working merino stud established in 1841 – and Geralka Rural Farm, a privately owned tourist attraction. South of Jamestown, *Bundaleer Forest Reserve* has camping and picnic grounds, and from nearby New Campbell Hill you look towards Mt Remarkable; in Ororoo you can picnic or barbecue beside Pekina Creek and walk along the creek to see Aboriginal rock carvings. *Rawnsley Park* is a good place for a base camp; there are walking trails, and horseriding, packhorse treks and four-wheel drive tours can be arranged. Before entering Flinders Ranges National Park you pass the turnoff to Arkaroo Rock, once a frequented Aboriginal campsite; subsequently the camping area at *Wilpena* gives access to the most spectacular single feature of the park – the vast rock bowl of Wilpena Pound, ringed with cliffs and jagged rocks and significant in Aboriginal lore. Beyond Wilpena is the Cazneaux Tree and the road to Sacred Canyon, another site of Aboriginal art, and near Bunyeroo Valley lookout the road crosses the famous Heysen trail; north of Bunyeroo is *Brachina Gorge*, where there are bush camping and picnic spots. You can choose to camp next at the ruins of *Aroona* (the first homestead in the Flinders Ranges) or at three following camping areas – *Slippery Dip, Trezona* and *Youncoona* – before turning off to Blinman and taking the road through Glass's Gorge to Parachilna. North of Parachilna is historic Beltana township, where the work of Rev. John Flynn led to his establishment of the Royal Flying Doctor Service.

The terrain of the Gammon Ranges is difficult and often inaccessible; walking off the beaten track is recommended only for the experienced and you should advise the ranger of your itinerary. Before leaving the ranges, detour to award-winning *Arkaroola*: this is a privately owned wildlife sanctuary and tourist resort and a mecca for fossickers, with a caravan park and camping area; drive to the waterholes of Nooldoonooldoona and Bararranna and the smelter ruins of Bolla Bollana, take the spectacular Ridge Top four-wheel drive tour or visit the observatory (by arrangement).

In Chambers Gorge, 9 kilometres off the road south from Balcanoona, the rock carvings are probably the finest in the ranges. There are no facilities in the gorge and bush camping is restricted; neither walking nor driving should be undertaken in the heat of summer and at all times water should be carried. From this point you continue south past Wirrealpa homestead,

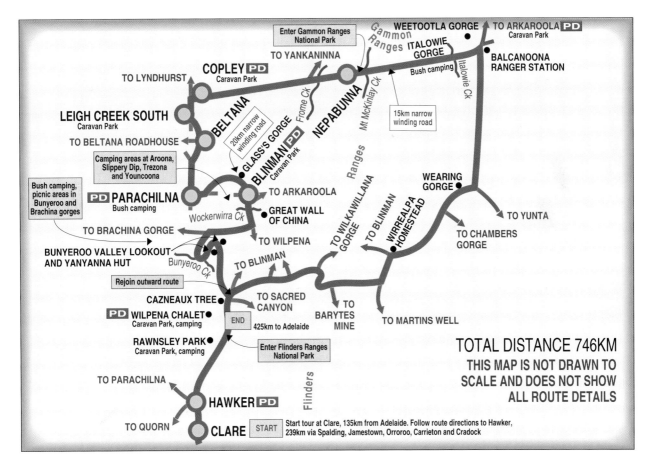

Enter Gammon Ranges National Park
TO YANKANINNA
WEETOOTLA GORGE
TO ARKAROOLA PD
Caravan Park
Gammon Ranges
ITALOWIE GORGE
BALCANOONA RANGER STATION
Bush camping
COPLEY PD
Caravan Park
TO LYNDHURST
Frome Ck
NEPABUNNA
15km narrow winding road
Italowie Ck
Mt McKinlay Ck
LEIGH CREEK SOUTH
Caravan Park
BELTANA
20km narrow winding road
TO BELTANA ROADHOUSE
GLASS'S GORGE
BLINMAN PD
Caravan Park
Ranges
Camping areas at Aroona, Slippery Dip, Trezona and Youncoona
WEARING GORGE
Bush camping, picnic areas in Bunyeroo and Brachina gorges
PD PARACHILNA
Bush camping
TO ARKAROOLA
GREAT WALL OF CHINA
TO WILKAWILLANA GORGE
TO BLINMAN
WIRREALPA HOMESTEAD
TO YUNTA
Wockerwirra Ck
TO BRACHINA GORGE
TO WILPENA
TO CHAMBERS GORGE
BUNYEROO VALLEY LOOKOUT AND YANYANNA HUT
Bunyeroo Ck
TO BLINMAN
Rejoin outward route
CAZNEAUX TREE
TO SACRED CANYON
TO BARYTES MINE
TO MARTINS WELL
PD WILPENA CHALET
Caravan Park, camping
END
425km to Adelaide
RAWNSLEY PARK
Caravan Park, camping
Enter Flinders Ranges National Park
Flinders
TO PARACHILNA

TOTAL DISTANCE 746KM
THIS MAP IS NOT DRAWN TO SCALE AND DOES NOT SHOW ALL ROUTE DETAILS

HAWKER PD
TO QUORN
CLARE START
Start tour at Clare, 135km from Adelaide. Follow route directions to Hawker, 239km via Spalding, Jamestown, Orroroo, Carrieton and Cradock

briefly re-enter Flinders Ranges National Park and re-join the outward route at the Brachina Gorge turnoff.

WARNINGS ▶ A potentially hostile region requiring care and preparation. Roads may be closed after rain. Contact RAA Touring Department Northern Roads Conditions Hotline, tel. (08) 11633, or local police. ▶ Check road conditions with NPWS authorities before entering national parks. Tracks not recommended for caravan towing. ▶ If doubt about public access on tracks off plotted route, contact landowner concerned or local police. ▶ Leave gates, roads and water supplies as found. Homesteads should be contacted only in real emergencies. ▶ Drive cautiously if water covers road; take extreme care at creek crossings. Corrugation a possible problem: best to maintain even speed. Dust also a hazard, especially passing vehicles. ▶ Always carry spare food, water and basic spare parts. ▶ Dry creekbeds subject to flash floods after rain. Check before camping. Except in designated areas, request permission to camp from the landowner concerned. No designated areas in national parks, but private facilities at Wilpena and Arkaroola. For bush camping in parks, contact NPWS ranger stations (***see Bookings and Per-***

mits). ▶ Observe fire regulations: check daily broadcasts, local police, the CFA or district councils. Total and permanent ban at Arkaroola except in caravan park. ▶ Shooters' permits obtainable from NPWS. Shooting banned in national parks and at Arkaroola sanctuary; written permission required from property owners. ▶ Between Copley and Wilpena fuel only at Arkaroola, 32 kilometres off plotted route, approximately 133 kilometres from Copley. ▶ Fossickers must take only samples for personal use.

BOOKINGS AND PERMITS ▶ Permit to enter and camp in Flinders and Gammon national parks obtainable from NPWS head office; also South Australian Desert Pass Package ($50.00), valid for one year and giving information on park usage. Short-term passes from ranger stations at Hawker, tel. (086) 48 4244; Wilpena, tel. (086) 48 0048 and Balcanoona, tel. (086) 48 4829. ▶ For Arkaroola Sanctuary contact Arkaroola Travel, 50 Pirie Street, Adelaide 5000; tel. (08) 212 1366, (008) 88 2318.

THE FLINDERS AND GAMMON RANGES

ROUTE DIRECTIONS

Depart Adelaide CBD via King William St/Rd, O'Connell St and Main North Rd to Clare (approx. 135 km).

START TOUR

0.0 km Zero trip meter adjacent to Clare Post Office. **SO**.

> **PD** *Caravan park in flora and fauna sanctuary. Historic town, centre for Clare Valley wineries. National Trust Museum. Sevenhill Cellars and monastery 7 km south.*

(1.2 km)

1.2 km S'post: Jamestown. **KR** along Main North Rd.

> *Blythe off to left.*

(6.5 km)

7.7 km S'post: Jamestown. **TR** off Main North Rd.

> *Bungaree 4 km straight on. Historic homestead.*

(17.8 km)

25.5 km Geralka Rural Farm on left. **SO**.

> *Caravan park. Copper mine, machinery museum, working Clydesdales, pony rides. Tours weekends and holidays or by arrangement.*

(14.2 km)

39.7 km Spalding council offices at town centre. **SO**.

> **PD** *Trout fishing; riverside barbecues.*

(0.1 km)

39.8 km S'post: Jamestown. **TL**.

(34.6 km)

74.4 km Crossroads in Jamestown. S'post: Ororoo. **SO**.

> **PD** *Caravan park. Gladstone off to left. Bundaleer Forest Reserve 9 km south.*

(0.6 km)

75.0 km Cross railway line and immediately s'post: Ororoo. **TR**.

(56.3 km)

131.3 km S'post: Hawker. **TR** along Railway Tce. Heavy vehicles bypass.

> *Ororoo town centre straight ahead.* **PD** *Caravan park. Yesteryear Costume Gallery. Pekina Creek scenic walk – Aboriginal rock carvings.*

(1.4 km)

132.7 km S'post: Hawker. **TR**.

(0.2 km)

132.9 km Cross railway line.

(28.6 km)

161.5 km Gravel.

(7.4 km)

168.9 km Bitumen.

(0.5 km)

169.4 km In Carrieton, s'post: Hawker. **TL**. **P**

(0.1 km)

169.5 km S'post: Hawker. **TR**.

> *Wilmington off to left.*

(0.4 km)

169.9 km S'post: Hawker. **KL**.

> *Belton off to right. Aboriginal rock carvings 5 km.*

(0.1 km)

170.0 km Gravel.

(0.3 km)

170.3 km S'post: Hawker. **TR**.

(43.7 km)

214.0 km Bitumen through Cradock.

> *No facilities in the town.*

(0.6 km)

214.6 km Gravel.

(25.2 km)

239.8 km Bitumen into Hawker.

(1.0 km)

240.8 km Hawker town centre. S'post: Wilpena.

> **PD** *Caravan park and supplies. NPWS office in Hawker District Council building. Historic walk through town. Jarvis Hill walking trail and lookout 5 km south-west. Yourambulla Caves 11 km south. For local 4WD tours see Information Office.*

0.0 km Zero trip meter at town centre. **TR**.

> *Parachilna off to left.*

(34.2 km)

34.2 km S'post: Rawnsley Park.

> *Rawnsley Park 3 km off to left. Private facility. Camping, caravan park, 4WD tours, walking trails, horseriding.*

0.0 km Zero trip meter at above s'post. **SO**.

(8.9 km)

8.9 km Sign: Flinders Ranges National Park. **SO**.

> *Contact ranger for camping permit.*

(8.5 km)

Old stone church at Cradock

Imposing cliff face, Gammon Ranges

Italowie Gorge

17.4 km S'post: Blinman.

> *Wilpena Chalet 3 km off to left.* **PD** *Caravan park, camping (private facility). 4WD tours, scenic flights, walking trails, bush camping (consult ranger).*

0.0 km Zero trip meter at above s'post. **SO**.
(0.2 km)
0.2 km Gravel.
(0.4 km)
0.6 km Intersection.

> *Cazneaux tree 300 m off to left. 500-m walk to set used in making the film* Robbery Under Arms.

0.0 km Zero trip meter at above intersection. **SO**.
(0.6 km)
0.6 km Intersection.

> *Sacred Canyon 14 km off to right. Aboriginal carvings.*

0.0 km Zero trip meter at above intersection. **SO** and immediately cross Wilpena Creek.
(3.6 km)
3.6 km S'post: Brachina Gorge. **TL**.

> *Blinman 55 km straight ahead.*

(12.9 km)
16.5 km Intersection.

> *Yanyanna Hut straight ahead.*

0.0 km Zero trip meter at above intersection. **KR**.
(2.2 km)
2.2 km Bunyeroo Valley lookout on left. **SO**.

> *Spectacular views of valley and Wilpena Pound.*

(2.8 km)
5.0 km Intersection. **KR**.

> *Carpark and lookout on left.*

(0.5 km)
5.5 km Bunyeroo Creek. Follow creekbed. Cross and recross creek for next 1.5 km through Bunyeroo Gorge.

> *Picnic and bush camping areas.*

(1.6 km)
7.1 km Bunyeroo Gorge walking trail on left. **SO**.
(10.5 km)
17.6 km Intersection. S'post: Blinman.

THE FLINDERS AND GAMMON RANGES

> Brachina Gorge 1 km off to left. 21 km to Main North Rd. Picnic and bush camping areas.

0.0 km Zero trip meter at above intersection. **TR.**
        (0.7 km)

0.7 km Intersection.

> Aroona ruins off to left. 6.4 km to Aroona camping sites (on right). Toilets, water. 6.7 km to Aroona hut and bore. Ruins and spring a 5-min. walk from carpark.

0.0 km Zero trip meter at above intersection. **SO.**
        (1.9 km)

1.9 km Slippery Dip camping area on right. **SO.**

> Toilets, water.

        (2.2 km)

4.1 km Intersection. **SO.**

> Trezona camping area on left. Toilets, water.

        (3.2 km)

7.3 km Intersection. **SO.**

> Youncoona camping area to left. Toilets, water.

        (3.3 km)

10.6 km Intersection. S'post: Blinman. **TL.**

> Wilpena off to right.

        (14.3 km)

24.9 km Cross Wockerwirra Creek.

> Great Wall of China east of road in this section.

        (10.5 km)

35.4 km S'post: Blinman. **SO.**

> Arkaroola off to right.

        (2.6 km)

38.0 km S'post: Blinman town centre. **SO.**

> Scenic drive to Parachilna via Angorichina on left.

        (0.2 km)

38.2 km Blinman town centre, North Blinman Hotel. **SO.**

> **PD** Caravan park. Early copper-mining area.

        (0.2 km)

38.4 km S'post: Scenic drive to Parachilna via Glass's Gorge.

> Blinman Mine off to right.

0.0 km Zero trip meter at above s'post. **KL.**
        (5.8 km)

5.8 km S'post: Glass's Gorge. **SO.**

> Sign: Narrow winding road next 20 km. Brilliant wildflowers after spring rains.

        (20.3 km)

26.1 km Cross cattle grid.

> Sign: Private property. No shooting. No camping.

        (2.6 km)

28.7 km S'post: Parachilna. **TR.**

> Blinman off to left.

        (11.4 km)

40.1 km T intersection.

> Parachilna settlement straight ahead. Bush camping. Historic bush pub. **PD**

0.0 km Zero trip meter at above intersection. **TR** onto bitumen.
        (20.7 km)

20.7 km S'post: Beltana Historic Village. **TR** onto gravel.
        (15.8 km)

36.5 km Crossroads. S'post: Leigh Creek South.

> Beltana historic town 1 km off to right. Original base of Royal Flying Doctor Service, 1911. Beltana Roadhouse 10 km off to left (tourist information service).

0.0 km Zero trip meter at above crossroads. **SO.**
        (17.0 km)

17.0 km Cross railway line.
        (1.9 km)

18.9 km T intersection. **TR** onto bitumen.
        (9.5 km)

28.4 km S'post: Lyndhurst.

> Leigh Creek South off to left. **PD** Caravan park (limited facilities). Brown coal mining; tours during school holidays.

0.0 km Zero trip meter at above s'post. **SO.**
        (4.5 km)

4.5 km S'post: Copley/Arkaroola. **TR.**

> Lyndhurst straight ahead.

        (0.2 km)

4.7 km S'post: Arkaroola. **SO** along gravel and cross railway line.

> Copley off to left. **PD** Caravan park. Next fuel Wilpena (269 km), or 133 km via Arkaroola, 32 km off route.

        (45.4 km)

50.1 km S'post: Balcanoona. **SO.**

> Yankaninna off to left.

(2.0 km)

52.1 km Cross Frome Creek.

(16.0 km)

68.1 km Nepabunna town centre, adjacent Health Clinic. **SO.**

(1.9 km)

70.0 km Sign: Gammon Ranges National Park. **SO.**

> Bushwalking in park recommended for experienced walkers only.

(4.2 km)

74.2 km Cross Mt McKinlay Creek.

> Narrow, winding road for next 15 km.

(15.2 km)

89.4 km Sign: Italowie Gorge. **SO.**

> Bush camping, no facilities.

(1.1 km)

90.5 km Information board on left.

0.0 km Zero trip meter at information board. **SO.**

(7.8 km)

7.8 km Cross Italowie Creek.

(6.8 km)

14.6 km S'post: Yunta.

> Arkaroola straight ahead. 0.7 km to intersection. Balcanoona ranger station 0.7 km straight ahead; toilets, water, permits and information centre. Arkaroola 32 km to left. From intersection, 2.0 km to Weetootla Gorge turnoff on left. 5 km through gorge; picnic and bush camping areas. From Weetootla turnoff, straight ahead to Arkaroola village. **PD** Caravan park. Camping area. Total fire ban in Arkaroola (Mt Painter) Wildlife Sanctuary except in caravan park. 4WD tours. Fossicking permitted. Scenic flights. Astronomical observatory (booking essential).

0.0 km Zero trip meter at above s'post. **TR.**

(38.5 km)

38.5 km S'post: Blinman. **TR.**

> Yunta straight ahead.

(9.0 km)

47.5 km Sign: Wearing Gorge. **SO.**

(14.9 km)

62.4 km S'post: Wirrealpa.

> Chambers Gorge 9 km off to left. Camping, bushwalking, no facilities. Fine Aboriginal carvings. Advisable to carry water; avoid in summer.

0.0 km Zero trip meter at above s'post. **SO.**

(28.9 km)

28.9 km S'post: Erudina. **TL.**

> Blinman 35 km straight ahead. Wirrealpa homestead on right.

(23.8 km)

52.7 km S'post: Flinders Ranges National Park. **TR.**

> Martins Well straight ahead.

(13.2 km)

65.9 km T intersection. S'post: Oraparinna H.S. **TR.**

> Barytes Mine 2 km off to left. No access.

(2.3 km)

68.2 km Sign: Flinders Ranges National Park. **SO.**

(2.6 km)

70.8 km Intersection.

> Wilkawillana Gorge 7 km to right. Bush camping and picnic sites throughout.

0.0 km Zero trip meter at above intersection. **SO.**

(12.6 km)

12.6 km Intersection. **SO.**

> Alternative route to Blinman off to right.

(5.9 km)

18.5 km T intersection. **TL.**

> Blinman off to right.

(12.4 km)

30.9 km S'post: Wilpena. **SO.**

> Brachina Gorge off to right. Rejoin outward route here.

(4.7 km)

35.6 km Bitumen.

(0.2 km)

35.8 km At Wilpena, s'post: Hawker 51. Zero trip meter.

> Wilpena Chalet off to right. **PD**

END TOUR

Return to Adelaide along outward route via Hawker, Clare and Main North Rd (approx. 425 km).

TOURS OUT OF MELBOURNE

The small area of the Garden State is an advantage to the four-wheel explorer, as tour destinations can be quickly and easily accessed via the excellent road system. Our tours cover a variety of terrain and touring attractions; several combine forest tracks, pastoral scenery and dramatic coastline in one. Victoria has a temperate climate which, however, can be extremely volatile especially in coastal regions. Spring, late summer and autumn are the best times to make these trips.

THE UPPER YARRA VALLEY (a day tour: 163 kilometres). An interesting and sometimes challenging drive through the forest tracks and over the lower slopes of the Great Dividing Range, still largely unspoilt, although so close to Melbourne. There are attractive picnic and bush camping spots to break the journey.

THE OTWAY RANGES (tour over 2 days: 253 kilometres). A mixture of rugged coastline and steep bush

Spring in the Grampians

tracks make this a varied drive, with possible stops to extend the tour according to your interests: bushwalking, fishing, swimming or wildlife observation. We have suggested several coastal camping areas.

CROAJINGOLONG NATIONAL PARK (tour over 3 days: 120 kilometres). Although the actual plotted route is short, it starts a fair distance from Melbourne and is almost all unsealed. The tour takes in the coastal heathlands and rainforest of south-east Gippsland and plenty of hilly, sandy tracks make an interesting drive.

VICTORIA'S NATIONAL, STATE AND FOREST PARKS

Most national parks, state forests, state parks, reserves and other public lands in Victoria are administered by the Department of Conservation and Environment (DCE), who publish excellent information sheets about all these areas which include camping facilities, the special attractions of the area, activities and whether permits or bookings are required. When planning your trips contact DCE head office at 240 Victoria Parade, East Melbourne VIC 3002; tel. (03) 412 4011. Addresses and phone numbers for local and regional offices are given in the tour descriptions. When using public land, remember the following rules.

▶ *No domestic pets in national parks. Dogs are allowed in some state parks and coastal reserves, provided they are on a leash. Dogs are allowed in state forests without a leash.*
▶ *Firearms are not permitted in national and most state parks. For information about taking firearms into state forests, contact local DCE offices.*
▶ *Drive only on formed roads.*

▶ *All native animals and plants are protected. Do not remove or disturb.*
▶ *Take out all rubbish that has not been completely burned.*
▶ *Camp at least 30 metres from the edge of any stream, lake or water supply.*
▶ *No detergents or pollutants in streams, lakes and water supplies.*
▶ *Portable generators are prohibited in most national, state and coastal parks.*
▶ *Keep noise to a minimum to avoid disturbing others.*
▶ *Portable stoves are preferable to open fires. Do not cut down trees or shrubs for wood. In camping areas, fires must be lit only in the fireplaces provided and in other areas they must be contained in a receptacle, fireplace or trench. Never leave a fire unattended, make sure it is properly extinguished before you leave. Be aware of total fire ban days! For detailed regulations, see DCE information sheets.*
▶ *Leave your campsite clean and keep the bush beautiful.*

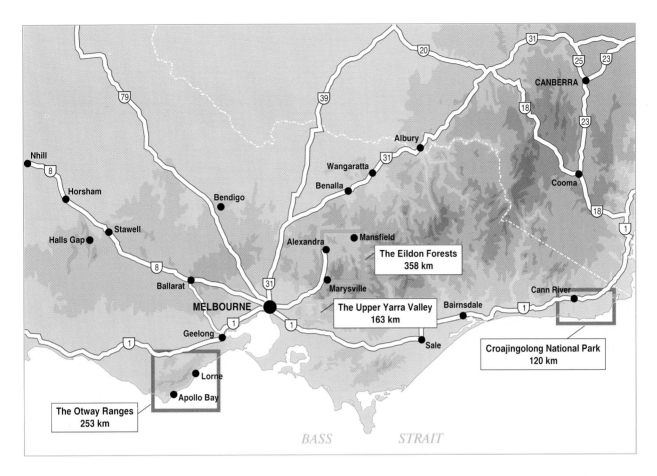

There are several inlet campsites.

THE EILDON FORESTS (tour over 2 or 3 days: 358 kilometres). A challenging drive through high forest country around picturesque Lake Eildon. There are difficult four-wheel sections on forest tracks and great camping and fishing opportunities.

THE GRAMPIANS (tour over 3 or 4 days: 224 kilometres). Superb mountain vistas are a dramatic backdrop to this often difficult and always changing drive. Take plenty of time to camp and explore the region. *For route directions and information on this tour, see 'Adelaide to Melbourne: Nhill to the Grampians National Park', in the Treks Around Australia.*

BEFORE YOU SET OUT ▶ Read the tour description carefully. ▶ Check that you have obtained any necessary permits. ▶ Check weather conditions with local authorities or Bureau of Meteorology. ▶ Make sure you have the appropriate maps and information for the tour. ▶ Check that your vehicle is in good order for the conditions ahead. Have you the necessary spare parts? ▶ If you are camping, have you the right equipment?

USEFUL INFORMATION

For touring information contact:
Victorian Travel Centre, 230 Collins Street
Melbourne 3000, (03) 790 2211.

For motoring information contact:
Royal Automobile Club of Victoria (RACV)
422 Little Collins Street, Melbourne 3000
(03) 790 2211.

For four-wheel driving information contact:
Victorian Four Wheel Drive Clubs Association Inc.
552 Whitehorse Road, Mitcham 3132, (03) 872 4610
PO Box 401C, Melbourne 3001.

For licences and information on fishing regulations contact:
Department of Conservation and Environment
240 Victoria Parade, East Melbourne 3002
(03) 412 4011.

THE UPPER YARRA VALLEY

START POINT Map page 50, E4

TOTAL KM 163. Does not include 41 km Melbourne to start point and 50 km end point to Melbourne. *See Route Directions.*
UNSEALED KM 122.
DEGREE OF DIFFICULTY Moderate *See Warnings.*
DRIVING TIME A day tour. Allow time to/from start/end points. *See Route Directions.*
LONGEST DISTANCE NO FUEL 87 km (Warburton to Gembrook).
TOPOGRAPHIC MAP Auslig 1:100 000 series: *Healesville.*
LOCAL/SPECIALITY MAP DCE map: *Yarra Valley and Gembrook Forest.*
OTHER USEFUL INFORMATION Yarra Valley and Dandenong Ranges Tourism Board booklet: *Spend Time in the Yarra Valley and Dandenong Ranges*; DCE information sheet: *Upper Yarra Valley.*
BEST TIME OF YEAR TO TRAVEL October–March. Some tracks are subject to seasonal closure or impassable after heavy rain or snow. *See Warnings.*

TOUR DESCRIPTION This interesting day tour winds through the picturesque forests of the upper Yarra Valley and the lower heights of the Great Dividing Range, areas largely under DCE management. Although you are never really far from civilisation, the region is still apparently remote and beautiful. There is plenty of challenge for four-wheel drivers and a chance to put driving skills into practice on steep track sections with ruts and occasional washaways which need careful negotiation.

Throughout the tour, you pass through scenic forests of mountain ash, brown and messmate stringybark and silvertop. Magnificent tree ferns line the creeks and gullies. You can spot remains of the old timber tramways which carried huge logs to the sawmills in the forests and then transported the timber to the railhead at Yarra Junction, once the thriving centre of the local timber industry. These tramways were gently graded so that horsepower, and later steam and motor engines could pull the log bogies over the steep terrain. Walking trails now follow many of these disused routes and offer a chance to see native flora and fauna at close range if you have the time and patience. The region is home to wombats, kangaroos, platypus, echidnas and lyrebirds.

At the start of the tour, a visit to the Upper Yarra Historic Museum in Yarra Junction will give you an idea of how the early timber workers lived. You then head off on forest tracks through Yarra State Forest around Mt Tugwell and Mt Bride. There is an attractive picnic spot at Starlings Gap; other picnic areas are at Big Pats Creek and on the banks of the Yarra halfway through the trip. The route traverses the Bump, an historic landmark which was tunnelled to allow the timber tramway to pass through it. Around this area you'll also see the evidence of the disastrous Ash Wednesday bushfires of 1983 which destroyed much of the native forest, now slowly regenerating. Bush camping is allowed in forest areas if you wish to make more than a day of this tour; there is a caravan park and camping area in *Warburton.*

WARNINGS ▶ Sections of tracks closed 1 June–30 September or later. Some tracks impassable after snow and heavy rain. Minor tracks also subject to closure. Check with DCE office at Powelltown, Main Road, Powelltown VIC 3797; tel. (059) 66 7204 on road conditions and possible track closures. ▶ This tour not suitable for caravans. ▶ Camping and picnicking allowed in state forests but use existing fireplaces and observe DCE fire, waste disposal and litter regulations at all times.

BOOKINGS AND PERMITS ▶ For information on camping and use of forest areas contact DCE offices at 240 Victoria Parade, East Melbourne 3002; tel. (03) 412 4011. ▶ For tourism information contact the Yarra Valley and Dandenong Ranges Tourism Board, PO Box 590, Healesville VIC 3777; tel. (059) 62 4022.

ROUTE DIRECTIONS

Depart Melbourne CBD via Bridge Rd, High St, Cotham Rd, Whitehorse Rd and Maroondah Hwy to Warburton Hwy and Maroondah Hwy intersection (approx. 41 km).
START TOUR

0.0 km Zero trip meter at s'post: Warburton. **TR** onto Warburton Hwy.
(16.4 km)

16.4 km S'post: Warburton. **SO** through Woori Yallock township.

> **PD** *Healesville off to left, Pakenham off to right.*

(5.7 km)

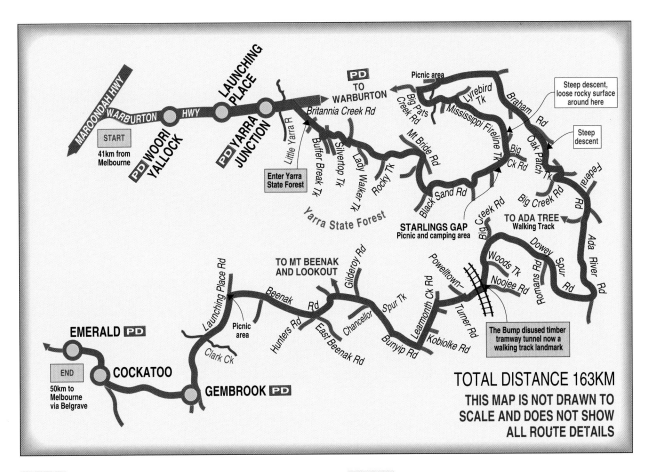

TOTAL DISTANCE 163KM
THIS MAP IS NOT DRAWN TO
SCALE AND DOES NOT SHOW
ALL ROUTE DETAILS

22.1 km S'post: Warburton. **SO** through Launching Place township past Launching Place Hotel.
(2.9 km)

25.0 km S'post: Warburton. **SO** through Yarra Junction township past Yarra Junction Hotel.

> **PD** *Interesting glimpses into the lives of early timberworkers displayed at Yarra Valley Historical Museum. Powelltown 16 km off to right.*

(1.4 km)

26.4 km Little Yarra River. Cross bridge.
(1.2 km)

27.6 km S'post: Britannia Creek Rd. **TR**.
(2.1 km)

29.7 km

S'post: Britannia Creek Rd. **SO** onto gravel.

> *Sign: Yarra State Forest. Britannia Falls off to left. Guidehouse Rd on right.*

(0.4 km)

30.1 km T intersection. **TL** along Britannia Creek Rd.
(1.3 km)

31.4 km

Intersection. **KR** then **KL** at Silvertop Track intersection.
(1.2 km)

32.6 km Intersection. **KR**.

> *Justice Track on left.*

(1.2 km)

33.8 km Intersection. **SO**.

> *Lady Walker Track on right.*

(2.0 km)

35.8 km S'post: Britannia Creek Rd. **SO**.

> *Rocky Track on right.*

(4.3 km)

40.1 km T intersection. **TR** onto Mt Bride Rd.
(0.5 km)

40.6 km Intersection. **KR**.
(0.3 km)

Steep descent, Mississippi Track, Yarra Valley

40.9 km Intersection. **SO**.

> Britannia Range Track on right.

(3.9 km)

44.8 km S'post: Black Sand Rd. **TL**.

(4.2 km)

49.0 km T intersection. **TL**.

> Fitzpatrick Rd on right.

(2.4 km)

51.4 km Intersection. **SO**.

> Road joins on right.

(0.8 km)

52.2 km Starlings Gap Picnic Area on right. **SO**.

(1.3 km)

53.5 km S'post: Mississippi Track. **TL**.

(1.3 km)

54.8 km Y intersection. **KL**.

> Logging track enters on right.

(2.9 km)

57.7 km Steep descent. **SO**.

> Caution: loose rocky surface.

(4.1 km)

61.8 km Intersection. **TL** onto Big Pats Creek Rd.

> Lyrebird Track on right.

(0.9 km)

62.7 km Big Pats Creek. Cross wooden bridge.

> Big Pats Creek Camping Ground and Picnic Area on right. Picnic tables, barbecues.

(2.7 km)

65.6 km T intersection. **TR** onto Riverside Drive.

(0.6 km)

66.2 km T intersection.

> Picnic ground on left on banks of Yarra River. Picnic tables, barbecues. Warburton township 4 km off to left. **PD** Caravan park.

0.0 km Zero trip meter at above intersection. **TR** onto Warburton–Woods Point Rd.

(5.8 km)

5.8 km S'post: Braham Rd. **TR** onto gravel.

(8.2 km)

14.0 km Intersection. **SO**.

> Mississippi Rd on right.

(1.2 km)

15.2 km Intersection. **SO** along Oat Patch Track.

> Caution: steep section for next 500 m.

(3.6 km)

18.8 km T intersection. **TR** onto Braham Rd.

(0.5 km)

19.3 km T intersection. S'post: Big Creek Rd. **TR**.

(0.3 km)

19.6 km S'post: Federal Short Cut. **TL**.

(3.0 km)

22.6 km S'post: Federal Rd. **TR**.

(0.6 km)

23.2 km Intersection. **SO**.

> New Turkey Spur Track on left.

(0.8 km)

24.0 km S'post: Ada River Rd. **SO**.

> Track on right for walkers only, 2 km to view Ada Tree.

(4.4 km)

Tree ferns, Yarra Valley

28.4 km Ada River. Cross bridge.
(0.4 km)
28.8 km S'post: Dowey Spur Rd. **KR**.

> *Ada River Rd continues to left.*

(2.6 km)
31.4 km Intersection. **SO**.

> *Romans Creek Rd on left.*

(5.9 km)
37.3 km S'post: Big Creek Rd. **TL**.
(2.9 km)
40.2 km Intersection. **KR**.

> *Woods Track on left.*

(3.2 km)
43.4 km T intersection. **TR** onto bitumen.

> *The Bump. Timber tramline once ran beneath this hill.*

(2.4 km)
45.8 km S'post: Turner Rd. **TL** onto gravel.
(2.7 km)
48.5 km S'post: Learmonth Creek Rd. **TL**.
(3.1 km)
51.6 km S'post: Kobiolke Rd. **SO**.
(0.9 km)
52.5 km T intersection. **TR** onto Bunyip Rd.
(4.3 km)
56.8 km Intersection. **SO**.

> *Chancellor Spur Track enters on left.*

(2.5 km)
59.3 km Intersection. **SO**.

> *Gilderoy Rd on right.*

(1.4 km)

60.7 km Intersection. **SO**.

> *Mt Beenak on right. Fire tower.*

(0.5 km)
61.2 km S'post: Basan Corner. **KL**.
(3.0 km)
64.2 km S'post: Gembrook. **TR** onto Beenak Rd.

> *East Beenak Rd on left. Hunters Rd straight ahead.*

(5.1 km)
69.3 km S'post: Gembrook. **SO** along Beenak Rd.

> *Road enters on left.*

(2.5 km)
71.8 km Intersection. **TL** onto bitumen: Launching Place Rd.

> *Ewart Park Reserve on right. Picnic tables, barbecue, toilets.*

(5.2 km)
77.0 km Cross bridge.

> *Picnic area and swimming hole on left.*

(5.9 km)
82.9 km S'post: Cockatoo. **TR** and enter Gembrook township.

> **PD** *Pakenham off to left. Gembrook straight ahead.*

(6.8 km)
89.7 km T intersection. S'post: Emerald. **TR** onto Healesville–Kooweerup Rd.

> *Pakenham off to left.*

(0.7 km)
90.4 km S'post: Emerald. **SO** at roundabout.

> *Healesville off to right.*

(5.3 km)
95.7 km S'post: Belgrave. **SO** at roundabout through Emerald. **PD**
(0.1 km)
95.8 km S'post: Belgrave. **SO** at roundabout through Emerald.
(0.5 km)
96.3 km S'post: Melbourne. **SO** at roundabout through Emerald. Zero trip meter.
END TOUR
Follow s'posts to return to Melbourne (approx. 50 km) by various routes.

THE OTWAY RANGES

START POINT Map page 53, Q8.

TOTAL KM 253. Does not include 89 km Melbourne to start point and 240 km end point to Melbourne via Great Ocean Road and Princes Highway. **See Route Directions.**
UNSEALED KM 175.
DEGREE OF DIFFICULTY Difficult. **See Warnings.**
DRIVING TIME Tour over 2 days. Allow time to/from start/end points. **See Route Directions.**
LONGEST DISTANCE NO FUEL 134 km (Gellibrand to Apollo Bay via Blanket Bay).
TOPOGRAPHIC MAPS Auslig 1:100 000 series: *Colac* and *Otway*.
LOCAL/SPECIALITY MAP DCE map: *The Otways*.
OTHER USEFUL INFORMATION Geelong Otway Tourism booklet: *Geelong Otway Official Visitors Guide*; DCE information sheets on *Angahook–Lorne State Park* and *Otway National Park*.
BEST TIME OF YEAR TO TRAVEL November–April as heavy rain in spring and winter makes sections of the unsealed tracks impassable, and some are subject to seasonal closure.

TOUR DESCRIPTION This exciting tour winds through the ridges and valleys of the Otway Ranges and offers plenty of four-wheel drive challenges on forest tracks. The route also incorporates sections of the Great Ocean Road, built by returned soldiers to honour those who died in the First World War. This spectacular coastal road gives you the opportunity to visit the resort towns of Lorne, Aireys Inlet (on the old Cobb & Co coach route) and, on the return journey, Apollo Bay (once a whaling station). You can sample the delights of the fabulous surfing spots along the way and there is good fishing from the ledges along the rocky coastline and in the creeks which run from the steep hills down to the ocean. Walking enthusiasts will need strong shoes as many well-marked trails criss-cross the national and state parks in the area; some follow the routes of the old narrow gauge tramways once used to transport timber through the ranges.

Starting out from the town of Moriac, you cover gravel tracks (often boggy in sections) through the Alcoa Mining Lease and the Angahook–Lorne State Park. The swampy heathland areas bloom with wildflowers in spring and early summer. Expect to see swamp wallabies, echidnas and many species of birds including, if you are lucky, the endangered peregrine falcon. You will also notice forest areas slowly regenerating after the Ash Wednesday bushfires of 1983. There are breathtaking views over Anglesea from high vantage points, and the Moggs Creek Picnic Area is near the route as you wind down into Fairhaven.

Further south through Lorne and the Otway State Forest, the vegetation changes as the climate is wetter. Tall forests of mountain ash, messmate, manna and blue gum alternate with magnificent rainforest gullies. Take time to visit the Erskine Falls, which cascade over one of the highest drops in the ranges. Nearby Blanket Leaf Picnic Area is another pleasant stop. The timber industry brought settlement to the Otways, and you pass many small towns such as Forrest, situated on the remains of the timber tramway to Colac, Gellibrand and Beech Forest, once the hub of the timber industry, now a quiet tourist destination. Off our route, but worth a visit, are the giant tree ferns of Melba Gully State Park, near Lavers Hill. Glow-worms light the walking paths at night.

The Otway National Park has a variety of walking trails and rugged beaches. A short diversion from the route takes you to Cape Otway Lighthouse, the oldest on the Victorian mainland, which guides ships through the treacherous waters of Bass Strait. The tour finishes at Point Lewis on scenic Blanket Bay. Return to the Great Ocean Road via the same track and then on to Apollo Bay, Geelong and Melbourne; or take the inland route through Forrest to Colac.

Camping in Lorne–Angahook State Park is limited to areas at *Salt Creek* and *Hammonds Creek* (in the north) and near *Allanvale*. These are bush campsites. In the Otway National Park camp at areas on the banks of the *Aire River* and at *Blanket Bay* at the end of the tour. (Fresh water is usually available from Blanket Bay Creek.) Camp in the Otway State Forest at designated areas at *Stevensons Falls* and *Aire Valley Road* or choose your own bush site. There are also camping areas and caravan parks at a number of other coastal and bush locations in the Otway area: at *Lavers Hill*, *Forrest*, *Lorne*, *Aireys Inlet*, *Skenes Creek*, *Wye River*, *Apollo Bay* and the *Cumberland River Reserve*, 5 kilometres south of Lorne.

WARNINGS ▶ Do not attempt this tour after heavy rain as tracks quickly become boggy and sometimes impassable. Sections of track are subject to seasonal closure, usually from 31 May–end October. For information about

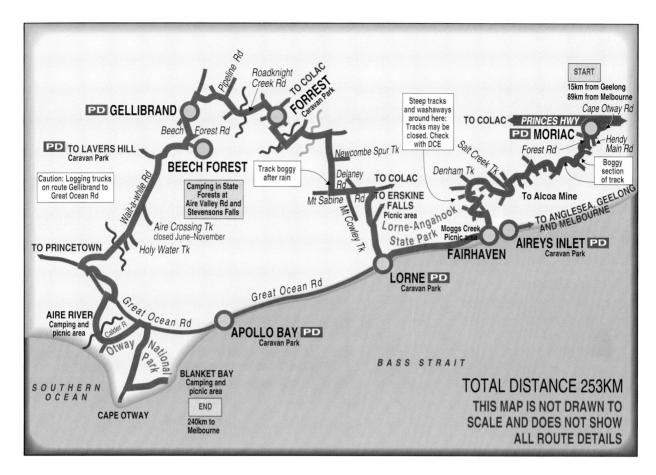

closures and road conditions, check with DCE offices at Colac, 83 Gellibrand Street, Colac VIC 3250; tel. (052) 33 5533; Geelong, cnr Fenwick and Little Malop streets, Geelong VIC 3220; tel. (052) 26 4667; or Melbourne, 49 Spring Street, Melbourne 3000; tel. (03) 651 3038. ▶ This tour is not suitable for caravans. ▶ No open fires in Angahook–Lorne, take portable gas stoves. Light fires only in fireplaces provided in Otway National Park. ▶ No pets or firearms. ▶ In the Otway State Forest observe regulations on rubbish removal, lighting of fires and use of firearms. ▶ Be careful of strong seas and incoming tides when fishing off rock ledges along the coast.

BOOKINGS AND PERMITS ▶ No permit required to traverse state parks or forests in the tour. ▶ Camping in the Angahook–Lorne State Park and Otway National Park at designated areas only (no charge). For detailed camping information for the Otway area contact DCE offices listed above or the rangers at Lorne, (052) 89 1732, or Apollo Bay, (052) 37 6889. ▶ Remember an amateur fishing licence is required to fish inland waters. Contact DCE offices for information. ▶ Check with Cape Otway Lighthouse before visiting. Ring (052) 37 9240. ▶ For general touring information on the Otway region, contact the

Geelong Otway Tourist Information Centre, National Wool Museum, cnr Moorabool and Brougham streets, Geelong VIC 3220; tel. (052) 37 9240; or the Melbourne Travel Centre, 230 Collins Street, Melbourne 3000; tel. (03) 619 9600.

ROUTE DIRECTIONS

Depart Melbourne CBD via Westgate Bridge and Princes Hwy to Geelong (approx. 74 km). Follow Princes Hwy west through Geelong for 15 km to Princes Hwy and Cape Otway Rd intersection.
START TOUR

0.0 km   Zero trip meter at s'post: Moriac. **TL** onto Cape Otway Rd.

> Colac straight ahead.

(5.6 km)

5.6 km   Cross railway line and immediately **TL** onto Hendy Main Rd at s'post: Torquay 23/Anglesea 30.

| Cape Otway Rd straight ahead. Moriac town centre straight ahead. **PD** |

(3.8 km)
9.4 km S'post: Larcombe Rd. **TR**.
(1.0 km)
10.4 km S'post: Forest Rd. **TL**.
(9.2 km)
19.6 km S'post: Gum Flats Rd. **TR**.
(1.2 km)
20.8 km S'post: Harrison Track (obscured). **TL** onto gravel.
(0.1 km)
20.9 km Intersection. **SO**.

| Another track enters on left. |

(3.6 km)
24.5 km
Intersection of tracks through boggy swamp area.

| All tracks lead back into main track. |

(2.4 km)
26.9 km Intersection. **KR** on main track at top of hill.
(0.1 km)
27.0 km
Boggy stretch then intersection.

| This section can be difficult and is often impassable after rain. A narrow track skirts around to the left avoiding the worst sections of the bog. |

0.0 km Zero trip meter at above intersection. **KR**.

| Another track leads ahead and to left. |

(0.2 km)
0.2 km Intersection. **SO**.

| Another track enters on left. |

(2.4 km)
2.6 km T intersection. **TR** and immediately cross causeway over swamp. T intersection. **TL**.
(0.9 km)
3.5 km Intersection. **TL** and **SO** to short steep jump up. **TR** at apex.

| Dam at top of jump up. |

(0.3 km)
3.8 km Intersection. **KR**.

View from Lorne–Angahook Park

| Alcoa Mine on left. Views of Anglesea in background. |

(3.0 km)
6.8 km T intersection. **TL**.
(1.5 km)
8.3 km Intersection. **SO** along Bald Hills Rd.

| Salt Creek Track on right. |

(1.4 km)
9.7 km Intersection. **SO**.

| Road enters on left. |

(1.3 km)
11.0 km S'post: No. 2 Rd. **KR** at Y intersection.

| Anglesea off to left. |

(0.3 km)
11.3 km Y intersection. **KR**.
(1.4 km)
12.7 km S'post: No. 2 Rd. **SO**.

| Denham Track on right. |

(3.3 km)
16.0 km S'post: Angahook State Forest. **SO** and immediately **KR** along No. 2 Rd.

| Bushland and walking trails. Batson Track on right. |

(4.8 km)
20.8 km S'post: Bambra Rd. **SO** at crossroads.

| Bambra Rd on left. Breakfast Creek Rd on right. Gate. Subject to seasonal closure. **See Warnings**. |

(1.5 km)
22.3 km S'post: Ironbark Spur Track. **TL**.

Sign: dry weather road only. Take care. Steep decline with ruts and washaways. If Ironbark Spur Track is closed, retrace to intersection with Breakfast Creek Rd and follow Bambra Rd, Seaview Rd and Gentle Annie Track to Moggs Creek Picnic Area. Pick up route directions.

(5.2 km)

27.5 km Creek crossing.

Take care. Steep ascent. Badly rutted with deep washaways.

(1.7 km)

29.2 km Gate.

Seasonally closed. **See Warnings.**

(0.1 km)

29.3 km T intersection. **TL** onto Rennicks Track.

Seasonally closed. **See Warnings.**

(5.4 km)

34.7 km Y intersection. **KR.**

(0.1 km)

34.8 km Intersection. **SO.**

Another track on right.

(0.6 km)

35.4 km Intersection. **KR.**

Another track on left.

(0.2 km)

35.6 km Intersection. **SO.**

Tracks on left and right.

(0.3 km)

35.9 km T intersection.

Track on right to Moggs Creek Picnic Area 1 km. No camping. Many bush walks from this picnic ground. Barbecues and toilets.

0.0 km Zero trip meter at above intersection. **TL.**

(0.7 km)

0.7 km S'post: Old Coach Rd. **TR.**

(0.7 km)

1.4 km T intersection. **TR** onto Great Ocean Rd in Fairhaven.

Aireys Inlet 3 km off to left. **PD** *Supplies and caravan park.*

(16.7 km)

18.1 km Erskine River in Lorne. Cross bridge.

PD *Supplies and caravan park.*

(0.8 km)

18.9 km Intersection. S'post: Forest Park/Erskine Falls.

0.0 km Zero trip meter at above s'post. **TR** in Lorne.

(8.6 km)

8.6 km Gravel.

(1.6 km)

10.2 km Intersection. **SO.**

Erskine Falls 1 km off to right. Magnificent rainforest and walking trails. Picnic area, barbecues and toilets.

(4.6 km)

14.8 km S'post: Mt Sabine Road/Forrest. **TL.**

S'post: Dry Weather Rd only. Colac off to right.

(3.3 km)

18.1 km Intersection. **KL.**

Delaney Rd on right.

(1.9 km)

20.0 km Intersection. **SO.**

Mt Cowley Track on left.

(7.3 km)

27.3 km S'post: Thompson Rd/Forrest 12. **TR.**

Seasonal closure. **See Warnings.**

(0.6 km)

27.9 km Track section boggy after rain.

(10.4 km)

38.3 km Intersection. **SO.**

Newcombe Spur Track on right.

(1.2 km)

39.5 km T intersection. **TL.**

(1.5 km)

41.0 km Cross bridge.

(0.6 km)

41.6 km T intersection. **TL** onto bitumen.

(0.6 km)

42.2 km Gravel.

(1.1 km)

43.3 km Intersection. **TR.**

(0.7 km)

44.0 km Creek. Cross bridge.

(0.4 km)

44.4 km S'post: Station St. **TR** onto bitumen.

(0.6 km)

Congram Creek, Otway Ranges

Otway pastures

45.0 km   T intersection.

> *Forrest Caravan Park and Forrest Hotel.*

0.0 km   Zero trip meter at above intersection. **TL** adjacent to caravan park and hotel.
(0.1 km)

0.1 km   S'post: Colac. **SO** over crossroads.
(2.7 km)

2.8 km   S'post: Roadknight Creek Rd. **TL** onto gravel.
(2.9 km)

5.7 km   Cross wooden bridge.
(6.8 km)

12.5 km   Intersection. **KR** at s'post: Ridge Rd (obscured).

> *Stevenson Falls Camping and Picnic Area off to left. Barbecue, toilets.*

(2.1 km)

14.6 km   Intersection. **SO.**

> *Pipeline Rd on right.*

(8.8 km)

23.4 km   S'post: Gellibrand. **TR.**
(4.7 km)

28.1 km   T intersection. **TL** onto bitumen.
(1.4 km)

29.5 km   Gellibrand River. Cross bridge, enter Gellibrand.
(0.8 km)

30.3 km   Gellibrand General Store. **PD**

0.0 km   Zero trip meter at store. **SO.**
(1.5 km)

1.5 km   S'post: Gellibrand East Rd. **TL.** S'post: Gellibrand Pottery. **TR** at T intersection onto gravel.

> *Lavers Hill straight ahead.*

(0.2 km)

1.7 km   S'post: Beech Forest 14. **SO.**

> *Gellibrand East Rd on left. Beware logging trucks next 45 km (to Great Ocean Rd).*

(3.3 km)

5.0 km   Gellibrand Pottery Gallery on left. **SO.**
(13.4 km)

18.4 km   S'post: Apollo Bay. **KL** onto bitumen.

> *Lavers Hill off to right.*

(0.3 km)

18.7 km T intersection.

> Beech Forest on left. Old timber town. Camping in state forest 6 km along Aire Valley Rd. Barbecues, toilets.

0.0 km Zero trip meter at above intersection. **TR**.
(14.0 km)
14.0 km S'post: Wait-A-While Rd. **TL** onto gravel.

> Lavers Hill straight ahead. Old timber town. **PD** Supplies, caravan park. Stands of rainforest found in creek beds near Wait-A-While Rd.

(5.6 km)
19.6 km S'post: Wait-A-While Rd. **SO**.

> Trees become smaller as you descend this track. Aire Crossing Track on left. Closed June–November.

(4.5 km)
24.1 km Intersection. **SO**.

> Holy Water Track on left.

(2.5 km)
26.6 km Y intersection. **KR**.
(3.2 km)
29.8 km Ford River. Cross bridge.
(1.5 km)
31.3 km Bitumen.
(0.4 km)
31.7 km T intersection. **TL** onto Great Ocean Rd.
(0.5 km)
32.2 km S'post: Old Ocean Rd. **TL** onto gravel.

> Blue gum forest. Trees smaller as you descend the track.

(8.4 km)
40.6 km S'post: Lavers Hill. **TR** onto Great Ocean Rd and onto bitumen.

> Apollo Bay off to left.

(0.5 km)
41.1 km S'post: Sand Rd. **TL** onto gravel.
(0.2 km)
41.3 km Gate.

> Leave gate as found. S'post: Access to Otway National Park.

(1.6 km)
42.9 km Y intersection. **KL**.
(1.9 km)
44.8 km Gate.

> Leave as found.

(2.4 km)
47.2 km Sign: Otway National Park.
(0.4 km)
47.6 km Aire River. Cross wooden bridge.

> Camping areas on river bank. Barbecues, toilets.

(1.6 km)
49.2 km Intersection. **TL**.
(2.3 km)
51.5 km Bitumen.
(0.7 km)
52.2 km Cross wooden bridge.
(2.5 km)
54.7 km S'post: Apollo Bay. **TR** onto Great Ocean Rd.
(3.9 km)
58.6 km S'post: Cape Otway. **TR** onto gravel.

> Otway National Park.

(9.0 km)
67.6 km Intersection. **SO**.

> Bimbi Park off to right. Private camping facility.

(2.0 km)
69.6 km Intersection.

> Track straight ahead leads 2.6 km to Cape Otway Lighthouse Reserve. No camping. 3.5 km to Cape Otway Lighthouse carpark.

0.0 km Zero trip meter. **TL** at above intersection.
(1.4 km)
1.4 km Gate. Cross bridge then **KL**.

> Leave gate as found.

(5.9 km)
7.3 km Blanket Bay camping area. Zero trip meter.

> Barbecues, toilets, water from Blanket Bay Creek. Approx. 40 km to Apollo Bay. **PD** Supplies.

END TOUR
Return to Great Ocean Rd by same track and then on to Melbourne (approx. 240 km) via Apollo Bay, Lorne and Torquay along Great Ocean Rd and Princes Hwy, or take inland route to Forrest and Princes Hwy.

CROAJINGOLONG NATIONAL PARK

START POINT Map page 61, M11.

TOTAL KM 120. Does not include approx. 480 km Melbourne to start point and approx. 550 km end point to Melbourne. **See Route Directions.**
UNSEALED KM 111.
DEGREE OF DIFFICULTY Easy.
DRIVING TIME Tour over 3 days. Allow time to/from start/end points. **See Route Directions.**
LONGEST DISTANCE NO FUEL 120 km (Cann River to Mallacoota).
TOPOGRAPHIC MAPS Auslig 1:1 000 000 series: *Eden; Mallacoota; Cann.*
LOCAL/SPECIALITY MAP Vic Roads administrative series: *Mallacoota 282014.*
OTHER USEFUL INFORMATION DCE visitors' information sheet: *Croajingolong National Park*; booklet: *Where to Camp in the Great Outdoors.* For all local information contact the DCE Cann River Information Centre or Mallacoota park office. (**See Bookings and Permits.**)

TOUR DESCRIPTION This trip takes in the coastal country of Victoria's south east and the state's most unusual national park – Croajingolong, with striking scenic contrasts in almost undisturbed rainforest, woodland and heath, together with ocean beaches, rocky promontories, inlets and coves. It is a naturalist's delight and a wonderful place in which to relax; the abundant wildlife includes rare species, and wildflowers are magnificent in spring. However, the very attractions of the remote wilderness make it necessary to choose your time to travel very carefully (**see Warnings; Bookings and Permits**).

The country is hilly and in parts sandy, but tracks are relatively easy provided recent weather has been dry; there is some overgrowth in early sections. In the park there are four coastal camping sites and picnic areas: *Thurra River, Mueller River, Wingan Inlet* and *Shipwreck Creek.* Ocean beaches are generally treacherous and swimming is recommended for experienced surfers only.

To reach the start point from Melbourne requires a long drive (approximately 6 hours), but an early departure should enable you to comfortably reach the first camping area in Croajingolong – Thurra River, set in unspoilt forest. Here you can relax in the bush or on the beach, or walk on the dunes where scrubs and heaths are the habitat of the rare eastern bristlebird and the ground parrot.

Returning to the route, you pass the turnoff to Mt Everard – from the summit you have a broad view of the park – then follow Cicada Trail to West Wingan Road, with Wingan Inlet campsite off to the right. Wingan offers fishing in surf, estuary and river; trails include a nature walk from camp to ocean beach, and at the day's end nocturnal marsupials such as possums, gliders and bandicoots can be seen by torchlight.

From West Wingan Road you leave the park and take a winding course through beautiful state forest, crossing the Wingan River and Hard To Seek Creek before re-entering Croajingolong and following Betka Track to the coast and the Shipwreck Creek campsite. On a leisurely walk you can explore the heathlands towards Mallacoota or Seal Creek; extending your stay, a day's trek will take you to the Benedore River. Before setting off on the long drive back to Melbourne, why not visit the beach at Mallacoota to fish or swim?

WARNINGS ▶ Legislation under discussion at the time of writing may result in closure of some four-wheel drive access tracks. Check with Information Centre at Cann River (**see Bookings and Permits**). ▶ Essential to contact Information Centre before departing from Melbourne; road conditions are unpredictable and sections may be closed at short notice. Two creek crossings fill after heavy rain. ▶ Certain sections (in particular, approaches to camps) are unsuitable for towing caravans. ▶ Camping at designated areas only in the park; bush camping is possible in state forest. ▶ It is advisable to carry emergency water supplies. ▶ Ocean beaches are dangerous: swimming is not recommended.

BOOKINGS AND PERMITS ▶ Advance booking essential at Christmas and Easter and in school holidays; minimum one week at all campsites at these times. Booking opens 1 September (Christmas) and 1 January (Easter). Contact DCE Information Centre, Princes Highway, Cann River VIC 3890; tel. (051) 58 6351. ▶ National park branch office at Genoa Rd, Mallacoota VIC 3892; tel. (051) 58 0263. ▶ Amateur fishing licence (AFL) is required to fish the Wingan River. Contact the DCE offices for information.

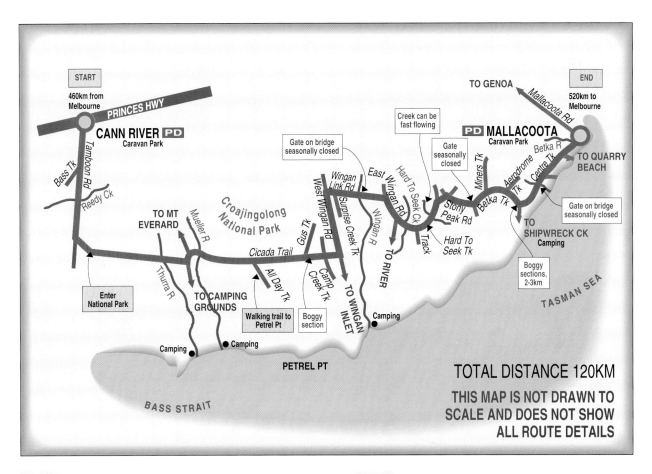

TOTAL DISTANCE 120KM

THIS MAP IS NOT DRAWN TO
SCALE AND DOES NOT SHOW
ALL ROUTE DETAILS

ROUTE DIRECTIONS

Depart Melbourne CBD via St Kilda Rd, Dandenong Rd and Princes Hwy to Cann River (approx. 460 km).

START TOUR

0.0 km   Zero trip meter in Cann River township at s'post: Tamboon Inlet/Pt Hicks. **TR** onto Tamboon Rd.

> **PD** *Caravan park and supplies. Next fuel Mallacoota (120 km).*

   (3.6 km)

3.6 km   Gravel.

   (4.4 km)

8.0 km   Y intersection. **KL**.

   (1.1 km)

9.1 km   Reedy Creek. Cross bridge.

   (7.2 km)

16.3 km   Y intersection. S'post: Pt Hicks. **KL**.

   (5.2 km)

21.5 km   Sign: Croajingolong National Park.

   (8.6 km)

30.1 km   Thurra River. Cross bridge.

   (6.3 km)

36.4 km   S'post: Mt Everard/Cicada Trail.

> *Thurra River and Mueller River camping areas straight ahead. Pit toilets, fireplaces and picnic facilities at both. At Thurra River: bush and beach walks, sand dunes; fresh water from river upstream from bridge. Further 5 km to Mueller River: access to inlet and beach; no fresh water. Surf beaches treacherous; for experienced swimmers only. Advance bookings required at both for holiday periods.*

0.0 km   Zero trip meter at above s'post. **TL**.

   (0.4 km)

0.4 km   Intersection. **SO**. Sign: Road closed 1 June to 30 September.

> *Mt Everard off to left, approx. 2 km up track and 1-km walk. Good views.*

   (1.1 km)

1.5 km   Cross Mueller River.

   (6.5 km)

At the Wingan River

Boggy track, Croajingolong

Spot the goanna

8.0 km S'post: Cicada Trail. **KL**.

> *Carpark. All Day Track to right: walking trail to beach near Petrel Pt.*

(5.0 km)

13.0 km Intersection. **SO**.

> *Gus Track off to left.*

(1.5 km)

14.5 km Boggy section. **SO**.

(5.2 km)

19.7 km Crossroads. S'post: Cicada Trail. **SO** over Camp Creek Track.

(1.4 km)

21.1 km T intersection: West Wingan Rd (good surface).

> *Wingan Inlet camping area approx. 10 km to right. Road unsuitable for caravans. Barbecues, toilets, picnic facilities. Fresh water in visitors' day area; information board. Access to beach and inlet; bushwalking; boating (limited) and canoeing; fishing (licence required for river). Advance booking necessary in holiday periods.*

0.0 km Zero trip meter at above intersection. **TL**.

(7.8 km)

7.8 km S'post: Wingan Link Rd. **TR**.

(0.6 km)

8.4 km Intersection. **SO**.

> *Surprise Creek Track on right.*

(11.7 km)

20.1 km Wingan River. Cross wooden bridge.

> *Gate on bridge may be closed.*

(2.3 km)

22.4 km T intersection. **TR** onto East Wingan Rd.

(0.2 km)

22.6 km Intersection. **KR**.

> *Track on left.*

(0.4 km)

23.0 km Intersection. **KL**.

> *Track on right: 4 km to river.*

(1.0 km)

24.0 km Hard To Seek Creek. Cross bridge.

(2.5 km)

26.5 km Intersection. **SO**.

> *Track on right.*

(3.0 km)

29.5 km Cross creek: cement causeway and rocky creekbed.

> *Creek can be fast-flowing.*

(2.9 km)

32.4 km Y intersection. **KR.**

(0.1 km)

32.5 km Crossroads. S'post: Stony Peak Rd. **TR.**

(6.0 km)

38.5 km S'post: Betka Track. **TL** through gate.

> *Seasonally closed.*

(2.6 km)

41.1 km S'post: Betka Track. **SO.**

> *Miners Track on left. 4WD only.*

(5.2 km)

46.3 km S'post: Betka Track/Shipwreck Creek. **KR.**

> *Aerodrome Track on left. Mallacoota 9 km. Next 2–3 km can be boggy in sections.*

(2.9 km)

49.2 km T intersection.

> *Shipwreck Creek camping area to right (5 sites). Approach unsuitable for caravans. Barbecues, pit toilet, picnic facilities. Fresh water from creek about 1 km upstream. Bush and beach walks; 500-m walk to surf beach; swimming for experienced surfers only.*

0.0 km Zero trip meter at above intersection. **TL** onto Centre Track.

(2.8 km)

2.8 km Creek. Cross wooden bridge.

> *Gate seasonally closed.*

(1.7 km)

4.5 km Y intersection. S'post: Centre Track. **KR.**

(1.2 km)

5.7 km Cross wooden bridge.

(0.3 km)

6.0 km Y intersection. **KL.**

> *Track on right.*

(0.7 km)

6.7 km Airstrip on left. **SO.**

(0.3 km)

7.0 km Cross wooden bridge.

Creek crossing, Croajingolong National Park

> *Track to Quarry Beach on right.*

(1.0 km)

8.0 km Bitumen.

(2.0 km)

10.0 km Betka River. Cross bridge.

(2.8 km)

12.8 km Roundabout in Mallacoota town centre. Maurice Ave and Betka Rd intersection. S'post: Genoa. Zero trip meter.

> **PD** *Caravan park and supplies. Beaches, good fishing.*

END TOUR

TL onto Maurice Ave–Main Mallacoota Rd. Return to Melbourne via Genoa and Princes Hwy (approx. 520 km).

THE EILDON FORESTS

START POINT Map page 50, F3.

TOTAL KM 358. Does not include 60 km Melbourne to start point and 60 km end point to Melbourne. *See Route Directions.*

UNSEALED KM 174.

DEGREE OF DIFFICULTY Difficult.

DRIVING TIME Tour over 2 or 3 days. Allow extra time to get to/from start/end points. *See Route Directions.*

LONGEST DISTANCE NO FUEL Fuel at Healesville, Alexandra, Mansfield, Jamieson, Marysville.

TOPOGRAPHIC MAP Auslig 1:250 000 series: *Warburton.* See also 1:100 000 series.

LOCAL/SPECIALITY MAPS Broadbent tourist map: *Lake Eildon and District*; DCE maps: *Toolangi–Black Range Forests*; *Eildon–Big River Forest.*

OTHER USEFUL INFORMATION DCE information sheets: *Eildon State Park*; *Fraser National Park*; *Big River Valley*; *Lady Talbot Forest Drive*; DCE booklet: *Where to Camp in Victoria's Great Outdoors.*

BEST TIME OF YEAR TO TRAVEL November–April, to avoid snow in winter and track closures.

TOUR DESCRIPTION This tour is through the high forest country to the north-east of Melbourne and traverses the Toolangi–Black Range and Eildon–Big River state forests. The forests are under DCE management and are zoned for various uses: timber production, nature conservation, recreation and education. Messmate, mountain ash and radiata pine plantations are logged in the area, and you can see some towering stands of giant mountain ash along the route. Rainbow and brown trout are abundant in the many streams and the area is a paradise for bushwalkers and gold fossickers and a habitat for native animals and birds.

You can camp in state forests and there are designated campsites which have some facilities in the *Murrindindi Scenic Reserve* and at *Stockmans Reward*, *Big River Camp*, *Frenchmans Creek*, *Cumberland Falls* and *Steavenson Falls*. The route allows access to *Fraser National Park* and *Eildon State Park*, both on the shores of man-made Lake Eildon, constructed to irrigate a vast stretch of northern Victoria and to provide hydro-electric power. If you wished to extend your tour there are plenty of opportunities to camp for a day or two in

Track near Marysville

attractive lakeside settings. There are also numerous private facilities along our route offering camping and accommodation.

WARNINGS ▶ Tracks on this tour may be closed by the DCE due to snow and wet weather; at least one section is closed June–November. Some tracks are certainly impassable after rain. If in doubt check with DCE offices at Healesville or Alexandra, see *Bookings and Permits.* ▶ Do not attempt Mt Terrible Track after wet weather. This section best undertaken in company with another vehicle. If in doubt, bypass the section, *see Route Directions*. ▶ Most parts of this tour not suitable for caravans and trailers. ▶ Beware logging trucks on all forest tracks. ▶ Observe regulations on lighting of fires, locations of campsites, litter disposal and sanitation when picnicking or camping in state forests, state parks and national parks. ▶ An amateur fishing licence required to fish inland waters, contact DCE offices for information.

BOOKINGS AND PERMITS ▶ Bush camping is allowed in state forests except where otherwise indicated. No permits or bookings are necessary but obtain information and regulations from DCE head office or offices at Healesville: Maroondah Highway, Healesville VIC 3777; tel. (059) 62 4900; Alexandra: 46 Aitken Street, Alexandra, VIC 3714; tel. (057) 72 1633; Marysville: Lyell Street, Marysville VIC 3779; tel. (059) 63 3306. ▶ Permits to camp are necessary in Fraser National Park and Eildon State Park. Obtain information from DCE offices in Melbourne or Alexandra, or write to Fraser National Park, PO Box 153, Alexandra VIC 3714; tel. (057) 72 1293.

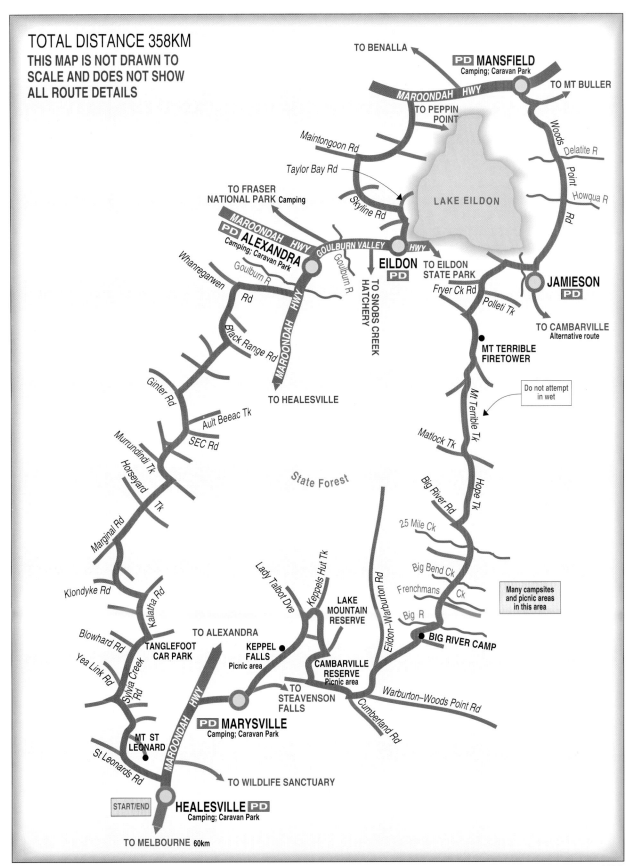

TOTAL DISTANCE 358KM
THIS MAP IS NOT DRAWN TO
SCALE AND DOES NOT SHOW
ALL ROUTE DETAILS

TO BENALLA

PD MANSFIELD
Camping; Caravan Park

TO MT BULLER

MAROONDAH HWY

TO PEPPIN POINT

Maintongoon Rd

Woods

Delatite R

Point

Howqua R

Rd

Taylor Bay Rd

LAKE EILDON

TO FRASER
NATIONAL PARK Camping

Skyline Rd

MAROONDAH HWY

PD ALEXANDRA
Camping; Caravan Park

Goulburn R

GOULBURN VALLEY HWY

EILDON PD

TO EILDON STATE PARK

JAMIESON PD

Whanreganwen Rd

Goulburn R

TO SNOBS CREEK HATCHERY

Fryer Ck Rd

Polleti Tk

TO CAMBARVILLE
Alternative route

Black Range Rd

MAROONDAH HWY

TO HEALESVILLE

MT TERRIBLE
FIRETOWER

Ginter Rd

Do not attempt
in wet

Ault Beeac Tk

Mt Terrible Tk

SEC Rd

Matlock Tk

Hope Tk

Murrundindi Tk

State Forest

Horseyard Tk

Big River Rd

25 Mile Ck

Marginal Rd

Big Bend Ck

Klondyke Rd

Lady Talbot Dve

Keppels Hut Tk

Frenchmans Ck

Kalatha Rd

Eildon–Warburton Rd

Big R

Many campsites
and picnic areas
in this area

TO ALEXANDRA

LAKE
MOUNTAIN
RESERVE

Blowhard Rd

TANGLEFOOT
CAR PARK

KEPPEL
FALLS
Picnic area

BIG RIVER CAMP

Yea Link Rd

Sylvia Creek Rd

CAMBARVILLE
RESERVE
Picnic area

TO
STEAVENSON
FALLS

Warburton–Woods Point Rd

MAROONDAH HWY

PD MARYSVILLE
Camping; Caravan Park

Cumberland Rd

MT ST
LEONARD

St Leonards Rd

TO WILDLIFE SANCTUARY

START/END

HEALESVILLE PD
Camping; Caravan Park

TO MELBOURNE 60km

THE EILDON FORESTS

ROUTE DIRECTIONS

Depart Melbourne north via Maroondah Hwy to Healesville Post Office (approx. 60 km).

> **PD** *Caravan park, camping and supplies.*

START TOUR

0.0 km Zero trip meter in Healesville opposite post office. Proceed north along hwy.
(0.7 km)

0.7 km S'post: St Leonards Rd to Myers Creek Rd. **TL** off Maroondah Hwy.
(7.1 km)

7.8 km Sign: Myers Creek Scenic Reserve. **SO**.

> *Picnic area.*

(4.1 km)

11.9 km S'post: Monda Track. **TR** onto gravel road.

> *Information board: Toolangi–Black Range Forest Drive.*

(3.4 km)

15.3 km Intersection. **SO**.

> *Mt St Leonards Lookout on right.*

(0.6 km)

15.9 km S'post: Quarry Rd. **TL**.

> *Sign: road closed 15 June–31 October.*

(3.9 km)

19.8 km **SO** through quarry.

> *Tanglefoot Carpark via Myrtle Gully off to right. Walking track only.*

(0.3 km)

20.1 km S'post: Sylvia Creek Rd. **TR** at T intersection.
(0.4 km)

20.5 km Intersection. **KR**.

> *Yea Link Rd on left.*

(3.8 km)

24.3 km Intersection. **SO**.
S'post: Blowhard Rd on left.
(1.0 km)

25.3 km Tanglefoot Carpark and Picnic Area on right.
(0.9 km)

26.2 km S'post: Kalatha Rd. **TL**.
(3.6 km)

29.8 km Intersection. **SO**.

> *Kalatha Link Rd on left.*

(0.1 km)

29.9 km S'post: Klondyke Rd. **TL**.
(2.1 km)

32.0 km Y intersection. **KR**.
(0.6 km)

32.6 km Intersection. **SO**.

> *Track enters on right.*

(4.0 km)

36.6 km S'post: Marginal Rd. **TR** at T intersection.
(4.3 km)

40.9 km Crossroads. **SO** over Horseyard Track.
(4.2 km)

45.1 km S'post: Murrindindi Track. **TL** at T intersection.

> *Murrindindi Scenic Reserve and Wilhelmina Falls off to right. Camping, pit toilets, barbecues. Easy walking track to falls from carpark.*

(1.1 km)

46.2 km Intersection. **TR**.
(1.5 km)

47.7 km Intersection. **SO**.
(2.6 km)

50.3 km Sign: Black Range State Forest. **SO**.
(0.5 km)

50.8 km S'post: Ginters Rd. **SO**.

> *SEC By-Pass Rd on right.*

(0.5 km)

51.3 km S'post: WP 22. **SO** along Ginters Rd.

> *Ault Beeac Track on right.*

(0.3 km)

51.6 Ault Beeac Picnic Area on right. **SO**.

> *Barbecue, picnic tables.*

(2.3 km)

53.9 km S'post: Tratford Break. **TR**.
(2.4 km)

56.3 km S'post: Tratford Break. **SO** over crossroads.
(0.8 km)

57.1 km Y intersection. **KR**.
(1.7 km)

58.8 km S'post: Black Range Rd. **TL** at T intersection.
(6.6 km)

65.4 km Intersection. **SO**.

> *Track enters on right.*

(3.7 km)

69.1 km S'post: to Whanregarwen Rd. **SO** along
Scrubby Creek Rd.
(2.6 km)

71.7 km T intersection. **TR** onto bitumen:
Whanregarwen Rd.
(8.7 km)

80.4 km S'post: Alexandra. **TL** onto Maroondah Hwy.

> *Healesville via Maroondah Hwy to right.*

(1.0 km)

81.4 km Goulburn River. Cross bridge.
(2.5 km)

83.9 km Crossroads. S'post: Eildon. Maroondah
Hwy on left.

> **PD** *Caravan park, supplies in Alexandra.
> Farming town and base for alpine activities.*

0.0 km Zero trip meter at above intersection. **SO**
over crossroads onto Goulburn Valley Hwy.

> *Sign: road unsuitable for caravans and trailers.*

(1.9 km)

1.9 km S'post: Eildon. **SO** along Goulburn Valley
Hwy.

> *Fraser National Park off to left.*

(7.4 km)

9.3 km Goulburn River. Cross bridge.
(3.1 km)

12.4 km S'post: Eildon. **SO** through Thornton.

> *Turn now for Healesville and Melbourne.*

(8.5 km)

20.9 km Intersection. **SO**.

> *Snobs Creek Fish Hatchery on right. Research
> centre open daily to visitors 10 am–4 pm.*

(3.6 km)

24.5 km Eildon Pondage Picnic Area on left.

> *Fireplaces, toilets.*

(1.1 km)

25.6 km Intersection. S'post: Taylor Bay.

> *Eildon town centre.* **PD** *Supplies, caravan
> park and camping area. Access to Lake
> Eildon: boating and fishing. Access to Eildon
> State Park and Jerusalem Creek Camping
> Area 8 km straight ahead. Permit required to
> camp. Barbecues, toilets, fresh water.*

0.0 km Zero trip meter at above intersection. **TL**.
(0.1 km)

0.1 km Intersection. **KR** along Centre Ave.

> *Riverside Drive on left.*

(0.3 km)

0.4 km S'post: Taylor Bay. **TL** onto High St at crossroads.
(0.9 km)

1.3 km S'post: Taylor Bay. **SO** through roundabout.

> *Thornton off to left.*

(0.7 km)

2.0 km S'post: Taylor Bay. **TL** onto Skyline Rd.
(9.7 km)

11.7 km S'post: Bonnie Doon. Take 2nd exit at
roundabout and continue along Skyline Rd.

> *Alexandra off to left. Fraser National Park
> on right. Camping, toilets, gas barbecues.
> Permit required to camp.*

(2.2 km)

13.9 km Gravel.
(6.4 km)

20.3 km T intersection. S'post: Maintongoon Rd. **TR**.
(5.0 km)

25.3 km Intersection. **SO**.

> *Sonenberg Rd on right.*

(6.0 km)

31.3 km S'post: Mansfield. **SO**.

> *Peppin Point off to right.*

(1.4 km)

32.7 km Bitumen.
(7.0 km)

39.7 km S'post: Mansfield. **TR** onto Maroondah Hwy.

> *Turn left to Bonnie Doon and Melbourne.*

(8.1 km)

47.8 km S'post: Mansfield. **SO** along Maroondah Hwy.

> *Benalla/Midland Link Hwy on left.*

(12.3 km)

60.1 km Mansfield town centre opposite post office.

> **PD** *Caravan park and camping. Supplies.
> Timber and resort town.*

0.0 km Zero trip meter at above point. **SO** through
Mansfield.
(0.5 km)

0.5 km S'post: Jamieson. **TR**.

> *Whitfield straight ahead.*

(0.7 km)

THE EILDON FORESTS

Keppel Falls, near Marysville

1.2 km T intersection. S'post: Jamieson. **TL**.
(2.4 km)

3.6 km S'post: Jamieson. **TR** onto Woods Point Rd.

> Road to Mt Buller straight ahead.

(9.0 km)

12.6 km Delatite River. Cross bridge.
(10.2 km)

22.8 km Howqua River. Cross bridge.
(12.5 km)

35.3 km S'post: Eildon. **TR** and immediately cross Goulburn River.

> Jamieson straight ahead. **PD** Alternative route south to The Triangle then west to Cambarville if conditions not good enough to try Mt Terrible Track. Pick up route directions at Cambarville.

(10.4 km)

45.7 km S'post: Mt Terrible Lookout. **TL** onto gravel at Bald Hill Gap.
(6.9 km)

52.6 km Intersection. **SO** along Mt Terrible Track.

> Fryers Creek Rd on right.

(2.0 km)

54.6 km S'post: Mt Terrible Track. **SO**.

> Polleti Track on left.

(5.1 km)

59.7 km T intersection. **TL**.
(0.4 km)

60.1 km Mt Terrible Fire Tower on left. **SO**.

> Refuge hut 50 m.

(0.5 km)

60.6 km Y intersection. **KR** down hill.
(0.4 km)

61.0 km S'post: Mt Terrible Track. **TL**.

> Track with gate on right.

(8.8 km)

69.8 km T intersection. **TL** onto Matlock Track. 30 m to s'post: Hope Track. **KR**.

> Matlock Track on left.

(3.1 km)

72.9 km S'post: Big River Rd. **TL** at T intersection.
(2.6 km)

75.5 km Cross Twenty-five Mile Creek.
(0.6 km)

76.1 km Intersection. **KL**.

> Twenty-five Mile Track on right.

(3.9 km)

80.0 km Big Bend Creek. Cross wooden bridge.

> Camping and picnic area on right. Barbecues.

(3.2 km)

83.2 km Intersection. **SO**.

> Vennells Campsite on right. Barbecues.

(2.6 km)

85.8 km Frenchmans Creek. Cross wooden bridge.

> Camping and picnic area on right. Barbecues.

(5.5 km)

91.3 km Intersection. **SO** along Big River Rd.

> Frenchmans Spur track on left.

(0.6 km)

91.9 km Big River. Cross bridge.

> Camping and picnic area on right. Barbecues.

(7.8 km)

99.7 km T intersection. **TR** along Big River Rd.

> Big River Camp on left. Barbecues.

(0.1 km)

99.8 km Intersection. **KL** onto Eildon–Warburton Rd.

> Road to Eildon on right.

(5.9 km)

105.7 km T intersection. **TR** onto bitumen: Warburton–Woods Point Rd.

> Woods Point off to left.

(0.8 km)

106.5 km S'post: Marysville. **TR** onto Cumberland Rd.

Warburton off to left.

(1.8 km)
108.3 km Intersection. **SO.**

Cambarville Recreation and Picnic Area on right. Barbecues, toilets and picnic tables. Relics of old sawmill and town.

(1.2 km)
109.5 km **SO** onto gravel.

Big Culvert historic site and walking track on left.

(5.5 km)
115.0 km S'post: Lake Mountain. **TR** onto bitumen.

Marysville straight ahead.

(0.6 km)
115.6 km Cascades Picnic Area on left. **SO.**

Barbecues, water, toilets, shelters.

(7.8 km)
123.4 km S'post (obscured): Upper Taggerty Rd. **TL** onto gravel.

Lake Mountain Resort straight ahead.

0.0 km Zero trip meter at above intersection.
(2.3 km)
2.3 km Y intersection. **KR.**

Bantick Rd on left.

(6.2 km)
8.5 km T intersection. S'post: Keppels Hut Track. **TL.**
(0.3 km)
8.8 km T intersection. S'post: Talbot Drive. **TL.**
(1.9 km)
10.7 km Intersection. **KR.**

Bantick Rd on left.

(5.3 km)
16.0 km Keppel Falls Scenic Reserve on right. **SO.**

Picnic area: toilets. Myrtle Loop Walking Track .

(1.2 km)
17.2 km Taggerty River. Cross bridge.

Picnic area on right. Fireplaces.

(2.7 km)
19.9 km Keppel Falls Lookout on right. **SO.**

View of falls on Taggerty River.

(0.8 km)
20.7 km Keppel Falls Walking Track on right. **SO.**
(0.5 km)

21.2 km Y intersection. **KL.**

Road to Phantom Falls on right.

(2.1 km)
23.3 km Athols Abbey Picnic Area on right. **SO.**
(3.9 km)
27.2 km Taggerty River Picnic Area on left. **SO.**

Information board, barbecues, toilets.

(2.1 km)
29.3 km Bitumen.
(0.4 km)
29.7 km T intersection. **TR** onto Cumberland Rd.
(0.5 km)
30.2 km S'post: Healesville. **TL** over Steavenson River into Marysville.
(0.1 km)
30.3 km Marysville town centre opposite general store.

PD *Caravan park and camping area. Supplies. Many bushwalking tracks in area.*

0.0 km Zero trip meter at above location.
(0.1 km)
0.1 km S'post: Healesville. **KR.**

Steavenson Falls off to left. Picnic area, toilets, barbecues. Walking tracks.

(6.9 km)
7.0 km Acheron River. Cross bridge.
(2.5 km)
9.5 km S'post: Melbourne. **TL** onto Maroondah Hwy.
(13.4 km)
22.9 km Watts River. Cross bridge.

Fernshaw Park on left: barbecues, toilets, picnic tables.

(7.5 km)
30.4 km Maroondah Reservoir on right. **SO.**

Picnic area, toilets, barbecues.

(3.2 km)
33.6 km Intersection. **SO.**

Badger Creek Road on left to Healesville Wild Life Sanctuary, open daily. A variety of native animals live in bushland setting.

(0.4 km)
34.0 km Healesville town centre opposite post office.
END TOUR
Return to Melbourne via Maroondah Hwy (approx. 60 km).

In the Franklin–Gordon Wild Rivers National Park

TOURS AROUND TASMANIA

Of all the Australian states Tasmania, with its early founding as a penal colony, its physical isolation from the mainland and its relatively small area, has retained the greatest proportion of untouched or restored historic sites and buildings. These bring added interest to treks through the coastlands and mountain forests of this most beautiful island.

The tours range from short and extremely difficult to long and easy, with plenty of variety in between, and although many of the roads are not restricted to four-wheel driving we take you often into non-frequented regions. Climatic conditions vary from the temperate east to the rugged, windswept west, and these extremes are paralleled by the varied and spectacular scenery. The mountain regions receive heavy winter snowfall.

THE WELLINGTON RANGE (a day tour: 40 kilometres). This is a most unusual tour: very short, but extremely difficult. Crossing the Wellington Range – although it is only a quick drive from Hobart – the terrain is rocky and inhospitable, requiring low-range four-wheel drive almost throughout and allowing an average of only 7 kilometres an hour. It is exciting, unique and memorable!

THE EAST COAST AND FORESTS (a day tour: 175 kilometres). Here is a change to the gentle conditions of the east coast – the holiday coast – much of the trip being through tall forests; in the coastal townships there are contrasting opportunities for deep-sea fishing and underwater exploration. Most particularly it gives access to the unique and unforgettable Maria Island National Park, well worth a camping stop to extend this otherwise fairly short tour to the historic village of Campbell Town.

THE FRANKLIN-GORDON WILDERNESS (a day tour: 86 kilometres). Here is an example of a wonderful experience crammed into a short space of both time and dis-

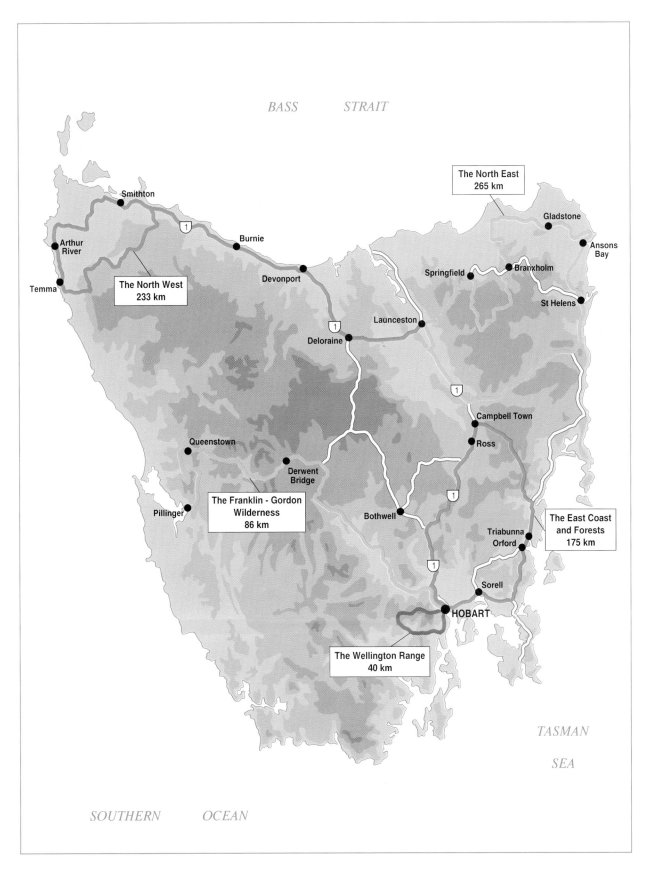

BASS STRAIT

The North East
265 km

Smithton

Gladstone

Burnie

Ansons
Bay

Arthur
River

Devonport

Springfield

Branxholm

The North West
233 km

St Helens

Temma

Launceston

Deloraine

Queenstown

Campbell Town

Derwent
Bridge

Ross

Pillinger

The Franklin - Gordon
Wilderness
86 km

The East Coast
and Forests
175 km

Bothwell

Triabunna
Orford

Sorell

HOBART

The Wellington Range
40 km

TASMAN

SEA

SOUTHERN   OCEAN

tance. Much of Tasmania's wild regions is inaccessible to vehicles; in fact, the final part of the track to Macquarie Harbour can be done only on foot and you must return to Queenstown the way you came. This is no hardship, however; even such a brief glimpse of the Wild Rivers National Park makes the trip one not to be missed.

THE NORTH WEST (a day tour: 223 kilometres). This

is your introduction to the rugged north-west coast and forests around the Arthur-Pieman Protected Area, named for the two rivers that mark its north and south extremes. Part of the coast road is through sand-dune country; then, south of Temma, you turn inland across marshy heathland and through vast forest reserves, working your way north-east. The environment is varied, from ancient rainforest and eucalypts to blackwood swamps and open plains, and the keen observer can discover equally varied wildlife.

THE NORTH EAST (tour over 2 days: 265 kilometres).

This is the longest of the Tasmanian tours; generally of moderate difficulty, it includes 3 sections for which alternative routes are given in case weather conditions or personal preference precludes their use. The north east is a popular tourist region; it takes in the beautiful Bay of Fires Coastal Reserve and Mt William National Park, and from there takes a wide sweep south to the tip of Ben Lomond National Park, where the adventurous can take the steep and narrow road to the mountain top. The route then ends in the agricultural Scottsdale country.

BEFORE YOU SET OUT ▶ Read the tour description

carefully. ▶ Check that you have obtained any necessary permits. ▶ Check weather conditions with local authorities or the Bureau of Meteorology. ▶ Make sure you have the appropriate maps and information for the tour. ▶ Check that your vehicle is in good order for the conditions ahead. Have you the necessary spare parts? ▶ If you are camping, have you the right equipment?

▼▼▼▼▼▼▼

TAKE CARE

● Don't take short cuts over virgin ground. You will destroy the vegetation. Stick to tracks open for use.

Bog on Mt McCall Road

USEFUL INFORMATION

For touring information contact:
Tasmanian Travel Centre
80 Elizabeth Street
Hobart 7000
(002) 30 0250.

For motoring and touring information contact:
Royal Automobile Club of Tasmania
 (RACT)
Cnr Patrick and Murray Streets
Hobart 7000
(002) 38 2200.

For four-wheel driving information contact:
Tasmanian Recreational Vehicles Association
22 Elliott Road
Glenorchy TAS 7010.

The World Heritage Area of the south west

TASMANIA'S NATIONAL PARKS AND FOREST RESERVES

The Department of Parks, Wildlife and Heritage manages the state's national parks and many other sites that include the Wilderness World Heritage area in the south west. On these tours you will encounter Maria Island, Mt William and Ben Lomond national parks, the Arthur-Pieman Protected Area and many forest reserves; all are covered in the DPWH booklet *Tasmania's National Parks and Reserves: a Visitors Guide.* For additional information contact DPWH head office, 134 Macquarie Street, Hobart 7000; tel. (002) 33 8011; or regional offices, given in the route directions.

Many of Tasmania's wild areas are accessible only to walkers, to whom the DPWH gives this advice.

▶ *Leave a walk plan with a responsible person, clearly indicating the time of your return.*

▶ *Make sure you have the right gear; Tasmania's weather can turn from sun to snow in a matter of hours.*

▶ *Use toilets where possible; bury waste 15 centimetres deep and 100 metres from campsites or watercourses.*

▶ *Keep your group small; a maximum of 8 is best.*

For information on forest reserves, contact the Tasmanian Forestry Commission, 134 Macquarie Street, Hobart 7000; tel. (002) 33 8011; or regional offices given in the route directions.

Please observe the following code.

▶ *Check with appropriate authorities regarding domestic animals; they are not allowed in national parks, but may be taken into certain other areas.*

▶ *Do not bring firearms into parks or reserves.*

▶ *If possible, light fires in fireplaces provided; if there are none, clear the surrounding area to not less than 3 metres, never leave a fire unattended, extinguish it carefully before you leave and be sure to observe total fire ban periods. Fires may not be lit in areas of peat or of grassed sand dunes.*

▶ *Keep to formed roads at all times.*

▶ *Use rubbish bins provided, or take your rubbish with you.*

▶ *Do not disturb or remove native plants or animals; all are protected.*

THE WELLINGTON RANGE

START POINT Map page 63, L6.

TOTAL KM 40. Does not include 8 km Hobart to start point and 30 km end point to Hobart. ***See Route Directions.***
UNSEALED KM 26.
DEGREE OF DIFFICULTY Extreme.
DRIVING TIME 3 hours. Allow time to/from start/end points. ***See Route Directions.***
LONGEST DISTANCE NO FUEL No fuel this tour.
TOPOGRAPHIC MAP Tasmap 1:100 000 series: *Derwent.*
LOCAL/SPECIALITY MAP Tasmap 1:25 000 series: *Collinsvale.*
BEST TIME OF YEAR TO TRAVEL November–March, but never in rain or fog.

TOUR DESCRIPTION This is an exciting drive through a spectacular, rocky landscape alternately revealing and concealing stunning views. It is short, but definitely for the true four-wheel drive enthusiast, climbing and crossing the range to the east of Hobart; you will need a key to open 2 gates kept permanently locked (***see Bookings and Permits***). The terrain is steep and unforgiving and for the most part requires continuous use of low-range four-wheel drive; the tracks are stony and often loose and slippery – the difficulty in creek crossings lies not in the level or speed of the water but in the rocks that form the creekbeds. In contrast, you emerge from the range onto undulating, green pastureland with great views over the Huon Valley, taking the Crabtree Road to Grove and the homeward run along the Southern Outlet.

Of additional interest on the road to the start point is the Cascade Brewery in South Hobart; this is the oldest continuously operated manufacturing enterprise in Australia and has been working since 1824; in a picturesque setting, it is well worth a visit.

WARNING ▶ Do not attempt after morning fog or rain.

BOOKINGS AND PERMITS ▶ Permission to enter and key to open gates should be obtained in person from DPWH, 134 Macquarie Street, Hobart 7000; tel. (002) 33 8011. ▶ For tourist information contact Tasmanian Travel Centre, 80 Elizabeth Street, Hobart 7000; tel. (002) 30 8250.

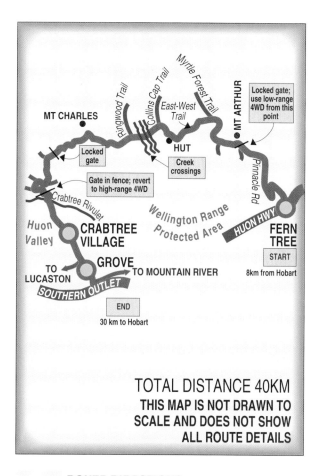

TOTAL DISTANCE 40KM
THIS MAP IS NOT DRAWN TO SCALE AND DOES NOT SHOW ALL ROUTE DETAILS

ROUTE DIRECTIONS

Depart Hobart south-east via Davey St (A6) and Huon Hwy (B64) to intersection at s'post: Mt Wellington in Fern Tree (approx. 8 km).

> *Before leaving, obtain key from DPWH (**see Bookings and Permits**).*

START TOUR

0.0 km Zero trip meter at above intersection. **TR** along Pinnacle Rd (C616).
(9.5 km)

9.5 km Intersection. **TR** through boom gate onto gravel (key required).

> *From this point, use low-range 4WD.*

(1.7 km)

11.2 km Intersection. **KR** downhill.
(3.5 km)

14.7 km Intersection. **TL** onto East West Trail.

> *Myrtle Forest Trail straight on.*

(3.2 km)

17.9 km Hut on left.
(1.1 km)
19.0 km Intersection. **SO**.

> *Collins Cap Trail on right.*

(0.7 km)
19.7 km Several creek crossings in quick succession.
(1.3 km)
21.0 km Intersection. **SO**.

> *Ringwood Trail on right.*

(7.6 km)
28.6 km Gate (key required).
(0.2 km)
28.8 km T intersection. **TL**.
(1.5 km)
30.3 km Intersection. **KR**.
(0.2 km)
30.5 km Intersection. **KL**.
(1.1 km)
31.6 km Gate in fence. **SO**.
(0.6 km)
32.2 km Crabtree Rivulet. Cross bridge.
(0.1 km)
32.3 km T intersection. **TL**.
(2.8 km)
35.1 km Bitumen. **SO** through Crabtree village.
(1.8 km)
36.9 km S'post: Grove (C618). **SO**.

> *Lucaston off to right.*

(2.7 km)
39.6 km T intersection. S'post: To A6. **TR**.

> *Mountain River off to left.*

(0.2 km)
39.8 km T intersection. S'post: Kingston/Hobart
(A6). Zero trip meter.
END TOUR
TL onto Southern Outlet (A6). Return to
Hobart (approx. 30 km).

Snow in the Huon Valley – an old machinery shed

Apple picking in the Huon Valley

Huon pine forest

THE EAST COAST AND FORESTS

START POINT Map page 63, N6.

TOTAL KM 175. Does not include 25 km Hobart to start point and 135 km end point to Hobart or 69 km end point to Launceston. *See Route Directions.*

UNSEALED KM 92.

DEGREE OF DIFFICULTY Easy.

DRIVING TIME A day tour. Allow time to/from start/end points. *See Route Directions.*

LONGEST DISTANCE NO FUEL 111 km (Triabunna to Campbell Town).

TOPOGRAPHIC MAPS Auslig 1:250 000 series: *South East*; *North East*.

LOCAL/SPECIALITY MAPS Forestry Commission Tasmania: *Forest Reserves, Southern Tasmania*; *Forest Reserves, Northern Tasmania*.

OTHER USEFUL INFORMATION Suncoast Regional Tourism Association booklet: *Tasmania's Suncoast ... from Bridport to Buckland.*

BEST TIME OF YEAR TO TRAVEL October–April, but possible at any time.

TOUR DESCRIPTION In this tour you leave the far south and drive through beautiful eastern coastland and forest, mainly on Forestry Commission tracks; bush camping is permitted in forest reserves. There are picnic areas and lookouts along the road from Sorell and through Sandspit Reserve, and walking trails in the reserve. You take a recently developed road to Orford, on the Prosser River estuary, and Triabunna, once a garrison town and whaling station, trees in this area are mainly blue gums that may grow to some 50 metres, and the view across Mercury Bay to Maria Island is wonderful. If you can extend the trip – temporarily forgoing four-wheel driving, since no tourist vehicles are permitted on the island – a ferry trip takes you to this former penal settlement that predates Port Arthur and is now perhaps the most fascinating of Tasmania's national parks: peaceful and pollution-free, with unusual ruins, it is also a fauna reserve where threatened mainland species have been introduced, and marine habitats can be explored by scuba diving or snorkelling. There is a campsite at *Darlington* with barbecues and toilets; others at *Frenchs Farm* and *Encampment Cove* have pit toilets only.

From Triabunna the road moves inland across Brook-

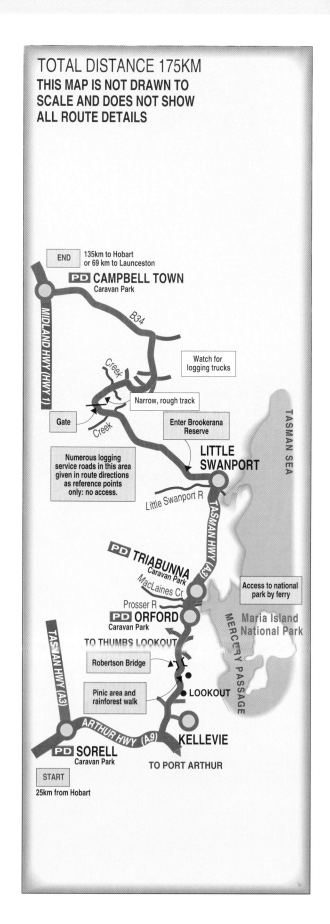

TOTAL DISTANCE 175KM
THIS MAP IS NOT DRAWN TO SCALE AND DOES NOT SHOW ALL ROUTE DETAILS

END — 135km to Hobart or 69 km to Launceston

PD CAMPBELL TOWN Caravan Park

MIDLAND HWY (HWY 1)

B34

Creek

Watch for logging trucks

Narrow, rough track

Gate

Enter Brookerana Reserve

Creek

LITTLE SWANPORT

Numerous logging service roads in this area given in route directions as reference points only: no access.

Little Swanport R

TASMAN HWY (A3)

TASMAN SEA

PD TRIABUNNA Caravan Park

MacLaines Cr

Prosser R

PD ORFORD Caravan Park

TO THUMBS LOOKOUT

Access to national park by ferry

Maria Island National Park

MERCURY PASSAGE

Robertson Bridge

Pinic area and rainforest walk

● **LOOKOUT**

TASMAN HWY (A3)

ARTHUR HWY (A9)

KELLEVIE

PD SORELL Caravan Park

TO PORT ARTHUR

START — 25km from Hobart

erana and Tooms White Gums reserves to historic Campbell Town in the midlands, a centre for the fine wool industry since the early 1820s.

WARNING ▶ Watch for timber trucks using forestry roads.

BOOKINGS AND PERMITS ▶ No permits required for forest reserves. ▶ For information on Maria Island National Park contact Ranger, Maria Island, c/- Post Office, Triabunna TAS 7273; tel. (002) 57 1420. ▶ For information on forest reserves, contact Forestry Commission office, Victoria Street, Triabunna TAS 7190; tel. (002) 57 3243. ▶ For tourist information contact Suncoast Regional Tourism Association, 20 Cecilia Street, St Helens TAS 7216; tel. (003) 76 1329.

ROUTE DIRECTIONS

Depart Hobart east via Tasman Bridge and Tasman Hwy (A3) to Sorell (approx. 25 km).

START TOUR

0.0 km Zero trip meter at Sorell Post Office. **SO**.

PD *Caravan park.*

(0.2 km)

0.2 km T intersection. S'post: Dunalley (A9). **TR**.
(21.5 km)

21.7 km S'post: Nugent (C335). **TL**.
(0.7 km)

22.4 km Gravel.
(1.9 km)

24.3 km S'post: Kellevie. **SO**.
(2.1 km)

26.4 km Intersection. **KR**.
(1.5 km)

27.9 km S'post: Thumbs Lookout. **KL**.
(2.4 km)

30.3 km Scenic lookout on right.
(6.3 km)

36.6 km Picnic area on right. **SO**. At 150 m, cross Robertson Bridge.
(9.5 km)

46.1 km Intersection. **SO**.

Road enters on right.

(0.5 km)

46.6 km Intersection. **KL**.
(5.6 km)

52.2 km Intersection.

Thumbs Lookout off to left. Picnic area 2 km.

Chinamans Bay, Maria Island

0.0 km Zero trip meter at above intersection. **SO**.
(3.9 km)

3.9 km Bitumen.
(0.2 km)

4.1 km T intersection. **TL** into Orford.

PD *Supplies, caravan park.*

(0.9 km)

5.0 km T intersection. **TR** onto Tasman Hwy (A3). Prosser River. Cross bridge.
(3.2 km)

8.2 km Intersection. **SO**.

Maria Island Ferry off to right. No vehicles permitted in national park; no supplies. Walking, swimming, scuba diving, camping. Historic ruins of penal settlement.

(3.6 km)

11.8 km Maclaines Creek. Cross bridge.

Triabunna town centre off to right. PD *Supplies, caravan park.*

(22.1 km)

33.9 km Little Swanport River. Cross bridge.
(0.9 km)

34.8 km Intersection. **TL**.
(0.3 km)

35.1 km Gravel.
(7.4 km)

42.5 km Intersection. **SO**.

Road on left. Watch for timber trucks next 40 km. The forestry tracks indicated in directions are service roads for timber work, included as reference points only; do not use. This is all natural timber country in sequential regeneration; you drive through an avenue of forest.

(2.9 km)

45.4 km Intersection. **SO.**

> *Road off to left.*

(0.8 km)

46.2 km Intersection. **SO.**

> *Road off to right. Sign: Brookerana Forest Reserve. Stand of Rocka Rivulet gums, rare in this area.*

(1.5 km)

47.7 km Intersection. **SO.**

> *Road on left.*

(7.0 km)

54.7 km Intersection. **SO.**

> *Road on left.*

(1.9 km)

56.6 km Intersection. **SO.**

> *Road on right.*

(0.4 km)

57.0 km Intersection. **SO.**

> *Road on left.*

(2.3 km)

59.3 km Intersection. **SO.**

> *Staggered crossroads.*

(2.2 km)

61.5 km Intersection. **SO.**

> *Road off to right.*

(0.9 km)

62.4 km Y intersection. **KL.**

(1.3 km)

63.7 km Y intersection. **KR.**

(0.8 km)

64.5 km Y intersection. **KR.**

(0.6 km)

65.1 km Y intersection. **KR.**

(1.1 km)

66.2 km Intersection. **KL.**

(1.2 km)

67.4 km Creek. Cross bridge.

(0.8 km)

68.2 km Grid.

(1.0 km)

69.2 km Intersection. **SO.**

> *Road on left.*

(0.7 km)

69.9 km Intersection. **SO.**

> *Road on right.*

(0.9 km)

70.8 km Gate.

> *Leave as found.*

(1.1 km)

71.9 km Intersection. **TR.**

> *Narrow, rougher track.*

(0.7 km)

72.6 km Intersection. **TL.**

(2.4 km)

75.0 km Intersection. **KR.**

(1.0 km)

76.0 km Creek. Cross bridge.

(0.4 km)

76.4 km Intersection. **SO.**

> *Road off to right.*

(1.0 km)

77.4 km T intersection. **TR.**

(2.9 km)

80.3 km Intersection. **SO.**

> *Road enters on left.*

(1.8 km)

82.1 km Crossroads. Sign: give way. **TL.**

(1.9 km)

84.0 km Intersection. **SO.**

> *Road on left.*

(9.4 km)

93.4 km T intersection. **TL** onto bitumen (B34).

(29.5 km)

122.9 km T intersection. Midland Hwy (Hwy 1) in Campbell Town. Zero trip meter.

> **PD** *Supplies, caravan park. Historic town. Wool growing and stud sheep centre; many National Trust buildings; nearby Evansville Game Farm.*

END TOUR

Return via Midland Hwy to Hobart (approx. 135 km) or Launceston (approx. 69 km).

THE FRANKLIN-GORDON WILDERNESS

START POINT Map page 62, E1.

TOTAL KM 86. Does not include 255 km Hobart to/from Queenstown or 252 km Launceston to/from Queenstown. *See Route Directions.*
UNSEALED KM 36.
DEGREE OF DIFFICULTY Moderate.
DRIVING TIME A day tour. Allow time to/from Queenstown. *See Route Directions.*
LONGEST DISTANCE NO FUEL No fuel this tour.
TOPOGRAPHIC MAP Auslig 1:250 000 series: *South West.*
LOCAL/SPECIALITY MAP Tasmap: 1:100 000 series: *Franklin; Lyell Highway: Map and Notes between Derwent Bridge and Strahan.*
BEST TIME OF YEAR TO TRAVEL November–April.

TOUR DESCRIPTION So much has been written and spoken about the Franklin-Lower Gordon Wild Rivers National Park that little remains to be said, but nothing you have heard can equal the experience of seeing this magnificent and awe-inspiring country with its dramatic waterways and towering gorges. This is the central portion of the World Heritage Area that extends right to the south coast; the short but memorable tour can be conveniently approached from either Launceston or Hobart.

As you complete the run along the Lyell Highway and descend the steep slope of Mt Owen you see the spectacular Queenstown hills, stripped of timber to fuel the copper-mining operations, that in certain lights appear in subtle shades of pink and gold; in Queenstown itself you can learn the history of the district at The Gallery.

The short trip – you must return the way you came – takes the Mt McCall Track to Bird River; there are breathtaking views of the wilderness area across Crotty Dam before you continue south to the picnic ground at the end of the track. From here you take the difficult but exciting walk to the Kelly Basin and the abandoned Pillinger settlement and perhaps look out across Macquarie Harbour, in this now tranquil setting, to once-infamous Sarah Island, a historic site.

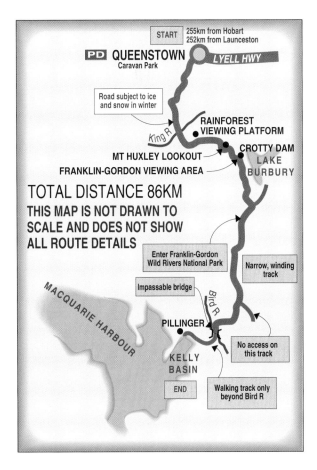

WARNING ▶ The last part of the track is rough, steep and often wet and slippery; in winter may be icy or snow-covered. Check conditions with Queenstown police, tel. (004) 71 1877.

BOOKINGS AND PERMITS ▶ For national park information contact DPWH office, PO Box 21, Queenstown TAS 7467; tel. (004) 71 2511. ▶ For tourist information contact Tourism Tasmania, 39–41 Orr Street, Queenstown TAS 7467; tel. (004) 71 1099.

ROUTE DIRECTIONS

Depart Hobart north-east via Lyell Hwy (approx. 255 km) or Launceston east via Bass, Marlborough and Lyell hwys (approx. 252 km) to Queenstown.
START TOUR

| **PD** *Information Centre and ranger.* |

0.0 km Zero trip meter at BP service station opposite Empire Hotel in McNamara St. **SO**. **(1.4 km)**

1.4 km Intersection. **SO**.

THE FRANKLIN-GORDON WILDERNESS

World Heritage country – the Bird River region

> *Caravan park off to right.*

(8.9 km)

10.3 km King River. Cross bridge.

> *Sign: road ahead subject to ice and snow in winter.*

(0.8 km)

11.1 km Rainforest viewing platform on left. **SO.**
(6.9 km)

18.0 km Mt Huxley lookout on left. **SO.**
(0.9 km)

18.9 km Franklin-Gordon viewing area over Crotty Dam on left. **SO.**
(6.9 km)

25.8 km Gravel.
(1.1 km)

26.9 km T intersection. **TR.**
(3.6 km)

30.5 km Sign: Franklin-Gordon Wild Rivers National Park. **SO.**

> *Narrow, winding track.*

(7.5 km)

38.0 km S'post: Mt McCall/Kelly Basin/Bird River. **TR.**

> *Locked barrier straight ahead. No access.*

(5.4 km)

43.4 km End track; impassable bridge.

> *Picnic area, not suitable for camping. 3-hr return walk to abandoned Pillinger Settlement and Kelly Basin on Macquarie Harbour.*

Return to Queenstown via same track (43 km). Zero trip meter.
END TOUR
Return to Launceston or Hobart (see start of tour).

THE NORTH WEST

START POINT Map page 64, D3.

TOTAL KM 223. Does not include 225 km Launceston to start point and 202 km end point to Launceston.
UNSEALED KM 176.
DEGREE OF DIFFICULTY Moderate.
DRIVING TIME Tour over 2 days. Allow time to/from start/end points.
LONGEST DISTANCE NO FUEL No fuel this tour.
TOPOGRAPHIC MAP Auslig 1:250 000 series: *North West.*
LOCAL/SPECIALITY MAPS Tasmap 1:100 000 series: *Welcome*; Forestry Commission Tasmania: *The Smithton District Forest Reserves.*
OTHER USEFUL INFORMATION Wilderness Getaway Tourism Association brochure: *Tasmania's West North West.*
BEST TIME OF YEAR TO TRAVEL November–April.

TOUR DESCRIPTION Tasmania's west is well known for its wild coast beaten by the Roaring Forties across the Southern Ocean and part of this tour parallels that coast, yet the north west also has some of the state's richest farmland and is an important forestry area. The tour begins at Smithton, a fishing industry town that contains as well Tasmania's most modern dairy farm, and from this district also comes much of the state's distinctive leatherwood honey.

Turn off the Bass Highway to Marrawah, then take the Arthur River Road south to the *Arthur-Pieman Protected Area*; you can camp here, but permission must be obtained from the ranger at Arthur River. Before reaching Temma you reach Rebecca Road: this is the alternative route east to use if the formidable Balfour Track is impassable; the Balfour Track is only for the experienced and adventurous, and before attempting it you should contact the Arthur River ranger. Rebecca Road is rejoined north of Balfour and Blackwater Road followed to Kanunnah Bridge; you can picnic there, or a little farther on if you wish to follow the rainforest walk in Julius River Reserve. A short distance beyond that is the 10-kilometre detour to the flooded limestone sinkhole, Lake Chisholm, and there you may just be lucky enough to catch a platypus unawares. At Tayatea Bridge the Arthur River is crossed again near another picnic ground, and you continue through forest to Mawbanna Road and the Bass Highway, to return to Launceston.

WARNING ▶ Before attempting the Balfour Track, contact Ranger, Arthur-Pieman Protected Area, c/- Post Office, Marrawah TAS 7330; tel. (004) 57 1225.

Bridge over the Rapid River

BOOKINGS AND PERMITS ▶ Permit to camp in Arthur River Protected Area from ranger at Arthur River (*see Warning*). ▶ For information on forests contact Forestry Commission office, PO Box 63, Smithton TAS 7330; tel. (004) 52 1317. ▶ For tourist information contact Wilderness Gateway Tourism Association, PO Box 973, Burnie TAS 7320; tel. (004) 31 1033.

ROUTE DIRECTIONS

Depart Launceston via Bass Hwy to Smithton (approx. 225 km).

> **PD** *Centre of Circular Head district.*

START TOUR

0.0 km Zero trip meter at Smith and Emmett streets intersection. S'post: Montagu (C215). **SO.**
(0.2 km)

0.2 km Traffic lights. S'post: Montagu (C215). **SO.**
(11.3 km)

11.5 km S'post: Marrawah. **TL** onto gravel: Barcoo Rd.
(2.1 km)

13.6 km Intersection. **KR.**

> *Edwards Rd on left.*

(1.1 km)

14.7 km Intersection. **SO.**

> *Williams Rd on left.*

(0.1 km)

14.8 km Intersection. **KL.**
(17.8 km)

32.6 km S'post: Marrawah. **TL** onto bitumen: Park Rd.
(3.7 km)

36.3 km T intersection. S'post: Marrawah. **TR** onto Bass Hwy (A2).
(20.1 km)

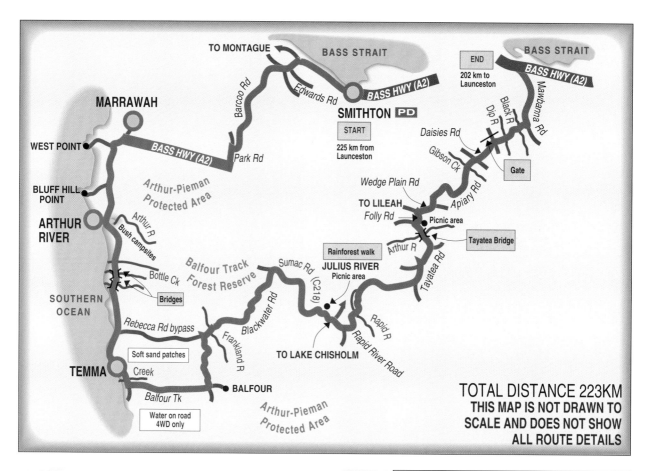

TOTAL DISTANCE 223KM
THIS MAP IS NOT DRAWN TO
SCALE AND DOES NOT SHOW
ALL ROUTE DETAILS

56.4 km T intersection. S'post: Arthur River (C214). **TL.**

> *Marrawah township off to right.*

(1.7 km)
58.1 km Gravel.

> *Sign: Arthur-Pieman Protected Area.*

(0.2 km)
58.3 km Intersection. **SO.**

> *West Point off to right.*

(7.5 km)
65.8 km Intersection.

> *Bluff Hill Point and lighthouse off to right.*

0.0 km Zero trip meter at above intersection. **SO.**
(4.7 km)
4.7 km Arthur River village.

> *DPWH office. Contact ranger for camping permit and condition of Balfour Track.*

0.0 km Zero trip meter at ranger office. **SO.**
(0.3 km)
0.3 km Intersection. **TL.** Arthur River. Cross bridge.

> *Camping area.*

(0.6 km)
0.9 km Intersection. **SO.**

> *Arthur Beach off to right.*

(1.2 km)
2.1 km Camping grounds on right. **SO.**
(5.5 km)
7.6 km Bottle Creek. Cross bridge.
(1.7 km)
9.3 km Cross bridge.
(1.4 km)
10.7 km Cross bridge.
(4.7 km)
15.4 km Crossroads. S'post: Temma.

> *Kanunnah Bridge off to left.*

0.0 km Zero trip meter at above intersection. **SO.**

> *Alternative route to left via Rebecca Rd avoids Balfour Track; joins plotted route at next zero trip meter.*

(7.8 km)

7.8 km **SO** through Temma.

> *Soft, sandy stretches in following section.*

(1.7 km)

9.5 km **KR** over sand dune.

(0.3 km)

9.8 km Cross bridge and grid.

(2.4 km)

12.2 km Cross bridge.

(0.6 km)

12.8 km Intersection. **KR**.

(1.0 km)

13.8 km Keep right across creek. **TL**.

(0.2 km)

14.0 km Intersection. **KL**.

> *S'post: Balfour, partly obscured, on tree in V of intersection. Following section includes many ground-water patches, usually with hard sand base; 4WD only. Check depth if in doubt.*

(14.1 km)

28.1 km Crossroads. **TL** onto main road.

> *Balfour village straight ahead.*

(8.8 km)

28.5 km S'post: Smithton.

0.0 km Zero trip meter at above intersection. **TR**.

> *Rebecca Rd bypass rejoins route. Occasional bitumen sections in next 90 km.*

(1.6 km)

1.6 km Frankland River. Cross bridge.

(15.8 km)

17.4 km T intersection. S'post: Tayatea Bridge (C218). **TR**.

(1.8 km)

19.2 km Sumac Lookout Carpark on left. **SO**.

> *View over Arthur River.*

(7.5 km)

26.7 km Intersection. **SO**.

> *Julius River Reserve on left. Barbecue, picnic tables. 30-min. return walk through rainforest.*

(2.9 km)

29.6 km Intersection.

> *Lake Chisholm off to left; 10 km return. 15-min. walk to lake from carpark.*

0.0 km Zero trip meter at above intersection. **KR**.

(2.8 km)

2.8 km S'post: Tayatea Bridge (C218). **KL** onto Rapid River Rd.

(4.1 km)

6.9 km Rapid River. Cross bridge.

(13.5 km)

20.4 km T intersection. S'post: Tayatea Bridge. **TL** onto Tayatea Rd.

(3.1 km)

23.5 km S'post: Tayatea Bridge. **SO**.

> *Road enters on left.*

(2.6 km)

26.1 km S'post: Tayatea Bridge. **SO**.

> *Road enters on right.*

(3.3 km)

29.4 km Arthur River. Cross Tayatea Bridge.

> *Picnic area, barbecue on right.*

(3.0 km)

32.4 km S'post: Folly Rd. **TR**.

(1.8 km)

34.2 km S'post: Wedge Plain Rd. **KR**.

> *Lileah off to left.*

(2.2 km)

36.4 km S'post: Apiary Rd. **TL**.

(10.3 km)

46.7 km Cross Gibson Creek.

(1.0 km)

47.7 km T intersection. **TR**. S'post: Daisies Rd. **TL**.

(5.2 km)

52.9 km Crossroads. **SO**.

> *Gate on left.*

(0.4 km)

53.3 km S'post: Mawbanna. **TL**.

> *Exit Daisies Rd.*

(1.0 km)

54.3 km Dip River. Cross bridge. **TL**.

(2.4 km)

56.7 km T intersection. S'post: Mawbanna. **TL**. Black River. Cross bridge.

(2.0 km)

58.7 km T intersection. S'post: Bass Hwy (A2). **TL** onto bitumen: Mawbanna Rd.

(10.4 km)

69.1 km Intersection. Bass Hwy. Zero trip meter.

END TOUR

TR onto Bass Hwy to return to Launceston (approx. 202 km).

THE NORTH EAST

START POINT Map page 65, Q6.

TOTAL KM 265. Does not include 167 km Launceston to start point and 57 km end point to Launceston. *See Route Directions.*

UNSEALED KM 202.

DEGREE OF DIFFICULTY Moderate.

DRIVING TIME Tour over 2 days. Allow time to/from start/end points. *See Route Directions.*

LONGEST DISTANCE NO FUEL 102 km (Ringarooma to Scottsdale).

TOPOGRAPHIC MAP Auslig 1:250 000 series: *North East.*

LOCAL/SPECIALITY MAP Forestry Commission Tasmania: *Forest Reserves in North-East Tasmania.*

OTHER USEFUL INFORMATION DPWH brochure: *Mt William National Park* (includes map); Suncoast Regional Tourism Association booklet: *Tasmania's Suncoast ... from Bridport to Buckland.*

BEST TIME OF YEAR TO TRAVEL November–April.

TOUR DESCRIPTION This is a tour through the northern part of Tasmania's Suncoast and the inland mountain forests, touching Mt William and Ben Lomond national parks and a number of forest reserves and including 3 challenging but rewarding alternatives. The forestry roads are generally well-made but slippery when wet, and in certain sections the track to follow will be the one avoiding a bog or a washaway. There are several campsites along or near the route, and bush camping is possible in forest areas.

Take time to explore the St Helens district before setting out on the major part of the tour, the climate here is milder than in other parts of the state and excellent for fishing, surfing and swimming. You can camp in the *Point State Recreation Area*, where there are wide beaches, huge sand dunes and pleasant walks, and the Georges Bay estuary is a sanctuary; in the township, visit the award-winning History Room and Museum. A few kilometres farther on there is a bush camping area at *Binalong Bay* – which claims to have the whitest sand in the world – and another at *Policemans Point* that gives access to the surf-fishing beaches of Ansons Bay; here also is the chance to do some deep-sea fishing and scuba diving, while the less energetic could enjoy a houseboat cruise. If you take the route that

North of Ansons Bay in Mt William National Park

enters Mt William National Park through the coastal heathlands north of Ansons Bay – which provides wonderful views of the rugged shoreline – make time to visit the historic lighthouse at Eddystone Point, so called for the resemblance to its famous English namesake. In the north of the park, the more venturesome can follow Forester Kangaroo Drive through an area famous for large numbers of these kangaroos and for the Bennetts wallaby.

A roughly south-westerly route through pastureland and forest brings you to the campsite in *Ben Lomond National Park* and to the tour's third alternative: the difficult climb to the Peak up the narrow road known as Jacobs Ladder. This magnificent area is best known as a ski field and Jacobs Ladder is certain to be snow-covered in winter, but although Ben Lomond is cold the alpine summer is beautiful, with a carpet of wildflowers. Finally, from wild Ben Lomond the forest roads lead you north again to the rich agricultural region around *Scottsdale* and a junction with the Tasman Highway for the return to Launceston.

WARNING ▶ Section to Eddystone Point may be impassable after rain; check conditions at Ansons Bay service station and general store.

BOOKINGS AND PERMITS ▶ No permits needed to traverse parks and forests. For information on Mt William National Park, contact the park office, Musselroe Road entrance, tel. (003) 57 2108; for Ben Lomond, contact DPWH Northern Region office, Bass Highway, Prospect TAS 7250; tel. (003) 41 5312. ▶ For information on forest reserves, contact Forestry Commission office, 24 King Street, Scottsdale TAS 7260; tel. (003) 52 2466. ▶ For tourist information contact Suncoast Regional Tourism Association, 20 Cecilia Street, St Helens TAS 7216; tel. (003) 76 1329.

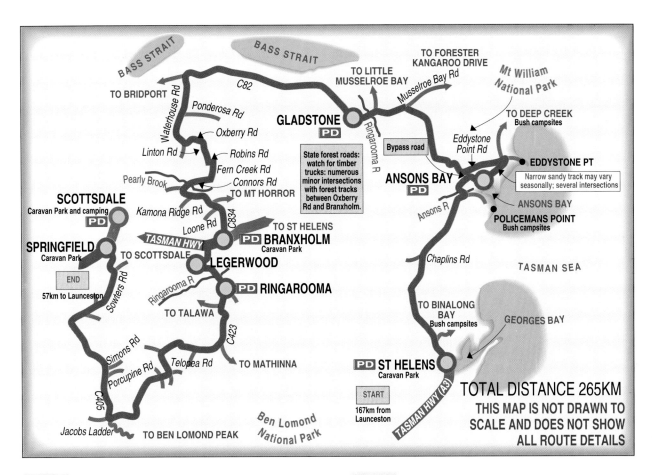

ROUTE DIRECTIONS

Depart Launceston CBD via Midland Hwy (Hwy 1), A4, A3 to St Helens (approx. 167 km).

> **PD** *Caravan park. Boating, fishing, surfing, water skiing, scuba diving; bushwalking. History Room and Museum; St Helens Point Recreation Area includes campsites.*

START TOUR

0.0 km Zero trip meter in Cecilia St, opposite post office, heading north on A3.
(0.3 km)
0.3 km S'post: Scottsdale (A3). **TL** into Tully St.
(1.0 km)
1.3 km S'post: Scottsdale (A3). **TR**.
(0.9 km)
2.2 km S'post: Priory (C843). **TR**.
(2.1 km)
4.3 km S'post: Priory/Ansons Bay.

> *Binalong Bay (C849) off to right; no through road. Camping area, no facilities.*

0.0 km Zero trip meter at above s'post: **SO**.
(5.0 km)
5.0 km Gravel.
(9.9 km)
14.9 km S'post: Ansons Bay. **SO**.

> *Chaplins Rd on left.*

(0.9 km)
15.8 km Intersection. **SO**.

> *Road enters on left.*

(15.6 km)
31.4 km S'post: Ansons Bay (C843).

> *Policemans Point 5 km off to right. Camping area; no facilities.*

0.0 km Zero trip meter at above s'post. **SO**.
(1.0 km)
1.0 km Ansons River. Cross causeway.
(4.0 km)
5.0 km S'post: Ansons Bay.

> *Gladstone off to left.*

0.0 km Zero trip meter at above s'post. **TR**.

THE NORTH EAST

> *Gladstone road to left bypasses the 4WD heathlands section north of Ansons Bay; joins plotted route at Eddystone Point Rd.*

(2.6 km)

2.6 km   Sign: Store. **KL** in Ansons Bay.

(0.3 km)

2.9 km   Intersection. **SO**.

> *Boobyalla Drive on right.*

(0.5 km)

3.4 km   Ansons Bay General Store on right.

> **PD** *Supplies. Beautiful beaches; diving, windsurfing, fishing; houseboat cruises. No camping on foreshores.*

(1.0 km)

3.5 km   Intersection. **TL** onto narrow, sandy track.

> *Tracks in this area may vary seasonally; keep to those most clearly defined by recent use.*

(0.1 km)

3.6 km   Intersection. **KL**.

(0.3 km)

3.9 km   Intersection. **KL**.

(1.7 km)

5.6 km   Sign on right: keep to main tracks. **SO**.

(0.4 km)

6.0 km   Intersection. **KL**.

(3.6 km)

9.6 km   Intersection.

> *Eddystone Lighthouse off to right; circular, granite tower classified as historic building. Deep Creek campsite straight ahead. This is the southernmost part of Mt William National Park.*

0.0 km   Zero trip meter at above intersection. **TL** onto Eddystone Point Rd.

(9.4 km)

9.4 km   T intersection. S'post: Gladstone.

0.0 km   Zero trip meter at above intersection. **TR**.

> *Bypass from Ansons Bay turnoff rejoins here.*

(16.5 km)

16.5 km   Bitumen.

(1.7 km)

18.2 km   S'post: Gladstone (C843).

> *Musselroe Bay Rd (C845) on right leads to Forester Kangaroo Drive (approx. 9 km) in Mt William National Park. Campsites on coast, some facilities. Inland site near Mt William.*

0.0 km   Zero trip meter at above s'post. **TL**.

(1.9 km)

1.9 km   Gravel.

(4.2 km)

6.1 km   Intersection. Sign: give way. **KL** onto bitumen.

> *Little Musselroe Bay off to right.*

(0.7 km)

6.8 km   Ringarooma River. Cross bridge.

(1.2 km)

8.0 km   Crossroads in Gladstone township. S'post: Bridport (C82). **SO**. **PD**

(4.8 km)

12.8 km   Gravel.

(14.7 km)

27.5 km   Bitumen.

(17.6 km)

35.1 km   Intersection: Waterhouse Rd. **TL** onto gravel.

> *Bridport straight ahead.*

(8.0 km)

43.1 km   Intersection. **SO**.

> *Ponderosa Rd on left.*

(4.9 km)

48.0 km   S'post: Oxberry Rd. **TL**.

> *Begins section of State Forest roads, well maintained but basically unmapped. Keep to charted tracks and watch for timber trucks. Take extra care after rain.*

(2.7 km)

50.7 km   Intersection. **SO**.

> *Road off to right.*

(0.3 km)

51.0 km   Intersection. **SO**.

> *Road off to left.*

(1.0 km)

52.0 km   Intersection. **SO**. Road on right.

(0.9 km)

52.9 km   S'post: Linton Rd. **TR**.

(1.0 km)

Broken bridge near St Helens

53.9 km Crossroads. **SO.**
(0.6 km)
54.5 km Intersection. **SO.**

Road on right.

(0.7 km)
55.2 km Intersection. **SO.**

Road on right.

(0.1 km)
55.3 km Intersection. **SO.**

Road on left.

(0.7 km)
56.0 km Intersection. **SO.**

Road enters on left.

(1.9 km)

57.9 km

Intersection. **KR.**
(0.7 km)
58.6 km Intersection. **SO.**

Road on right.

(0.7 km)
59.3 km S'post: Robins Rd. **TL.**
(1.6 km)
60.9 km S'post: Fern Creek Rd. **TR.**
(0.7 km)

61.6 km

Intersection. **KL.**
(1.8 km)
63.4 km Intersection. **KR** over crest.
(1.1 km)
64.5 km T intersection. **TR** onto Connors Rd.
(0.3 km)
64.8 km Intersection. **SO.**

Road on right.

(0.9 km)
65.7 km S'post: Base Rd. **TL.**
(0.2 km)
65.9 km S'post: Branxholm. **TL.**
(0.8 km)
66.7 km Pearly Brook. Cross bridge.
(0.4 km)
67.1 km Intersection. **KL** onto C834.
(0.4 km)
67.5 km Intersection. **SO.**

Kamona Ridge Rd on right.

(2.1 km)
69.6 km Intersection. **SO.**

Mt Horror off to left.

(2.9 km)
72.5 km S'post: Branxholm. **SO.**

Tasman Hwy off to right.

(0.5 km)
73.0 km S'post: Branxholm (C834). **KR.**
(1.2 km)
74.2 km T intersection. S'post: Branxholm. **TR.**
(1.0 km)
75.2 km Intersection. **SO.**

Loone Rd on right.

(3.0 km)
78.2 km Bitumen.
(2.1 km)
80.3 km T intersection in Branxholm. S'post: Scottsdale (A3).

THE NORTH EAST

| | Supplies, caravan park. Former mining town; now vegetable and dairying centre. |

0.0 km Zero trip meter at above intersection. **TR.**

| St Helens off to left. |

(1.1 km)

1.1 km S'post: Scottsdale. **SO.**

| C424 on left. |

(3.3 km)

4.4 km S'post: Ringarooma (C423). **TL.**

(3.0 km)

7.4 km T intersection in Legerwood. S'post: Ringarooma (C423). **TL.**

(3.5 km)

10.9 km Ringarooma River. Cross bridge.

(1.3 km)

12.2 km Ringarooma township, opposite post office. **SO.**

| | Farming and timber-milling centre. Views from nearby Mathinna Hill. Extensive pine plantations in Ringarooma-Scottsdale area. |

(1.8 km)

14.0 km S'post: Mathinna (C423). **TR.**

(3.6 km)

17.6 km Intersection. S'post: Mathinna. **SO.**

(1.9 km)

19.5 km Gravel.

(4.9 km)

24.4 km S'post: Targa. **TR.**

(7.0 km)

31.4 km Intersection. **KR.**

(9.2 km)

40.6 km S'post: Upper Blessington. **TL** onto Telopea Rd.

(2.1 km)

42.7 km S'post: Telopea Rd. **SO.**

| Upper Esk Rd on left. |

(3.0 km)

45.7 km Crossroads. S'post: Upper Blessington Rd. **TR.**

(2.7 km)

48.4 km Crossroads. **SO.**

(7.1 km)

55.5 km Bitumen.

(4.5 km)

60.0 km T intersection. S'post: Ben Lomond (C401). **TR.**

(3.4 km)

63.4 km S'post: White Hills (C401).

| Ben Lomond National Park to left; camping. Steep climb up Jacobs Ladder on gravel to Ben Lomond Peak. Magnificent scenery, wildflowers in spring and summer, snow in winter. Shelter, toilet facilities only at peak. Alpine village open during ski season. Road closed after heavy snow falls. |

0.0 km Zero trip meter at above s'post. **SO.**

(0.3 km)

0.3 km S'post: Camden Rd (C405 to A3). **TR.**

(0.7 km)

1.0 km Gravel.

(7.4 km)

8.4 km Intersection. **KL.**

| Porcupine Rd on right. |

(2.1 km)

10.5 km S'post: Camden Rd. **SO.**

| Simons Rd on right. |

(12.6 km)

23.1 km S'post: Diddleum Rd. **SO.**

(2.7 km)

25.8 km S'post: Scottsdale. **TL** onto Sowters Rd.

(3.5 km)

29.3 km Intersection. **KR.**

(6.7 km)

36.0 km

Intersection. **KR.**

(0.2 km)

36.2 km

Intersection. **KL.**

(0.4 km)

36.6 km

Intersection. **KR.**

(1.2 km)

37.8 km Bitumen.

(3.2 km)

41.0 km T intersection (C407). **TL.** S'post: Springfield. **TR.**

(2.4 km)

43.4 km T intersection: Tasman Hwy (A3). Zero trip meter.

| Scottsdale 7 km off to right. | Caravan park, camping area. |

END TOUR

Return to Launceston via Tasman Hwy (A3, approx. 57 km).

TREKS AROUND AUSTRALIA

The complete trip around Australia is divided into a number of treks, starting and ending at major population centres, so you can join in or leave when you wish. There are reverse directions for people travelling in the opposite direction. Treks are divided into sections, usually corresponding to a day's travel.

Each section has its own sketch map, detailed route directions and camping and permits information and is cross-referenced to the Australia-wide map coverage section of the book.

Tall timbers

THE COASTAL FORESTS

SYDNEY

«»

BRISBANE

1295 KILOMETRES

SYDNEY «» GLOUCESTER	319 km
GLOUCESTER «» KEMPSEY	284 km
KEMPSEY «» GRAFTON	244 km
GRAFTON «» BRISBANE	448 km

Taking an unusual route between the New South Wales and Queensland capitals, this trek gives an unrivalled opportunity to discover the forests of the Great Dividing Range running north from Sydney to the border. It is a beautiful trip and for the most part not a difficult one, allowing for the fact that mountain roads are usually steep and frequently narrow. It can be undertaken at virtually any time of the year but should be avoided after periods of heavy rain, whatever the season: roads can then be very slippery and creeks on occasion impassable. Always check conditions with officers of the New South Wales Forestry Commission, which manages the greater part of the region through which the route is plotted.

In addition to the beauty of the mountain landscape and the contrasting farming and grazing lands, this land is historically rich both in the pastoral country and in the forests that have been logged since the time of the nineteenth-century cedar-getters. The local maps recommended in the route directions include comprehensive descriptions of regional backgrounds, tree species, forest preservation and logging, and there are so many walks, reserves and vantage points both on and off the plotted route that we suggest you contact Forestry Commission regional offices before beginning each section.

178

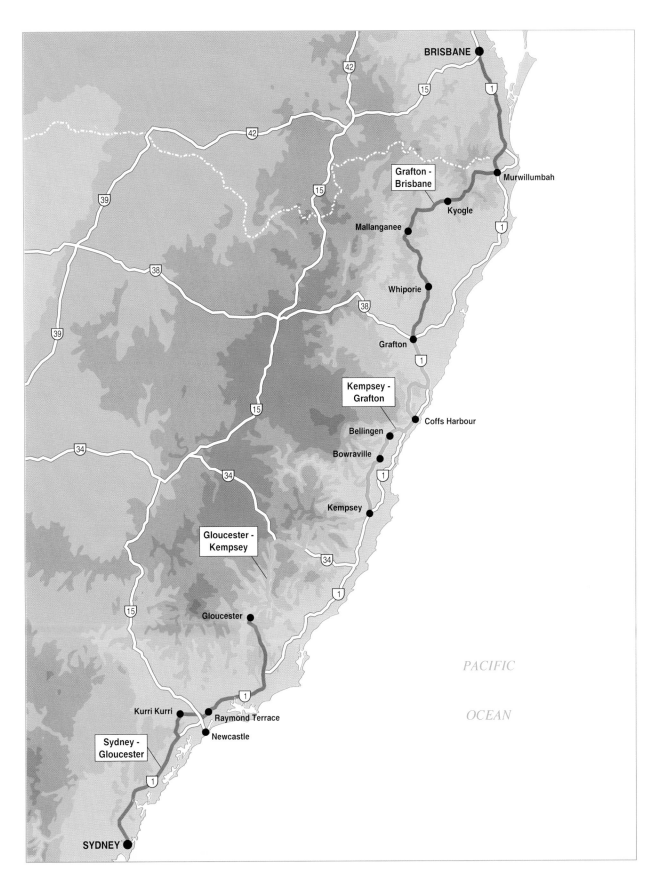

USEFUL INFORMATION

For touring information contact:
New South Wales Travel Centre
19 Castlereagh Street
Sydney 2000
(02) 231 4444.

For motoring and touring information contact:
National Roads and Motorists' Association (NRMA)
151 Clarence Street
Sydney 2000
(02) 9222.

For four-wheel driving information contact:
Four Wheel Drive Clubs Association of New South
   Wales and Australian Capital Territory
GPO Box 3870
Sydney 2001.

In the Myall River Forest

BEFORE YOU SET OUT ▶ Read the section description carefully. ▶ Check that you have obtained any necessary permits. ▶ Check weather conditions with local authorities or the Bureau of Meteorology. ▶ Make sure you have the appropriate maps and information for the trek. ▶ Check that your vehicle is in good order for the conditions ahead. Have you the necessary spare parts? ▶ If you are camping, do you have the right equipment?

NEW SOUTH WALES STATE FORESTS AND NATIONAL PARKS

By far the greater part of this trek runs through the state forests of north-east New South Wales. Most roads are well-maintained and the Forestry Commission has established a number of picnic areas with essential facilities. There are not many designated campsites, but bush camping is permitted anywhere in the forests – a handy guide for campers is cited in the route directions. For all information, contact the Forestry Commission of New South Wales, Building 2, 423 Pennant Hills Road, Pennant Hills NSW 2120; tel. (02) 980 4100; or regional offices, given in the route directions.

The plotted route does not enter a national park, but more than one is within easy reach. For information, contact National Parks and Wildlife Service, 43 Bridge Street, Hurstville NSW 2220; tel. (02) 585 6333.

To help maintain and preserve the forests for everyone, please observe the following code.

▶ *Camp at least 20 metres from any watercourse.*
▶ *Use existing clearings; do not remove or damage vegetation.*
▶ *Do not camp in established picnic areas.*
▶ *Use rubbish bins provided, or take your rubbish with you.*
▶ *When bush camping, make sure that latrines are at least 50 metres from streams or rivers and are well covered when you leave.*
▶ *In bush camps, light fires only in properly constructed fireplaces and never within 4.5 metres of a tree or a log. Flammable material should be cleared to at least 1.5 metres, and a fire must never be left unattended. The Forestry Commission suggests you do not enter forests at all during periods of total fire ban.*
▶ *Do not disturb native plants or animals; all are protected.*
▶ *Some areas are privately leased; respect owners' property.*
▶ *Fossicking is prohibited, except in certain specified areas.*

SYDNEY
«»
GLOUCESTER

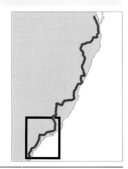

START POINT
Map page 3, K8.

TOTAL KM 319.
UNSEALED KM 77.
DEGREE OF DIFFICULTY Moderate.
DRIVING TIME 6 hours (Freemans Waterholes to Gloucester).
LONGEST DISTANCE NO FUEL Petrol 105 km (Booral to Gloucester); diesel 145 km (Raymond Terrace to Gloucester).
TOPOGRAPHIC MAP Auslig 1:250 000 series: *Newcastle.*
LOCAL/SPECIALITY MAPS NSW Forestry Commission: *Bulahdelah State Forests*; CMA: *Touring Map of the Hunter Area*; *Tourist Map of Barrington Tops and Gloucester Districts*; NRMA: *Newcastle and District*; *Lower North Coast*; *Sydney–Newcastle Freeway*.
OTHER USEFUL INFORMATION NSW Forestry Commission brochure: *Camping and Recreation in State Forests.*

DESCRIPTION The drive north from Sydney takes you through the eastern slopes of the Great Dividing Range with magnificent views of both the mountains and the coastal regions. It is a trip of generally moderate difficulty, but one or two sections need more care after rain and parts of the track through Myall River Forest are overgrown. Also in this forest are a number of creek crossings; each is through shallow water over a firm base but may be subject to flash flooding, although the floods recede quite quickly. In unfavourable weather the forest section can be avoided by taking the Bulahdelah–Gloucester road, approaching Bulahdelah either directly from the Pacific Highway or across from Booral.

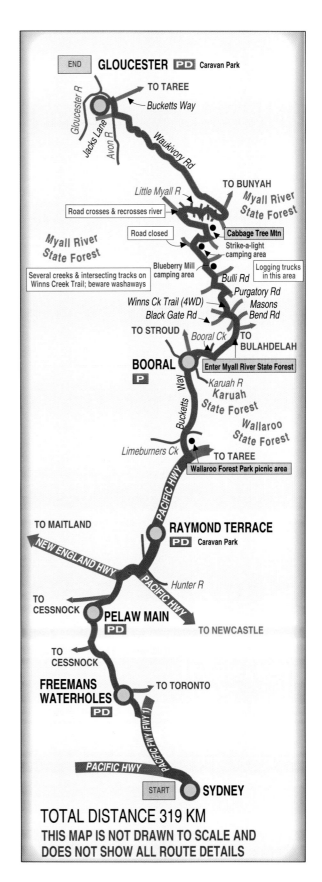

181

North-east of Raymond Terrace you briefly cross sections of Wallaroo and Karuah forests, then go through Booral to the possibly difficult but very beautiful four-wheel drive run through Myall River Forest; there are two forest campsites, *Blueberry Mill* and *Strike-a-Light*. At Blueberry Mill – site of an abandoned sawmill – you will be bush camping, but it's an excellent base for bushwalking; Strike-a-Light, in a rugged terrain with many mountain streams, has facilities for campers.

The mountain forests give way to lush dairying country as you follow the road to Gloucester, and about 16 kilometres west of this town is the little village of Copeland, well worth a visit. It was a booming goldfield town in the 1870s and the richest mine was the Mountain Maid; rainforest now covers the goldfield, but the Mountain Maid has been privately restored and visitors can see much of the original machinery in working order. There is a camping area at *Copeland Common*, and another at *Barrington Reserve*, on the road from Gloucester.

WARNINGS ▶ Watch for logging trucks in state forests. ▶ Some forest areas subject to thick mists in the colder months; be prepared for sudden changes in weather. ▶ Road through Myall River Forest four-wheel drive only. ▶ Creek crossings subject to flash floods. Check conditions at Forestry Commission offices (*see Bookings and Permits*).

BOOKINGS AND PERMITS ▶ No permits required to traverse or camp in state forests. For information, contact Forestry Commission regional offices: 184 Parry Street, Newcastle NSW 2300; tel. (049) 61 1771; 10 McKenzie Street, Bulahdelah NSW 2423; tel. (049) 97 4206. ▶ For local information contact Newcastle Tourist Information Centre, King Street, Newcastle NSW 2300; tel. (049) 29 9299; Gloucester Tourist Information Centre, Queen Street, Gloucester NSW 2422; tel. (065) 58 1408.

ROUTE DIRECTIONS

Depart Sydney CBD north via Harbour Bridge, Pacific Hwy, Pacific Fwy (Fwy 1); take Taree/Cessnock exit along Freeman Drive to Freemans Waterholes (approx. 125 km).

0.0 km Zero trip meter at roundabout. S'post: Taree.

PD *Memorial Mining Museum.*

(11.5 km) Opp. dir. s'post: Wyong. ▲ 48.6 km

11.5 km S'post: Kurri Kurri. **SO.**

Cessnock off to left.

(6.8 km) Opp. dir. s'post: Sydney. ▲ 37.1 km

18.3 km Pelaw Main centre, adjacent to BP service station. **SO.** PD
(0.6 km) ▲ 30.3 km
18.9 km In Kurri Kurri, s'post: Taree. **TR** into Railway St.
(0.3 km) ▲ 29.7 km
19.2 km At roundabout, s'post: Taree. **TR.**

Cessnock off to left.

(15.1 km) ▲ 29.4 km
34.3 km At roundabout, s'post: Taree. **SO.**
(1.2 km) Opp. dir. s'post: Sydney. ▲ 14.3 km
35.5 km S'post: Taree. **TR** onto New England Hwy.

Maitland off to left.

(4.0 km) Opp. dir. s'post: Sydney. ▲ 13.1 km
39.5 km S'post: Taree. **KL.** Immediately bridge over Hunter River.

Newcastle straight ahead.

(9.1 km) ▲ 9.1 km
48.6 km S'post: Taree.

Raymond Terrace town centre to left. PD *Supplies, caravan park. Historic homes and churches; Hunter Regional Botanic Gardens.*

0.0 km Zero trip meter at above s'post. **SO** along Pacific Hwy.
(17.9 km) ▲ 0.0 km
▲ 82.8 km
17.9 km S'post: Gloucester. **TL** onto Bucketts Way.

Taree straight ahead.

(4.8 km) Opp. dir. s'post: Newcastle. ▲ 64.9 km
22.7 km Walleroo Forest Park Picnic Area on right. **SO.**

Barbecues, picnic tables.

(1.7 km) ▲ 60.1 km
24.4 km Limeburners Creek. Cross bridge.
(16.0 km) ▲ 58.4 km
40.4 km Karuah River in Booral. Cross bridge. P
(1.2 km) ▲ 42.4 km
41.6 km S'post: Bulahdelah. **TR.**

Stroud straight ahead.

(3.1 km) Opp. dir. s'post:Newcastle. ▲ 41.2 km
44.7 km Booral Creek. Cross bridge.
(12.7 km) ▲ 38.1 km
57.4 km S'post: Jarrah Rd. **TL** onto gravel.

Signs: Myall River State Forest; sanctuary – no firearms. Logging trucks in this area.

(4.8 km) Bitumen. ▲ 25.4 km

62.2 km S'post: Jarrah Rd. **SO.**

> *Masons Bend Rd on right.*

(2.7 km) ▲ 20.6 km

64.9 km S'post: Jarrah Rd. **SO.**

> *Gorong Rd on left.*

(1.5 km) ▲ 17.9 km

66.4 km S'post: Jarrah Rd. **SO.**

> *Purgatory Rd on right.*

(0.9 km) ▲ 16.4 km

67.3 km S'post: Winns Creek Trail. **TR.**

> *Black Gate Rd on left. Sign: 4WD to Crawford Rd.*

(1.9 km) ▲ 15.5 km

69.2 km Cross creek.

> *Steep exit; some washaways.*

(0.8 km) ▲ 13.6 km

70.0 km Cross creek.

(0.8 km) ▲ 12.8 km

70.8 km Intersection. **SO.**

> *Road enters on right.*

(0.1 km) ▲ 12.0 km

70.9 km Cross creek.

(0.1 km) ▲ 11.9 km

71.0 km Cross creek.

(0.3 km) ▲ 11.8 km

71.3 km Cross creek.

(0.5 km) ▲ 11.5 km

71.8 km Intersection. **SO.**

> *Track enters on left.*

(0.5 km) ▲ 11.0 km

72.3 km Intersection. **SO.**

> *Track enters on left.*

(0.3 km) ▲ 10.5 km

72.6 km Cross creek.

(0.1 km) ▲ 10.2 km

72.7 km T intersection. **TL.** Continue along Winns Creek Trail.

(3.1 km) ▲ 10.1 km

75.8 km T intersection. **TL** onto Crawford Rd.

(3.7 km) Opp. dir. s'post: Winns Creek Trail. ▲ 7.0 km

79.5 km S'post: Johnsons Creek Rd. **SO.**

> *Jarrah Rd on left.*

(1.8 km) Opp. dir. s'post: Crawford Rd. ▲ 3.3 km

81.3 km S'post: Johnsons Creek Rd. **KL.**

Crossing a bridge in the Myall River Forest

> *Bulli Forest Rd on right.*

(1.5 km) ▲ 1.5 km

82.8 km Blueberry Mill Camping Area on right.

> *Bush camp; no facilities. Many walking trails.*

0.0 km Zero trip meter at camping area. **SO.**

(0.4 km) ▲ 0.0 km
▲ 2.5 km

0.4 km Intersection. **SO.**

> *Blueberry Rd on right.*

(2.1 km) ▲ 2.1 km

2.5 km Strike-a-Light Camping Area on right. **SO.**

> *Barbecues, pit toilets, picnic tables, fresh water from creek.*

0.0 km Zero trip meter at camping area. **SO.**

(0.1 km) ▲ 0.0 km
▲ 59.6 km

0.1 km Cross wooden bridge.

(0.7 km) ▲ 59.5 km

0.8 km Intersection. **TR** onto Archs Camp Rd.

Clearing the track

	Johnsons Creek Rd straight on. Road closed.
(0.6 km)	▲ 58.8 km
1.4 km	Intersection. **SO.**
	Cabbage Tree Trail on right.
(3.4 km)	▲ 58.2 km
4.8 km	T intersection. **TL** onto Cabbage Tree Rd.
(2.0 km)	Opp. dir. s'post: Archs Camp Rd. ▲ 54.8 km
6.8 km	Cabbage Tree Mountain on right. **SO.**
	Radio towers. Drive to mountain top.
(1.2 km)	▲ 52.8 km
8.0 km	Y intersection. **KR.**
(1.9 km)	▲ 51.6 km
9.9 km	S'post: Little River Rd. **KR.**
(4.8 km)	▲ 49.7 km
14.7 km	Cross creek.
	Road crosses and recrosses sections of Little Myall River.
(0.1 km)	▲ 44.9 km

14.8 km	Cross creek.
(0.1 km)	▲ 44.8 km
14.9 km	Double creek crossing.
(0.1 km)	▲ 44.7 km
15.0 km	Cross wooden bridge.
(0.1 km)	▲ 44.6 km
15.1 km	Cross creek.
(0.5 km)	▲ 44.5 km
15.6 km	Cross creek.
(0.4 km)	▲ 44.0 km
16.0 km	Cross creek.
(0.1 km)	▲ 43.6 km
16.1 km	Cross creek.
(0.3 km)	▲ 43.5 km
16.4 km	Cross creek.
(0.6 km)	▲ 43.2 km
17.0 km	Cross creek.
(1.5 km)	▲ 42.6 km
18.5 km	Cross creek.
(0.5 km)	▲ 41.1 km
19.0 km	Cross causeway.
(0.1 km)	▲ 40.6 km
19.1 km	T intersection. **TL** onto Waukivory Rd.
(1.1 km)	▲ 40.5 km
20.2 km	S'post: Gloucester. **SO.**
	Bunyah off to right.
(29.0 km)	Opp. dir. s'post: Bulahdelah. ▲ 39.4 km
49.2 km	Bitumen.
(5.0 km)	Gravel. ▲ 10.4 km
54.2 km	S'post: Gloucester. **TR.**
	Jacks Lane straight on.
(4.1 km)	Opp. dir. s'post: Bulahdelah. ▲ 5.4 km
58.3 km	S'post: Gloucester. **TL** onto Bucketts Way.
	Taree off to right.
(0.3 km)	Opp. dir. s'post: Waukivory. ▲ 1.3 km
58.6 km	Avon River. Cross bridge.
(1.0 km)	▲ 1.0 km
59.6 km	S'post: Gloucester Shopping Centre. **TR** into Gloucester township.

PD *Caravan park. Fishing, canoeing, fossicking. St Clement's Historic Park, Folk Museum; timber mill inspection by appointment. Copeland 16 km west of township.*

Opp. dir. s'post: Taree. ▲ 0.0 km
REVERSE DIRECTIONS START

GLOUCESTER
«»
KEMPSEY

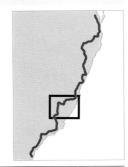

START POINT
Map page 5, L13.

TOTAL KM 284.
UNSEALED KM 212.
DEGREE OF DIFFICULTY Easy.
DRIVING TIME 8 hours.
LONGEST DISTANCE NO FUEL Next fuel Kempsey.
TOPOGRAPHIC MAPS Auslig 1:250 000 series: *Newcastle*; *Hastings*.
LOCAL/SPECIALITY MAPS NSW Forestry Commission: *Bulahdelah State Forests*; *Port Macquarie State Forests*; CMA: *Kempsey District Tourist Map*.
OTHER USEFUL INFORMATION NSW Forestry Commission brochure: *Camping and Recreation in State Forests*.

DESCRIPTION This is a fairly long trip but generally an easy one, continuing through the coastal mountain forests; the tracks rise and fall continuously from ridge peak to valley bed, and from the former there are often breathtaking views. There are 3 designated campsites: at *Maxwells Flat*, and about 100 kilometres beyond that there are 2 idyllic spots on the *Wilson River*.

Once on Knodingbul Road you drive almost entirely through state forest, leaving it briefly on the Oxley Highway, crossing the Hastings River, re-entering at Mt Boss and continuing to within 20 kilometres or so of Kempsey. In Dingo Tops Forest Park there are 2 walking trails and a picnic area; farther on, a short diversion to Blue Knob Lookout gives splendid views. On the left as you turn onto Hastings Forest Drive is A-Tree Blackbutt Natural Area, containing a magnificent stand of untouched blackbutt. Following a southern sweep, you reach Cobrabald Forest Park and the Wilson River camping areas, *Bluff* and *Wild Bull*.

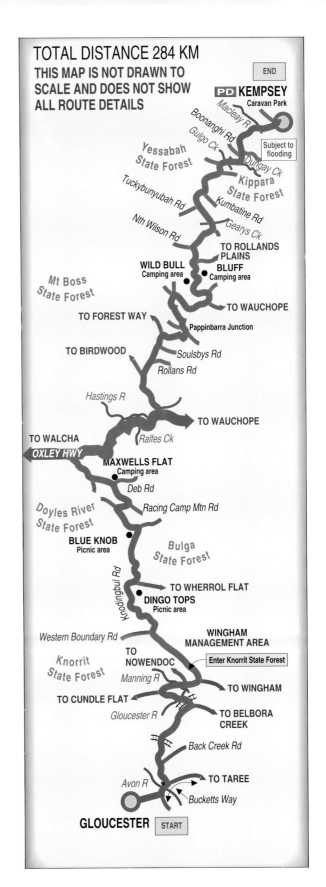

A slippery track

A pause in *Kempsey* brings a further opportunity to camp and swim. Kempsey is also a base for numerous day trips, notably the drive to historic Trial Bay Gaol at South West Rocks. Set in the Arakoon Recreation Area, this is witness to an abortive attempt at penal reform late last century – the trial, however, referring not to the penal service but to the first of many shipwrecks on this now historic section of the New South Wales coast.

WARNING ▶ Observe warnings given in previous section.

BOOKINGS AND PERMITS ▶ For information on state forests contact NSW Forestry Commission regional offices: 14 Queen Street, Gloucester NSW 2422; tel. (065) 58 1005; 27 Elbow Street, Kempsey NSW 2440; tel. (065) 62 1341. ▶ For local information contact Kempsey Tourist Information Centre, South Kempsey Park, South Kempsey 2440; tel. (065) 63 1555.

ROUTE DIRECTIONS

0.0 km Zero trip meter in Gloucester at Queen and Church streets intersection. S'post: Taree/Bucketts Way. **SO** along Queen St.
(0.4 km)   Opp. dir. s'post: Scone. ▲ 81.9 km

0.4 km S'post: Taree. **TR**.
(0.1 km)   Opp. dir. s'post: Scone. ▲ 81.5 km

0.5 km S'post: Taree. **TL**.

> *Newcastle via Bucketts Way straight ahead.*

(1.1 km)   Opp. dir. s'post: Scone. ▲ 81.4 km

1.6 km Avon River. Cross bridge.
(3.3 km)   ▲ 80.3 km

4.9 km S'post: Bundook. **TL**.

> *Taree straight ahead.*

(4.5 km)   Opp. dir. s'post: Gloucester. ▲ 77.0 km

9.4 km S'post: Bundook. **TL**. Immediately cross railway bridge.

> *Back Creek Rd straight ahead.*

(3.4 km)   Opp. dir. s'post:Gloucester. ▲ 72.5 km

12.8 km Cross railway line. Gravel.
(15.2 km)   Bitumen. ▲ 69.1 km

28.0 km S'post: Mt George. **TL**.

> *Belbora Creek straight ahead.*

(0.7 km)   Opp. dir. s'post: Gloucester. ▲ 53.9 km

28.7 km Cross railway bridge.
(2.5 km)   ▲ 53.2 km

31.2 km Gloucester River. Cross bridge.
(6.5 km)   ▲ 50.7 km

37.7 km S'post: Mt George. **TR**.

> *Cundle Flat straight ahead.*

(2.5 km)   Opp. dir. s'post: Gloucester. ▲ 44.2 km

40.2 km Manning River. Cross bridge.
(1.9 km)   ▲ 41.7 km

42.1 km Bitumen.
(0.1 km)   Gravel. ▲ 39.8 km

42.2 km S'post: Wingham. **TR**.

> *Nowendoc off to left.*

(6.0 km)   Opp. dir. s'post: Gloucester. ▲ 39.7km

48.2 km S'post: Knodingbul Forest Rd/Oxley. **TL** onto gravel.

> *Wingham straight ahead.*

(4.1 km)   Bitumen. ▲ 33.7 km

52.3 km Sign: Wingham Forest Management Area. **SO**.

> *Enter Knorrit Forest; route passes turnoff to old Connollys Creek tramline: walking trail. Continues through Dingo, Bulga and Doyles River state forests.*

(9.3 km)   ▲ 29.6 km
61.1 km Intersection. **SO**.

> *Western Boundary Rd on left.*

(20.3 km)   ▲ 20.3 km
81.9 km S'post: Oxley Hwy.

> *Wherrol Flat off to right. Dingo Tops Picnic Area. Barbecues, toilets, picnic tables.*

Opp. dir. s'post: Mt George.

0.0 km Zero trip meter at above s'post. **KL** along Knodingbul Rd.

> *Route passes Browns Lookout turnoff and Rowleys Rock Flora Reserve on right. Walking track to Rowleys Peak.*

(13.1 km)   ▲ 0.0 km
▲ 131.3 km
13.1 km S'post: Oxley Hwy. **TL** along Knodingbul Rd.

> *Blue Knob off to left. Panoramic views; picnic area.*

(6.3 km)   Opp. dir. s'post: Wingham. ▲ 118.2 km
19.4 km S'post: Causeway Rd. **KR**.
(3.1 km)   ▲ 111.9 km
22.5 km Cross causeway. Immediately **KL** along Causeway Rd.

> *Racing Camp Mountain Rd on right.*

(2.5 km)   ▲ 108.8 km
25.0 km Cross bridge.
(3.0 km)   ▲ 106.3 km
28.0 km Intersection. **SO**.

> *Deb Rd on right.*

(0.2 km)   ▲ 103.3 km
28.2 km Maxwells Flat Camping Area. **SO**.

> *Barbecues, toilets.*

(6.9 km)   ▲ 103.1 km
35.1 km T intersection. **TR** onto Knodingbul Rd.
(9.0 km)   Opp. dir. s'post: Causeway Rd. ▲ 96.2 km
44.1 km S'post: Wauchope. **TR** onto bitumen: Oxley Hwy.

> *Walcha off to left.*

(22.9 km)   Gravel. Opp.dir. s'post: Doyles River. ▲ 87.2 km

67.0 km Ralfes Creek. Cross bridge.
(6.1 km)   ▲ 64.3 km
73.1 km S'post: Birdwood. **TL**.

> *Wauchope straight ahead.*

(1.0 km)   Opp. dir. s'post: Walcha. ▲ 58.2 km
74.1 km Hastings River. Cross bridge.
(6.5 km)   ▲ 57.2 km
80.6 km Gravel.
(2.0 km)   Bitumen. ▲ 50.7 km
82.6 km S'post: Inlet Rd. **TR**.
(4.4 km)   ▲ 48.7 km
87.0 km S'post: Inlet Rd. **KL**.

> *Rollans Rd on right. Route traverses Mt Boss, Bellangry, Kippara and Yessabah state forests.*

(3.9 km)   ▲ 44.3 km
90.9 km Intersection. **KL** along Inlet Rd.

> *Soulsbys Rd on right.*

(1.8 km)   ▲ 40.4 km
92.7 km S'post: Cooks Rd/Pappinbarra. **TR**.

> *Forest Way straight ahead.*

(7.2 km)   Opp. dir. s'post: Inlet Rd. ▲ 38.6 km
99.9 km T intersection. S'post: Pappinbarra Junction. **TL**.
(0.5 km)   Opp. dir. s'post: Cooks Rd. ▲ 31.4 km
100.4 km S'post: Pappinbarra Rd Right Arm. **TR**.

> *Field Studies Centre off to left. Track follows the line of the valley, which is dotted with small farming properties.*

(0.2 km)   ▲ 30.9 km
100.6 km Cross bridge.
(4.4 km)   ▲ 30.7 km
105.0 km Cross bridge.
(2.0 km)   ▲ 26.3 km
107.0 km Cross bridge.
(4.3 km)   ▲ 24.3 km
111.3 km Crossroads. S'post: Hastings Forest Way. **TR**.

> *A-Tree Blackbutt Natural Area on left. Wilson River Reserve on left. Mackays Ridge straight ahead.*

(11.0 km)   Opp. dir. s'post: Pappinbarra. ▲ 20.0 km
122.3 km S'post: Cobrabald Recreation Area. **TL**.

> *Wauchope straight ahead.*

(0.9 km)   Opp. dir. s'post: Wilson River Reserve. ▲ 9.0 km
123.2 km Y intersection. S'post: Cobrabald Rd. **KL**.
(8.1 km)   ▲ 8.1 km

On a mountain track

131.3 km S'post: Bluff Picnic Area.

> *Sign: Cobrabald Recreation Area. Wild Bull Park off to left. Camping and picnic area. Barbecues, toilets, picnic tables, fresh water from river both at Wild Bull and nearby Bluff Picnic Area. Swimming holes.*

0.0 km Zero trip meter at above s'post. **KR**.
(1.3 km)   ▲ 0.0 km
                                              ▲ 1.3 km

1.3 km Wilson River. Cross bridge. S'post: Bobs Ridge Rd.

> *Bluff Picnic and Camping Area on right.*

0.0 km Zero trip meter at above s'post. **SO**.
(5.0 km)   ▲ 0.0 km
                                              ▲ 69.9 km

5.0 km Y intersection. **KL**.
(4.5 km)   ▲ 64.9 km

9.5 km S'post: North Wilson Rd. **TL**.

> *Rollands Plains straight ahead.*

(3.4 km)   Opp. dir. s'post:
                Cobrabald Recreation Area. ▲ 60.4 km

12.9 km S'post: Marowin Brook Rd. **TR**.

> *North Wilson Rd straight on.*

(13.1 km)   Opp. dir. s'post: Rollands Plains. ▲57.0 km
26.0 km S'post: Gearys Flat Rd. **TL**.
(1.1 km)   Opp. dir. s'post:
                        Tuckybunyubah Rd. ▲43.9 km
27.1 km Gearys Creek. Cross bridge.
(3.0 km)   ▲ 42.8 km
30.1 km S'post: Gearys Flat Rd. **SO**.

> *Tuckybunyubah Rd on left.*

(4.2 km)   ▲ 39.8 km
34.3 km Intersection. **SO** along Bears Rd.

> *Kumbatine Rd on right.*

(8.2 km)   ▲ 35.6 km
42.5 km S'post: Davis Rd. **TL**.

> *Bears Rd straight on.*

(2.4 km)   Opp. dir. s'post: Bears Rd. ▲ 27.4 km
44.9 km T intersection. **TR**.
(1.5 km)   Opp. dir. s'post: Davis Rd. ▲ 25.0 km
46.4 km Cross Gulgo Creek.
(2.6 km)   ▲ 23.5 km
49.0 km Dungay Creek. Cross causeway.

> *Causeway subject to flooding. Check depth.*

(0.3 km)   ▲ 20.9 km
49.3 km Intersection. **SO**.

> *Boonanghi Rd on left.*

(1.7 km)   ▲ 20.6 km
51.0 km Intersection. **SO**.

> *Clarkes Rd on right.*

(2.3 km)   Opp. dir. s'post: Dungay Creek Rd. ▲18.9 km
53.3 km Bitumen.
(5.3 km)   Gravel. ▲ 16.6 km
58.6 km Macleay River. Cross bridge.
(5.8 km)   ▲ 11.3 km
64.4 km S'post: Kempsey. **TR**.

> *Armidale off to left.*

(5.5 km)   Opp. dir. s'post: Sherwood. ▲ 5.5 km
69.9 km West Kempsey Post Office.

> *Kempsey town centre 2 km straight ahead.* **PD** *Supplies, caravan park. Wildlife Sanctuary and Nursery. Many interesting day trips in surrounding region.*

REVERSE DIRECTIONS START ▲ 0.0 km

KEMPSEY
«»
GRAFTON

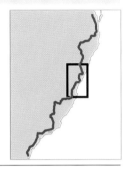

START POINT
Map page 5, N10.

TOTAL KM 244.
UNSEALED KM 98.
DEGREE OF DIFFICULTY Difficult.
DRIVING TIME 8 hours.
LONGEST DISTANCE NO FUEL 78 km (Kempsey to Bowraville).
TOPOGRAPHIC MAPS Auslig 1:250 000 series: *Hastings*; *Dorrigo*; *Coffs Harbour*; *Grafton*.
LOCAL/SPECIALITY MAPS NSW Forestry Commission: *Kempsey State Forests*; *Coffs Harbour State Forests*; CMA: *Coffs Harbour District Map*.
OTHER USEFUL INFORMATION NSW Forestry Commission brochure: *Camping and Recreation in State Forests*; Coffs Harbour Tourism booklet: *Discover Coffs Harbour*.

DESCRIPTION This trip is described as difficult only because of a short section in Wedding Bells State Forest: Boyds Road going towards Marys Waterhole Road is steep, with a loose gravel surface and many washaways. The remaining part is an easy drive that continues to follow the ridges, crystal streams and valleys of the eastern Great Dividing Range, combining this with dairy pastureland and thickly wooded forests. In the south-east of Ingalba State Forest is Cedar Park Reserve, where several large red cedars are preserved and groves of young trees have been planted in recent years.

There are no designated campsites on the plotted route, but – as in all the state forests, and particularly in Tamban and Ingalba – there are many places for bush camping off the beaten track; alternatively, there are caravan parks at *Coffs Harbour*, splendidly situated on the coast and backed by magnificent, timbered mountains. A stop at

Northern rainforest

Coffs Harbour offers surfing, fishing, canoeing, bushwalking and many tourist attractions – not forgetting the biggest banana in the world. Just north of the town is the noted Bruxner Park Flora Reserve with vegetation ranging from dry hardwood to rainforest; sample the walking tracks or enjoy great views with a picnic at Sealy Lookout.

The last stretch of the trip is a run up the Pacific Highway from Corindi Beach and through forest and pastureland to Grafton, centre of a rich farming and grazing district and a city of parks where, if you have timed your arrival for early November, you could be part of the famous Jacaranda Festival.

WARNING ▶ Observe forest warnings given for the first section of the trek.

BOOKINGS AND PERMITS ▶ For information on state forests, contact NSW Forestry Commission regional office: Cnr High and Hood Streets, Coffs Harbour Jetty NSW 2451; tel. (066) 52 8677. ▶ For local information contact Clarence River Tourist Association, Box 555, Grafton NSW 2460; tel. (066) 42 4677.

189

ROUTE DIRECTIONS

0.0 km Zero trip meter adjacent to West Kempsey Post Office, heading west along River St.
    (4.0 km) ▲ 34.5 km

4.0 km S'post: Spooners Ave/Frederickton. **TR**.

> *Armidale straight ahead.*

    (3.9 km) Opp. dir. s'post: Kempsey. ▲ 30.5 km

7.9 km Gravel.
    (0.1 km) Bitumen. ▲ 26.6 km

8.0 km S'post: Frederickton. **SO**.

> *Collombatti off to left.*

    (4.4 km) Opp. dir. s'post: Kempsey. ▲ 26.5 km

12.4 km Railway line. Cross bridge.
    (1.0 km) ▲ 22.1 km

13.4 km S'post: Collombatti Rd. **TL** onto bitumen.

> *Frederickton off to right.*

    (4.9 km) Gravel. Opp. dir. s'post: Spooners Ave. ▲ 21.1 km

18.3 km Gravel.
    (0.3 km) Bitumen. ▲ 16.2 km

18.6 km Y intersection. S'post: To Tamban Forest Drive. **KL**.

> *Seven Hills Rd on right.*

    (0.3 km) ▲ 15.9 km

18.9 km Railway line. Cross bridge.
    (0.5 km) Sign: Tamban State Forest. ▲ 15.6 km

19.4 km Y intersection. S'post: Range Rd. **KL**.
    (5.8 km) ▲ 15.1 km

25.2 km Y intersection. S'post: Forest Drive/Buds Crossing Rd. **KL**.

> *Range Rd on right.*

    (3.5 km) Opp. dir. s'post: Kempsey. ▲ 9.3 km

28.7 km Eungai Creek. Cross causeway.

> *Route now traverses Ingalba State Forest.*

    (2.0 km) ▲ 5.8 km

30.7 km T intersection. S'post: Stockyard Creek Rd/Cedar Park Forest Drive.

> *Stockyard Creek Rd on left.*

    (1.3 km) Opp. dir. s'post: Buds Crossing Rd. ▲ 3.8 km

32.0 km Y intersection. S'post: Stockyard Creek Rd. **KL**.

> *Sanders Rd on right.*

    (0.1 km) ▲ 2.5 km

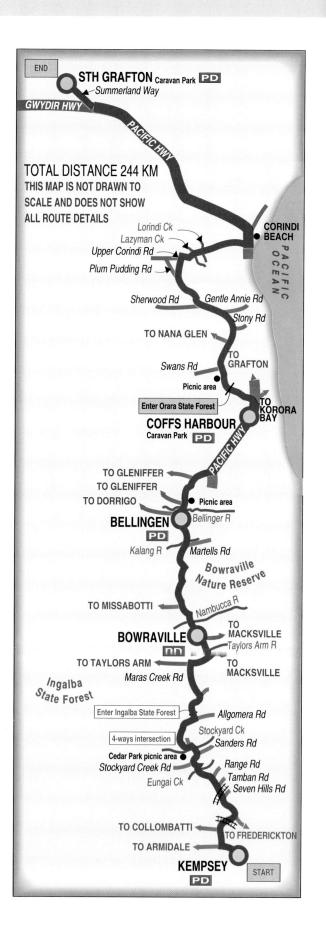

TOTAL DISTANCE 244 KM
THIS MAP IS NOT DRAWN TO SCALE AND DOES NOT SHOW ALL ROUTE DETAILS

Wooden bridge over swollen river

32.1 km	Y intersection. **KL**.	
	Calhouns Rd on right.	
	(0.9 km)	▲ 2.4 km
33.0 km	Cross Stockyard Creek.	
	(0.4 km)	▲ 1.5 km
33.4 km	Y intersection. S'post: Jacks Rd. **KL**.	
	Stockyard Creek Rd on right.	
	(1.1 km)	▲ 1.1 km
34.5 km	S'post: Jacks Rd.	
	Cedar Park 200 m off to left. Barbecues, fresh water.	
0.0 km	Zero trip meter at above s'post. **SO**.	
	(2.3 km)	▲ 0.0 km
		▲ 43.2 km
2.3 km	S'post: Eungai. **TR** onto Wittigs Rd.	
	(0.3 km)	▲ 40.9 km
2.6 km	4-ways intersection. S'post: Allgomera Rd. **KL** (hard left).	
	McKays Rd on right. Stockyard Creek Rd hard right.	
	(1.7 km)	Opp. dir. s'post: Wittigs Rd. ▲ 40.6 km

4.3 km	Intersection. **KR**.	
	(0.7 km)	▲ 38.9 km
5.0 km	Cross bridge.	
	(1.1 km)	▲ 38.2 km
6.1 km	Cross bridge.	
	(1.2 km)	▲ 37.1 km
7.3 km	Cross bridge.	
	(4.7 km)	▲ 35.9 km
12.0 km	Cross bridge.	
	(0.3 km)	▲ 31.2 km
12.3 km	S'post: Range Rd. **TL**.	
	(0.6 km)	▲ 30.9 km
12.9 km	Sign: Ingalba State Forest. **SO**.	
	(4.5 km)	▲ 30.3 km
17.4 km	Y intersection. S'post: Maras Creek Rd. **TL**.	
	(0.6 km)	▲ 25.8 km
18.0 km	Intersection. **SO**.	
	Teagues Knob Rd on right.	
	(0.2 km)	▲ 25.2 km
18.2 km	Intersection. **SO**.	
	(2.5 km)	▲ 25.0 km

20.7 km Cross bridge.
(3.3 km) ▲ 22.5 km
24.0 km Bitumen.
(0.2 km) Gravel. ▲ 19.2 km
24.2 km T intersection. **TR.**
(1.2 km) Opp. dir. s'post: Maras Creek Rd. ▲19.0 km
25.4 km T intersection. S'post: Macksville. **TR.**

> Taylors Arm off to left.

(6.0 km) Opp. dir. s'post: Utungun Hall. ▲ 17.8 km
31.4 km S'post: Bowraville. **TL** onto Congarinni North Rd. Immediately Taylors Arm River. Cross bridge.

> Macksville straight ahead.

(0.3 km) Opp. dir. s'post: Taylors Arm. ▲ 11.8 km
31.7 km Gravel.
(2.4 km) Bitumen. ▲ 11.5 km
34.1 km T intersection. S'post: Bowraville. **TL.**
(5.6 km) ▲ 9.1 km
39.7 km T intersection. S'post: Bowraville. **TL** onto bitumen: Wilson Rd.

> Macksville off to right.

(2.9 km) Gravel. ▲ 3.5 km
42.6 km S'post: High St. **TR** into Bowraville town centre.
(0.6 km) Opp. dir. s'post: Macksville. ▲ 0.6 km
43.2 km Bowraville town centre, adjacent to State Bank. **PD**
0.0 km Zero trip meter at State Bank. **SO.**
(0.7 km) ▲ 0.0 km
▲ 31.5 km
0.7 km Nambucca River. Cross Lanes bridge.
(0.3 km) ▲ 30.8 km
1.0 km S'post: Bellingen. **TL** onto Bowraville Rd.

> Macksville off to right.

(5.7 km) Opp. dir. s'post: Bowraville. ▲ 30.5 km
6.7 km Y intersection. S'post: Bellingen. **KR.**

> Missabotti off to left.

(0.9 km) ▲ 24.8 km
7.6 km Cross bridge onto gravel.

> This section skirts Bowraville Nature Reserve.

(13.3 km) Bitumen. ▲ 23.9 km
20.9 km Bitumen.
(0.4 km) Gravel. ▲ 10.6 km
21.3 km T intersection. S'post: Bellingen. **TL.**

> Martells Rd on right.

(1.8 km) Opp. dir. s'post: Bowraville. ▲ 10.2 km

23.1 km Spicketts Creek. Cross bridge.
(0.5 km) ▲ 8.4 km
23.6 km Kalang River. Cross bridge.
(7.8 km) ▲ 7.9 km
31.4 km S'post: Coffs Harbour. **TR** into Bellingen.

> Dorrigo off to left.

(0.1 km) ▲ 0.1 km
31.5 km In Bellingen, s'post: Gleniffer. **PD**
Opp. dir. s'post: Dorrigo.
0.0 km Zero trip meter at above s'post. **TL** into Wharf St.
(0.1 km) ▲ 0.0 km
▲ 34.3 km
0.1 km Bellinger River. Cross bridge.

> *Picnic ground on far side of river. Barbecues, tables.*

(0.6 km) ▲ 34.2 km
0.7 km Roundabout. S'post: Valery. **TR.**

> Gleniffer off to left.

(1.0 km) ▲ 33.6 km
1.7 km S'post: Hydes Creek/Valery. **TL.**

> North Bank straight ahead.

(3.6 km) Opp. dir. s'post: Bellingen. ▲ 32.6 km
5.3 km Cross bridge.
(2.2 km) ▲ 29.0 km
7.5 km T intersection. S'post: Gleniffer–Valery road.

> Gleniffer off to left.

(4.0 km) ▲ 26.8 km
11.5 km T intersection. **TR** onto gravel.
(5.1 km) Bitumen. ▲ 22.8 km
16.6 km Bitumen.
(1.7 km) Gravel. ▲ 17.7 km
21.3 km T intersection. **TL** onto Pacific Hwy.
(13.0 km) Opp. dir. s'post: Valery. ▲ 13.0 km
34.3 km Coffs Harbour town centre, adjacent to post office.

> **PD** *Supplies, caravan park. Surfing, fishing, boating, bushwalking. Kumbaingeri Wildlife Park; Arms, Armour and Militaria Museum; Pet Porpoise Pool; Storyland Gardens.*

0.0 km Zero trip meter at post office. **SO** along Pacific Hwy.
(4.7 km) ▲ 0.0 km
▲ 9.3 km

4.7 km S'post: Bruxner Park. **TL.**

Korora Bay off to right. Grafton straight ahead.

(3.6 km) ▲ 4.6 km

8.3 km Sign: Orara State Forest.
(0.2 km) ▲ 1.0 km

8.5 km S'post: Wedding Bells Forest Drive. **SO.**

Bruxner Park Flora Reserve on left. Sealy Lookout 2 km to left; views across Coffs Harbour.

(0.8 km) ▲ 0.8 km

9.3 km Picnic area on right.

Barbecues, tables. Walking trails.

0.0 km Zero trip meter adjacent to picnic area. **SO.**
(1.0 km) ▲ 0.0 km
▲ 1.0 km

1.0 km Intersection.

Swans Rd on left. Park Creek Picnic Ground on left. Walking trails.

0.0 km Zero trip meter at above intersection. **SO.**
(2.5 km) ▲ 0.0 km
▲ 90.8 km

2.5 km Intersection. **KR** and immediately cross bridge.

Mt Corambra off to left.

(6.3 km) ▲ 88.3 km

8.8 km S'post: Pacific Hwy. **TR** onto Nana Glen Rd; immediately **TL** onto gravel.

Nana Glen off to left.

(0.6 km) Bitumen. Opp. dir. s'post: Bruxner Park. ▲ 82.0 km

9.4 km Intersection. **KL.**

Eno Rd on right.

(0.5 km) ▲ 81.4 km

9.9 km Intersection. **SO.**

Link Rd on right. Route traverses Wedding Bells and Conglomerate state forests.

(1.5 km) ▲ 80.9 km

11.4 km Intersection. **SO.**

Broken Rd on right.

(0.6 km) ▲ 79.4 km

12.0 km Intersection. **SO.**

Stony Rd on right.

(1.6 km) ▲ 78.8 km

13.6 km T intersection, oblique angle. **TR** onto Marys Waterhole Rd.
(0.5 km) Opp. dir. s'post: Boyds Rd. ▲ 77.2 km

14.1 km Y intersection. S'post: Marys Waterhole Rd. **KL.**

Track on right.

(3.2 km) ▲ 76.7 km

17.3 km T intersection. **TL** onto Gentle Annie Rd.
(0.1 km) ▲ 73.5 km

17.4 km T intersection. **TL** along Gentle Annie Rd.
(0.7 km) ▲ 73.4 km

18.1 km S'post: Sherwood Rd. **SO.**

Sign: Conglomerate State Forest. Sherwood Rd continues on left.

(2.9 km) Opp. dir. s'post: Gentle Annie Rd. ▲72.7 km

21.0 km Y intersection. **KR.**
(0.1 km) ▲ 69.8 km

21.1 km S'post: Plum Pudding Rd. **TR.**

Sherwood Rd on left.

(2.4 km) Opp. dir. s'post:Sherwood Rd. ▲ 69.7 km

23.5 km S'post: Plum Pudding Rd. **KR.**

Parberrys Spur Rd on left.

(2.5 km) ▲ 67.3 km

26.0 km S'post: Andersons Mountain Rd. **TR.**

Plum Pudding Rd straight on.

(4.8 km) ▲ 64.8 km

30.8 km T intersection. **TR** onto Upper Corindi Rd.
(2.2 km) Opp. dir. s'post: Andersons Mountain Rd. ▲ 60.0 km

33.0 km Lazyman Creek. Cross bridge.
(1.0 km) ▲ 57.8 km

34.0 km Lorindi Creek. Cross Boyles Bridge.
(0.6 km) ▲ 56.8 km

34.6 km Bitumen.
(6.7 km) Gravel. ▲ 56.2 km

41.3 km S'post: Grafton. **TL** onto Pacific Hwy.

Coffs Harbour off to right.

(49.5 km) Opp. dir. s'post: Corindi. ▲ 49.5 km

90.8 km Pacific Hwy/Summerland Way/Gwydir Hwy intersection.**SO** along Summerland Way into Grafton.

PD *Supplies, caravan park. Centre for Clarence Valley district. Sailing, canoeing, water skiing. Susan Island Recreation Reserve; Grafton Walking Track; Jacaranda Festival in November.*

REVERSE DIRECTIONS START ▲ 0.0 km

GRAFTON
«»
BRISBANE

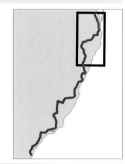

START POINT
Map page 5, O5.

TOTAL KM 448.
UNSEALED KM 186.
DEGREE OF DIFFICULTY Difficult.
DRIVING TIME 8 hours (Grafton to Murwillumbah).
LONGEST DISTANCE NO FUEL 94 km (Grafton to Whiporie).
TOPOGRAPHIC MAPS Auslig 1:250 000 series: *Grafton*; *Warwick*; *Tweed Heads*; *Brisbane*.
LOCAL/SPECIALITY MAPS NSW Forestry Commission: *Coffs Harbour State Forests*; *Casino State Forests*; CMA: *Grafton and District Map*; *A Touring Map of the Holiday Coast – New England*.
OTHER USEFUL INFORMATION NSW Forestry Commission brochures: *Camping and Recreation in State Forests*; *State Forests of the Far North Coast*; Shire of Tweed brochure: *The Tweed and its World Heritage National Parks*.

DESCRIPTION The difficult part of this otherwise easy trip is what is known as the Sportsmans Creek Trail, reached about 52 kilometres after leaving Grafton. For the rest, the countryside throughout is amazingly diverse, ranging from steep hills to rolling pastures; it is almost always green and lush, but particularly so after rain. The trip is quite long, but can be broken either by bush camping in places of your own choice or at any of 3 designated campsites on or near the route: *Pikapene*, *Peacock Creek* and *Mebbin Forest*.

The difficult section begins as you leave Fortis Creek State Forest and enter Banyabba Nature Reserve, turning east and then north to join the Banyabba Fire Trail and pass through Banyabba Forest, turning along Summerland Way and through Whiporie. Pikapene, 5 kilo-

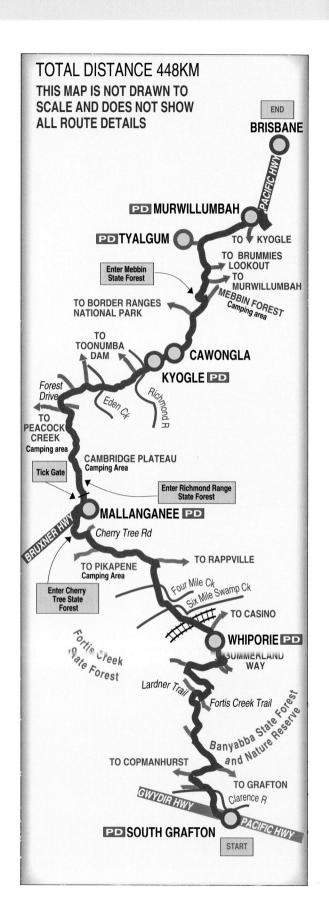

TOTAL DISTANCE 448KM
THIS MAP IS NOT DRAWN TO SCALE AND DOES NOT SHOW ALL ROUTE DETAILS

metres off the road, is set on a grassy creek flat in a spectacular hoop pine forest. The drive is then through Cherry Tree Forest, Mallanganee Flora Reserve and the Richmond Range; this section skirts Cambridge Plateau Flora Reserve, largely a subtropical rainforest region. Peacock Creek camp is to your left in the northern Richmond Ranges; you then leave the forest and trek across country through Kyogle to Mebbin Forest and the third camping ground, where there are many roads and trails to explore. A short diversion in Wollumbin Forest leads to Brummies Lookout and magnificent views of the west face of Mt Warning.

From Tyalgum, you roughly follow and cross the Oxley River on the way to Murwillumbah in the Tweed Valley, then rejoin the Pacific Highway and travel the Sunshine Coast to Brisbane.

WARNING ▶ Observe forest warnings given in the first section of the trek.

BOOKINGS AND PERMITS ▶ For information on state forests contact NSW Forestry Commission regional offices: Cnr Walker and Canterbury Streets, Casino NSW 2470; tel. (066) 62 1688; 135 Murwillumbah Street, Murwillumbah NSW 2484; tel. (066) 72 1213. ▶ For local information contact Tweed Visitors Centre, Pacific Highway, Murwillumbah NSW 2484; tel. (066) 72 1340.

ROUTE DIRECTIONS

0.0 km	Zero trip meter in South Grafton at s'post: Gwydir Hwy on Pacific Hwy, heading west.	
	(0.2 km)	▲ 138.8 km
0.2 km	Roundabout. S'post: Gwydir Hwy. **SO.**	
	(6.3 km)	▲ 138.6 km
6.5 km	S'post: Copmanhurst. **TR.**	

> Glen Innes straight ahead.

	(0.8 km) Opp. dir. s'post: Grafton.	▲ 132.3 km
7.3 km	S'post: Copmanhurst. **SO.**	

> Eastonville off to left.

	(7.1 km) Opp. dir. s'post: Grafton.	▲ 131.5 km
14.4 km	Clarence River. Cross bridge.	
	(3.9 km)	▲ 124.4 km
18.3 km	S'post: Whiteman Creek Rd. **TR** onto gravel.	
	(3.5 km) Bitumen.	▲ 120.5 km
21.8 km	Bitumen.	
	(0.3 km) Gravel.	▲ 117.0 km

22.1 km	T intersection. **TR** and immediately cross bridge.	
	(8.3 km)	▲ 116.7 km
30.4 km	S'post: Coaldale. **TL.**	

> Grafton straight ahead.

	(9.0 km) Opp. dir. s'post: Copmanhurst.	▲ 108.4 km
39.4 km	S'post: Fortis Creek. **TR** onto gravel.	

> This section passes through Fortis Creek State Forest.

	(12.4 km) Bitumen.	▲ 99.4 km
51.8 km	Y intersection. **KR.**	
	(0.5 km)	▲ 87.0 km
52.3 km	S'post: Fortis Creek Trail. **KR.**	

> Sign: Banyabba Nature Reserve. Lardner Trail on left.

	(2.7 km)	▲ 86.5 km
55.0 km	S'post: Sportsmans Creek Trail. **TL.**	

> Fortis Creek Trail on right.

	(5.2 km)	▲ 83.8 km
60.2 km	S'post: Sportsmans Creek Trail. **SO.**	

> Saltwater Trail on right.

	(1.6 km)	▲ 78.6 km
61.8 km	Rocky creek crossing.	
	(0.3 km)	▲ 77.0 km
62.1 km	Cross rough wooden bridge.	
	(14.2 km)	▲ 76.7 km
76.3 km	S'post: Banyabba Trail. **TR.**	
	(5.2 km)	▲ 62.5 km
81.5 km	Enter Banyabba State Forest. **SO.**	
	(0.5 km) Opp. dir. s'post: Banyabba Trail.	▲ 57.3 km
82.0 km	Intersection. **TL.**	
	(5.2 km)	▲ 56.8 km
87.2 km	Crossroads. **SO.**	

> Old Coach Rd on right.

	(0.8 km)	▲ 51.6 km
88.0 km	T intersection. **TL** onto bitumen: Summerland Way.	

> A number of pine plantations in this area.

	(4.2 km) Gravel.	▲ 50.8 km
92.2 km	Cross New Dight Bridge.	
	(1.3 km)	▲ 46.6 km
93.5 km	Whiporie village. **PD**	
	(2.6 km)	▲ 45.3 km
96.1 km	S'post: Camira Creek. **TL.**	

> Casino straight ahead.

	(3.0 km) Opp. dir. s'post: Grafton.	▲ 42.7 km

Rough wooden bridge in the Banyabba Forest

99.1 km Cross railway line onto gravel.
(12.2 km) Bitumen. ▲ 39.7 km
111.3 km Six Mile Swamp Creek. Cross bridge.
(5.1 km) ▲ 27.5 km
116.4 km Four Mile Creek. Cross bridge onto bitumen.
(6.6 km) Gravel. ▲ 22.4 km
123.0 km S'post: Tabulam. **SO**.

> *Rappville off to right.*

(8.6 km) Opp. dir. s'post: Whiporie. ▲ 15.8 km
131.6 km Gravel.
(3.1 km) Bitumen.▲ 7.2 km
134.7 km Intersection. **SO**.

> *North Belmore Rd on left.*

(4.1 km) ▲ 4.1 km
138.8 km S'post: Tabulam.

> *Pikapene off to left. 5.2 km to camp and picnic area in hoop pine forest. Barbecues, toilets, water, shelters.*

Opp. dir. s'post: Rappville.

0.0 km Zero trip meter at above s'post. **SO** across grid at fence line.
(0.9 km) ▲ 0.0 km
▲ 56.6 km
0.9 km Cross wooden bridge.
(1.1 km) ▲ 55.7 km
2.0 km Sign: Cherry Tree State Forest. **SO**.
(2.0 km) ▲ 54.6 km
4.0 km Intersection. **KL**.

> *Cherry Tree Rd on right.*

(0.2 km) ▲ 52.6 km
4.2 km Intersection. Tick gate. **KR**.
(7.9 km) ▲ 52.4 km
12.1 km S'post: Mallanganee. **KR** onto bitumen.
(8.2 km) Gravel. Opp. dir. s'post: Busbys Flat. ▲ 44.5 km
20.3 km T intersection. **TR** onto Bruxner Hwy.
(1.0 km) Opp. dir. s'post: Deep Creek. ▲ 36.3 km
21.3 km Mallanganee township to right. **SO**.

> **PD** *Road skirts Mallanganee Flora Reserve.*

(2.3 km) ▲ 35.3 km
23.6 km Tick gate. 100 m to s'post: Forest Drive. **TL** onto gravel.
(6.7 km) Bitumen. ▲ 33.0 km
30.3 km Sign: Richmond Range State Forest. **SO**.
(5.6 km) ▲ 26.3 km
35.9 km Cambridge Plateau Picnic Area. **SO**.

> *Barbecues, toilets, water, shelters. Views of Richmond River valley. Cambridge Plateau Flora Reserve: subtropical rainforest.*

(3.9 km) ▲ 20.7 km
39.8 km Intersection. **KR**.
(16.8 km) ▲ 16.8 km
56.6 km S'post: Forest Drive.

> *Peacock Creek Camping Area 2.7 km off to left. Water, toilets, shelters.*

Opp. dir. s'post: Forest Drive.
0.0 km Zero trip meter at above s'post. **TR**.
(0.1 km) ▲ 0.0 km
▲ 37.5 km
0.1 km S'post: Forest Drive. **TL**.

> *Casino straight ahead.*

(6.7 km) Opp. dir. s'post: Forest Drive. ▲ 37.4 km
6.8 km Cross wooden bridge.
(1.3 km) ▲ 30.7 km
8.1 km S'post: Kyogle. **SO**.

	Forest Drive on left.

(4.5 km)   Opp. dir. s'post: Forest Drive. ▲ 29.4 km

12.6 km   S'post: Kyogle. **SO**.

	Toonumba Dam off to left.

(7.3 km)   Opp. dir. s'post: Bonalbo. ▲ 24.9 km

19.9 km   Cross bridge onto bitumen.

(5.1 km)   Gravel. ▲ 17.6 km

25.0 km   Eden Creek. Cross bridge.

(9.0 km)   ▲ 12.5 km

34.0 km   T intersection. **TR**.

	Toonumba Dam off to left.

(2.4 km)   Opp. dir. s'post:
Bonalbo via Mt Brown. ▲ 3.5 km

36.4 km   Richmond River. Cross bridge.

(0.6 km)   ▲ 1.1 km

37.0 km   T intersection. **TL**.

(0.5 km)   Opp. dir. s'post: Geneva. ▲ 0.5 km

37.5 km   T intersection. **TR** into Kyogle; immediately s'post: Murwillumbah. **PD**

Opp. dir. s'post: Geneva.

0.0 km   Zero trip meter at above s'post. **TL**.

(1.8 km)   ▲ 0.0 km
    ▲ 43.3 km

1.8 km   S'post: Murwillumbah. **TR**.

	Green Pigeon straight ahead.

(7.2 km)   Opp. dir. s'post: Kyogle. ▲ 41.5 km

9.0 km   Gravel.

(3.5 km)   Bitumen. ▲ 34.3 km

12.5 km   Bitumen.

(1.3 km)   Gravel. ▲ 30.8 km

13.8 km   Cawongla. **SO**.

(1.0 km)   ▲ 29.5 km

14.8 km   Gravel.

(10.3 km)   Bitumen. ▲ 28.5 km

25.1 km   S'post: Murwillumbah. **SO**.

	Border Ranges National Park off to left.

(4.6 km)   Opp. dir. s'post: Kyogle. ▲ 18.2 km

29.7 km   Bitumen.

(2.2 km)   Gravel. ▲ 13.6 km

31.9 km   S'post: Cadell Rd. **TL** onto gravel.

(3.3 km)   Bitumen. ▲ 11.4 km

35.2 km   Sign: Mebbin State Forest. **SO**.

(8.1 km)   ▲ 8.1 km

43.3 km   Mebbin Forest Picnic and Camping Area.

	Barbecues, toilets, water, shelters. Giant ironbark, believed to be the world's oldest, about 3 km south.

0.0 km   Zero trip meter adjacent to camping area. **SO**.

(1.6 km)   ▲ 0.0 km
    ▲ 8.4 km

1.6 km   S'post: Tyalgum. **KL**.

	Murwillumbah off to right.

(2.3 km)   Opp. dir. s'post: Mebbin Forest. ▲ 6.8 km

3.9 km   S'post: Condowie Rd. **KR**.

	Route continues through Wollumbin Forest.

(4.5 km)   ▲ 4.5 km

8.4 km   T intersection. S'post: Brummies Rd.

	Brummies Lookout off to right. Magnificent view towards Mt Warning. Amaroo Flora Reserve off to right: subtropical rainforest.

Opp. dir. s'post: Condowie Rd.

0.0 km   Zero trip meter at above s'post. **TL**.

(5.7 km)   ▲ 0.0 km
    ▲ 5.7 km

5.7 km   T intersection.

	Tyalgum township on left. **PD**

Opp. dir. s'post: Swifts Rd.

0.0 km   Zero trip meter at above intersection. **TR** onto bitumen.

(11.0 km)   Gravel. ▲ 0.0 km
    ▲ 22.7 km

11.0 km   Oxley River. Cross bridge.

(6.7 km)   ▲ 11.7 km

17.7 km   S'post: Murwillumbah. **TL**.

	Kyogle off to right.

(3.9 km)   Opp. dir. s'post: Tyalgum. ▲ 5.0 km

21.6 km   S'post: Tweed Heads. **TR**.

(0.4 km)   Opp. dir. s'post: Kyogle. ▲ 1.1 km

22.0 km   Roundabout. **SO** through Murwillumbah.

	PD Supplies, caravan park. Base for exploration of 4 World Heritage National Parks: Mt Warning, Border Ranges, Nightcap and Lamington.

(0.7 km)   ▲ 0.7 km

22.7 km   T intersection. **TL** onto Pacific Hwy. Follow Pacific Hwy to Brisbane (approx. 135 km) to pick up route directions for next trek, Brisbane to Cairns.

REVERSE DIRECTIONS START ▲ 0.0 km

INTO THE TROPICS
BRISBANE «» CAIRNS
3464 KILOMETRES

BRISBANE «» BOONDOOMA DAM   228 km

BOONDOOMA DAM
«» ISLA GORGE NATIONAL PARK   341 km

ISLA GORGE NATIONAL PARK
«» CARNARVON GORGE   392 km

CARNARVON GORGE
«» BLACKDOWN TABLELAND NATIONAL PARK
290 km

BLACKDOWN TABLELAND NATIONAL PARK
«» CLAIRVIEW   293 km

CLAIRVIEW «» MACKAY   183 km

MACKAY
«» EUNGELLA NATIONAL PARK   119 km

EUNGELLA NATIONAL PARK
«» BURDEKIN FALLS DAM   275 km

BURDEKIN FALLS DAM
«» CHARTERS TOWERS   165 km

CHARTERS TOWERS
«» PORCUPINE GORGE   282 km

PORCUPINE GORGE «» THE LYND   208 km

THE LYND «» CARDWELL   289 km

CARDWELL «» CAIRNS   399 km

This trek covers a diverse slice of Queensland, from the mountainous picture-postcard terrain of the south east, through the dry, flat central plains, to the lush tropical far north. Dramatic Carnarvon Gorge is reached from the south across the Great Dividing Range through sparse grazing country. Much further north and typical of

QUEENSLAND'S NATIONAL PARKS

The majority of national parks have good facilities for camping and where appropriate we suggest you use their designated campsites. Fees are reasonable. Contact national park head office for information when planning your trips. Permits are necessary to camp in all parks and, although self-registration is possible at many parks, it is advisable to book ahead at busy holiday periods. Contact Queensland National Parks and Wildlife Service (QNPWS), 160 Ann Street, Brisbane 4000; PO Box 155, North Quay 4002; tel. (07) 227 8185.

Regional offices:
QNPWS Northern Regional Centre
Marlow Street
Pallarenda QLD;
PO Box 5391
Townsville Mail Centre
QLD 4810
(077) 74 1211.

QNPWS Far Northern Regional Centre
10-12 McLeod Street
Cairns QLD;
PO Box 2066
Cairns QLD 4870
(070) 52 3093.

Local national parks offices are listed in the route directions.
When using national parks, obey the following rules.
▶ *Drive only on roads and identifiable tracks and obey all notices.*
▶ *No domestic animals are allowed.*
▶ *When walking, keep to the tracks. Shortcutting causes erosion.*
▶ *Don't disturb or feed native animals; all are protected.*
▶ *Leave all plants, living or dead, undamaged.*
▶ *Don't collect firewood from the park. Bring your own or – preferably – use a fuel stove.*
▶ *No firearms, generators, petrol-engined fridges or chainsaws allowed.*
▶ *Never leave a campfire unattended and put your fire out with water.*
▶ *Take your rubbish with you or leave in the bins provided. Leave your campsite clean.*

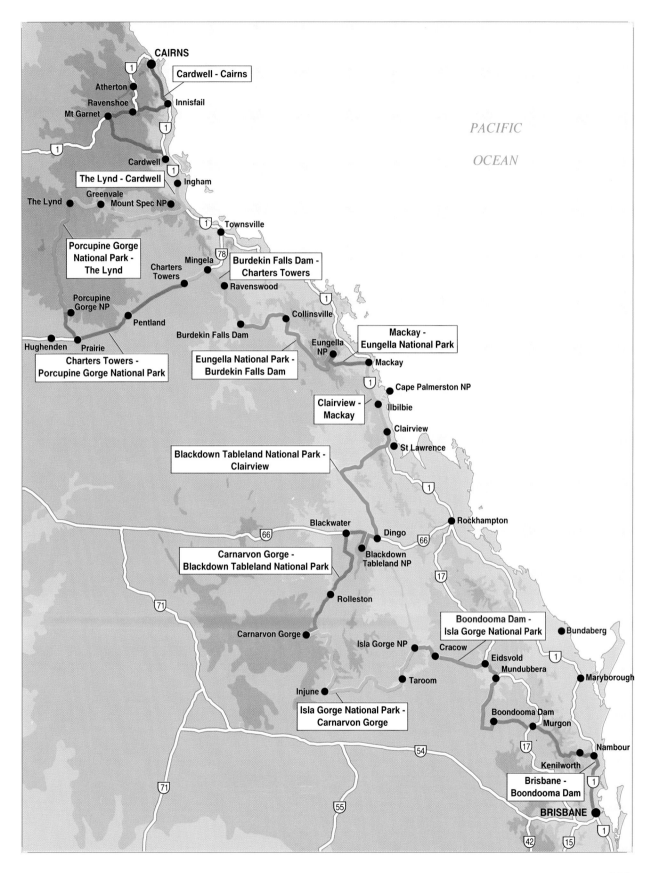

CAIRNS

Cardwell - Cairns

Atherton
Ravenshoe
Mt Garnet
Innisfail

PACIFIC

OCEAN

Cardwell

The Lynd - Cardwell
Ingham

Greenvale
The Lynd
Mount Spec NP

Townsville

Porcupine Gorge
National Park -
The Lynd

Mingela
Charters
Towers

Burdekin Falls Dam -
Charters Towers

Ravenswood

Porcupine
Gorge NP

Collinsville

Pentland

Burdekin Falls Dam

Eungella
NP

Mackay -
Eungella National Park

Hughenden
Prairie

Charters Towers -
Porcupine Gorge National Park

Eungella National Park -
Burdekin Falls Dam

Mackay

Cape Palmerston NP

Ilbilbie

Clairview -
Mackay

Clairview
St Lawrence

Blackdown Tableland National Park -
Clairview

Blackwater
Dingo
Rockhampton

Carnarvon Gorge -
Blackdown Tableland National Park

Blackdown
Tableland NP

Rolleston

Boondooma Dam -
Isla Gorge National Park

Bundaberg

Carnarvon Gorge

Isla Gorge NP
Cracow

Eidsvold
Mundubbera

Maryborough

Injune

Taroom

Isla Gorge National Park -
Carnarvon Gorge

Boondooma Dam
Murgon

Nambour

Kenilworth

Brisbane -
Boondooma Dam

BRISBANE

Millaa Millaa Falls, Atherton Tableland

Blackdown Tableland

the rich, coastal rainforests in this region, lies Mt Spec National Park; the last part of the trip to this park offers the four-wheel drive enthusiast an interesting drive via Hidden Valley and Paluma. Only a few hours on is Cardwell, a serene fishing village, and on the way to Cairns you have the option to explore the Atherton Tableland at leisure. Cairns is an ideal base for cruises to the islands which line the Great Barrier Reef. It is also the gateway to Cape York and the starting point of your trek across the top of Australia.

This trek north can be made at any time of year, but do not attempt to travel after heavy rain as unsealed roads quickly become impassable. Spring and autumn are probably the most comfortable travelling times.

Driving conditions vary greatly on this trek, ranging from easy (between Brisbane and Boondooma Dam) to more gruelling (the Mia Mia State Forest track between Mackay and Eungella National Park). Alternative routes are always indicated where there are difficult sections of road. One of the more taxing but rewarding drives is the optional loop tour to Cape Palmerston National Park (between Clairview and Mackay). Creek crossings are numerous on the trek, and some, such as the Tartrus Weir causeway and the Herbert River, can offer an interesting challenge. The route skirts and crosses the Great Dividing Range, so take care on narrow and winding roads.

BEFORE YOU SET OUT ▶ Read the section description carefully. ▶Check that you have obtained any necessary permits. ▶ Check weather conditions with local authorities or Bureau of Meteorology. ▶ Make sure you have the appropriate maps and information for the trek. ▶ Check that your vehicle is in good order for the conditions ahead. Have you the necessary spare parts? ▶ If you are camping, do you have the right camping equipment?

USEFUL INFORMATION

For touring information contact:
Queensland Government Travel Centre
196 Adelaide Street
Brisbane 4000
(07) 221 6111.

For motoring and touring information contact:
Royal Automobile Club of Queensland (RACQ)
300 St Pauls Terrace
Brisbane 4000
(07) 253 2444.

For four-wheel driving information contact:
Queensland Association of Four Wheel Drive
  Clubs Inc.
PO Box 174
Brisbane Markets QLD 4000
(07) 379 9129.

BRISBANE
«»
BOONDOOMA DAM

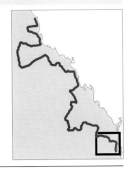

START POINT
Map page 13, N4

TOTAL KM 228. Does not include 96 km from Brisbane to Nambour exit. *See Route Directions.*

UNSEALED KM 99.

DEGREE OF DIFFICULTY Easy. Section of road between Mapleton and Kenilworth not suitable for caravans. *See Warnings.*

DRIVING TIME 6 hours. Allow time from Brisbane to Nambour exit. *See Route Directions.*

LONGEST DISTANCE NO FUEL 125 km (Kenilworth to Murgon).

TOPOGRAPHIC MAP Auslig 1:250 000 series: *Gympie.*

LOCAL/SPECIALITY MAPS Sunmap: *South-east Queensland; Outback Queensland.*

OTHER USEFUL INFORMATION QNPWS brochure: *South-east Queensland*; QNPWS visitor information sheets: *Kondalilla* and *Mapleton Falls* national parks; Department of Forestry booklets: *Jimna/Conondale/Mary Valley* and *Brisbane/Sunshine Coast* regions; Lions Club brochure: *Blackall Range.*

DESCRIPTION This trek section includes mountainous country close to the Sunshine Coast, the spectacular rainforest of the Blackall Range and the lush grazing country of south-east Queensland. The village of Montville is the craft capital of the region: you could spend a whole day browsing in the art and craft galleries and sampling food served in Montville's restaurants and tearooms. Worth visiting are Kondalilla and Mapleton Falls national parks, valuable wildlife habitats which protect remnants of rainforest and eucalypt that once grew throughout

the Blackall Range. Both these parks have picnic facilities but camping is not permitted.

Overnight camping is available at *Charlie Moreland State Forest Park, Peach Trees State Forest Park, Landcruiser Mountain Park*, and at *Boondooma Dam*. Charlie Moreland is an open grassy forest camping ground with a large rock pool for swimming and good hiking tracks. From Peach Trees State Forest Park you can explore the forests, lookouts, waterfalls and creeks of the Jimna and Conondale ranges.

Landcruiser Mountain Park has 250 kilometres of four-wheel drive tracks (easy to difficult). Camp anywhere on this private property, avoid creek banks; campsites at Cowah Falls and Trakka Terrace have bush toilets but no other facilities.

Boondooma Dam, surrounded by open ironbark forest, offers excellent water-skiing and fishing, and there is abundant wildlife. Camping areas are near the water. This huge dam was filled by heavy rain within one week in 1983, instead of an anticipated 18 months.

WARNING ▶ A section of the road between Mapleton and Kenilworth is not suitable for full-sized caravans. Detour via Maleny.

BOOKINGS AND PERMITS ▶ Driving in state forests is permitted only on designated forest drives. Obtain a permit to drive on other forestry roads. ▶ Contact the Kenilworth Forest Office, Maleny–Kenilworth Road; tel. (074) 46 0925, for information and to obtain a permit to camp at Charlie Moreland State Forest Park. Self-registration is also available on site. ▶ To book a campsite at Peach Trees State Forest Park contact the Jimna Forest Office, Kilcoy–Murgon Road, Jimna, QLD 4515; tel. (074) 97 3133. ▶ The removal of flora and fauna, and the use of firearms and archery, are not permitted at Landcruiser Mountain Park. The permit charge (covering entry, four-wheel drive tracks and camping) may be paid on arrival. Self-register if the office is unattended. To book write to Landcruiser Mountain Park, Elgin Vale via Nanango, QLD 4615; tel. (071) 68 8181. ▶ Book ahead to camp at Boondooma Dam in peak holiday periods; tel. (071) 68 9133. Register with the supervisor in person between 7.30 am– 4.30 pm at the camping ground or write to the Storage Supervisor, Boondooma Dam, PO Box 21, Proston QLD 4613.

BRISBANE ‹›› BOONDOOMA DAM

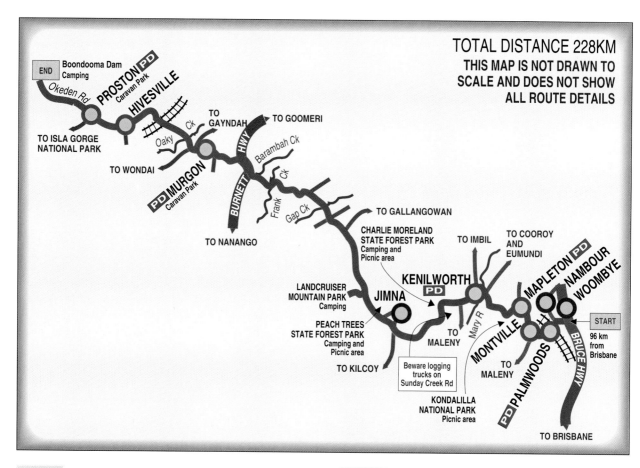

TOTAL DISTANCE 228KM
THIS MAP IS NOT DRAWN TO
SCALE AND DOES NOT SHOW
ALL ROUTE DETAILS

ROUTE DIRECTIONS

Depart Brisbane north via Bruce Hwy approx.
96 km. Take Nambour exit. Stop at intersection
of Nambour Rd and Montville Rd.

0.0 km Zero trip meter at above intersection. **TL.**
(0.3 km)
▲ 0.0 km
▲ 16.4 km

0.3 km S'post: Palmwoods/Montville. **KL.**
(2.9 km)
▲ 16.1 km

3.2 km Pass under railway bridge then **TL.** S'post:
Montville. **SO** through Palmwoods. **PD**
(9.9 km)
▲ 13.2 km

13.1 km S'post: Mapleton. **TR.**

*Full-sized caravans are not suited to
section of road beyond Mapleton. Detour
here to Kenilworth via Maleny.*

(0.4 km)
▲ 3.3 km

13.5 km Montville village. **SO.**

*Montville is the craft capital of south-east
Queensland.*

(2.9 km)
▲ 2.9 km

16.4 km S'post: Mapleton.

*Kondalilla National Park and Kondalilla
Falls on left. Day use only: picnic tables,
barbecues, toilets. Walking tracks through
rainforest: piccabeen palms and bunya
pines. Swimming hole above the 80-metre
high falls.*

0.0 km Zero trip meter at above s'post. **SO.**
(5.5 km)
▲ 0.0 km
▲ 26.7 km

5.5 km Mapleton 60 km/h sign. **PD**
(0.6 km)
▲ 21.2 km

6.1 km S'post: Kenilworth 21. **TL.**
(3.1 km)
▲ 20.6 km

9.2 km Gravel.
(7.4 km)
Bitumen. ▲ 17.5 km

16.6 km Bitumen.
(9.1 km)
Gravel. ▲ 10.1 km

25.7 km S'post: Kenilworth 1. **TL.**
(0.3 km)
▲ 1.0 km

26.0 km Mary River. Cross bridge.
(0.7 km)
▲ 0.7 km

26.7 km S'post: Maleny.

> *Travellers towing caravans pick up directions here.*

0.0 km Zero trip meter at above intersection. **TL.**
(0.6 km)   ▲ 0.0 km
                                            ▲ 11.4 km

0.6 km Kenilworth town centre. **SO.** PD
(3.5 km)   ▲ 10.8 km

4.1 km Bellbird Creek. Cross bridge.
(2.7 km)   ▲ 7.3 km

6.8 km S'post: Kenilworth State Forest. **TR** onto gravel.
(4.6 km)   Bitumen. ▲ 4.6 km

11.4 km Enter Charlie Moreland State Forest Park.

> *Camping and picnic tables, barbecues, toilets, water (no showers). Bellbird habitat. Walking tracks, swimming.*

0.0 km Zero trip meter at self-registration hut. **SO** through park.
(0.1 km)   ▲ 0.0 km
                                            ▲ 154.7 km

0.1 km Grid followed by Sunday Creek Rd: gravel.

> *Caution: beware logging trucks along Sunday Creek Rd. Steep climb. Watch for wildlife in this section.*

(11.5 km)   Bitumen. ▲ 154.6 km
11.6 km S'post: Jimna 21. **SO.**
(16.4 km)   ▲ 143.1 km
28.0 km Bitumen.
(1.3 km)   Gravel. ▲ 126.7 km
29.3 km S'post: Jimna 4. **TR.**
(2.4 km) Opp. dir. s'post: Sunday Creek Rd/Kenilworth.
                                            ▲ 125.4 km

31.7 km S'post: Goomeri 80. **KL** onto gravel.

> *Peach Trees State Forest Park approx. 1 km ahead. Camping area, picnic tables, barbecues, toilets. Walking tracks. Swimming hole.*

(14.4 km)   Bitumen. ▲ 123.0 km
46.1 km Jiggera Creek. Cross bridge.
(1.8 km)   ▲ 108.6 km
47.9 km Intersection. **SO.**

> *Landcruiser Mountain Park on left. 4WD and wilderness area. Day use and camping. No facilities except bush toilets. 250 km 4WD tracks (easy to difficult).*

(16.4 km)   ▲ 106.8 km

64.3 km Y intersection. **KL.**

> *Gallangowan off to right.*

(7.3 km)   ▲ 90.4 km
71.6 km S'post: Goomeri 40. **SO** over crossroads.
(4.0 km)   ▲ 83.1 km
75.6 km Gap Creek. Cross bridge.
(5.4 km)   ▲ 79.1 km
81.0 km Intersection. S'post: Goomeri. **TL.**
(2.4 km)   Opp. dir. s'post: Kilcoy. ▲ 73.7 km
83.4 km Peenam Creek. Cross bridge.
(2.3 km)   ▲ 71.3 km
85.7 km Frank Creek. Cross bridge.
(5.2 km)   ▲ 69.0 km
90.9 km Bitumen.
(0.3 km)   Gravel. ▲ 63.8 km
91.2 km Intersection. S'post: Goomeri 21. **SO.**
(2.3 km)   Opp. dir. s'post: Kilcoy. ▲ 63.5 km
93.5 km Barambah Creek. Cross bridge.
(3.8 km)   ▲ 61.2 km
97.3 km S'post: Goomeri 14. **TR** onto Burnett Hwy.
(2.8 km)   Opp. dir. s'post: Kilcoy. ▲ 57.4 km
100.1 km S'post: Murgon. **TL.**
(8.9 km)   Opp. dir. s'post: Nanango. ▲ 54.6 km
109.0 km S'post: Murgon. **TR.**
(3.1 km)   Opp. dir. s'post: Goomeri. ▲ 45.7 km
112.1 km Sawpit Creek. Cross Burtons Bridge.
(2.6 km)   ▲ 42.6 km
114.7 km Murgon town centre: Anzac monument.

> PD *Supplies, caravan park. Murgon, settled in 1843, is surrounded by rich land used for agriculture, dairying and beef cattle. Visit the SBD Cheese Factory to see champion cheddar cheese being made.*

(1.5 km)   ▲ 40.0 km
116.2 km S'post: Wondai. **SO.**

> *Gayndah off to right. Queensland's oldest town once vied for the title of State capital. Gayndah oranges are export quality.*

(1.9 km)   ▲ 38.5 km
118.1 km S'post: Byee. **TR.**
(3.7 km)   Opp. dir. s'post: Murgon. ▲ 36.6 km
121.8 km Oaky Creek. Cross bridge.
(3.1 km)   ▲ 32.9 km
124.9 km Cross railway line.
(1.2 km)   Opp. dir. s'post: Wondai. ▲ 29.8 km
126.1 km Crossroads. S'post: Silverleaf 4. **SO.**
(7.6 km)   Opp. dir. s'post: Gayndah. ▲ 28.6 km
133.7 km S'post: Hivesville. **KL.**
(0.3 km)   Opp. dir. s'post: Murgon. ▲ 21.0 km

Hivesville Hotel

Boondooma Dam

134.0 km S'post: Hivesville. **KL.**
(2.1 km) ▲ 20.7 km
136.1 km S'post: Hivesville 10.
(2.1 km) ▲ 18.6 km
138.2 km S'post: Hivesville. **SO.**
(6.3 km) Opp. dir. s'post: Murgon. ▲ 16.5 km
144.5 km S'post: Proston. **TR.**

> Hivesville town centre.

(7.8 km) Opp. dir. s'post: Cloyna. ▲ 10.2 km
152.3 km Intersection. S'post: Proston 3. **SO.**
(2.4 km) Opp. dir. s'post: Wondai. ▲ 2.4 km
154.7 km Crossroads. S'post: Boondooma Dam 20.

> Proston town centre on left. **PD** Supplies,
> caravan park. Settled in 1910 by a group of
> English migrants. Sidcup Castle, a town
> landmark, was built as a replica of the
> owner's childhood home in Kent, England.

0.0 km Zero trip meter at above crossroads. **TR** onto
Okeden Rd. **SO.**
(18.5 km) ▲ 0.0 km
▲ 18.5 km
18.5 km Boondooma Dam Camping Area entrance.

> Barbecues, toilets, hot showers.
> Water-skiing, windsurfing, fishing.
> Camping permit required.

REVERSE DIRECTIONS START ▲ 0.0 km

TREAD LIGHTLY!
On Public and Private Land

■ Leave gates as you found them – open or shut.

■ Stay off roads and tracks when they are wet and easily
cut up.

■ Ford creeks at designated crossings.

■ Travel only where allowed: get permission to cross
private land and obtain permits where necessary.

BOONDOOMA DAM «» ISLA GORGE NATIONAL PARK

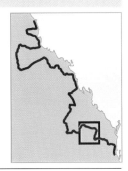

START POINT

Map page 13, K2.

TOTAL KM 341.

UNSEALED KM 88.

DEGREE OF DIFFICULTY Easy.

DRIVING TIME 6 hours.

LONGEST DISTANCE NO FUEL 219 km (Eidsvold to Taroom, next section).

TOPOGRAPHIC MAPS Auslig 1:250 000 series: *Taroom.*

LOCAL/SPECIALITY MAPS Sunmap: *South-east Queensland*; *Central Queensland*.

OTHER USEFUL INFORMATION QNPWS visitor information sheet: *Isla Gorge National Park*.

DESCRIPTION This section takes in Mundubbera, Queensland's citrus-growing capital on the banks of the Burnett River, and grazing country around Eidsvold, where the state's best quality beef is produced. Watch for bottle trees near the Boyne River and the oasis of native palms along Delusion Creek and the Dawson River, on the Isla–Delusion Road. Situated close to the Burnett Highway, *Isla Gorge* is a little known national park of great beauty: a mass of gorges, delicately coloured sandstone cliffs and pinnacles. The camping area is near the lookout. Bush camping is also allowed. There are good walking tracks and from the lookout you will sometimes spot wallabies and kangaroos.

WARNING ▶ Stick to formed walking tracks to avoid getting lost.

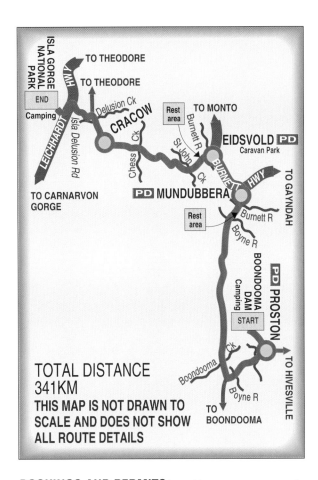

TOTAL DISTANCE 341KM

THIS MAP IS NOT DRAWN TO SCALE AND DOES NOT SHOW ALL ROUTE DETAILS

BOOKINGS AND PERMITS ▶ Self-register on site at Isla Gorge. For advance bookings or information contact QNPWS, Park Lane Plaza, Tank Street, Gladstone QLD 4680; PO Box 315, Gladstone QLD 4680; tel. (079) 76 0766; or QNPWS, PO Box 175, Taroom QLD 4420; tel. (076) 27 3358.

ROUTE DIRECTIONS

0.0 km Zero trip meter at entrance to Boondooma Dam Camping Area. **TR.**

(18.5 km) ▲ 0.0 km

▲ 18.5 km

18.5 km Proston town centre adjacent to ambulance station. **PD**

0.0 km Zero trip meter at Proston Ambulance Station. **SO** towards Mundubbera.

(36.6 km) ▲ 0.0 km

▲ 132.8 km

36.6 km Boyne River. Cross bridge.

Large bottle trees on either side of road.

(4.7 km) ▲ 96.2 km

41.3 km S'post: Mundubbera. **TR.**

(9.2 km) Opp. dir. s'post: Proston. ▲ 91.5 km

BOONDOOMA DAM «» ISLA GORGE NATIONAL PARK

Isla Gorge

50.5 km	Boondooma Creek. Cross bridge.	
	(61.8 km)	▲ 82.3 km
112.3 km	Derri Derra Creek. Cross bridge.	
	(8.1 km)	▲ 20.5 km
120.4 km	Boyne River. Cross bridge.	
	(11.4 km)	▲ 12.4 km
131.8 km	Burnett River. Cross bridge.	

> Rest area with toilets

	(1.0 km)	▲ 1.0 km
132.8 km	S'post: Eidsvold 37. **SO.**	

> Mundubbera off to left. **PD** Supplies. Centre of a major citrus-growing area.

	Opp. dir. s'post: Dalby 212.	
0.0 km	Zero trip meter at above s'post. **SO.**	
	(2.0 km)	▲ 0.0 km
	Opp. dir. s'post: Mundubberra.	▲ 190.0 km
2.0 km	Burnett Hwy. S'post: Eidsvold. **TL.**	
	(14.4 km)	▲ 188.0 km
16.4 km	O'Bil Bil Creek. Cross bridge.	
	(23.7 km)	▲ 173.6 km

40.1 km	Harkness Boundary Creek. Cross bridge.	
	(0.3 km)	▲ 149.9 km
40.4 km	S'post: Cracow in Eidsvold township. **TL** into Moreton St.	

> **PD** Supplies, caravan park. Eidsvold Historical Museum houses a superb collection of rocks, gems and fossils. Next fuel Taroom (218 km).

	(7.3 km)	▲ 149.6 km
47.7 km	Burnett River. Cross bridge.	

> Rest area with toilets.

	(8.6 km)	▲ 142.3 km
56.3 km	Washpool Creek. Cross bridge.	
	(3.7 km)	▲ 133.7 km
60.0 km	Springer Creek. Cross bridge.	
	(3.5 km)	▲ 130.0 km
63.5 km	Little Morrow Creek. Cross bridge.	
	(0.3 km)	▲ 126.5 km
63.8 km	Morrow Creek. Cross bridge.	
	(5.7 km)	▲ 126.2 km

Bottle trees near Proston

Delusion Creek

▼▼▼▼▼▼▼▼

TAKE CARE

- In a bushfire, drive to an open area away from trees, stay in the vehicle, cover all bare skin with non-flammable clothing, preferably wool, or a woollen blanket, and keep low.

- Don't take short cuts over virgin ground. You will destroy the vegetation. Stick to tracks open for use.

- Four-wheel drive tracks are subject to closure; if in doubt, check with local authorities such as national parks or forestry departments.

69.5 km St John Creek. Cross bridge.
(7.1 km) ▲ 120.5 km
76.6 km Fiery Creek. Cross bridge.
(10.0 km) ▲ 113.4 km
86.6 km Gravel.
(3.2 km) Bitumen. ▲ 103.4 km
89.8 km Redbank Creek. Cross bridge.
(4.9 km) ▲ 100.2 km
94.7 km S'post: Theodore 91. **SO**.
(14.3 km) Opp. dir. s'post: Eidsvold 52. ▲ 95.3 km
109.0 km Chess Creek. Cross bridge.
(12.3 km) ▲ 81.0 km
121.3 km S'post: Theodore 65. **SO**.

Banana 111 km off to right.

(15.2 km) ▲ 68.7 km
136.5 km Cracow. **TR** onto bitumen in town.

General store.

(0.3 km) Gravel. ▲ 53.5 km
136.8 km S'post: Theodore. **TL**.
(1.5 km) Opp. dir. S'post: Eidsvold. ▲ 53.2 km
138.3 km Gravel.
(17.5 km) Bitumen. ▲ 51.7 km
155.8 km Delusion Creek. Cross bridge and immediately **TL** onto Isla–Delusion Rd.
(3.3 km) Opp. dir. s'post: Cracow. ▲ 34.2 km
159.1 km Y intersection. **KR**.
(15.4 km) ▲ 30.9 km
174.5 km T intersection. **TL** onto bitumen: Leichhardt Hwy.
(14.2 km) Gravel. Opp. dir. s'post: Isla–Delusion Rd. ▲ 15.5 km
188.7 km S'post: Isla Gorge Lookout 1.4. **TR** onto gravel.
(1.3 km) Bitumen.▲ 1.3 km
190.0 km Isla Gorge Lookout and Camping Ground entrance.

Camping permit required. Self-register on site. Bush camping allowed. Picnic tables, barbecues, toilets, water. Fabulous walking tracks and views.

REVERSE DIRECTIONS START ▲ 0.0 km

ISLA GORGE NATIONAL PARK
«»
CARNARVON GORGE

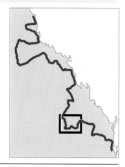

START POINT
Map page 15, K13.

TOTAL KM 392.
UNSEALED KM 220.
DEGREE OF DIFFICULTY Easy.
DRIVING TIME 6 hours.
LONGEST DISTANCE NO FUEL Petrol: 164 km (Taroom to Injune). Diesel: 257 km (Injune to Rolleston, next section).
TOPOGRAPHIC MAP Auslig 1:250 000 series: *Taroom*.
LOCAL/SPECIALITY MAPS Sunmap: *Central Queensland*; QNPWS Park Guide: *Carnarvon National Park*.
OTHER USEFUL INFORMATION QNPWS visitor information sheet: *Carnarvon Gorge*.

DESCRIPTION This section crosses the tablelands of the Great Dividing Range through dry central Queensland grazing country and the cattle town of Injune, to the extraordinary *Carnarvon Gorge*. There is a lot of bitumen and good quality gravel to cover, and at almost 400 kilometres it is a long day.

Carnarvon National Park, in the central highlands sandstone belt, is Queensland's most popular inland park. Much of this reserve is inaccessible high, dry plateau country with eucalypt-covered hills. Carnarvon Creek flows through the main deep sandstone gorge (Carnarvon) lined with moist eucalypts, palms and ferns. It is a haven for birds and wildlife, including platypus and grey kangaroos.

Vehicle on Taroom–Injune road

Walking tracks lead from the ranger's office to ancient Aboriginal rock art sites, lookouts and fern-lined ravines. There is a camping area near the gorge entrance. *Big Bend* is a less developed campsite 10 kilometres from the nearest carpark (toilets only). Alternatively, the privately owned *Oasis Lodge* is situated near the gorge entrance – its cabins have a five-star rating.

WARNINGS ▶ The Carnarvon Gorge road is impassable after heavy rains. Contact the Carnarvon Ranger on (079) 84 4505 from Injune, and check before leaving the gorge. ▶ In case of wet weather bring extra food and suitable camping gear.

BOOKINGS AND PERMITS ▶ A camping permit is required for Carnarvon Gorge. To book and pay in advance contact the Ranger, Carnarvon Gorge, Carnarvon National Park, via Rolleston QLD 4702; tel. (079) 84 4505. ▶ Advance bookings (with deposit) are required at Oasis Lodge; tel. (079) 84 4503, or Brisbane (07) 25 25411.

ISLA GORGE NATIONAL PARK «» CARNARVON GORGE

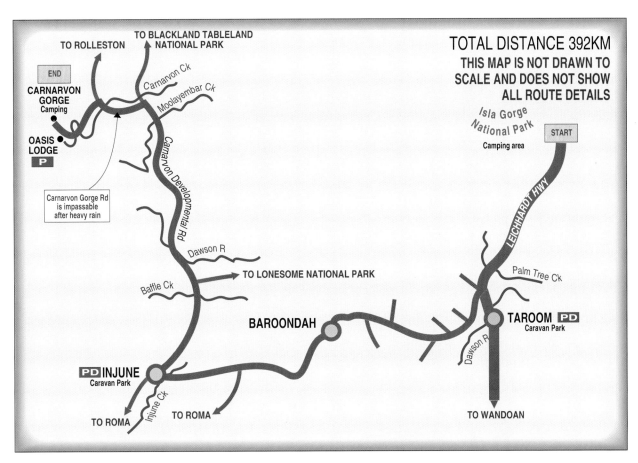

TOTAL DISTANCE 392KM
THIS MAP IS NOT DRAWN TO SCALE AND DOES NOT SHOW ALL ROUTE DETAILS

ROUTE DIRECTIONS

0.0 km Zero trip meter at entrance to Isla Gorge picnic area. **SO** along track to Leichhardt Hwy intersection.
(1.3 km) ▲ 391.6 km

1.3 km Bitumen. **TR** onto Leichhardt Hwy.
(49.4 km) Gravel. ▲ 390.3 km

50.7 km Palm Tree Creek. Cross bridge.
(0.6 km) ▲ 340.9 km

51.3 km S'post: Taroom 18. **TL**.
(17.6 km) ▲ 340.3 km

68.9 km S'post: Injune 158. **TR** onto gravel.

> Taroom straight ahead 1 km on Leichhardt Hwy. **PD** Supplies.

(6.6 km) Bitumen. ▲ 322.7 km

75.5 km Y intersection. **KL**.
(11.1 km) ▲ 316.1 km

86.6 km Intersection. S'post: Injune Rd. **TL**.
(4.9 km) ▲ 305.0 km

91.5 km S'post: Injune Rd. **KR**.
(20.9 km) ▲ 300.1 km

112.4 km Intersection. S'post: Injune Rd. **KL**.

> Broadmere Rd on right.

(7.9 km) ▲ 279.2 km

120.3 km S'post: Injune. **KR**.
(27.4 km) Opp. dir. s'post:Taroom. ▲ 271.3 km

147.7 km Causeway.
(1.8 km) ▲ 243.9 km

149.5 km Intersection. S'post: Injune. **SO**.

> Yebna off to right.

(46.9 km) Opp. dir. s'post: Taroom. ▲ 242.1 km

196.4 km Intersection. S'post: Injune 34. **SO**.

> Roma off to left.

(14.0 km) Opp. dir. s'post: Taroom. ▲ 195.2 km

210.4 km Bitumen.
(19.8 km) Gravel. ▲ 181.2 km

230.2 km Injune Creek. Cross bridge.
(0.6 km) ▲ 161.4 km

230.8 km S'post: Rolleston 171. **TR** in Injune. **SO** through town. **PD**

> Supplies, caravan park.

(1.4 km) ▲ 160.8 km

Carnarvon Creek, Carnarvon Gorge

232.2 km	S'post: Carnarvon Gorge. **KR**.	
	(32.7 km)	▲ 159.4 km
264.9 km	Baffle Creek. Cross bridge.	
	(26.2 km)	▲ 126.7 km
291.1 km	Dawson River. Cross bridge.	
	(23.0 km)	▲ 100.5 km
314.1 km	Gravel.	
	(4.4 km)	Bitumen. ▲ 77.5 km
318.5 km	Bullaroo Creek. Cross bridge.	
	(16.9 km)	▲ 73.1 km
335.4 km	Moolayember Creek. Cross bridge.	
	(10.7 km)	▲ 56.2 km
346.1 km	S'post: Carnarvon Gorge. **TL**.	
	(16.5 km)	Opp. dir. s'post: Injune 116. ▲ 45.5 km
362.6 km	Carnarvon Creek Causeway.	

Caution: fast-flowing creek subject to flooding, impassable after heavy rain. If in doubt about condition of creek, phone the Carnarvon Ranger (079) 84 4505, from Injune.

	(2.2 km)	▲ 29.0 km
364.8 km	T intersection. S'post: Carnarvon. **TL**.	

Rolleston off to right.

	(10.2 km)	Opp. dir. s'post: Injune 131. ▲ 26.8 km
375.0 km	Carnarvon Creek Causeway.	

Caution: fast-flowing creek subject to flooding, impassable after heavy rain. See above.

	(13.2 km)	▲ 16.6 km
388.2 km	Oasis Lodge on left. **SO**.	

P *Supplies at general store. Private five-star cabin accommodation, dining room, laundry. Book in advance.*

	(3.4 km)	▲ 3.4 km
391.6 km	Carnarvon Gorge Camping Area.	

Picnic tables, barbecues, toilets, cold water showers, telephones. Aboriginal rock art sites, waterfalls, swimming hole; 21 km of walking tracks. Register at ranger's office. Advance booking required.

REVERSE DIRECTIONS START ▲ 0.0 km

CARNARVON GORGE
«»
BLACKDOWN TABLELAND NATIONAL PARK

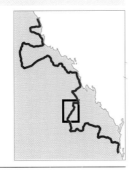

START POINT
Map page 14, H12.

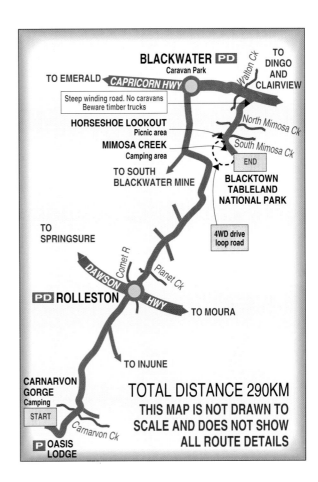

TOTAL DISTANCE 290KM
THIS MAP IS NOT DRAWN TO SCALE AND DOES NOT SHOW ALL ROUTE DETAILS

TOTAL KM 290 (not including option).
UNSEALED KM 196.
DEGREE OF DIFFICULTY Easy. The optional loop tour in Blackdown Tableland National Park is difficult.
DRIVING TIME 5 hours.
LONGEST DISTANCE NO FUEL 126 km (Rolleston to Blackwater).
TOPOGRAPHIC MAPS Auslig 1:250 000 series: *Taroom; Duaringa.*
LOCAL/SPECIALITY MAP Sunmap: *Central Queensland.*
OTHER USEFUL INFORMATION QNPWS visitor information sheet: *Blackdown Tableland National Park.*

DESCRIPTION On good quality roads, this five-hour drive takes you across hot, dry plains through Blackwater (the 'coal capital' of Queensland) to the lush natural splendour of Blackdown Tableland National Park. The majestic sandstone plateau is dissected by deep gorges, streams and waterfalls. The tableland has a moister, colder climate than the surrounding plains and is covered in heath, wattle and tall eucalypt forests. Be prepared for cool nights even in summer.

Blackdown has plenty of gently graded walking tracks, as well as longer hiking tracks through rugged gorges for the dedicated bushwalker. Most of the walks range between 2 and 4 kilometres (round trip) and give you the chance to see wildflowers, birdlife, clifflines, waterfalls and rocky pools. The Mimosa Culture Circuit leads through old cattle yards to an Aboriginal art site. The longest hike, to Stony Creek Gorge, is 5 kilometres each way, but worth it for the dramatic views of the deep gorge and steep waterfall. Take fresh drinking water. The walking track to the gorge is only accessible from the park's loop road. From here the road is suitable only for four-wheel drive vehicles. It continues to Charlevue Lookout before returning, via a steep incline, to the main track. ***See Warnings.***

The camping ground at *Mimosa Creek* has a picnic area and there is another picnic area for day visitors at Horseshoe Lookout. The nearest caravan parks are at *Dingo* (approximately 30 kilometres from the park on the Capricorn Highway) and *Blackwater.*

WARNINGS ▶ The road leading to Blackdown Tableland from the Capricorn Highway is steep, winding and unsuitable for caravans. Access may be restricted during wet weather or times of high-fire danger. Be cautious of timber trucks. ▶ Take care around cliffs and waterfalls. ▶ The optional loop

211

Waterfall, Blackdown Tableland

road in the park has sections of deep sand and exposed rock. Be cautious on the steep incline after Charlevue Lookout.

BOOKINGS AND PERMITS ▶ A permit is required to camp at Mimosa Creek. Self-register on site during off-peak times but book ahead (up to 12 months in advance) in peak holiday season. Contact the Ranger, Blackdown Tableland National Park, via Dingo, QLD 4702; tel. (079) 86 1964; or QNPWS Central Regional Centre, Royal Bank Building, 194 Quay Street, Rockhampton QLD 4700; tel. (079) 27 6511.

ROUTE DIRECTIONS

0.0 km	Zero trip meter at ranger station, Carnarvon Gorge Camping Area. **SO** towards Oasis Lodge.
(3.4 km)	▲ 259.0 km
3.4 km	Oasis Lodge.

> **P** *Supplies.*

(13.2 km)	▲ 255.6 km
16.6 km	Carnarvon Creek. Causeway.

> *Caution: road may be flooded after heavy rain.*

(10.2 km)	▲ 242.4 km
26.8 km	S'post: Rolleston 69. **SO.**
(49.7 km)	Opp. dir. s'post: Carnarvon National Park.
	▲ 232.2 km
76.5 km	Bitumen. S'post: Rolleston 19. **TL.**
(19.6 km)	Gravel. Opp. dir. s'post: Carnarvon National Park. ▲ 182.5 km
96.1 km	S'post: Rolleston. **SO.**
(0.1 km)	Opp. dir. s'post: Carnarvon National Park. ▲ 162.9 km

CARNARVON GORGE «» BLACKDOWN TABLELAND NP

96.2 km Comet River. Cross bridge and enter Rolleston.
(0.4 km) ▲ 162.8 km

96.6 km Rolleston town centre. **SO.** PD
(0.1 km) ▲ 162.4 km

96.7 km S'post: Blackwater. **TR.**
(0.6 km) ▲ 162.3 km

97.3 km S'post: Blackwater 121. **TL.**
(3.1 km) Opp. dir. s'post: Rolleston. ▲ 161.7 km

100.4 km Gravel.
(10.4 km) Bitumen. ▲ 158.6 km

110.8 km Planet Creek. Cross bridge.
(2.9 km) ▲ 148.2 km

113.7 km Bitumen.
(3.0 km) Gravel. ▲ 145.3 km

116.7 km Gravel.
(12.0 km) Bitumen. ▲ 142.3 km

128.7 km Intersection. S'post: Blackwater 88. **SO.**
(15.2 km) Opp. dir. s'post: Rolleston 32. ▲ 130.3 km

143.9 km Intersection. S'post: Blackwater 73. **SO.**
(31.9 km) Opp. dir. s'post: Rolleston 47. ▲ 115.1 km

175.8 km Bitumen.
(0.3 km) Gravel. ▲ 83.2 km

176.1 km Gravel.
(15.8 km) Bitumen. ▲ 82.9 km

191.9 km S'post: Blackwater. **TR** onto bitumen.
(30.5 km) Gravel.
Opp. dir. s'post: Rolleston. ▲ 67.1 km

222.4 km S'post: Duaringa. **TR** onto Capricorn Hwy and enter Blackwater. **SO.**

> *Blackwater business centre immediately on left.* PD *Supplies, caravan park.*

(20.1 km) Opp. dir. s'post: Rolleston. ▲ 36.6 km

242.5 km Bluff town centre. **SO.**

> P *Supplies.*

(6.5 km) ▲ 16.5 km

249.0 km Walton Creek. Cross bridge.
(10.0 km) ▲ 10.0 km

259.0 km S'post: Blackdown Tableland National Park.

> *Caution: steep, winding road to Blackdown Tableland National Park camping area. Road not suitable for full-sized caravans.*

Opp. dir. s'post: Blackwater.

0.0 km Zero trip meter at above intersection. **TR** off Capricorn Hwy onto gravel. **SO.**
(28.6 km) ▲ 0.0 km
▲ 31.3 km

28.6 km North Mimosa Creek. Causeway.
(2.6 km) ▲ 2.7 km

Mimosa Creek, Blackdown Tableland

31.2 km South Mimosa Creek. Causeway.
(0.1 km) ▲ 0.1 km

31.3 km S'post: Mimosa Creek Camping Area. **TR.**

> *Picnic tables, fireplaces, toilets, drinking water. Excellent choice of walking tracks to lookouts, waterfalls, rockpools. Self-register on site. Book in advance for peak holiday periods.*

REVERSE DIRECTIONS START ▲ 0.0 km

Option: 4WD loop trip through park.

0.0 km Zero trip meter at above s'post. Optional 4WD loop drive from campsite is 28 km. Start from camping area. Head south.
(4.2 km)

4.2 km Intersection. **TR.**
(4.2 km)

8.4 km Intersection. **KR.**
(1.1 km)

9.5 km Intersection. **SO.**

> *Walking track 5 km each way. Take fresh water. Views of 240-m deep sandstone gorge. Spectacular waterfall after heavy rain.*

(6.7 km)

16.2 km Y intersection. **KR.**
(3.1 km)

19.3 km Charlevue Lookout 100 m off to left. **SO.**

> *Views across a valley to Arthurs Bluff (state forest). Caution: steep incline after leaving lookout.*

(6.5 km)

25.8 km T intersection. **TR** to rejoin main track and return to camping area.
End option.

BLACKDOWN TABLELAND NATIONAL PARK
«»
CLAIRVIEW

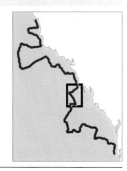

START POINT
Map page 15, J9, 10.

TOTAL KM 293.
UNSEALED KM 139.
DEGREE OF DIFFICULTY Easy.
DRIVING TIME 6 hours.
LONGEST DISTANCE NO FUEL 248 km (Dingo to Clairview).
TOPOGRAPHIC MAPS Auslig 1:250 000 series: *Duaringa; St Lawrence.*
LOCAL/SPECIALITY MAP Sunmap: *Central Queensland.*
OTHER USEFUL INFORMATION QNPWS visitor information sheet: *Blackdown Tableland National Park.*

DESCRIPTION An easy six-hour drive, this trek section has an interesting topography. Near Dingo the countryside is dry and flat, with views of Boomer Range to the right. Beef and wheat are the main industries in this area and you pass through Royles and Tartrus cattle stations. There are a number of creek crossings along the Marlborough–Sarina Road, which skirts the Broadsound Range. From the turnoff to St Lawrence along Croydon Road you head east towards the Coral Sea coast, with a steep descent down Connors Range.

You may want to take a quick look at the old port town of St Lawrence before taking the Bruce Highway to the tiny coastal village of Clairview, at the southern end of Queensland's sugar cane belt. Located right near the beach, the *Golden Mermaid Caravan Resort* is a perfect base from which to fish, crab, sail and swim. An added

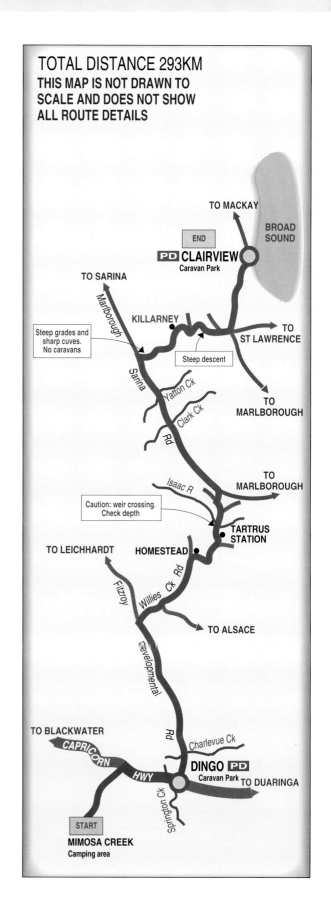

TOTAL DISTANCE 293KM
THIS MAP IS NOT DRAWN TO SCALE AND DOES NOT SHOW ALL ROUTE DETAILS

214

BLACKDOWN TABLELAND NATIONAL PARK «» CLAIRVIEW

attraction is the view of Wild Duck Island and other islands in the Broad Sound (named by Captain Cook). Golden Mermaid has a swimming pool and a tropical shelter. You will also find a caravan park at *Clairview Creek* 14 km south of Clairview. You can fish and swim in the creek next to the park, which has a picnic area.

WARNINGS ▶ Sections of both the Fitzroy Developmental Road and the Marlborough–Sarina Road are prone to flooding. Check in Dingo before proceeding. ▶ Caution should be taken when crossing the Tartrus Weir: the road is covered with flowing water. Check the depth before proceeding. ▶ A section of Croydon Road (between the Marlborough–Sarina Road and the Bruce Highway) crosses the Great Dividing Range; steep grades and sharp curves make this section unsuitable for full-sized caravans.

BOOKINGS AND PERMITS ▶ Book in advance for both the caravan parks at Clairview: Golden Mermaid Caravan Resort, tel. (079) 560 190; Clairview Creek Caravan Park, tel. (079) 560 143.

Crossing Tartrus Weir

ROUTE DIRECTIONS

0.0 km Zero trip meter at Mimosa Creek Camping Ground and main road intersection. **TL** towards Capricorn Hwy.
(31.1 km) ▲ 293.2 km

31.1 km S'post: Duaringa. **TR** onto Capricorn Hwy: bitumen.
(10.8 km) Gravel. Opp. dir. s'post: Blackdown Tableland National Park. ▲ 262.1 km

41.9 km Springton Creek. Cross bridge.
(2.0 km) ▲ 251.3 km

43.9 km S'post: Dysart. **TL** into Dingo town centre.

> **PD** *Supplies, caravan park.*

(1.0 km) Opp. dir. s'post: Blackwater. ▲ 249.3 km

44.9 km S'post: Dysart. **KR** in Dingo on Dingo–Mt Flora road.
(4.8 km) ▲ 248.3 km

49.7 km Charlevue Creek. Cross bridge.
(45.2 km) ▲ 243.5 km

94.9 km S'post: Willies Creek Road. **TR** onto gravel.
(12.4 km) Bitumen. ▲ 198.3 km

107.3 km T intersection. **TL**.
(18.5 km) ▲ 185.9 km

125.8 km Intersection. Royles Road on left. **KR**.
(4.1 km) ▲ 167.4 km

129.9 km Y intersection. **KL**.
(1.8 km) ▲ 163.3 km

131.7 km Grid. **SO**.

> *Royles Homestead on left.*

(3.2 km) ▲ 161.5 km

134.9 km Intersection. **TL**.

> *Road follows fence line.*

(9.4 km) ▲ 158.3 km

144.3 km Cross Tartrus Weir.

> *Caution: flowing water. Check depth. Proceed with caution.*

(1.9 km) ▲ 148.9 km

146.2 km Tartrus Station. **TL**.

> *Private property.*

(0.6 km) ▲ 147.0 km

146.8 km Y intersection. **KR**.

> *Follow fence line.*

(2.2 km) ▲ 146.4 km

149.0 km Cross causeway.
(6.9 km) ▲ 144.2 km

Back road near Clairview

155.9 km Cross causeway.
    (1.4 km) ▲ 137.3 km
157.3 km Cross causeway.
    (1.7 km) ▲ 135.9 km
159.0 km T intersection. **TL** onto Marlborough–Sarina
    Road: bitumen.
    (7.8 km)   Gravel. Opp. dir. s'post: Tartrus. ▲ 134.2 km
166.8 km Clements Creek. Cross bridge.
    (13.0 km) ▲ 120.4 km
179.8 km Stockyard Creek. Cross bridge.
    (9.9 km) ▲ 113.4 km
189.7 km Grave Gully. Cross bridge.
    (1.0 km) ▲ 103.5 km
190.7 km Clark Creek. Cross bridge.
    (11.9 km) ▲ 102.5 km
202.6 km Yatton Creek. Cross bridge.
    (12.8 km) ▲ 90.6 km
215.4 km S'post: St Lawrence 55. **TR** onto gravel:
    Croydon Rd.

> *Warning: road crosses Connors Range. Not suitable for full-sized caravans. Steep grades and sharp curves.*

    (5.9 km)   Bitumen. ▲ 77.8 km
221.3 km Main Creek. Cross bridge.
    (15.8 km) ▲ 71.9 km
237.1 km Killarney property on left. **SO.**
    (4.2 km) ▲ 56.1 km
241.3 km Intersection. S'post: St Lawrence. **SO.**

> *Collaroy off to left.*

    (3.7 km)   Opp. dir. s'post: Croydon. ▲ 51.9 km
245.0 km Bitumen.

> *Caution: steep descent.*

    (2.8 km)   Gravel. ▲ 48.2 km
247.8 km Gravel.
    (3.9 km)   Bitumen. ▲ 45.4 km
251.7 km S'post: Beaconsfield. **SO.**
    (1.9 km) ▲ 41.5 km
253.6 km Creek crossing.
    (1.1 km) ▲ 39.6 km
254.7 km Creek crossing.
    (6.7 km) ▲ 38.5 km
261.4 km Crossroads. S'post: Mackay 155. **TL** onto
    Bruce Hwy.

> *Old port town of St Lawrence 5 km ahead. Open air museum.*

    (17.9 km)   Opp. dir. s'post: Croydon 45. ▲ 31.8 km
279.3 km Clairview Creek Service Station and
    Caravan Park on left. **SO.**

> **PD** *Supplies. Caravan park on creek: picnic tables, barbecues, toilets, hot showers, laundry. Swimming and fishing.*

    (13.2 km) ▲ 13.0 km
292.5 km S'post: Clairview 1. **TR.**
    (0.7 km) ▲ 0.7 km
293.2 km Clairview Golden Mermaid Caravan Resort
    on right.

> **PD** *Supplies. Caravan resort on beach. Clairview is renowned for fishing, crabbing and sailing. Views of off-shore islands in Broad Sound. Resort has swimming pool, tropical shelter with tables and barbecues, toilets, hot showers and laundry.*

REVERSE DIRECTIONS START ▲ 0.0 km

CLAIRVIEW
«»
MACKAY

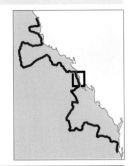

START POINT
Map page 15, J6.

TOTAL KM 183 (including option).

UNSEALED KM 43.

DEGREE OF DIFFICULTY Optional trek to Cape Palmerston National Park is extremely difficult. Clairview to Mackay direct is easy.

DRIVING TIME 6 hours (including optional return trip to Cape Palmerston National Park).

LONGEST DISTANCE NO FUEL 52 km (Ilbilbie return via Cape Palmerston).

TOPOGRAPHIC MAP Auslig 1:250 000 series: *Mackay*.

LOCAL/SPECIALITY MAP Sunmap: *Central Queensland*.

OTHER USEFUL INFORMATION QNPWS visitor information sheet: *Cape Palmerston National Park*; Tourism Mackay Inc. booklet: *Destination Mackay Holiday Guide*.

DESCRIPTION The tropical city of Mackay is only an hour's drive north of Clairview via the Bruce Highway. For a challenge on the way, detour from Ilbilbie to the isolated and very beautiful Cape Palmerston National Park. Accessible only by four-wheel drive, you can reach the cape by an inland track along swamplands, or by a beach track which skirts the coastal sand dunes. It takes nearly 2 hours to negotiate the 15-kilometre inland track, an indication of how difficult this route can be. The beach track is quicker and smoother, but still requires skill and care.

Once at the cape you can bushwalk or swim and fish on the beach. The lookout at the top of Cape Palmerston gives you views of the Northumberland Isles and Mt Funnel, an extinct volcanic crater. Birdwatchers will find plenty to see, including sea eagles, swallows and

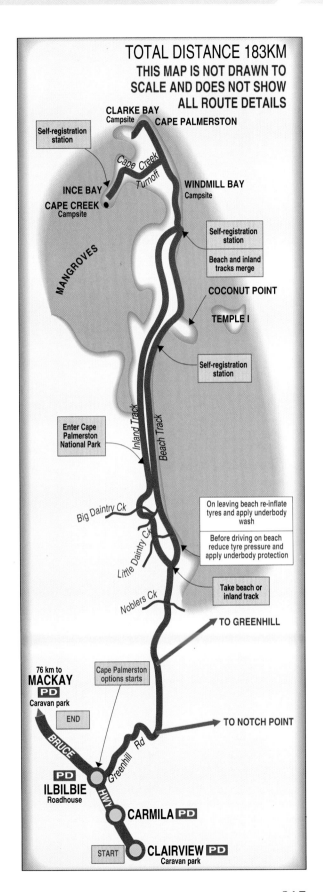

TOTAL DISTANCE 183KM
THIS MAP IS NOT DRAWN TO
SCALE AND DOES NOT SHOW
ALL ROUTE DETAILS

Victoria Street, Mackay

Blacks Beach, Mackay

finches. Overnight visitors can pitch a tent under the sheoaks at the *Windmill Bay* or *Cape Creek* bush campsites. Cape Creek, a popular destination for local anglers, is the best spot to fish. Campers should be self-sufficient with food, water, fuel and insect repellent. There are no facilities.

You may want to plan for more than an overnight stay in Mackay, a sunny, attractive city where lorikeets sing in the palms which line the main street and the beaches. Close to rainforests and the Great Barrier Reef, Mackay is the centre of a rich sugar, coal and grain-producing district.

The region is renowned for reef, ocean and island fishing. Crab, prawns and other seafood are available in Mackay's restaurants. If you are camping you can purchase fresh seafood to barbecue at one of the aquaculture farms in Sarina, 39 kilometres from Ilbilbie.

Day and extended cruises leave Mackay Harbour to Credlin Reef and some of the Cumberland and Whitsunday islands. You can hire snorkelling and scuba-diving equipment, or just swim and explore. Camping is allowed on some of the island national parks near Mackay. Check with the Mackay QNPWS office. You can also camp at a number of beachfront caravan parks in and around *Mackay*.

WARNINGS ▶ The optional trip to Cape Palmerston is extremely difficult. Do not attempt with trailers or caravans. The inland track may be impassable for several weeks after heavy rain. Check track conditions and weather reports with the Mackay QNPWS, Cnr River and Wood Streets, Mackay QLD 4740; tel. (079) 51 8788. Office hours are 8 am–5 pm. ▶ The alternative beach route is quicker and smoother but the tide height should be half-tide or lower. Check with the QNPWS Mackay office. ▶ Before taking beach route, spray vehicle with underbody protection (oil spray). Use underbody wash after leaving the beach. ▶ Tyre pressure should be 15–20 psi for beach travel. ▶ Swimmers, beware box jellyfish during summer. ▶ Do not destroy native flora. Use driftwood from the beach. ▶ Remove all rubbish from the park.

BOOKINGS AND PERMITS ▶ A Cape Palmerston map and an information sheet are available at Ilbilbie Roadhouse. ▶ Obtain a camping permit from one of the self-registration stations in Cape Palmerston National Park. ▶ For details about permits and camping on island national parks near Mackay, contact the Mackay QNPWS office. ▶ Tourist information and details about caravan parks and other accommodation is available from Tourism Mackay Inc., The Mill, 320 Nebo Road, Mackay QLD 4740; tel. (079) 52 2677.

ROUTE DIRECTIONS

0.0 km Zero trip meter in Clairview at Bruce Hwy intersection. **TR** towards Mackay. **SO** along Bruce Hwy. **PD**

(21.5 km) ▲ 55.3 km

21.5 km Exotic Fruit Garden Cafe on right. **SO**.

> *Picnic area and playground. Cafe in orchard setting.*

(7.7 km) ▲ 33.8 km

29.2 km Carmila township and beach off to right. **SO**. **PD**

(26.1 km) ▲ 26.1 km

55.3 km Intersection. S'post: Greenhill 11.

> *Ilbilbie Roadhouse off to left.* **PD** *Supplies. QNPWS map and information about Cape Palmerston National Park avail. at roadhouse. Cape Palmerston is an idyllic place to fish, swim, bushwalk and birdwatch.*

Cape Palmerston National Park

Start optional trek or continue on Bruce Hwy to Mackay (75 km).

▲ 0.0 km

Opp dir: start optional trek or continue on Bruce Hwy to Clairview (55.3 km)

0.0 km Zero trip meter at above intersection. **TR** onto Greenhill Road.
(4.6 km)

4.6 km Y intersection. **KL** onto gravel.

Notch Point off to right.

(2.5 km)

7.1 km Bush track. **TL.**

Track entrance is obscured and not signposted. Greenhill is straight ahead. Engage 4WD.

(2.6 km)

9.7 km Cross Noblers Creek.
(1.4 km)

11.1 km Y junction. **KL** to take inland track to Cape Creek or Windmill Bay campsites. **KR** to take beach track.

Inland track: approx. 15 km and approx. 2 hours drive.

Extremely difficult, sometimes impassable. Check track condition with QNPWS Mackay.

Beach track: a quicker, smoother route to campsites.

Tide should be half-tide or lower. Check with QNPWS Mackay. Tyre pressure should be at 15–20 psi. Take underbody protection and wash.

Return to Bruce Hwy and **TR. SO** to Mackay (approx. 75 km).

PD *Supplies, caravan parks. Beaches. Access to national park islands and the Great Barrier Reef.*

REVERSE DIRECTIONS START ▲ 0.0 km
Take Bruce Hwy from Mackay 75 km to Ilbilbie Roadhouse. **TL** onto Greenhill Rd for Cape Palmerston option or continue **SO** along Bruce Hwy 55 km to Clairview.

MACKAY
«»
EUNGELLA NATIONAL PARK

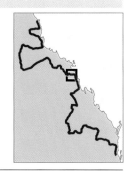

START POINT
Map page 15, J4.

TOTAL KM 119.
UNSEALED KM 65.
DEGREE OF DIFFICULTY Difficult. The optional route via Finch Hatton and Eungella is easy.
DRIVING TIME 5 hours.
LONGEST DISTANCE NO FUEL 82 km (Gargett to Eungella).
TOPOGRAPHIC MAP Auslig 1:250 000 series: *Mackay.*
LOCAL/SPECIALTY MAP Sunmap: *North Queensland.*
OTHER USEFUL INFORMATION QNPWS visitor information sheet: *Eungella National Park.*

DESCRIPTION Eungella National Park lies 80 kilometres west of Mackay in the majestic, high-altitude Clarke Range. Originally called 'land of clouds' by the Aborigines, the range is covered in rainforest except for the north-west section – an area of open, drier forest and deep gorges. To reach the park from Mackay you have two choices. The challenging, plotted route through Mia Mia State Forest takes 5 hours. It is a scenic drive in which you climb the Clarke Range before traversing its summit through eucalypt and rainforest. Skill and experience are needed to negotiate this route.

Inexperienced four-wheel drivers are advised to take the easier, shorter option. Take the Eungella turnoff and follow the Mackay–Eungella Road through the Pioneer Valley before climbing steeply up the Clarke Range, via Finch Hatton, to Eungella. You may like to detour into Finch Hatton Gorge, a secluded area of the park, where you can swim, watch platypus, and explore rainforest on walking tracks. The longest track climbs to the peak of Mt Dalrymple, Queensland's third highest mountain.

Apart from Finch Hatton Gorge and Broken River, most of the park is inaccessible. The QNPWS ranger's office, a picnic area and camping ground are at Broken River, 6 kilometres south of Eungella. From the walkway and platforms over the river you can watch duck-billed platypus (best at sunrise and sunset during summer).

The Eungella honeyeater, day frog and orange sided skink are unique to the park. Take the Palm Walk along the edge of the range to lookouts with views across cane farms in Pioneer Valley to the bulk sugar terminal in Mackay's harbour, and the islands offshore. The Broken River walking trail winds along the river through tranquil rainforest.

Fern Flat camping ground and picnic area is half a kilometre from the ranger's office, adjacent to the river, and minutes from the nearest swimming hole. If you take the Finch Hatton/Eungella route you may prefer to camp at Finch Hatton Gorge in the privately owned *Platypus Bush Camp.* There are a small number of huts and campsites (toilets only, no showers). Private chalet accommodation is available in *Eungella* and the town has several caravan parks.

WARNINGS ▶ The route through Mia Mia State Forest is very difficult and should not be attempted by the inexperienced four-wheel driver. There are many creek crossings, and after heavy rain washaways and landslides are common. ▶ During major rainfall dense fog occurs on the range. ▶ Caravans are unsuited to the forest track and take care on the steep, winding section of the Mackay–Eungella Road between Finch Hatton and Eungella.

BOOKINGS AND PERMITS ▶ Obtain a permit for the Mia Mia State Forest track from the Mackay District Forestry Office, Michelmores Building, Cnr Wood and River Streets, Mackay QLD 4740; PO Box 582, Mackay QLD 4740; tel. (079) 51 8747. ▶ During peak holiday periods book in advance to camp at Eungella National Park. Self-register at other times. Contact the QNPWS, Cnr Wood and River Streets, Mackay QLD 4740; PO Box 623, Mackay QLD 4740; tel. (079) 51 8788; or the Ranger, Eungella National Park c/- Post Office, Dalrymple Heights QLD 4740; tel. (079) 58 4552. ▶ For enquiries about Platypus Bush Camp, tel. (079) 58 3204.

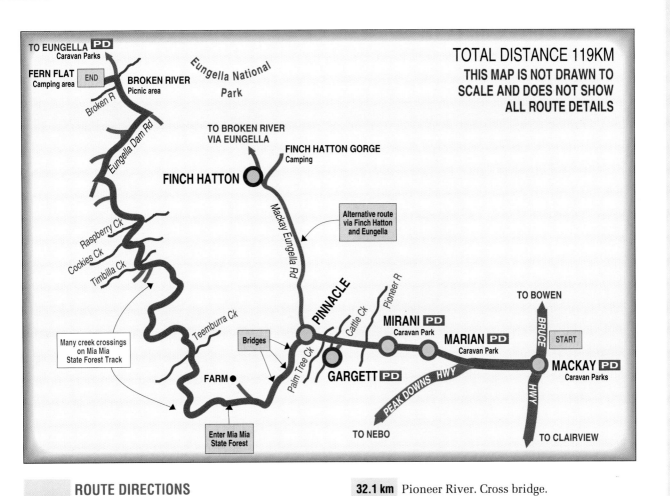

TOTAL DISTANCE 119KM
THIS MAP IS NOT DRAWN TO SCALE AND DOES NOT SHOW ALL ROUTE DETAILS

ROUTE DIRECTIONS

0.0 km Zero trip meter at intersection Bruce Hwy and Peak Downs Hwy in Mackay facing west towards Nebo. S'post: Nebo/Eungella. **SO** along Peak Downs Hwy.

> **PD** *Supplies in Mackay.*

(0.4 km) ▲ 119.2 km

0.4 km S'post: Eungella National Park 77. **SO.**

(5.9 km) ▲ 118.8 km

6.3 km S'post: Eungella. **TR** off hwy onto Mackay–Eungella Rd.

(16.7 km) ▲ 112.9 km

23.0 km Marian town centre. **SO.**

> **PD** *Supplies, caravan park.*

(8.8 km) ▲ 96.2 km

31.8 km Mirani town centre. **SO.**

> **PD** *Supplies, caravan park. Museum in the town library houses artefacts from the Pioneer Valley.*

(0.3 km) ▲ 87.4 km

32.1 km Pioneer River. Cross bridge.

(13.3 km) ▲ 87.1 km

45.4 km Cross railway line.

> *Gargett township off to left.* **PD** *Supplies.*

(1.3 km) ▲ 73.8 km

46.7 km Cattle Creek. Cross bridge.

> *Small picnic area.*

(0.8 km) ▲ 72.5 km

47.5 km Palm Tree Creek. Cross bridge.

(1.2 km) ▲ 71.7 km

48.7 km S'post: Septimus 6. **TL. SO** towards Septimus and Eungella.

> *An alternative route to the park is to continue on Mackay–Eungella Rd through Finch Hatton to Eungella. Broken River is 6 km south along Eungella–Broken River Rd.*

(0.3 km) ▲ 70.5 km

Pioneer Valley

49.0 km   Intersection. **SO**.

> *Pinnacle St on right.*

(0.4 km)   ▲ 70.2 km
49.4 km   Cross wooden single-lane bridge.
(2.5 km)   ▲ 69.8 km
51.9 km   Cross single-lane concrete bridge.
(1.4 km)   ▲ 67.3 km
53.3 km   Cross single-lane wooden bridge.
(0.5 km)   ▲ 65.9 km
53.8 km   Y intersection. **TR** onto gravel track.

> *Turnoff is immediately before a single-lane
> bridge.*

(0.1 km)   Bitumen. ▲ 65.4 km
53.9 km   Y intersection. Private s'post: Captains
Crossing/Teemburra Creek. **KL**.
(0.2 km)   ▲ 65.3 km
54.1 km   Creek crossing.
(0.4 km)   ▲ 65.1 km
54.5 km   Cattle grid.
(0.5 km)   ▲ 64.7 km

55.0 km   Cross grid. S'post: Mia Mia State Forest. **SO**.

> *Warning: dry weather road. Restricted
> vehicle access, 4WD only. Permit required.
> Narrow and winding section up Clarke
> Range.*

(2.7 km)   ▲ 64.2 km
57.7 km   Creek crossing.
(1.1 km)   ▲ 61.5 km
58.8 km   McLeans Creek. Cross causeway.
(1.5 km)   ▲ 60.4 km
60.3 km   Cherrytree Creek. Cross causeway.
(2.3 km)   ▲ 58.9 km
62.6 km   Teemburra Creek/Captains Crossing.

> *Caution: possible washaway ahead.*

(7.7 km)   ▲ 56.6 km
70.3 km   Creek crossing.
(1.0 km)   ▲ 48.9 km
71.3 km   Creek crossing.
(1.1 km)   ▲ 47.9 km
72.4 km   Endeavour Creek crossing.

> *Caution: difficult. Take care.*

(0.1 km)   ▲ 46.8 km
72.5 km   Intersection to detour. **TL**.

> *Caution: washaway ahead.*

(0.2 km)   ▲ 46.7 km
72.7 km   Creek crossing.

> *Caution: steep entry and egress on Clarke
> Range. Landslides and washaways after
> heavy rain. Track can be slippery.*

(2.3 km)   ▲ 46.5 km
75.0 km   Creek crossing.
(0.7 km)   ▲ 44.2 km
75.7 km   Creek crossing.

> *Look for King Orchids in bloom high in the
> treetops, in spring.*

(13.6 km)   ▲ 43.5 km
89.3 km   Creek crossing.
(1.2 km)   ▲ 29.9 km
90.5 km   Intersection. **SO**.
(1.0 km)   ▲ 28.7 km
91.5 km   Cattle grid. **SO**.
(2.8 km)   ▲ 27.7 km
94.3 km   Intersection. **SO**.
(6.1 km)   ▲ 24.9 km
100.4 km Timbilla Creek crossing.
(1.4 km)   ▲ 18.8 km

Broken River, Eungella National Park

101.8 km Cockies Creek crossing.
(1.3 km)   ▲ 17.4 km

103.1 km Raspberry Creek crossing.
(2.8 km)   ▲ 16.1 km

105.9 km Intersection. **SO**.
(1.6 km)   ▲ 13.3 km

107.5 km Cattle grid. **SO**.
(1.8 km)   Opp. dir. sign: dry weather road only.
                Restricted vehicle access. 4WD only. ▲ 11.7 km

109.3 km T intersection. **TR**.
(2.0 km)   Opp. dir. s'post:
                          Crediton State Forest. ▲ 9.9 km

111.3 km Intersection. **SO** on Eungella Dam Rd.
(1.8 km)   ▲ 7.9 km

113.1 km Intersection. **KR**.
(1.0 km)   Opp. dir. s'post:
                   Eungella Dam/Collinsville. ▲ 6.1 km

114.1 km T intersection. S'post: Eungella 10. **TL**.
(4.9 km)   Opp. dir. s'post: Eungella Dam 23. ▲ 5.1 km

119.0 km Bitumen.
(0.2 km)   Gravel. ▲ 0.2 km

119.2 km Eungella National Park: Broken River
Picnic Ground.

> *Ranger station, kiosk, information centre.*
> *Self-register if unattended. Take internal*
> *road on left of office 0.5 km to Fern Flat*
> *Camping Area (adjacent to river). Picnic*
> *tables, barbecues, toilets, hot showers. Palm*
> *Walk and Broken River walking tracks,*
> *swimming holes. Abundant wildlife.*

REVERSE DIRECTIONS START ▲ 0.0 km

EUNGELLA NATIONAL PARK

«»

BURDEKIN FALLS DAM

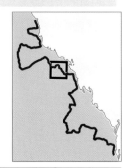

START POINT
Map page 14, I3.

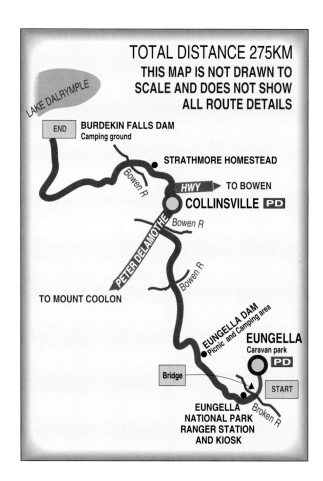

TOTAL DISTANCE 275KM
THIS MAP IS NOT DRAWN TO SCALE AND DOES NOT SHOW ALL ROUTE DETAILS

TOTAL KM 275.
UNSEALED KM 243.
DEGREE OF DIFFICULTY Moderate.
DRIVING TIME 7 hours.
LONGEST DISTANCE NO FUEL 200 km (Collinsville to Ravenswood, next section).
TOPOGRAPHIC MAP Auslig 1:250 000 series: *Mt Coolon*.
LOCAL/SPECIALITY MAP Sunmap: *North Queensland*.
OTHER USEFUL INFORMATION *See Bookings and Permits.*

DESCRIPTION Long stretches of unsealed road make this a tiring trip. Just 20 kilometres from Eungella National Park you pass Eungella Dam, an important water storage area and fauna sanctuary – a peaceful spot to fish, swim or sail. From here you cross huge tracts of cattle country, past a number of homesteads. The only town on this trip is Collinsville, a coal mining town in the Bowen River coal basin.

The drive across the Burdekin Falls Dam spillway at the edge of Lake Dalrymple is exciting (and safe, the access gates are closed if the level is overflowing). Almost four times the size of Sydney Harbour, this massive lake is the largest water storage area in Queensland, supplying water to the Townsville and Burdekin Delta region. It is a popular location for water sports and fishing, particularly barramundi. Burdekin Falls is a short walk downstream from the spillway. The Burdekin Falls Dam Camping Ground and picnic area are right near the dam wall, with good views.

WARNINGS ▶ After heavy rain sections of unsealed road are impassable and creek crossings are prone to flooding. Check the Eungella–Collinsville section with the Eungella QNPWS Ranger, (070) 88 1033; and the Collinsville–Burdekin Falls Dam section with Collinsville Police, (077) 85 5377; or the dam supervisor, (077) 70 3177. ▶ For information on crossing the dam spillway, contact the dam supervisor. ▶ Beware, crocodiles may inhabit waterways in this area.

BOOKINGS AND PERMITS ▶ Advance bookings to camp at Burdekin Falls Dam are required in peak holiday periods. Register with the supervisor on site. For enquiries tel. (077) 70 3177. ▶ For tourist information contact Townsville Enterprise Ltd, Enterprise House, 3 The Strand, Townsville QLD 4810; tel. (077) 71 3061.

Burdekin Falls Dam spillway

ROUTE DIRECTIONS

0.0 km Zero trip meter at Broken River bridge adjacent to Eungella National Park s'post, heading towards Eungella Dam. **SO**.

> **PD** *Supplies at Eungella.*

(0.1 km) ▲ 275. 2 km

0.1 km Eungella National Park ranger station and kiosk on right.

(0.2 km) ▲ 275.1 km

0.3 km Gravel.

(2.9 km) Bitumen. ▲ 274.9 km

3.2 km S'post: Eungella Dam 25. **KR**.

(2.0 km) Opp. dir. s'post: Eungella 8. ▲ 272.0 km

5.2 km S'post: Eungella Dam 23. **TR**.

(1.0 km) Opp. dir. s'post: Eungella 10. ▲ 270.0 km

6.2 km S'post: Eungella Dam/Collinsville. **KL**.

(18.4 km) ▲ 269.0 km

24.6 km Eungella Dam Camping Ground and boat ramp on right. **SO**.

> *Fauna sanctuary. Fishing, canoeing, windsurfing, water skiing, sailing and swimming.*

(1.1 km) ▲ 250.6 km

25.7 km Eungella Dam Picnic Area on right. **SO**.

> *Picnic tables, barbecues, toilets.*

(0.4 km) ▲ 249.5 km

26.1 km S'post: Collinsville 121. **TL**.

(0.4 km) ▲ 249.1 km

26.5 km Mt Barker Lookout turnoff on right.

> *Excellent views over Eungella Dam.*

(1.2 km) ▲ 248.7 km

27.7 km Gate.

> *Leave as found.*

(6.2 km) ▲ 247.5 km

33.9 km Gate.

> *Leave as found.*

(0.8 km) ▲ 241.3 km

EUNGELLA NATIONAL PARK «» BURDEKIN FALLS DAM

34.7 km S'post: Collinsville. **KL.**
(8.1 km) ▲ 240.5 km
42.8 km Creek crossing.
(3.5 km) ▲ 232.4 km
46.3 km Cattle grid.

> *Homestead on right.*

(0.3 km) ▲ 228.9 km
46.6 km S'post: Collinsville. **KR.**
(0.9 km) Opp. dir s'post: Eungella Dam. ▲ 228.6 km
47.5 km Y intersection. **KR.**
(4.3 km) ▲ 227.7 km
51.8 km Causeway.
(8.6 km) ▲ 223.4 km
60.4 km Bowen River.

> *Wide causeway.*

(6.1 km) ▲ 214.8 km
66.5 km Intersection. **SO.**

> *Exmoore Station off to right.*

(15.7 km) ▲ 208.7 km
82.2 km Gate.

> *Leave as found.*

(7.0 km) ▲ 193.0 km
89.2 km Gate.

> *Leave as found.*

(0.3 km) ▲ 186.0 km
89.5 km Homestead on right.
(9.5 km) ▲ 185.7 km
99.0 km Concrete bridge.
(14.2 km) ▲ 176.2 km
113.2 km T intersection. **TR.**
(0.1 km) ▲ 162.0 km
113.3 km Bitumen. Bowen River. Cross bridge.
(19.5 km) ▲ 161.9 km
132.8 km Pelican Creek. Cross bridge.
(3.5 km) ▲ 142.4 km
136.3 km S'post: Bowen 87. **KL.**
(0.7 km) ▲ 138.9 km
137.0 km Collinsville Post Office.

> **PD** *Supplies. Next fuel Ravenswood (200 km). Open-cut coal mine and power station in this area in the Bowen River basin.*

(0.2 km) ▲ 138.2 km
137.2 km S'post: Bowen 88. **TR.**
(3.9 km) ▲ 138.0 km

Cattle in creek near Burdekin Falls Dam

Burdekin Falls Dam Camping Ground

Fallen tree, back road

EUNGELLA NATIONAL PARK «» BURDEKIN FALLS DAM

141.1 km S'post: Strathmore 23. **TL** onto gravel.
    (1.3 km)   Bitumen. Opp. dir. s'post:
                    Collinsville 4. ▲ 134.1 km

142.4 km S'post: Burdekin Falls Dam 117. **SO.**
    (0.6 km)   ▲ 132.8 km

143.0 km Causeway.
    (10.6 km)   ▲ 132.2 km

153.6 km Causeway.
    (6.2 km)   ▲ 121.6 km

159.8 km Causeway.
    (4.4 km)   ▲ 115.4 km

164.2 km Strathmore Homestead on right.
    (8.6 km)   ▲ 111.0 km

172.8 km Bowen River. Cross bridge.
    (1.1 km)   ▲ 102.4 km

173.9 km Blue Valley/Mt Wickham off to right. **SO.**
    (1.8 km)   ▲ 101.3 km

175.7 km Causeway.
    (5.0 km)   ▲ 99.5 km

180.7 km Y intersection. **KL.**

> *Panhandle off to right.*

    (0.3 km)   ▲ 94.5 km

181.0 km Causeway.
    (3.1 km)   ▲ 94.2 km

184.1 km Causeway.
    (19.3 km)   ▲ 91.1 km

203.4 km Bitumen.
    (1.2 km)   Gravel. ▲ 71.8 km

204.6 km Gravel.
    (17.7 km)   Bitumen. ▲ 70.6 km

222.3 km S'post: Burdekin Falls Dam. **KL.**
    (7.3 km)   ▲ 52.9 km

229.6 km Nuggety Gully. Causeway.
    (6.2 km)   ▲ 45.6 km

235.8 km Causeway.
    (1.1 km)   ▲ 39.4 km

236.9 km Y intersection. S'post: Burdekin Falls Dam.
    KR.
    (24.1 km)   Opp. dir. s'post:
            Bowen via Strathmore. ▲ 38.3 km

261.0 km Intersection. **SO.**

> *Glendon Station off to right.*

    (4.6 km)   ▲ 14.2 km

265.6 km Cross causeway.
    (6.3 km)   ▲ 9.6 km

271.9 km Burdekin Falls Dam spillway. **KR** adjacent
    to dam wall onto bitumen.
    (0.2 km)   Opp. dir. s'post:
       Collinsville via Strathmore 134. ▲ 3.3 km

Broken River Range

272.1 km Gate. S'post: warning – road subject to
    flooding. **SO.**
    (2.8 km)   ▲ 3.1 km

274.9 km Burdekin Falls Dam Camping Ground on
    left.
    (0.1 km)   ▲ 0.3 km

275.0 km S'post: Queensland Water Resources
    Commission Office. **TL.**
    (0.2 km)   Opp. dir. s'post: Collinsville. ▲ 0.2 km

275.2 km Information Centre.

> *Register at centre. Camping ground adjacent to the dam wall overlooking Lake Dalrymple. Water skiing, windsurfing, fishing, swimming, sailing, canoeing. Camping ground has motel units, picnic tables, barbecues, water, toilets, hot showers and a laundry.*

REVERSE DIRECTIONS START ▲ 0.0 km

BURDEKIN FALLS DAM «» CHARTERS TOWERS

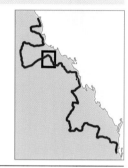

START POINT
Map page 14, F2.

TOTAL KM 165.
UNSEALED KM Nil.
DEGREE OF DIFFICULTY Easy.
DRIVING TIME REQUIRED 3 hours.
LONGEST DISTANCE NO FUEL 43 km (Ravenswood to Mingela).
TOPOGRAPHIC MAPS Auslig: 1:250 000 series: *Bowen; Charters Towers.*
LOCAL/SPECIALITY MAP Sunmap: *North Queensland.*
OTHER USEFUL INFORMATION *See Bookings and Permits.*

DESCRIPTION This three-hour drive through hot, dry, cattle country is easy, leaving you time to sightsee in Charters Towers, once known locally as 'The World'. Take a short detour to the old goldrush town of Ravenswood on the way, once the first major town in north Queensland, now only a few inhabitants remain. The headstones in the cemetery reveal a lot about this ghost town's history.

Beef and boarding schools, not gold, are now the lifeblood of Charters Towers. Queensland's second largest city in 1877, most of its original buildings have been restored: Royal Arcade, the Stock Exchange building and the post office are classic examples of colonial architecture. Visit in the first week of May to catch the annual country music festival, or in late July when the annual show and rodeo are held. There are a number of caravan parks in *Charters Towers.*

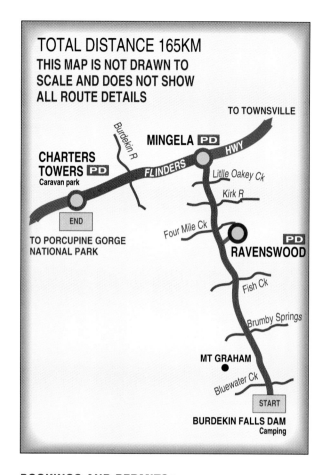

TOTAL DISTANCE 165KM
THIS MAP IS NOT DRAWN TO SCALE AND DOES NOT SHOW ALL ROUTE DETAILS

BOOKINGS AND PERMITS ▶ For tourist information contact National Trust, Charters Towers Branch, Stock Exchange Arcade, Mosman Street, Charters Towers QLD 4820; tel. (077) 87 2374; or Townsville Enterprise Limited, Enterprise House, 3 The Strand, Townsville QLD 4810; tel. (077) 71 3061.

ROUTE DIRECTIONS

0.0 km	Zero trip meter at Burdekin Falls Dam Camping Ground exit. **TL.**	
	(0.1 km)	▲ 164.8 km
0.1 km	S'post: Ravenswood. **TR.**	
	(4.0 km)	Opp. dir. s'post: Collinsville/Glendon ▲ 164.7 km
4.1 km	Bluewater Creek. Cross bridge.	
	(4.0 km)	▲ 160.7km
8.1 km	Mt Graham on left.	
	(26.0 km)	▲ 156.7 km
34.1 km	Brumby Springs. Cross bridge.	
	(26.8 km)	▲ 130.7 km
60.9 km	Fish Creek. Cross bridge.	
	(20.0 km)	▲ 103.9 km
80.9 km	S'post: Mingela 39. **SO.**	

Charters Towers City Hall

Church in Ravenswood

Historic gold-rush town of Ravenswood 2 km off to right. **PD**	
(2.7 km)	▲ 83.9 km
83.6 km Four Mile Creek. Cross bridge.	
(15.9 km)	Opp. dir. s'post: Burdekin Falls Dam ▲ 81.2 km
99.5 km Kirk River. Cross bridge.	
(11.6 km)	▲ 65.3 km
111.1 km Little Oakey Creek. Cross bridge.	
(8.5 km)	▲ 53.7 km
119.6 km T intersection in Mingela. **TL**.	

PD *General store. The annual Mingela Rodeo and Race Day is held in the first week of May.*

(0.8 km)	▲ 45.2 km
120.4 km S'post: Charters Towers 47. **TL** onto Flinders Hwy.	
(25.4 km) Opp. dir. s'post:Mingela 1. ▲ 44.4 km	
145.8 km Burdekin River. Cross bridge.	
(19.0 km)	▲ 19.0 km

164.8 km Charters Towers 60 km/h sign. **SO** to town centre.

PD *Supplies, caravan parks, private accommodation. Tourist information at National Trust shop in Stock Exchange Arcade.*

REVERSE DIRECTIONS START ▲ 0.0 km

CHARTERS TOWERS
«»
PORCUPINE GORGE NATIONAL PARK

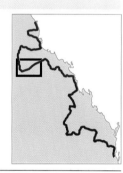

START POINT
Map page 14, D1.

TOTAL KM 282.
UNSEALED KM 76.
DEGREE OF DIFFICULTY Easy.
DRIVING TIME REQUIRED 5 hours.
LONGEST DISTANCE NO FUEL 287 km (Prairie to The Lynd, next section).
TOPOGRAPHIC MAP Auslig 1:250 000 series: *Hughenden*.
LOCAL/SPECIALITY MAP Sunmap: *North Queensland*.
OTHER USEFUL INFORMATION QNPWS visitor information sheet: *Porcupine Gorge National Park*.

DESCRIPTION The first 206 kilometres of this five-hour trip take you along the Flinders Highway through grazing district broken by the small towns of Balfes Creek, Homestead, Pentland and Prairie. After Prairie the route deviates from the highway onto unsealed road, across 30 kilometres of plains, sparsely covered with eucalypts and acacias. Once on the Kennedy Developmental Road you can not miss the Porcupine Gorge National Park. The vibrantly coloured sandstone walls of this 'mini Grand Canyon' rise suddenly out of the plains on your right, about 45 kilometres north of Hughenden.

The Kennedy Developmental Road runs parallel to the western side of the gorge. Stop at the viewing platform at Porcupine Gorge Lookout before entering

Pyramid, Porcupine Gorge

the park from Pyramid Lookout at the northern end of the gorge. A gently descending walking track takes you down into the gorge. It is an easy walk downstream along flat sandstone rocks which line Porcupine Creek, where tortoises swim in deep pools lined with sheoaks and paperbarks. Black ducks and rock wallabies are a common sight. At sunset, the sound of parrots and currawongs echo in the gorge. There are campsites at the *Pyramid* and a pit toilet and shelter shed is provided (no water or showers).

WARNING ▶ The detour from the Flinders Highway onto Kennedy Developmental Road should not be attempted after wet weather: the Flinders River becomes impassable. The alternative, via Hughenden, adds about 40 km to the trip.

BOOKINGS AND PERMITS ▶ Campers can self-register at the Pyramid or obtain a permit from QNPWS, Great Barrier Reef Wonderland Office, Box 5391, Townsville Mail Exchange, Townsville QLD 4810; tel. (077) 21 2399; or QNPWS, Natal Downs Road, Charters Towers QLD 4820; PO Box 187, Charters Towers QLD 4820; tel. (077) 87 3388.

230

CHARTERS TOWERS «» PORCUPINE GORGE NP

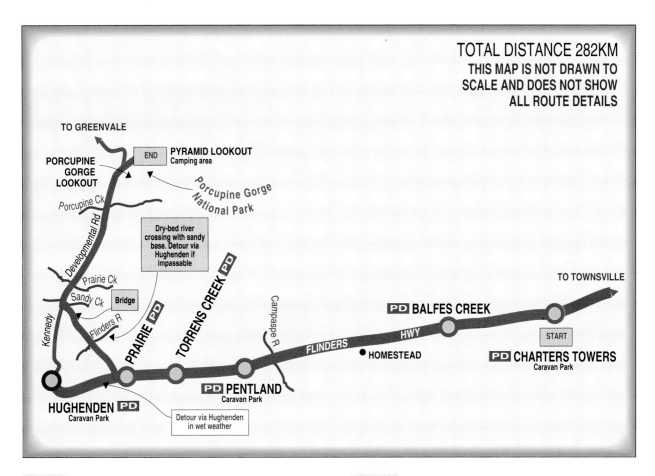

TOTAL DISTANCE 282KM
THIS MAP IS NOT DRAWN TO
SCALE AND DOES NOT SHOW
ALL ROUTE DETAILS

TO GREENVALE

END PYRAMID LOOKOUT
Camping area

PORCUPINE
GORGE
LOOKOUT

Porcupine Gorge
National Park

Porcupine Ck

Dry-bed river
crossing with sandy
base. Detour via
Hughenden if
impassable

Developmental Rd

Prairie Ck

Sandy Ck **Bridge**

PRAIRIE PD

TORRENS CREEK PD

Campaspe R

TO TOWNSVILLE

PD BALFES CREEK

Kennedy

Flinders R

FLINDERS HWY

HOMESTEAD

START

PD CHARTERS TOWERS
Caravan Park

PD PENTLAND
Caravan Park

HUGHENDEN **PD**
Caravan Park

Detour via Hughenden
in wet weather

ROUTE DIRECTIONS

0.0 km Zero trip meter outside Charters Towers on Hughenden Rd at 80 km/h sign. **SO** towards Hughenden.
(2.3 km) ▲ 271.4 km

2.3 km S'post: Hughenden. **KR** on Flinders Hwy.
(39.0 km) ▲ 269.1 km

41.3 km Balfes Creek town centre.
PD
(31.5 km) ▲ 230.1 km

72.8 km Homestead town centre.
(15.9 km) ▲ 198.6 km

88.7 km Campaspe River. Cross bridge.

Picnic area on left.

(17.0 km) ▲ 182.7 km

105.7 km Pentland town centre.

PD *Caravan park.*

(52.0 km) ▲ 165.7 km

157.7 km Torrens Creek town centre.
PD
(45.4 km) ▲ 113.7 km

203.1 km Prairie Post Office.

PD *Locals praise the 'Prairie sausage', reputedly Australia's tastiest. Next fuel The Lynd (287 km).*

(2.7 km) ▲ 68.3 km

205.8 km S'post: Glendower. **TR** onto gravel.

Following wet weather detour via Hughenden by continuing on the Flinders Hwy and taking the Kennedy Developmental Rd.

(9.8 km) Bitumen. ▲ 65.6 km

215.6 km Gate.

Leave as found.

(4.1 km) ▲ 55.8 km

219.7 km Intersection. **SO.**
(3.3 km) ▲ 51.7 km

223.0 km Creek crossing.

100 m to Flinders River: dry-bed river crossing with sandy base. Detour via Hughenden in wet weather.

(1.6 km) ▲ 48.4 km

231

224.6 km Y intersection. **KR**. Gate.

> *Leave as found.*

(3.2 km) ▲ 46.8 km

227.8 km Gate.

> *Leave as found.*

(1.2 km) ▲ 43.6 km

229.0 km Causeway.

(6.9 km) ▲ 42.4 km

235.9 km Gate.

> *Leave as found.*

(0.6 km) ▲ 35.5 km

236.5 km T intersection. **TR** onto Kennedy Developmental Rd.

(0.8 km)   Opp. dir. s'post: Glentor Rd. ▲ 34.9 km

237.3 km Sandy Creek. Cross bridge.

(5.7 km) ▲ 34.1 km

243.0 km Cross Prairie Creek.

(3.3 km) ▲ 28.4 km

246.3 km Porcupine Creek. Cross bridge.

(25.1 km) ▲ 25.1 km

271.4 km S'post: Porcupine Gorge 1.5.

> *Turn right to view Porcupine Gorge from lookout. Return to Kennedy Developmental Rd and turn right.*

0.0 km Zero trip meter on Kennedy Developmental Rd opposite turnoff to Porcupine Gorge Lookout. **SO**.

(3.5 km) ▲ 0.0 km
    ▲ 10.6 km

3.5 km S'post: Pyramid Lookout 7. **KR**.

(4.6 km)   Opp. dir. s'post: Hughenden 64. ▲ 7.1 km

8.1 km Y intersection. S'post: Pyramid Lookout 2.5. **KR**.

(2.5 km) ▲ 2.5 km

10.6 km Pyramid Camping Area.

> *Gorge walks and swimming holes. Picnic tables, shelter shed, pit toilet (no water or showers). Self-register on site.*

REVERSE DIRECTIONS START ▲ 0.0 km

Prairie Hotel

Porcupine Gorge

TREAD LIGHTLY!
On Public and Private Land

■ Take your rubbish home with you. Do not bury it.

■ Leave your campsite as you found it.

■ Leave gates as you found them – open or shut.

■ Don't disturb livestock – slow down or stop.

■ Stay off roads and tracks when they are wet and easily cut up.

PORCUPINE GORGE NATIONAL PARK
«»
THE LYND

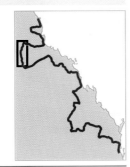

START POINT
Map page 21, N2.

TOTAL KM 208.
UNSEALED KM 200.
DEGREE OF DIFFICULTY Easy.
DRIVING TIME 5 hours.
LONGEST DISTANCE NO FUEL Fuel at The Lynd.
TOPOGRAPHIC MAPS Auslig 1:250 000 series: *Clarke River; Einasleigh.*
LOCAL/SPECIALITY MAP Sunmap: *North Queensland.*

DESCRIPTION This is a long, easy haul on predominantly good quality unsealed road through dry, open ironbark forest. Much of the land was once volcanic, leaving jagged ridges of basalt and granite. The days are very hot in summer and pleasantly warm in winter. In good seasons properties in the region carry high stock loads of cattle. Watch for them on the roads. Arrive in The Lynd at Easter or in July to catch their country race meeting. *The Oasis Caravan Park,* with powered sites and cabins, is located next to The Oasis Roadhouse on Kennedy Developmental Road. Ask about road conditions at the roadhouse, where you can also pick up tourist information.

WARNING ▶ Watch for cattle crossing.

BOOKINGS AND PERMITS ▶ Book in advance if staying at The Oasis Caravan Park over Easter or in July. Write to The Oasis Roadhouse and Caravan Park, c/- PO Mt Garnet QLD 4872; or tel. (070) 62 5291.

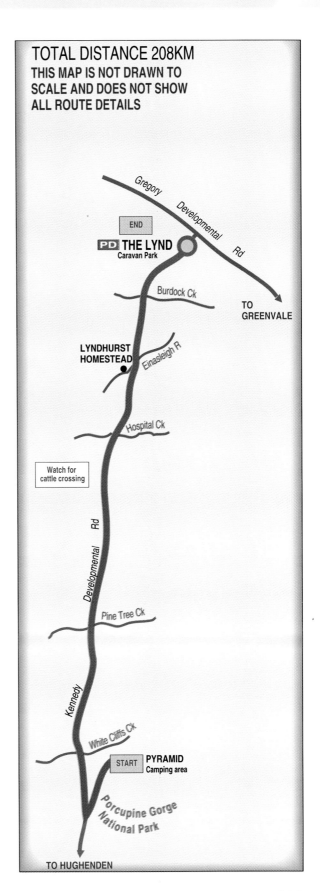

TOTAL DISTANCE 208KM
THIS MAP IS NOT DRAWN TO SCALE AND DOES NOT SHOW ALL ROUTE DETAILS

Sunset, north-western Queensland

ROUTE DIRECTIONS

0.0 km Zero trip meter at the Pyramid Camping Area. Return to Kennedy Developmental Rd. **TR.**
(7.3 km) ▲ 207.7 km

7.3 km S'post: The Lynd 203. **SO.**
(1.0 km)
Pyramid Lookout 7. ▲ 200.4 km

8.3 km White Cliffs Creek. Cross causeway.
(31.4 km) ▲ 199.4 km

39.7 km S'post: The Lynd 153.
(17.2 km) Opp. dir. s'post: Hughenden 103. ▲ 168.0 km

56.9 km Bitumen.
(0.4 km) Gravel. ▲ 150.8 km

57.3 km Pine Tree Creek. Cross bridge.
(3.0 km) ▲ 150.4 km

60.3 km Gravel.
(70.2 km) ▲ 147.4 km

130.5 km Hospital Creek. Cross bridge.
(28.4 km) ▲ 77.2 km

158.9 km S'post: The Lynd 48. **SO.**
(1.0 km) ▲ 48.8 km

159.9 km Einasleigh River. Cross causeway.

> *Lyndhurst Homestead on left.*

(5.6 km) ▲ 47.8 km

165.5 km Bitumen.
(3.7 km) Gravel. ▲ 42.2 km

169.2 km Gravel.
(0.5 km) Bitumen. ▲ 38.5 km

169.7 km Burdock Creek. Cross causeway.
(1.4 km) ▲ 38.0 km

171.1 km Crossroads. **SO.**
(25.9 km) ▲ 36.6 km

197.0 km Bitumen.
(0.6 km) Gravel. ▲ 10.7 km

197.6 km Gravel.
(9.1 km) Bitumen. ▲ 10.1 km

206.7 km S'post: The Lynd 1. **SO.**
(1.0 km) Opp. dir. s'post: Hughenden 284. ▲ 1.0 km

207.7 km The Oasis Roadhouse and Caravan Park.

> **PD** *Supplies, caravan park. Tourist information. Picnic tables, barbecues, toilets, hot showers, laundry.*

REVERSE DIRECTIONS START ▲ 0.0 km

THE LYND
«»
CARDWELL

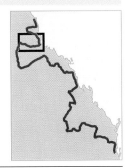

Cardwell Pier

START POINT

Map page 17, J11.

TOTAL KM 289.

UNSEALED KM 144.

DEGREE OF DIFFICULTY Plotted route via Mt Spec National Park is difficult after wet weather. The Lynd to Cardwell via Ingham and bypassing Mt Spec is the easier route. *See Warnings.*

DRIVING TIME 8 hours (The Lynd to Mt Spec National Park). Easier route 5 hours.

LONGEST DISTANCE NO FUEL 243 km (The Lynd to Hidden Valley).

TOPOGRAPHIC MAPS Auslig 1:250 000 series: *Einasleigh; Ingham.*

LOCAL/SPECIALTY MAPS Sunmaps: *North Queensland; Townsville and District.*

OTHER USEFUL INFORMATION QNPWS visitor information sheets: *Mt Spec National Park; North Queensland National Parks.*

DESCRIPTION From The Lynd you recross the Great Dividing Range to Mt Spec National Park, on Paluma Range north of Townsville. The park, with eucalypt woodland on the foothills and lush rainforest around the summit, has an annual rainfall 3 times the average of the flood plains below. There is a camping ground and picnic area at *Paradise Waterhole* on Big Crystal Creek with a number of good swimming holes. Look for cassowary, birds of paradise and tropical fruit pigeons. Collect your camping permit and park information at the QNPWS ranger's office in Paluma, high in the rainforest on the way to the campsite. Have a devonshire tea, or browse in the pottery and craft galleries and the butterfly and insect museum, before descending the range. This road is very steep, narrow and winding and can be difficult after heavy rain. On the way to Paradise Waterhole, the range road passes McClellands Lookout and Little Crystal Creek, a picturesque swimming and picnic spot on the margin of the rainforest. From Mt Spec it is an easy 90 kilometres up the Bruce Highway to *Cardwell* on the shore of the Coral Sea. As well as offering caravan parks and excellent fishing in Hinchinbrook Channel, this serene village is the starting point for cruises to many tropical islands including *Hinchinbrook Island*, the world's largest island national park.

WARNINGS ▶ Mt Spec Road, from Paluma to the Bruce Highway, is steep, narrow and winding. Experience and care are required, particularly after heavy rain. Do not attempt with caravans or trailers. The alternative is to continue on the Blue Range Road to Ingham then proceed north 52 kilometres to Cardwell. ▶ Swimmers beware marine stingers at beaches, saltwater creeks and estuaries November–April.

BOOKINGS AND PERMITS ▶ Obtain a camping permit for Mt Spec National Park at the QNPWS, c/- Main Street, Paluma QLD 4816; tel. (077) 70 8526; or Great Barrier Reef Wonderland Information Centre, PO Box 5391, Townsville QLD 4810; tel. (077) 21 2399. ▶ Obtain permits for Hinchinbrook Island and other island national parks from QNPWS, Cardwell Information Centre, Bruce Highway, Cardwell QLD 4816; PO Box 74, Cardwell QLD 4816; tel. (070) 66 8601.

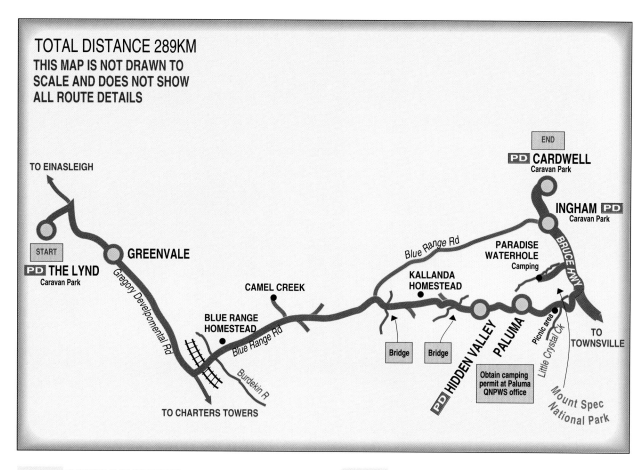

TOTAL DISTANCE 289KM
THIS MAP IS NOT DRAWN TO
SCALE AND DOES NOT SHOW
ALL ROUTE DETAILS

ROUTE DIRECTIONS

0.0 km Zero trip meter at The Oasis Roadhouse on Kennedy Developmental Rd. **SO** towards The Lynd Junction.
(1.6 km) ▲ 54.2 km

1.6 km S'post: Charters Towers. **KR** at Y intersection onto Gregory Developmental Rd.
(52.6 km) Opp. dir. s'post: The Lynd. ▲ 52.6 km

54.2 km S'post: Charters Towers 204.

> Greenvale on left.

Opp. dir. s'post: Mt Garnet.

0.0 km Zero trip meter at above intersection on Gregory Developmental Rd heading towards Charters Towers. **SO**.
(1.2 km) ▲ 0.0 km
▲ 234.6 km

1.2 km Redbank Creek. Cross bridge.
(34.1 km) ▲ 233.4 km

35.3 km Marble Creek. Cross bridge.
(23.3 km) ▲ 199.3 km

58.6 km S'post: Blue Range 6. **TL** onto gravel: Blue Range Rd.
(3.5 km) Bitumen. ▲ 176.0 km

62.1 km Cross railway line.
(3.6 km) ▲ 172.5 km

65.7 km Cross Burdekin River.
(0.5 km) ▲ 168.9 km

66.2 km Blue Range Homestead on left. **SO**.
(39.4 km) ▲ 168.4 km

105.6 km S'post: Gadarra. **KR**.

> Camel Creek off to left.

(2.9 km) Opp. dir. s'post: Greenvale. ▲ 129.0 km

108.5 km S'post: Ingham. **KL**.
(3.2 km) Opp. dir. s'post: Greenvale. ▲ 126.1 km

111.7 km Y intersection. **KR**.
(18.6 km) ▲ 122.9 km

130.3 km Intersection. **SO**.

> Kangaroo Hills off to right.

(0.8 km) Opp. dir. s'post:Camel Creek. ▲ 104.3 km

131.1 km Bitumen.
(0.4 km) Gravel. ▲ 103.5 km

131.5 km Intersection. S'post: Kallanda/Hidden Valley. **TR** onto gravel: Husseys Rd.

> *Alternatively, continue on bitumen (Blue Range Rd) and follow s'posts to Ingham (approx. 56 km). Proceed north on the Bruce Highway to Cardwell (approx. 52 km).*

    (5.2 km)   ▲ 103.1 km

136.7 km Creek crossing. Cross grid bridge.
    (4.4 km)   ▲ 97.9 km

141.1 km Intersection. **KL.**
    (6.9 km)   ▲ 93.5 km

148.0 km Kallanda Homestead on left.
    (4.8 km)   ▲ 86.6 km

152.8 km Intersection. **KR.**
    (0.6 km)   ▲ 81.8 km

153.4 km Intersection. **SO.**
    (14.5 km)   ▲ 81.2 km

167.9 km Intersection. **SO.**
    (0.6 km)   ▲ 66.7 km

168.5 km Creek crossing. Cross grid bridge.
    (17.3 km)   ▲ 66.1 km

185.8 km Gate.

> *Leave as found.*

    (1.0 km)   ▲ 48.8 km

186.8 km T intersection. **TL.**
    (0.9 km)   ▲ 47.8 km

187.7 km Intersection. **SO** over bridge.
    (0.4 km)   ▲ 46.9 km

188.1 km Intersection. **SO.**
    (0.5 km)   ▲ 46.5 km

188.6 km Intersection. **SO.**

> *Hidden Valley Cabins off to left.* **PD** *Supplies. Private log cabin resort on cattle station. 4WD tracks.*

    (13.4 km)   ▲ 46.0 km

202.0 km Intersection. **SO.**
    (1.3 km)   ▲ 32.6 km

203.3 km Bitumen.
    (3.1 km)   Gravel. ▲ 31.3 km

206.4 km Intersection. **SO.**
    (3.9 km)   Opp. dir. s'post: Hidden Valley 19. ▲ 28.2 km

210.3 km Paluma town centre.

> *Tea house, art and craft galleries, butterfly and insect museum. QNPWS Ranger's Office. Obtain camping permit, park information.*

    (0.6 km)   ▲ 24.3 km

210.9 km Intersection. S'post: Ingham 63. **SO.**

Paradise Waterhole

> *Caution: 18 km steep, narrow winding road. Scenic drive past McClellands Lookout and Little Crystal Creek. Lookout has panoramic views of Halifax Bay, walking tracks, and a picnic area with tables, barbecues, toilets, water. Little Crystal Creek has an excellent swimming hole, picnic tables, barbecues, toilets and water.*

    (17.3 km)   ▲ 23.7 km

228.2 km T intersection. **TL** onto Bruce Hwy: bitumen.
    (2.1 km)   Gravel. Opp. dir. s'post: Paluma 18. ▲ 6.4 km

230.3 km S'post: Big Crystal Creek Camping Area. **TL** off Bruce Hwy.
    (2.0 km)   ▲ 4.3 km

232.3 km Gravel.
    (2.3 km)   Bitumen. ▲ 2.3 km

234.6 km S'post: Big Crystal Creek. Paradise Waterhole Camping Ground on right.

> *Picnic tables, barbecues, toilets, water, showers. Permit required. Swimming hole. Rainforest walks. The wet tropical rainforest in Mt Spec National Park is listed as a World Heritage Area.*

Return to Bruce Hwy. **TL.** Proceed north to Cardwell (90 km).

> **PD** *Supplies, caravan parks, private accommodation. Popular fishing village. Cruises to Hinchinbrook Island and other offshore national parks.*

Proceed south from Cardwell
along Bruce Hwy to Mt Spec National Park
turnoff (90 km approx.)
REVERSE DIRECTIONS START ▲ 0.0 km

CARDWELL
‹›
CAIRNS

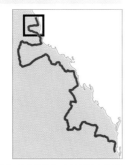

START POINT
Map page 17, L10.

TOTAL KM 399.
UNSEALED KM 169.
DEGREE OF DIFFICULTY Easy.
DRIVING TIME 6 hours (Cardwell to Kennedy Hwy and Tully Falls Rd intersection).
LONGEST DISTANCE NO FUEL 186 km (Cardwell to Mt Garnet).
TOPOGRAPHIC MAPS Auslig 1:250 000 series: *Ingham; Innisfail.*
LOCAL/SPECIALITY MAPS Sunmaps: *Cardwell to Port Douglas; North Queensland.*
OTHER USEFUL INFORMATION QNPWS visitor information sheet: *North Queensland National Parks.* QNPWS brochure: *Atherton Tableland National and Environmental Parks.* Department of Forestry, Queensland: *Recreation in State Forests: Ingham – Cardwell – Tully Region; Recreation in State Forests: Atherton Tableland Region.*

DESCRIPTION The highways and roads in this trek section thread through, and past, pockets of protected tropical rainforest. This is an enviable trip with plenty of options to consider. From Cardwell there are beautiful coastal views as you climb the Cardwell Range. You have a choice of two short detours to see the wild Blencoe Falls, before crossing the fast-flowing Herbert River. After linking onto the Kennedy Highway you pass through the old copper-mining town of Mt Garnet, then Innot Hot Springs, where the road-weary can relax in thermal mineral pools. See Millstream Falls, the widest in the state, before taking your preferred route to Cairns.

From the crossroads of the Kennedy Highway and Tully Falls Road near Ravenshoe, take the coastal route to Cairns via Millaa Millaa and Innisfail, or explore Atherton

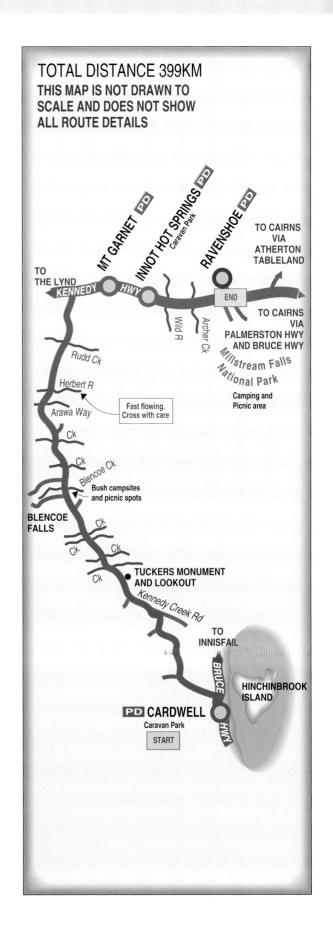

TOTAL DISTANCE 399KM
THIS MAP IS NOT DRAWN TO SCALE AND DOES NOT SHOW ALL ROUTE DETAILS

Vehicle crossing Herbert River

Tableland before heading to Cairns. This ancient volcanic plateau is covered in a patchwork of rolling green farmlands and dense tropical rainforest. It is an extremely attractive touring area, with cascading waterfalls, fast-flowing rivers and over a dozen national parks. Two of these are the extinct volcanic crater lakes, Barrine and Eacham. Walking tracks through rainforest surrounding the lakes may give you glimpses of the blue Ulysses butterfly, musky rat kangaroos, carpet pythons, forest dragon lizards, or saw-shelled tortoise.

With the Great Barrier Reef to the east, Atherton Tableland to the west and palm-fringed beaches to the north and south, Cairns is the gateway to far north Queensland. Right on the foreshore of Trinity Bay, it is a city of tropical parks and gardens, with a harbour which plays host to international cruise ships and yachts, to pleasure craft and big game-fishing vessels. Cairns is also the starting point for the Cape York adventure and the trek across the Gulf Savannah to Darwin.

Camping is permitted in a number of national parks close to *Cairns* and there is a wide range of caravan parks, budget and quality accommodation. Camping is not permitted in national parks on *Atherton Tableland* but several of the *state forest parks* have camping areas (permit required).

WARNINGS ▶ The Herbert River is fast-flowing. Cross with care. After heavy rain check with the QNPWS, Cardwell Information Centre, Bruce Highway, Cardwell QLD 4816; tel. (070) 66 8601. ▶ The two detour tracks to Blencoe Falls are not suitable for caravans and trailers. ▶ Swimmers: beware box jellyfish in summer months.

BOOKINGS AND PERMITS ▶ For national park camping permits contact: QNPWS Far Northern Regional Centre, 10–12 McLeod Street, Cairns QLD 4870; PO Box 2066, Cairns QLD 4870; tel. (070) 52 3093. ▶ Obtain permits and information about camping and driving in State Forests from: Queensland Department of Forestry, Atherton District Office, 83 Main Street, Atherton QLD 4883; tel. (070) 91 1844. ▶ For general tourist information contact: Far North Queensland Promotion Bureau Ltd, 36–38 Aplin Street, Cairns QLD 4870; tel. (070) 51 3588. Information about Atherton Tableland is available from: Atherton Tableland Promotion Bureau, PO Box 257, Atherton QLD 4883; tel. (070) 91 3608.

Blencoe Falls

Abandoned homestead, Atherton Tableland

ROUTE DIRECTIONS

0.0 km	Zero trip meter opposite war memorial monument in Cardwell facing north. **SO** along Bruce Hwy.	
	(4.5 km)	▲ 74.5 km
4.5 km	S'post: Ellerbeck Rd. **TL** off Bruce Hwy.	
	(0.4 km)	▲ 70.0 km
4.9 km	Gravel.	
	(2.7 km)	Bitumen. ▲ 69.6 km
7.6 km	Cross wooden bridge.	
	(1.1 km)	▲ 66.9 km
8.7 km	Cross wooden bridge.	
	(2.8 km)	▲ 65.8 km
11.5 km	Y intersection. **KR.**	
	(0.2 km)	▲ 63.0 km
11.7 km	Cross wooden bridge onto bitumen.	
	(0.5 km)	Gravel. ▲ 62.8 km
12.2 km	Y intersection. **KR** on bitumen.	
	(0.3 km)	▲ 62.3 km
12.5 km	S'post: Hamilton Rd. **TL.**	
	(1.2 km)	▲ 62.0 km
13.7 km	Gravel.	
	(2.6 km)	Bitumen. ▲ 60.8 km
16.3 km	Cross wooden bridge.	
	(0.8 km)	▲ 58.2 km
17.1 km	S'post: Meacham Rd. **TR.**	
	(0.8 km)	▲ 57.4 km
17.9 km	Cross wooden bridge.	
	(0.3 km)	▲ 56.6 km
18.2 km	T intersection. **TL** onto bitumen: Kennedy Creek Rd.	
	(0.1 km)	Gravel. ▲ 56.3 km
18.3 km	S'post: Kirrama Rd. **TR** onto gravel.	
	(10.4 km)	Bitumen. Opp. dir. s'post: Kennedy 6. ▲ 56.2 km
28.7 km	Tuckers Monument and Lookout. **SO.**	
	(12.0 km)	▲ 45.8 km
41.0 km	Cross causeway. **SO.**	
	(3.5 km)	▲ 33.5 km
44.5 km	Cross causeway. **SO.**	
	(10.6 km)	▲ 30.0 km
55.1 km	Cross causeway.	
	(1.2 km)	▲ 19.4 km
56.3 km	Cross causeway.	
	(1.6 km)	▲ 18.2 km
57.9 km	S'post: Mt Garnet 160/Blencoe Falls 19. **KL.**	
	(16.6 km)	▲ 16.6 km
74.5 km	S'post: Blencoe Falls Lookout.	

> *Turn left for 10 km return trip to spectacular Blencoe Falls. 4WD only. Do not take caravans or trailers down this track.*

0.0 km Zero trip meter at above intersection. **SO** towards Mt Garnet.
(2.8 km) ▲ 0.0 km
▲ 3.9 km

2.8 km Blencoe Creek. Cross wooden bridge.

> *Picnic spots. Bush campsites.*

(1.1 km) ▲ 1.1 km
3.9 km Intersection.

> *Turn left to view Blencoe Falls (10 km return trip). 4WD only. Do not take caravans or trailers down this track.*

0.0 km Zero trip meter at above intersection. **SO**.
(4.9 km) ▲ 0.0 km
▲ 152.7 km

4.9 km Cross causeway.
(9.3 km) ▲ 147.8 km
14.2 km Cross causeway.
(0.2 km) ▲ 138.5 km
14.4 km S'post: Mt Garnet. **TL**.

> *Homestead entrance road on right.*

(11.3 km) Opp. dir. s'post: Townsville. ▲ 138.3 km
25.7 km Arawa Way causeway.
(2.2 km) ▲ 127.0 km
27.9 km Herbert River crossing.

> *Warning: fast flowing. Cross with care.*

(23.9 km) ▲ 124.5 km
51.8 km Intersection. **SO**.
(21.3 km) ▲ 100.9 km
73.1 km Cross wooden bridge.
(3.5 km) ▲ 79.6 km
76.6 km Rudd Creek. Cross wooden bridge.
(8.9 km) ▲ 76.1 km
85.5 km Bitumen.
(6.6 km) Gravel. ▲ 67.2 km
92.1 km Gravel.
(11.7 km) Bitumen. ▲ 60.6 km
103.8 km S'post: Mt Garnet 4. **TR** onto Kennedy Hwy: bitumen.
(4.0 km) Gravel. Opp. dir. s'post: Gunnawarra Rd. ▲ 48.9 km
107.8 km Mt Garnet Post Office. **SO**.

> **PD** *Mt Garnet's rodeo and country race meeting are held each May Day weekend.*

(15.7 km) ▲ 44.9 km
123.5 km Innot Hot Springs town centre. **SO**.

> **PD** *Caravan park. Hot mineral springs.*

(5.6 km) ▲ 29.2 km
129.1 km Wild River. Cross bridge.
(7.7 km) ▲ 23.6 km
136.8 km Archer Creek. Cross bridge.

> *Archer Creek Camping Ground on right. Picnic tables, toilets, water.*

(12.1 km) ▲ 15.9 km
148.9 km Intersection. **SO**.

> *Millstream Falls National Park off to right. Queensland's widest waterfall. Spans 65 m after heavy rain. Walking tracks. Swimming holes. Campsites, picnic tables, barbecues, toilets, tank water.*

(3.8 km) ▲ 3.8 km
152.7 km Crossroads. **SO** along Kennedy Hwy. **KR** onto Palmerston Hwy and follow hwy (approx. 85 km) through Millaa Millaa to Innisfail. **PD** Take Bruce Hwy north (past Bellenden Ker National Park) to Cairns (approx. 83 km).

> *To explore Atherton Tableland proceed (approx. 53 km) straight along Kennedy Hwy to Atherton. **PD** From Atherton take the Gillies Hwy (58 km) to Gordonvale, and the Bruce Hwy (26 km) to Cairns. **PD** Supplies, caravan parks. Access to Green Island and other national parks. Scenic train trip through Barron River Gorge National Park. Daily reef cruises. Fishing, scuba-diving, snorkelling, swimming, whitewater rafting, hang-gliding.*

Opp. dir. s'post: Mt Garnet 46 at Kennedy Hwy and Tully Falls Rd intersection near Ravenshoe.
REVERSE DIRECTIONS START ▲ 0.0 km

THE FAR NORTH
CAPE YORK PENINSULA
2463 KILOMETRES

CAIRNS » COOKTOWN 258 km

**COOKTOWN
» LAKEFIELD NATIONAL PARK** 197 km

**LAKEFIELD NATIONAL PARK
» THE ARCHER RIVER** 259 km

**THE ARCHER RIVER
» IRON RANGE NATIONAL PARK** 130 km

**IRON RANGE NATIONAL PARK
» THE WENLOCK RIVER** 102 km

THE WENLOCK RIVER » BAMAGA 264 km

BAMAGA » THE DULHUNTY RIVER 162 km

THE DULHUNTY RIVER » WEIPA 214 km

WEIPA » COEN 259 km

COEN » LAURA 252 km

LAURA » MAYTOWN 77 km

MAYTOWN » CAIRNS 289 km

Car and trailer, Frenchmans Gap Road, Iron Range

If you draw a line from Cairns on the east coast to Karumba on the Gulf of Carpentaria, you have a geographic triangle of which Cape York, Australia's northernmost point, is the apex. The area within this triangle is larger than the State of Victoria and, during the wet season, with the exception of a few permanent pockets of population, largely uninhabited. It includes an extraordinary mix of country. The east coast is tropical rainforest and mountainous, the beginning of the Great Dividing Range, but west of the ranges the land is flat and scrubby until you reach the rich river grazing land of the Carpentaria coast.

From November to May the monsoonal rains make roads impassable to all vehicles and waterways cover the land. But in the dry season, the cape undergoes a sudden population explosion when the tracks are open to four-wheel drive vehicles. Indeed, if there were such a thing as a four-wheel drivers' Mecca, Cape York would probably be it.

Adventurers come north for a variety of reasons. The fishing, which is spectacularly good, is one (especially for barramundi). Others come for the scenery, which ranges from dense green rainforest, through woodlands and

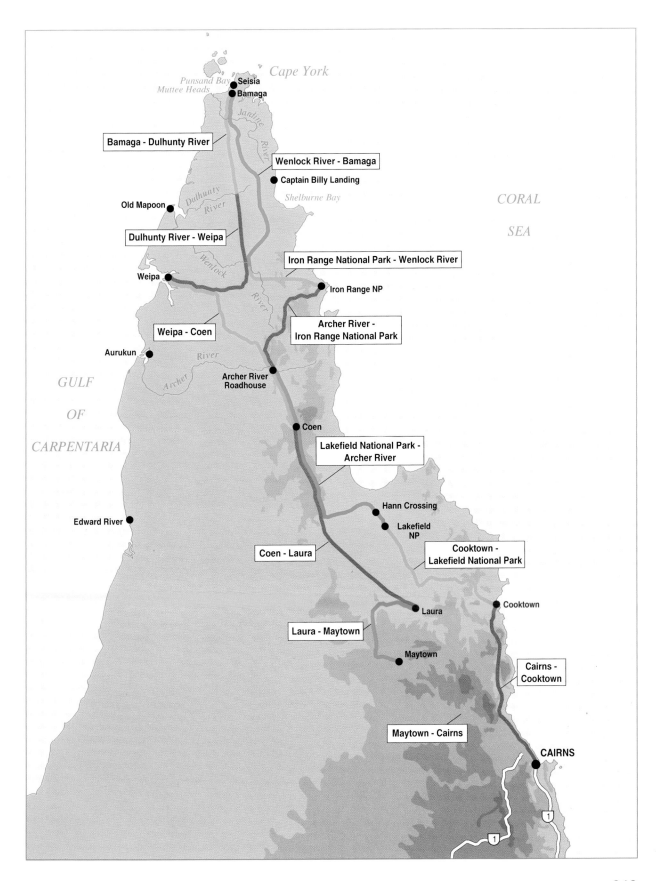

Cape York

Punsand Bay
Muttee Heads
Seisia
Bamaga

Bamaga - Dulhunty River

Wenlock River - Bamaga

Captain Billy Landing

Shelburne Bay

CORAL

SEA

Old Mapoon

Dulhunty River - Weipa

Iron Range National Park - Wenlock River

Iron Range NP

Weipa

Archer River -
Iron Range National Park

Weipa - Coen

Aurukun

Archer River
Roadhouse

GULF

OF

CARPENTARIA

Coen

Lakefield National Park -
Archer River

Hann Crossing

Lakefield
NP

Edward River

Cooktown -
Lakefield National Park

Coen - Laura

Laura

Laura - Maytown

Cooktown

Cairns -
Cooktown

Maytown

Maytown - Cairns

CAIRNS

forest, to massive sand dunes. There are thousands of kilometres of white beaches, rivers, creeks and wild shoreline, which are host to an interesting mixture of plant and animal life; some species are not found anywhere else in Australia. Many people come simply to escape from civilisation, while others come for the challenge and pleasure of the drive itself, which is tough, demanding and sometimes heartbreaking.

At Weipa, Comalco have converted a bauxite mining town into a major stopover for visitors. You can tour the mines and there is excellent fishing from Weipa. From Bamaga, at the tip of Cape York, you can make fishing and boating trips and explore the surrounding beaches.

There are vast areas of the peninsula which are not open to motor vehicles of any kind and we hope they remain that way. Some are privately owned and controlled grazing properties. Other sections of the cape are owned by the descendants of the original Aboriginal tribes who inhabited the region as long as 40 000 years ago. The land has been transferred to their care again by deed of gift. Of these, the Bamaga, Seisia and Injunu Communities, at the very tip, and the Kowanyama Community in the south-west, welcome visitors and are becoming increasingly well-equipped to deal with them. Communities at Aurukun and Edward River are gearing up to handle tourism, and the community at Lockhart River already helps to host and provide services to visitors to the Iron Range National Park on the Coral Sea coast.

ROADS AND ROUTES There are a number of ways you can visit Cape York, but there is only one way to really see it and that is by four-wheel drive vehicle. We have mapped and charted the route as a special one-way loop here. Although you don't have to religiously follow the series of maps and charts, doing so will guarantee you will see the peninsula to best advantage. Be well prepared to camp out; there is a plethora of great opportunities. And remember, do not attempt this trip other than in the dry season: May – November.

Our charts begin north of Cairns. Head along the coastal track to Cooktown and then traverse the Lakefield National Park to link up with the Peninsula Developmental Road at Musgrave. This track is a good introduction to the region because some of it is indeed hard going and indicative of the rough patches to come.

Continue north to the Weipa turnoff where the nature of the track changes somewhat to become the Old Telegraph Road, named for obvious reasons. When this track was first cut, it simply took the shortest route north up the centre of the peninsula, through creeks and rivers. More recently a new track has been made which takes advantage of the ridges and avoids creek crossings as much as possible.

The trek follows the new road north, breaking away from the Old Telegraph Road past the Wenlock River, to rejoin it briefly some 60 kilometres south of the Jardine River. You then follow another new section, to cross the Jardine by vehicle ferry. It is possible to travel north via the Old Telegraph Road all the way to Bamaga but it is extremely difficult in many sections (impossible for some vehicles) and more than likely to cause damage. The trek makes use of the Old Telegraph Road to return south, however, but only after using the new section of road to cross the Jardine. You should not cross on the line of the old road except at the end of the dry season when the water is at its lowest, and even then only with great care and some knowledge.

Divert east briefly and bypass the Heathlands property, once a cattle station, now owned by the QNPWS and with a ranger station, in order to avoid Gunshot Creek which requires a winch to negotiate its steep southern bank.

There are several major diversions. The first tracks into the rainforests of Iron Range National Park on the Pacific coast and we have charted this diversion into the trek going north. The second heads west to the Gulf coast at Weipa and this is a feature of the southbound journey.

Last, but certainly not least, there are the more southerly diversions into the splendid Rokeby National Park and then the full-on adventure of the Laura to Maytown Cobb & Co. coach road, to be undertaken before returning to the Atherton Tablelands or Cairns, where you can pick up route directions for the next trek, Cairns to Darwin.

It must be said that all roads on the peninsula are difficult and some are far more difficult than others. As with other trips through the far north, some special planning is necessary before you embark.

Your vehicle should be prepared to cope with a variety of difficult unsealed road conditions: potholes, washaways, ruts and bulldust patches. Leave excess baggage behind, and caravans should be left at Cairns. There are many creek crossings on the trip, so check your winch is in good working order. North of Cooktown, emergency breakdown services, supplies and fuel are available at Weipa, Bamaga and Coen; fuel, supplies and minor repairs are available at Musgrave Station, Archer River and Hann River, but you should carry the appropriate spare parts.

ROYAL FLYING DOCTOR SERVICE As this is a remote area you should carry high-frequency radio. Before you leave, register with the RFDS and obtain the guide listing bases, call signs and broadcast frequencies. For information, contact RFDS, PO Box 345, Hurstville NSW 2220; tel. (02) 580 9711.

USEFUL INFORMATION

For national parks information contact:
QNPWS
239 George Street
Brisbane 4000
(07) 22 4414.

QNPWS
10–12 McLeod Street
Cairns QLD 4870
(07) 98 2188.

For touring information contact:
Far North Queensland Promotion Bureau
36–38 Aplin Street
Cairns QLD 4870
(070) 51 3588.

For information on road conditions contact:
Royal Automobile Club of Queensland (RACQ)
(070) 51 6711.

For emergency medical assistance ring:
Royal Flying Doctor Service
(070) 53 1952 (base)
(070) 53 5419 (medical assistance).

HOW TO BE CROCODILE-WISE

Of the two crocodile species found in Australia's north, the saltwater or estuarine crocodile is dangerous. It lives in salt water and fresh water, usually in tidal sections of rivers and creeks, floodplain waterholes and freshwater swamps and is found as far inland as 100 kilometres. The freshwater crocodile, while not dangerous, can deliver a savage bite if disturbed. Treat all crocodiles longer than 1.5 metres as dangerous, and obey the following rules.

▶ *Seek local advice before swimming, camping, fishing or boating.*
▶ *Swim, canoe and use small boats only in shallow rapids.*
▶ *Watch children and pets in the water or at the water's edge where large crocodiles might live.*
▶ *Fill a bucket with water and prepare food or clean fish at least 5 metres from the water's edge.*
▶ *Do not lean from boats or hang articles over the edge.*
▶ *When fishing stand at least a few metres back from the water's edge and do not stand on overhanging logs.*
▶ *Burn or remove from your campsite food scraps, fish offal and other wastes.*

CODE OF ETHICS FOR CAPE YORK

▶ *Make sure you observe all private property signs and do not enter unless there is real emergency.*
▶ *Be scrupulous in observing local Aboriginal community regulations. Courtesy requires a telephone call or visit to community offices before you explore these areas. Permits are required to camp. Do not photograph anyone without their permission. Cape York is rich in relics and evidence of past Aboriginal habitation. Do not touch or disturb anything.*
▶ *Permits required to camp in all national parks. No pets or firearms in national parks; fishing is prohibited in most parks. Obtain information about Cape York national parks before you set out from the head office in Brisbane or Cairns regional office.*

▶ *Leave all gates as found.*
▶ *Gear your thinking to the concept of carrying your rubbish with you, as there probably won't be receptacles at your campsite. Do not bury rubbish. Take fresh food where possible rather than tins or bottles. There are rubbish disposal points at Mount Carbine, Cooktown, Lakeland, Laura, Musgrave, Coen, Archer River Roadhouse, Weipa, the Wenlock and Jardine rivers and Bamaga.*
▶ *Dig deep to dispose of human waste and do not pollute waterways. Take great care to extinguish fires completely.*
▶ *Drive cautiously and stick to formed tracks to cause minimal environmental damage. Leave nothing behind you to lessen the enjoyment of others.*

CAIRNS
»
COOKTOWN

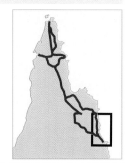

START POINT
Map page 17, K6

TOTAL KM 258.
UNSEALED KM 145.
DEGREE OF DIFFICULTY Moderate.
DRIVING TIME 6 hours.
LONGEST DISTANCE NO FUEL 74 km (Wujal Wujal to Cooktown).
TOPOGRAPHIC MAPS Auslig 1:250 000 series: *Mossman*; *Cooktown*. See also 1:100 000 series.
LOCAL/SPECIALITY MAPS Sunmaps: *North Queensland*; *Cardwell to Port Douglas*.
OTHER USEFUL INFORMATION QNPWS visitor information sheets: *Daintree* and *Cape Tribulation* national parks.

DESCRIPTION Head north from Cairns and Port Douglas via Mossman, and briefly divert from route at the spectacular Mossman River Gorge, in the Daintree National Park. The accessible lower reaches of the gorge allow visitors to explore the lowland rainforest and a scenic walking track follows the bank of the river leading to cool swimming holes and a view of the rapids. You can picnic here but no camping allowed.

From Mossman, enter the Cape Tribulation National Park by way of the ferry over the Daintree River. The Daintree-Bloomfield track, pushed through in 1984 in the face of opposition from the green movement, leads past Cape Tribulation through dense World Heritage rainforests, boulder-strewn creek gullies and along the edge of sandy beaches, offering many opportunities to walk, explore and observe the diverse plant and animal life. The track itself is a mixture of good bitumen and good and bad gravel and in places is very steep.

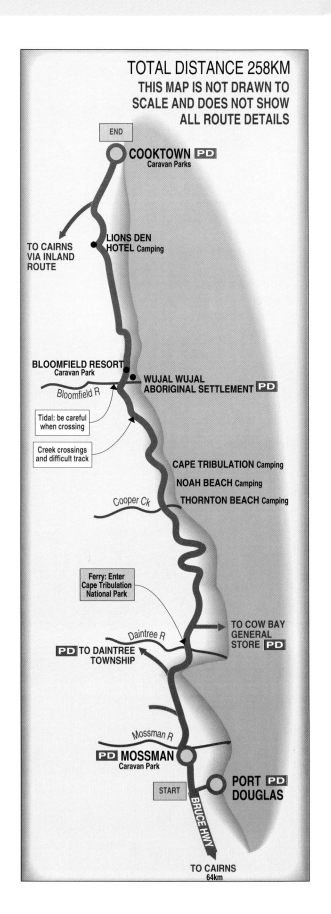

TOTAL DISTANCE 258KM
THIS MAP IS NOT DRAWN TO SCALE AND DOES NOT SHOW ALL ROUTE DETAILS

END
COOKTOWN **PD**
Caravan Parks

TO CAIRNS VIA INLAND ROUTE

LIONS DEN HOTEL Camping

BLOOMFIELD RESORT
Caravan Park
Bloomfield R
WUJAL WUJAL ABORIGINAL SETTLEMENT **PD**

Tidal: be careful when crossing

Creek crossings and difficult track

CAPE TRIBULATION Camping
NOAH BEACH Camping
THORNTON BEACH Camping

Cooper Ck

Ferry: Enter Cape Tribulation National Park

TO COW BAY GENERAL STORE **PD**

Daintree R
PD TO DAINTREE TOWNSHIP

Mossman R
PD MOSSMAN
Caravan Park

START

PORT **PD** DOUGLAS

BRUCE HWY

TO CAIRNS
64km

The Daintree River, on the way to Cape Tribulation

The park boundary abuts the Great Barrier Reef and extends north to the Bloomfield River. There is a designated national park camping area at *Noah Beach*, 8 kilometres south of Cape Tribulation; a public camping area at *Thornton Beach*; private camping facilities at *Myall Creek, Cape Tribulation, Lions Den Hotel* and a picnic area at Cape Tribulation. After crossing the Bloomfield you pass the Aboriginal mission township of Wujal Wujal and Cedar Bay National Park. You will see Black Mountain, an extraordinary formation of black granite, as you turn into the main Cooktown road. This old goldrush town was the first white settlement in Australia – James Cook and his party camped here for nearly three months while the *Endeavour* was repaired after being holed on the Great Barrier Reef – and it is worth spending a day exploring the area.

WARNINGS ▶ The Daintree ferry operates only between 6 am and 6 pm. ▶ The Bloomfield River is sometimes impassable at high tide, check depth of water and tide charts obtainable at local stores and service stations before attempting to cross. ▶ Crocodiles inhabit coastline, the Daintree and Bloomfield rivers and all inland waterways in Australia's north. Be crocodile-wise. Do not swim. ▶ Marine stingers make swimming in the sea dangerous October–April. ▶ Some sections of the Daintree-Bloomfield track are steep and slippery after heavy rain; the Cape Tribulation–Bloomfield section is four-wheel drive only, do not take caravans or trailers. For more information contact the QNPWS ranger, Cape Tribulation National Park, cnr Front and Johnston Streets, Mossman QLD 4873; PO Box 251; tel. (070) 98 2188. ▶ The beach, reefs and coastal waters in this area are protected marine park; no fishing or collecting from Cape Tribulation north to Bloomfield. Limited fishing by line is allowed south of Cape Tribulation.

BOOKINGS AND PERMITS ▶ No camping in Daintree National Park; self-register on site at Noah Beach. For more information on Cape Tribulation National Park contact either QNPWS, Cairns Regional centre, 10–12 McLeod Street, Cairns QLD 4870; PO Box 2066; tel. (070) 52 3093, or the Mossman QNPWS office. ▶ For information on private camping facilities contact the Far North Queensland Promotion Bureau Ltd, 36–38 Aplin Street, Cairns QLD 4870; PO Box 865; tel. (070) 51 3588.

Mossman River

Cape Tribulation National Park

ROUTE DIRECTIONS

Depart Cairns north towards Port Douglas via Cook Hwy for approx. 64 km.

0.0 km Zero trip meter at Bruce Hwy and Port Douglas intersection at s'post: Mossman 14. **SO** to Mossman.

(13.9 km)

13.9 km Mossman. **SO**.

> **PD** *Supplies, caravan park. Mossman Gorge 4 km off to left. Beautiful waterholes and rainforest walks.*

(1.2 km)

15.1 km Mossman River. Cross bridge.

(1.3 km)

16.4 km S'post: Daintree 38. **KR**.

(5.7 km)

22.1 km S'post: Daintree. **KR**.

(18.0 km)

40.1 km Sign: Cape Tribulation National Park. **TR** onto gravel: Daintree Ferry road.

> *Daintree township straight ahead.* **PD**

(3.8 km)

43.9 km Daintree River. Ferry crossing.

> *Ferry operates 6 am–6 pm.*

(10.7 km)

54.6 km Y intersection. **KR**.

(0.3 km)

54.9 km S'post: Buchanan Creek. **SO**.

> **PD** *Supplies at Cow Bay, 2.5 km off to right.*

(1.1 km)

56.0 km Cross wooden bridge.

(7.3 km)

63.3 km Cooper Creek. Cross causeway.

> *Thornton Beach off to right. Camping, toilets, kiosk.*

(3.5 km)

66.8 km Bouncing Stones beach on right. **SO**.

(3.5 km)

70.3 km Cross wooden bridge.

> *Noah Beach Camping Area off to right. Fresh water, toilets. Permit necessary, register on site.*

(6.2 km)

76.5 km Coconut Beach Rainforest Resort on right. **SO**.

Crossing the Bloomfield River

> *Private facility.*

(2.8 km)
79.3 km Cape Tribulation kiosk and rainforest information centre on left. **SO.**

> *Next section of track to Bloomfield River difficult. 4WD only.*

(1.2 km)
80.5 km S'post: Bloomfield Crossing 32.

> *Cape Tribulation 100 m off to right.*

0.0 km Zero trip meter at above s'post. **SO.**
(5.6 km)
5.6 km Creek crossing.
(2.1 km)
7.7 km Creek crossing.
(21.5 km)
29.2 km Creek crossing.
(9.1 km)
38.3 km Bloomfield River. Cross and immediately **TR**. S'post Wujal Wujal.

> *Caution: tidal river. Check depth before crossing.*

(0.6 km)
38.9 km S'post: Douglas Street. **KL.**

> *Wujal Wujal village 200 m off to right.* **PD**

(2.4 km)
41.3 km Causeway.
(6.3 km)
47.6 km Bloomfield River Resort and Caravan Park on right. **SO.**

> *Private facility.*

(30.8 km)
78.4 km Wallaby Creek. Cross wooden bridge.
(3.2 km)
81.4 km Lions Den historic hotel and camping area on left. **SO.**
(0.6 km)
82.0 km Mungumby Creek. Cross wooden bridge.
(4.0 km)
86.0 km S'post: Cooktown 28. **TR** onto bitumen.
(3.9 km)
89.9 km Gravel.
(2.8 km)
92.7 km Trevethan Creek. Cross wooden bridge.
(10.0 km)
102.7 km Bitumen.
(2.8 km)
105.5 km Annan River. Cross bridge onto gravel.
(5.2 km)
110.7 km Bitumen, then 100 m to Cooktown 60 km/h sign.
(2.4 km)
113.1 km T intersection. **TL** into Hope Street.
(0.2 km)
113.3 km Cooktown centre.

> **PD** *Supplies, camping and caravan parks.*

COOKTOWN » LAKEFIELD NATIONAL PARK

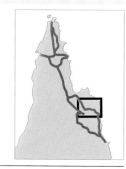

START POINT
Map page 17, K3.

TOTAL KM 197.
UNSEALED KM 186.
DEGREE OF DIFFICULTY Moderate.
DRIVING TIME 5 hours.
LONGEST DISTANCE NO FUEL 246 km (Endeavour Falls Caravan Park to Musgrave Station, next section).
TOPOGRAPHIC MAPS Auslig 1:250 000 series: *Cooktown*; *Cape Melville*; *Ebagoola*. See also 1:100 000 series.
LOCAL/SPECIALITY MAPS Sunmap: *North Queensland*; QNPWS map: *Lakefield National Park*.
OTHER USEFUL INFORMATION QNPWS visitor information sheets: *Far North Queensland, Cape York Peninsula* and *Lakefield* national parks; *Hann Crossing, Laura Homestead*; Mike Foulkes' *Cape York Peninsula Overlanders Guide*; Ron and Viv Moon's *Cape York: an Adventurer's Guide*.

DESCRIPTION The next section of the trek leaves the coast at Cooktown to head inland across harsh grazing country via Battlecamp – a true four-wheel drive track which will give you a good idea of the road conditions on Cape York. There is no town at Battlecamp, but you can visit the ruins of the old Battlecamp property homestead so named after the explorer Edmund Kennedy fought a pitched battle against Aborigines here in 1878. Ahead lies Lakefield National Park, the second largest in Queensland and comprising what were the grazing properties of Laura and Lakefield.

The old Laura homestead is interesting because of its association with the establishment of the Cape York

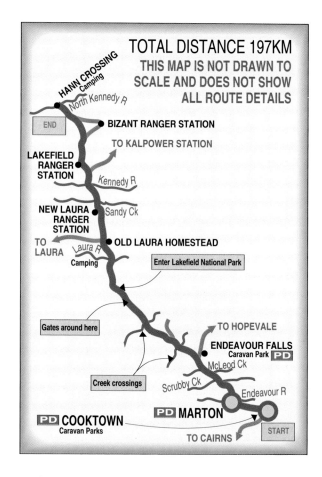

TOTAL DISTANCE 197KM
THIS MAP IS NOT DRAWN TO SCALE AND DOES NOT SHOW ALL ROUTE DETAILS

cattle industry and with the Palmer River goldfields. Once in disrepair, it has now been restored and the unique buildings are worth inspection.

Lakefield is largely covered by grasslands and woodlands, with mudflats and mangroves along the coast and estuaries of the Normanby and North Kennedy Rivers. Vast areas are covered in water during the wet season and in the dry season there are many creeks, lagoons and waterholes which provide a habitat for a great variety of birds and wildlife. Fishing is permitted. Lakefield is a key area for estuarine crocodile conservation in Queensland; information about their habitat and safety precautions which you should observe is available from the park rangers.

Bush camping (no facilities) is permitted at a number of sites in Lakefield; enlist the rangers' help to choose. We found *Hann Crossing*, named after William Hann, who explored much of Cape York and discovered the Palmer River Goldfields, a good spot to camp. Here the North Kennedy River is shallow, with scoured rock forming a rough natural crossing. Downstream there is a small waterfall, and upstream the river divides into two. The walking track along both branches is a pleasant way to explore.

Magpie geese nesting, Lakefield National Park

WARNING ▶ Crocodiles inhabit coastline and all inland waterways on Cape York Peninsula. Be crocodile-wise. Do not swim.

BOOKINGS AND PERMITS ▶ Permits required to camp anywhere in Lakefield National Park and you should register with a park ranger on arrival if intending to camp. Book ahead through QNPWS in Cairns, 10–12 McLeod Street, Cairns, QLD 4870; PO Box 2066; tel. (070) 52 3093; or contact the ranger, Lakefield National Park, PMB 29, Cairns Mail Centre, QLD 4870; tel. (070) 60 2162. Permits can also be obtained from the park rangers at Lakefield, New Laura or Bizant. *See Route Directions.*

ROUTE DIRECTIONS

0.0 km Zero trip meter adjacent to Cooktown Post Office facing west on Charlotte Street. **SO.**
(1.2 km)
1.2 km S'post: Hope Vale along McIvor River Rd. **KR** to Marton.

Cairns off to left.

(9.6 km)
10.8 km Marton General Store. **SO.** **PD**
(0.3 km)
11.1 km Endeavour River. Cross wooden bridge.
(0.3 km)
11.4 km Gravel.

Airport on right.

(6.3 km)
17.7 km Scrubby Creek. Cross wooden bridge.
(4.0 km)
21.7 km McLeod Creek. Cross wooden bridge.
(11.3 km)
33.0 km Endeavour Falls Caravan Park on right.

PD *Next fuel Musgrave Station (246 km).*

(4.4 km)
37.4 km S'post: Battlecamp. **KL.**

Hopevale Mission off to right.

(5.6 km)

COOKTOWN » LAKEFIELD NATIONAL PARK

43.0 km Creek crossing.

> *Check depth before proceeding.*

(2.7 km)

45.7 km Y intersection. **KL.**

(20.1 km)

65.8 km Creek crossing.

(4.5 km)

70.3 km Gate.

> *Leave as found.*

(5.4 km)

75.6 km Gate.

> *Leave as found.*

(7.6 km)

83.3 km Gate.

> *Leave as found.*

(5.0 km)

88.3 km S'post: Lakefield National Park. **SO.**

(23.7 km)

112.0 km Cross Laura River.

> *Check depth before proceeding. Bush camping.*

(0.4 km)

112.4 km Old Laura Homestead historic site. **SO.**

(0.7 km)

113.1 km S'post: New Laura Ranger Station. **TR.**

> *Laura off to left.*

(23.9 km)

137.0 km New Laura Ranger Station on left.

> *Obtain permits for all campsites south of Old Faithful Waterhole.*

0.0 km Zero trip meter at ranger station. **SO.**

(11.0 km)

11.0 km Sandy Creek. Cross wooden bridge.

(1.5 km)

12.5 km Kennedy River. Cross wooden bridge.

(20.6 km)

33.1 km S'post: Lakefield. **KL.**

> *Kalpower Station off to right.*

(1.5 km)

34.6 km Lakefield Ranger Station. **SO.**

> *Obtain permits for campsites south of Hann Crossing.*

(5.0 km)

Gate, leave as found

Sunset, North Kennedy River

39.6 km S'post: Hann Crossing 20. **KL.**

> *Bizant Ranger Station 22 km off to right. Obtain permits for campsites north of Hann Crossing.*

(5.3 km)

44.9 km Y intersection, take either track.

> *Gibson Lake on left.*

(14.7 km)

59.6 km S'post: Musgrave 85. **TL.**

> *Hann Crossing. Permit required to camp. Campsites on both sides of river. Rocky crossing, take care.*

LAKEFIELD NATIONAL PARK
»
THE ARCHER RIVER

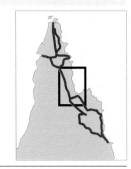

START POINT
Map page 18, F13

TOTAL KM 259.
UNSEALED KM 256.
DEGREE OF DIFFICULTY Easy but *see Warnings.*
DRIVING TIME 6 hours.
LONGEST DISTANCE NO FUEL 111 km (Musgrave Station to Coen).
TOPOGRAPHIC MAPS Auslig 1:250 000 series: *Ebagoola*; *Coen*. See also 1:100 000 series.
LOCAL/SPECIALITY MAPS Sunmap: *North Queensland*; QNPWS map: *Lakefield National Park*; Croc Shop map: *Cape York.*
OTHER USEFUL INFORMATION Mike Foulkes' *Cape York Peninsula Overlanders Guide*; Ron and Viv Moon's *Cape York: An Adventurer's Guide.*

DESCRIPTION This part of the trek covers the northern section of the Lakefield National Park and links with the Peninsula Developmental Road at historic Musgrave Station. The road from Lakefield to Musgrave is generally reasonable quality gravel. Musgrave was originally a telegraph station. Built in 1887, it now offers a welcome break and meals, accommodation and fuel. The route north passes through Coen, a major centre with stores and a hotel and hospital. Mechanical repairs are available here. There are many options for camping along the way, including those with facilities near *Musgrave* and *Coen* but the *Archer River* is a relatively easy destination in a day and the wide sandy banks are perfect for an overnight stop. Good camping facilities are available also at the nearby *Archer River Roadhouse*, and fuel, supplies and limited mechanical repairs.

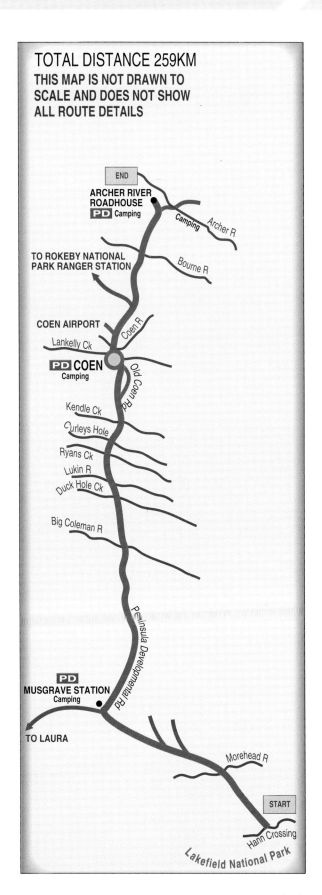

TOTAL DISTANCE 259KM
THIS MAP IS NOT DRAWN TO SCALE AND DOES NOT SHOW ALL ROUTE DETAILS

END

ARCHER RIVER ROADHOUSE
PD Camping

Camping   Archer R

TO ROKEBY NATIONAL PARK RANGER STATION

Bourne R

COEN AIRPORT

Coen R

Lankelly Ck

PD COEN
Camping

Old Coen Rd

Kendle Ck

Curleys Hole

Ryans Ck

Lukin R

Duck Hole Ck

Big Coleman R

Peninsula Developmental Rd

PD
MUSGRAVE STATION
Camping

TO LAURA

Morehead R

START

Hann Crossing

Lakefield National Park

Cars outside Musgrave Station

WARNINGS ▶ Crocodiles inhabit coastline and all inland waterways on Cape York Peninsula. Be crocodile-wise. Do not swim. ▶ The Peninsula Developmental Road north of Musgrave to the Archer River is quite good but there are bad corrugations and potholes as well as sharp dips and creek crossings between Musgrave and Coen. Drive with great care.

BOOKINGS AND PERMITS ▶ For more information on camping and facilities in this section of the route contact Musgrave Station, tel. (070) 60 3229; Clarke's General Store and Garage in Coen, tel (070) 60 1144; Archer River Roadhouse, tel. (070) 60 3266. ▶Croc Shop map is obtainable from Cairns shop, 10E Shield Street, Cairns QLD; tel. (070) 31 1477.

ROUTE DIRECTIONS

0.0 km Zero trip meter north side of the rocky section of Hann Crossing. **SO** towards Musgrave.
(0.1 km)

0.1 km S'post: Musgrave 85. **SO**.
(13.4 km)

13.5 km Cross Morehead River.

> *Rocky crossing, usually dry.*

(25.9 km)

39.4 km S'post: Musgrave. **KL** at Y intersection.
(1.5 km)

40.9 km Intersection. **KL**.
(41.4 km)

82.3 km T intersection on curve. S'post: Coen 109. **TR** onto Peninsula Developmental Rd.

> *Musgrave Station.* **PD** *Supplies, hot showers, toilets and meals. Minor repairs. Rubbish disposal.*

0.0 km Zero trip meter at above intersection facing north. **SO**.
(26.1 km)

26.1 km Cross Big Coleman River.

> *Normally dry.*

(21.9 km)

48.0 km Cross Duck Hole Creek.

> *Normally dry.*

(1.8 km)

49.8 km Cross Lukin River.

> *Normally dry.*

(14.2 km)

64.0 km Cross Ryans Creek.

> *Normally dry.*

(3.3 km)

67.3 km Cross Curleys Hole.

> *Normally dry.*

(3.0 km)

70.3 km Kendle Creek. Cross bridge.

(12.3 km)

82.6 km Intersection. **SO**.

> *Road on right is old Coen road.*

(26.4 km)

109.0 km Bitumen.

(1.7 km)

110.7 km S'post: Weipa. **TR**.

> *Coen business centre straight ahead.* **PD** *Supplies, camping. Mechanical repairs. Rubbish disposal.*

(0.7 km)

111.4 km Lankelly Creek. Cross bridge.

(0.6 km)

112.0 km Coen River. Cross bridge.

(0.3 km)

112.3 km Gravel.

(1.2 km)

113.5 km Intersection. **SO**.

> *The Bend Camping Area on right. Toilets. Campsites on the banks of the Coen River.*

(18.9 km)

132.4 km Y intersection. S'post: Weipa. **KR**.

> *Coen Airport off to left.*

(2.8 km)

White herons on lagoon, Lakefield National Park

Waterlilies, Lakefield National Park

135.2 km Intersection. **SO**.

> *Rokeby National Park Ranger Station 70 km off to left. Some sharp bends in road.*

(15.9 km)

151.1 km Cross Bourne Creek.

(25.2 km)

176.3 km Archer River Roadhouse.

> **PD** *Hot meals and supplies, camping and hot showers. Limited facilities for repairs, welding and tyre changes. River campsites 100 m (toilets). Good camping on sandy river banks.*

THE ARCHER RIVER » IRON RANGE NATIONAL PARK

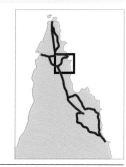

START POINT
Map page 18, D9.

TOTAL KM 130.
UNSEALED KM 130.
DEGREE OF DIFFICULTY Moderate.
DRIVING TIME 5 hours.
LONGEST DISTANCE NO FUEL 496 km (Archer River to Bamaga via Iron Range National Park).
TOPOGRAPHIC MAPS Auslig 1:250 000 series: *Coen*; *Cape Weymouth*. See also 1:100 000 series.
LOCAL/SPECIALITY MAPS Sunmap: *North Queensland*; Croc Shop map: *Cape York*.
OTHER USEFUL INFORMATION Mike Foulkes' *Cape York Peninsula Overlanders Guide*; Viv and Ron Moon's *Cape York: an Adventurer's Guide*; QNPWS visitor information sheet: *Far North Queensland National Parks*.

DESCRIPTION This diversion from the main route north takes travellers into the remote Iron Range National Park, the largest area of tropical lowland rainforest remaining in Australia, which supports a variety of unusual plant and animal species; for example, the cuscus, palm cockatoo and pitcher plant are also found in Papua New Guinea but nowhere else in Australia. The first half of the trip is over reasonable quality gravel. This deteriorates steadily towards the coast; there are some steep creek crossings and substantial washaways as the track winds through the range. Visitors to Iron Range must be self-sufficient; call on the ranger station before setting up camp, as campsites are under constant revision and offer a choice of beach front or rainforest. There is a good national park campsite near the junction of the *Portland Roads* and *Lockhart River* roads and another at *Chilli Beach* on the coast.

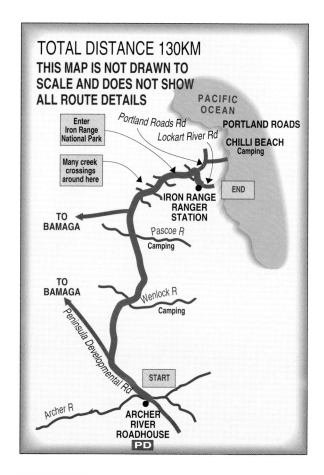

WARNINGS ▶ Crocodiles inhabit coastline and inland waterways on Cape York Peninsula. Be crocodile-wise. Do not swim. ▶ Fuel is not available on this section or on the journey north to Bamaga. Take extra fuel for 500 km minimum at Archer River.

BOOKINGS AND PERMITS ▶ Obtain permits to camp in Iron Range National Park from the ranger on site at King Park Homestead, or book ahead through King Park PMB, Cairns Mail Centre, QLD 4871; tel. (070) 60 7170.

ROUTE DIRECTIONS

0.0 km Zero trip meter at s'post: Archer River at Bill Hansen Bridge on north side of river. **SO** on Peninsula Developmental Rd.
(20.5 km)

20.5 km S'post: Iron Range National Park 99/Lockhart River 120. **TR**.
(26.0 km)

46.5 km Creek crossing.
(34.0 km)

80.5 km Creek crossing.
(12.1 km)

Chilli Beach sunset

92.6 km	Creek crossing.
	(9.8 km)
102.4 km	Creek crossing.
	(12.3 km)
114.7 km	S'post: Iron Range National Park. **SO**.
	(6.7 km)
121.4 km	Creek crossing.
	(0.6 km)
122.0 km	Creek crossing.
	(4.9 km)
126.9 km	Cross bridge.
	(0.6 km)
127.5 km	Y intersection. **KR** at airport s'post.
	(2.7 km)
130.2 km	King Park Homestead: Iron Range National Park Ranger Station.

> *Contact ranger who will advise campsite availability and provide permits. Allow a further hour to locate campsite. Excellent campsite with barbecues and toilets at Portland Roads/Lockhart River roads intersection. Beach camping at Chilli Beach.*

▼▼▼▼▼▼▼▼

TAKE CARE

- Be crocodile-wise. Dangerous estuarine crocodiles may inhabit rivers, beaches and inland waterways of Australia's north.

- In outback Australia long distances separate some towns. Take care to ensure your vehicle is roadworthy before setting out and carry adequate supplies of petrol, water and food.

- In Australia's north, during the wet season (October–May) roads become impassable. Check conditions before setting out.

IRON RANGE NATIONAL PARK
»
THE WENLOCK RIVER

START POINT
Map page 18, E7.

TOTAL KM 102.
UNSEALED KM 102.
DEGREE OF DIFFICULTY Difficult.
DRIVING TIME 5 hours.
LONGEST DISTANCE NO FUEL No fuel this section. Next fuel Bamaga (264 km from Wenlock River).
TOPOGRAPHIC MAPS Auslig 1:250 000 series: *Coen*; *Cape Weymouth*; *Orford Bay*. See also 1:100 000 series.
LOCAL/SPECIALITY MAPS Sunmap: *North Queensland*; Croc Shop map: *Cape York*.
OTHER USEFUL INFORMATION Mike Foulkes' *Cape York Peninsula Overlanders Guide*; Viv and Ron Moon's *Cape York: an Adventurer's Guide*; QNPWS visitor information sheet: *Far North Queensland National Parks*.

DESCRIPTION This section of trek returns you to the Peninsula Developmental Road via the secondary track known as Frenchmans Gap Road. The track is rough and potholed and you cross the Pascoe River and Wenlock River twice which makes it hard going. The country is diverse, ranging from the lowland rainforest near the coast through woodland and heathlands further inland. Bush campsites are available on the banks of the *Wenlock River*.

WARNINGS ▶ Crocodiles inhabit coastline and inland waterways on Cape York Peninsula. Be crocodile-wise. Do not swim. ▶ Drive with great care on difficult

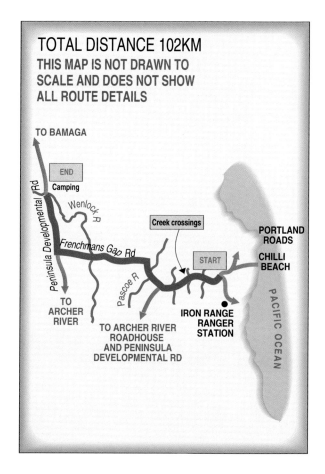

TOTAL DISTANCE 102KM
THIS MAP IS NOT DRAWN TO SCALE AND DOES NOT SHOW ALL ROUTE DETAILS

sections of track along Frenchmans Gap Road. ▶ Care needed in managing steep sandy exit from Pascoe River and boggy section immediately following the Wenlock River first crossing.

ROUTE DIRECTIONS

0.0 km Zero trip meter at Portland Roads and Lockhart River roads intersection, facing west at airport s'post. **SO**.
 (0.6 km)
0.6 km Cross bridge.
 (3.6 km)
4.2 km Creek crossing.
 (1.4 km)
5.6 km Creek crossing.
 (1.1 km)
6.7 km Creek crossing.
 (3.2 km)
9.9 km Creek crossing.
 (7.2 km)
17.1 km Creek crossing.
 (8.3 km)

258

IRON RANGE NATIONAL PARK » THE WENLOCK RIVER

Iron Range coast

25.4 km	Creek crossing.
	(2.2 km)
27.6 km	Intersection. **TR** onto Frenchmans Gap Rd.
	(10.5 km)
38.1 km	Cross Pascoe River.

> *Check depth before crossing. Engage 4WD. Steep sandy exit, washaways.*

(4.0 km)

42.7 km	Intersection. **KL**.
	(24.4 km)
67.1 km	Cross Wenlock River.

> *Check depth before crossing. Engage 4WD. Narrow exit with washaways and sharp corners. The Wenlock River has wide sandy banks suitable for camping.*

(0.6 km)

67.7 km	Multiple intersection. **KR**.
	(12.5 km)

80.2 km	T intersection. **TR** onto Peninsula Developmental Rd.
	(22.0 km)
102.2 km	Cross Wenlock River.

> *Check depth before crossing and engage 4WD. Numerous campsites on north shore of river. This can become extremely crowded: some sites avail. above bank.*

TREAD LIGHTLY!
On Public and Private Land

■ Take your rubbish home with you. Do not bury it.

THE WENLOCK RIVER » BAMAGA

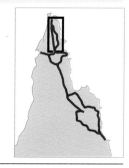

START POINT
Map page 18, C7.

TOTAL KM 264.
UNSEALED KM 264.
DEGREE OF DIFFICULTY Moderate.
DRIVING TIME 7 hours.
LONGEST DISTANCE NO FUEL Fuel at Bamaga.
TOPOGRAPHIC MAPS Auslig 1:250 000 series: *Orford Bay*; *Cape York*; *Jardine River*; *Thursday Island*. See also 1:100 000 series.
LOCAL/SPECIALITY MAPS Sunmap: *North Queensland*; Croc Shop map: *Cape York*.
OTHER USEFUL INFORMATION Mike Foulkes' *Cape York Peninsula Overlanders Guide*; Viv and Ron Moon's *Cape York: an Adventurer's Guide*; QNPWS visitor information sheet: *Jardine River National Park*.

DESCRIPTION The rest of the trek to the tip of the Australian mainland at Cape York provides a marvellous diversity of countryside including rainforest, woodlands, heathlands, mangroves and scrub. This route is an alternative to the Old Telegraph Road and gives access to areas that the old road does not. You head across the Heathlands Reserve, once the site of an experiment in pastoral development by Comalco, now under QNPWS management. Riverside camping and access to beach front camping at *Shelburne Bay* is available through Shelburne Station. This is a private facility, call at the homestead for further information. Alternatively, you can bush camp at *Captain Billy Landing*, on the coast a little further north; the access track winds through dense jungle. Another worthwhile diversion from the plotted route is a visit to the spec-

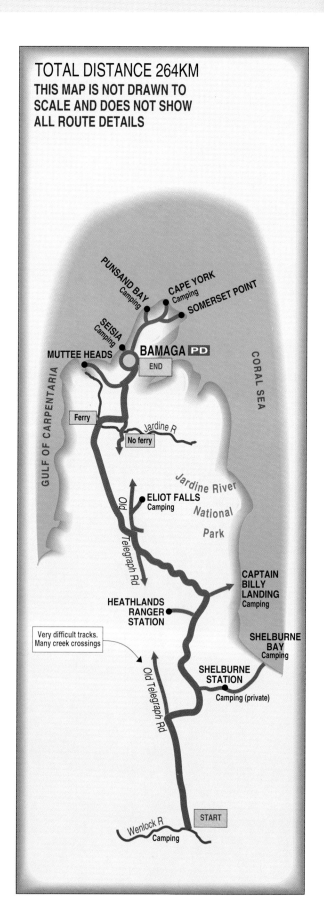

TOTAL DISTANCE 264KM
THIS MAP IS NOT DRAWN TO
SCALE AND DOES NOT SHOW
ALL ROUTE DETAILS

tacular Fruit Bat Falls, 6 kilometres up the Old Telegraph Road. You can camp nearby at *Eliot Falls*; this area is all part of the Jardine River National Park. Back on the new track north, cross the Jardine by ferry, and then it's a short distance to Bamaga and the tip of the top!

At the Islander community of Bamaga you can obtain fuel, supplies and mechanical repairs. Camp only within prescribed areas: *Seisia* camping resort (Red Island Point) and *Cowal Creek* both offer excellent facilities including showers, fresh water and toilets. You must get advice and permission from the Community Services Office in Bamaga should you wish to visit other communities in the area.

From Bamaga, explore the white beaches of *Punsand Bay*, where there is a camping resort and kiosk (with toilets, showers, fresh water). Access to the tip of Cape York is near *Cape York Wilderness Lodge* which, in addition to four-star accommodation, has a camping resort with all facilities and a kiosk.

Other expeditions should include the excellent fishing at *Muttee Heads* at the north of the Jardine River (bush camping only). Visits to historic Somerset, the site of the early Jardine Homestead, and to Fly Point should be day trips as no camping is allowed.

WARNINGS ▶ Crocodiles inhabit coastline and inland waterways on Cape York. Be crocodile-wise. Do not swim. ▶ Road conditions on this trek section vary from good to poor depending on maintenance, time of year and weather but expect some passages of soft bulldust, lengthy sections of corrugated gravel, occasional washaways and awkward creeks to cross. Often the road is narrow and twisting. Keep well to the left and exercise caution always. ▶ Around Bamaga, travel only on marked roads. No shooting in the area. Camp only in prescribed areas.

BOOKINGS AND PERMITS ▶ QNPWS permits required to camp at Eliot Falls and Captain Billy Landing. Obtain from the ranger at Heathlands Reserve; tel. (070) 60 3241 or from QNPWS, Far Northern Regional Office, PO Box 2066, Cairns QLD 4871; tel. (070) 52 3093. ▶ Permission required to camp at Shelburne Station. Obtain from the homestead, radio call sign 8QRD, or write to PMB 44, Cairns Mail Centre, Cairns QLD 4870. ▶ Permit required from Injinu Community at Cowal Creek to camp at Muttee Heads. ▶ For information and booking at Seisia tel. (070) 69 3243 and for Cowal Creek, tel. (070) 69 3252. ▶ Write to the Punsand Bay resort at Punsand Bay Private Reserve Pty Ltd, Wilderness Base Camp, Punsand Bay, via Bamaga QLD 4876; tel. (070) 69 1722. ▶ Contact the Cape York Wilderness Lodge by writing C/- Post Office, Bamaga QLD 4876; tel. (070) 69 1444.

ROUTE DIRECTIONS

0.0 km Zero trip meter on north shore of Wenlock River at s'post: Bamaga. **SO**.

> *Moreton Station on right.*

(10.4 km)

10.4 km Creek crossing.

(31.0 km)

41.4 km Cross Barrie Creek.

(0.7 km)

42.1 km Y intersection. **KR**.

> *The Old Telegraph Rd north is straight ahead. This track is very difficult with many creek crossings, washaways and a broken road surface. It is not maintained, and an option for only the most adventuresome. Be warned.*

(11.9 km)

54.0 km Creek crossing.

(9.6 km)

63.6 km Intersection.

> *Shelburne Homestead 13 km off to right (easy track). Riverside camping on property and access to beach frontage camping at Shelburne Bay. Obtain further information and pay fees at homestead.*

0.0 km Zero trip meter at above intersection. **SO**.

(12.0 km)

12.0 km Microwave tower on left. **SO**.

(22.6 km)

34.6 km S'post: Bamaga 161. **KR**.

> *Heathlands Ranger Station 13 km off to left. Obtain information and camping permits for Captain Billy Landing and Eliot Falls.*

0.0 km Zero trip meter at above s'post. **KR**.

(10.9 km)

10.9 km S'post: Bamaga/Cape York. Captain Billy Landing 27 km off to right.

> *Bush camping, no facilities, permit required. Water obtainable from creek 5 km from beach.*

0.0 km Zero trip meter at above s'post. **KL**.

(45.0 km)

45.0 km Intersection. **KR**.

> *Old Telegraph Rd joins on left.*

(7.2 km)

Heathlands track

Frangipani Beach, at the tip of Cape York

52.2 km Y intersection. Use either track.
(2.2 km)
54.2 km S'post: Bamaga Ferry (Jardine River). **KL**.

> *Old Telegraph Rd continues straight ahead with many creek crossings and no ferry service at the Jardine River (which may not be fordable). However, a short 6-km detour along this track brings you to attractive campsites at Eliot Falls (toilets, barbecues). Permit required to camp.*

(53.5 km)
107.9 km Jardine River Ferry.

> *Substantial fee payable on board.*

(33.1 km)
141.0 km T intersection. **TR**.

> *Track to left goes 26 km to Muttee Heads at the entrance of the Jardine River.*

(7.4 km)
148.4 km WW2 DC-3 crash site. **SO**.
(0.2 km)
148.6 km S'post: Bamaga. **TL**.

> *Bamaga Airport on right.*

(4.6 km)
153.2 km Intersection. **SO**.

> *Turnoff on right to Punsand Bay (25 km) and Cape York (30 km). Somerset, Albany Passage and Fly Point also accessible off this track.*

(1.4 km)
154.6 km S'post: Bamaga. **TR**.

> *Seisia 7 km off to left.*

(0.4 km)
155.0 km Bamaga General Store.

> **PD** *Supplies, mechanical repairs. Camp only in prescribed areas. Call at Council Office to obtain information.*

BAMAGA
»
THE DULHUNTY RIVER

START POINT
Map page 18, C3.

TOTAL KM 162.
UNSEALED KM 162.
DEGREE OF DIFFICULTY Difficult. *See Warnings.*
DRIVING TIME 6 hours.
LONGEST DISTANCE NO FUEL 376 km (Bamaga to Weipa, next section).
TOPOGRAPHIC MAPS Auslig 1:250 000 series: *Cape York*; *Thursday Island*; *Jardine River*; *Orford Bay*; *Weipa*; *Cape Weymouth*. See also 1:100 000 series.
LOCAL/SPECIALITY MAPS Sunmap: *North Queensland*; Croc Shop map: *Cape York*.
OTHER USEFUL INFORMATION Mike Foulkes' *Overlanders Guide to Cape York*; Viv and Ron Moon's *Cape York: an Adventurer's Guide*; QNPWS visitor information sheet: *Jardine River National Park*.

DESCRIPTION At first this section simply reverses the northbound journey on the new road as far as the Shelburne Bay turnoff; but then the adventurous can branch off onto the Old Telegraph Road, a difficult track involving many creek crossings. *See Warnings.* We have plotted a detour via Heathlands to avoid Gunshot Creek, which is virtually impassable except by winching.

The option to making the trip along the Old Telegraph Road is to continue south along the new road from the Shelburne Bay turnoff, again reversing the northbound route of the previous trek section. There are good bush campsites on the banks of the *Dulhunty River* at the end of the section.

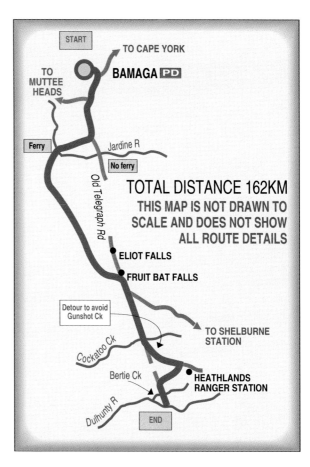

WARNINGS ▶ Crocodile inhabit coastline and all inland waterways on Cape York. Be crocodile-wise. Do not swim. ▶ Section of road includes hazardous creek crossings. Detour via Heathlands to avoid Gunshot Creek. ▶ No fuel this section. Take on enough fuel at Bamaga for 376 km.

ROUTE DIRECTIONS

0.0 km   Zero trip meter at Bamaga General Store. **PD** Next fuel Weipa (376 km).
(0.4 km)
0.4 km   S'post: Cairns. **TL.**
(1.4 km)
1.8 km   S'post: Punsand/Cape York. **SO.**
(4.6 km)
6.4 km   Intersection. **TR.**

> *Bamaga Airport straight ahead.*

(0.2 km)
6.6 km   Site of WW2 DC-3 crash on left. **SO.**
(7.5 km)
14.1 km   S'post: Cairns. **TL.**

Swimming at Fruit Bat Falls

	Muttee Heads straight ahead.
(23.2 km)	
37.3 km	Intersection. **KR**.
	Old Telegraph Rd on left. No ferry across the Jardine River on this road.
(0.1 km)	
37.4 km	Y intersection. **KR**.
(9.7 km)	
47.1 km	Jardine River Ferry.
	Substantial fee payable on board.
(53.7 km)	
100.8 km	T intersection. **TR** onto Old Telegraph Rd.
(9.3 km)	
110.1 km	Y intersection. **KR**.
	New road via Shelburne Station on left: alternative route south.
(20.2 km)	
130.3 km	Cross Cockatoo Creek.
(0.6 km)	

130.9 km	Y intersection. **TL** to Heathlands.
	Old Telegraph Rd straight ahead but Gunshot Creek impassable other than by winching. Detour through Heathlands.
(12.0 km)	
142.9 km	Intersection. **TR**.
	Heathlands Ranger Station straight ahead.
(12.0 km)	
154.9 km	Intersection. **TL**.
	Rejoin Old Telegraph Rd.
(3.4 km)	
158.3 km	Cross Bertie Creek.
	Check course and depth.
(3.5 km)	
161.8 km	Cross Dulhunty River.
	Bush campsites available in vicinity.

THE DULHUNTY RIVER
»
WEIPA

START POINT
Map page 18, C6.

TOTAL KM 214.
UNSEALED KM 204.
DEGREE OF DIFFICULTY Moderate.
DRIVING TIME 6 hours.
LONGEST DISTANCE NO FUEL Fuel at Weipa.
TOPOGRAPHIC MAPS Auslig 1:250 000 series: *Weipa*; *Cape Weymouth*. See also 1:100 000 series.
LOCAL/SPECIALITY MAPS Sunmap: *North Queensland*; Croc Shop map: *Cape York*; Comalco map: *Weipa Township*; Marpoona Community maps of routes to *Mapoon* and *Pennefather River*.
OTHER USEFUL INFORMATION Mike Foulkes' *Overlanders Guide to Cape York*; Viv and Ron Moon's *Cape York: an Adventurer's Guide*.

DESCRIPTION The road to Weipa is fairly typical hard Cape York driving up to the point where the Peninsula Developmental Road joins the Batavia track, after which it is excellent quality gravel and bitumen into Weipa township. Weipa is a major town on Cape York and the centre of the Comalco bauxite mining operations. From the town you can join a tour of the mine operation, or enjoy river cruises. There are a number of good fishing spots in the vicinity, predominantly along the Mission, Embla and Hay rivers. You can make at least two enjoyable camping trips from Weipa; to the mouth of the *Pennefather River* (approximately 70 kilometres to the north) and to *Old Mapoon* at Port Musgrave, at the entrance of the Wenlock River (79 kilometres). The tracks to both are rough with very soft sand at the conclusion

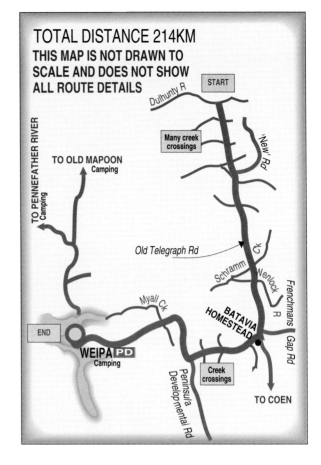

points. Camping in Weipa itself is permitted only at the *Pax Haven Camping Ground*.

WARNINGS ▶ Crocodiles inhabit coastline and all inland waterways on Cape York. Be crocodile-wise. Do not swim. ▶ Beware of loose stock on the Batavia track. ▶ Beware of bauxite trucks close to Weipa and give way to these vehicles at all times. Do not drive on Comalco haul roads marked private.

BOOKINGS AND PERMITS ▶ Permits required to camp and visit at Old Mapoon and Pennefather River. Obtain information from Marpoona Community Corporation in Weipa; tel. (070) 69 7468. ▶ Advance bookings for Pax Haven Camping Ground on (070) 69 7871. ▶ For information on Comalco operations and tours contact the Comalco Public Liaison Officer at Lorim Point; tel. (070) 69 7101.

THE DULHUNTY RIVER » WEIPA

Road section near the Wenlock River

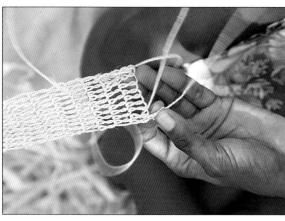

Aurukun craft

ROUTE DIRECTIONS

0.0 km   Zero trip meter at Dulhunty River on south shore.
(38.0 km)

38.0 km   Intersection. **SO.**

> *New road joins on left.*

(0.8 km)

38.8 km   Cross Barrie Creek.
(31.0 km)

69.8 km   Cross Schramm Creek.
(10.3 km)

80.1 km   Cross Wenlock River.

> *Check depth before crossing and engage low-range 4WD.*

(22.1 km)

102.2 km   Intersection. **SO.**

> *Frenchmans Gap Rd to Portland Roads on left.*

(1.6 km)

103.8 km   Intersection. **TR** at airstrip onto North Weipa road via Batavia Station.
(1.2 km)

105.0 km   Batavia Homestead on left. **SO.**
(0.4 km)

105.4 km   Creek crossing.

> *Check depth, engage 4WD.*

(23.3 km)

128.7 km   Creek crossing.

> *Steep exit.*

(10.2)

138.9 km   Creek crossing.
(5.0 km)

143.9 km   Intersection. **TR** onto Peninsula Developmental Rd.
(15.5 km)

159.4 km   Myall Creek. Cross wooden bridge.
(44.6 km)

204.0 km   Bitumen.
(1.1 km)

205.1 km   S'post: Weipa. **TR.**

> *Airport road on left.*

(9.1 km)

214.2 km   S'post: Weipa Camping Ground. **TL.**

> *Shopping centre on right. Pax Haven Camping Ground behind the shopping centre.* **PD** *Supplies and mechanical repairs avail. in Weipa.*

WEIPA » COEN

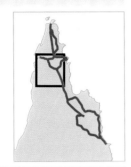

START POINT
Map page 18, B7.

TOTAL KM 259.
UNSEALED KM 249.
DEGREE OF DIFFICULTY Moderate.
DRIVING TIME 5 hours.
LONGEST DISTANCE NO FUEL 195 km (Weipa to Archer River Roadhouse).
TOPOGRAPHIC MAPS Auslig 1:250 000 series: *Weipa*; *Cape Weymouth*; *Aurukun*; *Coen*. See also 1:100 000 series.
LOCAL/SPECIALITY MAPS Sunmap: *North Queensland*; Croc Shop map: *Cape York*.
OTHER USEFUL INFORMATION Mike Foulkes' *Cape York Peninsula Overlanders' Guide*; Viv and Ron Moon's *Cape York: an Adventurer's Guide*; QNPWS visitor information sheet: *Rokeby National Park*.

DESCRIPTION The route follows the Peninsula Developmental Road which has a good quality gravel surface over its entire length to the major peninsula town of Coen, where there is an attractive camping area 3 kilometres north of the town on the sandy banks of the *Coen River*. Fuel, mechanical repairs and stores are available in Coen. If you choose to stop at *Archer River*, the licensed roadhouse can supply fuel and most needs, including limited mechanical repairs. Camping facilities are available or alternatively you can camp nearby on the banks of the Archer. North of Coen, there is an opportunity to detour from the trek to the wildlife and wilderness area of Rokeby National Park. The ranger station is about 70 kilometres from the Peninsula Developmental Road; call here for information and permits to bush camp. Rokeby offers a huge variety of plant and bird species and many opportunities for walks for the serious hiker, but you must be completely self-sufficient as there are no facilities.

WARNINGS ▶ Crocodiles inhabit coastline and inland waterways on Cape York. Be crocodile-wise. Do not

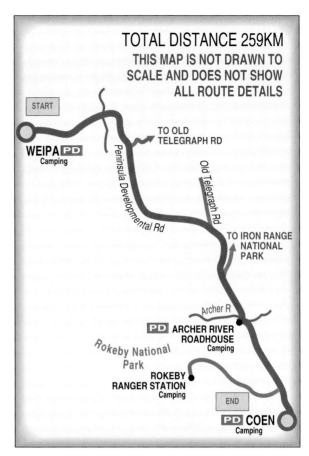

Moonscape of termite mounds, Cape York Peninsula

swim. ▶ Carry spare water and make sure you are self-sufficient to visit Rokeby National Park. ▶ Fishing prohibited in Rokeby National Park.

BOOKINGS AND PERMITS ▶ Obtain permits to camp in Rokeby National Park from the ranger at Rokeby, tel. (070) 60 3256; or write to QNPWS, PMB 28, Cairns Mail Centre, QLD 4870. ▶ Contact the Archer River Roadhouse on (070) 60 3266 for information about camping.

The Archer River

Archer River campsites

ROUTE DIRECTIONS

0.0 km Depart Weipa on Peninsula Developmental Rd and follow signposts for 145 km (approx. 2 hrs) to intersection with the Old Telegraph Rd which joins from the north.
(145.0 km)

145.0 km S'post: Coen.

0.0 km Zero trip meter at above s'post. Proceed south.
(29.8 km)

29.8 km Intersection. **SO**.

> *Iron Range National Park turnoff on left.*

(20.5 km)

50.3 km Cross Archer River.

> *Archer River Roadhouse on south bank.* **PD** *Hot meals, toilets, showers. Limited supplies and some mechanical repairs. Camping available at roadhouse or on banks of the Archer River.*

(41.7 km)

92.0 km Intersection. **SO**.

> *Rokeby National Park turnoff on right, 66 km to ranger station. Bush camping at designated sites. Permit required, contact ranger.*

(21.5 km)

113.5 km S'post: camping.

> *Coen River Camping Area on left. Toilets. Coen 2 km.* **PD** *Supplies and mechanical repairs.*

▼▼▼▼▼▼▼▼

TAKE CARE

● In outback Australia long distances separate some towns. Take care to ensure your vehicle is roadworthy before setting out and carry adequate supplies of petrol, water and food.

● Permits are required if you want to divert off public roads within Aboriginal Land areas.

● In Australia's north, during the wet season (October–May) roads become impassable. Check conditions before setting out.

COEN » LAURA

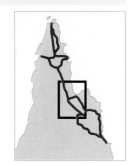

START POINT
Map page 18, E10.

TOTAL KM 252.
UNSEALED KM 252.
DEGREE OF DIFFICULTY Moderate.
DRIVING TIME 5 hours.
LONGEST DISTANCE NO FUEL 112 km (Coen to Musgrave Station).
TOPOGRAPHIC MAPS Auslig 1:250 000 series: *Coen*; *Ebagoola*; *Hann River*; *Cooktown*. See also 1:100 000 series.
LOCAL/SPECIALITY MAPS Sunmap: *North Queensland*; Croc Shop map: *Cape York*.
OTHER USEFUL INFORMATION Mike Foulkes' *Cape York Peninsula Overlanders' Guide*; Viv and Ron Moon's *Cape York: an Adventurer's Guide*.

DESCRIPTION The route south from Coen retraces our northbound trek as far as Musgrave Station; from here you can return to Cooktown and Cairns across Lakefield National Park. But if you head south to the ridge country around Laura, you then have several interesting options. One is to continue on the Peninsula Developmental Road via Mount Carbine to Cairns or Mareeba. A visit to the Aboriginal rock art site at Split Rock, 13 kilometres south of Laura on the Peninsula Developmental Road, is worthwhile. There are thousand-year-old paintings of animals, birds, fish and human and spirit figures. A further choice, mapped and charted in the next section, is to retrace 1.8 kilometres north from Laura along the Peninsula Developmental Road to the turnoff on the left, which follows the historic Laura–Maytown Cobb & Co. coach road through the abandoned gold-mining town of Maytown. This is a real four-wheel drive experience – if you feel you need it! You can rejoin the Peninsula Developmental Road further south to return to Cairns or Mareeba. This route allows you to visit Jowalbinna Station and make a day trip to the famous Quinkan Aboriginal rock

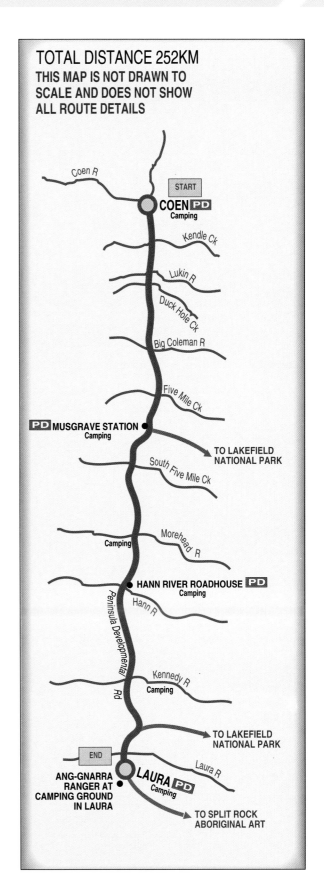

TOTAL DISTANCE 252KM
THIS MAP IS NOT DRAWN TO SCALE AND DOES NOT SHOW ALL ROUTE DETAILS

Coen R

START

COEN **PD**
Camping

Kendle Ck

Lukin R

Duck Hole Ck

Big Coleman R

Five Mile Ck

PD MUSGRAVE STATION
Camping

TO LAKEFIELD NATIONAL PARK

South Five Mile Ck

Morehead R

Camping

HANN RIVER ROADHOUSE **PD**
Camping

Hann R

Peninsula Developmental Rd

Kennedy R
Camping

TO LAKEFIELD NATIONAL PARK

END

ANG-GNARRA RANGER AT CAMPING GROUND IN LAURA

LAURA **PD**
Camping

Laura R

TO SPLIT ROCK ABORIGINAL ART

Aboriginal rock paintings, Quinkan Reserve

art sites. You can bush camp at *Jowalbinna* if you wish to stay longer.

Along the road from Coen to Laura there are several good camping spots: the *Morehead* and *Kennedy* river crossings are attractive places and the *Hann River Roadhouse* has a pleasant camping ground. At *Laura*, where you can get fuel and supplies, and limited mechanical repairs, there is an excellent camping ground, and there is also a good bush camping spot at the *Little Laura* crossing, 12 kilometres north of the town.

WARNINGS ▶ Crocodiles inhabit coastline and inland waterways on Cape York. Be crocodile-wise. Do not swim. ▶ South of Coen the Peninsula Developmental Road is generally badly corrugated, has many sharp dips and bends and creek crossings. Drive with great care.

BOOKINGS AND PERMITS ▶ Permits to visit Split Rock Aboriginal art site and to traverse Quinkan Reserve available from the ranger at the Ang-Gnarra Corporation office in Laura; tel. (070) 60 3214. The corporation also runs the camping ground in Laura.

▶ For information and camp bookings at Hann River Roadhouse write to PMB 88, Mail Centre, Cairns QLD 4870; tel. (070) 60 3242. ▶ For information on Jowalbinna, call at Quinkan Hotel in Laura or contact the Trezise Bush Guide Service, PO Box 106, Freshwater, Cairns QLD 4870; tel. (070) 55 1865.

▼▼▼▼▼▼▼▼

TAKE CARE

● In outback Australia long distances separate some towns. Take care to ensure your vehicle is roadworthy before setting out and carry adequate supplies of petrol, water and food.

● Permits are required if you want to divert off public roads within Aboriginal Land areas.

ROUTE DIRECTIONS

0.0 km Zero trip meter at exit to Coen River Camping Area.
(1.3 km)

1.3 km Coen River. Cross bridge.
(0.6 km)

1.9 km Lankelly Creek. Cross bridge.
(1.1 km)

3.0 km S'post: Laura. **TL**.

> *Coen town centre on right.* **PD** *Supplies and caravan park.*

(40.7 km)

43.7 km Cross Kendle Creek.
(18.8 km)

62.5 km Cross Lukin River.
(1.8 km)

64.3 km Cross Duck Hole Creek.
(21.8 km)

86.1 km Cross Big Coleman River.
(17.3 km)

103.4 km Cross Five Mile Creek.
(8.7 km)

112.1 km Intersection. S'post: Laura.

> *Musgrave Station on right.* **PD** *Hot meals, limited supplies and camping area. Lakefield National Park turnoff on left: optional return route to Cooktown.*

0.0 km Zero trip meter at above s'post. **SO**.
(0.2 km)

0.2 km Cross Saltwater Creek.
(9.3 km)

9.5 km Cross South Five Mile Creek.
(10.3 km)

19.8 km Cross Windmill Creek.
(3.3 km)

23.1 km Cross Fifteen Mile Creek.
(5.9 km)

29.0 km Cross Noorko Creek.
(1.9 km)

30.9 km Cross Marys Creek.
(3.2 km)

34.1 km Morehead River. Cross bridge.

> *Good camping, toilets and shelters.*

(8.6 km)

42.7 km Cross Deadhorse Creek.
(10.8 km)

53.5 km Cross Healy Creek.
(4.5 km)

Jowalbinna Bush Camp

58.0 km Cross Codroy Creek.
(5.3 km)

63.3 km **SO** and immediately cross bridge over Hann River.

> *Hann River Roadhouse on left.* **PD** *Camping, hot meals, showers.*

(4.4 km)

67.7 km Cross Rocky Creek.
(9.2 km)

76.9 km Cross Weiss Creek.
(2.8 km)

79.7 km Cross North Kennedy River.
(17.1 km)

96.8 km Cross Laker Creek.
(9.2 km)

106.0 km Kennedy River. Cross bridge.

> *Good camping, toilets and shelters.*

(21.5 km)

127.5 km Little Laura River. Cross bridge.

> *Good camping.*

(4.9 km)

132.4 km Cross Sandy Creek.
(5.9 km)

138.3 km Intersection. **SO**.

> *Lakefield National Park off to left.*

(0.5 km)

138.8 km Laura River. Cross bridge.
(0.9 km)

139.7 km Intersection.

> *Laura township.* **PD** *Ang-Gnarra Corporation Ranger Station and Camping Ground. Famous Quinkan Hotel 100 m on left.*

LAURA
»
MAYTOWN

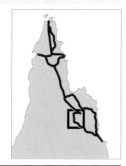

START POINT
Map page 16, I3.

TOTAL KM 77.
UNSEALED KM 77.
DEGREE OF DIFFICULTY Extreme.
DRIVING TIME 6 hours.
LONGEST DISTANCE NO FUEL 224 km (Laura to Mt Carbine, next section).
TOPOGRAPHIC MAPS Auslig 1:250 000 series: *Cooktown*; *Mossman*. See also 1:100 000 series.
LOCAL/SPECIALITY MAPS Sunmap: *North Queensland*; QNPWS and Dept of Resource Industries: *Gold'n Palmer Reserve Heritage Map*.
OTHER USEFUL INFORMATION QNPWS visitor information sheet: *Palmer Goldfields Reserve*; Trezise Bush Guide Service brochures: *Jowalbinna* and *Quinkan Country*; Mike Foulkes' *Cape York Peninsula Overlanders' Guide*; Viv and Ron Moon's *Cape York: an Adventurer's Guide*.

DESCRIPTION This trek follows the historic Cobb & Co. coach road to Maytown, the abandoned site of the major town on the Palmer River Goldfields. For most of its relatively short length the route is extremely difficult, crossing and following the ridges of the Great Dividing Range over rocky escarpments and numerous creek crossings. The road was cut with hand-held implements in the 1870s and this is evident along the journey.

When alluvial gold was discovered along the Palmer in 1873, the area quickly became a mecca for European and Chinese miners, despite its isolation and the extremes of climate. The local Aborigines, faced with the destruction of their traditional hunting grounds, clashed with the new settlers and there were bloody

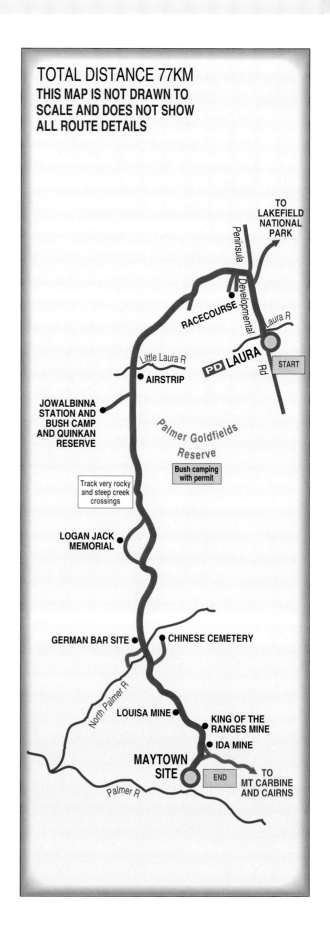

TOTAL DISTANCE 77KM
THIS MAP IS NOT DRAWN TO SCALE AND DOES NOT SHOW ALL ROUTE DETAILS

The notorious Cobb & Co. coach road to Old Maytown

reprisals. When the alluvial gold petered out, the Maytown reefs were mined, which meant the importation of expensive equipment to work the hard rock. Financial difficulties led to the virtual abandoning of the Palmer. Now you see only the remains of the old mines and relics of habitation. You can spend days exploring but you must be self-sufficient to camp as there are no facilities.

WARNINGS ▶ Crocodiles inhabit coastline and inland waterways on Cape York. Be crocodile-wise. Do not swim. ▶ Take great care on Laura–Maytown road. This rough track requires skill and experience with four-wheel driving. ▶ When in the Palmer Goldfields Reserve, keep to the tracks defined on the QNPWS map. Other tracks are closed to the public. Beware dangerous open shafts. No mining or prospecting. ▶ No fuel at Maytown. Take enough fuel at Laura for 224 km.

BOOKINGS AND PERMITS ▶ Permit required to traverse a section of the Quinkan Reserve. Obtain from Ang-Gnarra Corporation office in Laura, tel. (070) 60 3214. ▶ Permit required to camp in the Maytown area and Palmer Goldfields Reserve. Obtain from QNPWS

in Cairns, 10–12 McLeod Street, Cairns; PO Box 2066; Cairns QLD 4870; tel. (070) 52 3093 or QNPWS in Chillagoe, PO Box 38, Chillagoe QLD 4871; tel. (070) 94 7163 ▶ Information and bookings for Jowalbinna Bush Camp and Rock Art Trek from PO Box 106, Freshwater, Cairns QLD 4870; tel. (070) 55 1865.

ROUTE DIRECTIONS

0.0 km   Zero trip meter at Laura township turnoff on Peninsula Developmental Road heading north.

> **PD** *Next fuel Mt Carbine (224 km).*

(0.9 km)

0.9 km   Laura River. Cross bridge.

(0.6 km)

1.5 km   Intersection. **SO**.

> *Lakefield National Park off to right.*

(0.3 km)

1.8 km   Intersection. **TL**.

(0.2 km)

Old Maytown, a ghost town

2.0 km   Intersection. **KR** around Laura Racetrack and Rodeo Grounds.
(0.1 km)

2.1 km   Intersection. **KR** as above.
(4.9 km)

7.0 km   Intersection. **KR**.
(20.7 km)

27.7 km   Cross Little Laura River.

> *Rocky crossing.*

(4.0 km)

31.7 km   Airstrip on left. **SO**.
(2.3 km)

34.0 km   Intersection. S'post: Maytown. **TL**.

> *Jowalbinna Station straight ahead. Jowalbinna Bush Camp (4 km) is available only to those who have booked walks with Trezise Bush Guide Service.*

0.0 km   Zero trip meter at above s'post. **SO**.
(0.2 km)

0.2 km   Creek crossing.

> *Steep exit.*

(0.5 km)

0.7 km   S'post: Quinkan Reserve. **SO**.

> *No camping or lighting fires in this area. Permit required to traverse if you leave the track.*

(17.7 km)

18.4 km   S'post: Palmer Goldfields Reserve. **SO**.
(0.2 km)

18.6 km   Intersection. **SO**.

> *Logan Jack Memorial Cairn off to right.*

(5.6 km)

24.2 km   Intersection. **TL**.

> *Logan Jack track rejoins on right.*

(8.2 km)

32.4 km   Intersection. **KR**.

> *Mine site track on left.*

(4.1 km)

36.5 km S'post: German Bar/North Palmer Crossing. **SO** to North Palmer River.

> *Track on right leads 500 m to site of German Bar township.*

(0.9 km)

37.4 km Intersection. **KL.**

> *Palmer River Crossing off to right.*

(0.3 km)

37.7 km S'post: Maytown. **TR.**

> *Chinese Cemetery 1.9 km straight ahead.*

(1.5 km)

39.2 km Intersection. **KR.**

(0.4 km)

39.6 km Intersection. **KL.**

(0.1 km)

39.7 km Louisa Mine relics on right. **SO.**

(1.0 km)

40.7 km S'post: King of the Ranges Mine. **SO.**

(0.9 km)

41.6 km S'post: Maytown 2.3. **KR.**

> *Ida Mine 500 m off to left.*

(0.5 km)

42.1 km S'post: Maytown. **SO.**

> *Palmer River Crossing via Dog Leg Creek and route to Cairns on left.*

(0.2 km)

42.3 km S'post: Maytown. **SO.**

> *Charcoal Burners off to right.*

(0.9 km)

43.2 km Intersection. **SO.**

> *Cemetery off to left.*

(0.1 km)

43.3 km Maytown site.

> *Explore region at leisure. Bush camping available, permit required. No facilities.*

Peninsula Developmental Road, south of Laura

Palmer Goldfields sign

Kim at work in camp

MAYTOWN
»
CAIRNS

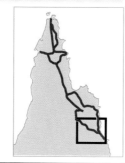

START POINT
Map page 16, I5.

TOTAL KM 289.
UNSEALED KM 79.
DEGREE OF DIFFICULTY Difficult.
DRIVING TIME 6 hours.
LONGEST DISTANCE NO FUEL Fuel at Mt Carbine (147 km from Maytown).
TOPOGRAPHIC MAPS Auslig 1:250 000 series: *Mossman*; *Cairns*. See also 1:100 000 series.
LOCAL/SPECIALITY MAPS Sunmap: *North Queensland*; QNPWS map: *Gold'n Heritage*.

DESCRIPTION This linking section returns from the Palmer River Goldfields to the Peninsula Developmental Road and on to Mt Carbine, Mossman and Cairns. The track from Maytown is narrow, and twists and winds through the Great Dividing Range past gold-mining sites. Constantly rising and falling, it provides 360-degree views over the surrounding country. Road quality is reasonable but drive slowly and watch for oncoming traffic on the narrow track.

WARNINGS ▶ Crocodiles inhabit coastline and all inland waterways in far north Queensland. Be crocodile-wise. Do not swim. ▶ Watch for oncoming traffic on narrow winding track Maytown to Peninsula Developmental Road.

BOOKINGS AND PERMITS ▶ For information on accommodation and camping in and around Cairns contact QNPWS, 10–12 McLeod Street; PO Box 2066, Cairns QLD 4870; tel. (070) 52 3093 or Far North Queensland Promotion Bureau, 36–38 Aplin Street; PO Box 865, Cairns QLD 4870; tel. (070) 51 3588.

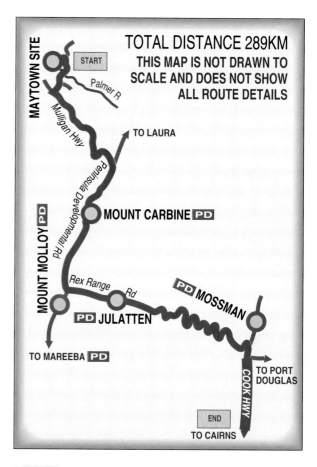

TOTAL DISTANCE 289KM
THIS MAP IS NOT DRAWN TO SCALE AND DOES NOT SHOW ALL ROUTE DETAILS

ROUTE DIRECTIONS

From Maytown retrace 1 km to s'post: Palmer River Crossing via Dog Leg Creek/Cairns.

0.0 km Zero trip meter at above s'post. Proceed south.
(4.2 km)

4.2 km S'post: Palmer River Crossing 3.5. **SO**.

| *Queen Mill 1.3 km off to left.* |

(3.7 km)

7.9 km Cross Palmer River.
(3.2 km)

11.1 km Intersection. **KR**.
(1.5 km)

12.6 km Crossroads. **TL** onto Mulligan Hwy.
(0.8 km)

13.4 km S'post: Mt Carbine. **SO**.
(26.4 km)

39.8 km Cross airstrip. **SO**.
(16.6 km)

View from ranges towards Cairns

56.4 km   Gate.

> *Leave as found.*

(22.9 km)

79.3 km   Intersection. **TR** onto bitumen: Peninsula Developmental Rd.

(67.6 km)

146.9 km   Mt Carbine town centre. **SO**.

> **PD** *Supplies.*

(29.1 km)

176.0 km   S'post: Mossman.

> *Rex Range Rd on left. Spectacular views over ranges.*

TL to return to Mossman and Cairns via Rex Range Rd and Cook Hwy (113 km approx.) to pick up route directions for next trek Cairns to Darwin. Alternatively, **SO** to Mt Molloy and Mareeba (41 km approx.) and join the next trek there.

TREAD LIGHTLY!
On Public and Private Land

■ Take your rubbish home with you. Do not bury it.

■ Leave gates as you found them – open or shut.

■ Do not damage swamps, steep hills or creekbanks which can be easily scarred by churning wheels.

■ Ford creeks at designated crossings.

ACROSS THE TOP
CAIRNS «» DARWIN
3507 KILOMETRES

CAIRNS «» THE EINASLEIGH RIVER   393 km

THE EINASLEIGH RIVER «» UNDARA LAVA LODGE   298 km

UNDARA LAVA LODGE «» CHILLAGOE   180 km

CHILLAGOE «» DORUNDA STATION   417 km

DORUNDA STATION «» KARUMBA   186 km

KARUMBA «» BURKETOWN   297 km

BURKETOWN «» LAWN HILL NATIONAL PARK   219 km

LAWN HILL NATIONAL PARK «» HELLS GATE ROADHOUSE   217 km

HELLS GATE ROADHOUSE «» BORROLOOLA   322 km

BORROLOOLA «» NATHAN RIVER STATION   184 km

NATHAN RIVER STATION «» THE ROPER RIVER BAR   192 km

THE ROPER RIVER BAR «» DARWIN   602 km

Southern rockhole, Nitmiluk (Katherine Gorge) National Park

Only a few major arterial roads link the tropical cities of Cairns and Darwin. In between lies the Gulf Savannah, stretching west of Cairns to the Northern Territory (NT) border. The trek crosses into Territory Gulf country after Hells Gate and follows the Gulf of Carpentaria coastline past vast cattle stations into the heart of the Never Never, around Mataranka. There are more rivers than roads across this outback by the sea. Fed by Gulf waters, these magnificent tidal rivers thread through mangrove wetlands and saltflats, into immense grassed plains. The dry season (April – October) is the best time to travel across the top. When the monsoons hit during the wet, generally November – March,

road conditions change dramatically with flash flooding. Even in the dry it is advisable to check road conditions and weather reports regularly. Most roads are unsealed and in reasonable condition, with some corrugated sections and patches of bulldust and potholes. The plains are parched and brown at the end of the dry season and it can be particularly dusty, but after the monsoons the country is lush and green.

Take fishing gear because many of your overnight stops, some at bush campsites beside rivers, others in national parks or on cattle stations, are excellent fishing spots. The Gulf region (and the Territory in general) is renowned for barramundi and saratoga. Try your hand at reef and game fishing at Karumba and Darwin. There is a bag limit on barramundi and other rules and regulations apply for recreational fishing. The NT Department of Primary Industry and Fisheries has arranged a scheme with several private pastoral properties which allows visitors access to fishing spots. Check route directions for details and conditions. Remember to be crocodile-wise when fishing and camping.

The country we traverse is ancient and pristine with unique wildlife and only a small and scattered population in outback towns, remote cattle stations and Aboriginal settlements. You can experience station life at Dorunda and Escott stations and, with permits, stay on Aboriginal settlements at Kowanyama and Doomadgee. (Never enter Aboriginal land beyond unrestricted areas without a permit.) Northern Australia is rich in Aboriginal legend and culture and evidence of their presence at Lawn Hill National Park dates back over 17,000 years. Their paintings adorn rock art sites both here and at Nitmiluk (Katherine Gorge) National Park. Canoeing and bushwalking at both these parks, and at Elsey National Park near Mataranka, reveal amazing aquatic wildlife and gorges, waterfalls and rockpools of indescribable beauty. Some of the most geologically fascinating areas to explore on this trip (such as the Undara lava tubes

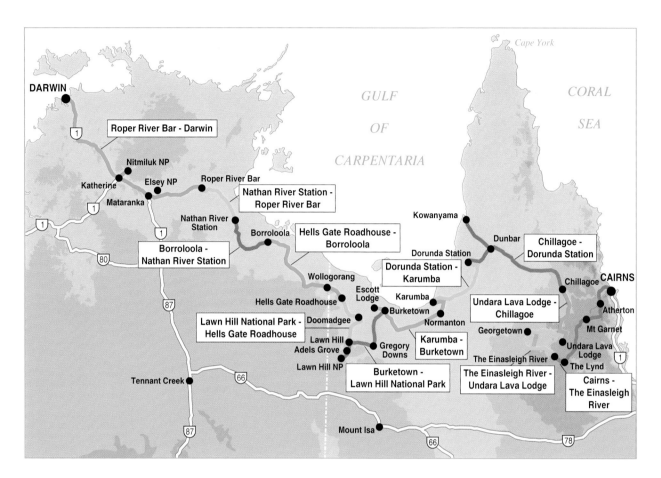

and Tallaroo Hot Springs) are within station properties where access is restricted unless accompanied by a Savannah Guide. These guides are the official protectors, and have an intimate knowledge, of their specific wilderness areas.

This is not Sunday driving country. You should carry high-frequency radio. Before you leave, register with the Royal Flying Doctor Service and obtain the guide listing bases, radio call signs and broadcast frequencies. Plan ahead, take sensible precautions and make your trek across the top a complete four-wheel drive adventure.

HOW TO BE CROCODILE-WISE

Of the two crocodile species found in Australia's north, the saltwater or estuarine crocodile is dangerous. It lives in salt water and fresh water, usually in tidal sections of rivers and creeks, floodplain waterholes and freshwater swamps and is found as far inland as 100 kilometres. The freshwater crocodile, while not dangerous, can deliver a savage bite if disturbed. Treat all crocodiles longer than 1.5 metres as dangerous and obey the following rules.

▶ *Seek local advice before swimming, camping, fishing or boating.*

▶ *Swim, canoe and use small boats only in shallow rapids.*
▶ *Watch children and pets in the water or at the water's edge where large crocodiles might live.*
▶ *Fill a bucket with water and prepare food or clean fish at least 5 metres from the water's edge.*
▶ *Do not lean from boats or hang articles over the edge.*
▶ *When fishing stand at least a few metres back from the water's edge and do not stand on overhanging logs.*
▶ *Burn or remove from your campsite food scraps, fish offal and other wastes.*

279

TIPS FOR OUTBACK DRIVING

▶ *Plan ahead: ensure your vehicle is fully serviced and equipped and have it regularly serviced on long trips; obtain relevant maps; book your campsites or accommodation in advance, where applicable.*

▶ *Carry basic spare parts and water, food and fuel.*

▶ *Check road conditions and weather reports before each departure.*

▶ *Stay on the plotted route. Do not deviate for off-road exploration.*

▶ *Always remain with your vehicle if it breaks down. If lost or stranded, stay with your vehicle and conserve water.*

▶ *Station properties are often unfenced in the outback: watch for cattle and wildlife on roads and avoid night driving.*

▶ *Be alert for bulldust, soft sand and mud. Negotiate in a reasonably high gear and speed after studying the hazard. Reduce tyre pressure for deep sand.*

▶ *Cattle grids are a potential hazard. Approach with caution.*

▶ *Do not enter dips at a high speed. Brake on entry and accelerate again as you exit to give maximum clearance and to prevent springs from bottoming out.*

▶ *Check tracks across creeks for clear passage and water depth. If passage is possible, drive through in low range, second gear or high range, first gear and clear the opposite embankment before stopping.*

▶ *Do not camp in dry creeks in case of flash flooding.*

▶ *Give road trains a wide berth. Slow down and if there is an escort vehicle watch for signals. If you move off the road, reduce speed and watch for guide posts and soft edges.*

USEFUL INFORMATION

For information on road conditions contact:

Gulf Local Authorities Development Association (GLADA)
55 McLeod Street
PO Box 2312, Cairns QLD 4870
(070) 51 4658/31 1631.

Etheridge Shire Council
St George Street, Georgetown
QLD 4871, (070) 62 1233.

Carpentaria Shire Council
Landsborough Street
Normanton QLD 4890
(077) 45 1268/45 1166.

Burke Shire Council
Musgrave Street, Burketown
QLD 4830, (077) 45 5100.

Automobile Association of Northern Territory Inc. (AANT)
MLC Building, 79–81 Smith St
Darwin 0800, (089) 81 3837.

For touring information contact:

GLADA
55 McLeod Street, Cairns
QLD 4870, (070) 51 4658.

Katherine Region Tourist Association
Stuart Highway cnr Lindsay Street
PO Box 555,
Katherine NT 0851
(089) 72 2650.

For national parks information contact:

QNPWS
10–12 McLeod Street,
Cairns QLD 4870
(070) 98 2188.

Northern Territory Conservation Commission (NTCC)
Giles Street, PO Box 344
Katherine NT 0850
(089) 72 8770.

For information on Aboriginal land contact:

Doomadgee Aboriginal Council
South Street, Doomadgee
QLD 4830, (077) 45 8188.

Community Ranger
Kowanyama Aboriginal Land
PO Box Kowanyama
QLD 4871, (070) 60 5187.

Northern Land Council
9 Rowling Street, PO Box 42921
Casuarina, NT 0810, (089) 81 7011.

For emergency medical assistance contact:

Royal Flying Doctor Service
1 Junction Street, Cairns QLD 4870
(070) 53 1952 (base)
(070) 53 5419 (emergency).

Aerial Medical Services
(089) 22 8888 (Darwin Hospital)
(089) 72 9211 (Katherine Hospital).

CAIRNS
«»
THE EINASLEIGH RIVER

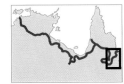

START POINT
Map page 17, L6.

TOTAL KM 393.
UNSEALED KM 35.
DEGREE OF DIFFICULTY Easy.
DRIVING TIME 5 hours (Smithfield to the Einasleigh River).
LONGEST DISTANCE NO FUEL 166 km (Mount Garnet to The Lynd).
TOPOGRAPHIC MAPS Auslig 1:250 000 series: *Atherton*; *Einasleigh*. See also 1:100 000 series.
LOCAL/SPECIALITY MAPS Sunmap: *Gulf Savannah*; Auslig: *Northern Australia*.
OTHER USEFUL INFORMATION Queensland Tourist and Travel Corporation (QTTC) booklet: *Gulf Savannah*; Gulf Local Authorities Development Association Inc. (GLADA) booklet: *Gulf Savannah Factfinder*.

DESCRIPTION Virtually all of this fascinating trip is via the Kennedy Highway. It traverses the lush Atherton Tableland via Kuranda, Mareeba and Atherton, and brings you down across the eastern edge of the Gulf Savannah. Here the highway passes through Ravenshoe, Innot Hot Springs and Mount Garnet before slicing through 40 Mile Scrub National Park – a mix of rare vine thicket and grassy woodland – home to possums, wallabies and a variety of birds. This park lies on the edge of the McBride Volcanic Province, an area with over 150 extinct volcanic craters. Conclude your day's journey on the banks of the *Einasleigh River* where you can take your pick of bush campsites (no facilities). *Archer Creek* (near Mount Garnet) is also ideal for bush camping (toilets only). There are plenty of caravan

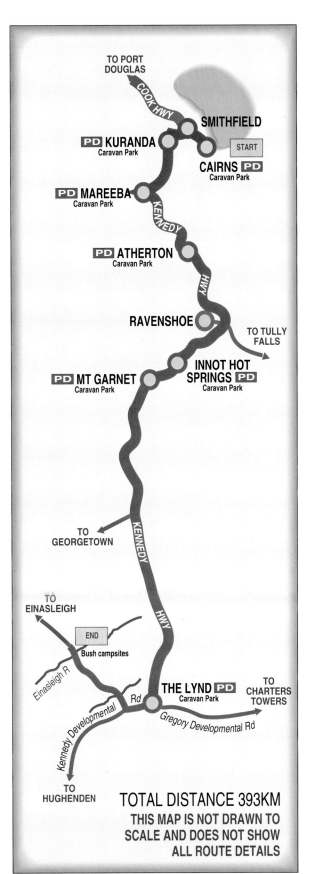

TOTAL DISTANCE 393KM
THIS MAP IS NOT DRAWN TO SCALE AND DOES NOT SHOW ALL ROUTE DETAILS

281

CAIRNS «» THE EINASLEIGH RIVER

Blue Ulysses butterfly at Australian Butterfly Sanctuary, Kuranda

parks between Cairns and Mount Garnet and you will find *The Oasis Caravan Park* at The Lynd.

WARNINGS ▶ Many bush campsites are on private property. Do not leave formed tracks or trespass for off-road exploration. ▶ Crocodiles inhabit coastlines and inland waterways in the Gulf Savannah. Be crocodile-wise. Do not swim.

BOOKINGS AND PERMITS ▶ Information about the Gulf Savannah is obtainable from GLADA, 55 McLeod Street, Cairns QLD; PO Box 2312, Cairns QLD 4870; tel. (070) 51 4658/31 1631.

ROUTE DIRECTIONS

Depart Cairns CBD north via Cook Hwy, approx. 15 km to Smithfield.

0.0 km Zero trip meter at s'post: Mareeba/Kuranda on Cook Hwy in Smithfield. **TL** onto Kennedy Hwy.
(12.7 km) ▲ 377.8 km
12.7 km Barron River. Cross bridge.

(1.4 km) ▲ 365.1 km
14.1 km Intersection. S'post: Mareeba. **SO**.

Kuranda off to left. **PD** *Supplies, caravan park. Rainforest village on Macalister Range. Nocturnal zoo, large butterfly sanctuary. Street markets. Access to Barron Falls.*

(35.0 km) ▲ 363.7 km
49.1 km S'post: Atherton 32. **SO**.
(1.0 km) ▲ 328.7 km
50.1 km Intersection. S'post: Atherton. **TL** on Kennedy Hwy.

Mareeba township off to right. **PD** *Supplies, caravan park. Mareeba Rodeo is held each July.*

(25.8 km) ▲ 327.7 km
75.9 km Tolga town centre.

Peanut-growing area. Visit Tolga Woodworks showroom and factory.

(4.1 km) ▲ 301.9 km

80.0 km Atherton 60 km/h sign. **SO** along Kennedy Hwy.
(0.5 km) ▲ 297.8 km
80.5 km S'post: Ravenshoe/Herberton. **SO** through roundabout and Atherton CBD.

> **PD** *Supplies, caravan park. Farming hamlet and hub of the Atherton Tableland. Annual Maize Festival each September.*

(0.8 km) ▲ 297.3 km
81.3 km S'post: Ravenshoe. **TL.**
(0.6 km) ▲ 296.5 km
81.9 km S'post: Ravenshoe. **SO.**
(2.9 km) Opp. dir. s'post: Atherton. ▲ 295.9 km
84.8 km S'post: Ravenshoe. **SO.**

> *Malanda off to left.*

(24.7 km) Opp. dir. s'post: Atherton. ▲ 293.0 km
109.5 km S'post: Ravenshoe. **SO.**

> *Herberton off to right. Historic tin mining town.*

(23.0 km) ▲ 268.3 km
132.5 km Intersection. S'post: Mt Garnet. **SO.**

> *Ravenshoe off to right. Annual Torimba Forest Festival each October.*

(0.6 km) ▲ 245.3 km
133.1 km S'post: Mt Garnet. **SO.**

> *Tully Falls off to left. Ravenshoe off to right.*

(15.8 km) ▲ 244.7 km
148.9 km Archer Creek. Cross bridge.
(7.6 km) ▲ 228.9 km
156.5 km Wild River. Cross bridge.
(5.5 km) ▲ 221.3 km
162.0 km Innot Hot Springs town centre.

> **PD** *Caravan park. Hot mineral springs.*

(11.3 km) ▲ 215.8 km
173.3 km Big Dinner Creek. Cross bridge.
(4.0 km) ▲ 204.5 km
177.3 km Mount Garnet town centre.

> **PD** *Supplies, caravan park.*

(1.9 km) ▲ 200.5 km
179.2 km S'post: The Lynd 163. **SO.**
(2.7 km) ▲ 198.6 km
181.9 km S'post: The Lynd 159. **SO.**
(64.3 km) Opp. dir. s'post: Mt Garnet 4. ▲ 195.9 km
246.2 km S'post: The Lynd. **SO.**

> *Georgetown off to right.*

Barron Falls

(66.3 km) Opp. dir. s'post: Mt Garnet. ▲ 131.6 km
312.5 km Eight Mile Creek. Cross bridge.
(28.8 km) ▲ 65.3 km
341.3 km S'post: The Lynd. **KR** onto Kennedy Developmental Rd.

> *Charters Towers off to left along Gregory Developmental Rd.*

(1.8 km) ▲ 36.5 km
343.1 km The Lynd. **SO.**

> **PD** *Supplies. The Oasis Roadhouse and Caravan Park on left. Ask about road conditions.*

(0.9 km) ▲ 34.7 km
344.0 km S'post: Einasleigh 73. **TR.**
(4.0 km) Opp. dir. s'post: The Lynd 2. ▲ 33.8 km
348.0 km ND Creek. Cross causeway.
(29.8 km) ▲ 29.8 km
377.8 km Einasleigh River. Cross concrete bridge.

> *Ideal bush campsites along river bank. No facilities.*

REVERSE DIRECTIONS START ▲ 0.0 km

THE EINASLEIGH RIVER «» UNDARA LAVA LODGE

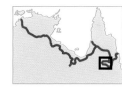

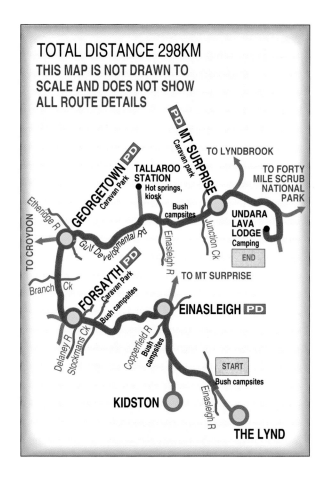

TOTAL DISTANCE 298KM
THIS MAP IS NOT DRAWN TO SCALE AND DOES NOT SHOW ALL ROUTE DETAILS

TO LYNDBROOK

TO CROYDON

Etheridge R

GEORGETOWN PD
Caravan Park

Gulf Developmental Rd

MT SURPRISE PD
Caravan park

TALLAROO STATION
Hot springs, kiosk

Bush campsites

Einsleigh R

Junction Ck

TO FORTY MILE SCRUB NATIONAL PARK

UNDARA LAVA LODGE
Camping
END

FORSAYTH PD
Caravan Park

Bush campsites

Branch Ck

TO MT SURPRISE

EINASLEIGH PD

Delaney R

Stockmans Ck

Copperfield R
Bush campsites

START
Bush campsites

KIDSTON

Einasleigh R

THE LYND

START POINT
Map page 16, I11.

TOTAL KM 298.
UNSEALED KM 166.
DEGREE OF DIFFICULTY Easy.
DRIVING TIME 5 hours. Allow plenty of time for fossicking and sightseeing.
LONGEST DISTANCE NO FUEL 234 km (Mount Surprise to Chillagoe, next section).
TOPOGRAPHIC MAPS Auslig 1:250 000 series: *Einasleigh*; *Georgetown*.
LOCAL/SPECIALITY MAPS Sunmap: *Gulf Savannah*; Auslig: *Northern Australia*.
OTHER USEFUL INFORMATION QTTC booklet: *Gulf Savannah*, GLADA booklet. *Gulf Savannah Footfinder* leaflets on Undara and Tallaroo Stations, available from Etheridge Shire Council, tel. (070) 62 1233 or GLADA.

DESCRIPTION This easy drive on good quality roads is a must for those with an interest in geology and history, and a yen to explore. There are at least 5 bush campsites where you may choose to break your trip. Continuing on what is known as the 'Undara Loop' (which starts at 40 Mile Scrub National Park) along the Gregory Developmental Road, you pass through Einasleigh, an old copper mining town perched on the eastern edge of the Newcastle Range among unusual flat top hills. From Einasleigh's old bush pub it is an easy walk to Einasleigh Gorge, a sheer drop to the Copperfield River. Between Einasleigh and Forsayth,

the road climbs over the Newcastle Range with views of the surrounding granite country. Gold nuggets are still found at Forsayth, one of the few remaining gold mining towns which sprang up during the late 1800s boom. You can explore the abandoned mines behind the town (but with extreme caution). Keen fossickers can deviate 103 kilometres south from Forsayth to ruggedly beautiful Agate Creek where there is a range of coloured agates at the mineral reserve.

From Forsayth the loop joins with the Gulf Developmental Road at Georgetown, set amongst rolling hills and wooded savannah grasslands. Fifty-two kilometres over the Newcastle Range from Georgetown is Tallaroo Station, a working cattle property with bubbling hot mineral springs. You can take a rejuvenating dip beneath the melaleucas in a natural spa fed by the springs, stroll along the Einasleigh River (where the Jardines camped on their way to Cape York in 1864), or go on a guided tour of this historic property. From here it is just a quick trip through Mount Surprise (another gem fossicking spot) to Undara Lava Lodge, situated close to the remarkable Undara lava tubes. This lava field in the Great Dividing Range high country consists of tubes which snake their way underground beneath grazing

Hot springs on Tallaroo Station

land. As big as train tunnels and winding for over 100 kilometres, these tubes were formed by lava flows from the Undara crater almost 200 000 years ago. A Savannah Guide conducts full and half day tours from the lodge. Abseil or rock climb, enjoy an aerial flight over the lava field, or go on a guided tour of nearby cattle properties. The *Lava Lodge* offers unusual and comfortable private accommodation in restored railway carriages. There are also caravan and campsites.

WARNING ▶ Crocodiles inhabit coastlines and inland waterways in the Gulf Savannah. Be crocodile wise. Do not swim.

BOOKINGS AND PERMITS ▶ To book ahead for a guided tour at Tallaroo Station, write to Tallaroo Station, PO Mount Surprise QLD 4871; tel. (070) 62 1221. ▶ Book in advance to tour the Undara lava tubes and to stay either at Lava Lodge or the camping area: Lava Lodge, Undara, Mount Surprise QLD 4871; tel. (070) 97 1411. ▶ No permits are required for bush campsites along the Undara Loop.

ROUTE DIRECTIONS

0.0 km Zero trip meter at Einasleigh River west bank. **SO** towards Einasleigh.
(4.6 km) ▲ 204.2 km

4.6 km Boree Creek. Cross causeway.
(13.4 km) ▲ 199.6 km

18.0 km Intersection. **KR**.
(3.0 km) ▲ 186.2 km

21.0 km S'post: Einasleigh 21. **SO**.

Kidston off to left.

(21.6 km) Opp. dir. s'post: The Lynd 56. ▲ 183.2 km

42.6 km Copperfield River. Cross causeway.

Bush campsites along river bank.

(0.2 km) ▲ 161.6 km

42.8 km Einasleigh town centre. S'post: Forsayth. **SO**.

PD *Supplies at Einasleigh. Old copper mining town on the south-eastern edge of the Undara lava field.*

(0.2 km) ▲ 161.4 km

285

Undara lava tube

43.0 km S'post: Forsayth 70. **TL.**
(0.4 km) Opp. dir. s'post: Kidston. ▲ 161.2 km
43.4 km S'post: Forsayth 70. **TR.**
(5.4 km) Opp. dir. s'post: Kidston. ▲ 160.8 km
48.8 km Intersection. **KR.**
(10.2 km) ▲ 155.4 km
59.0 km Cross Stockmans Creek.

> Bush campsites along creek bank.

(41.0 km) ▲ 145.2 km
100.0 km Intersection. **KL.**
(10.9 km) ▲ 104.2 km
110.9 km Delaney River. Cross bridge.
(0.5 km) ▲ 93.3 km
111.4 km Forsayth town centre. S'post: Georgetown 40. **TR.**

> **PD** Supplies, caravan park at Forsayth. Collection of agates and thundereggs on display at the Goldfields Tavern.

(0.8 km) Opp. dir. s'post: Einasleigh ▲ 92.8 km
112.2 km Intersection. **SO.**

> Agate Creek off to left.

(7.1 km) ▲ 92.0 km
119.3 km Branch Creek. Cross causeway.

> Bush campsites along creek bank.

(31.8 km) ▲ 84.9 km
151.1 km Bitumen. 60 km/h sign.
(1.0 km) Gravel. ▲ 53.1 km
152.1 km Georgetown Post Office. **SO.**

> **PD** Supplies, caravan park. Gold fossicking at the Etheridge Goldfield.

(0.2 km) ▲ 52.1 km

152.3 km S'post: Mt Garnet 216. **TR** onto Gulf Developmental Rd and immediately cross Etheridge River.

> Croydon 149 km off to left.

(51.9 km) Opp. dir. s'post: Forsayth 40. ▲ 51.9 km
204.2 km Intersection. Tallaroo Hot Springs 9 km ott to left.

> Kiosk. No camping. Open daily (except Saturday) April–September. Spring tours and spa pool.

0.0 km Zero trip meter at above intersection. **SO** along Gulf Developmental Rd.
(4.5 km) ▲ 0.0 km
  ▲ 94.1 km
4.5 km Einasleigh River. Cross bridge.

> Bush campsites on river bank.

(27.2 km) ▲ 89.6 km
31.7 km Junction Creek. Cross bridge.

> Bush campsites on creek bank.

(8.7 km) ▲ 62.4 km
40.4 km Mount Surprise town centre. **SO.**

> **PD** Supplies, caravan park. Next fuel Chillagoe (234 km).

(38.8 km) ▲ 53.7 km
79.2 km S'post: Undara Lava Lodge. **TR** through gate onto gravel.
(5.8 km) Bitumen. ▲ 14.9 km
85.0 km S'post: Undara Lava Lodge 9. **TR.**
(4.8 km) ▲ 9.1 km
89.8 km Gate.

> Leave as found.

(4.3 km) ▲ 4.3 km
94.1 km Entrance to Undara Lava Lodge complex. **TR.**

> Lodge accommodation, caravan and campsites. Kiosk, restaurant and bar. Barbecues, toilets, hot showers, laundry. Book ahead. Daily guided tours to lava tubes.

REVERSE DIRECTIONS START ▲ 0.0 km

UNDARA LAVA LODGE
«»
CHILLAGOE

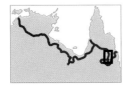

START POINT
Map page 17, J9.

TOTAL KM 180.
UNSEALED KM 156.
DEGREE OF DIFFICULTY Easy.
DRIVING TIME 5 hours.
LONGEST DISTANCE NO FUEL Fuel at Chillagoe.
TOPOGRAPHIC MAPS Auslig 1:250 000 series:
Einasleigh; Atherton. See also 1:100 000 series.
LOCAL/SPECIALITY MAPS Sunmap: *Gulf Savannah*;
Auslig: *Northern Australia.*
OTHER USEFUL INFORMATION QNPWS park guide:
Chillagoe-Mungana Caves National Parks.

DESCRIPTION From Undara Lava Lodge it is an easy five-hour trek through grazing country to Chillagoe, situated on a limestone and marble belt believed to be 400 million years old. Marble is mined here and Dome Rock – a mass of white marble – can be spotted 2 kilometres east of Chillagoe's town centre. Chillagoe was once a copper mining town and the museum and disused smelter ruins (the old heart of the town), are worth visiting.

Australia's oldest limestone caves are located only ten minutes from town in a series of small national parks known as the Chillagoe-Mungana Caves National Parks. Rugged limestone outcrops (some up to 70 metres high) house a wonderland of colourful caves decorated with lime crystals. You can explore several of the major caves by torchlight on regular guided tours and there are caves where you can take self-guided walks. At Pompeii Cave rock wallabies and possums can sometimes be seen. In Royal Arch Cave (the main

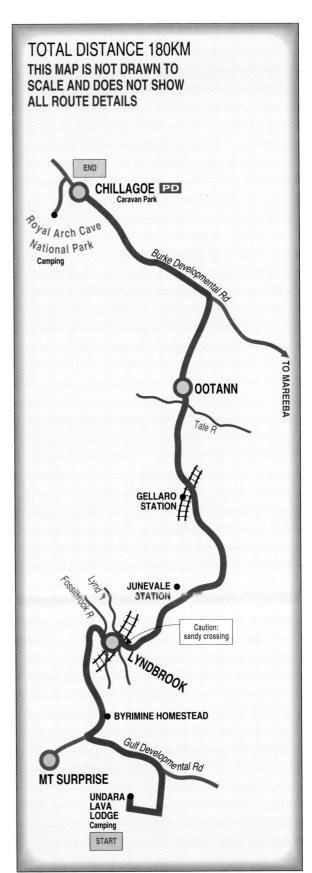

TOTAL DISTANCE 180KM
THIS MAP IS NOT DRAWN TO
SCALE AND DOES NOT SHOW
ALL ROUTE DETAILS

END

CHILLAGOE PD
Caravan Park

Royal Arch Cave
National Park
Camping

Burke Developmental Rd

TO MAREEBA

OOTANN

Tate R

GELLARO
STATION

Lynd R

Fossilbrook R

JUNEVALE
STATION

Caution:
sandy crossing

LYNDBROOK

BYRIMINE HOMESTEAD

Gulf Developmental Rd

MT SURPRISE

UNDARA
LAVA
LODGE
Camping

START

Fairy Grotto, Donna Cave

guided tour) hand-held lamps add to the fun. A small camping area is situated near *Royal Arch Cave* and *Chillagoe* has a caravan park.

WARNINGS ▶ Creek crossings subject to flooding. Enquire at Undara Lava Lodge (070) 97 1411; or Mount Surprise Police Station (070) 62 3120 ▶ Do not enter caves before contacting the QNPWS ranger. Obtain information on guided tours and self-guided cave walks from the QNPWS Chillagoe office.

BOOKINGS AND PERMITS ▶ For information, advance bookings, tour tickets and a camping permit, contact the QNPWS, Cathedral Street, Chillagoe; PO Box 38, Chillagoe QLD 4871; tel. (070) 94 7163.

ROUTE DIRECTIONS

Exit Undara Lava Lodge and **TL** onto gravel. **SO** to Gulf Developmental Rd.

0.0 km   Zero trip meter at intersection of Undara Lava Lodge road and Gulf Developmental Road. **TL.**
  (24.6 km)   ▲ 180.2 km

24.6 km S'post: Springfield. **TR** onto gravel.
  (1.8 km)   Bitumen. ▲ 155.6 km

26.4 km S'post: Springfield. **KL.**
  (15.9 km)   ▲ 153.8 km

42.3 km Y intersection. **KL.**

> *Homestead on right.*

  (9.9 km)   ▲ 137.9 km

52.2 km Y intersection. **SO.**
  (3.7 km)   ▲ 128.0 km

55.9 km Intersection. **SO.**
  (6.0 km)   ▲ 124.3 km

61.9 km S'post: Burlington. **TR** and immediately cross Fossilbrook causeway.
  (0.9 km)   Opp. dir. s'post: Mt Surprise. ▲ 118.3 km

62.8 km Gate.

> *Leave as found. Burlington Homestead off to right.*

(2.2 km) ▲ 117.4 km

65.0 km Cross causeway.

(3.3 km) ▲ 115.2 km

68.3 km Railway crossing.

> *Lyndbrook Railway Station on right.*

(0.5 km) ▲ 111.9 km

68.8 km Cross Lynd River.

> *Sandy crossing.*

(13.9 km) ▲ 111.4 km

82.7 km Intersection. **SO**.

> *Junevale Station off to left.*

(9.0 km) ▲ 97.5 km

91.7 km Cross causeway.

(9.3 km) ▲ 88.5 km

101.0 km Y intersection. **KL**.

(1.0 km) ▲ 79.2 km

102.0 km Rocky Tate River. Cross causeway.

(18.1 km) ▲ 78.2 km

120.1 km Cross railway line.

> *Gellaro Station off to left.*

(12.7 km) ▲ 60.1 km

132.8 km Tate River. Cross causeway.

(9.2 km) ▲ 47.4 km

142.0 km S'post: Almaden. **SO**.

(8.1 km) Opp. dir. s'post: Mt Surprise. ▲ 38.2 km

150.1 km S'post: Chillagoe. **TL** onto Burke Developmental Road.

(30.1 km) Opp. dir. s'post: Mt Surprise. ▲ 30.1 km

180.2 km Chillagoe town centre.

> **PD** *Supplies, caravan park. Royal Arch Cave National Park 7 km south-west of Chillagoe. Small camping area: picnic tables, barbecues, water, no showers. Obtain information, camping permit and tickets for guided cave tours from QNPWS Chillagoe office in Cathedral St.*

REVERSE DIRECTIONS START ▲ 0.0 km

Limestone formations, Chillagoe Caves National Park

▼ ▼ ▼ ▼ ▼ ▼ ▼

TAKE CARE

● Be crocodile-wise. Dangerous estuarine crocodiles may inhabit rivers, beaches and inland waterways of Australia's north.

● In outback Australia long distances separate some towns. Take care to ensure your vehicle is roadworthy before setting out and carry adequate supplies of petrol, water and food.

● Permits are required if you want to divert off public roads within Aboriginal Land areas.

● In Australia's north, during the wet season (October–May) roads become impassable. Check conditions before setting out.

● Carry additional water in desert areas: 5 litres per person per day is recommended, plus extra for the radiator.

● Don't take short cuts over virgin ground. You will destroy the vegetation. Stick to tracks open for use.

● Four-wheel drive tracks are subject to closure; if in doubt, check with local authorities such as national parks or forestry departments.

CHILLAGOE
«»
DORUNDA STATION

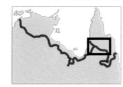

The lagoon on Dorunda Station

START POINT
Map page 16, I7.

TOTAL KM 417.
UNSEALED KM 417.
DEGREE OF DIFFICULTY Moderately difficult. *See Warnings.*
DRIVING TIME 7 hours.
LONGEST DISTANCE NO FUEL 417 km (Fuel at Dorunda Station).
TOPOGRAPHIC MAPS Auslig 1:250 000 series: *Atherton*; *Walsh*; *Galbraith*. See also 1:100 000 series.
LOCAL/SPECIALITY MAPS Sunmap: *Gulf Savannah*; Auslig: *Northern Australia*.
OTHER USEFUL INFORMATION GLADA booklet: *Gulf Savannah Factfinder*; QTTC booklet: *Gulf Savannah*.

DESCRIPTION This trek section is a long haul across the base of Cape York Peninsula on the Burke Developmental Road. Although unsealed this road is generally good, except for a section near the Lynd River (*see Warnings*). There are bush campsites beside the *Walsh* and *Lynd* rivers and your other options for camping are *Kowanyama* or *Dorunda Station*.

Kowanyama (a two-hour drive from the turnoff on the Burke Developmental Road) is an Aboriginal community situated 18 kilometres from the Gulf of Carpentaria coast on the Mitchell River delta. The community still hunt and fish within the trust area – over 300 kilometres of marine savannah grassland plains, freshwater wetlands and dune woodlands. It is a popular fishing destination and there are 3 bush campsites (no facilities) at fresh and saltwater locations (for example *Topsy Creek* on the coast). Kowanyama has an eight-roomed guest house. Fuel is available through the Kowanyama Council Depot and there is a general store and supermarket.

Avid anglers will find it hard to bypass Dorunda Station, one of the world's largest wilderness areas. Dorunda's lake and lagoons, and the Staaten and Wyaaba rivers which mark the station's boundaries, teem with barramundi, bream and the sought-after saratoga. This private cattle property is home to a rare albino crocodile, a flying fox colony, dingoes, wild pigs and other wildlife. Observe cattle mustering and branding, go on a guided safari, or explore the property on horseback. *Dorunda Lodge* has a swimming pool and a licensed restaurant. You may prefer to camp at the designated site near the lodge, with access to lodge facilties. There are bush campsites near the lake's edge (no facilities). Hire boats and fishing rods are available, as are petrol and diesel.

WARNINGS ▶ There are no fuel stops between Chillagoe and Dorunda Station. ▶ Several river and creek crossings are impassable after heavy rain. Check before proceeding by phoning GLADA in Cairns; tel. (070) 51 4658. ▶ Take care on the Burke Developmental Road 83 km past the Lynd River. There is a long section of deep bulldust and potholes. ▶ Crocodiles inhabit coastline and inland waterways in the Gulf Savannah. Be crocodile-wise. Do not swim.

BOOKINGS AND PERMITS ▶ Book at least three weeks in advance to stay at Kowanyama (day visits are not recommended). Contact the Community Ranger, Kowanyama Aboriginal Land and Natural Resource Management, c/- PO Kowanyama QLD 4871; tel. (070) 60 5187. Camping fee/accommodation charge apply. Follow all Kowanyama management regulations. ▶ Advance bookings are necessary at Dorunda. Write to Dorunda

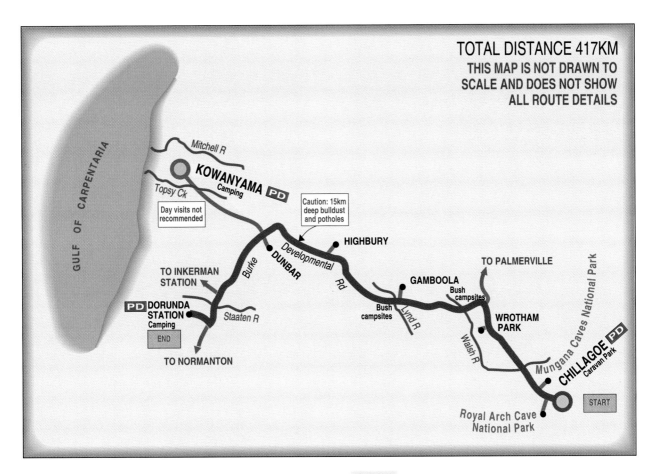

TOTAL DISTANCE 417KM
THIS MAP IS NOT DRAWN TO
SCALE AND DOES NOT SHOW
ALL ROUTE DETAILS

Station, PMB 16, Via Normanton QLD 4890; tel. Cairns (070) 53 4500 (quote Dorunda). Camping fee/lodge accommodation charge apply. Rates on application.

ROUTE DIRECTIONS

0.0 km Zero trip meter opposite the Post Office Hotel, Queen Street, Chillagoe, facing west. **SO** to Burke Developmental Rd.

> **PD** *Next fuel Dorunda Station, 417 km.*

(0.1 km) ▲ 304.1 km

0.1 km S'post: Mungana National Park 15. **SO**.

(0.8 km) ▲ 304.0 km

0.9 km Intersection. S'post: Mungana National Park. **SO**.

> *Old State Smelters off to right.*

(0.5 km) ▲ 303.2 km

1.4 km Intersection. S'post: Mungana National Park/Wrotham Park 83. **KR**.

> *Royal Arch Cave off to left.*

(14.4 km) ▲ 302.7 km

15.8 km S'post: Normanton. **SO**.

(0.6 km) ▲ 288.3 km

16.4 km Intersection. **SO**.

> *Mungana Caves National Park off to right.*

(15.9 km) ▲ 287.7 km

32.0 km Walsh River. Cross causeway.

(49.2 km) ▲ 271.8 km

81.5 km Cross causeway.

(2.9 km) ▲ 222.6 km

84.4 km Gate then s'post: Gamboola. **SO**.

> *Leave gate as found. Wrotham Park off to left. Airstrip on left.*

(1.4 km) ▲ 219.7 km

85.8 km Gate.

> *Leave as found.*

(4.4 km) ▲ 218.3 km

90.2 km Gate.

> *Leave as found.*

(6.0 km) ▲ 213.9 km

291

Bulldust on the Burke Developmental Road

96.2 km Intersection. S'post: Mt Mulgrave/Palmerville. **SO**.
(14.7 km)   Opp. dir. s'post: Chillagoe 95. ▲207.9 km
110.9 km Gate.

> *Leave as found.*

(10.3 km)   ▲ 193.2 km
121.2 km Walsh River. Cross causeway.

> *Bush campsites on river bank.*

(11.8 km)   ▲ 182.9 km
133.0 km S'post: Dunbar. **KL**.

> *Gamboola off to right.*

(46.0 km)   Opp. dir. s'post: Chillagoe. ▲ 171.1 km
179.0 km Lynd River. Cross causeway.

> *Bush campsites on river bank.*

(21.1 km)   ▲ 125.1 km
200.1 km S'post: Kowanyama 187. **SO**.

> *Highbury off to right.*

> *Caution: deep bulldust and potholes 62 km ahead for a 15-km stretch.*

(104.0 km)   ▲ 104.0 km
304.1 km Intersection. S'post: Normanton.

> *Kowanyama Aboriginal community 103 km off to right.* **PD** *Supplies. Bush campsites and guest house. Book in advance. Day visits not recommended. Call at the Kowanyama Community Council Office on arrival for directions to bush campsites and further information. Fresh and saltwater fishing.*

0.0 km Zero trip meter at above intersection. **KL** along Burke Developmental Rd.
(3.5 km)   ▲ 0.0 km
    ▲ 112.8 km

3.5 km Intersection. **SO**.

> *Dunbar Station off to left.*

(2.6 km)   ▲ 109.3 km
6.1 km Gate.

> *Leave as found.*

(26.2 km)   ▲ 106.7 km
32.3 km Gate.

> *Leave as found.*

(21.0 km)   ▲ 80.5 km
53.3 km S'post: Normanton 212. **SO**.

> *Inkerman Station off to right.*

(18.8 km)   Opp. dir. s'post: Chillagoe 350. ▲59.5 km
72.1 km Staaten River. Cross bridge.
(15.6 km)   ▲ 40.7 km
87.7 km S'post: Dorunda. **TR** through gate.

> *Leave as found.*

(10.8 km)   ▲ 25.1 km
98.5 km Gate.

> *Leave as found.*

(11.2 km)   ▲ 14.3 km
109.7 km Gate.

> *Leave as found.*

(2.5 km)   ▲ 3.1 km
112.2 km Gate.

> *Leave as found.*

(0.6 km)   ▲ 0.6 km
112.8 km Dorunda Homestead on right.

> **PD** *Working cattle station: safaris, fishing, boat hire. Camping and lodge accommodation. Campers have access to lodge facilities: swimming pool, restaurant, bar, toilet, showers, laundry. Bush campsites near lake (no facilities). Book ahead.*

REVERSE DIRECTIONS START ▲ 0.0 km

DORUNDA STATION «» KARUMBA

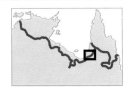

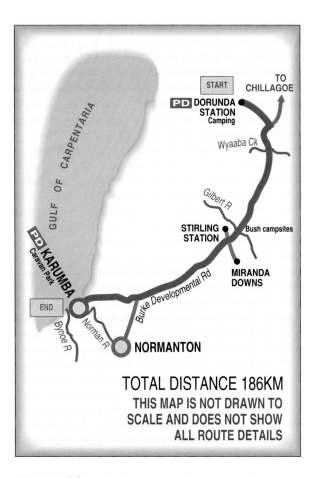

TOTAL DISTANCE 186KM
THIS MAP IS NOT DRAWN TO SCALE AND DOES NOT SHOW ALL ROUTE DETAILS

START POINT
Map page 16, D6.

TOTAL KM 186.
UNSEALED 145.
DEGREE OF DIFFICULTY Easy.
DRIVING TIME 4 hours.
LONGEST DISTANCE NO FUEL 186 km (Dorunda Station to Karumba).
TOPOGRAPHIC MAP Auslig 1:250 000 series: *Normanton*. See also 1:100 000 series.
LOCAL/SPECIALITY MAPS Sunmap: *Gulf Savannah*; Auslig: *Northern Australia*.
OTHER USEFUL INFORMATION GLADA booklet: *Gulf Savannah Factfinder*, QTTC booklet: *Gulf Savannah*.

DESCRIPTION An easy four-hour drive brings you to the fascinating frontier port town of Karumba, at the mouth of the Norman River. As the centre of the Gulf of Carpentaria's prawning and fishing industry, and the only access point to the vast, remote gulf waters, Karumba is a popular destination for professional and amateur anglers. Charter vessels and hire dinghies are available for those tempted by the exquisite variety of fish abundant in the Arafura Sea. The town is surrounded by exotic wetlands extending 30 kilometres inland, home to saltwater crocodiles and flocks of brolgas, cranes and black swans. These tidal estuaries are also a resting area for migratory birds from south-east Asia. Overnight visitors can choose between the *Gulf Country Caravan Park* or the *Karumba Lodge Hotel* which has sea views and a seafood restaurant.

WARNINGS ▶ Check road conditions with GLADA or nearest shire council office. ▶ Crocodiles inhabit coastline and inland waterways in the Gulf Savannah. Be crocodile-wise. Do not swim.

BOOKINGS AND PERMITS ▶ Book in advance with the Gulf Country Caravan Park, Yappar Street, Karumba, PO Box 184 Karumba QLD 4891; tel. (077) 45 9148. ▶ Advance bookings required for the Karumba Lodge Hotel, Yappar Street, Karumba; PO Box 19, Karumba QLD 4891; tel. (077) 45 9379.

TAKE CARE

● Don't take short cuts over virgin ground. You will destroy the vegetation. Stick to tracks open for use.

293

ROUTE DIRECTIONS

0.0 km Zero trip meter at intersection of Burke Developmental Rd and Dorunda Station turnoff facing south. **SO.**

(6.8 km) ▲ 185.9 km

6.8 km Gate.

> *Leave as found.*

(1.2 km) ▲ 179.1 km

8.0 km Wyaaba Creek. Cross causeway.

(31.5 km) ▲ 177.9 km

39.5 km S'post: Normanton 136. **SO.**

(5.8 km) Opp. dir. s'post: Chillagoe 434. ▲146.4 km

45.3 km Gate.

> *Leave as found.*

(26.1 km) ▲ 140.6 km

71.4 km Gilbert River. Cross causeway.

> *Bush campsites along river bank.*

(2.7 km) ▲ 114.5 km

74.1 km Gate.

> *Leave as found.*

(4.0 km) ▲ 111.8 km

78.1 km S'post: Normanton 97. **SO.**

> *Miranda Downs off to left. Stirling Station off to right.*

(3.8 km) Opp. dir. s'post: Chillagoe. ▲ 107.8 km

81.9 km Gate.

> *Leave as found.*

(25.6 km) ▲ 104.0 km

107.5 km Gate.

> *Leave as found.*

(37.3 km) ▲ 78.4 km

144.8 km Bitumen. S'post: Karumba. **TR** after 100 m.

> *Normanton straight ahead along Burke Developmental Rd.*

(39.3 km) Gravel. ▲ 41.1 km

184.1 km Karumba 60 km/h sign.

(1.8 km) ▲ 1.8 km

185.9 km Karumba town centre.

> **PD** *Supplies. Caravan park, hotel/motel. Prawn and barramundi fishing. Charter boats for fishing and exploration of the Gulf.*

REVERSE DIRECTIONS START ▲ 0.0 km

Prawn trawlers on the Norman River, Karumba

Cockatoos in the main street, Karumba

Camping at Karumba

KARUMBA
«»
BURKETOWN

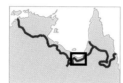

START POINT
Map page 19, H8.

TOTAL KM 297.
UNSEALED KM 208.
DEGREE OF DIFFICULTY Easy.
DRIVING TIME 6 hours.
LONGEST DISTANCE NO FUEL 229 km (Normanton to Burketown).
TOPOGRAPHIC MAPS Auslig 1:250 000 series: *Normanton; Burketown.* See also 1:100 000 series.
LOCAL/SPECIALITY MAPS Sunmap: *Gulf Savannah;* Auslig: *Northern Australia.*
OTHER USEFUL INFORMATION GLADA booklet: *Gulf Savannah Factfinder.*

DESCRIPTION The road from Karumba through Normanton to Burketown was once known as 'The Great Top Road' which transported prospectors and other travellers by Cobb & Co. coach to the Cape York gold fields. The countryside is typical of the Gulf Savannah: flat, featureless and often transformed into an inland sea during a big wet season. The Western Savannah was originally called the 'Plains of Promise'. Its wetlands play host to crocodiles, pelicans, fish (even prawns), while the grasslands abound with kangaroos, emus and all sorts of wildlife.

Burketown sits on the Albert River, dividing the wetlands from the grass plains to the south. This isolated town 25 kilometres from the coast was the first Gulf settlement. It was a wild place where law and order was maintained by the Native Mounted Police. During 1866 an epidemic of typhoid ('Gulf Fever') forced settlers to evacuate to Sweers Island. Burketown's cemetery gives you an insight into the town's troubled history. You can stay overnight at the *Burketown Caravan Park* or camp

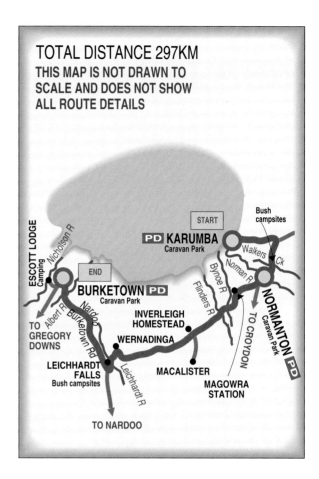

next to *Leichhardt Falls* at a bush campsite (no facilities).

Alternatively, head 17 kilometres west of Burketown to *Escott Lodge* on Escott cattle station. Choose between lodge or bush cabin accommodation, or camp in the station's camping grounds. There are also a number of bush campsites (no facilities) along a creek bank. The station, on the Nicholson River, is well known for barramundi fishing. Hire boats are available. Tours and joy flights, bushwalking and horseriding, all enable you to witness station life.

WARNINGS ▶ Check road conditions with GLADA or nearest shire council office. ▶ Crocodiles inhabit coastline and inland waterways in the Gulf Savannah. Be crocodile-wise. Do not swim.

BOOKINGS AND PERMITS ▶ Book in advance to stay at Escott Station. Contact Escott Lodge, PO Burketown QLD 4830; tel. (077) 45 5108.

Welcome to Burketown

ROUTE DIRECTIONS

0.0 km   Zero trip meter at 80 km/h sign departing Karumba. **SO**.
(39.3 km)   ▲ 68.7 km

39.3 km   S'post: Normanton 30. **SO**.
(1.1 km)   Opp. dir. s'post: Karumba. ▲ 29.4 km

40.4 km   Walkers Creek. Cross bridge.

> *Bush campsites along creek bank.*

(27.2 km)   ▲ 28.3 km

67.6 km   Norman River. Cross bridge.
(1.1 km)   ▲ 1.1 km

68.7 km   Normantown town centre.

> **PD** *Supplies, caravan park, mechanical repairs. Historic central town of the Gulf Savannah on the Norman River.*

0.0 km   Zero trip meter at Normanton Post Office on Landsborough St heading south. **SO** onto Burke Developmental Rd.
(5.6 km)   ▲ 0.0 km
                                 ▲ 228.6 km

5.6 km   Intersection. S'post: Burketown. **TR** onto gravel.
(18.8 km)   Bitumen. Opp. dir. s'post: Normanton 5. ▲ 223.0 km

24.4 km   Y intersection. **SO**.

> *Magowra Station off to right.*

(13.0 km)   ▲ 204.2 km

37.4 km   S'post: Burke & Wills Campsite No. 119. **SO**.

> *Take access track on left 1.5 km to the most northerly campsite of the ill-fated Burke and Wills trans-continental expedition.*

(0.3 km)   ▲ 191.2 km

37.7 km   Bynoe River. Cross causeway.
(2.6 km)   ▲ 190.9 km

40.3 km   Re-cross Bynoe River.
(2.9 km)   ▲ 188.3 km

43.2 km   Flinders River. Cross causeway.
(0.4 km)   ▲ 185.4 km

43.6 km   Y intersection. **SO**.
(27.6 km)   ▲ 185.0 km

71.2 km   Intersection. **SO**.

> *Inverleigh Homestead off to right. Macalister off to left.*

(66.1 km)   ▲ 157.4 km
137.3 km Y intersection. **SO**.
(10.0 km)   ▲ 91.3 km
147.3 km Intersection. **SO**.

> *Wernadinga off to right.*

(6.5 km)   ▲ 81.3 km
153.8 km Cross Leichhardt River.

> *Wide rocky crossing.*

(0.5 km)   ▲ 74.8 km
154.3 km Gate.

> *Leave as found.*

(0.1 km)   ▲ 74.3 km
154.4 km Y intersection. **KR** onto Nardoo–Burketown Rd.
(2.1 km)   ▲ 74.2 km
156.5 km Leichhardt River. Cross causeway.

> *Bush campsites adjacent to Leichhardt Falls on river bank. Caution: crocodiles.*

(0.6 km)   ▲ 72.1 km
157.1 km Intersection. **SO**.

> *Frederick Walker Monument off to left: burial site of the Native Mounted Police Commandant who led a search party for Burke and Wills.*

(56.6 km)   ▲ 71.5 km
213.7 km Bitumen. **SO**.
(11.7 km)   Gravel. ▲ 14.9 km
225.4 km Albert River. Cross bridge.
(3.2 km)   ▲ 3.2 km
228.6 km Burketown town control.

> **PD** *Supplies, caravan park, mechanical repairs. Small town on the Albert River. Annual Burketown Races held second Saturday in July. Barramundi fishing championships held each Easter.*

Option: Overnight stop at Escott Lodge.
Head 5 km south from Burketown along Wills Developmental Rd. Take Escott Station turnoff on right, 12 km to Escott Lodge cattle station /resort.

> *Lodge accommodation with licensed restaurant, swimming pool. Camping ground has toilets, hot showers, laundry. Access to bush campsites on Nicholson River (no facilities). Barramundi fishing, bushwalking, boat hire, scenic tours, joy flights.*

REVERSE DIRECTIONS START ▲ 0.0 km

Carpentaria Shire Council Office, Normanton

The Great Top Road

Leichhardt River

BURKETOWN
«»
LAWN HILL
NATIONAL PARK

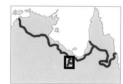

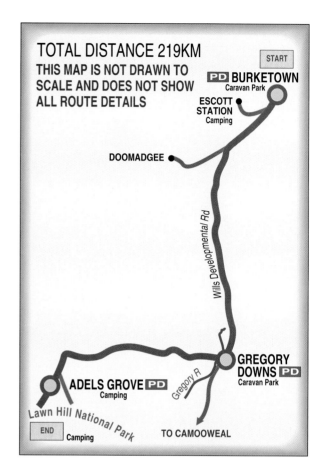

TOTAL DISTANCE 219KM
THIS MAP IS NOT DRAWN TO SCALE AND DOES NOT SHOW ALL ROUTE DETAILS

START
PD BURKETOWN
Caravan Park
ESCOTT STATION
Camping
DOOMADGEE
Wills Developmental Rd
GREGORY DOWNS PD
Caravan Park
ADELS GROVE PD
Camping
Gregory R
Lawn Hill National Park
END Camping
TO CAMOOWEAL

START POINT
Map page 19, E9.

TOTAL KM 219.
UNSEALED KM 219.
DEGREE OF DIFFICULTY Easy.
DRIVING TIME 4 hours.
LONGEST DISTANCE NO FUEL 115 km (Burketown to Gregory Downs).
TOPOGRAPHIC MAPS Auslig: 1:250 000 series: *Burketown*; *Lawn Hill*. See also 1:100 000 series.
LOCAL/SPECIALITY MAPS Sunmap: *Gulf Savannah*; Auslig: *Northern Australia*.
OTHER USEFUL INFORMATION GLADA booklet: *Gulf Savannah Factfinder*; QNPWS visitor information sheet: *Lawn Hill National Park*.

DESCRIPTION This short, easy drive takes you across the flat, semi-arid grass plains of the Western Savannah. From Burketown head south to Gregory Downs, a small town on the Gregory River. This fast-flowing river, spring-fed from the Georgina Basin, has wide sandy banks often used as bush campsites. The annual canoe race championships each May are well attended as the Gregory River is regarded as one of the best canoe courses in Australia. From here the route takes you west to *Adels Grove*, known locally as 'The Frenchman's Garden'. You can tour the stand of exotic tropical trees planted in the 1930s by a French botanist, Albert De Lestang. The property has a store and camping ground with campsites and on site caravans.

Lawn Hill National Park lies just 5 kilometres away. From Adels Grove you will see the towering sandstone escarpment of the Constance Range which juts dramati-

cally above the sparse grasslands. Hidden within the range lies Lawn Hill Gorge, a surprising tropical oasis. The red and grey gorge walls rise up to 60 metres above Lawn Hill Creek, fringed with tropical plants – the remnants of wet rainforest which covered the entire area about 15 million years ago. The Waanyi Aboriginal tribe occupied the gorge for at least 17 000 years and the park lies within their 'Rainbow Serpent' country. Ochre paintings on the gorge walls at Wild Dog and Rainbow Dreaming art sites are within pleasant walking distance of the grassed, shady campground next to the creek. There are some 20 kilometres of walking tracks which lead along the gorge around Island Stack to Indarri Falls and a natural spa waterhole. Canoes and inflatable boats are a good way to explore the magic of the gorge. Take binoculars to see the prolific wildlife which includes freshwater crocodiles, tortoises, wallabies and bats.

WARNINGS ▶ Check road conditions with GLADA or nearest shire council office. ▶ Day temperatures during summer can exceed 40 degrees while mid-winter nights can be near 0 degrees. Bring appropriate clothing. ▶ Crocodiles inhabit coastline and inland water-

Waterfall, Lawn Hill National Park

ways in the Gulf Savannah. Be crocodile-wise. Do not swim. ▶ Advise the QNPWS ranger if bushwalking outside the gorge area.

BOOKINGS AND PERMITS ▶ For information and bookings at Adels Grove, contact Savannah Guide Post, Adels Grove, PMB 2, Mt Isa QLD 4825; tel. (077) 43 7887 and ask for Adels Grove (delays are frequent). ▶ To ensure a campsite at Lawn Hill, book 6–12 weeks in advance by writing to: The Ranger, Lawn Hill National Park, PMB 12, Mt Isa QLD 4825. Self-register on site between October and February. Direct telephone enquiries to the QNPWS Mount Isa Area Office; tel. (077) 43 2055.

ROUTE DIRECTIONS

Depart Burketown on Wills Developmental Rd 5 km south-west to the Escott Station turnoff.

0.0 km Zero trip meter at above intersection. **SO.**
(20.8 km) ▲ 213.7 km
20.8 km S'post: Gregory Downs 86. **SO.**

> Doomadgee Aboriginal community off to right.

(1.3 km) Opp. dir. s'post: Burketown 24. ▲192.9 km
22.1 km Beames Brook. Cross bridge.
(93.2 km) ▲ 191.6 km
115.3 km S'post: Lawn Hill National Park 100. **TR.**

> Gregory Downs 50 m straight ahead. **PD**
> Supplies, caravan park. Minor mechanical
> repairs. The Gregory Downs Hotel is an old
> Cobb & Co. coach house.

(0.5 km) ▲ 98.4 km
115.8 km Gregory River. Cross bridge.

299

> *Site of the annual May canoe races. Wide sandy river bank. Swimming, bush camping (no facilities).*

(73.4 km) ▲ 97.9 km
189.2 km S'post: Lawn Hill National Park. **TL.**
(0.5 km) ▲ 24.5 km
189.7 km Gate.

> *Leave as found.*

(9.5 km) ▲ 24.0 km
199.2 km Intersection. S'post: Lawn Hill National Park 15. **SO.**
(4.9 km) ▲ 14.5 km
204.1 km S'post: Lawn Hill National Park 10. **SO.**

> *Adels Grove 400 m straight ahead on right.* **PD** *Supplies, minor mechanical repairs. Botanical tours of exotic and native plants and trees in 'The Frenchman's Garden'. Caravan and campsites: barbecues, toilets, hot showers, laundry. Swimming in waterhole and creek. Canoe and dinghy hire.*

(6.4 km) ▲ 9.6 km
210.5 km Lawn Hill National Park entrance. **SO.**
(3.2 km) ▲ 3.2 km
213.7 km Lawn Hill National Park Camping Area and Ranger Station.

> *Shady, grassed camping ground bounded by gorges next to Lawn Hill Creek: picnic tables, barbecues, toilets, hot showers, laundry tubs. Permit required. Book in advance or self-register on site, October–February. Bushwalking, canoeing and swimming. Aboriginal art sites.*

REVERSE DIRECTIONS START ▲ 0.0 km

Canoeing on Lawn Hill Creek

Lawn Hill Gorge

LAWN HILL NATIONAL PARK «» HELLS GATE ROADHOUSE

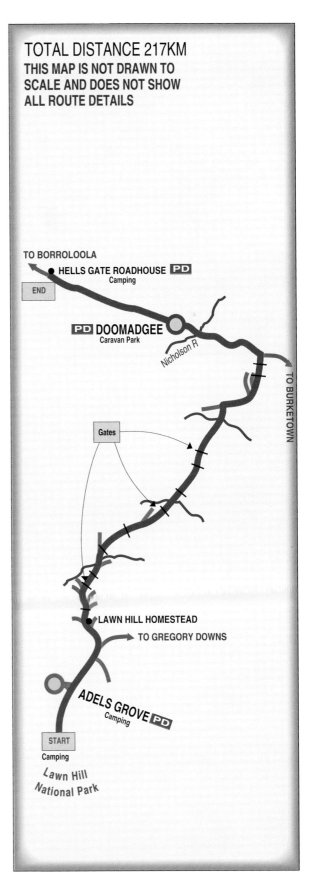

TOTAL DISTANCE 217KM
THIS MAP IS NOT DRAWN TO SCALE AND DOES NOT SHOW ALL ROUTE DETAILS

TO BORROLOOLA

HELLS GATE ROADHOUSE **PD**
Camping

END

PD DOOMADGEE
Caravan Park

Nicholson R

TO BURKETOWN

Gates

LAWN HILL HOMESTEAD

TO GREGORY DOWNS

ADELS GROVE **PD**
Camping

START
Camping

Lawn Hill National Park

START POINT
Map page 19, C11.

TOTAL KM 217.
UNSEALED KM 217.
DEGREE OF DIFFICULTY Moderate.
DRIVING TIME 4 hours.
LONGEST DISTANCE NO FUEL 135 km (Adels Grove to Doomadgee).
TOPOGRAPHIC MAPS Auslig 1:250 000 series: *Lawn Hill*; *Westmoreland*. See also 1:100 000 series.
LOCAL/SPECIALITY MAPS Sunmap: *Gulf Savannah*; Auslig: *Northern Australia*.
OTHER USEFUL INFORMATION GLADA booklet: *Gulf Savannah Factfinder*; QTTC booklet: *Gulf Savannah*.

DESCRIPTION For most of this trip you traverse the vast Lawn Hill Station property on a bush track of reasonable quality, although there are some sections of deep bulldust (**see Warnings**). On leaving this property you head north-west through the Aboriginal township of *Doomadgee* in an Aboriginal Trust Area. The town has a caravan park, guest house and a small retail area but access into the wider trust area is restricted (**see Bookings and Permits**). There is a camping ground at *Hells Gate Roadhouse*, 81 kilometres from Doomadgee. Fishing expeditions to 8 Mile Beach on the Gulf (Macassan) coast leave from the roadhouse with a Savannah Guide. Before European occupation fishing crews from the Celebes in Indonesia sailed the monsoonal winds to fish these waters.

WARNINGS ▶ Some sections of the track through Lawn Hill Station are deep bulldust. Check road conditions with GLADA or nearest shire council office. ▶ Crocodiles inhabit coastlines and waterways in the Gulf Savannah. Be crocodile-wise. Do not swim.

BOOKINGS AND PERMITS ▶ No camping, fishing or shooting on Lawn Hill Station. Leave gates as found. ▶ For information and a permit to camp and fish within Doomadgee Aboriginal Community Council Trust Area call into the office of the Doomadgee Aboriginal Community Council, South Street, Doomadgee or tel. (077) 45 8188 (operator connected call). ▶ To book at the Doomadgee Guest House tel. (077) 45 8230. ▶ Advance booking required to stay at Hells Gate Roadhouse, PMB 2, Burketown QLD 4830; tel. (077) 43 7887 (operator connected).

ROUTE DIRECTIONS

Depart Lawn Hill National Park 5 km to Adels Grove turnoff.

0.0 km Zero trip meter at the Adels Grove turnoff heading north. **SO.**

> Adels Grove 400 m off to left. **PD**

(4.9 km) ▲ 135.2 km
4.9 km Intersection. **KL.**

> Road to right is the old road to Tennant Creek.

(9.4 km) ▲ 130.3 km
14.3 km Gate.

> Leave as found.

(0.4 km) ▲ 120.9 km
14.7 km Intersection. **KL.**

> Gregory Downs 74 km off to right.

(1.5 km) Opp. dir. s'post: Gorge. ▲ 120.5 km
16.2 km S'post: Doomadgee. **KL.**

> Follow yellow homemade signs through the paddocks of Lawn Hill Station. Warning: no camping, fishing or shooting.

(0.2 km) ▲ 119.0 km
16.4 km S'post: Doomadgee. **KR** at Lawn Hill Homestead.

> Lawn Hill Homestead on right.

(0.2 km) ▲ 118.8 km
16.6 km S'post: Doomadgee. **KL** through gate then **KL** again.

> Leave gate as found.

(0.2 km) ▲ 118.6 km
16.8 km S'post: Doomadgee. **KR.** 50 m to s'post: Doomadgee. **KR** through gate.

(1.1 km) ▲ 118.4 km
17.9 km Gate.

> Leave gate as found.

(0.1 km) ▲ 117.3 km
18.0 km S'post: Doomadgee. **KL.**

(0.2 km) ▲ 117.2 km
18.2 km Cross Lawn Hill Creek.

(0.2 km) ▲ 117.0 km
18.4 km S'post: Doomadgee. **KR** then through gate.

> Leave as found.

(6.4 km) ▲ 116.8 km
24.8 km Gate.

> Leave as found.

(5.6 km) ▲ 110.4 km
30.4 km Intersection. **KR.**

(3.6 km) ▲ 104.8 km
34.0 km Gate.

> Leave as found.

(0.1 km) ▲ 101.2 km
34.1 km Creek crossing.

(4.9 km) ▲ 101.1 km
39.0 km Gate.

> Leave as found.

(12.6 km) ▲ 96.2 km
51.6 km Gate.

> Leave as found.

(6.5 km) ▲ 83.6 km
58.1 km Creek crossing.

(0.2 km) ▲ 77.1 km
58.3 km Gate.

> Leave as found.

(11.9 km) ▲ 76.9 km
70.2 km Creek crossing.

(13.2 km) ▲ 65.0 km
83.4 km T intersection. **TR.**

> Bowthorn Station 26 km off to left.

(33.2 km) ▲ 51.8 km
116.6 km Intersection. **KR.**

(3.2 km) ▲ 18.6 km

Road train on a Gulf Savannah road

119.8 km Y intersection. **KR.**
(3.5 km)   ▲ 15.4 km
123.3 km Y intersection. **KR.**
(0.6 km)   ▲ 11.9 km
123.9 km Gate.

Leave as found.

(0.1 km)   ▲ 11.3 km
124.0 km Y intersection. **KR.**
(2.6 km)   ▲ 11.2 km
126.6 km Gate then **KR.**

Leave gate as found.

(0.2 km)   Opp. dir. s'post: Lawn Hill Station.
No camping, fishing or shooting allowed. ▲ 8.6 km
126.8 km T intersection. **TL.**
(4.5 km)   Opp. dir. s'post: Bowthorn 72. ▲ 8.4 km
131.3 km Nicholson River. Cross causeway.
(0.4 km)   ▲ 3.9 km
131.7 km S'post: Doomadgee Aboriginal Council
Trust Area. **SO.**
(3.5 km)   ▲ 3.5 km
135.2 km Intersection. S'post: Borroloola. **SO.**

Doomadgee Caravan Park on left. Doomadgee town centre 1 km off to left. **PD** *Supplies, guest house. Permit from Doomadgee Aboriginal Community Council required to camp within the trust area.*

Opp. dir. s'post: Burketown.
0.0 km Zero trip meter at above intersection. **SO.**
(81.3 km)   ▲ 0.0 km
▲ 81.3 km
81.3 km Hells Gate Roadhouse on right.

PD *Limited supplies. Camping ground: barbecues, toilets, hot showers. Book ahead. Fishing expeditions with Savannah Guide to the Gulf shore. Enquire at roadhouse.*

REVERSE DIRECTIONS START ▲ 0.0 km

HELLS GATE ROADHOUSE «» BORROLOOLA

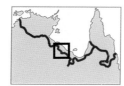

START POINT
Map page 19, C8.

TOTAL KM 322.
UNSEALED KM 322.
DEGREE OF DIFFICULTY Moderately difficult.
DRIVING TIME 7 hours.
LONGEST DISTANCE NO FUEL 263 km (Wollogorang to Borroloola).
TOPOGRAPHIC MAPS Auslig 1:250 000 series: *Westmoreland*; *Calvert Hills*.
LOCAL/SPECIALITY MAPS Sunmap: *Gulf Savannah*; DPIF: *Northern Territory Fishing Map*; Auslig: *Northern Australia*.
OTHER USEFUL INFORMATION NTTC booklet: *Tracks of Australia's Northern Territory: A Guide for Four Wheel Drivers*; DPIF booklet: *Northern Territory Fishing & Boating Guide*; RACQ booklet: *Northern Territory Guide*.

DESCRIPTION The track from Hells Gate to the Northern Territory border winds among sand palms and is liable to break into stretches of bulldust in the dry season. The road improves after the border crossing but is still subject to seasonal changes. There are bush campsites on the *Calvert*, *Robinson* and *Wearyan* rivers and fishing is permitted (**see Bookings and Permits**) at three pastoral properties en route: Pungalina, Seven Emu and Manangoora.

The small town of Borroloola is on Narwinbi Aboriginal Land. Barramundi, reef fish and mudcrabs attract anglers to the McArthur River. The Borroloola Fishing Classic is held each Easter. Borroloola Museum, oppo-

site the *McArthur River Caravan Park*, is the oldest surviving example of an outback police station.

WARNINGS ▶ Check road conditions with GLADA or the nearest shire council office. ▶ The track from Hells Gate to the border may have patches of bulldust. ▶ The track to Pungalina Station is ungraded and dangerous. Do not attempt without prior permission and advice from owners.

BOOKINGS AND PERMITS ▶ For permission to fish on Pungalina Station write to: Pungalina Station, PMB 171, Katherine NT 0851; or tel. (089) 75 8742 (BH); (089) 75 8741 (AH). ▶ Advance permission is not required to fish on Seven Emu Station or Manangoora Station. Call at homesteads on arrival. ▶ Observe DPIF rules and regulations on fishing and read DPIF's *Northern Territory Fishing Map* carefully.

ROUTE DIRECTIONS

0.0 km	Zero trip meter adjacent to Hells Gate Roadhouse. **SO.**
	(54.2 km) ▲ 322.3 km
54.2 km	Gate. Northern Territory border.
	Leave gate as found. Adjust watches to Northern Territory time.
	(5.1 km) ▲ 268.1 km
59.3 km	Gate.
	Leave as found. Wollogorang Roadhouse on right after gate. **PD** *Supplies, camping ground.*
	(1.1 km) ▲ 263.0 km
60.4 km	Gate.
	Leave as found.
	(0.3 km) ▲ 261.9 km
60.7 km	Cross Settlement Creek.
	(11.0 km) ▲ 261.6 km
71.7 km	Gate.
	Leave as found. Turnoff to Pungalina Station approx. 36 km on right at grid. No access without prior permission. Warning: dangerous ungraded track to station. Do not attempt without owner's advice.
	(45.6 km) ▲ 250.6 km
117.3 km	S'post: Borroloola/Cape Crawford. **KR.**

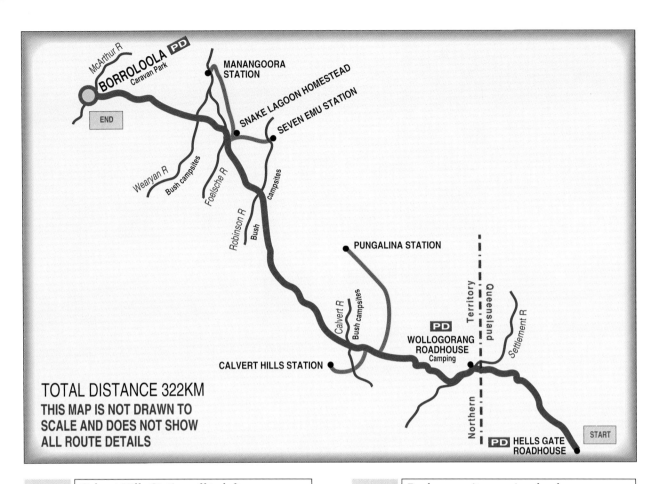

TOTAL DISTANCE 322KM
THIS MAP IS NOT DRAWN TO
SCALE AND DOES NOT SHOW
ALL ROUTE DETAILS

Calvert Hills Station off to left.

(23.0 km) Opp. dir. s'post:
Wollogorang/Qld border. ▲ 205.0 km
140.3 km Cross Calvert River.

Bush campsites on river bank.

(71.1 km) ▲ 182.0 km
211.4 km Cross Robinson River.

Bush campsites on river bank.

(36.4 km) ▲ 110.9 km
247.8 km Intersection. S'post: Borroloola 69. **TL**.

*Manangoora Station 19 km off to right.
Seven Emu Station 49 km off to right. Call
at either homestead on arrival for
permission to fish.*

(0.1 km) Opp. dir. s'post: Wollogorang. ▲ 74.5 km
247.9 km Cross Foelsche River.
(14.8 km) ▲ 74.4 km
262.7 km Cross Wearyan River.

Bush campsites on river bank.

(54.3 km) ▲ 59.6 km
317.0 km McArthur River. Cross causeway.
(1.7 km) ▲ 5.3 km
318.7 km S'post: Borroloola. **TR**.
(2.1 km) ▲ 3.6 km
320.8 km McArthur River Caravan Park on right.

*Borroloola Museum opposite caravan
park. Mechanical repairs at workshop
behind museum.*

(1.5 km) ▲ 1.5 km
322.3 km Borroloola town centre.

PD *Supplies, motel. Small town on
McArthur River on Narwinbi Aboriginal
land. Fishing and boating.*

REVERSE DIRECTIONS START ▲ 0.0 km

BORROLOOLA «» NATHAN RIVER STATION

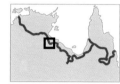

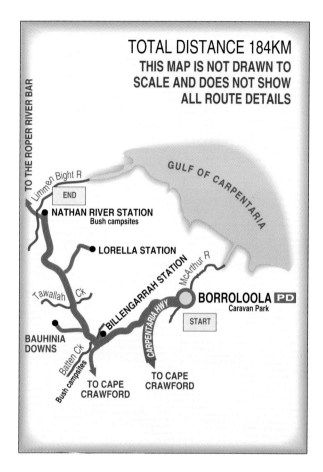

TOTAL DISTANCE 184KM
THIS MAP IS NOT DRAWN TO SCALE AND DOES NOT SHOW ALL ROUTE DETAILS

START POINT

Map page 27, O3

TOTAL KM 184.
UNSEALED KM 158.
DEGREE OF DIFFICULTY Easy.
DRIVING TIME 4 hours.
LONGEST DISTANCE NO FUEL No fuel this section.
Next fuel Roper Bar (376 km).
TOPOGRAPHIC MAPS Auslig 1:250 000 series: *Bauhnia Downs*; *Mount Young*.
LOCAL/SPECIALITY MAPS DPIF: *Northern Territory Fishing Map*; Auslig: *Northern Australia*.
OTHER USEFUL INFORMATION NTTC booklet: *Tracks of Australia's Northern Territory: A Guide for Four Wheel Drivers*; RACQ booklet: *Northern Territory Guide*; DPIF booklet: *Northern Territory Fishing & Boating Guide*.

DESCRIPTION Patches of scrub and rocky escarpments break the sparse, undulating country between Borroloola and Nathan River Station. Bush camping (no facilities) is permitted at *Batten Creek* on Billengarrah Station. As you head north from here the Tawallah Range is on your right. The rock escarpments change with every bend in the road and there are many billabongs and streams, typical of Gulf country. Bush camping and fishing are permitted at *Lorella Station* (35 kilometres off the route) with advance permission (*see Bookings and Permits*). *Nathan River Station* has no facilities but bush camping is permitted. Call at the homestead on arrival. On Nathan River Station there are magnificent rock formations known as the 'Hidden City' – said to date back over a billion years.

Unfortunately there is no access to the 'Hidden City' at present, although there are plans to include it in a future national park. There are bush campsites and plenty of spots to fish along the Limmen Bight River.

WARNINGS ▶ Road impassable after heavy rain. For information on road conditions contact the nearest police station or the AANT; tel. (089) 81 3837. ▶ Crocodiles inhabit coastline and inland waterways in the Northern Territory. Be crocodile-wise. Do not swim.

BOOKINGS AND PERMITS ▶ No camping on Bauhinia Downs. ▶ Camping and fishing are permitted on Lorella Station only with advance permission. Write to Lorella Station, c/- 7 Mahoney Street, Palmerston NT 0830; or tel. (089) 32 3174. ▶ Call at the Nathan River Homestead on arrival at the station for permission to camp or fish; tel. (089) 75 9940.

ROUTE DIRECTIONS

0.0 km Zero trip meter at s'post: Cape Crawford adjacent to Borroloola turnoff on Carpentaria Hwy. **SO.**

(26.1 km) Opp. dir. s'post: Wollogorang. ▲ 183.8 km

26.1 km S'post: Roper Bar. **TR** onto gravel.

(46.5 km) Bitumen. Opp. dir. s'post: Borroloola. ▲ 157.7 km

72.6 km Intersection. **SO.**

> *Cape Crawford 95 km straight ahead.*

(2.2 km) ▲ 111.2 km

74.8 km Intersection. **SO.**

> *Billengarrah Homestead 5 km off to right.*

(2.9 km) ▲ 109.0 km

77.7 km S'post: Roper Bar. **TR.**

(3.5 km) Opp. dir. s'post: Borroloola. ▲ 106.1 km

81.2 km Cross Batten Creek.

> *Bush camping on creek bank.*

(6.9 km) ▲ 102.6 km

88.1 km Intersection. **SO.**

> *Bauhinia Downs Station off to left. No camping.*

(8.4 km) ▲ 95.7 km

96.5 km Gate.

> *Leave as found.*

(15.1 km) ▲ 87.3 km

111.6 km Cross Tawalla Creek.

(4.0 km) ▲ 72.2 km

115.6 km Gate.

> *Leave as found.*

(18.6 km) ▲ 68.2 km

134.2 km Intersection. **SO.**

> *Lorella Springs Station 35 km off to right. Camping and fishing are permitted in designated areas. Advance notification required.*

(26.8 km) ▲ 49.6 km

161.0 km Gate.

> *Leave as found.*

(21.9 km) ▲ 22.8 km

182.9 km Entrance to Nathan River Station. **KR** to homestead.

A natural sentinel watches over the 'Hidden City' on Nathan River Station

> *Airstrip on left.*

(0.8 km) ▲ 0.9 km

183.7 km Gate.

> *Leave as found.*

(0.1 km) ▲ 0.1 km

183.0 km Nathan River Homestead on right.

> *Fishing spots and bush camping along Limmen Bight River. Call at homestead on arrival.*

REVERSE DIRECTIONS START ▲ 0.0 km

NATHAN RIVER STATION «» THE ROPER RIVER BAR

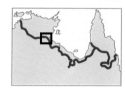

Roper River Bar

START POINT
Map page 25, M12.

TOTAL KM 192.
UNSEALED KM 192.
DEGREE OF DIFFICULTY Easy.
DRIVING TIME 4 hours.
LONGEST DISTANCE NO FUEL Fuel at Roper Bar.
TOPOGRAPHIC MAP Auslig 1:250 000 series: *Urapunga*. See also 1:100 000 series.
LOCAL/SPECIALITY MAPS DPIF: *Northern Territory Fishing Map*; Auslig: *Northern Australia*.
OTHER USEFUL INFORMATION NTTC booklet: *Tracks of Australia's Northern Territory: A Guide for Four Wheel Drivers*; DPIF booklet: *Northern Territory Fishing & Boating Guide*; RACQ booklet: *Northern Territory Guide*.

DESCRIPTION Running parallel to the Gulf coast, the unsealed road between Nathan River Station and the Roper River Bar is in reasonable condition but may be impassable during the wet season. It crosses the *Limmen Bight*, *Cox*, *Towns* and *Hodgson* rivers, past billabongs and swamps covered in waterlilies. There are bush campsites (no facilities) along all these rivers. The Gulf coast is accessible at Limmen Bight River Fishing Camp and Port Roper, both excellent fishing spots (**see Bookings and Permits**). Once you reach the abandoned ruins of St Vidgeon Station, past Lomarieum and Wadamunga lagoons, you are on the border of Marra Aboriginal Land to the east, and Arnhem Land to the north. The Roper River flows eastwards through wet-

lands to Port Roper in the Gulf. At the end of the wet season the fish almost jump onto your line downstream from the town of *Roper Bar*. There is a caravan park in the town and bush campsites (no facilities) high on the embankment at the *Roper River Bar*. The rock bar divides the tidal from the freshwater Roper and both river and bar were named after John Roper, a member of Ludwig Leichhardt's 1845 expedition.

WARNINGS ▶ Road impassable after heavy rain. For information on road conditions contact the nearest police station or the AANT; tel. (089) 81 3837. ▶ Crocodiles inhabit coastline and inland waterways in the Northern Territory. Be crocodile-wise. Do not swim. ▶ Observe DPIF rules and regulations on fishing.

BOOKINGS AND PERMITS ▶ Bush camping is permitted on the Limmen Bight River only with permission from Nathan River Station; tel. (089) 75 9940. No permits are required for bush camping near the Cox, Towns and Hodgson rivers. ▶ Fishing without a permit at Port Roper is allowed only at Roper River No. 1 and No. 2 Landings.

ROUTE DIRECTIONS

0.0 km	Zero trip meter at Nathan River Homestead heading north. **SO.**	
	(1.1 km)	▲ 192.3 km
1.1 km	Intersection. **KR** onto Roper Bar Rd.	
	(10.6 km)	▲ 191.2 km
11.7 km	Limmen Bight River. Cross causeway.	

Bush campsites on river bank. Permission from Nathan River Station.

	(21.4 km)	▲ 180.6 km

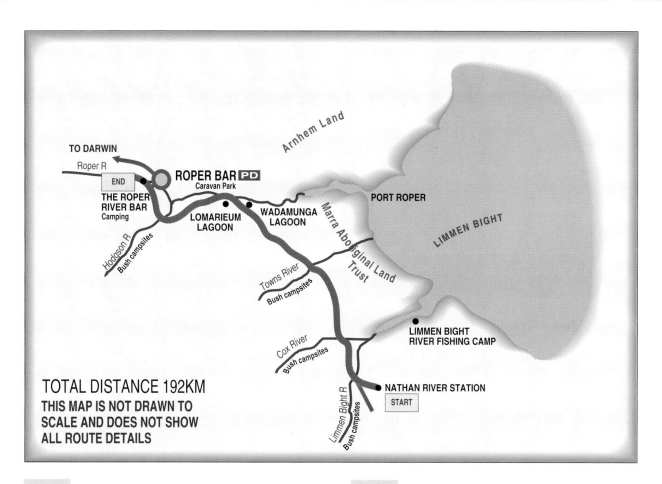

TOTAL DISTANCE 192KM

THIS MAP IS NOT DRAWN TO SCALE AND DOES NOT SHOW ALL ROUTE DETAILS

33.1 km Cox River. Cross causeway.

Bush campsites on river bank. Boat ramp. Limmen Bight River Fishing Camp off to right. Call at camp headquarters on arrival.

(38.2 km) ▲ 159.2 km

71.3 km Towns River. Cross causeway.

Bush campsites on river bank. Boat ramp.

(30.9 km) ▲ 121.0 km

102.2 km S'post: Roper Bar 90. **TL**.

Port Roper (on Marra Aboriginal Land) 42 km off to right. Public access restricted to Roper River No. 1 and No. 2 Landings.

(65.8 km) Opp. dir. s'post: Borroloola. ▲ 90.1 km

168.0 km Hodgson River. Cross causeway.

Bush campsites on river bank. Boat ramp.

(21.6 km) ▲ 24.3 km

189.6 km S'post: Roper Bar. **TR**.

Mataranka off to left.

(1.1 km) ▲ 2.7 km

190.7 km Intersection. **SO**.

Roper Bar 2 km off to right. **PD** *Supplies, caravan park.*

(1.6 km) ▲ 1.6 km

92.3 km Roper River Bar.

Limited bush campsites high on river embankment. Barramundi and saratoga fishing.

REVERSE DIRECTIONS START ▲ 0.0 km

THE ROPER RIVER BAR «» DARWIN

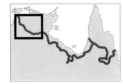

Mataranka thermal pool, Elsey National Park

START POINT
Map page 25, L10.

TOTAL KM 602.
UNSEALED KM 40.
DEGREE OF DIFFICULTY Easy.
DRIVING TIME 4 hours (The Roper River Bar to Katherine).
LONGEST DISTANCE NO FUEL 182 km (Roper Bar to Mataranka).
TOPOGRAPHIC MAPS Auslig 1:250 000 series: *Urupunga*; *Katherine*. See also 1:100 000 series.
LOCAL/SPECIALITY MAPS DPIF: *Northern Territory Fishing Map*; Auslig: *Northern Australia.*
OTHER USEFUL INFORMATION Katherine Region Tourist Association booklet: *Katherine Region*; DPIF booklet: *Northern Territory Fishing & Boating Guide*; Northern Territory Conservation Commission (NTCC) brochure: *Australia's Northern Territory Parks.*

DESCRIPTION From Roper Bar the Roper Highway takes you deep into the Never Never – a belt of land between the top end and the tablelands, immortalised in Mrs Aeneas Gunn's classic, *We of the Never Never.* Just south of Mataranka, on the outskirts of serene *Elsey National Park,* is a replica of the Gunn homestead at the *Mataranka Homestead Resort.* There is a caravan park and camping ground here, set among flame trees and another – 12 Mile Yards – beside the Roper River within the park. Take binoculars on riverbank walks through pockets of rainforest because the birdlife is phenomenal.

From Mataranka it is only an hour's drive on the Stuart Highway past Beswick Aboriginal Land and Cutta Cutta Caves to *Katherine.* One of the Territory's earliest settlements, Katherine is the commercial centre for cattle stations and Aboriginal communities in the Elsey, Gulf and Victoria River

districts. *Nitmiluk (Katherine Gorge) National Park* is only 30 kilometres north-east via a sealed road. The park preserves a system of 13 gorges separated by rapids and carved in a zig-zag course through the sandstone plateau by the Katherine River. A guided boat trip up the river, past rugged gold and grey gorge cliffs, reveals Aboriginal paintings, rainforest plants and fascinating wildlife, including freshwater crocodiles, turtles and pythons.

The park has a Visitors Centre, kiosk, picnic and camping ground. Enquire about bush campsites at the Visitors Centre. The park has over 100 kilometres of signposted walking tracks, ranging from short strolls to a five-day hike to *Edith Falls*, on the north-western border of the park. There is a picnic and camping area here, and the large pandanus fringed rockpool is a safe place to swim.

Route directions for the next trek to Kununurra start in Katherine. If you plan to visit Kakadu or enjoy other Darwin-based tours, head up the Stuart Highway 315 kilometres to *Darwin* – a port city with a relaxed tropical charm. Darwin has a wide range of accommodation.

WARNINGS ▶ For information on road conditions contact the nearest police station or the AANT; tel. (089) 81 3837. ▶ Crocodiles inhabit coastline and inland waterways in the Northern Territory. Be crocodile-wise. ▶ Box jellyfish are prevalent in the sea and coastal creeks October to May. Do not swim.

BOOKINGS AND PERMITS ▶ Book a campsite at Elsey National Park by contacting the Roper River District Office, NTCC, PMB 188, Katherine NT 0851; tel. (089) 75 4560. ▶ To book a campsite at Nitmiluk (Katherine Gorge) National Park or Edith Falls contact Katherine Regional Office, NTCC, Giles Street, Katherine; PO Box 344, Katherine NT 0851; tel. (089) 89 4411; or ring the Nitmiluk (Katherine Gorge) National Park Visitor Information Centre; tel. (089) 72 1886.

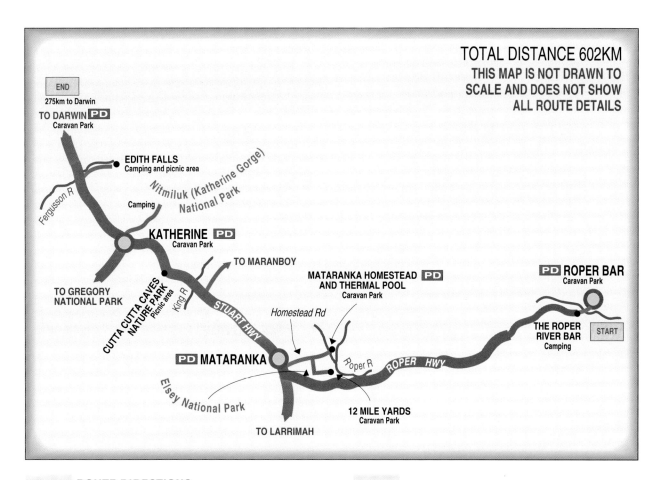

TOTAL DISTANCE 602KM
THIS MAP IS NOT DRAWN TO
SCALE AND DOES NOT SHOW
ALL ROUTE DETAILS

ROUTE DIRECTIONS

0.0 km Zero trip meter at s'post: Mataranka at Roper Bar turnoff heading west. **SO**.
(39.5 km) ▲ 179.7 km
39.5 km Bitumen.
(135.2 km) Gravel. ▲ 140.2 km
174.7 km S'post: Katherine. **TR** onto Stuart Hwy.
(5.0 km) Opp. dir. s'post: Roper Bar. ▲ 5.0 km
179.7 km Intersection.

> Elsey National Park 8 km off to right along Homestead Rd. **PD** Caravan park and thermal pool at Mataranka Homestead Resort, just outside the park. 12 Mile Yards camping ground along the Roper River in the park has tent and caravan sites, picnic tables, fireplaces, toilets, showers. Riverbank walks, canoeing. Swimming and fishing at Mataranka Falls and in the Waterhouse and Roper rivers at designated spots.

▲ 0.0 km

0.0 km Zero trip meter at above intersection.
S'post: Katherine. **SO** along Stuart Hwy.
(1.8 km) ▲ 107.1 km

1.8 km Mataranka town centre. **SO** along Stuart Hwy.

> **PD** Supplies. Cutta Cutta Caves Nature Park 84 km north on the hwy has unique tropical limestone caves: home to the rare Ghost Bat. Cave tours. Picnic area with tables, water.

(105.3 km) ▲ 105.3 km
107.1 km Katherine town centre.

> **PD** Supplies, caravan park. Regional centre for Aboriginal communities, cattle stations and mining camps. Annual show, camp draft and rodeo each July. Nitmiluk (Katherine Gorge) National Park 29 km north-east of town. Visitor Centre, kiosk, picnic area and camping ground: tables, barbecues, toilets, hot showers. Bush campsites: portable toilets, water.

The route directions for the next trek to Kununurra start in Katherine. To visit Darwin take the Stuart Hwy 315 km to Darwin.

REVERSE DIRECTIONS START ▲ 0.0 km

WEST OF THE NEVER NEVER
DARWIN
«»
KUNUNURRA
1421 KILOMETRES

DARWIN «» TIMBER CREEK   603 km

TIMBER CREEK «» BULLITA OUTSTATION   129 km

BULLITA OUTSTATION «» THE WICKHAM RIVER   84 km

THE WICKHAM RIVER «» KALKARINDJI   133 km

KALKARINDJI «» KUNUNURRA   472 km

Rocky section of track, Gregory National Park

Mesa country near Mistake Creek Station

The trek from Darwin to Kununurra is relatively short with challenging sections in Gregory National Park on the Bullita Stockroute and Humbert tracks. This remote park, south of the Victoria Highway in the heart of the Victoria River district cattle country, has an unusual mixture of tropical and semi-arid vegetation, dramatic gorges, ranges and flat-topped hills. There are only a few small towns on our route and you will need to carry extra supplies of food, water and fuel between Timber Creek and the Aboriginal township of Kalkarindji. We then head west past Inverway and Mistake Creek cattle stations, to join the Duncan Highway which winds north and links back onto the Victoria Highway 3 kilometres from the Western Australian border. Kununurra, on the banks of the Ord River in the Kimberley region, is just half an hour's drive from here but Keep River National Park and Lake Argyle Tourist Village are tempting diversions. The park, nestled on the Northern Territory side of the border, is significant in Aboriginal Dreamtime legend. The turnoff to Lake Argyle, a massive body of water created by the Ord River Irrigation Scheme, is 10 kilometres over the border.

River and creek crossings are common on this track so avoid travelling in the wet season. Rocky river beds present an exciting driving challenge: negotiate with caution. The many rivers banks are ideal bush camp-sites but do remember that this is crocodile country. Carry high-frequency radio and guide listing Radphone call signs and frequencies.

TREAD LIGHTLY!
On Public and Private Land

■ Ford creeks at designated crossings.

■ Travel only where allowed: get permission to cross private land and obtain permits where necessary.

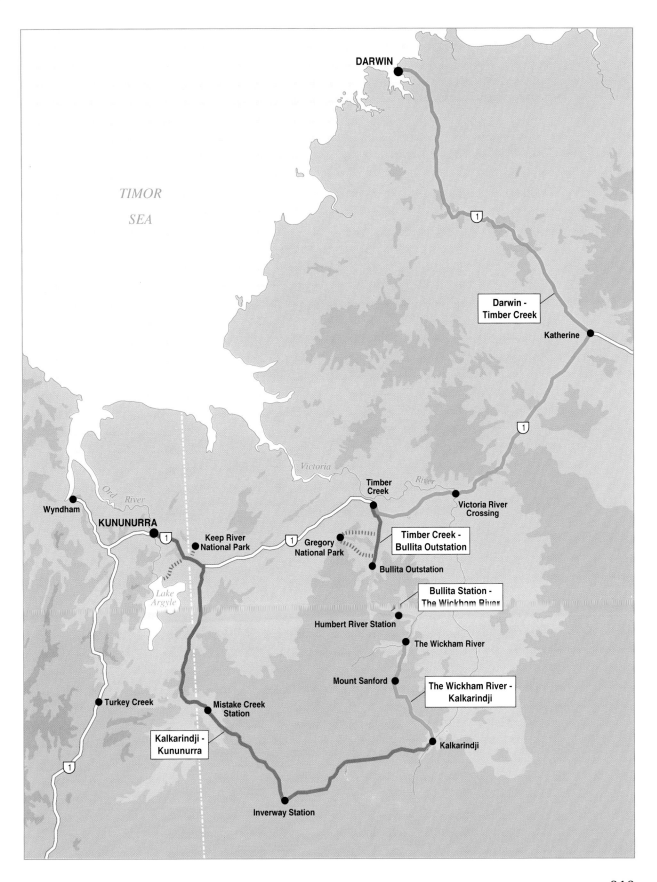

DARWIN

Darwin - Timber Creek

Katherine

TIMOR SEA

Victoria River

Timber Creek

Victoria River Crossing

Timber Creek - Bullita Outstation

Wyndham

Ord River

KUNUNURRA

Keep River National Park

Gregory National Park

Bullita Outstation

Lake Argyle

Bullita Station - The Wickham River

Humbert River Station

The Wickham River

Mount Sanford

The Wickham River - Kalkarindji

Turkey Creek

Mistake Creek Station

Kalkarindji - Kununurra

Kalkarindji

Inverway Station

GREGORY AND KEEP RIVER NATIONAL PARKS

Both parks feature open woodland dissected by rugged escarpments and deep gorges carved by rivers which form part of the mighty river system weaving through the top end of this state. There are excellent marked walking tracks within these parks. You will need a permit to traverse the Bullita and Humbert tracks in Gregory National Park and you must notify either the Timber Creek or Bullita Outstation ranger of the completion of your trek through the park. The telephone numbers of both ranger stations are given in the route directions. For general information contact the Northern Territory Conservation Commission (NTCC), Giles Street, Katherine; PO Box 344, Katherine NT 0850; tel. (089) 72 8770.

Help protect these parks.

▶ *Keep to designated roads and tracks.*
▶ *Camp only at designated areas.*
▶ *Carry rubbish away with you if bins are not provided.*
▶ *Carry drinking water on bush walks.*
▶ *Use park fireplaces and collect firewood outside park boundaries. Bring a gas stove if possible.*
▶ *Firearms and pets are prohibited.*
▶ *Respect native plants and animals.*
▶ *Do not touch Aboriginal art sites.*

HOW TO BE CROCODILE-WISE

Of the two crocodile species found in Australia's north, the saltwater or estuarine crocodile is dangerous. It lives in salt water and fresh water, usually in tidal sections of rivers and creeks, floodplain waterholes and fresh water swamps and is found as far inland as 100 kilometres. The fresh water crocodile, while not dangerous, can deliver a savage bite if interfered with. Treat all crocodiles longer than 1.5 metres as dangerous, and obey the following rules.

▶ *Seek local advice before swimming, camping, fishing or boating.*

▶ *Swim, canoe or use small boats only in shallow rapids.*
▶ *Watch children and pets in the water or at the water's edge where large crocodiles might live.*
▶ *Fill a bucket with water and prepare food or clean fish at least 5 metres from the water's edge.*
▶ *Do not lean from boats or hang articles over the edge.*
▶ *When fishing stand at least a few metres back from the water's edge. Do not stand on overhanging logs.*
▶ *Burn or remove from your campsite food scraps, fish offal and other wastes.*

USEFUL INFORMATION

For touring information contact:
Katherine Region Tourist Association
Stuart Highway cnr Lindsay Street
PO Box 555, Katherine NT 0851
(089) 72 2650.

Ord Tourist Bureau
75 Coolibah Drive, PO Box 466
Kununurra NT 6743, (089) 68 1177.

Department of Conservation and Land Management (CALM)
Kimberley Regional Office
Messmate Way, PO Box 942, Kununurra WA 6743
(091) 68 0200.

For motoring information contact:
Automobile Association of Northern
  Territory Inc. (AANT)
MLC Building, 79–81 Smith Street
Darwin NT 0800, (089) 81 3837.

For emergency medical assistance contact:
Aerial Medical Services
(089) 22 8888 (Darwin Hospital)
(089) 72 9211 (Katherine Hospital).

DARWIN
«»
TIMBER CREEK

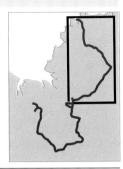

START POINT
Map page 24, E5.

TOTAL KM 603 (all sealed).
DEGREE OF DIFFICULTY Easy.
DRIVING TIME 7 hours.
LONGEST DISTANCE NO FUEL 195 km (Katherine to Victoria River Crossing).
TOPOGRAPHIC MAP Auslig 1:250 000 series: *Delamere*. See also 1:100 000 series.
LOCAL/SPECIALITY MAPS DPIF: *Northern Territory Fishing Map*; Auslig: *Northern Territory*.
OTHER USEFUL INFORMATION Conservation Commission of the Northern Territory (CCNT) visitor information sheet: *Gregory National Park*.

DESCRIPTION After reaching Katherine via the Stuart Highway from Darwin we swing south-west along the narrow Victoria Highway towards Gregory National Park. The park, with spectacular ranges and tropical and semi-arid plants, lies in the Victoria River district cattle country and includes land originally part of various cattle stations. Victoria River Crossing (195 kilometres from Katherine) is a tiny community located where the Victoria River crosses the highway. The Victoria River Gorge is accessible from here and there are a number of excellent fishing spots close to the *Victoria River Inn*, which has caravan and campsites. From the crossing you drive past the Fitzroy and Stokes ranges to the township of *Timber Creek*, located on the northern perimeter of the larger sector of the park. The park was named in honour of Augustus Charles Gregory who led the first expedition of the area in 1855 and named Timber Creek after repairing his vessel with local timber. Fishing is popular at *Big Horse Creek Camping Area* on the banks of the Victoria River, not

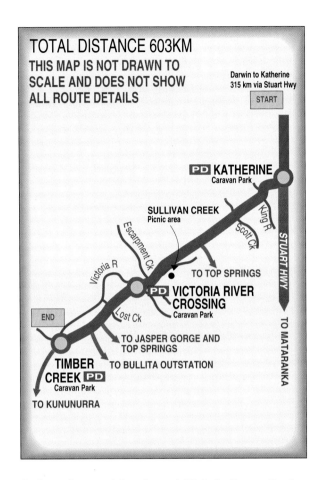

TOTAL DISTANCE 603KM
THIS MAP IS NOT DRAWN TO SCALE AND DOES NOT SHOW ALL ROUTE DETAILS

Darwin to Katherine
315 km via Stuart Hwy
START

PD KATHERINE
Caravan Park

SULLIVAN CREEK
Picnic area

Escarpment Ck

King R

Scott Ck

Victoria R

TO TOP SPRINGS

PD VICTORIA RIVER CROSSING
Caravan Park

STUART HWY

TO MATARANKA

END

Lost Ck

TO JASPER GORGE AND TOP SPRINGS

TO BULLITA OUTSTATION

TIMBER CREEK **PD**
Caravan Park

TO KUNUNURRA

far from the town's hotel motel. Visit the Ranger Station for park information.

WARNINGS ▶ Give way to road trains on the Victoria Highway. ▶ Crocodiles inhabit coastline and inland waterways in the Northern Territory. Be crocodile-wise. Do not swim.

BOOKINGS AND PERMITS ▶ For information on Gregory National Park and permits for the Bullita and Humbert tracks, contact the CCNT Katherine Regional Office, Giles Street, Katherine NT; PO Box 344, Katherine NT 0851; tel. (089) 72 8770; or the CCNT Ranger, Gregory National Park, Victoria Highway, Timber Creek NT 0851; tel. (089) 75 0888; or the CCNT Ranger, Bullita Outstation; tel. (089) 75 0833.

Victoria River crossing

Escarpment along the Victoria River

ROUTE DIRECTIONS

Depart Darwin along Stuart Hwy to Katherine (approx. 315 km).

> **PD** *Supplies, caravan park.*

0.0 km Zero trip meter at Stuart Hwy and Victoria Hwy intersection in Katherine. **SO** along Victoria Hwy.
(34.8 km) ▲ 195.1 km
34.8 km King River. Cross bridge.
(36.0 km) ▲ 160.3 km
70.8 km Scott Creek. Cross bridge.
(55.8 km) ▲ 124.3 km
126.6 km Intersection. S'post: Kununurra. **SO**.

> *Top Springs 166 km off to left.*

(36.7 km) Opp. dir. s'post: Katherine. ▲ 68.5 km

163.3 km Sign: Gregory National Park.

> *Sullivan Creek Picnic and Camping Area 15 km ahead on left: tables, barbecues.*

(23.1 km) ▲ 31.8 km
186.4 km Escarpment Creek. Cross bridge.
(8.3 km) ▲ 8.7 km
194.7 km Victoria River. Cross bridge.
(0.4 km) ▲ 0.4 km
195.1 km Victoria River Crossing.

> **PD** *Caravan park, motel. Access to the Victoria River Gorge. Fishing.*

0.0 km Zero trip meter opposite inn. **SO** along Victoria Hwy.
(1.8 km) ▲ 0.0 km
▲ 92.9 km
1.8 km Track. **SO**.

> *Walking trail on left is an escarpment walk over steep, loose, rocky terrain (1 hr return).*

(6.5 km) ▲ 91.1 km
8.3 km Intersection. **SO**.

> *Victoria River access track off to right. Canoeing, fishing.*

(4.3 km) ▲ 84.6 km
12.6 km Exit Gregory National Park.
(4.2 km) Opp. dir. sign:
Gregory National Park. ▲ 80.3 km
16.8 km Lost Creek. Cross bridge.
(48.8 km) ▲ 76.1 km
65.6 km Intersection. S'post: Kununurra. **SO**.

> *Top Springs 219 km off to left.*

(16.8 km) ▲ 27.3 km
82.4 km Intersection. **SO**.

> *Bullita Outstation 52 km off to left.*

(10.5 km) ▲ 10.5 km
92.9 km Timber Creek town centre.

> **PD** *Supplies, caravan park, mechanical repairs. Annual race meeting each September. Camping at Big Horse Creek 8 km west of the town: picnic tables, barbecues, pit toilets. Enquire about picnic areas and fishing spots at the Timber Creek Information Centre or the CCNT Timber Creek Ranger Station. Permit required to traverse Gregory National Park.*

REVERSE DIRECTIONS START ▲ 0.0 km

TIMBER CREEK
«»
BULLITA OUTSTATION

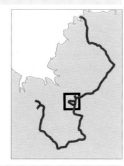

START POINT
Map page 26, E2.

TOTAL KM 129.
UNSEALED KM 119.
DEGREE OF DIFFICULTY Extreme. *See Warnings.*
DRIVING TIME 8 hours.
LONGEST DISTANCE NO FUEL 346 km (Timber Creek to Kalkarindji, 2 sections on).
TOPOGRAPHIC MAPS 1:250 000 series: *Delamere*; *Victoria River Downs*. See also 1:100 000 series.
LOCAL/SPECIALITY MAPS DPIF: *Northern Territory Fishing Map*; Auslig: *Northern Australia*.
OTHER USEFUL INFORMATION CCNT visitor information sheets: *Gregory National Park*; *Gregory National Park: Bullita Sector*.

DESCRIPTION This trip penetrates into the remote interior of Gregory National Park. Sparsely covered by eucalypts and tall grasses, the country is broken by limestone hills, jagged sandstone escarpments and flat-topped ranges. *Limestone Gorge Camping Area*, 59 kilometres from Timber Creek, is set among flinty limestone blocks and karsts. There is a scenic walking track along one of the rugged ridges and a swimming hole on Limestone Creek. *Bullita Outstation* is situated 17 kilometres from the gorge on the East Baines River which stops running early in the dry season leaving a chain of waterholes. There is a shady camping ground near the old homestead, now the Bullita Ranger Station. Ask the ranger for information on the Bullita Stockroute loop track which starts and ends at the homestead. Sections of this track are extremely difficult and a permit is required (*see Warnings* and *Bookings and*

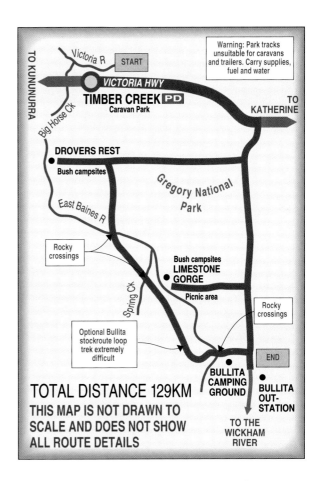

TOTAL DISTANCE 129KM
THIS MAP IS NOT DRAWN TO SCALE AND DOES NOT SHOW ALL ROUTE DETAILS

Permits). The easier option is to return to the Victoria Highway and continue 228 kilometres to Kununurra, via Timber Creek.

The Bullita Stockroute loop track follows the old route used by stockmen droving cattle herds to the Wyndham Meatworks. It crosses the East Baines River before descending into Spring Valley past boab and nut trees and terraced limestone hills. Wild donkeys, brumbies, cattle, buffalo and noisy Little Corella parrots are a common sight. The park's rich pastoral history is evident at the Spring Creek cattle yards, and at the junction of Spring Creek and the East Baines River where the 'Oriental Hotel' boab trees bears the carving of a stockman who named the tree and campsite after his favourite hotel. There is a bush campsite next to the billabong at *Drovers Rest* where the Auvergne and Bullita stockroutes converged. From here the route heads eastwards into the Barrabarrac Valley to meet up with the Bullita–Victoria Highway road. You can either return to the highway and continue on to Kununurra, or return to Bullita Outstation to follow our next 3 plotted routes. These head southwards to the Wickham River and Kalkarindji before looping back to the Victoria Highway, 36 kilometres from Kununurra.

317

'Oriental Hotel' boab tree on the Bullita Stockroute track

WARNINGS ▶ There are no fuel stops between Timber Creek and Kalkarindji. Take on enough fuel for 400 kilometres minimum at Timber Creek. ▶ Carry adequate supplies of food and water. ▶ Bullita Stockroute loop track is poorly defined and extremely difficult. Follow the picket markers and cairns. During the wet season the track may be closed, particularly December–February ▶ No caravans or trailers in the park. ▶ Crocodiles inhabit coastline and inland waterways in the Northern Territory. Be crocodile-wise. Do not swim.

BOOKINGS AND PERMITS ▶ A permit is required to traverse tracks in Gregory National Park. Obtain at least a month in advance from the CCNT Ranger, Gregory National Park, Victoria Highway, Timber Creek NT 0851; tel. (089) 75 0888; or the CCNT Ranger, Bullita Sector, Gregory National Park, PMB 124, Katherine NT 0851; tel. (089) 75 0833. ▶ Before taking the Bullita Stockroute track call in at the Bullita Ranger Station. Supply details of the intended completion date of your trip. Notify either the Timber Creek or Bullita ranger once you have completed the loop trek. ▶ Camp only in designated areas. Take rubbish with you and observe all park regulations.

ROUTE DIRECTIONS

0.0 km Zero trip meter adjacent to Timber Creek Store on Victoria Hwy facing east. **PD** S'post: Katherine. **SO** along hwy.

Next fuel Kalkarindji (346 km).

(10.0 km) ▲ 50.2 km
10.0 km S'post: Bullita. **TR** onto gravel.
(6.6 km) ▲ 40.2 km
16.6 km Intersection. S'post: Gregory National Park. **SO**.

Warning: park tracks suitable for 4WD vehicles only. No trailers or caravans. Carry drinking water.

(33.6 km) ▲ 33.6 km
50.2 km Intersection. **SO**.

Limestone Gorge 9 km off to right. Camping and picnic area in an eroded limestone landscape. Ridge walking track with scenic lookouts. Swimming hole in Limestone Creek. Picnic tables, barbecues, pit toilet, drinking water. Self-register.

318

0.0 km Zero trip meter at above intersection. **SO.**
  (6.7 km) ▲ 0.0 km
  ▲ 7.9 km

6.7 km S'post: Bullita Homestead. **KR.**
  (0.6 km) ▲ 1.2 km
7.3 km Intersection. **SO.**

Bullita Camping Ground 300 m to right on East Baines River. Picnic area: tables, barbecues, pit toilet, drinking water.

  (0.6 km) ▲ 0.6 km
7.9 km Bullita Homestead Ranger Station.

  ▲ 0.0 km

Obtain information and permit for Bullita Stockroute loop trek. Caution: the Bullita loop track is rated extremely difficult. Carry extra supplies of food, water and fuel.

Option: Bullita Stockroute loop trek.
Zero trip meter at Bullita Homestead.
Return to Bullita Camping Ground turnoff.
  (0.6 km)
0.6 km S'post: Camping Ground. **TL.**

Camping ground is 300 m on left.

  (0.3 km)
0.9 km **KL** into East Baines River crossing.

Caution: dry, rocky limestone river bed. Follow markers.

  (21.3 km)
22.2 km Intersection. **KR.**

Giant boab tree marked 'Oriental Hotel' 100 m ahead on right at junction Spring Creek and East Baines River. Old campsite and meeting place used by drovers and musterers, chosen for its good shade and proximity to water.

  (0.1 km)
22.3 km Cross Spring Creek.

Caution: sharp entry, rocky bottom.

  (10.8 km)
33.1 km Cross East Baines River.

Caution: very rocky. Take extreme care. Use low range 4WD.

  (8.1 km)
41.2 km Intersection. S'post: Timber Creek 58.

Tall grass on the Bullita Stockroute track

Drovers Rest 13 km off to left along moderately difficult track. Bush campsites beside billabong. Barbecues only. Fishing.

0.0 km Zero trip meter at above intersection. **TR.**
  (5.0 km)
5.0 km Intersection. **KR.**
  (6.4 km)
11.4 km Intersection. **SO.**
  (17.9 km)
29.3 km T intersection.

Timber Creek 34 km off to left. Bullita Ranger Station 20 km off to right.

Return to Bullita Outstation to link with next trek section or take the Victoria Hwy to Timber Creek and continue 228 km to Kununurra. Notify Ranger at Timber Creek or Bullita of completion of Bullita Stockroute loop.
End option.
Either pick up optional Bullita Stockroute loop trek directions or take the main park road and **TL** to Timber Creek (58 km).
REVERSE DIRECTIONS START ▲ 0.0 km

BULLITA OUTSTATION «» THE WICKHAM RIVER

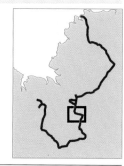

START POINT
Map page 26, E3.

TOTAL KM 84.
UNSEALED KM 84.
DEGREE OF DIFFICULTY Difficult.
DRIVING TIME 5 hours.
LONGEST DISTANCE NO FUEL No fuel this section.
TOPOGRAPHIC MAPS Auslig 1:250 000 series: *Victoria River Downs*; *Waterloo*. See also 1:100 000 series.
LOCAL/SPECIALITY MAPS DPIF: *Northern Territory Fishing Map*; Auslig: *Northern Australia*.
OTHER USEFUL INFORMATION CCNT visitor information sheet: *Gregory National Park: Bullita Sector*.

DESCRIPTION From Bullita Outstation the Humbert Track heads south along the old packhorse trail which connected Bullita with Humbert River Station in the 1940s. It is a difficult and poorly defined track that passes fascinating mesa-topped hills and negotiates rugged limestone ridges through thick scrub before taking you out of Gregory National Park to the banks of the *Wickham River*, where you can choose a bush campsite.

WARNINGS ▶ There are no fuel stops this section. Next fuel Kalkarindji. ▶ The Humbert Track is poorly defined and difficult. Follow the picket markers. No caravans or trailers. ▶ Carry adequate supplies of food and water. ▶ Take all rubbish with you. Observe all park regulations.

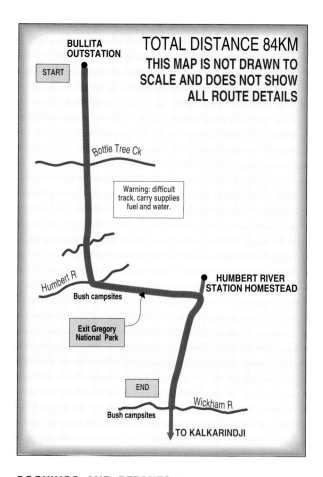

BOOKINGS AND PERMITS ▶ Obtain a permit to traverse the Humbert Track from CCNT Ranger, Gregory National Park, Victoria Highway, Timber Creek NT 0851; tel. (089) 75 0888; or CCNT Ranger, Bullita Sector, Gregory National Park, PMB 124, Katherine NT 0851; tel. (089) 75 0833.

ROUTE DIRECTIONS

0.0 km Zero trip meter at Bullita Homestead Ranger Station. Depart on track as advised by ranger.
(0.3 km) ▲ 84.0 km
0.3 km Fence line at edge of airstrip. **TR**.
(1.0 km) ▲ 83.7 km
1.3 km Intersection. **TR** onto Humbert Track.
(2.7 km) ▲ 82.7 km
4.0 km Rocky creek crossing.
(4.9 km) ▲ 80.0 km
8.9 km Intersection. **TL** before fenceposts.
(4.3 km) ▲ 75.1 km
13.2 km Cross Bottle Tree Creek.

Creek banks lined with boab trees.

(28.7 km) ▲ 70.8 km

Wild donkeys in Gregory National Park

41.9 km Wide rocky creek crossing.
(3.9 km) ▲ 42.1 km
45.8 km Cross Humbert River.

> *Riverbank bush campsites. River runs a few months in the late wet season leaving waterholes. Fishing, wildlife.*

(19.5 km) ⊥ 39.3 km
65.3 km Gate. Exit Gregory National Park.

> *Leave gate as found.*

(2.4 km) ▲ 18.7 km
67.7 km Gate then **KR**.

> *Humbert River Homestead off to left.*

(0.1 km) ▲ 16.3 km
67.8 km Gate.

> *Leave as found.*

(0.3 km) ▲ 16.2 km
68.1 km Intersection. **KR**.

> *Airstrip on left.*

(5.6 km) ▲ 15.9 km
73.7 km Gate.

> *Leave as found.*

(4.0 km) ▲ 10.3 km
77.7 km Intersection, **KR**,
(5.7 km) ▲ 6.3 km
83.4 km Gate.

> *Leave as found.*

(0.6 km) ▲ 0.6 km
84.0 km Cross Wickham River.

> *Riverbank bush campsites. Fishing. Abundant wildlife.*

REVERSE DIRECTIONS START ▲ 0.0 km

THE WICKHAM RIVER «» KALKARINDJI

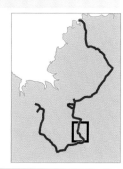

START POINT
Map page 26, E5.

TOTAL KM 133.
UNSEALED KM 126.
DEGREE OF DIFFICULTY Difficult.
DRIVING TIME 5 hours.
LONGEST DISTANCE NO FUEL Fuel at Kalkarindji.
TOPOGRAPHIC MAPS Auslig 1:250 000 series: *Waterloo*; *Wave Hill*. See also 1:100 000 series.
LOCAL/SPECIALITY MAP DPIF: *Northern Territory Fishing Map*; Auslig: *Northern Australia*.
OTHER USEFUL INFORMATION RACQ: *Northern Territory Guide*.

DESCRIPTION This trip continues south through Humbert River and Mt Sanford cattle stations to the small Aboriginal township of Kalkarindji, on Daguragu Aboriginal Land. The first 60 kilometres are difficult as the track is seldom used and often follows creek beds and embankments. At Mt Sanford Station the track joins a well-maintained gravel road to complete the drive into Kalkarindji.

WARNING ▶ The track from the Wickham River to Mt Sanford Homestead is poorly defined, following creek beds and embankments.

BOOKINGS AND PERMITS ▶ Do not enter Daguragu Aboriginal community without a permit, obtainable from: Central Land Council, PMB 47, Kalkarindji NT 0851; tel. (089) 75 0855. ▶ To book at Kalkarindji Service Station Caravan Park tel. (089) 75 0788.

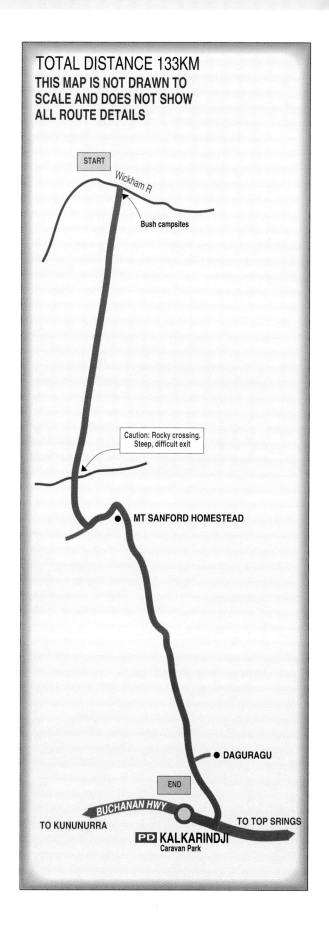

TOTAL DISTANCE 133KM
THIS MAP IS NOT DRAWN TO SCALE AND DOES NOT SHOW ALL ROUTE DETAILS

START

Wickham R

Bush campsites

Caution: Rocky crossing. Steep, difficult exit

● MT SANFORD HOMESTEAD

● DAGURAGU

END

BUCHANAN HWY

TO KUNUNURRA

TO TOP SRINGS

PD KALKARINDJI
Caravan Park

ROUTE DIRECTIONS

0.0 km Zero trip meter on southern embankment of Wickham River heading south. **SO**.

(0.4 km) ▲ 133.0 km

0.4 km Y intersection. **KR**.

(2.7 km) ▲ 132.0 km

3.1 km Gate.

> Leave as found.

(7.0 km) ▲ 130.0 km

10.1 km Gate.

> Leave as found.

(2.1 km) ▲ 123.0 km

12.2 km Gate.

> Leave as found.

(13.2 km) ▲ 120.9 km

25.4 km Cross creek.

> Caution: rocky bed. Difficult steep exit.

(1.2 km) ▲ 107.7 km

26.6 km Gate.

> Leave as found.

(33.7 km) ▲ 106.5 km

60.3 km Gate.

> Leave as found.

(1.9 km) ▲ 72.8 km

62.2 km Gate.

> Leave as found. Airstrip on right.

(0.2 km) ▲ 70.9 km

62.4 km T intersection. **TL**.

> Mt Sanford Homestead off to right.

(0.1 km) ▲ 70.7 km

62.5 km Gate.

> Leave as found.

(3.6 km) ▲ 70.6 km

66.1 km Gate.

> Leave as found.

(8.2 km) ▲ 67.0 km

74.3 km Gate.

> Leave as found.

(3.3 km) ▲ 58.8 km

77.6 km Gate.

Mt Sanford

> Leave as found.

(16.2 km) ▲ 55.5 km

93.8 km Gate.

> Leave as found.

(0.4 km) ▲ 39.3 km

94.2 km Gate.

> Leave as found.

(14.5 km) ▲ 38.9 km

108.7 km Gate.

> Leave as found. Daguragu Aboriginal community off to left. Vehicles not permitted to carry alcohol.

(16.8 km) ▲ 24.4 km

125.5 km T intersection. **TR** onto bitumen.

(7.5 km) Gravel ▲ 7.6 km

133.0 km T intersection. **TR** onto Buchanan Hwy. **SO**.

(0.1 km) ▲ 0.1 km

133.1 km Kalkarindji Service Station Caravan Park.

> **PD** Supplies, caravan park. Small aboriginal community. Gemstone prospecting at Wave Hill Station No. 22 Bore, 9 km from Kalkarindji. Ask for details at service station.

REVERSE DIRECTIONS START ▲ 0.0 km

KALKARINDJI
«»
KUNUNURRA

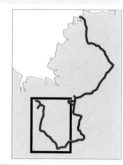

START POINT
Map page 26, E6.

TOTAL KM 472.
UNSEALED KM 426.
DEGREE OF DIFFICULTY Easy.
DRIVING TIME 8 hours.
LONGEST DISTANCE NO FUEL Fuel at Kununurra.
TOPOGRAPHIC MAPS Auslig 1: 250 000 series: *Umbunya*; *Auvergne*; *Cambridge Gulf*. See also 1:100 000 series.
LOCAL/SPECIALITY MAPS Auslig: *Northern Australia*.
OTHER USEFUL INFORMATION CCNT visitor information sheet: *Keep River National Park*; Western Australian Tourism Commission booklet: *Western Australia's Unique North*.

DESCRIPTION Magnificent flat-topped (mesa) hills border the road as you approach Mistake Creek Station from Kalkarindji. This is a long trip on unsealed roads of good quality. Once on the Victoria Highway (3 kilometres before the Western Australian border) you are offered a diversion into Keep River National Park, noted for its rugged escarpments and striking sandstone formations. It is an area significant in the Dreamtime legends of the Mirriwung and Gadjerong Aborigines. The park road takes you past Cockatoo Lagoon, Nganalam art site and Keep River Gorge, to *Gurrandalng* and *Jarrnarm* camping areas. Bush camping is permitted with approval from the ranger.

Just over the border is the turnoff to the Argyle Downs Homestead Museum and *Lake Argyle Tourist Village*. The museum was once the home of the pioneering Durack family who were the area's first settlers in the late 1800s. Massive Lake Argyle is the main storage reservoir for the Ord River Irrigation Scheme which harnesses the waters of Kimberley region rivers for irrigation. The caravan park and motel overlook the lake which is dotted with islands and fringed

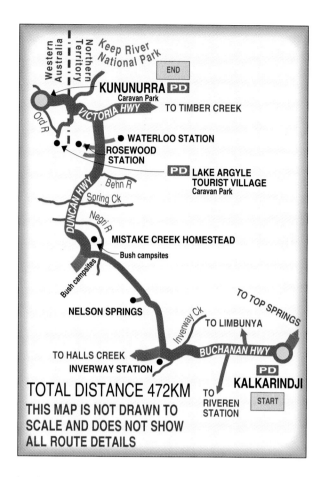

TOTAL DISTANCE 472KM
THIS MAP IS NOT DRAWN TO
SCALE AND DOES NOT SHOW
ALL ROUTE DETAILS

by the rugged red slopes of mountains that covered the area before the lake and dam were built. Take a cruise on one of the largest constructed lakes in the southern hemisphere.

Kununurra (meaning 'big water') sits alongside Lake Kununurra on the Ord River and is the administrative and residential centre for the Argyle Diamond Mine and the Ord River Irrigation Scheme. The town has a number of caravan parks. Hidden Valley National Park, 2.5 kilometres east of the town, is for day visitors only.

WARNINGS ▶ Observe quarantine regulations when entering Western Australia. ▶ Crocodiles inhabit coastline and inland waterways in the Northern Territory and Western Australia. Be crocodile-wise. Do not swim.

BOOKINGS AND PERMITS ▶ A camping permit is required at Keep River National Park. Obtain at Ranger Station or self-register. For advance information contact the Ranger, Keep River National Park; tel. (091) 67 8827. ▶ To book at Lake Argyle contact Lake Argyle Tourist Village, PO Box 111, Kununurra NT 6743; tel. (091) 68 7360; or Ord Tourist Bureau, 75 Coolibah Drive, Kununurra; PO Box 446, Kununurra NT 6743; tel. (091) 68 1177.

Nganalam art site, Keep River National Park

ROUTE DIRECTIONS

0.0 km   Zero trip meter adjacent to Kalkarindji Service Station on Buchanan Hwy heading west. **SO**.
      (0.9 km)   ▲ 426.6 km
0.9 km   Gravel.
      (85.0 km)   Bitumen. ▲ 425.7 km
85.9 km   Intersection. **SO**.

> Limbunya 60 km off to right.

      (10.3 km)   ▲ 340.7 km
96.2 km   Intersection. **SO**.

> Riveren Station 42 km off to left.

      (55.4 km)   ▲ 330.4 km
151.6 km   Cross Inverway Creek.

> Inverway Station off to left.

      (0.9 km)   ▲ 275.0 km
152.5 km   S'post: Nelsons Springs. **TR**.
      (11.3 km)   ▲ 274.1 km

163.8 km   Gate.

> Leave as found.

      (7.2 km)   ▲ 262.8 km
171.0 km   Gate.

> Leave as found.

      (5.6 km)   ▲ 255.6 km
176.6 km   Intersection. **KL**.
      (58.0 km)   ▲ 250.0 km
234.6 km   Intersection. **SO**.

> Nelson Springs 2 km off to left.

      (19.4 km)   ▲ 192.0 km
254.0 km   Intersection. **KL**.
      (4.6 km)   ▲ 172.6 km
258.6 km   Cross Negri River.

> Riverbank bush campsites.

      (3.0 km)   ▲ 168.0 km
261.6 km   T intersection. **TR** onto Duncan Rd.
      (14.4 km)   Opp. dir. s'post: Inverway 105. ▲165.0 km
276.0 km   Intersection. **SO**.

Brolga Dreaming Camping Area, Keep River National Park

Mistake Creek Station off to right.	
(6.2 km)	▲ 150.6 km

282.0 km Negri River. Cross causeway.

Riverbank bush campsites.	
(42.4 km)	▲ 144.4 km

324.6 km Spring Creek. Cross causeway.
(27.6 km) ▲ 102.0 km

352.2 km Behn River. Cross causeway.
(6.0 km) ▲ 74.4 km

358.2 km Intersection. **SO.**

Argyle Downs Homestead 6 km off to left.	
(10.9 km)	▲ 68.4 km

369.1 km Intersection. **SO.**

Rosewood Station 3 km off to left.	
(1.5 km)	▲ 57.5 km

370.6 km Intersection. **SO.**

Waterloo Station 38 km off to right.	
(45.1 km)	▲ 56.0 km

415.7 km S'post: Kununurra. **TL** onto bitumen: Victoria Hwy.
(10.9 km) Gravel. ▲ 10.9 km
▲ 0.0 km

426.6 km Intersection.
Option: Keep River National Park.

0.0 km Zero trip meter at above intersection on Victoria Hwy. **TR.**
(2.1 km)

2.1 km Cockatoo Lagoon Walking Track on right.
(0.5 km)

2.6 km Intersection. **SO.**

Ranger Station 100 m on right: park information. Ask about location of drinking water.

(12.3 km)

14.9 km Intersection. **SO.**

Gurrandalng Camping Area 3 km off to left: picnic tables, barbecues, pit toilets. Walking tracks. Self-register.

(7.7 km)

22.6 km Intersection. **SO**.

> *Keep River Gorge 1 km off to right. Good walking track through sandstone gorge.*

(3.1 km)

25.7 km Car park on left. **SO**.

> *Ten-minute walk to Nganalam Aboriginal art site.*

(5.5 km)

31.2 km Jarrnarm Camping Area.

> *Walking tracks. Picnic tables, barbecues, pit toilets.*

Return to Victoria Hwy via the same route.
End option.

0.0 km Zero trip meter at Keep River National Park turnoff on Victoria Hwy heading west. **SO**.
(3.0 km)   ▲ 0.0 km
                                 ▲ 9.8 km

3.0 km Western Australia border. **SO**.

> *Observe quarantine regulations. Adjust watches.*

(6.8 km)   ▲ 6.8 km
                                 ▲ 0.0 km

9.8 km Intersection.
Option: Lake Argyle Tourist Village.

0.0 km Zero trip meter at above intersection on Victoria Hwy. **TL**.
(23.8 km)

23.8 km Ray Walkers Bush Camp.

> *Private accommodation.*

(9.1 km)

32.9 km Argyle Downs Homestead Museum.

> *Reconstructed pioneer homestead, relocated when Ord River Dam was built. Historical museum serves as a memorial to the Duracks, the Kimberley region's first settlers. Patsy Durack finished building Argyle Downs in 1895.*

(1.3 km)

34.2 km Lake Argyle Tourist Village.

> **PD** *Caravan park, hotel/motel overlooking Lake Argyle. Cruises and fishing trips on Australia's largest constructed lake: the Ord River Scheme's main reservoir.*

Return to Victoria Hwy via the same route.
End option.

Lake Argyle

0.0 km Zero trip meter at Lake Argyle Tourist Village turnoff on Victoria Hwy heading west. **SO**.
(35.7 km)   ▲ 0.0 km
                                  ▲ 35.7 km

35.7 km Kununurra.

> **PD** *Caravan parks, supplies, mechanical repairs. Small town near Lake Kununurra on the Ord River originally settled to service the Ord River irrigation project. Cruises on the lake and upstream past the Everglades and magnificent rugged gorges. Access to Kellys Knob scenic lookout and Hidden Valley National Park: day visits only. Ord River Festival is held each August.*

REVERSE DIRECTIONS START ▲ 0.0 km

THE KIMBERLEY
KUNUNURRA
«»
BROOME
2501 KILOMETRES

Emma Gorge

KUNUNURRA «» PURNULULU   616 km

KUNUNURRA «» EL QUESTRO STATION   222 km

EL QUESTRO STATION «» MINERS POOL   290 km

Saltwater (estuarine) crocodile

MINERS POOL «» MITCHELL FALLS   188 km

MITCHELL FALLS «» ADCOCK GORGE   393 km

ADCOCK GORGE «» BROOME   792 km

Freshwater crocodile

The Kimberley is a timeless and varied land that requires at least 2 weeks to explore. You have to be totally self-sufficient and your vehicle well equipped. Read our route directions carefully before setting out; check your winch and spare parts. Most importantly, do not attempt this trek during the wet season, November–March, when unsealed roads become impassable, national parks and natural attractions inaccessible. Travel only during the dry season, April–October, preferably as soon after the end of the wet as is possible to take a vehicle along the few accessible tracks. During the dry season the region progressively dries out and becomes harsher until around mid-October when water is very scarce and the country takes on a lean, brown look.

Our trek covers the Kimberley's 3 main geographical districts commencing with Purnululu National Park in the south-east, a transition zone between the desert and the north Kimberley. We then wind across the north from Kununurra and the tidal flats of Wyndham to the

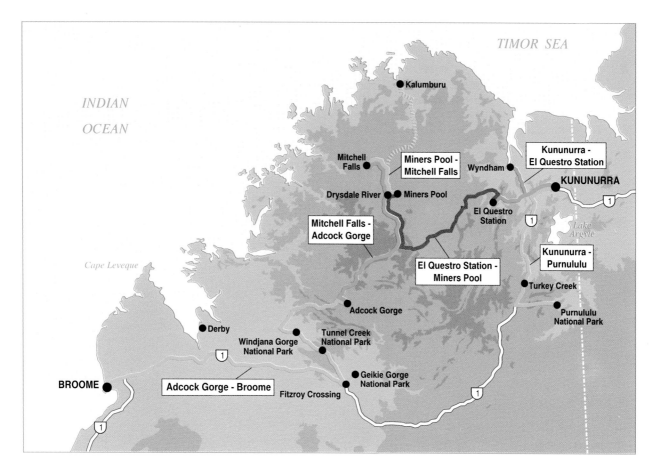

Drysdale River and Mitchell Plateau areas and, optionally, Kalumburu Aboriginal Reserve on the coast. The north is a combination of sandstone ranges, ancient volcanic rocks, open woodlands, mangrove swamps and lush vegetation around watercourses. Finally we move on to the west where an ancient limestone barrier reef has eroded to form many of the gorges and caves for which the Kimberley is famous. Nowhere else in Australia is there such a concentration of diverse gorges – pockets of cool water within magnificent ranges. Some gorges are located in national parks, others on private property in which case landowners usually allow camping for a small fee. We leave the western district at the large sandy plains of Broome and the Dampier Peninsula, an extension of the Great Sandy Desert.

HOW TO BE CROCODILE-WISE

Of the two crocodile species found in Australia's north, the saltwater or estuarine crocodile is dangerous. It lives in salt water and fresh water, usually in tidal sections of rivers and creeks, floodplain waterholes and freshwater swamps and is found as far inland as 100 kilometres.

The freshwater crocodile, while not dangerous, can deliver a savage bite if interfered with. Treat all crocodiles longer than 1.5 metres as dangerous, and obey the following rules.

▶ *Seek local advice before swimming, camping, fishing or boating.*

▶ *Swim, canoe and use small boats only in shallow rapids.*
▶ *Watch children and pets in the water or at the water's edge where large crocodiles might live.*
▶ *Fill a bucket with water and prepare food or clean fish at least 5 metres from the water's edge.*
▶ *Do not lean from boats or hang articles over the edge.*
▶ *When fishing stand at least a few metres back from the water's edge. Do not stand on overhanging logs.*
▶ *Burn or remove from your campsite food scraps, fish offal and other wastes.*

CAMPING Fortunately, beautiful campsites are plentiful in the Kimberley because once you leave behind the townships at each end there are neither caravan parks nor motels along the way. Some sections of road are unsuitable for caravans and/or trailers. The national parks have neither powered caravan sites nor hot water but some have campsites. Some landowners provide campsites, homestead accommodation and/or tours to the more remote regions.

ROADS Two major roads traverse the Kimberley. The Great Northern Highway skirts around the southern boundary and is bitumen all the way. The Gibb River Road cuts across the centre and is a formed natural-earth road, therefore more demanding. It is a beef route linking the ports of Derby and Wyndham. Maintenance is better early in the dry season, than later, when corrugations and occasional bulldust patches appear. Our long option to Kalumburu Mission and the spectacular Kimberley coastline is via another red-earth road, Gibb River–Kalumburu Road. Heavy rain usually makes these unsealed roads impassable bogs or flowing creeks.

FUEL Fuel at the townships is reasonably cheap, but at the homesteads and roadhouses it can be very expensive – $1 or more per litre. For the option to Kalumburu, fuel is available only at Drysdale River

CODE OF ETHICS FOR THE KIMBERLEY

We do not venture into the most wild and remote places in the Kimberley that constitute Australia's last great wilderness. They are extremely fragile and sensitive to human disturbance and are important refuges for a multitude of animals and plants. Patches of rainforest are the most biologically sensitive areas. During your visit you should, however, treat the whole Kimberley region as ecologically fragile.

Many Aboriginal people live in small communities and on reserves and missions. You must obtain a permit before visiting the Kalumburu Reserve, check at Mt Barnett Roadhouse before visiting the Kupingarri community, and ring the various Dampier Peninsula communities before visiting them. Remember, too, that much of the outback Kimberley is privately owned cattle country. The following code of ethics applies universally to national parks, public land and private property.

▶ *Many Aboriginal sites have deep cultural and historical significance; never touch, damage or remove anything.*

▶ *Drive along formed roads and tracks, follow signs and do not make your own path through the bush.*

▶ *Bushwalk only along defined tracks and be especially careful not to trample sensitive areas with sand-dune plants, steep slopes or sparse vegetation.*

▶ *Preferably bring your portable gas stove and do not light fires except in barbecues or established fireplaces. Extinguish fires completely.*

▶ *Camp only in designated camping areas and camp away from watercourses to avoid erosion, compaction and pollution of soil.*

▶ *Bathe, brush your teeth and wash dishes at least 50 metres away from creeks and lakes. Use sand instead of detergent to wash dishes.*

▶ *In a national park use pit toilets if provided. Otherwise bury your waste in a 15-centimetre deep hole at least 100 metres away from campsite and water.*

▶ *Place rubbish in bins provided or take it away with you. Do not throw rubbish or food scraps into rivers or creeks.*

▶ *Pets, firearms and spearguns are prohibited in national parks. A permit is required to keep or move wildlife and flora. Beware wildlife on roads.*

▶ *Fishing regulations apply in national parks. Do not fish in sanctuary zones, and conserve fish numbers by taking enough only for your immediate needs.*

▶ *When driving on roads passing through pastoral leases beware livestock on roads.*

▶ *Call at homesteads to obtain landowners' permission before leaving main roads to enter pastoral leases. Keep off station roads when wet.*

▶ *Leave all gates as found and do not cut, remove or drive over fences.*

▶ *Obtain landowners' permission before shooting animals or taking dogs onto properties.*

▶ *Obtain landowners' permission before lighting fires on properties.*

▶ *Do not interfere with livestock or their watering facilities.*

▶ *Do not swim in private water tanks.*

USEFUL INFORMATION

For touring information contact:
Western Australian Tourist Centre
Albert Facey House
Cnr Forrest Place and Wellington Street
Perth 6000
(09) 483 1111.

(Addresses and telephone numbers for the local touring information centres are included in route directions.)

For information about national parks and nature reserves contact:
CALM Kimberley Regional Office
Messmate Way
PO Box 942, Kununurra WA 6743
(091) 68 0200.

CALM West Kimberley District Office
Herbert Street
PO Box 65, Broome WA 6725
(091) 92 1036.

For motoring information contact:
The Royal Automobile Club of Western Australia
   Inc. (RAC)
228 Adelaide Terrace
Perth 6000
(09) 421 4444.

For four-wheel driving information contact:
Western Australian Association of Four Wheel
   Drive Clubs Inc.
PO Box 6029, East Perth 6004

For medical attention contact:
Royal Flying Doctor Service
60 Clarendon Street
PO Box 52, Derby WA 6728
(091) 91 1211.

Wyndham District Hospital
1270 Minderoo Street
PO Box 230, Wyndham WA 6740
(091) 61 1104.

Traditional Aboriginal dancers, Kimberley

Lower Manning Gorge

Homestead and Kalumburu town centre. For the trek sections that start and end at Mitchell Falls, Drysdale River Homestead is the only fuel stop – there is no fuel on the Mitchell Plateau.

ROYAL FLYING DOCTOR SERVICE As this is a remote area you should carry high frequency radio. Before you leave, register with the RFDS, and obtain the guide listing bases, radio call signs and broadcast frequencies. For information, contact RFDS, PO Box 345, Hurstville NSW 2220; tel. (02) 580 9711.

KUNUNURRA
«»
PURNULULU

START POINT
Map page 37, R5.

TOTAL KM 616.
UNSEALED KM 106.
DEGREE OF DIFFICULTY Moderate.
DRIVING TIME 10 hours over minimum 4 days.
LONGEST DISTANCE NO FUEL 216 km (Turkey Creek Roadhouse to Purnululu and return).
TOPOGRAPHIC MAPS Auslig 1:250 000 series: *Cambridge Gulf; Lissadell; Dixon Range*. See also 1:100 000 series.
LOCAL/SPECIALITY MAPS StreetSmart Touring Map: *East Kimberley; Robinson's Western Australia*.
OTHER USEFUL INFORMATION Western Australian Tourism Commission booklet: *Western Australia's Unique North*; CALM booklet: *North-West Bound: From Shark Bay to Wyndham*; CALM brochure: *Bungle Bungle National Park*.

DESCRIPTION Our first Kimberley trek section leaves the 'Around Australia' route for an optional diversion to Purnululu National Park with its amazing Bungle Bungle massif and gorge system. Access to the park's most spectacular features is extremely limited and many people choose to see them by helicopter or fixed-wing aircraft. However, the four-wheel drive venture into the park is well worth the effort.

This national park is a remote wilderness covering 3000 square kilometres. It has no facilities and requires total self-sufficiency. *Bellburn* and *Kurrajong* campsites are popular. You could also camp overnight at *Cathedral Gorge* after an easy walk or, if an adventurous and fit backpacker, at *Piccaninny Gorge* after 2 days of exploration.

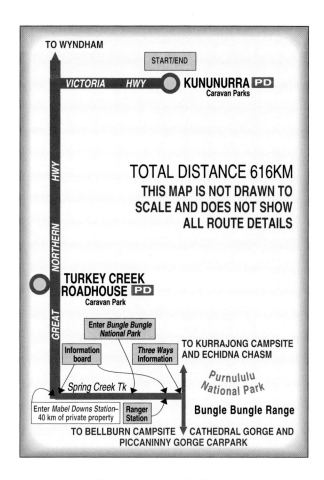

TO WYNDHAM

START/END

VICTORIA HWY ○ **KUNUNURRA** PD
Caravan Parks

NORTHERN HWY

TOTAL DISTANCE 616KM
THIS MAP IS NOT DRAWN TO SCALE AND DOES NOT SHOW ALL ROUTE DETAILS

GREAT

○ **TURKEY CREEK ROADHOUSE** PD
Caravan Park

Enter Bungle Bungle National Park

Information board

Three Ways Information

TO KURRAJONG CAMPSITE AND ECHIDNA CHASM

Purnululu National Park

Spring Creek Tk

Enter *Mabel Downs Station*– 40 km of private property | *Ranger Station*

Bungle Bungle Range

TO BELLBURN CAMPSITE ▼ CATHEDRAL GORGE AND PICCANINNY GORGE CARPARK

Approached from an aircraft the Bungle Bungle massif is an imposing sight: orange and black tiger stripes across beehive-like mounds encased in a silica and lichen skin. Euros and nabarleks are rumoured to live on top of the massif. Elsewhere in the park you will see nailtail wallabies, green tree frogs and more than 130 bird species including rainbow bee-eaters and budgerigars.

In the Kija language 'Purnululu' means sandstone, and the Purnululu Aboriginal camp was re-established in the area several years ago. Many Aboriginal artworks and burial sites date back millennia.

WARNINGS ▶ Camping and fires prohibited on Mabel Downs Station 40 kilometres from Great Northern Highway to national-park boundary. ▶ Spring Creek Track leading to national park unsuitable for caravans and trailers. ▶ Do not embark during wet season; national park closed January–March or longer, depending on weather. ▶ Bushwalks to most significant gorges require overnight camping; advise ranger before setting out. Carry your own water. Wear hat and apply sunscreen. ▶ No facilities in national park; be totally self-sufficient. ▶ Ord River and many creeks dry most

Vehicle bogged in sand, Piccaninny Creek Road

of year; little running water for swimming except occasional rock pools. ► Stay on established tracks and camp only in designated areas to prevent erosion. ► Access at massif restricted to creek beds. Climbing 'beehives' prohibited. ► Do not touch fragile and easily damaged rock formations. ► Do not touch, damage or remove any item you encounter at Aboriginal sites.

BOOKINGS AND PERMITS ► Entry and camping fees apply at national park; pay at ranger station on site. ► For information about Purnululu National Park and helicopter tours from Kurrajong Campsite contact CALM Kimberley Regional Office, Messmate Way, Kununurra WA 6743; PO Box 942, Kununurra WA 6743; tel. (091) 68 0200. ► For information about helicopter and fixed-wing aircraft tours of national park from Kununurra contact Kununurra Visitors Centre, Coolibah Drive, Kununurra WA 6743; tel. (091) 68 1177. ► For information about national park and Halls Creek region contact Halls Creek Information Centre, Great Northern Highway, Halls Creek WA 6770; tel. (091) 68 6262 May–September; tel. (091) 68 6164 October–April.

▼▼▼▼▼▼▼▼

TAKE CARE

● Permits are required if you want to divert off public roads within Aboriginal Land areas.

● Carry additional water in desert areas: 5 litres per person per day is recommended, plus extra for the radiator.

● In Australia's north, during the wet season (October–May) roads become impassable. Check conditions before setting out.

● Don't take short cuts over virgin ground. You will destroy the vegetation. Stick to tracks open for use.

333

ROUTE DIRECTIONS

0.0 km Zero trip meter at Messmate Way and Victoria Hwy intersection in Kununurra. S'post: Wyndham. **SO** along Victoria Hwy heading west.

> **PD** *Supplies, caravan parks. Helicopter and fixed-wing aircraft tours to Purnululu National Park.*

(45.6 km)

45.6 km S'post: Halls Creek. **TL** onto Great Northern Hwy.

(154.5 km)

200.1 km Turkey Creek Roadhouse on right. **SO**.

> **PD** *Caravan park, accomm., meals.*

(54.8 km)

254.9 km S'post: Purnululu (Bungle Bungle) National Park 53. **TL** onto gravel: Spring Creek Track.

> *4WD track only. Caravans and trailers prohibited.*

(0.3 km)

255.2 km Information board on right. **SO**.

> *Enter Mabel Downs Station, 40 km of private property. Camping and fires prohibited; use only portable gas stove for cooking.*

(40.0 km)

295.2 km Sign: Purnululu (Bungle Bungle) National Park. **SO**.

(11.8 km)

307.0 km Information board on left. **SO**.

> *Ranger station off to right.*

(1.0 km)

308.0 km Three Ways intersection.

> *Information, running water, pit toilets. Turn right 12.6 km to Bellburn Campsite, easy drive. Fresh water, pit toilets. Turn right 26.9 km to Piccaninny Gorge carpark, slow drive along sandy track. Two-day bushwalk. Camp overnight. Bushwalk to Cathedral Gorge 2.5-km return. Camp overnight. Turn left 6 km to Kurrajong Campsite, easy drive. Fresh water, bush shower, pit toilets. Helicopter tours of park. Turn left 19 km to Echidna Chasm carpark, easy drive. No facilities. Easy 3-km return bushwalk.*

Return to Kununurra 308 km via same route for start of next trek section.

Water pump, Bellburn Campsite

Purnululu National Park

KUNUNURRA

«»

EL QUESTRO STATION

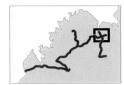

START POINT
Map page 37, R5.

TOTAL KM 222.
UNSEALED KM 115.
DEGREE OF DIFFICULTY Difficult.
DRIVING TIME 5 hours.
LONGEST DISTANCE NO FUEL 121 km (Wyndham to El Questro Station).
TOPOGRAPHIC MAP Auslig 1:250 000 series: *Cambridge Gulf.* See also 1:100 000 series.
LOCAL/SPECIALITY MAPS StreetSmart Touring Map: *East Kimberley; Robinson's Western Australia.*
OTHER USEFUL INFORMATION Western Australian Tourism Commission booklets: *Western Australia's Unique North* and *Drive North*; CALM booklet: *North-West Bound: From Shark Bay to Wyndham; El Questro Station, East Kimberley* information folder.

DESCRIPTION This trek section takes you across the mud flats of the King and Pentecost rivers and around the outskirts of the Cockburn Range. From Kununurra to Wyndham the road winds through magnificent ancient gorge country.

Wyndham is the state's most northerly town and safest port harbour, as well as an important centre for the east Kimberley pastoral and mining-exploration areas. The town greets you with a 'Big Croc' sculpture symbolising the saltwater crocodiles that inhabit Cambridge Gulf.

Along King River Road you can visit natural-ochre Aboriginal cave paintings of spiritual figures and animals and picnic in the small clearing at Moochalabra Dam. The Prison Tree that marks the beginning of Old

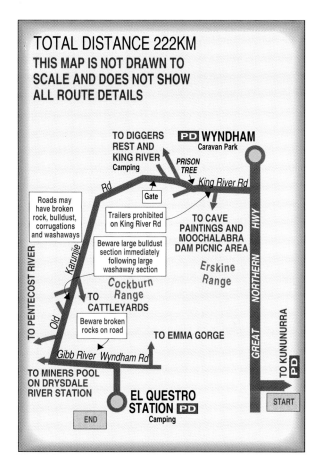

Karunjie Road is an impressive 8 metre-high boab tree. The hole at its base was originally cut to allow entry to the hollow interior, once used by local police as a natural lockup.

Diggers Rest is a small private cattle station that was once a meatworks and pumping station. Enjoy camping or homestead accommodation, horseriding treks, fishing in the King River and tributaries, birdwatching around the billabongs and in May–June, the cattle muster. You then skirt around the Cockburn Range and cattleyards and move on to Gibb River–Wyndham Road, a 667-kilometre road-train route that carries beef cattle from isolated stations to Derby and Wyndham ports.

In the heart of the Kimberley outback, the stunning *El Questro Station* private resort takes you by surprise. Set in lush vegetation, the homestead has several types of accommodation including camping and a caravan park. The fresh water of the Pentecost River is suitable for swimming, boating and fishing, and you can bushwalk up the red-rock escarpments of El Questro Gorge. Emma Gorge, still part of El Questro Station, is a few kilometres further along Gibb River–Wyndham Road and the site of another private resort.

335

Zebedee Springs, El Questro Station

WARNINGS ▶ King River and Old Karunjie roads are little used and difficult four-wheel drive tracks with sections of broken rock, bulldust and washaways. Contact Wyndham police station (091) 61 1055, for information about road conditions. Bogging most likely during wet–hot season December–March. ▶ Trailers prohibited on King River Road due to steep inclines on creek banks. ▶ Gibb River–Wyndham Road traverses northern section of El Questro Station: beware livestock on track. ▶ Gibb River–Wyndham Road a gravel surface: broken rocks may puncture tyres. Have spare tyres ready. ▶ Crocodiles inhabit coastline and inland waterways including King and Pentecost rivers. Be crocodile-wise. Do not swim. ▶ No swimming, boating, fishing or camping at Moochalabra Dam – Wyndham's water supply. ▶ Fresh water scarce during dry season April–September; bring drinking water.

BOOKINGS AND PERMITS ▶ For all information, contact Kununurra Visitors Centre, PO Box 446, Kununurra WA 6743; tel. (091) 68 1177 or Wyndham Tourist Information Centre, Old Port Post Office, O'Donnell Street, Wyndham Port WA 6741; tel. (091) 61 1054.

ROUTE DIRECTIONS

Depart Kununurra south-west 45 km via Victoria Hwy. **PD** Turn right at T intersection onto Great Northern Hwy 56 km to Wyndham East.

0.0 km Zero trip meter at Great Northern Hwy and Welch St intersection in Wyndham East. **SO** along Great Northern Hwy heading south.

> **PD** *Supplies, caravan park. Post office on left, adjacent to Koolinda Street.*

(5.9 km) ▲ 24.0 km
5.9 km S'post: King River Rd. **TR** onto gravel.
(18.1 km) Bitumen. ▲ 18.1 km
24.0 km Intersection. S'post: Cave Paintings 0.6/Moochalabra Dam 1.2.

> *Turn left 0.6 km to cave paintings and 1.2 km to dam, picnic area and barbecues. No picnic tables or toilets. Swimming, boating, fishing and camping prohibited.*

0.0 km   Zero trip meter at above intersection. **SO**.

       (5.0 km) ▲ 0.0 km

       ▲ 97.3 km

5.0 km   S'post: Prison Tree. **KR**.

> *No through road on left.*

       (0.6 km) ▲ 92.3 km

5.6 km   Prison Tree on right. **SO** onto Old Karunjie Rd.

       (0.2 km) ▲ 91.7 km

5.8 km   Y intersection. **KR**.

       (2.1 km) ▲ 91.5 km

7.9 km   Y intersection. Homemade s'post: Pentecost River. **KL**.

> *Homemade s'post on right: Diggers Rest. Camping and accomm.*

       (1.7 km) ▲ 89.4 km

9.6 km   Intersection. **KL** through gate.

       (28.6 km) ▲ 87.7 km

38.2 km   Y intersection. **KR**.

> *Road on left leads to cattleyards.*

       (7.7 km) ▲ 59.1 km

45.9 km   Y intersection. **KL**.

> *Beware large bulldust section immediately following large washaway section.*

       (6.7 km) ▲ 51.4 km

52.6 km   Intersection. **KL**.

       (3.3 km) ▲ 44.7 km

55.9 km   Intersection. **KL**.

> *Track on right leads to Pentecost River.*

       (0.2 km) ▲ 41.4 km

56.1 km   **SO** through gate.

> *Leave as found.*

       (1.2 km) ▲ 41.2 km

57.3 km   T intersection. **TL** onto Gibb River–Wyndham Rd.

       (24.0 km) ▲ 40.0 km

81.3 km   Intersection. S'post: El Questro Station Homestead 16. **TR**.

       (16.0 km) ▲ 16.0 km

97.3 km   El Questro Station Homestead.

> **PD** *Limited supplies, caravan park. Private cattle-station resort. Camping on Pentecost River, other accomm. Straight ahead along Gibb River–Wyndham Rd 12 km to Emma Gorge. Walk on left to private resort. Supplies, accomm.*

REVERSE DIRECTIONS START ▲ 0.0 km

Wandjina rock paintings, Chamberlain Gorge

Blue Pool, Emma Gorge

EL QUESTRO STATION «» MINERS POOL

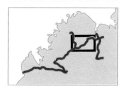

START POINT
Map page 37, Q5.

TOTAL KM 290.
UNSEALED KM 290.
DEGREE OF DIFFICULTY Moderate.
DRIVING TIME 6 hours.
LONGEST DISTANCE NO FUEL 178 km (Durack River Homestead to Drysdale River Homestead).
TOPOGRAPHIC MAPS Auslig 1:250 000 series: *Cambridge Gulf; Ashton; Drysdale*. See also 1:100 000 series.
LOCAL/SPECIALITY MAPS StreetSmart Touring Map: *East Kimberley; Robinson's Western Australia.*
OTHER USEFUL INFORMATION Western Australian Tourism Commission booklets: *Western Australia's Unique North* and *Drive North*; CALM booklet: *North-West Bound: From Shark Bay to Wyndham.*

DESCRIPTION On this trek section you penetrate deep into the Kimberley pastoral region. At the El Questro Station turnoff you travel west along Gibb River–Wyndham Road, part of the 667-kilometre beef route. The rugged country it traverses is regularly punctuated by shady campsites, gorges, creeks and waterholes. You then take Gibb River–Kalumburu Road as far north as Miners Pool on Drysdale River Station. This natural-earth road continues to the Kalumburu Aboriginal Reserve on the Mitchell Plateau; see option in next trek section.

The condition of the roads, all unsealed, depends on how recently they were serviced by a grader, and servicing takes place once a year, in June or July. On average the condition is reasonable, though, with long patches of corrugation and only small patches of bulldust. There are, however, many river and creek crossings that are negotiable only during the dry season April–September. *See Warnings.*

All 10 optional campsites are on private property, either close to homesteads or on river and creek banks. Homestead camping and accommodation is at *Home Valley Homestead, Jacks Waterhole* on *Durack River Homestead, Pentecost Downs Homestead* on *Karunjie Station* and *Drysdale River Homestead.* There are bush campsites and picnic spots on the banks of the *Durack* and *Gibb* rivers, *Campbell* and *Plain* creeks and other tributaries, and at *Miners Pool.*

Home Valley and Durack River homesteads conduct four-wheel drive tours, and you can enjoy horseriding, cattle mustering and scenic flights by arrangement with some of the landholders. Durack River Homestead, once the residence of the famous pioneering Durack family, re-creates life as it once was in the Kimberley.

WARNINGS ▶ Do not embark during wet–hot season December–March. Flooding rivers may make roads totally impassable and cause their closure. ▶ Gibb River–Wyndham Road a gravel surface: broken rocks may puncture tyres. Have spare tyres ready. Check road conditions by contacting Main Roads Western Australia, PMB 159, Derby WA 6728; tel. (091) 91 1133. ▶ Beware livestock on roads. ▶ Fresh water scarce during dry season from April to September; bring drinking water. ▶ Fuel prices at homesteads along Gibb River–Wyndham Road usually very high: up to $1 per litre. ▶ Crocodiles inhabit all inland waterways. Be crocodile-wise. Do not swim.

BOOKINGS AND PERMITS ▶ Obtain permission from landholders before camping on private property. Not necessary to book ahead to camp, but book ahead to stay in homesteads. For Home Valley, Durack River and Pentecost Downs homesteads, contact Pentecost Downs (Karunjie), PO Box 833, Kununurra WA 6743; tel. (091) 61 4322. For Drysdale River Homestead and Miners Pool, contact Drysdale River Station, PMB 9, via Wyndham WA 6740; tel. (091) 61 4326. ▶ For all information, contact Kununurra Visitors Centre, PO Box 446, Kununurra WA 6743; tel. (091) 68 1177 or Wyndham Tourist Information Centre, Old Port Post Office, O'Donnell Street, Wyndham Port WA 6741; tel. (091) 61 1054.

ROUTE DIRECTIONS

0.0 km Zero trip meter at El Questro Station Homestead heading north. **SO. PD**
(16.0 km) ▲ 48.9 km

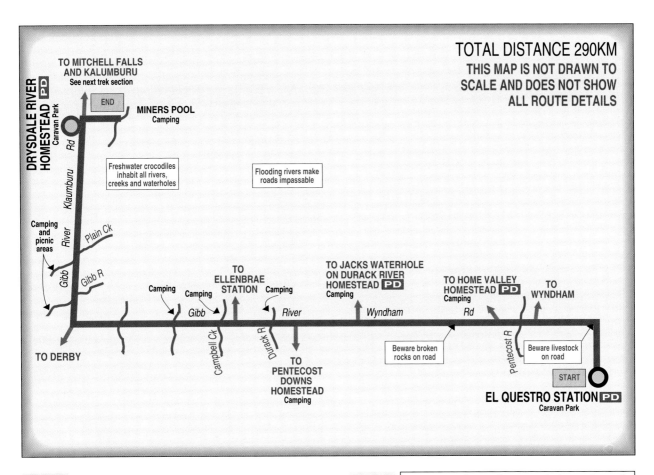

TOTAL DISTANCE 290KM
THIS MAP IS NOT DRAWN TO
SCALE AND DOES NOT SHOW
ALL ROUTE DETAILS

16.0 km   T intersection. **TL** onto Gibb
River–Wyndham Rd.
(24.0 km)   ▲ 32.9 km

40.0 km   Intersection. **SO.**

> *Old Karunjie Rd–King River Rd on right
> continues to Great Northern Hwy leading
> to Wyndham.*

(0.2 km)   ▲ 8.9 km

40.2 km   Pentecost River crossing. **SO.**
(8.7 km)   ▲ 8.7 km

48.9 km   Intersection.

> *Sign on right: Home Valley Homestead
> 1 km.* PD *Supplies, minor mechanical
> repairs. Camping, homestead accomm.,
> hot showers, toilets. 4WD tours, scenic
> flights, fishing, boating, swimming.*

0.0 km   Zero trip meter at above intersection. **SO.**
(58.1 km)   ▲ 0.0 km
     ▲ 58.1 km

58.1 km   Intersection.

> *Sign on right: Jacks Waterhole on Durack
> River Homestead 800 m.* PD *Supplies,
> minor mechanical repairs. Camping,
> homestead accomm., hot showers, toilets.
> 4WD tours, fishing, boating, swimming.*

0.0 km   Zero trip meter at above intersection. **SO.**
(23.0 km)   ▲ 0.0 km
     ▲ 23.0 km

23.0 km   Intersection.

> *Sign on left: Pentecost Downs Homestead/
> Durack Wilderness Retreat on Karunjie Station
> 48 km along Karunjie Homestead Rd. Camping,
> homestead accomm. Fishing, boating,
> swimming, horseriding, cattle mustering.*

0.0 km   Zero trip meter at above intersection. **SO.**
(5.0 km)   ▲ 0.0 km
     ▲ 160.4 km

5.0 km   Durack River crossing. **SO.**

> *Bush campsites on river banks. No
> facilities. Seasonal drinking water.*

(20.8 km)   ▲ 155.4 km

339

Pentecost River crossing, Gibb River–Wyndham Road

25.8 km Intersection. **SO.**

> *Sign on right: Ellenbrae Station.*

(3.0 km) ▲ 134.6 km

28.8 km Campbell Creek crossing. **SO.**

> *Bush campsites on creek banks. No facilities. Seasonal drinking water.*

(23.8 km) ▲ 131.6 km

52.6 km Creek crossing. **SO.**

> *Bush campsites on creek banks. No facilities. Seasonal drinking water.*

(20.0 km) ▲ 107.8 km

72.6 km Creek crossing. **SO.**

(23.3 km) ▲ 87.8 km

95.9 km T intersection. S'post: Kalumburu. **TR** onto Gibb River–Kalumburu Rd.

> *Derby off to left.*

(3.1 km) Opp. dir. s'post: Kununurra/Wyndham. ▲ 64.5 km

99.0 km Gibb River crossing. **SO.**

> *Bush campsites and picnic areas on river banks. No facilities.*

(13.1 km) ▲ 61.4 km

112.1 km Plain Creek crossing. **SO.**

> *Bush campsites and picnic areas on creek banks. No facilities.*

(43.1 km) ▲ 48.3 km

155.2 km Intersection. **SO.**

> *Sign on left: Drysdale Station Homestead 1 km.* **PD** *Supplies. Camping, homestead accomm.*

(2.2 km) ▲ 5.2 km

157.4 km S'post: Miners Pool/camping area 3.5. **TR.**

(3.0 km) ▲ 3.0 km

160.4 km Miners Pool bush camping and picnic area on right.

> *No facilities. Fresh water in Drysdale River.*

REVERSE DIRECTIONS START ▲ 0.0 km

MINERS POOL
«»
MITCHELL FALLS

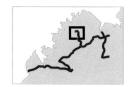

START POINT
Map page 37, N5.

TOTAL KM 188. Option to Kalumburu Aboriginal Reserve is 211 kilometres from Mitchell Falls carpark, plus return.

UNSEALED KM 188 and an extra 127 kilometres for option to Kalumburu Aboriginal Reserve from Gibb River–Kalumburu Road and Port Warrender Road intersection.

DEGREE OF DIFFICULTY Moderate.

DRIVING TIME 6 hours (over a minimum of 3 days). Option to Kalumburu Aboriginal Reserve takes approximately 3 hours more from Mitchell Falls carpark. Allow extra time to return to Mitchell Falls for start of next trek section.

LONGEST DISTANCE NO FUEL 226 km (Drysdale Station Homestead to Kalumburu town centre if option is taken; otherwise there is no fuel on the Mitchell Plateau).

TOPOGRAPHIC MAPS Auslig 1:250 000 series: Drysdale; Montague Sound. See also 1:100 000 series.

LOCAL/SPECIALITY MAPS StreetSmart Touring Map: East Kimberley; Robinson's Western Australia.

OTHER USEFUL INFORMATION Western Australian Tourism Commission booklets: Western Australia's Unique North and Drive North; CALM booklet: North-West Bound: From Shark Bay to Wyndham.

DESCRIPTION You venture into the remote coastal regions of the far-north Kimberley on this trek section. Access is often by plane, which is clear when you see the many airstrips that dot the region. It is a timeless land, one of the world's virgin wilderness areas, and you need at least 3 days to fully explore it. Even the walks around the Mitchell Plateau, an elevated laterite-

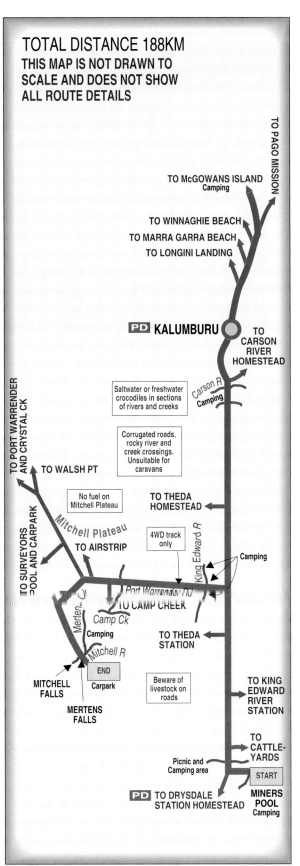

TOTAL DISTANCE 188KM
THIS MAP IS NOT DRAWN TO SCALE AND DOES NOT SHOW ALL ROUTE DETAILS

Kimberley coastline, Talbot Bay

capped plain, require a return journey of about 4 or 5 hours. Well worth the extra time and distance is the option to Kalumburu which ends at McGowans Island, the most northern point in the Kimberley covered by the treks.

Vegetation in the Mitchell Falls area comprises small patches of rainforest on steep slopes. Valleys and creek lines have open woodlands of grey box and white gum, and paperbarks and pandanus grow along watercourses. Unique tropical plants such as the fan palm are a dominant feature.

Bush campsites and picnic spots are plentiful along the banks of the *Drysdale* and *King Edward* rivers and *Camp, Crystal* and *Mertens* creeks, most of which permanently supply drinking water. The King Edward River crossing campsite near Port Warrender Road is located at the first major watercourse encountered on the Mitchell Plateau track. The Camp Creek campsite is a good base camp for day trips to other sections of the plateau.

Kalumburu Reserve and Catholic Mission has been accessible to tourists only in recent years. The mission building nestles amid giant mango trees and coconut palms, and further north is the abandoned Pago Mission. The community permits camping around the *Carson River* crossing, no fee, and beach camping at *McGowans Island* where a small fee applies. A cattle operation is the main business of the reserve, as well as fishing, trekking trips and scenic flights that let you experience the wonders of the Kimberley coastline.

WARNINGS ▶ Total self-sufficiency required in very remote and isolated Mitchell Plateau area. No fuel there; take your own for 226 kilometres between Drysdale Station Homestead and Kalumburu town centre. ▶ Permanent drinking water in most rivers and creeks, but fresh water scarce during dry season from April to September. Bring your own water. ▶ Totally unsealed road surface extensively corrugated; rocky river and creek crossings. Roads unsuitable for caravans. Have spare tyres ready. Check road conditions by contacting Main Roads Western Australia, PMB 159, Derby WA 6728; tel. (091) 91 1133. ▶ Both freshwater and saltwater crocodiles inhabit rivers, creeks and waterholes; be cautious. ▶ Walk to Mitchell Falls over rough country. Track marked and well worn but if in doubt, walk close

to creek. Be careful when close to the many cliffs.
▶ Beware livestock on roads.

BOOKINGS AND PERMITS ▶ If option to Kalumburu taken, permit required. Apply in writing, at least 4 weeks before embarking, to the Chairman, Kalumburu Aboriginal Community, via Wyndham WA 6740; tel. (091) 61 4300. Not necessary to book ahead for beach camping at McGowans Island but fee applicable and payable on site. ▶ For all information about the far-north Kimberley region, contact Kununurra Visitors Centre, PO Box 446, Kununurra WA 6743; tel. (091) 68 1177 or Wyndham Tourist Information Centre, Old Port Post Office, O'Donnell Street, Wyndham Port WA 6741; tel. (091) 61 1054.

ROUTE DIRECTIONS

0.0 km Zero trip meter at Miners Pool campsite heading west. **SO.**
(3.0 km) ▲ 103.0 km

3.0 km T intersection. **TR** onto Gibb River–Kalumburu Rd.

> *Drysdale Station Homestead turnoff 2.2 km off to left.* **PD** *Next fuel Kalumburu town centre (226 km). Road unsuitable for caravans beyond this point.*

(0.1 km) ▲ 100.0 km
3.1 km Cattleyards on right. **SO.**
(0.4 km) ▲ 99.9 km
3.5 km Drysdale River crossing. **SO.**

> *Camping and picnic area on river bank on left.*

(34.8 km) ▲ 99.5 km
00.0 km Gate.

> *Leave as found.*

(2.7 km) ▲ 64.7 km
41.0 km Intersection. **SO.**

> *King Edward River Homestead on right.*

(8.9 km) ▲ 62.0 km
49.9 km Gate.

> *Leave as found.*

(15.0 km) ▲ 53.1 km
64.9 km Gate.

> *Leave as found.*

(22.9 km) ▲ 38.1 km

87.8 km Intersection. **SO.**

> *Theda Station off to left.*

(15.2 km) ▲ 15.2 km
103.0 km Intersection. Handmade sign: Mitchell Plateau. ▲ 0.0 km
Option: Kalumburu Aboriginal Reserve.

0.0 km Zero trip meter at Gibb River–Kalumburu Rd and Port Warrender Rd intersection. **SO** along Gibb River–Kalumburu Rd heading north.
(34.2 km)
34.2 km Gate.

> *Leave as found.*

(1.8 km)
36.0 km Gate.

> *Leave as found. Theda Homestead 600 m off to left.*

(27.2 km)
63.2 km Gate.

> *Leave as found.*

(3.1 km)
66.3 km Creek crossing. **SO.**
(18.1 km)
84.4 km Carson River crossing. **SO.**

> *Bush campsites on river banks. No facilities.*

(0.5 km)
84.9 km T intersection. **TL.**

> *Carson River Rd on right leads to Carson River Homestead.*

(1.9 km)
86.8 km Gate.

> *Leave as found.*

(13.4 km)
100.2 km Gate.

> *Leave as found.*

(4.9 km)
105.1 km Kalumburu town centre, adjacent to mission building on left and store on right. **TR.**

> **PD** *Supplies.*

(0.9 km)
106.0 km Intersection. **KL.**

MINERS POOL «» MITCHELL FALLS

Airstrip on right.

(4.0 km)
110.0 km Intersection. **KR**.

Road on left leads to Longini Landing.

(6.6 km)
116.6 km Intersection. **KR**.

Marra Garra Beach off to left.

(2.2 km)
118.8 km Intersection. **KR**.
Winnaghie Beach off to left.
(1.5 km)
120.3 km Intersection. Handmade s'post: McGowans Island. **KL**.

Keep right to Pago Mission ruins and other beach camping areas.

(6.2 km)
126.5 km McGowans Island camping area.

Campsites (fee) along beach. Showers. Fishing, tours.

Return to Gibb River–Kalumburu Road and Port Warrender Road intersection by same route and pick up route directions.
End option.

0.0 km Zero trip meter at above intersection. **TL** if coming from Miners Pool, **TR** if returning from Kalumburu, onto Port Warrender Rd.

4WD track only.

(5.2 km) ▲ 0.0 km
▲ 67.0 km
5.2 km Various bush campsites along banks of King Edward River. **SO**.

No facilities. Permanent drinking water.

(1.3 km) ▲ 61.8 km
6.5 km King Edward River crossing. **SO**.

Bush campsites on river banks. No facilities. Permanent drinking water.

(59.6 km) ▲ 60.5 km
66.1 km S'post: Mitchell Falls. **KL**.
(0.5 km) ▲ 0.9 km
66.6 km Creek crossing. **SO**.

Abandoned mining campsites immediately following crossing.

(0.2 km) ▲ 0.4 km

66.8 km S'posts: Airstrip 5.0, Mitchell Falls t/o 4.5, Surveyors Pool t/o 24, Camping site t/o 0.6. **SO**.
(0.2 km) ▲ 0.2 km
67.0 km Intersection.

Turn left 8.0 km to Camp Creek Campsite. No facilities. Permanent drinking water. Turn left 6.4 km to mining weather gauge on right and various tracks to bush campsites on creek banks.

0.0 km Zero trip meter at above intersection. **SO**.
(2.8 km) ▲ 0.0 km
▲ 17.9 km
2.8 km Y intersection. **KL**.

Airstrip off to right.

(0.6 km) ▲ 15.1 km
3.4 km Y intersection. S'post: Mitchell Falls 12. **TL**.

Track on right leads to Surveyors Pool and Port Warrender. Straight ahead to Surveyors Pool turnoff 19 km, then turn left 6.5 km to carpark and to begin 4 km return walk to Surveyors Pool. Drinking water. Straight ahead at Surveyors Pool turnoff along difficult track 33 km to Y intersection: turn left 12 km to Crystal Creek bush campsites at Port Warrender; track on right leads part way to Walsh Point before ending at a washaway.

(4.5 km) ▲ 14.5 km
7.9 km Y intersection. **KL**.
(0.5 km) ▲ 10.0 km
8.4 km T intersection. **TL**.
(9.5 km) ▲ 9.5 km
17.9 km Mitchell Falls carpark.

Begin walks to Mitchell Falls 4 hr, Mertens Falls 2.5 hr, Little Mertens Falls 1.5 hr. Campsites and drinking water at Mertens Creek.

REVERSE DIRECTIONS START ▲ 0.0 km

MITCHELL FALLS
«»
ADCOCK GORGE

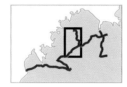

START POINT
Map page 37, M4.

TOTAL KM 393.
UNSEALED KM 393.
DEGREE OF DIFFICULTY Moderate from Mitchell Falls to Drysdale River Homestead, then easy.
DRIVING TIME 6 hours.
LONGEST DISTANCE NO FUEL 172 km (Drysdale Station Homestead to Mt Barnett Roadhouse). If option to Kalumburu was taken in previous trek section, last fuel Kalumburu town centre to Drysdale Station Homestead (226 km); otherwise no fuel on the Mitchell Plateau.
TOPOGRAPHIC MAPS Auslig 1:250 000 series: *Drysdale*; *Ashton*; *Mt Elizabeth*. See also 1:100 000 series.
LOCAL/SPECIALITY MAPS StreetSmart Touring Map: *East Kimberley*; *Robinson's Western Australia*.
OTHER USEFUL INFORMATION Western Australian Tourism Commission booklets: *Western Australia's Unique North* and *Drive North*; CALM booklet: *North-West Bound: From Shark Bay to Wyndham*.

DESCRIPTION In the heart of cattle country, you pass from the shire of Wyndham–East Kimberley to that of Derby–West Kimberley along a route that is easy to negotiate after the first and moderately difficult section between Mitchell Falls and Drysdale Station Homestead.

Derby–Gibb River Road, the long western section of the beef road, opens up some spectacular sights. To your left are the Gibb, Barnett and Phillips ranges, and there are four gorges – Barnett, Manning, Galvans and Adcock – along the way, all excellent for swimming and bushwalking; Manning River and gorge also have good fishing. Adcock Gorge is a particularly pretty

Frill-necked lizard

spot: a waterfall cascading over rock terraces into a little pool, next to an Aboriginal burial site.

The Kupingarri Aboriginal Community lives on Mt Barnett Station, opposite the roadhouse. Visitors are not encouraged to enter this area; if you wish to visit, report to the roadhouse office first. Galvans Gorge contains a small Aboriginal art gallery featuring sacred rock paintings of the Wandjina spirit beings. Photography is permitted, but do not touch or disturb the paintings.

During the first part of the trek there are bush campsites and picnic areas at the *Plain Creek* and *Gibb River* crossings along Gibb River–Kalumburu Road. Thereafter a fee applies to camp on two private properties, *Mt Elizabeth Station* and *Manning Gorge on Mt Barnett Station*, but the campsite at *Adcock Gorge* does not entail a fee. You can stay at the homestead or tour the 200 000 hectares of picturesque Mt Elizabeth Station. The other working cattle station, Mt Barnett, has fuel and several very good service facilities.

WARNINGS ▶ Totally unsealed roads can be undermined along edges after rain. Derby–Gibb River Road

345

MITCHELL FALLS «» ADCOCK GORGE

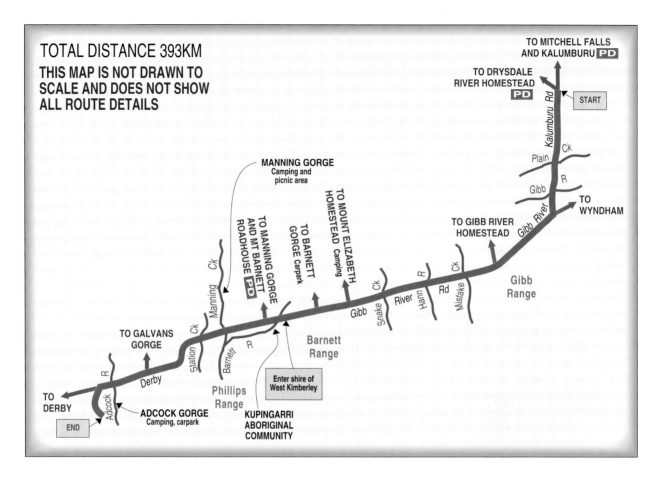

TOTAL DISTANCE 393KM

THIS MAP IS NOT DRAWN TO SCALE AND DOES NOT SHOW ALL ROUTE DETAILS

graded once a year in May or later. Some river and creek crossings may be rocky. Caravans possible from Drysdale Station Homestead onwards. To check road conditions contact Main Roads Western Australia, PMB 159, Derby WA 6728; tel. (091) 91 1133. ▶ Fresh water scarce during dry season from April to September/November; bring your own drinking water. ▶ Crocodiles inhabit coastline and inland waterways. Be crocodilewise. Do not swim. ▶ Beware livestock on roads. ▶ Do not touch or disturb Aboriginal rock paintings at Galvans Gorge and burial site at Adcock Gorge.

BOOKINGS AND PERMITS ▶ Book ahead for homestead accommodation and tours, but not camping, at Mt Elizabeth Station. Contact Mt Elizabeth Station, via Derby WA 6728; tel. (091) 91 4644. ▶ Book ahead for Easter peak season to camp at Manning Gorge; groups of 10 or more also book ahead. Contact Mt Barnett Roadhouse, PMB, via Derby WA 6728; tel. (091) 91 7007. ▶ For all information about east Kimberley region contact Kununurra Visitors Centre, Coolibah Drive, Kununurra WA 6743; PO Box 446, Kununurra WA 6743; tel. (091) 68 1177 or Wyndham Tourist Information Centre, Old Port Post Office, O'Donnell

Street, Wyndham Port WA 6741; tel. (091) 61 1054. ▶ For all information about west Kimberley region contact Derby Tourist Bureau, 1 Clarendon Street, Derby WA 6728; PO Box 48, Derby WA 6728; tel. (091) 91 1426.

ROUTE DIRECTIONS

Depart Mitchell Falls carpark north 15 km approx. to Port Warrender Rd T intersection. Turn right 70 km approx. to Gibb River–Kalumburu Rd T intersection. Turn right 102 km approx. to Drysdale Station Homestead intersection.

0.0 km Zero trip meter at Drysdale Station Homestead intersection. **SO.**

> *Sign on right: Drysdale Station Homestead 1.0.* PD *Supplies. Camping, homestead accomm. Roads suitable for caravans again from this point onwards.*

(43.1 km)   ▲ 0.0 km
                                        ▲ 59.3 km

43.1 km Plain Creek crossing. **SO.**

Signpost, Gibb River– Kalumburu Road

> Bush campsites and picnic areas on creek banks. No facilities.

(13.1 km) ▲ 16.2 km

56.2 km Gibb River crossing. **SO.**

> Bush campsites and picnic areas on river banks. No facilities.

(3.1 km) ▲ 3.1 km

59.3 km Intersection. S'post: Derby 373.

> Gibb River–Wyndham Rd on left.

Opp. dir. s'post: Kununurra 333/Wyndham 292.

0.0 km Zero trip meter at above intersection. **SO.**
(40.1 km) ▲ 0.0 km
▲ 70.0 km

40.1 km Gibb River Homestead on right. **SO** onto Derby–Gibb River Rd.

> Private property – no entry.

(1.5 km) ▲ 29.9 km
44.6 km Mistake Creek crossing. **SO.**
(9.2 km) ▲ 25.4 km
53.8 km Hann River crossing. **SO.**
(7.0 km) ▲ 16.2 km
60.8 km Snake Creek crossing. **SO.**
(9.2 km) ▲ 9.2 km
70.0 km Intersection.

> Mt Elizabeth Homestead 30 km off to right. Camping, accomm., limited supplies, tours.

0.0 km Zero trip meter at above intersection. **SO.**
(9.6 km) ▲ 0.0 km
▲ 9.6 km

9.6 km Intersection.

> Barnett Gorge carpark 5 km off to right. Walk 300 m to gorge and swimming hole.

0.0 km Zero trip meter at above intersection. **SO.**
(14.7 km) ▲ 0.0 km
▲ 28.5 km

14.7 km Sign: Welcome to Shire of West Kimberley. **SO.**
(12.8 km) ▲ 13.8 km

27.5 km Barnett River crossing. **SO.**
(1.0 km) ▲ 1.0 km

28.5 km Mt Barnett Roadhouse and homestead on right.

> **PD** Supplies, minor mechanical repairs. Meals, takeaway food, showers, laundry, toilets, running water. Walk 7 km to Manning Gorge and river. Camping. Barbecues, toilets. Swimming, bushwalking. Kupingarri Aboriginal Community on left: do not visit before reporting to roadhouse.

0.0 km Zero trip meter at Mt Barnett Roadhouse. **SO.**
(1.4 km) ▲ 0.0 km
▲ 14.3 km

1.4 km Station Creek crossing. **SO.**
(12.9 km) ▲ 12.9 km

14.3 km Intersection.

> Galvans Gorge 1 km off to right. Walk 300 m to main pool, waterfall and small Aboriginal art gallery: treat with respect. Swimming, bushwalking.

0.0 km Zero trip meter at above intersection. **SO.**
(13.7 km) ▲ 0.0 km
▲ 23.8 km

13.7 km Adcock River crossing. **SO.**
(5.0 km) ◆ 10.1 km

19.0 km S'post: Adcock Gorge 5. **TL.**
(4.8 km) ▲ 4.8 km

23.8 km Adcock Gorge carpark.

> Camping. Barbecues. Walk 300 m to gorge, waterfall, swimming hole and Aboriginal burial site: treat with respect.

REVERSE DIRECTIONS START ▲ 0.0 km

ADCOCK GORGE
«»
BROOME

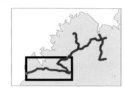

START POINT
Map page 37, M6.

TOTAL KM 762.

UNSEALED KM 302.

DEGREE OF DIFFICULTY Moderate from Adcock Gorge to Geikie Gorge, easy from Fitzroy Crossing to Broome.

DRIVING TIME 13 hours.

LONGEST DISTANCE NO FUEL 311 km (Mt House Homestead to Fitzroy Crossing).

TOPOGRAPHIC MAPS Auslig 1:250 000 series: *Mt Elizabeth*; *Lennard River*; *Derby*; *Broome*. See also 1:100 000 series.

LOCAL/SPECIALITY MAPS StreetSmart Touring Map: *West Kimberley*; *Robinson's Western Australia*.

OTHER USEFUL INFORMATION Western Australian Tourism Commission booklets: *Western Australia's Unique North* and *Drive North*; CALM booklet: *North-West Bound: From Shark Bay to Wyndham*; CALM geological survey by Phillip Playford: *Geology of Windjana Gorge, Geikie Gorge and Tunnel Creek National Parks*; CALM brochure: *Devonian Reef National Parks: Geikie Gorge, Windjana Gorge, Tunnel Creek*; Derby Tourist Bureau brochure: *At Derby ... One Day Tours: Windjana Gorge and Tunnel Creek*.

DESCRIPTION This long trek takes you into the Kimberley's ancient coral reefs once submerged by a vast tropical sea. The 3 national parks you visit – Windjana Gorge, Tunnel Creek and Geikie Gorge – were carved deeply by the flooding of 3 rivers. Exposed cross-sections of fossil layers and limestone strata open a fascinating window on life before the evolution of reptiles or mammals.

The 5 gorges – Bell, Lennard, Windjana, Tunnel Creek

and Geikie – all offer something unique. Vegetation along the river banks includes paper-barked cadjeputs, river gums, freshwater mangroves, pandanus, native figs, reeds and wild passionfruit. Fruit bats and many waterbirds and tropical aquatic lifeforms share their habitat with the ubiquitous freshwater crocodile.

In Windjana Gorge National Park in the dry season the Lennard River forms pockets of cool water surrounded by trees and shrubs. The only way to see most of the gorge is via a 3.5 kilometre-long trail that winds from the campsite along the water's edge.

Tunnel Creek is part of the state's oldest cave system. A walk through to the other side of the range is broken up about halfway by a roof collapse, you have to wade through several permanent freshwater pools to experience the wonders of the fossil reef. Aborigines decorated the north entrance with paintings, and once made stone axes out of the black dolorite and basalt rocks found at the other end.

Geikie Gorge was carved by the Fitzroy River. The short return walk to the western wall is a pleasant ramble and a ranger-conducted boat tour to the other sheer walls is worthwhile. Sunrise and sunset are the best times to enjoy the brilliant colours of the gorge's galleried walls mirrored in the still waters.

You can camp at *Bell Gorge* and *Windjana Gorge*, which also has a caravan park and a picnic area. Geikie Gorge National Park is for picnicking and day use only, but nearby *Fitzroy Crossing* has caravan parks.

The roads on this long section comprise two parts: mainly good-quality gravel for the 346 kilometres between Adcock Gorge and Geikie Gorge, and highway bitumen for the 396 kilometres between Fitzroy Crossing and Broome.

WARNINGS ▶ Do not embark during wet season when flooding rivers make national parks and natural attractions inaccessible. ▶ For an adventurous walk through Tunnel Creek wear shoes and shorts/bathers and be prepared to get cold and wet. Protect your camera and take your own torch or lamplight. ▶ No electricity at Windjana National Park; portable generators permitted in marked area during indicated hours. ▶ Do not touch or disturb Aboriginal cave and rock paintings at Windjana and Tunnel Creek national parks. ▶ Camping and fires strictly prohibited at Lennard Gorge, Tunnel Creek and Geikie Gorge. ▶ Along road between Adcock Gorge and Geikie Gorge beware short sharp dips, bulldust patches and corrugations. ▶ Crocodiles inhabit gorges and river systems. Be crocodile-wise. Do not swim. ▶ At Geikie Gorge National Park both river banks are a sanctuary; do not go within 200 metres of

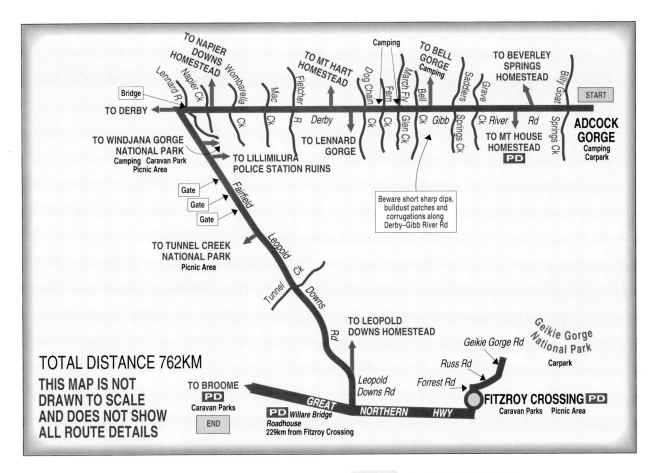

TO NAPIER DOWNS HOMESTEAD
TO MT HART HOMESTEAD
Camping
TO BELL GORGE
Camping
TO BEVERLEY SPRINGS HOMESTEAD

START

Bridge
Lennard R.
Napier Ck
Wombarella
TO DERBY
Mac Ck
Fletcher R.
Derby
Dog Chain Ck
Fern Ck
March Fly
Glen Ck
Bell Ck
Gibb
Saddlers Ck
Grave Ck
River Rd
Billy Goat Springs Ck

ADCOCK GORGE
Camping Carpark

TO WINDJANA GORGE NATIONAL PARK
Camping Caravan Park Picnic Area

TO LILLIMILURA POLICE STATION RUINS

TO LENNARD GORGE

Springs Ck
TO MT HOUSE HOMESTEAD PD

Gate
Gate
Gate

Fairfield

Beware short sharp dips, bulldust patches and corrugations along Derby–Gibb River Rd

TO TUNNEL CREEK NATIONAL PARK
Picnic Area

Leopold Ck

Tunnel
Downs Rd

TO LEOPOLD DOWNS HOMESTEAD

Geikie Gorge National Park
Geikie Gorge Rd
Carpark

Russ Rd
Forrest Rd

TO BROOME
PD
Caravan Parks

Leopold Downs Rd

TO BROOME
PD
Caravan Parks
END

PD Willare Bridge Roadhouse
229km from Fitzroy Crossing

GREAT NORTHERN HWY

FITZROY CROSSING PD
Caravan Parks Picnic Area

TOTAL DISTANCE 762KM

THIS MAP IS NOT DRAWN TO SCALE AND DOES NOT SHOW ALL ROUTE DETAILS

either bank, except permitted area along west bank from southern boundary to beginning of gorge's west wall. Tickets available on site for boating tours. Launch fee and restrictions apply to private boats; check with ranger before launching. ▶ Beware livestock and wild-life on roads.

BOOKINGS AND PERMITS ▶ No prior permits re-quired to camp at Bell Gorge or Windjana Gorge but small camping fee applies at Windjana; pay ranger on site. ▶ For information about camping and caravan areas at Windjana Gorge National Park contact CALM West Kimberley District Office, Herbert Street, Broome WA 6725; PO Box 65, Broome WA 6725; tel. (091) 92 1036. ▶ For information about Fitzroy Crossing cara-van parks and west Kimberley region contact Derby Tourist Bureau, 1 Clarendon Street, Derby WA 6728; PO Box 48, Derby WA 6728; tel. (091) 91 1426.

ROUTE DIRECTIONS

0.0 km Zero trip meter at Adcock Gorge carpark heading north. **SO**.
(4.8 km) ▲ 0.0 km
▲ 58.9 km

4.8 km T intersection. **TL** onto Derby–Gibb River Rd.
(6.4 km) ▲ 54.1 km

11.2 km Billy Goat Springs Creek crossing. **SO**.
(9.9 km) ▲ 47.7 km

21.1 km Intersection. **SO**.

> *Beverley Springs Homestead off to right along Beverley Springs Rd. Group tours.*

(3.8 km) ▲ 37.8 km

24.9 km Intersection. **SO**.

> *Mt House Homestead 10 km off to left along Mornington Rd. PD Limited supplies, ice.*

(20.4 km) ▲ 34.0 km

45.3 km Grave Creek crossing. **SO**.
(4.3 km) ▲ 13.6 km

Windjana Gorge

49.6 km Saddlers Springs Creek crossing. **SO.**
(9.3 km) ▲ 9.3 km
58.9 km Intersection.

> *Bell Gorge 30 km off to right along Silent Grove Rd: rough track. Camping. No facilities. Swimming, fishing. Walk from camping area to spectacular gorge.*

0.0 km Zero trip meter at above intersection. **SO.**
(3.6 km) ▲ 0.0 km
▲ 23.0 km
3.6 km Bell Creek crossing. **SO.**

> *Bush campsite on right along creek bank. Permanent water.*

(5.9 km) ▲ 19.4 km
9.5 km March Fly Glen Creek crossing. **SO.**

> *Bush campsite on right along creek bank just before crossing. Permanent water.*

(5.6 km) ▲ 13.5 km
15.1 km Fern Creek crossing. **SO.**
(5.6 km) ▲ 7.9 km

20.7 km Dog Chain Creek crossing. **SO.**

> *Bush campsite on right along creek bank just before crossing.*

(2.3 km) ▲ 2.3 km
23.0 km Three-way intersection.

> *Lennard Gorge carpark 7 km along second turnoff on left: good-quality gravel and small rocky creek crossing. Walk 200 m to spectacular gorge lookout. Camping and fires prohibited. Swimming. Millie Windie Rd first turnoff on left.*

0.0 km Zero trip meter at above intersection. **SO.**
(6.8 km) ▲ 0.0 km
▲ 72.4 km
6.8 km Intersection. **SO.**

> *Mt Hart Homestead off to right along Mt Hart Rd.*

(21.6 km) ▲ 65.6 km
28.4 km Fletcher River crossing. **SO.**
(7.9 km) ▲ 44.0 km

36.3 km Mac Creek. Cross bridge.
(14.8 km) ▲ 36.1 km

51.1 km Wombarella Creek crossing. **SO.**
(11.2 km) ▲ 21.3 km

62.3 km Napier Creek crossing immediately after intersection. **SO.**

> *Napier Downs Homestead off to right along Napier Downs Rd.*

(9.7 km) ▲ 10.1 km

72.0 km Lennard River. Cross bridge.
(0.4 km) ▲ 0.4 km

72.4 km Intersection. S'post: Windjana Gorge National Park 23.

> *Straight ahead 125 km to Derby.*

Opp. dir. s'post: Gibb River 249.

0.0 km Zero trip meter at above intersection. **TL** onto Fairfield–Leopold Downs Rd.
(20.2 km) ▲ 0.0 km
▲ 20.2 km

20.2 km S'post: Fitzroy Crossing 154.

> *Windjana Gorge National Park on left. Walk 100 m to camping area and caravan park. Picnic tables, barbecues, pit toilets, running water, showers. Information. Easy return walk through gorge.*

Opp. dir. s'post: Derby 150.

0.0 km Zero trip meter at above s'post. **SO.**
(3.8 km) ▲ 0.0 km
▲ 3.8 km

3.8 km Intersection.

> *Lillimilura police-station ruins 100 m off to left.*

0.0 km Zero trip meter at above intersection. **SO.**
(12.6 km) ▲ 0.0 km
▲ 32.4 km

12.6 km Gate. **SO.**

> *Leave as found.*

(5.9 km) ▲ 19.8 km

18.5 km Gate. **SO.**

> *Leave as found.*

(5.9 km) ▲ 13.9 km

24.4 km Gate. **SO.**

> *Leave as found.*

(8.0 km) ▲ 8.0 km

32.4 km Intersection.

> *Tunnel Creek National Park on right. Camping and fires prohibited. Adventurous return walk through cave includes wading in small pools.*

0.0 km Zero trip meter at above intersection. **SO.**
(30.5 km) ▲ 0.0 km
▲ 135.1 km

30.5 km Tunnel Creek crossing. **SO.**
(0.5 km) ▲ 104.6 km

31.0 km Intersection. **SO.**
(28.8 km) ▲ 104.1 km

59.8 km T intersection. **TR.**
(11.1 km) Opp. dir. s'post: Tunnel Creek. ▲ 75.3 km

70.9 km T intersection. S'post: Fitzroy Crossing 42. **TL** onto bitumen: Great Northern Hwy.
(43.9 km) Gravel. Opp. dir. s'post:
Tunnel Creek. ▲ 64.2 km

114.8 km Intersection. S'post: Geikie Gorge National Park 18. **TL** through Fitzroy Crossing along Forrest Rd.

> **PD** *Supplies, caravan parks. Accomm., minor mechanical repairs.*

(2.3 km) ▲ 20.3 km

117.1 km Intersection. S'post: Geikie Gorge. **TR** onto Russ Rd.
(16.5 km) ▲ 18.0 km

133.6 km Intersection. Sign: Geikie Gorge National Park. **TL** onto Geikie Gorge Rd.

> *Straight ahead 200 m to ranger's office.*

(1.5 km) ▲ 1.5 km

135.1 km Geikie Gorge carpark.

> *Camping and fires prohibited. Gas barbecues, toilets, running water. Information. Boat tours, bushwalking. Swimming best at junction of Margaret and Fitzroy rivers where large sand bank usually develops.*

Depart Geikie Gorge carpark south 20 km to Great Northern Hwy T intersection. Turn right 396 km to Broome for start of next trek.

> **PD** *Willare Bridge Roadhouse 229 km from Fitzroy Crossing.*

REVERSE DIRECTIONS START ▲ 0.0 km

NORTH-WEST FRONTIERS
BROOME «» PERTH
4287 KILOMETRES

Broome beach sunset

BROOME «» EIGHTY MILE BEACH 378 km

EIGHTY MILE BEACH «» MARBLE BAR 235 km

MARBLE BAR «» HAMERSLEY RANGE 320 km

HAMERSLEY RANGE «» WITTENOOM 170 km

WITTENOOM «» ROEBOURNE 346 km

ROEBOURNE «» ONSLOW 314 km

ONSLOW «» EXMOUTH 358 km

EXMOUTH «» CARNARVON 438 km

CARNARVON «» CAPE PERON «» DENHAM 442 km

DENHAM «» STEEP POINT «» KALBARRI 695 km

KALBARRI «» PERTH 591 km

On this long trek you move on from Broome and the west Kimberley for an adventure through the Great Sandy Desert and the Pilbara, Gascoyne and mid-west regions, finishing at the state capital, a thriving metropolis in the south west. Many places visited are accessible only to four-wheel drive vehicles, so some challenging driving is combined with much easier gravel sections and long bitumen linking sections.

The Pilbara region is the largest area in Australia, a hot dry land rich in iron ore and mining history. Highlights of our trek include the Marble Bar region, Hamersley Range National Park – the state's second-largest national park – and Millstream–Chichester National Park, an oasis and a welcome contrast. The best times to travel are the cooler months of April –

October, to avoid the hottest time of year, and to enjoy the wildflowers that bloom in early spring.

From Onslow at the west-coast end of the Pilbara you move on to the Gascoyne coast to explore the regions around Exmouth, Coral Bay, Carnarvon and Denham. Driving through Cape Range National Park you can enjoy views of the beautiful Ningaloo Reef Marine Park and continue on to the blue-water paradise of Coral Bay.

A diversion from Denham on the Peron Peninsula to the world-famous dolphins at Monkey Mia is followed by a stay in one of the state's newest national parks, Francois Peron. At Australia's westernmost extremity, there is an opportunity to visit Edel Land and the wild coast south of Steep Point. The warm winter–early spring months of May–October is the best time to travel, to see the early-spring wildflowers and avoid the high and constant winds that often sweep the coast between November and February.

The mid-west sections take you through the coastal gorges of Kalbarri National Park and down to Geraldton, then there is a long highway linking section all the way south to Perth. Again it is best to embark during the warm winter months of May–October, for the early-spring wildflowers and to avoid the coastal winds that occur later.

BEFORE YOU SET OUT ▶ Read the section description carefully. ▶ Check weather conditions with local authorities or Bureau of Meteorology. ▶ Make sure you have the appropriate maps and information for the trek. ▶ Check that your vehicle is in good order for the conditions ahead. Have you the necessary spare parts? ▶ If you are camping, do you have the right camping equipment? ▶ If you are fishing, obtain any necessary licences and find out about regulations.

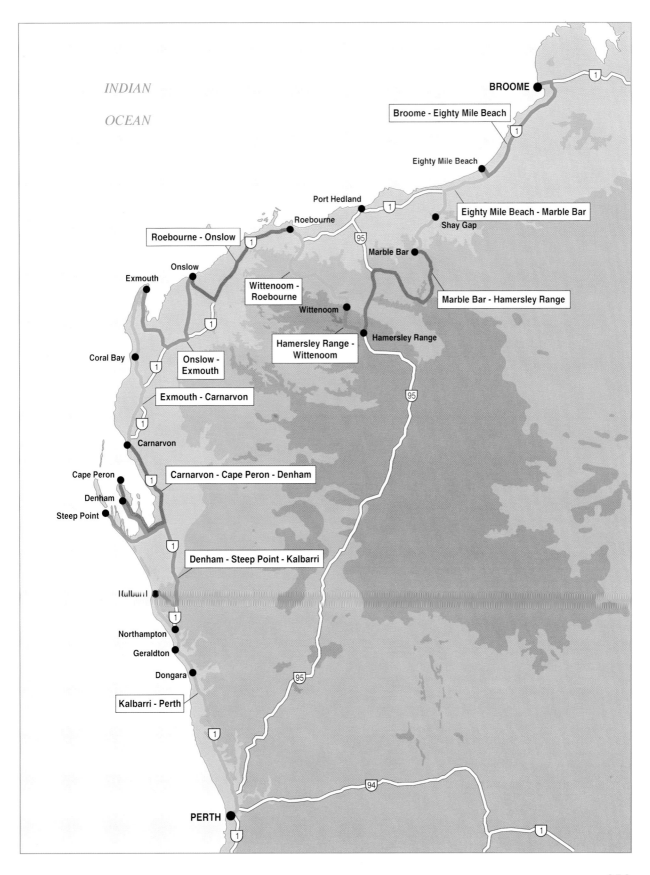

INDIAN

OCEAN

BROOME

Broome - Eighty Mile Beach

Eighty Mile Beach

Port Hedland

Roebourne

Eighty Mile Beach - Marble Bar

Shay Gap

Roebourne - Onslow

Marble Bar

Onslow

Exmouth

Wittenoom -
Roebourne

Wittenoom

Marble Bar - Hamersley Range

Hamersley Range

Coral Bay

Hamersley Range -
Wittenoom

Onslow -
Exmouth

Exmouth - Carnarvon

Carnarvon

Cape Peron

Carnarvon - Cape Peron - Denham

Denham

Steep Point

Denham - Steep Point - Kalbarri

Kalbarri

Northampton

Geraldton

Dongara

Kalbarri - Perth

PERTH

WESTERN AUSTRALIA'S NATIONAL PARKS AND NATURE RESERVES

In Western Australia all national parks and reserves are managed by the Department of Conservation and Land Management (CALM). Most national parks have good facilities for camping and where appropriate we suggest you use their designated campsites. No prior permits are required to traverse national parks and fees are reasonable; self-register or pay the ranger on site as appropriate. To stay in the more popular and established parks it is advisable to book ahead for peak holiday periods. For information when planning your trips contact the relevant district or regional CALM office as stated in the route directions, or head office in Perth: CALM State Operations Headquarters, 50 Hayman Road, Como WA 6152; PO Box 104, Como WA 6152; tel. (09) 367 0333.

When using national parks and nature reserves, obey the following rules.

▶ *Drive along formed roads and tracks, follow signs and do not make your own path through the bush.*
▶ *Bushwalk only along defined tracks and be especially careful not to trample sensitive areas with sand-dune plains, steep slopes or sparse vegetation.*

▶ *Preferably bring your portable gas stove and do not light fires except in barbecues or established fireplaces. Extinguish fires completely. Do not collect firewood from the park unless permitted by ranger.*
▶ *Camp only in designated camping areas and camp away from watercourses to avoid erosion, compaction and pollution of soil.*
▶ *Bathe, brush your teeth and wash dishes at least 50 metres away from creeks and lakes. Use sand instead of detergent to wash dishes.*
▶ *Use pit toilets if provided. Otherwise bury your waste in a 15 centimetre hole at least 100 metres away from campsite and water.*
▶ *Place rubbish in bins provided or take it away with you. Do not throw rubbish or food scraps into rivers or creeks.*
▶ *Pets, firearms and spearguns are prohibited. A permit is required to keep or move wildlife and flora. Beware wildlife on roads.*
▶ *Fishing regulations apply. Do not fish in sanctuary zones, and conserve fish numbers by taking enough only for your immediate needs.*
▶ *Never touch, damage or remove anything you find at Aboriginal sites.*

USEFUL INFORMATION

For touring information contact:
Western Australian Tourist Centre
Albert Facey House
Cnr Forrest Place and Wellington Street
Perth 6000, (09) 483 1111.
Addresses and telephone numbers for the local touring information centres are included in route directions.

For four-wheel driving information contact:
Western Australian Association of
 Four Wheel Drive Clubs Inc.
PO Box 6029
East Perth 6000.

For motoring information contact:
The Royal Automobile Club of
 Western Australia Inc. (RAC)
228 Adelaide Terrace
Perth 6000, (09) 421 4444.

For fishing licences and regulations contact:
The Fisheries Department of
 Western Australia
108 Adelaide Terrace
East Perth 6004
(09) 220 5333.

BROOME
«»
EIGHTY MILE BEACH

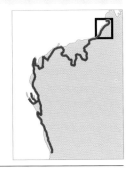

START POINT
Map page 36, H8.

TOTAL KM 378.
UNSEALED KM 9.
DEGREE OF DIFFICULTY Easy.
DRIVING TIME 5 hours.
LONGEST DISTANCE NO FUEL 290 km (Roebuck Roadhouse to Sandfire Roadhouse).
TOPOGRAPHIC MAPS Auslig 1:250 000 series: *Broome*; *Lagrange*; *Munro*; *Mandora*. See also 1:100 000 series.
LOCAL/SPECIALITY MAPS StreetSmart touring maps: *West Kimberley* and *Pilbara*; *Robinson's Western Australia*.
OTHER USEFUL INFORMATION Western Australian Tourism Commission booklet: *Western Australia's Unique North*; CALM booklet: *North-West Bound! From Shark Bay to Wyndham*; MAPco of Western Australia booklet: *Northern Western Australia*.

DESCRIPTION Our first Broome to Perth trek section is a relocation stage between the west Kimberley and Pilbara regions. The bitumen Great Northern Highway, the only way south to Eighty Mile Beach, crosses the Great Sandy Desert – a desolate but starkly beautiful land of spinifex and sandhills.

Campsites do not feature along the way but there are caravan parks at *Broome*, *Port Smith*, *Sandfire Roadhouse* and *Eighty Mile Beach*.

If you missed it during the previous trek, stop off at Broome Bird Observatory where over 220 species live in acacia bushland next to Roebuck Bay. Further along the route, the caravan park at Port Smith is right next to a park

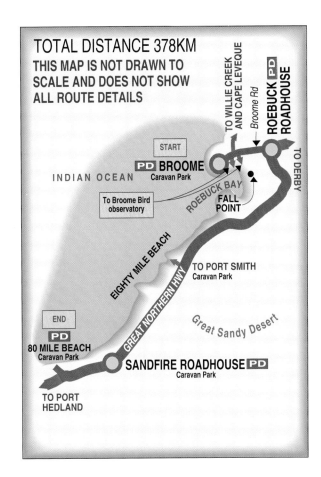

full of exotic birds as well as a tropical garden. The bird park contains parrots, pigeons, finches, lorikeets and cockatoos, and the tropical garden has 140 species of palms from Australia and around the world. Port Smith is a tidal lagoon, so swimming and fishing are both excellent, and the beach beckons four-wheel drivers.

At the end of an easy day you should still have time to go swimming and shell collecting at popular Eighty Mile Beach; the shells there are huge, luminous and beautiful to behold.

WARNINGS ▶ Camping prohibited at Port Smith and Eighty Mile Beach. ▶ Net fishing prohibited at Port Smith.

BOOKINGS AND PERMITS ▶ For information about caravan parks at Broome, Port Smith, Sandfire Roadhouse and Eighty Mile Beach contact Broome Tourist Bureau, Cnr Bagot Road and Great Northern Highway, Broome WA 6725; PO Box 352, Broome WA 6725; tel. (091) 92 2222. ▶ For horseriding on Eighty Mile Beach contact Broome Tourist Bureau. ▶ For information about the natural environment and the Great Sandy Desert contact CALM West Kimberley District Office, Herbert Street, Broome WA 6725; PO Box 65, Broome WA 6725; tel. (091) 92 1036.

355

ROUTE DIRECTIONS

0.0 km Zero trip meter adjacent to Broome Post Office in Hamersley St. **SO** heading east.

> **PD** *Supplies, caravan parks.*

(4.2 km) ▲ 4.2 km

4.2 km Intersection.

> *Broome Bird Observatory 15 km off to right along Crab Creek Rd.*

0.0 km Zero trip meter at above intersection. **SO** along Broome Rd.

(5.7 km) ▲ 0.0 km
 ▲ 141.1 km

5.7 km Intersection. **SO.**

> *Willie Creek and Cape Leveque off to left along Beagle Bay–Broome Rd. Broome Bird Observatory 12 km off to right.*

(24.3 km) ▲ 135.4 km

30.0 km Roebuck Roadhouse on left. **SO.**

> **PD** *Supplies.*

(0.2 km) ▲ 111.1 km

30.2 km S'post: Port Hedland 580. **TR** onto Great Northern Hwy.

> *Straight ahead to Derby.*

(110.9 km) Opp. dir. s'post: Broome 34. ▲ 110.9 km

141.1 km Intersection.

> *Turn right onto gravel 23 km to Port Smith. Caravan park 22 km then turn left. Limited supplies and fuel. No powered sites. Portable generators permitted. Bird park and gardens straight ahead a further 800 m. Turn right at bird park 300 m to Port Smith Lagoon. Fishing. Netting prohibited. Swimming. Camping prohibited.*

0.0 km Zero trip meter at above intersection. **SO.**

(178.6 km) ▲ 0.0 km
 ▲ 232.9 km

178.6 km Sandfire Roadhouse on left. **SO.**

> **PD** *Limited supplies, caravan park. Meals, accomm.*

(45.1 km) ▲ 54.3 km

223.7 km Intersection. S'post: 80 Mile Beach. **TR** onto gravel.

(9.2 km) Bitumen. ▲ 9.2 km

Shell collecting, Eighty Mile Beach

Sign at Port Smith

232.9 km S'post at entrance: 80 Mile Beach Caravan Park.

> *Limited food supplies. Beach camping prohibited. Swimming, fishing, shell collecting, horseriding.*

REVERSE DIRECTIONS START ▲ 0.0 km

EIGHTY MILE BEACH ‹› MARBLE BAR

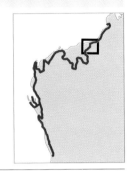

START POINT
Map page 36, E12.

TOTAL KM 235.
UNSEALED KM 124.
DEGREE OF DIFFICULTY Easy.
DRIVING TIME 5 hours.
LONGEST DISTANCE NO FUEL 116 km (Shay Gap to Marble Bar).
TOPOGRAPHIC MAPS Auslig 1:250 000 series: *Mandora*; *Yarrie*; *Port Hedland*; *Marble Bar*. See also 1:100 000 series.
LOCAL/SPECIALITY MAPS StreetSmart touring map: *Pilbara*; *Robinson's Western Australia*.
OTHER USEFUL INFORMATION Western Australian Tourism Commission booklet: *Western Australia's Unique North*; MAPco of Western Australia booklet: *Northern Western Australia*; Marble Bar Information Centre brochures: *Marble Bar: Be Surprised* and *Marble Bar: Australia's Hottest Town*; East Pilbara Shire Newsletter.

DESCRIPTION Departing the coastline, you pass through some fascinating mesa and semi-arid country to the rich mineral region of the East Pilbara. This shire is the largest area in Australia, an eroded sun-drenched land of red and purple rocks, golden spinifex and tremendous gorges.

On this section the road is excellent and well maintained. There are no campsites along the way, but you can stay in caravan parks at *Shay Gap* – a tiny mining-service township, and at *Marble Bar*.

Marble Bar township derives its name from a unique and extraordinarily colourful jasper bar that pioneers mistook for marble. The town has been a centre for gold and mineral mining and the pastoral industry since 1891. The Government Building, constructed of

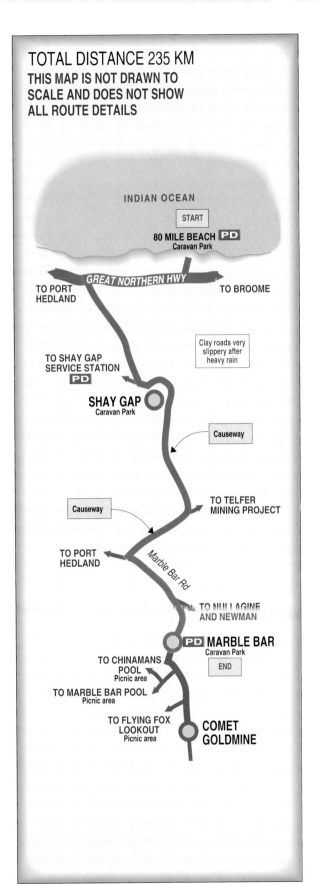

Welcome to Marble Bar

stone in 1895 and still in use, is its most impressive piece of architecture.

Chinamans Pool is one of the region's many natural attractions that are ideal for swimming and picnicking. Marble Bar Pool, where the jasper bar crosses the Congan River, is the best place to see the bar. Flying Fox Lookout affords a magnificent view of the Congan valley, and Comet Goldmine, a functioning mine-tailings works where there is a comprehensive gemstone and jewellery display featuring samples of the beautiful Pilbara jade, is worth a visit.

WARNINGS ▶ Clay roads very slippery after heavy rain. Before departure ring Marble Bar police station on (091) 76 1005 to check road conditions. ▶ Best not to embark December–March when Marble Bar becomes Australia's hottest town due to consistently high temperatures of 38 degrees or more. For mild days and cool nights travel April–November. ▶ Marble Bar Pool an A-class reserve: chipping of jasper bar prohibited. Take samples instead from jasper deposit on road to Comet Goldmine.

BOOKINGS AND PERMITS ▶ For information about caravan parks, sightseeing tours, gemstone fossicking, four-wheel drive excursions and fishing charters contact Marble Bar Information Centre, BP Service Station and Towing Service, Francis Street, Marble Bar WA 6760; tel. (091) 76 1041. ▶ For information about Pilbara Regional Office contact CALM Pilbara Regional Office, SGIO Building, Welcome Road, Karratha WA 6714; PO Box 835, Karratha WA 6714; tel. (091) 86 8288.

ROUTE DIRECTIONS

0.0 km Zero trip meter at 80 Mile Beach Caravan Park exit.
(9.2 km)   ▲ 118.5 km
9.2 km T intersection. **TR** onto bitumen: Great Northern Hwy.

> Broome off to left.

(51.6 km)   Gravel. ▲ 109.3 km
60.8 km Intersection. S'post: Shay Gap/Marble Bar 172. **TL** onto gravel.

> *Port Hedland off to right.*

(57.7 km)   Bitumen. Opp. dir. s'post: Broome. ▲ 57.7 km

118.5 km T intersection.

> *Turn right 100 m to Shay Gap Service Station.* **PD** *Minor mechanical repairs.*

0.0 km Zero trip meter at above T intersection. **TL** onto bitumen.
(2.4 km)   Gravel. ▲ 0.0 km
    ▲ 56.7 km

2.4 km Intersection. S'post: Marble Bar. **TL** onto gravel.

> *Straight ahead to Shay Gap. Supplies, caravan parks.*

(25.7 km)   Bitumen. ▲ 54.3 km
28.1 km Causeway. **SO.**
(28.6 km)   ▲ 28.6 km
56.7 km T intersection. S'post: Marble Bar.

> *Telfer mining project off to left.*

    Opp. dir. s'post: Shay Gap 56.

0.0 km Zero trip meter at above T intersection. **TR.**
(23.9 km)   ▲ 0.0 km
    ▲ 59.6 km

23.9 km Causeway. **SO.**
(1.0 km)   ▲ 35.7 km
24.9 km T intersection. S'post: Marble Bar 32. **TL** onto Marble Bar Rd.

> *Port Hedland off to right.*

(26.4 km)   Opp. dir. s'post: Shay Gap 70. ▲ 34.7 km
51.3 km Y intersection. S'post: Marble Bar 8. **KR** onto bitumen.

> *Nullagine and Newman off to left.*

(8.3 km)   Gravel. Opp. dir. s'post: Port Hedland. ▲ 8.3 km
59.6 km Marble Bar town centre, adjacent to post office–general store on Francis St.

> **PD** *Supplies, caravan park, accomm., service facilities. Historic buildings. Information at BP Service Station and Towing Service on Francis St. Next fuel Auski Roadhouse (263 km).*

Option: Marble Bar Pool, Chinamans Pool, Comet Goldmine.

0.0 km Zero trip meter at post office–general store on Francis St heading south. **SO** along General St.
(0.6 km)   ▲ 0.0 km
    ▲ 1.4 km

Marble Bar Pool

0.6 km Intersection. S'post: Wittenoom/Marble Bar Pool. **TL.**
(0.8 km)   Opp. dir. s'post: Town centre. ▲ 0.8 km
1.4 km Intersection. S'post: Marble Bar Pool and Chinamans Pool.

> *Turn right 2 km to s'post: Chinamans Pool then turn right 400 m to picnic area and swimming hole. Camping prohibited. Straight ahead 900 m from s'post: Chinamans Pool to Marble Bar Pool, picnic area and swimming hole. Camping and chipping of jasper bar prohibited.*

0.0 km Zero trip meter at above intersection. **SO** onto gravel.
(3.6 km)   ▲ 0.0 km
    ▲ 3.6 km

3.6 km Intersection.

> *Turn right 1.1 km to Flying Fox Lookout. Picnic area, barbecues.*

0.0 km Zero trip meter at above intersection. **SO.**
(3.2 km)   ▲ 0.0 km
    ▲ 3.2 km

3.2 km Comet Goldmine on right.

> *Minerals and jewellery display. Souvenirs.*

End option.
Return to Marble Bar town centre by same route or start next trek section at Comet Goldmine.

    REVERSE DIRECTIONS START ▲ 0.0 km

MARBLE BAR «» HAMERSLEY RANGE

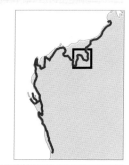

START POINT
Map page 34, E2.

TOTAL KM 320.
UNSEALED KM 198.
DEGREE OF DIFFICULTY Easy.
DRIVING TIME 5.5 hours.
LONGEST DISTANCE NO FUEL 263 km (Marble Bar to Auski Roadhouse).
TOPOGRAPHIC MAPS Auslig 1:250 000 series: *Marble Bar; Roy Hill; Mt Bruce.* See also 1:100 000 series.
LOCAL/SPECIALITY MAPS StreetSmart touring map: *Pilbara; Robinson's Western Australia.*
OTHER USEFUL INFORMATION Western Australian Tourism Commission booklet: *Western Australia's Unique North* and brochure: *Hamersley Range National Park, Millstream–Chichester National Park*; MAPco of Western Australia booklet: *Northern Western Australia*; CALM booklet: *North-West Bound: From Shark Bay to Wyndham*; Wittenoom Tourist Association brochure: *Wittenoom: Central to Hamersley Gorges.*

DESCRIPTION This section penetrates deeply into the rich iron-ore country of the Hamersley Range and begins an exploration of the gorge system around Wittenoom. The geology of Hamersley Range National Park is striking: spectacular mountains, gorges, watercourses and plateaus. As well as being the traditional home of the Banjima and Innawonga Aboriginal people, the park is home to a wealth of Pilbara animals such as spinifex pigeons, ring-tailed dragons and red kangaroos. Wildflowers grow in abundance and vary with the seasons.

Entering the park via Yampire Gorge Road you pass through an area once used for asbestos mining. There is still a small risk of inhaling microscopic asbestos-dust particles, especially if the tailings are disturbed; *see Warnings.* Along this approach to *Yampire* camping area you will see some unusual sights: tram tracks, a well, buses and old boilers. There are giant termite mounds en route to Fortescue Falls, the park's only permanent waterfall.

Circular Pool campsite and the base of Dales Gorge are the end points of this section. Streams, pools, waterfalls and ferns provide a colourful contrast to steep terraced cliffs of loose red rock.

WARNINGS ▶ Gravel roads may be slippery and treacherous after heavy rain; be cautious. ▶ Take on enough fuel at Auski Roadhouse for 227 kilometres to Wittenoom. ▶ Blue asbestos used to be important commodity in Wittenoom region. Some mine tailings potentially dangerous; avoid tailings heaps. When entering national park via Yampire Gorge Road keep car windows closed and observe warning signs. ▶ Be careful and notify ranger before commencing longer walks. Extremely hazardous gorges recommended only for physically fit walkers. ▶ Hamersley Range also has Banjima name, Karijini, and national park has much evidence of early Aboriginal occupation. Do not touch, disturb or remove anything at Aboriginal sites. ▶ Fires prohibited in park. Use only fireplaces and gas barbecues provided or preferably bring your portable gas stove. ▶ Gathering of rocks and picking of flowers prohibited in national park; all flora, fauna and rock formations protected.

BOOKINGS AND PERMITS ▶ No prior permits required to traverse national park. Camp only in designated areas, self-register and pay fees on site. ▶ For all information about camping and national park ring ranger on (091) 89 8157 or contact CALM Pilbara Regional Office, SGIO Building, Welcome Road, Karratha WA 6714; PO Box 835, Karratha WA 6714; tel. (091) 86 8288. ▶ For information about Wittenoom, gorges and national park contact Wittenoom Tourist Shop, Sixth Avenue, Wittenoom WA 6752; PO Box 24, Wittenoom WA 6752; tel. (091) 89 7096.

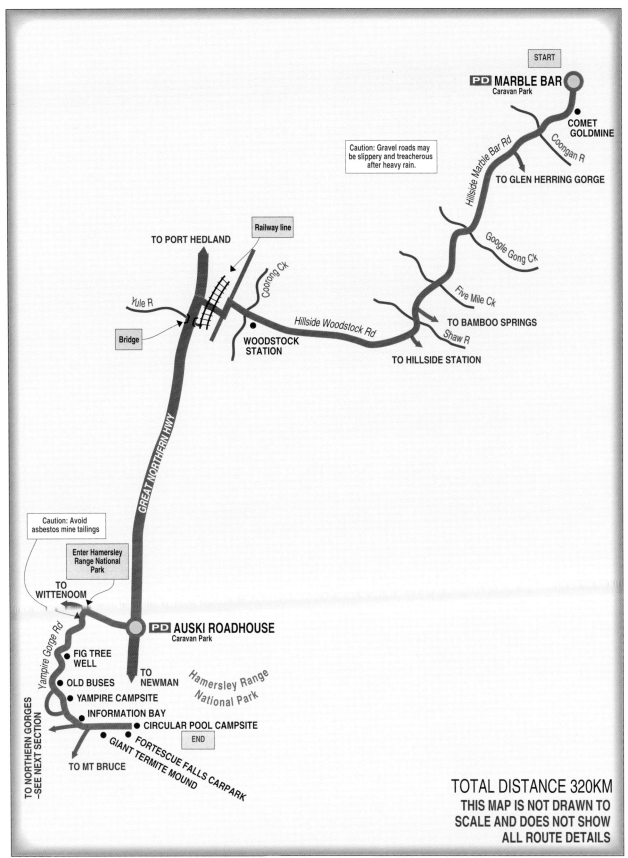

START

PD MARBLE BAR
Caravan Park

COMET
GOLDMINE

Coongan R

Hillside Marble Bar Rd

TO GLEN HERRING GORGE

Caution: Gravel roads may
be slippery and treacherous
after heavy rain.

Google Gong Ck

Five Mile Ck

TO BAMBOO SPRINGS

Shaw R

TO HILLSIDE STATION

Railway line

TO PORT HEDLAND

Coorong Ck

Yule R

Hillside Woodstock Rd

Bridge

WOODSTOCK
STATION

GREAT NORTHERN HWY

Caution: Avoid
asbestos mine tailings

Enter Hamersley
Range National
Park

TO
WITTENOOM

PD AUSKI ROADHOUSE
Caravan Park

Yampire Gorge Rd

FIG TREE
WELL

TO
NEWMAN

Hamersley Range
National Park

OLD BUSES

YAMPIRE CAMPSITE

INFORMATION BAY

CIRCULAR POOL CAMPSITE

END

TO NORTHERN GORGES
–SEE NEXT SECTION

FORTESCUE FALLS CARPARK

GIANT TERMITE MOUND

TO MT BRUCE

TOTAL DISTANCE 320KM
THIS MAP IS NOT DRAWN TO
SCALE AND DOES NOT SHOW
ALL ROUTE DETAILS

Dales Gorge at base of Circular Pool

Asbestos-tailings warning sign

ROUTE DIRECTIONS

Depart Marble Bar town centre south 8.2 km to Comet Goldmine (see *Route Directions* for previous section).

> *Next fuel Auski Roadhouse 263 km.*

0.0 km   Zero trip meter at Comet Goldmine heading south. **SO.**
     (8.3 km)   ▲ 84.0 km

8.3 km   Coongan River causeway. **SO.**
     (14.1 km)   ▲ 75.7 km

22.4 km   Intersection. **SO.**

> *Glen Herring Gorge 32 km off to left along rough 4WD track.*

     (33.5 km)   ▲ 61.6 km

55.9 km   Google Gong Creek crossing. **SO.**
     (23.3 km)   ▲ 28.1 km

79.2 km   Five Mile Creek crossing. **SO.**
     (4.8 km)   ▲ 4.8 km

84.0 km   Y intersection. S'post: Wittenoom.

> *Bamboo Springs off to left.*

0.0 km   Zero trip meter at above Y intersection. **KR.**
     (0.5 km)   ▲ 0.0 km
         ▲ 75.3 km

0.5 km   Shaw River crossing. **SO.**

> *Hillside Station off to left immediately after Shaw River crossing.*

     (57.0 km)   ▲ 74.8 km

57.5 km   Coorong Creek crossing. **SO.**

> *Woodstock Station on left immediately before Coorong Creek crossing.*

     (7.1 km)   ▲ 17.8 km

64.6 km   S'post: Wittenoom. **TL.**
     (0.9 km)   Opp. dir. s'post: Marble Bar. ▲ 10.7 km

65.5 km   S'post: Wittenoom 143. **TR.**
     (0.9 km)   Opp. dir. s'post: Marble Bar. ▲ 9.8 km

66.4 km   Cross railway line.
     (8.9 km)   ▲ 8.9 km

75.3 km   T intersection. S'post: Wittenoom.

> *Port Hedland 168 km off to right.*

     Opp. dir. s'post: Marble Bar 164.

0.0 km   Zero trip meter at above T intersection. **TL** onto bitumen: Great Northern Hwy.
     (3.5 km)   Gravel. ▲ 0.0 km
         ▲ 95.5 km

3.5 km Yule River. Cross bridge.
(92.0 km)   ▲ 92.0 km

95.5 km Crossroads. S'post: Wittenoom 41/Hamersley Range National Park.

> *Auski Roadhouse at crossroads.* **PD** *Limited supplies, caravan park. Next fuel Wittenoom (227 km). Straight ahead to Newman.*

    Opp. dir. s'post: Port Hedland 261.

0.0 km Zero trip meter at above crossroads. **TR** onto Roy Hill–Wittenoom Rd.
(18.3 km)   ▲ 0.0 km
    ▲ 40.7 km

18.3 km Intersection. S'post: Yampire Gorge/Hamersley Range National Park. **TL** onto gravel: Yampire Gorge Rd.

> *Keep car windows closed in disused asbestos mine-tailings area indicated by warning sign. Straight ahead 24 km to Wittenoom.*

(0.5 km)   Bitumen. Opp. dir. s'post: Port Hedland. ▲ 22.4 km

18.8 km Sign: Hamersley Range National Park. **SO**.

> *Camp in designated areas only.*

(11.4 km)   ▲ 21.9 km
30.2 km Fig Tree Well on left. **SO**.

> *Historic well used originally by Afghan cameleers and later for watering horses.*

(4.8 km)   ▲ 10.5 km
35.0 km Two old buses on left. **SO**.

> *Buses used as accomm. by geologists prospecting for iron ore in 1960s.*

(5.7 km)   ▲ 5.7 km
40.7 km Intersection.

> *Doug Francis Drive on right: a 3-km loop track, no purpose.*

0.0 km Zero trip meter at above intersection. **SO**.
(1.4 km)   ▲ 0.0 km
    ▲ 16.1 km

1.4 km Yampire camping area on left.

> *Fireplaces, gas barbecues, pit toilets. Portable generators permitted. Limited shade.*

(3.8 km)   ▲ 14.7 km
5.2 km Information board on left.

> *Overhead freshwater tank 10 m from information board.*

Giant termite mound, near Mt Bruce

(0.3 km)   ▲ 10.9 km
5.5 km Intersection. S'post: Dales Gorge. **SO**.

> *Northern gorges off to right.*

(0.2 km)   Opp. dir. s'post: Yampire Gorge. ▲ 10.6 km
5.7 km Intersection. S'post: Dales Gorge. **TL** onto Joffre Falls Rd.

> *Giant termite mound 1 km on right. Straight ahead to Mt Bruce.*

(9.5 km)   ▲ 10.4 km
15.2 km Fortescue Falls carpark on right. **SO**.

> *Camping prohibited. Pit toilets. Steep 400 m return walk to falls and pool. Swimming.*

(0.9 km)   ▲ 0.9 km
16.1 km Circular Pool campsite.

> *Fireplaces, gas barbecues, pit toilets. Portable generators not permitted. Steep descent then easy ramble 800 m return to hidden gardens of Circular Pool and base of Dales Gorge.*

REVERSE DIRECTIONS START ▲ 0.0 km

HAMERSLEY RANGE «» WITTENOOM

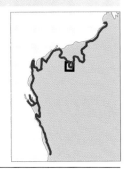

START POINT
Map page 34, C5.

TOTAL KM 170.
UNSEALED KM 163.
DEGREE OF DIFFICULTY Easy.
DRIVING TIME 3 hours.
LONGEST DISTANCE NO FUEL 227 km (Auski Roadhouse to Wittenoom).
TOPOGRAPHIC MAP Auslig 1:250,000 series: *Mt Bruce*. See also 1:100 000 series.
LOCAL/SPECIALITY MAPS StreetSmart touring map: *Pilbara; Robinson's Western Australia.*
OTHER USEFUL INFORMATION Western Australian Tourism Commission booklet: *Western Australia's Unique North* and brochure: *Hamersley Range National Park, Millstream–Chichester National Park*; CALM booklet: *North-West Bound: From Shark Bay to Wyndham*; MAPco of Western Australia booklet: *Northern Western Australia*; Wittenoom Tourist Association brochure: *Wittenoom: Central to Hamersley Gorges.*

DESCRIPTION On this section you explore the more spectacular and famous gorges at the northern end of Australia's second-largest national park. Though the distance covered is short, this beautiful rust-red and green country deserves at least a full day's stopover: enjoy walking, swimming in the crystal pools, and the wildflowers: yellow cassias and wattles, northern bluebells and purple mulla-mullas. Your first walk is a steep, hard climb to the top of Mt Bruce.

The park's rolling hillsides hide small and usually dry creeks that suddenly plunge into vertical chasms up to 100 metres deep. *Weano Gorge* has a camping area

Joffre Falls, dry

and a walk trail that takes you down into the gorge itself and through its base to Handrail Pool after which various tracks lead to swimming holes or views of Red, Weano and Hancock gorges. There is also camping at *Joffre Gorge* and a short track leads to a lookout over the falls and pool. Lookouts over Knox Gorge can also be reached after several short walks. Kalamina Gorge has a picnic area and a choice of walks into the gorge's lush, shaded pool or along a creek and small ponds within the gorge itself.

Wittenoom, on the northern escarpment of the range, was a major centre for the blue-asbestos mining industry between 1947 and 1966; **see Warnings.** Since the mine closed Wittenoom has changed from the largest settlement in the north west to a small town catering for the many visitors to the gorges each year.

WARNINGS ▶ Gravel roads may be slippery and treacherous after heavy rain; be cautious. ▶ Avoid potentially dangerous asbestos-mine tailings especially around Wittenoom township and Wittenoom Gorge. Keep car windows closed, observe warning signs and avoid tailings heaps. ▶ Most walks extremely

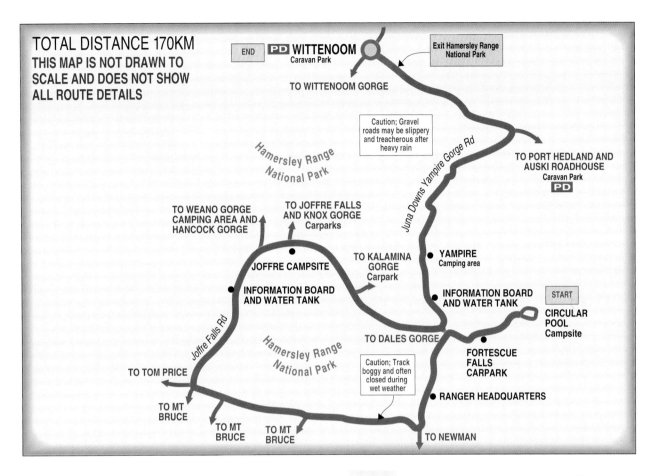

TOTAL DISTANCE 170KM
THIS MAP IS NOT DRAWN TO
SCALE AND DOES NOT SHOW
ALL ROUTE DETAILS

END | **PD WITTENOOM** Caravan Park

Exit Hamersley Range National Park

TO WITTENOOM GORGE

Caution; Gravel roads may be slippery and treacherous after heavy rain

Hamersley Range National Park

TO PORT HEDLAND AND AUSKI ROADHOUSE
Caravan Park **PD**

Juna Downs Yampire Gorge Rd

TO WEANO GORGE CAMPING AREA AND HANCOCK GORGE

TO JOFFRE FALLS AND KNOX GORGE Carparks

JOFFRE CAMPSITE

YAMPIRE Camping area

TO KALAMINA GORGE Carpark

INFORMATION BOARD AND WATER TANK

INFORMATION BOARD AND WATER TANK

START

CIRCULAR POOL Campsite

Joffre Falls Rd

Hamersley Range National Park

TO DALES GORGE

TO TOM PRICE

Caution; Track boggy and often closed during wet weather

FORTESCUE FALLS CARPARK

TO MT BRUCE

RANGER HEADQUARTERS

TO MT BRUCE | TO MT BRUCE

TO NEWMAN

---

hazardous and strenuous; top physical fitness required. Notify ranger before undertaking all walks. ▶ Do not touch, disturb or remove anything you find at Aboriginal sites. ▶ Fires prohibited; use only cooking facilities provided or preferably bring portable gas stove. ▶ Do not gather rocks or pick wildflowers.

BOOKINGS AND PERMITS ▶ Camp only in designated areas, self-register and pay fees on site. ▶ See previous trek section for where to find information about camping, Wittenoom gorge region and Hamersley Range National Park.

ROUTE DIRECTIONS

0.0 km   Zero trip meter at end of one-way track exit to Circular Pool campsite in Hamersley Range National Park.
   (0.5 km)   ▲ 41.1 km
0.5 km   Intersection. Fortescue Falls carpark on left. **SO**.
   (9.5 km)   ▲ 40.6 km

10.0 km   T intersection. S'post: Mt Bruce. **TL**.

> *Wittenoom and Weano gorges off to right.*

   (11.2 km)   Opp. dir. s'post: Dales Gorge. ▲ 31.1 km
21.2 km   Ranger headquarters on left. **SO**.
   (2.3 km)   ▲ 19.9 km
23.5 km   Y intersection. **KR**.

> *Keep left to Newman.*

   (17.6 km)   ▲ 17.6 km
41.1 km   Y intersection.
0.0 km   Zero trip meter at above Y intersection. **KR**.

> *Track boggy and often closed during wet weather. Left track slightly longer but rejoins after passing Mt Bruce.*

   (13.5 km)   ▲ 0.0 km
                ▲ 14.8 km
13.5 km   Mt Bruce on left. **SO**.
   (1.3 km)   ▲ 1.3 km
14.8 km   Y intersection.
0.0 km   Zero trip meter at above Y intersection. **KR**.

> *Mt Bruce off to left. Track continues 1.6 km to carpark at base of mountain. Commence 3-km return walk: steep hard climb to stunning views at top.*

(6.6 km) ▲ 0.0 km
▲ 32.6 km

6.6 km Crossroads. S'post: Wittenoom. **TR**.

> *Loop road around Mt Bruce commences on left. Straight ahead to Tom Price.*

(25.2 km) Opp. dir. s'post: Mt Bruce. ▲ 26.0 km

31.8 km Information board and overhead water tank on left. **SO**.

(0.8 km) ▲ 0.8 km

32.6 km Intersection. S'post: Wittenoom/Dales Gorge.

> *Straight ahead 9 km to Y intersection s'post: Weano Gorge. Keep right a further 4 km to Weano Gorge camping area on left. Fireplaces, gas barbecues, pit toilets. Portable generators not permitted. Straight ahead a further 200-m to Weano Gorge walk trail on left, a 300-m return walk to Handrail Pool at base of gorge. Straight ahead a further 300 m to information board at end of track. Details on 6 walking tracks commencing from this point: 2 enter freshwater swimming holes within gorge; 4 lead to views of Red, Weano and Hancock gorges.*

Opp. dir. s'post: Tom Price.

0.0 km Zero trip meter at above intersection. **TR**.

(2.5 km) ▲ 0.0 km
▲ 2.5 km

2.5 km Intersection. S'post: Wittenoom. Joffre campsite on right.

> *Fireplaces, gas barbecues, pit toilets. Portable generators permitted. Turn left 1.4 km to Joffre Falls carpark on left. Walk 50 m to lookout. Straight ahead a further 4.2 km to Knox Gorge carpark. Commence several short walks to lookouts over Knox Gorge.*

Opp. dir. s'post: Tom Price.

0.0 km Zero trip meter at above intersection. **SO**.

(10.7 km) ▲ 0.0 km
▲ 10.7 km

10.7 km Intersection. S'post: Circular Pool campsite.

> *Turn left 6 km to Kalamina Gorge carpark. Picnic tables, pit toilets. Camping prohibited. Commence 30-min. return walk to Kalamina Falls and pool or 3-hr return walk within gorge along creek and ponds.*

Opp. dir. s'post: Joffre campsite.

0.0 km Zero trip meter at above intersection. **SO**.

(18.7 km) ▲ 0.0 km
▲ 68.5 km

18.7 km T intersection. S'post: Wittenoom. **TL**.

> *Dales Gorge off to right. Information board and water tank 100 m off to right.*

(3.8 km) Opp. dir. s'post: Weano Gorge 46. ▲ 49.8 km

22.5 km Yampire camping area on right. **SO**.

(23.8 km) ▲ 46.0 km

46.3 km T intersection. S'post: Wittenoom. **TL** onto bitumen: Roy Hill–Wittenoom Rd.

> *Auski Roadhouse off to right.* **PD** *Caravan park. Port Hedland off to right.*

(5.8 km) Gravel. Opp. dir. s'post: Yampire Gorge. ▲ 22.2 km

52.1 km Gravel. **SO**.

(9.0 km) Bitumen. ▲ 16.4 km

61.1 km Exit national park.

(6.4 km) Opp. dir. s'post: Hamersley Range National Park. ▲ 7.4 km

67.5 km Bitumen. **SO**.

(1.0 km) Gravel. ▲ 1.0 km

68.5 km T intersection. S'post: Tom Price. Wittenoom township on left. Caravan park on immediate right across T intersection.

> **PD** *Supplies, caravan park, hospital. Tours of gorges and iron-ore mines. Historic buildings, gallery, gem display. Turn left at T intersection to Wittenoom Gorge Scenic Drive, 12 km bitumen. See Warnings about asbestos-tailings health risk.*

REVERSE DIRECTIONS START ▲ 0.0 km

WITTENOOM
«»
ROEBOURNE

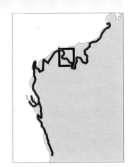

START POINT
Map page 34, C4.

TOTAL KM 346.
UNSEALED KM 300.
DEGREE OF DIFFICULTY Easy.
DRIVING TIME 6 hours.
LONGEST DISTANCE NO FUEL 346 km (Wittenoom to Roebourne).
TOPOGRAPHIC MAPS Auslig 1:250,000 series: *Mt Bruce*; *Pyramid*; *Yarraloola*; *Roebourne*; *Dampier*. See also 1:100 000 series.
LOCAL/SPECIALITY MAPS StreetSmart touring map: *Pilbara*; *Robinson's Western Australia*.
OTHER USEFUL INFORMATION Western Australian Tourism Commission booklet: *Western Australia's Unique North* and brochure: *Hamersley Range National Park, Millstream–Chichester National Park*; CALM booklet: *North-West Bound: From Shark Bay to Wyndham* and information sheet: *Millstream–Chichester National Park*; MAPco of Western Australia booklet: *Northern Western Australia*.

DESCRIPTION On this section you follow the Hamersley Range north west through pastoral country settled in the late nineteenth century by the Wittenoom and Hancock families. Views of the range are constant and beautiful for the first half, and the red earth comes alive with wildflowers and stockfeed in early spring and following rainfall.

The second half takes you through Millstream–Chichester National Park: 200 000 hectares of basalt ranges and clay tablelands. Millstream on the Fortescue River is a tropical paradise of ferns, cadjeputs, native palms, date palms planted by Afghan cameleers, lily ponds and permanent freshwater pools. A diversity of rare wildlife includes dragonflies and damselflies, fruit bats and spec-

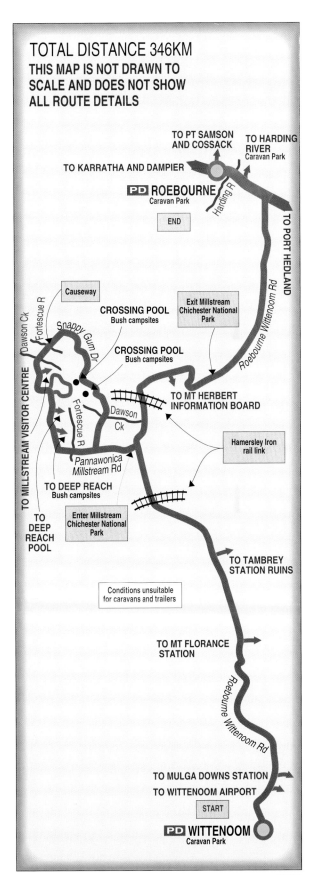

TOTAL DISTANCE 346KM
THIS MAP IS NOT DRAWN TO
SCALE AND DOES NOT SHOW
ALL ROUTE DETAILS

Lily pond, Millstream

tacular birds. Chinderwarriner Pool is a lush oasis that was once a campsite for the Yinjibarndi Aboriginal people. Camping is ideal under tall melaleucas at *Crossing Pool* and *Deep Reach* where you can swim, canoe and enjoy a range of interesting bushwalks.

You then cross the second part of the national park, the Chichester Range, a dramatically different landscape of sandy watercourses, huge knobs of red rock, spiky spinifex and white snappy gums. A strenuous walk up Mt Herbert rewards you with breathtaking views of the bronzed coastal plains, and the old camel track takes you through a rugged section of the range. Python Pool, at the foot of a wonderfully etched rock face, is a refreshing stop-off point for a swim.

Established in 1864, Roebourne is the oldest town on the north-west coast and was once the centre for the Pilbara's early mining and pastoral industries. The special character of the township and the old port of Cossack is preserved in their many stone buildings, and access is provided to several pleasant spots along the coast. You can stay at the caravan park on *Samson Road* as well as one near the *Harding River* between the national park and Roebourne.

WARNINGS ▶ Conditions in Millstream–Chichester National Park unsuitable for caravans or trailers. ▶ Sites at Millstream and Chinderwarrier Pool remain very important to Yinjibarndi Aboriginal people, and Python Pool in Chichester Range section of national park has Aboriginal rock carvings. Do not touch, disturb or remove anything you find at Aboriginal sites in either section of park. ▶ Fires prohibited in park. Use only gas barbecues provided or preferably bring your portable gas stove. ▶ Gathering of rocks and picking of flowers prohibited in park.

BOOKINGS AND PERMITS ▶ No prior permits necessary to traverse national park. Camp only in designated areas; self-register on site. ▶ For all information about camping and national park ring ranger on (091) 84 5144 or (091) 84 5125, or contact CALM Pilbara Regional Office, SGIO Building, Welcome Road, Karratha WA 6714; PO Box 835, Karratha WA 6714; tel. (091) 86 8288. ▶ For information about Roebourne district contact Roebourne Tourist Bureau, 173 Roe Street, Roebourne WA 6718; tel. (091) 82 1060.

368

ROUTE DIRECTIONS

0.0 km   Zero trip meter in Wittenoom at caravan-park entrance. S'post: Roebourne 287. **SO** onto Roebourne–Wittenoom Rd.

> **PD** *Supplies, caravan park.*

(1.0 km)   ▲ 181.0 km
1.0 km   S'post: Roebourne. **SO**.
(0.3 km)   Opp. dir. s'post: Wittenoom. ▲ 180.0 km
1.3 km   Gravel. **SO**.
(9.7 km)   Bitumen. ▲ 179.7 km
11.0 km   Intersection. **SO** onto bitumen.

> *Wittenoom Airport off to right. Bitumen crosses Fortescue River floodplain.*

(2.6 km)   Gravel. ▲ 170.0 km
13.6 km   Intersection. **SO**.

> *Mulga Downs Station off to right. Birthplace of late mining magnate Lang Hancock. Spectacular views of Hamersley Range from intersection.*

(2.9 km)   ▲ 167.4 km
16.5 km   Gravel. **SO**.
(68.9 km)   Bitumen. ▲ 164.5 km
85.4 km   Intersection. **SO**.

> *Mt Florance Station off to right.*

(35.0 km)   ▲ 95.6 km
120.4 km   Intersection. **SO**.

> *Track on right leads to Tambrey Station ruins. Main homestead building constructed of crushed and tamped termite mounds.*

(17.0 km)   ▲ 60.6 km
137.4 km   S'post: Millstream. Cross railway line and railway service road.

> *Railway line link between Tom Price and Dampier. Used exclusively for shipment of iron ore. Some freight trains a kilometre long.*

(28.5 km)   Opp. dir. s'post: Wittenoom. ▲ 43.6 km
165.9 km   Intersection. S'post: Millstream 21. **TL** onto Pannawonica–Millstream Rd.

> *Enter Millstream–Chichester National Park.*

(11.6 km)   Opp. dir. s'post: Wittenoom. ▲ 15.1 km
177.5 km   Intersection. S'post: Crossing Pool. **TR**.

> *Millstream straight ahead.*

(3.5 km)   Opp. dir. s'post: Wittenoom 180. ▲ 3.5 km

181.0 km   Dawson Creek crossing.
0.0 km   Zero trip meter at Dawson Creek crossing. **SO**.
(3.8 km)   ▲ 0.0 km
                                                ▲ 3.8 km

3.8 km   Crossing Pool on left. S'post: Crossing Pool main camping area.

> *Camping, gas barbecues, pit toilets. Portable generators not permitted. Swimming, canoeing. Main camping area further on.*

0.0 km   Zero trip meter at Crossing Pool. **SO**.
(0.4 km)   ▲ 0.0 km
                                                ▲ 0.4 km

0.4 km   Intersection. S'post: Snappy Gum Drive.

> *Straight ahead 300 m to Crossing Pool main camping area. Gas barbecues, pit toilets. Portable generators permitted. Swimming, canoeing, bushwalking. Shady campsites.*

0.0 km   Zero trip meter at above intersection. **TR** onto Snappy Gum Drive.
(5.7 km)   ▲ 0.0 km
                                                ▲ 9.2 km

5.7 km   T intersection. **TL**.

> *No access on right.*

(0.1 km)   Opp. dir. s'post: Crossing Pool 5. ▲ 3.5 km
5.8 km   Fortescue River causeway. **SO**.

> *Pipeline runs alongside road.*

(2.6 km)   ▲ 3.4 km
8.4 km   Millstream Depot water authority on right. **SO**.
(0.4 km)   ▲ 0.8 km
8.8 km   Crossroads. **SO** and immediately cross Dawson Creek, then immediately **TL** at intersection. S'post: Millstream.

> *Pipeline continues straight ahead.*

(0.4 km)   ▲ 0.4 km
9.2 km   Intersection. S'post: Deep Reach picnic area.

> *Millstream Homestead Visitor Centre on left. Gas barbecues, pit toilets, running water. Ranger, information shelter, telephone. Commence several walking trails. Easy walk to Chinderwarriner Pool. Easy 3.5-km walk along Murlunmunyjurna Trail to Crossing Pool. One-way 8-km walk along rugged Chichester Range Camel Trail.*

0.0 km   Zero trip meter at above intersection. **SO**.
(0.8 km)   ▲ 0.0 km
                                                ▲ 1.4 km

0.8 km   T intersection. **TR.**
(0.6 km)   ▲ 0.6 km
1.4 km   Intersection.

Turn left along loop road 4.8 km to cliff lookout over Fortescue River and surrounding pools.

0.0 km   Zero trip meter at above intersection. **SO.**
(0.2 km)   ▲ 0.0 km
                                            ▲ 0.2 km
0.2 km   Intersection.

Cliff-lookout loop road rejoins on left.

0.0 km   Zero trip meter at above intersection. **SO.**
(2.6 km)   ▲ 0.0 km
                                            ▲ 2.6 km
2.6 km   Intersection.

Turn left 300 m to Deep Reach picnic area. Gas barbecues, pit toilets. Swimming, canoeing. Camping prohibited; camping area further on.

0.0 km   Zero trip meter at above intersection. **SO.**
(1.4 km)   ▲ 0.0 km
                                            ▲ 1.4 km
1.4 km   Intersection.

Turn left 500 m to Deep Reach camping area. Gas barbecues, pit toilets. Portable generators permitted. Swimming, canoeing.

0.0 km   Zero trip meter at above intersection. **SO.**
(1.3 km)   ▲ 0.0 km
                                            ▲ 57.6 km
1.3 km   T intersection. S'post: Main Rd. **TL** onto Pannawonica–Millstream Rd.
(2.2 km)   Opp. dir. s'post:Deep Reach 2. ▲ 56.3 km
3.5 km   Fortescue River crossing. **SO.**
(1.1 km)   ▲ 54.1 km
4.6 km   Intersection. S'post: Roebourne 140. **SO.**

Crossing Pool off to left.

(11.6 km)   Opp. dir. s'post: Deep Reach. ▲ 53.0 km
16.2 km   T intersection. S'post: Roebourne. **TL** onto Roebourne–Wittenoom Rd.

Wittenoom off to right.

(19.7 km)   Opp. dir. s'post: Millstream 221. ▲41.4 km
35.9 km   Cross railway line.
(10.7 km)   ▲ 21.7 km
46.6 km   Bitumen. **SO.**
(2.7 km)   Gravel. ▲ 11.0 km

49.3 km   Intersection. **SO.**

Turn right along track 100m to Mt Herbert and information board. Three walking tracks. Camel Track 16-km return. Mt Herbert Trail 600-m return steep walk to panoramic views. McKenzie Spring 4.5-km walk to old camel watering place.

(8.3 km)   ▲ 8.3 km
57.6 km   Intersection.

Turn right 300 m to Python Pool. Camping prohibited. Gas barbecues, pit toilets. Short walk to good swimming spot. Aboriginal rock carvings.

0.0 km   Zero trip meter at above intersection. **SO** onto gravel.
(60.7 km)   Bitumen. ▲ 0.0 km
                                            ▲ 88.3 km
60.7 km   T intersection. S'post: Roebourne. **TL** onto bitumen: North West Coastal Hwy.

Port Hedland off to right.

(26.7 km)   Gravel. Opp. dir. s'post: Wittenoom. ▲27.6 km
87.4 km   Intersection. **SO.**

Turn right 1 km to caravan park.

(0.2 km)   ▲ 0.9 km
87.6 km   Harding River. Cross bridge.
(0.4 km)   ▲ 0.7 km
88.0 km   Intersection. S'post: Roebourne town centre/Karratha. **TR** onto Carnarvon Tce.
(0.3 km)   Opp. dir. s'post: Port Hedland. ▲ 0.3 km
88.3 km   Roebourne police station, cnr Carnarvon Tce and Queen St.

PD Supplies, caravan park. Many historic stone buildings in town and old port of Cossack. Access to Dampier, Cape Lambert and Pt Samson: major port for Roebourne district at turn of century, now small fishing settlement. Swimming, fishing, boating, beachwalking.

REVERSE DIRECTIONS START ▲ 0.0 km

ROEBOURNE
«»
ONSLOW

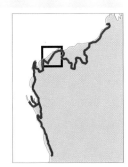

START POINT
Map page 38, H1.

TOTAL KM 314.
UNSEALED KM 65.
DEGREE OF DIFFICULTY Easy.
DRIVING TIME 5 hours.
LONGEST DISTANCE NO FUEL 170 km (Fortescue Roadhouse to Onslow).
TOPOGRAPHIC MAPS Auslig 1:250 000 series: *Roebourne*; *Dampier*; *Yarraloola*; *Wyloo*; *Onslow*. See also 1:100 000 series.
LOCAL/SPECIALITY MAPS StreetSmart touring maps: *Pilbara*; *Robinson's Western Australia*.
OTHER USEFUL INFORMATION Western Australian Tourism Commission booklet: *Western Australia's Unique North* and brochure: *Onslow: For Sun and Lazy Days*; CALM booklet: *North-West Bound: From Shark Bay to Wyndham*; MAPco of Western Australia booklet: *Northern Western Australia*.

DESCRIPTION For much of this section the only possible route is along the bitumen North West Coastal Hwy. The short dirt road that links the highway with Onslow Road is flat and well graded during the dry periods. It is relatively featureless plains country except for an interesting section after Peedamullah Station where there is a massive field of termite mounds completely exposed on the grassy land. There are no campsites along the way, but you can camp on some of the islands around *Onslow* and stay in caravan parks at *Roebourne* and *Onslow* and, optionally, at *Karratha*.

The section finishes in the pretty coastal holiday village of Onslow. In 1925 constant cyclones forced the townsite to be moved from the mouth of the Ashburton River to Beadon Bay; you visit and camp at the

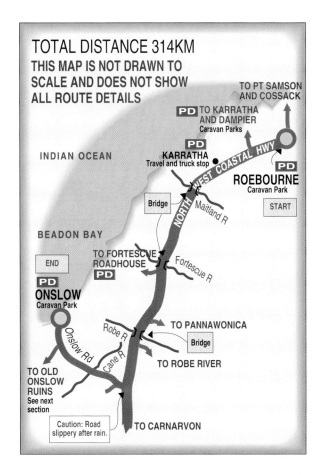

Old Onslow ruins at the beginning of the next trek section. In the late nineteenth century Onslow was a bustling pearling centre, then gold was discovered. It is now the supply base for the oilfields off the coast at Barrow Island, and for the Saladin oilfields.

Onslow's lifestyle is lazy and low-key, and fishing is its greatest attraction. Boating, water-sport and marine-life enthusiasts can enjoy offshore islands, coral reefs, bays and inlets amid safe waters. Around town there are popular picnic and fishing spots at Ashburton River, Four Mile Creek and Beadon Creek Groyne. Native animals abound in tidal-creek mangrove swamps, coastal dunes and riverine woodlands, and beautiful wildflowers such as the Sturt Desert Pea and wild hibiscus bloom in spring and after rain.

WARNINGS ▶ Short gravel section linking North West Coastal Highway and Onslow Road very flat; retains water for long time after heavy rain, very slippery and boggy when wet. Before departure ring Onslow police station on (091) 84 6000 or Ashburton Shire Council in Onslow on (091) 84 6001 to check road conditions. ▶ Do not embark during December–February: hot summer months feature occasional dust

Caravan park, Onslow

storms, cyclonic winds and torrential rain. Travel only during winter months March–November when temperatures average 25–30 degrees Celsius.

BOOKINGS AND PERMITS ▶ For information about touring in Karratha region contact NorWest Tourist Centres, City Shopping Centre, Welcome Road, Karratha WA 6714; tel. (091) 85 2474. ▶ For information about touring in Onslow region, boat charters and camping on islands contact Elaine's Souvenirs, Second Avenue, Onslow WA 6710; tel. (091) 84 6161. ▶ For information about natural environment contact CALM Pilbara Regional Office, SGIO Building, Welcome Road, Karratha WA 6714; PO Box 835, Karratha WA 6714; tel. (091) 86 8288.

ROUTE DIRECTIONS

Depart Roebourne Post Office heading north via Carnarvon Tce, Roe St and Clearville Rd. Straight ahead heading west along North West Coastal Hwy 39 km to Karratha turnoff.

0.0 km Zero trip meter at North West Coastal Hwy and Karratha Rd intersection. S'post: Carnarvon. **SO**.

> *Karratha off to right.* **PD** *Supplies, caravan parks.*

(8.9 km) Opp. dir. s'post: Roebourne. ▲ 275.1 km

8.9 km Karratha Travel and Truck Stop on right. **SO**. **PD**

(19.7 km) ▲ 266.2 km

28.6 km Maitland River. Cross bridge.

(76.9 km) ▲ 246.5 km

105.5 km Fortescue River. Cross bridge.

> *Fortescue Roadhouse 500 m on right.* **PD**

(41.9 km) ▲ 169.6 km

147.4 km Intersection. S'post: Carnarvon. **SO**.

> *Pannawonica off to left.*

(3.0 km) Opp. dir. s'post: Karratha. ▲ 127.7 km

150.4 km Robe River. Cross bridge.

> *Track on left immediately after bridge leads to river and picnic area.*

(39.0 km) ▲ 124.7 km

189.4 km Intersection. S'post: Peedamullah 7. **TR** onto gravel.

> *Straight ahead to Carnarvon.*

(6.5 km) Bitumen. ▲ 85.7 km

195.9 km Y intersection. **KR**.

> *Keep left along track to Peedamullah Station.*

(25.4 km) ▲ 79.2 km

221.3 km Cane River causeway. **SO**.

(33.2 km) ▲ 53.8 km

254.5 km T intersection. **TR** onto bitumen: Onslow Rd.

(2.3 km) Gravel. Opp. dir. s'post: Peedamullah. ▲ 20.6 km

256.8 km Intersection. S'post: Onslow. **SO**.

> *Turn left along Twitchin Rd 27 km to Old Onslow ruins.*

(16.6 km) ▲ 18.3 km

273.4 km Information board on left. **SO**.

(1.7 km) ▲ 1.7 km

275.1 km Onslow Post Office, cnr Second Ave and Simpson St.

> **PD** *Supplies, caravan park. Fishing, boating, swimming, windsurfing, diving and snorkelling around islands. Camping on some islands.*

REVERSE DIRECTIONS START ▲ 0.0 km

ONSLOW
«»
EXMOUTH

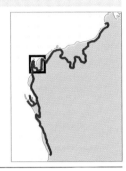

START POINT
Map page 38, E2.

TOTAL KM 358.
UNSEALED KM 209.
DEGREE OF DIFFICULTY Easy.
DRIVING TIME 6 hours.
LONGEST DISTANCE NO FUEL 334km (Onslow to Exmouth).
TOPOGRAPHIC MAPS Auslig 1:250 000 series: *Onslow*; *Yarraloola*; *Wyloo*; *Yanrey*; *Ningaloo*. See also 1:100 000 series.
LOCAL/SPECIALITY MAPS Department of Land Administration Perth tourist map: *Gascoyne Coast*; Exmouth Tourist Bureau maps: *Exmouth Town Map* and *North West Cape*; *Robinson's Western Australia*.
OTHER USEFUL INFORMATION Western Australian Tourism Commission booklet: *Western Australia's Unique North* and brochure: *Onslow: For Sun and Lazy Days*; CALM booklets: *North-West Bound: From Shark Bay to Wyndham* and *Birds of Cape Range National Park and Ningaloo Marine Park*; MAPco of *Western Australia booklet: Northern Western Australia*; Minderoo Station information sheet for Three Mile Pool Caravan–Camping Ground; Exmouth Tourist Bureau brochure: *Exmouth, Western Australia: Where It's Summer All Year Round* and information sheet: *The Attractions*.

DESCRIPTION Departing the Pilbara region for the Gascoyne coast, you follow coastal pastoral country through Ashburton and Exmouth shires along mostly good-quality and maintained gravel roads. The only camping stopover is *Three Mile Pool Caravan-Camping Ground* on the Ashburton River, Minderoo Station near Old Onslow ruins, after which there are caravan parks at *Kailis Prawn Fishery* and *Exmouth*.

At North West Cape you take a worthwhile detour into Cape Range National Park, which is explored in more detail during the next trek section. The park has many contrasts: rugged sandstone canyons and gorges carved over millions of years, high-plateau eucalypt woodlands, flat coastal plains with terraces of ancient fossil reefs, coastal dunes, rocky shores and white sandy beaches. The animals are well adapted to living in harsh conditions and the plants are an unusual mixture of Pilbara, south-west and northern species.

Charles Knife Road affords panoramic views of the Cape Range, and Shothole Canyon Road takes you into the heart of canyon country. Between the two roads is Badjirrajirra Trail, a walk over the top of the range, and Lightfoot Heritage Trail is a loop walk through the rugged limestone formation. Camping areas are not featured until the next trek section, but you can picnic at Shothole Canyon.

Exmouth was founded in 1967 as a support town for the joint Australian–United States naval communications station 'Harold E. Holt'. Excellent fishing and weather conditions make it popular all year round, and the surrounding waters at the edge of the Continental Shelf are the scene of many gamefishing records. Other activities include diving, snorkelling, boating, bushwalking, birdwatching and four-wheel drive safaris.

WARNINGS ▶ Gravel roads often treacherous and boggy after rain. Before departure ring Ashburton Shire Office on (091) 84 6001 or Onslow police station on (091) 84 6000 to check road conditions. ▶ Do not embark November–April when cyclones most common along Gascoyne coast, flood damage can make roads impassable. ▶ Rivers and creeks usually dry, often drought conditions; carry sufficient drinking water. ▶ Beware livestock and wild life crossing unfenced roads. ▶ Do not embark October–March when conditions particularly harsh in Cape Range National Park and temperatures can soar to over 50 degrees Celsius. Attempt bushwalks only April–September. Wear suitable footwear and notify ranger before setting out. ▶ On Cape Range peninsula do not touch shell middens and other relics of past Aboriginal occupation. When shell collecting leave live coral alone, put rocks and coral back in place, do not disturb shells with eggs, and collect only shells you wish to keep.

BOOKINGS AND PERMITS ▶ No camping fee for Three Mile Pool Caravan–Camping Ground on Minderoo Station near Old Onslow ruins. Caretaker in residence during peak season May–October. Check in on arrival, camp only in designated areas and adhere to station-management guidelines set out on information sheet. For all information contact Minderoo Station, Onslow WA 6710; tel. (091) 84 6044. ▶ For accommodation at Giralia Homestead contact Giralia Station, Bul-

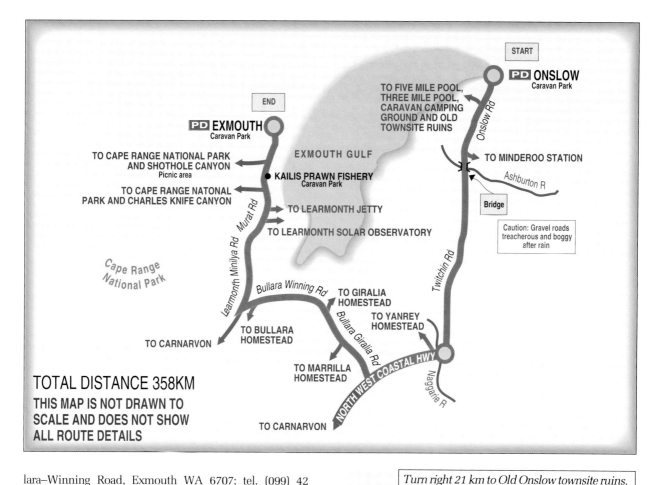

END

PD EXMOUTH
Caravan Park

TO CAPE RANGE NATIONAL PARK
AND SHOTHOLE CANYON
Picnic area

TO CAPE RANGE NATONAL
PARK AND CHARLES KNIFE CANYON

KAILIS PRAWN FISHERY
Caravan Park

TO LEARMONTH JETTY

TO LEARMONTH SOLAR OBSERVATORY

EXMOUTH GULF

START

PD ONSLOW
Caravan Park

TO FIVE MILE POOL,
THREE MILE POOL,
CARAVAN CAMPING
GROUND AND OLD
TOWNSITE RUINS

Onslow Rd

TO MINDEROO STATION

Ashburton R

Bridge

Caution: Gravel roads
treacherous and boggy
after rain

Learmonth Minilya Rd
Murat Rd

Cape Range
National Park

Bullara Winning Rd

TO GIRALIA
HOMESTEAD

Twitchin Rd

TO BULLARA
HOMESTEAD

TO CARNARVON

Bullara Giralia Rd

TO YANREY
HOMESTEAD

TO MARRILLA
HOMESTEAD

NORTH WEST COASTAL HWY

Naggarie R

TO CARNARVON

TOTAL DISTANCE 358KM

**THIS MAP IS NOT DRAWN TO
SCALE AND DOES NOT SHOW
ALL ROUTE DETAILS**

lara–Winning Road, Exmouth WA 6707; tel. (099) 42 5937. ▶ For information about activities in Cape Range National Park and Exmouth region contact Exmouth Tourist Bureau, Thew Street, Exmouth WA 6707; PO Box 149, Exmouth WA 6707; tel. (099) 49 1176 and (099) 49 1779.

ROUTE DIRECTIONS

0.0 km   Zero trip meter at Onslow Post Office, cnr Simpson St and Second Ave. **SO** along Second Ave and Onslow Rd heading south east.

> PD *Supplies, caravan park.*

(1.7 km)   ▲ 23.9 km
1.7 km   Information board on right. **SO**.
(16.6 km)   ▲ 22.2 km
18.3 km Intersection. S'post: Twitchin Rd/Old Onslow 27. **TR** onto gravel.
(5.6 km)   Bitumen. Opp. dir. s'post: Onslow. ▲ 5.6 km
23.9 km Intersection.

> *Turn right 21 km to Old Onslow townsite ruins. Five Mile Pool 11.1 km on left. Swimming, fishing. Camping prohibited. Three Mile Pool Caravan–Camping Ground on banks of Ashburton River, Minderoo Station, a further 4.4 km on left. Caretaker on site. Swimming, fishing. Straight ahead a further 500 m to sign: Old Onslow at intersection. Uralla off to left. Camping prohibited beyond this point. Straight ahead a further 4.6 km to Y intersection. Keep right to Old Cemetery. Keep left 400 m to Old Onslow ruins. Camping, shooting and removal of building materials prohibited. Beach straight ahead along track.*

0.0 km   Zero trip meter at above intersection. **SO**.
(17.3 km)   ▲ 0.0 km
                                                       ▲ 300.0 km

17.3 km Ashburton River. Cross bridge.

> *Minderoo Station off to left immediately before bridge.*

(103.4 km)   ▲ 282.7 km

120.7 km T intersection. **TR** onto bitumen: North West Coastal Hwy.

(2.2 km)   Gravel. Opp. dir. s'post: Twitchin Rd. ▲ 179.3 km

122.9 km Naggarie River. Cross bridge.

(3.5 km)   ▲ 177.1 km

126.4 km Intersection. **SO.**

> *Yanrey Station off to right.*

(36.1 km)   ▲ 173.6 km

162.5 km Intersection. S'post: Exmouth 168. **TR** onto gravel: Bullara–Giralia Rd.

(29.2 km)   Bitumen. ▲ 137.5 km

191.7 km Intersection. **SO** onto Bullara–Winning Rd.

> *Marrilla Homestead off to left.*

(14.9 km)   ▲ 108.3 km

206.6 km Intersection. **SO.**

> *Track on right leads to Giralia Homestead. Accomm.*

(33.6 km)   ▲ 93.4 km

240.2 km Intersection. S'post: Exmouth. **SO.**

> *Track on left leads to Bullara Homestead.*

(5.0 km)   ▲ 59.8 km

245.2 km T intersection. S'post: Exmouth. **TR** onto bitumen: Learmonth–Minilya Rd.

> *Carnarvon off to left.*

(54.3 km)   Gravel. Opp. dir. s'post: Giralia. ▲ 54.8 km

299.5 km Intersection. **SO.**

> *Learmonth Solar Observatory off to right.*

(0.5 km)   ▲ 0.5 km

300.0 km Intersection.

> *Learmonth Jetty 500 m off to right. Good fishing.*

0.0 km Zero trip meter at above intersection. **SO** onto Murat Rd.

(10.5 km)   ▲ 0.0 km
     ▲ 10.5 km

10.5 km Intersection.

Warning sign, Bullara–Giralia Road

> *Turn left along Charles Knife Rd to Cape Range National Park and Charles Knife Canyon. Gravel after 3.7 km. Straight ahead a further 2.9 km to sign: Cape Range National Park. Straight ahead a further 4 km to sign: Lookout 1km off to right. Commence 8-km return walk along Badjirrajirra Trail. Straight ahead a further 900m to Capped Oilwell. Commence 7-km return walk along Lightfoot Heritage Trail.*

0.0 km Zero trip meter at above intersection. **SO.**

(0.1 km)   ▲ 0.0 km
     ▲ 0.1 km

0.1 km Intersection. Kailis Prawn Fishery on right.

> *Caravan park. Prawns and fish for sale.*

0.0 km Zero trip meter at above intersection. **SO.**

(6.8 km)   ▲ 0.0 km
     ▲ 6.8 km

6.8 km Intersection.

> *Turn left along gravel Shothole Canyon Rd 10.7 km to sign: Cape Range National Park. Straight ahead 1.7 km to Shothole Canyon picnic area. Camping prohibited. Picnic tables, gas barbecues, pit toilets. Lookout.*

0.0 km Zero trip meter at above intersection. **SO.**

(15.8 km)   ▲ 0.0 km
     ▲ 16.3 km

15.8 km Intersection. S'post: Maidstone Crescent. **TL** into Exmouth town centre.

(0.5 km)   ▲ 0.5 km

16.3 km Exmouth police station on right.

> **PD** *Supplies, caravan parks. All services, major mechanical repairs, hospital.*

REVERSE DIRECTIONS START ▲ 0.0 km

EXMOUTH «» CARNARVON

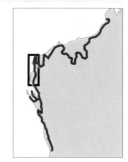

START POINT

Map page 38, C3.

TOTAL KM 438.

UNSEALED KM 146.

DEGREE OF DIFFICULTY Moderate; easy from Coral Bay to Carnarvon.

DRIVING TIME 5 hours (Exmouth to Coral Bay).

LONGEST DISTANCE NO FUEL 177 km (Lighthouse Caravan Park to Coral Bay).

TOPOGRAPHIC MAPS Auslig 1:250 000 series: *Onslow*; *Ningaloo*; *Minilya*; *Quobba*. See also 1:100 000 series.

LOCAL/SPECIALITY MAPS Department of Land Administration Perth tourist map: *Gascoyne Coast*; Exmouth Tourist Bureau maps: *Exmouth Town Map* and *North West Cape*; *Robinson's Western Australia*.

OTHER USEFUL INFORMATION Western Australian Tourism Commission booklet: *Western Australia's Unique North*; CALM booklets: *North-West Bound: From Shark Bay to Wyndham* and *Birds of Cape Range National Park and Ningaloo Marine Park*, brochure: *Parks of the Coral Coast: Visitor Guide to Ningaloo Marine Park and Cape Range National Park* and information sheet: *The Importance of Coastal Dunes*; MAPco of Western Australia booklet: *Northern Western Australia*; Exmouth Tourist Bureau information sheet: *The Attractions*; Peoples Park Caravan Park Coral Bay brochure: *Ningaloo Reef Coastal Guide*.

DESCRIPTION After heading north from Exmouth you turn south through Cape Range National Park all the way to Coral Bay, driving only 100 metres behind a line of sand dunes just off the beach. Through countryside that is all sparse low scrubland you enjoy repeated views of the magnificent Ningaloo Reef just offshore

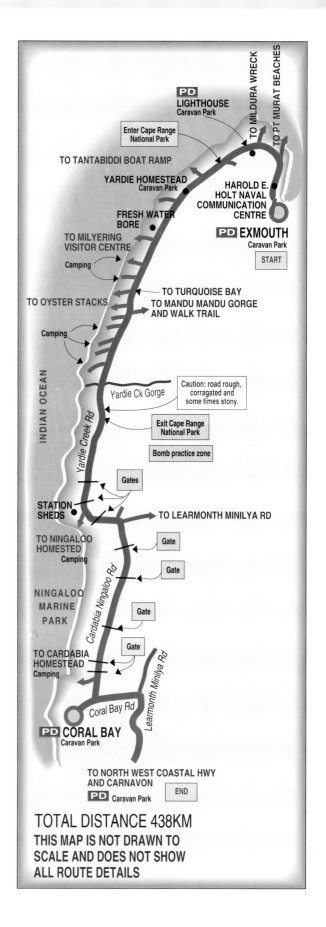

TOTAL DISTANCE 438KM
THIS MAP IS NOT DRAWN TO SCALE AND DOES NOT SHOW ALL ROUTE DETAILS

and turquoise waters inshore. Up to Yardie Creek near the southern end of the national park the road is good-quality gravel, and a large bitumen section links Coral Bay with Carnarvon.

Explore Mandu Mandu Gorge and Yardie Creek on foot: the former is the bed of an ancient river that carved the gorge's vertical red-sandstone walls over millions of years. Near T Bone Bay camping area is Milyering Visitor Centre, made from rammed earth and run by solar power, with an impressive array of materials on the unique natural environment. The route directions include the 8 camping areas within the park. There are also campsites on private property accessible from side tracks. Caravan parks are located at *Vlaming Head Lighthouse* on the tip of North West Cape, *Yardie Homestead, Coral Bay* and *Carnarvon.*

Coral Bay is a small idyllic resort town with a fringing coral-reef system of crystal-clear water, perfect for snorkelling or viewing coral formations and marine life from glass-bottomed boats. From here you drive on to Carnarvon, a much larger and fully serviced town, from where you commence the next trek section.

Coral Bay beach

WARNINGS ▶ *See Warnings* in previous trek section. ▶ National park has neither powered sites nor water except one fresh-water bore; bring your own drinking water. ▶ Private powered boats prohibited on Yardie Creek Gorge. ▶ Road after Yardie Creek Sand Bar rough, narrow and sometimes stoney. ▶ Section of coastal plains immediately south of national park used by RAAF as bomb practice zone and may be closed. Check this and other local information at Milyering Visitor Centre in national park. ▶ Do not interfere with or remove any material from historical shipwrecks; protected by law. ▶ Coral Bay a marine reserve; fishing prohibited. For fishing regulations in Ningaloo Marine Park contact CALM Exmouth District Office, Lot 391 Thew Street, Exmouth WA 6707; PO Box 201, Exmouth WA 6707; tel. (099) 49 1676 or Fisheries Department in Perth

BOOKINGS AND PERMITS ▶ No prior permits required to traverse Cape Range National Park but camping fee applicable; pay resident caretaker during peak season April–September or ranger October–March. Camp only in designated areas and check in with ranger at Milyering Visitor Centre on site. Limit stay to 28 days. For all information about Cape Range National Park and Ningaloo Marine Park contact Milyering Visitor Centre or CALM Exmouth District Office. ▶ Campsites along beach south of national park on private property. For sites on Ningaloo Station obtain permis-

sion from landowner in person; for Cardabia Station ring (099) 42 5935. ▶ Book Coral Bay caravan parks in advance for school-holiday peak seasons. ▶ For all information about national parks, Exmouth and Coral Bay contact Exmouth Tourist Bureau, Thew Street, Exmouth WA 6707; PO Box 149, Exmouth WA 6707; tel. (099) 49 1176 or (099) 49 1779. ▶ For information about Carnarvon region contact Carnarvon District Tourist Bureau, Robinson Street, Carnarvon WA 6701; tel. (099) 41 1146.

▼▼▼▼▼▼▼
TAKE CARE

● In outback Australia long distances separate some towns. Take care to ensure your vehicle is roadworthy before setting out and carry adequate supplies of petrol, water and food.

● Permits are required if you want to divert off public roads within Aboriginal Land areas.

● In Australia's north, during the wet season (October–May) roads become impassable. Check conditions before setting out.

● Carry additional water in desert areas: 5 litres per person per day is recommended, plus extra for the radiator.

● Don't take short cuts over virgin ground. You will destroy the vegetation. Stick to tracks open for use.

ROUTE DIRECTIONS

0.0 km   Zero trip meter at Exmouth police station. **SO** along Maidstone Crescent heading north.

> **PD** *Supplies, caravan parks. All services, major mechanical repairs.*

    (0.4 km)   ▲ 11.4 km

0.4 km   T intersection. S'post: Lighthouse 17. **TL** onto Murat Rd.

    (5.4 km)   ▲ 11.0 km

5.8 km   Harold E. Holt naval communications station on left. **SO**.

    (5.6 km)   ▲ 5.6 km

11.4 km   Intersection. S'post: Cape Range National Park.

> *Straight ahead 4.6 km to Pt Murat beaches. Swimming, snorkelling.*

0.0 km   Zero trip meter at above intersection. **TL** onto Yardie Creek Rd.

    (4.4 km)   ▲ 0.0 km
     ▲ 4.4 km

4.4 km   Intersection.

> *Turn right along gravel Mildura Wreck Rd 4.1 km to wreck of S.S. Mildura, visible from beach. Vessel wrecked in 1907 while carrying cattle from Kimberley.*

0.0 km   Zero trip meter at above intersection. **SO**.

    (2.1 km)   ▲ 0.0 km
     ▲ 2.7 km

2.1 km   Lighthouse Caravan Park on left at Vlaming Head. **SO**.

> **PD** *Supplies. Next fuel Coral Bay 177 km.*

    (0.6 km)   ▲ 0.6 km

2.7 km   Intersection.

> *Turn left along steep gravel Johnson Rd. 1 km to lighthouse and panoramic views of cape and Exmouth.*

0.0 km   Zero trip meter at above intersection. **SO**.

    (14.3 km)   ▲ 0.0 km
     ▲ 29.8 km

14.3 km   Yardie Homestead Chalet and Caravan Park on left. **SO**.

    (4.3 km)   ▲ 15.5 km

18.6 km   Tantabiddi boat ramp on right. **SO**.

> *Camping prohibited. Pit toilets. Swimming.*

    (3.2 km)   ▲ 11.2 km

21.8 km   Sign: Cape Range National Park. **SO**.

    (2.9 km)   ▲ 8.0 km

24.7 km   Gravel. **SO**.

    (5.1 km)   Bitumen. ▲ 5.1 km

29.8 km   Intersection.

> *Turn right 1 km to Neds Camp on right. Barbecues, pit toilets. Boat ramp. Mesa Camp 3 km. Barbecues, pit toilets.*

0.0 km   Zero trip meter at above intersection. **SO**.

    (0.1 km)   ▲ 0.0 km
     ▲ 3.1 km

0.1 km   Intersection. **SO**.

> *Freshwater bore off to left.*

    (3.0 km)   ▲ 3.0 km

3.1 km   Intersection.

> *Turn right 200 m to Milyering Visitor Centre. Information, ranger. Pit toilets. T Bone Bay camping area a further 500 m on right. Picnic tables, pit toilets. Lakeside camping area a further 3 km off to left. Pit toilets.*

0.0 km   Zero trip meter at above intersection. **SO**.

    (6.3 km)   ▲ 0.0 km
     ▲ 6.3 km

6.3 km   Intersection.

> *Turn right 700 m to Tulki Beach camping area. Pit toilets.*

0.0 km   Zero trip meter at above intersection. **SO**.

    (3.3 km)   ▲ 0.0 km
     ▲ 3.3 km

3.3 km   Intersection.

> *Turn right 500 m to Turquoise Bay. Camping prohibited.*

0.0 km   Zero trip meter at above intersection. **SO**.

    (3.2 km)   ▲ 0.0 km
     ▲ 3.2 km

3.2 km   Intersection.

> *Turn right 500 m to Oyster Stacks. Camping prohibited.*

0.0 km   Zero trip meter at above intersection. **SO**.

    (1.1 km)   ▲ 0.0 km
     ▲ 1.1 km

1.1 km   Intersection.

> *Turn left along Mandu Mandu Gorge Track 500 m to carpark and gorge walk: moderately easy, 1-hr return.*

Boat tour of Yardie Creek Gorge, Cape Range National Park

0.0 km	Zero trip meter at above intersection. **SO.** (0.2 km) ▲ 0.0 km ▲ 0.2 km
0.2 km	Intersection.

> Turn right 500 m to Mandu Mandu North camping ground.

0.0 km	Zero trip meter at above intersection. **SO.** (0.7 km) ▲ 0.0 km ▲ 0.7 km
0.7 km	Intersection.

> Turn right 500 m to Mandu Mandu South camping ground.

0.0 km	Zero trip meter at above intersection. **SO.** (5.9 km) ▲ 0.0 km ▲ 5.9 km
5.9 km	Intersection.

> Turn right to Pilgramunnu Bay camping ground. Pit toilets.

0.0 km	Zero trip meter at above intersection. **SO.** (4.9 km) ▲ 0.0 km ▲ 4.9 km
4.9 km	Intersection.

> Turn right 200 m to Sandy Bay picnic area. Camping prohibited. Picnic tables, barbecues, pit toilets.

0.0 km	Zero trip meter at above intersection. **SO.** (0.9 km) ▲ 0.0 km ▲ 0.9 km
0.9 km	Intersection.

> Turn right 500 m to Osprey Bay camping ground. Barbecues, pit toilets.

0.0 km	Zero trip meter at above intersection. **SO.** (9.7 km) ▲ 0.0 km ▲ 9.7 km
9.7 km	Yardie Creek carpark, picnic area and small-tents-only camping area on right.

Picnic tables, barbecues, pit toilets. Walk: initially easy then harder when enters range. Boat tours into Yardie Creek Gorge. Access by 4WD only from this point onwards.

0.0 km Zero trip meter at Yardie Creek carpark. **SO.**
(0.1 km) ▲ 0.0 km
▲ 106.8 km

0.1 km Yardie Creek Sand Bar crossing. **SO** onto Ningaloo–Yardie Creek Rd.

Reduce tyre pressures for soft sand.

(7.1 km) ▲ 106.7 km
7.2 km Exit Cape Range National Park.

Increase tyre pressures.

(14.3 km) Opp. dir. s'post:
Cape Range National Park. ▲ 99.6 km
21.5 km Gate. **SO.**

Leave as found.

(12.6 km) ▲ 85.3 km
34.1 km Gate. **SO** and immediately **KL.**

Leave as found. Track on right leads to beach.

(8.2 km) ▲ 72.7 km
42.3 km Gate. **SO.**

Leave as found.

(1.3 km) ▲ 64.5 km
43.6 km Station sheds on right. **SO.**
(0.3 km) ▲ 63.2 km
43.9 km Y intersection. **KL** onto Ningaloo Rd.

Turn right to Ningaloo Homestead. Camping.

(1.7 km) ▲ 62.9 km
45.6 km Y intersection. **KL** and immediately **SO** through gate.

Leave as found.

(5.7 km) ▲ 61.2 km
51.3 km Intersection. **TR** onto Cardabia–Ningaloo Rd.

Straight ahead 25 km to Learmonth–Minilya Rd.

(3.1 km) ▲ 55.5 km
54.4 km Gate. **SO.**

Leave as found.

(7.0 km) ▲ 52.4 km
61.4 km Gate. **SO.**

Leave as found.

(21.5 km) ▲ 45.4 km
82.9 km Gate. **SO.**

Leave as found.

(1.1 km) ▲ 23.9 km
84.0 km Y intersection. **KL.**
(12.3 km) ▲ 22.8 km
96.3 km Gate. **SO.**

Leave as found.

(2.5 km) ▲ 10.5 km
98.8 km Gate. **SO.**

Leave as found.

(1.0 km) ▲ 8.0 km
99.8 km Cardabia Homestead on right. **SO.**

Camping.

(0.3 km) ▲ 7.0 km
100.1 km Y intersection. **KL.**
(1.5 km) ▲ 6.7 km
101.6 km T intersection. **TR** onto bitumen: Coral Bay Rd.

Turn left 8.8 km to Learmonth–Minilya Rd.

(5.2 km) ▲ 5.2 km
106.8 km Coral Bay town centre, adjacent to Coral Bay Hotel carpark, Ningaloo Reef Resort.

PD *Supplies, caravan parks. Next fuel Minilya Roadhouse (100 km).*

REVERSE DIRECTIONS START ▲ 0.0 km
Depart Coral Bay Hotel carpark heading east via Coral Bay Rd 14 km to Learmonth–Minilya Rd T intersection. **TR** 78 km to North West Coastal Hwy intersection. **SO** 8 km to Minilya Roadhouse and caravan park on Minilya River on left. **SO** along highway to Robinson St intersection outside Carnarvon. **SO** along Robinson St 7 km to Carnarvon Post Office on left for start of next trek section.

CARNARVON
«»
CAPE PERON
«»
DENHAM

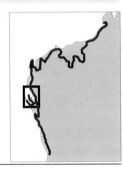

START POINT
Map page 38, C8

TOTAL KM 442.

UNSEALED KM 106.

DEGREE OF DIFFICULTY Difficult; easy from Carnarvon to Overlander Roadhouse.

DRIVING TIME 4 hours (Overlander Roadhouse to Cape Peron and return to Denham).

LONGEST DISTANCE NO FUEL 125 km (Carnarvon to Wooramel Roadhouse). No fuel after Denham on Peron Peninsula.

TOPOGRAPHIC MAPS Auslig 1:250 000 series: *Quobba*; *Wooramel*; *Yaringa*; *Edel*; *Shark Bay*. See also 1:100 000 series.

LOCAL/SPECIALITY MAPS Department of Land Administration Perth tourist map: *Gascoyne Coast*; Shark Bay Tourist Centre map: *Peron Peninsula*, *Robinson's Western Australia*.

OTHER USEFUL INFORMATION Western Australian Tourism Commission booklet: *Western Australia's Unique North* and brochure: *Shark Bay, Western Australia*; CALM booklets: *North-West Bound: From Shark Bay to Wyndham* and *Wildflower Country*, brochures: *Before You Meet the Dolphins of Monkey Mia* and *Francois Peron National Park* and information sheet: *Francois Peron National Park: Things You Need to Know*; MAPco of Western Australia booklet: *Northern Western Australia*; WA Heritage Committee brochure: *Shark Bay Heritage Trail*; Hamelin Pool information sheet: *Shark Bay: Historic Hamelin Pool, Telegraph Station and Post Office*.

DESCRIPTION The arid coastal scrubland of this section and its diversions have extraordinary appeal and you have to remind yourself that the Indian Ocean is at times only 100 metres away. The sand country dominates both the large bitumen-highway section linking Carnarvon with the Overlander Roadhouse and the roads of the Peron Peninsula on Shark Bay.

You visit Hamelin Pool Marine Nature Reserve with its stromatolites: incredible dome-shaped structures formed by primitive single-celled organisms dating back 3.5 billion years. A few kilometres further on is the turnoff to Useless Loop and Steep Point along the Edel Land 'prong'; see next trek section. Nanga Bay Resort, built from blocks of compacted shell mined from a nearby quarry, is on a huge sheep station, and Shell Beach comprises about 60 kilometres of countless tiny shells up to 10 metres deep. At Eagle Bluff you might see ospreys (sea-eagles), or green turtles and dugongs (sea-cows) feeding in shallow seagrass beds, wild goats, and, across the reach, the salt stockpile at the Useless Loop saltworks.

Denham is the major town of the Shark Bay region and Australia's most westerly town. Pearling and fishing have been surpassed by the world-famous dolphins at nearby Monkey Mia as its most popular attraction: wild bottlenose dolphins come to shore to be fed.

The natural features of Francois Peron National Park, one of the state's newest parks, include a dramatic red-cliff coastline, white beaches, dense coastal scrub, colourful wildflowers in season and gypsum salt pans called birridas; *see Warnings*. Kangaroos, euros, emus and reptiles abound on land, and both sides of Cape Peron teem with marine life including whales, sharks and rock lobsters. The route directions for the park include four camping areas, and there are caravan parks along the way at *Wooramel Roadhouse, Overlander Roadhouse, Hamelin Pool, Nanga Bay Station, Denham* and *Monkey Mia*.

WARNINGS ▶ Peron Road suitable for two-wheel drive but four-wheel drive essential after Peron Homestead; low-clearance vehicles have difficulty. ▶ Sand drifts sometimes very soft especially on side tracks leading to shoreline: reduce tyre pressures. ▶ Follow designated tracks; do not drive onto unused tracks or sites undergoing revegetation. ▶ Track towards Cape Peron skirts around birridas. Do not drive onto them: quicksand-like mire below hard thin crust causes bogging. Also avoid degradation of vegetation caused by vehicle tracks. ▶ If bathing in artesian bore at Peron Homestead beware very hot and deep water and slippery sides of tank. Do not drink water: salt content too

381

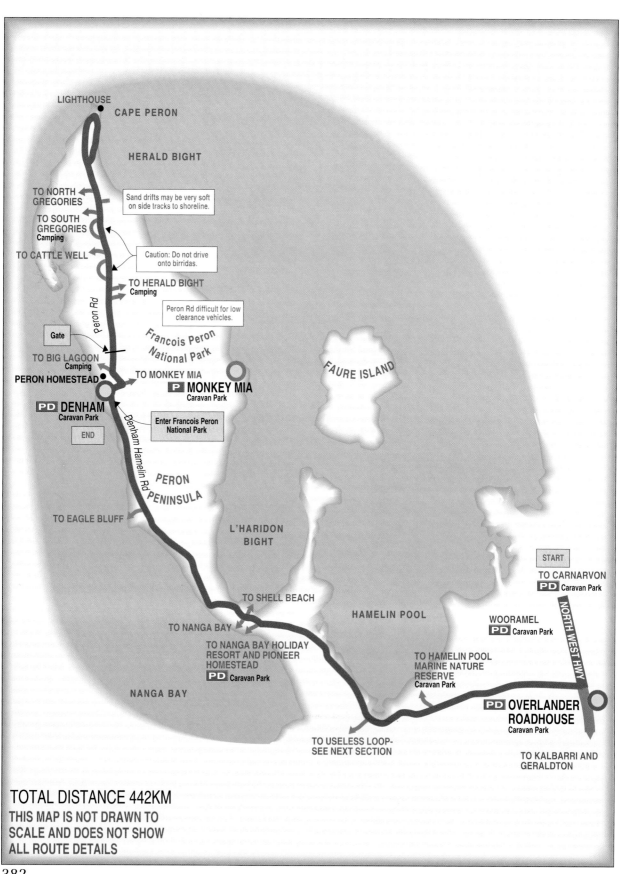

LIGHTHOUSE • CAPE PERON

HERALD BIGHT

TO NORTH GREGORIES

Sand drifts may be very soft on side tracks to shoreline.

TO SOUTH GREGORIES
Camping

TO CATTLE WELL

Caution: Do not drive onto birridas.

TO HERALD BIGHT
Camping

Peron Rd difficult for low clearance vehicles.

Peron Rd

Francois Peron National Park

FAURE ISLAND

Gate

TO BIG LAGOON
Camping

PERON HOMESTEAD •

TO MONKEY MIA

P MONKEY MIA
Caravan Park

PD DENHAM
Caravan Park

Denham Hamelin Rd

Enter Francois Peron National Park

END

PERON PENINSULA

TO EAGLE BLUFF

L'HARIDON BIGHT

START

TO CARNARVON
PD Caravan Park

TO SHELL BEACH

HAMELIN POOL

WOORAMEL
PD Caravan Park

NORTH WEST HWY

TO NANGA BAY

TO NANGA BAY HOLIDAY RESORT AND PIONEER HOMESTEAD
PD Caravan Park

TO HAMELIN POOL MARINE NATURE RESERVE
Caravan Park

PD OVERLANDER ROADHOUSE
Caravan Park

NANGA BAY

TO USELESS LOOP-
SEE NEXT SECTION

TO KALBARRI AND GERALDTON

TOTAL DISTANCE 442KM

THIS MAP IS NOT DRAWN TO SCALE AND DOES NOT SHOW ALL ROUTE DETAILS

high. Limit bathing time to prevent energy loss. ▶ Be wary of crumbling edges and strong wind around cliff area in national park. ▶ Light fires only in fire rings provided; preferably bring your portable gas stove. Use limited firewood sparingly and do not collect it, to help prevent degradation of vegetation and dune systems. ▶ No fresh water in region; carry your own drinking water.

BOOKINGS AND PERMITS ▶ For information about attractions and caravan rest area at Hamelin Pool Marine Nature Reserve ring (099) 42 5905. ▶ For information about attractions and caravan parks at Nanga Bay Holiday Resort and Denham contact Shark Bay Tourist Centre, Knight Terrace, Denham WA 6537; tel. (099) 48 1253. ▶ Fee applicable to visit Monkey Mia; pay at entrance gate to main parking area. For information about dolphins and caravan park contact ranger at Dolphin Information Centre, Shire of Shark Bay, Denham WA 6537; tel. (099) 48 1366. ▶ No prior permits required to traverse Francois Peron National Park but day-use and camping fees applicable; camp only in designated areas and pay at honesty box at entrance gate near Peron Homestead. For all information about national park and region contact CALM Shark Bay District Office, Knight Terrace, Denham WA 6537; tel. (099) 48 1208.

ROUTE DIRECTIONS

Depart Carnarvon Post Office heading north-east via Robinson St 7 km to North West Coastal Hwy intersection.

> **PD** *Supplies, caravan parks. All services. Next fuel Wooramel Roadhouse (118 km).*

TR onto highway 118 km to Wooramel Roadhouse and caravan park on Wooramel River on right. **SO** 76 km to Denham–Hamelin Rd intersection on right.

> *Straight ahead 200 m to Overlander Roadhouse.* **PD** *Caravan park.*

0.0 km Zero trip meter at Denham–Hamelin Rd and North West Coastal Hwy intersection. S'post: Shark Bay. **TR** onto Denham–Hamelin Rd.
(26.8 km) ▲ 26.8 km
26.8 km Intersection.

> *Turn right to historic telegraph station and Hamelin Pool Marine Nature Reserve on private property. Gate at 900 m: leave as found and immediately turn left. Y intersection a further 500 m. Keep right 2.7 km to gate: leave as found. Y intersection a further 5.2 km. Keep right 200 m to telegraph station, post office and stromatolite information centre. Keep left 200 m to Hamelin Pool and a further 100 m to view stromatolites. Caravan rest area, gas barbecues, tearooms, souvenirs.*

0.0 km Zero trip meter at above intersection. **SO.**
(14.8 km) ▲ 0.0 km
▲ 14.8 km
14.8 km Intersection. S'post: Denham.

> *Useless Loop off to left along Useless Loop Rd. See next trek section.*

0.0 km Zero trip meter at above intersection. **SO.**
(36.6 km) ▲ 0.0 km
▲ 36.6 km
36.6 km Intersection. S'post: Denham.

> *Turn left onto gravel 3 km to Nanga Bay Holiday Resort and Caravan Park.* **PD** *Supplies. Restaurant, accomm. Swimming, fishing, station tours. Pioneer Homestead Museum at Freshwater Camp.*

0.0 km Zero trip meter at above intersection. **SO.**
(7.1 km) ▲ 0.0 km
▲ 7.1 km
7.1 km Crossroads.

> *Turn right onto gravel 1 km to Shell Beach. Turn left to Nanga Bay.*

0.0 km Zero trip meter at above crossroads. **SO.**
(25.6 km) ▲ 0.0 km
▲ 25.6 km
25.6 km Intersection.

> *Turn left onto gravel 4.5 km to Eagle Bluff.*

0.0 km Zero trip meter at above intersection. **SO.**
(18.6 km) ▲ 0.0 km
▲ 18.6 km
18.6 km Intersection. S'post: Monkey Mia.

> *Straight ahead 1 km to Denham.* **PD** *Supplies, caravan parks, all services. Boat tours, museum.*

CARNARVON «» CAPE PERON «» DENHAM

0.0 km Zero trip meter at above intersection. **TR** onto Monkey Mia Rd.
(4.1 km) ▲ 0.0 km
▲ 4.1 km

4.1 km Intersection. S'post: Francois Peron National Park.

> *Straight ahead 21.5 km to Monkey Mia.* 🅿 *Supplies, caravan park. Pay area-use fee at ranger station. Information at Dolphin Welfare Centre. No alcohol.*

0.0 km Zero trip meter at above intersection. **TL** onto gravel: Peron Rd.
(6.2 km) Bitumen. ▲ 0.0 km
▲ 6.2 km

6.2 km Gate and intersection. Peron Homestead on left.

> *Pay park-use fee at this point. Artesian bore at homestead. Turn left 11.4 km to Big Lagoon. Camping, fishing, boating.*

0.0 km Zero trip meter at above gate and intersection. **SO**.
(23.4 km) ▲ 0.0 km
▲ 23.4 km

23.4 km Y intersection.

> *Turn right 5.8 km to Herald Bight. Camping, fishing, boating.*

0.0 km Zero trip meter at above Y intersection. **KL**.
(2.3 km) ▲ 0.0 km
▲ 2.3 km

2.3 km Intersection.

> *Herald Bight off to right along side track.*

0.0 km Zero trip meter at above intersection. **SO**.
(0.6 km) ▲ 0.0 km
▲ 4.9 km

0.6 km Y intersection. **KR**.

> *Loop track around birrida commences on left.*

(1.5 km) ▲ 4.3 km
2.1 km Intersection. **SO**.

> *Loop track rejoins on left.*

(2.8 km) ▲ 2.8 km
4.9 km Y intersection.

> *Keep left 1 km to Cattle Well. Very soft sand near shoreline at end of track.*

0.0 km Zero trip meter at above Y intersection. **KR**.
(0.9 km) ▲ 0.0 km
▲ 2.2 km

0.9 km Y intersection. **KR**.

> *Loop track commences on left.*

(0.9 km) ▲ 1.3 km
1.8 km Intersection. **SO**.

> *Loop track rejoins on left.*

(0.4 km) ▲ 0.4 km
2.2 km Intersection.

> *Turn left 1 km to South Gregories. Camping, fishing, boating.*

0.0 km Zero trip meter at above intersection. **SO**.
(0.5 km) ▲ 0.0 km
▲ 2.7 km

0.5 km Intersection. **SO**.

> *Track commences on right.*

(2.2 km) ▲ 2.2 km
2.7 km Intersection.

> *Turn left 1 km to North Gregories. Camping, boating, fishing.*

0.0 km Zero trip meter at above intersection. **SO**.
(4.6 km) ▲ 0.0 km
▲ 10.7 km

4.6 km Y intersection. **KL**.

> *Loop track to Cape Peron and lighthouse commences on right.*

(4.8 km) ▲ 6.1 km
9.4 km Cape Peron. **TR**.
(1.3 km) ▲ 1.3 km
10.7 km T intersection.

> *Turn left 100 m to lighthouse.*

TR onto loop track 3.5 km to main-track intersection. **TL** to return to Monkey Mia Rd and Denham–Hamelin Rd intersection via same route 50.4 km. **SO** along Denham–Hamelin Rd 1 km to Denham police station on left for start of next trek section.

REVERSE DIRECTIONS START ▲ 0.0 km

DENHAM
«»
STEEP POINT
«»
KALBARRI

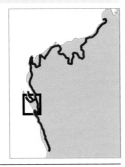

START POINT
Map page 38, B10.

TOTAL KM 685.
UNSEALED KM 309.
DEGREE OF DIFFICULTY Difficult from Useless Loop Road turnoff to Steep Point and return, otherwise easy.
DRIVING TIME 4 hours (Denham–Hamelin Road and Useless Loop Road intersection to Steep Point).
LONGEST DISTANCE NO FUEL 388 km (Nanga Bay Holiday Resort to Overlander Roadhouse). No fuel on Edel Land after Denham–Hamelin Road and Useless Loop Road intersection.
TOPOGRAPHIC MAPS Auslig 1:250 000 series: *Shark Bay*; *Edel*; *Yaringa*; *Ajana*. See also 1:100 000 series.
LOCAL/SPECIALITY MAPS Department of Land Administration Perth tourist map: *Gascoyne Coast*; StreetSmart touring map: *Batavia Coast*; Shark Bay Tourist Centre map: *Shark Bay*; *Robinson's Western Australia*.
OTHER USEFUL INFORMATION Western Australian Tourism Commission booklet: *Western Australia's Unique North*; CALM booklet: *North-West Bound: From Shark Bay to Wyndham*; MAPco of Western Australia booklet: *Northern Western Australia*; WA Heritage Committee brochure: *Shark Bay Heritage Trail*; Carrarang Station location map–information sheet.

DESCRIPTION This section explores Edel Land and Steep Point on Australia's westernmost extremity and traverses rough, arid pastoral and salt-mining country. There are 2 large bitumen linking sections. The first is 89 kilometres from Denham down to the Useless Loop Road turnoff, followed by four-wheel drive gravel all the way to Steep Point and back to the turnoff via coastal tracks. The second bitumen section is 288 kilometres from the turnoff to Kalbarri, the popular resort town on the mouth of the Murchison River from where you commence the next trek section.

Most of the plotted route directions take you through two private properties, *Tamala* and *Carrarang* stations. Bush campsites are managed by the ranger at Steep Point. Four-wheel drive explorers are urged to proceed with care and caution through this fragile natural environment.

Follow the new signposted road to Steep Point – do not visit the Useless Loop solar salt operation and gypsum mine which is closed to tourists. Stay in caravan parks along the bitumen linking sections at *Nanga Bay Holiday Resort*, *Overlander Roadhouse*, *Billabong Roadhouse* and *Kalbarri*.

Features of the wild arid coastland include huge wind-driven sand dunes and protected bays along the eastern shore of Edel Land facing Shark Bay. The magnificent limestone Zuytdorp Cliffs, named after the Dutch merchant ship that was wrecked below them in 1712, rise vertically to 170 metres above sea level for 260 kilometres south of Steep Point.

With a good swell, the deafening Thunder Bay blowholes punch jets of spume 20 metres into the air. Fishing is excellent, and in spring a profusion of desert wildflowers doubly enhances the area's extraordinary beauty.

WARNINGS ▶ Do not embark November–April when constant south-westerly winds make travel in region unpleasant. ▶ Privately employed ranger checks that visitors conform with conditions of entry. ▶ Dispose of litter in bins provided or at designated tip sites. Indiscriminate litterers given on-the-spot fines. ▶ When fishing do not exceed bag limits or take undersize reef fish and rock lobsters. Fishing activity subject to inspection and imposition of fines by ranger. ▶ Drive only on designated tracks, do not sidetrack around difficult hills, and do not enter areas barred from vehicle access to allow revegetation. ▶ Do not drive on beach at Crayfish Bay: sand very soft. ▶ Reduce tyre pressures to no more than 20 psi in sand-dune area. ▶ Firewood very limited. Take your own, take or purchase from ranger, or preferably bring your portable gas stove. ▶ No fresh water or supplies in Edel Land

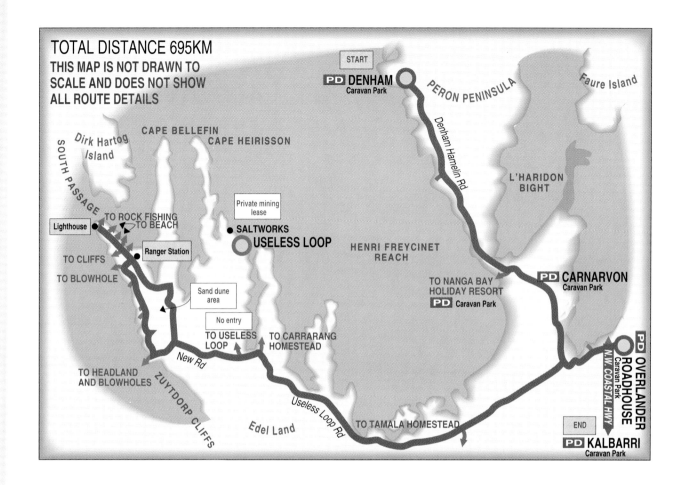

TOTAL DISTANCE 695KM
THIS MAP IS NOT DRAWN TO SCALE AND DOES NOT SHOW ALL ROUTE DETAILS

region; take all your own. ▶ No fuel in region; take in enough at Nanga Bay Holiday Resort for 388 km to Overlander Roadhouse.

BOOKINGS AND PERMITS ▶ Before bush camping on Tamala Station contact manager at homestead in person. ▶ Before bush camping on Carrarang Station ring station manager on (099) 48 3997 or ranger at Steep Point on (099) 48 3993. Camp only in areas designated by rubbish bins and pay camping fee when checking in at ranger station. ▶ Amateur Fisherman's Licence required for net fishing and catching rock lobsters; available from Fisheries Department offices in Geraldton, Denham, Carnarvon and Perth. ▶ For all information about activities in Edel Land region contact Shark Bay Tourist Centre, Knight Terrace, Denham WA 6537; tel. (099) 48 1253. ▶ For information about natural environment contact CALM Shark Bay District Office, Knight Terrace, Denham WA 6537; tel. (099) 48 1208. ▶ For information about Kalbarri region contact Kalbarri Travel Service, Grey Street, Kalbarri WA 6536; tel. (099) 37 1049.

ROUTE DIRECTIONS

Depart Denham police station on Denham–Hamelin Road heading north east then south east 51 km.

> *Turn right to Nanga Bay Holiday Resort.* **PD** *Caravan park. Next fuel Overlander Roadhouse (388 km).*

SO 38 km.

0.0 km Zero trip meter at Denham–Hamelin Rd and Useless Loop Rd intersection. S'post: Useless Loop. **TR** onto gravel: Useless Loop Rd.

(43.1 km)   Bitumen. ▲ 128.6 km

43.1 km Intersection. **SO**.

> *Turn left onto Tamala Rd to Tamala Homestead. Bush camping, track leading to beach.*

(4.0 km)   ▲ 85.5 km

47.1 km Baba Bight on right. **SO**.

> *Views of bight at southern end of Henri Freycinet Reach.*

Blowhole at Thunder Bay

(28.5 km) ▲ 81.5 km
75.6 km Intersection. **SO**.

> *Turn right onto Carrarang Rd to Carrarang Homestead. Bush camping.*

(5.0 km) ▲ 53.0 km
80.6 km Sign: No access to Useless Loop. **SO** onto new road.

> *Engage 4WD. Useless Loop off to right along Useless Loop Rd. Private mining lease. No services or tourist access.*

(37.0 km) ▲ 48.0 km
117.6 km T intersection. **TR**.

> *Engage 2WD. False Entrance and Crayfish Bay off to left along west-coast track system explored during return from Steep Point.*

(11.0 km) ▲ 11.0 km
128.6 km Intersection. S'post: Steep Pt.

> *Clough Bar on right. No access.*

0.0 km Zero trip meter at above intersection. **SO**.

> *Reduce tyre pressures and engage 4WD.*

(2.5 km) ▲ 0.0 km
▲ 30.4 km
2.5 km Y intersection. **KR**.

(2.3 km) ▲ 27.9 km
4.8 km Intersection. **SO**.

(3.1 km) ▲ 25.6 km
7.9 km Y intersection. **KL**.

> *Loop track commences on right.*

(0.2 km) ▲ 22.5 km
8.1 km Y intersection. **KL**.

> *Loop track rejoins on right.*

(1.4 km) ▲ 22.3 km
9.5 km Intersection. **SO**.

> *Thunder Bay and blowholes off to left. West-coast track system from False Entrance and Crayfish Bay rejoins at this point: explored during return from Steep Point.*

(12.6 km) ▲ 20.9 km

387

Zuytdorp Cliffs

22.1 km Ranger station and telephone box on right. **SO**.
(2.9 km) ▲ 8.3 km
25.0 km Intersection. **SO**.

| Turn left to Zuytdorp Cliffs. |

(0.8 km) ▲ 5.4 km
25.8 km T intersection. **TL**.

| Track on right continues 100 m to beach. |

(0.6 km) ▲ 4.6 km
26.4 km Intersection. S'post: Steep Pt. **SO**.

| Track on right continues 100 m to beach. |

(0.1 km) ▲ 4.0 km
26.5 km Y intersection. S'post: Keep left. **KL**.
(0.1 km) ▲ 3.9 km
26.6 km Y intersection. **KL**.

| Loop track commences on right. |

(1.0 km) ▲ 3.8 km
27.6 km Intersection. **SO**.

| Loop track rejoins on right. |

(0.1 km) ▲ 2.8 km
27.7 km Intersection. **SO**.

| Track on right continues 100 m to beach. |

(0.8 km) ▲ 2.7 km
28.5 km Y intersection. **KL**.

| Track on right continues 100 m to beach. |

(1.3 km) ▲ 1.9 km
29.8 km S'post: Steep Pt. Lighthouse on left. **SO**.
(0.4 km) ▲ 0.6 km
30.2 km Y intersection. **KL**.

| Turn right for rock fishing. |

(0.2 km) ▲ 0.2 km
30.4 km Steep Pt.
Return from Steep Pt via same route 21 km.
0.0 km Zero trip meter at intersection. S'post: Thunder Bay blowholes. **TR**.
(5.2 km) ▲ 0.0 km
▲ 21.3 km
5.2 km Intersection. **TL**.

| Straight ahead 500 m to T intersection at cliff edge. Turn right 1 km to Thunder Bay blowholes. |

(1.8 km) ▲ 16.1 km
7.0 km Y intersection. **KL**.

| Keep right 1 km to south end of Thunder Bay. |

(3.1 km) ▲ 14.3 km
10.1 km Y intersection. **KL**.

| Keep right to north end of Crayfish Bay. |

(3.5 km) ▲ 11.2 km
13.6 km Y intersection. **KL**.

| Keep right along beach towards headland. |

(4.5 km) ▲ 7.7 km
18.1 km South end of Crayfish Bay. **SO**.
(0.2 km) ▲ 3.2 km
18.3 km Intersection. False Entrance on right. **TL**.

| Straight ahead to headland and blowholes. |

(3.0 km) ▲ 3.0 km
21.3 km Intersection.
To return via earlier route: **TR** 118 km to Denham–Hamelin Rd turnoff. **TR** onto Denham–Hamelin Rd 41 km to North West Coastal Hwy T intersection. **TR** onto highway.

| Overlander Roadhouse 200 m on left. **PD** Caravan park. |

SO 45 km.

| Billabong Roadhouse on right. **PD** Caravan park. Next fuel Kalbarri (202 km). |

SO 134 km. **TR** onto Ajana–Kalbarri Rd 66 km. **SO** onto Clotworthy St in Kalbarri 400 m. **TL** at Grey St T intersection 1 km to Kalbarri Motor Hotel, cnr Porter St on left, for start of next trek section.

| **PD** Supplies, caravan parks. |

REVERSE DIRECTIONS START ▲ 0.0 km

KALBARRI
«»
PERTH

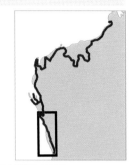

START POINT
Map page 38, C13.

TOTAL KM 591.
UNSEALED KM 97.
DEGREE OF DIFFICULTY Moderate.
DRIVING TIME 2 hours (Kalbarri to Northampton).
LONGEST DISTANCE NO FUEL 76 km (Red Bluff Caravan Park to Port Gregory).
TOPOGRAPHIC MAPS Auslig 1:250 000 series: *Ajana*; *Geraldton*. See also 1:100 000 series.
LOCAL/SPECIALITY MAPS StreetSmart touring map: *Batavia Coast*; *Robinson's Western Australia*.
OTHER USEFUL INFORMATION Western Australian Tourism Commission booklet: *Western Australia's Unique North*; Geraldton Tourist Bureau booklet: *Geraldton–Greenough Visitors Guide to the Friendliest City in the West*.

DESCRIPTION This short section takes in the spectacular Kalbarri National Park coastal gorges south of Kalbarri through coastal scrub country that in spring is transformed into a carpet of brilliant wildflowers. The mutiny on the Dutch trading vessel *Batavia* took place in 1629 during the period in which many Dutch ships visited the west coast; at Wittecarra Creek near Red Bluff an historic cairn marks the spot where 2 mutineers were set ashore as punishment and therefore are believed to be Australia's first white settlers.

A coastal walk takes in Mushroom Rock – actually a series of rocks shaped by natural elements – and Rainbow Valley, a fascinating spectrum in stone. Another walk takes you from Pot Alley Gorge via Eagle Gorge to Natural Bridge where the cliffs are eroded into some unusual shapes. Shell House Gorge, Grandstand Rock and Island Rock were once part of the mainland but became

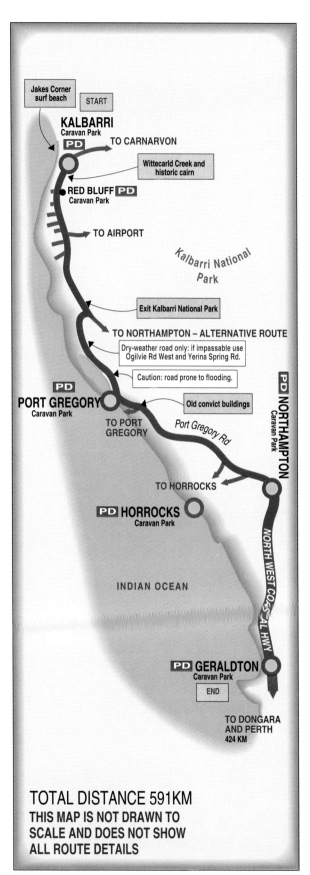

TOTAL DISTANCE 591KM
THIS MAP IS NOT DRAWN TO SCALE AND DOES NOT SHOW ALL ROUTE DETAILS

389

detached by the continual pounding of the Indian Ocean. Though you cannot camp in the park you can stay in the caravan park at *Red Bluff* and in caravan parks further south at *Port Gregory, Horrocks, Northampton* and *Geraldton*.

South of the national park a sandy track skirts Hutt Lagoon west of where Leonard Casley proclaimed Hutt River Province when he seceded from the Commonwealth of Australia in 1970. Port Gregory is a pretty tourist haven with a spectacular natural harbour and excellent fishing, and Horrocks is another very worthwhile fishing–holiday stopover. The plotted route directions finish at Northampton, one of the oldest settlements outside Perth with an abundance of colonial architecture. From Northampton it is an easy but long drive along highway bitumen to Geraldton and on to Perth.

WARNINGS ▶ Camping prohibited in Kalbarri National Park. ▶ Do not embark November–February when region subject to high and constant winds. ▶ Grey Road south of national park swampy, subject to flooding and possibly boggy. Before embarking after rain ring Kalbarri police station on (099) 37 1006 or contact park rangers in person to check road condition. If road impassable proceed to Northampton via Ogilvie Road West and Yerina Spring Road, bypassing Port Gregory turnoff. ▶ Be extremely careful around hazardous coastal cliff region of national park. ▶ Do not take any species of coral in waters within three-kilometre radius of service jetty at end of Port Street, Port Gregory. ▶ Beware sharp coral, sea snakes, stone fish, stingrays, cone shells and sharks in coastal waters.

BOOKINGS AND PERMITS ▶ For information about natural environment of Kalbarri National Park contact CALM Greenough–Gascoyne Regional Office, Seventh Floor Town Towers, Geraldton WA 6530; PO Box 72, Geraldton WA 6530; tel. (099) 21 5955. ▶ For information about caravan parks in Kalbarri township and national park contact Kalbarri Travel Service, Grey Street, Kalbarri WA 6536; tel. (099) 37 1049. ▶ For information about caravan parks at Port Gregory, Horrocks and Northampton contact Northampton Tourist Cafe, North West Coastal Highway, Northampton WA 6535; tel. (099) 34 1495. ▶ For information about caravan parks in Geraldton contact Geraldton Tourist Bureau, Bill Sewell Complex, Chapman Road, Geraldton WA 6530; tel. (099) 21 3999.

ROUTE DIRECTIONS

0.0 km Zero trip meter in Kalbarri at Kalbarri Motor Hotel, cnr Porter St and Grey St. **SO** heading west along Grey St then south along Red Bluff Rd.

> **PD** *Supplies, caravan parks.*

(3.2 km)   ▲ 4.4 km
3.2 km Rainbow Jungle Tropical Rainforest and Bird Park on left. **SO.**

> *An exotic sandstone complex of waterfalls, creeks and ponds. Jakes Corner on right, one of state's premier surf beaches.*

(1.0 km)   ▲ 1.2 km
4.2 km Wittecarra Creek and historic cairn on right. **SO.**
(0.2 km)   ▲ 0.2 km
4.4 km Intersection. S'post: Kalbarri National Park coastal gorges.

> *Straight ahead 200 m to Red Bluff Caravan Park on left.* **PD** *Straight ahead a further 200 m to Red Bluff Beach. Fishing, swimming, surfing.*

0.0 km Zero trip meter at above intersection. **TL** onto gravel: Grey Rd.
(1.0 km)   Bitumen. ▲ 0.0 km
      ▲ 1.0 km
1.0 km Intersection. S'post: Mushroom Rock.

> *Turn right 300 m to Red Bluff carpark. Commence easy 800-m return walk to headland.*

0.0 km Zero trip meter at above intersection. **SO.**
(0.2 km)   ▲ 0.0 km
      ▲ 0.2 km
0.2 km Intersection.

> *Turn right 300 m to Mushroom Rock carpark. Commence leisurely 2-hr loop walk via Rainbow Valley.*

0.0 km Zero trip meter at above intersection. **SO.**
(0.6 km)   ▲ 0.0 km
      ▲ 0.6 km
0.6 km Intersection.

> *Turn right 300 m to Rainbow Valley carpark. Walk trail from Mushroom Rock rejoins.*

0.0 km Zero trip meter at above intersection. **SO.**
(0.3 km)   ▲ 0.0 km
      ▲ 0.3 km

0.3 km Intersection.

> *Turn right 500 m to Pot Alley Gorge carpark. Commence 8-km coastal walk to Natural Bridge via Eagle Gorge.*

0.0 km Zero trip meter at above intersection. **SO**.
(0.9 km) ▲ 0.0 km
▲ 1.8 km

0.9 km Intersection. **SO**.

> *Airport off to left.*

(0.9 km) ▲ 0.9 km
1.8 km Intersection.

> *Turn right 1.7 km to Eagle Gorge carpark. Panoramic views. Beach at base of gorge.*

0.0 km Zero trip meter at above intersection. **SO**.
(2.8 km) ▲ 0.0 km
▲ 2.8 km

2.8 km Y intersection. S'post: Port Gregory.

> *Keep right along Natural Bridge Rd 1.5 km to intersection then turn right 700 m to Shell House and Grandstand Rock. Straight ahead at turnoff a further 1.6 km then right 500 m to Island Rock. Straight ahead at turnoff a further 2.3 km to Natural Bridge and end of coastal walk from Pot Alley Gorge.*

Opp. dir. s'post: Kalbarri.

0.0 km Zero trip meter at above Y intersection. **KL** along Grey Rd.
(8.9 km) ▲ 0.0 km
▲ 64.0 km

8.9 km Exit national park.
(18.0 km) Opp. dir. s'post:
Kalbarri National Park. ▲ 55.1 km

26.9 km Intersection. S'post: Port Gregory Caravan Park. **TR**.

> *Dry-weather road only.*

(8.7 km) ▲ 37.1 km
35.6 km Hutt Lagoon commences on right.

> *Caution: this section of road skirts swamp and is prone to flooding.*

(28.4 km) ▲ 28.4 km
64.0 km Intersection. S'post: Northampton.

> *Turn right 5 km to Port Gregory.* **PD** *Supplies, caravan park. Fishing, rock-lobster fishing.*

Opp. dir. s'post: Grey Rd.

0.0 km Zero trip meter at above intersection. **SO** onto Port Gregory Rd.
(2.7 km) ▲ 0.0 km
▲ 42.5 km

2.7 km Old convict buildings on left. **SO**.
(23.5 km) ▲ 39.8 km
26.2 km S'post: Northampton 16. **SO** onto bitumen.
(7.1 km) Gravel. Opp. dir. s'post:
Port Gregory. ▲ 16.3 km

33.3 km Intersection. S'post: Northampton. **SO**.

> *Turn right to T intersection then turn right 17 km to Horrocks.* **PD** *Supplies, caravan park. Fishing, swimming, surfing.*

(4.9 km) Opp. dir. s'post: Port Gregory. ▲ 9.2 km
38.2 km Intersection. S'post: Northampton. **SO** onto Stephen St.

> *Turn right onto Horrocks Rd 19.5 km to Horrocks.*

(4.3 km) Opp. dir. s'post: Port Gregory. ▲ 4.3 km
42.5 km T intersection. S'post: Geraldton. Northampton shire office and library on left.

> **PD** *Supplies, caravan park. Colonial buildings.*

TR onto Hampton St–North West Coastal Hwy 44 km to Chapman Valley Rd turnoff. **SO** 5 km to the Rotary, cnr Brand Hwy in Geraldton. **SO** along Brand Hwy to Perth (424 km) for start of next trek.

> **PD** *Supplies, caravan parks.*

REVERSE DIRECTIONS START ▲ 0.0 km

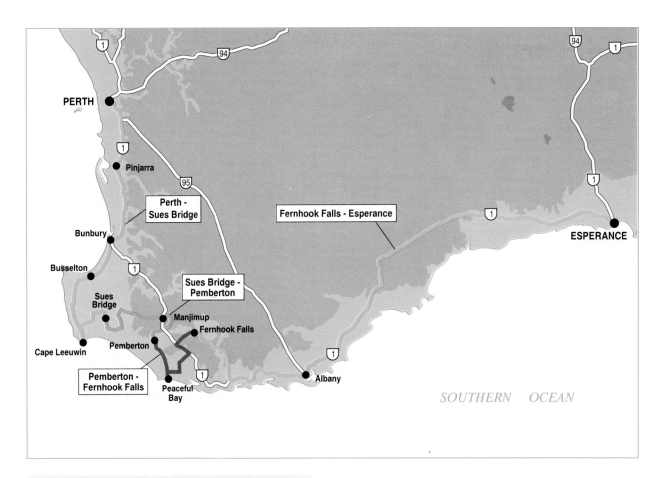

THE SOUTH WEST
PERTH «» ESPERANCE
1482 KILOMETRES

PERTH «» SUES BRIDGE   445 km

SUES BRIDGE «» PEMBERTON   196 km

PEMBERTON «» FERNHOOK FALLS   175 km

FERNHOOK FALLS «» ESPERANCE   665 km

The best time of year to embark on this trip is spring–summer, when the forests and coastal regions offer welcome coolness, and an amazing array of wild-flowers are in bloom. Avoid travelling after heavy rains when some forest and coastal roads become impassable, and in winter, June–August, when cold weather makes the region unpleasant.

It is an easy journey south of Perth through rolling dairy country into the jarrah forests and pine plantations of the lush south-west corner. You can visit the rugged and beautiful Leeuwin–Naturaliste National Park, a very popular surfing region; Cape Leeuwin, the land's end of the south west, is where the wild Southern and Indian oceans meet.

The trek then follows the Blackwood River inland through tall forests of jarrah and marri to the popular camping and picnic area at Sues Bridge. Passing through the picturesque timber towns of Pemberton and Northcliffe you enter Warren National Park and Northcliffe Forest Park where the trees are some of the oldest and largest in Australia. The passage down to Denmark on the south coast is through the beautiful karri and tingle forests of Walpole–Nornalup National Park. Thereafter it is a short bitumen sprint to Albany, the state's first settlement and then a longer haul on to Esperance, set in a region of white beaches, dark headlands and scores of sparkling islands.

Canal Rocks, Leeuwin – Naturaliste National Park

BEFORE YOU SET OUT ▶ Read the section description carefully. ▶ Check weather conditions with local authorities or Bureau of Meteorology. ▶ Make sure you have the appropriate maps and information for the trek. ▶ Check that your vehicle is in good order for the conditions ahead. Have you the necessary spare parts? ▶ If you are camping, do you have the right equipment? ▶ If you are fishing, obtain any necessary licences and find out about regulations.

TREAD LIGHTLY!
On Public and Private Land

■ Take your rubbish home with you. Do not bury it.

■ Leave gates as you found them – open or shut.

■ Don't disturb livestock – slow down or stop.

■ Do not damage swamps, steep hills or creekbanks which can be easily scarred by churning wheels.

■ Comply with signs and closures.

WESTERN AUSTRALIA'S NATIONAL PARKS AND NATURE RESERVES

In Western Australia all national parks and reserves are managed by the Department of Conservation and Land Management (CALM). Most national parks have good facilities for camping and where appropriate we suggest you use their designated campsites. No prior permits are required to traverse national parks and fees are reasonable; self-register or pay the ranger on site as appropriate. To stay in the more popular and established parks it is advisable to book ahead for peak holiday periods. For information when planning your trips contact the relevant district or regional CALM office as stated in the route directions, or head office in Perth: CALM State Operations Headquarters, 50 Hayman Road, Como WA 6152; PO Box 104, Como WA 6152; tel. (09) 367 0333.

When using national parks and nature reserves, obey the following rules.

▶ Drive along formed roads and tracks, follow signs and do not make your own path through the bush.

▶ Bushwalk only along defined tracks and be especially careful not to trample sensitive areas with sand-dune plains, steep slopes or sparse vegetation.

▶ Preferably bring your portable gas stove and do not light fires except in barbecues or established fireplaces. Extinguish fires completely. Do not collect firewood from the park unless permitted by ranger.

▶ Camp only in designated camping areas and camp away from watercourses to avoid erosion, compaction and pollution of soil.

▶ Bathe, brush your teeth and wash dishes at least 50 metres away from creeks and lakes. Use sand instead of detergent to wash dishes.

▶ Use pit toilets if provided. Otherwise bury your waste in a 15–centimetre hole at least 100 metres away from campsite and water.

▶ Place rubbish in bins provided or take it away with you. Do not throw rubbish or food scraps into rivers or creeks.

▶ Pets, firearms and spearguns are prohibited. A permit is required to keep or move wildlife and flora. Beware wildlife on roads.

▶ Fishing regulations apply. Do not fish in sanctuary zones, and conserve fish numbers by taking enough only for your immediate needs.

▶ Never touch, damage or remove anything you find at Aboriginal sites.

USEFUL INFORMATION

For touring information contact:
Western Australian Tourist Centre
Albert Facey House
Cnr Forrest Place
  and Wellington Street
Perth 6000
(09) 483 1111.

Addresses and telephone numbers for the local touring information centres are included in route directions.

For motoring information contact:
The Royal Automobile Club of
  Western Australia Inc. (RAC)
228 Adelaide Terrace
Perth 6000
(09) 421 4444.

For four-wheel driving information contact:
Western Australian Association of
  Four Wheel Drive Clubs Inc.
PO Box 6029
East Perth 6000.

For fishing licences and regulations contact:
The Fisheries Department of Western Australia
108 Adelaide Terrace
East Perth 6004
(09) 220 5333.

PERTH
«»
SUES BRIDGE

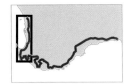

Point Road Camping and Picnic Area

START POINT
Map page 30, D7.

TOTAL KM 445 km.
UNSEALED KM 91.
DEGREE OF DIFFICULTY Moderate.
DRIVING TIME 5 hours (Margaret River to Sues Bridge).
LONGEST DISTANCE NO FUEL 222 km (Karridale to Manjimup).
TOPOGRAPHIC MAPS Auslig 1:250 000 series: *Busselton*; *Augusta*. See also 1:100 000 series.
LOCAL/SPECIALITY MAPS StreetSmart touring maps: *South West Western Australia* and *South West Corner*; RAC map: *Lower South West*; Robinson's *Western Australia*.
OTHER USEFUL INFORMATION Western Australian Tourism Commission booklet: *Western Australia's Southern Wonders*; CALM Discover series booklet: *Wild Places, Quiet Places: a Guide to the Natural Highlights of the South West*.

DESCRIPTION This section is exciting, full of interest and spectacle, and its many possible activities deserve at least 3 days. It is well worth exploring the many wineries of the rich dairy, cattle and timber region between Busselton and Margaret River. You could also tour the 3 underground limestone caves – Mammoth, Lake and Jewel – before driving on to Augusta for an overnight stay.

Much of the coastline is part of the Leeuwin–Naturaliste National Park and is rugged, beautiful and very popular for surfing. Conto Spring Picnic Area as well as *Contos Field* and *Point Road* camping and picnic areas are on this part of the route. Just back from the shoreline you traverse the Boranup Karri State Forest with its choice of shady picnic spots and the *Boranup Forest Camping and Picnic Area*. Down at the state's southernmost tip is Augusta, a lovely town in a perfect setting of trees and tranquil Blackwood River estuary waters, and Cape Leeuwin, where the wild waters of the Indian and Southern oceans meet.

Heading inland again you follow the Blackwood River to pass through Karridale township and into the Blackwood State Forest. Here you can camp and picnic under tall stands of jarrah and marri at *Alexandra Bridge* or *Sues Bridge*, the popular camping, picnic and caravan site which is the end point of the section. There are caravan parks throughout the trip at *Busselton*, *Margaret River*, *Hamelin Bay*, *Augusta* and *Kudardup*.

WARNINGS ▶ Do not embark after rain when region may be too wet for creek crossings and boggy sections. Check conditions with ranger at Margaret River on (097) 57 2322. ▶ Forest tracks in second half of section boggy after rain; tracks cross 5 small creeks sometimes in minor flood. ▶ Concrete causeway crosses often fast flowing Blackwood River; check water depth and flow before crossing. If river impassable at flood time use Blackwood Road track to Sues Road turnoff and turn left along Sues Road to Sues Bridge Camping and Picnic Area. ▶ Tracks little used and often blocked by fallen trees or branches. ▶ Tracks around Conto Spring very narrow; beware oncoming vehicles. ▶ Take on enough fuel at Karridale for 222 kilometres to Manjimup in next section. ▶ When rock fishing around Cape Freycinet beware freak waves and swells. ▶ Bring your own drinking water to Sues Bridge Camping and Picnic Area. ▶ Observe fire-danger warnings.

BOOKINGS AND PERMITS ▶ No prior permits required to traverse Leeuwin–Naturaliste National Park or Boranup Karri and Blackwood River state forests.

395

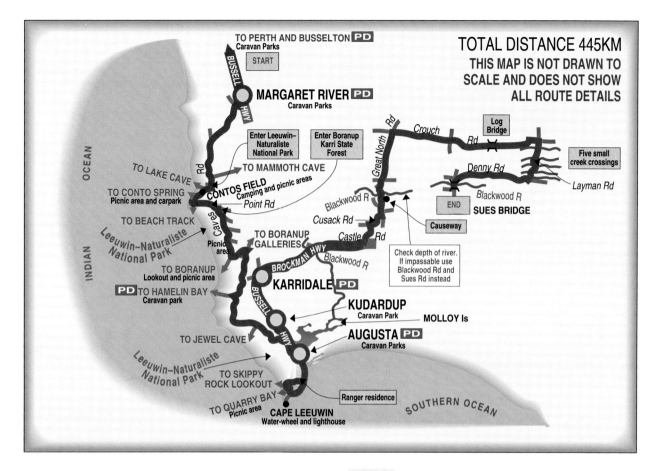

TO PERTH AND BUSSELTON **PD**
Caravan Parks
START

TOTAL DISTANCE 445KM
THIS MAP IS NOT DRAWN TO
SCALE AND DOES NOT SHOW
ALL ROUTE DETAILS

BUSSELL HWY

MARGARET RIVER **PD**
Caravan Parks

Crouch Rd

Log Bridge

Enter Leeuwin–
Naturaliste
National Park

Enter Boranup
Karri State
Forest

Rd

Great North

Five small
creek crossings

TO MAMMOTH CAVE

TO LAKE CAVE

Denny Rd

Layman Rd

Rd

CONTOS FIELD

Camping and picnic areas

TO CONTO SPRING
Picnic area and carpark

Point Rd

Blackwood R

END

Blackwood R

SUES BRIDGE

Causeway

TO BEACH TRACK

Caves

Cusack Rd

Leeuwin–Naturaliste
National Park

Picnic
area

TO BORANUP
GALLERIES

Castle Rd

Blackwood R

Check depth of river.
If impassable use
Blackwood Rd and
Sues Rd instead

BROCKMAN HWY

OCEAN

INDIAN

TO BORANUP
Lookout and picnic area

KARRIDALE **PD**

PD TO HAMELIN BAY
Caravan park

BUSSELL

KUDARDUP
Caravan Park

MOLLOY Is

HWY

TO JEWEL CAVE

AUGUSTA **PD**
Caravan Parks

Leeuwin–Naturaliste
National Park

TO SKIPPY
ROCK LOOKOUT

Ranger residence

TO QUARRY BAY
Picnic area

CAPE LEEUWIN
Water-wheel and lighthouse

SOUTHERN OCEAN

Camp in all forest areas, except pine plantations, for maximum 3 nights. For information about camping and caravan sites in park and forests contact CALM Busselton District Office, 14 Queen Street, Busselton WA 6280; tel. (097) 52 1677. ▶ Fee applicable to camp around Alexandra Bridge at Blackwood River crossing; caretaker collects on site. ▶ For information about caravan parks in Margaret River and tours of Mammoth Cave and Lake Cave contact Margaret River Tourist Bureau, cnr Tunbridge Road and Bussell Highway, Margaret River WA 6285; tel. (097) 57 2911. ▶ For information about caravan parks in Hamelin Bay, Augusta and Kudardup, and tours of Jewel Cave and Cape Leeuwin lighthouse, contact Augusta Information Centre, Leeuwin Souvenirs, Blackwood Avenue, Augusta WA 6290; tel. (097) 58 1695.

ROUTE DIRECTIONS

Depart Perth from WA Tourist Centre and GPO in Forrest Place via Wellington, Plain and Hay sts. **SO** along Shepparton Rd, Albany Hwy and South Western Hwy to Bunbury (approx. 169 km). Head south along Bussel Hwy via Busselton to Margaret River (approx. 100 km).

0.0 km Zero trip meter at Margaret River Hotel, cnr Willmott Ave and Bussell Hwy heading south east. **SO** along Bussell Hwy.

PD *Supplies, caravan parks. accomm.*

(1.1 km) ▲ 18.2 km
1.1 km Intersection. S'post: Boodjidup St. **TR**.
(7.6 km) ▲ 17.1 km
8.7 km T intersection. S'post: Caves Rd. **TL**.
(6.1 km) ▲ 9.5 km
14.8 km Intersection. S'post: Lake Cave. **SO**.

Turn left to Mammoth Cave. Tours.

(3.0 km) Opp. dir. s'post: Margaret River. ▲ 3.4 km
17.8 km Intersection. S'post: Lake Cave. **TR**.

Enter Leeuwin–Naturaliste National Park.

(0.4 km)   Opp. dir. s'post: Yallingup. ▲ 0.4 km
18.2 km Intersection. S'post: Conto Rd.

Straight ahead 200 m to Lake Cave and tearooms. Tours.

0.0 km Zero trip meter at above intersection. **TR** onto gravel.
(1.7 km)   Bitumen. ▲ 0.0 km
                              ▲ 1.7 km

1.7 km S'post: Beach access. Contos Field Camping Area on left.

Turn left to picnic area. Barbecues, toilets.

0.0 km Zero trip meter at above point. **SO.**
(1.8 km)   ▲ 0.0 km
                              ▲ 1.8 km

1.8 km Intersection. S'post: Cape Freycinet.

Keep right 500 m to Conto Spring Picnic Area and carpark. Picnic tables, barbecues, toilets. Tracks leading to beach. Beware oncoming vehicles along narrow tracks. Many access points along coastal track to rock-fishing areas: beware freak waves and swells.

0.0 km Zero trip meter at above intersection. **TL.**
(1.1 km)   ▲ 0.0 km
                              ▲ 1.1 km

1.1 km Intersection. S'post: Point Rd.

Straight ahead 400 m to beach track.

0.0 km Zero trip meter at above intersection. **TL.**
(2.1 km)   ▲ 0.0 km
                              ▲ 2.1 km

2.1 km Point Rd Camping and Picnic Area.

Barbecues, toilets.

0.0 km Zero trip meter at above point. **SO** along Love Spring Rd.
(4.0 km)   ▲ 0.0 km
                              ▲ 15.3 km

4.0 km Crossroads. **TR** onto Boranup Drive.

Enter Boranup Karri State Forest. Allan Rd straight ahead.

(0.8 km)   Opp. dir. s'post: Point Rd. ▲ 11.3 km
4.8 km Intersection. **KL.**

Turn right 100 m to picnic area. Picnic tables, barbecues.

(2.1 km)   ▲ 10.5 km

6.9 km Intersection. **SO.**

Turn left 100 m to picnic area. Picnic tables, barbecues.

(3.1 km)   ▲ 8.4 km
10.0 km Y intersection. **KR.**

Douglas Rd on left.

(0.9 km)   ▲ 5.3 km
10.9 km Picnic area on right. **SO.**

Picnic tables, barbecues.

(4.4 km)   ▲ 4.4 km
15.3 km Intersection. S'post: Caves Rd.

Straight ahead 100 m to Boranup Lookout and picnic area. Picnic tables, barbecues.

0.0 km Zero trip meter at above intersection. **TL.**
(0.5 km)   ▲ 0.0 km
                              ▲ 1.0 km

0.5 km Y intersection. **KL.**
(0.5 km)   ▲ 0.5 km

1.0 km Boranup Forest Camping and Picnic Area on right.

Picnic tables, barbecues, toilets. Information.

0.0 km Zero trip meter at above point. **SO.**
(1.5 km)   ▲ 0.0 km
                              ▲ 8.1 km

1.5 km Intersection. S'post: Augusta. **TR** onto bitumen: Caves Rd.

Turn left to Boranup Galleries. Rammed-earth gallery displaying locally made furniture and fine art.

(6.6 km) Gravel. Opp. dir. s'post: Boranup Drive. ▲ 6.6 km
8.1 km Intersection. S'post: Caves Rd.

Straight ahead along Hamelin Bay West Rd 2 km to Hamelin Bay holiday–fishing village. **PD** *Caravan park. Telephone, toilets. Swimming, fishing, boating.*

0.0 km Zero trip meter at above intersection. **TL.**
(8.4 km)   ▲ 0.0 km
                              ▲ 8.4 km

8.4 km Intersection.

Turn right 300 m to Jewel Cave. Tours.

0.0 km Zero trip meter at above intersection. **SO.**
(5.1 km)   ▲ 0.0 km
                              ▲ 16.1 km

397

5.1 km Intersection. S'post: Augusta. **TR** onto Bussell Hwy.

> *Enter Augusta township. Margaret River off to left.*

(3.4 km)   ▲ 11.0 km

8.5 km Augusta Post Office on right. **SO** along Blackwood Ave–Leeuwin Rd.

> **PD** *Supplies, caravan parks. Accomm., hospital, all services.*

(3.9 km)   Opp. dir. s'post: Yallingup. ▲ 7.6 km

12.4 km Sign: Leeuwin–Naturaliste National Park. Ranger residence on right. **SO.**

(3.7 km)   ▲ 3.7 km

16.1 km Intersection. S'post: Quarry Bay/Skippy Rock.

> *Straight ahead 1 km to Cape Leeuwin, land's end at junction of Indian and Southern oceans. Historic water-wheel and lighthouse. Tours.*

0.0 km Zero trip meter at above intersection. **TR** onto gravel.

(0.2 km)   Bitumen. ▲ 0.0 km

          ▲ 0.2 km

0.2 km Intersection.

> *Turn right 1.2 km to Skippy Rock Lookout. Bushwalking, fishing.*

0.0 km Zero trip meter at above intersection. **SO.**

(0.6 km)   ▲ 0.0 km

          ▲ 0.6 km

0.6 km Intersection.

> *Turn right 200 m to Quarry Bay Picnic Area. Picnic tables, toilets.*

0.0 km Zero trip meter at above intersection. **SO.**

(4.6 km)   ▲ 0.0 km

          ▲ 8.9 km

4.6 km T intersection. **TL** onto bitumen: Leeuwin Rd.

(4.3 km)   Gravel. ▲ 4.3 km

8.9 km S'post: Margaret River. Augusta Post Office on left.

0.0 km Zero trip meter at post office. **SO** along Bussell Hwy.

(3.5 km)   ▲ 0.0 km

          ▲ 25.4 km

3.5 km Intersection. S'post: Margaret River. **SO.**

> *Yallingup off to left along Caves Rd.*

Fallen log on forest road

(3.5 km)   Opp. dir. s'post: Augusta. ▲ 21.9 km

7.0 km Intersection. **SO.**

> *Turn right along Molloy Rd 8 km to Molloy Caravan Park at Kudardup on Blackwood River.*

(5.6 km)   ▲ 18.4 km

12.6 km Intersection. S'post: Margaret River. **SO.**

> *Hamelin Bay off to left.*

(2.1 km)   Opp. dir. s'post: Augusta. ▲ 12.8 km

14.7 km Intersection. S'post: Nannup. **TR** onto Brockman Hwy in Karridale township.

> **PD** *Next fuel Manjimup (222 km). Margaret River straight ahead.*

(10.1 km)   Opp. dir. s'post: Augusta. ▲ 10.7 km

24.8 km Blackwood River. Cross Alexandra Bridge.

(0.6 km)   ▲ 0.6 km

25.4 km Intersection.

Lighthouse at Cape Leeuwin, land's end

Crossing Blackwood River causeway

> *Turn left along Clark Drive 1.6 km to Alexandra Bridge Camping and Picnic Area on Blackwood River on right. Picnic tables, barbecues. Caretaker on site. Outstanding spot under towering jarrah trees.*

0.0 km Zero trip meter at above intersection. **SO.**
　　　　(5.6 km)　　　　　　　　　　　▲ 0.0 km
　　　　　　　　　　　　　　　　　　　▲ 66.7 km

5.6 km Intersection. S'post: Castle Rd. **TL** onto gravel.
　　　　(3.2 km)　　　　　Bitumen. ▲ 61.1 km

8.8 km T intersection. **TR** onto Cusack Rd.
　　　　(1.6 km)　　　　　　　　　　　▲ 57.9 km

10.4 km T intersection. **TL.**
　　　　(1.6 km)　　　　　　　　　　　▲ 56.3 km

12.0 km Intersection. **KL.**

> *Blackwood Rd on right.*

　　　　(1.0 km)　　　　　　　　　　　▲ 54.7 km

13.0 km Intersection. S'post: Great North Rd. **TR.**

> *Schroeder Rd on left.*

　　　　(3.0 km)　　　　　　　　　　▲ 53.7 km

16.0 km Blackwood River causeway and culverts on ford at Hut Pool. **SO.**

> *Check depth before crossing fast-flowing river; if impassable use alternative route to Sues Bridge via Blackwood Rd and Sues Rd. Canoeing. Swimming prohibited. Picnic area on northern bank. Barbecues.*

　　　　(1.6 km)　　　　　　　　　　▲ 50.7 km

17.6 km Intersection. **SO.**
　　　　(0.7 km)　　　　　　　　　　▲ 49.1 km

18.3 km Crossroads. S'post: Great North Rd. **SO.**

> *Denny Rd on left and right.*

　　　　(7.7 km)　　　　　　　　　　▲ 48.4 km

26.0 km Crossroads. S'post: Crouch Rd. **TR.**
　　　　(8.7 km)　　　　　　　　　　▲ 40.7 km

34.7 km Crossroads. S'post: Crouch Rd. **SO.**

> *Sues Rd on left and right.*

　　　　(4.8 km)　　　　　　　　　　▲ 32.0 km

39.5 km Cross log bridge.
　　　　(8.1 km)　　　　　　　　　　▲ 27.2 km

47.6 km Crossroads. S'post: Layman Rd. **TR.**
　　　　(1.0 km)　　　　　　　　　　▲ 19.1 km

48.6 km First small creek crossing. **SO.**
　　　　(2.0 km)　　　　　　　　　　▲ 18.1 km

50.6 km Second small creek crossing. **SO.**
　　　　(0.9 km)　　　　　　　　　　▲ 16.1 km

51.5 km Third small creek crossing. **SO.**
　　　　(1.7 km)　　　　　　　　　　▲ 15.2 km

53.2 km Fourth small creek crossing. **SO.**
　　　　(0.6 km)　　　　　　　　　　▲ 13.5 km

53.8 km Fifth small creek crossing. **SO.**
　　　　(0.1 km)　　　　　　　　　　▲ 12.9 km

53.9 km T intersection. S'post: Denny Rd. **TR.**
　　　　(11.6 km)　　　　　　　　　▲ 12.8 km

65.5 km Crossroads. **TL** onto Sues Rd.
　　　　(0.9 km)　　　　　　　　　　▲ 1.2 km

66.4 km Blackwood River. Cross Sues Bridge.
　　　　(0.3 km)　　　　　　　　　　▲ 0.3 km

66.7 km Intersection. S'post: Sues Bridge Camping Area and Picnic Ground.

> *Turn right along Sues Bridge Camping Area Rd to camping ground, caravan park and picnic area. Picnic tables, barbecues, toilets. Swimming, fishing, canoeing.*

REVERSE DIRECTIONS START ▲ 0.0 km

SUES BRIDGE «» PEMBERTON

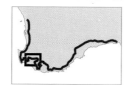

One Tree Bridge near Manjimup

START POINT
Map page 31, G9

TOTAL KM 196.
UNSEALED KM 135.
DEGREE OF DIFFICULTY Moderate.
DRIVING TIME 5 hours.
LONGEST DISTANCE NO FUEL Next fuel Manjimup (145 km from Sues Bridge).
TOPOGRAPHIC MAPS Auslig 1:250 000 series: *Augusta*; *Pemberton*. See also 1:100 000 series.
LOCAL/SPECIALITY MAPS StreetSmart touring maps: *South West Western Australia*; *South West Corner* and *Southern Forests*; RAC map: *Lower South West*; *Robinson's Western Australia*.
OTHER USEFUL INFORMATION Western Australian Tourism Commission booklet: *Western Australia's Southern Wonders*; CALM Discover series booklet: *Wild Places, Quiet Places: a Guide to the Natural Highlights of the South West* and brochure: *Trees of the Southern Forests*; Pemberton Tourist Centre brochure: *Pemberton–Northcliffe: What to Do, What to See in Big Tree Country*; Natrali Promotions bi-annual free guide: *Pemberton and Northcliffe: Kingdom of the Karri*; Pemberton Fishing Spot information sheet: *Catching Your Own King Trout at Pemberton Fishing Spot*.

DESCRIPTION After a brief drive through coastal lowlands, most of this section is spent in magnificent forests of jarrah, marri and karri typical of the south west. Picnic in cool forest settings at Cane Break, Four Aces, One Tree Bridge and Big Brook Arboretum picnic areas. Though camping is not a feature of our trip you can camp in some state-forest areas around Pemberton; *see Bookings and Permits*. Otherwise stay in caravan parks at *Manjimup* and *Pemberton* townships.

Manjimup is the gateway to southern tall-timber country and is also the centre for research into forest fires and native animals. A fauna conservation area in the Perup jarrah–wandoo forest is one of the few known places where endangered species such as numbats, woylies and chuditches survive and breed. The living forest dominates life in and around Pemberton: huge karri trees, permanent waters for trout and marron fishing, large waterways for canoeing adventures, old railway formations once used for hauling timber. In the next section your exploration of this fascinating region moves on to Pemberton's Warren National Park along the Warren River and the scenic recreation area around Northcliffe.

WARNINGS ▶ Some sections of forest tracks boggy and slippery after heavy rain. Beware oncoming traffic along very narrow tracks and watch out for sections partially blocked by fallen trees and branches. ▶ Observe fire-danger warnings.

BOOKINGS AND PERMITS ▶ No prior permits required to traverse parks or forest areas. ▶ Camping in Pemberton state-forest areas with no facilities permitted for up to three nights. For information about suitable sites contact CALM Pemberton District Office, Kennedy Street, Pemberton WA 6260; tel. (097) 76 1200. ▶ For information about caravan parks and activities in Manjimup region contact Manjimup Tourist Bureau, cnr Rose and Edward Streets, Manjimup WA 6258; tel. (097) 71 1831. ▶ For information about caravan park and activities in Pemberton region contact Pemberton Tourist Centre, Brockman Street, Pemberton WA 6260; tel. (097) 76 1133. ▶ For information about Manjimup forest regions contact CALM Manjimup Regional and District Offices, Brain Street, Manjimup WA 6258; tel. (097) 71 1988. ▶ For information about licence and regulations for catching marron in Donnelly River contact Fisheries Department.

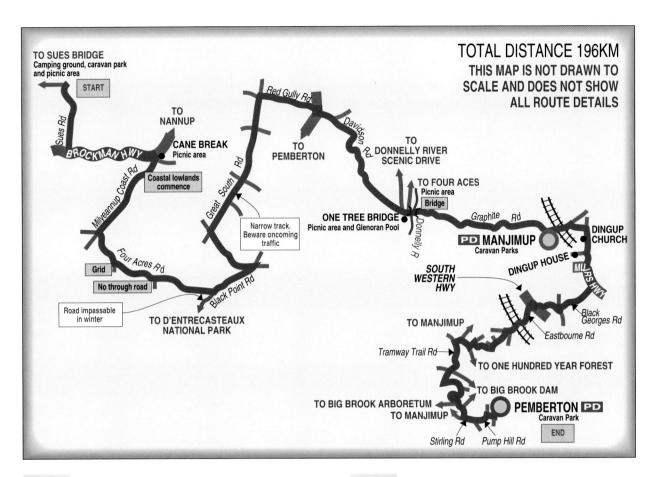

TOTAL DISTANCE 196KM
THIS MAP IS NOT DRAWN TO
SCALE AND DOES NOT SHOW
ALL ROUTE DETAILS

ROUTE DIRECTIONS

0.0 km Zero trip meter at Sues Rd and Sues Bridge Camping Area Rd intersection heading south. **SO** along Sues Rd.

Next fuel Manjimup 145 km.

(9.3 km) ▲ 123.0 km

0.0 km Crossroads. TL onto bitumen Brockman Hwy.

Chester Rd straight ahead.

(13.1 km) Gravel. Opp. dir. s'post: Sues Rd/Sues Bridge Camp Area. ▲113.7 km

22.4 km Intersection. S'post: To Stewart Rd. Cane Break Picnic Area on left. **TR** onto Milyeannup Coast Rd.

Picnic tables, barbecues, toilets. Nannup straight ahead.

(1.0 km) Opp. dir. s'post: Margaret River. ▲100.6 km

23.4 km Intersection. **SO**.

Stewart Rd on left.

(2.0 km) Opp. dir. s'post: Nannup. ▲ 99.6 km

25.4 km Gravel. **SO**.

Country becomes coastal lowlands.

(11.3 km) Bitumen. ▲ 97.6 km

36.7 km Crossroads. S'post: Four Acres Rd. **TL**.

Governor Broome Rd on right.

(4.3 km) ▲ 86.3 km

41.0 km Intersection and grid. **SO**.

Don Rd on right: no through road.

(16.7 km) ▲ 82.0 km

57.7 km T intersection. S'post: Black Point Rd. **TL**.

Road on right continues 15 km to western coastal section of D'Entrecasteaux National Park. Impassable in winter and subject to blockage by fallen trees and branches.

(5.4 km) ▲ 65.3 km

63.1 km T intersection. S'post: Stewart Rd. **TL**.

(7.5 km) ▲ 59.9 km

70.6 km Intersection. S'post: Great South Rd. **TR**.

Narrow track: beware oncoming traffic.

(4.6 km) ▲ 52.4 km

75.2 km Intersection. S'post: Great South Rd. **SO**.

Coate Rd on right.

(3.5 km) ▲ 47.8 km

78.7 km Crossroads. **SO**.

Darradup Rd on left and right.

(7.1 km) ▲ 44.3 km

85.8 km Crossroads. **SO**.

Blackwood Rd on left and right.

(4.8 km) ▲ 37.2 km

90.6 km Crossroads. S'post: Red Gully Rd. **TR**.

(8.4 km) Opp. dir. s'post: Great South Rd. ▲ 32.4 km

99.0 km T intersection. **TR** onto bitumen: Vasse Hwy.

(1.4 km) Gravel. ▲ 24.0 km

100.4 km Intersection. S'post: Davidson Rd. **TL**.

Pemberton straight ahead.

(0.7 km) Opp. dir. s'post: Nannup. ▲ 22.6 km

101.1 km Gravel. **SO**.

(2.0 km) Bitumen. ▲ 21.9 km

103.1 km Intersection. **KR**.

Mt Leeuwin Rd on left.

(15.9 km) ▲ 19.9 km

119.0 km Bitumen. **SO**.

(3.4 km) Gravel. ▲ 4.0 km

122.4 km Intersection. **SO**.

Turn left for Donnelly River Scenic Drive, 30-km drive through karri–marri forest.

(0.6 km) ▲ 0.6 km

123.0 km Intersection.

Turn left to Four Aces Picnic Area. Picnic tables, toilets. Educational display on karri forests. Commence short walk through karri forest.

0.0 km Zero trip meter at above intersection. **SO**.

(1.0 km) ▲ 0.0 km

▲ 1.0 km

1.0 km One Tree Bridge Picnic Area on right.

Picnic tables, barbecues, toilets. Fishing. Straight ahead a further 200 m to Glenoran Pool Picnic Area. Good swimming hole.

0.0 km Zero trip meter at above point. **SO** onto Graphite Rd.

(0.1 km) ▲ 0.0 km

▲ 21.0 km

0.1 km Donnelly River. Cross bridge.

(20.9 km) ▲ 20.9 km

21.0 km Intersection.

Turn right to Manjimup township. **PD** Supplies, caravan parks. Timber tours, Timber Park, Diamond Tree Tower fire-lookout, Bunnings Diamond Mill, Deanmill, vineyard.

0.0 km Zero trip meter at above intersection. **SO**.

(0.1 km) ▲ 0.0 km

▲ 33.5 km

0.1 km Cross railway line and **SO** at s'post: Perup Rd.

(3.2 km) Opp. dir. s'post: Nannup. ▲ 33.4 km

3.3 km Intersection. S'post: Morgans Rd. **TR** onto gravel.

(2.4 km) Bitumen. ▲ 30.2 km

5.7 km Intersection. S'post: Balbarrup Rd. **TR**.

(0.9 km) Opp. dir. s'post: Morgans Rd. ▲ 27.8 km

6.6 km Historic Dingup Church on right. **SO**.

Built in 1897 as a home, then used as a school and later as a church.

(2.4 km) ▲ 26.9 km

9.0 km Intersection. S'post: Balbarrup Rd. Historic Dingup House on right. **SO**.

Built in 1870. Dingup Rd on right.

(1.9 km) ▲ 24.5 km

10.9 km T intersection. **TL** onto Muirs Hwy.

(2.1 km) Opp. dir. s'post: Balbarrup Rd. ▲ 22.6 km

13.0 km Intersection. S'post: Black Georges Rd. **TR** onto gravel.

(7.1 km) Bitumen. ▲ 20.5 km

20.1 km T intersection. **TL** onto bitumen: Middlesex Rd.

(0.1 km) Gravel. Opp. dir. s'post: Black Georges Rd. ▲ 13.4 km

20.2 km Intersection. S'post: Pipe Clay Gully Rd. **TR** onto gravel.

(4.1 km) Bitumen. ▲ 13.3 km

24.3 km T intersection. **TR** onto bitumen: South Western Hwy.

(0.7 km) Gravel. Opp. dir. s'post: Pipe Clay Gully Rd. ▲ 9.2 km

25.0 km Intersection. S'post: Eastbourne Rd. **TL**.

Enter Diamond State Forest.

(4.1 km) Opp. dir. s'post: South Western Hwy. ▲ 8.5 km

29.1 km Cross railway line.
(0.1 km)   ▲ 4.4 km
29.2 km Intersection. **TR** onto gravel: Ridge Rd.
(0.2 km)   Bitumen. ▲ 4.3 km
29.4 km Intersection. S'post: Farrs Rd. **TL**.
(1.7 km)   ▲ 4.1 km
31.1 km Intersection. **KL**.
(0.7 km)   ▲ 2.4 km
31.8 km Y intersection. **KL**.
(1.0 km)   ▲ 1.7 km
32.8 km Intersection. **SO**.
(0.3 km)   ▲ 0.7 km
33.1 km T intersection. **TL** onto Smiths Rd.
(0.4 km)   ▲ 0.4 km
33.5 km Intersection. S'post: Manjimup.

> *Turn left to One Hundred Year Forest, comprising 70 m-tall karri trees. Site originally cleared in 1865 for wheat production that failed; later regenerated by fire that induced seedfall from other trees.*

0.0 km Zero trip meter at above intersection. **SO**.
(2.3 km)   Opp. dir. s'post: Pemberton. ▲ 0.0 km
                                              ▲ 9.8 km
2.3 km Intersection. S'post: Channybearup Rd. **TL**.

> *Manjimup off to right.*

(0.6 km)   Opp. dir. s'post:
                         Smiths Rd/100 Year Forest. ▲ 7.5 km
2.9 km Intersection. S'post: Tramway Trail Rd. **TL**.
(3.3 km)   ▲ 6.9 km
6.2 km Crossroads. S'post: Tramway Trail. **SO**.

> *Brook Rd on left and right. Turn left 3.5 km to Big Brook Dam. Easy 3.5-km walk around dam gives excellent views across water. Trout fishing.*

(3.3 km)   ▲ 3.6 km
9.5 km Intersection. S'post: Rainbow Trail. **TL**.

> *Historic Tramway and Rainbow trails scenic rail lines through marri–karri forests.*

(0.2 km)   ▲ 0.3 km
9.7 km Intersection. S'post: Pemberton. **SO** along Sequoia Rd.
(0.1 km)   Opp. dir. s'post: Manjimup. ▲ 0.1 km
9.8 km Intersection. S'post: Rainbow Trail.

> *Turn right 200 m to Big Brook Arboretum. Commence easy 1.2-km circuit walk from barbecue site through delightful karri grove.*

0.0 km Zero trip meter at above intersection. **KL**.
(0.2 km)   ▲ 0.0 km
                                              ▲ 0.2 km
0.2 km Intersection. S'post: Rainbow Trail.

> *Big Brook Dam off to left.*

0.0 km Zero trip meter at above intersection. **SO**.
(1.5 km)   ▲ 0.0 km
                                              ▲ 7.8 km
1.5 km Intersection. S'post: Pemberton. **TL** onto bitumen: Stirling Rd.

> *Manjimup off to right.*

(3.1 km)   Gravel. ▲ 6.3 km
4.6 km Intersection. S'post: Pump Hill Rd. **SO**.

> *Stirling Rd on right.*

(2.4 km)   ▲ 3.2 km
7.0 km Intersection. S'post: Club Rd. **TR**.
(0.2 km)   ▲ 0.8 km
7.2 km Intersection. S'post: Brockman St. **TL**.

> *Enter Pemberton township.*

(0.6 km)   ▲ 0.6 km
7.8 km Pemberton Post Office on right, cnr Ellis St.

> **PD** *Supplies, caravan park. Hospital, all services. Pioneer Timber Museum, sawmill, art and craft shops, wineries. Beedelup Falls, trout and marron hatchery. Fishing.*

REVERSE DIRECTIONS START ▲ 0.0 km

▼▼▼▼▼▼▼▼
TAKE CARE

● In a bushfire, drive to an open area away from trees, stay in the vehicle, cover all bare skin with non-flammable clothing, preferably wool, or a woollen blanket, and keep low.

● Don't take short cuts over virgin ground. You will destroy the vegetation. Stick to tracks open for use.

● Four-wheel drive tracks are subject to closure; if in doubt, check with local authorities such as national parks or forestry departments.

PEMBERTON
«»
FERNHOOK FALLS

Signs on Heartbreak Trail

START POINT
Map page 30, E12.

TOTAL KM 175.
UNSEALED KM 111.
DEGREE OF DIFFICULTY Extreme.
DRIVING TIME 5 hours.
LONGEST DISTANCE NO FUEL 182 km (Northcliffe to Peaceful Bay, next section).
TOPOGRAPHIC MAP Auslig 1:250 000 series: *Pemberton*. See also 1:100 000 series.
LOCAL/SPECIALITY MAPS StreetSmart touring maps: *South West Western Australia, Southern Forests* and *The South Coast*; RAC map: *Lower South West*; *Robinson's Western Australia*.
OTHER USEFUL INFORMATION Western Australian Tourism Commission booklet: *Western Australia's Southern Wonders*; CALM Discover series booklet: *Wild Places, Quiet Places: a Guide to the Natural Highlights of the South West* and brochures: *Walpole National Parks and Forests: Where Karri Meets the Coast* and *Trees of the Southern Forests*; Northcliffe Tourist Information Centre brochure: *Pemberton–Northcliffe: What to Do, What to See in Big Tree Country*; Natrali Promotions bi-annual free guide: *Pemberton and Northcliffe: Kingdom of the Karri.*

DESCRIPTION Giant karri forests dominate the first part of this section around the picturesque timber towns of Pemberton and Northcliffe. *Warren National Park* covers about 1400 hectares of magnificent uncut karri in the Warren River valley, which can be viewed from the Heartbreak and Maiden Bush trails; there are picnic and camping spots near the river. Northcliffe Forest Park on the edge of *Northcliffe* township contains some of Australia's tallest and oldest trees which you can see when exploring the forest on foot. Stay in the caravan park in Northcliffe, the gateway to a scenic area ideal for camping, boating, fishing and swimming.

You then head south towards the Southern Ocean coastline to emerge at *Windy Harbour*, a tiny fishing–resort community at Point D'Entrecasteaux. From there you undertake a real four-wheel drive adventure – *see Warnings* – which can be extended by stopping over at the campsite at the mouth of the *Gardner River* alongside some fishing shanties. Back on Chesapeake Road you head east to conclude the section at *Fernhook Falls*, a beautiful camping and picnic area just north of Denmark township.

WARNINGS ▶ Steep and rough roads in Warren National Park unsuitable for caravans and trailers. ▶ Take on enough fuel at Northcliffe for 182 kilometres to Peaceful Bay in next section. ▶ Do not embark after heavy rain when Lower Gardner Road, extremely difficult section of low-lying coastal wetlands between Windy Harbour and Chesapeake Road, becomes waterlogged. Check depth of Blackwater Creek before crossing. Keep to main track when traversing firm section of track to avoid bogging. Long sections of track overgrown with vegetation and very narrow: beware damage to vehicle's paintwork. To avoid adventuresome track, return from Windy Harbour to Chesapeake Road turnoff and rejoin route where Lower Gardner Road track exits onto Chesapeake Road at approximately 10 kilometres. ▶ Windy Harbour has no facilities other than a caravan park. ▶ Observe fire-danger warnings.

BOOKINGS AND PERMITS ▶ No prior permits required to traverse Warren, Brockman or D'Entrecasteaux national parks or Northcliffe Forest Park reserve. ▶ For information about camping, conditions and natural environment of national parks and Fern-

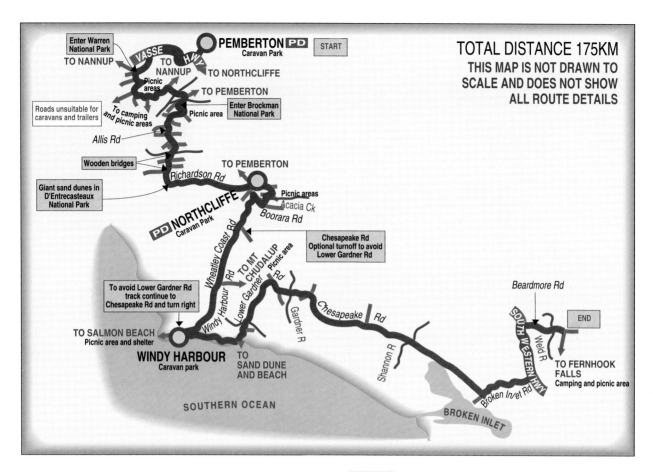

TOTAL DISTANCE 175KM
THIS MAP IS NOT DRAWN TO SCALE AND DOES NOT SHOW ALL ROUTE DETAILS

hook Falls site contact CALM Pemberton District Office, Kennedy Street, Pemberton WA 6260; tel. (097) 76 1200. ▶ For information about caravan parks in Northcliffe and Windy Harbour contact Northcliffe Tourist Information Centre, adjacent to Pioneer Museum, Northcliffe WA 6262; tel. (097) 76 7203. ▶ For information about licence and regulations for catching marron contact Fisheries Department.

ROUTE DIRECTIONS

0.0 km Zero trip meter at Pemberton Post Office, cnr Brockman St and Ellis St heading south west. **SO** along Brockman St.

> **PD** *Supplies, caravan park.*

(3.0 km) ▲ 19.0 km

3.0 km Intersection. S'post: Nannup. **TR** onto Vasse Hwy.

> *Northcliffe straight ahead.*

(8.9 km) Opp. dir. s'post: Pemberton. ▲ 16.0 km

11.9 km Intersection. S'post: Warren National Park. **KL** onto gravel.

(0.5 km) Bitumen. ▲ 7.1 km

12.4 km Crossroads. S'post: Northcliffe. **TL** onto Old Vasse Rd.

> *Enter Warren National Park. Nannup off to right.*

(2.8 km) ▲ 6.6 km

15.2 km Intersection. **SO.**

> *Turn right along Hawke Rd to Swamp Willow Craft Shop.*

(1.1 km) ▲ 3.8 km

16.3 km Intersection. S'post: Heartbreak Trail. **TR.**

> *Slow, scenic drive. Caution: slippery when wet. Buses, caravans and trailers prohibited.*

(2.7 km) ▲ 2.7 km

19.0 km Intersection. Sign: One-way traffic.

> *Turn right 100 m to camping and picnic area. Picnic tables, barbecues.*

0.0 km Zero trip meter at above intersection. **SO.**

(0.1 km) ▲ 0.0 km
▲ 8.7 km

405

0.1 km Intersection. S'post: Maiden Bush Trail Scenic Drive. **TL.**
(1.2 km) ▲ 8.6 km
1.3 km Camping area on right. **SO.**

> *Picnic tables, barbecues, toilets. Fishing on Warren River.*

(1.6 km) ▲ 7.4 km
2.9 km Intersection. **SO.**

> *Turn right 100 m to camping and picnic area. Picnic tables, barbecues, toilets. Fishing on Warren River.*

(1.5 km) ▲ 5.8 km
4.4 km Picnic area on left. **SO.**

> *Picnic tables, barbecues.*

(0.9 km) ▲ 4.3 km
5.3 km Picnic area on right. **SO.**

> *Picnic tables, barbecues.*

(1.3 km) ▲ 3.4 km
6.6 km Intersection. S'post: Northcliffe. **TR.**

> *Nannup off to left.*

(1.8 km) ▲ 2.1 km
8.4 km Bitumen. **SO.**
(0.2 km) Gravel. ▲ 0.3 km
8.6 km Treen Brook. Cross bridge.
(0.1 km) ▲ 0.1 km
8.7 km King Trout Farm on right.

> *Trout and marron fishing and sales. Rod hire. Restaurant.*

0.0 km Zero trip meter at above point. **SO.**
(0.1 km) ▲ 0.0 km
▲ 32.2 km
0.1 km Intersection. S'post: Northcliffe. **TR** onto Pemberton–Northcliffe Rd.

> *Pemberton off to left.*

(1.4 km) Opp. dir. s'post: Old Vasse Rd. ▲ 32.1 km
1.5 km Warren River. Cross bridge.
(0.6 km) ▲ 30.7 km
2.1 km Intersection. **SO.**

> *Enter Brockman National Park. Calcup Rd on right.*

(1.2 km) ▲ 30.1 km
3.3 km Picnic area on left. **SO.**

Fernhook Falls

> *Picnic tables, barbecues.*

(1.2 km) ▲ 28.9 km
4.5 km Intersection. S'post: Allis Rd. **TR** onto gravel.
(1.2 km) Bitumen. ▲ 27.7 km
5.7 km Crossroads. **SO.**
(0.7 km) ▲ 26.5 km
6.4 km Intersection. S'post: Calcup Rd. **SO.**

> *Calcup Rd commences on right.*

(0.1 km) Opp. dir. s'post: Allis Rd. ▲ 25.8 km
6.5 km Crossroads. S'post: Calcup Rd. **SO.**

> *Barker Rd on left and right.*

(1.1 km) ▲ 25.7 km
7.6 km Intersection. S'post: Malimup Track. **SO.**

> *Calcup Rd on right.*

(0.6 km) Opp. dir. s'post: Calcup Rd. ▲ 24.6 km
8.2 km Crossroads. S'post: MalimupTrack. **SO.**

> *Plantation Rd on left and right.*

(3.2 km) ▲ 24.0 km
11.4 km Dombakup River. Cross wooden bridge.

> *Ford on right.*

(0.3 km) ▲ 20.8 km
11.7 km Crossroads. S'post: Malimup Track. **SO.** Nineteen Rd on left and right.
(1.2 km) ▲ 20.5 km
12.9 km Intersection. S'post: Richardson Rd. **SO.**

> *Malimup Rd on left.*

(1.0 km) ▲ 19.3 km
13.9 km Cross wooden bridge.
(0.2 km) ▲ 18.3 km

14.1 km   Intersection. S'post: Richardson Rd. **SO**.

> *Lewis Rd on right.*

(4.2 km)   ▲ 18.1 km

18.3 km   Giant sand dunes on right. **SO**.

> *A section of D'Entrecasteaux National Park.*

(4.3 km)   ▲ 13.9 km

22.6 km   Bitumen. **SO**.

(8.8 km)   Gravel. ▲ 9.6 km

31.4 km   Intersection. S'post: Windy Harbour. **TR** onto Pemberton–Northcliffe Rd.

> *Pemberton off to left.*

(0.8 km)   Opp. dir. s'post: Richardson Rd. ▲ 0.8 km

32.2 km   Intersection. S'post: Forest Park.

> *Windy Harbour off to right.*

0.0 km   Zero trip meter at above intersection. **TL** onto Wheatley–Windy Harbour Rd.

> *Enter Northcliffe township.* **PD** *Supplies, caravan park. Timber mill, Pioneer Museum, Jubilee Park museum complex and eucalypt arboretum. Next fuel Peaceful Bay (182 km).*

(0.9 km)   Opp. dir. s'post: Pemberton. ▲ 0.0 km
                                  ▲ 23.1 km

0.9 km   Cross railway line.

(0.1 km)   ▲ 22.2 km

1.0 km   Intersection. S'post: Northcliffe Forest Park. **TR** onto gravel.

(1.1 km)   Bitumen. ▲ 22.1 km

2.1 km   Information board. **SO**.

> *Commence several walks of length approx. 1 km. Reserve includes some of Australia's largest and oldest trees, amazing hollow-butt karri and twin karri, and a wildflower display in season.*

(1.8 km)   ▲ 21.0 km

3.9 km   Picnic area on right. **SO**.

> *Picnic tables, barbecues, shelter.*

(0.4 km)   ▲ 19.2 km

4.3 km   Intersection. S'post: Northcliffe. **TR** onto bitumen.

(0.3 km)   Gravel. ▲ 18.8 km

4.6 km   Intersection. S'post: Acacia Rd. **TL** onto gravel.

(0.0 km)   Bitumen. ▲ 18.5 km

4.6 km   Intersection. S'post: Acacia Rd. **KR**.

(1.0 km)   ▲ 18.5 km

5.6 km   Acacia Rd Picnic Area on right. **SO**.

Huge karri tree, Northcliffe Forest Park

> *Picnic tables, barbecues, toilets.*

(0.2 km)   ▲ 17.5 km

5.8 km   Acacia Creek. Cross bridge.

(1.1 km)   ▲ 17.3 km

6.9 km   T intersection. **TR** onto bitumen: Boorara Rd.

(0.8 km)   Gravel. ▲ 16.2 km

7.7 km   T intersection. **TL** onto Wheatley Coast Rd.

(5.6 km)   Opp. dir. s'post: Boorara Rd. ▲ 15.4 km

13.3 km   Intersection. **SO**.

> *Chesapeake Rd on left: optional turnoff to avoid Lower Gardner Rd track which joins approx. 10 km further on.*

(9.8 km)   ▲ 9.8 km

23.1 km   Intersection.

> *Turn left 200 m to Mt Chudalup Picnic Area. Picnic tables, barbecues. Walking trail to lookout at top of Mt Chudalup, granite dome, with unobstructed views of up to 30 km.*

0.0 km Zero trip meter at above intersection. **SO** onto Windy Harbour Rd.
(11.3 km) ▲ 0.0 km
▲ 11.3 km

11.3 km Intersection.

> Turn right onto gravel 3.5 km to Salmon Beach Picnic Area and shelter. Scenic spot backed by 60 m-high sand dunes. 4WD access only.

0.0 km Zero trip meter at above intersection. **SO** onto gravel.
(0.5 km) Bitumen. ▲ 0.0 km
▲ 0.5 km

0.5 km Windy Harbour settlement.

> Caravan park. No facilities. Sandy beach, safe swimming and snorkelling.

0.0 km Zero trip meter at above point. Return to Salmon Beach turnoff and **SO** along Windy Harbour Rd heading north.

> To avoid Lower Gardner Rd track continue to Chesapeake Rd and turn right.

(1.0 km) ▲ 0.0 km
▲ 80.7 km

1.0 km Intersection. S'post: Rubbish tip. **TR** onto gravel: Lower Gardner Rd.
(0.3 km) Bitumen. ▲ 79.7 km

1.3 km S'post: Sand track – 4WD only. **SO.**

> S'post is at far end of rubbish-tip area.

(0.0 km) ▲ 79.4 km
1.3 km Y intersection. **KL.**

> Caution: road very narrow.

(8.5 km) ▲ 79.4 km
9.8 km T intersection. **TL.**

> Sand dune and beach off to right.

(0.2 km) ▲ 70.9 km
10.0 km Cleared area suitable for camping. **SO.**

> Beach shanties on section of Gardner Beach. Swimming, fishing. Track on right leads to mouth of Gardner River. Homemade sign: To river. Canoeing in river.

(0.2 km) ▲ 70.7 km
10.2 km Y intersection. **KR.**
(1.0 km) ▲ 70.5 km
11.2 km Blackwater Creek crossing. **SO.**

> Established track with firm base runs across creek; check depth before crossing. Track may have a lot of water on it for next 10 km, but track firmer than surrounding country. Beware possible scratching of vehicle along very narrow track.

(9.3 km) ▲ 69.5 km
20.5 km Y intersection. **KR** over hill.
(0.1 km) ▲ 60.2 km
20.6 km T intersection. **TR** onto Chesapeake Rd.
(2.0 km) ▲ 60.1 km
22.6 km Intersection. S'post: Chesapeake Rd. **SO.**

> Marringup Rd on right.

(2.2 km) ▲ 58.1 km
24.8 km Gardner River. Cross bridge.
(3.4 km) ▲ 55.9 km
28.2 km Crossroads. S'post: Chesapeake Rd. **SO.**

> Gardner River Rd on left and right.

(10.4 km) ▲ 52.5 km
38.6 km Intersection. S'post: Chesapeake Rd. **SO.**

> Deeside Coast Rd on left.

(6.8 km) ▲ 42.1 km
45.4 km Shannon River. Cross bridge.
(12.8 km) ▲ 35.3 km
58.2 km T intersection. S'post: Broken Inlet Rd. **TL.**

> Road on right continues to Broken Inlet.

(8.1 km) Opp. dir. s'post: Chesapeake Rd. ▲22.5 km
66.3 km Intersection. S'post: Manjimup. **TL** onto bitumen: South Western Hwy.
(8.5 km) Gravel. Opp. dir. s'post: Broken Inlet. ▲ 14.4 km

74.8 km Intersection. S'post: Fernhook Drive. **TR** onto gravel: Beardmore Rd.
(4.6 km) Bitumen. ▲ 5.9 km

79.4 km Weld River. Cross bridge.
(1.3 km) ▲ 1.3 km
80.7 km Intersection. S'post: Fernhook Falls.

> Turn right to camping and picnic area. Picnic tables, barbecues, toilets. Magnificent waterfall and picnic area.

REVERSE DIRECTIONS START ▲ 0.0 km

FERNHOOK FALLS
«»
ESPERANCE

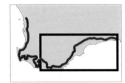

START POINT
Map page 30, F12

TOTAL KM 665.
UNSEALED KM 57.
DEGREE OF DIFFICULTY Easy.
DRIVING TIME 4 hours (Fernhook Falls to Albany).
LONGEST DISTANCE NO FUEL 174 km (Albany to Jerramangup).
TOPOGRAPHIC MAPS Auslig 1:250 000 series: *Pemberton*; *Mt Barker*; *Albany*. See also 1:100 000 series.
LOCAL/SPECIALITY MAPS StreetSmart touring maps: *South West Western Australia* and *The South Coast*; Western Australian tourist map: *Rainbow Coast*; *Robinson's Western Australia*.
OTHER USEFUL INFORMATION Western Australian Tourism Commission booklet: *Western Australia's Southern Wonders*; CALM Discover series booklets: *Wild Places, Quiet Places: a Guide to the Natural Highlights of the South West* and *Walpole National Parks and Forests: Where Karri Meets the Coast*; Rainbow Coast Tourism Directorate booklet: *1791–1991: The Rainbow Coast WA Anniversary Souvenir Edition*.

DESCRIPTION This section heads towards Denmark on the south coast through karri–tingle forests and cleared rolling pasturelands. It is an easy drive through extraordinarily beautiful country and there are ample opportunities to picnic or browse through craft shops and wineries.

Mt Frankland National Park covers 30 000 hectares of uncut forest surrounding Mt Frankland, a granite monadnock once used as a fire-lookout post. You pass through the aptly named Valley of the Giants, a rare forest comprising giant stands of red tingles and karris. Walpole–Nornalup National Park covers 18 000 hec-

tares surrounding the Walpole and Nornalup inlets and protects a variety of forest and coastal environments, plants and animals. Both national parks have camping areas though camping is not included in our route directions.

Caravan parks are located at *Peaceful Bay, Denmark, Albany* and *Esperance*. The state's first settlement and ex-whaling capital, Albany is now a leading holiday centre: fishing is excellent in its harbours, rivers and estuaries, and there is much to see and do when visiting the town, its spectacular coastal scenery, beaches and nearby national parks. The trek ends with a long stretch to Esperance, on the edge of the Nullarbor Plain.

WARNING ▶ Observe fire-danger warnings especially during summer months December–February.

BOOKINGS AND PERMITS ▶ No prior permits required to traverse Mt Frankland or Walpole–Nornalup national parks. ▶ For information about camping in national parks contact CALM Walpole District Office, South West Highway, Walpole WA 6398; tel. (098) 40 1027. ▶ For information about caravan park at Peaceful Bay contact Walpole Tourist Bureau, Pioneer Cottage, Pioneer Park, Walpole WA 6398; tel. (098) 40 1111. ▶ For information about caravan park in Denmark contact Denmark Tourist Bureau, Strickland Street, Denmark WA 6333; tel. (098) 48 1265. ▶ For information about caravan parks in Albany contact Albany Tourist Bureau, Peels Place, Albany WA 6330; tel. (098) 41 1088. ▶ For information about licence and regulations for catching marron contact Fisheries Department.

ROUTE DIRECTIONS

0.0 km Zero trip meter at Beardmore Rd and Fernhook Falls Camping Area intersection heading east. **SO** along Beardmore Rd.

Next fuel Peaceful Bay (67 km).

(0.3 km) ▲ 12.1 km
0.3 km Deep River. Cross bridge.

Fernhook Falls on right.

(6.8 km) ▲ 11.8 km
7.1 km Intersection. S'post: Beardmore Rd. **SO**.

Doug Rd on right.

(5.0 km) ▲ 5.0 km
12.1 km Y intersection. S'post: Walpole.

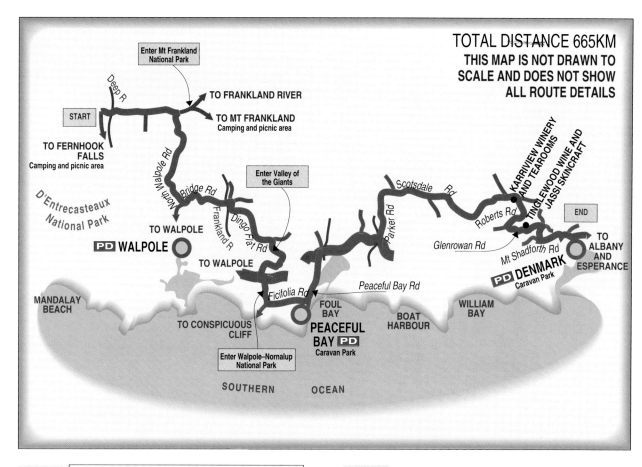

TOTAL DISTANCE 665KM
THIS MAP IS NOT DRAWN TO
SCALE AND DOES NOT SHOW
ALL ROUTE DETAILS

Keep left to North Walpole Rd crossroads. Enter Mt Frankland National Park. Straight ahead a further 4.9 km to Y intersection. Keep right 2 km to Mt Frankland Camping and Picnic Area. Toilets. 1.5 km walk to Mt Frankland summit. Keep left along Caldyanup Rd 4.2 km to Frankland River. Canoeing.

0.0 km Zero trip meter at above Y intersection. **KR.**
(0.2 km)   ▲ 0.0 km
                                                ▲ 14.1 km

0.2 km T intersection. **TR** onto North Walpole Rd.
(5.0 km)   ▲ 13.9 km

5.2 km Bitumen. **SO.**
(8.9 km)   Gravel. ▲ 8.9 km

14.1 km Intersection. S'post: Bridge Rd.

Straight ahead approx. 5 km to Walpole settlement. PD Supplies.

0.0 km Zero trip meter at above intersection. **TL.**
(6.9 km)   ▲ 0.0 km
                                                ▲ 32.0 km

6.9 km Frankland River. Cross bridge.
(1.5 km)   ▲ 25.1 km

8.4 km Intersection. S'post: Hazelvale Rd. **SO.**

Hazelvale North Rd on left.

(0.2 km)   ▲ 23.6 km

8.6 km Intersection. S'post: Dingo Flat Rd. **TR** onto gravel.

Hazelvale Rd straight ahead.

(10.1 km)   Bitumen. ▲ 23.4 km

18.7 km Intersection. S'post: Valley of the Giants Rd. **TR** onto bitumen.
(2.9 km)   Gravel. ▲ 13.3 km

21.6 km Sign: You are now entering the Valley of the Giants. **SO.**

Rare forest of giant karri and red tingle trees with distinctive buttressed roots and massive trunks. Information shelter.

(0.4 km)   ▲ 10.4 km

22.0 km Valley of the Giants Picnic Area on left. **SO.**

Picnic tables, barbecues, toilets.

(5.1 km)   ▲ 10.0 km

27.1 km Intersection. S'post: Denmark. **TL** onto South Coast Hwy.

> *Walpole off to right.*

(1.0 km) Opp. dir. s'post: Valley of the Giants. ▲ 4.9 km

28.1 km Intersection. S'post: Conspicuous Cliff. **TR** onto gravel.

(1.9 km) Bitumen. ▲ 3.9 km

30.0 km Sign: Walpole–Nornalup National Park. **SO.**

(2.0 km) ▲ 2.0 km

32.0 km Intersection. S'post: Peaceful Bay.

> *Turn right 2.5 km to Conspicuous Cliff. Wild coastline.*

0.0 km Zero trip meter at above intersection. **SO** along Ficifolia Rd.

> *Large area of red-flowering gum trees.*

(6.7 km) Opp. dir. s'post: Nornalup. ▲ 0.0 km
▲ 6.7 km

6.7 km Intersection. S'post: Bow Bridge.

> *Turn right 2.5 km to Peaceful Bay.* **PD** *Caravan park, accomm., fishing.*

0.0 km Zero trip meter at above intersection. **TL** onto bitumen: Peaceful Bay Rd.

(6.5 km) Gravel. Opp. dir. s'post: Ficifolia Rd. ▲ 0.0 km
▲ 68.6 km

6.5 km Intersection. S'post: Denmark. **TR** onto South Coast Hwy.

> *Walpole off to left.*

(0.4 km) Opp. dir. s'post: Peaceful Bay. ▲ 62.1 km

6.9 km Intersection. **SO.**

> *Valley of the Giants Rd on left.*

(0.1 km) ▲ 61.7 km

7.0 km Bow River. Cross bridge.

> *Bow River Roadhouse on left.* **PD** *Supplies.*

(6.8 km) ▲ 61.6 km

13.8 km Intersection. **SO.**

> *Tindale Rd on left.*

(2.1 km) ▲ 54.8 km

15.9 km Kent River. Cross bridge.

(0.7 km) ▲ 52.7 km

16.6 km Intersection. S'post: Kentdale. **TL** onto gravel: Parker Rd.

(8.8 km) Bitumen. ▲ 52.0 km

25.4 km Intersection. **SO.**

(5.3 km) Opp. dir. s'post: Kentdale. ▲ 43.2 km

30.7 km Bitumen. **SO.**

(0.1 km) Gravel. ▲ 37.9 km

30.8 km Intersection. S'post: Scotsdale Rd. **SO.**

> *Kordabup Rd on right.*

(14.0 km) ▲ 37.8 km

44.8 km Intersection. **SO.**

> *Harewood Rd on left.*

(3.4 km) ▲ 23.8 km

48.2 km Intersection. S'post: Roberts Rd. **TR** onto gravel.

> *Karriview Winery and Tearooms on right.*

(3.6 km) Bitumen. ▲ 20.4 km

51.8 km Intersection. S'post: Glenrowan Rd. **TL.**

(3.5 km) ▲ 16.8 km

55.3 km Tinglewood Wines and Jassi Skincraft on left. **SO.**

(2.0 km) ▲ 13.3 km

57.3 km Crossroads. S'post: Turner Rd. **TR.**

> *Walter Rd on left.*

(2.0 km) Opp. dir. s'post: Glenrowan Rd. ▲ 11.3 km

59.3 km Intersection. S'post: Mt Shadforth Rd. **TL** onto bitumen.

(9.2 km) Gravel. Opp. dir. s'post: Turner Rd. ▲ 9.3 km

68.5 km Intersection. **TR** onto Strickland St.

> *Enter Denmark township.*

(0.1 km) ▲ 0.1 km

68.6 km Crossroads.

> *High St on left and right. Straight ahead 200 m to Denmark Post Office on left, cnr Bent St.* **PD** *Supplies, caravan park.*

REVERSE DIRECTIONS START : 0.0 km

Turn left at above crossroads onto High St and **SO** along South Coast Hwy approx. 50 km to Albany Hwy and Chester Pass Rd intersection in Albany.

> **PD** *Supplies, caravan parks. Albany Whaleworld whaling museum, picnic areas. Swimming, fishing.*

From Albany, take South Coast Hwy to Esperance (approx. 481 km) for start of next trek.

> **PD** *Supplies, caravan park. Fishing, seal viewing from tanker jetty.*

ACROSS THE NULLARBOR

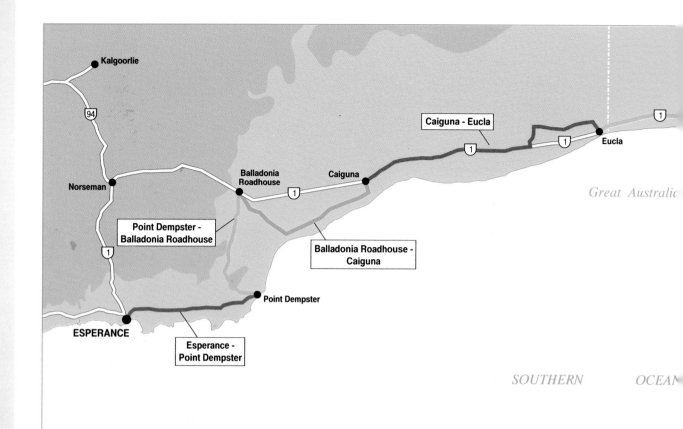

ACROSS THE NULLARBOR
ESPERANCE «» ADELAIDE
2543 KILOMETRES

ESPERANCE «» POINT DEMPSTER   207 km

POINT DEMPSTER
«» BALLADONIA ROADHOUSE   185 km

BALLADONIA ROADHOUSE «» CAIGUNA   241 km

CAIGUNA «» EUCLA   374 km

EUCLA «» FOWLERS BAY   610 km

FOWLERS BAY «» ADELAIDE   926 km

This trek to a great extent avoids the usual interstate route along the Eyre Highway – although in the latter sections the highway serves as a link – and runs through isolated and desolate regions of the southern Australian coast. Offsetting the difficulties encountered are the magnificent scenery of Cape Le Grand and Cape Arid, the always spectacular cliffs of the Great Australian Bight, the magic of a night on the Nullarbor Plain and the beautiful and geologically unique wilderness of the Gawler Ranges. Contrasting with rugged mountain and desert driving are wide saltbush plains and the lonely sidings of the Transcontinental Railway line. The best time to travel is spring or autumn, to avoid the heat of summer and the winter rains and to catch the spring wildflowers in the ranges.

Conditions from Point Dempster to Caiguna are extremely difficult and at no point off the highway is this an easy trek. There is no fuel in the sections from Esperance to Balladonia and fresh water only early on the route at Lucky Bay and at Orleans Bay Caravan Park; once off the highway after leaving Balladonia there is neither fuel nor fresh water before Caiguna – indeed, it is advisable to carry ample supplies of water at all times. There are few designated camping areas,

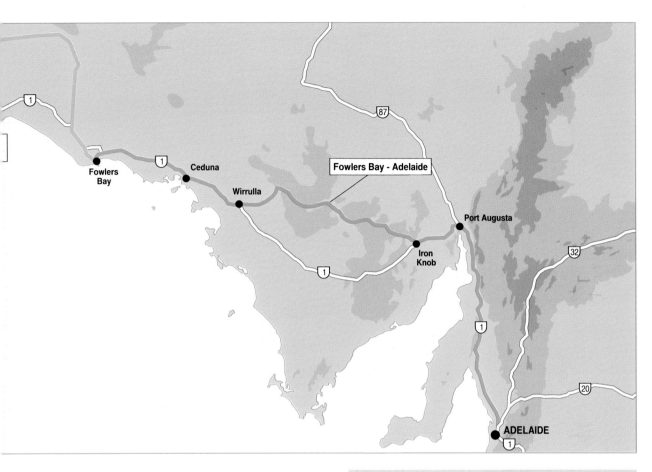

but bush camping is possible. For the experienced four-wheel driver, this is indeed a remarkable trek.

BEFORE YOU SET OUT ▶ Read the section description carefully. ▶Check that you have obtained any necessary permits. ▶ Check weather conditions with local authorities or the Bureau of Meteorology. ▶ Make sure you have the appropriate maps and information for the trek. ▶ Check that your vehicle is in good order for the conditions ahead. Have you the necessary spare parts? ▶ If you are camping, do you have the right camping equipment?

TREAD LIGHTLY!
On Public and Private Land

■ Take your rubbish home with you. Do not bury it.

■ Leave gates as you found them – open or shut.

■ Don't disturb livestock – slow down or stop.

■ Stay off roads and tracks when they are wet and easily cut up.

■ Ford creeks at designated crossings.

■ Observe firelighting regulations and total fire ban days.

NATIONAL PARKS OF WESTERN AND SOUTH AUSTRALIA

In Western Australia you pass through Cape Le Grand and Cape Arid national parks and Nuytsland Nature Reserve – both national parks notable for dramatic coastal scenery and Cape Arid for challenging inland four-wheel driving. Immediately over the state border is Nullarbor National Park, also with a magnificent, lonely coast of cliffs and dunes where southern right whales may be observed in the breeding season. The treeless limestone plain is just a small part of the park, the majority being a vast, low, open woodland; the nearest NPWS office is at Ceduna. Camping areas in parks are given in route directions.

For all information contact CALM, 50 Hayman Road, Como WA 6152; tel. (09) 367 0333; NPWS Information Centre, 55 Grenfell Street, Adelaide 5000; tel. (08) 207 2300.

Regional offices:
CALM District Office
92 Dempster Street
Esperance WA 6450
(090) 71 3733.

NPWS Far West Regional Office
11 McKenzie Street
Ceduna SA 5690
(086) 25 3144.

National park regulations are similar in both states; please observe the following code.

▶ *Stay on formed tracks, observe all notices and follow signs.*
▶ *Use litter bins provided, or take rubbish with you.*
▶ *Light fires only in fireplaces provided, or use portable stoves.*
▶ *Do not disturb, collect or damage animals, wildflowers, vegetation, earth or rock formations; all wildlife is protected.*
▶ *Contact local rangers where permits are required.*
▶ *In Cape Arid, observe precautions regarding dieback problem.*

USEFUL INFORMATION

For touring information contact:

WA Tourist Centre
Albert Facey House
Cnr Forrest Place and
  Wellington Street
Perth 6000
(09) 483 1111.

Tourism South Australia
1 King William Street
Adelaide 5000
(08) 212 1505
(008) 88 2092.

For motoring and touring information contact:

Royal Automobile Club of
  Western Australia Inc. (RAC)
228 Adelaide Terrace
Perth 6000
(09) 421 4444.

Royal Automobile Association of
  South Australia Inc. (RAA)
41 Hindmarsh Square
Adelaide 5000
(08) 223 4555.

For four-wheel driving information contact:
Western Australian Association
  of FWDC
PO Box 6029
East Perth WA 6004.

South Australian Association of
  FWDC
GPO Box 178
Blair Athol SA 5084.

South Australian authorities are extremely concerned about unauthorised use of private roads and private property. Take particular care if driving off the plotted route.

ESPERANCE
«»
POINT DEMPSTER

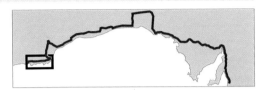

START POINT
Map page 32, H12.

TOTAL KM 207.
UNSEALED KM 164.
DEGREE OF DIFFICULTY Difficult.
DRIVING TIME 6 hours.
LONGEST DISTANCE NO FUEL No fuel this section. Next fuel Balladonia (392 km).
TOPOGRAPHIC MAPS Auslig 1:250 000 series: *Esperance*; *Malcolm*. See also 1:100 000 series.
LOCAL/SPECIALITY MAPS Dept of Lands Administration StreetSmart: *Esperance*.
OTHER USEFUL INFORMATION CALM information sheet: *Cape Arid and Eucla National Parks*.

DESCRIPTION This section borders the great Southern Ocean, taking Merivale and Fisheries roads south of the Eyre Highway and focusing on the national parks at Cape Le Grand and Cape Arid; the landscape of the parks is superb. Tracks are of good-surface gravel until you reach the last 80 kilometres; from there to Point Dempster you are in true four-wheel drive country (*see Warnings*), but to view the remote, secluded countryside makes the difficult drive well worth while. There are camping areas in both national parks: in Cape Le Grand at *Le Grand Beach* and *Lucky Bay* and in Cape Arid at *Thomas River*, *Thomas Fishery*, *Seal Creek* and *Jorndee Creek*.

In Cape Le Grand the white, sandy beaches between rocky headlands are set against a background of rugged granite peaks, culminating in Mt Le Grand; inland, several large caves run below the peaks and rich heaths, swamps and freshwater pools cover undulating sandplains. Wildlife includes kangaroos, wallabies, possums, bandicoots and many seabirds, penguins among them. Dense thickets of banksias dot the plains and mallee the granite hills, and the spring wildflowers are a wonderful sight. There is a spectacular trail well marked with walks of from 1 hour to 1 day, many good fishing spots, good swimming and surfing (but beware rips) and picnic facilities at Rossiter Bay and Hellfire Bay.

An alternative place to break your journey is the *Orleans Bay Caravan Park*, 15 kilometres south of Merivale Road on the shore of Duke of Orleans Bay. It is near beautiful beaches, and again you can fish and swim. At the crossing of Tagon Road you enter the aptly named Cape Arid National Park; here too the scenery is dramatic, most notably with stunning beaches, vivid seas and rocky headlands. In late winter and early spring whales can often be seen off the coast, and land dwellers include the Cape Barren goose and the endangered ground parrot. This park is infected with dieback (*see Warnings*); bushwalkers can help to combat this by cleaning mud and soil from shoes before entering the park.

WARNINGS ► No fuel on this or following trek and no fresh water beyond Orleans Bay Caravan Park; be completely self-sufficient. ►Check road conditions after rain; contact CALM rangers for Cape Le Grand (*see Bookings and Permits)* and Cape Arid, PO Box 185, Esperance WA 6450; tel. (090) 75 0055. ► Firewood very scarce: portable gas stove recommended. ► Camp in designated areas only. ► Beaches at Cape Le Grand treacherous for vehicles; consult ranger about surface conditions and tides. ► Dieback problems cause periodic closure of roads; essential to keep to formed tracks as vehicles spread the fungus. ► Last 80 kilometres include sand and bog patches, are narrow and rough and mostly single track. ► Exercise great care when passing Daringdella Lake; apparently firm crust can conceal bog. Keep away from lake edge.

BOOKINGS AND PERMITS ► Camping fee payable at Cape Le Grand ranger office, tel. (090) 75 9022. ► Orleans Bay Caravan Park, Howick WA; tel. (090) 75 0033. ► Recreational fishing regulations apply. Contact park ranger or Esperance Fisheries Department, Port Authority Building, The Esplanade, Esperance WA 6450; tel. (090) 71 1839.

ESPERANCE «» POINT DEMPSTER

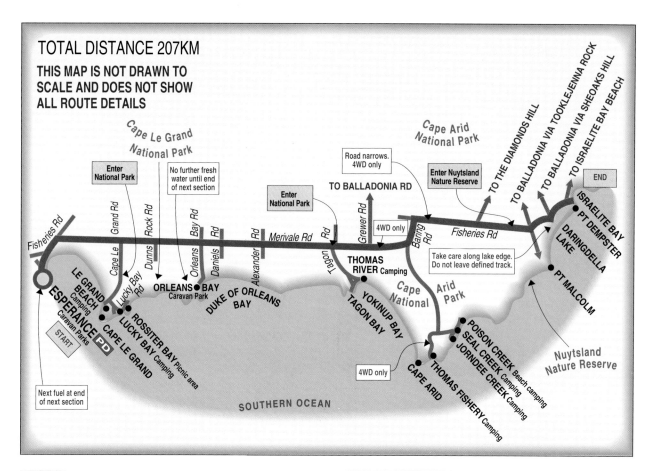

TOTAL DISTANCE 207KM

THIS MAP IS NOT DRAWN TO SCALE AND DOES NOT SHOW ALL ROUTE DETAILS

ROUTE DIRECTIONS

0.0 km Zero trip meter adjacent to Tourist Information Centre in Dempster St, Esperance, facing north. **SO.**

> *No fuel this section. Next fuel Balladonia Roadhouse, approx. 392 km not including diversions.*

(1.3 km) ▲ 34.7 km

1.3 km S'post: Goldfields Rd/Cape Le Grand. **TR.**
(3.8 km) ▲ 33.4 km

5.1 km S'post: Cape Le Grand. **TR** onto Fisheries Rd.
(3.6 km) Opp. dir. s'post: Goldfields Rd. ▲ 29.6 km

8.7 km S'post: Cape Le Grand. **TR** onto Merivale Rd.
(26.0 km) Opp. dir. s'post: Fisheries Rd. ▲ 26.0 km

34.7 km S'post: Duke of Orleans Bay.

> *Cape Le Grand off to right. 11.2 km: enter National Park. 11.7 km: information and ranger station on left; pay camping fees here. 19.3 km: intersection. Le Grand Beach 4 km straight ahead.*

> *To left: Lucky Bay 9 km, Rossiter Bay 15 km. Camping areas, barbecues, toilets, water, showers at Cape Le Grand and Lucky Bay. Picnic area at Rossiter Bay; no camping.*

Opp. dir. s'post: Esperance.

0.0 km Zero trip meter at above s'post. **SO.**
(7.6 km) ▲ 0.0 km
▲ 31.2 km

7.6 km Intersection. **SO** onto gravel.

> *Dunns Rock Rd on right.*

(23.6 km) Bitumen. ▲ 23.6 km

31.2 km Crossroads: Orleans Bay Rd.

> *Orleans Bay Caravan Park 15 km off to right.*

0.0 km Zero trip meter at above crossroads. **SO.**
(11.9 km) ▲ 0.0 km
▲ 40.6 km

11.9 km Crossroads: Daniels Rd. **SO.**
(8.6 km) ▲ 28.7 km

20.5 km Crossroads: Alexander Rd. **SO.**
(20.1 km) ▲ 20.1 km

40.6 km Crossroads (offset): Tagon Rd. S'post: Cape Arid National Park.

> *Tagon Bay off to right. 6.2 km: information station on left. 6.5 km: intersection. Tagon Bay off to right. Yokinup Bay straight ahead. Walking trail from Tagon Bay 7 km return, approx. 4 hrs; views of coastline. Thomas River camping areas approx. 9 km off to left. Picnic tables, fireplaces, toilets, water (not drinkable).*

0.0 km Zero trip meter at above crossroads. **SO.**
(13.3 km) ▲ 0.0 km
▲ 23.1 km

13.3 km Intersection. **SO.**

> *Grewer Rd on left, linking with Balladonia Rd (4WD only) via Mt Ragged.*

(3.1 km) ▲ 9.8 km
16.4 km Sign: 4WD only. **SO.**
(6.7 km) ▲ 6.7 km
23.1 km Intersection: Baring Rd.

> *Poison Creek off to right. 17.9 km: intersection. Poison Creek straight ahead; Thomas Fishery Track (4WD) on right to camp area, approx 7 km. From intersection, straight ahead for 6.3 km, then Jorndee Creek to right, Seal Creek and Poison Creek to left. 1.7 km to Jorndee Creek camping area; gas barbecue, toilets, picnic tables. 1.5 km to Seal Creek camping and picnic areas; gas barbecue, toilets, water (not drinkable). 4.1 km to Poison Creek picnic area; beach camping, no facilities.*

0.0 km Zero trip meter at above intersection. **SO** along Baring Rd.
(7.8 km) ▲ 0.0 km
▲ 59.6 km

7.8 km T intersection. **TR** onto Fisheries Rd.
(4.4 km) Opp. dir. s'post:
Poison Creek/Baring Rd. ▲ 51.8 km

12.2 km Sign: Road narrows. 4WD only. No water. No fuel. **SO.**
(20.9 km) ▲ 47.4 km
33.1 km Intersection. **SO.**

> *The Diamonds Hill approx. 10 km off to left. Mt Ragged visible to left of hill.*

(19.1 km) ▲ 26.5 km

The beach at Cape Arid

52.2 km National park boundary. **SO.**
(7.4 km) Opp. dir. s'post:
Cape Arid National Park. ▲ 7.4 km
59.6 km Crossroads. S'post: Israelite Bay.

> *Pt Malcolm 15 km off to right. Balladonia via Tooklejenna Rock to left.*

Opp. dir. s'post: Esperance.
0.0 km Zero trip meter at above s'post. **SO.**
(8.6 km) ▲ 0.0 km
▲ 17.3 km
8.6 km Crossroads. **SO** along edge of salt lake.

> *Track on left links with Old Balladonia Track, via Sheoaks Hill. Daringdella Lake 100 m to right. Stay on defined track. Lake edge can be soft and saltpans very boggy.*

(5.7 km) ▲ 8.7 km
14.3 km Y intersection. **KL** away from lake edge.
(1.5 km) ▲ 3.0 km
15.8 km Y intersection. **KR.**

> *Israelite Bay beach to left.*

(0.5 km) ▲ 1.5 km
16.3 km Pioneer graves on left. **SO.**
(1.0 km) ▲ 1.0 km
17.3 km Glencoe Telegraph Station ruins on left.

> *Numerous campsites here and in immediate vicinity of Pt Dempster. Glencoe ruins classified by National Trust. Unsafe to enter.*

REVERSE DIRECTIONS START ▲ 0.0 km

POINT DEMPSTER
«»
BALLADONIA ROADHOUSE

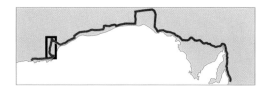

START POINT
Map page 33, K11.

TOTAL KM 185.
UNSEALED KM 185.
DEGREE OF DIFFICULTY Extreme.
DRIVING TIME 6 hours.
LONGEST DISTANCE NO FUEL Fuel at Balladonia
Roadhouse.
TOPOGRAPHIC MAP Auslig 1:250 000 series: *Malcolm, Balladonia*. See also 1:100 000 series.
LOCAL/SPECIALITY MAP Dept. of Land Administration StreetSmart: *Esperance*.
OTHER USEFUL INFORMATION CALM information
sheet: *Cape Arid and Eucla National Parks* (includes
map).

DESCRIPTION First retracing your steps from the coast
at Point Dempster, this section takes you up the Wylie
Scarp and through the northern part of Cape Arid
National Park to pass *Mt Ragged*, highest point in the
Russell Range. These mountains were islands about 40
million years ago, and wave-cut platforms can still be
discerned on their upper slopes. Here you can camp
and, if enterprising, take a strenuous walk to the top of
Tower Peak to be rewarded with spectacular views of
the coastline and surrounding country.

The track to *Balladonia*, where there is a caravan
park, is very rough, and at times so narrow that damage
may be done to vehicles' paintwork; it improves somewhat after leaving Mt Ragged, but this is all serious
four-wheel drive country from the western shore of the
Great Australian Bight to the edge of the Nullarbor
Plain.

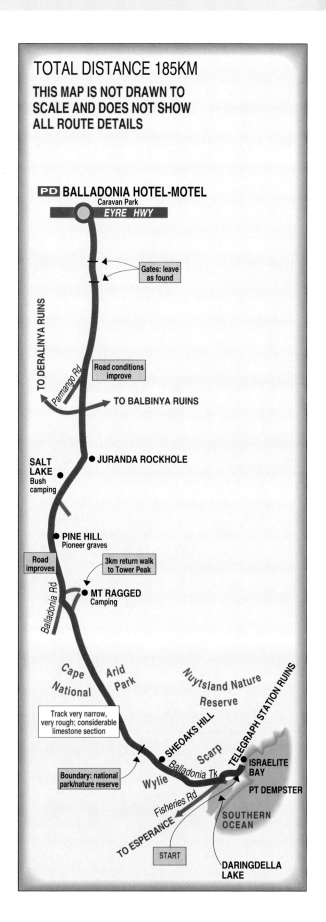

TOTAL DISTANCE 185KM
THIS MAP IS NOT DRAWN TO
SCALE AND DOES NOT SHOW
ALL ROUTE DETAILS

PD BALLADONIA HOTEL-MOTEL
Caravan Park
EYRE HWY

Gates: leave
as found

TO DERALINYA RUINS

Parmango Rd

Road conditions
improve

TO BALBINYA RUINS

JURANDA ROCKHOLE

SALT LAKE
Bush camping

PINE HILL
Pioneer graves

Road improves

3km return walk
to Tower Peak

Balladonia Rd

MT RAGGED
Camping

Cape Arid
National Park

Nuytsland Nature
Reserve

TELEGRAPH STATION RUINS

Track very narrow,
very rough; considerable
limestone section

SHEOAKS HILL

Scarp

Balladonia Tk

ISRAELITE BAY

Boundary: national
park/nature reserve

Wylie

PT DEMPSTER

Fisheries Rd

SOUTHERN OCEAN

TO ESPERANCE

START

DARINGDELLA LAKE

Mount Ragged

It is a historic region, too: pioneers' graves and ruined buildings bear silent witness to the trials of early settlement. Coastal vegetation is a mix of southern sandheaths and mallee, extending inland as far as Mt Ragged; to the north there is a transition to woodland dominated by saltbush and bluebush. All in all, this is a trek that demands slow but steady progress – a true adventure through spectacular terrain.

WARNINGS ▶ No fuel or fresh-water in this section; be completely self-sufficient. ▶ Track to Balladonia very rough, narrow, with patches of bog, sand and limestone. Always check possible road closure and conditions after rain; contact Cape Arid CALM office, PO Box 185, Esperance WA 6450; tel. (090) 75 0055. ▶ As in previous section, dieback problem in national park. Keep to formed roads. ▶ No permit required to camp in Cape Arid National Park.

BOOKINGS AND PERMITS ▶ Balladonia Caravan Park, Eyre Highway (limited facilities; overnight stop only); tel. (090) 39 3456. ▶ Balladonia Hotel-Motel, Eyre Highway; tel. (090) 39 3453.

ROUTE DIRECTIONS

0.0 km Zero trip meter at old telegraph station ruins; return via entrance track.
(0.3 km) ▲ 48.2 km
0.3 km Y intersection. **KR**.
(0.7 km) ▲ 47.9 km
1.0 km Pioneer graves on right.
SO.
(0.5 km) ▲ 47.2 km
1.5 km Intersection. **SO**.

Israelite Bay to right.

(1.3 km) ▲ 46.7 km
2.8 km Y intersection. **KR**.
(5.6 km) ▲ 45.4 km
8.4 km Track leads off lake shore slightly, towards scrub.
(0.2 km) ▲ 39.8 km
8.6 km Crossroads. **TR** onto Balladonia Track via Sheoaks Hill.

419

The old telegraph station ruins at Glencoe

Fisheries Road, impassable in the wet

> *Esperance straight ahead. Daringdella Lake 100 m to left. Track climbs Wylie Scarp for next 10 km.*

(14.8 km) ▲ 39.6 km

23.4 km Sign: Cape Arid National Park. **SO.**

> *Track very narrow and rough, with considerable limestone section.*

(24.8 km) ▲ 24.8 km

48.2 km Intersection.

> *Track to base of Mt Ragged on right.*

0.0 km Zero trip meter at above intersection. **SO.**
(3.7 km) ▲ 0.0 km
▲ 136.8 km

3.7 km T intersection. **TR** onto Balladonia Rd.

> *Road improves.*

(0.1 km) ▲ 133.1 km

3.8 km Intersection. **SO.**

> *Track to Mt Ragged camp base area on right. Barbecue, picnic facilities, toilets. From here a 3-km return walk to Tower Peak.*

(18.1 km) ▲ 133.0 km

21.9 km Pine Hill pioneer grave sites on right. **SO.**
(4.5 km) ▲ 114.9 km

26.4 km Intersection. **SO.**
(7.6 km) Opp. dir. s'post:
Cape Arid National Park. ▲ 110.4 km

34.0 km Salt Lake on left. **SO.**

> *Bush camping.*

(0.3 km) ▲ 102.8 km

34.3 km Juranda Rockhole. **SO.**
(16.1 km) ▲ 102.5 km

50.4 km Crossroads. **SO.**

> *Balbinya ruins approx. 12 km to right. Deralinya ruins approx. 7 km to left.*

(12.7 km) ▲ 86.4 km

63.1 km Intersection. **SO.**

> *Parmango Rd enters on left. Road conditions improve.*

(36.7 km) Opp. dir. s'post: Road impassable
in wet conditions. ▲ 73.7 km

99.8 km Gate.

> *Leave as found.*

(13.6 km) ▲ 37.0 km

113.4 km Gate.

> *Leave as found.*

(23.2 km) ▲ 23.4 km

136.6 km T intersection. **TL** onto bitumen: Eyre Hwy.
(0.2 km) Gravel. ▲ 0.2 km

136.8 km Balladonia Hotel-Motel and Roadhouse.

> **PD** *Caravan park, camping. Picnic area at nearby Neumann Rocks.*

REVERSE DIRECTIONS START ▲ 0.0 km

BALLADONIA ROADHOUSE «» CAIGUNA

START POINT
Map page 33, K9.

TOTAL KM 241.
UNSEALED KM 155.
DEGREE OF DIFFICULTY Extreme.
DRIVING TIME 7 hours.
LONGEST DISTANCE NO FUEL Fuel at Caiguna.
TOPOGRAPHIC MAPS Auslig 1:250 000 series: *Balladonia*; *Culver*. See also 1:100 000 series.
LOCAL/SPECIALITY MAP RAC, Western Australia: *Perth to Adelaide via Eyre Highway*.
OTHER USEFUL INFORMATION Leisure Time Publications book: *Across Australia* (Eyre Highway route).

DESCRIPTION The Eyre Highway between Balladonia and Caiguna includes one of the longest straight stretches of roadway in the world. In this section you start along it, but soon turn south through another true four-wheel drive region to find the coast and the spectacular Baxter Cliffs that form the southern boundary of the Nuytsland Nature Reserve, stretching along the shore of the Great Australian Bight. This is a bush-camping-only section.

East and south of Balladonia you are in plains country; the track is narrow and the plains are grazed by many kangaroos that may appear from nowhere and can be something of a hazard. It is a slow and rough haul across the considerable area of limestone escarpment leading down into the nature reserve and to the coast, but the magnificent spectacle revealed with startling suddenness is its own reward. There are myriad tracks along the Baxter Cliffs; your route

The Baxter Cliffs

is a rocky, narrow and overgrown trail east along the scarp, moving gradually inland until it meets the track leading to the memorial to John Baxter, Eyre's explorer companion who was killed there by Aborigines in 1841.

At this point you leave the coast road, turning north to meet the highway again at *Caiguna* where there is a caravan park. The truly intrepid could continue along the coast via the Baxter memorial to the Eyre Bird Sanctuary, but this should be approached with added caution and only with extra supplies of water and fuel.

WARNINGS ▶ No fuel or fresh water in this section after leaving the highway; be completely self-sufficient. ▶ Track extremely rough, particularly over limestone; narrow, overgrown sections can result in damage to paintwork. ▶ Once off Eyre Hwy, watch for kangaroos crossing.

BOOKINGS AND PERMITS ▶ Caiguna Caravan Park, Eyre Highway, Caiguna WA 6443; tel. (090) 39 3459 (minimum booking all times).

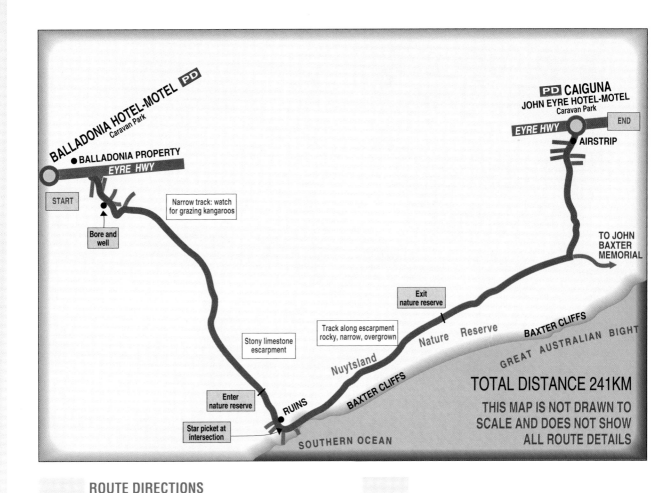

BALLADONIA HOTEL-MOTEL **PD**
Caravan Park
● BALLADONIA PROPERTY
EYRE HWY
START
Bore and well
Narrow track: watch for grazing kangaroos

PD CAIGUNA
JOHN EYRE HOTEL-MOTEL
Caravan Park
EYRE HWY
END
● AIRSTRIP

TO JOHN BAXTER MEMORIAL

Exit nature reserve

Stony limestone escarpment

Track along escarpment rocky, narrow, overgrown

Nuytsland   Nature   Reserve   BAXTER CLIFFS
GREAT AUSTRALIAN BIGHT

Enter nature reserve
RUINS
BAXTER CLIFFS

Star picket at intersection
SOUTHERN OCEAN

TOTAL DISTANCE 241KM

THIS MAP IS NOT DRAWN TO
SCALE AND DOES NOT SHOW
ALL ROUTE DETAILS

ROUTE DIRECTIONS

0.0 km Zero trip meter adjacent to Balladonia Roadhouse, heading east along Eyre Hwy.

> **PD** *Refuel suggested; next fuel Caiguna (241 km).*

(27.8 km) ▲ 86.1 km

27.8 km Balladonia property entrance on left. **SO.**

(58.3 km) ▲ 58.3 km

86.1 km S'post: Water/BBQ Area.

0.0 km Zero trip meter at above s'post. **TR** onto gravel, running parallel to Eyre Hwy.

(0.2 km) Bitumen. ▲ 73.5 km

0.2 km Intersection. **TR** and follow track.

> *Track continues parallel to Eyre Hwy.*

(0.3 km) ▲ 73.3 km

0.5 km Intersection. **KL.**

(1.2 km) ▲ 73.0 km

1.7 km Intersection. **SO.**

> *Track enters on left.*

(0.4 km) ▲ 71.8 km

2.1 km Intersection. **SO.**

> *Track enters on left.*

(8.0 km) ▲ 71.4 km

10.1 km Intersection. **SO.**

> *Old bore and well on right.*

(0.8 km) ▲ 63.4 km

10.9 km Y intersection. **KR.**

(10.8 km) ▲ 62.6 km

21.7 km Intersection. **KR.**

> *Track enters on left.*

(41.9 km) ▲ 51.8 km

63.6 km Sign: Nuytsland Nature Reserve. **SO.**

(5.9 km) ▲ 9.9 km

69.5 km Ruins on left. **SO.**

(0.3 km) ▲ 4.0 km

69.8 km Intersection. **SO.**

> *Track enters on right.*

(1.4 km) ▲ 3.7 km

71.2 km Intersection. **KL.**

A disused bore along the route

Shingle-back lizards

Track along the Baxter Cliffs

	Track enters on right.	
	(2.3 km)	▲ 2.3 km
73.5 km	Intersection.	
	Star picket in middle of intersection. Baxter Cliffs 500 m to right. Views of Great Australian Bight.	
0.0 km	Zero trip meter at above intersection. **SO.**	
	(1.4 km)	▲ 0.0 km
		▲ 1.4 km
1.4 km	Y intersection.	
	Baxter Cliffs to right, as above.	
0.0 km	Zero trip meter at above intersection. **KL.**	
	(28.1 km)	▲ 0.0 km
		▲ 80.0 km
28.1 km	Reserve boundary. **SO.**	
	(28.7 km)	Opp. dir. s'post:
		Nuytsland Nature Reserve. ▲ 51.9 km
56.8 km	Intersection. **TL.**	
	John Baxter Memorial, on Baxter Cliffs, approx. 20 km straight ahead.	
	(15.0 km)	▲ 23.2 km
71.8 km	Intersection. **SO.**	
	Track enters on right.	
	(1.7 km)	▲ 8.2 km
73.5 km	Intersection. **SO.**	
	(1.5 km)	▲ 6.5 km
75.0 km	Intersection. **SO.**	
	Track enters on left.	
	(1.8 km)	▲ 5.0 km
76.8 km	Intersection. **SO.**	
	Track enters on left.	
	(1.1 km)	▲ 3.2 km
77.9 km	**KR** onto airstrip at stop sign.	
	(1.3 km)	▲ 2.1 km
79.2 km	**SO** off airstrip at stop sign.	
	(0.8 km)	▲ 0.8 km
80.0 km	Bitumen: Eyre Hwy. John Eyre Hotel-Motel, Caiguna.	
	PD *Caravan park. Track enters at rear of hotel on Eyre Hwy. Route directions for next section start at Madura Pass Roadhouse, approx. 160 km along Eyre Hwy.*	

REVERSE DIRECTIONS START Gravel. ▲ 0.0 km

CAIGUNA
«»
EUCLA

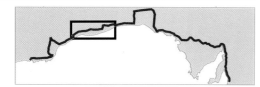

Chowilla Doline

START POINT
Map page 33, M9.

TOTAL KM 374.
UNSEALED KM 95.
DEGREE OF DIFFICULTY Moderate.
DRIVING TIME 5 hours (Madura Pass Roadhouse to Eucla).
LONGEST DISTANCE NO FUEL 118 km (Madura Pass Roadhouse to Mundrabilla).
TOPOGRAPHIC MAPS Auslig 1:250 000 series: *Madura*; *Eucla*. See also 1:100 000 series.
LOCAL/SPECIALITY MAP RAC, Western Australia: *Perth to Adelaide via Eyre Highway.*
OTHER USEFUL INFORMATION CALM information sheet: *Cape Arid and Eucla National Parks* (includes map); Leisure Time Publications book: *Across Australia* (Eyre Highway route).

DESCRIPTION This part of the Nullarbor Plain is famous for its rockholes, dolines and caves, some of which are visited; the country is much more typical of the Nullarbor than the land you see from the highway. The route is not as difficult as in the previous two sections, but it does need careful navigation as there are many crisscrossing tracks along the way; it is a good idea to carry a compass and to establish a general idea of their direction. The tracks are generally in good condition; the usual proviso regarding wet weather applies, although heavy rain is unusual in the area. There are no designated camping or picnic spots, but *Mundrabilla* has a caravan park (now able to provide unlimited water for showers); of interest there is the nearby animal and bird park in which you can see examples of local fauna as diverse as camels, emus and finches.

To continue the trek, take the road north across the Hampton Tableland and then turn east. Notable points

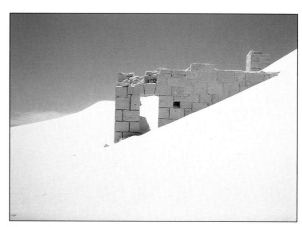

The old telegraph station, Eucla

along the way are first Wileura Rockhole and then Chowilla Doline, the latter a large limestone sinkhole. At this point you can detour to Abrakurrie Cave and Kutowilla Doline in a region typical of that traversed before recrossing the tableland to end the trip at Eucla. Take time here to see the old telegraph station before it finally disappears beneath the sand – and perhaps spend a while at Eucla National Park, an area of mallee scrub and heathland near the state border. Wilson Bluff, in the park, is another excellent vantage point from which to view the sea cliffs of the Bight.

WARNINGS ► Careful navigation required; advisable to carry a compass. ► Tracks may become impassable after heavy rain. ► Be completely self-sufficient in section Mundrabilla to Eucla.

BOOKINGS AND PERMITS ► No permits required. ► Mundrabilla Caravan Park, Eyre Highway, Mundrabilla WA 6443; tel. (090) 39 3465. ► Hospitality Inn (inc. caravan facility), Eyre Highway, Madura WA 6483; tel. (090) 39 3464.

424

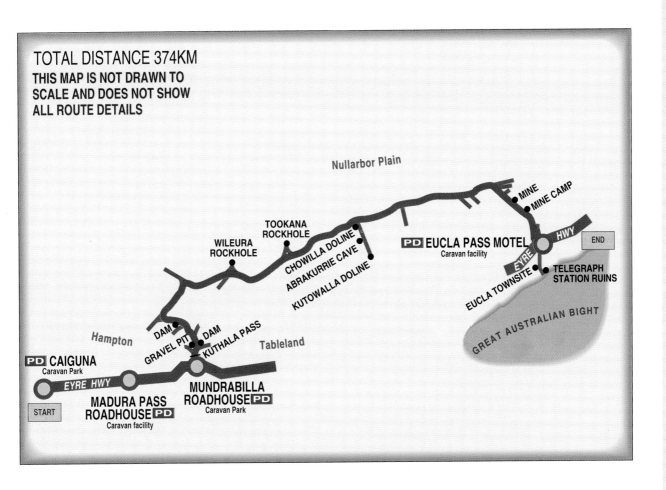

TOTAL DISTANCE 374KM
**THIS MAP IS NOT DRAWN TO
SCALE AND DOES NOT SHOW
ALL ROUTE DETAILS**

ROUTE DIRECTIONS

Depart Caiguna east along Eyre Hwy to
Madura Pass Roadhouse (approx. 160 km).

> **PD** *Caravan facility. Adjust watches to
> appropriate time.*

0.0 km Zero trip meter on Eyre Hwy adjacent to
roadhouse. **SO**.
(118.1 km) ▲ 118.1 km

118.1 km Mundrabilla Motel and Roadhouse on
left.

> **PD** *Caravan park.*

0.0 km Zero trip meter at roadhouse. **SO**.
(0.2 km) ▲ 0.0 km
▲ 50.5 km

0.2 km Intersection. **TL** onto gravel.
(2.0 km) Bitumen. ▲ 50.3 km

2.2 km Y intersection. **KR** at gravel pit.
(0.3 km) ▲ 48.3 km

2.5 km Y intersection. **KL** around dam.
(2.0 km) ▲ 48.0 km

4.5 km Y intersection. **KL**.
(1.8 km) ▲ 46.0 km

6.3 km Y intersection. **KR** around dam.
(7.3 km) ▲ 44.2 km

13.6 km

Intersection. **TR**.
(7.7 km) ▲ 36.9 km

21.3 km

T intersection. **TR**.
(8.0 km) ▲ 29.2 km

29.3 km Y intersection. **KR**.

> *Wileura Rockhole 200 m to left.*

(0.2 km) ▲ 21.2 km

29.5 km Intersection.

> *Road enters on right.*

(0.7 km) ▲ 21.0 km

30.2 km Wileura Rockhole track rejoins on left. **SO**.
(9.9 km) ▲ 20.3 km

425

Looking south towards Mundrabilla Roadhouse from Kuthala Pass

40.1 km Intersection. **SO.**

> *Tookana Rockhole 200 m off to left. Track then rejoins main route.*

(10.4 km)   ▲ 10.4 km

50.5 km Intersection.

> *Off to right: Chowilla Doline immediately; Abrakurrie Cave 2.2 km; Kutowalla Doline 4.9 km.*

0.0 km Zero trip meter at above intersection. **SO.**
(9.5 km)   ▲ 0.0 km
                                      ▲ 45.3 km

9.5 km Intersection. **SO.**

> *Track enters on right.*

(17.4 km)   ▲ 35.8 km

26.9 km Intersection. **KL.**
(1.9 km)   ▲ 18.4 km

28.8 km Intersection. **KL.**
(2.1 km)   ▲ 16.5 km

30.9 km Intersection. **KR.**
(1.4 km)   ▲ 14.4 km

32.3 km Intersection. **KR.**
(0.8 km)   ▲ 13.0 km

33.1 km Intersection. **SO.**

> *Track enters on left.*

(3.9 km)   ▲ 12.2 km

37.0 km Mine on left. **SO.**
(3.1 km)   ▲ 8.3 km

40.1 km Mine camp on left. **SO.**
(3.6 km)   ▲ 5.2 km

43.7 km T intersection. **TL.**
(1.3 km)   ▲ 1.6 km

45.0 km T intersection. **TR** onto bitumen: Eyre Hwy.
(0.2 km)   Gravel. ▲ 0.3 km

45.2 km S'post: Old Telegraph Station. **TL.**
(0.1 km)   ▲ 0.1 km

45.3 km S'posts: Eucla Pass Motel/Caravan Park and Amber Motel/Service Station.

> **PD** *Old telegraph station and townsite 5 km off to right.*

REVERSE DIRECTIONS START ▲ 0.0 km

EUCLA
«»
FOWLERS BAY

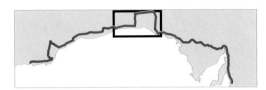

Night camp on the Nullarbor

START POINT
Map page 44, A8.

TOTAL KM 610.
UNSEALED KM 422.
DEGREE OF DIFFICULTY Difficult.
DRIVING TIME 10 hours.
LONGEST DISTANCE NO FUEL 313 km (Cook to Nundroo).
TOPOGRAPHIC MAPS Auslig 1:250 000 series: *Coompana*; *Nullarbor*; *Fowler*. See also 1:100 000 series.
LOCAL/SPECIALITY MAPS RAA regional series: *Upper Eyre Peninsula and Far West Coast*; Gregorys State Road Map 520: *South Australia*; Tourism South Australia: *South Australia Touring Map*; RAC, Western Australia: *Perth to Adelaide via Eyre Highway*.
OTHER USEFUL INFORMATION NPWS information sheet: *Nullarbor National Park* (Get Out and About series); Eyre Peninsula Tourism Association booklet: *Eyre Peninsula, South Australia*; Leisure Time Publications book: *Across Australia* (Eyre Highway route).

DESCRIPTION This section sees the transition from the Nullarbor Plain to the sandhill and salt-flat country of central and northern South Australia. Leaving the Eyre Highway west of the township of Nullarbor the route first traverses *Nullarbor National Park*, a low, flat, featureless region scattered with saltbush and other low-growing vegetation.

There are no designated camping areas in the park – or anywhere in this section before reaching Nundroo – but bush camping is possible (permit required), as it is on the exposed Nullarbor Plain; however, before thinking of camping near the Transcontinental Railway line remember that there is a considerable stream of railway traffic throughout the night. In fact, for about 140 kilometres – from Cook, a railway service town, through the sidings of Fisher, Watson and O'Malley to Ooldea – the route runs parallel to the line, well-known as including the world's longest completely straight stretch of track.

The road north to Cook is excellent gravel, but deteriorates markedly to a twisting, rough, stony and little-used track as it follows the line east to Ooldea, known for its association with the legendary Daisy Bates. Heading back to the highway road conditions improve again, passing through predominantly mallee scrub country with sections of red sand and saltpans.

This is a long trip but it takes you through a region fascinating in its sheer magnitude, and to know the absolute solitude of a night spent out on the plain is a unique experience.

WARNINGS ▶ Fuel outlet at Cook does not operate continuously at weekends; advance notice of arrival at such time is appreciated; tel. (086) 41 8506. ▶ No retail outlets for fuel or supplies between Cook and Nundroo; be self-sufficient.

BOOKINGS AND PERMITS ▶ Permit required to bush camp in Nullarbor National Park. No ranger on site: contact NPWS regional office, 11 McKenzie Street, Ceduna SA 5690; tel. (086) 25 3144. No permit required to traverse park only. ▶ Permit required to travel on Yalata Aboriginal Land. Contact Yalata Roadhouse; tel. (086) 25 6990. Community includes caravan park. ▶ Nundroo Caravan Park, Eyre Highway; tel. (086) 25 6120. ▶ For general information contact Ceduna Gateway Tourist Centre, 58 Poynton Street, Ceduna SA 5690; tel. (086) 25 2780.

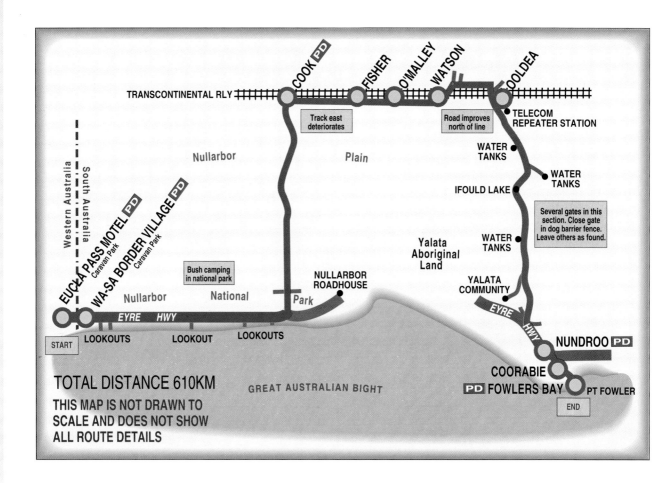

TRANSCONTINENTAL RLY

COOK **PD** FISHER O'MALLEY WATSON OOLDEA

Track east deteriorates

Road improves north of line

TELECOM REPEATER STATION

WATER TANKS

WATER TANKS

IFOULD LAKE

Nullarbor   Plain

Western Australia

South Australia

EUCLA PASS MOTEL **PD** Caravan Park

WA-SA BORDER VILLAGE **PD** Caravan Park

Several gates in this section. Close gate in dog barrier fence. Leave others as found.

WATER TANKS

Yalata Aboriginal Land

Bush camping in national park

NULLARBOR ROADHOUSE

YALATA COMMUNITY

Nullarbor   National   Park

EYRE HWY

EYRE HWY

LOOKOUTS   LOOKOUT   LOOKOUTS

START

NUNDROO PD

COORABIE

PD FOWLERS BAY PT FOWLER

TOTAL DISTANCE 610KM

GREAT AUSTRALIAN BIGHT

END

THIS MAP IS NOT DRAWN TO SCALE AND DOES NOT SHOW ALL ROUTE DETAILS

ROUTE DIRECTIONS

Depart Eucla east along Eyre Hwy to WA-SA Border Village (approx. 13 km).

0.0 km Zero trip meter adjacent to BP hotel-motel. **SO**.

> **PD** *Supplies, caravan park. Remember to adjust watches.*

(0.3 km)   ▲ 252.9 km

0.3 km S'post: Nullarbor. **SO**.
(12.8 km)   ▲ 252.6 km

13.1 km Lookout on right. **SO**.

> *Lookouts give panoramic views of Bight and coastline.*

(3.5 km)   ▲ 239.8 km

16.6 km Lookout on right. **SO**.
(59.5 km)   ▲ 236.3 km

76.1 km Lookout on right. **SO**.
(36.3 km)   ▲ 176.8 km

112.4 km Lookout on right. **SO**.
(22.1 km)   ▲ 140.5 km

134.5 km Lookout on right. **SO**.
(11.2 km)   ▲ 118.4 km

145.7 km S'post: Cook 107. **TL** onto gravel.

> *Enter Nullarbor National Park. Bush camping (permit required); caving with permission from NPWS district office.*

(10.1 km)   Bitumen. ▲ 107.2 km

155.8 km Crossroads. **SO**.
(97.1 km)   ▲ 97.1 km

252.9 km T intersection on outskirts of Cook township.

> **PD** *(See Warnings.) No other facilities. The Transcontinental Railway runs through Cook. The track east runs south of the line.*

0.0 km Zero trip meter at above intersection. **TR** skirting back of housing.
(1.3 km)   ▲ 0.0 km
                                             ▲ 54.9 km

1.3 km Intersection. **SO** at railway crossing.

The real Nullarbor

	Road deteriorates, continuing south of railway line.
(53.6 km) ▲ 53.6 km	
54.9 km Sign: Fisher Railway Siding.	
	Track leads off back to Eyre Hwy.
0.0 km Zero trip meter at above sign. **SO.**	
(54.1 km) ▲ 0.0 km ▲ 54.1 km	
54.1 km Railway crossing stop sign.	
	Watson Railway Siding ahead.
0.0 km Zero trip meter at above sign. Cross railway line.	
(0.1 km) ▲ 0.0 km ▲ 235.4 km	
0.1 km Intersection immediately after railway crossing. **TR** through Watson Siding community.	
	No facilities or services.
(0.6 km) ▲ 235.3 km	

0.7 km Intersection. **SO.**	
	Road improves on north side of line.
(31.8 km) ▲ 234.7 km	
32.5 km Intersection. **KR.** After 50 m, cross railway line. Again **KR.**	
	Ooldea Railway Siding and Telecom Repeater Station on left after railway crossing.
(24.2 km) ▲ 202.9 km	
56.7 km Water tanks on right. **SO.**	
(32.8 km) ▲ 178.7 km	
89.5 km Intersection. **KR.**	
	Tracks to water tanks on left.
(5.5 km) ▲ 145.9 km	
95.0 km Cross Ifould Lake.	
	Large saltpan lake.
(26.2 km) ▲ 140.4 km	
121.2 km Tanks on right. **SO.**	
(16.5 km) ▲ 114.2 km	

Eyre Highway

137.7 km Gate.

> *Leave as found.*

(12.1 km) ▲ 97.7 km
149.8 km Y intersection. **KL**.

> *Track on right to Eyre Hwy via Yalata Community.*

(3.7 km) ▲ 85.6 km
153.5 km Gate.

> *Leave as found.*

(6.6 km) ▲ 81.9 km
160.1 km Gate.

> *Leave as found.*

(7.4 km) ▲ 75.3 km
167.5 km Gate.

> *Dog barrier fence. Leave gate closed.*

(8.1 km) ▲ 67.9 km
175.6 km Intersection. **SO**.

> *Track enters on right.*

(0.9 km) ▲ 59.8 km
176.5 km Gate.

> *Leave as found.*

(1.1 km) ▲ 58.9 km
177.6 km Gate.

> *Leave as found.*

(0.5 km) ▲ 57.8 km
178.1 km Intersection. **KR**. At 500 m, pass shearing sheds.

> *Track on left to homestead.*

(0.8 km) ▲ 57.3 km
178.9 km Gate. **TL** immediately onto bitumen: Eyre Hwy.
(24.6 km) Gravel. ▲ 56.5 km
203.5 km Nundroo Roadhouse. **SO**.

> **PD** *Supplies, caravan park.*

(4.9 km) ▲ 31.9 km
208.4 km S'post: Fowlers Bay. **TR** onto gravel.

> *Ceduna straight ahead.*

(9.7 km) Bitumen. Opp. dir. s'post.
Nundroo. ▲ 27.0 km
218.1 km S'post: Fowlers Bay. **TL**.

> *Coorabie on right.*

(17.3 km) Opp. dir. s'post: Nundroo. ▲ 17.3 km
235.4 km Fowlers Bay town centre.

> **PD** *Caravan park. Excellent fishing. Route directions for the next section start at Wirrulla, approx. 231 km via Eyre Hwy. Ceduna (139 km) is the checkpoint for animal and plant quarantine regulations.*

REVERSE DIRECTIONS START ▲ 0.0 km

FOWLERS BAY
«»
ADELAIDE

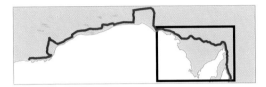

Salt lake, near Wirrulla

START POINT
Map page 45, K9.

TOTAL KM 926.
UNSEALED KM 305.
DEGREE OF DIFFICULTY Moderate.
DRIVING TIME 7 hours (Wirrulla to Port Augusta).
LONGEST DISTANCE NO FUEL 188 km (Wirrulla to Mt Ive Station).
TOPOGRAPHIC MAPS Auslig 1:250 000 series: *Streaky Bay*; *Yardea*; *Port Augusta*. See also 1:100 000 series.
LOCAL/SPECIALITY MAPS RAA regional series: *Upper Eyre Peninsula and Far West Coast*; Tourism South Australia: *South Australia Touring Map*; Dept of Lands Landsmap: *Tourist Guide to Outback and Central South Australia*; RAC, Western Australia: *Perth to Adelaide via Eyre Highway*.
OTHER USEFUL INFORMATION Eyre Peninsula Tourist Association booklet: *Eyre Peninsula, South Australia*; Leisure Time Publications book: *Across Australia*.

DESCRIPTION This section includes almost the entire length of the Gawler Ranges, South Australia's great wilderness area and a region of spectacular beauty combining grasslands, saltbush and mallee, for the most part grazing land and consisting partly of pastoral leaseholds. In spring the ranges are covered with wildflowers – here in 1839 Eyre first reported seeing Sturt's Desert Pea – and supports more than 140 species of birdlife; red and western grey kangaroos are to be seen, and also euros. There are exhilarating views, excellent picnic spots and interesting geological formations.

Leaving Wirrulla, service centre for a cereal-growing and grazing area, the route crosses part of a salt lake and heads directly north, then turning east through the hills to Yardea and passing quite near the southernmost reaches of Lake Gairdner. The journey can be broken at *Mt Ive Station*, which has a camping area and gives access to land bordering Lake Gairdner; at the centre you can discover the unique flora, fauna and geology of the region. Just before rejoining the Eyre Highway, near Iron Knob the road passes by Corunna Station, where scenes in the film *The Sundowners* were shot, and Iron Knob itself is worth visiting. This was the birthplace of the Australian steel industry, iron ore being discovered in 1894. Here is one of the nation's largest collections of gems and minerals and also the fascinating BHP Mining Museum, and guided tours through the iron-ore quarries can be arranged. Ending the plotted route at Port Augusta, don't miss seeing Wadlata Outback Centre – where interpretive displays include geological history, Aboriginal culture and early exploration – and observing a centre of the remarkable School of the Air in operation.

WARNINGS ▶ Road conditions can vary greatly with weather and vehicular wear; signposting and general visitors' amenities are limited; advice on immediate local conditions from Wudinna, (086) 80 2002; Kimba, (086) 47 2026; or Gawler Ranges Wilderness Safari office, (086) 80 2045. ▶ Area subject to flash flooding; may be impassable after heavy rain. Contact NPWS Ceduna regional office, tel. (086) 25 3144. ▶ Camping or driving on private property only with permission. Do not camp near homesteads or watering points.

BOOKINGS AND PERMITS ▶ Mt Ive Tourist Centre, tel. (086) 48 1817. ▶ Iron Knob Community Tourist Centre, tel. (086) 46 2129 (follow 'i' signs from Eyre Highway). ▶ Port Augusta Tourist Information Centre, 41 Flinders Terrace, Port Augusta SA 5700; tel. (086) 41 0793. ▶ Eyre Peninsula Tourism Association, 50 Liverpool St, Port Lincoln SA 5606; tel. (086) 82 4688.

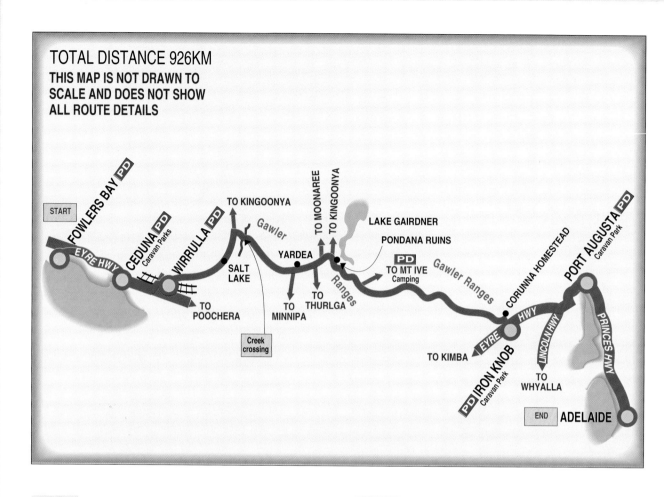

TOTAL DISTANCE 926KM
THIS MAP IS NOT DRAWN TO SCALE AND DOES NOT SHOW ALL ROUTE DETAILS

ROUTE DIRECTIONS

Depart Fowlers Bay to rejoin Eyre Hwy, heading east to Wirrulla, via Ceduna (approx. 231 km).

> *Ceduna is the checkpoint for animal and plant quarantine regulations.* PD

0.0 km Zero trip meter at s'post: Kingoonya on Eyre Hwy. **TL.**

> *Poochera 47 km straight ahead.*

    (0.1 km)   Opp. dir. s'post: Ceduna. ▲ 375.1 km

0.1 km Cross railway line and immediately **TR** into township.
    (0.2 km)   ▲ 375.0 km

0.3 km Intersection. **TL** through township.
    (0.2 km)   ▲ 374.8 km

0.5 km Wirrulla town centre, adjacent to general store. S'post: Kingoonya. **SO.** PD
    (0.2 km)   Opp. dir. s'post: Ceduna. ▲ 374.6 km

0.7 km Gravel.
    (38.9 km)   Bitumen. ▲ 374.4 km

39.6 km Salt lake on left. **SO.**
    (8.9 km)   ▲ 335.5 km

48.5 km Cross salt lake.
    (19.9 km)   ▲ 326.6 km

68.4 km Intersection. S'post: Iron Knob/Yardea. **TR.**

> *Kingoonya straight ahead.*

    (8.0 km)   Op. dir. s'post: Wirrulla. ▲ 306.7 km

76.4 km Creek crossing.
    (44.3 km)   ▲ 298.7 km

120.7 km Intersection. S'post: Iron Knob.

> *Minnipa off to right.*

    (18.6 km)   Opp. dir. s'post: Wirrulla. ▲ 254.4 km

139.3 km Intersection. **SO.**

> *Thurlga off to right.*

    (4.2 km)   Opp. dir. s'post: Yardea. ▲ 235.8 km

143.5 km Intersection. S'post: Mt Ive. **SO.**

> *Moonaree off to left.*

    (10.5 km)   Opp. dir. s'post: Yardea. ▲ 231.6 km

154.0 km Intersection. S'post: Iron Knob. **TR.**

Ancient rock formation, Gawler Ranges

Kingoonya off to left. Pondana stone ruins ahead.

(27.6 km)   Opp. dir. s'post: Yardea. ▲ 221.1 km
181.6 km S'post: Iron Knob. **SO**.

Mt Ive homestead 6 km to left. **PD** *Camping, accommodation.*

(50.5 km)   Opp. dir. s'post: Yardea ▲ 193.5 km
232.1 km S'post: Port Augusta. **SO**.
(68.4 km)   Opp. dir. s'post: Yardea ▲ 143.0 km
300.5 km Corunna homestead on left. **SO**.
(5.0 km)   ▲ 74.6 km
305.5 km Eyre Hwy. S'post: Port Augusta. **TL** onto bitumen.

Kimba off to right. Iron Knob Roadhouse straight ahead. **PD** *Caravan park. BHP Mining Museum; quarry tours.*

(43.1 km)   Gravel. Opp. dir. s'post: Yardea. ▲ 69.6 km
348.6 km S'post: Port Augusta. **TL**.

Whyalla off to right.

(25.6 km)   Opp. dir. s'post: Ceduna. ▲ 26.5 km
374.2 km Cross bridge into Port Augusta.
(0.9 km)   ▲ 0.9 km
375.1 km Port Augusta town centre, Eyre Hwy and Flinders Tce intersection.

PD *Caravan park. Wadlata Outback Centre; School of the Air.*

Follow Princes Hwy to Adelaide (approx. 320 km) to pick up route directions for next trek, Adelaide to Melbourne.

REVERSE DIRECTIONS START ▲ 0.0 km

THROUGH THE GRAMPIANS
ADELAIDE
«»
MELBOURNE
965 KILOMETRES

ADELAIDE «» NHILL   415 km

NHILL «» THE GRAMPIANS   210 km

THE GRAMPIANS «» MELBOURNE   340 km

This trek linking Adelaide and Melbourne takes you through 2 of Victoria's most remarkable and contrasting regions: the vast, undulating mallee of the Big Desert and the stern and rugged Grampian Ranges at the western extremity of the Great Dividing Range. The route approaches the desert from the Ouyen Highway at Murrayville, taking the Yanac Track that runs almost parallel to the eastern boundary of the Big Desert Wilderness Area and on to the township of Nhill. From there you take the Western Highway to Horsham and so to the Grampians and the national park, describing a long curve through the central and northern ranges – the outback Grampians – to emerge near Stawell, via Halls Gap and the north shore of Lake Lonsdale. In both regions animal life is plentiful, varied and in some cases rare; one desert inhabitant is the mound-building mallee fowl, while the high places are sanctuary for the endangered peregrine falcon.

The best time to travel is in spring and autumn; in the mountains – which can be extremely hot in summer and bleak in winter, with snow in the higher peaks – spring is the time to see the flowers at their best, and the desert track should not be attempted in summer heat. Part of the route from Horsham to Strachans Camping Area is extremely difficult; in fact, considerable care is needed generally to traverse both regions, but the rewards are great and unforgettable.

BEFORE YOU SET OUT ▶ Read the section description carefully. ▶ Check that you have obtained any necessary permits. ▶ Check weather conditions with local authorities or the Bureau of Meteorology. ▶ Make sure you have the appropriate maps and information for the trek. ▶ Check that your vehicle is in good order for the conditions ahead. Have you the necessary spare parts? ▶ If you are camping, do you have the right equipment?

USEFUL INFORMATION

For touring information contact:
Tourism South Australia
  Travel Centre
1 King William Street
Adelaide 5000
(08) 212 1505
(008) 88 2092.

Victorian Travel Centre
230 Collins Street
Melbourne 3000
(03) 790 2211.

For motoring and touring information contact:
Royal Automobile Association
  of South Australia Inc. (RAA)
41 Hindmarsh Square
Adelaide 5000
(08) 223 4555.

Royal Automobile Club of Victoria (RACV)
422 Little Collins Street
Melbourne 3000
(03) 790 2211.

For four-wheel driving information contact:
South Australian Association
  of Four Wheel Drive Clubs
GPO Box 178
Blair Athol 5084.

Victoria Association of Four
  Wheel Drive Clubs Inc.
552 Whitehorse Road
Mitcham 3132
(03) 872 4610.

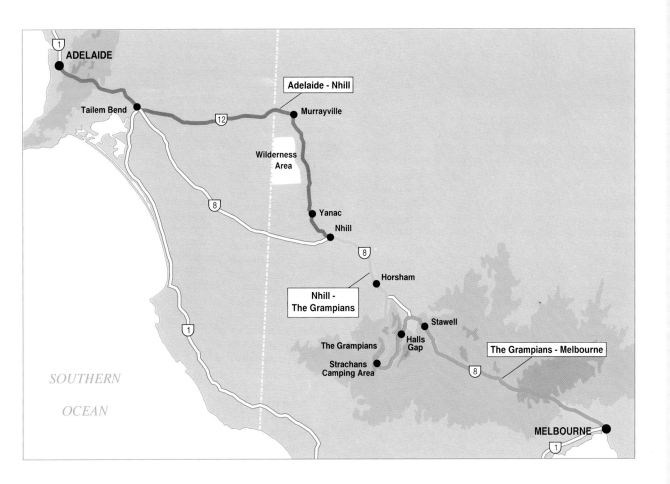

NATIONAL PARKS OF VICTORIA

The Grampians National Park is Victoria's second-largest and one of the finest, being part of the ancient and precipitous sandstone mountains known to Aboriginal tribes as Gariwerd and possessing, as well as its wonderful natural attraction, Victoria's richest store of rock art. Camping facilities are generally basic – barbecues, picnic tables, pit toilets and rubbish collection – but bush camping is permitted away from designated sites except in specifically prohibited areas. For all information contact Department of Conservation and Environment regional offices; these are noted in the route directions.

To help protect and maintain the park, please observe the following code.

▶ *Drive only on formed public roads.*
▶ *Leave dogs, cats and other domestic pets at home.*

▶ *Don't bring firearms to the park.*
▶ *Set up bush camps at least 1 kilometre from any designated campsite, 50 metres from a sealed road and 30 metres from any stream, lake or water supply. Use natural clearings; do not disturb vegetation.*
▶ *Don't bathe or wash dishes in creeks or lakes. Take water to camp in containers.*
▶ *At campsites, light fires only in fireplaces provided. Observe standard fire regulations.*
▶ *In bush camps, set your fire in a trench at least 30 centimetres deep (which is filled after use) and at least 7.5 metres from any log, tree or stump; flammable material should be cleared to 3 metres.*
▶ *Remove all rubbish not completely burnt.*
▶ *Remember that all native animals and plants are protected.*

ADELAIDE «» NHILL

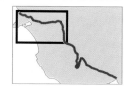

Big Billy Bore

START POINT
Map page 41, L8.

TOTAL KM 415.
UNSEALED KM 81.
DEGREE OF DIFFICULTY Moderate.
DRIVING TIME 6 hours.
LONGEST DISTANCE NO FUEL 143 km (Murrayville to Nhill).
TOPOGRAPHIC MAPS Auslig 1:250 000 series: *Ouyen*; *Horsham*; Auslig 1:100 000 series: *Danyo*; *Wallowa*.
LOCAL/SPECIALITY MAPS Rudi Paoletti: *Big Desert Adventure*; Tourism South Australia: *South Australia Touring Map*; RACV: *Victoria*.
OTHER USEFUL INFORMATION DCE information sheet: *Big Desert Wilderness*; DCE booklets: *Victoria's Desert Country – Touring Guide*; *Where to Camp in the Great Outdoors*.

DESCRIPTION Outstanding in this section are the Big Desert, and Victoria's first declared wilderness area which it encloses. One of the rare places remaining virtually undisturbed by human presence, the impression is of a timeless solitude. A fairly long but easy drive from Adelaide along the Ouyen Highway brings you to *Murrayville*, where you can camp before setting out on the Yanac road through the desert. This is a dry-weather track only and may be subject to washaways (*see Warnings*); bush camping areas along the way are at *Big Billy Bore*, *the Springs*, *Moonlight Tank* and *Broken Bucket*, with water at the first and last of these and pit toilets at Broken Bucket. There are no tracks into the wilderness, which lies 5 kilometres west of the road and roughly parallel to it; access is on foot only and extreme care should be taken in attempting to explore – map and compass are essential items of equipment (*see Warnings*). The desert landscape consists of sand ridges interspersed with flat, sandy plains where the greatest profusion of wildflowers can be found; vegetation is chiefly heath, mallee heath and scrub mallee, but the variety of shrubs is wide and includes cypress pines on the dunesides. Among the fauna are the rare western whipbird and the bustard, and this is the best place in Victoria to observe native snakes and lizards.

Leaving the desert, the route continues to the wheat-growing centre of Nhill, which claims to have the largest single-bin silo in the southern hemisphere and where you can visit the cottage of one of Australia's best known poets, John Shaw Neilson.

WARNINGS ▶ Murrayville–Yanac dry-weather track only. Check conditions before attempting with caravan. Advisable to carry emergency water supplies. ▶ No vehicular access to wilderness and no facilities or water; walkers must be completely self-sufficient; ability to use map and compass vital. For overnight walks, inform ranger (*see Bookings and Permits*) and complete trip intention form. ▶ Observe fire regulations as for national parks. Use portable stove in preference to fire. ▶ At the time of writing, special investigation of state wilderness areas included Big Desert. Check current regulations with ranger.

BOOKINGS AND PERMITS ▶ No permits required. For information on conditions contact Ranger in Charge, Post Office, Underbool VIC 3509; tel. (050) 94 6267 or DCE regional offices: 253 Eleventh Street, Mildura VIC 3500; tel. (050) 22 3000; PO Box 61, Murrayville VIC 3512; tel. (050) 95 2161. ▶ Bethune Caravan Park (limited facilities), Reed Street, Murrayville VIC 3512; tel. (050) 95 2290. ▶ Nhill Tourist Information Centre, Victoria Street, Nhill VIC 3418; tel. (053) 91 1811.

436

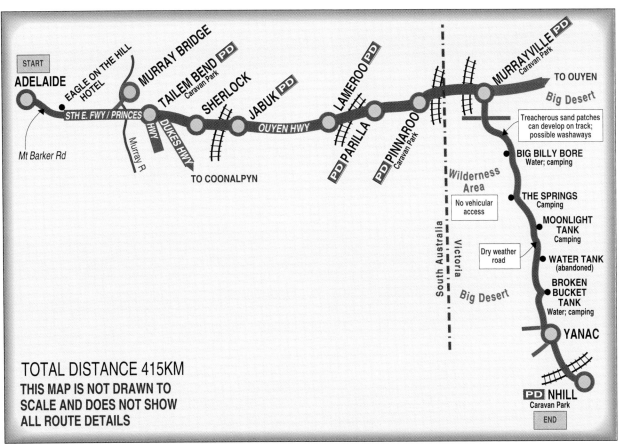

TOTAL DISTANCE 415KM

THIS MAP IS NOT DRAWN TO SCALE AND DOES NOT SHOW ALL ROUTE DETAILS

ROUTE DIRECTIONS

Depart Adelaide CBD south-east via Glen Osmond Rd–Mt Barker Rd to Eagle on the Hill Hotel (approx. 11 km).

0.0 km Zero trip meter adjacent to hotel. S'post: Murray Bridge. **SO.**

> *Continue along South Eastern Fwy.*

(60.3 km) ▲ 261.4 km

60.3 km S'post: Tailem Bend. **SO.**

> *Murray Bridge off to left. Continue onto Princes Hwy.*

(7.8 km) ▲ 201.1 km

68.1 km Murray River. Cross bridge.

(18.9 km) ▲ 193.3 km

87.0 km S'post: Lameroo. **SO.**

> *Tailem Bend town centre off to left.* **PD** *Caravan park.*

(5.3 km) ▲ 174.4 km

92.3 km S'post: Pinnaroo. **TL.**

> *Coonalpyn straight ahead.*

(29.9 km) Opp. dir. s'post: Tailem Bend. ▲ 169.1 km

122.2 km Sherlock general store. **SO.**

> *Route now follows Ouyen Hwy to Murrayville.*

(23.1 km) ▲ 139.2 km

145.3 km Cross railway line.

(3.4 km) ▲ 116.1 km

148.7 km Jabuk general store on right. **PD**

(44.0 km) ▲ 112.7 km

192.7 km Lameroo township. S'post: Pinnaroo. **TR.**

(0.4 km) ▲ 68.7 km

193.1 km S'post: Pinnaroo. **TL.**

(0.2 km) ▲ 68.3 km

193.3 km Lameroo town centre, adjacent to post office. **PD**

(9.1 km) ▲ 68.1 km

202.4 km Cross railway line.

(5.7 km) ▲ 59.0 km

Gum Tree Flats

On the Nhill road

208.1 km Parilla township, adjacent to general store. **PD**
(25.8 km) ▲ 53.3 km
233.9 km S'post: Ouyen. **KR.**

> *Pinnaroo town centre to left.* **PD** *Supplies, caravan park.*

(6.3 km) ▲ 27.5 km
240.2 km Cross railway line.

> *Immediately cross state border. Adjust watches.*

(20.0 km) ▲ 21.2 km
260.2 km Cross railway line.
(1.2 km) ▲ 1.2 km
261.4 km Murrayville town centre adjacent to Murrayville Hotel, McKenzie and Reed streets intersection.

> **PD** *Caravan park (limited facilities).*

0.0 km Zero trip meter at above intersection. **SO.**
(0.3 km) ▲ 0.0 km
▲ 143.0 km

0.3 km S'post: Nhill. **TR.**

> *Dry-weather road only. Ouyen straight ahead.*

(6.5 km) Opp. dir. s'post: Pinnaroo. ▲ 142.7 km
6.8 km Crossroads. **SO** onto gravel.
(27.2 km) Bitumen. ▲ 136.2 km
34.0 km Big Billy Bore on right. **SO.**

> *Water, picnic tables, fireplace. Bush camping. Wilderness boundary approx. 5 km west of route. Access on foot only. Exercise extreme care.*

(15.0 km) ▲ 109.0 km
49.0 km The Springs on right. **SO.**

> *Picnic tables. Bush camping.*

(25.0 km) ▲ 94.0 km
74.0 km Disused water tank on left. **SO.**
(14.1 km) ▲ 69.0 km
88.1 km Broken Bucket tank on left. Approx. 100 m to bitumen. **SO.**

> *Water, pit toilets. Bush camping.*

(19.9 km) Gravel. ▲ 54.9 km
108.0 km S'post: Nhill. **TL.**
(2.0 km) ▲ 35.0 km
110.0 km T intersection in Yanac. S'post: Nhill. **TR** onto Nhill–Yanac road.
(3.1 km) ▲ 33.0 km
113.1 km S'post: Nhill. **KL.**
(23.4 km) Opp. dir. s'post: Yanac. ▲ 29.9 km
136.5 km Cross railway line.
(6.5 km) ▲ 6.5 km
143.0 km Nhill town centre, adjacent to post office.

> **PD** *Supplies, caravan park.*

REVERSE DIRECTIONS START ▲ 0.0 km

NHILL
⟪⟫
THE GRAMPIANS

START POINT
Map page 54, E7.

TOTAL KM 210.
UNSEALED KM 95.
DEGREE OF DIFFICULTY Extreme.
DRIVING TIME 5 hours.
LONGEST DISTANCE NO FUEL Diesel: 205 km (Horsham to Halls Gap); petrol: 144 km (Happy Wanderer to Halls Gap).
TOPOGRAPHIC MAPS Auslig 1:250 000 series: *Hamilton*; *Horsham*.
LOCAL/SPECIALITY MAPS DCE: *The Grampians*; VICMAP Outdoor Leisure series: *Northern Grampians*.
OTHER USEFUL INFORMATION Victorian Tourism Commission booklet: *The Grampians (Gariwerd)*; Algona Publications booklet: *The Grampian Ranges by Road and Track*; DCE various information sheets: *Grampians National Park*; DCE booklets: *Grampians (Gariwerd) National Park Touring Guide*; *Where to Camp in Victoria's Great Outdoors*.

DESCRIPTION In this section you drive first from Nhill to Horsham – unofficial capital of the Wimmera – through some of the state's major wheatlands. The route then turns south along Pohlners Road through the craggy, forested Grampian Ranges to *Strachans Camping Area*. It is an extremely difficult track, but along the way you can enjoy magnificent scenery, many and varied bushwalks, delightful picnic spots and recreational fishing; bird and animal watchers will be in their element and the ranges are a photographer's paradise. The unusually diverse flora, some species of which are endemic, derive from the variety of soils and climate extending from sandy heathland to bleak subalpine country; the spring flowering is nationally famous.

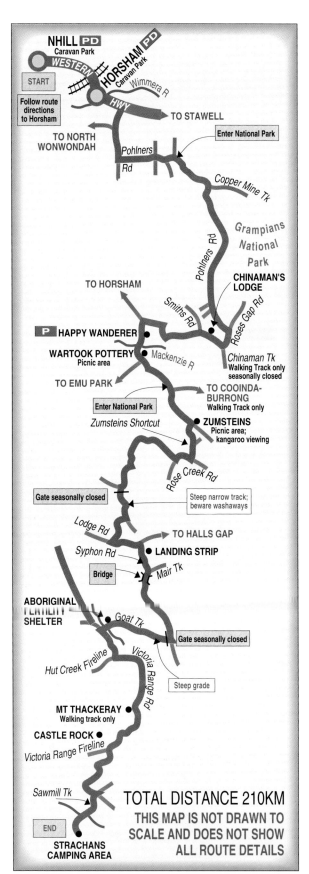

TOTAL DISTANCE 210KM

THIS MAP IS NOT DRAWN TO SCALE AND DOES NOT SHOW ALL ROUTE DETAILS

Strachans is the only designated campsite on the plotted route (note that Zumsteins is now open for day use only), but bush camping is possible except in specifically prohibited areas; there are also sites slightly off the route that could be useful – for instance, *Troopers Creek* on Roses Gap Road and *Buandik* near Glenisla Shelter. Roads in the mountains are a mixture of bitumen, good gravel, rough gravel and difficult steep, stony tracks – the last presenting a definite challenge. It is advisable to check with rangers regarding conditions (**see Warnings**).

There are so many beautiful places to be seen that a brief introduction can barely touch upon them: to plan this fascinating trip to best advantage we suggest you contact the appropriate regional DCE office.

WARNINGS ▶ No diesel between Horsham and Halls Gap (205 km). ▶ Some roads seasonally closed; in Goat Track/Victoria Range Road area tracks both rough and steep in parts. ▶ Watch out for wildlife, particularly on narrow tracks. ▶ Possibility of fallen branches or small trees; an axe or a bow saw is useful equipment. ▶ If planning an overnight walk, advisable to discuss with ranger and if possible complete trip intention form.

BOOKINGS AND PERMITS ▶ No permit required to traverse national park. Permits for self-registration at campsites from DCE regional office, 21 McLachlan Street, Horsham VIC 3400; tel. (053) 81 1255; also from Horsham Tourist Information Office, 20 O'Callaghans Parade, Horsham VIC 3400; tel. (053) 82 1832. Permits do not guarantee specific sites. ▶ Horsham Caravan Park, Firebrace Street, Horsham VIC 3400; tel. (053) 82 3476, (008) 03 2217. ▶ Inland fishing licence from DCE office, Dunkeld Road, Halls Gap VIC 3381; tel. (053) 56 4381; or at Zumsteins.

ROUTE DIRECTIONS

0.0 km Zero trip meter at Nhill Post Office, Nelson St. S'post: Melbourne. **SO.** 🅿️
(2.9 km) ▲ 75.1 km

2.9 km S'post: Horsham. **SO.**

Wyperfeld National Park off to left.

(11.4 km) ▲ 72.2 km

14.3 km Kiata township. S'post: Horsham. **SO.**

Little Desert National Park off to right.

(18.6 km) ▲ 60.8 km

32.9 km Wimmera River. Cross bridge.
(3.8 km) ▲ 42.2 km

36.7 km S'post: Melbourne. **SO.**

Wyperfeld National Park/Jeparit off to left. Little Desert National Park/Dimboola off to right.

(37.5 km) ▲ 38.4 km

74.2 km Cross railway line into Horsham.
(0.9 km) ▲ 0.9 km

75.1 km Firebrace St and Baillie St (Western Hwy) intersection. S'post: Ballarat. **SO.**

Horsham town centre on right. 🅿️ *Supplies, caravan park. Olde Horsham Village; fishing in Wimmera River. Next diesel Halls Gap (205 km).*

0.0 km Zero trip meter at above intersection. **SO.**
(0.5 km) ▲ 0.0 km
▲ 70.6 km

0.5 km S'post: Ballarat. **TR** into McPherson St (Western Hwy).

Warracknabeal via Henty Hwy off to left.

(1.3 km) ▲ 70.1 km

1.8 km Roundabout. S'post: Ballarat. **SO** and immediately cross Wimmera River.
(1.3 km) ▲ 68.8 km

3.1 km S'post: Ballarat. **SO** along Western Hwy.

Hamilton off to right.

(2.9 km) ▲ 67.5 km

6.0 km S'post: Stawell 62. **SO** along Western Hwy.

Grampians Tourist Area off to right.

(12.0 km) Opp. dir. s'post: Horsham. ▲ 64.6 km

18.0 km S'post: Zumsteins. **TR** off highway.

Stawell straight ahead.

(9.0 km) Opp. dir. s'post: Horsham. ▲ 52.6 km

27.0 km S'post: Laharum. **SO.**

North Wonwondah off to right; road merges.

(2.2 km) Opp. dir. s'post: Western Hwy. ▲ 43.6 km

29.2 km S'post: Pohlners Rd. **TL** onto gravel.
(3.0 km) Bitumen. ▲ 41.4 km

32.2 km Crossroads. **SO.**
(0.8 km) ▲ 38.4 km

33.0 km Intersection. **SO.**
(0.7 km) ▲ 37.6 km

33.7 km S'post: Pohlners Rd. **SO.**

Road enters on left. Enter national park.

(4.1 km) ▲ 36.9 km

37.8 km S'post: Pohlners Rd. **SO.**

> *Copper Mine Track on left.*

(10.0 km) ▲ 32.8 km
47.8 km Intersection. **KL**.
(0.4 km) ▲ 22.8 km
48.2 km Intersection. **KL**.
(2.6 km) ▲ 22.4 km
50.8 km S'post: Roses Gap Rd. **TR**.
(1.2 km) Opp. dir. s'post: Pohlners Rd. ▲ 19.8 km
52.0 km S'post: Roses Gap Rd. **SO**.

> *Chinaman Track on left. Walkers only. Seasonally closed.*

(1.5 km) Opp. dir. s'post: Roses Gap Rd. ▲ 18.6 km
53.5 km Chinaman's Lodge on right. **SO**.

> *Private facility.*

(1.0 km) ▲ 17.1 km
54.5 km S'post: Laharum. **KL**.

> *Smiths Rd on right.*

(5.7 km) Opp. dir. s'post: Roses Gap. ▲ 16.1 km
60.2 km S'post: Zumsteins. **KL**.

> *Horsham off to right.*

(0.1 km) ▲ 10.4 km
60.3 km S'post: Zumsteins. **TL** onto bitumen.
(0.4 km) Gravel. Opp. dir. s'post: Roses Gap Rd. ▲ 10.3 km
60.7 km Happy Wanderer Holiday Resort. **SO**.

> *Private facility.* 🅿 *Caravans on site; camping (1 site), accommodation. Next fuel Halls Gap (144 km).*

(1.2 km) ▲ 9.9 km
61.9 km Mackenzie River. Cross bridge.
(0.4 km) ▲ 8.7 km
62.3 km Wartook Pottery and Art Gallery on left. **SO**.
(1.1 km) ▲ 8.3 km
63.4 km Intersection. **SO**.

> *Emu Park Holiday Park 2 km off to right.*

(3.2 km) ▲ 7.2 km
66.6 km Intersection. **SO**.

> *Cooinda–Burrong 1 km off to left. Walking track only. Sign: Grampians National Park.*

(4.0 km) ▲ 4.0 km
70.6 km Zumsteins picnic area. S'post: Zumsteins Track.

> *Area frequented by kangaroos; do not feed. No camping. Zumsteins Mackenzie River walking trail (4 km).*

Mackenzie Falls

Kangaroos at Zumsteins

0.0 km   Zero trip meter at above s'post: **TR** onto gravel.
(2.2 km)   Bitumen. ▲ 0.0 km
                                         ▲ 64.3 km

2.2 km   Intersection. **SO**.

> *Road enters on left.*

(1.7 km)   ▲ 62.1 km
3.9 km   S'post: Rose Creek Rd. **TR**.
(1.6 km)   Opp. dir. s'post:
                    Zumsteins Shortcut. ▲ 60.4 km
5.5 km   S'post: Wallaby Rocks. **TR**.
(10.0 km)   Opp. dir. s'post:
                    Rose Creek Road. ▲ 58.8 km
15.5 km Intersection. **TL** and immediately through gate posts.

> *Gate seasonally closed. Track is narrow and steep; can be rough going. Beware washaways and large rocks.*

(2.2 km)   ▲ 48.8 km
17.7 km Intersection. **TR**.
(2.9 km)   ▲ 46.6 km
20.6 km S'post: Lodge Rd. **TL**.
(2.7 km)   Opp. dir. s'post: Hines Tk. ▲ 43.7 km
23.3 km S'post: Syphon Rd. **TR**.

> *Halls Gap straight ahead.*

(0.4 km)   Opp. dir. s'post: Henty Hwy. ▲ 41.0 km
23.7 km Landing strip on left. **SO**.
(2.0 km)   ▲ 40.6 km
25.7 km S'post: Syphon Rd. **KR** and immediately cross wooden bridge.

> *Mair Track on left.*

(6.4 km)   ▲ 38.6 km
32.1 km S'post: Goat Track. **TR**.

> *Gate seasonally closed. Steep grade. Syphon Rd straight on.*

(6.9 km)   Opp. dir. s'post: Syphon Rd. ▲ 32.2 km
39.0 km Intersection. **SO**.

> *5-min walk on right to Aboriginal Fertility Shelter.*

(0.9 km)   ▲ 25.3 km
39.9 km Cross creek.
(0.1 km)   ▲ 24.4 km
40.0 km S'post: Victoria Range Rd. **TL**.

> *Goat Track straight on.*

(2.8 km)   Opp. dir. s'post: Goat Track. ▲ 24.3 km

Rocky bluffs in the Grampians

42.8 km Intersection. **SO**.

> *Hut Creek Fireline Track on right.*

(7.5 km)   ▲ 21.5 km
50.3 km Mt Thackeray summit off to right. **SO**.

> *Walking trail.*

(5.7 km)   ▲ 14.0 km
56.0 km Intersection. **SO** along Victoria Range Rd.

> *Victoria Range Fireline Track on right. 500 m to unmarked track to Castle Rock (the Fortress).*

(4.7 km)   ▲ 8.3 km
60.7 km Crossroads. S'post: Sawmill Track. **TR**.

> *Victoria Range Rd straight on.*

(1.8 km)   ▲ 3.6 km
62.5 km Cross creek.
(1.8 km)   ▲ 1.8 km
64.3 km Strachans Camping Area.

> *Barbecues, toilets. Self-registration for camping.*

REVERSE DIRECTIONS START ▲ 0.0 km

THE GRAMPIANS
«»
MELBOURNE

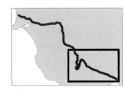

Grampians wildflowers

START POINT
Map page 52, I2.

TOTAL KM 340.
UNSEALED KM 65.
DEGREE OF DIFFICULTY Difficult.
DRIVING TIME 4 hours (Strachans Camping Area to Stawell).
LONGEST DISTANCE NO FUEL Next fuel Halls Gap.
TOPOGRAPHIC MAPS Auslig 1:250 000 series: *Horsham, Hamilton, Ballarat*.
LOCAL/SPECIALITY MAPS DCE: *The Grampians.* VICMAP Outdoor Leisure series: *Northern Grampians.*
OTHER USEFUL INFORMATION Victorian Tourism Commission booklet: *The Grampians (Gariwerd)*; Algona Publications booklet: *The Grampian Ranges by Road and Track*; DCE various information sheets: *Grampians National Park*; DCE booklets: *Grampians (Gariwerd) National Park Touring Guide*; *Where to Camp in Victoria's Great Outdoors.*

DESCRIPTION From Strachans Camping Area you take Jensens Road and briefly leave the national park, passing Mirranatwa and crossing Dwyer Creek to strike north again along Henham Track. Shortly before leaving the track there are a number of minor creek crossings, and as you turn onto Silverband Road you pass *Mt Rosea* camping ground; a stop here gives access to the walks branching from Sundial Turntable through the southern part of the Wonderland Range, considered a major highlight of the Grampians. Before reaching Halls Gap another offshoot, from Mt Victory Road, leads to the Wonderland Turntable, starting point of the track to the spectacular Grand Canyon and the Whale's Mouth rock.

Halls Gap, crouched between Mt William and Wonderland ranges and the focal point for yet more diverse walking tracks, annually in spring holds an exhibition of the wildflowers for which the Grampians are renowned. Brambuk Centre gives a vivid and unique view of local Aboriginal culture and nearby is Wallaroo Wildlife Park, where some of the inhabitants are friendly enough to be handfed.

Beyond Halls Gap the route leaves the national park, crosses north-flowing Fyans Creek and skirts the sandy beaches of *Lake Lonsdale*; the lake shore is another possible campsite (no facilities) with a chance to enjoy some water sports – but check conditions first: lake waters are used for summer irrigation and levels may be reduced. From this point Ledcourt Road takes you to the Western Highway and an easy drive to Melbourne.

WARNINGS ▶ Some roads seasonally closed. Check before starting out. ▶ Watch out for wildlife, particularly on narrow tracks. ▶ Possibility of fallen branches or small trees; an axe or a bow saw is useful equipment. ▶ If planning an overnight walk, advise discussion with ranger and if possible completion of trip intention form.

BOOKINGS AND PERMITS ▶ No permit required to traverse national park. Permits for self-registration at campsites from DCE regional offices: Dunkeld Road, Halls Gap VIC 3381; tel. (053) 56 4381; PO Box 201, Stawell VIC 3380; tel. (053) 58 1588; also from Stawell and Grampians Information Centre, 54 Western Highway, Stawell VIC 3380; tel. (053) 58 2314. Permits do not guarantee specific sites. ▶ Halls Gap Caravan Park, Dunkeld Road, Halls Gap VIC 3381; tel. (053) 56 4251. ▶ Inland fishing licence from Halls Gap DCE office (see above).

443

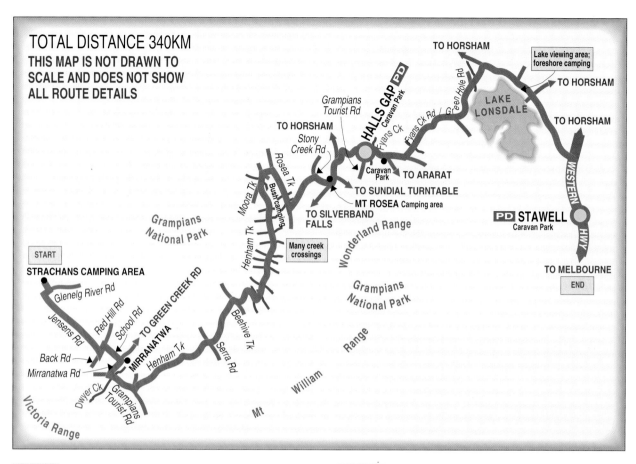

TOTAL DISTANCE 340KM
THIS MAP IS NOT DRAWN TO
SCALE AND DOES NOT SHOW
ALL ROUTE DETAILS

ROUTE DIRECTIONS

0.0 km   Zero trip meter at Strachans Camping Area, adjacent to bark hut.
   (0.4 km)   ▲ 62.6 km

0.4 km   T intersection. **TR** onto Glenelg River Rd; immediately s'post: Jensens Rd. **TL**.
   (10.0 km)   Opp. dir. s'post: Sawmill Tk. ▲ 62.2 km

10.4 km   T intersection. **TL** onto bitumen.
   (0.7 km)   Gravel. Opp. dir. s'post: Jensens Rd. ▲ 52.2 km

11.1 km   S'post: Mirranatwa. **KR** on bitumen.

> *Gravel straight on: Red Hill Rd.*

   (3.0 km)   ▲ 51.5 km

14.1 km   T intersection. **TR**.

> *Green Creek Rd off to left.*

   (2.1 km)   Opp. dir. s'post: Mirranatwa School. ▲ 48.5 km

16.2 km   T intersection. S'post: Halls Gap. **TL**.
   (0.1 km)   Opp. dir. s'post: Mirranatwa. ▲ 46.4 km

16.3 km   Dwyer Creek. Cross bridge.
   (3.8 km)   ▲ 46.3 km

20.1 km   S'post: Henham Track. **TL** onto gravel.
   (0.2 km)   Bitumen. ▲ 42.5 km

20.3 km   Y intersection. **KR**.
   (9.4 km)   ▲ 42.3 km

29.7 km   Crossroads. S'post: Henham Track. **SO** over Serra Rd.
   (4.9 km)   ▲ 32.9 km

34.6 km   T intersection. **TR** along Henham Track.

> *Beehive Track on left.*

   (0.8 km)   ▲ 28.0 km

35.4 km   Y intersection. **KL**.
   (2.6 km)   ▲ 27.2 km

38.0 km   Cross creek.
   (0.1 km)   ▲ 24.6 km

38.1 km   Cross creek.
   (1.1 km)   ▲ 24.5 km

39.2 km   Cross creek.
   (2.3 km)   ▲ 23.4 km

41.5 km   Cross creek.
   (0.9 km)   ▲ 21.1 km

42.4 km   Cross creek.
   (0.4 km)   ▲ 20.2 km

42.8 km Cross creek.
(1.2 km) ▲ 19.8 km
44.0 km Cross creek.
(1.2 km) ▲ 18.6 km
45.2 km Cross creek.
(0.3 km) ▲ 17.4 km
45.5 km Cross creek.
(0.7 km) ▲ 17.1 km
46.2 km Cross creek.
(3.4 km) ▲ 16.4 km
49.6 km S'post: Henham Track. **TR**.

Moora Track on left.

(0.2 km) ▲ 13.0 km
49.8 km Cross creek.
(0.1 km) ▲ 12.8 km
49.9 km Intersection. **TR** off Henham Track.
(0.2 km) ▲ 12.7 km
50.1 km Intersection. **KL**.

Bush camping area on right. Seasonal track.

(1.0 km) ▲ 12.5 km
51.1 km Lookout on right. **SO**.
(0.8 km) ▲ 11.5 km
51.9 km T intersection. **TR** onto Rosea Track.
(2.1 km) ▲ 10.7 km
54.0 km Cross creek.
(0.8 km) ▲ 8.6 km
54.8 km Cross creek.
(5.0 km) ▲ 7.8 km
59.8 km T intersection. S'post: Stony Creek Rd. **TR**.
(2.3 km) Opp. dir. s'post: Rosea Tk. ▲ 2.8 km
62.1 km T intersection. **TL** onto bitumen.

Mt Rosea campsite area on left. Barbecues, toilets, water. Self-registration. Silverband Falls 3 km off to right.

(0.5 km) Gravel. ▲ 0.5 km
62.6 km S'post: Halls Gap.

Sundial Turntable 1.2 km off to right. Walking trails.

0.0 km Zero trip meter at above s'post. **SO**.
(2.5 km) ▲ 0.0 km
▲ 44.2 km
2.5 km S'post: Halls Gap 6. **TR**.

Horsham off to left.

(5.1 km) Opp. dir. s'post: Halls Gap 16. ▲ 41.7 km
7.6 km S'post: Stawell. **TL** onto Grampians Rd.

Halls Gap town centre off to right. **PD** Caravan park. Many walking trails. Brambuk Aboriginal Cultural Centre; Wallaroo Wildlife Park.

(0.8 km) Opp. dir. s'post: Zumsteins. ▲ 36.6 km
8.4 km Delleys Bridge. Cross Fyans Creek.
(1.7 km) ▲ 35.8 km
10.1 km S'post: Stawell. **SO**.

Ararat off to right. **PD** Caravan park immediately on right.

(2.0 km) Opp. dir. s'post: Halls Gap. ▲ 34.1 km
12.1 km S'post: Fyans Creek. **TL**.
(1.3 km) ▲ 32.1 km
13.4 km Fyans Creek. Cross bridge.
(6.0 km) ▲ 30.8 km
19.4 km Y intersection. **KL** onto gravel.
(4.2 km) Bitumen. ▲ 24.8 km
23.6 km Y intersection. **KR**.
(0.2 km) ▲ 20.6 km
23.8 km Mt William Creek. Cross bridge.
(1.6 km) ▲ 20.4 km
25.4 km S'post: Stawell. **SO**.

Horsham off to left.

(2.8 km) Opp. dir. s'post: Halls Gap. ▲ 18.8 km
28.2 km Intersection. **SO**.

Lake Lonsdale viewing area off to right. Camping along lake foreshore (permit required). No facilities. Water sports permitted.

(3.5 km) ▲ 16.0 km
31.7 km Crossroads. S'post: Stawell. **SO** onto bitumen.

Horsham off to left. Lake Lonsdale off to right.

(7.5 km) Gravel. Opp. dir. s'post: Green Hole Outlet. ▲ 12.5 km
39.2 km S'post: Stawell. **TR** onto Western Hwy.

Horsham off to left.

(5.0 km) ▲ 5.0 km
44.2 km S'post: Stawell town centre 2 km off to right.

PD Caravan park.

REVERSE DIRECTIONS START ▲ 0.0 km
Follow Western Hwy to Melbourne (approx. 233 km) to pick up route directions for next trek, Melbourne to Sydney.

Towards snow-capped Mt Bogong in the Victorian Alps

OVER THE ALPS
MELBOURNE
«»
SYDNEY
1236 KILOMETRES

MELBOURNE «» BRIGHT	361 km
BRIGHT «» NATIVE DOG FLAT	234 km
NATIVE DOG FLAT «» COOMA	211 km
COOMA «» SYDNEY	430 km

This is not a difficult trek; it allows you ample time to enjoy the magnificent mountain country along a route that in each section reveals vista after vista at almost every turn; however, many mountain roads are narrow, twisting, steep and sometimes rough, and particular care is needed if you are towing a caravan. There are wonderful opportunities for fishing in mountain streams and lakes, but don't forget an inland fishing licence is required in Victoria, while New South Wales has local seasonal and bag restrictions; you can also enjoy river swimming, bushwalking and water sports, and there is endless scope for photographers. In the Victorian Alps you will find heathlands, grasslands and bogs in the harsh environment above the sturdy snow-gum treeline, and in the lower forests there are many eucalypt species – notably one of the tallest, the majestic alpine ash. In a few places can be found the only exclusively alpine marsupial in the world – the rare mountain pygmy possum. Over the border, the mountains in Kosciusko National Park give way to the coastal ranges and the wet sclerophyll forests of the New South Wales highlands. The trek should be undertaken November–May since although the last section

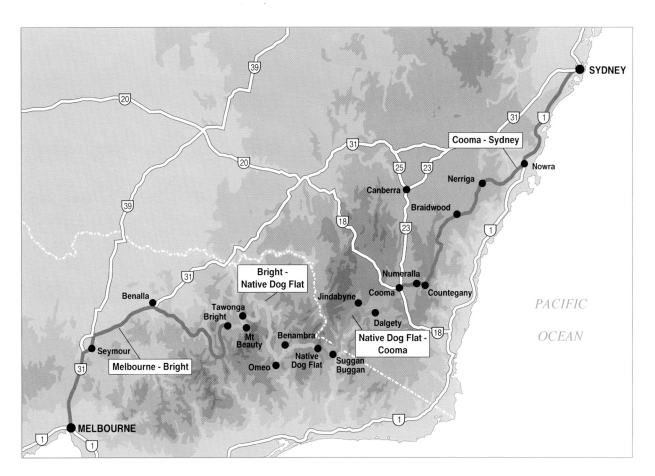

can be attempted at any time, many of the alpine roads followed are inaccessible in winter. Camping facilities in the Victorian Alps are basic, with toilets and fireplaces at relatively few places; prepare to be self-sufficient between major stopping places.

Shortly after leaving Benalla you enter state forest, then cross sections of Victoria's rambling Alpine National Park, enter Kosciusko National Park at the state border and cross its southernmost arm. From there the route continues north-east through the Great Dividing Range to Cooma and through historic Braidwood to Nowra, completing the trek on the Princes Highway along the beautiful Illawarra Coast to Sydney.

BEFORE YOU SET OUT ▶ Read the section description carefully ▶ Check that you have obtained any necessary permits. ▶ Check weather conditions with local authorities or the Bureau of Meteorology. ▶ Make sure you have the appropriate maps and information for the trek. ▶ Check that your vehicle is in good order for the conditions ahead. Have you the necessary spare parts? ▶ If you are camping, do you have the right equipment?

USEFUL INFORMATION

For touring information contact:
Victorian Travel Centre, 230 Collins Street
Melbourne 3000, (03) 790 2211.
New South Wales Travel Centre
19 Castlereagh Street, Sydney 2000
(02) 231 4444.

For motoring and touring information contact:
Royal Automobile Club of Victoria (RACV)
422 Little Collins Street, Melbourne 3000
(03) 790 2211.
National Roads & Motorists' Association (NRMA)
151 Clarence Street, Sydney 2000, (02) 260 9222.

For four-wheel driving information contact:
Victoria Four Wheel Drive Association Inc.
552 Whitehorse Road, Mitcham VIC 3132
(03) 872 4610.
FWDC Association of NSW & ACT
GPO Box 3870, Sydney 2001.

NATIONAL PARKS OF VICTORIA AND NEW SOUTH WALES

On this trek you visit Mt Buffalo National Park, Victoria's Alpine National Park (which now comprises several smaller, formerly individual parks such as Cobberas-Tingaringy), Kosciusko National Park and Morton National Park, passing also within easy reach of Deua National Park in the last section. A code of ethics applying to all is given below, but for the alpine parks there are special aspects to be considered. Mountain weather can be deceptive; it can change without warning and travellers – particularly when bushwalking – should always carry warm clothing and supplies of sustaining food, even in summertime. Note also that the mountain distress call is three long whistle or torch signals, repeated at one-minute intervals.

For information on Victorian national parks contact DCE, 240 Victoria Parade, East Melbourne VIC 3002, tel. (03) 412 4795; for New South Wales, contact NPWS Head Office, 43 Bridge Street, Hurstville NSW 2220; tel. (02) 585 6333; or regional offices in both states, given in the route directions. Note that particular regulations apply to four-wheel driving in New South Wales parks.

To help protect and maintain these areas, please observe the following code.

▶ *Keep to defined walking tracks or formed roads.*
▶ *Carry out what you carry in.*
▶ *Camp at least 20 metres from any watercourse.*
▶ *Do not bathe or wash dishes in lakes or streams; carry water to camp.*
▶ *Where there are no toilet facilities, bury waste at least 100 metres from any stream or campsite.*
▶ *Cutting living trees is prohibited; use only fallen timber for firewood and clear flammable material to at least 3 metres; preferably use a portable stove. Never leave a fire unattended. In Morton National Park open fires are permitted only in constructed metal fireplaces.*
▶ *Remember that all native animals and plants, geological features and archaeological sites are protected.*
▶ *Do not bring domestic pets into parks.*
▶ *Firearms are permitted only for deer hunting in designated areas in Victoria.*

Upper cataract of Eurobin Falls, Mt Buffalo National Park

Sunset over the Bogong High Plains

MELBOURNE
«»
BRIGHT

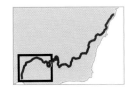

START POINT
Map page 50, C4.

TOTAL KM 361.
UNSEALED KM 89.
DEGREE OF DIFFICULTY Moderate.
DRIVING TIME 5 hours (Benalla to Bright).
LONGEST DISTANCE NO FUEL 104 km (Whitfield to Porepunkah).
TOPOGRAPHIC MAP Auslig 1:250 000 series: *Wangaratta*.
LOCAL/SPECIALITY MAPS RACV: *Victoria*; DCE: *Victoria's Alpine Area*; Auslig Ausmap series: *Australian Alps National Parks Touring Map*.
OTHER USEFUL INFORMATION DCE booklet: *Where to Camp in Victoria's Great Outdoors*; information sheets: *Victoria's Alpine National Park*; *Mt Buffalo National Park* (various); *Roads and Vehicle Access*.

DESCRIPTION A smooth trip up the Hume Freeway brings you to Benalla in the Kelly country; from here you begin a traverse of the Victorian Alps through state forest in the high country where the southern tip of the Great Dividing Range turns westward. The tracks are steep and rough but otherwise not difficult, and for the most part the views are stunning, with wildflowers and wild berries along the road and changing vistas at each climb, descent and turn. Some of the best mountain walking country in Australia is to be found here.

Offshoots just past Cheshunt take you to Lake William Hovell and to Paradise Falls, both beautiful picnic areas. There is a camping ground at *Whitfield* and camping is permitted in state forest, but the only designated bush campsite on the route is near *Upper Buckland Junction*. However, a short diversion on reaching Porepunkah leads you to Mt Buffalo National

Park and the camping area at *Lake Catani*, a place ideal also for fishing, walking, swimming or boating; the road from Porepunkah gives splendid views of the park and of more distant Victorian alpine peaks. The national park is a spectacular region in which massive, steep-sided granite tors rise above a plateau; there are planned nature walks, a nature drive and – for the intrepid – some of the hardest rock climbs in Australia, especially in The Gorge above Eurobin Falls. Returning to the plotted route, the section ends in the beautiful and historic goldfields town of Bright, in the Ovens Valley.

WARNINGS ▶ Tracks accessible only in summer; some may be temporarily closed. ▶ Be prepared for sudden, extreme and unpredictable changes in mountain weather. Always carry warm clothing, even in summer, and extra food supplies. ▶ Mountain sunlight burns, even in cool weather. Take precautions. ▶ Before bushwalking, advise responsible person of planned itinerary; if possible, complete intentions form. Carry drinking water; mountain water frequently unsuitable.

BOOKINGS AND PERMITS ▶ Booking advisable at Lake Catani in holiday periods. Contact DCE Regional Office, Bakers Gully Road, Bright VIC 3741; tel. (057) 55 1577. ▶ Mt Buffalo Park Office, PO Box 72, Porepunkah VIC 3740; tel. (057) 55 1466. ▶ Bright Tourist Information, la Delany Avenue, Bright VIC 3741 ▶ Deer hunting is permitted subject to certain regulations; contact DCE.

ROUTE DIRECTIONS

Depart Melbourne CBD north via Elizabeth St, Royal Pde, Sydney Rd, Hume Fwy to Benalla (approx. 192 km).

> **PD** *Caravan park, bird sanctuary. Costume and Pioneer Museum, Kelly Museum; Ledger collection of Australian paintings.*

0.0 km Zero trip meter in Bridge St (Hume Hwy), adjacent to post office. **SO.**
(0.1 km) ▲ 58.2 km

0.1 km Intersection: traffic lights. S'post: Yarrawonga. **SO.**
(1.3 km) ▲ 58.1 km

1.4 km S'post: Tatong. **TR** onto Samaria Rd.

> *Benalla Airport on left.*

(0.9 km) ▲ 56.8 km

2.3 km S'post: Greta South. **TL** onto Kilfeera Rd.

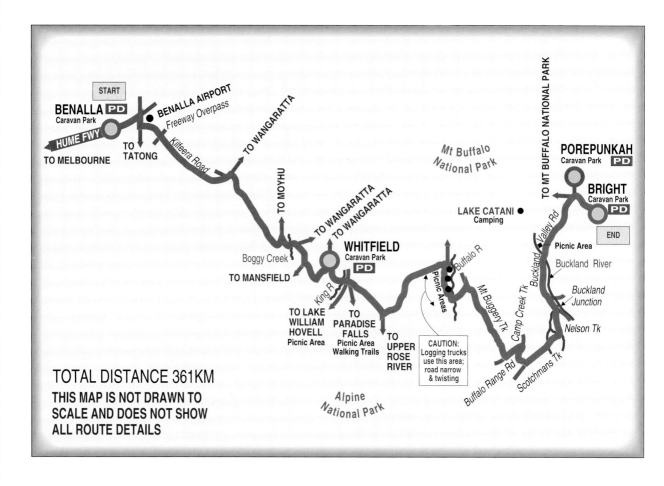

TOTAL DISTANCE 361KM

THIS MAP IS NOT DRAWN TO SCALE AND DOES NOT SHOW ALL ROUTE DETAILS

	Tatong straight ahead.
	(2.0 km) ▲ 55.9 km
4.3 km	Cross freeway overpass.
	(22.1 km) ▲ 53.9 km
26.4 km	S'post: Whitfield. **KR.**
	Road enters on left.
	(0.1 km) ▲ 31.8 km
26.5 km	Y intersection. S'post: Whitfield. **KR.**
	Wangaratta off to left.
	(17.7 km) ▲ 31.7 km
44.2 km	S'post: Whitfield. **TR** onto gravel.
	Moyhu straight ahead.
	(1.9 km) Bitumen. Opp. dir. s'post: Benalla. ▲14.0 km
46.1 km	Boggy Creek. Cross wooden bridge.
	(0.9 km) ▲ 12.1 km
47.0 km	Y intersection. S'post: Whitfield. **KR.**
	Wangaratta off to left.
	(4.0 km) Opp. dir. s'post: Benalla. ▲ 11.2 km

51.0 km	T intersection. S'post: Whitfield. **TL** onto bitumen.
	Mansfield off to right.
	(4.6 km) Gravel. Opp. dir. s'post: Benalla. ▲7.2 km
55.6 km	Cross wooden bridge.
	(2.6 km) ▲ 2.6 km
58.2 km	Whitfield township. S'post: Cheshunt.
	PD *Supplies, caravan park, camping. Fishing, swimming. Dairying and tobacco centre.*
0.0 km	Zero trip meter at above s'post. **TR.**
	(4.1 km) ▲ 0.0 km
	▲ 4.6 km
4.1 km	King River. Cross bridge.
	(0.5 km) ▲ 0.5 km
4.6 km	Crossroads. S'post: Rose River.
	Lake William Hovell off to right. Picnic tables, toilets. Boat ramp.
	Opp. dir. s'post: Whitfield.

0.0 km Zero trip meter at above crossroads. **SO.**
(1.6 km)   ▲ 0.0 km
                                                 ▲ 1.6 km

1.6 km Intersection.

> *Paradise Falls off to right. Picnic tables, fireplace, toilets. Walking trails.*

0.0 km Zero trip meter at above intersection. **SO.**
(4.2 km)   ▲ 0.0 km
                                                 ▲ 104.2 km

4.2 km Gravel.
(8.4 km)   Bitumen. ▲ 100.0 km
12.6 km S'post: Myrtleford. **SO.**

> *Upper Rose River off to right.*

(17.0 km)   ▲ 91.6 km
29.6 km S'post: Abbeyards. **TR.**

> *Myrtleford off to left. Signs: caution – logging trucks in area; no thru road. Road narrow and twisting.*

(2.9 km)   Opp. dir. s'post: Whitfield. ▲ 74.6 km
32.5 km Picnic area on left. **SO.**

> *Picnic facilities, barbecues on Buffalo River bank at this and 2 following points.*

(2.4 km)   ▲ 71.7 km
34.9 km Picnic area on left. **SO.**
(1.2 km)   ▲ 69.3 km
36.1 km Mannagum Picnic Area on left.
(1.7 km)   ▲ 68.1 km
37.8 km S'post: Durling Track. **TL** and immediately cross Buffalo River.

> *Track partially concealed. Easy river crossing with hard, rocky base.*

(4.1 km)   ▲ 66.4 km
41.9 km T intersection. **TR** onto Mt Buggery Track.
(15.6 km)   Opp. dir. s'post: Durling Track. ▲ 62.3 km
57.5 km S'post: Camp Creek Track. **TL.**
(3.0 km)   Opp. dir. s'post:
                                Mt Buggery Track. ▲ 46.7 km
60.5 km T intersection. **TR** onto Buffalo Range Rd.
(3.8 km)   Opp. dir. s'post:
                                Camp Creek Track. ▲ 43.7 km
64.3 km T intersection. S'post:Scotchmans Track. **TL.**
(4.6 km)   ▲ 39.9 km
68.9 km Cross creek.
(2.6 km)   ▲ 35.3 km
71.5 km T intersection. **TL** onto Nelson Track.
(0.1 km)   Opp. dir. s'post:
                                Scotchmans Track. ▲ 32.7 km

Winter at Lake Catani, Mt Buffalo National Park

71.6 km Cross creek.
(3.1 km)   ▲ 32.6 km
74.7 km T intersection. **TL** onto Buckland Valley Rd.
(0.3 km)   ▲ 29.5 km
75.0 km Cross bridge.

> *Bush campsite on right.*

(3.4 km)   Opp. dir. sign:
                          Upper Buckland Junction. ▲ 29.2 km
78.4 km Intersection. **SO.**

> *Road enters on right.*

(7.2 km)   Opp. dir. s'post:
                             Buckland Valley Rd. ▲ 25.8 km
85.6 km Buckland River. Cross bridge onto bitumen.

> *Picnic area, barbecue on left.*

(12.2 km)   Gravel. ▲ 18.6 km
97.8 km Roundabout. S'post: Bright. **TR** onto Ovens Hwy.

> *Mt Buffalo National Park off to left. 500 m straight ahead to Porepunkah township.* **PD** *Supplies, caravan park. Bushwalking, fishing, gold prospecting, river swimming.*

(6.4 km)   ▲ 6.4 km
104.2 km Bright town centre, adjacent to State Bank in Gavan St.

> **PD** *Supplies, caravan park. Bushwalking, fishing, gold prospecting. Historical museum; historic buildings. Autumn festival (late April).*

REVERSE DIRECTIONS START ▲ 0.0 km

451

BRIGHT
«»
NATIVE DOG FLAT

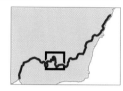

START POINT
Map page 60, B6.

TOTAL KM 234.
UNSEALED KM 138.
DEGREE OF DIFFICULTY Moderate.
DRIVING TIME 7 hours.
LONGEST DISTANCE NO FUEL 158 km (Tawonga to Benambra).
TOPOGRAPHIC MAPS Auslig 1:250 000 series: *Wangaratta*; *Tallangatta*.
LOCAL/SPECIALITY MAPS RACV: *Victoria*; DCE: *Victoria's Alpine Area*; Auslig Ausmap series: *Australian Alps National Parks Touring Map*.
OTHER USEFUL INFORMATION DCE information sheets: *Victoria's Alpine National Park*; *Roads and Vehicle Access*; booklet: *Where to Camp in Victoria's Great Outdoors*.

DESCRIPTION The tracks in this section are a mixture of good and bad; there is only one moderately difficult four-wheel drive section, but all except the bitumen surfaces are very narrow and require great care. Crossing the Ovens River not far from Bright, the route runs eastwards through state forest towards Mt Beauty, in the Upper Kiewa Valley; established at the foot of Mt Bogong to accommodate construction workers on the Kiewa Hydroelectric Scheme, the township is true to its name and well worth a visit that could be followed by a night camp at *Tawonga*. At *Mountain Creek Camping Area* comes the first brief drive in the Alpine National Park before a swing north across Granite Flats Spur joins the Omeo Highway, twisting and turning south again through Mt Wills Historic Area to cross a neck of the park; you leave it again just beyond *Anglers Rest Camping Area*.

Gold–washing channel near Omeo, dug by Chinese miners

Omeo, lying just below the southernmost point of the route, is a former gold-mining centre; the Oriental Claims Historic Area is a reminder of its association with Chinese miners in the last century. Off the Omeo Highway, Benambra is the place to stock up on fuel and provisions for the rest of this section and part of the next, since *Native Dog Flat* has no facilities; while at Benambra, don't miss visiting the lookout.

The final leg of the trip briefly joins the Bicentennial National Trail, which a company of riders followed from Melbourne to Canberra in Australia's year of celebration.

WARNINGS ▶ Watch for logging trucks on weekdays and for kangaroos and wallabies, particularly at dawn and dusk. ▶ Observe general warnings, particularly concerning weather, given in previous section.

BOOKINGS AND PERMITS ▶ For local information contact Chamber of Commerce, Mt Beauty VIC 3699; tel. (057) 57 2133; Administration Centre, Falls Creek Alpine Resort; tel. (057) 58 3224.

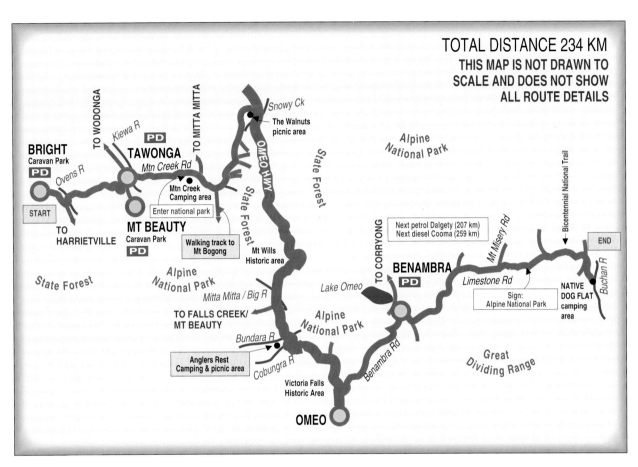

TOTAL DISTANCE 234 KM
THIS MAP IS NOT DRAWN TO
SCALE AND DOES NOT SHOW
ALL ROUTE DETAILS

ROUTE DIRECTIONS

0.0 km Zero trip meter in Gavan St, Bright, adjacent to State Bank. S'post: Mt Hotham. **SO**.
(5.4 km) ▲ 40.0 km

5.4 km S'post: Tawonga/Mt Beauty. **TL**.

> Harrietville straight ahead.

(0.1 km) Opp. dir. s'post: Bright. ▲ 34.6 km

5.5 km Ovens River. Cross bridge.
(21.5 km) ▲ 34.5 km

27.0 km T intersection. S'post: Tawonga. **TL**.

> Mt Beauty off to right. **PD** Caravan park. Fishing, water sports.

(2.3 km) Opp. dir. s'post: Bright. ▲ 13.0 km

29.3 km In Tawonga, s'post: Mountain Creek Rd. **TR**.

> Wodonga straight ahead.

(1.3 km) Opp. dir. s'post: Mt Beauty. ▲ 10.7 km

30.6 km Kiewa River. Cross bridge.
(6.4 km) ▲ 9.4 km

37.0 km Gravel.

> Road narrows. Sign: caution – logging trucks frequent this road.

(2.9 km) Bitumen. ▲ 3.0 km

39.9 km Sign: Alpine National Park. **SO**.
(0.1 km) ▲ 0.1 km

40.0 km S'post: Trappers Gap.

> Mountain Creek Camping and Picnic Area. Barbecues, toilets, water. Walking trails.

0.0 km Zero trip meter at above s'post. **KL**.
(6.7 km) ▲ 0.0 km
▲ 38.5 km

6.7 km 5-ways junction. S'post: Eskdale Spur. **TR** and immediately through gate; **KR** up hill.

> Mitta Mitta off to left.

(3.9 km) Opp. dir. s'post: Trappers Creek. ▲ 31.8 km

10.6 km S'post: Camp Creek Track. **TR**.

> Trappers Spur Track on left.

(1.6 km) ▲ 27.9 km

12.2 km Intersection. **KL**.

> *Eskdale Spur/Mt Bogong 4 km off to right. Walking track.*

(1.5 km) ▲ 26.3 km

13.7 km Cross creek.

(1.8 km) ▲ 24.8 km

15.5 km Intersection. **KL** (hard left).

(4.3 km) Opp. dir. s'post: Camp Creek Track. ▲ 23.0 km

19.8 km Intersection. **TL** (hard left).

(3.2 km) ▲ 18.7 km

23.0 km Intersection. **SO**.

> *Road enters on right.*

(13.2 km) ▲ 15.5 km

36.2 km T intersection. **TR** onto Omeo Hwy.

(2.2 km) Opp. dir. s'post: The Hollow Way. ▲ 2.3 km

38.4 km Snowy Creek. Cross bridge.

(0.1 km) ▲ 0.1 km

38.5 km The Walnuts Picnic Area on right.

> *Barbecues, picnic tables, water.*

0.0 km Zero trip meter at picnic area. **SO**.

(5.2 km) ▲ 0.0 km
▲ 89.5 km

5.2 km Bitumen.

(17.9 km) Gravel. ▲ 84.3 km

23.1 km Gravel.

> *Route passes through Mt Wills Historic Area.*

(26.0 km) Bitumen. ▲ 66.4 km

49.1 km Mitta Mitta/Big River. Cross bridge onto bitumen.

(4.1 km) Gravel. ▲ 40.4 km

53.2 km Intersection. **SO**.

> *Falls Creek/Mt Beauty off to right.*

(1.9 km) ▲ 36.3 km

55.1 km Gravel.

(7.2 km) Bitumen. ▲ 34.4 km

62.3 km Bundara River. Cross bridge.

(1.8 km) ▲ 27.2 km

64.1 km Anglers Rest Camping and Picnic Area. **SO**.

> *Barbecues, toilets, picnic tables, water.*

(0.5 km) ▲ 25.4 km

64.6 km Cobungra River. Cross bridge.

(17.8 km) ▲ 24.9 km

82.4 km Bitumen.

(7.1 km) Gravel. ▲ 7.1 km

The Kiewa River near Tawonga

89.5 km S'post: Benambra.

> *Omeo 4 km straight ahead. Bushwalking, canoeing, river swimming, fishing, gold prospecting. Oriental Claims Historic Area.*

Opp. dir. s'post: Tallangatta

0.0 km Zero trip meter at above s'post. **TL**.

(18.8 km) ▲ 0.0 km
▲ 66.2 km

18.8 km In Benambra, s'post: Foster St. **TR**.

> **PD** *General store. Corryong straight ahead. Next petrol Dalgety (207 km); next diesel Cooma (259 km).*

(3.0 km) Opp. dir. s'post: Omeo. ▲ 47.4 km

21.8 km Intersection. **KL**.

(6.7 km) ▲ 44.4 km

28.5 km Gravel.

(6.2 km) Bitumen. ▲ 37.7 km

34.7 km S'post: Limestone Rd. **KR**.

(7.3 km) Opp. dir. s'post: Benambra Rd. ▲ 31.5 km

42.0 km S'post: Limestone Rd. **SO**.

> *Mt Misery Rd on left.*

(10.6 km) ▲ 24.2 km

52.6 km Sign: Alpine National Park. **SO**.

(13.6 km) ▲ 13.6 km

66.2 km Native Dog Flat Camping Area, Buchan River.

> *Numerous campsites; fresh water; no other facilities.*

REVERSE DIRECTIONS START ▲ 0.0 km

NATIVE DOG FLAT
«»
COOMA

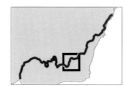

START POINT
Map page 60, G7.

TOTAL KM 211.
UNSEALED KM 122.
DEGREE OF DIFFICULTY Easy.
DRIVING TIME 5 hours.
LONGEST DISTANCE NO FUEL Next diesel Cooma (211 km from Native Dog Flat); next petrol Dalgety (160 km).
TOPOGRAPHIC MAPS Auslig 1:250 000 series: *Tallangatta*; *Bega*.
LOCAL/SPECIALITY MAPS DCE: *Victoria's Alpine Area*; Auslig Ausmap series: *Australian Alps National Parks Tourist Map*; CMA: *Snowy Kosciusko*.
OTHER USEFUL INFORMATION Cooma-Monaro and Snowy River councils booklet: *Snowy Mountains: Monaro Country*; Forestry Commission information sheet: *Camping and Recreation in State Forests*; NSW NPWS information sheet: *Kosciusko National Park – Bushwalking and Camping*.

DESCRIPTION Although this is an easy section in that it requires no true four-wheel driving, conditions can be difficult and demanding – Barry Way, for instance, is narrow, twisting, steep and often rough, and can be very slippery after rain. Leaving Native Dog Flat, Black Mountain Road takes you through the historic *Suggan Buggan* area, where you can camp or picnic, to the state border; here also there are camping grounds.

In New South Wales, the alpine country east of Mt Kosciusko is magnificent and for some distance the route follows the extraordinarily beautiful *Snowy River*; on the banks there are a number of excellent campsites. The plotted route just bypasses Jindabyne, in the heart of the Snowy Mountains and an excellent stopping place for

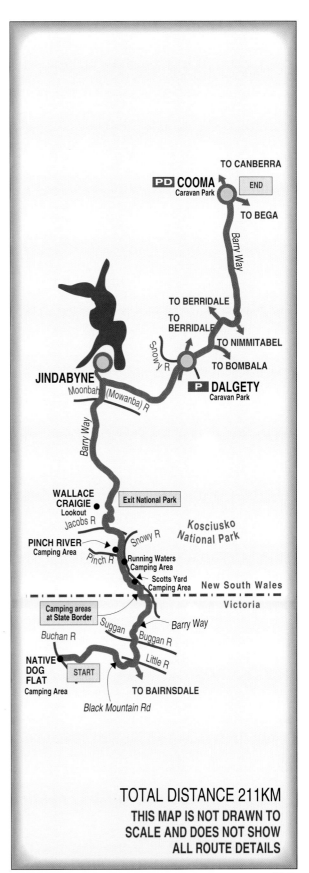

TOTAL DISTANCE 211KM
THIS MAP IS NOT DRAWN TO SCALE AND DOES NOT SHOW ALL ROUTE DETAILS

455

Lake Jindabyne

trout fishermen and those who practise water sports. Between Jindabyne and Cooma there is some amazing high-plains grazing country to be seen, and another opportunity to camp at *Dalgety*. The section ends at Cooma, perhaps most closely associated with the Snowy Mountains Scheme; particularly striking is the International Avenue of Flags in Centennial Park, created as a lasting memorial to the men and women from many countries who worked to construct the nation's greatest engineering achievement.

WARNINGS ▶ Observe weather warnings given in first section. ▶ Watch for logging trucks in state forests. Camping may be restricted in certain areas and at certain times. Contact NSW Forestry Commission office, 24 Berry Street, PO Box 25, Nowra NSW 2541; tel. (044) 21 8833.

BOOKINGS AND PERMITS ▶ No permits required to traverse national park. For information, contact Jindabyne Information Centre, PO Box 215, Jindabyne NSW 2627; tel. (064) 56 2444. ▶ For local information, contact Cooma Tourist Information Centre, 119 Sharp Street, Cooma NSW 2630; tel. (064) 50 1742.

ROUTE DIRECTIONS

0.0 km Zero trip meter at Buchan River crossing, Native Dog Flat, heading east along Black Mountain Rd.
(30.4 km) ▲ 96.8 km
30.4 km S'post: Jindabyne. **TL** onto Barry Way.

> *Bairnsdale off to right.*

(0.3 km) Opp. dir. s'post: Benambra. ▲ 66.4 km
30.7 km Little River. Cross bridge.
(11.7 km) ▲ 66.1 km
42.4 km Suggan Buggan River. Cross bridge.

> *Camping area on left. Barbecues, toilets, picnic tables, water. Historic site.*

(19.3 km) ▲ 54.4 km
61.7 km New South Wales border.

> *Sign: Kosciusko National Park. Picnic and camping area. Barbecues, toilets, picnic tables, water from Snowy River.*

(3.1 km) ▲ 35.1 km

456

Looking towards Mt Kosciusko

64.8 km Scott's Yard Camping and Picnic Area. **SO**.

All camping and picnic areas on the route through Kosciusko National Park have barbecues, toilets, picnic tables and water.

(7.8 km) ▲ 32.0 km

72.6 km Running Waters Camping and Picnic Area. **SO**.

Route passes between Byadbo and Pilot wilderness areas.

(2.6 km) ▲ 24.2 km

75.2 km Pinch River. Cross bridge.

Pinch River Camping and Picnic Area.

(5.2 km) ▲ 21.6 km

80.4 km Halfway Flat Picnic Area. **SO**.
(1.6 km) ▲ 16.4 km

82.0 km Jacobs River Camping and Picnic Area. **SO**
(2.9 km) ▲ 14.8 km

84.9 km Jacobs River. Cross bridge.
(9.5 km) ▲ 11.9 km

94.4 km Wallace Craigie Lookout on left. **SO**.
(2.4 km) ▲ 2.4 km

96.8 km National park boundary.

Opp. dir. sign: Kosciusko National Park.

0.0 km Zero trip meter at boundary. **SO**.
(11.1 km) ▲ 0.0 km
▲ 114.5 km

11.1 km Bitumen.
(18.7 km) Gravel. ▲ 103.4 km

29.8 km Moonbah (Mowamba) River. Cross bridge.
(3.7 km) ▲ 84.7 km

33.5 km S'post: Dalgety. **TR**.

Jindabyne straight ahead. Trout fishing, boating, water skiing on Lake Jindabyne.

(6.7 km) Opp. dir. s'post: Buchan. ▲ 81.0 km

40.2 km Gravel.
(2.8 km) Bitumen. ▲ 74.3 km

43.0 km Bitumen.
(19.5 km) Gravel. ▲ 71.5 km

62.5 km Intersection. **SO**.

Road enters on right.

(0.2 km) Opp. dir. s'post: Jindabyne. ▲ 52.0 km

62.7 km Snowy River. Cross bridge.
(0.2 km) ▲ 51.8 km

62.9 km In Dalgety, s'post: Berry Farm. **TL**.

P *General store. Caravan park, camping.*

(0.3 km) Opp. dir. s'post: Jindabyne. ▲ 51.6 km

63.2 km S'post: Bombala. **TR**.

Berridale straight ahead.

(6.6 km) Opp. dir. s'post: Jimenbuen. ▲ 51.3 km

69.8 km S'post: Bobundara. **TL** onto gravel.

Bombala straight ahead.

(6.9 km) Bitumen. Opp. dir. s'post: Dalgety. ▲44.7 km

76.7 km T intersection. S'post: Bobundara. **TR**.

Berridale off to left.

(4.8 km) ▲ 37.8 km

81.5 km S'post: Cooma. **SO** onto bitumen.

Nimmitabel off to right.

(32.0 km) Gravel. Opp. dir. s'post: Berridale. ▲33.0 km

113.5 km S'post: To Monaro Hwy. **TL** into Cooma.

Bega off to right.

(0.9 km) Opp. dir. s'post: Bobundara. ▲ 1.0 km

114.4 km Roundabout. **SO**.
(0.1 km) ▲ 0.1 km

114.5 km S'post: Monaro Hwy. **TR** into Cooma town centre.

PD *Jindabyne off to left. Canberra off to right. Centre for Snowy Mountains Scheme. Travellers' Rest Pioneer Museum, Southern Cloud Memorial, International Avenue of Flags, Time Walk, Snowy Alpine Nature and Deer Park, many National Trust buildings.*

REVERSE DIRECTIONS START ▲ 0.0 km

COOMA
«»
SYDNEY

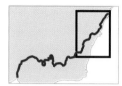

START POINT
Map page 10, D9.

TOTAL KM 430.
UNSEALED KM 175.
DEGREE OF DIFFICULTY Easy.
DRIVING TIME 6 hours (Cooma to Nowra).
LONGEST DISTANCE NO FUEL 143 km (Cooma to Braidwood).
TOPOGRAPHIC MAPS Auslig 1:250 000 series: *Bega*; *Canberra*; *Ulladulla*; *Wollongong*.
LOCAL/SPECIALITY MAPS CMA: *A Touring Map of the South Coast Area in New South Wales*; Forestry Commission of New South Wales: *Nowra State Forests*; Broadbent Johns: *Weekend Sydney Maps* (Nowra–Sydney section).
OTHER USEFUL INFORMATION Shoalhaven City Council booklet: *Shoalhaven*; Cooma-Monara and Snowy River councils booklet: *Snowy Mountains: Monaro Country*; NSW Forestry Commission information sheet: *Camping and Recreation in State Forests*; NSW NPWS information sheets: *Morton National Park Visitor Guide* and *Camping Information*.

DESCRIPTION This is an easy and relaxing trip off the usual tourist route; it runs through rolling pasture land and mountain scenery to the Pacific coast. Near Countegany, just east of Numeralla, you pass the road to the *Cascades*; this is a four-wheel drive track only and leads to a campsite and picnic area. Settlements along the route are rare, but do stop at Braidwood, on Jillamatong Creek. Once principal town of the southern goldfields, Braidwood echoes the early days of gold mining and of bushranging in the 1860s; the National Trust has classified the entire centre of the town. Before reaching Braidwood the route passes close by Deua

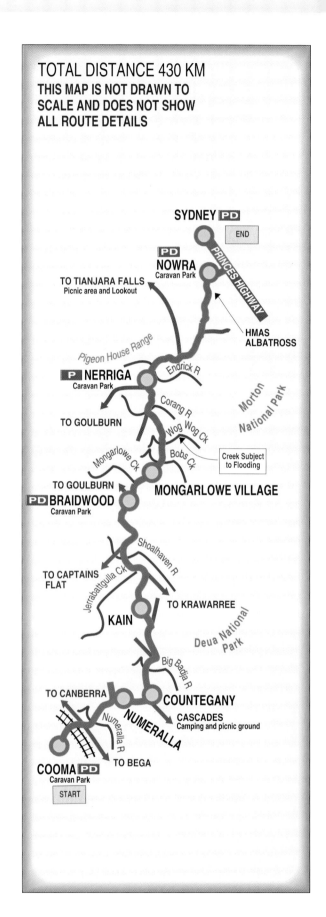

TOTAL DISTANCE 430 KM
THIS MAP IS NOT DRAWN TO
SCALE AND DOES NOT SHOW
ALL ROUTE DETAILS

National Park, a wild and scenic region; near the Braidwood road it shows unusual features formed by a belt of limestone: rocky outcrops, cave systems and the striking Big Hole. It is a place for remote bushwalking and bush camping; there are no facilities. From Nerriga you cross the Endrick River and briefly enter Morton National Park along Pigeon House Range and past the turnoff to Tianjara Falls. This is a landscape of colourful cliffs and cataracts falling to forested valleys; bush camping and walking will tempt the enthusiast, with trails – many of them marked – of varying difficulty.

Of particular interest as you approach Nowra is Australia's only naval air station, HMAS *Albatross*, where the Naval Aviation Museum is open to visitors. Nowra (incidentally the home of the first Melbourne Cup winner, Archer) is the centre of the Shoalhaven district and another excellent place for fishing and water sports; visit Nowra Animal Park, set in rainforest, and Hanging Rock lookout. The trip ends with a winding drive along the Princes Highway between the southern highlands and the sea up the beautiful Illawarra coast to Sydney.

WARNINGS ▶ Watch for logging trucks in state forests. Camping may be restricted in certain areas and at certain times; contact NSW Forestry Commission office, 24 Berry Street, PO Box 25, Nowra NSW 2541; tel. (044) 21 8833.

BOOKINGS AND PERMITS ▶ For touring information contact Braidwood Tourist Information Centre, 186 Wallace Street, Braidwood NSW 2622; tel. (048) 42 2310; Shoalhaven City Tourist Centre, 254 Princes Highway, Bomaderry NSW 2541; tel. (044) 21 0778. ▶ NPWS regional offices: for Deua National Park, PO Box 282, Narooma NSW 2546; tel. (044) 76 2888; for Morton National Park, 24 Berry Street, PO Box 707, Nowra NSW 2541; tel. (044) 21 9969.

ROUTE DIRECTIONS

0.0 km Zero trip meter in Cooma at Bombala and Sharp streets intersection. S'post: Monaro Hwy/Canberra. **SO** along Sharp Street.
(0.6 km) ▲ 34.8 km

0.6 km S'post: Bradley St. **TR**.
(0.6 km) ▲ 34.2 km

1.2 km S'post: Polo Flat/Numeralla. **TR** onto Yareen Rd.

| *Canberra straight ahead.* |

(0.1 km) ▲ 33.6 km

1.3 km Cross railway line.
(1.5 km) ▲ 33.5 km

2.8 km Crossroads. S'post: Numeralla. **SO**.

| *Canberra off to left. Bega off to right.* |

(19.5 km) Opp. dir. s'post: Cooma. ▲ 32.0 km

22.3 km Numeralla River. Cross bridge. Continue through Numeralla.
(0.3 km) ▲ 12.5 km

22.6 km S'post: Countegany. **SO**.

| *Peakview off to left.* |

(6.4 km) ▲ 12.2 km

29.0 km Gravel.
(5.8 km) Bitumen. ▲ 5.8 km

34.8 km Intersection.

| *Cascades off to right. From intersection take following route, 4WD only. At 3.2 km, enter Badja State Forest. At 4.5 km, turn right onto Tuross River road. At 5.9 km and 10.4 km, s'posts to Cascades; turn right at each one. It is then 2.5 km to picnic and camping area.* |

0.0 km Zero trip meter at above intersection. **SO**.
(6.1 km) ▲ 0.0 km
▲ 108.3 km

6.1 km Big Badja River. Cross bridge.
(4.6 km) ▲ 102.2 km

10.7 km Intersection. S'post: Braidwood. **KR**.
(30.9 km) Opp. dir. s'post: Cooma. ▲ 97.6 km

41.6 km Bitumen.
(2.2 km) Gravel. ▲ 66.7 km

43.8 km Gravel.
(8.3 km) Bitumen. s 64.5 km

52.1 km Bitumen.
(4.2 km) Gravel. ▲ 56.2 km

56.3 km S'post: Kain. **TL** onto gravel.
(9.3 km) Bitumen. ▲ 52.0 km

65.6 km Jerrabattgulla Creek. Cross causeway.
(6.3 km) ▲ 42.7 km

71.9 km Jerrabattgulla Creek. Cross bridge.
(5.3 km) ▲ 36.4 km

77.2 km T intersection. **TL** onto bitumen.

| *Krawarree off to right.* |

(0.2 km) Gravel. Opp. dir. s'post: Jerrabattgulla. ▲ 31.1 km

77.4 km Jerrabattgulla Creek. Cross bridge.
(6.2 km) ▲ 30.9 km

83.6 km S'post: Braidwood. **SO** onto gravel.

459

| Captains Flat off to left. |

(1.8 km) — Bitumen. ▲ 24.7 km
85.4 km Bitumen.
(0.2 km) — Gravel. ▲ 22.9 km
85.6 km Shoalhaven River. Cross bridge.
(1.7 km) — ▲ 22.7 km
87.3 km Gravel.
(1.3 km) — Bitumen. ▲ 21.0 km
88.6 km Bitumen.
(17.1 km) — Gravel. ▲ 19.7 km
105.7 km S'post: Braidwood. **TL**.

| Araluen off to right. |

(1.6 km) — Opp. dir. s'post: Captains Flat/Cooma. ▲ 2.6 km
107.3 km S'post: Braidwood. **TR** across creek.
(0.3 km) — ▲ 1.0 km
107.6 km S'post: Goulburn. **TL** into Braidwood.
(0.3 km) — ▲ 0.7 km
107.9 km Crossroads. S'post: Goulburn. **SO**.

| Batemans Bay off to right. |

(0.4 km) — ▲ 0.4 km
108.3 km Braidwood town centre, adjacent to post office.

| **PD** Supplies, caravan park. Historic town; former gold-mining centre. Bushwalking, trout fishing. Braidwood Trout Hatchery. |

0.0 km Zero trip meter at s'post: Mongarlowe, 50 m from post office. **TR** into Wilson St.
(13.4 km) — ▲ 0.0 km
— ▲ 127.6 km
13.4 km Mongarlowe River. Cross bridge.
(0.1 km) — ▲ 114.2 km
13.5 km Mongarlowe village. S'post: Nerriga. **SO**.
(0.8 km) — Opp. dir. s'post: Braidwood. ▲ 114.1 km
14.3 km Gravel.
(6.5 km) — Bitumen. ▲ 113.3 km
20.8 km Bobs Creek. Cross causeway.
(18.9 km) — ▲ 106.8 km
39.7 km Cross Wog Wog Creek.

| Sign: subject to flooding. |

(2.4 km) — ▲ 87.9 km
42.1 km T intersection. **TR**.
(4.5 km) — Opp. dir. s'post: Mongarlowe. ▲ 85.5 km
46.6 km Corang River. Cross bridge.
(8.1 km) — ▲ 81.0 km
54.7 km Bitumen.
(0.2 km) — Gravel. ▲ 72.9 km

54.9 km S'post: Nerriga. **SO**.

| Goulburn off to left. |

(3.7 km) — Opp. dir. s'post: Braidwood. ▲ 72.7 km
58.6 km Nerriga town centre, adjacent to general store. **SO**.

| **P** Supplies, caravan park. |

(0.1 km) — ▲ 69.0 km
58.7 km Gravel.
(4.4 km) — Bitumen. ▲ 68.9 km
63.1 km Endrick River. Cross bridge.
(24.3 km) — ▲ 64.5 km
87.4 km Creek. Cross bridge.
(0.1 km) — ▲ 40.2 km
87.5 km Tianjara Falls off to left. **SO**.

| Lookout and picnic area; barbecues. Great views of Morton National Park. |

(16.2 km) — ▲ 40.1 km
103.7 km S'post: Nowra. **TL**.

| Huskisson straight ahead. |

(13.4 km) — Opp. dir. s'post: Braidwood. ▲ 23.9 km
117.1 km Bitumen.

| Naval air station on right. Aviation Museum. |

(3.1 km) — Gravel. ▲ 10.5 km
120.2 km T intersection. **TL**.
(7.0 km) — ▲ 7.4 km
127.2 km Roundabout in Nowra. **SO** along Kalandar Rd.
(0.4 km) — ▲ 0.4 km
127.6 km Intersection. S'post: Nowra. **TL** onto Princes Hwy, to Nowra town centre.

| **PD** Caravan park. Shoalhaven Shire centre. Fishing, water sports. Hanging Rock lookout; Nowra Animal Park. Batemans Bay off to right. |

Follow the Princes Hwy to Sydney (approx. 159 km) to pick up route directions for the next trek (Sydney to Brisbane).

REVERSE DIRECTIONS START ▲ 0.0 km

THE DESERT TREKS

The desert treks may be undertaken individually or linked together. Each has its own sketch map, detailed route directions and camping and permits information, and is cross referenced to the Australia-wide map coverage section of the book.

THE DESERT TREKS

BIRDSVILLE «» MT DARE	770 km	
MT DARE «» ALICE SPRINGS	438 km	
ALICE SPRINGS «» PALM VALLEY	306 km	
ALICE SPRINGS «» HALLS CREEK	1097 km	
WILUNA «» ULURU	1410 km	
MARLA «» MARREE	621 km	
MARREE «» BIRDSVILLE	519 km	
BIRDSVILLE «» INNAMINCKA	419 km	
INNAMINCKA «» TIBOOBURRA	362 km	

The desert treks take you through a wide range of Australia's central desert and semi-desert regions, with degrees of difficulty ranging from easy to extreme. Although most sections of the tracks are now well-established motor-vehicle routes, others are accessible to four-wheel drive vehicles only. Most tracks pass through the uniquely harsh environment of Australia's outback and should be approached with extreme caution and respect; read all route directions carefully. Study the road-map section of the book to plan your access to the trek start points. Each trek may be undertaken individually, as part of other desert treks, or as part of other treks and tours. All information relevant to a specific desert trek is contained within that trek.

Our first trek leaves from the tiny outback town of Birdsville. Take the Birdsville Outside Track and the Rig Road through the red sands of the Simpson Desert to Witjira National Park and Mt Dare Homestead, a stopover point near the South Australian–Northern Territory border. The next trek is along the Old Andado Track through the red dunes, forest scrub, clay pans and sandstone ranges between Mt Dare and Alice Springs, the heart of the Red Centre.

Alice Springs to Palm Valley is an easy return trip through the beautiful MacDonnell Ranges to Finke Gorge National Park where the rare palm trees and Finke River landforms are some of Australia's most ancient natural attractions.

Red sand dunes of the Simpson Desert

It is a lengthy and moderately difficult but strikingly beautiful journey through the Tanami Desert from Alice Springs to Halls Creek via the Tanami Track, passing through the MacDonnells and red-desert scrub, with an enjoyable detour to Wolfe Creek Crater National Park on the other side of the Northern Territory–Western Australia border.

We chose not to tackle the Canning Stock Route, a 1750-kilometre journey from Halls Creek to Wiluna through the inhospitable red sand-dune country of the Great Sandy, Little Sandy and Gibson deserts. It was last used by drovers in 1958 but is becoming increasingly popular with four-wheel drive enthusiasts. You should not attempt it alone. For the Canning Stock Route, equip yourself and your party extremely well for desert travel, allow a travelling time of 2 weeks at a leisurely pace, and register your intended route with Halls Creek and Wiluna police stations.

Instead, to link up with Wiluna and our next trek, take the much less direct but infinitely easier Great Northern Highway from Halls Creek to Meekatharra, then head east.

The aptly named Gunbarrel Highway bisects the Gibson and Great Sandy deserts on its eastward path from Wiluna to Uluru (Ayers Rock), the world's largest monolith. This long stretch requires total self-sufficiency and careful preparation, but once committed to it you will find the desert landscape surprisingly beautiful and diverse. The last section via the Laverton–Warburton Road to Uluru National Park is much less of a challenge.

Route directions for the easy trek along the Oodnadatta Track commence at Marla and end at Marree, both in South Australia. To link up with Marla from Uluru, take the Lasseter Highway east, then the Stuart Highway south; see the relevant road map for northern South Australia. The relatively busy Oodnadatta Track closely follows the old Ghan railway line, named at the turn of the

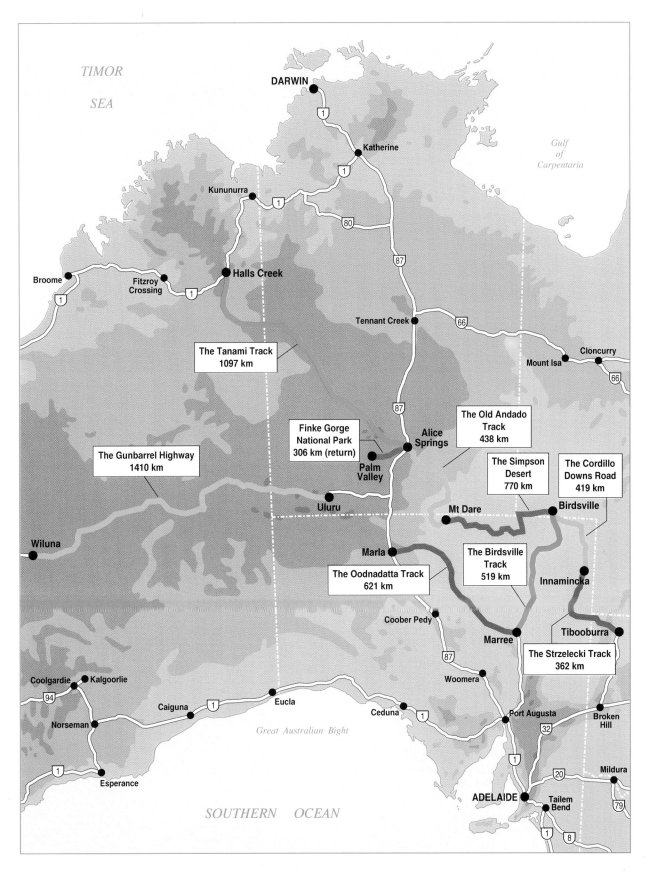

ESSENTIAL ADVICE ON DESERT CROSSINGS

▶ Learn about the natural environment of the deserts you plan to trek though, in order to better understand them. When appropriate in an individual trek we include relevant addresses and telephone numbers for the following conservation authorities: Queensland National Parks and Wildlife Service (QNPWS); South Australian National Parks and Wildlife Service (SANPWS); Australian National Parks and Wildlife Service (ANPWS); Conservation Commission of the Northern Territory (CCNT); CALM (Conservation and Land Management).

▶ Travel only in the cooler months April–September, never the summer months October–March when desert temperatures can soar above 50 degrees Celsius.

▶ Vehicles approaching from opposite directions can be obscured by high sand dunes. Equip your vehicle, or the lead vehicle in your convoy, with a long antenna, preferably with a flag at the top, in order to make sure the vehicle is visible as it approaches the top of a dune.

▶ Before departure, check road and track conditions. See **Warnings** in individual treks for contacts.

▶ Before departure, advise a responsible person of your intended route and, while travelling, regularly inform him/her of your whereabouts. Police stations at the start/end points of trek routes are the best contacts.

▶ In desert conditions, vehicles use about 30 per cent more fuel. Remember this when estimating your fuel requirements, and carry an additional 20 litres per vehicle as a safeguard. Check distances between fuel stops in individual treks.

▶ Carry at least 2 spare wheels and tyres, as well as 2 spare tubes and a puncture-repair kit. Practise how to remove an old tyre from the rim and replace it with a new one. Lower tyre pressures to about 20 psi, perhaps lower, when traversing very soft sand dunes, but run normal pressures until low pressures can no longer be avoided. Increase tyre pressures again as soon as possible.

▶ Carry at least 5 litres of drinking water per person for each day of travel: dehydration can cause disorientation, confusion and panic, which are very dangerous in remote areas. If your vehicle has the capacity, carry an additional 10–12 litres per person per day for bathing, cooking, and washing clothes and dishes. Keep in mind that it is possible to go for three days without bathing and that many foods can be prepared without water. Set aside a separate quantity of water equivalent to the capacity of the engine cooling system in case a leak caused by damage to the radiator or radiator hose occurs. Carry reserve supplies of water in case you experience unexpected delays due to storm activity, dust storms, vehicle breakdowns, a wrong turn, or poor road conditions.

▶ Carry adequate warm clothing for very cold desert nights.

▶ Whenever possible, stay at the designated campsites in national parks or along the track, or in caravan parks; otherwise set up alongside the track. Most towns and settlements included in the route directions have alternative forms of accommodation.

▶ Do not use soap or detergents in water sources, particularly ancient artesian bores and mound springs that are home to rare aquatic life. Use sand instead of detergent to wash dishes. Do not throw rubbish or food scraps into creeks, rivers or lakes.

▶ In areas without toilets, bury your toilet wastes in a 15-centimetre hole at least 100 metres away from camp and any water.

▶ Use bins or tips if provided, do not bury rubbish, and take all non-combustible rubbish away with you when leaving campsites.

▶ Dead wood is in short supply in desert regions and is also home to many small desert creatures; do not collect it for campfire fuel. Preferably bring your portable gas stove, and use only established barbecues and fireplaces.

▶ Do not take animals, pets or firearms into national parks and nature reserves, and beware wildlife crossing tracks.

▶ Many desert areas are part of traditional Aboriginal trade and travel routes or are designated Aboriginal lands. Never touch, damage or remove anything you find at Aboriginal sites, and treat Aboriginal communities with respect. See individual treks for information about permits required to visit Aboriginal lands.

▶ For all information about tours, attractions and accommodation see **Bookings and Permits** in individual treks or contact capital-city travel centres.

Animal bones in the Simpson Desert

Enjoying a dip in Dalhousie Springs

century in honour of the region's large population of Afghan cameleers. Many old railway ruins and ancient mound springs make this trek an historical adventure.

The Birdsville Track from Marree to Birdsville follows the old and infamous stock route that is nowadays an easy journey taking in old homesteads, artesian bores and the Sturt Stony Desert. When the Birdsville Inside Track branches off, take the easier Outside Track, also plotted in the Birdsville to Mt Dare trek.

The trek from Birdsville to Innamincka via the Cordillo Downs Road takes you through some interesting historical country made famous by explorers such as Sturt, Burke and Wills. You see evidence of their early and difficult explorations as you traverse the Sturt Stony Desert and the naturally irrigated pasturelands known as channel country.

Between Innamincka and Tibooburra we take the old Strzelecki Track stock route south through the orange and red sands of the Strzelecki Desert, then turn east along the Cameron Corner Road to Sturt National Park and Tibooburra in the corner country of north-western New South Wales.

COMMUNICATIONS

Some form of communication is absolutely essential in remote desert regions. Arrange for a top supplier and installer to equip your vehicle with a radio transceiver, and carry a high-frequency (HF) single sideband radio to contact the network of Royal Flying Doctor Service (RFDS) bases all around Australia and the Australia-wide Australian and Overseas Telecommunications Corporation (AOTC) Radphone network.

For information about radio operator's licences and appropriate radio bases and their frequencies, contact your local office of the Commonwealth Department of Transport and Communications. It has offices in every state capital which are listed in the front of the White Pages of the telephone directory.

ROYAL FLYING DOCTOR SERVICE

For information about all the services offered by the RFDS, contact the Australian Council of the Royal Flying Doctor Service of Australia, Level 5, 15-17 Young Street, NSW 2000; telephone (02) 241 2411.

Before you depart, contact the appropriate RFDS office to register your name, home or base address and radio call sign with them. Take the RFDS guide that sets out all the bases, radio call signs and broadcast frequencies.

In an emergency requiring RFDS assistance it will be necessary for service staff to know exactly where you are. In some cases the RFDS will direct you to the nearest airstrip for evacuation, if an aircraft is needed. The RFDS may arrange a helicopter charter if it is impossible for you to reach an airstrip. In this case, staff have to be able to locate you, so give your position as precisely as you can and consider lighting an oily fire, which will give off dense black smoke, to help them find you. See individual trek **Warnings** for the RFDS bases closest to the start and end point of each trek.

Portable transceiver sets are available for hire from the RFDS bases at Charleville, Jandakot and Broken Hill. These sets include an emergency call button which automatically transmits an emergency signal to RFDS bases. The addresses and telephone numbers of these bases are: Old Cunnamulla Road, Charleville QLD 4470; (076) 54 1233; 3 Eagle Drive, Jandakot Airport WA 6164; (09) 332 7733; Airport, Broken Hill NSW 2880; (080) 88 0777.

THE SIMPSON DESERT
BIRDSVILLE
«»
MT DARE

START POINT
Map page 22, D2.

TOTAL KM 770.
UNSEALED KM 770.
DEGREE OF DIFFICULTY Extreme.
DRIVING TIME 3 or 4 days.
LONGEST DISTANCE NO FUEL 770 km (Birdsville to Mt Dare Homestead).
TOPOGRAPHIC MAPS Auslig 1:250 000 series: *Birdsville*; *Panda Panda*; *Pollyanna*; *Dalhousie*. See also 1:100 000 series.
LOCAL/SPECIALITY MAPS Westprint Heritage map: *Dalhousie and Simpson Desert*; Sunmap: *Outback Queensland*.
OTHER USEFUL INFORMATION SANPWS brochure: *Parks of the Far North of South Australia*; Northern Territory Tourist Commission booklet: *Tracks of Australia's Northern Territory: a Guide for Four Wheel Drivers*; Gregorys Consumer Guide: *4WD Great Treks*; Mt Dare Information Centre brochure: *Mount Dare Homestead, Witjira National Park, SA* and information sheet: *Mount Dare Homestead: For Aircraft Information.*

DESCRIPTION This trek is rated extremely difficult because of the remoteness of the Simpson Desert region, but it is possible to complete it without mishap if you exercise reasonable skill and consideration; see *Warnings* and *Essential Advice on Desert Crossings* in the introduction to the desert treks.

The direction of our chosen route is east–west, more difficult than west–east due to the steeper sand dunes on the eastern approach. We do, however, use the easiest of all tracks: the Birdsville Outside Track and the Rig Road. The Rig Road is about 250 kilometres longer than the more difficult French Line, but both routes include most of the desert's 1300 sand-dune crossings ranging from easy to difficult. Track conditions always dictate which route you will take: if the Rig Road is used you will also have to use either the Inside or Outside Birdsville track, depending on availability, and following rains in the north the French Line may be blocked by water which floods Eyre Creek west of Birdsville. Sometimes weather conditions make crossing impossible from any direction.

Birdsville is a real outback town that was a thriving settlement at the turn of the century until a toll on cattle crossing the nearby border was abolished after Federation in 1901. Every August–September its famous hotel becomes the centre of the Birdsville Race Carnival celebrations when the town's population swells from under 200 to about 3000. Here at the eastern end of the trek you can camp in the caravan park; at the western end there are campsites in Witjira National Park, both at *Dalhousie Springs,* a series of therapeutic mound springs in a desert oasis, and in bush settings around *Mt Dare Homestead,* an original outback homestead. In the Simpson Desert there are no designated campsites but you can set up anywhere at the side of the track.

WARNINGS ▶ Preferably travel in convoy of 2, 3 or 4 vehicles. ▶ Don't cross sand dunes 'blind'. Walk ahead and survey the terrain. ▶ Before departure ring Birdsville police, (0071) 78 220, to let them know your intended route, and during trek regularly inform them of your whereabouts. ▶ If travelling east–west, before departure ring Birdsville police to check condition and availability of tracks; if travelling west–east contact Alice Springs Royal Flying Doctor Service, Stuart Terrace, Alice Springs NT 0870; tel. (089) 52 5355 and ask for Mt Dare Homestead (7STW), or contact Hamilton Station, Alice Springs NT 0870; tel. (089) 56 8530. ▶ Use normal tyre pressures until first sequence of soft-sand dunes which require lowering of pressures to about 20 psi. ▶ At entrance to Witjira National Park track crosses large salt pan that may be boggy after rain. ▶ Dispose of rubbish at dumps near Birdsville and Dalhousie Springs. ▶ Do not use soap or detergents at Dalhousie Springs waters. ▶ Beware camels crossing tracks. ▶ For emergency help contact RFDS base at Charleville, (076) 54 1233, or Port Augusta, (086) 42 2044.

BOOKINGS AND PERMITS ▶ Necessary to advise QNPWS of intention to use Queensland section of Simpson Desert National Park. Contact QNPWS, 160 Ann Street, Brisbane 4000; tel. (07) 227 8185. ▶ Necessary to obtain Desert Parks Pass to use South Australian

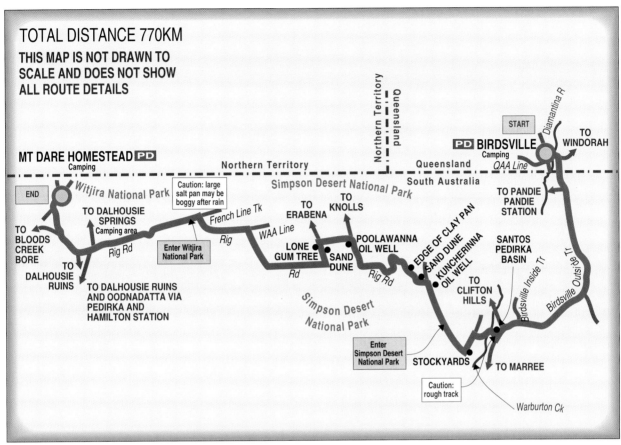

TOTAL DISTANCE 770KM
THIS MAP IS NOT DRAWN TO
SCALE AND DOES NOT SHOW
ALL ROUTE DETAILS

section of park. Fee applicable, pass valid for one year and entitles holder to traverse and camp in all South Australian desert parks. Contact South Australian Department of Environment and Planning, Information Centre, 55 Grenfell Street, Adelaide 5000; tel. (08) 207 2300, or SANPWS Far North Region Office, 60 Elder Terrace, Hawker SA 5434; tel. (086) 48 4244. ▶ For accommodation in Birdsville Hotel book in advance, (076) 56 3244. ▶ For homestead accommodation at Mt Dare Homestead book in advance by writing to Mt Dare Homestead, Far North South Australia, PMB Alice Springs NT 0872 or ring telephone number in *Warnings.*

ROUTE DIRECTIONS

0.0 km   Zero trip meter in Birdsville, adjacent to Birdsville Hotel. **SO** onto Birdsville Developmental Rd, heading east.

> **PD** *Supplies, caravan park. Mechanical repairs, meals, accom., post agency, medical centre. Hot artesian-bore water. Generator electricity. Next fuel Mt Dare Homestead (770 km).*

(2.7 km)   ▲ 233.3 km

2.7 km   Diamantina River crossing. **SO.**
(1.4 km)   ▲ 230.6 km
4.1 km   Intersection. S'post: Marree. **TR.**

> *Windorah straight ahead.*

(9.3 km)   Opp. dir. s'post: Birdsville. ▲ 229.2 km
13.4 km   Queensland–South Australian border. **SO.**
(15.2 km)   ▲ 219.9 km
28.6 km   Intersection. **SO.**

> *Pandie Pandie Homestead off to right.*

(94.5 km)   ▲ 204.7 km
123.1 km   Intersection. **SO.**

> *Track on left.*

(58.4 km)   ▲ 110.2 km
181.5 km   Intersection. **SO.**

> *Junction of Inside Track on right.*

(13.8 km)   ▲ 51.8 km
195.3 km   Intersection. Clifton Hills Homestead on right. **SO.**

Clifton Hills Station off to right. Pedirka Basin straight ahead.

(11.0 km) ▲ 38.0 km

206.3 km Intersection. S'post: Santos Pedirka Basin. **TR**.

Track deteriorates to rough quality for next 26 km through Clifton Hills Station. Marree straight ahead.

(8.9 km) ▲ 27.0 km

215.2 km Warburton Creek crossing. **SO**.

Creek bed usually dry.

(18.1 km) ▲ 18.1 km

233.3 km T intersection.

0.0 km Zero trip meter at above T intersection. **TL**.

(19.5 km) ▲ 0.0 km
▲ 225.9 km

19.5 km Intersection. Stockyards on left. **SO**.

(0.5 km) ▲ 206.4 km

20.0 km Road begins to bear right heading north west. **SO**.

(58.5 km) ▲ 205.9 km

78.5 km Sign: Kuncherinna. **SO**.

(0.7 km) ▲ 147.4 km

79.2 km Intersection. **KL** onto Rig Rd and immediately cross sand dune.

(9.4 km) ▲ 146.7 km

88.6 km **KR** heading north along eastern edge of clay pan.

(92.8 km) ▲ 137.3 km

181.4km Intersection. Poolawanna Oil Well on left. **SO**.

(4.2 km) ▲ 44.5 km

185.6 km Intersection. Homemade sign: Rig Rd.

Homemade sign: Line to Knolls on right.

(33.8 km) ▲ 40.3 km

219.4 km Intersection. **SO**.

Erabena Track on right.

(6.5 km) ▲ 6.5 km

225.9 km Lone Gum Tree on right.

The Simpson Desert's only eucalypt.

0.0 km Zero trip meter at above point. **SO** along Rig Rd.

(11.1 km) ▲ 0.0 km
▲ 142.6 km

11.1 km Track bears right and immediately crosses sand. **SO**.

(48.2 km) ▲ 131.5 km

59.3 km Track bears right. **SO**.

(33.8 km) ▲ 83.3 km

93.1 km T intersection. **TL** along Rig Rd.

WAA Line on right.

(49.5 km) ▲ 49.5 km

142.6 km T intersection.

French Line on right.

0.0 km Zero trip meter at above T intersection. **TL** along Rig Rd.

Enter Witjira National Park. Caution: track crosses large salt pan that may be boggy after rain.

(98.7 km) ▲ 0.0 km
▲ 98.7 km

98.7 km Intersection. S'post: Mt Dare Homestead 67.

Turn right to Dalhousie Springs Camping Area. Swimming in thermal pool. Straight ahead 8.5 km to Dalhousie ruins and Oodnadatta via Pedirka and Hamilton Station.

0.0 km Zero trip meter at above intersection. **TR**.

(2.1 km) ▲ 0.0 km
▲ 69.1 km

2.1 km Intersection. S'post: Mt Dare Homestead. **SO**.

Dalhousie ruins off to left.

(32.4 km) ▲ 67.0 km

34.5 km Intersection. S'post: Mt Dare Homestead 33. **TR**.

Bloods Creek Bore straight ahead.

(25.2 km) ▲ 34.6 km

59.7 km Intersection. S'post: Mt Dare 9. **TR**.

(9.4 km) ▲ 9.4 km

69.1 km Mt Dare Homestead, adjacent to Binjis Bar.

PD *Camping , minor mechanical repairs, breakdown service, meals, accomm., ice, information, airstrip.*

REVERSE DIRECTIONS START ▲ 0.0 km

THE OLD ANDADO TRACK
MT DARE
«》
ALICE SPRINGS

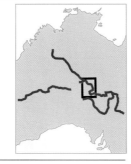

START POINT
Map page 29, M13.

TOTAL KM 438.
UNSEALED KM 423.
DEGREE OF DIFFICULTY Difficult.
DRIVING TIME 10 hours over 1 or 2 days
LONGEST DISTANCE NO FUEL 438 km (Mt Dare Homestead to Alice Springs).
TOPOGRAPHIC MAPS Auslig 1:250 000 series: *Dalhousie*; *McDills*; *Hale River*; *Rodinga*; *Alice Springs*. See also 1:100 000 series.
LOCAL/SPECIALITY MAPS Westprint Heritage map: *Alice Springs–Finke–Andado*; Central Australian Tourism Industry Association (CATIA) map: *Alice Springs and Central Australia.*
OTHER USEFUL INFORMATION SANPWS brochure: *Parks of the Far North of South Australia*; Northern Territory Tourist Commission booklet: *Tracks of Australia's Northern Territory: a Guide for Four Wheel Drivers*; Gregorys Consumer Guide: *4WD Great Treks*; Mt Dare Homestead information sheet: *Mt Dare to Alice Springs via Old Andado.*

DESCRIPTION The Old Andado Track follows the old station track from Mt Dare Homestead to Alice Springs through spectacular desert and range country. The southern section of the track between Mt Dare and Old Andado homesteads is slow and sandy and twists through stands of small trees, shrubs and clay pans. Although *Old Andado Station* is relatively close to Mt Dare it is an ideal stopover point en route to Alice Springs, especially if you choose to undertake the long drive over more than one day. You can camp on the property and stay at the

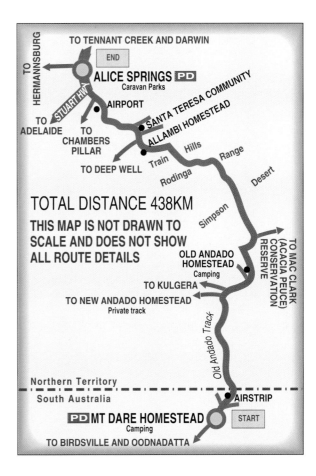

TOTAL DISTANCE 438KM
THIS MAP IS NOT DRAWN TO SCALE AND DOES NOT SHOW ALL ROUTE DETAILS

homestead, built in 1921 and possibly the best of its type remaining in the Northern Territory.

After Old Andado most of the drive to Alice Springs is easier, along wide sweeping plains past the Mac Clark (*Acacia Peuce*) Reserve and high ranges, Allambi Station and the Santa Teresa Community. *Alice Springs* is considered to be the 'capital' of central Australia and has several caravan parks and many historical and scenic attractions both in the town and its environs.

Before setting out on this trek see **Warnings** and **Essential Advice on Desert Crossings** in the introduction to the desert treks.

WARNINGS ▶ Remote Old Andado Track requires total self-sufficiency. Before departure from either Mt Dare or Alice Springs check track conditions by ringing Alice Springs Royal Flying Doctor Service, Stuart Terrace, Alice Springs NT 0870; tel. (089) 52 5355 and ask for Mt Dare Homestead (7STW). ▶ For emergency help contact RFDS base at Port Augusta, (086) 42 2044, or Alice Springs.

BOOKINGS AND PERMITS ▶ Necessary to obtain Desert Parks Pass to use sections of Witjira National Park. Fee applicable, pass valid for 1 year and entitles holder to traverse and camp in all South Australian desert parks. Contact South Australian Department of Environment and Planning, Information Centre, 55 Grenfell Street, Adelaide 5000; GPO Box 667, Adelaide 5001; tel. (08) 207 2300, or SANPWS Far North Region Office, 60 Elder Terrace, Hawker SA 5434; PO Box 102, Hawker SA 5434; tel. (086) 48 4244. ▶ See *Warnings* for contact point for booking accommodation at Mt Dare Homestead. ▶ Book camping and homestead accommodation at Old Andado Station in advance by ringing (089) 56 0812. ▶ For information on caravan parks and attractions in Alice Springs region contact CATIA, PO Box 2227, Alice Springs NT 0871; tel. (089) 52 5199.

A typical central Australian landscape

ROUTE DIRECTIONS

0.0 km Zero trip meter at Mt Dare Homestead, adjacent to Binjis Bar. **SO** heading north.

> **PD** *Limited supplies, minor mechanical repairs, breakdown service. Camping in bush setting. Homestead accomm., information, meals, takeaway food, ice. Airstrip. Next fuel Alice Springs (438 km).*

(0.1 km) ▲ 107.4 km

0.1 km Intersection. **KL.**

(0.6 km) ▲ 107.3 km

0.7 km Intersection. Base of airstrip. **KR.**

(6.5 km) ▲ 106.7 km

7.2 km S'post: Alice Springs. **SO.**

(81.9 km) ▲ 100.2 km

89.1 km Intersection. **KR.**

> *Private track on left leads to New Andado Homestead.*

(1.9 km) ▲ 18.3 km

91.0 km Intersection. **SO.**

> *Kulgera off to left.*

(16.2 km) ▲ 16.4 km

107.2 km Intersection. **SO.**

> *Track on left.*

(0.2 km) ▲ 0.2 km

107.4 km Old Andado Station on left.

> *Camping. Homestead accomm., meals. No fuel.*

0.0 km Zero trip meter at above point. **SO.**

(39.2 km) ▲ 0.0 km
▲ 227.0 km

39.2 km Intersection. **TL.**

> *Straight ahead 8 km to Mac Clark (Acacia Peuce) Conservation Reserve on left, one of very few stands of Acacia peuce in world. Very old variety of hardwood once valued for fence posts until species realised to be rare.*

(107.5 km) Opp. dir. s'post: Kulgera via Old Andado. ▲ 187.8 km

146.7 km S'post: Santa Teresa 96. **SO.**

(74.1 km) Opp. dir. s'post: Andado 142. ▲ 80.3 km

220.8 km S'post: Santa Teresa. **SO.**

(6.2 km) Opp. dir. s'post: Andado. ▲ 6.2 km

227.0 km Allambi Homestead on left.

0.0 km Zero trip meter at above point. **SO.**

> *Straight ahead 50 m to s'post: Alice Springs.*

(7.7 km) Opp. dir. s'post: Andado. ▲ 0.0 km
▲ 103.3 km

7.7 km Intersection. S'post: Alice Springs. **SO.**

> *Deep Well off to left.*

(10.5 km) Opp. dir. s'post: Allambi 7. ▲ 95.6 km

18.2 km Intersection. **SO.**

> *Track on right.*

(0.8 km) ▲ 85.1 km

19.0 km Santa Teresa Community on right. **SO.**

(0.4 km) ▲ 84.3 km

19.4 km T intersection. S'post: Alice Springs 70. **TL.**

(69.0 km) Opp. dir. s'post: Allambi. ▲ 83.9 km

88.4 km Bitumen. **SO.**

(1.0 km) Gravel. ▲ 14.9 km

89.4 km Roundabout. Airport on left. **SO.**

(2.7 km) ▲ 13.9 km

Alice Springs-bound

92.1 km Intersection. S'post: Alice Springs. **SO**.

> *Chambers Pillar 149 km off to left via 4WD-only track.*

(0.3 km)   Opp. dir. s'post: Airport. ▲ 11.2 km

92.4 km Intersection. S'post: Alice Springs. **SO** onto Stuart Hwy.

> *Adelaide off to left via Stuart Hwy.*

(5.7 km)   Opp. dir. s'post: Airport. ▲ 10.9 km

98.1 km Alice Springs information board on left. **SO**.
(5.2 km)   ▲ 5.2 km

103.3 km Intersection. S'post: Alice Springs town centre on right.

> **PD** *Supplies, caravan parks. Hospital, RFDS base, hotel–casino, restaurants, sports grounds, swimming pool, golf course, shops, Aboriginal art galleries. Annual events May–August. Hermannsburg off to left. Tennant Creek and Darwin straight ahead.*

REVERSE DIRECTIONS START ▲ 0.0 km

▼▼▼▼▼▼▼▼

TAKE CARE

● In outback Australia long distances separate some towns. Take care to ensure your vehicle is roadworthy before setting out and carry adequate supplies of petrol, water and food.

● Permits are required if you want to divert off public roads within Aboriginal Land areas.

● Carry additional water in desert areas: 5 litres per person per day is recommended, plus extra for the radiator.

● Don't take short cuts over virgin ground. You will destroy the vegetation. Stick to tracks open for use.

FINKE GORGE NATIONAL PARK
ALICE SPRINGS
«»
PALM VALLEY

START POINT
Map page 29, J9.

TOTAL KM 306.
UNSEALED KM 116.
DEGREE OF DIFFICULTY Easy.
DRIVING TIME 5 hours.
LONGEST DISTANCES NO FUEL 115 km (Alice Springs to Wallace Rockhole Community); 231 km (Wallace Rockhole Community to Alice Springs). No fuel at Palm Valley.
TOPOGRAPHIC MAPS Auslig 1:250 000 series: *Alice Springs*; *Hermannsburg*; *Henbury*. See also 1:100 000 series.
LOCAL/SPECIALITY MAP Central Australian Tourism Industry Association (CATIA) map: *Alice Springs and Central Australia*.
OTHER USEFUL INFORMATION CCNT information sheet: *Finke Gorge National Park*.

DESCRIPTION This easy day tour takes you west of Alice Springs via Larapinta Drive through the spectacular purple–reds of the West MacDonnells to the high red canyon walls of the northern end of Finke Gorge. Finally there is the unique Palm Valley where rare cycad and red-cabbage palms, survivors there for 10 000 years, replace the more common eucalypts.

Finke Gorge National Park and Palm Valley are home to arid-zone wildlife species such as euros, dingoes, rock wallabies, echidnas and lizards. The Finke River, one of the world's oldest watercourses, was traditionally a major trade and travel route for local desert Aboriginal tribes. The park and its envi-

Cycad palms, Palm Valley

rons contain sites that remain culturally significant to Aborigines as well as evidence of early European settlement. Our tour visits memorials to the great Aboriginal artist Albert Namatjira and the pioneer church figure John Flynn, and passes through the old Hermannsburg Mission area that in 1982 was returned to the traditional Western Arrente Aboriginal owners.

Our route directions include camping areas at the *Wallace Rockhole Community* and *Palm Valley* as well as caravan parks at *Alice Springs* and *White Gums Park*.

WARNINGS ▶ Slow and rocky track into Palm Valley follows sandy bed of Finke River and may be impassable after rain. Before departure contact Northern Territory Emergency Service, (089) 52 3833, or recorded report, (089) 52 7111, to check road conditions. ▶ If tackling very difficult track running along length of Finke Gorge, whether driving north–south or south–north, travel in convoy of at least 2 vehicles. ▶ Light fires only in barbecues provided and collect dead wood from river bed only sparingly. ▶ Do not use generators. ▶ Contact ranger on site

472

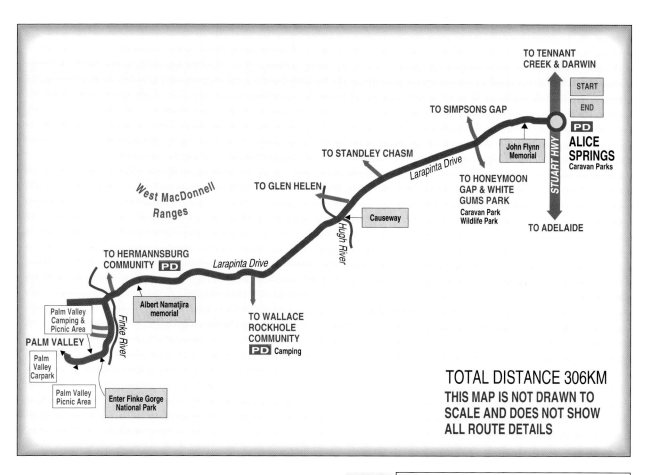

TO TENNANT
CREEK & DARWIN

START

END

PD

**ALICE
SPRINGS**
Caravan Parks

TO SIMPSONS GAP

TO STANDLEY CHASM

Larapinta Drive

John Flynn
Memorial

STUART HWY

TO GLEN HELEN

TO HONEYMOON
GAP & WHITE
GUMS PARK
Caravan Park
Wildlife Park

TO ADELAIDE

Causeway

Hugh River

West MacDonnell
Ranges

TO HERMANNSBURG
COMMUNITY PD

Larapinta Drive

Albert Namatjira
memorial

Finke River

Palm Valley
Camping &
Picnic Area

PALM VALLEY

Palm
Valley
Carpark

Palm Valley
Picnic Area

Enter Finke Gorge
National Park

TO WALLACE
ROCKHOLE
COMMUNITY
PD Camping

TOTAL DISTANCE 306KM
**THIS MAP IS NOT DRAWN TO
SCALE AND DOES NOT SHOW
ALL ROUTE DETAILS**

before leaving on longer walks through wilderness areas. ▶ For emergency help contact RFDS base at Alice Springs, (089) 52 5355.

BOOKINGS AND PERMITS ▶ Permit required to camp in Finke Gorge National Park. Self-register on site at Palm Valley Camping and Picnic Area, the only designated campsite in park. ▶ For information on national park contact ranger on site or CCNT Alice Springs Regional Office, South Stuart Highway, Alice Springs NT 0871; PO Box 1046; tel. (089) 51 8211. ▶ For information on Wallace Rockhole Community and caravan parks in Alice Springs and White Gums Park contact CATIA, PO Box 2227, Alice Springs NT 0871; tel. (089) 52 5199.

ROUTE DIRECTIONS

0.0 km Zero trip meter in Alice Springs at Larapinta Drive and Stuart Hwy intersection. S'post: Hermannsburg. **SO** onto Larapinta Drive heading west.

PD *Supplies, caravan parks. RFDS base, Aboriginal art and craft galleries, museums, old gaol, restaurants, casino, arid-zone botanic garden, annual events May–August. Adelaide off to left. Tennant Creek and Darwin off to right. Next fuel Wallace Rockhole Community (115 km).*

(0.9 km)
0.9 km Roundabout. **SO**.
(5.7 km)
6.6 km John Flynn memorial on left. **SO**.
(0.8 km)
7.4 km Sign: Simpsons Gap National Park. **SO**.
(9.2 km)
16.6 km Intersection. S'post: Hermannsburg.

Turn right to Simpsons Gap. Turn left to Honeymoon Gap. Turn left 1 km to White Gums Park. Caravan park. Tearooms, wildlife park, scenic walks, lookout.

0.0 km Zero trip meter at above intersection. **SO**.
(24.9 km)

24.9 km Intersection.

> Turn right to Standley Chasm. Kiosk, picnic area.

0.0 km Zero trip meter at above intersection. **SO**.
(6.5 km)

6.5 km Intersection. S'post: Hermannsburg.

> Glen Helen off to right along Namatjira Drive.

0.0 km Zero trip meter at above intersection. **SO**.
(2.8 km)

2.8 km Hugh River causeway. **SO**.
(44.2 km)

47.0 km Gravel. **SO**.
(0.3 km)

47.3 km Intersection.

> Turn left 20 km to Wallace Rockhole Community. **PD** Camping. Aboriginal art and craft for sale. Next fuel Alice Springs (231 km).

0.0 km Zero trip meter at above intersection. **SO**.
(32.4 km)

32.4 km Albert Namatjira memorial on left. **SO**.
(2.6 km)

35.0 km Intersection. S'post: Areyonga/Palm Valley. **SO**.

> Turn right to Hermannsburg Community. **PD**

(0.9 km)

35.9 km Finke River crossing. **SO**.

> Usually a dry river bed.

(0.6 km)

36.5 km Intersection. S'post: Palm Valley. **TL**.

> 4WD track only.

(7.3 km)

43.8 km Intersection. **SO**.

> Track on right.

(1.0 km)

44.8 km Intersection. **SO**.

> Track on right. Sign: Closed – restricted area.

(3.7 km)

48.5 km Sign: Finke Gorge National Park. **SO**.
(4.7 km)

53.2 km Intersection. Palm Valley Camping and Picnic Area on right. **SO**.

MacDonnell Ranges

Finke River country

> Picnic tables, wood barbecues, toilets. Showers, water. Walk along creek bed via palms, cycads and sandstone cliffs towards carpark.

(0.5 km)

53.7 km Intersection. Palm Valley Picnic Area on left. **SO**.

> Picnic tables, wood barbecues, toilets. Water.

(3.8 km)

57.5 km Palm Valley carpark.

> Camping prohibited. Walk along creek bed via palms, cycads and sandstone cliffs, to Palm Bend and Amphitheatre area. Western end of national park has longer wilderness walks through rugged sandstone uplands and gullies.

Return to Alice Springs via same route (153 km).

THE TANAMI TRACK
ALICE SPRINGS
«»
HALLS CREEK

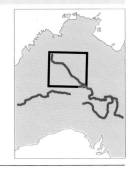

START POINT
Map page 29, J9.

TOTAL KM 1097.
UNSEALED KM 936.
DEGREE OF DIFFICULTY Moderate.
DRIVING TIME 12 to 14 hours over 2 days.
LONGEST DISTANCES NO FUEL 329 km (Yuendumu Community to Rabbit Flat Roadhouse); 339 km (Rabbit Flat Roadhouse to Carrunya Homestead).
TOPOGRAPHIC MAPS Auslig 1:250 000 series: *Alice Springs*; *Hermannsburg*; *Napperby*; *Mt Doreen*; *Mt Theo*; *The Granites*; *Tanami*; *Billiluna*; *Gordon Downs*. See also 1:100 000 series.
LOCAL/SPECIALITY MAPS Central Australian Tourism Industry Association (CATIA) map: *Alice Springs and Central Australia*; *Gregorys Western Australia*.
OTHER USEFUL INFORMATION Northern Territory Tourist Commission booklet: *Tracks of Australia's Northern Territory: a Guide for Four Wheel Drivers*; Western Australian Tourism Commission booklet: *Western Australia's Unique North*; CALM booklet: *North-West Bound: From Shark Bay to Wyndham*.

DESCRIPTION The Tanami Desert is more populated and its tracks used more than most of the other deserts, but it is a harsh environment and should be approached with caution and respect; see *Warnings* and *Essential Advice on Desert Crossings* in the introduction to the desert treks. The track's quality is reasonably good for most of the distance, and you pass through landscapes of considerable beauty, from the purple–red MacDon-

nell Ranges at the Alice Springs end to the red sands and desert scrub further along.

Towards the top end of the trek the detour to Wolfe Creek Crater National Park is well worthwhile: the meteorite crater is 850 metres wide and 49 metres deep. From the national park you drive on to Halls Creek, located at the edge of the Great Sandy Desert in the heart of east Kimberley country. Western Australia's first gold discovery was made there.

Camp under the extraordinarily beautiful desert stars at any number of suitable sites along the track. Our route directions also include camping areas at *Tilmouth Well Roadhouse*, the *rest stop* past the Chilla Well turnoff, and *Wolfe Creek Crater.* Caravan parks are located at *Alice Springs* and *Halls Creek*, or *Fitzroy Crossing* if you choose to turn left at the Great Northern Highway T intersection (274 kilometres) to explore part of the west Kimberley region.

WARNINGS ▶ Before departure contact Alice Springs police, cnr Bath and Parson streets, to advise them of intended departure time and proposed arrival time. Also notify Halls Creek police on arrival at Halls Creek police station. ▶ Rabbit Flat Roadhouse, 627 kilometres from Alice Springs, never open for business on Tuesdays, Wednesdays or Thursdays. ▶ Beware washaways and sand drifts, especially after crossing into Western Australia where track deteriorates dramatically. Before departure check track condition by contacting Northern Territory Department of Transport and Works, (089) 51 5542, or recorded report, (089) 52 7111, or Main Roads Department Western Australia, (09) 323 4354. ▶ Possible to complete trek in a day but more sensible to break it up into two. ▶ For emergency help contact RFDS base at Alice Springs, (089) 52 5355, or Derby, (091) 191 1211.

BOOKINGS AND PERMITS ▶ No permits required to use Tanami Track but permit required to refuel at Yuendumu Community. Before departure contact Central Land Council, 31–33 Stuart Highway, Alice Springs NT 0871; PO Box 3321; tel. (089) 51 6320. ▶ For information on caravan parks in Alice Springs and camping at Tilmouth Well Roadhouse contact CATIA, PO Box 2227, Alice Springs NT 0871; tel. (089) 52 5199. ▶ For information on Wolfe Creek Crater National Park and caravan park in Halls Creek contact Halls Creek Information Centre, Great Northern Highway, Halls Creek WA 6770; tel. (091) 68 6262 May–September, (091) 68 6164 other times. ▶ For information on east Kimberley region contact CALM Kimberley Regional Office, PO Box 942. Kununurra WA 6743; tel.

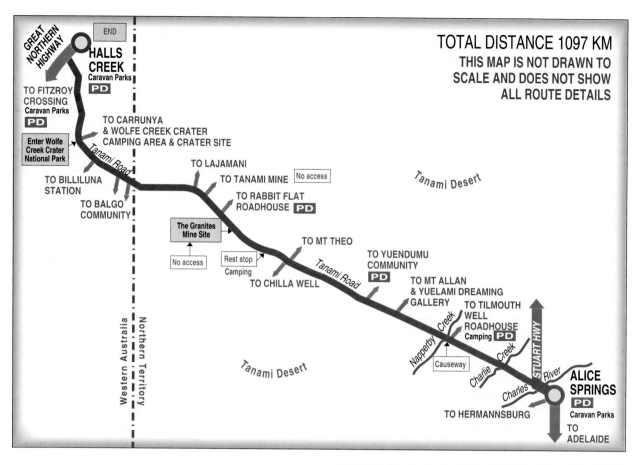

TOTAL DISTANCE 1097 KM
THIS MAP IS NOT DRAWN TO
SCALE AND DOES NOT SHOW
ALL ROUTE DETAILS

(091) 68 0200 or CCNT Alice Springs Regional Office, South Stuart Highway, Alice Springs NT 0871; PO Box 1046; tel. (089) 51 8211.

ROUTE DIRECTIONS

0.0 km Zero trip meter in Alice Springs at Stuart Hwy and Larapinta Drive intersection. S'post: Darwin. **SO** onto Stuart Hwy heading north.

> **PD** *Supplies, caravan parks. RFDS base, Aboriginal art and craft galleries, museums, old gaol, restaurants, casino, arid-zone botanic garden, annual events May–August. Hermannsburg off to left. Alice Springs town centre on right. Next fuel Tilmouth Well Roadhouse (195 km).*

(7.2 km)   Opp. dir. s'post: Kulgera. ▲ 195.2 km
7.2 km Charles River. Cross bridge.
(13.8 km)   ▲ 188.0 km
21.0 km Intersection. S'post: Tanami Rd/Yuendumu. **TL**.

> *Tennant Creek and Darwin straight ahead.*

(101.8 km)   Opp. dir. s'post: Alice Springs. ▲174.2 km
122.8 km Charlie Creek causeway. **SO**.
(21.8 km)   ▲ 72.4 km
144.6 km Gravel. **SO**.
(50.6 km)   Bitumen. ▲ 50.6 km
195.2 km Intersection.

> *Turn left to Tilmouth Well Roadhouse.* **PD** *Supplies, camping. Meals.*

0.0 km Zero trip meter at above intersection. **SO**.
(0.3 km)   ▲ 0.0 km
                    ▲ 67.7 km
0.3 km Napperby Creek causeway. **SO**.
(67.4 km)   ▲ 67.4 km
67.7 km Intersection.

> *Turn right 31 km to Yuelami Dreaming Gallery at Mt Allan.*

0.0 km Zero trip meter at above intersection. **SO**.
(38.8 km)   ▲ 0.0 km
                    ▲ 38.8 km
38.8 km Intersection.

> Turn right 2 km to Yuendumu Community.
> **PD** Supplies. Food. Next fuel Rabbit Flat
> Roadhouse (329 km).

0.0 km Zero trip meter at above intersection. **SO.**
(130.8 km)   ▲ 0.0 km
                              ▲ 268.0 km

130.8 km Intersection. **SO.**

> Mt Theo off to right.

(1.1 km)   ▲ 137.2 km

131.9 km Intersection. **SO.**

> Chilla Well off to left.

(35.7 km)   ▲ 136.1 km

167.6 km Rest stop on left. **SO.**

> Possible campsite. Barbecue, water, shelter.

(100.4 km)   ▲ 100.4 km

268.0 km The Granites Mine Site on left, adjacent to windmill, abandoned buildings and tailings pile.

> No access; mine in full operation.

0.0 km Zero trip meter at above point. **SO.**
(57.2 km)   ▲ 0.0 km
                              ▲ 57.2 km

57.2 km Intersection.

> Turn right 2 km to Rabbit Flat Roadhouse.
> **PD** Supplies. Meals, water, toilets. Not open
> Tuesdays, Wednesdays and Thursdays. Next
> fuel Carrunya Homestead (339 km).

0.0 km Zero trip meter at above intersection. **SO.**
(44.3 km)   ▲ 0.0 km
                              ▲ 128.8 km

44.3 km Intersection. **SO.**

> Tanami Mine off to right. No access; mine
> in full operation.

(2.6 km)   ▲ 84.5 km

46.9 km S'post: WA border. **SO.**

> Lajamani off to right.

(81.9 km)   Opp. dir. s'post: Yuendumu. ▲ 81.9 km

128.8 km Sign: Western Australian border.

0.0 km Zero trip meter at above point. **SO.**
(88.5 km)   ▲ 0.0 km
                              ▲ 207.7 km

88.5 km Intersection. **SO.**

> Balgo Community off to left.

(25.4 km)   ▲ 119.2 km

Tanami termite mounds

113.9 km Intersection. S'post: Halls Creek. **SO.**

> Balgo Community off to left.

(47.3 km)   Opp. dir. s'post: Alice Springs. ▲ 93.8 km

161.2 km Intersection. **SO** along Tanami Rd.

> Billiluna Station off to left.

(46.5 km)   ▲ 46.5 km

207.7 km Intersection.

> Turn right to Carrunya Homestead and store.
> **PD** Supplies. Next fuel Halls Creek (134 km).
> Enter Wolfe Creek Crater National Park.
> Camping area, picnic tables and information
> shelter 16 km; crater site 7 km from camping
> area.

0.0 km Zero trip meter at above intersection. **SO.**
(116.9 km)   ▲ 0.0 km
                              ▲ 134.0 km

116.9 km T intersection. S'post: Halls Creek 18. **TR**
onto bitumen; Great Northern Hwy.

> Fitzroy Crossing 274 km off to left. **PD**
> Caravan park.

(17.1 km)   Gravel. Opp. dir. s'post:
                   Alice Springs 1040. ▲ 17.1 km

134.0 km Halls Creek town centre, adjacent to police
station.

> **PD** Supplies, caravan park. Accomm.
> Mud-brick ruins of Old Halls Creek; China
> Wall: natural white-quartz vein 6 km north
> near Old Halls Creek.

REVERSE DIRECTIONS START ▲ 0.0 km

THE GUNBARREL HIGHWAY
WILUNA
«»
ULURU

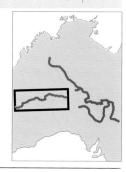

START POINT
Map page 34, F11.

TOTAL KM 1410.
UNSEALED KM 1361.
DEGREE OF DIFFICULTY Extreme.
DRIVING TIME 4 or 5 days.
LONGEST DISTANCES NO FUEL 725 km (Carnegie Homestead to Warrakurna Roadhouse); 491 km (Carnegie Homestead to Warburton Community); 351 km (Wiluna to Carnegie Homestead); 231 km (Docker River Community to Yulara Resort).
TOPOGRAPHIC MAPS Auslig 1:250 000 series: *Wiluna*; *Kingston*; *Robert*; *Browne*; *Bentley*; *Rawlinson*; *Scott*; *Petermann Ranges*; *Ayers Rock*. See also 1:100 000 series.
LOCAL/SPECIALITY MAPS RAC Western Australia map: *Perth to Alice Springs ... via 'Gunbarrel Highway' or 'Warburton Road'*; *Gregorys Western Australia*.
OTHER USEFUL INFORMATION Western Australian Tourism Commission booklet: *Western Australia's Unique North*; CALM booklet: *North-West Bound: From Shark Bay to Wyndham*; Northern Territory Tourist Commission booklet: *Tracks of Australia's Northern Territory: a Guide for Four Wheel Drivers*; ANPWS brochure: *Uluru (Ayers Rock/Mt Olga) National Park Visitor Guide* and booklet: *An Insight into Uluru: the Mala Walk and the Mutitjulu Walk*.

DESCRIPTION The Gunbarrel Highway is one of Australia's toughest long-haul treks. The distance is considerable and the area extremely remote, so be even more meticulous when organising all the usual desert trek precautions, as outlined in ***Essential Advice on Desert Crossings*** in the introduction to the desert treks. Also see ***Warnings***, and prepare the vehicle to handle constantly changing conditions. Once you have made the commitment, however, the journey is most rewarding.

The Gunbarrel was first surveyed and opened up by Len Beadell and his team during the 1950s and 1960s, effectively bisecting Western Australia's Gibson and Great Victoria deserts. It is very beautiful and diverse country and usually unlike what you would expect in a desert region, especially after rains. Our route directions follow the Beadell line all the way except a long-abandoned section between the Warburton Community and Giles Meteorological Station used only by four-wheel drivers. Interestingly, the road surface there is probably the best part of the track and passes through beautiful groves of desert sheoaks in shallow depressions between sand dunes.

Our start point, Wiluna, boasted the largest goldmine in the Southern Hemisphere and a population of 9000 at the peak of the mining boom. Our end point is Uluru National Park which consists of Kata Tjuta (The Olgas), a rambling chain of polished domes divided by gorges and valleys, and Uluru (Ayers Rock), Australia's famous sandstone monolith. Take time to walk the tracks and lookouts to see the fascinating dryland plants and animals that survive in the harsh environment of this unique biosphere reserve.

You can camp anywhere along the track or at established campsites at *Harry Johnston Water*, *Carnegie Homestead*, *Camp Beadell* and *Lasseters Cave (Tjunti)*. There are caravan parks at *Wiluna* and *Warrakurna Roadhouse*, and *Yulara Resort* has several levels of accommodation including a caravan and camping ground.

WARNINGS ▶ Travel in convoy of at least 2 vehicles. ▶ Track includes corrugations, ruts, washaways, stones, sand and, depending on seasonal conditions, mud. Before departure contact Wiluna police station, Thompson Street, Wiluna WA 6646; tel. (099) 81 7024 and Yulara police station, Lasseter Highway, Yulara NT 0872; tel. (089) 56 2166 to check track conditions and register intended route. ▶ Do not attempt to drive more than about 300 kilometres per day. ▶ Be totally self-sufficient with food, water and fuel and equip vehicle for all foreseeable emergencies. ▶ For emergency help contact RFDS base at Meekatharra, (099) 81 1107, or Alice Springs, (089) 52 5355.

BOOKINGS AND PERMITS ▶ Permits required to traverse Aboriginal lands. No fees applicable but include restrictions on movement; for example, into communities except to refuel. Allow at least 2 weeks for permits to be issued. For Western Australia, including refuel-

Car in watercourse after rain on the Gunbarrel Highway

Harry Johnston water-camp, Gunbarrel Highway

ling at Warburton Community, contact Aboriginal Lands Trust, 35 Havelock Street, West Perth 6005; tel. (09) 483 1333. For Northern Territory, including visiting Docker River Community and Lasseters Cave, contact Central Land Council, 31–33 Stuart Highway, Alice Springs NT 0871; PO Box 3221; tel. (089) 51 6320. ▶ For information on caravan park and accommodation in Wiluna con-

tact Wiluna Shire Office, Scotia Street, Wiluna WA 6646; tel. (099) 81 7010. ▶ For information on Carnegie Homestead contact Carnegie Station, Gunbarrel Highway via Wiluna; tel. (099) 63 5809. ▶ For information on Uluru, the Olgas and Yulara Resort contact Central Australian Tourism Industry Association (CATIA), PO Box 2227, Alice Springs NT 0871; tel. (089) 52 5199.

ROUTE DIRECTIONS

0.0 km   Zero trip meter in Wiluna at Gunbarrel Hwy and Wotton St intersection. S'post: Gunbarrel Hwy. **SO** heading east.

> **PD** *Supplies, caravan park. Accomm., post office, RFDS nurses' post. Next fuel Carnegie Homestead (351 km).*

(5.3 km)   ▲ 194.2 km
5.3 km   Intersection. **SO.**

> *Wiluna Emu Farm off to left. Wiluna Goldmine off to right.*

(5.3 km)   ▲ 188.9 km
10.6 km   Millibillillie Homestead on right. **SO.**
(12.1 km)   ▲ 183.6 km
22.7 km   Rocky causeway. **SO.**
(19.4 km)   ▲ 171.5 km
42.1 km   Intersection. **SO.**

> *Track on left leads to Lake Violet, Earaheedy and Glenayle homesteads and rejoins highway further on.*

(10.4 km)   ▲ 152.1 km
52.5 km   Intersection. **SO.**

> *Roche Bros Mine off to left. No access. Beware road trains exiting.*

(2.3 km)   ▲ 141.7 km
54.8 km   Intersection. **SO.**

> *Track on left.*

(3.4 km)   ▲ 139.4 km
58.2 km   Intersection. S'post: Carnegie. **KL.**

> *Windmill on left. Barwidgee Homestead to right.*

(22.0 km)   ▲ 136.0 km
80.2 km   Windmill and stockyards on left. **SO.**
(63.6 km)   ▲ 114.0 km
143.8 km   Intersection. Windmill on right. **SO.**

THE GUNBARREL HIGHWAY

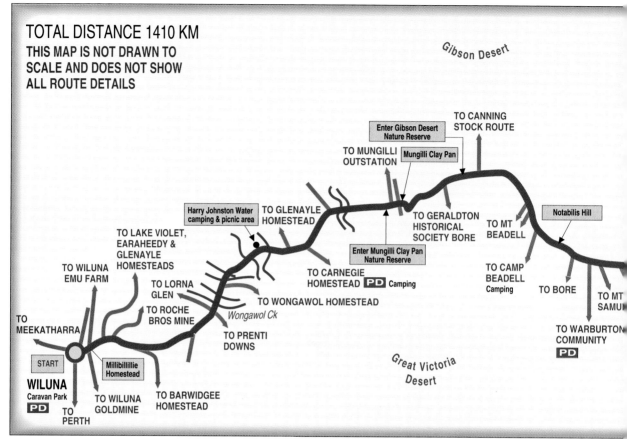

TOTAL DISTANCE 1410 KM
THIS MAP IS NOT DRAWN TO
SCALE AND DOES NOT SHOW
ALL ROUTE DETAILS

Gibson Desert

TO CANNING
STOCK ROUTE

Enter Gibson Desert
Nature Reserve

TO MUNGILLI
OUTSTATION

Mungilli Clay Pan

TO GERALDTON
HISTORICAL
SOCIETY BORE

TO MT
BEADELL

Notabilis Hill

Harry Johnston Water
camping & picnic area

TO GLENAYLE
HOMESTEAD

Enter Mungilli Clay Pan
Nature Reserve

TO CAMP
BEADELL
Camping

TO BORE

TO MT
SAMU

TO LAKE VIOLET,
EARAHEEDY &
GLENAYLE
HOMESTEADS

TO CARNEGIE
HOMESTEAD **PD** Camping

TO WILUNA
EMU FARM

TO LORNA
GLEN

TO WONGAWOL HOMESTEAD

Wongawol Ck

TO WARBURTON
COMMUNITY
PD

TO ROCHE
BROS MINE

TO
MEEKATHARRA

TO PRENTI
DOWNS

*Great Victoria
Desert*

START

Millibillillie
Homestead

WILUNA
Caravan Park
PD

TO WILUNA
GOLDMINE

TO BARWIDGEE
HOMESTEAD

TO
PERTH

Track on right.	
(12.5 km) ▲ 50.4 km	
156.3 km Stockyards and windmill on right. **SO**.	
(37.9 km) ▲ 37.9 km	
194.2 km Crossroads.	

Lorna Glen off to left. Prenti Downs off to right.

0.0 km Zero trip meter at above crossroads. **SO**.
(10.0 km) ▲ 0.0 km
▲ 157.0 km
10.0 km Wongawol Creek crossing. **SO**.
(4.2 km) ▲ 147.0 km
14.2 km Creek crossing. **SO**.
(14.3 km) ▲ 142.8 km
28.5 km Intersection. **KL**.

Track on right leads to Wongawol Homestead.

(7.3 km) ▲ 128.5 km
35.8 km Creek crossing. **SO**.
(7.6 km) ▲ 121.2 km
43.4 km Creek crossing. **SO**.
(0.5 km) ▲ 113.6 km

43.9 km Windmill on left. **SO**.
(28.0 km) ▲ 113.1 km
71.9 km Creek crossing. **SO**.
(0.8 km) ▲ 85.1 km
72.7 km Windmill on left. **SO**.

Stockyards on right.

(15.8 km) ▲ 84.3 km
88.5 km Intersection. **SO** and immediately cross creek.

Harry Johnston Water camping area on left. Picnic table, barbecue, shelter. Waterhole. Private property. Good campsite.

(38.1 km) ▲ 68.5 km
126.6 km Windmill on right. **SO**.

Track on left leads to Glenayle Homestead.

(29.8 km) ▲ 30.4 km
156.4 km Y intersection. **KR** into Carnegie Homestead.
(0.6 km) ▲ 0.6 km
157.0 km Carnegie Homestead.

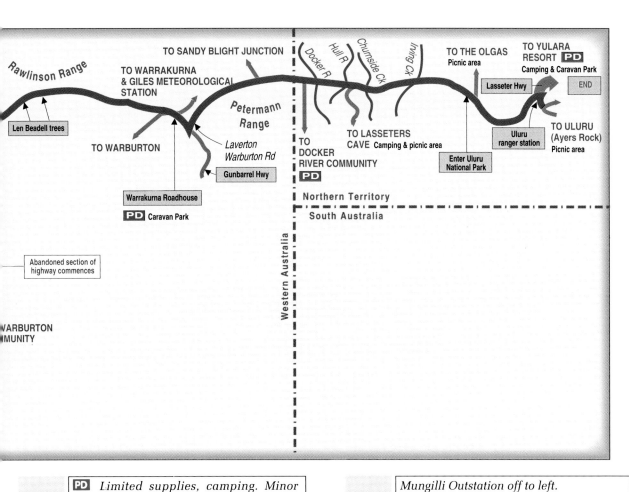

PD *Limited supplies, camping. Minor mechanical repairs, hot showers, homestead accomm. Next fuel Warburton Community (491 km) or Warrakurna Roadhouse (725 km).*

0.0 km Zero trip meter at exit to Carnegie Homestead. S'post: Gunbarrel Hwy. **SO.**
(18.3 km) ▲ 0.0 km
▲ 151.3 km

18.3 km Windmill on right. **SO.**
(14.5 km) ▲ 133.0 km

32.8 km Intersection. **SO.**

Track on left.

(41.9 km) ▲ 118.5 km

74.7 km Creek crossing. **SO.**
(0.7 km) ▲ 76.6 km

75.4 km Creek crossing. **SO.**
(75.5 km) ▲ 75.9 km

150.9 km Sign: Mungilli Clay Pan Nature Reserve. **SO.**
(0.2 km) ▲ 0.4 km

151.1 km Intersection. **KR.**

Mungilli Outstation off to left.

(0.2 km) ▲ 0.2 km

151.3 km Crossroads.

Eagle Rd on left and right.

0.0 km Zero trip meter at above crossroads. **SO.**

Mungilli Clay Pan straight ahead, occasionally impassable after heavy rain. If impassable, detour around clay pan but beware soft ground.

(55.2 km) ▲ 0.0 km
▲ 55.2 km

55.2 km Intersection. S'post: Water.

Turn right to Geraldton Historical Society Bore. Capped artesian bores, water accessible at 30 m.

0.0 km Zero trip meter at above intersection. **SO.**
(1.1 km) ▲ 0.0 km
▲ 87.1 km

1.1 km Sign: Gibson Desert Nature Reserve on right. **SO**.
(30.7 km) ▲ 86.0 km

31.8 km Intersection. Len Beadell plaque on right. **SO**.

> *Gary Hwy on left leads to Canning Stock Route.*

(40.8 km) ▲ 55.3 km

72.6 km Exit Gibson Desert Nature Reserve.
(14.5 km) Opp. dir. s'post:
Gibson Desert Nature Reserve. ▲ 14.5 km

87.1 km Intersection.

> *Loop road to Mt Beadell commences on right.*

0.0 km Zero trip meter at above intersection. **KL**.
(0.9 km) ▲ 0.0 km
▲ 0.9 km

0.9 km Intersection.

> *Loop road to Mt Beadell rejoins on right.*

0.0 km Zero trip meter at above intersection. **SO**.
(5.3 km) ▲ 0.0 km
▲ 5.3 km

5.3 km Intersection.

> *Turn right 500 m to Camp Beadell. Good shady campsite, artesian bore.*

0.0 km Zero trip meter at above intersection. **SO**.
(24.7 km) ▲ 0.0 km
▲ 54.7 km

24.7 km Notabilis Hill and cairn on left. **SO**.
(5.0 km) ▲ 30.0 km

29.7 km Artesian bore on right. **SO**.
(25.0 km) ▲ 25.0 km

54.7 km Intersection. Len Beadell tree and plaque on left.

> *Desert sheoak. Turn right 500 m to artesian bore.*

0.0 km Zero trip meter at above intersection. **SO**.
(10.8 km) ▲ 0.0 km
▲ 10.8 km

10.8 km Intersection.

> *Turn right onto Heather Hwy 126 km to Warburton Community. **PD** Alternative route to Uluru.*

0.0 km Zero trip meter at above intersection. **SO**.
(5.7 km) Opp. dir. s'post: Wiluna 720. ▲ 0.0 km
▲ 82.2 km

5.7 km Intersection. **KL**.

> *Keep right 100 m to cairn on top of hill and lookout at Mt Samuel.*

(26.8 km) ▲ 76.5 km

32.5 km Intersection. **SO**.

> *Track on right.*

(2.9 km) ▲ 49.7 km

35.4 km Intersection. **SO**.

> *Track on right alternative route to Warburton Community.*

(0.8 km) ▲ 46.8 km

36.2 km Intersection. **SO**.

> *Track on left.*

(46.0 km) ▲ 46.0 km

82.2 km T intersection. S'post: Giles.

> *Warburton Community off to right.*

0.0 km Zero trip meter at above T intersection. **TL**.

> *Sign: Road closed – unsafe from this point. Abandoned section of Gunbarrel Hwy commences.*

(89.7 km) Opp. dir. s'post: Carnegie. ▲ 0.0 km
▲ 163.7 km

89.7 km Intersection. **SO**.

> *Track on left.*

(74.0 km) ▲ 74.0 km

163.7 km Len Beadell tree on right.

> *Desert sheoak; plaque removed.*

0.0 km Zero trip meter at above point. **SO**.
(12.7 km) ▲ 0.0 km
▲ 113.4 km

12.7 km Len Beadell tree on right. **SO**.

> *Desert sheoak; plaque removed.*

(84.3 km) ▲ 100.7 km

97.0 km T intersection. **TL** onto Laverton–Warburton Rd.

> *Warburton Community off to right.*

(16.1 km) ▲ 16.4 km

113.1 km Intersection. S'post: Yulara. **TR**.

> *Warrakurna and Giles Meteorological Station straight ahead.*

(0.3 km) ▲ 0.3 km

113.4 km Warrakurna Roadhouse on right.

> **PD** *Supplies, caravan park. Water. Next fuel Docker River Community (104 km).*

0.0 km Zero trip meter at above point. **SO.**
(29.3 km)
▲ 0.0 km
▲ 103.5 km

29.3 km Intersection. S'post: Yulara. **TL.**

> *Gunbarrel Hwy on right.*

(49.1 km) Opp. dir. s'post: Giles. ▲ 74.2 km
78.4 km Intersection. S'post: Docker River/Yulara. **TR.**

> *Sandy Blight Junction off to left.*

(17.1 km) Opp. dir. s'post: Giles. ▲ 25.1 km
95.5 km Western Australia–Northern Territory border. **SO.**

> *Sign: Permit required to enter Aboriginal land. Camping prohibited for next 50 km except at Lasseters Cave.*

(8.0 km) ▲ 8.0 km
103.5 km Intersection. S'post: Yulara.

> *Turn right to Docker River Community.* **PD** *Supplies. Next fuel Yulara Resort (231 km).*

0.0 km Zero trip meter at above intersection. **SO.**
(1.8 km) Opp. dir. s'post: Giles. ▲ 0.0 km
▲ 40.6 km

1.8 km Docker River crossing. **SO.**
(38.7 km) ▲ 38.8 km
40.5 km Hull River crossing. **SO.**
(0.1 km) ▲ 0.1 km
40.6 km Intersection.

> *Turn right 700 m to Lasseters Cave (Tjunti). Camping. Picnic tables, barbecues, water.*

0.0 km Zero trip meter at above intersection. **SO.**
(26.3 km) ▲ 0.0 km
▲ 141.5 km

26.3 km Churnside Creek crossing. **SO.**
(34.2 km) ▲ 115.2 km
60.5 km Irving Creek crossing. **SO.**
(77.5 km) ▲ 81.0 km
138.0 km Sign: Uluru National Park. **SO.**
(3.5 km) ▲ 3.5 km
141.5 km T intersection. S'post: Uluru.

> *Turn left 1 km to The Olgas (Kata Tjuta). Picnic tables, toilets, water. No camping.*

Lasseters Cave and sign

The Olgas

0.0 km Zero trip meter at above T intersection. **TR** onto bitumen.
(40.4 km) Gravel. Opp. dir. s'post: Giles/Docker River. ▲ 0.0 km
▲ 40.4 km

40.4 km T intersection. S'post: Uluru.

> *Turn left onto Lasseter Hwy 8.2 km to Yulara Resort.* **PD** *Camping, caravan park. Accomm.*

0.0 km Zero trip meter at above T intersection. **TR.**
(8.4 km) Opp. dir. s'post: Kata Tjuta. ▲ 0.0 km
▲ 8.4 km

8.4 km Uluru ranger station on right.

> *Picnic tables, gas barbecues, toilets, water. Information, kiosks, arts and crafts. Straight ahead to Uluru (Ayers Rock).*

REVERSE DIRECTIONS START ▲ 0.0 km

THE OODNADATTA TRACK
MARLA ◀◀▶ MARREE

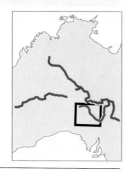

START POINT
Map page 47, N5.

TOTAL KM 621.
UNSEALED KM 617.
DEGREE OF DIFFICULTY Easy.
DRIVING TIME 2 to 3 days.
LONGEST DISTANCES NO FUEL 214 km (Marla to Oodnadatta); 202 km (Oodnadatta to William Creek); 205 km (William Creek to Marree).
TOPOGRAPHIC MAPS Auslig 1:250 000 series: *Wintinna*; *Oodnadatta*; *Warrina*; *Lake Eyre*; *Curdimurka*; *Marree*. See also 1:100 000 series.
LOCAL/SPECIALITY MAPS Westprint Heritage map: *Oodnadatta Track*; Pink Roadhouse, Oodnadatta mud maps: *Lake Eyre North – from William Creek* and *Coward Springs*.
OTHER USEFUL INFORMATION Flinders Ranges and Outback of South Australia Regional Tourist Association booklet: *Flinders Ranges and Outback South Australia: Official Visitors Guide*; Pink Roadhouse, Oodnadatta information sheets: *Oodnadatta–Warrina– Oodnadatta, Peake Ruins* and *William Creek– Curdimurka–William Creek*; Coward Springs Camel Station brochure: *Oodnadatta Track –Coward Springs Campground*; Tourism South Australia brochure: *Outback South Australia: Every Day a New Discovery*.

DESCRIPTION The Oodnadatta Track takes you on an historical adventure along mostly good-quality graded gravel roads, closely following the old Ghan railway line that ran between Adelaide and Alice Springs. The ruins of settlements and stone-fettlers' cottages, water tanks, viaducts, rail bridges and sid-

ings appear regularly in this area of mound springs and artesian bores that figure significantly in Aboriginal history and mythology. You can camp at *Algebuckina Waterhole* and *Curdimurka ruins* or at *Coward Springs Campground*, an oasis in this driest part of Australia's arid zone, set amid wetlands and shrublands in the shade of tamarisks and date palms.

You can also stay in caravan parks at the four towns visited. *Marla* is a major service centre on the Stuart Highway midway between Coober Pedy and the Northern Territory border. *Oodnadatta*, or 'Utnadata': blossom of the mulga, was an important Ghan railhead from 1891 to 1929 and retains much of its original outback character. *William Creek* lies within Anna Creek, one of South Australia's largest cattle stations, and is Australia's smallest town. *Marree*, Aboriginal for possum, used to be the staging post for camel trains and is now a small service centre and starting point for the Oodnadatta and Birdsville tracks.

Though this road is relatively straightforward, take note of **Warnings** and **Essential Advice on Desert Crossings** in the introduction to the desert treks.

WARNINGS ▶ Before departure contact Marla police, (086) 70 7020, and Marree police, (086) 75 8346, to register intended route; contact Oodnadatta police, (086) 70 7805, or Pink Roadhouse Oodnadatta, (086) 70 7822, or Northern South Australia Road Condition Report, (08) 11 633, to check road conditions. ▶ Be cautious and avoid occasional sharp dips and ruts. Watch for road surfaces that may be loose. ▶ For emergency help contact RFDS base at Port Augusta, (086) 42 2044, or Broken Hill, (080) 88 0777, if reception is poor.

BOOKINGS AND PERMITS ▶ No permits required to use Oodnadatta Track. ▶ For information on caravan park in Marla contact Marla Hotel Motel, Stuart Highway, Marla SA 5724; tel. (086) 70 7001. ▶ For information on caravan park in Oodnadatta contact Pink Roadhouse, Oodnadatta Track, Oodnadatta SA 5734; tel. (086) 70 7822. ▶ For information on caravan park in William Creek ring William Creek Hotel and Caravan Park, (086) 70 7880. ▶ Coward Springs Campground open May–October. Self-register. For information write to Coward Springs Camel Station, PO Box 56, Kingscote, Kangaroo Island SA 5223. ▶ For information on caravan park at Marree contact Marree Tourist Park and Caravan Park, cnr Oodnadatta and Birdsville tracks, Marree SA 5733; tel. (086) 75 8371.

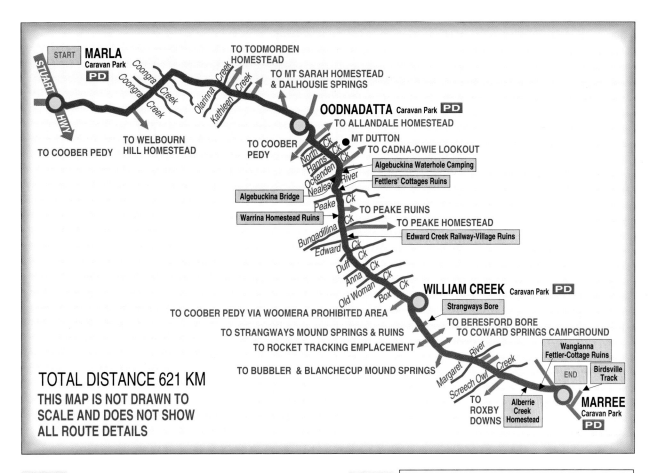

TOTAL DISTANCE 621 KM

THIS MAP IS NOT DRAWN TO
SCALE AND DOES NOT SHOW
ALL ROUTE DETAILS

ROUTE DIRECTIONS

Zero trip meter in Marla at Marla Hotel Motel
on Stuart Hwy. **SO** heading south east.

> **PD** Supplies, caravan park. Mechanical
> repairs, accomm., medical clinic, police
> station. Next fuel Oodnadatta (214 km).

(4.0 km)   Opp. dir. s'post: Alice Springs. ▲ 213.5 km
4.0 km   Intersection. S'post: Oodnadatta Track. **TL**.

> Coober Pedy straight ahead.

(43.3 km)   ▲ 209.5 km
47.3 km   Y intersection. S'post: Oodnadatta. **KL**.

> Welbourn Hill Homestead off to right.

(36.9 km)   ▲ 166.2 km
84.2 km   Coongra Creek crossing. **SO**.
(5.1 km)   ▲ 129.3 km
89.3 km   Coongra Creek crossing. **SO**.
(26.0 km)   ▲ 124.2 km
115.3 km   Olarinna Creek crossing. **SO**.
(11.6 km)   ▲ 98.2 km
126.9 km   Intersection. **SO**.

> Todmorden Homestead 9 km off to left.

(2.6 km)   ▲ 86.6 km
129.5 km   Kathleen Creek crossing. **SO**.
(7.1 km)   ▲ 84.0 km
136.6 km   Intersection. **SO**.

> Todmorden Homestead 10 km off to left.

(59.3 km)   ▲ 76.9 km
195.9 km   Intersection. **SO**.

> Mt Sarah Homestead 64 km off to left;
> Dalhousie Springs a further 106 km.

(17.6 km)   Opp. dir. s'post:
          Alice Springs via Marla. ▲ 17.6 km
213.5 km   Oodnadatta town centre, adjacent to Pink
          Roadhouse.

> **PD** Supplies, caravan park. Mechanical
> repairs, accomm., information, meals, medical
> services, post office, police station, telephone,
> airstrip. Railway-station museum. Swimming
> in Neales River permanent waterholes. Annual
> Picnic Race Meeting held in May. Next fuel
> William Creek (202 km).

0.0 km Zero trip meter at above point. **SO.**
(5.5 km)

▲ 0.0 km

▲ 202.3 km

5.5 km Intersection. S'post: Marree/Oodnadatta Track. **TL.**

| *Coober Pedy straight ahead.* |

(13.5 km)   ▲ 196.8 km

19.0 km Intersection. **SO.**

| *Allandale Homestead 10 km off to left.* |

(9.7 km)   ▲ 183.3 km

28.7 km North Creek crossing. **SO.**

| *Old Ghan rail bridge on left.* |

(4.8 km)   ▲ 173.6 km

33.5 km Hanns Creek crossing. **SO.**
(6.1 km)   ▲ 168.8 km

39.6 km Intersection. **SO.**

| *Turn left to Cadna-owie Lookout.* |

(3.6 km)   ▲ 162.7 km

43.2 km Intersection. S'post: Mt Dutton. **SO.**

| *Turn left to Mt Dutton ruins: stone-fettlers' cottages on Allandale Station. Private property; do not touch.* |

(3.9 km)   ▲ 159.1 km

47.1 km Ockenden Creek crossing. **SO.**

| *Old Ghan bridge on left.* |

(10.2 km)   ▲ 155.2 km

57.3 km Neales River crossing. **SO.**

| *Algebuckina Waterhole on left. Large permanent waterhole. Camping. Algebuckina Bridge on right.* |

(0.7 km)   ▲ 145.0 km

58.0 km Intersection. **SO.**

| *Algebuckina Waterhole off to left.* |

(14.1 km)   ▲ 144.3 km

72.1 km Intersection. Fettlers' cottages ruins on left. **SO.**
(1.0 km)   ▲ 130.2 km

73.1 km Peake Creek crossing. **SO.**
(17.3 km)   ▲ 129.2 km

90.4 km Giles memorial cairn on left. **SO.**

| *Track behind cairn leads to Peake ruins.* |

(5.1 km)   ▲ 111.9 km

Old Ghan rail bridge

Signs along the Oodnadatta Track

95.5 km Warrina Homestead ruins and Elders memorial on left. **SO.**
(9.2 km)   ▲ 106.8 km

104.7 km Bungadillina Creek crossing. **SO.**
(1.4 km)   ▲ 97.6 km

106.1 km Intersection. **SO.**

| *Peake Homestead off to left. Sidney Kidman Co. property.* |

(5.0 km)   ▲ 96.2 km

111.1 km Intersection. Edward Creek railway-village ruins on left. **SO.**

| *Desalination plant towers over fettlers' cottages ruins, water tanks, windmill and artesian bore.* |

(0.6 km)   ▲ 91.2 km

111.7 km Edward Creek crossing. **SO.**
(22.3 km)   ▲ 90.6 km

134.0 km Duff Creek crossing. **SO.**
(13.7 km)   ▲ 68.3 km

147.7 km Anna Creek crossing. **SO.**
(9.5 km) ▲ 54.6 km
157.2 km Old Woman Creek crossing. **SO.**
(1.1 km) ▲ 45.1 km
158.3 km Box Creek crossing. **SO.**
(38.7 km) ▲ 44.0 km
197.0 km Intersection. S'post: William Creek. **SO.**

> *Coober Pedy 168 km off to right via Woomera prohibited area.*

(5.3 km) ▲ 5.3 km
202.3 km William Creek, adjacent to William Creek Hotel on left.

> **PD** *Limited supplies, caravan park. Minor mechanical repairs, accomm., meals, ice, telephone. Next fuel Marree (205 km).*

0.0 km Zero trip meter at above point. **SO.**
(37.1 km) ▲ 0.0 km
▲ 73.8 km

37.1 km Intersection. **SO.**

> *Strangways Bore and historical railway siding on left. Strangways Mound Springs and ruins off to right.*

(12.5 km) ▲ 36.7 km
49.6 km Crossroads. **SO.**

> *Turn left to Beresford Bore (flowing) and historical railway siding. Turn right to concrete tower: historical rocket-tracking emplacement used 1950–60 for Woomera tests.*

(24.2 km) ▲ 24.2 km
73.8 km Intersection.

> *Turn left to Coward Springs Campground and historical railway siding. Generators not permitted. Showers, toilets, water. Flowing artesian bore, wetlands, camel safaris.*

0.0 km Zero trip meter at above intersection. **SO.**
(0.7 km) ▲ 0.0 km
▲ 0.7 km

0.7 km Intersection.

> *Turn right 6 km to Bubbler and Blanchecup mound springs.*

0.0 km Zero trip meter at above intersection. **SO.**
(24.4 km) ▲ 0.0 km
▲ 130.4 km

24.4 km Margaret River crossing. **SO.**
(4.8 km) ▲ 106.0 km

Old Marree rail siding

29.2 km Intersection. **SO.**

> *Turn left to Curdimurka ruins. Camping. Water, toilets.*

(8.5 km) ▲ 101.2 km
37.7 km Intersection. **SO.**

> *Turn left to lookout over Lake Eyre South.*

(19.6 km) ▲ 92.7 km
57.3 km Screech Owl Creek crossing. **SO.**
(4.8 km) ▲ 73.1 km
62.1 km Intersection. S'post: Marree. **SO.**

> *Roxby Downs off to right along Borefield Rd.*

(16.0 km) Opp. dir. s'post: William Creek. ▲ 68.3 km
78.1 km Alberrie Creek Homestead on right. **SO.**

> *Once a fettler cottage used by railway; now owned and used by Finniss Springs Station.*

(17.1 km) ▲ 52.3 km
95.2 km Wangianna fettler cottage ruins on right. **SO.**
(35.2 km) ▲ 35.2 km
130.4 km Marree town centre, adjacent to general store and post office.

> **PD** *Supplies, caravan park. Mechanical repairs, accomm., information, meals, hospital, post office, police station, telephone. Annual Picnic Race Meeting and Gymkhana held in June.*

REVERSE DIRECTIONS START ▲ 0.0 km

THE BIRDSVILLE TRACK
MARREE
«»
BIRDSVILLE

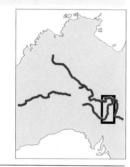

START POINT
Map page 22, B11.

TOTAL KM 519.
UNSEALED KM 519.
DEGREE OF DIFFICULTY Easy.
DRIVING TIME 7 hours.
LONGEST DISTANCES NO FUEL 315 km (Mungerannie Roadhouse to Birdsville); 204 km (Marree to Mungerannie Roadhouse).
TOPOGRAPHIC MAPS Auslig 1:250 000 series: *Marree*; *Kopperamanna*; *Gason*; *Pandie Pandie*; *Birdsville*. See also 1:100 000 series.
LOCAL/SPECIALITY MAPS Westprint Heritage map: *Birdsville and Strzelecki Tracks*; Flinders Ranges and Outback of South Australia Regional Tourist Association map: *Outback South Australia*.
OTHER USEFUL INFORMATION Flinders Ranges and Outback of South Australia Regional Tourist Association booklet: *Flinders Ranges and Outback South Australia Official Visitors Guide*.

DESCRIPTION The fabled Birdsville Track was developed in the 1880s as one of Australia's first major north–south cattle routes, and has claimed the lives of many people who attempted to traverse the Sturt Stony Desert. Today the journey is a relatively easy drive along a well-maintained gravel road, and easily completed in a day.

The small service centre of Marree was once an important railhead as well as a staging post for the Afghan cameleers who supplied the channel-country stations.

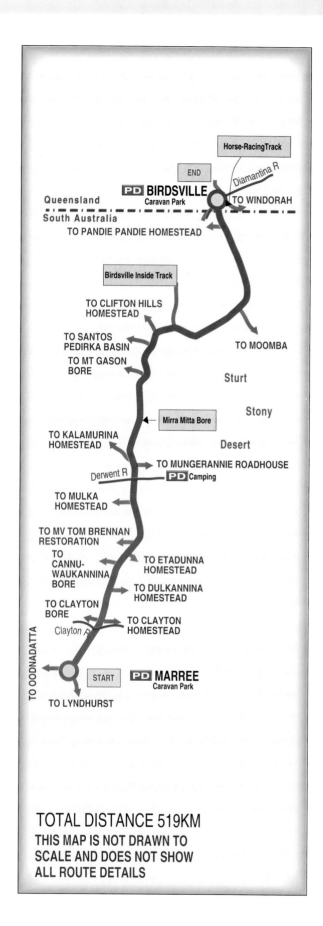

TOTAL DISTANCE 519KM
THIS MAP IS NOT DRAWN TO SCALE AND DOES NOT SHOW ALL ROUTE DETAILS

Lake Harry ruins

From there the track follows the old stock route past scattered homesteads and flowing artesian bores to Mt Gason Bore and the Sturt Stony Desert. This gibber-strewn expanse, with its immense parallel sand dunes, divides the Cooper and Diamantina rivers' drainage systems. North of Clifton Hills Homestead the Birdsville Inside Track branches off from the main Outside track. Because it crosses the Goyder Lagoon floodplain, this wetter and slightly more difficult route was ideal for stock movement, but it is also often impassable and therefore less commonly used.

Known as Diamantina Crossing until 1882, Birdsville originated as a depot for state-border surveyors working in the Simpson Desert. It rapidly became a thriving outback centre but is now a tiny isolated town famous only for its one remaining hotel and annual Race Carnival celebrations held in August–September.

Our route directions include the caravan parks at *Birdsville* and *Marree* as well as the camping area at *Mungerannie Roadhouse* near the Derwent River. Before trekking through this remote desert region see **Warnings** and **Essential Advice on Desert Crossings** in the introduction to the desert treks.

WARNINGS ▶ Sections of track sometimes impassable after heavy rain, especially Birdsville Inside Track. Before departure ring Marree police, (086) 75 8346, and Birdsville police, (0071) 78 220, to check condition and availability of tracks and to register your intended route. ▶ Beware occasional broken edges and soft sections of bulldust that may trap vehicle. ▶ Be careful if collecting water from flowing artesian bores: water temperature near boiling point. ▶ Dispose of rubbish at rubbish dump near Birdsville. ▶ For emergency help contact RFDS base at Port Augusta, (086) 42 2044, or Charleville, (076) 54 1233.

BOOKINGS AND PERMITS ▶ Necessary to obtain Desert Parks Pass to traverse South Australian desert regions; pass valid for 1 year and entitles holder to traverse and camp in all South Australian desert parks. Contact South Australian Department of Environment and Planning, Information Centre, 55 Grenfell Street, Adelaide 5000; GPO Box 667, Adelaide 5001; tel. (08) 207 2300 or SANPWS, Far North Region Office, 60 Elder Terrace, Hawker SA 5434; PO Box 102; tel. (086) 48 4244. ▶ For information on caravan park in Marree contact Marree Tourist Park and Caravan Park, cnr Oodnadatta and Birdsville tracks, Marree SA 5733; tel. (086) 75 8371. ▶ Book accommodation at Birdsville Hotel in advance, (076) 56 3244.

ROUTE DIRECTIONS

0.0 km Zero trip meter in Marree at Oodnadatta Track, Birdsville Track and Lyndhurst Rd intersection. S'post: Birdsville. **SO** onto Birdsville Track heading north east.

> **PD** *Supplies, caravan park. Mechanical repairs, accomm., information, meals, hospital, post office, police station, telephone. Annual Picnic Race Meeting and Gymkhana held in June. Oodnadatta off to left. Lyndhurst off to right. Next fuel Mungerannie Roadhouse (204 km).*

(30.0 km) Opp. dir. s'post: Lyndhurst. ▲ 204.1 km
30.0 km Lake Harry ruins on right. **SO**.

> *1860 site of experimental date-palm plantation.*

(12.1 km) ▲ 174.1 km
42.1 km Dog proof fence. **SO**.

> *Actually a grid to keep dingoes off pastoral lands. World's longest human-made barrier.*

(9.9 km) ▲ 162.0 km
52.0 km Clayton River crossing. **SO**.
(0.7 km) ▲ 152.1 km
52.7 km Crossroads. **SO**.

> *Clayton Bore off to left. Clayton Homestead off to right.*

(30.1 km) ▲ 151.4 km
82.8 km Intersection. **SO**.

> *Dulkaninna Homestead off to right.*

(27.6 km) Opp. dir. s'post: Marree. ▲ 121.3 km

489

110.4 km Intersection. **SO.**

> *Cannuwaukaninna Bore off to left.*

(10.9 km) ▲ 93.7 km

121.3 km Intersection. **SO.**

> *Etadunna Homestead off to right.*

(12.7 km) ▲ 82.8 km

134.0 km Intersection. **SO.**

> *Turn left to MV Tom Brennan Cooper Creek supply-barge restoration.*

(31.3 km) ▲ 70.1 km

165.3 km Intersection. **SO.**

> *Mulka Homestead 2 km off to left.*

(38.7 km) ▲ 38.8 km

204.0 km Derwent River crossing. **SO.**

(0.1 km) ▲ 0.1 km

204.1 km Intersection.

> *Turn right to Mungerannie Roadhouse.* **PD** *Camping. Meals. Next fuel Birdsville (315 km).*

0.0 km Zero trip meter at above intersection. **SO.**

(2.3 km) ▲ 0.0 km

▲ 133.8 km

2.3 km Intersection. S'post: Birdsville. **SO.**

> *Kalamurina Homestead off to left.*

(33.5 km) Opp. dir. s'post: Marree 207. ▲ 131.5 km

35.8 km Mirra Mitta Bore on right. **SO.**

(46.3 km) ▲ 98.0 km

82.1 km Intersection. **SO.**

> *Mt Gason Bore 4 km off to left.*

(26.8 km) ▲ 51.7 km

108.9 km Intersection. **SO.**

> *Santos Pedirka Basin off to left.*

(11.0 km) ▲ 24.9 km

119.9 km Intersection. **SO.**

> *Clifton Hills Homestead off to left.*

(13.9 km) Opp. dir. s'post: Pedirka Basin. ▲13.9 km

133.8 km Intersection.

> *Junction of Birdsville Inside Track: dry-weather track only.*

0.0 km Zero trip meter at above intersection. **SO.**

(58.4 km) ▲ 0.0 km

▲ 181.5 km

Diamantina River, just outside Birdsville

58.4 km Intersection. **SO.**

> *Track on right leads to Moomba.*

(94.5 km) ▲ 123.1 km

152.9 km Intersection. **SO.**

> *Pandie Pandie Homestead off to left.*

(15.2 km) ▲ 28.6 km

168.1 km South Australia–Queensland border. **SO.**

(9.3 km) ▲ 13.4 km

177.4 km T intersection. S'post: Birdsville. **TL.**

> *Birdsville racecourse on right. Windorah off to right.*

(1.4 km) Opp. dir. s'post: Marree. ▲ 4.1 km

178.8 km Diamantina River crossing. **SO.**

(2.7 km) ▲ 2.7 km

181.5 km Birdsville town centre, adjacent to Birdsville Hotel.

> **PD** *Supplies, caravan park. Mechanical repairs, meals, accomm., post-office agency, medical centre, police station, telephone, airport. Royal Hotel ruins. Hot artesian-bore water. Generator electricity.*

REVERSE DIRECTIONS START ▲ 0.0 km

THE CORDILLO DOWNS ROAD
BIRDSVILLE
«»
INNAMINCKA

START POINT
Map page 22, D2.

TOTAL KM 419.
UNSEALED KM 419.
DEGREE OF DIFFICULTY Difficult.
DRIVING TIME 7 to 8 hours.
LONGEST DISTANCE NO FUEL 419 km (Birdsville to Innamincka).
TOPOGRAPHIC MAPS Auslig 1:250 000 series: *Birdsville*; *Betoota*; *Cordillo*; *Innamincka*. See also 1:100 000 series.
LOCAL/SPECIALITY MAPS Westprint Heritage map: *Birdsville and Strzelecki Tracks*; Flinders Ranges and Outback of South Australia Regional Tourist Assocation map: *Outback South Australia*.
OTHER USEFUL INFORMATION Flinders Ranges and Outback of South Australia Regional Tourist Association booklet: *Flinders Ranges and Outback South Australia Official Visitors Guide*; SANPWS brochure: *Parks on the Far North of South Australia*.

DESCRIPTION This track is known as Cordillo Downs Road because it passes the historic Cordillo Downs Homestead; in its heyday as Australia's largest sheep station it ran 85 000 head of sheep. Our trek is rated difficult mainly because the road is rough and not well maintained, but its surface is generally firm; see *Warnings* and *Essential Advice on Desert Crossings* in the introduction to the desert treks.

From *Birdsville*, where you can stay in the caravan park, you head east along the Birdsville Developmental Road before turning south onto the Cordillo Downs Road, where the track begins to deteriorate. After passing the Cadelga Homestead ruins it skirts around the Lamamour Plateau on the left, with the Sturt Stony Desert on the right, and crosses a myriad of usually dry creek beds that lie within channel country: a huge area of naturally irrigated pasture. The explorer Charles Sturt called this a desolate region, but it has an extraordinary arid beauty that changes constantly.

Once in the Innamincka Regional Reserve, worthwhile detours can be made to the fabulous Coongie Lakes region, or to Gidgealpa via Cooper Creek, and out to Nappa Merrie to see the famous Burke and Wills Dig Tree. Innamincka, a corruption of the Aboriginal work 'Yidniminckanie', sprang up around a hotel that catered for pioneer Strzelecki Track drovers and was a thriving custom-duty post before Federation in 1901. You can bush camp at several areas at waterholes on the banks of *Cooper Creek*, where the fishing is excellent.

WARNINGS ▶ Sections of road sometimes impassable after rain. Watch for many unexpected washaways that may destroy vehicle's suspension components, and occasional bulldust patches. ▶ Before departure contact Birdsville police, (0071) 78 220, and Innamincka Hotel, (086) 75 9901, to check road conditions and register intended route. ▶ For emergency help contact RFDS base at Charleville, (076) 54 1233, or Broken Hill, (080) 88 0777.

BOOKINGS AND PERMITS ▶ Necessary to obtain Desert Parks Pass to traverse South Australian desert regions including Innamincka Regional Reserve; pass valid for 1 year and entitles holder to traverse and camp in all South Australian desert parks. Contact South Australian Department of Environment and Planning, Information Centre, 55 Grenfell Street, Adelaide 5000; GPO Box 667, Adelaide 5001; tel. (08) 207 2300 or SANPWS Far North Region Office, 60 Elder Terrace, Hawker SA 5434; PO Box 102; tel. (086) 48 4244. ▶ Book accommodation at Birdsville Hotel in advance, (076) 56 3244. ▶ For information on camping, accommodation and tours in Innamincka region contact Innamincka Hotel, PMB 3, Innamincka SA 5731; tel. (086) 75 9901 or Trading Post general store, Innamincka; tel. (086) 75 9900.

ROUTE DIRECTIONS

0.0 km Zero trip meter in Birdsville at Birdsville Hotel. **SO** onto Birdsville Developmental Rd heading east.

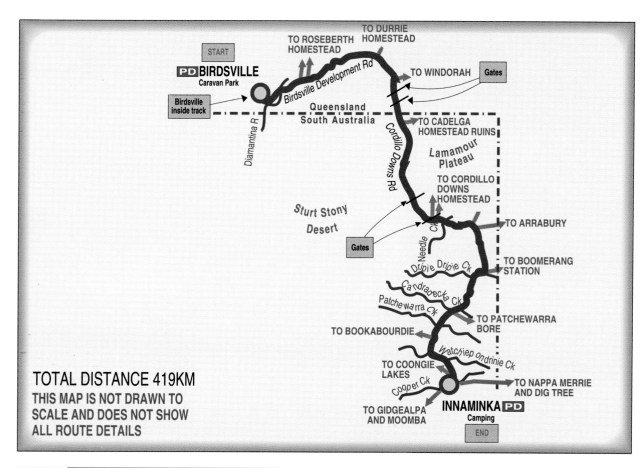

TOTAL DISTANCE 419KM
THIS MAP IS NOT DRAWN TO
SCALE AND DOES NOT SHOW
ALL ROUTE DETAILS

PD *Supplies, caravan park. Mechanical repairs, meals, accomm., post-office agency, medical centre, police station, telephone, airport. Royal Hotel ruins. Hot artesian-bore water. Generator-supplied electricity. Next fuel Innamincka (419 km).*

(2.7 km) ▲ 110.0 km
2.7 km Diamantina River crossing. **SO.**

(1.4 km) ▲ 107.3 km
4.1 km Intersection. S'post: Windorah. **SO.**

Marree off to right via Birdsville Outside Track.

(29.3 km) Opp. dir. s'post: Birdsville. ▲ 105.9 km
33.4 km Intersection. **SO.**

Roseberth Homestead off to left.

(0.4 km) ▲ 76.6 km
33.8 km Intersection. S'post: Betoota. **SO.**

Roseberth Homestead off to left.

(71.0 km) Opp. dir. s'post: Birdsville. ▲ 76.2 km

104.8 km Intersection. S'post: Betoota. **SO.**

Durrie Homestead off to left.

(5.2 km) Opp. dir. s'post: Birdsville. ▲ 5.2 km
110.0 km Intersection. S'post: Cordillo Downs.

Windorah straight ahead.

0.0 km Zero trip meter at above intersection. **TR** onto Cordillo Downs Road.

(12.7 km) Opp. dir. s'post: Birdsville. ▲ 0.0 km
▲ 43.7 km

12.7 km Gate. **SO.**

Leave as found.

(18.6 km) ▲ 31.0 km
31.3 km Gate. **SO.**

Leave as found.

(12.4 km) ▲ 12.4 km
43.7 km Intersection. S'post: Cordillo Downs 86.

Cadelga Homestead ruins off to left.

0.0 km Zero trip meter at above intersection. **SO** for 200 m and cross Cadelga Creek.
(76.7 km) Opp. dir. s'post: Birdsville. ▲ 0.0 km
▲ 123.1 km

76.7 km Gate. **SO.**

> *Leave as found.*

(10.4 km) ▲ 46.4 km
87.1 km Intersection. **SO.**

> *Cordillo Downs Homestead off to left.*

(0.3 km) ▲ 36.0 km
87.4 km Gate. **SO.**

> *Leave as found.*

(1.5 km) ▲ 35.7 km
88.9 km Intersection. S'post: Innamincka. **SO.**

> *Track on left to Cordillo Downs Homestead.*

(2.0 km) Opp. dir. s'post: Birdsville. ▲ 34.2 km
90.9 km Needle Creek crossing. **SO.**
(27.3 km) ▲ 32.2 km
118.2 km Intersection. S'post: Innamincka 152. **SO.**

> *Track on left.*

(4.9 km) ▲ 4.9 km
123.1 km T intersection.

> *Arrabury off to left.*

0.0 km Zero trip meter at above intersection. **TR.**
(9.4 km) Opp. dir. s'post: Birdsville. ▲ 0.0 km
▲ 142.1 km

9.4 km Sign: Innamincka Regional Reserve. **SO.**
(24.7 km) ▲ 132.7 km
34.1 km Intersection. S'post: Innamincka. **SO.**

> *Track on left leads to Boomerang Station.*

(1.3 km) Opp. dir. s'post: Arrabury. ▲ 108.0 km
35.4 km Leap Year Bore on left. **SO.**
(11.5 km) ▲ 106.7 km
46.9 km Dripie Dripie Creek crossing. **SO.**
(14.0 km) ▲ 95.2 km
60.9 km Candradecka Creek crossing. **SO.**
(23.4 km) ▲ 81.2 km
84.3 km Intersection. **SO** and immediately cross Patchewarra Creek.

> *Patchewarra Bore off to left.*

(25.3 km) ▲ 57.8 km
109.6 km Intersection. S'post: Innamincka. **SO.**

> *Bookabourdie off to right.*

Sturt Stony Desert

Cooper Creek at Innaminka

(15.4 km) Opp. dir. s'post: Cordillo Downs. ▲ 32.5 km
125.0 km Watchiepondrinie Creek crossing. **SO.**
(14.2 km) ▲ 17.1 km
139.2 km Intersection. **SO.**

> *Coongie Lakes 103 km off to right.*

(2.3 km) ▲ 2.9 km
141.5 km Cooper Creek causeway. **SO.**
(0.6 km) ▲ 0.6 km
142.1 km Intersection. Innamincka town centre, adjacent to Innamincka Hotel and Trading Post general store.

> **PD** *Supplies, bush camping at Cooper Creek waterholes. Minor mechanical repairs, accomm., meals. Nappa Merrie and Burke and Wills Dig Tree off to left across Queensland border. Memorial cairns for Sturt and Burke and Wills, Kings Marker memorial to John King, Inland Mission hostel ruins, Yantrwantas rock carvings.*

REVERSE DIRECTIONS START ▲ 0.0 km

493

THE STRZELECKI TRACK

INNAMINCKA

«»

TIBOOBURRA

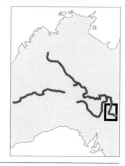

START POINT
Map page 22, G6.

TOTAL KM 362.
UNSEALED KM 362.
DEGREE OF DIFFICULTY Moderate.
DRIVING TIME 6 hours.
LONGEST DISTANCES NO FUEL 222 km (Innamincka to Cameron Corner); 140 km (Cameron Corner to Tibooburra).
TOPOGRAPHIC MAPS Auslig 1:250 000 series: *Innamincka*; *Strzelecki*; *Milparinka*. See also 1:100 000 series.
LOCAL/SPECIALITY MAPS Westprint Heritage map: *Birdsville and Strzelecki Tracks*; Flinders Ranges and Outback of South Australia Regional Tourist Association map: *Outback South Australia*.
OTHER USEFUL INFORMATION Flinders Ranges and Outback of South Australia Regional Tourist Association booklet: *Flinders Ranges and Outback South Australia Official Visitors Guide*; NSW National Parks and Wildlife Service (NPWS) brochure: *Park Guide: Sturt National Park*.

DESCRIPTION For the first 113 kilometres of this trek we use the old Strzelecki Track, a stock route pioneered in 1870 when cattle-duffer Harry Redford stole a whole herd and drove it south to the Adelaide markets. Motor-vehicle traffic has increased steadily since the 1960s when natural gas was discovered in the Cooper Basin and the gas field was established at Moomba. In this first section the track's condition ranges from average to poor; see *Warnings* and *Essential Advice on Desert Crossings* in the introduction to the desert treks.

In the Strzelecki Desert you see mostly pale orange–red sand dunes with occasional dunes of pure soft sand in

Sign along the Strzelecki Track

vivid red: striking next to the bright-blue skies and green grasses of the Australian outback. Turning east along Cameron Corner Road the track's quality improves, and at the famous Cameron Corner, named after government surveyor John Cameron who surveyed the border, you are standing in South Australia, Queensland and New South Wales all at the same time.

The track continues west–east into New South Wales across many sand dunes and traverses Sturt National Park, 188 000 hectares of semi-desert with intriguing geology and wildlife. Surrounded by granite outcrops and known to early goldminers as the Granites, Tibooburra derives its name from an Aboriginal word meaning 'heaps of boulders'.

Our route directions include bush camping at waterholes along the banks of *Cooper Creek* at Innamincka, and camping at *Cameron Corner* and *Fort Grey Camping Area* in Sturt National Park; there is also a caravan park at *Tibooburra*.

WARNINGS ▶ Before departure ring Innamincka Hotel, (086) 75 9901, and NPWS District Office, Tibooburra, (080) 91 3308, to register intended route and ring Innamincka Hotel, or Northern South Australia Road Condition Report, (08) 11 633, to check road conditions. ▶ Some sections of

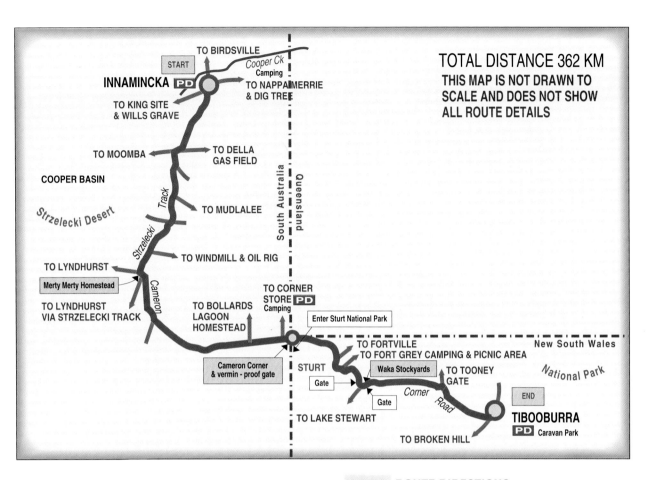

TOTAL DISTANCE 362 KM
THIS MAP IS NOT DRAWN TO
SCALE AND DOES NOT SHOW
ALL ROUTE DETAILS

track may be impassable after heavy rain. ▶ When crossing sand dunes in last west–east section to Tibooburra, keep hard left to avoid possible oncoming traffic. ▶ Carry extra drinking water and fuel. ▶ For emergency help contact RFDS base at Broken Hill, (080) 88 0777.

BOOKINGS AND PERMITS ▶ Obtain Desert Parks Pass to traverse South Australian sections of desert. Fee applicable, pass valid for 1 year and entitles holder to traverse and camp in all South Australian desert parks. Contact SA Department of Environment and Planning, 55 Grenfell Street, Adelaide 5000; GPO Box 667, Adelaide 5001; tel. (08) 207 2300, or SANPWS Far North Region Office, 60 Elder Terrace, Hawker SA 5434; PO Box 102; tel. (086) 48 4244. ▶ For information on Innamincka region contact Innamincka Hotel, PMB 3, Innamincka SA 5731; tel. (086) 75 9901, or Trading Post general store, Innamincka, (086) 75 9900. ▶ For information on desert environment contact SANPWS Far North Region Office. ▶ Self-register at Fort Grey Camping Area and 3 other campsites in Sturt National Park. For information on national park and Tibooburra region contact NSWNPWS District Office, Briscoe Street, Tibooburra NSW 2880; tel. (080) 91 3308.

ROUTE DIRECTIONS

0.0 km Zero trip meter in Innamincka at Strzelecki Track intersection. S'post: Wills Grave. **SO** onto Strzelecki Track heading south west.

> **PD** *Supplies, bush camping at Cooper Creek waterholes. Minor mechanical repairs, accomm., meals. Nappa Merrie and famous Burke and Wills Dig Tree off to left across Queensland border. Memorial cairns for Sturt and Burke and Wills, Kings Marker memorial to John King, Inland Mission hostel ruins, Yantrwantas rock carvings. Local tours, fishing, charter boat. Next fuel Cameron Corner (222 km).*

(1.3 km)   Opp. dir. s'post: Birdsville 422. ▲1.3 km
1.3 km Intersection. S'post: Lyndhurst.

> *Turn right 7 km to King site; Wills grave a further 12 km. Alternative route to Lyndhurst via Moomba.*

0.0 km Zero trip meter at above intersection. **SO**.
(44.1 km)   ▲ 0.0 km
                                               ▲ 111.5 km

495

44.1 km   T intersection. S'post: Lyndhurst. **TR.**

> *Track on left leads to Della Gas Field.*

(0.5 km)   Opp. dir. s'post: Innamincka. ▲ 67.4 km

44.6 km   Intersection. S'post: Lyndhurst. **TL.**

> *Track straight ahead leads to Moomba.*

(6.1 km)   ▲ 66.9 km

50.7 km   Y intersection. **KR.**

(19.1 km)   ▲ 60.8 km

69.8 km   Intersection. **SO.**

> *Mudlalee off to left.*

(6.3 km)   ▲ 41.7 km

76.1 km   Crossroads. **SO.**

(22.6 km)   ▲ 35.4 km

98.7 km   Intersection. **SO.**

> *Windmill and oil rig off to left.*

(12.8 km)   ▲ 12.8 km

111.5 km   T intersection. S'post: Bollards Lagoon Homestead.

> *Merty Merty Homestead on right. Lyndhurst off to right.*

0.0 km   Zero trip meter at above T intersection. **TL** off Strzelecki Track onto Cameron Corner Road.

> *Strzelecki Track to Lyndhurst continues from 600 m on right.*

(25.6 km)   Opp. dir. s'post: Innamincka. ▲ 0.0 km
    ▲ 108.9 km

25.6 km   Intersection. **SO.**

> *Track on right.*

(68.8 km)   ▲ 83.3 km

94.4 km   Intersection. S'post: Tibooburra 177. **SO.**

> *Bollards Lagoon Homestead off to left.*

(14.5 km)   Opp. dir. s'post:
    Merty Merty Homestead. ▲ 14.5 km

108.9 km   Intersection.

> *Turn left to Corner Store and homestead at Cameron Corner.* **PD** *Bush camping. Light refreshments, toilets. Next fuel Tibooburra (140 km).*

0.0 km   Zero trip meter at above intersection. **KR.**

(0.3 km)   ▲ 0.0 km
    ▲ 31.0 km

0.3 km   Vermin-proof gate at South Australia–Queensland–New South Wales border. **SO**

through Cameron Corner along Cameron Corner Road.

> *Close gate after entering NSW and Sturt National Park. Vermin-proof fences built during 1880s rabbit plague.*

(21.5 km)   ▲ 30.7 km

21.8 km   Intersection. S'post: Tibooburra 120. **SO.**

> *Fortville off to left.*

(9.2 km)   Opp. dir. s'post:
    Cameron Corner 21. ▲ 9.2 km

31.0 km   Intersection. S'post: Tibooburra.

> *Turn left 1 km to Fort Grey Camping Area. Picnic tables, gas barbecues, toilets. Water, shelter. Fires prohibited.*

0.0 km   Zero trip meter at above intersection. **SO.**

(28.8 km)   Opp. dir. s'post: Cameron Corner. ▲ 0.0 km
    ▲ 109.7 km

28.8 km   Gate. **SO.**

> *Leave as found.*

(1.2 km)   ▲ 80.9 km

30.0 km   T intersection. S'post: Tibooburra. **TL.**

> *Lake Stewart 10 km off to right.*

(0.2 km)   Opp. dir. s'post:
    Cameron Corner 50. ▲ 79.7 km

30.2 km   Gate. **SO.**

> *Leave as found. Waka Stockyards 500 m on left.*

(35.0 km)   ▲ 79.5 km

65.2 km   T intersection. S'post: Tibooburra. **TR.**

> *Tooney Gate off to left.*

(42.9 km)   Opp. dir. s'post:
    Cameron Corner 85. ▲ 44.5 km

108.1 km   T intersection. S'post: Tibooburra 1. **TL.**

> *Broken Hill off to right. RFDS base.*

(1.6 km)   Opp. dir. s'post: Cameron Corner. ▲1.6 km

109.7 km   Tibooburra town centre, adjacent to police station.

> **PD** *Supplies, caravan park. Accomm., all services. Many historic buildings of local stone. Nearby goldfields, Sturt cairn, Poole grave, Golden Gully scenic walk. Gymkhana and rodeo held on NSW Labour Day weekend in early October.*

REVERSE DIRECTIONS START ▲ 0.0 km

ROAD MAPS

Freeway with Freeway Route Number................	═══🄵🄴═══
Freeway under construction...............................	════════════
Highway sealed with National Route Number....	━━🄷31━━
Highway sealed with Metroad Route Number....	━━⬡1━━
Highway unsealed with Tasmania Route Number	═══A10═══
Highway under construction...............................	▪▪▪▪▪▪▪▪▪▪
Major road sealed with State Route Number.......	━━156━━
Major road unsealed...	───────
Major road under construction...........................	───────
Distributor road, with Tourist Route....................	─────
Distributor road unsealed..................................	───────
Minor road..	─────
Minor road unsealed...	───────
Vehicle track..	───────
Walking Track...	··········
Railway with station..	┼┼┼●┼┼ Paratoo
Total kilometres between two points..................	▼ 114 ▼
Intermediate kilometres......................................	▼ 77 ▼
State border..	─ ─ ─ ─
Major fence line...	vermin-proof fence
State capital city..	**DARWIN**
Town, over 50 000 inhabitants...........................	**GEELONG** ○
Town, 10 000-50 000 inhabitants........................	**Bairnsdale** ○
Town, 5 000-10 000 inhabitants.........................	Hamilton ○
Town, 1 000-5 000 inhabitants...........................	Maffra ○
Town, 200-1 000 inhabitants..............................	Omeo ○
Town, under 200 inhabitants..............................	Eskdale ○
Locality, suburb..	BUNGALLA
Pastoral station homestead...............................	*Alroy Downs* ■
Closed Aboriginal town......................................	Murgenella ○
Roadhouse..	Fortesque 🄷
Commercial airport...	✈
Place of interest...	•
Landmark feature..	•
Hill, mountain...	+
Lighthouse..	★
Route destination...	*TO GOULBURN*
Lake..	
Intermittent lake...	
Aboriginal land...	
Prohibited areas...	
National parks..	
Adjoining page number.......................................	**56**

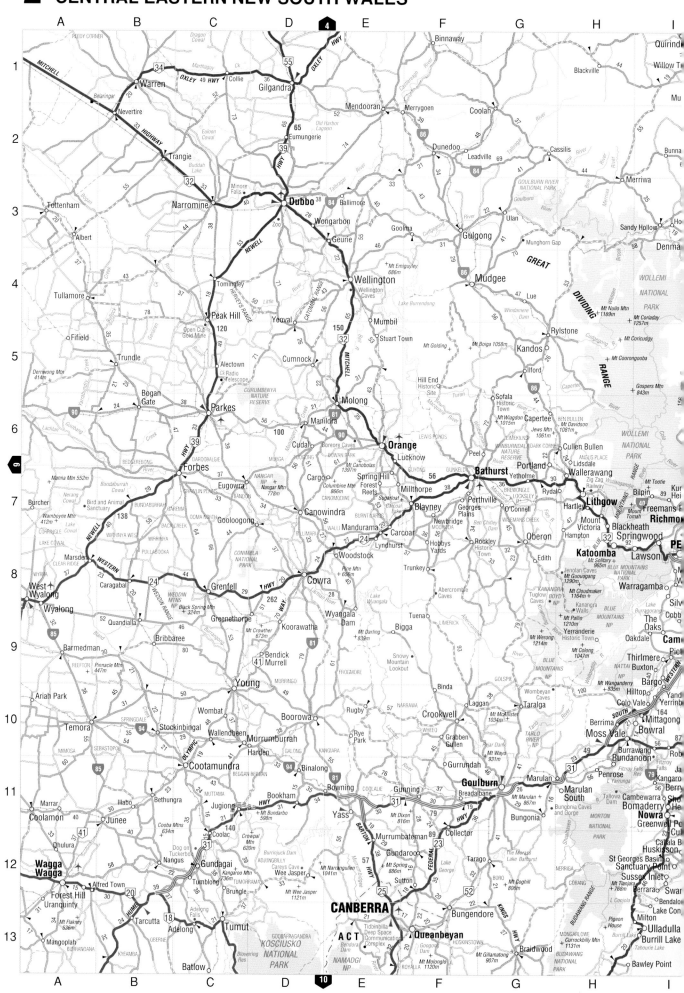

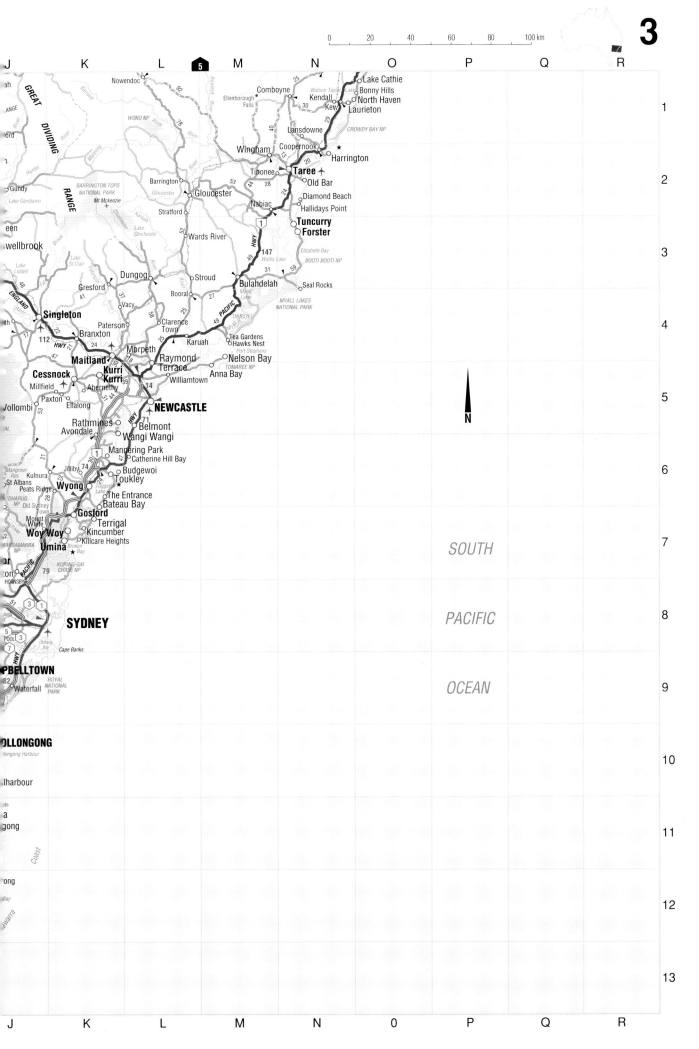

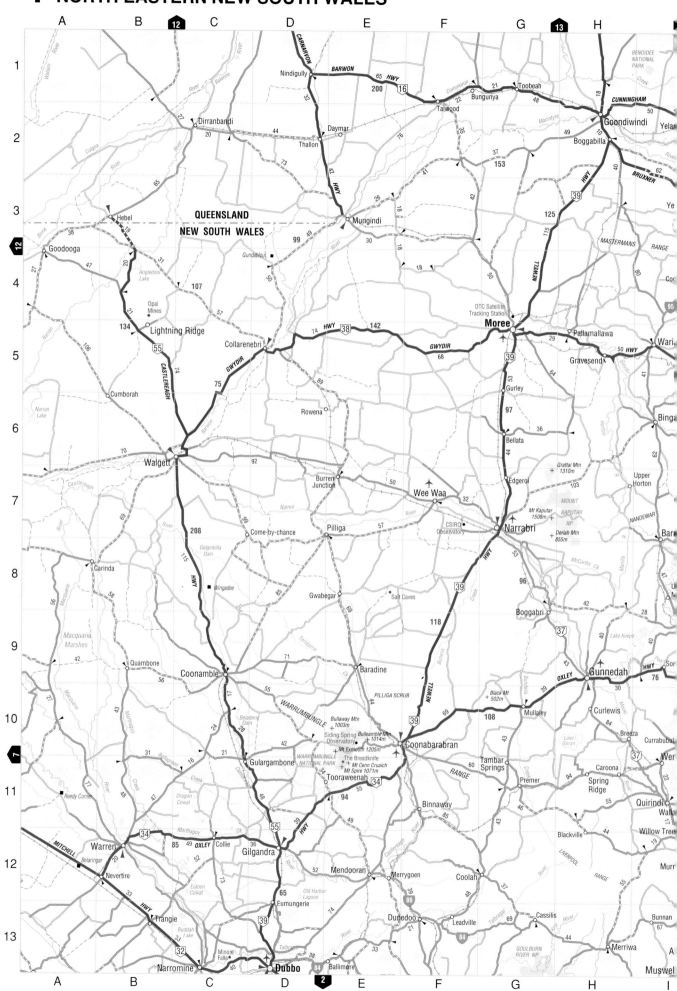

0 20 40 60 80 100 km

J K L M N O P Q R

13

1

Karara
GREAT
200 40
Mt Burrabaranga 794m
Lake Leslie
Warwick
15 HWY
Tannymorel
Killarney
MAIN RANGE NP
Rathdowney
MT BARNEY NP
Hillview
Springbrook
Tumbulgum
Tweed Heads
Banora Point
Kingscliff
Bogangar
Pottsville Beach

20
Coolmunda Dam
60
Legume
Woodenbong
Urbenville
Tyalgum
Murwillumbah
MT WARNING NP
Uki
Burringbar
29
33
Ocean Shores
Brunswick Heads

21
Dalveen
Pozieres
Thulimbah
142
45
63
LAMINGTON NP
BORDER RANGES NP
91
Kyogle
Nimbin
Mullumbimby
110
Cape Byron
Byron Bay

34
Mt Bullaganang 629m
Amiens
113
Appleethorpe
Stanthorpe
Severnlea
Haystack Mtn 878m
RICHMOND RANGE
43
Bangalow
Clunes
Newrybar
Lennox Head

2

QUEENSLAND
Glen Aplin
Ballandean
SUNDOWN NP
GIRRAWEEN NP
BALD ROCK NP
BOONOO BOONOO NP
Bonalbo
Mummulgum
190
45
Casino
44 31
Lismore
Alstonville
33
48
36
Ballina

Texas
24
Glenlyon Dam
Wallangarra
Drake
81
Tabulam
Mallanganee
47
Coraki
Wardell
Broadwater
BROADWATER NP

247
95
DIVIDING
HWY
44
Tenterfield
15
Mt Belmore 650m
55
91
HIGHWAY
Woodburn
1
Evans Head

3

NEW SOUTH WALES
RANGE
Torrington
Mt Bajimba 1446m
Baryulgil
112
Mt Marsh 501m
Lawrence Road
Chatsworth
The Broadwater
130
Iluka
BUNDJALUNG NATIONAL PARK

4

61
Emmaville
Deepwater
91
ENGLAND
65 12
GIBRALTAR RANGE NATIONAL PARK
162
38
GWYDIR
136
HWY
Carrs Creek Junction
Maclean
Yamba
Angourie

56
KINGS PLAINS NP
Inverell
38
Glen Innes
26
28
NYMBOIDA NP
Copmanhurst
Ulmarra
Tyndale
Brooms Head

5

67
Red Range
161
Power Station
Grafton
41
YURAYGIR NP
N

98
Gilgai
Glencoe
The Black Mtn 591m
Boyd River
Nymboida
Coutts Crossing
48
Minnie Water
Lake Hiawatha

6

Tingha
Ben Lomond
88
Glenreagh
82
1
Red Rock
North Solitary Island
North West Solitary Island
Wooli

46
NEW
15
GUY FAWKES RIVER NATIONAL PARK
Mt Hyland 1439m
Arrawarra
Woolgoolga
Groper Island
Emerald Beach
South Solitary Island

7

Llangothlin
Guyra
36
28
31
Coramba
Moonee Beach
Split Solitary Island
Coffs Harbour
Muttonbird Island
Coffs Harbour
SOUTH

53
48
Thunderbolt's Cave
RANGE
48
Ebor Falls
46
Dorrigo
DORRIGO NP
Sawtell

8

Bundarra
37
Armidale
78
Hillgrove
Wollomombi Falls
CATHEDRAL ROCK NP
Ebor
78
Bellingen
Mylestom
Urunga
Valla Beach
165
Nambucca Heads

26
Uralla
40
Wollomombi
NEW ENGLAND NATIONAL PARK
56
Bowraville

111
48
Dangars Falls
Mihi Falls
108
Taylors Arm
49
Macksville
Scotts Head
Stuarts Point

9

15
HWY
25
Walcha Road
41
OXLEY WILD RIVERS NATIONAL PARK
Bellbrook
Willawarrin
34
South West Rocks
Trial Bay Gaol
PACIFIC

24
42
Walcha
OXLEY
31
Apsley Falls
Stoney Ck Falls
Frederickton
Smithtown
Gladstone
Hat Head
HAT HEAD NP

10

Dungowan
48
Tia Falls
Yarrowitch Falls
WERRIKIMBE NATIONAL PARK
1
Kempsey
Crescent Head

33
Niangala
70
264
Mt Seaview
120
Point Plomer
Telegraph Point
LIMEBURNERS CREEK NATURE RESERVE

11

Nundle
53
Tuggolo
26
Mt Seaview
34 HWY
Long Flat
Beechwood
23
Wauchope
Port Macquarie
OCEAN

Nowendoc
Ellenborough
25
24
Lake Cathie
Kew
Bonny Hills
North Haven
Laurieton

86
Combyne
30
Kendall
74
27

12

WOKO NATIONAL PARK
44
Lansdowne
Wingham
Coopernook
Harrington
CROWDY BAY NP
Crowdy Head

GREAT
DIVIDING
BARRINGTON TOPS NATIONAL PARK
Mt Mckenzie
Barrington
Tinonee
55
Taree
Old Bar
Diamond Beach
Hallidays Point

13

RANGE
Gloucester
Stratford
Nabiac
24
Tuncurry
Forster
1

3

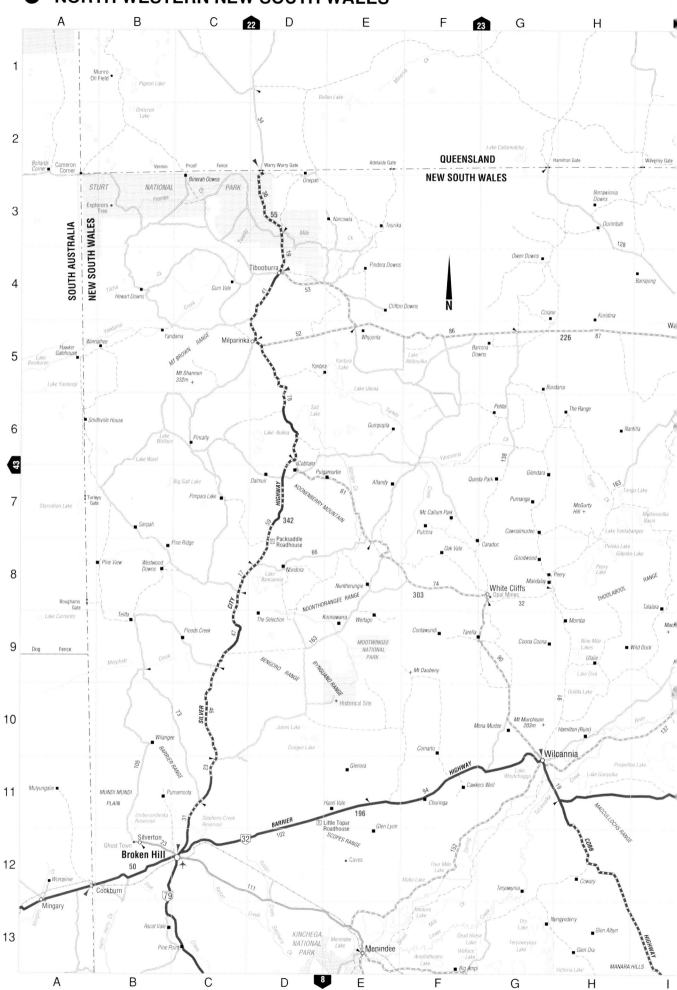

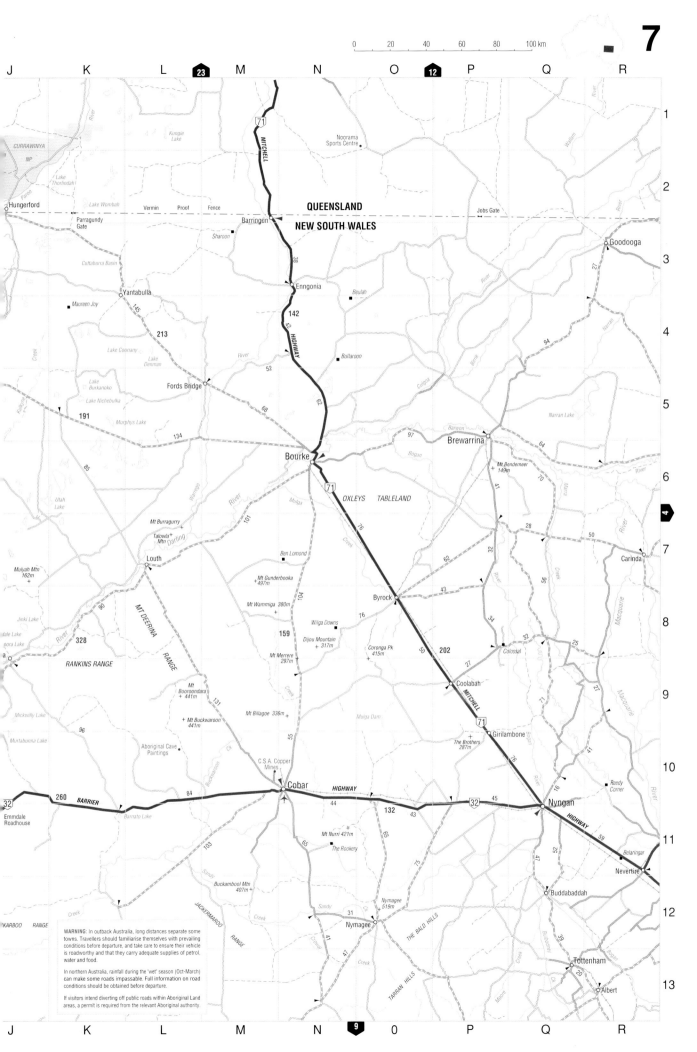

0 20 40 60 80 100 km

1

CURRAWINYA
NP

Kungie
Lake

Noorama
Sports Centre

2

Lake
Thorlindah

Paroo

Lake Wombah

Hungerford

QUEENSLAND

Vermin   Proof   Fence

Barringun

Jobs Gate

NEW SOUTH WALES

3

Parragundy
Gate

38

Sharoon

Enngonia

Beulah

Goodooga

27

Cuttaburra Basin

4

Maureen Joy

Yantabulla

145

142

42

Bullaroon

94

213

Lake Coonany

HIGHWAY

River

52

5

191

Lake
Burkanoko

134

Lake Nichebulka

Murphys Lake

68

62

Barwon

Brewarrina

97

Bogan

Narran Lake

64

Narran

6

85

Utah
Lake

Fords Bridge

Bourke

71

OXLEYS   TABLELAND

Mt Bendemeer
149m

41

70

4

Warrego

101

76

62

32

28

50

7

Mulyah Mtn
162m

Mt Burragurry

Talowla
Mtn *Darling*

Louth

Ben Lomond

Mt Gunderbooka
497m

River

43

56

Carinda

90

Jinki Lake

MT DEERINA

104

Mt Wammiga 380m

76

Byrock

202

34

32

25

8

oora Lake

328

RANKINS RANGE

RANGE

159

Wilga Downs

Dijou Mountain
+ 317m

50

27

Colossal

Mt Merrere
297m

Coronga Pk
415m

a

131

Mt
Booroondara
+ 441m

Mt Billagoe 336m

Muiga Dam

Coolabah

27

9

Mickwilly Lake

96

+ Mt Buckwaroon
441m

MITCHELL

71

The Brothers
287m

Girilambone

41

Murtabunna Lake

Aboriginal Cave
Paintings

55

76

10

260 *BARRIER*

84

C.S.A. Copper
Mines

Buckwaroon *Ck*

16

Reedy
Corner

32

32

Emmdale
Roadhouse

Barnato Lake

Cobar

HIGHWAY

44

132   43

32

45

Nyngan

HIGHWAY

11

103

65

65

Mt Nurri 421m

75

59

Belaringar

47

52

Sandy

The Rookery

Nevertire

KARBOO   RANGE

Sandy

JACKERMAROO

Buckambool Mtn
407m

Creek

Sandy

Nymagee 519m

31

THE BALD HILLS

Buddabaddah

39

12

41

47

Nymagee

Crowl

TARRAN HILLS

20

Tottenham

13

Albert

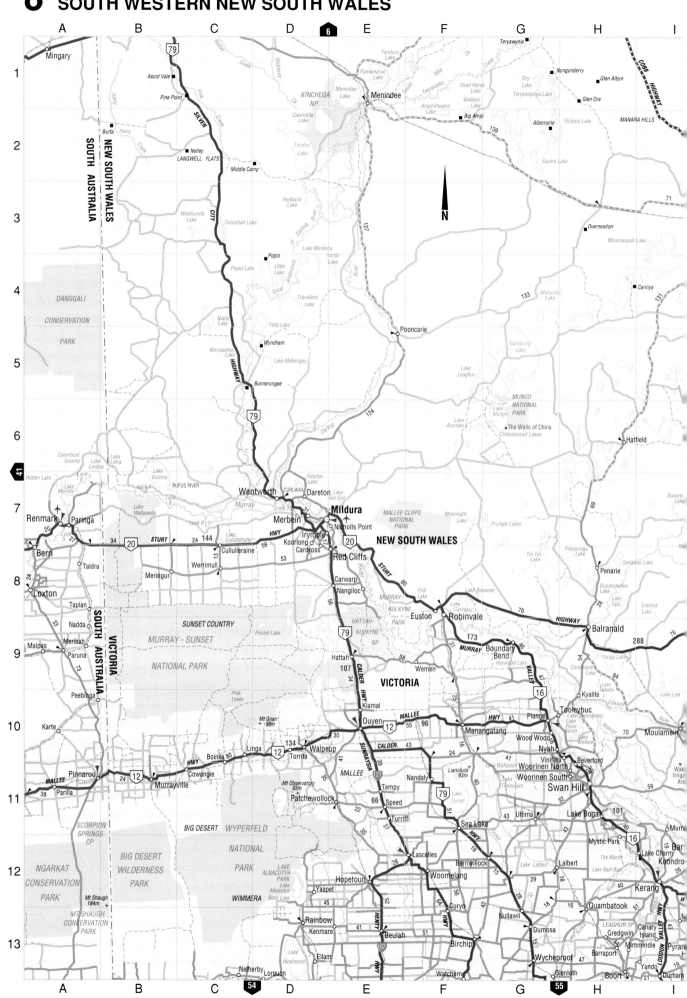

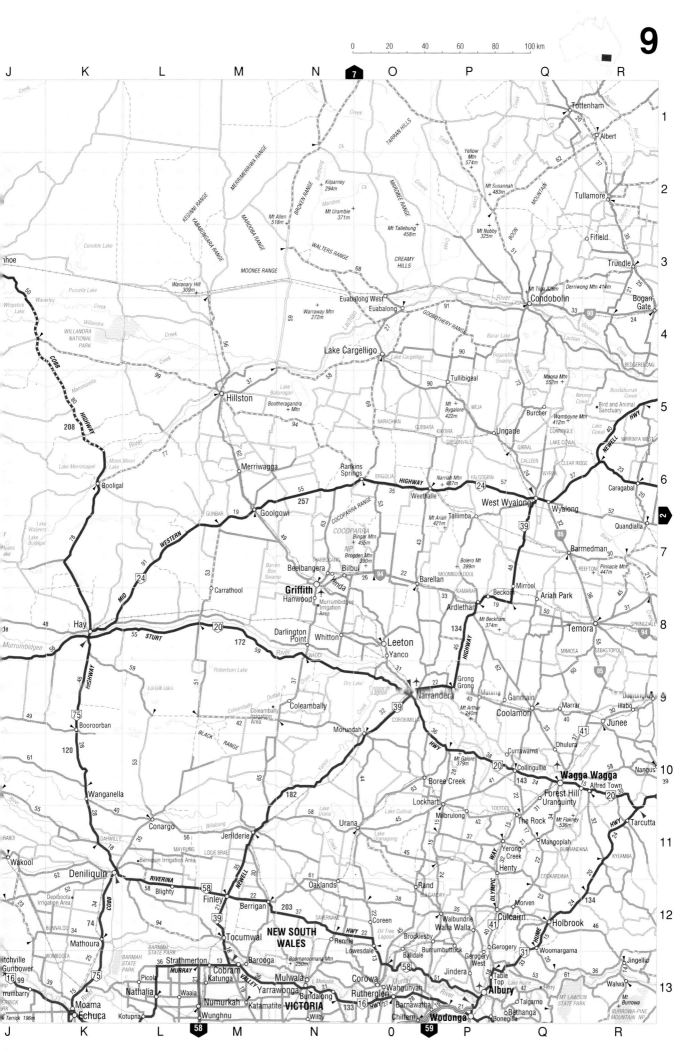

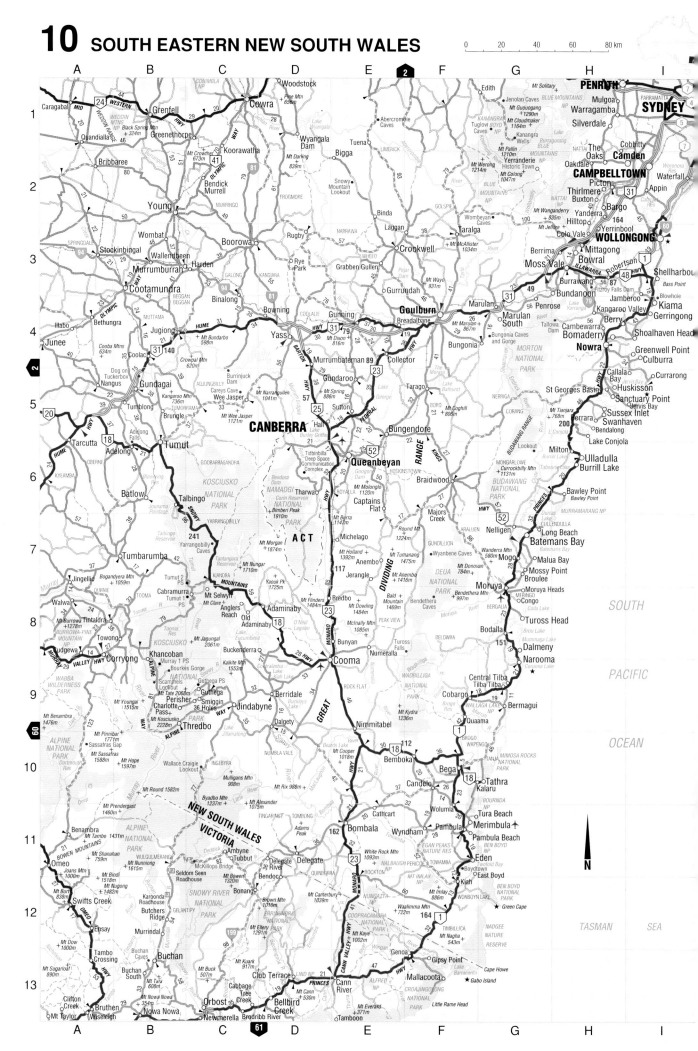

0   20   40   60   80 km

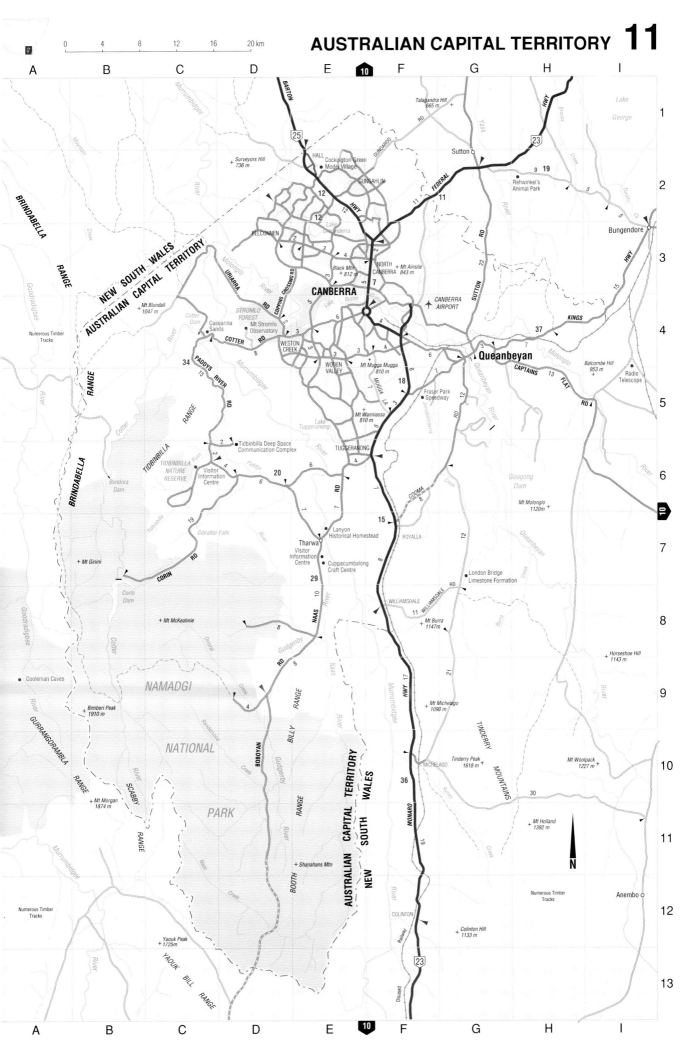

0   4   8   12   16   20 km

A   B   C   D   E   F   G   H   I

BRINDABELLA

RANGE

NEW SOUTH WALES

AUSTRALIAN CAPITAL TERRITORY

Numerous Timber Tracks

Goodradigbee

Murrumbidgee

+ Mt Blundall 1047 m

BRINDABELLA RANGE

Cotter Dam

Casuarina Sands

Bendora Dam

+ Mt Ginini

Corin Dam

Cooleman Caves

NAMADGI

Bimberi Peak 1910 m

GURRANGORAMBLA RANGE

+ Mt Morgan 1874 m

SCABBY RANGE

NATIONAL

PARK

Murrumbidgee

Yaouk Peak 1725 m

YAOUK BILL RANGE

BARTON

10

25

HALL

+ Surveyors Hill 736 m

Cockington Green Model Village

GUNGAHLIN

12

12

12

BELCONNEN

Lake Ginninderra

URIARRA RD

Molonglo River

STROMLO FOREST

Mt Stromlo Observatory

WESTON CREEK

COPPINS CROSSING RD

CANBERRA

Black Mtn 812 m

NORTH CANBERRA

+ Mt Ainslie 843 m

Lake Burley Griffin

7

COTTER RD

PADDYS RIVER

34

15

RANGE

RD

Murrumbidgee

WODEN VALLEY

+ Mt Mugga Mugga 810 m

Lake Tuggeranong

+ Mt Wanniassa 810 m

MUGGA LA

18

3

TUGGERANONG

TIDBINBILLA NATURE RESERVE

Tidbinbilla Deep Space Communication Complex

Visitor Information Centre

2

4

20

6

Paddys River

Gibraltar Falls

19

CORIN RD

+ Mt McKeahnie

NAAS RD

10

7

7

RD

Lanyon Historical Homestead

Tharwa Visitor Information Centre

Cuppacumbalong Craft Centre

29

Gudgenby River

8

8

Naas River

4

BOBOYAN RD

BILLY RANGE

Gudgenby River

Orroral River

BOOTH RANGE

+ Shanahans Mtn

AUSTRALIAN CAPITAL TERRITORY

NEW SOUTH WALES

COLINTON

Railway

Dissed

23

GUNDAROO

RD

Talagandra Hill 665 m

Sutton

FEDERAL HWY

11

11

Yass River

Rehwinkel's Animal Park

9   19

5

5

5

23

Bungendore

HWY

SUTTON RD

22

CANBERRA AIRPORT

Queanbeyan

Queanbeyan River

KINGS

37

CAPTAINS

13

FLAT RD

Balcombe Hill 953 m

Radio Telescope

6

7

Fraser Park Speedway

Jerrabomberra

RD

12

Googong Dam

Mt Molonglo 1120m

10

15

COOMA

8

ROYALLA

RD

12

London Bridge Limestone Formation

8

WILLIAMSDALE

11

WILLIAMSDALE RD

+ Mt Burra 1147m

Burra Creek

21

Murrumbidgee River

HWY 17

MONARO

36

19

MICHELAGO

+ Mt Michelago 1090m

Tinderry Peak 1618 m

TINDERRY

MOUNTAINS

Queanbeyan River

+ Horseshoe Hill 1143 m

+ Mt Woolpack 1227 m +

30

+ Mt Holland 1392 m

Creek

River

Numerous Timber Tracks

Anembo

+ Colinton Hill 1133 m

N

1

2

3

4

5

6

7

8

9

10

11

12

13

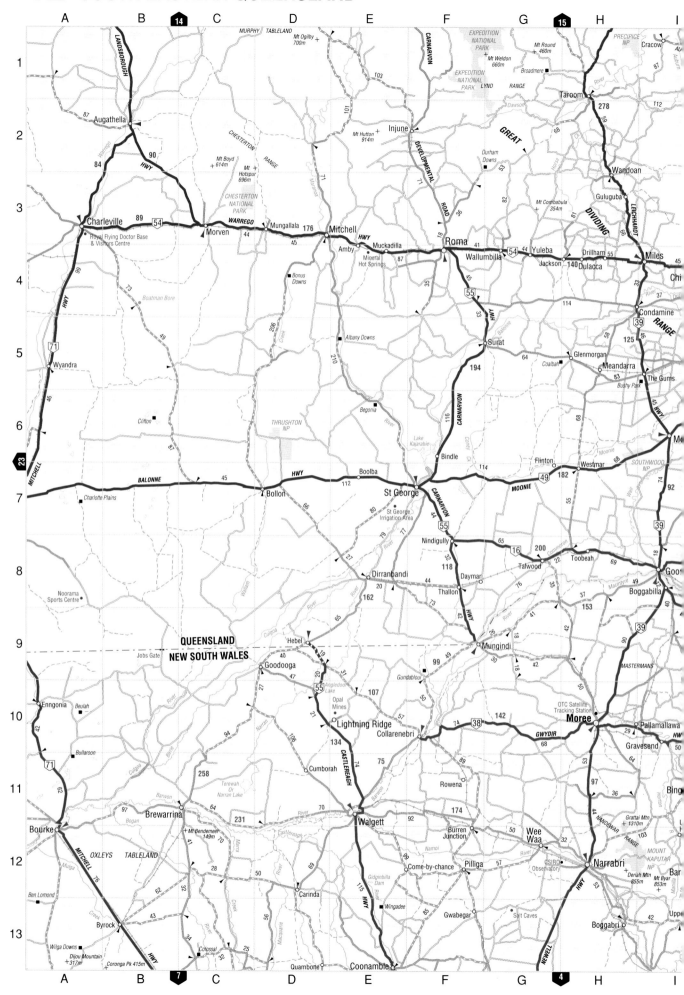

0 20 40 60 80 100 km

J K L M N O P Q R

N

SOUTH

PACIFIC

OCEAN

1

2

3

4

5

6

7

8

9

10

11

12

13

Eidsvold
Mundubbera
Binjour
Gayndah
44
37
17
109
Dallarnil
Biggenden
Broweena
Coalstoun Lakes
WALSH NP
Childers
Buxton Toogoom
Howard
Torbanlea
Hervey Bay
FRASER
ISLAND
GREAT SANDY
NATIONAL PARK
Maryborough
Eurong
Mungar
Maaroom
Tuan
Owanyilla
Tiaro
Gundiah
Bauple
Tin Can
Bay
Rainbow Beach
Double Island Point
Wide Bay Military
Training Area
Miva
Neerdie
Gunalda
BRUCE
Tansey
Woolooga
Kilkivan
Gympie
Cooran
COOLOOLA
NATIONAL
PARK
Lake Cootharaba
COOLOOLA COAST
Proston
Murgon
Wondai
Goomeri
Tingoora
Memerambi
Gallangowan
Borumba
Resvr
Imbil
Kenilworth
Noosa Heads
Peregian Beach
Coolum Beach
Cooroy
Eumundi
Bli Bli
Tewantin
SUNSHINE COAST
Kingaroy
Taabinga
Kumbia
Brooklands
Nanango
Yarraman
Linville
Harlin
Maidenwell
Dangore Mtn
599m
Widgee Mtn
688m
Nambour
Witta
Maroochydore
Buderim
169
Blackbutt
Moore
Woodford
Wamuran
Beerwah
Glass House
Mountains
Caloundra
CONONDALE
NATIONAL
PARK
D'AGUILAR
Bell
Kaimkillenbun
Moola
Maclagan
Cooyar
Toogoolawah
Esk
Kilcoy
Caboolture
Burpengary
Limbah
Bongaree
MORETON
ISLAND NP
Dalby
Kulpi
Haden
Brymaroo
Goombungee
Hampton
Crows Nest
Cabarlah
Murphys Creek
Cominya
Lowood
Fernvale
Samford
STRATHPINE
Deception Bay
Redcliffe
Moreton
Bay
MORETON ISLAND
SOUTH
Point Lookout
Dunwich
NORTH
STRADBROKE
ISLAND
TOOWOOMBA
Oakey
Kingsthorpe
Gatton
Grantham
Laidley
Rosewood
IPSWICH
BRISBANE
Victoria Point
Redland Bay
Beenleigh
SOUTH STRADBROKE
ISLAND
Springside
Pittsworth
Southbrook
Greenmount
Thornton
Rosevale
Peak Crossing
Jimboomba
Tamborine
Village
Oxenford
Southport
Pittsworth
Nobby
Clifton
Kalbar
Aratula
Boonah
Roadvale
Beaudesert
Nerang
103
SURFERS PARADISE
Leyburn
Pratten
Allora
Clintonvale
Mt Alford
Maroon
Hillview
Mudgeeraba
Springbrook
Burleigh Heads
CURRUMBIN
Coolangatta
GOLD COAST
Warwick
Tannymorel
Rathdowney
Tweed Heads
Banora Point
Kingscliff
Karara
Killarney
Woodenbong
Murwillumbah
MT WARNING NP
UKI
Bogangar
Pottsville Beach
Legume
Mulli Mulli
Urbenville
Tyalgum
Burringbar
Dalveen
Pozieres
Amiens
Thulimbah
Appletthorpe
Haystack Mtn
878m
Kyogle
Nimbin
Mullumbimby
Ocean Shores
Brunswick Heads
Cape Byron
QUEENSLAND
Severnlea
Glen Aplin
Stanthorpe
Boonoo
Boonoo
Falls
RICHMOND RANGE
Bangalow
Clunes
Byron Bay
Newrybar
Texas
Ballandean
GIRRAWEEN NP
Bonalbo
Lismore
Lennox Head
Ballina
Wallangarra
SUNDOWN NP
Tabulam
Mummulgum
Casino
Alstonville
Tenterfield
Drake
Mallanganee
Coraki
Wardell
Broadwater
BROADWATER NP
NEW SOUTH WALES
Woodburn
Evans Head
Torrington
Mt Bajimba
1446m
Baryulgil
Mt Marsh
501m
BUNDJALUNG
NP
Emmaville
Deepwater
GIBRALTAR
RANGE NP
Chatsworth
Maclean
Iluka
Yamba
Lawrence
Brooms Head
Copmanhurst
Carrs Creek Junction
Ulmarra
Grafton
Minnie Water
Inverell
Glen Innes
Red Range
Coutts
Crossing
Wooli
Gilgai
Glencoe
Balancing Rock
The Black Mtn
591m
GUY
FAWKES
NP
Nymboida
Glenreagh
Red Rock
Arrawarra
Woolgoolga
Emerald Beach
Moonee Beach
Tingha
Ben Lomond
Mt Hyland
1439m
Bundarra
Llangothlin
Guyra
Coramba
Coffs Harbour
Sawtell
Thunderbolts
Cave
Ebor
Falls
Dorrigo
NEW
ENGLAND
NP
Bellingen
Mylestone
Urunga
Valla Beach
Nambucca Heads
Armidale
Hillgrove
Wollomombi
Falls
Bowraville
Macksville
Scotts Head
Stuarts Point
South West Rocks

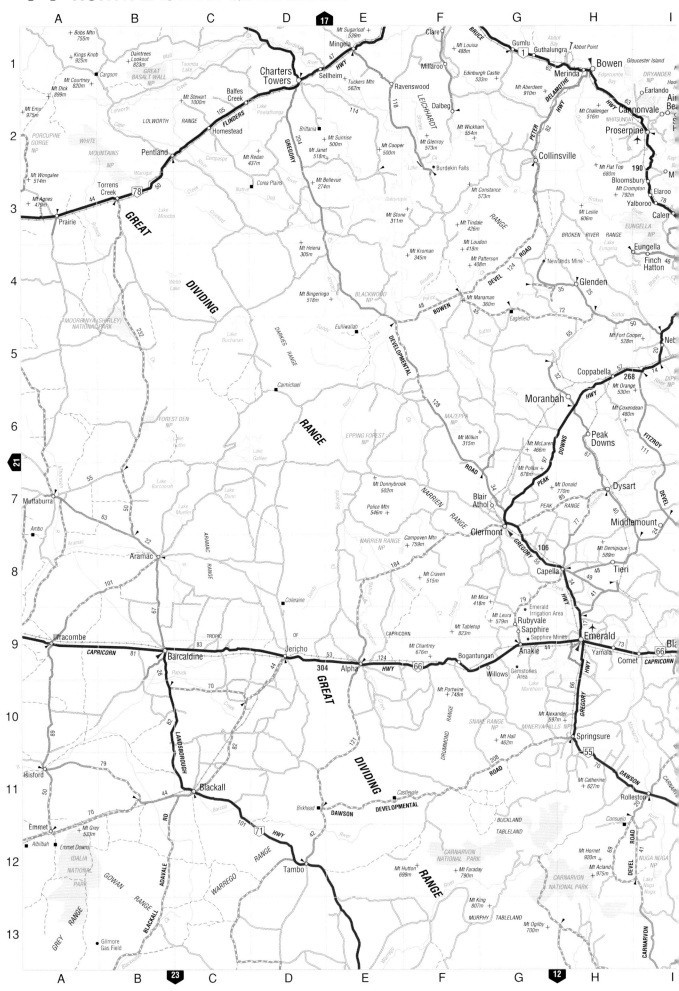

0 20 40 60 80 100 km

J K L M N O P Q R

N

1

2

THE WHITSUNDAYS

3

Island
SUNDAY ISLANDS
GROUP
TIONAL PARK
nd

Island

Brampton Island

Island
TSUNDAY ISLANDS
GROUP
ATIONAL PARK

oal Point
ucasia
enella
Mackay
ton
kers Creek
Half Tide
Grasstree
Sarina Beach
Armstrong Beach

4

GREAT

Koumala
Ilbilbie

CAPE PALMERSTON
NATIONAL PARK

Middle Island

NORTHUMBERLAND

South Island

SOUTH ISLAND
NATIONAL PARK

SOUTH

5

1

Carmila
aggy Rock

WEST HILL
NATIONAL PARK

ISLES

BARRIER

ite Bluff Mtn
522m
334

Broad
Sound

Quail Island

PACIFIC

6

Mt Edward
171m

Mt Price
164m

Mt Westall
550m

St Lawrence

Shoalwater
Bay

Military

Training

Mt Joss
421m

Mt Phillip
393m

Pine Mtn
375m

Double Mtn
747m

Area

7

Mt Buffalo
518m

Ogmore

Mt Wellington
528m

Mt Mulgrave
655m

REEF

OCEAN

Mt Bora
350m

74

Mt Magog
575m

Mt Atherton
438m

BRUCE

Marlborough

Kunwarara

BYFIELD
NATIONAL
PARK

8

82

Mt Gardiner
450m

Clifton

79

HWY

Glen Geddes

51

Apis Creek

izona

Round Mtn
146m

1

Yaamba
South Yaamba
Ridgelands

The Caves

40

Yeppoon

Mulambin

Great Keppel Island

Fitzroy River

32

Parkhurst

Kinka
Emu Park

9

263

Dingo
Wallaroo

Duaringa

66

Goganga

ROCKHAMPTON
Gracemere
Warren

Stanwell

Keppel Sands

Joskeleigh

TROPIC

Heron Island

OF

CAPRICORN

FOLEYVALE
ABORIGINAL
COMMUNITY

Woolwood

HWY

Midgee

Broadmount
405m

Mt Barker

DAWSON

RANGE

62

54

Mt Battery
486m

17

Boulercombe

Marmor

Scrubby Mtn
333m

CURTIS
ISLAND

BOTTLE ISLAND
NATIONAL PARK

CAPRICORN

10

50

Mt Wheal
606m

**Mount
Morgan**

39

Raglan

107

Southend

Mt Helen
633m

Dululu

Mt Hope
458m

Ambrose

33

WOORABINDA
ABORIGINAL
COMMUNITY

145

Wowan

Cedric Mtn
699m

Mount Larcom
Yarwun

Gladstone
Boyne Island
Tannum Sands

Lady Musgrave Island

Mt Dawson
317m

Rannes

36

30

Mt Redshirt
597m

108

DAWSON

66

Calliope

19

RODDS PENINSULA
NP

Bustard
Bay

Lady Elliott Island

53

Baralaba

33

Mt Ramsay
445m

Govigen

Jambin

Argoon

HWY

36

Specimen Hill
671m

Callide Coal Mine
& Power Station

Bororen

1

BRUCE

EURIMBULA
NP

Town of
Seventeen Seventy
Agnes Water

DEEPWATER
NP

11

Barranga

46

Banana

BANANA

Bruno Hill

Biloela
Thangool

42

Callide Dam

KROOMBIT
TOPS
NP

Nagoorin

Ubobo

Miriam
Vale

HWY

Mt Dromedary
477m

48

Baffle Creek

Bauhinia Downs

19

HWY

54

Moura

19

RANGE

Mt Graarbi
800m

Many
Peaks

Lake
Lania

Builyan

Lowmead

215

Rosedale

25

Yandaran

Moore Park

Burnett Heads
Bargara

Sandy Cape

GREAT

Mt Bodromen
330m

17

Blue Mtn
640m

97

CANIA GORGE
NP

Kalpowar

Mt Molangul
769m

Lake
Monduran

1

37

Avondale
Bucca

Rooney Point

SANDY

Platypus
Bay

Orchid Beach

Theodore

36

Mt Kandoonan
561m

257

Monto

Moonford

31

Mungungo

Bancroft

60

Mt Gaeta
542m

River

Goodwood

38

Bundaberg
Elliott Heads

37

Coonarr

Hervey

KINKUNA
NP

Bay

NP

FRASER

Mt Mungungal
568m

49

Mulgildie

44

37

55

Gin Gin

53

Buxton

Burrum Heads

12

112

PALM GROVE
NP

AUBURN

62

Abercorn

20

34

26

Wallaville

Mount Perry

Cordalba

Booyal

Childers

27

Woodgate

Howard

ISLA
GORGE
NP

RANGE

Cracow

37

45

Eidsvold

61

44

17

54

17

Dallarnil

29

35

Toogoom

Torbaniea

Hervey Bay

13

Mt Round
460m

PRECIPICE
NP

Mt Shaw
449m

Mt Mungungal

Quaggy Mtn
493m

ISLAND

Broadmere

J K L M N O P Q R

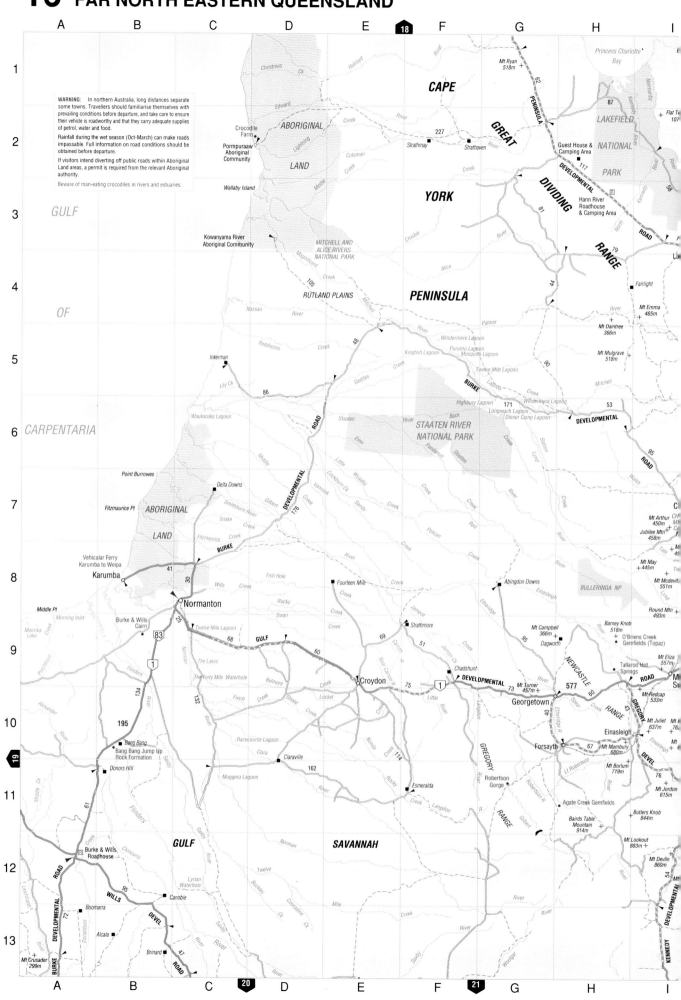

16 FAR NORTH EASTERN QUEENSLAND

A B C D E F G H I

1 2 3 4 5 6 7 8 9 10 11 12 13

18

CAPE

GREAT

Christmas Ck

Edward

River

Holroyd

Creek

Mt Ryan
518m

62

PENINSULA

Princess Charlotte
Bay

Kennedy

Normanby

87

LAKEFIELD

Flat T.
107

ABORIGINAL

Crocodile
Farm

Pormpuraaw
Aboriginal
Community

LAND

Lightning

Creek

Coleman

Creek

River

227

Strathmay

Strathaven

River

YORK

117

DIVIDING

Guest House &
Camping Area

81

Hann River
Roadhouse
& Camping Area

NATIONAL

PARK

58

Wallaby Island

Kowanyama River
Aboriginal Community

MITCHELL AND
ALICE RIVERS
NATIONAL PARK

Crosbie

River

79

RANGE

ROAD

La

79

RUTLAND PLAINS

105

Creek

Magnificent

Creek

Mitchell

PENINSULA

Palmer

River

Windermere Lagoon

44

Fairlight

Mt Emma
465m

Mt Daintree
366m

Nassau

River

Reddisons

Creek

48

Kingfish Lagoon

Purumu Lagoon

Mosquito Lagoon

90

Mt Mulgrave
518m

5 Inkerman

86

Geddes

Creek

Twelve Mile Lagoon

BURKE

Mitchell

Lily Ck

Waukanaka Lagoon

Staaten

River

Highbury Lagoon

Back

171

Longreach Lagoon

Dinner Camp Lagoon

53

Mitchell

6 **CARPENTARIA**

ROAD

Emu

Staaten

**STAATEN RIVER
NATIONAL PARK**

Windermere Lagoon

Lynd

Station

DEVELOPMENTAL

95

Walsh

ROAD

Point Burrowes

Delta Downs

DEVELOPMENTAL

Little

Vanrook

Cockburn Ck

Wyanta

Sandy

Creek

Creek

Creek

River

Red

Creek

Creek

Tate

Mt Arthur
450m

Jubilee Mtn
458m

7 Fitzmaurice Pt

ABORIGINAL

LAND

Smithburn River

Snake

Creek

Gilbert

176

Fitzmaurice

Creek

Pelican

Creek

River

Mt May
445m

Mt Mcdevit
551m

Vehicular Ferry
Karumba to Weipa

BURKE

41

Wills

Creek

Fish Hole

Fourteen Mile

Creek

Jampot

Creek

Abingdon Downs

Einasleigh

BULLERINGA NP

Round Mtn
493m

8 Karumba

30

Normanton

Rocky

Swan

Creek

Etheridge

Barney Knob
518m

Middle Pt

Morning Inlet

Burke & Wills
Cairn

83

25

Twelve Mile Lagoon

GULF

68

60

69

51

Strathmore

Jamin Ck

Mt Campbell
366m

Dagworth

95

O'Briens Creek
Gemfields (Topaz)

Tallaroo Hot
Springs

Mt Eliza
557m

9

Manrika
Lake

1

Flinders

The Lakes

60

Creek

Near Carron R.

1

Chadshunt

73

Mt Turner
457m

DEVELOPMENTAL

River

60

NEWCASTLE

577

40

Georgetown

GREGORY

Mt Redcap
533m

ROAD

M
S

Croydon

75

Carron

Jardin Ck

Etheridge R.

43

Alexander

134

River

The Forty Mile Waterhole

Belmore

Sheep

Locket

Creek

Little

River

Langdon

RANGE

Spear

Creek

Mt Juliet
637m

10

195

132

Racecourse Lagoon

Finch

Creek

Nonda

Rocky

ROAD

GREGORY

Forsayth

67

Einasleigh

Mt Mambury
680m

DEVEL

76

Bang Bang

Bang Bang Jump Up
Rock Formation

Clara

Claraville

Creek

114

Creek

Esmeralda

Robertson
Gorge

Robertson R.

Mt Borlum
719m

Mt Jordon
615m

Donors Hill

162

Langdon

GREGORY

Agate Creek Gemfields

RANGE

11

61

Flinders

Muggera Lagoon

River

Creek

Norman

Creek

R.

Gilbert

Bairds Table
Mountain
914m

Butlers Knob
844m

GULF

SAVANNAH

Mt Lookout
883m

12

ROAD

DEVELOPMENTAL

Burke & Wills
Roadhouse

Cloncurry

Lyrian
Waterhole

Twelve

Buckey

Mile

River

Creek

Mt Devlin
860m

54

95

WILLS

Canobie

Saxby

Cooramine

Creek

River

72

Boomarra

DEVEL

47

13 Mt Crusader
299m

BURKE

Alcala

Brinard

ROAD

River

Saxby

River

Weogar

Creek

KENNEDY

DEVELOPMENTA

19

20

21

J   K   L   M   N   O   P   Q   R

0   20   40   60   80   100 km

N

1

2

/ILLE NP
Point

Howick Island

LIZARD
ISLAND
NP

CORAL

3

ckey (Numbargulme)
479m

83

STARCKE NP

Cape Flattery

Lizard
Island

Hope Vale
Aboriginal Community

Cape Bedford

GREAT

Mt Piebald
117m
35

ENDEAVOUR RIVER
NATIONAL PARK

ack

Cooktown

4

Mt Mccormack
518m

28

Mt Byerley
445m

Black Mtn
475m

Helenvale
Rossville

BARRIER

CORAL

n Galleries
al Paintings)

54

Mt Finnigan
1148m

CEDAR BAY NP

KELAND

Mt Misery 869m
Mt Boolbun South
999m

Ayton

46

Mt Eyklin
595m

Mt Amy
869m

Wujal Wujal

CAPE
TRIBULATION
NP

Mt Mcdowall
548m

Mt Halycon
874m

5

Palmer River
Roadhouse

Mt Hemmant
1092m

Cape Tribulation

DAINTREE

Mt Alexandra
483m

NATIONAL
PARK

Daintree

SEA

46

Mt Elephant
1046m

Mt Spurgeon
1341m

Miallo

Trinity Bay

51

Cooya Beach

Mossman

Mount Carbine

Mossman
Gorge

Port Douglas

6

Maryfarms

Mt Frazer
1155m

Julatten

PEBBLY BEACH

Hodgkinson R

Mount Molloy

Ellis Beach

GREEN ISLAND NP
Green Island

HANN
TABLELAND NP

42

Clifton Beach

lligan

Lake
Mitchell

Kuranda

Smithfield

Mareeba-Dimbula
Irrigation Area

51

Biboohra

CAIRNS

BARRIER

Mt Mcleod
808m

New
Northcote

BARRON
GORGE NP

FITZROY ISLAND NP
Fitzroy Island

7

Arringunna Mtn
599m

Mt White
764m

33

Mareeba

Edmonton

Caves
t Alexander
0m

Dimbulah

Collins Weir

Gordonvale

Aloomba
Fishery
Falls

High Island

naden

65

Reholds
Blue Mtn
868m

Tolga

Tinaroo
Falls

50

Kai

Deeral

Petford

Atherton

BARTLE FRERE
NP

RUSSELL RIVER NP

Hermit Hill
885m

Irvinebank

Herberton

133

38

Malanda

Babinda

Bramston Beach

8

Geebung Hill
897m

Kalunga

Millaa

Topaz

Miriwinni

PALMERSTON

Millaa Millaa Falls

Flying Fish Point

79

Tumoulin

Millaa

BARTLE FRERE

EUBENANGEE SWAMP NP

Nymbool

Ravenshoe

HWY

Innisfail

Seven Mile Hill
767m

47

Innot Hot
Springs

Mt Koolmoon
1177m

79

Mena
Creek

Mourilyan

Mt Bear
841m

Mount
Garnet

Millstream
Falls

Mt Pandanus
1103m

Tulley
Falls

Mt Pope
808m

Silkwood

21

Inarlinga

HWY

Kurrimine Beach

66

Tiger Hill
868m

El Arish

Bingil Bay

HWY

Koombooloomba
Reservoir

25

Mission Beach

Dunk Island

9

FORTY MILE
SGRUR NP

Euramo

Tully

DUNK ISLAND NP

HULL RIVER NP
Bedarra Island

4n
UNDARA
NP

Mt Sharples
810m

Murray Falls

EDMUND KENNEDY NP
Rockingham Bay

REEF

Commissioners Cap
1028m

G W Knob
764m

258

Mt Garrachan
762m

Cape Richards
Cape Sandwich

62

Mt Mcbride
911m

Herbert River
Falls

Cardwell

Mt Pitt
722m

HINCHINBROOK
ISLAND

Mt Bowen
1119m

10

220

Princess Hills
Lake

Walters Plains
Lake

LUMHOLTZ
NP

52

BRUCE

Mt Graham
834m

Mt Diamantina
1000m

Kinrara

River

LUMHOLTZ

HINCHINBROOK ISLAND NP

Lake Lucy

Abergowrie

Lucinda-Dungeness

CTION

Saltern Lagoon

Mt Farquharson
548m

Halifax

Pelorus Island (Yanooa)
Orpheus Island (Goolboddi)

HWY

Cassady Beach

ORPHEUS ISLAND NP

Conjuboy

Trebonne

Ingham

adhouse
envale Nickel
Mine

Mt Lee
829m

Toobanna

11

GREGORY

159

Mt Fox
811m

43

Allingham

Great Palm Island Aboriginal Community

Great Palm Island

Extinct Volcano

Jourama Falls

Mt SPEC/
CRYSTAL CREEK NP

Mt Spec
990m

Bagal Beach

Blue Water Springs
Roadhouse

Mt Zero
1036m

Rollingstone

Lookouts

Magnetic
Island

MAGNETIC ISLAND NP

12

Clarke River

DEVELOPMENTAL

Mt Halifax 1063m

Bluewater

Jalloonda

Nelly Bay

HERVEYS

RANGE

DEVEL

RD

Pallarenda

Mt Cataract
873m

TOWNSVILLE

THURINGOWA

Cape Bowling Green

Round Mtn
375m

BOWLING GREEN

BOWLING GREEN BAY NP

ROAD

93

136

Mt Stuart
582m

BOWLING
BAY
NP

Alligator Creek

Alva

Dotswood

Ross
River
Resvr

Giru

Cungulla

Mtn

Mt Louisa
671m

Mt Flagstone
590m

78

Mt Elliot
1234m

Brandon

Seaforth

37

Ayr

13

Kings Knob
925m

Daintrees
Lookout
823m

GREAT
BASALT WALL NP

Mt Sugarloaf
539m

46

Burdekin River
Irrigation Area

Home Hill

BRUCE

53

CAPE UPSTART NP

Abbot
Bay

Cargoon

Mingela

Haughton

Clare

Mt Louisa
488m

Gumlu

HWY

1

Guthalungra

Abbot Point

Sellheim

Ck

Hann

Millaroo

J   K   L   M   N   14   O   P   Q   R

0   20   40   60   80   100 km

A B C D E F G H I

1

TORRES STRAIT

BADU ISLAND
Mulgrave Hill 209m

Mt Augustus 399m

MOA ISLAND

High Island

2

Thursday Island
Horn Island

Cape York Wilderness Lodge

PRINCE OF WALES ISLAND

Endeavour Strait

Cape York

Newcastle Bay

N

3

Bamaga

Parslow Pt

GULF OF

Left Hill 108m

Vrilya Point

Vehicle Ferry

JARDINE RIVER NATIONAL PARK

Orford Bay

4

Puddingpan Hill 123m

Jardine River

RICHARDSON RANGE

ABORIGINAL

Cridland Hill 112m

Helby Hill 150m

CAPTAIN BILLY LANDING

CARPENTARIA

LAND

Messum Hill 87m

Shelburne Bay

CORAL

5

412

250

Creek

Conical Hill 86m

Cape Grenville

Mapoon Aboriginal Community

Port Musgrave Bay

Ducie River

Palm

Briscoe Hill 147m

6

Bertiehaugh

Temple Bay

Glennie 299m

GREAT

Wenlock

Moreton Telegraph Station

Huxley Hill 283m

Kennedy Hill 518m

DIVIDING

Barret Hill 366m

Weymouth Bay

SEA

7

Duyfken Point

Albatross Bay

Mission

R

Batavia Downs 40

Mt Dobson 495m

IRON RANGE NP

Portland Roads

Cape Weymouth

GREAT

Weipa

65

48

Bowden 345m

Mt Tozer 545m

Lockhart River Aboriginal Community

Vehicular Ferry Weipa to Karumba

PENINSULA

EMBLEY

RANGE

249

Wenlock River

RANGE

Cape Direction

Direction Hill 146m

8

Pera Head

70

Lagoon Creek

Iguana Mtn 244m

Mt Carter 671m

GEIKE

Jacks Knob 411m

Night Island

Merkunga Creek

DEVELOPMENTAL

Bald Hill 441m

Table Mtn 458m

Aurukun Aboriginal Community

ARCHER BEND

RANGE

Archer

Cape Sidmouth

9

NATIONAL

112

Archer River Roadhouse

Birthday Mtn 438m

MCILWRAITH

Whale Hill 306m

BARRIER

ROKEBY

Round Mtn 321m

PARK

NATIONAL

RANGE

ABORIGINAL

River

PARK

Double Hill 411m

Claremont Isles

REEF

10

CAPE

Mt Croll 488m

Coen

LAND

Silver Plains

Mt White 449m

Port Stewart

53

FLINDERS GROUP NP

Flinders Group Is

Pipon Island

Cape Melville

St Pauls Hill 418m

11

45

Kintore 405m

Princess Charlotte Bay

Bathurst Bay

CAPE MELVILLE NP

Bay Hill 432m

Barrow Point

YORK

Kendall

River

Mt Ryan 518m

62

CAPE MELVILLE NP

Howick Island

Christmas Ck

Holroyd

River

Normanby

LIZARD ISLAND NP

12

227

Flat Top Hill 107m

Saddle Hill 508m

Lizard Island

Crocodile Farm

Pormpuraaw Aboriginal Community

Edward

River

Strathmay

Strathaven

GREAT

LAKEFIELD

NATIONAL

Kennedy River

Mt Stuckey (Numbargulme) 479m

Cape Flattery

Lightning

Coleman

Creek

PENINSULA

90

Guest House & Camping Area

PARK

58

STARCKE NP

MT WEBB NP

13

Wallaby Island

DIVIDING

Hann River Roadhouse & Camping Area

River

Mt Jack 213m

83

Hope Vale Aboriginal Community

Cape Bedford

Mottle Creek

MITCHELL AND ALICE RIVERS NATIONAL PARK

Crosbie Creek

RANGE

Kennedy River

Mt Piebald 117m

ENDEAVOUR RIVER NATIONAL PARK

Kowanyama Aboriginal Community

A B C D E F G H I

16 17

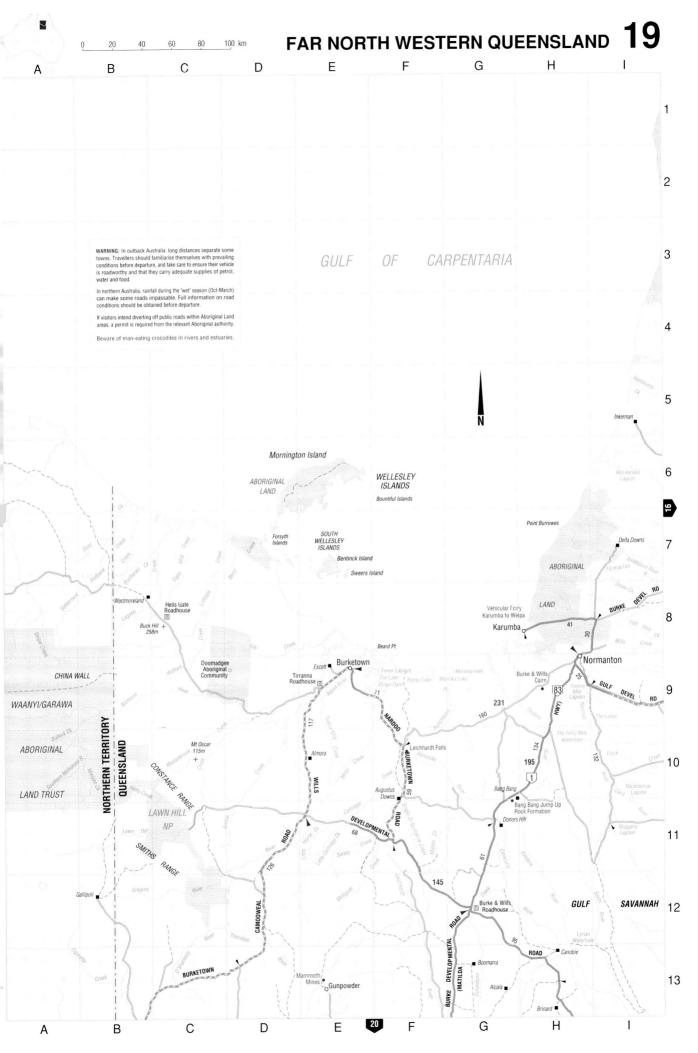

0 20 40 60 80 100 km

A B C D E F G H I

GULF OF CARPENTARIA

WARNING: In outback Australia, long distances separate some towns. Travellers should familiarise themselves with prevailing conditions before departure, and take care to ensure their vehicle is roadworthy and that they carry adequate supplies of petrol, water and food.

In northern Australia, rainfall during the "wet" season (Oct-March) can make some roads impassable. Full information on road conditions should be obtained before departure.

If visitors intend diverting off public roads within Aboriginal Land areas, a permit is required from the relevant Aboriginal authority.

Beware of man-eating crocodiles in rivers and estuaries.

N

Inkerman

Mornington Island

ABORIGINAL LAND

WELLESLEY ISLANDS

Bountiful Islands

Watukanaka Lagoon

16

Point Burrowes

Delta Downs

Forsyth Islands

SOUTH WELLESLEY ISLANDS

ABORIGINAL

Bentinck Island

Sweers Island

LAND

Fitzmaurice R.

Smithburn River

Snake Ck

BURKE DEVEL RD

Westmoreland

Hells Gate Roadhouse

Vehicular Ferry Karumba to Weipa

41

30

Fish Hole Ck

Wills Ck

Buck Hill 258m

Beard Pt

Karumba

Normanton

CHINA WALL

Doomadgee Aboriginal Community

Escott

Burketown

Timor Lagoon

The Lake

Morning Inlet

Burke & Wills Cairn

83

GULF DEVEL RD

WAANYI/GARAWA

Tirranna Roadhouse

Dingo Dam

Rocky Lake

Manrika Lake

Twenty Mile Lagoon

ABORIGINAL

71

160

231

The Forty Mile Waterhole

132

NORTHERN TERRITORY

QUEENSLAND

117

NARDOO

134

LAND TRUST

Mt Oscar 115m

Almora

BURKETOWN

Leichhardt Falls

195

1

Finch Ck

Bang Bang

Muggera Lagoon

CONSTANCE RANGE

WILLS

ROAD

Augustus Downs

65

Bang Bang Jump Up Rock Formation

Racecourse Lagoon

LAWN HILL NP

Donors Hill

SMITHS RANGE

68

DEVELOPMENTAL

Gregory River

126

Cloncurry River

145

61

Gallipoli

CAMODWEAL

Burke & Wills Roadhouse

GULF SAVANNAH

ROAD

Lynan Waterhole

BURKETOWN

95

ROAD

Canobie

BURKE DEVELOPMENTAL (MATILDA)

Boomarra

Mammoth Mines

Gunpowder

Alcala

Brinard

A B C D E F G H I

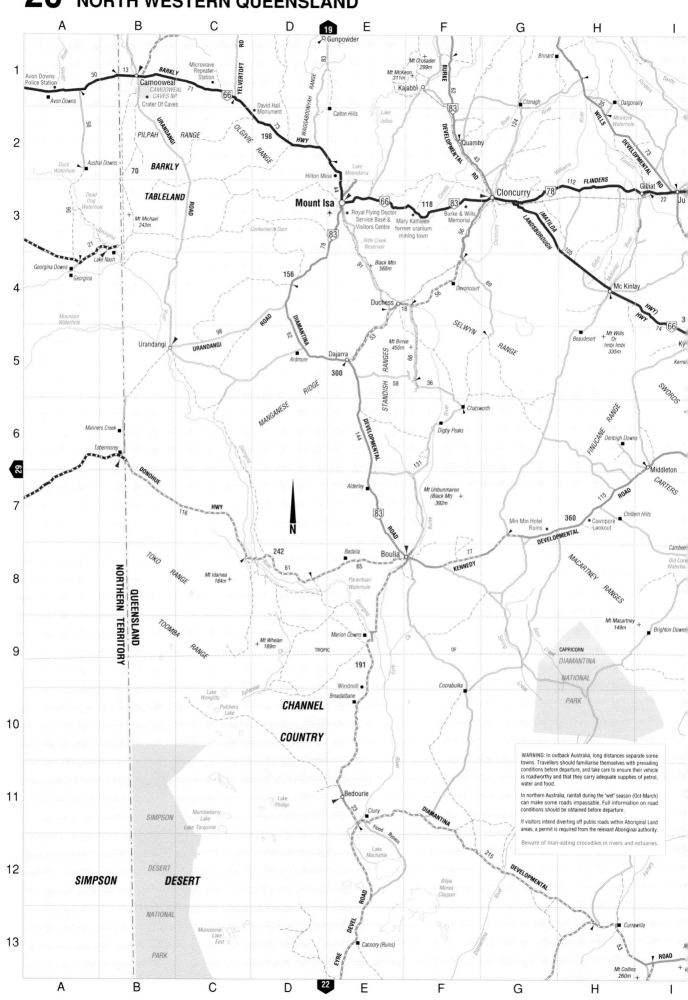

19

A B C D E F G H I

Gunpowder

Avon Downs Police Station
James River
Avon Downs
30
13
Camooweal
BARKLY
Microwave Repeater Station
YELVERTOFT RD
CAMOOWEAL CAVES NP
Crater Of Caves
71
66
David Hall Monument
WAGGABOONYAH RANGE
Mt Crusader 299m
Mt McKeon 311m
Brinard
BURKE
Kajabbi
83
Calton Hills
Clonagh
Dalgonally
35
McIntyre Waterhole
WILLS
56
URANDANGI RANGE
PILPAH
OLGIVIE RANGE
198
73
HWY
Lake Julius
63
Quamby
43
124
DEVELOPMENTAL
WILLIAMS
73
DEVELOPMENTAL
Austral Downs
Duck Waterhole
70
BARKLY
TABLELAND
198
Hilton Mine
Lake Moondarra
RD
Cloncurry
112
FLINDERS
78
Giliat
22
Ju
Dead Dog Waterhole
56
Mt Michael 243m
Conkerberry Dam
Mount Isa
66
118
83
Burke & Wills Memorial
LANDSBOROUGH
IMATILDA
105
Georgina Downs
21
Lake Nash
Georgina
78
83
Royal Flying Doctor Service Base & Visitors Centre
Mary Kathleen former uranium mining town
56
Selwyn
3
Georgina River
Rifle Creek Reservoir
91
Black Mtn 568m
69
Devoncourt
Mc Kinlay
HWY
74
66
3
156
Duchess
18
56
Ky
Mountain Waterhole
98
ROAD
62
DIAMANTINA
53
Mt Birnie 450m
66
SELWYN RANGE
Beaudesert
Mt Wills Or Imbi Imbi 335m
Kerrs
Urandangi
URANDANGI
Ardmore
Dajarra
300
58
36
FINUCANE RANGE
SWORDS
Manners Creek
MANGANESE
Georgina River
144
STANDISH RANGES
Chatsworth
Digby Peaks
Denbigh Downs
29
Tobermorey
DONOHUE
RIDGE
DEVELOPMENTAL
131
Mt Unbunmaroo (Black Mt) 392m
Middleton
CARTERS
116
HWY
Alderley
83
Min Min Hotel Ruins
115
ROAD
Chiltern Hills
242
Badalia
65
Boulia
ROAD
77
360
Cawnpore Lookout
Cambee
61
KENNEDY
MACARTNEY RANGES
Old Cork Waterho
TOKO RANGE
Mt Idamea 184m
Paravituari Waterhole
Georgina River
TOOMBA RANGE
Mt Whelan 189m
Marion Downs
TROPIC
OF
Mt Macartney 149m
Brighton Downs
QUEENSLAND
NORTHERN TERRITORY
N
CHANNEL
191
Windmill
Breadalbane
Coorabulka
Eyre Creek
CAPRICORN
DIAMANTINA
NATIONAL
Lake Wongitta
Sylvester Creek
COUNTRY
Pulchera Lake
Spring Creek
Gum Creek
PARK
SIMPSON
Mumbleberry Lake
Lake Torquinie
Lake Phillipi
Bedourie
23
Cluny
Flood
DIAMANTINA
DEVELOPMENTAL
SIMPSON
DESERT
DESERT
Lake Machattie
215
Bilpa Morea Claypan
NATIONAL
ROAD
DEVEL
EYRE
Cacoory (Ruins)
Currawilla
53
ROAD
PARK
Muncoonie Lake East
Mt Collins 260m

WARNING: In outback Australia, long distances separate some towns. Travellers should familiarise themselves with prevailing conditions before departure, and take care to ensure their vehicle is roadworthy and that they carry adequate supplies of petrol, water and food.

In northern Australia, rainfall during the "wet" season (Oct-March) can make some roads impassable. Full information on road conditions should be obtained before departure.

If visitors intend diverting off public roads within Aboriginal Land areas, a permit is required from the relevant Aboriginal authority.

Beware of man-eating crocodiles in rivers and estuaries.

22

A B C D E F G H I

0 20 40 60 80 100 km

J K 16 L M N O P 17 Q R

1

GREAT

KENNEDY

Sandy River
Elmore
Mt Louisa 671m
Bobs Mtn 755m
Kings Knob 925m
Daintrees Lookout 823m
GREAT BASALT WALL NP
Cargoon
Wall
Toomba Lake
Ck
Hann Ck
Charters Towers
Sellheim

2

73
Clutha
Burleigh
GRAMPIAN HILLS
DEVELOPMENTAL
Mt Courtney 820m
Mt Dick 899m
Mt Emu 975m
WHITE MOUNTAINS NP
Lolworth
Mt Stewart 1000m
Balfes Creek
Homestead
105
HWY
243
LOLWORTH RANGE
Cape
Campaspe
Mt Redan 437m
Corea Plains
Mt Sunrise 500m
Brittania
Mt Janet 518m

3

Nelia 49 Nonda
390
Maxwelton
Richmond
57
48
HWY
Compton Downs
Alderley
Mt Desolation 579m
ROAD
Mt Wongalee 514m
64
Hughenden
Mt Agnes 479m
Prairie
44
Torrens Creek
FLINDERS
50
Warrigal
Lake Moocha
Native
Creek
Dog
Ck
Mt Helena 305m
Mt Bellevue 274m

4

Flinders
Coleraine
Essex Downs
147
62
Mt Walker 479m
Arrara
44
106
Bullock Creek
DIVIDING
MOORRINYA (SHIRLEY) NP
Webb Lake
Crooked
Capsize

5

LANDSBOROUGH
84
Albion Downs
Dagworth
72m
Stamford
212
67
DEVELOPMENTAL
Microwave Station
Barenya
232
Lake Buchanan
DARKIES RANGE
Sandy Creek

6

168
Mt Booka Booka 251m
Corfield
83
KENNEDY
Microwave Station
Bonnie Downs
100
FOREST DEN NP
Ck
Lake Huffer
Lake Galilee
Carmichael
RANGE
14

7

Opal Fields
80
Microwave Station
1st Flying Surgeon Service 1958
Winton
Lorraine Station
109
HWY
Muttaburra
91
55
63
50
Lake Barcoorah
Lake Dunn
Lake Mueller

8

CORYS RANGE
Mt Williams 263m
Clyde
(MATILDA
Evesham
65
Morella
281
Darra
119
Elmore
Ambo
116
101
Aramac
22
ARAMAC
RANGE
Coleraine
Sandy

9

Cork
Mt Davy 294m
2m
LARK QUARRY ENVIRONMENTAL PARK
FORSYTH
Velson Pk
66
Opalton
67
Mt Booroom 263m
BLADENSBURG NP
RANGE
Manero
Oondooroo
TROPIC
Dalkeith
Mayne
OF
Thomson
Longreach
Ilfracombe
27
CAPRICORN
81
Barcaldine
83
Jericho
HWY
53
Alpha

10

WINTON
MOUNTAINS 228
JUNDAH
38
89
ROAD
THOMSON
DEVELOPMENTAL
100
89
ROAD
CAPRICORN
26
71
70
82
44
LANDSBOROUGH
121

11

RANGES
37
56
Stonehenge
49
Bimerah
Isisford
50
79
82
Birkhead
Blackall
44
101

12

74
68
52
Emmet
Mt Grey 533m
Emmet Downs
IDALIA NATIONAL PARK
GOWAN RANGE
ADAVALE
ROAD
HWY
42
Tambo
WARREGO RANGE
Barcoo

13

Berrimpa
Jundah
95
WELFORD NATIONAL PARK
50
Yaraka
MACEDON RANGE
GREY RANGE
BLACKALL RANGE
79
94
Budgerygar
Gilmore Gas Field
Windorah

J K L 23 M N O P Q R

0 20 40 60 80 100 km

J K L M N O P Q R

Windorah

JUNDAH QUILPIE RD
79
50
51
Clifton
38
134
DIAMANTINA
CHEVIOT RANGE
Budgerygar
HELL HOLE GORGE NP
GREY RANGE
Gilmore Gas Field
GOWAN RANGE ROAD
21
LANDSBOROUGH
71
River
87
Augathella
71
84

ADAVALE
BLACKALL
Adavale
ADAVALE
Ambathala
CHARLEVILLE ROAD
179
MARIALA NP
Lake Dartmouth
Charleville
Royal Flying Doctor Base & Visitors Centre
54
71
199

COLEMAN RANGE
103
Cornwall
Earlstoun
Bull Creek Opal Field
Kyabra
97
Boothulla
DEVELOPMENTAL ROAD
Numerous Opal Fields
Mt Bellalie 216m
Oil Fields
Quilpie
36
Cheepie
210
Cooladdi
99
Mt Prara +309m
HWY
(MATILDA
Wyandra
46
MCGREGOR RANGE
Eromanga
Congie
234
Oil Fields
76
RD
Coongoola
54
Clifton
87
GREY RANGE
NORLEY RANGE
THARGOMINDAH
Toompine
35
Opal Mines
82
QUILPIE
127
MITCHELL
RANGE
122
Repeater Station
cundra
Thargomindah
BULLOO
LAKE BINDEGOLLY NP
130
Blackgate Opal Field
Yowah Opal Field
198
68
Cunnamulla
BALONNE ROAD
134
49
HWY
Charlotte Plains
71
DEVELOPMENTAL ROAD
Mud Springs
Eulo
118
146
Noorama Sports Centre
MITCHELL
CURRAWINYA NP
Lake Wyara
Lake Numalla
Kungie Lake

WARNING: In outback Australia, long distances separate some towns. Travellers should familiarise themselves with prevailing conditions before departure, and take care to ensure their vehicle is roadworthy and that they carry adequate supplies of petrol, water and food.

In northern Australia, rainfall during the 'wet' season (Oct-March) can make some roads impassable. Full information on road conditions should be obtained before departure.

If visitors intend diverting off public roads within Aboriginal Land areas, a permit is required from the relevant Aboriginal authority.

Adelaide Gate
Hamilton Gate
Waverley Gate
Hungerford
Vermin Proof Fence
Parragundy Gate
QUEENSLAND
NEW SOUTH WALES
Jobs Gate
Lake Callamulcha
Teurika
Berawinnia Downs
Ourimbah
128
Barringun
Sharoon
38
101
Maureen Joy
145
Enngonia
Beulah
142
Pindera Downs
Owen Downs
Barrajong
213
Bullaroon
HWY
42
Clifton Downs
86
226
Colane
Koridina
Wanaaring
57
Fords Bridge
52
71
97
Brewarrina
Whyjonta
87
River
68
63
Barrona Downs
191
Murphys Lake
Bourke
Mt Bendemeer 149m
Bundarra
134
OXLEYS TABLELAND
Turkey Ck
Petita
Nantilla
Noonamah
85
MITCHELL
76
Bogan
41
Gumgoopla
138
Questa Park
Glendara
163
Utah Lake
Tonga Lake
MT DEERINA RANGE
Louth
Ben Lomond
101
62
28
Allandy
Qulchra
Purnanga
Cawnalmurtee
Peery Lake
Lake Poloka Yanlabangee
Mt Mulyah 162m
Jinki Lake
Darling River
Mt Wammiga 380m
Wilga Downs
32
43
Oak Vale
Goodwood
74
Polocara
THOOLABOOL RANGE
Byrock
HWY
Opal Mines
White Cliffs
32
Mandalay

J K 6 L M N O 7 P Q R

1 2 3 4 5 6 12 7 8 0 10 11 12 13

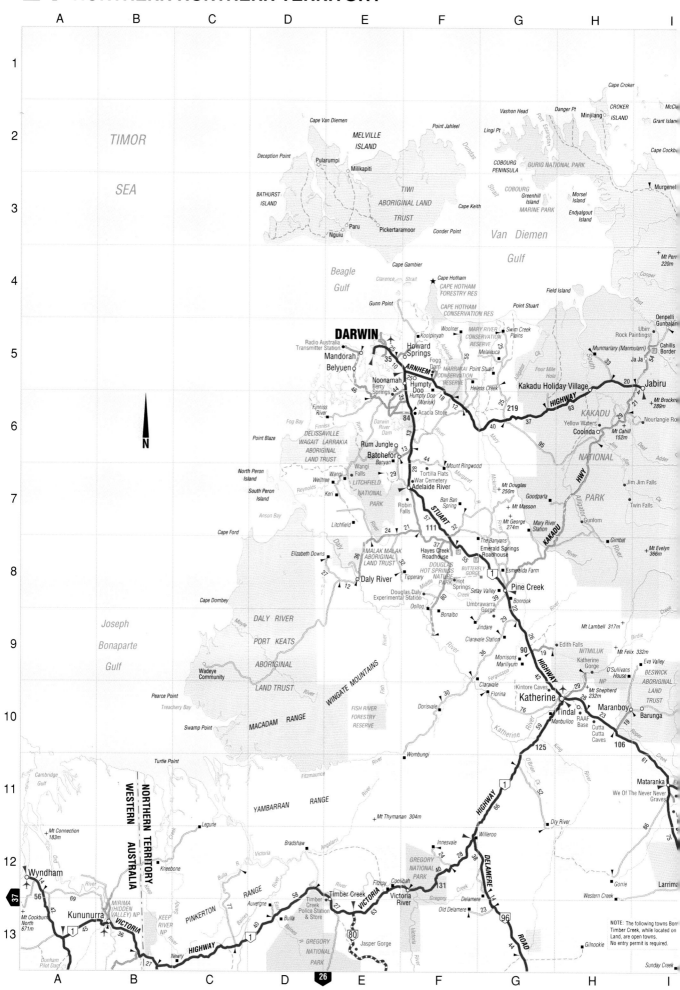

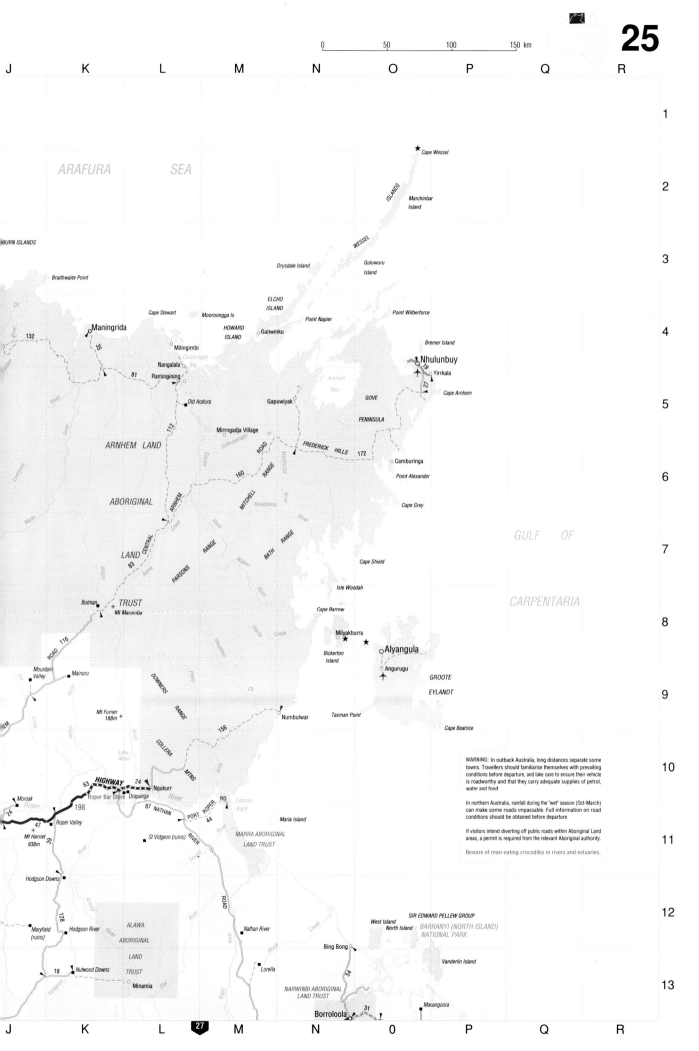

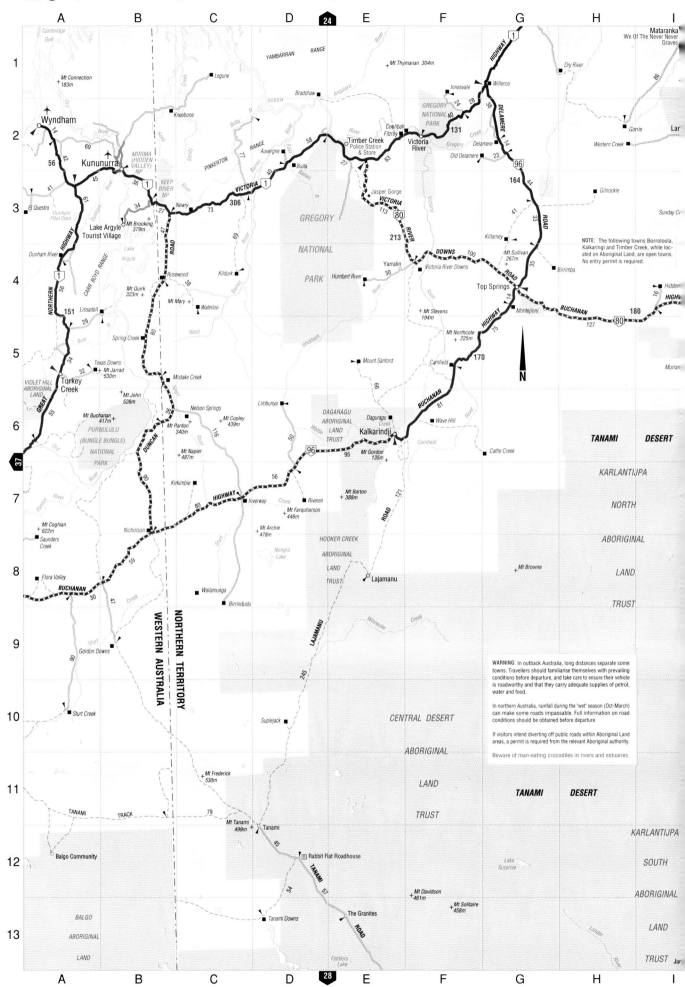

26 CENTRAL NORTHERN TERRITORY

24

A B C D E F G H I

1

Cambridge Gulf

Mt Connection +183m

YAMBARRAN RANGE

+ Mt Thymanan 304m

Dry River

Matarank We Of The Never Never Graves

Legune

Kneebone

Bradshaw

Victoria River

Innesvale

Willeroo

Highway 1

Gorrie

Lar

2

Wyndham

14

Kununurra

56 42

69

MIRIMA (HIDDEN VALLEY) NP

PINKERTON RANGE

77

Auvergne

East River

Baines River

58

Timber Creek Police Station & Store

27

Coolibah Fitzroy

Victoria River

63

GREGORY NATIONAL PARK

24 28

131

Gregory Creek

Old Delamere

Delamere

40

38

DELAMERE

14

23

96

Western Creek

3

El Questro

41

45

36

1

KEEP RIVER NP

34

Mt Brooking 379m

Newry

73

VICTORIA 1 306

Bulla

Baines R

GREGORY

Jasper Gorge

VICTORIA 80 213

113

River

DOWNS

Victoria

164

44

41

33

ROAD

Killarney

Mt Sullivan + 267m

Gilnockie

Sunday Cr

NOTE: The following towns Borroloola, Kalkaringi and Timber Creek, while located on Aboriginal Land, are open towns. No entry permit is required.

4

Lake Argyle Tourist Village

NORTHERN HIGHWAY

Dunham River

1

56

151

61

CARR BOYD RANGE

Lissadell

29

Lake Argyle

Rosewood

38

Kildurk

Mt Quirk 323m +

Mt Mary +

Waterloo

West River

Humbert River

Yarralin

30

Victoria River Downs

+ Mt Stevens 194m

100

Top Springs

14

Montejinni

Birrimba

BUCHANAN

80 180

127

Hidden HIGH

5

34

Texas Downs

32 + Mt Jarrad 530m

Spring Creek

80

Mistake Creek

Wickham River

Mount Sanford

66

Camfield

170

Murran

N

6

VIOLET HILL ABORIGINAL LAND

Turkey Creek

55

GREAT

Ord R

Mt Buchanan 417m +

PURNULULU (BUNGLE BUNGLE) NATIONAL PARK

Mt John 526m

DUNCAN

36

Mt Panton 340m

Nelson Springs

116

+ Mt Copley 439m

Limbunya

50

Wattie Creek

DAGARAGU ABORIGINAL LAND TRUST

Dagaragu

Kalkarindji

96

95

BUCHANAN

81

Camfield River

Wave Hill

TANAMI DESERT

KARLANTIJPA

7

37

Panton River

Mt Napier + 487m

58

Kirkimbie

80

HIGHWAY

Inverway

56

Riveren

Mt Gordon 135m +

Mt Barton + 388m

ROAD 121

Cattle Creek

NORTH

ABORIGINAL

8

Flora Valley

BUCHANAN

30

Mt Coghlan + 622m

Saunders Creek

47

Creek

Nicholson

Sturt River

59

Wallamunga

Birrindudu

Mt Farquharson 446m

Mt Archie 478m

Nongra Lake

HOOKER CREEK ABORIGINAL LAND TRUST

Lajamanu

Whinnecka Creek

+ Mt Browne

LAND

TRUST

9

Gordon Downs

90

Sturt Creek

LAJAMANU

245

WARNING: In outback Australia, long distances separate some towns. Travellers should familiarise themselves with prevailing conditions before departure, and take care to ensure their vehicle is roadworthy and that they carry adequate supplies of petrol, water and food.

10

Sturt Creek

Suplejack

CENTRAL DESERT

ABORIGINAL

In northern Australia, rainfall during the "wet" season (Oct-March) can make some roads impassable. Full information on road conditions should be obtained before departure.

11

Balgo Community

TANAMI TRACK

79

Mt Frederick 530m

LAND

TRUST

TANAMI DESERT

KARLANTIJPA

If visitors intend diverting off public roads within Aboriginal Land areas, a permit is required from the relevant Aboriginal authority.

Beware of man-eating crocodiles in rivers and estuaries.

12

WESTERN AUSTRALIA

NORTHERN TERRITORY

Mt Tanami 499m

Tanami

45

Rabbit Flat Roadhouse

TANAMI

54

57

Mt Davidson + 461m

Mt Solitaire 458m

Lake Surprise

SOUTH

ABORIGINAL

13

BALGO ABORIGINAL LAND

Tanami Downs

The Granites

ROAD

Fiddlers Lake

Lander River

LAND

TRUST

Jar

A B C D E F G H I

28

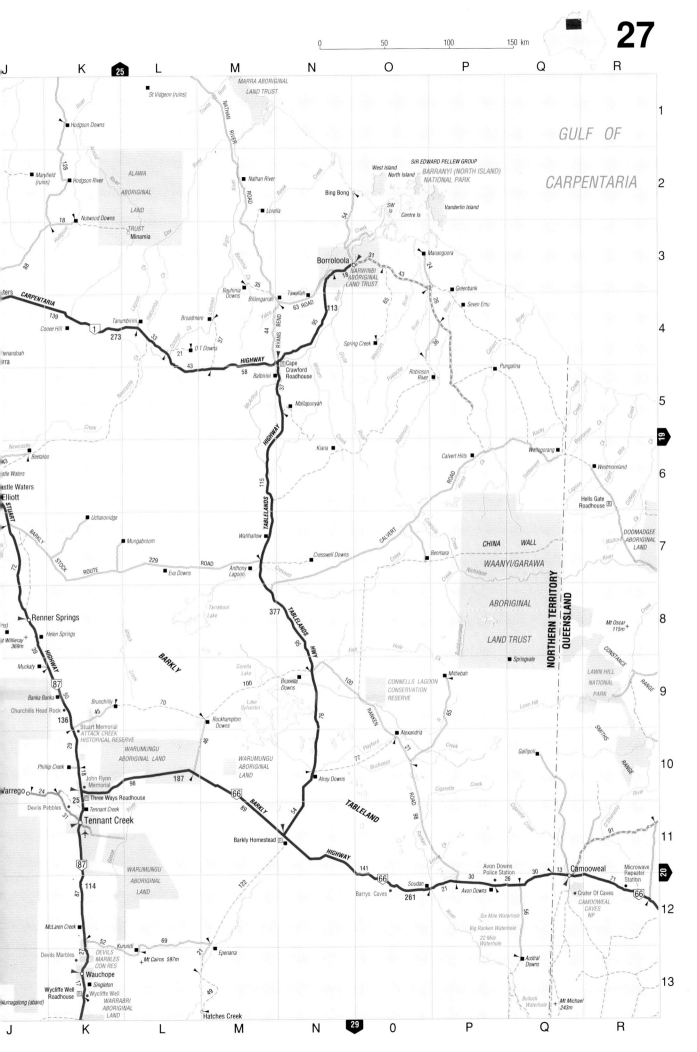

GULF OF

CARPENTARIA

J   K   L   M   N   O   P   Q   R

25

19

20

29

MARRA ABORIGINAL
LAND TRUST

St Vidgeon (ruins)

Hodgson Downs

Maryfield
(ruins)

128

Hodgson River

ALAWA

ABORIGINAL

LAND

18   Nutwood Downs

TRUST
Minamia

Nathan River

Lorella

Bing Bong

SIR EDWARD PELLEW GROUP

West Island
North Island

BARRANYI (NORTH ISLAND)
NATIONAL PARK

Vanderlin Island

SW
Is

Centre Is

Manangoora

Borroloola   31

18   NARWINBI
ABORIGINAL
LAND TRUST

Greenbank

Seven Emu

54

43

24

26

36

CARPENTARIA

139

Cooee Hill

Tanumbirini

273

1

33

O T Downs

21

43

58

Bauhinia
Downs

35

Billengarrah

Tawallah

Broadmere

RYANS BEND

44

63 ROAD

95

113

HIGHWAY

Cape
Crawford
Roadhouse

Balbirini

37

Mallapunyah

Spring Creek

65

Clyde

River

Foelsche

Robinson
River

Pungalina

HIGHWAY

Kiana

Robinson

Calvert Hills

Wollogorang

Westmoreland

Hells Gate
Roadhouse

DOOMADGEE
ABORIGINAL
LAND

115

TABLELANDS

Wallhallow

CALVERT

CHINA   WALL

WAANYI/GARAWA

Mt Oscar
115m

Beetaloo

Elliott

STUART

72

BARKLY

STOCK

ROUTE

229

ROAD

Ucharonidge

Mungabroom

Eva Downs

Cresswell Downs

Benmara

Nicholson

ABORIGINAL

LAND TRUST

Springvale

NORTHERN TERRITORY
QUEENSLAND

LAWN HILL
NATIONAL
PARK

CONSTANCE

RANGE

Anthony
Lagoon

Cresswell

377   TABLELANDS   HWY

Renner Springs

Helen Springs

Mt Willieray
369m

38

HIGHWAY

Muckaty

87

Banka Banka

50

Churchills Head Rock

136

Stuart Memorial
ATTACK CREEK
HISTORICAL RESERVE

62

Phillip Creek

John Flynn
Memorial

18

BARKLY

Tarrabool
Lake

Corella
Lake

100

95

Brunchilly

70

45

WARUMUNGU

ABORIGINAL

LAND

Lake
Sylvester

Rockhampton
Downs

46

WARUMUNGU
ABORIGINAL
LAND

Brunette
Downs

100

76

Fish

Hole

CONNELLS LAGOON
CONSERVATION
RESERVE

Mittiebah

Buddijurraw

Lawn Hill

SMITHS

RANGE

Gallipoli

O'Shanessy

98   24

Warrego

25

Three Ways Roadhouse

Devils Pebbles

31

Tennant Creek

87

WARUMUNGU

ABORIGINAL

LAND

114   87

McLaren Creek

Devils Marbles

52

Kurundi

69

27

DEVILS
MARBLES
CON RES

Mt Cairns 597m

21

Epenarra

49

Wauchope

Singleton

Wycliffe Well
Roadhouse

Wycliffe Well

WARRABRI
ABORIGINAL
LAND

Numagalong (aband)

Hatches Creek

RANKEN

98   187

66   BARKLY

89   54

Alroy Downs

Barkly Homestead

HIGHWAY

141

66

Soudan

261

Barrys Caves

21

122

TABLELAND

ROAD

Playford   77

Alexandria   21

Buchanan

ROAD

98

Ranken

Lorne

Avon Downs
Police Station

30

26

30   13

Avon Downs

Cigarette

Camooweal

91

71

Microwave
Repeater
Station

66

20

56

Six Mile Waterhole

Big Ranken Waterhole

22 Mile
Waterhole

Austral
Downs

Bullock
Waterhole

Mt Michael
243m

Crater Of Caves

CAMOOWEAL
CAVES
NP

J   K   L   M   N   O   P   Q   R

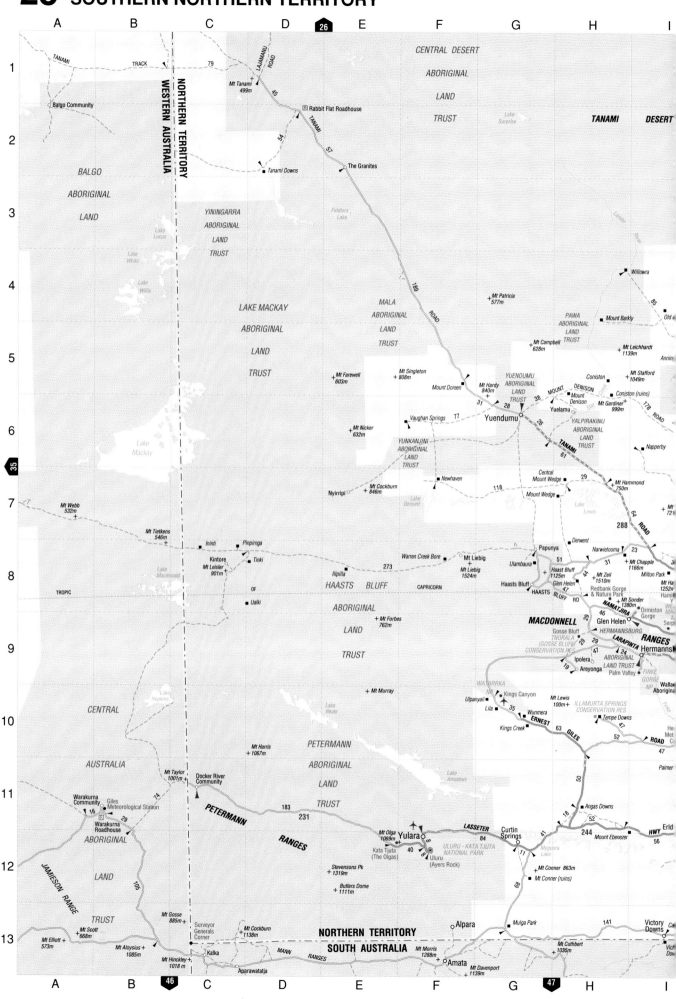

0 50 100 150 km

J K L M N O P Q R

WARUMUNGU ABORIGINAL LAND

27

Barkly Homestead

BARKLY

141

66

261

Soudan

21

30

Avon Downs Police Station

26

30 13

Camooweal

Microwave Repeater Station

66

71

Crater Of Caves

CAMOOWEAL CAVES NP

122

Barrys Caves

Avon Downs

Six Mile Waterhole

Big Ranken Waterhole

22 Mile Waterhole

Austral Downs

95

70

McLaren Creek

27

52 Kurundi

69

Epenarra

21

DEVILS MARBLES CON RES

Mt Cairns 597m

Devils Marbles

Wauchope

Singleton

49

Hatches Creek

56

Bullock Waterhole

Mt Michael 243m

Numagalong (Aband)

Wycliffe Well Roadhouse

19

Wycliffe Well

HIGHWAY

21 Ali-Curung

23

WARRABRI ABORIGINAL LAND TRUST

33

Murray Downs

Elkedra

95

Elkedra River

147

HIGHWAY

21

Lake Nash Ck

Georgina

110

41

Mt Nelson +554m

Tara

ALYAWARRA ABORIGINAL LAND TRUST

80

24

OORATIPPRA ABORIGINAL LAND

Annitowa

37

SANDOVER

Georgina Downs

Georgina

Stokes

Mountain Waterhole

Mt Stirling +575m

30

Barrow Creek

Wilora

Mt Tops +705m

HIGHWAY

Ammaroo

579

157

10

15

Argadargada

Urandangi

90

44

Mt Octy 696m

ANGARAPA ABORIGINAL LAND TRUST

Oratippra

Sandover River

Mt Hogarth 338m

93

ee Store & Police Station

50

25

135

Sandover

Derry Downs

45

Manners Creek

Woola Downs

24

Mt Skinner 677m

Utopia

Bundey

43

Arapunya

Tobermorey

aggie

Chianina

Atartinga

Delmore Downs

14

MacDonald Downs

TARLTON DOWNS ABORIGINAL LAND

HIGHWAY

SANDOVER

82

Red Cliff 658m

Waite River

18

Delny

33

23

Lucy Creek

48

PLENTY

101

art

Mt Byrne 711m

Bushy Park

29

Mount Swan 633m

16

Dneiper

Mt Sainthill 549m

Baikal

95

Tarlton Downs

43

Marqua

116

13m

40

26

37

Huckitta

18

NORTHERN TERRITORY

DONOHUE

27

PLENTY

34

55

Mount Riddock

Harts Range Police Station

30

485

75

HIGHWAY

Jervois

QUEENSLAND

Mt Idamea 184m

Yambah

Mt Riddock 1102m

Mt Campbell 1051m

Mt Palmer

Quartz Hill

58

41

Atula

Mt Reinecke 283m

TOOMBA

19

72

The Garden

52

Claraville

RANGES

Mt Ruby 852m

Indiana

Mt Woods +265m

Mt Wooldridge 288m

RANGE

68

29

Bond Springs

Mt Sir Charles +877m

Atnarpa

TREPHINA GORGE NATURE PARK

ARLTUNGA HISTORICAL RES

RUBY GAP NATURE PARK

TROPIC

Carter Knoll

Mt Whelan 189m

55

20

Alice Springs

113

Ross River

Ross River Historic Homestead

Mt Winnecke 258m

OF

CAPRICORN

sons Gap

17

33

41

89

Lake Wongitta

bataka

Amoonguna

Ringwood

Springs

101

88

SANTA TERESA ABORIGINAL LAND TRUST

Todd River

62

Limbla

Numery

199

85

Ooraminna Rockhole

Mt Ooraminna 649m

Santa Teresa

17

Allambi

Todd River Downs

SIMPSON

Mumbleberry Lake

Deep Well

WARNING: In outback Australia, long distances separate some towns. Travellers should familiarise themselves with prevailing conditions before departure, and take care to ensure their vehicle is roadworthy and that they carry adequate supplies of petrol, water and food.

In northern Australia, rainfall during the 'wet' season (Oct-March) can make some roads impassable. Full information on road conditions should be obtained before departure.

If visitors intend diverting off public roads within Aboriginal Land areas, a permit is required from the relevant Aboriginal authority.

DESERT

Lake Torquinie

75

Maryvale

33

4WD

217

Chambers Pillar

Idracowra

NATIONAL

53

Horseshoe Bend

Muncoomie Lake East

Track

SIMPSON

DESERT

PARK

Andado

Old Andado

95

16

34

36

Finke

31

Mt Peebles 262m

New Crown

22

Mt Grundy 397m

60

22

147

Mirranponga Pongunna Lake

NORTHERN TERRITORY

Mt Wilyunpa +227m

Poeppel Corner

SOUTH AUSTRALIA

Mt Cecil 551m

Mt Parlue 478m

Mt Mead 376m

Mount Dare

Mt Alinerta 222m

WITJIRA NATIONAL PARK

SIMPSON

DESERT

CONSERVATION

PARK

Tieyon

J K L M N O P Q R

47 48

1 2 3 4 5 6 7 8 9 10 11 12 13

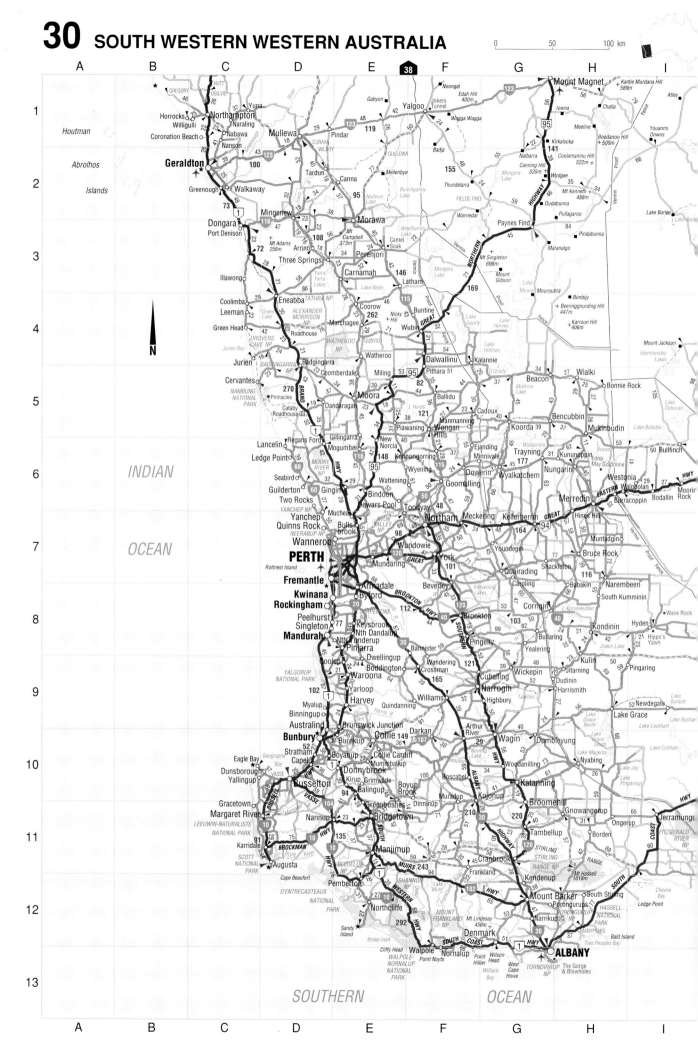

Map scale: 0 – 50 – 100 km

38

A B C D E F G H I

Houtman

Abrolhos

Islands

INDIAN

OCEAN

PERTH

Fremantle

Kwinana

Rockingham

Mandurah

Bunbury

Geraldton

Mount Magnet

Kantie Murdana Hill 589m

Atley

Youanmi Downs

ALBANY

SOUTHERN   OCEAN

1 2 3 4 5 6 7 8 9 10 11 12 13

A B C D E F G H I

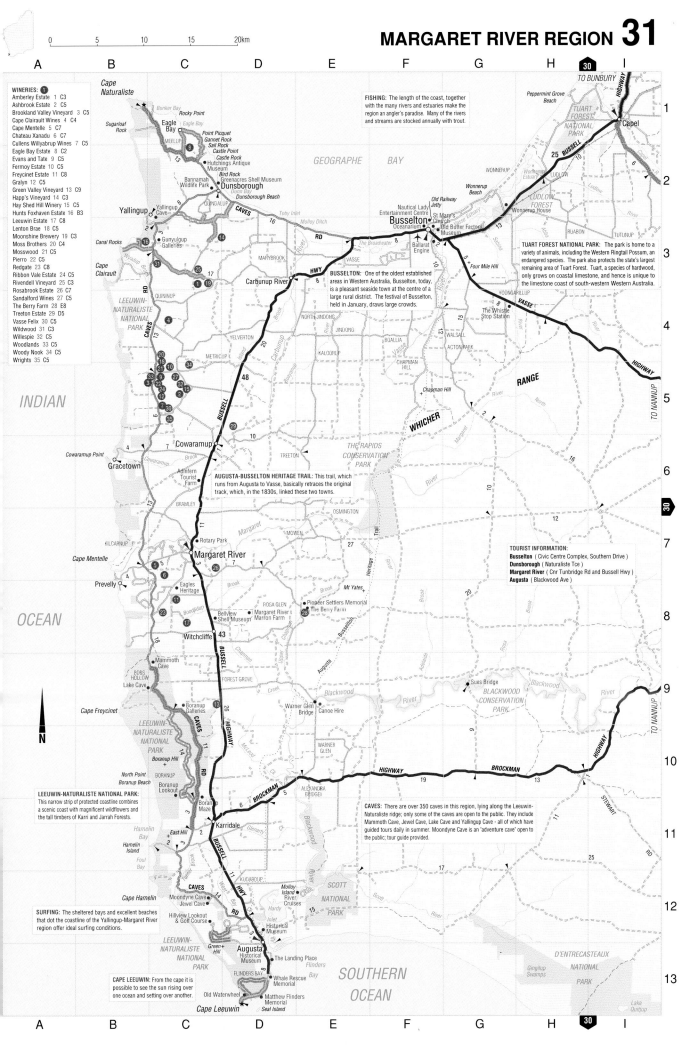

0   5   10   15   20km

WINERIES ❶

Amberley Estate 1 C3
Ashbrook Estate 2 C5
Brookland Valley Vineyard 3 C5
Cape Clairault Wines 4 C4
Cape Mentelle 5 C7
Chateau Xanadu 6 C7
Cullens Willyabrup Wines 7 C5
Eagle Bay Estate 8 C2
Evans and Tate 9 C5
Fermoy Estate 10 C5
Freycinet Estate 11 C8
Gralyn 12 C5
Green Valley Vineyard 13 C9
Happ's Vineyard 14 C3
Hay Shed Hill Winery 15 C5
Hunts Foxhaven Estate 16 B3
Leeuwin Estate 17 C8
Lenton Brae 18 C5
Moonshine Brewery 19 C3
Moss Brothers 20 C4
Mosswood 21 C5
Pierro 22 C5
Redgate 23 C8
Ribbon Vale Estate 24 C5
Rivendell Vineyard 25 C3
Rosabrook Estate 26 C7
Sandalford Wines 27 C5
The Berry Farm 28 E8
Treeton Estate 29 D5
Vasse Felix 30 C5
Wildwood 31 C3
Willespie 32 C5
Woodlands 33 C5
Woody Nook 34 C5
Wrights 35 C5

FISHING: The length of the coast, together with the many rivers and estuaries make the region an angler's paradise. Many of the rivers and streams are stocked annually with trout.

TUART FOREST NATIONAL PARK: The park is home to a variety of animals, including the Western Ringtail Possum, an endangered species. The park also protects the state's largest remaining area of Tuart Forest. Tuart, a species of hardwood, only grows on coastal limestone, and hence is unique to the limestone coast of south-western Western Australia.

BUSSELTON: One of the oldest established areas in Western Australia, Busselton, today, is a pleasant seaside town at the centre of a large rural district. The festival of Busselton, held in January, draws large crowds.

AUGUSTA-BUSSELTON HERITAGE TRAIL: This trail, which runs from Augusta to Vasse, basically retraces the original track, which, in the 1830s, linked these two towns.

TOURIST INFORMATION:
Busselton (Civic Centre Complex, Southern Drive)
Dunsborough (Naturaliste Tce)
Margaret River (Cnr Tunbridge Rd and Bussell Hwy)
Augusta (Blackwood Ave)

LEEUWIN-NATURALISTE NATIONAL PARK: This narrow strip of protected coastline combines a scenic coast with magnificent wildflowers and the tall timbers of Karri and Jarrah Forests.

CAVES: There are over 350 caves in this region, lying along the Leeuwin-Naturaliste ridge; only some of the caves are open to the public. They include Mammoth Cave, Jewel Cave, Lake Cave and Yallingup Cave - all of which have guided tours daily in summer. Moondyne Cave is an "adventure cave" open to the public; tour guide provided.

SURFING: The sheltered bays and excellent beaches that dot the coastline of the Yallingup-Margaret River region offer ideal surfing conditions.

CAPE LEEUWIN: From the cape it is possible to see the sun rising over one ocean and setting over another.

INDIAN OCEAN

SOUTHERN OCEAN

GEOGRAPHE BAY

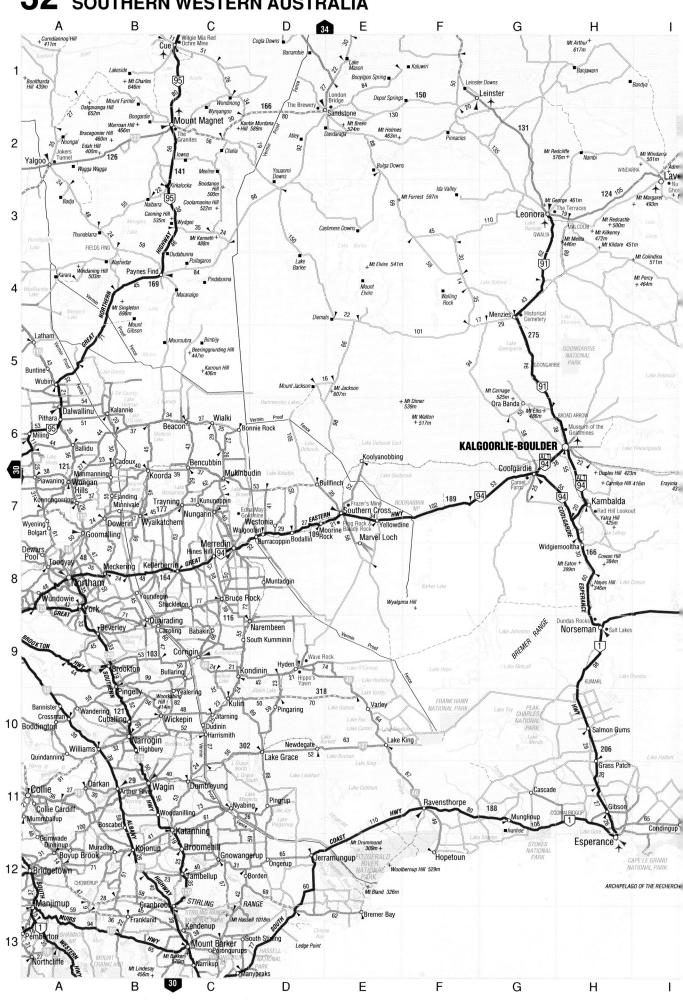

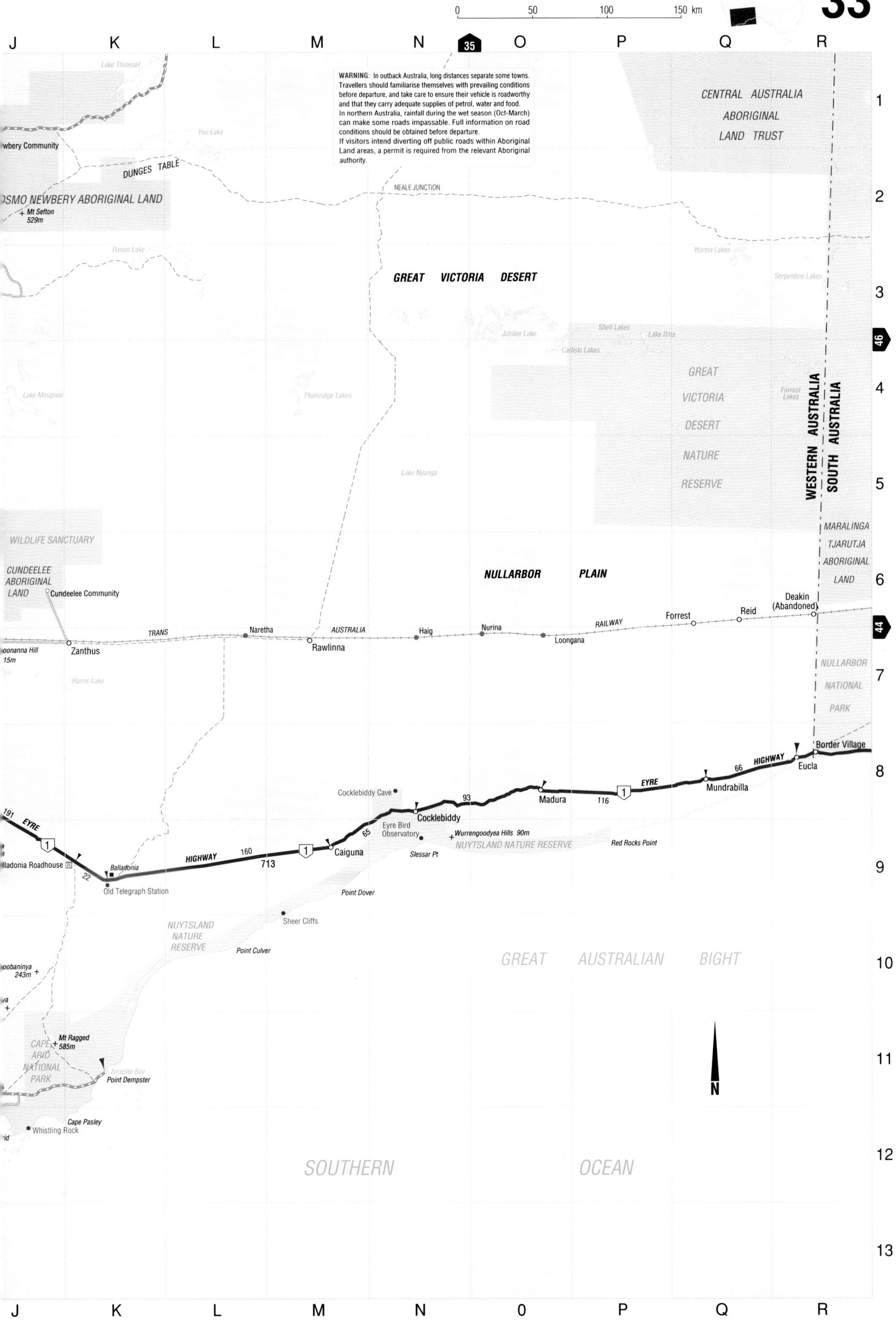

0   50   100   150 km

J   K   L   M   N   O   P   Q   R

Lake Throssel

wbery Community

Yeo Lake

DUNGES TABLE

NEALE JUNCTION

OSMO NEWBERY ABORIGINAL LAND

+ Mt Sefton
529m

Rason Lake

Wanna Lakes

Serpentine Lakes

GREAT   VICTORIA   DESERT

CENTRAL AUSTRALIA

ABORIGINAL

LAND TRUST

Lake Minigwal

Plumridge Lakes

Jubilee Lake

Shell Lakes   Lake Ilma

Carlisle Lakes

Forrest
Lakes

GREAT

VICTORIA

DESERT

NATURE

RESERVE

Lake Nyanga

WILDLIFE SANCTUARY

CUNDEELEE
ABORIGINAL
LAND   Cundeelee Community

NULLARBOR   PLAIN

Deakin
(Abandoned)

Forrest   Reid

MARALINGA

TJARUTJA

ABORIGINAL

LAND

TRANS   Naretha   AUSTRALIA   Haig   Nurina   RAILWAY

oonanna Hill
15m   Zanthus

Rawlinna

Loongana

Harris Lake

NULLARBOR

NATIONAL

PARK

Border Village

66 **HIGHWAY**   Eucla

Cocklebiddy Cave

93   Madura   116   Eyre   Mundrabilla

191   EYRE

EYRE

HIGHWAY   160   Caiguna

Cocklebiddy

65

Eyre Bird
Observatory

+ Wurrengoodyea Hills 90m
NUYTSLAND NATURE RESERVE

Red Rocks Point

lladonia Roadhouse

713

22   Balladonia
Old Telegraph Station

Slessar Pt

Point Dover

Point Dempster

NUYTSLAND
NATURE
RESERVE   Sheer Cliffs

Point Culver

GREAT   AUSTRALIAN   BIGHT

oobaninya +
243m

va +

CAPE
ARID
NATIONAL
PARK

+ Mt Ragged
585m

Israelite Bay

Cape Pasley

Whistling Rock

SOUTHERN   OCEAN

WESTERN AUSTRALIA
SOUTH AUSTRALIA

N

1   **2**   **3**   **4**   **5**   **6**   **7**   **8**   **9**   **10**   **11**   **12**   **13**

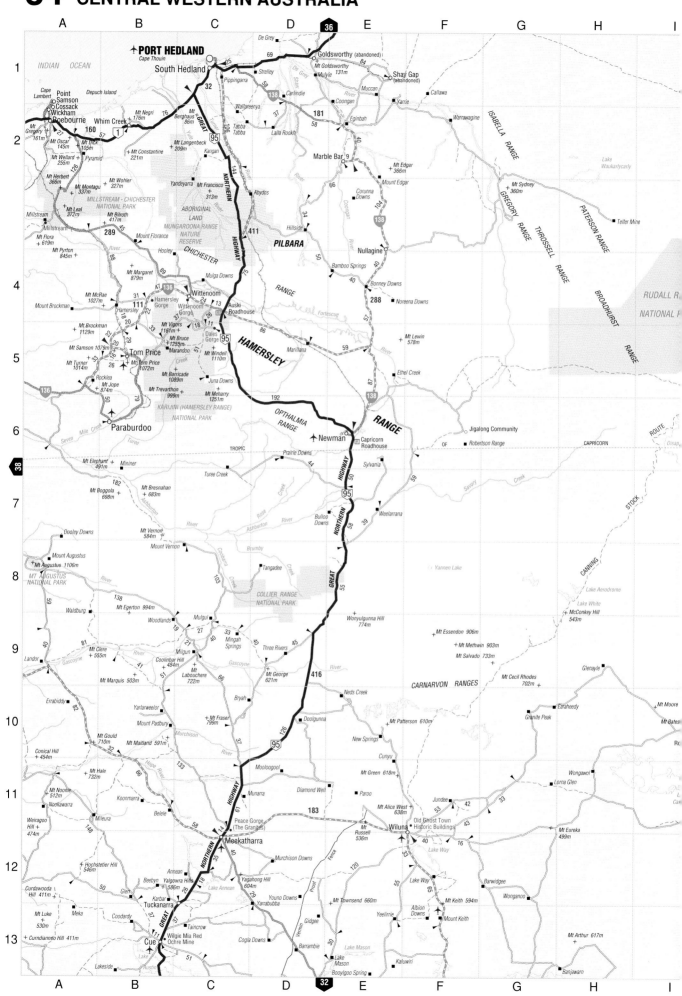

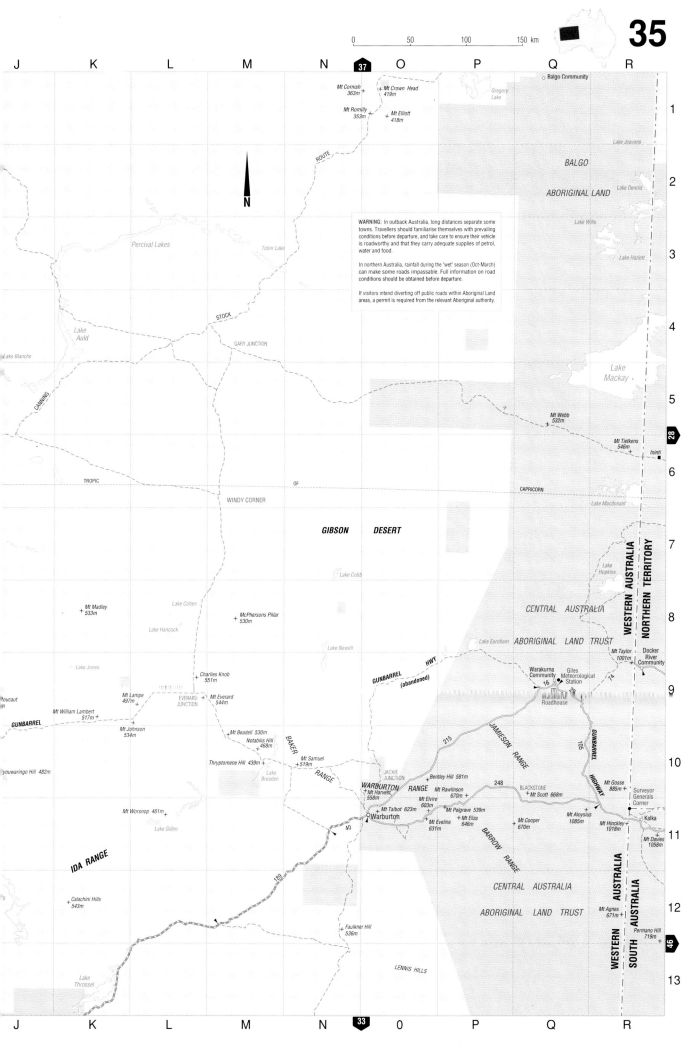

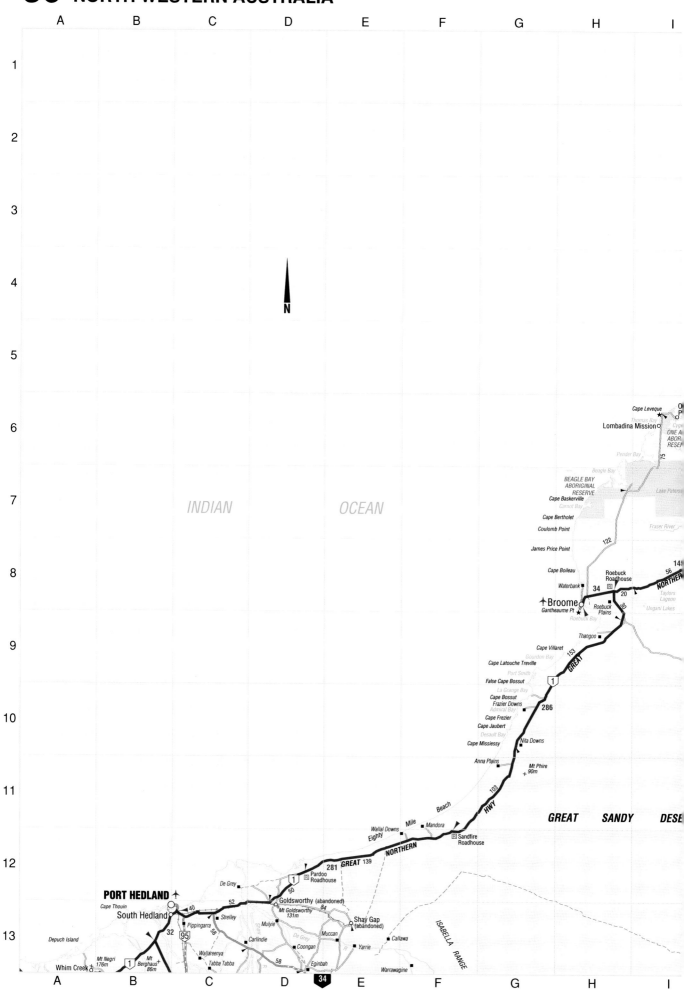

A B C D E F G H I

1

2

3

4

N

5

6
Cape Leveque
Lombadina Mission
Thomas Bay
Cygn
ONE A
ABOR
RESE

7
INDIAN OCEAN
BEAGLE BAY ABORIGINAL RESERVE
Cape Baskerville
Carnot Bay
Cape Bertholet
Coulomb Point
Pender Bay
Beagle Bay
75
Fraser River
122

8
James Price Point
Cape Boileau
Waterbank
Broome
Gantheaume Pt
Roebuck Roadhouse
34
20
NORTHER
56
14
Taylors Lagoon
Ungani Lakes
Roebuck Plains
Roebuck Bay

9
Cape Villaret
Gourdon Bay
Cape Latouche Treville
Port Smith
False Cape Bossut
La Grange Bay
Thangoo
GREAT
153
1

10
Cape Bossut
Frazier Downs
Admiral Bay
Cape Frezier
Cape Jaubert
Desault Bay
Cape Missiessy
Nita Downs
286

11
Anna Plains
Mt Phire
+ 90m
Beach
103
HWY
GREAT SANDY DESE

12
Wallal Downs
Eighty
Mile
Mandora
Sandfire Roadhouse
NORTHERN
GREAT 139
281
Pardoo Roadhouse
1
50
De Grey
52

13
PORT HEDLAND
Cape Thouin
South Hedland
Depuch Island
Mt Negri 176m
Whim Creek
Mt Berghaus 86m
1
32
95
40
Pippingarra
58
Strelley
Mulyie
Waljareenya
Tabba Tabba
Carlindie
58
Goldsworthy (abandoned)
Mt Goldsworthy 131m
84
Shay Gap (abandoned)
Muccan
Coongan
Eginbah
De Grey
Yarrie
Callawa
Warrawagine
ISABELLA RANGE

A B C D E 34 F G H I

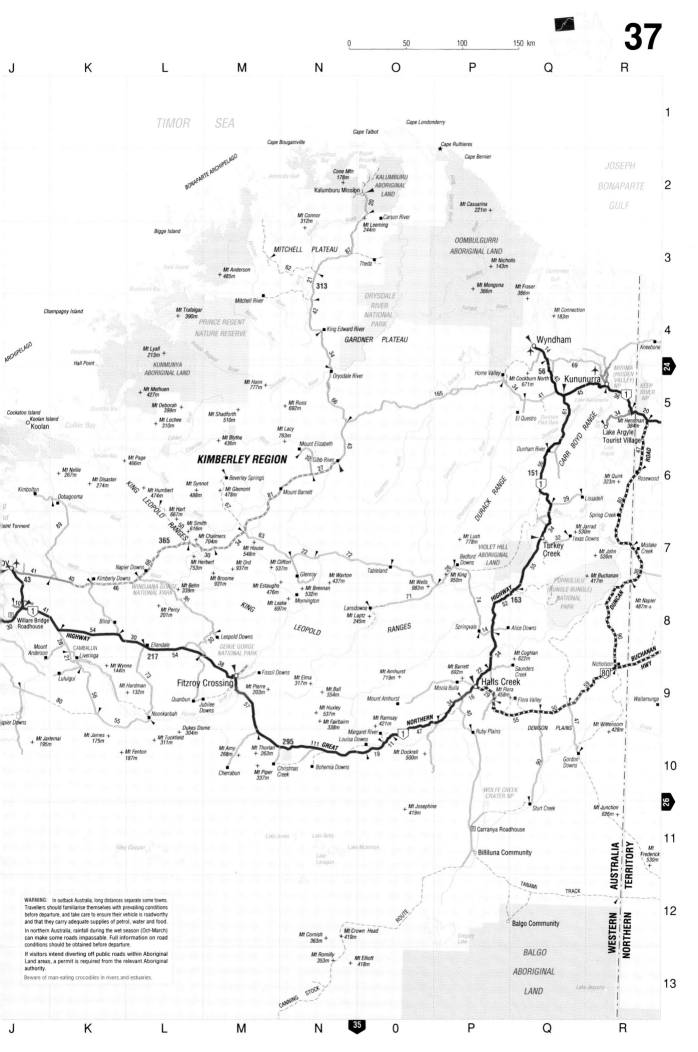

WARNING: In outback Australia, long distances separate some towns. Travellers should familiarise themselves with prevailing conditions before departure, and take care to ensure their vehicle is roadworthy and that they carry adequate supplies of petrol, water and food.

In northern Australia, rainfall during the wet season (Oct–March) can make some roads impassable. Full information on road conditions should be obtained before departure.

If visitors intend diverting off public roads within Aboriginal Land areas, a permit is required from the relevant Aboriginal authority.

Beware of man-eating crocodiles in rivers and estuaries.

0   50   100 km

INDIAN

OCEAN

Barrow Island

Montebello Islands

Cape Poivre

Sholl Island

Cape Preston

Regnard Bay

Dampier Karratha Point Samson Wickham
Karratha Roadhouse Roebourne
Mt Negri 176m
Whim Creek
Mt Langenbeck 209m
Mt Constantine 221m

ABORIGINAL LAND

Mt Potter 98m
Mt Leopold 250m
Mt Sholl 173m
Mt Roe 183m
Mt Wellard 255m
Pyramid
Mt McLeod 150m
Cooya Pooya
Mt Regal 169m

Fortescue Roadhouse

WEST NORTH

Yarraloola

Onslow

Beadon Point

Thevenard Island

Pannawonica

Millstream

MILLSTREAM - CHICHESTER NATIONAL PARK

Mt Herbert 366m
Mt Leal 372m Mt Richthofen 390m
Mt Bilroth 417m

MUNGAROONA RANGE NATURE RESERVE

Mt Enid 302m
Mt Florance
Hooley

PILBARA

North Murion Island

Wreck of SS 'Mildura'
False Island Cape
Low Point
Naval Communication Station
Point Murat - Restricted Area

NORTH WEST CAPE

CAPE RANGE NATIONAL PARK

Exmouth

Shothole Canyon

Mt Hollister 315m
LEARMONTH

Exmouth Gulf

Minderoo

Mt Minnie 218m
Cane River
Red Hill
Mt Dempster 372m
Mt Rica 565m
Mt Elvire 673m
Mt Flora

Mt Pyrton 845m

HAMERSLEY

Wittenoom
Hamersley Gorge
Mt Mcrae 1027m
Hamersley
Mt Stevenson 1020m
Mt Bruce 1255m

Koordarrie

Mt Mary 115m

Nanutarra Roadhouse

Mt Stuart 304m
Mt Farquhar 997m
Mount Brockman
Mt Brockman 1129m

Norwegian Bay

Ningaloo
Shipwrecks
Bullara

HIGHWAY

Mt Alexander 410m
Uaroo

Mt Edith 292m
Mt Elizabeth 275m Wyloo
Mt De Courcey 485m
Duck Creek

Mt Turner 1014m
Mt Tom Price 1072m
Rocklea

Tom Price
Marandoo
Mt Barricade 1089m

Coral Bay
Cardabia
Point Maud

WEST COASTAL

Marrilla
Nyang
Mt Forrest 145m
Towera

Mt Danvers 246m
Mt Clement 358m
Glenflorrie
Mt Wall 957m

Mt Jope 874m

KARIJINI (HAMERSLEY RANGE) NATIONAL PARK

Warroora
Bulbarli Point

NORTH

Mt Hamlet 248m

Mt Florry 482m
Kooline

RANGE

Paraburdoo

TROPIC

Cape Farquhar

Gnaraloo Bay

Minilya Roadhouse

Wandagee

Mt Tucker 265m
Maroonah

BARLEE RANGE NATURE RESERVE

Ashburton Downs

CAPRICORN

Mt Elephant 491m
Mininer

Gnaraloo

Manberry

Middalya

Lyndon

OF

Mangaroon

Mt Thomson 392m
Edmund

Wanna

Mt Boggola 698m
Mt Bresnahan 683m

Cape Cuvier

Lake Macleod

Hill Springs

Moogooree

Minnie Creek

Mt Agamemnon 337m
Gifford Creek

Dooley Downs

Mt Vernon 584m
Mount Vernon

H.M.A.S. 'Sydney' Memorial Cairn
Blowholes

Cooralya
Mardathuna

Eudamullah
Mt Sandiman 343m

Mt Augustus 1106m
MT AUGUSTUS NATIONAL PARK
Mount Augustus

Waldburg

Mt Egerton 994m
Woodlands

Bernier Island

Carnarvon
Gneedingarra
Meeragoolia

Lyons River

Yinnetharra

Mt Phillips
Mt Phillips 780m

Mt James 602m
Mt Gascoyne 789m
Mt Clere 555m

Milgun
Coolinbar Hill 484m

Dorre Island

Mooka

Gascoyne Junction

Mt Steere 469m
Mooloo Downs

Mt Marquis 503m

Shark Bay

Ella Valla
Yalbalgo

Mt Dalgety 520m
Mt Puckford 583m
Landor

Cape Peron North

Marron
Wahroonga Pimbee

Carey Downs

Glenburgh
Yalbra

Erong Springs
Errabiddy

Yarlarweelor
Mt Fraser 799m

Dirk Hartog Island

Monkey Mia
Dolphin Sightings
Monkey Mia

Meedo
Gilroyd

Mt Madeline 313m
Innouendy

Mt Gould 710m
Mount Padbury
Mt Maitland 591m

Denham

Wooramel Roadhouse
Yaringa North

Callytharra Springs

Wooramel

Mt Nairn 452m
Byro

Milly Milly

Mt Hale 732m
Conical Hill 454m

Mileura

Koonmarra
Belele

Eagle Bluff

COASTAL

Yalardy

Mt Dugel 461m

Milly Milly

Mt Noome 512m
Nookawarra

Useless Loop

Henri Freycinet Harbour

100 km Shell Beach
Nanga Bay Resort

Overlander Roadhouse

Muggon
Mount Narryer

Mt Narryer 514m

Weiragoo Hill 474m

Annean

Mt Elliot 418m

HIGHWAY

Muggon

Mt Murchison 503m
Mt Hochstetter Hill 546m

Lake Annean

Tamala
Zuytdorp Cliffs

Meadow

Billabong Roadhouse

Murchison

Wooleen
Boolardy
Meka
Coodardy

Annean
Yalgowra Hills
Karbar

ZUYTDORP NATIONAL PARK

Nerren Nerren

Vermin

NICHOLSON RANGE

Mt Luke 530m
Curndiannoo Hill 411m

Curdawooda Hill 411m
Glen

Tuckanarra

Proof

New Forest
Yallalong

Murgoo

Gnarowanna Hill 405m

Taincrow

KALBARRI NATIONAL PARK

Eurardy

Kalbarri

Yandi
Lake Nerramyne
Pinegrove
Bullardoo

Booltharda Hill 439m
Miljanna Hill 425m

Lakeside

Cue
Wilgie Mia Red Ochre Mine

Baline

Binnu

Vermin

Narloo
Yuin
Tardie

Eeradar Hill 326m

Dalgavanga Hill 652m
Mount Farmer
Bracegonier Hill 460m

Mount Magnet

GREAT

Warroon Hill 466m
Noongal
Wynnagoo
Wondinong

Boogardie
The Granites

N

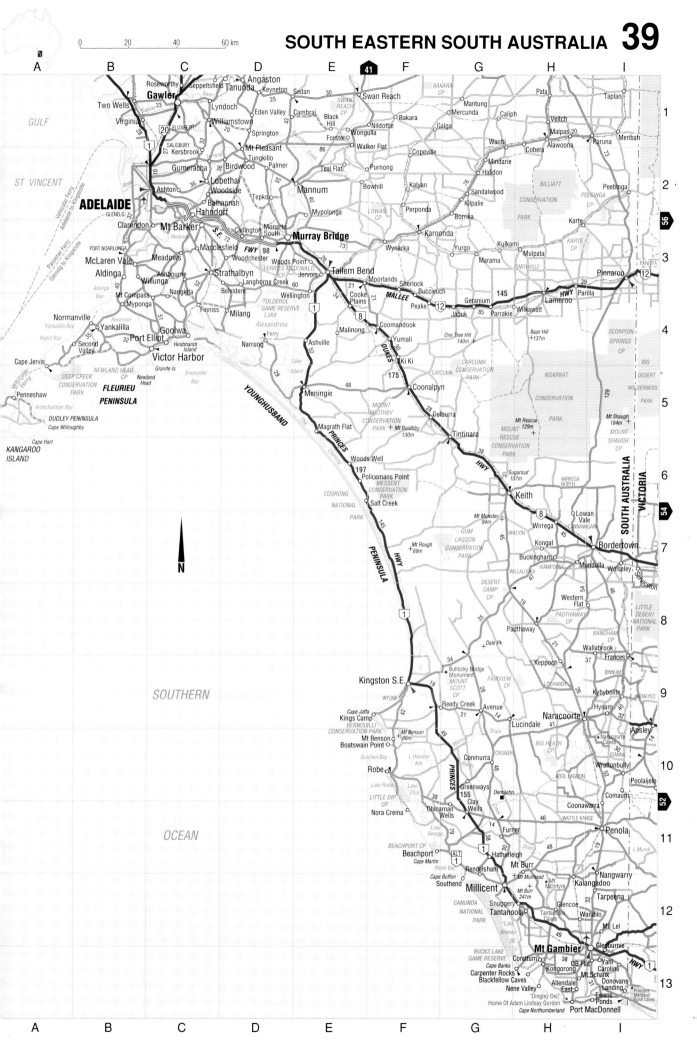

0   20   40   60 km

GULF

ST VINCENT

ADELAIDE
GLENELG

Two Wells
Virginia
Roseworthy
Gawler
Seppeltsfield
Tanunda
Angaston
Keyneton
Sedan
Swan Reach

Lyndoch
Williamstown
Eden Valley
Springton
Cambrai
Black Hill
Forster
Nildottie
Bakara
Galga
Mantung
Mercunda
Caliph
Veltch
Pata
Taplan

Kersbrook
Mt Pleasant
Palmer
Wongulla
Walker Flat
Copeville
Mindarie
Wanbi
Cobera
Alawoona
Malpas
Paruna
Meribah

Gumeracha
Birdwood
Tungkillo
Teal Flat
Purnong
Bowhill
Kalyan
Sandalwood
Halidon
Borrika
Karte
Peebinga

Lobethal
Woodside
Balhannah
Mannum
Perponda
Kilpalie
Karoonda
Kulkami
Mulpata

Clarendon
Mt Barker
Hahndorf
Callington
Monarto South
Murray Bridge
Wynarka
Yurgo
Marama
Smithville
Karte

Macclesfield
Woodchester
Woods Point
Tailem Bend
Moorlands
Sherlock
Buccleuch
Geranium
Parilla
Pinnaroo

McLaren Vale
Meadows
Ashbourne
Strathalbyn
Langhorne Creek
Belvidere
Wellington
Jervois
Cooke Plains
Peake
Jabuk
Parrakie
Wilkawatt
Lameroo

Aldinga
Willunga
Nangkita
Finniss
Milang
Ashville
Coomandook
Yumali
Ki Ki
Coonalpyn

Normanville
Yankalilla
Port Elliot
Goolwa
Narrung
Meningie
Magrath Flat
Gulburra
Tintinara
Keith
Wirrega
Bordertown
Wolseley

Cape Jervis
Victor Harbor
Woods Well
Policemans Point
Salt Creek

Penneshaw
Kingston S.E.
Reedy Creek
Avenue
Lucindale
Naracoorte
Hynam
Apsley

KANGAROO ISLAND
Cape Jaffa
Kings Camp
Mt Benson
Boatswain Point
Robe
Conmurra
Greenways
Wrattonbully
Comaum
Coonawarra

Nora Creina
Chinaman Wells
Clay Wells
Furner
Penola

Beachport
Hatherleigh
Mt Burr
Nangwarry
Kalangadoo
Tarpeena

Rendelsham
Millicent
Glencoe
Wandilo
Mil Lel

Southend
Snuggery
Tantanoola
Mt Gambier
Glenburnie

Corattum
OB Flat
Yahl
Caroline
Kongorong
Mt Schank
Donovans
Carpenter Rocks
Blackfellow Caves
Nene Valley
Allendale East
Ewens Ponds
Cape Northumberland
Port MacDonnell

SOUTHERN

OCEAN

N

A B C D **42** E F G H I

1

Minnipa
Yaninee
Wudinna Hill 260m
Wudinna Wudinna Hill
Turtle Rock
Peella Rocks
Polda Rocks
PINKAWILLINIE CONSERVATION PARK
Buckleboo
LAKE GILLES CONSERVATION PARK
Cooyerdoo Hill 269m
Mt Whyalla Se + 232m
WHYALLA CONSERVATION PARK
Iron Baron
Po
W

45
FLINDERS
Port Kenny
Lake Yaninee
49
KULLIPARU CONSERVATION PARK
MOUNT DAMPER
Samphire Flat
Kyancutta
Koongawa
1
88 EYRE HWY
Kimba
94
Mt Middleback + 446m
Iron Baron
Mt Young 136m
MIDDLEBACK RANGE
24
False Bay

2
Venus Bay
VENUS BAY CP
ALT 1
Talia
Warramboo
Darkes Memorial
Caralue Bluff + 484m
Caralue
Waddikee
85
Carpie Puntha Hill 479m
83
MURNINNIE BEACH
Granite Hill + 252m
MUNYAROO CONSERVATION PARK
Plank Point

3
Talia Caves
LAKE NEWLAND CP
Anxious Bay
Colton
31
56
Mt Wedge 247m
MOUNT WEDGE
Kappawanta Hill 99m
58
52
COCATA CONSERVATION PARK
HAMBIDGE CONSERVATION PARK
Lock
BARWELL CONSERVATION PARK
56
Carrappe Hill CP
Mt Darke Peak 448m
Darke Peak
KIELPA
73
YELDULKNIE CP
23
Mangalo
Mt Olinthus 453m
MULTALIE
YABMANA
MIDDLECAMP HILLS
Mt Geharty 277m
MINBRIE
PONDOOMA
ALT 1
Cowell
Lucky Bay
Shoalwater Point

4
Cape Finniss
Bramfield
Sheoak Hill 366m
Elliston
BASCOMBE WELL CONSERVATION PARK
HWY 104
Sheringa
Murdinga
HINCKS CONSERVATION PARK
Toolige Hill + 196m
82
Tooligie
EYRE
PENINSULA
24
Verran
Mt Priscilla 170m
Rudall
Cleve
Carpa
44
Arno Bay
277
Gibbon Point
HWY
Cape Driver
FRANKLIN HARBOR CONSERVATION PARK
Germein Point
Elbow Hill
Myponie Point
Point Riley
Wallaroo Bay
Wallaroo

5
Flinders Island
GREAT
Lake Hamilton
Karkoo
Wharminda
Mt Hill 197m
Butler Tanks
Port Neill
Cape Hardy
LINCOLN
SPENCER
Cape Elizabeth
Moonta Bay
Tiparra Bay
Moonta
Weetulta

6
AUSTRALIAN
Drummond Point
Mount Hope
Kapinnie
30
Yeelanna
Cockaleechie
URANNO
Cummins
STOKES
Ungarra
Lipson
Yallunda Flat
Tumby Bay
Tumby Bay
GULF
GOOSE ISLAND CP
Wardang Island
Pt. Pearce
Port Victoria
20
Balgowan
South Kilkerran
Urania
44
Wauraltee

7
BIGHT
Point Sir Isaac
Lookout
Coffin Bay
Warrow
Coulta
43
41
37
Edillilie
Koppio
Tod River Res.
White Flat
50
Louth Bay
Poonindie
Reevesby Island
SIR JOSEPH BANKS GROUP CONSERVATION PARK
Roxby Island
Sir Joseph Banks Group
Spilsby Island
Port Rickaby
YORKE
PENINSULA
M
Port Minlacowie
31

8
Point Whidbey
Lookout
Avoid Bay
COFFIN BAY NATIONAL PARK
Wanilla
Wangary
21
Coffin Bay
KELLIDIE BAY CP
North Shields
Boston Bay
Cape Donington
Flinders Monument
Boston Island
LINCOLN NATIONAL PARK
Taylor Island
Corny Point
Lookout
POINT SOUTTAR
LEVEN BEACH
Pt. Turton
30
Daly Head
Blowhole
CARRIBIE CP
Point Margaret
Hardwicke Bay
Hardwicke Bay
Warooka
50
Yorketown
Brentwood
S
Oakl
39
Coob
Edithb
MOOROWIE

9
Flinders Lookout
Sleaford Bay
Cape Carnot
Liguanea Island
Sleaford Mere
Stamford Hill 137m
Cape Tournefort
West Point
Hopkins Island
Flinders Tablet
Thistle Island
Albatross Island
Gambier Islands
Royston Head
INNES NP
Marion Bay
Pondalowie Bay
West Cape
The Ethel (shipwreck)
Cape Spencer
Stenhouse Bay
Inneston Historic Ruins
WARRENBEN CONSERVATION PARK
Point Yorke
Lookout
Hillock Point
POINT DAVENPORT
Point Davenport CONSERVATION PARK
Trou

10
Port Lincoln
North Neptunes
N
ALTHORPE ISLANDS CP
Althorpe Islands
INVESTIGATOR
STRAIT
Cape D'Estaing
Mt Marso 182m
Emu Bay
Ki
Bay

11
SOUTHERN
OCEAN
KANGAROO ISLAND
CAPE TORRENS CP
Cape Torrens
Cape Borda
Lookout
FLINDERS CHASE NATIONAL PARK
Vennachar Point
29
WEST END HWY
24
Kelly Hill Caves
Karatta
Parndana
PLAYFORD
35
HWY
43
Cygnet River
LATHAMI CP
WESTERN RIVER CP
Cape Dutton
Stokes Bay
Cape Cassini
Ki
Nepe
87
Sapp

12
Cape Bedout
Rocky River
Remarkable Rocks
Cape Du Couedic
Admirals Arch
Breakneck R.
Rocky R.
Kelly Hill
Seals
KELLY HILL CP
C. Younghusband
Kirkpatrick Point
Cape Rouget
Vivonne Bay
VIVONNE BAY CP
Mt Bloomfield
Seal Bay
107
Ellson
103
Murray Lagoon
Cape Kersaint
Cape Gantheaume
CAPE GANTHEAUME CONSERVATION PARK
Cape Gantheaume

13

A B C D E F G H I

0 20 40 60 80 100 km

Grid columns: J K L M N O P Q R
Grid rows: 1–13

ADELAIDE

Melrose, Booleroo Centre, Pekina, Nantabibbie, Oodla Wirra, Murray Town, Wirrabara, Appila, Tarcowie, Yatina, Peterborough, Napperby, Nelshaby, Hornsdale, Mannanarie, Yongala, Gumbowie, Laura, Caltowie, Jamestown, Terowie, Whyte Yarcowie, Gladstone, Georgetown, Hallett, Crystal Brook, Narridy, Canowie, Mount Bryan, Spalding, Booborowie, Burra, Redbanks, Blyth, Clare, Farrell Flat, Worlds End, Florieton, Bute, Bumbunga, Sevenhill, Meridin, Black Springs, Emu Downs, Balaklava, Auburn, Saddleworth, Morgan, Cadell, Weston Flat, Taylorville, Waterval, Leasingham, Marrabel, Hampden, Mount Mary, Renmark, Paringa, Berri, Owen, Tarlee, Kapunda, Truro, Blanchetown, Waikerie, Loxton, Gawler, Nuriootpa, Angaston, Tanunda, Swan Reach, Taldra, Virginia, Lyndoch, Williamstown, Eden Valley, Sedan, Cambrai, Bakara, Alawoona, Meribah, Elizabeth, Mount Pleasant, Birdwood, Palmer, Mannum, Purnong, Copeville, Peebinga, ADELAIDE, Hahndorf, Woodside, Balhannah, Tepko, Mypolonga, Bowhill, Kalyan, Perponda, Karte, Mt Barker, Clarendon, Macclesfield, Callington, Monarto South, Murray Bridge, Wynarka, Yurgo, Marama, Kulkami, Mulpata, McLaren Vale, Willunga, Strathalbyn, Langhorne Creek, Wellington, Tailem Bend, Moorlands, Sherlock, Buccleuch, Peake, Jabuk, Parrakie, Geranium, Wilkawatt, Lameroo, Pinnaroo, Aldinga, Mt Compass, Myponga, Nangkita, Finniss, Milang, Cooke Plains, Coomandook, Yumali, Coonalpyn, Marama, Normanville, Yankalilla, Goolwa, Port Elliot, Victor Harbor, Narrung, Ashville, Ki Ki, Culburra, Tintinara, Keith, Meningie, Magrath Flat, Woods Well, Policemans Point, Salt Creek, Bordertown, Wolseley, Serviceton, Mundulla, Kongal, Buckingham, Wampoony

DANGGALI CONSERVATION PARK, PANDAPPA CONSERVATION PARK, BROOKFIELD CONSERVATION PARK, POOGINOOK CONSERVATION PARK, MURRAY RIVER NP, BILLIATT CONSERVATION PARK, NGARKAT CONSERVATION PARK, MOUNT RESCUE CONSERVATION PARK, MOUNT BOOTHBY CONSERVATION PARK, MESSENT CONSERVATION PARK, COORONG NATIONAL PARK, GUM LAGOON CONSERVATION PARK, DEEP CREEK CONSERVATION PARK, NEWLAND HEAD CP, FLEURIEU PENINSULA, YOUNGHUSBAND PENINSULA, SOUTHERN OCEAN, GULF ST VINCENT

SOUTH AUSTRALIA / NEW SOUTH WALES
SOUTH AUSTRALIA / VICTORIA

MOUNT LOFTY RANGES, MOUNT BARRIER NORTH, TELOWIE GORGE CP

Highways: HWY 32, 64, 83, 20, 8, 12, 1, 98, STURT HWY, MALLEE HWY, DUKES HWY, PRINCES HWY, BARRIER HWY, 43, 39, 54, 175, 145

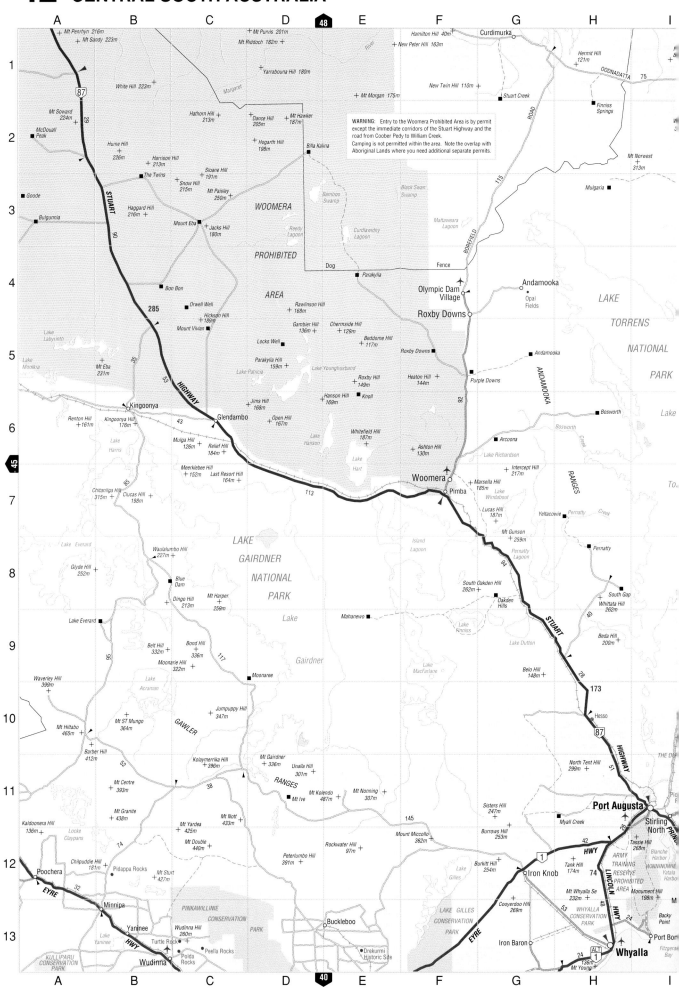

WARNING: Entry to the Woomera Prohibited Area is by permit except the immediate corridors of the Stuart Highway and the road from Coober Pedy to William Creek.
Camping is not permitted within the area. Note the overlap with Aboriginal Lands where you need additional separate permits.

0 20 40 60 80 100 km

J K L M N 49 O P Q R

WARNING: In outback Australia, long distances separate some towns. Travellers should familiarise themselves with prevailing conditions before departure, and take care to ensure their vehicle is roadworthy and that they carry adequate supplies of petrol, water and food.

In northern Australia, rainfall during the "wet" season (Oct-March) can make some roads impassable. Full information on road conditions should be obtained before departure.

If visitors intend diverting off public roads within Aboriginal Land areas, a permit is required from the relevant Aboriginal authority.

STRZELECKI REGIONAL RESERVE

1

Mundowdna

195

Macdonnell Creek

Mount Hopeless

Lake Callabonna

Winnathee

Wilpoorinna

Prospect Hill + 218m

Fence

Hawker Gate House

2

83

Farina (ruin)

Dog

Mt Gardiner + 374m

Mt Babbage + 369m

Moolawatana

Mount Fitton

Boolkaree Creek

Yandama

Smithville House

Tent Hill 247m

Mount Freeling

Mt Livingston 616m +

Mount Fitton

Mt Neil + 571m

3

Mt Lyndhurst 286m

Mount Lyndhurst

RANGES

Paralana Hot Springs

Dog

Wallace Ck

Avondale

TRACK

STRZELECKI

Mt Pitt 855m +

Mt Painter 790m

Fence

Starvation Lake

4

Lyndhurst

39

Mandarin Caps 655m

FLINDERS

GAMMON RANGES

Arkaroola

Wooltana

LAKE

Turleys Gate

Packsaddle

Mt Coffin 835m +

Mt Serle 933m

Mt Mckinlay 1051m +

NATIONAL

Weetootla Gorge

FROME

Pine View

5

Copley

Leigh Creek

Mt Jeffery 727m

Maynards Well

NORTH

PARK

Balcanoona

REGIONAL

RESERVE

272

Mt Deception + 685m

Mt Hack + 1083m

Lake Frome

Lake Culberta

Boughams Gate

6

Beltana Roadhouse

Beltana

Beltana

Sliding Rock Mine (Ruins)

Old Warraween A (Ruins)

Lake Karpi

Lake Carnanto

Teilta

Patawarta Hill 1009m

Narrina

Chambers Gorge

Mt Chambers 433m

Lake Moko

Dog Fence

65

Parachilna

32

Blinman

Wirrealpa

Lake Millyera

Lake Tarkarooloo

Eurinilla

Morphetts

7

Motpena

Angorichina Tourist Village

Great Wall of China

59

FLINDERS RANGES

Frome Downs

Lake Namba

Lake Yentaawena

SOUTH AUSTRALIA

Commodore

Oraparinna

Reaphook Hill + 388m

Benagerie

NEW SOUTH WALES

8

Mt Rupert 655m +

NATIONAL

Mt Caernarvon 920m

Martins Well

Wilpena

Erudina

Mooleulooloo

Mulyungarie

MUNDI MUNDI PLAIN

89

Moralana

Wilpena

RANGES

PARK

83

Burnett Hill 442m

Mt Aleck 1128m

Lookout

Wilpena Pound

Rawnsley Park

Willippa

Curnamona

9

Arkaba

52

Wilyerpa Hill 880m

Bibliando

Killawarra

Old Telechie

Umberumberka Reservoir

Ghost Town

Wonoka Historic Site (ruin)

Mt Plantagenet 949m

Siccus River

Baratta

47

FLINDERS

Hawker

Yourambulla Caves

Willow Waters (Ruins)

Mt Victor + 464m

Bimbowrie

Donata Ck

Wompinie

Cockburn

10

Hut Hill + 618m

107

Cradock

Plumbago

Outalpa Hill + 496m

Outalpa

HIGHWAY

32 68

Mingary

Tepco

Aroona

SOUTH

71

Belton

Marchant Hill 799m

Spotswood Hill

Weekeroo Hill 568m

Weekeroo

Olary

Ballara

11

Price Hill 756m

Wirra Downs

Waukaringa

Mannahill

223

Maldorky Hill 428m

Mutooroo

Burta

Carrieton

Johnberg

Meadow Downs

81

Tattawuppa Hill + 611m

Wadnaminga

Browns Hill 152m

Hammond

37

Ivy Glen

Eurelia

Yalpara

Yunta

Oulnina Hill 710m

Oulnina

BENDA RANGE

12

56

Willowie

50

Morchard

Pekina Hill 732m

BARRIER

Paratoo

74 Dare Hill + 452m

Oulnina Park

Booleroo

Orroroo

12

Nackara Hill 661m

Dawson

Nantabibbie

Nackara

Ocalla Ck

Melrose

Pekina

Black Rock

24

MINWALARA

Oodla Wirra

Murray Town

Tarcowie

Yatina

56

14

UCOLTA

Doughboy Hill + 602m

Alderman Reservoir

Wright Hill + 517m

13

Wirrabara

Hornsdale

Yongala

Peterborough

Appila

Mannanarie

Gumbowie

Mt Lock 743m +

Belalie North

Boiekevie Hill + 539m

Ironback Hill + 378m

DANGGALI CONSERVATION PARK

Stone Hut

J K L M 41 N O P Q R

N

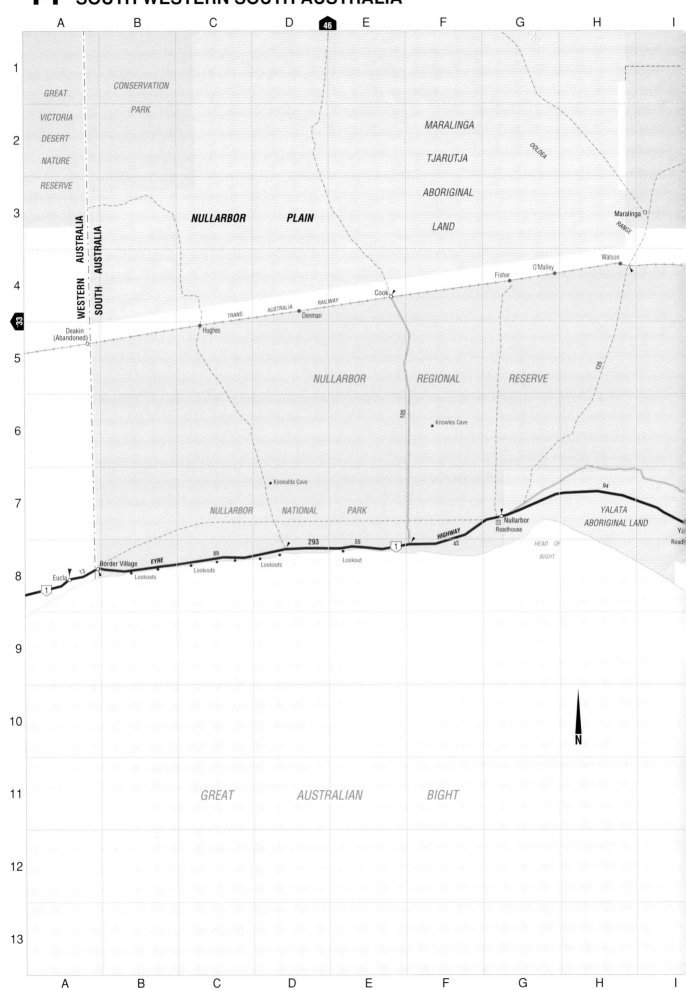

44 SOUTH WESTERN SOUTH AUSTRALIA

46

GREAT

CONSERVATION

VICTORIA

PARK

DESERT

MARALINGA

NATURE

TJARUTJA

RESERVE

ABORIGINAL

NULLARBOR   PLAIN

LAND

WESTERN AUSTRALIA
SOUTH AUSTRALIA

OOLDEA

Maralinga

RANGE

Watson

33

Fisher   O'Malley

Cook

TRANS   AUSTRALIA   RAILWAY

Denman

Hughes

Deakin
(Abandoned)

NULLARBOR   REGIONAL   RESERVE

125

105

Knowles Cave

Koonalda Cave

94

NULLARBOR   NATIONAL   PARK

YALATA
ABORIGINAL LAND

Nullarbor
Roadhouse

293   55   HIGHWAY   42

1   Ya
Road

Lookout   HEAD OF
BIGHT

89

Border Village   EYRE

13   Lookouts   Lookouts

Eucla

Lookouts

1

GREAT   AUSTRALIAN   BIGHT

N

0   20   40   60   80   100 km

J   K   L   M   N   **47**   O   P   Q   R

1

MARALINGA

Ingomar

Wilkinson Lakes

West Point Hill
230m

Mc Douall Peak

TJARUTJA

WOOMERA

2

ABORIGINAL

Lake Anthony

Half Moon
Lake

PROHIBITED

Muckanippie

Bulgunnia

LAND

Mulgathing

Carnes

3

Mt Christie
233m

AREA

Warrior

Gibraltar Rocks

Gibraltar
Rocks

PARTRIDGE RANGE

4

Bates

TRANS

Barton

AUSTRALIA

Mungala

Mount
Christie

Wynbring

RAILWAY

Malbooma

Wilgena Hill
253m

Lake
Moolkra

Lake
Labyrinth

Tarcoola

5

Ifould Lake

143

Mt Finke
361m

Bulpara Hill
237m

Renton Hill
161m

6

YELLABINNA   REGIONAL

RESERVE

Dog

42

7

Lake Everard

Culuna

YUMBARRA

Nuckulla Hill
264m

8

55

Roadhouse

CONSERVATION   PARK

Fence

Nundroo

202   EYRE

Dog   Fence

Bookabie School
Ruin

Cundilippy

Koonibba Hill
169m

OTC Satellite
Communication Station

PUREBA

Yaribrinda Hill

Waverley Hill
399m

9

Tallala Hill
84m

39

Bookabie

35

Cooper Hill
126m

Penong

1

73

HIGHWAY

Coppudurba Hill
147m

CONSERVATION   PARK

Bookabie Hill
149m

Woolshed Hill
134m

Fowlers Bay

Point Fowler

Nurka Hill
130m

Mt Hiltabo
465m

10

Fowlers Bay

Lake
MacDonnell

Ceduna

Thevenard

EYRE

92

Oak Hill
111m

Wallala Hill
166m

Barber Hill
412m

Point Bell

FLINDERS

173

Pimbaacla Hill
121m

67

St Peter Island

Smoky Bay

Carawa

Wirrulla

11

NUYTS
ARCHIPELAGO
CONSERVATION
PARK

Eyre Island

Smoky Bay

109

HIGHWAY

YANTANABIE

ISLES OF
ST FRANCIS
CP

ACRAMAN
CREEK
CP

Point De Mole

Haslam

Kaldoonera Hill
136m

Locke
Claypans

Point Brown

Streaky
Bay

49

Cungena

40

Cape Bauer

ALT
1

Chandada

Poochera

12

Olive Islands

Streaky Bay

62

33

Corvisart Bay

HIGHWAY

Minnipa

Point Westall

CALPATANNA
WATERHOLE
CP

Sceale Bay

Murphys Haystacks

Mt Cooper
672m

KULLIPARU
CONSERVATION
PARK

Monument

Calca

Mt Hall
208m

13

Searcy Bay

Sea Lion
Colony

Cape Radstock

VENUS BAY
CP

Port Kenny

MOUNT DAMPER

J   K   L   M   N   O   P   Q   **40**   R

WARNING: Entry to the Woomera Prohibited Area is by permit
except the immediate corridors of the Stuart Highway and the
road from Coober Pedy to William Creek.
Camping is not permitted within the area. Note the overlap with
Aboriginal Lands where you need additional separate permits.

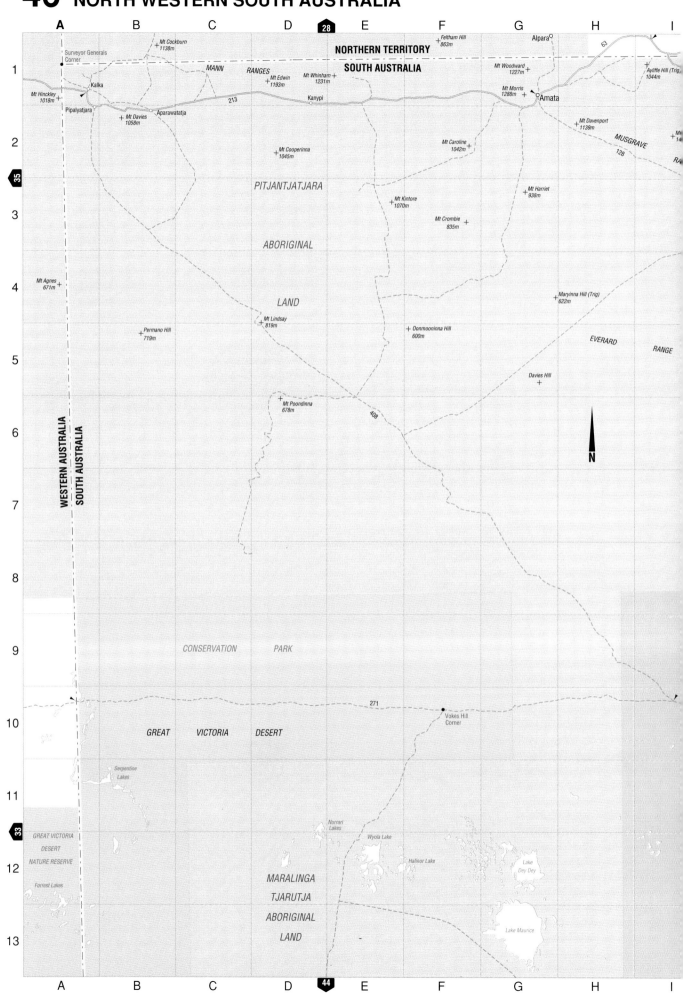

A **B** **C** **D** **28** **E** **F** **G** **H** **I**

Surveyor Generals Corner

+ Mt Cockburn 1138m

NORTHERN TERRITORY

+ Feltham Hill 863m

Alpara○

63

1

MANN RANGES

+ Mt Edwin 1193m

+ Mt Whinham 1231m

SOUTH AUSTRALIA

+ Mt Woodward 1227m

+ Ayliffe Hill (Trig) 1044m

Mt Hinckley 1018m +

Kalka

Kanypi

Mt Morris 1288m +

Amata○

Pipalyatjara

213

+ Mt Davies 1058m

Aparawatatja

+ Mt Davenport 1139m

MUSGRAVE

Mt 14

2

+ Mt Cooperinna 1045m

+ Mt Caroline 1042m

128

RA

35

PITJANTJATJARA

+ Mt Kintore 1070m

+ Mt Harriet 938m

3

+ Mt Crombie 835m

ABORIGINAL

4

Mt Agnes 671m +

LAND

+ Mt Lindsay 819m

+ Maryinna Hill (Trig) 622m

+ Permano Hill 719m

+ Oonmooninna Hill 600m

EVERARD

RANGE

5

Davies Hill +

+ Mt Poondinna 678m

6

408

N

7

8

9

CONSERVATION *PARK*

WESTERN AUSTRALIA

SOUTH AUSTRALIA

271

10

GREAT *VICTORIA* *DESERT*

Vokes Hill Corner●

Serpentine Lakes

11

Nurrari Lakes

33

GREAT VICTORIA

DESERT

NATURE RESERVE

Wyola Lake

Halinor Lake

Lake Dey Dey

12

Forrest Lakes

MARALINGA

TJARUTJA

ABORIGINAL

Lake Maurice

13

LAND

A **B** **C** **44** **E** **F** **G** **H** **I**

0   20   40   60   80   100 km

NORTHERN TERRITORY

SOUTH AUSTRALIA

Mount Cavenagh
24

Victory Downs
Victory Downs

Mt Cecil
551m

Mt Darling
544m

Mt Parlue
478m

Mt Mead
376m

Mt Hearne
306m

1

Sentinel Hill
910m

Marryat Creek

Tieyon

Eringa

Mt Barr
222m

2

Mt Warrabillinna
1125m

PITJANTJATJARA

ABORIGINAL

LAND

Echo Hill
604m

Mt Howe
519m

117

STUART

Hamilton Creek

Mt Britton
334m

3

na Hill (Trig)

regon

Marble Hill
523m

143

Alberga

Lambina
(ruin)

River

4

Mimili

Mt Ilibillee
917m

Chandler
Mt Chandler
551m

44

HIGHWAY

OODNADATTA

Todmorden

TRACK

5

EVERARD   RANGE

Mintabie

Marla

87

CENTRAL

83

Welbourn Hill

Neales   River

6

Ammaroodinna Hill
359m

AUSTRALIA

Wintinna

Arckaringa

48

7

Cadney
Homestead

Mount Willoughby

Mt Arckaringa
243m

Arckaringa

Creek

8

MARALINGA

TJARUTJA

ABORIGINAL

LAND

RAILWAY

Evelyn Downs

Evelyn Creek

Lora

Mount Barry

Creek

9

EMU JUNCTION

TALLARINGA

CONSERVATION

PARK

Pootnoura

153

Wooring Creek

Algebullcullia

Giddi-giddiona Creek

10

265

Dog   Fence

Creek

STUART

Oolgelima Ck

11

WOOMERA

Manguri

Log Creek

Coober Pedy

PROHIBITED

WARNING: Entry to the Woomera Prohibited Area is by permit
except the immediate corridors of the Stuart Highway and the
road from Coober Pedy to William Creek.
Camping is not permitted within the area. Note the overlap with
Aboriginal Lands where you need additional separate permits.

Mabel Creek

HIGHWAY

12

AREA

Wilkinson
Lakes

Dog   Fence

Lake
Phillipson

Wirrida

87

Mt Penrhyn
216m

13

A B C D **29** E F G H I

1 Mt Wilyunpa +227m
NORTHERN TERRITORY
Mirranponga Pongunna Lake
Poeppel

Mount Dare ■
Mt Apperda +245m
Mt Alinerta +222m
SOUTH AUSTRALIA
Larrys Hi +63m
Pillan Hill +60m

SIMPSON DESERT

2 Mt Weeahlakiminne +292m
WITJIRA
NATIONAL
SIMPSON DESERT
CONSERVATION PARK

Blood Creek Bore ●
Mt Hammersley +229m
Mt Barr +222m
PARK
REGIONAL
Poolowanna Lake

Mt Crispe ●+279m
Dalhousie Springs ●
Beale Hill +53m

3 Mt Emery +289m
Mt Dillon +234m
RESERVE
Peera Peera Poolanna Lake

SIMPSON   **DESERT**
Ephemeral Lakes

4 Hamilton ■
Mt Yangalee +244m
WARNING: Visitors planning to enter Desert Parks are required to contact the National Parks and Wildlife Service. A Desert Pass is necessary.
Lake Griselda

Mount Sarah ■
Mt Sarah +260m
Stevenson Creek
Umari

5 Mt Alexander +285m
Macumba
Kaltakoopah Creek

Alberga River
Willawilaninna Lake

6 **OODNADATTA**
Macumba ■
River
Pantoowarinna Lake

TRACK
Pialpotingoona Lake
Peeramudlayeppa Lake

7 Mt Carulina +211m
Oodnadatta ○
Mt Areebinna +245m
Hanns Hill +238m
Millyeewilpa Lake
Pompapillinna Lake
Warburton

Stewart Hill +180m
OODNADATTA
Lake Noolyeana

Mt Dutton +176m
Neales
Koolkooltinnie Lake

8 Arckaringa
TRACK
Mt Kingston North +209m
River
Peake

9 Mount Barry ■
Peake Creek
Mt Denison +238m
Peake ■
Lambing
Ricketts Hill +
Unbum Creek
LAKE EYRE
NATIONAL PA
Lake Eyre

Lora
Lake Conway
Hawker Creek
Creek
North

10 **WARNING:** Entry to the Woomera Prohibited Area is by permit except the immediate corridors of the Stuart Highway and the road from Coober Pedy to William Creek.
Camping is not permitted within the area. Note the overlap with Aboriginal Lands where you need additional separate permits.
203
Mt Margaret +412m
Nilpinna ■
Four Hills +105m
Davenport Creek

Mt Anna +265m
Douglas
Creek

11 **WOOMERA**
Lake Cadibarrawirracanna
Anna Creek ■
Ruby Hill +111m
William Creek ○
ELLIOT PRICE
CONSERVATION
PARK

12 **STUART**
PROHIBITED
Dog Creek
Batla Creek
Warriner Creek
127
Lake Eyre
LAKE EYRE
NATIONAL PARK
Lake France
Lake Ellen

HWY
[87]
AREA
Engenina Creek
Beresford Hill +71m
Lake Eyre South

13 Mt Penrhyn +216m
Mt Sandy +223m
Mt Woods +170m
Compeera Hill +158m
Wartariwidginna
Mt Purvis +201m
Bidna Boudna Hill +162m
Mt Riddoch +182m
Margaret River
New Peter Hill +163m
Hamilton Hill +40m
Curdimurka ○
Creek
Dog or Francois Creek
Fence

A B C D **42** E F G H

0 20 40 60 80 100 km

J K L M N O P Q R

22

Lake Nappanerica
Birdsville

QUEENSLAND
SOUTH AUSTRALIA

Haddon
Corner

Pandie Pandie

+ Frew Hill
123m

Lake Cooninnie

Moonda Lake

■ Cadelga

STRZELECKI

Lake Short

The West Lake

Stony Point
+ 195m

1

2

N

Lake Etamunbanie

Lake Moorayepe

Lake Uloowaranie

New Alton
Downs

+ Pulcara Hill
170m

3

DESERT

Goyder   Lagoon

Apawyilarranie Lake

+ Dickinna Hill
87m

■ Cordillo Downs

Arrabury

Koomarinna Lake

4

Clifton Hills

Diamantina   River

INNER

BIRDSVILLE
(Not Recommended)

Warburton   Creek

OUTER

BIRDSVILLE

312

TRACK

Leap Year
Bore

SOUTH AUSTRALIA   QUEENSLAND

5

STURT

Coongie

INNAMINCKA

Mulga
Bore

STONY

Lake Koodnanie

REGIONAL RESERVE

Patchawara
Bore

6

WARNING: In outback Australia, long distances separate some towns. Travellers should familiarise themselves with prevailing conditions before departure, and take care to ensure their vehicle is roadworthy and that they carry adequate supplies of petrol, water and food.

In northern Australia, rainfall during the "wet" season (Oct-March) can make some roads impassable. Full information on road conditions should be obtained before departure.

If visitors intend diverting off public roads within Aboriginal Land areas, a permit is required from the relevant Aboriginal authority.

DESERT

Cooper   Creek

Nappa
Merrie
Burke & Wills
Dig Tree

22

■ Cowarie

Lake Howitt

● Mirra Mitta Bore

Gidgealpa

Innamincka

Innamincka
Aboriginal
Rock Carvings

7

Kalamurina
Lake Miamiana

uthraootara Lake

BIRDSVILLE   TRACK

STRZELECKI

■ Mungerannie
■ Mungerannie
Roadhouse

8

Lake Kittakittaooloo

*Winthekarrinna
Waterhole*

Moomba Gasfield ●

TRACK   140

DESERT

Lake Wartakalanna

Lake Ngapakaldi

Creek

Lake Waipalyapeninna

Big Lake
Moomba

Creek

9

Mulka

Lake Hope

Lake Puntawolona

Flood By-pass Ferry

Cooper

Lake Killamperpunna

Flood By-pass Track

Lake Kopperekoppinna

Merty Merty

10

Lake Palankarinna

Etadunna

STRZELECKI

STRZELECKI

Lake Florence

Lake Gregory

REGIONAL   RESERVE

*STRZELECKI
CROSSING*

120

11

Dulkaninna

Bollards Lagoon

Cameron Corner

SOUTH AUSTRALIA   NEW SOUTH WALES

*STURT
NATIONAL
PARK*

Explorers
Tree ●

12

Clayton

Fence

*Lake
Blanche*

STRZELECKI

*STRZELECKI
REGIONAL RESERVE*

DESERT

13

J K L M N O P Q R

43

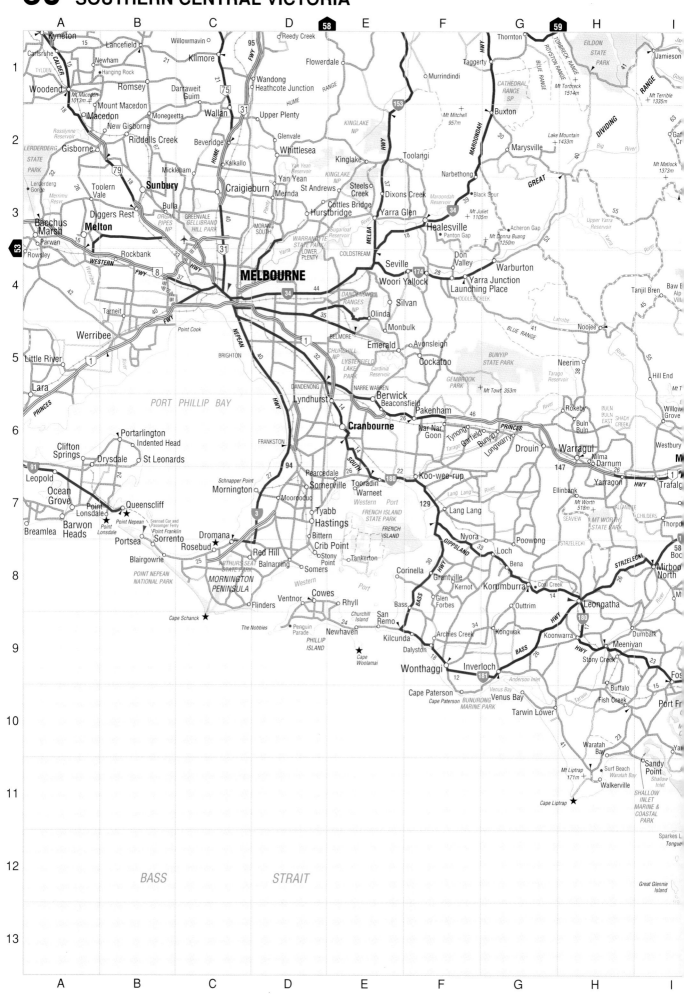

Kyneton
Carlsruhe
TYLDEN
CALDER
Woodend
Mt Macedon 1013m
Macedon
New Gisborne
Mount Macedon
Rosslynne Reservoir
Gisborne
LERDERDERG STATE PARK
Lerderderg Gorge
Parwan
Rowsley
Bacchus Marsh
Melton
Toolern Vale
Diggers Rest
Sunbury
Bulla
Rockbank
WESTERN HWY
Little River
Lara
PRINCES
Werribee
Tarneit

Lancefield
Newham
Hanging Rock
Romsey
Darraweit Guim
Monegeetta
Riddells Creek
Mickleham
Kalkallo
Craigieburn
Yan Yean
Mernda
Merrimu Resv

Willowmavin
Kilmore
Wandong
Heathcote Junction
Upper Plenty
Glenvale
Whittlesea
KINGLAKE NP
Yan Yean Reservoir
St Andrews
Steels Creek
Hurstbridge
Cottles Bridge
Sugarloaf Reservoir
WARRANDYTE STATE PARK
LOWER PLENTY
MORANG SOUTH
GREENVALE
GELLIBRAND HILL PARK
ORGAN PIPES NP

Reedy Creek
Flowerdale
HUME RANGE
KINGLAKE NP
Kinglake
Toolangi
Dixons Creek
MAROONDAH
Yarra Glen
Maroondah Reservoir
COLDSTREAM
Seville
Woori Yallock

Thornton
Taggerty
Murrindindi
Mt Mitchell 957m
Buxton
Narbethong
Black Spur
Mt Juliet 1105m
Healesville
Panton Gap
Acheron Gap
Mt Donna Buang 1250m
Don Valley
Warburton
Yarra Junction
Launching Place
HODDLES CREEK

EILDON STATE PARK
Jamieson
Mt Terrible 1335m
Mt Matlock 1373m
CATHEDRAL RANGE
BLUE RANGE
TORBRECK RANGE
ROYSTON RANGE
Mt Torbreck 1514m
Lake Mountain 1433m
Marysville
Big River
Upper Yarra Reservoir
GREAT DIVIDING RANGE
BLUE RANGE

MELBOURNE
Point Cook
BRIGHTON
PORT PHILLIP BAY
NEPEAN HWY
DANDENONG
FRANKSTON
Mornington
Schnapper Point
Mooroolbark
Silvan
Olinda
Monbulk
DANDENONG RANGES NP
Emerald
Avonsleigh
Cockatoo
BELMORE
CHURCHILL NP
LYSTERFIELD LAKE PARK
Cardinia Reservoir
NARRE WARREN
Lyndhurst
Berwick
Beaconsfield
Pakenham
Cranbourne
Nar Nar Goon
Tynong
Garfield
Bunyip
Longwarry
PRINCES
GEMBROOK PARK
Mt Towt 353m
BUNYIP STATE PARK
Neerim
Hill End
Noojee
Tarago Reservoir
BLUE RANGE
Latrobe River
Rokeby
Buln Buln
BULN BULN EAST
SHADY CREEK
Drouin
Warragul
Nilma
Darnum
Yarragon
Ellinbank
Mt Worth 518m
MT WORTH STATE PARK
SEAVIEW
STRZELECKI
CHILDERS
Westbury
Trafalgar
Thorpdale
Mirboo North
BOC
58

Portarlington
Indented Head
Clifton Springs
Drysdale
St Leonards
Leopold
Ocean Grove
Point Lonsdale
Queenscliff
Point Nepean
Searoad Car and Passenger Ferry
Point Franklin
Sorrento
Portsea
Blairgowrie
Rosebud
Dromana
ARTHURS SEAT STATE PARK
Red Hill
Balnarring
Somers
MORNINGTON PENINSULA
POINT NEPEAN NATIONAL PARK
Barwon Heads
Breamlea
Pearcedale
Somerville
Tyabb
Hastings
Bittern
Crib Point
Stony Point
Tooradin
Warneet
Western Port
FRENCH ISLAND STATE PARK
FRENCH ISLAND
Tankerton
Koo-wee-rup
Lang Lang
Nyora
Loch
Bena
Poowong
Koonwarra
Leongatha
Meeniyan
Dumbalk
Stony Creek
Buffalo
Fish Creek
Fos
Port Fr
GIPPSLAND HWY
BASS HWY
STRZELECKI HWY
Korumburra
Coal Creek
Kernot
Grantville
Corinella
Bass
Glen Forbes
Outtrim
Kongwak
Archies Creek
Dalyston
Kilcunda
Wonthaggi
Inverloch
Cape Paterson
Venus Bay
Venus Bay
BUNURONG MARINE PARK
Tarwin Lower
Waratah Bay
Sandy Point
Surf Beach
Mt Liptrap 171m
Walkerville
Cape Liptrap
SHALLOW INLET MARINE & COASTAL PARK
Waratah Bay

Ventnor
Cowes
Rhyll
San Remo
Newhaven
Churchill Island
Flinders
Cape Schanck
The Nobbies
Penguin Parade
PHILLIP ISLAND
Cape Woolamai
Cape Paterson

BASS STRAIT

Great Glennie Island
Sparkes L
Tongue

A | B | C | D | E | F | G | H | I

0   10   20   30   40   50 km

J   **K**   **59**   **L**   **M**   **N**   **O**   **P**   **60**   **Q**   **R**

Mt Mcdonald 1625m

SNOWY RANGE

ALPINE NATIONAL PARK

Wonnangatta

RANGE

DIVIDING

Dargo River

Mt Birregun 1463m

Swifts Creek

DOCTORS FLAT

Big Hill 675m

OMEO

17

GREAT

Mt Tamboritha 1640m

Mt Kent 1563m

Mt Wellington 1635m

Castle Hill 1448m

Dargo

Mt Delusion 1399m

BROOKVILLE

Mt Baldhead 1377m

Ensay

ENSAY SOUTH

REEDY FLAT

Murrindal

Wellington River

Lake Tarli Karng 1570m

Gable End 1570m

Mt Selma 1457m

Licola

River

35

Morris Peak 789m

Mt Djoandah 610m

195

Tambo Crossing

Mt Dow 1000m

Mt Elizabeth 942m

Buchan

Buchan Caves

Avon

MITCHELL RIVER NATIONAL PARK

53

HWY

Mt Useful 1432m

AVON WILDERNESS PARK

28

Mt Sugarloaf 890m

Little Dick 320m

Mt Tara 608m

erfeldy

Ben Cruachan 839m

River

40

Culloden

Woodglen

Bullumwaal

Mt Alfred 503m

DEPTFORD

33

Mt Nowa Nowa 354m

Wairewa

56

River

54

Lake Glenmaggie

Boisdale

Briagolong

Walpa

Wuk Wuk

Calulu

Lindenow

Clifton Creek

Mount Taylor

Wiseleigh

Sarstield

24

16

TAMBO UPPER

29

Bruthen

22

Nowa Nowa

Tostaree

BEARDMORE

BAW BAW NATIONAL PARK

Glenmaggie

Newry

17

FERNBANK

Mt Taylor 475m

Hillside

Wy Yung

Lucknow

22

Johnsonville

Swan Reach

1

Lake Tyers

Walhalla

Rawson

Seaton

Heyfield

Tinamba

Maffra

31

Stratford

PRINCES

69

32

HWY

1

20

Bairnsdale

Nicholson

14

Metung

Nungurner

Lake Tyers

Aboriginal Settlement

ica

Cowwarr

River

17

30

Meerlieu

14

34

Eagle Point

Lake King

Paynesville

Raymond Island

Lakes Entrance

Thomson

Toongabbie

21

Sale

Bengworden

GOON NURE

FORGE CREEK

Moondarra Reservoir

Lake Wellington

Loch Sport

THE LAKES NATIONAL PARK

Victoria

GIPPSLAND LAKES COASTAL PARK

Tyers

LaTrobe

HWY

26

Longford

30

Lake Coleman

Lake Reeve

Beach

YERS ARK

n

PRINCES

63

Rosedale

River

23

HOLEY PLAINS STATE PARK

24

30

Paradise Beach

Traralgon

HYLAND

HWY

20

33

Morwell

14

180

Flamingo Beach

Churchill

Callignee

Gormandale

HWY

Mile

Cut Mine

Hazelwood Cooling Pond

MORWELL NATIONAL PARK

TARRA - BULGA NATIONAL PARK

40

31

GIPPSLAND

Seaspray

Ninety

TASMAN   SEA

188

Woodside

19

SOUTH

Woodside Beach

Yarram

162

28

Alberton

Tarraville

McLoughlins Beach

Langsborough

Manns Beach

Welshpool

Port Albert

Port Welshpool

NOORAMUNGA MARINE AND WILDLIFE RESERVE

Inlet

Entrance Point

Mt Hunter 348m

WILSONS PROMONTORY MARINE PARK

oundback 314m

ONS

NTORY 7m

Vereker

PARK

t Latrobe 59m

beron

Mt Wilson 709m

N

South East Point

WILSONS PROMONTORY MARINE RESERVE

J   **K**   **L**   **M**   **N**   **O**   **P**   **Q**   **R**

1   2   3   4   5   6   7   8   9   10   11   12   13

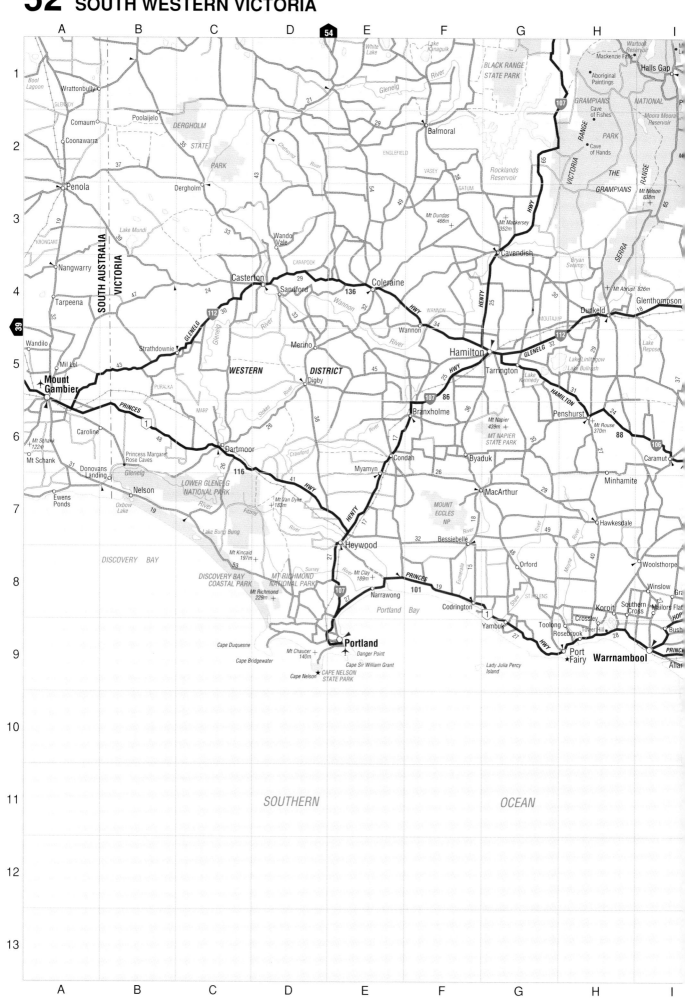

SOUTH WESTERN VICTORIA

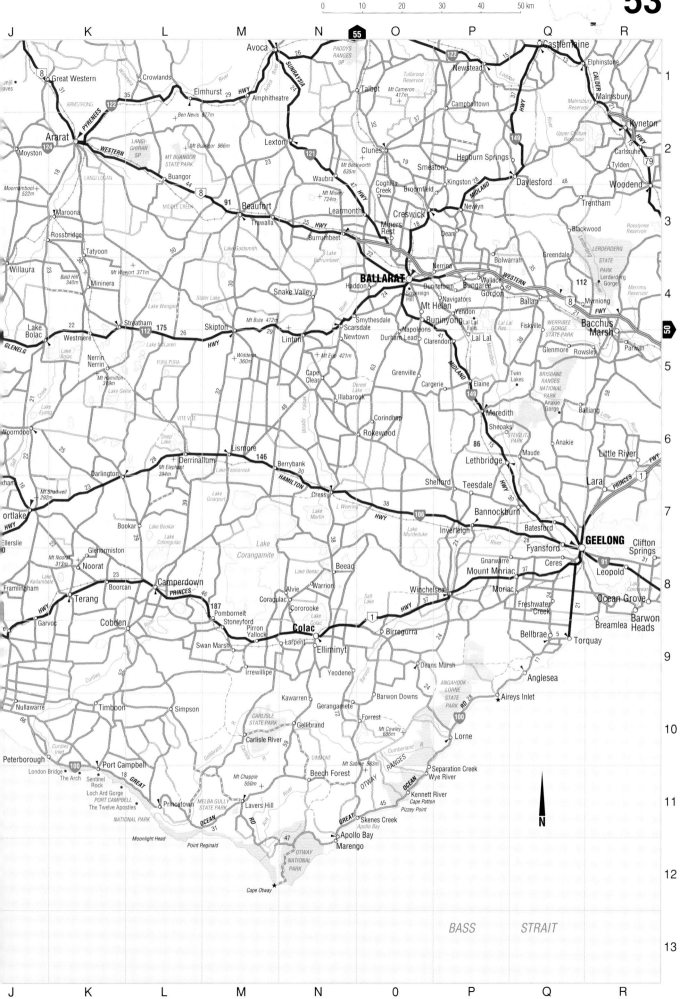

0 10 20 30 40 50 km

J K L M N O P Q R

Avoca
Great Western
Crowlands
Elmhurst 29
Amphitheatre
SUNRAYSIA
HWY
PADDYS
RANGES
SP
Newstead
Castlemaine
Elphinstone
CALDER
Ararat
Moyston
PYRENEES
WESTERN
Ben Nevis 877m
Mt Buangor 966m
LANGI-
GHIRAN
SP
MT BUANGOR
STATE PARK
Buangor
Lexton
Talbot
Mt Cameron
417m
Campbelltown
Malmsbury
Reservoir
Malmsbury
Kyneton
Carlsruhe
Tylden
Waubra
Learmonth
Clunes
Smeaton
Hepburn Springs
Kingston
Daylesford
Woodend
Beaufort
Trawalla
Burrumbeet
Mt Misery
724m
Coghills
Creek
Broomfield
Newlyn
MIDLAND
Trentham
Maroona
Rossbridge
Tatyoon
Mt Beckworth
635m
Creswick
Miners
Rest
Dean
Bolwarrah
Greendale
Blackwood
Rosslynne
Reservoir
Willaura
Bald Hill
340m
Minera
Mt Weejort 371m
Lake Goldsmith
Lake
Burrumbeet
Haddon
BALLARAT
Nerrina
Wallace
Bungaree
WESTERN
LERDERDERG
STATE
PARK
Lerderderg
Gorge
112
Merrimu
Reservoir
Lake
Bolac
Streatham
Skipton
Mt Bute 472m
Smythesdale
Sovereign
Hill
Dunnstown
Navigators
Gordon
Ballan
Myrniong
FWY
Bacchus
Marsh
GLENELG
Westmere
Nerrin
Nerrin
Mt Hamilton
319m
Lake Wongan
Slater Lake
Scarsdale
Napoleons
Newtown
Durham Leads
Mt Helen
Buninyong
Lal Lal
Falls
Lal Lal
Res
Fiskville
Lal Lal
WERRIBEE
GORGE
STATE PARK
Glenmore
Rowsley
Parwan
50
Lake McLaren
Linton
Clarendon
MIDLAND
Mt Ern 421m
Grenville
Cargerie
Elaine
Twin
Lakes
BRISBANE
RANGES
NATIONAL
PARK
Anakie
Gorge
Balliang
Woorndoo
Deep
Lake
Cape
Clear
Illabarook
Dereel
Lake
Grenville
Meredith
Sheoaks
Anakie
Little River
Darlington
Mt Elephant
394m
Derrinallum
Lismore
Berrybank
Rokewood
Corindhap
86
Lethbridge
STEIGLITZ
PARK
Maude
Lara
PRINCES
Ortlake
Mt Shadwell
292m
HAMILTON
Cressy
L Weering
Shelford
Teesdale
Bannockburn
Batesford
Geelong
Clifton
Springs
Bookar
Lake Bookar
Lake
Colongulac
Lake
Corangamite
Lake
Martin
Lake
Murdeduke
Inverleigh
Fyansford
Ceres
Leopold
Glenormiston
Mt Noorat
313m
Noorat
Boorcan
Camperdown
PRINCES
Beeac
Warrion
Gnarwarre
Mount Moriac
Ocean Grove
Terang
Garvoc
Cobden
Pomborneit
Stoneyford
Pirron
Yallock
Coragulac
Cororooke
Colac
Birregurra
Winchelsea
Moriac
Freshwater
Creek
Bellbrae
Torquay
Breamlea
Barwon
Heads
Swan Marsh
Larpent
Elliminyt
Irrewillipe
Yeodene
Deans Marsh
Anglesea
Nullawarre
Timboon
Simpson
Kawarren
Gerangamete
Forrest
Barwon Downs
ANGAHOOK-
LORNE
STATE
PARK
Aireys Inlet
Peterborough
Port Campbell
London Bridge
The Arch
Sentinel
Rock
Loch Ard Gorge
PORT CAMPBELL
The Twelve Apostles
NATIONAL
PARK
GREAT
CARLISLE
STATE PARK
Carlisle River
Gellibrand
Mt Cowley
686m
Lorne
Separation Creek
Wye River
OTWAY
Mt Chapple
550m
Beech Forest
Mt Sabine 583m
Cumberland R
Kennett River
Cape Patton
Pizzey Point
Princetown
MELBA GULLY
STATE PARK
Lavers Hill
OCEAN
RANGES
Skenes Creek
Apollo Bay
Moonlight Head
Point Reginald
OTWAY
NATIONAL
PARK
Marengo
Cape Otway

BASS   STRAIT

N

1
2
3
4
5
6
7
8
9
10
11
12
13

A B C D E F G H I

1 2 3 4 5 6 7 8 9 10 11 12 13

BIG DESERT

WYPERFELD

Mt Observatory
+ 93m

Patchewollock

Tempy

Speed

Turriff

22

35

27

SUNRAYSIA

Lascell

NATIONAL

SCORPION
SPRINGS
CP

BIG DESERT

WILDERNESS PARK

PARK

LAKE
ALBACUTYA
PARK

Lake
Albacutya

Hopetoun

Lake
Coorong

26

25

Mt Shaugh
184m +

MT SHAUGH
CONSERVATION
PARK

WIMMERA

Yaapet

Ross Lake

Rainbow

Kenmare

41

45

HWY

Beulah

107

GALAQUIL

SOUTH AUSTRALIA

VICTORIA

Lake
Hindmarsh

32

Ellam

45

HENTY

35

143

Yanac

21

Netherby

Lorquon

42

Jeparit

37

Warracknabea

39

Bordertown

8

Wolseley

43

Serviceton

WESTERN

Diapur

Miram

Kaniva

40

158

HWY

31

32

45

Nhill

8

Kiata

39

Gerang
Gerung

Antwerp

KATYIL

BORUNG

42

138

HWY

29

46

BANGHAM

SANDSMERE

45

48

LITTLE DESERT NATIONAL PARK

Wimmera

Dimboola

19

Wail

KALKEE

57

HENTY

HWY

Minyi

24

BANGHAM
CP

Frances

Lake
Oudute

Minimay

34

Goroke

Gymbowen

Mitre

Mitre
Lake

Lake
Wyn Wyn

Natimuk

MT ARAPILES-
TOOAN
STATE
PARK

Mt Arapiles
370m

Pimpinio

25

17

Jung

Murtoa

31

14

**WIMM
R**

Horsham

Binnum

31

Lake
Morea

18

32

HWY

Noradjuha

Haven

27

Taylors
Lake

60

Kybybolite

32

35

99

130

40

Clear Lake

40

Pine
Lake

41

WESTERN

W

Hynam

32

Apsley

21

WIMMERA

Edenhope

Lake
Wallace

North
Lake

Wombelano

Douglas

32

64

Toolondo
Reservoir

Mt Talbot 320m

THE BLACK

RANGE

HENTY

HWY

124

DIFFICULT RANGE

Flat Rock
Caves

Dadswells
Bridge

Mt Difficult
810m

Wartook
Reservoir

Mackenzie
Falls

61

Naracoorte

Naracoorte
Caves

30

40

14

Wrattonbully

Comaum

Coonawarra

Booi
Lagoon

GLENROY

Poolaijelo

DERGHOLM

STATE

32

34

White
Lake

Lake
Kanagulk

21

29

River

Balmoral

ENGLEFIELD

BLACK RANGE

STATE PARK

Aboriginal
Paintings

107

Rocklands
Reservoir

VICTORIA RANGE

GRAMPIANS

NATIONAL

Cave of Fishes

Lake
Bellfield

Cave of Hands

PARK

Ha

Mackenzie
River

Mt Mackenzie

Glenelg
River

Chetwynd
River

VASEY

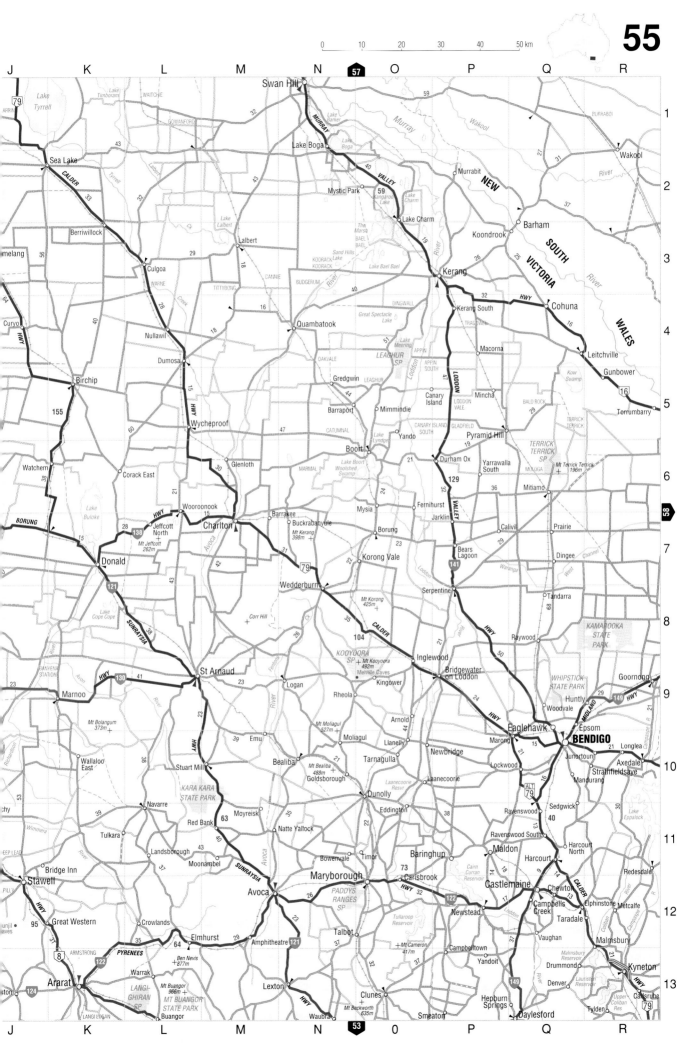

56 NORTH WESTERN VICTORIA

A   B   C   D   **8**   E   F   G   H   I

1

2

Coombool Swamp   *Lake Limbra*   *Lake Littra*   *Lake Victoria*

NEW SOUTH WALES

SILVER CITY HIGHWAY

79

Fletcher Lake

3

Murray   *Lock 6*   *Lock 7*   *RUFUS RIVER*   *Lock 8*   *River*   CURLWAA

Wentworth   Dareton

Lock 10   YELTA

Merbein   *Lake Gol Gol*

4

Paringa   *Lake Wallawalla*   **VICTORIA**   *Lock 9*   59   31   **Mildura**   Nichols Point   *MALLEE*

STURT   34   20   *HIGHWAY*   24   *Lake Cullulleraine*   Irymple   20   **STURT**

Cullulleraine   13   Koorlong   17

Taldra   KARAWINNA   Cardross   Red Cliffs

5   Meringur   Werrimull   53   YATPOOL   **CALDER**   80

Taplan

6   **SUNSET COUNTRY**   Carwarp   Nangiloc   *MURRAY-KULKYNE NATIONAL PARK*

107   56   NOWINGI   *Murray*

Nadda   *Rocket Lake*   HATTAH-KULKYNE

41   NATIONAL

7   Meribah   79   PARK   *Lake Bitterang*   *River*

Lake Lockie   HWY   58

MURRAY-SUNSET   Hattah

8   **NATIONAL PARK**   34

Peebinga

PEEBINGA CP

9   *Pink Lakes*   *Mt Gnarr 98m*   Kiamal

Ouyen   *MALLEE*

30

Linga   12   **HWY**   Torrita   Walpeup

10   134   80   Boinka   41   **MALLEE**   39

Pinnaroo   12   24   *MALLEE*   Cowangie   35   **121**

Dunt Peak   Tempy

11   Murrayville   *Mt Observatory 93m*   Patchewollock   22   Speed

Turriff

12   *SCORPION SPRINGS CP*   **BIG DESERT**   66   HWY

35   27

WYPERFELD NATIONAL PARK

13   *BIG DESERT WILDERNESS PARK*   Lascelle

A   B   C   D   **54**   E   F   G   H   I

SOUTH AUSTRALIA   VICTORIA

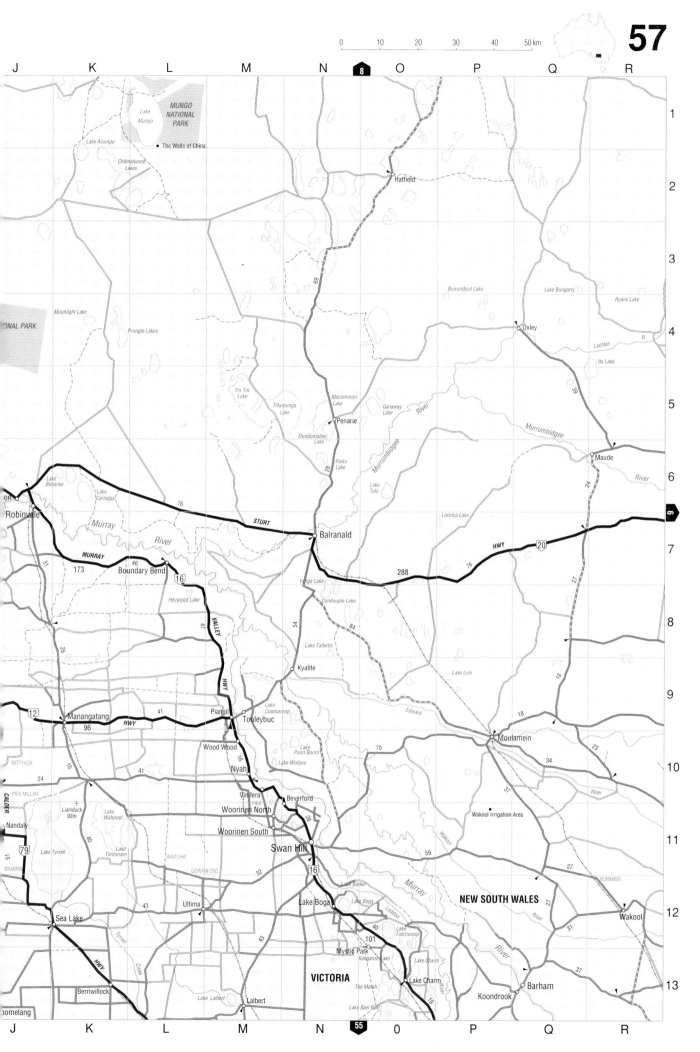

0 10 20 30 40 50 km

J K L M N 8 O P Q R

MUNGO
NATIONAL
PARK

Lake
Mungo

Lake Arumpo

Chibnalwood
Lakes

• The Walls of China

Hatfield

1

2

ONAL PARK

Moonlight Lake

Prungle Lakes

Bunumburt Lake

Lake Bungarry

Ryans Lake

Oxley

Lachlan

Ita Lake

3

4

69

Tin Tin
Lake

Pitarpunga
Lake

Macommon
Lake

Ganaway
Lake

River

Murrumbidgee

Maude

Penarie

28

Dundomallee
Lake

Paika
Lake

Lake
Tala

Murrumbidgee River

24

5

6

Lake
Benanee

Lake
Caringay

STURT

76

on

Robinvale

Murray

River

Balranald

Loorica Lake

HWY

20

9

288

76

27

7

MURRAY

31

173

46

Boundary Bend

16

Heywood Lake

54

Yanga Lake

Condouple Lake

8

47

VALLEY

25

84

Lake Talbetts

Lake Lyle

18

HWY

Kyalite

Edward

9

12

Manangatang

41

Piangil

Lake
Coomaroop

18

Moulamein

96

HWY

Tooleybuc

70

Lake
Poon Boom

23

MITTYACK

16

41

Wood Wood

Lake Wollare

34

37

River

24

PIER MILLAN

Nyah

10

Lianiduck
93m

Lake
Wahpool

Vinifera

Beverford

PIRA

Wakool Irrigation Area

11

Nandaly

Woorinen North

26

CALDER

40

Lake
Timboram

WAITCHIE

Woorinen South

Swan Hill

NEW SOUTH WALES

79

Lake Tyrrell

GOWANFORD

32

16

59

27

BURRABOI

NYARRIN

15

Ultima

Lake Batker

Murray

27

Wakool

43

Lake Boga

Loddon

31

12

Sea Lake

43

40

Lake
Tutchewop

River

Tyrrell Creek

101

Lake Charm

HWY

Mystic Park

Kangaroo Lake

Lake Charm

37

Barham

Berriwillock

Lake Lalbert

Lalbert

The Marsh

VICTORIA

Lake Charm

Koondrook

oomelang

Lake Bael Bael

55

19

13

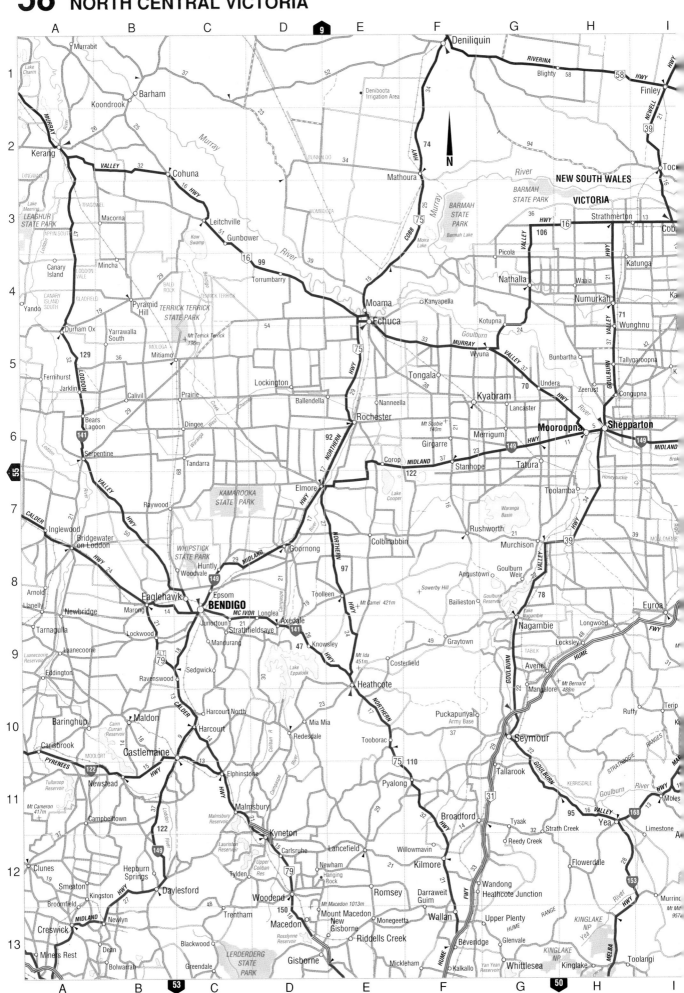

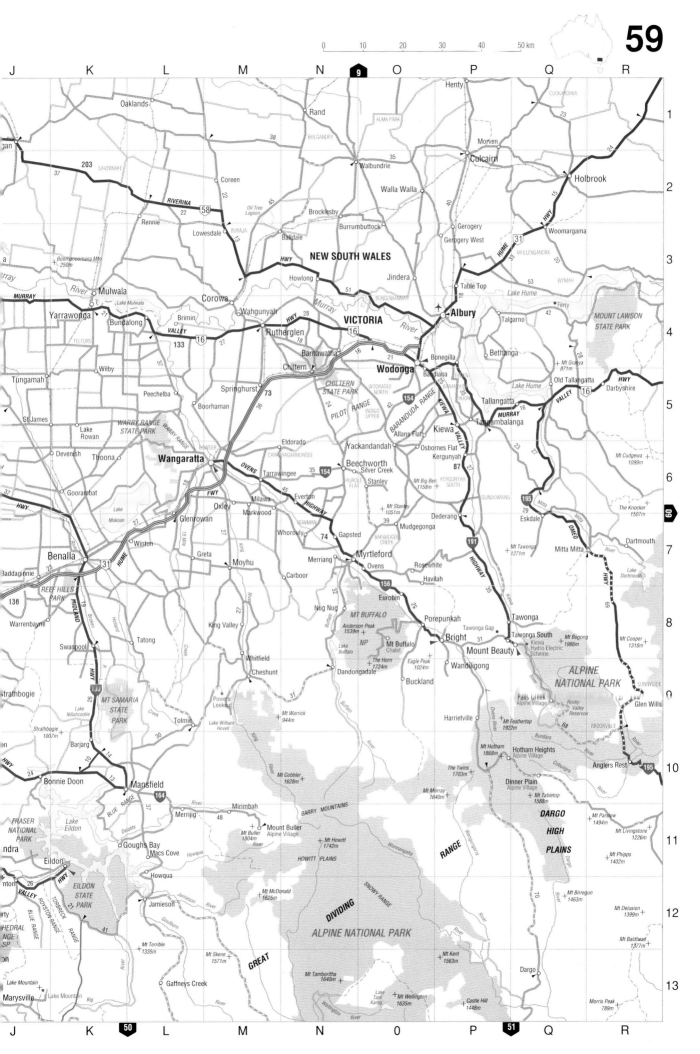

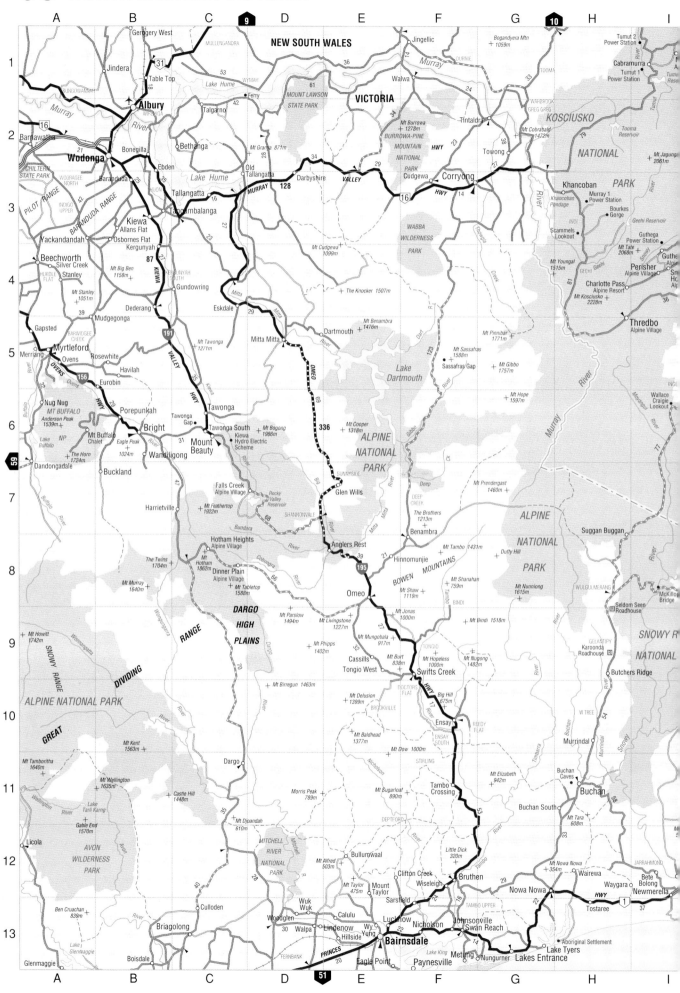

0 10 20 30 40 50 km

10

J K L M N O P Q R

ACT

SNOWY

Anglers Reach

Adaminaby

Old Adaminaby

O'Neill Lagoon

Mt Flinders 1484m

Bredbo

Mt Dowling 1198 m

Mt Anembo 1416m

Bald Mountain 1469m

DEUA NATIONAL PARK

Bendethera Caves

Bendethera Mtn 997m

Moruya

Moruya Heads

Congo

MERINGO

BERGALIA

TURLINJAH

Coila Lake

SNOWY

MOUNTAINS

HWY

MONARO

HWY

Lake Eucumbene

EUCUMBENE

Buckenderra

ROCKY PLAINS

Mtn 3m

Bunyan

Numeralla

CHAKOLA

McInally Mtn 1085m

PEAK VIEW

BADJA MILL

COUNTEGANY

BELOWRA

Tuross Falls

WADBILLIGA

NATIONAL

Tuross Head

Tuross Lake

Bodalla

Brou Lake

Eurobodalla

Dalmeny

Kianga

Narooma

Cootralantra Lake

Cooma

Kiah Lake

Berridale

Buckleys Lake

Lake Jindabyne

GREAT

DIVIDING

ROCK FLAT

Numeralla

River

WANDELLA

Peak Alone 954m

Mt Dromedary 806m

Central Tilba

CORUNNA

Corunna Lake

Montague Island

NATIONAL

PARK

Jindabyne

Snowy

Dalgety

Lake matong

River

SNOWY

Mt Cooper 1018m

Brown Mtn 1260m

MOUNTAINS

Mt Kydra 1236m

KYDRA

Brogo Reservoir

Tilba Tilba

Cobargo

Wallaga Lake

WALLAGA LAKE NATIONAL PARK

Bermagui

NUMBLA VALE

Nimmitabel

HWY

112

30

Bemboka

36

Quaama

Brogo

Murrah

ANGLEDALE

46

MIMOSA ROCKS

NATIONAL

Beards Lake

Mt Rix 988m

ANDO

22

NUMBUGGA

MORANS CROSSING

Bega

HWY

Tathra

PARK

Maclaughlin

River

BIBBENLUKE

KAMERUKA

26

Candelo

18

Kalaru

SOUTH

Mt Alexander 1075m

21

Cathcart

37

TOOTHDALE

14

Wolumla

Wallagoot Lake

BOURNDA NATIONAL PARK

TINGARINGY

CURROWONG

TOMBONG

Adams Pk

Bombala

20

32

28

20

Tura Beach

Merimbula

Pambula

PACIFIC

162

MILA

Wyndham

BURRAGATE

Pambula Beach

CRAIGIE

QUINBURRA

ROCKTON

White Rock Mtn 1093m

NALBAUGH NATIONAL PARK

EGAN PEAK NATIONAL PARK

52

TOWAMBA

Nullica

Eden

BEN BOYD NATIONAL PARK

OCEAN

Delegate River

Haydens Bog

Mt Delegate 1308m

Bendoc

Delegate

NEW SOUTH WALES

VICTORIA

PERICOE

Twofold Bay

Boydtown

East Boyd

DELLICKNORA

Bonang

Mt Canterbury 1039m

NUNGATTA NATIONAL PARK

Mt Poole 775m

MT IMLAY NATIONAL PARK

Mt Imlay 886m

Kiah

11

WONBOYN LAKE

Green Cape

BEN BOYD NATIONAL PARK

Brown Mtn 1010m

Mt Jersey 759m

Goongerah

Mt Ellery 1291m

ERRINUNDRA NATIONAL PARK

KOWAT

CHANDLERS CREEK

COOPRACAMBRA NATIONAL PARK

Mt Cooracambra 1000m

Mt Kaye 1002m

Waalimma Mtn 722m

60

164

HWY

32

TIMBILLICA

Mt Nagha 543m

NADGEE NATURE RESERVE

Cape Howe

COOMBIENBAR

58

VALLEY

HWY

Genoa

Wangarabell

Gipsy Point

Lake Barracoota

Mt Kuark 917m

Club Terrace

Noorinbee North

CANN

23

Noorinbee

PRINCES

21

Cann River

47

ALFRED NATIONAL PARK

KARLO CREEK

29

Mallacoota

Mallacoota Inlet

Gabo Island

FAIRHAVEN

CROAJINGOLONG NATIONAL PARK

Cabbage Tree Creek

19

Bellbird Creek

23

LIND NATIONAL PARK

Mt Cann 530m

Cann

35

dribb

Bemm River

Sydenham Inlet

Thurra

TAMBOON

Wingan Inlet

Point Ricardo

Cape Conran

Pearl Point

Tamboon Inlet

Point Hicks (Cape Everard)

Mt Everard 371m

Little Rame Head

Rame Head

TASMAN

SEA

N

J K L M N O P Q R

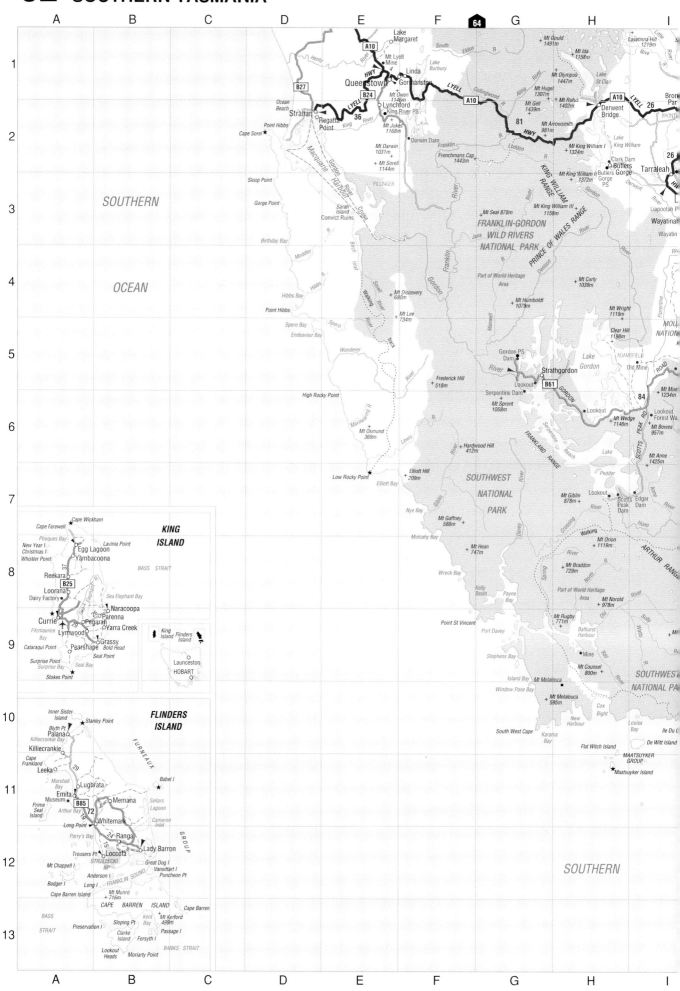

A B C D E F G H I

1

Lake Margaret
South Eldon R
Mt Gould 1491m +
Mt Ida + 1158m
Lavatinna Hill 1219m +
Little
Nive

A10
Mt Lyell Mine
Linda
Lake Burbury
Mt Olympus 1447m +
Lake St Clair

B27
HWY
Queenstown
Mt Owen 1146m
Gormanston
LYELL
Collingwood R
Mt Hugel 1307m +
Mt Rufus 1402m +
A10
LYELL
Bron Par
HWY

B24
LYELL
36
Strahan
Regatta Point
Lynchford
King River PS
A10
Alma R
Mt Gell 1439m +
Derwent Bridge
26
BRONTE

Ocean Beach
81
HWY
Mt Arrowsmith 981m +

2

Point Hibbs
Cape Sorell ★
Mt Jukes 1168m
Mt Darwin 1031m +
+ Mt Sorell 1144m
Darwin Dam
Franklin R
Loddon R
Mt King William I + 1324m
Clark Dam
Butlers Gorge
Butlers Gorge PS
Tarraleah
26
HWY

Frenchmans Cap 1443m +

3

Sloop Point
Gorge Point
Sarah Island Convict Ruins
Macquarie Harbour
Gordon River Cruise
PILLINGER
Franklin River
Mt Seal 878m +
Jane R
KING WILLIAM RANGE
Mt King William III 1158m +
Mt King William II + 1372m
Gordon R
Derwent R
Liapootah P
Wayatinah
Wayatin

Birthday Bay
Modder R
Gordon River
FRANKLIN-GORDON WILD RIVERS NATIONAL PARK
PRINCE OF WALES RANGE

4

Point Hibbs
Hibbs Bay
Hibbs R
Spero Bay
Spero R
Wanderer R
Birch Inlet
Wading River
Mt Discovery 680m +
Mt Lee 734m +
Denison R
Part of World Heritage Area
Mt Curly 1039m +
Mt Humboldt 1079m +
Mt Wright 1119m +
Clear Hill 1198m +
MOU NATION

5

Endeavour Bay
Franklin R
Maxwell R
Gordon PS Dam
Lake Gordon
ADAMSFIELD
Old Mine
SOUTHERN
OCEAN

6

High Rocky Point
Mainwaring R
Lewis R
Mt Osmund 369m +
Frederick Hill 518m +
Serpentine Dam
Mt Sprent 1058m +
Strathgordon
B61
Lookout
GORDON
Serpentine R
84
Lookout
Mt Mue 1234m +
Lookout Forest Wa
Mt Wedge 1146m +
Mt Bowes 957m +
Mt Anne 1425m +
Scotts Peak Rd
FRANKLAND RANGE
Roach R
Lake Pedder

7

Low Rocky Point ★
Elliott Bay
Elliott Hill 209m +
Hardwood Hill 412m +
SOUTHWEST NATIONAL PARK
Mt Giblin 878m +
Lookout
Scotts Peak Dam
Edgar Dam
ARTHUR RANG

Nye Bay
Gibbs R
Davey R
Mt Gaffney 588m +
Mt Hean 747m +
Crossing R
Walking
Mt Orion 1119m +
Huon R

8

Mulcahy Bay
Wreck Bay
Kelly Basin
Payne Bay
Mt Braddon 729m +
Part of World Heritage Area
Mt Norold 978m +
North R
Old R
Solly R
Watts R

9

Point St Vincent
Port Davey
Stephens Bay
Mt Rugby 771m +
Bathurst Harbour
Mine
Mt Counsel 800m +
SOUTHWES
NATIONAL PA

Island Bay
Window Pane Bay
Mt Melaleuca ■
Mt Melaleuca 595m +
Cox Bight
New Harbour
Louisa Bay
Ile Du C
De Witt Island

10

South West Cape
Karama Bay
Flat Witch Island
MAATSUYKER GROUP
Maatsuyker Island ★

KING ISLAND

Cape Wickham
Phoques Bay
Lavinia Point
New Year I
Christmas I
Whistler Point
Egg Lagoon
Yambacoona
BASS STRAIT
Reekara
B25
Loorana
Dairy Factory ●
Sea Elephant Bay
Naracoopa
Parenna
Currie ★
Pegarah
Yarra Creek
Fitzmaurice Bay
Lymwood
Grassy
Bold Head
Cataraqui Point
Pearshape
Seal Point
Surprise Point
Surprise Bay
Seal Bay
Stokes Point ★

King Island
Flinders Island
Launceston
HOBART

FLINDERS ISLAND

10

Inner Sister Island
Stanley Point ★
Blyth Pt
Palana
Killiecrankie Bay
Killiecrankie
Cape Frankland
Leeka
29
FURNEAUX
Lughrata
Babel I ★

11

Marshall Bay
Emita
Museum
Memana
Sellars Lagoon
Prime Seal Island
B85
Arthur Bay
72
Whitemark
Long Point
Cameron Inlet
Ranga
24
Lady Barron
Great Dog I
Trousers Pt
Loccota
15
STRZELECKI NP
FRANKLIN SOUND
Vansittart I
Puncheon Pt

12

Mt Chappell I
Badger I
Long I
Anderson I
Parry's Bay
Cape Barren Island
Mt Munro 716m +
CAPE BARREN ISLAND
Cape Barren
BANKS STRAIT
SOUTHERN

13

BASS STRAIT
Preservation I
Sloping Pt
Kent Bay
Mt Kerford 499m +
Clarke Island
Forsyth I
Passage I
Lookout Heads
Moriarty Point

A B C D E F G H I

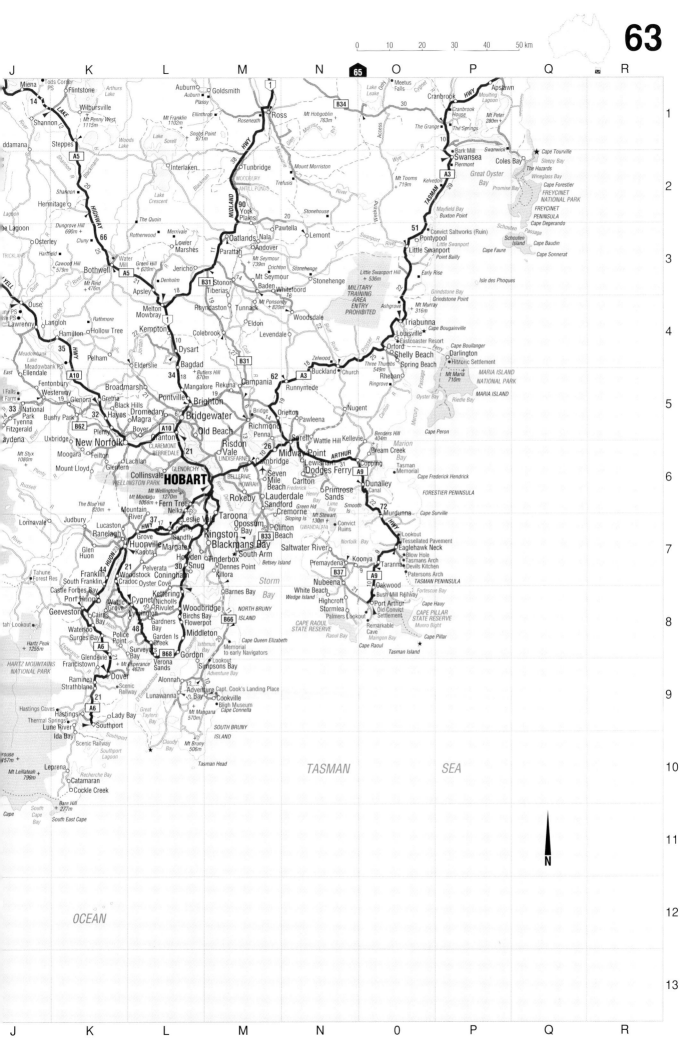

0 10 20 30 40 50 km

J K L M N O P Q R

Miena Tods Corner PS Flintstone Arthurs Lake Auburn Goldsmith Meetus Falls Cranbrook HWY Apslawn 1

14 Wilbursville Mt Franklin 1102m Roseneath Ross Mt Hobgoblin 763m Cranbrook House Mt Peter 280m B34

Shannon Mt Penny West 1115m Ellinthrop Plassy Access The Grange The Springs Swanwick Cape Tourville 2

Steppes A5 Woods Lake Interlaken Lake Sorell Tunbridge Mt Morriston Mt Tooms 719m Kelvedon Bark Mill Swansea Piermont Coles Bay The Hazards Sleepy Bay

Shannon 20 Lake Crescent Glen Trefusis Wye TASMAN Wineglass Bay Great Oyster Bay FREYCINET NATIONAL PARK

Hermitage HIGHWAY The Quoin Stonehouse 29 Mayfield Bay Buxton Point FREYCINET PENINSULA Cape Degerando 2

66 Rotherwood Merrivale MIDLAND 90 York Plains Pawtella Lemont Convict Saltworks (Ruin) Little Swanport Cape Baudin

Osterley Dungrove Hill 690m Cluny 23 Lower Marshes Andover Pontypool 51 Point Bailly Schouten Island Cape Sonnerat

Hartfield Cawood Hill 579m Water Mill Green Hill 620m Oatlands Nala Crichton Little Swanport Hill 536m Early Rise Isle des Phoques 3

Bothwell A5 Mt Reid 476m Jericho Denholm Mt Seymour 739m Stonehenge MILITARY TRAINING AREA ENTRY PROHIBITED Grindstone Bay

Apsley 18 Tiberias Mt Seymour Baden Whiteford Zelwood Ashgrove Mt Murray 316m Grindstone Point

Melton Mowbray Stonor B31 Rhyndaston Tunnack Eldon Woodsdale Triabunna Cape Bougainville 4

Kempton 1 Colebrook Levendale Three Thumbs 549m Orford Louisville Eastcoaster Resort Cape Boullanger Darlington Historic Settlement

35 Dysart Bagdad Butlers Hill 670m Campania A3 Buckland Church Rheban Shelly Beach Spring Beach MARIA ISLAND NATIONAL PARK Mt Maria 710m

Pelham 34 62 Rekuna Runnymede Ringrove MARIA ISLAND 5

A10 Broadmarsh Mangalore Nugent Oyster Bay Riedle Bay

33 Glenora Gretna Black Hills Pontville Brighton Bridge Orielton Pawleena Cape Peron

Bushy Park 32 Hayes Dromedary Old Beach Richmond Penna Sorell Wattle Hill Kellevie Benders Hill 404m Marion Bay Bream Creek 6

New Norfolk A10 Cranton Risdon Vale Cambridge 26 Midway Point Dodges Ferry Copping A9 Tasman Memorial Cape Frederick Hendrick

CLAREMONT BERRIEDALE 21 Seven Mile Beach Lewisham Dunalley FORESTIER PENINSULA

Collinsvale GLENORCHY BELLERIVE HOWRAH Primrose Sands 72 HWY Murdunna Cape Surville 7

HOBART Rokeby Lauderdale Sandford Cremorne Smooth Is Lookout Tessellated Pavement Eaglehawk Neck Blow Hole

Fern Tree Taroona Clifton Beach Saltwater River Koonya Tasmans Arch Devils Kitchen

Kingston Opossum Bay South Arm Premaydena B37 Taranna A9 Patersons Arch TASMAN PENINSULA 7

Huonville Blackmans Bay Howden Snug Tinderbox Dennes Point Nubeena Oakwood Bush Mill Railway 8

Franklin 44 Coningham Pelverata 30 Killora Barnes Bay White Beach Wedge Island Highcroft Port Arthur Old Convict Settlement CAPE PILLAR STATE RESERVE

Port Huon Woodstock Cradoc Kettering Cygnet Woodbridge Stormlea Palmers Lookout Cape Hauy

Geeveston Cairns Bay 48 Lymington Birchs Bay Flowerpot NORTH BRUNY ISLAND CAPE RAOUL STATE RESERVE Remarkable Cave Cape Pillar 8

Waterloo Surges Bay Gardners Bay Middleton Cape Queen Elizabeth Raoul Bay Maingon Bay Cape Raoul Tasman Island

A6 Glendevie Francistown B68 Gordon Verona Sands Simpsons Bay Bligh Museum 9

HARTZ MOUNTAINS NATIONAL PARK Raminea Strathblane Dover Alonnah Adventure Bay Capt. Cook's Landing Place Cookville Cape Connella

Hastings Caves 21 A6 Lady Bay Lunawanna Mt Mangana 570m SOUTH BRUNY ISLAND

Hastings Southport SOUTH BRUNY ISLAND 9

Thermal Springs Lune River Ida Bay Scenic Railway Mt Bruny 506m Tasman Head

Leprena Catamaran Cockle Creek Cloudy Bay TASMAN SEA 10

Bare Hill 277m South East Cape 11

N

OCEAN 12

13

J K L M N O P Q R

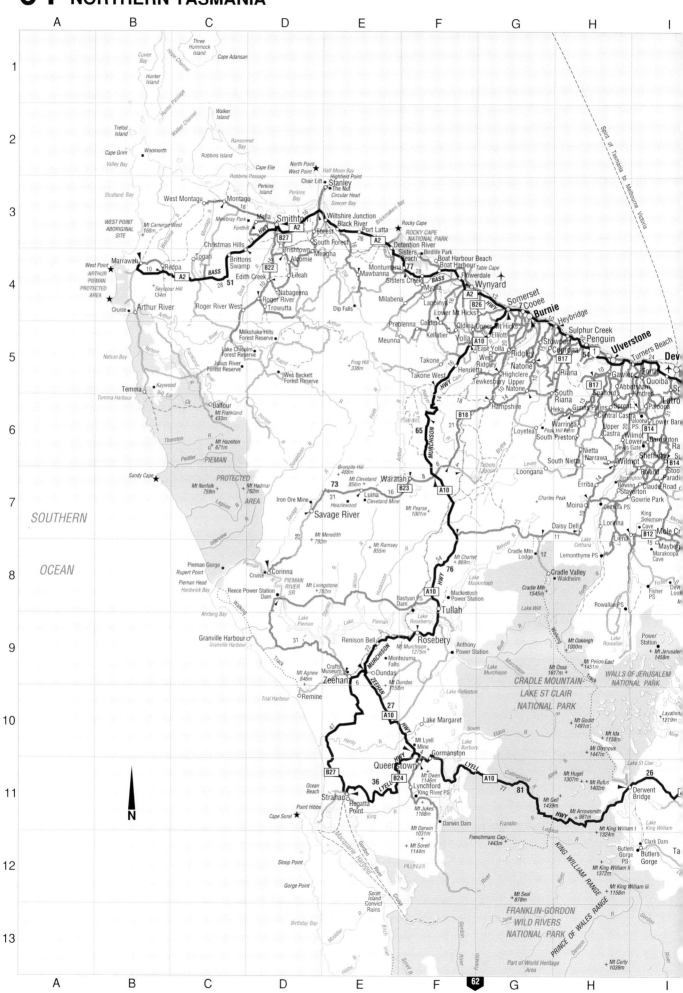

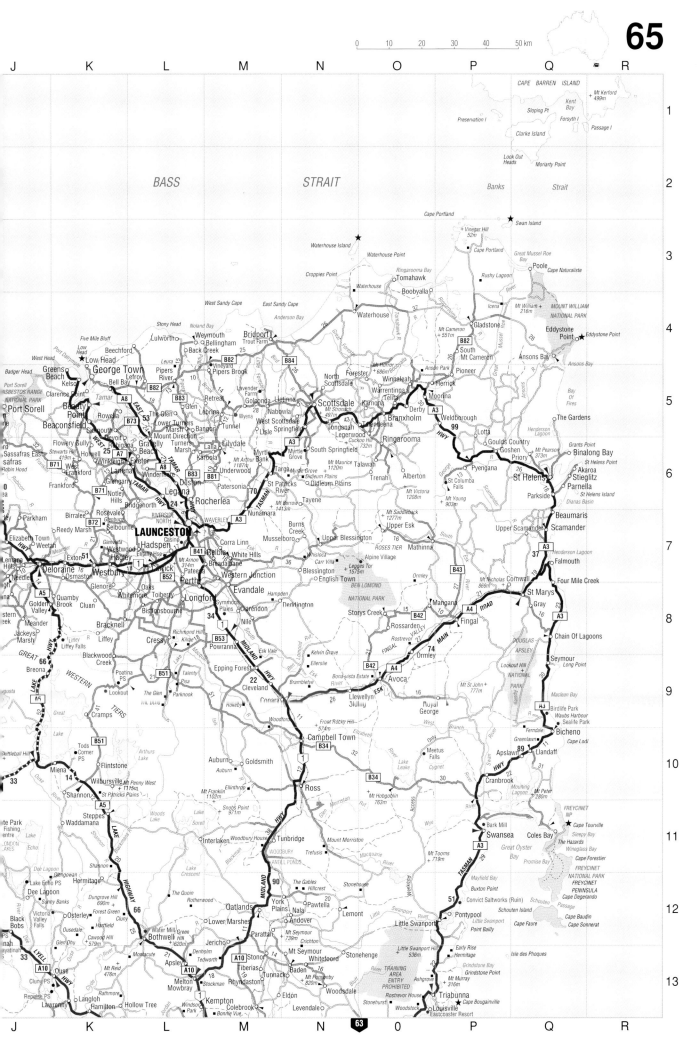

INDEX

The place names in this index are followed by two kinds of references. If a place appears on a map in the Road Maps section following page 497, the first reference or references, in **bold type**, will be the relevant map page and the grid reference. A page number in ordinary type following the bold map reference denotes a reference to the place in the ordinary text of the book. If a place has no bold type reference, just an ordinary page number, it does not appear on the maps but is mentioned in the text.

The alphabetical order followed in the index is 'word-by-word', where all entries under one word are grouped together. Where a place name consists of more than one word, the order is governed by the first and then the second word. For example:

Green Head

Green Island

Greendale

Greens Beach

Greenwell Point

Gregory Downs

Names beginning with St are indexed as Saint.

The following abbreviations are used in the index:

ACT   Australian Capital Territory
NSW   New South Wales
NT   Northern Territory
Qld   Queensland
SA   South Australia
St   Saint
Tas.   Tasmania
Vic.   Victoria
WA   Western Australia

References in **bold type** are map references to the Road Maps section of this book, following page 497.

Avoca Tas. **65 O9**
Avoca Vic. **53 M1, 55 M12**
Avon SA **41 K6**
Avon Valley National Park WA **30 E7**
Avondale NSW **3 K6**
Avondale Qld **15 O12**
Avonsleigh Vic. **50 F5**
Axedale Vic. **55 R10, 58 D9**
Ayers Rock NT *see* Uluru
Ayr Qld **17 O13**
Ayton Qld **17 K4**

Babakin WA **32 C9, 38 H8**
Babinda Qld **17 L8**
Bacchus Marsh Vic. **50 A3, 53 R5**
Back Creek Tas. **65 L4**
Baddaginnie Vic. **59 J7**
Baden Tas. **63 M3, 65 N13**
Badgingarra WA **30 D4**
Badgingarra Nat. Park WA **30 D4**, 105, 109
Badja State Forest NSW 459
Baffle Creek Qld **15 O11**
Bagdad Tas. **63 L4**
Bagot Well SA **41 M6**
Bailieston Vic. **58 F8**
Bairnsdale Vic. **51 P4, 60 E13**
Bakara SA **39 F1, 41 O7**
Bakara Conservation Park SA **39 F1, 41 O7**
Bakers Creek Qld **15 J4**
Baking Board Qld **12 I4**
Balaklava SA **41 K5**
Bald Island WA **30 H12**
Bald Rock National Park NSW **5 M3**
Balfes Creek Qld **14 C2, 21 Q2**, 230-1
Balfour Tas. **64 C6**, 171
Balgal Beach Qld **17 M11**
Balgo Community WA **37 P12**
Balgowan SA **40 I6**
Balhannah SA **39 C2, 41 L8**, 121
Balingup WA **30 E10**
Ball Bay Qld **14 I3**
Balladonia Roadhouse WA **33 K9**, 412, 416, 418-22
Ballan Vic. **53 Q4**
Ballandean Qld **5 L2, 13 L9**
Ballarat Vic. **53 O4**
Balldale NSW **9 O12, 59 M3**
Ballendella Vic. **58 E5**
Balliang Vic. **53 R4**
Ballidu WA **30 F5, 32 A6**
Ballimore NSW **2 E3, 4 E13**
Ballina NSW **5 P3, 13 O9**
Ballne WA **38 C13**
Balmoral Vic. **52 F2, 54 F13**
Balnarring Vic. **50 D8**
Balranald NSW **8 H9, 57 N7**
Bamaga Qld **18 C3**, 242, 244-5, 256, 258, 260-3
Banana Qld **15 L11**
Bancroft Qld **15 N12**
Bandiana Vic. **59 O5**
Bangalow NSW **5 P2, 13 O8**
Bangham Conservation Park SA **39 I8, 54 A9**
Bangor Tas. **65 L5**
Bannister WA **30 F8, 32 A10**
Bannockburn Vic. **53 Q7**
Banora Point NSW **5 P1, 13 O7**
Baradine NSW **4 E9**
Baralaba Qld **15 K10**
Baraduda Vic. **60 B3**

Barcaldine Qld **14 B9, 21 P9**
Barellan NSW **9 O7**
Bargara Qld **15 P12**
Bargo NSW **2 I9, 10 H2**
Barham NSW **8 I12, 55 Q3, 57 Q13, 58 B1**
Baringhup Vic. **55 P11, 58 A10**
Barjarg Vic. **59 K10**
Barkly Homestead NT **27 N11, 29 N1**
Barmedman NSW **2 A9, 9 Q7**
Barmera SA **41 Q6**
Barnawatha Vic. **9 P13, 59 N4, 60 A2**
Barnes Bay Tas. **63 M8**
Barooga NSW **9 M13, 59 J3**
Barraba NSW **4 I7, 12 I12**
Barradale Roadhouse WA 375
Barrakee Vic. **55 M7**
Barranyi (North Island) National Park NT **25 O12, 27 O2**
Barraport Vic. **8 H13, 55 N5**
Barrine National Park Qld 239
Barrington NSW **3 L2, 5 L13**
Barrington Tas. **64 I6**
Barrington Tops National Park NSW **3 K2, 5 K13**
Barringun NSW **7 M2, 23 P9**
Barron Gorge National Park Qld **17 L7**, 241
Barrow Creek NT **29 J4**
Barrow Island WA **38 E1**, 371
Bartle Frere National Park Qld **17 L7**
Barunga NT **24 I10**
Barunga Gap SA **41 J4**
Barwell Conservation Park SA **40 C3**
Barwon Downs Vic. **53 O10**
Barwon Heads Vic. **50 A7, 53 R9**
Baryulgil NSW **5 N4, 13 M10**
Bascombe Well Conservation Park SA **40 C3**
Bass Vic. **50 F8**
Batchelor NT **24 E6**, 79, 83
Bateau Bay NSW **3 K6**
Batemans Bay NSW **10 G7**, 45
Batesford Vic. **53 Q7**
Bathurst NSW **2 F7**, 47, 52
Bathurst Island NT **24 D3**
Batlow NSW **2 C13, 10 B6**
Battlecamp Qld 250
Bauple Qld **13 M2**
Baw Baw Alpine Village Vic. **50 I4**
Baw Baw National Park Vic. **51 J5**
Bawley Point NSW **2 H13, 10 H6**
Baxter Cliffs WA 421, 423
Bay of Fires Coastal Reserve Tas. 160
Beachport SA **39 F11**
Beachport Conservation Park SA **39 F11**
Beacon WA **30 G5, 32 C6**
Beaconsfield Tas. **65 K5**
Bealiba Vic. **55 N10**
Bears Lagoon Vic. **55 P7, 58 A6**
Beaudesert Qld **13 N7**
Beaufort SA **41 K5**
Beaufort Vic. **53 M3**
Beaumaris Tas. **65 Q7**
Beauty Point Tas. **65 K5**
Beckom NSW **9 P8**
Bedourie Qld **20 E11**
Beeac Vic. **53 N8**
Beech Forest Vic. **53 N11**, 142, 147
Beechford Tas. **65 L4**
Beechwood NSW **5 N11**
Beechworth Vic. **59 N6, 60 A4**
Beedelup National Park WA **30 E11**

Beelbangera NSW **9 N7**
Beenleigh Qld **13 N6**, 71
Beerwah Qld **13 N4**, 61
Bega NSW **10 F10, 61 P6**
Belair National Park SA **41 L8**
Belalie North SA **41 L2, 43 K13**
Belconnen ACT **11 D3**
Belgrave Vic. **50 E5**
Bell Qld **13 K4**
Bell Bay Tas. **65 K5**
Bell Gorge WA 348-50
Bellangry State Forest NSW 187
Bellata NSW **4 G6**
Bellbird Creek Vic. **10 D13, 61 K12**
Bellbrae Vic. **53 Q9**
Bellbrook NSW **5 N9**
Bellenden Ker National Park Qld 241
Bellerive Tas. **63 M6**
Bellingen NSW **5 O8, 13 M12**, 192
Bellingham Tas. **65 L4**
Bellthorpe State Forest Qld 58, 60
Belmont NSW **3 L5**
Beltana SA **22 C13, 43 K5**, 130, 134
Beltana Roadhouse SA **43 J5**
Belton SA **43 K10**
Belvidere SA **39 D3, 41 M9**
Belyuen NT **24 E5**
Bemboka NSW **10 F10, 61 O5**
Bemm River Vic. **61 K13**
Ben Boyd National Park NSW **10 G11, 61 P8**
Ben Lomond NSW **5 L6, 13 K11**
Ben Lomond National Park Tas. **65 O8**, 160-1, 172, 176
Bena Vic. **50 G8**
Benalla Vic. **59 K7**, 447, 449
Benambra Vic. **10 A11, 60 F8**, 452, 454
Bencubbin WA **30 G5, 32 C6**
Bendalong NSW **2 I12, 10 H5**
Bendemeer NSW **5 J9**
Bendick Murrell NSW **2 D9, 10 C2**
Bendidee National Park Qld **12 I7**
Bendigo Vic. **55 Q10, 58 C8**
Bendoc Vic. **10 D12, 61 K9**
Bengworden Vic. **51 O5**
Bermagui NSW **10 G9, 61 Q4**
Bernouilli Conservation Park SA **39 F9**
Berrara NSW **2 I12, 10 H5**
Berri SA **8 A8, 41 Q6**
Berridale NSW **10 D9, 61 K4**
Berriedale Tas. **63 L6**
Berrigan NSW **9 M12, 59 J1**
Berrima NSW **2 H10, 10 H3**
Berriwillock Vic. **8 G12, 55 K3, 57 K13**
Berry NSW **2 I11, 10 H4**
Berrybank Vic. **53 M6**
Berwick Vic. **50 E6**
Bessiebelle Vic. **52 F7**
Bete Bolong Vic. **60 I12**
Bethanga Vic. **9 Q13, 59 P4, 60 C2**
Bethany SA 120
Bethungra NSW **2 B11, 9 R9, 10 A4**
Betoota Qld **22 G2**
Beulah Tas. **64 I7**
Beulah Vic. **8 E13, 54 I5**
Beverford Vic. **8 H11, 57 N11**
Beveridge Vic. **50 C2, 58 F13**
Beverley WA **30 F7, 32 B9**
Biboohra Qld **17 K7**
Bicheno Tas. **65 Q10**

References in **bold type** are map references to the Road Maps section of this book, following page 497.

References in **bold type** are map references to the Road Maps section of this book, following page 497.

Broken Hill NSW **6 C12**
Bronte Park Tas. **62 I1, 65 J11**
Brookfield Conservation Park SA **41 N6**
Brooklands Qld **13 L4**
Brookton WA **30 F8, 32 B9**, 110, 113
Broome WA **36 H8**, 328-9, 348, 352, 355-6
Broomehill WA **30 G11, 32 C12**, 112
Broomfield Vic. **53 P3, 58 A12**
Brooms Head NSW **5 P5, 13 N10**
Brooweena Qld **13 L1**
Broulee NSW **10 G7**
Bruce Rock WA **30 H7, 32 C8**
Brucefield SA **40 I4**
Brungle NSW **2 C12, 10 B5**
Brunswick Heads NSW **5 P2, 13 O8**
Brunswick Junction WA **30 E9**
Bruthen Vic. **10 A13, 51 Q3, 60 F12**
Brymaroo Qld **13 K5**
Buangor Vic. **53 L2, 55 L13**
Bucasia Qld **15 J3**
Bucca Qld **15 O12**
Buccleuch SA **39 F3, 41 O9**
Buchan Vic. **10 B13, 51 R2, 60 H11**
Buchan South Vic. **60 H11**
Buckenderra NSW **10 D8, 61 K3**
Buckingham SA **39 H7, 41 Q13**
Buckland Tas. **63 N4**
Buckland Vic. **59 O9, 60 B7**
Buckleboo SA **40 E1, 42 E13**
Buckrabanyule Vic. **55 N7**
Budawang National Park NSW **2 H13, 10 G6**
Buddabaddah NSW **7 Q12**
Buderim Qld **13 N4**
Budgewoi NSW **3 K6**
Buffalo Vic. **50 H9**
Builyan Qld **15 N11**
Bulahdelah NSW **3 M3**, 181
Bulga State Forest NSW 187
Bulla Vic. **50 B3**
Bullaring WA **30 G8, 32 C9**, 110, 113
Bulleringa National Park Qld **16 H8**
Bullfinch WA **30 I6, 32 D7**
Bullita Outstation NT 312, 317-20
Bullsbrook WA **30 E7**
Bullumwaal Vic. **51 O3, 60 E12**
Buln Buln Vic. **50 H6**
Bumbunga SA **41 K4**
Bunbartha Vic. **58 H5**
Bunbury WA **30 D10**
Bundaberg Qld **15 P12**
Bundalong Vic. **9 N13, 59 L4**
Bundanoon NSW **2 H11, 10 H3**
Bundarra NSW **5 J7, 13 J12**
Bundjalung Nat. Park NSW **5 P4, 13 N10**
Bungaree Vic. **53 P4**
Bungendore NSW **2 F13, 10 E5, 11 I3**
Bungle Bungle National Park WA *see* Purnululu National Park
Bungonia NSW **2 G11, 10 G4**
Bungunya Qld **4 F1**
Buninyong Vic. **53 O4**
Bunnan NSW **2 I2, 4 I13**
Buntine WA **30 F4, 32 A5**
Bunya Mountains National Park Qld **13 K4**
Bunyan NSW **10 E8, 61 L2**
Bunyip Vic. **50 G6**
Bunyip State Park Vic. **50 G5**
Burcher NSW **2 A7, 9 Q5**

Burdekin Falls Dam Qld 198, 224, 227-8
Burekup WA **30 E10**
Burke and Wills Roadhouse Qld **16 A12, 19 G12**
Burketown Qld **19 E9**, 278, 295, 297-9
Burleigh Heads Qld **13 O7**
Burnett Heads Qld **15 P12**
Burnie Tas. **64 G4**
Burns Creek Tas. **65 N7**
Burpengary Qld **13 N5**
Burra SA **41 M4**
Burracoppin WA **30 H6, 32 D7**
Burrawang NSW **2 I10, 10 H3**
Burren Junction NSW **4 E7, 12 F12**
Burrill Lake NSW **2 I13, 10 H6**
Burringbar NSW **5 P1, 13 O8**
Burrowa-Pine Mountain National Park Vic. **9 R13, 10 A8, 60 E2**
Burrum Heads Qld **15 P13**
Burrumbeet Vic. **53 N3**
Burrumbuttock NSW **9 P12, 59 O3**
Bushfield Vic. **52 I9**
Bushy Park Tas. **63 K5**
Busselton WA **30 D10, 31 F3, 45 F3**, 395
Butchers Ridge Vic. **10 B12, 60 H9**
Bute SA **41 J4**
Butler Tanks SA **40 E5**
Butlers Gorge Tas. **62 H2, 64 I12**
Buxton NSW **2 I9, 10 H2**
Buxton Qld **13 M1, 15 P13**
Buxton Vic. **50 G2, 59 J13**
Byaduk Vic. **52 F6**
Byfield National Park Qld **15 M8**
Byford WA **30 E8**
Bylong NSW 47, 49
Byrock NSW **7 O8, 12 B13, 23 Q13**
Byron Bay NSW **5 Q2, 13 O8**

Cabarlah Qld **13 L5**
Cabbage Tree Creek Vic. **10 C13, 61 J12**
Caboolture Qld **13 N5**
Cabramurra NSW **10 C8, 60 I1**
Cadell SA **41 O5**
Cadney Homestead SA **47 P8**
Cadoux WA **30 F5, 32 B6**
Caiguna WA **33 M9**, 412, 421-3
Cairns Qld **17 L6**, 198, 200, 238-9, 241-2, 244, 246, 248, 269, 276-7, 282
Cairns Bay Tas. **63 K8**
Calca SA **45 P13**
Calder Tas. **64 F5**
Calen Qld **14 I3**
Caliph SA **39 G1, 41 P7**
Calivil Vic. **55 P7, 58 B6**
Callala Bay NSW **2 I12, 10 I5**
Callignee Vic. **51 K7**
Callington SA **39 D3, 41 M9**
Calliope Qld **15 N10**
Caloundra Qld **13 N4**
Calpatanna Waterhole Conservation Park SA **45 P13**
Caltowie SA **41 K2**
Calulu Vic. **51 O4, 60 E13**
Camballin WA **37 K8**
Cambewarra NSW **2 I11, 10 H4**
Cambrai SA **39 D1, 41 N7**
Cambridge Tas. **63 M6**
Camburinga NT **25 O6**
Camden NSW **2 I9, 10 I2**

Cameron Corner Qld 494, 496
Camooweal Qld **20 B1, 27 Q12, 29 Q1**
Camooweal Caves National Park Qld **20 B1, 27 Q12, 29 Q2**
Campania Tas. **63 M5**
Campbell Town Tas. **65 N10**, 158, 165-6
Campbells Creek Vic. **55 Q12**
Campbelltown NSW **3 J9, 10 I2**
Campbelltown Vic. **53 P1, 55 P13, 58 A11**
Camperdown Vic. **53 L8**
Canary Island Vic. **8 I13, 55 O5, 58 A4**
Canberra ACT **2 E13, 10 D5, 11 E3**
Candelo NSW **10 F10, 61 O6**
Cania Gorge National Park Qld **15 M12**
Cann River Vic. **10 E13, 61 M11**, 149
Canna WA **30 E2**
Cannonvale Qld **14 I2**
Canowie SA **41 L3**
Canowindra NSW **2 D7**
Canunda National Park SA **39 G12**
Cape Arid National Park WA **33 J11**, 412, 414-15, 417-20
Cape Barren Island Tas. **62 B13, 65 Q1**
Cape Clear Vic. **53 N5**
Cape Crawford Roadhouse NT **27 N4**
Cape Gantheaume Conservation Park SA **40 H12**
Cape Hotham Conservation Reserve NT **24 F4**
Cape Jervis SA **39 A4, 41 J10**
Cape Le Grand National Park WA **32 I12**, 412, 414-16
Cape Leeuwin WA 392, 395, 398
Cape Melville Nat Park Qld **17 J1, 18 G11, 18 H11**
Cape Palmerston National Park Qld **15 J5**, 200, 217-18
Cape Paterson Vic. **50 F10**
Cape Peron WA 352, 381
Cape Range National Park WA **38 B3**, 352, 373-8, 380
Cape Torrens Conservation Park SA **40 F11**
Cape Tribulation National Park Qld **17 K4**, 246-7, 249
Cape Upstart National Park Qld **17 P13**
Capel WA **30 D10, 31 I1, 45 I1**
Capella Qld **14 H8**
Capertee NSW **2 G6**
Capricorn Roadhouse WA **34 E6**
Captain Billy Landing Qld 261
Captains Flat NSW **10 E6**
Caragabal NSW **2 B8, 9 R6, 10 A1**
Caralue SA **40 E2**
Caramut Vic. **52 I6**
Carappee Hill Conservation Park SA **40 E2**
Carawa SA **45 P10**
Carboor Vic. **59 N8**
Carbunup River WA **31 D3, 45 D3**
Carcoar NSW **2 E7**
Carcuma Conservation Park SA **39 G4, 41 P10**
Cardross Vic. **8 D8, 56 G5**
Cardwell Qld **17 L10**, 198, 200, 235, 237-8, 240
Cargerie Vic. **53 P5**
Cargo NSW **2 E7**
Carinda NSW **4 A8, 7 R7, 12 D12**
Carisbrook Vic. **55 O12, 58 A10**
Carlisle River Vic. **53 M10**
Carlsruhe Vic. **50 A1, 53 R2, 55 R13, 58 D12**
Carlton Tas. **63 N6**
Carmila Qld **15 J5**
Carnamah WA **30 E3**

References in **bold type** are map references to the Road Maps section of this book, following page 497.

References in **bold type** are map references to the Road Maps section of this book, following page 497.

References in **bold type** are map references to the Road Maps section of this book, following page 497.

References in **bold type** are map references to the Road Maps section of this book, following page 497.

References in **bold type** are map references to the Road Maps section of this book, following page 497.

Goongarrie National Park WA **32 H5**
Goongerah Vic. **61 J10**
Goorambat Vic. **59 K6**
Goornong Vic. **55 R9, 58 D8**
Goose Island Conservation Park SA **40 H6**
Goovigen Qld **15 L10**
Gordon Tas. **63 L8**
Gordon Vic. **53 P4**
Gordonvale Qld **17 L7**, 241
Gormandale Vic. **51 K7**
Gormanston Tas. **62 E1, 64 F10**
Goroke Vic. **54 D9**
Gosford NSW **3 K7**
Goshen Tas. **65 P6**
Goughs Bay Vic. **59 K11**
Goulburn NSW **2 G11, 10 F4**
Goulburn River National Park NSW **2 G3, 4 G13**
Goulburn Weir Vic. **58 G8**
Goulds Country Tas. **65 P6**
Gowrie Park Tas. **64 I7**
Grabben Gullen NSW **2 F10, 10 E3**
Gracemere Qld **15 L9**
Gracetown WA **30 C11, 31 B6, 45 B6**
Grafton NSW **5 O5, 13 N11**, 189, 193-5
Graman NSW **5 J5, 13 J10**
Grampians National Park Vic. **52 H1, 54 H12**, 137, 434-5, 439-40, 443
Grantham Qld **13 L6**
Granton Tas. **63 L5**
Grantville Vic. **50 F8**
Granville Harbour Tas. **64 D9**
Grass Patch WA **32 H11**
Grassmere Vic. **52 I8**
Grasstree Qld **15 J4**
Grassy Tas. **62 B9**
Gravelly Beach Tas. **65 L6**
Gravesend NSW **4 H5, 12 I10**
Gray Tas. **65 Q8**
Graytown Vic. **58 F9**
Great Basalt Wall National Park Qld **14 B1, 17 K13, 21 P1**
Great Keppell Island Qld **15 M8**
Great Palm Island Aboriginal Community Qld **17 N11**
Great Sandy National Park Qld **15 Q12**
Great Wall of China 134
Great Western Vic. **53 J1, 55 J12**
Gredgwin Vic. **8 H13, 55 N5**
Green Head WA **30 C4**
Green Island Qld 241
Green Island National Park Qld **17 L6**
Greenbushes WA **30 E11**
Greendale Vic. **53 Q4, 58 C13**
Greenethorpe NSW **2 D9, 10 C1**
Greenmount Qld **13 L6**
Greenock SA **41 M6**
Greenough WA **30 C2**
Greens Beach Tas. **65 K5**
Greenvale Vic. **50 C3**
Greenways SA **39 G10**
Greenwell Point NSW **2 I11, 10 I4**
Gregory Downs Qld 298-9
Gregory National Park NT **24 D13, 24 F12, 26 D3, 26 F2**, 312, 314-17, 320-1
Grenfell NSW **2 C8, 10 B1**
Grenville Vic. **53 O5**
Gresford NSW **3 K3**
Greta Vic. **59 L7**

Gretna Tas. **63 K5**
Grevillia NSW 74
Griffith NSW **9 N7**
Grimwade WA **30 E10, 32 A12**
Grong Grong NSW **9 P9**
Groote Eylandt NT **25 O9**
Grove Tas. **63 L7**, 162
Guilderton WA **30 D6**
Gulargambone NSW **4 C11**
Gulgong NSW **2 F3**
Gulnare SA **41 K3**
Guluguba Qld **12 H3**
Gum Lagoon Conservation Park SA **39 G7, 41 P13**
Gumbowie SA **41 M1, 43 L13**
Gumeracha SA **39 C2, 41 M8**
Gumlu Qld **14 G1, 17 P13**
Gunalda Qld **13 M2**
Gunbower Vic. **9 J13, 55 R5, 58 C3**
Gundagai NSW **2 C12, 10 B5**
Gundaroo NSW **2 F12, 10 E5**
Gundiah Qld **13 M2**
Gundowring Vic. **60 C4**
Gundy NSW **3 J2, 5 J13**
Gungahlin ACT **11 E2**
Gunlom Falls NT 95
Gunnedah NSW **4 H9**
Gunning NSW **2 F11, 10 E4**
Gunns Plains Tas. **64 H6**
Gunpowder Qld **19 E13**
Gunshot Creek Qld 263-4
Gurig National Park NT **24 G2**, 76, 78, 84-7
Gurley NSW **4 G5**
Gurrundah NSW **2 F11, 10 E3**
Guthalungra Qld **14 G1, 17 P13**
Guthega NSW **10 C9, 60 I4**
Guy Fawkes River National Park NSW **5 M6, 13 M11**
Guyra NSW **5 L7, 13 K12**
Gwabegar NSW **4 E8, 12 F13**
Gymbowen Vic. **54 E9**
Gympie Qld **13 M3**, 66, 68

Haasts Bluff NT **28 G8**
Haddon Vic. **53 O4**
Haden Qld **13 L5**
Hadspen Tas. **65 L7**
Hagley Tas. **65 K7**
Hahndorf SA **39 C2, 41 L8**
Halbury SA **41 L5**
Half Tide Qld **15 J4**
Halidon SA **39 G2, 41 P8**
Halifax Qld **17 M10**
Hall ACT **11 E2**
Hallett SA **41 M3**
Hallidays Point NSW **3 N2, 5 N13**
Halls Creek WA **37 P9**, 462, 475, 477
Halls Gap Vic. **52 I1, 54 I12**, 434, 440, 443, 445
Hambidge Conservation Park SA **40 D2**
Hamelin Bay Holiday Village WA 397
Hamelin Pool Marine Nat. Res. WA 381, 383
Hamersley Range National Park WA *see* Karijini National Park
Hamilton SA **41 M5**
Hamilton Tas. **63 K4, 65 K13**
Hamilton Vic. **52 G5**
Hamilton Island Qld **15 J2**
Hamley Bridge SA **41 L6**

Hammond SA **43 J11**
Hampden NSW 42, 44
Hampden SA **41 M5**
Hampshire Tas. **64 G6**
Hampton NSW **2 H7**
Hampton Qld **13 L5**
Hann River Roadhouse Qld **16 H3, 18 F13**
Hann Tableland National Park Qld **17 K6**
Hansborough SA **41 M6**
Hanson SA **41 L4**
Hanwood NSW **9 N8**
Happy Valley Qld 67
Happy Wanderer Holiday Resort Vic. 441
Harcourt Vic. **55 Q11, 58 C10**
Harcourt North Vic. **55 Q11, 58 C10**
Harden NSW **2 D10, 10 C3**
Hardwicke Bay SA **40 I8**
Harford Tas. **65 J6**
Harlin Qld **13 M4**
Harrietville Vic. **59 P9, 60 C7**
Harrington NSW **3 N2, 5 N12**
Harrismith WA **30 H9, 32 C10**
Harrys Hut Qld 62, 66
Hart SA **41 K4**
Hartz Mountains National Park Tas. **63 J9**
Harvey WA **30 E9**, 102
Haslam SA **45 P11**
Hassell National Park WA **30 H12, 32 D13**
Hastings Tas. **63 K9**
Hastings Vic. **50 D7**
Hat Head NSW **5 O10**
Hat Head National Park NSW **5 O9**
Hatches Creek NT **27 M13, 29 M3**
Hatfield NSW **8 H6, 57 O2**
Hatherleigh SA **39 G11**
Hattah Vic. **8 E9, 56 H8**
Hattah-Kulkyne National Park Vic. **8 E8, 56 H7**
Haven Vic. **54 G10**
Havilah Vic. **59 O7, 60 B5**
Hawker SA **43 K9**, 130, 132, 135
Hawkesdale Vic. **52 H7**
Hawks Nest NSW **3 M4**
Hawley Beach Tas. **65 J5**
Hay NSW **9 K8**
Haydens Bog Vic. **61 K8**
Hayes Tas. **63 K5**
Hayes Creek Roadhouse NT **24 F8**
Healesville Vic. **50 F3**, 152, 154, 157
Healesville Sanctuary Vic. 157
Heathcote Vic. **58 E9**
Heathcote Junction Vic. **50 D1, 58 F12**
Heathlands Qld 263-4
Hebel Qld **4 B3, 12 D9**
Heka Tas. **64 H6**
Helenvale Qld **17 K4**
Hell Hole Gorge National Park Qld **23 M1**
Hells Gate Roadhouse Qld **19 C8, 27 R6**, 278, 301, 303-4
Henrietta Tas. **64 F5**
Henty NSW **9 P11, 59 P1**
Hepburn Springs Vic. **53 Q2, 55 Q13, 58 B12**
Herbert River Qld 239, 241
Herbert River National Park Qld **17 L10**
Herberton Qld **17 K8**, 283
Hermannsburg NT **28 I9**, 472, 474
Hermitage Tas. **63 K2, 65 K12**
Herrick Tas. **65 O5**
Hervey Bay Qld **13 N1, 15 Q13**

References in **bold type** are map references to the Road Maps section of this book, following page 497.

References in **bold type** are map references to the Road Maps section of this book, following page 497.

References in **bold type** are map references to the Road Maps section of this book, following page 497.

Lamington National Park Qld **5 O1, 13 N7**
Lancaster Vic. **58 G6**
Lancefield Vic. **50 B1, 58 E12**
Lancelin WA **30 D6**, 96, 103, 105-6
Landcruiser Mountain Park Qld 201, 203
Landsborough Vic. **55 L11**
Lanena Tas. **65 L6**
Lang Lang Vic. **50 F7**
Langhorne Creek SA **39 D3, 41 M9**
Langloh Tas. **63 J4, 65 K13**
Langsborough Vic. **51 K9**
Lansdowne NSW **3 N1, 5 N12**
Lapoinya Tas. **64 F4**
Lara Vic. **50 A5, 53 R7**
Larpent Vic. **53 N9**
Larrimah NT **24 I12, 26 I2**
Lascelles Vic. **8 F12, 54 I2, 56 I13**
Latham WA **30 E3, 32 A5**
Lathami Conservation Park SA **40 H11**
Latrobe Tas. **64 I6**
Lauderdale Tas. **63 M6**
Launceston Tas. **65 L7**, 166-7
Launching Place Vic. **50 F4**
Laura Qld **16 I3**, 242, 244-5, 250, 252, 269-73
Laura SA **41 K2**
Laurieton NSW **3 N1, 5 N12**
Lavers Hill Vic. **53 M11**, 142, 147
Laverton WA **32 I3**
Lawn Hill National Park Qld **19 C11, 27 R9**, 278, 298-302
Lawrence NSW **5 O5, 13 N10**
Lawrence Road NSW **5 O4**
Lawrenny Tas. **63 J4, 65 K13**
Lawson NSW **2 I8**
Leadville NSW **2 F2, 4 F13**
Learmonth Vic. **53 O3**
Leasingham SA **41 L5**
Lebrina Tas. **65 M5**
Ledge Point WA **30 D6**, 106
Leeka Tas. **62 A11**
Leeman WA **30 C4**
Leeton NSW **9 O8**
Leeuwin-Naturaliste National Park WA **30 C11, 31 B4, 31 B9, 31 C12, 45 B4, 45 B9, 45 C12**, 392, 395, 397
Lefroy Tas. **65 L5**
Legana Tas. **65 L6**
Legerwood Tas. **65 O5**
Legume NSW **5 M1, 13 L8**
Leigh Creek SA **22 C13, 43 K5**, 134
Leighton SA **41 L3**
Leinster WA **32 F1**
Leitchville Vic. **9 J13, 55 Q4, 58 C3**
Lemana Tas. **65 J7**
Lemont Tas. **63 N3, 65 N12**
Lennard Gorge WA 348, 350
Lennox Head NSW **5 Q3, 13 O9**
Leongatha Vic. **50 H8**
Leonora WA **32 G3**
Leopold Vic. **50 A7, 53 R8**
Leprena Tas. **63 K10**
Leslie Vale Tas. **63 L7**
Lesueur National Park WA 103, 105, 109
Lethbridge Vic. **53 P6**
Leven Beach Conservation Park SA **40 H8**
Levendale Tas. **63 N4, 65 N13**
Lewisham Tas. **63 N6**
Lexton Vic. **53 N2, 55 N13**

Leyburn Qld **13 K7**
Licola Vic. **51 K3, 60 A12**
Lidsdale NSW **2 H6**
Liena Tas. **64 I7**
Lietinna Tas. **65 N5**
Liffey Tas. **65 K8**
Lightning Ridge NSW **4 B5, 12 E10**
Lileah Tas. **64 D4**
Lilydale Tas. **65 M6**
Limestone Vic. **58 I12**
Limmen Bight River NT 308-9
Lincoln National Park SA **40 E8**
Lind National Park Vic. **10 D13, 61 L12**
Linda Tas. **62 F1**
Lindeman Island Qld **15 J2**
Lindenow Vic. **51 O4, 60 D13**
Lindisfarne Tas. **63 M6**
Linga Vic. **8 C10, 56 E10**
Linton Vic. **53 N5**
Linville Qld **13 L4**
Lipson SA **40 E6**
Lisle Tas. **65 M5**
Lismore NSW **5 P3, 13 N9**
Lismore Vic. **53 M6**
Litchfield National Park NT **24 E7**, 76, 78-83
Lithgow NSW **2 H7**
Little Desert National Park Vic. **39 I8, 54 D8**, 440
Little Dip Conservation Park SA **39 F10**
Little River Vic. **50 A5, 53 R6**
Little Swanport Tas. **63 O3, 65 P12**
Little Topar Roadhouse NSW **6 D11**
Lizard Island National Park Qld **17 K1, 18 I12**
Llandaff Tas. **65 Q10**
Llanelly Vic. **55 O10, 58 A8**
Llangothlin NSW **5 L7, 13 K12**
Llewellyn Siding Tas. **65 N9**
Lobethal SA **39 C2, 41 L8**
Loccota Tas. **62 B12**
Loch Vic. **50 G8**
Loch Sport Vic. **51 P5**
Lochiel SA **41 K4**
Lock SA **40 D3**
Lockhart NSW **9 P10**
Lockhart River Aboriginal Comm. Qld 244
Lockington Vic. **58 D5**
Locksley Vic. **58 H9**
Lockwood Vic. **55 Q10, 58 B9**
Logan Vic. **55 N9**
Long Beach NSW **10 G7**
Long Flat NSW **5 N11**
Long Plains SA **41 K6**
Longford Tas. **65 L8**
Longford Vic. **51 M6**
Longlea Vic. **55 R10, 58 D9**
Longley Tas. **63 L7**
Longreach Qld **21 N9**
Longwarry Vic. **50 G6**
Longwood Vic. **58 H9**
Lonnavale Tas. **63 J7**
Looma WA **37 K9**
Loongana Tas. **64 G6**
Loorana Tas. **62 A8**
Lorinna Tas. **64 H7**
Lorne Vic. **53 P10**, 142, 145, 147
Lorquon Vic. **8 D13, 54 E6**
Lost City NT 76, 79, 82
Lotta Tas. **65 P5**
Louisville Tas. **63 O4, 65 O13**

Louth NSW **7 L7, 23 O13**
Louth Bay SA **40 D7**
Loveday SA **41 Q6**
Low Head Tas. **65 K5**
Lowan Conservation Park SA **39 F2, 41 O8**
Lowan Vale SA **39 H7, 41 Q13**
Lowbank SA **41 P5**
Lower Barrington Tas. **64 I6**
Lower Beulah Tas. **64 I7**
Lower Glenelg National Park Vic. **52 C7**
Lower Marshes Tas. **63 L3, 65 M12**
Lower Mount Hicks Tas. **64 F4**
Lower Plenty Vic. **50 D4**
Lower Turners Marsh Tas. **65 L5**
Lowesdale NSW **9 O12, 59 M3**
Lowmead Qld **15 O11**
Lowood Qld **13 M6**
Loxton SA **8 A8, 41 Q6**, 125, 128
Loyetea Tas. **64 G6**
Lucaston Tas. **63 K7**, 163
Lucinda Qld **17 M10**
Lucindale SA **39 G9**
Lucknow NSW **2 E6**
Lucknow Vic. **51 P4, 60 D13**
Lucky Bay SA **40 H4**, 412
Lue NSW **2 G4**
Lughrata Tas. **62 A11**
Luina Tas. **64 E7**
Lulworth Tas. **65 L4**
Lumholtz National Park Qld **17 K10**
Lunawanna Tas. **63 L9**
Lune River Tas. **63 K9**
Lymington Tas. **63 L8**
Lymwood Tas. **62 A9**
Lynchford Tas. **62 E2, 64 F11**
Lyndhurst NSW **2 E8**
Lyndhurst SA **22 B12, 43 J3**
Lyndhurst Vic. **50 E6**
Lyndoch SA **39 C1, 41 M7**
Lyrup SA **41 Q6**

Maaroom Qld **13 N1**
Mabel Downs Station WA 332, 334
MacArthur Vic. **52 G7**
Macclesfield SA **39 C3, 41 L9**
McDermid Rock WA 110
Macedon Vic. **50 A2, 58 D13**
McGowans Island WA 342-4
Mackay Qld 198, 200, 217-21
McKinlay Qld **20 H4**
Macksville NSW **5 O9, 13 M13**
Maclagan Qld **13 K5**
McLaren Vale SA **39 B3, 41 L9**
Maclean NSW **5 P5, 13 N10**
McLoughlins Beach Vic. **51 L9**
Macorna Vic. **8 I13, 55 P4, 58 B3**
Macquarie Pass Nat. Park NSW 36, 42, 44
Macquarie Plains Tas. **63 K5**
Macs Cove Vic. **59 L11**
Madura WA **33 O8**
Madura Pass Roadhouse WA 425
Maffra Vic. **51 M5**
Maggea SA **41 P6**
Magnetic Island Qld **17 N11**
Magra Tas. **63 L5**
Magrath Flat SA **39 E5, 41 N11**
Maidenwell Qld **13 L4**

References in **bold type** are map references to the Road Maps section of this book, following page 497.

573

Mailors Flat Vic. **52 I8**
Main Range National Park Qld **5 M1, 13 L7**, 74
Maitland NSW **3 K4**
Maitland SA **40 I6**
Majors Creek NSW **10 F6**
Malanda Qld **17 L7**
Maldon Vic. **55 P11, 58 B10**
Maleny Qld 58, 60-1, 201-2
Malinong SA **39 E4, 41 N10**
Mallacoota Vic. **10 F13, 61 O11**, 148, 151
Mallala SA **41 L6**
Mallanganee NSW **5 N3, 13 M9**, 196
Mallee Cliffs National Park NSW **8 E7, 56 I4**
Malmsbury Vic. **53 R1, 55 R12, 58 C11**
Malpas SA **8 A9, 39 H1**
Malua Bay NSW **10 G7**
Mambray Creek SA **41 J1, 42 I13**
Manangatang Vic. **8 F10, 57 K9**
Manangoora Station NT 304-5
Mandorah NT **24 E5**
Mandurah WA **30 D8**
Mandurama NSW **2 E7**
Mandurang Vic. **55 Q10, 58 C9**
Mangalo SA **40 F3**
Mangalore Tas. **63 L5**
Mangalore Vic. **58 G9**
Mangana Tas. **65 O8**
Mangoplah NSW **2 A13, 9 Q11**
Manildra NSW **2 D6**
Manilla NSW **4 I9**
Maningrida NT **25 K4**
Manjimup WA **30 E11, 32 A13**, 395, 398, 400, 402
Manmanning WA **30 F5, 32 B7**
Mannahill SA **43 O11**
Mannanarie SA **41 L1, 43 K13**
Mannering Park NSW **3 K6**
Manning Gorge WA 345, 347
Manns Beach Vic. **51 L9**
Mannum SA **39 E2, 41 N8**, 125-6
Manoora SA **41 L5**
Mansfield Vic. **59 K10**, 152, 155
Mantung SA **39 G1, 41 P7**
Many Peaks Qld **15 N11**
Manypeaks WA **32 C13**
Mapleton Qld 201-2
Mapleton Falls National Park Qld 201
Maralinga SA **44 I3**
Marama SA **39 G3, 41 P9**
Maranboy NT **24 H10**
Marble Bar WA **34 E2**, 352, 357-9
Marchagee WA **30 E4**
Mareeba Qld **17 K7**, 269, 277, 281-2
Marengo Vic. **53 N12**
Margaret River WA **30 D11, 31 C7, 45 C7**, 395-6
Margate Tas. **63 L7**
Maria Island National Park Tas. **63 P5**, 158, 161, 164-5
Marian Qld 221
Mariala National Park Qld **23 O3**
Marino Conservation Park SA **40 F7**
Marion Bay SA **40 G9**
Markwood Vic. **59 M6**
Marla SA **47 N5**, 462, 484-5
Marlborough Qld **15 K7**
Marlo Vic. **61 J13**
Marmor Qld **15 M9**
Marnoo Vic. **55 K9**
Marong Vic. **55 Q10, 58 B8**

Maroochydore Qld **13 N4**
Maroon Qld **13 M7**
Maroona Vic. **53 K3**
Marrabel SA **41 M5**
Marrakai Conservation Reserve NT **24 F5**
Marramarra National Park NSW **3 J7**
Marrar NSW **2 A11, 9 Q9**
Marrawah Tas. **64 B4**, 169-70
Marree SA **22 B11, 43 J1**, 462, 484, 487-9
Marton Qld 251
Marulan NSW **2 H11, 10 G4**
Marulan South NSW **2 H11, 10 G4**
Marvel Loch WA **32 E8**
Mary Kathleen Qld **20 F3**
Mary River Conservation Reserve NT **24 F5**, 90
Maryborough Qld **13 M1**
Maryborough Vic. **55 O12**
Maryfarms Qld **17 K6**
Marysville Vic. **50 G2, 59 J13**, 152, 157
Maryvale Qld 73
Mataranka NT **24 I11, 26 I1**, 278, 310-11
Mathinna Tas. **65 O7**, 176
Mathoura NSW **9 K12, 58 F2**
Matong NSW **9 P9**
Maude NSW **9 J8, 57 R6**
Maude Vic. **53 Q6**
Mawbanna Tas. **64 E4**
Maxwelton Qld **21 K3**
Mayberry Tas. **64 I8**
Maydena Tas. **63 J5**
Maytown Qld 242, 244, 269, 272-3, 275-6
Mazeppa National Park Qld **14 F6**
Meadows SA **39 C3, 41 L9**
Meandarra Qld **12 H5**
Meander Tas. **65 J8**
Mebbin Forest NSW 195, 197
Meckering WA **30 F7, 32 B8**
Meekatharra WA **34 C12**
Meeniyan Vic. **50 H9**
Meerlieu Vic. **51 O5**
Melba Gully State Park Vic. 142
Melbourne Vic. **50 C4**
Mella Tas. **64 D3**
Melrose SA **41 K1, 43 J12**
Melton SA **41 J5**
Melton Vic. **50 A3**
Melton Mowbray Tas. **63 L4, 65 L13**
Melville Island NT **24 E2**
Memana Tas. **62 B11**
Memerambi Qld **13 L3**
Mena Creek Qld **17 L8**
Mendooran NSW **2 E2, 4 E12**
Mengha Tas. **64 D4**
Menindee NSW **6 E13, 8 E1**
Meningie SA **39 E5, 41 N11**
Menzies WA **32 G4**
Merbein Vic. **8 D7, 56 G4**
Mercunda SA **39 G1, 41 P7**
Meredith Vic. **53 P6**
Meribah SA **8 A9, 39 I1, 41 R7, 56 A7**
Merildin SA **41 L4**
Merimbula NSW **10 F11, 61 P7**
Merinda Qld **14 H1**
Meringur Vic. **8 B8, 56 C5**
Merino Vic. **52 D5**
Mernda Vic. **50 D3**
Merredin WA **30 H6, 32 C8**
Merriang Vic. **59 N7, 60 A5**

Merrigum Vic. **58 G6**
Merrijig Vic. **59 L11**
Merriton SA **41 K3**
Merriwa NSW **2 H3, 4 H13**
Merriwagga NSW **9 M6**
Merrygoen NSW **2 F2, 4 E12**
Merseylea Tas. **65 J6**
Merton Vic. **59 J10**
Messent Conservation Park SA **39 F6, 41 O12**
Metcalfe Vic. **55 R12**
Metung Vic. **51 Q4, 60 F13**
Meunna Tas. **64 F5**
Mia Mia Vic. **58 D10**
Mia Mia State Forest Qld 200, 220, 222
Miallo Qld **17 K5**
Michelago NSW **10 E7**
Mickleham Vic. **50 C2, 58 F13**
Middlecamp Hills Conservation Park SA **40 G3**
Middlemount Qld **14 I7**
Middleton Qld **20 I6**
Middleton Tas. **63 L8**
Midge Point Qld **14 I3**
Midgee Qld **15 L9**
Midway Point Tas. **63 M6**
Miena Tas. **63 J1, 65 K10**
Mil Lel SA **39 I12, 52 A5**
Milabena Tas. **64 F4**
Milang SA **39 D4, 41 M10**
Milawa Vic. **59 M6**
Milbrulong NSW **9 P11**
Mildura Vic. **8 E7, 56 G4**
Miles Qld **12 I4**
Milikapiti NT **24 E2**
Miling WA **30 E5, 32 A6**
Milingimbi NT **25 L4**
Millaa Millaa Qld **17 L8**, 238, 241
Millaroo Qld **14 F1, 17 O13**
Millfield NSW **3 K5**
Millicent SA **39 G12**
Millmerran Qld **13 K6**
Millstream Falls National Park Qld 238, 241
Millstream-Chichester National Park WA **34 A3, 38 H2**, 352, 367
Millthorpe NSW **2 E7**
Milparinka NSW **6 D5, 22 I11**
Milton NSW **2 I13, 10 H6**
Milyakburra NT **25 N8**
Mimili SA **47 L4**
Mimmindie Vic. **8 H13, 55 O5**
Mimosa Rocks National Park NSW **10 G10, 61 Q5**
Minamia NT **25 L13, 27 L3**
Mincha Vic. **8 I13, 55 P5, 58 B4**
Mindarie SA **39 G2, 41 P8**
Miners Pool WA 328, 338, 343
Miners Rest Vic. **53 O3, 58 A13**
Minerva Hills National Park Qld **14 G10**
Mingary SA **6 A12, 8 A1, 43 Q10**
Mingela Qld **14 E1, 17 N13**, 229
Mingenew WA **30 D2**
Minhamite Vic. **52 H6**
Minilya Roadhouse WA **38 C6**, 380
Minimay Vic. **54 C9**
Mininera Vic. **53 K4**
Minjilang NT **24 H2**
Minlaton SA **40 I7**
Minnie Water NSW **5 P6, 13 N11**
Minnipa SA **40 B1, 42 B13, 45 R12**
Minnivale WA **30 F6, 32 B7**

References in **bold type** are map references to the Road Maps section of this book, following page 497.

References in **bold type** are map references to the Road Maps section of this book, following page 497.

North Shields SA **40 D7**
North Stradbroke Island Qld **13 O6**
North Yunderup WA **30 E8**
Northam WA **30 F7, 32 A8**
Northampton WA **30 C1**, 390-1
Northcliffe WA **30 E12, 32 A13**, 392, 400, 404, 407
Northcliffe Forest Park WA 392, 404, 407
Northdown Tas. **65 J5**
Notley Hills Tas. **65 K6**
Notts Well SA **41 O6**
Nourlangie Rock NT 89, 93-4
Nowa Nowa Vic. **10 B13, 51 R4, 60 G12**
Nowendoc NSW **3 L1, 5 L11**
Nowra NSW **2 I11, 10 H4**, 42, 45, 447, 459-60
Nubeena Tas. **63 N7**
Nug Nug Vic. **59 N8, 60 A6**
Nuga Nuga National Park Qld **14 I12**
Nugent Tas. **63 N5**
Nullagine WA **34 E3**
Nullarbor National Park SA **33 R7, 44 C7**, 414, 427-8
Nullarbor Plain SA 427
Nullarbor Roadhouse SA **44 G7**
Nullawarre Vic. **53 J10**
Nullawil NSW **8 G13, 55 L4**
Nullica NSW **61 P8**
Numbulwar NT **25 N9**
Numeralla NSW **61 M2**
Numurkah Vic. **9 M13, 58 H4**
Nunamara Tas. **65 M6**
Nundle NSW **5 J11**
Nundroo SA **45 J8**, 427, 430
Nungarin WA **30 H6, 32 C7**
Nungatta National Park NSW **10 E12, 61 M9**
Nungurner Vic. **51 Q4, 60 G13**
Nuriootpa SA **41 M6**, 120, 122
Nuyts Archipelago Conservation Park SA **45 N10**
Nuytsland Nature Reserve WA 421-2
Nyabing WA **30 H10, 32 C11**
Nyah Vic. **8 G10, 57 M10**
Nyirripi NT **28 E7**
Nymagee NSW **7 O12**
Nymboida NSW **5 N6, 13 M11**
Nymboida National Park NSW **5 M5**
Nymbool Qld **17 J8**
Nyngan NSW **7 Q11**
Nyora Vic. **50 G7**

O'Connell NSW **2 G7**
O'Malley SA 427
Oakbank SA 120-1
Oakdale NSW **2 I9, 10 H2**
Oakey Qld **13 K5**
Oaklands NSW **9 N12, 59 L1**
Oaklands SA **40 I8**
Oaks Tas. **65 L8**
Oakwood Tas. **63 O8**
Oasis Roadhouse Qld **17 J11**, 234, 236, 283
Oatlands Tas. **63 M3, 65 M12**
OB Flat SA **39 I13**
Oberon NSW **2 G8**, 47, 53
Ocean Grove Vic. **50 A7, 53 R8**
Ocean Shores NSW **5 P2, 13 O8**
Oenpelli (Gunbalanya) NT **24 I5**
Ogmore Qld **15 K7**
Olary SA **43 P11**
Old Adaminaby NSW **10 C8, 61 J1**

Old Andado Station SA 469-70
Old Bar NSW **3 N2, 5 N13**
Old Beach Tas. **63 L5**
Old Tallangatta Vic. **59 Q5, 60 C3**
Oldina Tas. **64 F5**
Olgas, The NT *see* Kata Tjuta
Olinda Vic. **50 E4**
Olympic Dam Village SA **42 F4**
Omeo Vic. **10 A11, 60 E8**, 452, 454
One Arm Point WA **36 I6**
One Hundred Year Forest WA 403
Ongerup WA **30 H11, 32 D12**
Onslow WA **38 E2**, 352, 371-2, 374
Oodla Wirra SA **41 M1, 43 L13**
Oodnadatta SA **48 B7**, 484-5
Ooldea SA 427, 429
Ootann Qld **17 J8**
Opalton Qld **21 K8**
Opossum Bay Tas. **63 M7**
Ora Banda WA **32 G6**
Orange NSW **2 E6**
Orara State Forest NSW 193
Orbost Vic. **10 C13, 60 I12**
Orchid Beach Island Village Qld **15 R12**, 68
Orford Tas. **63 O4**, 164-5
Orford Vic. **52 G8**
Organ Pipes National Park Vic. **50 B3**
Orielton Tas. **63 M5**
Ormley Tas. **65 O8**
Orpheus Island National Park Qld **17 M10**
Ororoo SA **43 K12**, 130, 132
Osbornes Flat Vic. **59 O6, 60 B3**
Osmaston Tas. **65 K7**
Osterley Tas. **63 J3, 65 K12**
Otway National Park Vic. **53 N12**, 136, 142-3, 147
Ourimbah State Forest NSW 40
Ouse Tas. **63 J4, 65 K13**
Outtrim Vic. **50 G8**
Ouyen Vic. **8 E10, 56 H9**
Ovens Vic. **59 O7, 60 A5**
Overland Corner SA **41 Q5**
Overlander Roadhouse WA **38 D11**, 381, 383, 388
Owanyilla Qld **13 M1**
Owen SA **41 L6**
Oxenford Qld **13 N7**
Oxley NSW **8 I7, 57 Q4**
Oxley Vic. **59 M6**
Oxley Wild Rivers National Park NSW **5 L10**
Oyster Cove Tas. **63 L8**

Packsaddle Roadhouse NSW **6 D8, 22 I13**
Padthaway SA **39 H8**
Padthaway Conservation Park SA **39 H8**
Pakenham Vic. **50 F6**
Palana Tas. **62 A10**
Pallamallawa NSW **4 H5, 12 I10**
Pallarenda Qld **17 N12**
Palm Grove National Park Qld **15 J12**
Palm Valley NT 462, 472-4
Palmer SA **39 D2, 41 M8**
Palmer Goldfields Reserve Qld 272-5
Palmer River Roadhouse Qld **17 J5**
Palmwoods Qld 202
Paloona Tas. **64 I6**
Paluma Qld 200, 235, 237
Pambula NSW **10 F11, 61 P7**
Pambula Beach NSW **10 F11, 61 P7**

Pampas Qld **13 K6**
Pandappa Conservation Park SA **41 M2**
Panmure Vic. **53 J9**
Pannawonica WA **38 F2**
Papunya NT **28 G8**
Paraburdoo WA **34 B6, 38 H5**
Parachilna SA **43 K6**, 130, 134
Paradise Tas. **64 I7**
Paradise Beach Vic. **51 O7**
Paratoo SA **43 M12**
Parattah Tas. **63 M3, 65 M12**
Pardoo Roadhouse WA **36 D12**
Parenna Tas. **62 B9**
Parilla SA **8 A11, 39 H3, 41 Q9**, 438
Paringa SA **8 A7, 41 R5, 56 A4**
Parkers Corner Vic. **51 J5**
Parkes NSW **2 C6**
Parkham Tas. **65 J7**
Parkhurst Qld **15 L9**
Parkside Tas. **65 Q6**
Parndana SA **40 H11**
Parnella Tas. **65 Q6**
Parrakie SA **39 G4, 41 P10**
Parramatta NSW **3 J8**
Paru NT **24 E3**
Paruna SA **8 A9, 39 I1, 41 R7**, 129
Parwan Vic. **50 A3, 53 R5**
Pascoe River Qld 258-9
Paskeville SA **41 J5**
Pata SA **39 H1, 41 Q7**
Patchewollock Vic. **8 E11, 54 G1, 56 G11**
Pateena Tas. **65 L7**
Paterson NSW **3 L4**
Patersonia Tas. **65 M6**
Pawleena Tas. **63 N5**
Pawtella Tas. **63 M3, 65 N12**
Paxton NSW **3 K5**
Paynes Find WA **30 G3, 32 B4**
Paynesville Vic. **51 P5, 60 F13**
Peaceful Bay WA 409, 411
Peach Trees State Forest Park Qld 201, 203
Peak Charles WA 110, 116
Peak Charles National Park WA **32 G10**, 96, 110, 112, 116
Peak Crossing Qld **13 M6**, 72
Peak Downs Qld **14 H6**
Peak Eleanora WA 110
Peak Hill NSW **2 C4**
Peake SA **39 F4, 41 O10**
Pearcedale Vic. **50 E7**
Pearshape Tas. **62 A9**
Peats Ridge NSW **3 K6**
Peebinga SA **8 A10, 39 I2, 41 R8, 56 A9**
Peebinga Conservation Park SA **41 R8, 56 A9**, 129
Peechelba Vic. **59 L5**
Peel NSW **2 G6**
Peelhurst WA **30 D8**
Peep Hill SA **41 M5**
Pegarah Tas. **62 A9**
Pekina SA **41 L1, 43 K12**
Pelaw Main NSW 182
Pelham Tas. **63 K4**
Pelverata Tas. **63 L7**
Pemberton WA **30 E12, 32 A13**, 392, 400, 403-5
Pemberton National Park WA 400
Penarie NSW **8 H8, 57 N5**
Penguin Tas. **64 H5**
Penna Tas. **63 M5**

References in **bold type** are map references to the Road Maps section of this book, following page 497.

References in **bold type** are map references to the Road Maps section of this book, following page 497.

Redhill SA **41 K3**
Redland Bay Qld **13 N6**
Redpa Tas. **64 B4**
Reedy Creek SA **39 G9**
Reedy Creek Vic. **50 D1, 58 G12**
Reedy Marsh Tas. **65 K7**
Reef Hills Park Vic. **59 J8**
Reekara Tas. **62 A8**
Regans Ford WA **30 D6**
Regatta Point Tas. **62 D2, 64 E11**
Reid WA **33 Q6**
Rekuna Tas. **63 M5**
Relbia Tas. **65 M7**
Remine Tas. **64 D10**
Rendelsham SA **39 G11**
Renison Bell Tas. **64 E9**
Renmark SA **8 A7, 41 R5**
Renner Springs NT **27 J8**
Rennie NSW **9 N12, 59 L2**
Retreat Tas. **65 M5**
Rheban Tas. **63 O5**
Rheola Vic. **55 N9**
Rhyll Vic. **50 E8**
Rhyndaston Tas. **63 M4, 65 M13**
Rhynie SA **41 L5**
Riana Tas. **64 H5**
Richmond NSW **2 I7**
Richmond Qld **21 L3**
Richmond Tas. **63 M5**
Riddells Creek Vic. **50 B2, 58 E13**
Ridgelands Qld **15 L8**
Ridgley Tas. **64 G5**
Ringarooma Tas. **65 O6**, 176
Risdon Vale Tas. **63 M6**
Riverside North Tas. **65 L7**
Riverton SA **41 L5**
Roadvale Qld **13 M7**
Robbins Island Tas. **64 C2**
Robe SA **39 F10**
Robertson NSW **2 I10, 10 H3**, 36, 44
Robertstown SA **41 M5**
Robigana Tas. **65 L6**
Robinvale Vic. **8 F8, 57 J6**
Rocherlea Tas. **65 L6**
Rochester SA **41 K4**
Rochester Vic. **58 E6**
Rockbank Vic. **50 B4**
Rockhampton Qld **15 L9**
Rockingham WA **30 D8**
Rockley NSW **2 F8**
Rocky Cape National Park Tas. **64 F3**
Rodds Peninsula National Park Qld. **15 O10**
Roebourne WA **38 H1, 34 A2**, 352, 368, 370-1
Roebuck Roadhouse WA **36 H8**, 356
Roger River Tas. **64 D4**
Roger River West Tas. **64 C4**
Rokeby Tas. **63 M6**
Rokeby Vic. **50 H6**
Rokeby National Park Qld **18 D9**, 244, 267-8
Rokewood Vic. **53 O6**
Roland Tas. **64 I7**
Rolleston Qld **14 I11**, 213
Rollingstone Qld **17 M11**
Roma Qld **12 F4**
Romsey Vic. **50 B1, 58 E12**
Roper River Bar NT 278, 308-11
Rosebery Tas. **64 F9**
Rosebrook Vic. **52 H9**

Rosebud Vic. **50 C8**
Rosedale Qld **15 O12**
Rosedale Vic. **51 L6**
Rosevale Qld **13 M7**
Rosevale Tas. **65 K7**
Rosewhite Vic. **59 O7, 60 B5**
Rosewood Qld **13 M6**
Roseworthy SA **39 C1, 41 L7**
Ross Tas. **63 M1, 65 N10**
Ross River NT **29 K8**
Rossarden Tas. **65 O8**
Rossbridge Vic. **53 J3**
Rossville Qld **17 K4**
Rottnest Island WA **30 D7**
Rowella Tas. **65 K5**
Rowena NSW **4 D6, 12 F11**
Rowsley Vic. **50 A4, 53 R5**
Roxby Downs SA **42 F4**
Royal George Tas. **65 P9**
Royal National Park NSW **3 J9**
Rubyvale Qld **14 G9**
Rudall SA **40 E4**
Rudall River National Park WA **34 I4**
Ruffy Vic. **58 I10**
Rugby NSW **2 E10, 10 D3**
Rum Jungle NT **24 E6**, 79, 83
Runnymede Tas. **63 N5**
Rupanyup Vic. **54 I9**
Rushworth Vic. **58 F7**
Russell River National Park Qld **17 I7**
Rutherglen Vic. **9 O13, 59 M4**
Rydal NSW **2 H7**
Rye Park NSW **2 E10, 10 D3**
Rylstone NSW **2 G5**, 47, 49

Sacred Canyon SA 130, 133
Saddleworth SA **41 L5**
St Albans NSW **3 J6**
St Andrews Vic. **50 E3**
St Arnaud Vic. **55 L9**
St George Qld **12 F7**
St Georges Basin NSW **2 I12, 10 H5**
St Helens Tas. **65 Q6**, 172-3
St James Vic. **59 J5**
St Lawrence Qld **15 J6**, 214, 216
St Leonards Vic. **50 B6**
St Marys Tas. **65 Q8**
St Patricks River Tas. **65 M6**
Sale Vic. **51 M6**
Salisbury SA **39 C1, 41 L8**
Salmon Gums WA **32 H10**
Salt Creek SA **39 E6, 41 O12**
Salter Springs SA **41 L5**
Saltwater River Tas. **63 N7**
Samford Qld **13 N5**, 58-9
San Remo Vic. **50 E8**
Sanctuary Point NSW **10 H5**
Sandalwood SA **39 G2, 41 P8**
Sandfire Roadhouse WA **36 F12**, 355-6
Sandfly Tas. **63 L7**
Sandford Tas. **63 M6**
Sandford Vic. **52 D4**
Sandilands SA **40 I7**
Sandstone WA **32 E2**
Sandy Creek Falls NT 76
Sandy Hollow NSW **2 I3**
Sandy Island WA **30 E12**

Sandy Point Vic. **50 I11**
Santa Teresa NT **29 K9**
Sapphire Qld **14 G9**
Sapphiretown SA **40 I11**
Sarina Qld **15 J4**
Sarina Beach Qld **15 J4**, 218
Sarsfield Vic. **51 P4, 60 F13**
Sassafras Tas. **65 J6**
Sassafras East Tas. **65 J6**
Savage River Tas. **64 D7**
Sawtell NSW **5 O7, 13 N12**
Scamander Tas. **65 Q7**
Scarsdale Vic. **53 N4**
Scone NSW **3 J2, 4 I13**
Scorpion Springs Conservation Park SA **8 A11, 54 A1**
Scott National Park WA **30 C11, 31 E12, 45 E12**
Scotts Head NSW **5 O9, 13 N13**
Scottsdale Tas. **65 N5**, 60, 172, 175-6
Sea Lake Vic. **8 F11, 55 J2, 57 K12**
Seabird WA **30 D6**
Seaforth Qld **17 O12**
Seal Creek Vic. 148
Seal Rocks NSW **3 N3**
Seaspray Vic. **51 N8**
Seaton Vic. **51 K5**
Second Valley SA **39 B4, 41 K10**
Sedan SA **41 N7, 39 D1**
Sedgwick Vic. **55 Q11, 58 C9**
Selbourne Tas. **65 K7**
Seldom Seen Roadhouse Vic. **10 B11, 60 H9**
Sellheim Qld **14 D1, 17 M13, 21 R1**
Separation Creek Vic. **53 O11**
Seppeltsfield SA **39 C1, 41 M6**
Serpentine Vic. **55 P8, 58 A6**
Serpentine National Park WA **30 E8**
Serviceton Vic. **39 I7, 41 R13, 54 B7**
Seven Emu Station NT 304
Seven Mile Beach Tas. **63 M6**
Sevenhill SA **41 L4**
Severnlea Qld **5 L2, 13 L8**
Seville Vic. **50 F4**
Seymour Tas. **65 Q9**
Seymour Vic. **58 G10**
Shackleton WA **30 G7, 32 C8**
Shannon Tas. **63 J1, 65 K10**
Shannon National Park WA **30 F12, 32 A13**
Shark Bay WA 381, 385
Shaw Island National Park Qld **17 J0**
Shay Gap WA **34 E1, 36 E13**, 357, 359
Sheffield Tas. **64 I6**
Shelford Vic. **53 P7**
Shellharbour NSW **3 J10, 10 I3**
Shelly Beach Tas. **63 O4**
Sheoak Hill Conservation Park SA **40 F3**
Sheoaks Vic. **53 P6**
Shepparton Vic. **58 H6**
Sheringa SA **40 C4**
Sherlock SA **39 F3, 41 O9**
Shoal Point Qld **15 J3**
Shoalhaven Heads NSW **2 I11, 10 I4**
Shute Harbour Qld **14 I2**
Shutehaven Qld **14 I2**
Sidmouth Tas. **65 K5**
Silkwood Qld **17 L8**
Silvan Vic. **50 E4**
Silver Creek Vic. **59 N6, 60 A4**
Silverdale NSW **2 I8, 10 H1**

References in **bold type** are map references to the Road Maps section of this book, following page 497.

Silverton NSW **6 B12**
Simpson Vic. **53 L10**
Simpson Desert Conservation Park SA **20 B13, 22 B3, 29 Q12, 48 G2**
Simpson Desert National Park Qld **22 B1, 29 Q11, 48 G2**
Simpsons Bay Tas. **63 L9**
Simpsons Gap National Park NT 473
Singleton NSW **3 J4**
Singleton WA **30 D8**
Sir Joseph Banks Group Conservation Park SA **40 E7**
Sisters Beach Tas. **64 F4**
Sisters Creek Tas. **64 F4**
Skenes Creek Vic. **53 O11**, 142
Skipton Vic. **53 M4**
Smeaton Vic. **53 P2, 55 P13, 58 A12**
Smiggin Holes NSW **10 C9, 60 I4**
Smith Point NT 85-7
Smithfield Qld **17 L6**
Smithton Tas. **64 D3**, 169
Smithtown NSW **5 O10**
Smoky Bay SA **45 O11**
Smythesdale Vic. **53 N4**
Snake Range National Park Qld **14 G10**
Snake Valley Vic. **53 N4**
Snowtown SA **41 K4**
Snowy River National Park Vic. **10 C12, 60 I9**
Snug Tas. **63 L7**
Snuggery SA **39 H12**
Sofala NSW **2 G6**, 47, 50
Somers Vic. **50 D8**
Somerset Tas. **64 G4**
Somerton NSW **4 I9**
Somerville Vic. **50 D7**
Sorell Tas. **63 N6**, 164-5
Sorrento Vic. **50 B8**
South Arm Tas. **63 M7**
South Bruny Island Tas. **63 L9**
South Forest Tas. **64 D3**
South Franklin Tas. **63 K7**
South Hedland WA **34 C1, 36 B13**
South Island National Park Qld **15 L5**
South Kilkerran SA **40 I6**
South Kumminin WA **30 H8, 32 C9**
South Mount Cameron Tas. **65 P4**
South Nietta Tas. **64 H6**
South Preston Tas. **64 H6**
South Riana Tas. **64 G5**
South Springfield Tas. **65 N6**
South Stirling WA **30 H12, 32 C13**
South Stradbroke Island Qld **13 O6**
South West Rocks NSW **5 O9, 13 N13**, 186
South Yaamba Qld **15 L8**
Southbrook Qld **13 K6**
Southend Qld **15 N10**
Southend SA **39 G12**
Southern Cross Vic. **52 H8**
Southern Cross WA **32 E7**
Southport Qld **13 O7**
Southport Tas. **63 K9**
Southwest National Park Tas. **62 G7, 62 I9**
Southwood National Park Qld **12 H6**
Spalding SA **41 L3**, 132
Spalford Tas. **64 H6**
Speed Vic. **8 E11, 54 I1, 56 I12**
Split Rock Qld 270
Sprent Tas. **64 H6**

Spreyton Tas. **64 I5**
Spring Beach Tas. **63 O4**
Spring Hill NSW **2 E7**
Spring Ridge NSW **4 H11**
Springbrook Qld **5 P1, 13 N7**
Springfield Tas. **65 N5**
Springhurst Vic. **59 M5**
Springside Qld **13 K6**
Springsure Qld **14 H10**
Springton SA **39 D1, 41 M7**
Springwood NSW **2 I8**
Staaten River National Park Qld **16 F6**
Stamford Qld **21 M4**
Standley Chasm NT 474
Stanhope Vic. **58 F6**
Stanley Tas. **64 E3**
Stanley Vic. **59 O6, 60 A4**
Stansbury SA **40 I8**
Stanthorpe Qld **5 L2, 13 L8**
Stanwell Qld **15 L9**
Starcke National Park Qld **17 J2, 18 H13**
Staverton Tas. **64 H7**
Stawell Vic. **55 J12**, 434, 445
Steavenson Falls Vic. 157
Steels Creek Vic. **50 E3**
Steep Point WA 352, 381, 385
Stenhouse Bay SA **40 G9**
Steppes Tas. **63 K1, 65 K11**
Stevensons Falls Vic. 142, 146
Stieglitz Tas. **65 Q6**
Stirling North SA **42 I11**
Stirling Range National Park WA **30 G11, 32 C13**
Stockinbingal NSW **2 B10, 10 A3**
Stockwell SA **41 M6**
Stokes Bay SA **40 H11**
Stokes National Park WA **32 G12**
Stone Hut SA **41 K1, 43 J13**
Stonefield SA **41 N6**
Stonehenge Qld **21 L11**
Stonehenge Tas. **63 N3, 65 N13**
Stoneyford Vic. **53 M9**
Stonor Tas. **63 M3, 65 M13**
Stony Creek Vic. **50 H9**
Stony Creek Forest Park Qld 60
Stony Point Vic. **50 D8**
Stoodley Tas. **64 I6**
Stormlea Tas. **63 N8**
Storys Creek Tas. **65 O8**
Stowport Tas. **64 G5**
Strachans Camping Area Vic. 434, 439-40, 442-4
Strahan Tas. **62 D2, 64 E11**
Stratford NSW **3 L2, 5 L13**
Stratford Vic. **51 M5**
Strath Creek Vic. **58 G11**
Strathalbyn SA **39 C3, 41 M9**
Stratham WA **30 D10**
Strathblane Tas. **63 K9**
Strathbogie Vic. **59 J9**
Strathdownie Vic. **52 B5**
Strathfieldsaye Vic. **55 R10, 58 C9**
Strathgordon Tas. **62 G5**
Strathmerton Vic. **9 M13, 58 I3**
Streaky Bay SA **45 P12**
Streatham Vic. **53 K4**
Stroud NSW **3 L3**
Strzelecki National Park Tas. **62 B12**
Stuart Mill Vic. **55 M10**
Stuart Town NSW **2 E5**

Stuarts Point NSW **5 O9, 13 N13**
Sturt National Park NSW **6 A3, 22 H9, 49 R12**, 494-6
Sues Bridge WA 392, 395, 399, 401
Suggan Buggan Vic. **60 H7**, 455
Sulphur Creek Tas. **64 H5**
Sunbury Vic. **50 B3**
Sundown National Park Qld **5 L3, 13 K9**
Sunnyside Tas. **64 I6**
Sunnyvale SA **41 J5**, 128
Surat Qld **12 G5**
Surfers Paradise Qld **13 O7**
Surges Bay Tas. **63 K8**
Surveyors Bay Tas. **63 L8**
Sussex Inlet NSW **2 I12, 10 H5**
Sutherlands SA **41 N5**
Sutton NSW **2 F12**
Swan Hill Vic. **8 H11, 55 N1, 57 N11**
Swan Marsh Vic. **53 M9**
Swan Reach SA **39 E1, 41 N7**
Swan Reach Vic. **51 Q4, 60 F13**
Swan Reach Conservation Park SA **39 E1, 41 N7**
Swanhaven NSW **2 I12, 10 H5**
Swanpool Vic. **59 K8**
Swansea Tas. **63 P2, 65 P11**
Swifts Creek Vic. **10 A12, 51 P1, 60 F9**
Sydney NSW **3 K8**

Taabinga Qld **13 L4**
Table Top NSW **9 P13, 59 P3, 60 B1**
Tabletop Range NT 76
Tabulam NSW **5 N3, 13 M9**
Taggerty Vic. **50 G1, 59 J12**
Tailem Bend SA **39 E3, 41 N9**, 125, 129, 437
Takone Tas. **64 F5**
Takone West Tas. **64 F5**
Talawah Tas. **65 O6**
Talbingo NSW **10 B6**
Talbot Vic. **53 O1, 55 N12**
Taldra SA **8 A8, 41 R6, 56 A5**
Talgarno Vic. **9 Q13, 59 P4, 60 C2**
Talia SA **40 B2**
Tallangatta Vic. **59 Q5, 60 C3**
Tallaringa Conservation Park SA **47 N10**
Tallarook Vic. **58 G11**
Tallimba NSW **9 P7**
Tallygaroopna Vic. **58 H5**
Talwood Qld **4 F1, 12 G8**
Tamban State Forest NSW 189
Tambar Springs NSW **4 G11**
Tambellup WA **30 G11, 32 C12**
Tambo Qld **14 D12, 21 R12**
Tambo Crossing Vic. **10 A13, 51 Q2, 60 F11**
Tamboon Vic. **10 E13**
Tamborine Qld **13 N7**
Tamworth NSW **5 J10**
Tanami NT **26 D12, 28 D1**
Tandarra Vic. **55 Q8, 58 C6**
Tangambalanga Vic. **59 P5, 60 B3**
Tanjil Bren Vic. **50 I4**
Tanjil South Vic. **50 I6**
Tankerton Vic. **50 E8**
Tannum Sands Qld **15 N10**
Tannymorel Qld **5 M1, 13 L7**
Tansey Qld **13 L2**
Tantanoola SA **39 H12**
Tanunda SA **39 D1, 41 M7**, 120, 122

References in **bold type** are map references to the Road Maps section of this book, following page 497.

References in **bold type** are map references to the Road Maps section of this book, following page 497.

Tungkillo SA **39 D2, 41 M8**
Tunnack Tas. **63 M4, 65 N13**
Tunnel Tas. **65 M5**
Tunnel Creek National Park WA 348, 351
Tura Beach NSW **10 F11, 61 P7**
Turallin Qld **13 J6**
Turkey Creek WA **37 Q7, 39 D2**
Turkey Creek Roadhouse WA 334
Turners Beach Tas. **64 H5**
Turners Marsh Tas. **65 L6**
Tuross Head NSW **10 G8, 61 Q2**
Turriff Vic. **8 E11, 54 I1, 56 I12**
Tweed Heads NSW **5 P1, 13 O7**
Two Rocks WA **30 D6**, 105
Two Wells SA **39 B1, 41 L7**
Tyaak Vic. **58 G11**
Tyabb Vic. **50 D7**
Tyalgum NSW **5 P1, 13 N8**, 195
Tyenna Tas. **63 J5**
Tyers Vic. **51 J6**
Tyers Park Vic. **51 J6**
Tylden Vic. **55 R13**
Tyndale NSW **5 O5, 13 N10**
Tynong Vic. **50 F6**

Ubirr Rock NT 89, 93
Uobo Qld **15 N11**
Uki NSW **5 P1, 13 N8**, 75
Ulan NSW **2 G3**
Ulladulla NSW **2 I13, 10 H6**, 42, 46
Ulmarra NSW **5 O5, 13 N11**
Ultima Vic. **8 G11, 57 L12**
Uluru-Kata Tjuta National Park NT **28 F12**, 462,
    478, 482-3
Ulverstone Tas. **64 H5**
Umina NSW **3 K7**
Undalya SA **41 L5**
Undara Lava Tubes Qld 278, 284-5
Undera Vic. **58 G5**
Undara National Park Qld **17 J9**
Underwood Tas. **65 M6**
Ungarie NSW **9 P5**
Ungarra SA **40 E5**
Upper Blessington Tas. **65 N7**
Upper Castra Tas. **64 H6**
Upper Esk Tas. **65 O7**
Upper Horton NSW **4 H7, 12 I12**
Upper Manilla NSW **4 I8, 12 I13**
Upper Mount Hicks Tas. **64 F5**
Upper Natone Tas. **64 G5**
Upper Plenty Vic. **50 D2, 58 G13**
Upper Scamander Tas. **65 Q7**
Uralla NSW **5 K8**
Urana NSW **9 O11**
Urandangi Qld **20 B5, 29 R5**
Urania SA **40 I7**
Uranquinty NSW **2 A12, 9 Q10**
Urbenville NSW **5 N1, 13 M8**
Urunga NSW **5 O8, 13 N12**
Useless Loop WA **38 B10**
Uxbridge Tas. **63 K5**

Vacy NSW **3 K4**
Valla Beach NSW **5 O8, 13 N13**
Valley of the Giants WA 409-10
Van Diemen Gulf NT 88, 90

Varley WA **32 E10**
Vaughan Vic. **55 Q12**
Veitch SA **39 H1, 41 Q7**
Ventnor Vic. **50 D8**
Venus Bay SA **40 A2, 45 Q13**
Venus Bay Vic. **50 G10**
Venus Bay Conservation Park SA **40 A2, 45 Q13**
Verdun SA 120
Verona Sands Tas. **63 L8**
Verran SA **40 F4**
Victor Harbor SA **39 C4, 41 L10**
Victoria Point Qld **13 N6**
Victoria River NT **24 F12, 26 F2**, 315-16
Victoria Settlement NT 85, 87
Victory Downs NT **28 I13, 47 M1**
Vinifera Vic. **8 H10, 57 M10**
Violet Town Vic. **59 J8**
Virginia SA **39 B1, 41 L7**
Vivonne Bay SA **40 H12**
Vivonne Bay Conservation Park SA **40 H12**
Vlanning Head WA 378-9

Waaia Vic. **9 L13, 58 H4**
Wadbilliga National Park NSW **10 F9, 61 N3**
Waddamana Tas. **63 J1, 65 K11**
Waddikee SA **40 E2**
Wagga Wagga NSW **2 A12, 9 Q10**
Wagin WA **30 G10, 32 B11**, 112, 117
Wahgunyah Vic. **9 O13, 59 M4**
Waikerie SA **41 P5**, 125, 128
Wail Vic. **54 G8**
Wairewa Vic. **51 R3, 60 H12**
Wakool NSW **9 J11, 55 R2, 57 R12**
Wal Wal Vic. **54 I10**
Walbundrie NSW **9 P12, 59 N2**
Walcha NSW **5 K9**
Walcha Road NSW **5 K9**
Walgett NSW **4 C6, 12 E11**
Walgoolan WA **30 H6, 32 D7**
Walhalla Vic. **51 J5**
Walkaway WA **30 C2**
Walker Flat SA **39 E1, 41 N7**, 125, 127
Walkerston Qld **15 J4**
Walkerville Vic. **50 H11**
Walla Walla NSW **9 P12, 59 O2**
Wallabadah NSW **3 J1, 4 I11**
Wallabrook SA **39 I8**
Wallace Vic. **53 P4**
Wallace Rockhole Community NT **28 I9**, 472-4
Wallacia NSW **2 I8**
Wallaga Lake National Park NSW **10 F9, 61 P4**
Wallaloo East Vic. **55 K10**
Wallan Vic. **50 C2, 58 F13**
Wallangarra Qld **5 L3, 13 L9**
Wallaroo Qld **15 J9**
Wallaroo SA **40 I4**
Wallaville Qld **15 O13**
Wallendbeen NSW **2 C10, 10 B3**
Wallerawang NSW **2 H7**
Walls of Jerusalem National Park Tas. **64 H9**
Wallumbilla Qld **12 G4**
Walpa Vic. **51 O4, 60 D13**
Walpeup Vic. **8 D10, 56 G10**
Walpole WA **30 F12**, 410
Walpole-Nornalup National Park WA **30 E13**, 392,
    409
Walwa Vic. **9 R13, 10 A8, 60 F1**

Wampoony SA **41 Q13**
Wamuran Qld **13 N5**
Wanaaring NSW **6 I5, 23 M11**
Wanbi SA **39 G1, 41 P7**
Wandearah SA **41 J2**
Wandering WA **30 F8, 32 A10**
Wandiligong Vic. **59 P9, 60 B6**
Wandilo SA **39 H12, 52 A5**
Wando Vale Vic. **52 D3**
Wandoan Qld **12 H3**
Wandong Vic. **50 D1, 58 F12**
Wanganella NSW **9 K10**
Wangarabell Vic. **61 N10**
Wangaratta Vic. **59 M6**
Wangary SA **40 C7**
Wangi Wangi NSW **3 K5**
Wanilla SA **40 D7**
Wanneroo WA **30 D7**, 105
Wannon Vic. **52 F4**
Warakurna Community WA **28 B11, 35 Q9**
Warakurna Roadhouse WA **28 B11, 35 Q9**
Waratah Tas. **64 F7**
Waratah Bay Vic. **50 H10**
Warburton Vic. **50 G4**, 138, 140
Warburton WA **35 O11**, 478-9, 481-2
Wardell NSW **5 P3, 13 O9**
Wards River NSW **3 L3, 5 L13**
Warialda NSW **4 I5, 12 I10**
Warkworth NSW **3 J4**
Warneet Vic. **50 E7**
Warnertown SA **41 J2**
Warooka SA **40 H8**
Waroona WA **30 E9**
Warra Qld **13 J4**
Warrabah National Park NSW **5 J8**
Warracknabeal Vic. **54 H6**
Warragamba NSW **2 I8, 10 H1**
Warragul Vic. **50 H6**
Warrak Vic. **55 L13**
Warrakurna Roadhouse WA 478, 481, 483
Warramboo SA **40 D2**
Warrego NT **27 J10**
Warren NSW **2 B1, 4 B12**
Warren Qld **15 L9**
Warren National Park WA 392, 400, 404-5
Warrenbayne Vic. **59 J8**
Warrenben Conservation Park SA **40 H9**
Warrentinna Tas. **65 O5**
Warringa Tas. **64 H6**
Warrion Vic. **53 N8**
Warrnambool Vic. **52 I9**
Warrow SA **40 C6**
Warrumbungle National Park NSW **4 D10**
Warruwi NT **25 J3**
Warwick Qld **5 M1, 13 L7**
Washpool National Park NSW **5 M4**
Wasleys SA **41 L6**
Watarrka National Park NT **28 G9**
Watchem Vic. **8 F13, 55 K6**
Waterfall NSW **3 J9, 10 I2**
Waterhouse Tas. **65 N4**
Waterloo SA **41 M5**
Waterloo Tas. **63 K8**
Watervale SA **41 L5**
Watheroo WA **30 E4**
Watheroo National Park WA **30 D4**
Watson SA 427, 429
Wattening WA **30 F6, 32 A7**

References in **bold type** are map references to the Road Maps section of this book, following page 497.

582

References in **bold type** are map references to the Road Maps section of this book, following page 497.

References in **bold type** are map references to the Road Maps section of this book, following page 497.

ACCIDENT ACTION

UNCONSCIOUS PEOPLE CAN, AND DO, CHOKE TO DEATH

Blood, vomit, loose teeth or broken dentures can enter the airway, and the tongue can block the airway if an unconscious person is lying flat. THE VICTIM CAN ALSO BLEED TO DEATH. SIMPLE FIRST AID CAN SAVE A LIFE.

DON'T STAND BY AND LET THE VICTIM DIE

1 CLEAR AIRWAY
Lie victim on side and tilt head back.

2 CLEAR MOUTH
Quickly clear mouth, using fingers if necessary. If breathing, leave on side.

3 TILT
If not breathing, place victim on back. Tilt head back. Support the jaw, keeping fingers away from neck.

4 BLOW
Kneel beside head. Place your widely open mouth over victim's slightly open mouth, sealing nostrils with your cheek. Blow until victim's chest rises.
NOTE For an injured child, cover mouth and nose with your mouth. Blow until chest rises (20 times per minute).

5 LOOK, LISTEN
Watch chest fall. Listen for air escaping from mouth. Repeat steps 4 and 5, 15 times per minute.

6 RECOVERY POSITION
When breathing begins, place victim on side, head back, jaw supported, face pointing slightly towards ground.

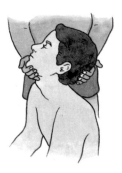

7 IF VICTIM IS TRAPPED
If victim is unconscious and is trapped e.g. in the car, still tilt head back and support the jaw.

SEND SOMEONE FOR HELP OR RADIO FOR HELP. IN ISOLATED AREAS DO NOT LEAVE YOUR CAR. DO NOT LEAVE AN UNCONSCIOUS PERSON.

THINK

▶ Has more than one person been hurt? Who needs help first? **Look after the unconscious victim first.**
▶ Stop bleeding by applying direct pressure over the wound.
▶ Send for help or an ambulance.
▶ Check for danger.
▶ Do not move casualties unnecessarily.